'This is an original, deeply researched and very readable book by the leading scholar of British fascism. It makes an extremely valuable contribution to our understanding of the British fascist tradition.'

Professor Roger Eatwell, University of Bath, UK

'By introducing a biographical approach to reveal the diversity of the visions of national rebirth adopted by six British fascists over nearly a century, Graham Macklin puts welcome flesh on the abstract formula and abstruse generalisations that have too often plagued fascist studies in the past, and simultaneously reveals the transnational nature of the fascist project in the minds of its most ardent believers. Hopefully, Macklin's impressively researched and thoughtful biographical study will inspire a new genre of fascist studies.'

Professor Roger Griffin, Oxford Brookes University, UK

'*Failed Führers* offers us something remarkable, a synoptic overview of the British far right firmly rooted in the granular detail of narrative biography. A maestro of British archives, Macklin brilliantly illuminates the shady saga of a rogues gallery of fanatics from Arnold Leese and Oswald Mosley to Colin Jordan and Nick Griffin. *Failed Führers* is a must read for anyone concerned about fascism, past, present, … and future?'

Kevin Coogan, author of Dreamer of the Day: Francis Parker Yockey and the Postwar Fascist International

'This is a readable and well-researched book from one of the leading scholars of British fascism. Dr Macklin's thesis centres on six meticulous case studies of leading British fascists, usefully setting their stories in a wider international context. With neo-fascism and the authoritarian and exclusionist populist right on the rise across the globe, this is an engaging and timely reminder to keep our eyes on the past, in order to better understand the unstable present.'

Dr David Baker, Warwick University, UK (Retired)

'With spectacular archival depth, *Failed Führers* convincingly shows how continuities in far right ideologies and movements are constructed and sustained as each generation's ideologues are shaped by trajectories of influence from key mentors to emergent protégés. A brilliant intervention into understandings of the historical and contemporary extreme right.'

Cynthia Miller-Idriss, American University, USA

'*Failed Führers* provides an important and timely contribution for historians, social scientists, and the general public by offering a comprehensive account of the historical evolution of the far right in Britain. His account is layered and nuanced reflecting a deep understanding of the topic. Macklin's manuscript is an important accomplishment and I highly recommend this book for anyone serious about understanding the far right.'

Peter Simi, Chapman University, USA

Failed Führers

This book provides a comprehensive history of the ideas and ideologues associated with the racial fascist tradition in Britain. It charts the evolution of the British extreme right from its post-war genesis after 1918 to its present-day incarnations, and details the ideological and strategic evolution of British fascism through the prism of its principal leaders and the movements with which they were associated.

Taking a collective biographical approach, the book focuses on the political careers of six principal ideologues and leaders, Arnold Leese (1878–1956); Sir Oswald Mosley (1896–1980); A.K. Chesterton (1899–1973); Colin Jordan (1923–2009); John Tyndall (1934–2005); and Nick Griffin (1959–), in order to study the evolution of the racial ideology of British fascism, from overtly biological conceptions of 'white supremacy' through 'racial nationalism' and latterly to 'cultural' arguments regarding 'ethno-nationalism'.

Drawing on extensive archival research and often obscure primary texts and propaganda as well as the official records of the British government and its security services, this is the definitive historical account of Britain's extreme right and will be essential reading for all students and scholars of race relations, extremism and fascism.

Graham Macklin is Assistant Professor/Postdoctoral Fellow at the Center for Research on Extremism (C-REX) at the University of Oslo, Norway. He has published extensively on extreme right-wing and anti-minority politics in Britain in both the inter-war and post-war periods including *Very Deeply Dyed in the Black: Sir Oswald Mosley and the Resurrection of British Fascism after 1945* (2007), *British National Party: Contemporary Perspectives* (2011) co-edited with Nigel Copsey, *Failed Führers: A History of Britain's Extreme Right* (2020), and *Researching the Far Right: Theory, Method and Practice* (2020) co-edited with Stephen Ashe, Joel Busher and Aaron Winter. Macklin co-edits 'Patterns of Prejudice: Fascism' and the 'Routledge Studies in Fascism and the Far Right' book series.

Routledge Studies in Fascism and the Far Right
Series editors: Nigel Copsey
Teesside University
and
Graham Macklin,
Center for Research on Extremism (C-REX), University of Oslo

This new book series focuses upon fascist, far right and right-wing politics primarily within a historical context but also drawing on insights from other disciplinary perspectives. Its scope also includes radical-right populism, cultural manifestations of the far right and points of convergence and exchange with the mainstream and traditional right.

Titles include:

The Far Right and the Environment
Politics, Discourse and Communication
Edited by Bernhard Forchtner

Vigilantism against Migrant and Minorities
Edited by Tore Bjørgo and Miroslav Mareš

Trumping Democracy
From Ronald Reagan to Alt-Right
Edited by Chip Berlet

A.K. Chesterton and the Evolution of Britain's Extreme Right, 1933–1973
Luke LeCras

Cumulative Extremism
A Comparative Historical Analysis
Alexander J. Carter

CasaPound Italia
Contemporary Extreme-Right Politics
Caterina Froio, Pietro Castelli Gattinara, Giorgia Bulli and Matteo Albanese

The International Alt-Right
Fascism for the 21st Century?
Patrik Hermansson, David Lawrence, Joe Mulhall and Simon Murdoch

Failed Führers
A History of Britain's Extreme Right
Graham Macklin

Failed Führers
A History of Britain's Extreme Right

Graham Macklin

LONDON AND NEW YORK

First published 2020
by Routledge
2 Park Square, Milton Park, Abingdon, Oxon OX14 4RN

and by Routledge
52 Vanderbilt Avenue, New York, NY 10017

Routledge is an imprint of the Taylor & Francis Group, an informa business

© 2020 Graham Macklin

The right of Graham Macklin to be identified as author of this work has been asserted by him in accordance with sections 77 and 78 of the Copyright, Designs and Patents Act 1988.

All rights reserved. No part of this book may be reprinted or reproduced or utilised in any form or by any electronic, mechanical, or other means, now known or hereafter invented, including photocopying and recording, or in any information storage or retrieval system, without permission in writing from the publishers.

Trademark notice: Product or corporate names may be trademarks or registered trademarks, and are used only for identification and explanation without intent to infringe.

British Library Cataloguing-in-Publication Data
A catalogue record for this book is available from the British Library

Library of Congress Cataloging-in-Publication Data
Names: Macklin, Graham, author.
Title: Failed führers : a history of Britain's extreme right / Graham Macklin.
Other titles: History of Britain's extreme right /
Description: Abingdon, Oxon ; New York : Routledge, 2020. | Series: Fascism and the far right | Includes bibliographical references and index. |
Identifiers: LCCN 2019052974 | ISBN 9780415627290 (hardback) | ISBN 9780415627306 (paperback) | ISBN 9781315697093 (ebook)
Subjects: LCSH: Fascists–Great Britain–Biography. | Right-wing extremists–Great Britain–Biography. | Right-wing extremists–Great Britain–History–20th century. | Fascism–Great Britain–History–20th century. | Great Britain–Race relations. | Great Britain–Politics and government–20th century.
Classification: LCC HN400.R3 M33 2020 | DDC 320.53/3–dc23
LC record available at https://lccn.loc.gov/2019052974

ISBN: 9780415627290 (hbk)
ISBN: 9780415627306 (pbk)
ISBN: 9781315697093 (ebk)

Typeset in Times New Roman
by Wearset, Boldon, Tyne and Wear

For Catherine

Contents

	Acknowledgements	x
	Introduction	1
1	Arnold Leese: The 'anti-jewish' camel doctor	22
2	Sir Oswald Mosley: From 'Britain First' to 'Europe-a-Nation'	92
3	A.K. Chesterton: From 'Fascist Revolutionary' to 'Jew-wise' conspiracy theorist	179
4	Colin Jordan: Dreaming of the Nazi 'Vanguard'	257
5	John Tyndall: In pursuit of the 'Anglo-Saxon Reich'	346
6	Nick Griffin: From the 'Third Position' to anti-Muslim 'populism'… and back again	435
	Conclusion	546
	Select bibliography	559
	Index	563

Acknowledgements

This book like almost every other is the product of collective endeavour. Whilst my name appears on the cover, I would not have completed it – indeed, I nearly did not – without the unstinting support and assistance of my family, friends and colleagues all of whom have helped me see the project through from its initial conception to final publication.

First and foremost, I must acknowledge the generous financial support of the Leverhulme Trust, who saw merit in the idea and granted me an Early Career Fellowship which enabled me to conduct much of the initial research underpinning the book. The initial funds provided by the Leverhulme Trust have since been augmented by a much-valued travel scholarship provided by the Foundation for Canadian Studies in the UK, for which I would like to thank its secretary Rick Bastani for providing me with the funds to undertake some invaluable research and experience a memorable trip to Canada.

I have been lucky enough to work alongside and become friends with a good many scholars at the various institutions in which I have worked over the years. Emeritus Professor Colin Holmes, whom I first met as an undergraduate, has given me invaluable long-term support and encouragement. Professor Nigel Copsey has been similarly supportive over the *longue durée*. Administrative happenstance resulted in my sharing an office for several years with Joel Busher, whose keen insight and friendship were immensely beneficial to my scholarship at a point in time when my interest in continuing an academic career was at a low ebb.

I have profited immeasurably from conversations with, and reading the work of, numerous academics, researchers, journalists and activists over the years including Cynthia Miller-Idriss, Hilary Pilkington, Fabian Virchow, Francis Beckett, Roger Griffin, Richard Thurlow, Tony Kushner, Barbara Rosenbaum, Jeff Bale, Martin Langebach, Jan Raabe, Daniel Koehler, Spencer Sunshine, Paul Jackson, Graeme Atkinson, Kim Knott, Matthew Francis, Ben Lee, Steve Woodbridge, Andrea Mammone, Gareth Harris and Donald Holbrook. David Baker, Roger Eatwell, Nigel Copsey and Kevin Coogan provided extremely valuable feedback on the final manuscript, though any mistakes are of course my own.

My former colleagues at Huddersfield University, Shaun McDaid and Professor Paul Thomas, went beyond the call of duty in their personal and professional support. So too did my Teesside colleagues, Ultán Gillen, Linsey Robb and Margaret Hems, who went out of their way to help me more than once. The Center for Research on Extremism (C-REX), at the University of Oslo, has provided me with an invigorating intellectual environment and peerless academic support (as well as politely putting up with me as I mangle the Norwegian language). I am particularly thankful to Tore Bjørgo, Anders Ravik Jupkås, Dagfinn Hagen, Pietro Castelli Gattinara, Jacob Ravndal, Eviane Leidig, Birgitte Haanshuus, Johannes Due Enstad, Cathrine Moe Thorleifsson, Catarina Froio, Lars Erik Bernstein, Astrid

Hauge Rambøl, Nina Høy-Peterson, Iris Beau Segers, Katrine Fangen, Rita Augestad Knudsen, Thomas Hegghammer, Elisabetta Cassina Wolf, Jørgen Axelson, Sofia Lygren, Yngvild Storli and last, but not least, Terje Emberland. Cas Mudde and Duncan McDonnell on their visits to C-REX both gave me timely words of encouragement, which I took to heart.

Archivists are the historian's best friend and this book would undoubtedly be the poorer were it not for their assistance. To my friends and former colleagues in the National Archives at Kew, I owe an ongoing debt. Karen Astwood, secretary of PHANZA was pivotal in helping me gain access to A.N. Field's papers in New Zealand whilst Daniel Jones of the Searchlight archive at the University of Northampton has been similarly helpful tracking down sources. Nor can one ignore the contribution given by a range of others in this regard. Martin Durham, Dan Trilling, Ryan Schaffer, Jess Chandler, Joe Mulhall, Alex Carter, Liam Liburd, Evan Smith and Pablo del Hierro all provided me with references I would never otherwise have found. Guy Walters also provided an extremely timely tip-off about the release of Werner Naumann's MI5 files.

For the historian, unearthing and reconstructing the extremist careers of secretive figures operating furtively and often clandestinely at the political margins of society can resemble an exercise in archaeology, reminiscent of A.J.A. Symons' *The Quest for Corvo*. There is, however, considerably more empirical evidence available lying closer to the surface than one might suppose. This study has benefited from toiling away in public archives on both sides of the Atlantic for several years, but I have also been lucky enough to gain access to several unique collections of private personal papers hitherto untapped by historians. I am very grateful to the late Kevan Bleach for granting me access to his personal archive relating to the British extreme right and for his insight into the personalities of those he knew. James Mason provided me with access to George Lincoln Rockwell's personal papers years before he publicly deposited them at the University of Kansas, where other researchers can now access them too. The willingness of nearly all the activists I approached for an interview, or have corresponded with over the years whilst researching this study, to discuss their recollections with me has also been beneficial to my understanding and I thank them for their time.

My editor at Routledge, Craig Fowlie, told me over drinks one evening that his own boss had once informed him that any editor thanked by an author in the acknowledgements for his/her 'patience' should be sacked. At the risk of costing Craig his job, I have marvelled at his forbearance as deadlines repeatedly came and went with a certain grim inevitability. I also owe Craig a huge debt for his advice, insight and friendship, not just whilst writing this book but on numerous other projects as well. Having taken an inordinate amount of time to deliver a much longer than originally agreed manuscript to him, the following paraphrased quote, often attributed to Blaise Pascal, feels apt by way of an apology: 'If I had more time, I would have written a shorter book.'

I would also like to thank Thérèse Wassily Saba, my copy editor and therefore an unsung hero, whose keen attention to detail in the final stages has helped to iron out some grammatical quirks that otherwise would have gone unnoticed.

I could not have asked for a better group of friends and their contribution has been no less important than that of my academic family and, of course, there is some overlap: Malcolm; Barney and Emily; Owen and Sarah; Christine and Jake; Shaun and Ania; Stevie and Susie; Polly; Alice; Duncan; Piers and Etala; Tom and Maria Laura; Catherine and Ian; Sara and Connor; Christine and Martin. Without their support, I probably would not have finished this book, or in all probability stuck with an academic career. Nowhere is this truer than the unfailing support and encouragement of my parents Hilary and Roger without whom I would not be where I am now. The same goes for my brothers, Stephen and Brian. This last sentence of the acknowledgements has been the hardest one of the whole book to write because I suddenly realise I have no absolutely idea how to put into words how unbelievably grateful I am to my best friend, Catherine, for putting up with this book (and me) for what must have seemed like an absolute eternity. 'Thank you' doesn't come close...

Introduction

This book details the ideological and strategic evolution of British fascism from its roots in the extreme right-wing and anti-Semitic *demi-monde* in the aftermath of the First World War, through a range of political parties and movements, to its present-day incarnations. While this volume does excavate unexplored areas of the British fascist tradition and draws, in multiple places, upon a raft of previously unseen archival sources, it makes no claims to being a comprehensive history. Instead of adopting the synoptic overview of previous classic historical accounts in the field,[1] the present study traces continuity and change within the British fascist tradition through a collective biographical approach, focusing upon the political careers of six principal ideologues and leaders: Arnold Leese (1878–1956), Sir Oswald Mosley (1896–1980), A.K. Chesterton (1899–1973), Colin Jordan (1923–2009), John Tyndall (1934–2005) and Nick Griffin (1959–).

These six biographical chapters, which can be read individually, or collectively, to illuminate the multifaceted nature of British fascism as it has evolved since the 1920s, pay particularly close attention to the transnational perspective that these individuals took both with regard their ideological visions but also in respect of their political organising too. The first chapter explores the 'Jew-wise' politicking of Arnold Leese – undoubtedly the UK's only self-proclaimed 'anti-Jewish camel doctor' – who led the Imperial Fascist League, a tiny but virulent pro-Nazi grouplet during the inter-war years. Although Leese was always a marginal political figure in the 1930s, his blend of rabid anti-Semitism, Nazi Nordicism and anti-Black racism had an outsized influence upon post-war generations of self-described 'racial nationalists' – a term which will be described in greater detail below. Chapter 2 examines the political career of Sir Oswald Mosley, a man reviled by Leese as a 'Kosher fascist'. Mosley led the British Union of Fascists (BUF), the pre-eminent fascist movement in inter-war Britain, the name of which he changed in 1937 to the British Union of Fascists and National Socialists to better reflect his own growing pro-Nazi stance. As discussed in more detail below, the existing historiography of British fascism has concentrated disproportionately on Mosley and the BUF.[2] This chapter focuses instead largely upon Mosley's post-war career as he transitioned from a straightforward 'Britain First' nationalism to the idea of 'Europe-a-Nation' which represented an ultimately unsuccessful attempt to redefine the parameters of the fascist vision for a post-fascist world.

Chapter 3 investigates the activities of A.K. Chesterton, one of Mosley's most vituperative anti-Jewish propagandists during the 1930s, who developed a career after 1945 as an internationally influential anti-Semitic conspiracy theorist. Chesterton held fast to the 'Britain First' credo of the BUF, carrying its torch forward through to the formation of the National Front in 1966. Chapter 4 surveys the career of the 'neo-Nazi godfather' Colin Jordan who evolved from being a 'Jew-wise' racial nationalist, like his mentor, Arnold

2 *Introduction*

Leese, to formulating a pan-Aryan 'universal' idea of Nazism that rejected the 'narrow' nationalism of the inter-war years altogether. Chapter 5 examines the life of John Tyndall, an ardent national socialist revolutionary who, having split from Jordan, espoused a mélange of racial nationalist ideas derived from Mosley and Chesterton, aimed at promoting a 'British' form of National Socialism. Within the extreme right milieu, Tyndall was one of its more notable political organisers, serving twice as National Front (NF) chairman, before founding the British National Party (BNP) in 1982. Chapter 6 concludes with an examination of the political career of Nick Griffin, a young racial nationalist who cut his teeth in Tyndall's NF, sticking with the group following its collapse in 1979, to become a leading light in its revolutionary nationalist 'political soldier' faction during the 1980s. Griffin established a reputation for himself as an ideological hardliner and voluble Holocaust denier, leading Tyndall to court him to join the BNP, a decision he was to rue. Griffin succeeded Tyndall as BNP leader in 1999, helped 'modernise' the party and embraced anti-Muslim racial 'populism', which helped propel the BNP to become the most successful racial nationalist organisation in British history before it politically imploded in 2010.

Methodology

Historians once regarded the biographical approach as somewhat unfashionable, many harbouring an ambivalent stance towards the genre, at best. Indeed, as one symposium on 'Historians and Biography' observed a decade ago, biography is the profession's 'unloved stepchild', often viewed as a 'lesser form of history' or a 'degraded form of historical writing'. This reasoning rests, in part, upon a common misapprehension that biography interprets the role of the individual in history as being, 'the only intellectual and analytical center of the argument.' This is rarely the case, however. Historians, generally speaking, use biography to explore the wider political, social, cultural and moral universe their subjects occupy and the two interact and illuminate one another.[3] Previous biographies of British fascists, and on Fascism and Nazism more generally, have provided keen insight into the individuals themselves and, arguably, some of the most sophisticated analysis of how the competing power bases of those 'working towards the Führer' ultimately energised the horrors of the Third Reich.[4] Biography serves us here as an analytical prism through which the broader ideological and organisational contours of the British fascist tradition, as it has evolved over the course of several generations, are refracted. This methodological approach has several distinct advantages, not least of which is to address the following lament:

> While scholars studying extreme right movements recently complained how less attention is paid to the ideology of these movements in contrast to the development of classificatory and explanatory models, even less attention is paid to those individuals who subscribe to, at times formulate and promote this ideology.[5]

This study seeks to redress this. In doing so, it also seeks to provide a broader contextual contemplation of the individuals who articulated and disseminated these ideas and the wider political environment in which they did so, whilst also focusing upon the political actions that resulted from those choices. As Sir Richard Evans observed in his magisterial history of the Third Reich, 'academic authors paint a somewhat bloodless, almost abstract picture of the Nazis, as if the theories and debates about them were more important than the people themselves.' Like Evans, this work, endeavours 'to put individuals back into the picture'[6] in order to give a fuller understanding of those promoting and producing the extreme right ideologies around which groups have mobilised.

Adopting a collective biographical approach – prosopography[7] – also offers a means of reinserting human agency into the broader structural explanations of history. Focusing on the role of these individuals within the broader racial nationalist milieu can help illuminate the broader historical processes which they helped to shape and which shaped them.[8] Historians recognise that people and parties are not simply hostages to fortune, buffeted by impersonal socio-economic 'drivers' without any means of recourse or redress. This is not to dismiss the salience of these factors. They are vital, of course, but so too is the need for a historically grounded approach that embeds individual actors, and the decisions and strategies they enact in pursuit of their political agendas, within this wider, structural context.[9] Karl Marx's oft-repeated aphorism succinctly summarises this interplay between human agency, impersonal structure and the burden of history:

> Men make their own history, but they do not make it just as they please; they do not make it under circumstances chosen by themselves, but under circumstances directly encountered, given, and transmitted from the past. The tradition of all the dead generations weighs like a nightmare on the brain of the living.[10]

Structuring the book in this manner, instead of adopting a more straightforward chronological approach to the history of British fascism, has several distinct analytical advantages.[11] Whilst acknowledging the collective biographical approach represents an artificial literary conceit, disaggregating these various ideologues avoids reifying British fascism as a monolithic tradition under a single leadership, since it illuminates the heterodox nature of fascist thought, a plurality erased by presenting fascism or 'right-wing extremism' as a uniform or indeed unitary phenomenon.[12] Highlighting the personal and political cleavages that have proliferated across its fractious and fissiparous history not only provides a sharper appreciation of how, and when, such conflicts have contributed to the political, organisational and tactical evolution of British fascism, but also emphasises that it was never a singular, homogenous social movement in the first place.[13] The prosopographic approach facilitates the elucidation of these nuances.

The collective biographical framework adopted by this study also refocuses our attention on the role of human agency within extreme right movements, something that is writ large within small *groupuscular* organisations. It also highlights that, above and beyond fomenting division – since human agency can also particularly destructive within miniscule political formations – individual activists, and the groups they form, are capable of adapting their ideologies to external circumstance (and, of course, their own personal peccadilloes), all the while remaining faithful to fascism's non-negotiable racial nationalist core. Whilst emphasising the ideological continuity of the milieu, the current work also establishes the central role of these ideologues and their activities in its perpetuation and longevity.[14] Indeed, whilst the book's structure serves to highlight the dynamic trajectories undertaken by these individuals over time and illuminates the broader ideological arc of their personal political development, it also seeks to locate their role in the evolution of the wider movement. This allows for a more detailed examination of the different strategies adopted by extreme right activists and the tensions between the 'mainstreamers' – who focus on legal, non-violent and electoral strategies – and the 'vanguardists' who take an extra-parliamentary approach often involving violence and illegality.[15]

Finally, this collective biographical approach addresses a glaring structural imbalance within the historiography of British fascism itself, which is virtually synonymous with the politics and personality of Oswald Mosley. Whilst understandable, this distorts our understanding of the movement's wider history.[16] Within this historiography, there is also a tendency within the literature towards personification, arguably borne out in the current work too. More to the point, many historians have tended to study the BUF precisely because it was the vehicle upon which Mosley squandered his supposedly considerable political talents: fascism as personal tragedy. This narrative, of wasted intellect squandered on gutter politics, has continued to endure though it obscures as much about British fascism as it reveals. Mosley was, of course, pivotal during the inter-war period but he was not always the most important or influential figure thereafter. Studying the pilot fish can tell us much about the whale and by situating Mosley alongside his political contemporaries, and their successors, – though he and his followers would baulk at such comparison – this book also provides a clearer understanding of Mosley's overall place within the British fascist pantheon.

Moving away from focusing solely upon Mosley, particularly during the inter-war period, also helps us to recalibrate our understanding of British fascism's periodisation. During the 1930s, Mosley's anti-fascist opponents mocked his movement's symbol, the flash and circle – symbolically depicting 'unity in action' – as a 'flash in the pan'.[17] In a wider historical sense, this was true. The BUF lasted a mere eight years: from 1932 to 1940. Yet despite the ultimately ephemeral nature of British fascism during the 'devil's decade', the historiography remains disproportionately weighted towards these eight years. Post-war British fascism has lasted over seventy years and is deserving of more scholarly interrogation.[18]

The current study extends the temporal frame of reference to encompass a full century of British fascism, with the caveat that the chapter on Mosley is weighted towards his post-1945 activities since these are lesser known. Although this study begins in the aftermath of the First World War, a conflict in which Leese, Mosley and Chesterton all served, this is not to imply that British fascism experienced the ideological equivalent of a virgin birth in 1918. There were many pre-war ideological and political tributaries that gradually coalesced into a body of thought that underpinned what became British fascist 'doctrine' during the early 1920s. Adumbrating the contours of British fascism's intellectual antecedents during the Edwardian era – social Darwinism, racism, eugenics, imperialism and jingoistic nationalism to name but a few – is beyond the scope of this study, though it would undoubtedly enhance our understanding of British fascism's domestic roots, which are often obscured by claims that it was little more than a foreign 'import'. That said, it is equally important not to downplay the radicalising effect that the contagious encounter with Italian Fascism and German National Socialism had upon native British fascists either. It is perhaps enough to remark at this juncture that the study of British fascism awaits its own Zeev Sternhell, whose work diligently traces 'proto-fascist' precursors in pre-1914 France.[19]

Having highlighted the analytic advantages of narrating British fascism's history through a biographical frame, it would be remiss not to issue a few caveats. It is hopefully already apparent that this is not a study of Thomas Carlyle's 'great men' bending history to their will, a viewpoint popular, for readily apparent reasons, with the fascists themselves.[20] If anything, it is the complete opposite – a narrative of marginal political actors vainly resisting the broader arc of global history. Nor is the focus upon 'leaders' intended as a definitive statement on the methodological prism through which we should understand British fascism not least because, as Paxton sagely observed of the 1930s: 'The image of the all-powerful dictator personalizes fascism, and creates the false impression that we can understand it fully by scrutinizing the leader alone.'[21] This observation is no less true regarding the post-war period. Furthermore, privileging the role played by these six leading ideologues risks mythologising the supposed centrality of their 'leadership' and, in doing so, crowding others off the stage, though, in keeping with Evan's injunction, I have endeavoured to locate these individual biographies within their social and political contexts.

In focusing upon these six ideologues, one might rightfully enquire whether there were other figures worthy of inclusion. Whilst the figures here are ideologues rather than intellectuals – a crucial distinction – there a number of elitist and anti-democratic thinkers, particularly Anthony Ludovici, who might have been considered for inclusion were it not for the fact that, despite the similarity of their core ideas, they personally never crossed the Rubicon to embrace fascism. Indeed such 'neo-Tories' – the intellectual counterparts of the Conservative Revolutionaries in Germany – viewed British fascism with elitist disdain, regarding it as distinctly plebeian. Sir Charles Petrie's remarks, after attending Mosley's 1934 Albert Hall meeting, were emblematic of the collective attitude of these neo-Tories: 'I agreed with about half he said, but the whole thing was very cheap and went against the grain with me.'[22] Indeed, despite their own marked sympathies for Nazism and Fascism, not to mention Franco's Spain, many 'neo-Tories' also viewed 'British fascism' as thoroughly 'un-British'.[23] This did not mean that their own contempt for liberal democracy was any less reactionary or that their panaceas were any less 'revolutionary' in intent. Indeed, as Stanley Payne observed 'The radical right ... often differed from fascism not by being more moderate, but simply by being more rightist'.[24]

Nor are the 'blood and soil' ruralists like William Sanderson, Viscount Lymington, Rolf Gardiner or Henry Williamson, subjected to in-depth scrutiny, despite their ecological preoccupations being an important tributary to British fascism, largely because they themselves did not lead 'political' organisations of any great note.[25] Perhaps the most obvious omission are the 'race thinkers' Roger Pearson and Robert Gayre – both of whom do feature, albeit only in passing, since neither man led a political movement and, moreover, because their efforts to resurrect 'scientific racism' after 1945 really requires a separate study.[26] Were this a study of the wider far right of British politics, particularly its anti-Muslim fringe, then figures like Stephen Yaxley-Lennon ('Tommy Robinson'), the former leader of the English Defence League (EDL), might conceivably qualify for inclusion but have been excluded from this study on the grounds that, whatever else they might be, they are not racial nationalists.[27]

Whilst consisting of six inter-related and interlocking biographies, the individual is neither the sole unit of analysis nor the interest of this study. The book makes no effort to illuminate the inner recesses of their interior lives or characters, addressing their personal lives only insofar as they have political consequences (or vice versa) or because it reveals something of note about the milieu they inhabit. Those seeking psychological insights will also be disappointed since this is neither a study of the 'authoritarian personality' nor 'charismatic leadership'. With the exception of Mosley,[28] most of these activists were notably absent this vital political ingredient, even though they undoubtedly possessed a measure of 'coterie charisma' necessary to weld together disparate groups of activists into something approaching a coherent political movement.[29]

Whilst this study utilises collective biography to chart the variegated ideological and strategic development of the fascist tradition, 'ideology' itself – defined succinctly as 'a more or less coherent set of ideas that proves the basis for organized political action, whether this is intended to preserve, modify or overthrow the existing system of power'[30] – is not without contestation. Indeed, scholars have failed to agree amongst themselves about its salience. In one corner, there are those who argue that British fascism was of interest precisely because it possessed a well-developed ideology compared to that of other minor European fascisms.[31] In the other, are those exemplified by solicitor advocate Anthony Julius who disparages British fascists as having

> contributed nothing to the understanding of their times; they included no thinkers or strategists of distinction or even mediocrity; there was nothing original or even engaging in their programmes; they produced nothing of political or cultural value; their newsletters and pamphlets were dreary, somewhat hysterical and most of all just *wrong* about the events they reported.[32]

There is merit in both viewpoints since they are not as contradictory as they first appear, though Julius ignores the essential point that ideas do not have to be 'original' or 'right' and still less of political and cultural 'value' for them to be adopted by, and believed in, by scores of people and *ergo* worthy of study. His comments reflect the wider perception of British fascism as a 'failure' – which, comparatively speaking, it self-evidently was. Space precludes rehashing why British fascism remained the 'ugly duckling'.[33] Suffice to say that even British fascism's own tacticians have understood their political tradition as a failure. 'So for the twenty years following the war', wrote one, looking back upon the past with a grimace, 'nationalism had not much to show for itself, save a few punch ups at Trafalgar Square, the odd riot, several unsuccessful electoral forays and a brace of convictions for sub-revolutionary activity'.[34]

'Ideology' evolves – not in a political vacuum – but in response to a dynamic interplay between ideologues and their followers and external circumstances that condition the choices and decisions they make regarding what points of ideology to emphasise and the strategies to employ to take advantage of perceived political opportunities. Whilst each of the ideologues discussed in the book were the official arbiters of orthodoxy within their respective movements, this is not to suggest that they espoused a finished 'ideology'. Even for these leading luminaries, 'ideology' came into focus only *after* they joined or formed political organisations, and, as these biographical case studies highlight, it continued to evolve thereafter.[35] One also needs to be mindful that fascism's followers and fellow travellers did not imbibe the 'official' ideology espoused by fascist leaders and ideologues without questioning it; there was dissent and disagreement, splits and fragmentation, as well as convergence and agreement. Nor can we take for granted that followers understood ideas and 'ideology' in the same fashion as did ideologues or indeed that it always 'mattered' in the same way, or at the same time, throughout the course of an activist's political career. This is not to imply a disjuncture between 'official' and 'unofficial' ideological interpretations. It is merely to suggest that activists who rallied to the fascist standard might have been attracted less by the finer points of the arcane, esoteric disputes about racial genealogy, Mendelian genetic inheritance or the Indo-European 'origins' of the 'Aryan' race, and more by the blunt, vulgar, racist messaging of fascist propaganda and its violent panaceas.[36] This is not necessarily a startlingly original observation. The 'esoteric' and 'exoteric' nature of fascist ideologies, arising from the 'conflict between ideological purity and the desire for a mass basis,' has long been evident to scholars.[37]

Whilst ideology defines the parameters of the group – and its enemies – 'ideology' in and of itself was not always the reason people joined, or remained active, in such groups. An apocryphal anecdote regarding Charlie Watts, a leading BUF activist, attests to this point. A young enthusiastic fascist he had recently recruited was once badgering Watts with political questions but was becoming increasing frustrated by Watts' terse responses. Pressed for his thoughts on Mosley's seminal tract, *The Greater Britain* (1932), the philosophical cornerstone of BUF ideology, Watts finally blurted out 'I don't know. I've never read it, I might disagree.'[38] Clearly, 'ideology' was of secondary importance even to some of those at the forefront of fascist movements which can prioritise 'feeling' and 'emotion' above intellect and thought, not to mention physical action over contemplation, though Mosley believed he could synthesise the two as the 'Thought-Deed Man'. Indeed 'ideology' also offers us limited insight into the dynamics of such groups, their social base or indeed their voters, many of whom were by no means 'fascist'.[39]

A fascist minimum?

There have been a number of productive scholarly debates in recent times which have attempted to define 'fascism' as a generic phenomenon but, as these are not the main focus of this book, they will only be discussed briefly here.[40] Amongst the most profitable approaches to defining fascism as a generic, ideal type, was the one pioneered by Roger Griffin who defined it as 'a genus of political ideology whose mythic core in its various permutations is a palingenetic form of populist ultranationalism' though, given the differences between 'populism' and 'fascism' as ideologies, his choice of the word 'populist' as a definitional feature compounded rather than relieved conceptual confusion.[41] That said, Griffin's core point, that the 'palingenetic myth' – a revival of the Greek term 'palingenesis' meaning rebirth of recreation – sat at the heart of fascism has been hugely influential. Roger Eatwell adopted a broadly analogous definition, albeit one which placed more emphasis on economic ideology and less on 'political religion', explaining fascism as an ideology that strives for 'social rebirth in order to forge a holistic-national radical Third Way.'[42] Regardless of their differences, however, both definitions capture the central notion of national rebirth and resurrection at the heart of fascism's nebulous promise.

All revolutionary movements contain within them such millenarian desires, however, what makes fascism distinctive is that 'it projects palingenetic longings onto the *nation*, conceived as an organic or racial entity.'[43] For many scholars, it was the intoxicating ideological synthesis of ultra-nationalism *with* 'palingenesis' that constituted the 'Fascist minimum' – the ideological essence of the phenomenon when shorn of its temporal trappings.[44] Griffin, in particular, argued for this method of philosophical abstraction as a means of identifying fascism as an 'ideal type'. Elaborating an ideal type is not the same as attempting to provide a definitive, *essentialist* statement about what fascism was, or is, in accordance with a 'template' or checklist of qualities since this produces only ossification. Instead, an 'ideal type' allows us to conceive of the liminal, fluid, aspects of fascist ideology – its core myths – which are not temporally bound, thereby allowing for the possibility that fascism does not have to return with the same external features for it to be recognised or understood as 'fascism'.[45]

Diffuse national contexts generate different forms of palingenetic myth since each has its own forms of 'nationalism' and nationalist readings of history, which further complicates the quest for a 'generic' fascism. British fascists, for their part, evolved their own specific understanding of the centrality of 'race' to their own national 'palingenesis' – national rebirth *was* racial rebirth and vice versa. Reflecting upon British fascism's ideological plurality, it is important to note, however, that insofar as racial biological determinism suffused myths of national rebirth, it did not animate everyone equally, in the same way, or indeed at the same time. Most notably, Mosley stood outside this tradition.[46] Race was also less of an all-consuming obsession for A.K. Chesterton, for whom the 'Menace of the Money Power' was the overarching concern. In terms of the political action that flowed from racial ideology, this was a question of degrees; since 'race' was a point of increasing ideological and political convergence around which all fascist and extreme right-wing groups coalesced from the 1950s onwards albeit underpinned by a conspiratorial anti-Semitism which, to a greater or lesser degree, was shared by all six political actors discussed here.

Post-war fascism?

It should be noted at this juncture that over seventy-five years after the military defeat of Fascism and Nazism historians remain deeply divided about whether 'fascism' continued to exist after 1945. Many historians of inter-war fascist history have refused to concede that fascism had any meaning or relevance beyond its 'epochal' significance. Ernst Nolte's *Der Faschismus in Seiner Epoche* (1963) set the stage, arguing that although a fascist residue had survived 1945, 'it cannot be said to have any real significance as far as the image of the era is concerned unless the term be stripped almost entirely of its traditional connotation.'[47] Fascism generated 'a world-historical moment' but that 'moment' has now 'passed'. Fascism was 'defeated, dead and buried' after 1945.[48] Any post-war recrudescence either was not 'fascism' at all or represented a 'mere coda'.[49]

The 'Age of Fascism' is over, that much is both incontestable and obvious. In Britain, the fascist 'epoch' was over rather sooner than elsewhere. May 1940 constituted the historical caesura – internment was the 'watershed' moment that halted British fascism to five years before National Socialism's own *Götterdämmerung* in 1945. Fascism, so the argument goes, cannot be understood, let alone adequately theorised outside of the unique conjuncture of structural conditions during the inter-war period that rendered it politically and historically significant. Those 'epochal' conditions ceased to exist after 1945. No historian worth his or her salt would argue otherwise. No phenomenon are supra-historical, however. Although post-war fascism lacks the broader economic and existential crisis from which it derived its 'significance' during the inter-war period, this does not mean that post-war variants have ceased to be 'fascism' simply because they now languish at the margins of European societies rather than occupying the central position they once did.

Ironically, there is far less resistance to conceptualising the periodisation of fascism's genesis *backwards* from 1919. Indeed, Sternhell has argued persuasively that: 'Fascism belonged not just to the interwar period but to the whole period of history that began with the modernization of the European continent at the end of the nineteenth century.'[50] If considering the 'roots' of Fascism and Nazism before 1919 is generally accepted, why then does treating fascism's continued survival, evolution and mutation, beyond the defeat of its regimes in 1945, as part of the same historical continuum, meet with disapproval? Jeffrey Bale detects a certain academic myopia in this regard, asserting the 'empirically incontestable observation' that:

> [A]lmost all of those scholars who eventually opted to devote the bulk of their own time and energy to researching neo-fascism had previously spent several years studying historic fascism, whereas most of the leading experts on classical fascism in Europe have spent little or no time studying its postwar (or extra European) variants and manifestations.[51]

Kallis argues for a 'qualified epochal' conception of fascism, acknowledging its significance within a specific, historical context, whilst granting that the 'general ideological current [which] gave birth to inter-war fascism has lingered on after the latter's demise, in the same way that it had predated it, long before the very term "fascism" had acquired any historic meaning.'[52] Less rigid categorisation seems eminently sensible, though doubtless the dispute will endure.

Roberts argues that conceptually stretching 'fascism' to encompass post-war phenomena dilutes its meaning and diminishes its historical importance. This is a valid point but by locking the correct application of the term 'fascism' within its epochal era, one runs the risk of legitimising the strategies of those contemporary organisations and parties who are deliberately decoupling their politics from the moral stigma of 'fascism' as a means of retaining and rehabilitating its central ideas.[53] Symptomatic of this decoupling is the refusal of most fascists to actually self-identify publicly as 'fascist' as they had openly done during the 1930s – though there were of course numerous figures who eschewed the term, notably José Antonio (Spain), Corneliu Codreanu (Romania) and Ferenc Szálasi (Hungary).

Latterly, historians of post-war fascism, frustrated by the *historicism* of some of their colleagues, have also had to contend with another issue: the *presentism* of some of their political science brethren who insist on a similar 'ontological distance' between 'historic' fascism and the contemporary 'populist radical right'.[54] Students of historical fascism and the contemporary extreme right are now, perhaps more than ever, 'increasingly distant from one another'.[55] Tracing the continuity between contemporary 'radical right' parties and fascism is not the focus of this study, suffice to say that not all far right groups or radical right 'populist' parties are 'fascist' for, whilst some like the NF and the BNP are a part of that tradition, others, like UKIP within a British context, were devoid of fascism's historical baggage and, moreover, its 'palingenetic' myth.[56]

This disciplinary disjuncture has led to scholars talking past one another; historians viewing post-war permutations of fascism through the prism of continuity with the inter-war years whilst political scientists, working within shorter time-frames, have adopted various neologisms to classify what they perceive as a quantifiably 'new' phenomenon.[57] 'Of course,' argues Copsey,

> it would be wrong to trace the ideological tradition of the contemporary extreme right only to fascism. But temporally focused on the present-day, political scientists are drawn far too readily to novelty, and pay insufficient attention to ways in which contemporary fascists recalibrate, conceal and supplement their fascism in the 'post-fascist' era … such an approach threatens to consign fascism to a museum.[58]

Recidivists or radicals: 'neo'-fascism?

On 4 July 1941, David Petrie, the Director-General of MI5, mused that although British fascism had been temporarily crippled,

> it is unlikely that it will not again raise its head with, maybe, some considerable difference in its slogans and outward trappings, though little in its essentially dangerous and subversive tendencies. There is a curious continuity in subversive and revolutionary movements and little ever occurs that cannot, somehow or other, be linked up with something that has gone before.[59]

Four years *before* the military destruction of Fascism and Nazism, Petrie's prescient observation anticipated post-war fascism as part of a fluid continuum. In the immediate aftermath of the war, journalists and anti-fascists alike also perceived the recrudescence of fascists and fascism, not as some historical disjuncture, but in terms of its direct connection to the pre-war period. In the British context 'neo-fascist' appeared in print almost immediately. *Fascism Inside England* (1946), authored by Frederic Mullally, an assistant editor of *Tribune*, was perhaps the first book to refer to the 'neo-fascist movement' in his survey of British fascism, written as Mosley's minions re-emerged in London's East End after the war. Mullally adopted the phrase to underwrite the continuity of the tradition rather than its disjuncture, however.[60]

Since then, however, the 'neo' prefix has become shorthand for distinguishing post-war fascism from its inter-war parent. Walter Laqueur accepted the notion of continuity inherent within the term but remarked upon its syntactic imbalance since '*neo* makes it clear that it is not identical with historical fascism, but *fascist* is the stronger part of the definition.' The two periods were nowhere near to being of same order of magnitude he felt compelled to point out, addressing the epochal debate.[61] Not everyone could see profit in utilising such terminology, however. A. James Gregor contemptuously dismisses 'neo-fascism' altogether since he finds it to be devoid of meaning.[62] From a different angle, political scientists have also largely dispensed with the term on the grounds that it no longer accurately described the 'radical' or 'extreme right' populist parties which had abandoned the fascist legacy by the 1980s, it was argued.[63]

Whilst historians and political scientists remain at odds terminologically, albeit for different reasons, few scholars have sought to clarify or elaborate upon what 'neo-fascism' might actually mean or indeed be. For political scientist Roger Karapin 'neo-fascist parties' were those 'which, in the post-war period, have substantially fascist goals and organizing methods.'[64] Whilst numerous parties have indeed continued to adhere to 'fascist goals' none have been able to rely upon the unbridled paramilitary violence characteristic of fascist 'organizing methods' during the 1930s. Roger Griffin has elaborated a more nuanced tripartite typology, subdividing 'post-war fascism' into the following categories: 'nostalgic Fascism/Neo-Nazism' represented by groups seeking to resurrect past movements; 'Mimetic Fascism/Neo-Nazism', that essentially Nazified indigenous traditions; and 'Neo-Fascism', which denoted a substantive modification of past forms. Griffin defines 'neo-fascism' as offering 'something new' with respect to its more ideologically ossified 'nostalgic' and 'mimetic' forms.[65] Stanley Payne found Griffin's taxonomy to be 'lucid and compelling' not to mention 'the only recent general interpretation of fascism in English that also includes a half chapter of analysis of the post-war organisations.' Returning to the question of significance, Payne concluded, however, that it all amounted to little more than a scholarly exercise analogous 'to the classification of obscure Amazonian languages rapidly undergoing extinction' unless of course a 'crisis' of one form or another rendered such doctrines relevant again.[66]

Whilst Griffin's typology is instructive, his definition of 'neo-fascism' is not altogether convincing. It privileges novelty over continuity, resulting from its baseline assumption that 'neo-fascism' was indeed 'offering something new with respect to interwar phenomena'. It is largely for this reason, in relation to the British context, which comprised of various 'nostalgic' and 'mimetic' movements after 1945, that this study eschews the term 'neo-fascism'. By way of self-justification, it is worth briefly exploring the 'new' permutations of post-war fascism that Griffin uses to justify his own ideal-typical subdivision: revolutionary nationalism, crypto-fascism, revisionism and conservative revolution. None of these permutations were 'new'. The emergence of each simply represented the rediscovery and recycling of previous forms of illiberal revolutionary nationalism sidelined by the rise of Hitler and Mussolini, revisited and repurposed by subsequent generations of activists as they struggled to circumnavigate the stigma and odium now attached to 'fascist' ideas. Efforts to fashion an acceptable, alternative form of 'fascist' politics that could be distanced from the self-corruption of fascism's revolutionary promise through accommodation and compromise, and the moral discredit its genocidal tyranny had wrought, was not simply a reaction to the vacuum created by the horrors of Nazism but an attempt to find a useable historical past. This turn towards 'purity' was already apparent as the fascist regimes decayed under the strain of 'total war' and industrialised killing, however. Indeed, the reversion to first principles reflected in the adoption of supposedly 'left-wing' revolutionary nationalism had actually begun with Mussolini's Salò Republic in September 1943 as the doomed dictator sought to put a 'revolutionary' gloss on his status as the Nazis' puppet in Northern Italy.

Nor was there anything particularly 'new' about another of the archetypal attributes of 'neo-fascism', its promulgation of Holocaust denial and historical 'revisionism' not least because it signalled the ongoing centrality of anti-Semitism to the tradition. Again, this development reflected an already extant trajectory. The Nazis themselves were the prototypical Holocaust deniers. Only a month after Mussolini's foundation of the Salò Republic, the Reichsführer-SS, Heinrich Himmler, stood before a gathering of SS officers in Posen in Nazi-occupied Poland on 4 October. Himmler spoke to his men 'quite frankly' about their role in the 'extermination of the Jewish race,' which for him was 'a page of glory in our history which has never been written and is never to be written.'[67] When the Nazis' efforts to annihilate the Jews proved unsuccessful, they turned to obliterating memory of their crimes, dynamiting the gas chambers, emptying the camps and murdering as many of the surviving inmates as possible through mass shootings and 'death marches' before the Allies liberated the camps, thereby publicly exposing the full extent of the Third Reich's perfidy. Therefore, when British fascists began denying the Holocaust, an extension of their interwar activities whitewashing the brutality of Nazism, their effusions paled into insignificance against the Nazis' own efforts to erase the evidence of their crimes.

Continuity in the British fascist tradition

Continuity rather than change also defines the internationalisation of 'neo-fascist' geopolitics which is often emphasised as a 'new' feature of the post-war period though, ironically, for this to be true the birth of 'neo-fascism' would have to be backdated to 1942 when the Third Reich purposefully began re-orientating its propaganda along a 'Europeanist axis'.[68] 'Total war' exacerbated this centrifugal process but even without it, from 1922 onwards, a dizzying array of international entanglements had already left an indelible mark upon interwar fascism and fascists.[69] Internationalisation was never a uniform process, however. Though Mosley was a key advocate for 'Europe-a-Nation' after 1945, his pan-European convocation created domestic tensions. A new generation of activists rejected his efforts to Europeanise fascist politics, which is not to argue that they rejected transnational activism. Similarly, a kaleidoscopic array of conflicting geopolitical panaceas for achieving racial salvation after 1945 existed too. Chesterton and his acolyte John Tyndall both rejected Mosley's vision of Europe as a 'Third Force', believing that Britain's imperial past offered deliverance. Jordan, meanwhile, rejected 'narrow' nationalism altogether in favour of a pan-Aryan Imperium. In terms of scale, Griffin moved to the other end of the spectrum, advocating micro-nationalist federation within a 'Europe of a thousand flags' and a 'new alliance' against neo-liberal globalisation with a variety of despotic regimes including, contemporaneously, Putin's Russia and its Syrian satrap. What underpinned and united each of these seemingly irreconcilable visions was a virulent 'Occidentalism' – a profound antipathy to Western, liberal modernity.[70]

Other scholars, writing in the 1990s, have pointed to the development of a 'concrete' anti-black racism after 1945, as the key differential between 'neo-fascism' and 'classic' inter-war fascism.[71] Insofar as British fascism is concerned, racism directed at people of colour, which played a 'minor role' during the inter-war years, certainly became 'much more significant in the revival of the tradition after the Second World War' since mass immigration amplified its importance.[72] Far from demarcating the two periods, the ongoing centrality of race, racism and anti-Semitism, within the racial nationalist tradition reinforced a seamless continuity. Anti-black racism was not the centrepiece of inter-war British fascist propaganda, eclipsed by an all-pervasive anti-Semitism, but it was certainly an ambient presence. Notions of 'whiteness' and by implication 'non-whiteness' which were 'forged in the crucible of the colonies' were clearly manifest in inter-war fascist propaganda.[73] The racialised imperial nostalgia that saturated such groups was, in part, a reflection of activists' personal experience. Mandle's 1966 study of the BUF leadership observed the prevalence of colonial and military backgrounds amongst the party's leaders, causing its author to remark: 'They roamed the empire and the world finding it less profitable then they had hoped, England less congenial than they wanted, each new job a disappointment.'[74]

Biologically sanctified racial essentialism came to (re)define British fascism's public platform in the post-war period. It was, just as it had been during the inter-war years, a fundamentally bio-political concern from which everything else sprang. 'Race' was not radial or contingent to 'palingenesis' or 'social rebirth' – they were one and the same. The solution to racial degeneracy was seen as its antithesis, racial renewal. The idea of race within fascist cosmology therefore differs from the xenophobic 'nativism' and crude racism that its propagandists seek to mobilise. British fascism's 'folkish' nationalism, although hard to commonly delineate since it varied in conception from ideologue to ideologue, is broadly analogous to the Germanic tradition of '*völkisch* nationalism', which played a pivotal role within Nazism. This had its own brand and style of romantic traditions, racial mysticism and nature worship, and similarly defined the 'people' in terms of an ineffable transcendental 'essence'. This 'essence' might be called 'nature', 'cosmos' or 'mythos', noted George Mosse, 'but in each instance it was fused to man's innermost nature, and represented the source of his creativity, the depth of feeling, his individuality, and his unity with other members of the "Volk".'[75]

Similar to the Germanic tradition, British fascist racial nationalism stressed the importance of 'blood' and of 'thinking with the blood', which provided an apparently insoluble bond linking each individual member to a wider *völkisch* community which simultaneously reached backwards into time immemorial and forward into a racially preordained future.[76] Whilst British fascists in the early twentieth century searched for the 'root' source of *völkisch* origins in an Indo-European 'Aryan' past, contemporaneously they searched for it through genetics, highlighting a similar obsession with points of origin in the hope of discovering the pure source of racial identity, undefiled and unsullied by materialistic modernity. This quest for racial purity harked back to a mythical moment in history when man – or more precisely the 'white man' – was not only supposedly racially 'pure' but also lived in a state of grace, where there was a mystical, organic union, of blood and soil and of man and nature. This atavistic utopia existed before capitalism, industrialisation, urbanisation, globalisation and the ubiquitous rootless cosmopolitan 'Jew' wrought racial ruination.

Structural changes in European societies, resulting from war and economic dislocation, catapulted anti-immigration politicking and anti-black racism to the forefront of fascist propaganda – becoming a new 'mobilizing passion'[77] in Paxton's parlance. It became the lightning rod around which activists reconstructed and resurrected their inter-war arguments about an existential threat to the biological integrity of race and nation. Indeed, both pre- and post-war forms of racist bio-politics united behind an eschatological belief in the preordained role of the white race as the engine of history and progress, which was facing an existential crisis thanks to a Jewish conspiracy aiming at white racial defilement. The overarching change of tone in racist propaganda, from self-confident calls for the maintenance of white supremacy at the beginning of the twentieth century, to increasingly shrill appeals to white victimhood and grievance at the commencement of the next, perhaps also reflected a sense within fascist and extreme right milieus that the imminence of racial apocalypse was moving ever closer.

Further highlighting that British fascist racial ideology was never preserved in aspic, but continued to morph reflexively in response to the political possibilities presented by changing social realities, was its embrace of a broader 'thematic shift'. Increasingly evident from the 1980s onwards was a 'new racism' that articulated 'culturally' defined forms of anti-Muslim prejudice that would come to supersede biological anti-black racism as the fulcrum of party platforms, particularly after 9/11. However, though it predominates in the public outpourings of such parties, it should be noted that this 'new' prejudice has simply been grafted onto a pre-existing racial nationalist framework rather than being truly transformative, making the nature of such 'cultural' arguments rather more transparent.[78]

Roberts' has inveighed upon historians not just to think about what survived as fascism but also 'to be clearer about what might have ended in 1945 – and about the implications of the ending of whatever it was'.[79] The changes in Europe since the war, not least of which was the entrenchment of liberal democracy, not only mitigated against the rise of totalitarian regimes but also against the factors that fuelled its rise and genocidal impulses in the first place. What did survive was fascism's palingenetic myth, which was granted a reprieve thanks to the collapse of European empires, the politicisation of migration and with it the racist and xenophobic sentiments that could be mobilised around the issue. What differed perhaps was the way in which the palingenetic myth manifested itself. No longer was it a brave vision of the future, confidently and openly proselytised. Instead, its anti-Semitic core, indivisible from British fascism's myth of racial rebirth, transmogrified into an 'esoteric' rather than 'exoteric' feature of its propaganda, though it is possible to overstate this.[80]

Paradoxically, race and immigration also cemented biological racism as an immutable centre of gravity insofar as British fascism's political nostrums were concerned. This had consequences. Symptomatic was the year 1968, which was of 'crucial importance' for the political and cultural development of the European extreme right as it engaged with the ideas of the French Nouvelle Droite (New Right) and meta-political struggle.[81] Contemporaneously, British fascists were oblivious to these developments.[82] They had their own '1968': Enoch Powell 'Rivers of Blood' speech. Powell's blood-drenched dystopia might have temporarily boosted British fascism's fortunes, offering its pariah politics a pathway out of the political ghetto, but seen retrospectively, the consequent reinforcement of 'race' only stymied its wider intellectual development. Reliant upon racist, anti-immigration politicking, both for mobilisation and support, the sophistication and 'quality' of British fascism's vision degenerated. Rather than developing a significant corpus of intellectual thought, something it conspicuously failed to do, British fascism became path dependent, regurgitating what boiled down to derivative, vulgarised versions of Nazi racial philosophy, which both reinforced its mimetic nature and contributed to its ongoing political marginalisation.

Indeed, post-war, with the exception of Mosley, British fascism produced no original thinkers and only belatedly engaged with the comparatively more sophisticated 'ethno-pluralist' arguments of French Nouvelle Droite ideologue Alain de Benoist but even these were a pale pastiche and never became deeply ingrained. This was partly because the tradition's intellectual development remained stunted due to its continued adherence to crude biological racism first articulated by figures like Arnold Leese. Arguably, British fascism's overt racist fulminations, coupled with its unsavoury historical baggage, not only delegitimised its own leaders and organisations but also soiled and stigmatised its own core concern as a political issue. British fascism's fixation with race ironically became counterproductive and highlighted too that there were limits to its ability to evolve beyond its core mobilising myths. The more self-reflective activists understood this. 'Those who talk of ensuring that the BNP remains at heart an ethno-nationalist party merely condemn it to failure,' noted one leading organiser. 'It is an example of breathtaking lack of subtlety and political gaucheness. Such an approach will also lead to ethnic destruction. This is the reality whether anyone likes it or not.'[83]

This all raises a legitimate question regarding the extent to which these avowedly racist movements remained 'fascist'. Mann, for instance, argues that 'the salience of their major issue, immigration, tends to undercut any general *Weltanschauung*, whether fascist or not' though he concludes that such groups 'are not seriously fascist.... It can make life unpleasant for immigrants but is unlikely to generate either fascism or any other totalizing ideology.'[84] As the present study argues, however, even when the voter base of these movements themselves have transcended such a definition, their leaders, who have continued to proselytise a totalising, revolutionary creed of palingenetic ultra-nationalism, have not.

Milieux and *groupuscule*

Whilst biographical in structure and ideological in focus, this study examines political organisation too. Moving beyond static taxonomies of inter-war fascism, which are rarely applicable to fascism's post-war forms, Griffin enjoins us to recognise instead that the two 'basic features' of post-war fascism are a tendency towards 'organizational complexity and ideological heterogeneity' and 'ideological and organizational innovation'.[85] This partly reflects a shift in scale. Mass movements and regimes define inter-war fascism's outer form. Looking through the other end of the telescope, however, post-war fascism with the exception of the NF, which for a brief moment in the 1970s became the fourth largest political party, and the BNP, which for an equally brief period in the 2000s exerted an outsized presence in certain localities, was largely characterised by its antithesis: the *groupuscule*, a political formation which, even when fully developed, 'has only a small, even minute active membership, a negligible following, and does not aspire to become a "player" in mainstream political culture'.[86] The majority of this seething profusion of grouplets are 'far too numerous to mention – and mostly too tiny to be worth mentioning'.[87] The concept of the *groupuscule* also moves us away from reifying the idea, promoted by these groups, that they are in fact rigid, hierarchical movements based upon unquestioned authority and slavish obedience. Such a misconception obscures the disorganised 'chaotic' reality of extreme right activism, the groups in question often resembling little more than 'transitory' street gangs as opposed to 'organized' entities. As Blee observes, 'chaos' is not simply a description of a group's membership; 'it is central to how many racial extremist groups operate in a liminal status between a strategic movement and a vaguely bounded subcultural network'.[88]

This is no less true of some of those groups operating in a British context, historically and contemporaneously, and the account of these groups that follows, has attempted to make sense of this 'chaos'. Seemingly ephemeral on their own terms, *groupuscules* structurally undergird this seemingly disorganised 'scene' and can – on occasion – coagulate into larger, more important political formations, the establishment of the National Front in 1966 being a case in point. This is important since, as Klandermans and Mayer observe 'Movement organizations are not conjured out of air; they do not build only on an ideological heritage but also on a structural one'.[89] Historically, these 'carriers groups' which transmitted both ideas and activists also served as 'abeyance' structures, performing a vital function for the ongoing diffusion and dissemination of the 'sacred flame' across the chasm of a hostile 'post-fascist' interregnum in which the possibility for 'mass' political action is otherwise extinguished.[90] Indeed, a reversion to *groupuscular* organisation reflected less a conscious choice than a response to the near complete dearth of available opportunities within the UK since 1945, stymied electorally by the first-past-the-post system and culturally by the widely held perception of British fascism as being on the wrong side of national history vis à vis the Second World War, which came to identify 'patriotism' with a defence of liberal democratic freedoms.[91]

Groupuscules can and do exhibit an array of organisational forms including microparties, leagues and fronts. These organisational forms are all evident throughout this study, each constituting a singular, loosely conceived 'node' operating within a wider political constellation, usefully defined as an 'amorphous, leaderless and centerless, cellular network of political ideology, organization and activism.' Griffin deploys the metaphor of the 'rhizome' to assist in visualising this organisational structure – resembling not so much a single organism (like a tree with a tap-root, branch and canopy) as a 'tangled root-system' (akin to a type of grass or tuber) that displays 'multiple starts and beginnings which intertwine and connect with each other'.[92] Griffin's metaphor finds its functional equivalent in Colin Campbell's sociological concept of the 'cultic milieu'[93] – society's permanent oppositional counter-cultural underground, which provides an invaluable conceptual tool for thinking about the nature of post-war fascism. The 'cultic milieu' functions, Campbell suggests, as an agent of cultural diffusion; cultural innovation; as a cultural gene pool; as an aid to societal adaption; whilst serving also as a negative reference group for cultural orthodoxy; and, finally, as an agent for the renewal of orthodoxy. Within the cultic milieu, ideas are 'fungible' rather than 'fixed' – rather like the amorphous, *groupuscular* carriers articulated by Griffin.[94] Participants within extreme right and 'fascist' milieus, insofar as they continue to adhere to the basic palingenetic premise, have been able to explore, debate and experiment with various strategies, ideas and philosophies, and to reject or assimilate them, either partially or completely. Through this ongoing process of ideological synthesis, a range of perspectives, beliefs and practices, a body of 'rejected' or 'stigmatised knowledge' which, in one way or another, explicitly rejects the legitimacy of liberal democracy, has been transmitted onwards through personal and political networks to ensure that fascism survived.[95]

The concept of the 'cultic milieu', back in vogue since it was first elaborated in the 1970s,[96] also enables us to contextualise post-war fascism in relation to the 'epochal' significance of its inter-war parent. Here Paxton's 'Five Stages of Fascism' is also useful, since it rejected the static essentialism of previous 'models' in favour of understanding fascism as a cycle of phases and processes through which historic fascist movements passed on their way to becoming regimes, or not. These five stages were: (1) the creation of movements; (2) their rooting in the political system; (3) their seizure of power; (4) the exercise of power; and (5) the long duration, during which the fascist regime choses either radicalisation or entropy. 'Though each stage is a prerequisite for the next, nothing requires a fascist movement to complete all of them, or even to move in only one direction.'[97]

The early history of 'proto-fascism' – stage one, analogous to the cultic milieu in many respects – was littered with myriad 'corpuscles of innovation' that provided alternative options for what fascism could be.[98] Post-war European fascism, returned to this stage after 1945. In Britain, fascism never ascended from 'stage one' in the first place. Regardless of its lack of wider political success, British fascism endured and evolved as a political tradition precisely because its activists could draw succour from their own 'cultic milieu', which provided fertile ground for a complex matrix of *groupuscular* activity.

Prior to 1945, Fascism and Nazism had been viewed by many Europeans as a movement of 'imminent possibility', and as a 'promising alternative' to liberalism and communism partially because 'it was not clear what such an alternative needed to entail.' After 1945, what this 'alternative' entailed was perfectly obvious to everyone. Greatly diminished as a political, cultural and social force due to the burden of having made common cause with Nazism and Fascism, British fascists persisted nonetheless, seeking to reinvent and redefine themselves through the emergence of immigration as a political issue.[99] Whilst British fascism was never an 'imminent possibility' either before or after 1945, it is to the ideologues and activists who struggled to ensure that it at least remained a 'continuing possibility' that we now turn.

Notes

1 Richard Thurlow, *Fascism in Britain: From Oswald Mosley's Blackshirts to the National Front* (London: I.B. Tauris, 1998).
2 Robert Benewick, *The Fascist Movement in Britain* (London: Allen Lane, 1972); Stephen Dorril, *Blackshirt: Sir Oswald Mosley and British Fascism* (London: Viking, 2006); Thomas Linehan, *East London for Mosley: The British Union of Fascists in East London and South-West Essex 1933–40* (London: Frank Cass, 1996); Thomas Linehan, *British Fascism, 1918–1939: Parties, Ideology and Culture* (Manchester: Manchester University Press, 2000); Martin Pugh, *Hurrah for the Blackshirts! Fascists and Fascism in Britain between the Wars* (London: Cape, 2005); and Robert Skidelsky, *Oswald Mosley* (London: Macmillan, 1975).
3 David Nasaw, 'AHR Roundtable: Historians and Biography – Introduction', *American Historical Review*, vol. 114, no. 3, 2009, p. 573.
4 For instance, Ian Kershaw, *Hitler: Hubris, 1889–1936* (London: Penguin, 2001); and Ian Kershaw, *Hitler: Nemesis, 1936–1945* (London: Penguin, 2001).
5 Matthew J. Goodwin, 'The Rise and Faults of the Internalist Perspective in Extreme Right Studies', *Representation*, vol. 42, no. 4, 2006, p. 354.
6 Richard Evans, *The Coming of the Third Reich* (London: Penguin, 2004), pp. xviii–xix.
7 Lawrence Stone, 'Prosopography', *Daedalus*, vol. 100, no. 1, 1971, p. 46 defines it as 'the investigation of the common background characteristics of a group of actors in history by means of a collective study of their lives.'
8 Alice Kessler-Harris, 'AHR Roundtable: Why Biography?' *American Historical Review*, vol. 114, no. 3, 2009, pp. 625–630 makes the same point.
9 For broader discussions, see Ian Kershaw, 'Personality and Power', *The Historian*, no. 83, Autumn 2004, pp. 8–19; and Lawrence Goldman, 'History and Biography', *Historical Research*, vol. 89, no. 245, 2016, pp. 399–411.

10 Karl Marx, *The Eighteenth Brumaire of Louis Bonaparte* (1852).
11 Clive Webb, *Rabble Rousers: The American Far Right in the Civil Rights Era* (Athens, GA: University of Georgia Press, 2010); and Caoimhe Nic Dháibhéid, *Terrorist Histories: Individuals and Political Violence since the 19th Century* (Abingdon: Routledge, 2017) take a similar approach.
12 Roger Eatwell, 'The Nature of the Right, 2: The Right as a Variety of "Styles of Thought"', in Roger Eatwell and Noël O'Sullivan (eds), *The Nature of the Right: European and American Politics and Political Thought since 1789* (London: Pinter, 1989), pp. 62–76 argues broadly the same point. Eatwell divides the wider 'Right' into five 'styles of thought': the reactionary right; the moderate right; the radical right; the extreme right; and the new right.
13 John F. Morrison, *The Origins and Rise of Dissident Irish Republicanism* (London: Bloomsbury, 2015) highlights a fruitful approach to understanding the role and impact of organisation splits which scholars of the extreme right might take note of.
14 David Art, *Inside Radical Right: The Development of Anti-Immigrant Parties in Western Europe* (Cambridge: Cambridge University Press, 2011), p. 107 argues that the causal mechanism 'is continuity of personnel rather than continuity of ideology.'
15 Leonard Zeskind, *Blood and Politics: The History of the White Nationalist Movement from the Margins to the Mainstream* (New York: Farrar, Straus & Giroux, 2009) explores the tensions between 'mainstreamers' and 'vanguardists' in the United States.
16 The present author is equally guilty of this sin, that is, Graham Macklin, *Very Deeply Dyed in Black: Sir Oswald Mosley and the Political Resurrection of British Fascism after 1945* (London: I.B. Tauris, 2007).
17 Nigel Jones, *Mosley* (London: Haus, 2004), p. 113.
18 For an overview, see Craig Fowlie, 'The British Far Right since 1967: A Bibliographic Survey', in Nigel Copsey and Matthew Worley (eds), *Tomorrow Belongs to Us: The British Far Right since 1967* (Abingdon: Routledge, 2018), pp. 224–267; and Graham Macklin, 'The Evolving Historiography of the Extreme Right in Britain', in Jennifer Craig-Norton, Christhard Hoffman and Tony Kushner (eds), *Migrant Britain: Histories and Historiographies: Essays in Honour of Colin Holmes* (Abingdon: Routledge, 2018), pp. 173–192.
19 Useful starting points are provided by Paul Kennedy and Anthony Nicholls (eds), *Nationalist and Racialist Movements in Britain and Germany before 1914* (London: Macmillan, 1981); Barbara Storm Farr, *The Development and Impact of Right-Wing Politics in Britain, 1903–1932* (New York: Garland, 1987); and Dan Stone, *Breeding Superman: Nietzsche, Race and Eugenics in Edwardian Interwar Britain* (Liverpool: Liverpool University Press, 2002).
20 For an early analysis, see J. Salwyn Schapiro, 'Thomas Carlyle, Prophet of Fascism', *The Journal of Modern History*, vol. 17, no. 2, June 1945, pp. 97–115.
21 Robert O. Paxton, *The Anatomy of Fascism* (London: Penguin, 2005), p. 9.
22 Bernhard Dietz, *Neo-Tories: The Revolt of British Conservatives against Democracy and Political Modernity (1929–1939)* (London: Bloomsbury, 2018), p. 22.
23 Sir Charles Petrie, *Chapters of Life* (London: Eyre & Spottiswoode, 1950) maintained, not altogether in jest, that had Mosley dressed his supporters in blue pullovers rather than blackshirts much would have been forgiven him.
24 Stanley Payne, *A History of Fascism, 1914–1945* (Madison, WI: University of Wisconsin Press, 1995), p. 19.
25 There is a large literature on this milieu, much of which remains to be synthesised into our understanding of British fascism's wider context. For an introduction, see Dan Stone, 'The Far Right and the Back-to-the-Land Movement', in Julie V. Gottlieb and Thomas P. Linehan (eds), *The Culture of Fascism: Visions of the Far Right in Britain* (London: I.B. Tauris, 2004), pp. 182–198; and Mike Tyldesly and Matthew Jeffries (eds), *Rolf Gardiner: Folk, Nature and Culture in Interwar Britain* (Abingdon: Routledge, 2010). See also Philip M. Coupland, *Farming, Fascism and Ecology: A Life of Jorian Jenks* (Abingdon: Routledge, 2017).
26 Their activities have not escaped scholarly scrutiny altogether, however. See, for instance, William H. Tucker, *The Science and Politics of Racial Research* (Chicago, IL: University of Illinois Press, 1994); William H. Tucker, *The Funding of Scientific Racism: Wickliffe Draper and the Pioneer Fund* (Chicago, IL: University of Illinois Press, 2002); and Kevin Coogan, *Dreamer of the Day: Francis Parker Yockey and the Postwar Fascist International* (New York: Autonomedia, 1999). In the British context, see also Bradley W. Hart, *George Pitt-Rivers and the Nazis* (London: Bloomsbury, 2015) for a biography of the eponymous anthropologist.

27 Anti-Muslim and xenophobic mobilisations, though they may mobilise fascist, extreme right and racist activists, are not *a priori* 'fascist' however and are therefore only discussed in passing in this present work. Joel Busher, *The Making of Anti-Muslim Protest: Grassroots activism in the English Defence League* (Abingdon: Routledge, 2016), pp. 20 and 21; and Hilary Pilkington, *Loud and Proud: Passion and Politics in the English Defence League* (Manchester: Manchester University Press, 2016), p. 4 support this view.
28 Mosley's heroic image was deliberately marketed by the BUF propaganda machine which purposefully magnified his personal attributes as 'Leader', on which, see Julie Gottlieb, 'The Marketing of Megalomania: Celebrity, Consumption and the Development of Political Technology in the British Union of Fascists', *Journal of Contemporary History*, vol. 41, no. 1, 2006, pp. 35–55.
29 Roger Eatwell, 'The Concept and Theory of Charismatic Leadership', *Totalitarian Movements and Political Religions*, vol. 7, no. 2, 2006, pp. 141–156.
30 Andrew Heywood, *Political Ideologies: An Introduction* (New York: Palgrave Macmillan, 2003), p. 12.
31 This is a view held by both Roger Eatwell and Richard Thurlow in their works on British fascism.
32 Anthony Julius, *Trials of the Diaspora: A History of Anti-Semitism in England* (Oxford: Oxford University Press, 2010), p. 309. Walter Laqueur, *Fascism: Past, Present and Future* (Oxford: Oxford University Press, 1996), p. 119 was similarly scornful in his refusal to study post-war British fascism, 'because it has not been very significant or in anyway original'.
33 Roger Griffin, 'British Fascism: The Ugly Duckling', in Mike Cronin (ed.), *The Failure of British Fascism: The Far Right and the Fight for Political Recognition* (Basingstoke: Macmillan, 1996), pp. 141–165.
34 *The Patriot*, no. 1, spring 1997.
35 James Aho, *The Politics of Righteousness: Idaho Christian Patriotism* (Seattle, WA: University of Washington Press, 1990), p. 187; and Kathy Blee, *Inside Organized Racism: Women in the Hate Movement* (Berkeley, CA: University of California Press, 2002), pp. 27–28 make similar observations.
36 Claudia Koonz, *The Nazi Conscience* (Cambridge, MA: Harvard University Press, 2003) also makes this point.
37 Michael Billig, *Fascists: A Social Psychological View of the National Front* (London: Academic Press, 1978), p. 124. Erving Goffman's 'Front and Back Regions of Everyday Life [1959]', in Erving Goffman, *The Presentation of Self in Everyday Life* (Harmondsworth: Penguin, 1990), pp. 111–121 was one of the first to theorise such a distinction between 'backstage' and 'frontstage' observing that, 'when one's activity occurs in the presence of other persons, some aspects of the activity are expressively accentuated and other aspects, which might discredit the fostered impression, are supressed.'
38 John Warburton, interview with the author, 21 April 1999.
39 For more on the importance of the emotional dynamics, see Mehr Latif, Kathleen Blee, Matthew DeMichele and Pete Simi, 'How Emotional Dynamics Maintain and Destroy White Supremacist Groups', *Humanity and Society*, vol. 42, no. 4, 2018, pp. 480–501.
40 Roger Griffin, *Fascism* (Cambridge: Polity, 2018) is a good recent summary.
41 For Roger Eatwell, 'Populism and Fascism', in Cristóbal Rovira Kaltwasser, Paul Taggart, Paulina Ochoa Espejo and Pierre Ostiguy (eds), *The Oxford Handbook of Populism* (Oxford: Oxford University Press, 2017), pp. 363–383 the core matrices of populism – defined as a 'thin' ideology – are the 'plain people', the 'self-serving elite', and 'rule by popular will', whilst fascism is defined by the 'holistic nation', a 'new man', and a 'third way authoritarian state'.
42 Roger Eatwell, *Fascism: A History* (London: Pimlico, 2003), p. 66.
43 Matthew Feldman, 'The Fascination of Fascism: A Concluding Interview with Roger Griffin', in Matthew Feldman (ed.), *A Fascist Century: Essays by Roger Griffin* (London: Palgrave, 2008), p. 207.
44 Roger Eatwell, 'On Defining the "Fascist Minimum": The Centrality of Ideology', *Journal of Political Ideologies*, vol. 1, no. 3, 1996, pp. 303–319.
45 Michael Freeden, 'Political Concepts and Ideological Morphology', *Journal of Political Philosophy*, vol. 2, no. 2, June 1994, pp. 140–165 convincingly demonstrates how ideologies, or at least those that wish to survive as anything other than a cargo cult, are protean and evolutionary, shedding time-bound 'peripheral' and 'adjacent' features, and absorbing new ones, in order to project forwards their 'core' components.

46 Thurlow, *Fascism in Britain* p. 224.
47 Ernst Nolte, *Three Faces of Fascism* (New York: Holt, Rinehart and Winston, 1966), p. 4.
48 Michael Mann, *Fascists* (Cambridge: Cambridge University Press, 2004), pp. 370 and 374.
49 For an interesting theoretical overview, see David D. Roberts, *Fascist Interactions: Proposals for a New Approach to Fascism and its Era* (New York: Berghahn, 2016), pp. 257–271.
50 Zeev Sternhell, *Neither Right nor Left: Fascist Ideology in France* (Princeton, NJ: Princeton University Press, 1995), p. 29. Sternhell's approach is not without its critics, however, see David D. Roberts, 'How not to Think about Fascism and Ideology, Intellectual Antecedents and Historical Meaning', *Journal of Contemporary History*, vol. 35, no. 2, April 2000, pp. 185–211.
51 Jeffrey M. Bale, '(Still) More on Fascist and Neo-Fascist Ideology and "Groupuscularity"', in Roger Griffin, Werner Loh and Andreas Umland (eds), *Fascism Past and Present, West and East: An International Debate on Concepts and Cases in the Comparative Study of the Extreme Right* (Stuttgart: ibidem-Verlag, 2006), pp. 292–293.
52 Aristotle A. Kallis, 'Studying Inter-War Fascism in Epochal and Diachronic Terms: Ideological Production, Political Experience and the Quest for "Consensus"', *European History Quarterly*, vol. 34, no. 1, 2004, p. 36. David D. Roberts, *Fascist Transactions*, p. 271 concedes 'we might find it possible to isolate some specifically fascist residuum transcending the epoch.'
53 Debates about the applicability of the term 'right-wing extremism' are essentially an extension of this conundrum. For Jérôme Jamin, 'Notes on Populism and the Extreme Right', in Andrea Mammone, Emmanuel Godin and Brian Jenkins (eds), *Varieties of Right-Wing Extremism in Europe* (Abingdon: Routledge, 2013), p. 39 labelling a group right-wing extremist, 'means indirectly situating it as part of the extension of fascism and its crimes, morally disqualifying it and excluding it from the democratic political arena.' Interestingly, given Jamin's concerns, Elisabeth Carter, 'Right-Wing Extremism/Radicalism: Reconstructing a Concept', *Journal of Political Ideologies*, vol. 23, no. 2, 2018, pp. 157–182 offers a 'minimal' definition of 'right-wing extremism' as 'an ideology that encompasses authoritarianism, anti-democracy and exclusionary and/or holistic nationalism', which is basically consonant with the 'fascist minimum' thereby highlighting an essential continuity between the two concepts. Sam Jackson, 'Non-Normative Political Extremism: Reclaiming a Concept's Analytical Utility', *Terrorism and Political Violence*, vol. 31, no. 2, 2019, pp. 244–259 offers a (non-pejorative) analytical framework for understanding 'extremism' as 'purposeful disruptive activity' which aims to 'replace or fundamentally alter the dominant political system.' Context is key to this definition for without it what is 'extreme' about 'extremism' vis-à-vis its stance towards the dominant form of politics cannot be properly understood. Pertinently, Jackson argues, 'we must not assert that racists are extremists and assume our readers will agree. To make this connection, we must describe how the racism of the alleged extremists seeks to disrupt some central features of the political system.' J.M. Berger, *Extremism* (Cambridge, MA: MIT Press, 2018), p. 170 provides a complementary definition of extremism as 'The belief that an in-group's success or survival can never be separated from the need for hostile action against an out-group.' Illustrating how this 'inseparability' of belief and action encompasses 'white nationalists', Berger observes (p. 45) the belief 'that white people can never be successful until nonwhites are removed from in-group society by means of segregation or extermination. This demand is definitional, non-negotiable and unconditional. To abandon the demand would be to abandon white nationalism.'
54 Nigel Copsey, 'Historians and the Contemporary Far Right: To Bring (or Not to Bring) the Past into the Present', in Stephen Ashe, Joel Busher, Graham Macklin and Arron Winter (eds), *Researching the Far Right* (Routledge: forthcoming 2020).
55 Matthew J. Goodwin, 'Grandpa's Fascism and the New Kids on the Block: Contemporary Approaches to the Dark Side of Europe', *Ethnopolitics*, vol. 6, no. 1, 2007, pp. 145–154.
56 Pietro Ignazi, 'The Extreme Right in Europe: A Survey', in Peter H. Merkl and Leonard Weinberg (eds), *The Revival of Right-Wing Extremism in the Nineties* (London: Frank Cass, 1997), p. 54. Federico Finchelstein, *From Fascism to Populism in History* (Oakland, CA: University of California Press, 2017), pp. xiii and xiv argues that populism and fascism are 'genealogically connected. They belong to the same history' and that populism 'occupied the place of fascism as it became a new "third way" between liberalism and communism.'
57 For examples of such 'terminological chaos', see Cas Mudde, *Populist Radical Right Parties in Europe* (Cambridge: Cambridge University Press, 2007), pp. 11–12.
58 Nigel Copsey, 'Fascism Studies (and the "Post-Fascist" Era): An Ideal Meeting Ground?', *Fascism*, vol. 1, no. 1, 2012, pp. 55–56. For a further call for academics to 'restate' the link

between the contemporary radical right and historic fascism, see Nigel Copsey, 'The Radical Right and Fascism', in Jens Rydgren (ed.), *The Oxford Handbook of the Radical Right* (Oxford: Oxford University Press, 2018), pp. 105–121.
59 David Petrie, 'Foreword', to *The British Union of Fascists* in TNA KV 4/241.
60 Frederic Mullally, *Fascism Inside England* (London: Claude Morris, 1946), p. 88.
61 Laqueur, *Fascism*, p. 7.
62 A. James Gregor, *The Search for Neofascism: The Use and Abuse of Social Science* (Cambridge: Cambridge University Press, 2006).
63 Elisabeth Carter, *The Extreme Right in Western Europe: Success or Failure* (Manchester: Manchester University Press, 2001), p. 21.
64 Roger Karapin, 'Radical-Right and Neo-Fascist Parties in Western Europe', *Comparative Politics*, vol. 30, no. 2, 1998, pp. 213–234.
65 Roger Griffin, *The Nature of Fascism* (Abingdon: Routledge, 1991), pp. 161–171. Roger Eatwell, *Fascism: A History* (London: Vintage, 1996), pp. 284–285 notes similarly that 'recidivist neo-fascists' predominated immediately after 1945 but have largely been replaced by a younger generation of 'radical neo-fascists'.
66 Stanley G. Payne, 'Historic Fascism and Neo-Fascism', *European History Quarterly*, vol. 23, 1993, pp. 69–75. Payne employs neo-fascism, defined along a similar axis to Griffin, in his magisterial tome, *A History of Fascism, 1914–1945* (London: University College London Press, 1995), p. 498.
67 'Translation of a Speech Excerpt in which Himmler Defines "Evacuation" of the Jews as "Extermination"', Official Translation from the War Crime Trials of Nazi Leaders Held at Nuernburg', available at https://catalog.archives.gov/id/305266 (accessed 5 January 2017).
68 Jean-Yves Camus and Nicolas Lebourg, *Far-Right Politics in Europe* (Cambridge, MA: Belknap Press: 2017), p. 38.
69 For a selection of recent scholarship, see Arnd Bauerkämper and Grzegorz Rossoliński-Liebe (eds), *Fascism without Borders: Transnational Connections between Movements and Regimes in Europe from 1918 to 1945* (New York: Berghahn, 2017).
70 Ian Buruma and Avishai Margalit, *Occidentalism: A Short History of Anti-Westernism* (London: Atlantic Books, 2004).
71 Diethelm Prowe, '"Classic" Fascism and the New Radical Right in Western Europe: Comparisons and Contrasts', *Contemporary European History*, vol. 3, no. 3, 1994, pp. 289–313.
72 Thurlow, *Fascism in Britain*, pp. 58–59.
73 Liam Liburd, 'Beyond the Pale: Whiteness, Masculinity and Empire in the British Union of Fascists, 1932–1940', *Fascism*, vol. 7, no. 2, 2018, pp. 275–296.
74 W.F. Mandle, 'The Leadership of the British Union of Fascists', *Australian Journal of Politics and History*, vol. 12, no. 3, 1966, pp. 360–383.
75 George Mosse, *The Crisis of German Ideology: Intellectual Origins of the Third Reich* (New York: Schocken, 1981), p. 4.
76 For fascist conceptions of temporality, see Roger Griffin, 'Fixing Solutions: Fascist Temporalities as Remedies for Liquid Modernity', *Journal of Modern European History*, vol. 13, no. 1, 2015, pp. 5–22.
77 Paxton, *The Anatomy of Fascism*, p. 41.
78 For an overview, see José Pedro Zúquete, 'The European Extreme-Right and Islam: New Directions?', *Journal of Political Ideologies*, vol. 13, no. 3, 2008, pp. 321–344. Hans-Georg Betz, 'Against the "Green Totalitarianism": Anti-Islamic Nativism in Contemporary Right-Wing Populism in Western Europe', in C.S. Liang (ed.), *Europe for the Europeans: The Foreign and Security Policy of the Populist Radical Right* (Aldershot: Ashgate, 2007), p. 42 also highlights that since that since 9/11 confrontation with Islam has become the 'central political issue' for all 'radical right' parties. In a similar fashion, Jens Rydgren, 'Is Extreme Right-Wing Populism Contagious? Explaining the Emergence of a New Party Family', *European Journal of Political Research*, vol. 44, no. 3, 2005, pp. 413–437 argues that this 'cultural racism' has become the new 'master frame' for the radical right.
79 Roberts, *Fascist Interactions*, p. 257.
80 Michael Billig, *Fascists: A Social Psychological View of the National Front* (London: Academic Press, 1978), pp. 124–126.
81 Andrea Mammone, 'The Transnational Reaction to 1968: Neo-Fascist Fronts and Political Cultures in France and Italy', *Contemporary European History*, vol. 17, no. 2, 2008, pp. 213–236.

82 For its limited impact, see Nigel Copsey, '*Au Revoir* to "Sacred Cows"? Assessing the Impact of the *Nouvelle Droite* in Britain', *Democracy and Security*, vol. 9, no. 3, 2013, pp. 287–303.
83 See Eddy Butler for Britain, March 2012, https://eddybutler.blogspot.com/2012/03/rise-and-fall-of-british-national-party.html (Accessed 5 June 2018).
84 Mann, *Fascists*, p. 370.
85 Griffin, *The Nature of Fascism*, pp. 161–171.
86 Roger Griffin, 'The Incredible Shrinking Ism: The Survival of Fascism in the Post-War Era', *Patterns of Prejudice*, vol. 36, no. 3, 2002, pp. 3–8. Pierre Milza had previously invoked the term 'groupuscule' in his work on French fascism.
87 Martin Blinkhorn, *Fascism and the Right in Europe*, 1919–1945 (Harlow: Pearson, 2000), p. 112.
88 Kathleen M. Blee, 'How the Study of White Supremacism is Helped and Hindered by Social Movement Research', *Mobilization*, vol. 22, no. 1, 2017, p. 5.
89 Bert Klandermans and Nonna Mayer (eds), *Extreme Right Activists in Europe: Through the Looking Glass* (Abingdon: Routledge, 2006), p. 11.
90 Roger Griffin, 'Interregnum or Endgame? The Radical Right in the "Post-Fascist" Era', *Journal of Politics Ideologies*, vol. 5, no. 2, 2000, pp. 163–178.
91 For the broader debate, see John Ramsden, *Don't Mention the War: The British and the Germans since 1890* (London: Little Brown, 2006). See also Daniele Caramani and Luca Manucci, 'National Past and Populism: The Re-Elaboration of Fascism and its Impact on Right-Wing Populism in Western Europe', *West European Politics*, vol. 6, no. 42, 2019, pp. 1159–1187.
92 Roger Griffin, 'From Slime Mould to Rhizome: An Introduction to the Groupuscular Right', *Patterns of Prejudice*, vol. 37, no. 1, 2003, pp. 27–50. Pedro D. Manrique, Minzhang Zheng, Zhenfeng Cao, Elvira Maria Restrepo and Neil F. Johnson, 'Generalized Gelation Theory Describes Onset of Online Extremist Support', *Physical Review Letters*, 121, 048301, published online 27 July 2018, gives credence to Griffin's 'slime mould' metaphor, suggesting that the growth of online extremist networks is analogous to the formation of gels.
93 Colin Campbell, 'The Cult, the Cultic Milieu and Secularization', *A Sociological Yearbook of Religion in Britain*, no. 5, 1972, pp. 119–136. In 'The Cultic Milieu Revisited' – a lecture given at the University of Leipzig on 12 June 2012 – Campbell questioned the applicability of his concept to the extreme right on the grounds that there was nothing inherently 'cultic' about protest groups that challenge the established order. 'In any case,' he wrote, 'people who are involved in protest groups cannot really be said to be "seekers after truth" for what they crave would appear to be power (or at least influence) rather than meaning.' Whilst this is true, and as Campbell reminds his readers, 'the adjective "cultic" has a religious, or at least spiritual, derivation,' the ideologues discussed herein, perhaps with the exception of Mosley, have all been keen to evangelise and fetishise esoteric beliefs about 'race' not simply in order to validate a particular biologically informed political platform, but also to bestow upon the human genome a sacred, spiritual value from which all higher meaning and purpose is supposedly derived. In this sense, the obsession with racial origins might also be viewed as being akin to a quest for 'truth' that deviates from broader societal norms.
94 Whilst he does not make explicit reference to the concept of the 'cultic milieu', Griffin ('Slime Mould', p. 28) gives a near identical description of extreme right groupuscularity 'as a latent or actual quality of all counter-cultural idioms of anti-systemic thought and activism in the modern age, especially when they are unable to form the nucleus of significant populist movements.'
95 Colin Campbell, 'The Cult, the Cultic Milieu and Secularization'. Michael Barkun, 'Conspiracy Theories as Stigmatized Knowledge', *Diogenes*, 2016, pp. 1–7 is also illuminating in this respect.
96 Campbell's original essay was reprinted in full in Jeffrey Kaplan and Heléne Lööw (eds), *The Cultic Milieu: Oppositional Subcultures in an Age of Globalisation* (Walnut Creek, CA: AltaMira Press, 2002), pp. 12–25, for example.
97 Robert O. Paxton, 'The Five Stages of Fascism', *The Journal of Modern History*, vol. 70, 1998, pp. 1–23. Paxton, *The Anatomy of Fascism*, p. 174, which extended his original arguments, implicitly endorsed this approach, conceding that it was 'relatively easy to admit the widespread continuation of Stage One – the founding stage – of radical Right movements with some explicit or implicit link to fascism.' Examples of Stage Two, wherein such movements become rooted in political systems as 'significant players and the bearers of important interests,' is not, however, a status that British groups have come close to attaining to date.
98 Roberts, *Fascist Interactions*, p. 260.
99 *Ibid.*, p. 274.

1 Arnold Leese
The 'anti-jewish' camel doctor

Barely remembered today, Arnold Leese was a pivotal figure in the development of British racial nationalism. Regarded as a 'pioneer' within the movement, Leese lived and died by the maxim that 'Race is the basis of all politics'. He was a vituperative anti-Semite for whom 'Democracy is Death' and whose views have led some scholars to judge him the nearest equivalent to an 'English Hitler'.[1] This assessment is unduly favourable to Leese. For one thing, Leese was no leader of men. He bore a far greater resemblance to the infamous Gauleiter of Franconia Julius Streicher, editor of *Der Stürmer*. Like Streicher, Leese was totally obsessed with and repelled by 'The Jew'. He openly advocated their extermination using a 'lethal chamber' years before the Nazis implemented their own 'Final Solution'. Leese was also a veterinarian specialising in diseases afflicting the 'one-humped camel' and as such was probably the only self-declared 'anti-Jewish camel doctor' in British history. From the late 1920s onwards, Leese campaigned relentlessly against the perceived perils of racial miscegenation, which he believed led to the degradation, decline and destruction of the white race. Ideologically puritanical, Leese was personally abstemious – he neither drank nor smoked – combining the two strands in his own individual epistemology: 'I think history records that England was at its best when it knew nothing of tobacco … and had no Jews,' he recorded in his autobiography.[2] Leese's belief in the sacred value of racial purity stimulated a profound desire for racial rebirth that could only be achieved by first segregating and then annihilating 'The Jew' – arch nemesis of the white race.

Arnold Spencer Leese was born on 16 November 1878 in Lytham St Annes, Lancashire. His father, Spencer Leese was a manufacturer and artist from a socially well-connected family. General Sir Oliver Leese was a second cousin. Another more distant relation was Richard Oastler, the Tory industrial reformer, known as the 'Factory King'.[3] The death of his father when Leese was a teenager left his family in dire financial straits, and compelled Leese to leave boarding school. He subsequently attended the Royal College of Veterinary Surgeons thanks to a financial subvention from his grandfather. Having graduated in 1903, Leese worked briefly as an 'equine clinician' in London before joining the Indian Civil Veterinary Department. He lived and worked in India for six years, largely along the North-West Frontier – 'far from the haunts of white men' – which prompted him to learn Hindustani. By his own account, Leese appears to have led an isolated existence working in 'the jungle and desert' with two assistants, a Muslim and a Sikh, whilst carving out a niche as an expert on camels.[4] His subsequent book, *A Treatise on the One-Humped Camel in Health and Disease* (1927), remains the seminal work on the subject. The camel parasite *Thelagia Leesei* was apparently named after him.[5] Transferred to East Africa, Leese was in Italian Somaliland when war was declared in 1914. During the First World War, in which his youngest brother John was killed at Gallipoli, Captain Leese served in East Africa with the Royal Army Veterinary Corps as a Camel Purchasing Officer to the Somaliland Remount Commission with the Camel Corps and in France as a Veterinary Officer to the Advanced Horse Transport Depot replacing horse-casualties in transport units at the front.[6]

During the war, Leese married May Winifred King, the daughter of his former landlord. She would become an ardent and vociferous supporter of his politics. When the war ended, Leese established a private veterinary practice in Stamford, Lincolnshire. His political views, coloured by the traditional racism of the age, in his case born of imperial service in India, were 'vaguely Conservative' and 'strongly individualist' – he particularly resented paying income tax. Leese detested Socialism 'in any form', viewing the rise of the Labour Party as a particular affront. Like many other right-wing Conservatives, Leese was mesmerised by Mussolini's 'bloodless revolution' in 1922, claiming it had saved the country from the 'chaos' into which 'liberalism' had plunged it. 'It appeared to me,' he recorded, 'that here was a movement which might end political humbug' in Britain too.[7] In April 1923, Leese wrote a short pamphlet praising Mussolini and highlighting the 'significance' of Fascism for Britain.[8]

The timing was apposite. In the following month, Rotha Lintorn-Orman, granddaughter of Field Marshall Sir John Lintorn Arabin Simmons, a former governor of Malta, founded the British Fascists (BF).[9] Driven by a misplaced interpretation of the depth of constitutional crisis surrounding Ulster and 'communism', the BF saw fascism not just an exercise in 'practical patriotism' but as an expression of national unity symbolised by the *fasces*.[10]

> Naturally we are trying to organise so as to prevent, if possible, the catastrophe of revolution, but our real aim is to bring into daily life the spirit of brotherhood and self-sacrifice that inspired the men in the trenches during the Great War,

wrote its president Brigadier-General R.B.D. Blakeney, a former deputy general manager of the Egyptian State Railways.[11] Blakeney saw the BF as an international organisation to fight 'subversive elements' and developed contacts and correspondents in Germany with similarly right-wing military figures surrounding General Erich Ludendorff, who was involved in several attempted coups against Germany's fledgling democracy, most recently, Hitler's Beerhall *putsch* in Munich in 1923. Blakeney's correspondents in such circles passed him information on 'communist matters'.[12]

Leese was an early member, founding its Stamford branch in March 1924. It gained eighty members 'but very few of these meant business'.[13] He came to deplore the fact that the party's acronym 'BF' invited the sobriquet 'Bloody Fools' and implored its leadership to change the name, but to no avail. He also came to see it as ideologically deficient. 'After a while,' he recalled, 'I found that there was no Fascism, as I understood it, in the organisation which was merely Conservatism with knobs on.'[14] Many historians would agree.[15] Leese abhorred its official policy of allowing former socialists and even Jews to become members. Indeed its lack of security meant that the BF was 'honeycombed' with communist infiltrators.[16] The BF Grand Council 'do not understand fascism at all,' Leese opined for whom 'Fascism' represented 'a revolt against democracy and a return to statesmanship' that would end the unrest and chaos induced by plebeian liberal democracy. What was required, he wrote, was a 'sane form of government, representative of an "aristocracy" of character and brains, and the scrapping of the silly universal equal suffrage'.[17] Later that year, he and Harry Simpson stood in the Stamford Town Council elections as 'Fascist candidates' in an effort to prevent the unchallenged election of two 'camouflaged Bolsheviks' from the Labour Party. They became Britain's first elected Fascist councillors. Ironically, the election intensified Leese's contempt for both democracy and the public. 'Many people I knew, voted for me because I had cured their pigs or pets and without the slightest idea what I stood for, beyond that,' he sneered.[18]

By 1925, Leese's dalliance with the BF was over.[19] He and Simpson joined a splinter group of approximately sixty disaffected activists, including several Jews, in founding the National Fascisti (NF), which, on 19 July 1926, changed its name to the British National Fascists (BNF).[20] For most of its brief, rancorous existence the group, which gained perhaps five hundred members, was led by Lieutenant-Colonel Henry Rippon-Seymour, 'a sort of adventurer who undoubtedly went into the organisation for his own financial ends'.[21] Rippon-Seymour's military credentials, not least his entitlement to wear the rows of medal-ribbons that festooned his chest, was doubtful. 'He is a well-known rascal,' noted MI5, 'and has, I think, several convictions for fraud and false pretences.'[22] The deception did not end there. Rippon-Seymour's second-in-command and live-in secretary was 'Colonel Victor Barker' who, it transpired during court proceedings in 1929 was actually a woman, Valerie Arkell-Smith.[23]

Rippon-Seymour believed that the revolution was at hand, writing to the *Daily Express* claiming that his organisation's 'Secret Service' had obtained 'documentary & photographic proof that a revolution *is* intended, & that the date is fixed' and that the Communists had already acquired the 'sinews of war'.[24] Communism – the 'creed of wild beasts' – required violent expurgation because 'wild beasts cannot be met with bare hands or gloves, they require more forceful and stronger weapons.'[25] The BNF, which urged 'deeds not words', readily resorting to violence to achieve its ends.[26] It acquired a drill hall and gymnasium, trained for direct action against political opponents and, in the process, became 'the first native fascist party to officially don the black shirt and apply political violence in a systematic manner.'[27] One statement from the group declared:

> We are anti-socialist, anti-Communist, and anti-Jewish...
> Ours is a broad, national policy of country before self...
> We are out to smash the reds and pinks.[28]

It called for the elimination of socialists from factories, the suppression of 'revolutionary' speakers and 'seditious' newspapers and demanded that the Red Flag be made 'illegal'. Socialist and communist movements were 'Jew-inspired, led and financed by Jewish Capitalism,' according to its 'Aims and Policy'. Perceiving a nation in racial decline, the BNF campaigned for the immediate cessation of 'alien' immigration and a revision of the Aliens Act and naturalisation laws. Trade licences for aliens were demanded as was an anti-alien tribunal, 'before which the alien wives of British subjects would be called'. Denying that it wished to overthrow parliamentary democracy, the BNF claimed it wished only to foster a 'truly national spirit' and a government led by 'men of British birth and breeding' with the will and power to govern.[29]

Described as 'a mixture of Ku-Klux Klan and undergraduate rag',[30] the BNF engaged in numerous acts of violent hooliganism against political opponents, including the theft and damage of a *Daily Herald* delivery van. This case became a minor *cause célèbre* owing to the leniency of the sentences handed to the four perpetrators. Despite one fascist being armed with an automatic pistol, the judge rather remarkably suggested, 'their efforts to be good and loyal citizens might be advanced by their joining the Police Reserve'.[31] Major-General Sir Wyndham Childs, the Metropolitan Police Assistant Commissioner was of a different mind, regarding the BNF as 'an intolerable nuisance' and 'not only valueless but a menace to the peace of this country'. Though he commended their patriotism as 'laudable', Childs lambasted their methods as 'damnable and illegal'. BNF efforts to foment violence against Communist meetings in Hyde Park were ineffectual, however, and invariably ended, 'in the black-shirts being chased down Oxford Street and eventually extricated from their troubles by the police'.[32] Its impact was further diminished due to the 'freakish military practices' of its members, which included 'parading outside its offices with drawn swords', which invited 'public ridicule'.[33] 'Its only accomplishment,' notes one historian 'was giving the British Fascisti a bad name, impugning its respectability, and thereby limiting its effectiveness as a voluntary organisation.'[34]

Leese was central to its endeavour to forge a more muscular and combative form of fascism, helping to shape the group into 'a militant, rigid, pseudo-Italian fascist party'.[35]

This was reflected in his pamphlet *Fascism* (1925), which glorified Mussolini and *squadristi* violence. It also claimed that 'true fascist spirit ... amounts almost to a religion raising them above creed and party'. Whilst lacking the crude racial evangelism for which he would later become infamous, and notably denouncing the Ku Klux Klan as a 'loathsome Secret Society', Leese's racial prejudices still shone through. Horrified by universal suffrage, Leese demanded the removal of those 'unfit to vote' from electoral rolls and the restriction of the franchise to those willing to sacrifice for the nation and, indeed, to pay for the privilege, through a 'voters income tax'. Leese also disenfranchised 'naturalised aliens of the first generation' and the Irish – 'always excepting the Loyalists'. Whilst he did not explicitly target Jews, Leese recorded his desire to 'get rid' of the 'large foreign element in our midst which is ousting our own people from employment'. His only statement specifically on 'race' affirmed simply that 'we National Fascists believe first and foremost in the splendid qualities of our own race'.[36] Leese's overarching conception of 'Fascism' was decidedly superficial, however. 'I have often heard people say that you cannot define Fascism,' he later recorded. 'I always said I could: a revolt against democracy and a return to statesmanship.'[37]

Leese took the Stamford BF branch over to the BNF and regularly wrote to the local press stressing the racial aspects of Fascism. 'Why does not the Government act against the Soviet?' asked one letter rhetorically. 'International Jews' was the answer. To arrest this process, Stamford's residents were asked to 'Support the National Fascists for a Nordic Revival'. Leese also organised fascist 'crusades' to spread the word to neighbouring towns and villages and in September 1926 invited Rippon-Seymour to address local members and the townspeople of Stamford. Following a tirade from Leese against the 'massed ignorance' induced by democracy as a precursor to Communism, Rippon-Seymour told the audience that Fascism would bring an end to class war and that a wise and benevolent dictator would govern with 'efficiency'. Furthermore, he stated, the 'alien question' was of pressing concern as the country was 'swarming with aliens and Jews'.[38]

The BNF disbanded in May 1927, shortly after Rippon-Seymour threatened several members with pistol and sword following their arrival at his Hammersmith offices to ventilate their disquiet at the fact that not only had he changed its constitution without consultation but had also 'systematically misappropriated' the organisation's funds.[39] Rippon-Seymour, who had previously been summoned for carrying firearms without a license, was subsequently fined £5 for assault.[40] Following the collapse of the BNF, Leese converted the remnants of the Stamford BNF into a 'Fascist League', a temporary structure through which to keep activists together. He remained a councillor but found democratic representation 'dull'. He stepped down in October 1927 having served a single term.[41] He retired in June 1928 and moved to 20 Pewley Hill, Guildford in Surrey, which, with a characteristically racist flourish, he rechristened the 'White House'.

Kitson and Beamish

His involvement with the BNF coincided with the effects of the Great Depression filtering through to Stamford and indeed the crystallisation of his own anti-Semitic interpretation of world events. The farming industry was hit severely by falling prices 'and my practice suffered a blow from which it never recovered,' Leese lamented. Against this backdrop, Leese struggled to understand how, 'although we had won the war, we seemed to be losing every yard of the peace which followed. Something, I felt, must be acting like a spanner in the works.'[42] His search for the source of this dislocation had already led Leese to the door of his neighbour, Arthur Kitson, inventor of the famous Kitson Lights, used for illuminating lighthouses. Kitson, who had worked with Thomas Edison on the original electric light and Alexander Graham Bell, inventor of the telephone, had another ruling passion: monetary reform. His critique of the banking system centred increasingly upon the role Jews supposedly played within it.[43] Whilst his work profoundly influenced social credit circles, Kitson's work was largely ignored by economists and politicians in Britain. He found a more receptive audience in Nazi Germany to which he was invited in September 1935 as a guest of the government 'and there he discussed the question of money with the Führer's representatives'.[44]

Kitson addressed a political meeting in Stamford. This was most likely at some point in late 1922. Leese was 'very much interested & went, after the meeting, to speak to him – & so it all began', recalled his widow in 1956.[45] 'I felt he knew something, goodness knows what, which others didn't, including myself,' Leese stated of his compulsion to call upon Kitson. Their subsequent friendship, which lasted until Kitson's death in 1937, was pivotal to Leese's political development. Kitson introduced Leese to the idea of the 'Jewish Menace' of which 'hitherto I had no knowledge'. It was not until he was forty-five, Leese later confessed that, 'I knew anything about what was going on behind the political scene.'[46] To aid his education, Kitson introduced his pupil to The Britons Publishing Society, a small anti-Semitic publishing house founded in 1919, from whom he obtained a copy of *The Protocols of the Elders of Zion*, a document purporting to reveal Jewish plans for world domination. In 1921, *The Times* Constantinople correspondent, Phillip Graves, exposed the book as a 'clumsy forgery' fabricated by the Tsarist secret police and based on Maurice Joly's anti-Bonapartist tract, *Dialogue aux Enfers entre Machiavel et Montesquieu, ou la Politique de Machiavel au XIX Siècle. Par un Contemporain* (1865).[47]

The Protocols' counterfeit provenance was immaterial to Leese. 'Everything in this little book rang true; I simply could not put it down until I had finished it.'[48] *The Protocols* was more than just the supposed template for Jewish world domination; it outlined the parameters of a global racial struggle between Aryan and Jew, waged eternally and universally, physically and metaphysically, until one was extinct. In essence, *The Protocols* put readers on notice of the magnitude of the conspiracy ranged against them in the hope that they would rage against their racial enemy.[49] Indeed, the second British imprint of *The Protocols*, published by The Britons as *The Jewish Peril* (1920), averred that the First World War and the subsequent Bolshevik revolution in 1917 was part of a 'Jew war' that represented 'nothing less than the extermination of Christians and the destruction of Christian nationality'. Unless the 'White Races' combined against the Jews 'and burst their usurious bonds, the enslavement of the nations will soon be irrevocable and compete.'[50] *The Protocols* and indeed The Britons newspaper, *The Hidden Hand or Jewry Ueber Alles*, were regarded by the police as 'scurrilous and anti-Semitic and are no doubt intended to lead to racial prejudice and pogroms in this country'.[51]

Leese internalised the doctrine of race war implicit at the heart of *The Protocols* as part and parcel of his development of a 'Nazi conscience' – an all-embracing, internally coherent set of ethical maxims that licensed any act against its racial foe, no matter how atrocious or barbaric, as part of a morally righteous war for racial survival.[52] No sooner had he finished *The Protocols* than Leese wrote to The Britons requesting further information. The Britons founder, Henry Hamilton Beamish, similarly 'lost no time', such was the urgency of their struggle. 'He appeared outside my door at Stamford on a motor-cycle side-car within two days of my application,' recalled Leese.[53] Unlike Kitson, Beamish was not even remotely interested in monetary reform, which he regarded as 'perfectly useless … until the Jew is entirely eliminated from the National life of the Aryan Races'.[54] Leese adopted the same view, though he never actually joined The Britons, preferring instead 'to paddle my own canoe'.[55]

Beamish, revered by Leese as an anti-Jewish 'pioneer', was the scion of a distinguished family, the third son of Rear Admiral H.H. Beamish, a former aide-de-camp to Queen Victoria. His brother, Rear Admiral Tufton Beamish, was twice Conservative MP for Lewes (1924–1931 and 1936–1945). Having left home at sixteen, Beamish, who was born in 1874, became a fur trader in Alaska, farmed wheat on the prairies and grew tea in Ceylon. He served in the Boer War during which time he 'discovered' that Jews ruled the world. Following a period in Rhodesia and South Africa and service in the First World War, Beamish returned to England, where he became involved in radical right-wing politics through the Vigilantes League led by Noel Pemberton Billing MP. Following a split within the League, he and Dr J.H. Clarke, a homeopath, founded The Britons in 1919. Together with another accomplice, Beamish also displayed a poster in London in March 1919 denouncing Sir Alfred Mond, the Jewish Commissioner for Works, as a traitor to his country. Mond sued and rather than pay the fine Beamish fled the country, returning only sporadically. Thereafter, he became something of a 'travelling salesman' for anti-Semitism, traversing the globe in the hope of raising public consciousness of the 'Jewish peril'.[56]

Unlike many of his colleagues who, in the wake of the First World War, were rabidly anti-German, Beamish's Aryan anti-Semitism compelled him towards collaboration with like-minded *völkisch* nationalists in Germany. In early 1923, he addressed a meeting of the Nationalsozialistische Deutsche Arbeiterpartei (NSDAP – National Socialist German Workers Party) in Munich. His speech was translated by the journalist Dietrich Eckart, a leading figure in the *Thule-Gesellschaft* (Thule Society), an occult *völkisch* society that served as an important ideological tributary to the Nazi party. Eckart was a mentor to the NSDAP leader, Adolf Hitler.[57] Though Eckart understood little English, he and Beamish 'understood one another by reason of their common ideals'.[58] The Britons newspaper, *The Hidden Hand*, subsequently delivered a glowing report on 'Germany's White Labour Party'. Its readers would 'be delighted' to learn that the 'Aryan spirit' was rising throughout the world in revolt against the power of Jewry, it reported. It also claimed Beamish had made Hitler's acquaintance and that, after studying the Nazis, 'was returning to England with the idea of starting a similar movement'.[59]

Contact between the *Thule-Gesellschaft* and The Britons persisted. The Bavarian activist Kurt Kerlen, with whom the group exchanged ideas and information, lectured The Britons on 12 July 1923.[60] Influenced by such contacts, The Britons executive committee voted on 15 September to form an 'Aryan Association' separate from its publishing activities.[61] The idea failed to take root, however. Nevertheless, in the following year, Kurt Lüdecke, one of Hitler's early supporters, visited The Britons in an effort to elicit funds for the fledgling Nazi party. Though the visit was financially unrewarding, Lüdecke gained 'real profit' from contact with his 'new allies'.[62] Lüdecke subsequently commended The Britons' newspaper, *British Guardian*, as 'an excellent co-worker in the Great Cause' adding that, 'we believe that only an international White League of Christians can fight the Jew successfully and decisively, and that a universal crusade is needed in order to exterminate the Jewish pest everywhere'.[63]

Imperial Fascist League

Such thinking was at the ideological heart of a new group that emerged in September 1928. The origins of the Imperial Fascist League (IFL) remain obscure. Initially, the group garnered about thirty members, from 'three genuine fascist groups' though principally from the BF.[64] The most high-profile BF recruit was Brigadier-General R.B.D. Blakeney. He was also involved with The Britons whose members were strongly represented in the IFL: Beamish became vice-president.[65] Leese was not, by one account, the original leader. He became so after replacing a man called 'Cole', who faded into obscurity thereafter. Leese lived in comparative isolation from London in provincial Guildford meaning that, as Harold Lockwood, an insurance salesman who later became one of Leese's closest collaborators, subsequently recalled, 'we did not get on to him until 1929'.[66] Leese soon became Director-General, running the organisation with Major J. Baillie, Leslie H. Sherrard and 'Brigadier-General' D. Erskine Tulloch, formerly the British Fascists 'Chief of Staff', whose military credentials MI5 questioned.[67] This triumvirate soon fell by the wayside, however, and by 1931 Leese was in sole control. His burgeoning racial anti-Semitism showed no restraint thereafter.[68]

Originally housed at 63 Chandos House, Buckingham Gate, in 1930 the IFL moved its offices to 16 Craven Street, Strand, described as 'two rooms without a telephone over a tailor's shop'.[69] In March 1929, Leese had begun publishing *The Fascist* – 'the organ of Fascist opinion' – its masthead emblazoned with the *fasces*, signalling its allegiance to Italian Fascism. *The Fascist* advocated the abolition of British democracy and its replacement with the Corporate State whose roots – 'those of the old Craft Guilds of Britain' – he believed to be universally applicable, though ultimately his enthusiasm for what he came to regard as a 'dull subject' waned.[70] Leese's fervour for Fascism as transnational concept endured slightly longer.

The Fascist's inaugural issue heralded Leese as the 'British correspondent' for the Swiss-based *Centre International d'Études sur la Fascisme* (CINEF – International Centre of Fascist Studies), which sought to 'export' Fascist ideas.[71] Major James S. Barnes was the secretary-general of this short-lived initiative. Barnes was a cousin of Lytton Strachey. He had been well connected with the Modernist avant-garde before becoming enamoured by Mussolini who had contributed a preface to his book, *The Universal Aspects of Fascism* (1928). Barnes was close to the anti-Semitic American poet Ezra Pound, perhaps *The Fascist*'s most high-profile subscriber, who considered the publication 'grand'.[72] That said, Pound also griped: 'too bad he [Leese] isn't exact with his facts. just jewphobia. amusing, lively but NOT practical.'[73] Barnes and Pound became 'Mussolini's most ardent and persistent Anglophone apostles', both men broadcasting for Fascist Italy during the Second World War including Mussolini's ill-fated Salò Republic. Barnes somehow escaped prosecution afterwards. Pound was confined to a mental institution.[74]

Such connections artificially amplified Leese's influence. The IFL remained the archetypal fascist *groupuscule*, its influence upon the wider public regarded as 'infinitesimal' by the authorities.[75] *The Fascist* had a steady circulation of around 3,000 copies, though a Mr Pope of Porthcawl, South Wales, purchased 1,000 copies sending the majority to South African sympathisers, leading Leese to claim that *The Fascist* was 'strongly entrenched' in the country 'from Cape Town to Durban to Northern Rhodesia'.[76] IFL membership was even smaller. MI5 observed in 1941 that it never exceeded 1,000 supporters and, at the time of its demise, had only 400 members.[77] Its activist base was considerably less. In January 1934, Special Branch reported the group was a mere 150-strong with another thirty to forty 'associate members' from abroad.[78] Furthermore, noted another source, practically all its London activities were carried out by 'about 50 enthusiasts' most of whom were activists in its 'Imperial Guard'.[79] Leese himself acknowledged that 'among our recruits we found that only one out of every ten has it in him to be a useful pioneer'. The other nine belonged to the category 'that hears a Fascist speaker or reads a Fascist pamphlet, gets excited, joins up, samples a bit of work, and then, like an "old soldier" simply fades away.' Retaining members, a perennial problem for fascist groups, did not bother Leese who was more interested in cultivating an 'Inner Circle' or racial elite.[80]

Despite its small size, the IFL had three grades of membership: The Graduates' Association, in which reposed the future 'governing aristocracy' of the Corporate State; the Fascist Legions, constituting the organisation's uniformed militia led initially by 'Commandant-General' Leslie H. Sherrard; and the Activist Confederations, the economic and industrial branch of the IFL.[81] Of these, only the Fascist Legions had any basis in reality and even this was slight. It was noted at a major IFL meeting in 1933 that the so-called Legions consisted of sixteen uniformed members who would have been hard pressed to fulfil their stated task of suppressing Bolshevik revolution.[82] In April 1933, *The Fascist* announced the formation of the 'Centre Detachment' or 'OC Detachment' as it was also known. This existed to carry out 'the activist part of the League's programme' primarily through uniformed street sales of the IFL newspaper. The secretary-general personally vetted all recruits. No 'recreation room' Fascists need apply, warned Leese.[83]

Perpetually short of money, the IFL had been founded with capital of £5, only once in its first five years of existence did its funds reach £100, approximately the amount required per annum to run the organisation.[84] The organisation was largely financed by Leese, supplemented by donations from a relatively small group of 'moderately well-to-do' elderly anti-Semites.[85] The most notable of these was Lieutenant-Colonel F.W.P. MacDonald, a retired Indian Army officer living in Brussels, who donated £5 a month to Leese and, on 25 November 1938, £50. MI5 speculated that MacDonald was a possible 'conduit-pipe' through which the Nazis channelled minor amounts of money to the IFL though, they conceded, 'we have no evidence about this'. More likely, they concluded, MacDonald simply subscribed to the IFL because of his 'shared outlook' with Leese.[86]

Leese and Mosley

Sir Oswald Mosley's conversion to Fascism in 1932 elicited a mixed response from early British fascists, which was at best ambivalent and at worst openly hostile. Leese had denounced Mosley's proto-fascist New Party as being under 'indirect Jewish control' since 1929. Undeterred, Mosley had tried to bring the IFL within his orbit, chairing a meeting at New Party headquarters on 27 April 1932, at which Leese and Beamish spoke on 'The Blindness of British Politics under the Jew Money-Power'. There were further meetings but, complained *The New Times*, 'as usual with the IFL the Jewish question seemed to them the only one worth their consideration'.[87] Mosley's encounter with the IFL was, his biographer asserted, the beginning of his education to the 'realities' as opposed to the 'surface realities' of modern life. Shortly afterwards, anti-Semitism featured in an early draft of *Greater Britain* (1932), the founding document of the British Union of Fascists (BUF), but was removed at the insistence of one of Mosley's collaborators.[88]

Leese resisted suggestions to merge with the New Party, suspicious both of Mosley's past socialism and his emerging 'fascism in theory'.[89] He responded to rumours that Mosley was about to 'go Fascist' by stating 'there is a much more profound process than the mere putting on of a black shirt.'[90] When Mosley founded the BUF in October 1932, Leese instructed his activists to wear swastika armbands to differentiate themselves from their rivals after the BUF adopted Blackshirts. Mosley, thought Leese, was an opportunistic popinjay and thus an undesirable leader for 'Nordic Fascism'. At root, however, his suspicion of Mosley was racial.[91] In May 1932, *The Fascist* reported 'Joseph Leiter, a Jew who cornered wheat profit to himself, died last month. He was the uncle of the wife of Sir Oswald Mosley'.[92] The Britons had highlighted this genealogy as early as March 1925.[93] Having read Lord Snowdon's autobiography, Leese convinced himself that Mosley himself was Jewish, subsequently listing him in his pamphlet, *Our Jewish Aristocracy: A Tale of Contamination* (1936).[94] He later simply observed that Mosley was a 'proper bastard',[95] who looked like a 'Dago'.[96]

Mosley dismissed Leese as 'absolutely certifiable'.[97] He also attacked the IFL as 'one of those little crank societies. They are mad about the Jews. They are a ridiculous and futile body. All their active members joined us long ago' – which was hardly a disavowal of anti-Semitism.[98] Mosley could not ignore Leese altogether though. From the sidelines Leese began claiming Mosley was a 'kosher fascist' whose 'British Jewnion of Fascists' only served to discredit genuine racial Fascism.[99] Leese made a point of differentiating between what he regarded as Mosley's hollow 'anti-Jewish attitude' and a genuine 'racial one'.[100] He also began claiming that Mosley's children were 'of Jewish blood' as a result of which he was 'savagely beaten up' by BUF activists at a public meeting on 24 November 1933, enduring the added humiliation of having his trousers torn off.[101] The attack had its intended effect. In the months afterwards, noted MI5, the IFL became 'moribund' with Leese, no doubt suitably chastened, concentrating instead upon the distribution of anti-Semitic propaganda.[102]

Mosley's 'muscling in' on British fascism 'took what little wind there was out of our sails for a time,' Leese conceded. The IFL activism recovered slowly, however, the anti-Semitic asperity of its East End activists serving as a recruiting standard for disillusioned BUF members.[103] As the BUF membership base began contracting after its peak in 1934, Leese added to the anxiety of the BUF leadership by poaching some of its activists in January 1935.[104] The IFL secretary James F. Rushbrook was despatched upon a country-wide tour targeting other disaffected Mosleyites leading to the formation of an IFL branch in Bristol in July but 'little progress' thereafter.[105]

Leese remained implacably opposed to Mosley for the remainder of his life, his animus fuelled by the belief that darker forces were seeking control of British Fascism. To this end, in May 1935, Leese published 'amazing exposures' that one of Mosley's lieutenants, Major-General J.F.C. Fuller, was involved with Aleister Crowley's occult activities, which, though it smacked of the absurd, was perfectly true.[106] Fuller threatened to sue but legal counsel, aware of the 'flood of unpleasant publicity' that would result for both the General and the BUF if his association with 'The Beast' became more widely known, dropped the proposed libel writ.[107] For Leese, the failure of the threatened libel action to materialise confirmed his view of the BUF's 'Armenoid mentality'.[108] It is unknown whether Leese was aware that Michael Hay, one of his own 'chief assistants' who had been expelled from the BUF for 'sodomy' was 'very friendly' with Fuller.[109]

Leese's relationship with other fascist *groupuscules* was no better. Under its new president, Lieutenant-Colonel H.C. Bruce Wilson, the BF had become increasingly anti-Semitic and pro-Nazi. In May 1934, Leese bemoaned that despite their programmatical propinquity the BF and IFL remained separate organisations. This was hardly surprising. Leese had already rejected a number of entreaties to work together and had attacked Wilson in print as a 'Freemason'.[110] Wilson refused to respond to this 'malevolent buffoonery' but retorted haughtily:

> It is not part of the programme of our Journal to waste its efforts in attempting to restrain a self-anointed Messiah of Fascism in this country from making a gratuitous exhibition before the public of his lack of the necessary qualifications for the very responsible position which he aspires to occupy.[111]

Leese attacked the BF again in the following month, his enmity heightened having discovered in the interim that the joint-editor of the BF journal, *British Fascism*, was one A.M. Sabine who, he alleged, had tried to split the IFL in 1929 and was compelled by a magistrate 'to return IFL property illegally detained by him'. Leese now flatly ruled out any possibility of future cooperation unless 'governed entirely' by the IFL.[112] Wilson simply mocked Leese's claim to be racial fascism's progenitor and advised him to read *Mein Kampf* in which 'there is no mention of Mr Arnold Leese'.[113]

Rejecting Leese, Wilson negotiated a merger with Mosley. He failed, however, to convince Lintorn-Orman of its merits. Having a controlling financial interest in the movement, Wilson was able to simply throw the BF out its headquarters, rented in his name, and take his supporters into the BUF.[114] When Lintorn-Orman died in May 1935, the remainder of the BF disintegrated.[115] Her adjutant Gordon Woods, who had applied for 'honorary membership' of the Nazi party, tried to arrange for an NSDAP delegation to attend her funeral. The organisation 'is so unimportant that it is not worth our while' responded Otto Bene, the Nazi *Ortsgruppenleiter* in Britain.[116] Woods and the remaining BF activists joined Leese. Woods subsequently became the IFL foreign liaison officer.[117]

The lure of Nazism

Leese's enthusiasm for Italian Fascism dissipated as his gaze fell upon Hitler's rising star, though he never personally visited Nazi Germany. In September 1930, Leese had applauded the Nazis after they became the second party in Saxony, though it was clear his ideological understanding was slight. 'Why on earth they call themselves "National Socialists" we do not know,' he lamented.[118] The lure of Nazism was more apparent in the following month when *The Fascist* published a front-page declaration regarding 'The German Fascists and Ourselves', which argued that the fundamental difference between the Fascism and Nazism was the question of 'Land' versus 'Race' whilst highlighting their 'sympathy' with Hitler's determination to rid Germany of 'aliens'.[119] Leese's enthusiasm grew even greater when Hitler was elected Chancellor. Having come to regard Mussolini as unsound on the 'Jewish question', Leese replaced the *fasces* with the swastika on *The Fascist*'s masthead in January 1933. 'We are backing Hitler, right from the word "Go", and we know we are on a certainty,' announced *The Fascist*. 'Hail Hitler and his Aryan policy'.[120] In March 1934, he rebranded *The Fascist* as 'the organ of racial Fascism'. As his enthusiasm for Nazism soared, Leese's admiration for Mussolini plummeted. Mussolini had 'ratted' and Fascist Italy had 'gone to the Jews', he claimed.[121] In retrospect, Leese argued that Mussolini had never had a hope of reviving the country. 'Rome was not made by men of the races which preponderate in Modern Italy', he declared.[122]

Leese's embrace of racial fascism quickly led to the establishment of direct contact with Nazi functionaries. From April 1931 onwards, *The Fascist* began featuring articles from Dr Hans Thost, London correspondent for *Völkischer Beobatcher*, the official NSDAP newspaper edited by Nazi ideologue Alfred Rosenberg, author of *Der Mythus des 20. Jahrhunderts* (1930). Thost, who had lived in England since October 1930, was later identified as 'the key man charged with building up the Nazi machine in Britain'.[123] In *The Fascist*, Thost argued that Nazi foreign policy sought only the revision of 'unjust treaties' and 'the unity of the Nordic Race against the penetration of international Jewish influence and in general to keep the White Races strong and free from pollution by the inferior elements of the human species'.[124] Thost addressed an IFL meeting on 3 June 1931 on 'The German National Socialists'[125] and in September helped establish the first Nazi Ortsgruppe in

London, becoming its initial Ortsgruppenleiter. Initially, this group was intimately linked to the IFL. 'The Ortsgruppe here has not yet developed very far,' wrote one member. 'Once a week we attend meetings of the Imperial Fascist League, which runs along the same lines as Herr Graefe, General Luddendorff, etc. Afterwards we get together at an Italian café where Dr Thost skilfully keeps the conversation flowing'.[126]

Leese remained in touch with Thost, complaining to him in November 1932 about the apparent discourtesy shown to an IFL member visiting the Nazi party.[127] The IFL had hoped Thost would act as their bridge to Rosenberg who had visited Britain in November 1931 and did so again in May 1933 as head of the newly established Aussenpolitische Amt (APA), the foreign policy office of the Nazi party.[128] Thost failed to oblige, however.[129] He had far more pressing tasks to attend to than pandering to Leese. His role as a Nazi propagandist was far more ambitious in its scope, leading, ultimately, to his expulsion from Britain in November 1935.[130]

Leese developed a more profitable relationship with Julius Streicher, editor of the rabidly anti-Semitic Nazi newspaper *Der Stürmer* who had organised the anti-Jewish boycott in April 1933 but had slipped out of favour within the Nazi hierarchy thereafter. Streicher praised Leese for his efforts to alert the 'schlafenden Engländer' ('sleeping Englishman') to 'die jüdische gefahr' ('the Jewish danger') and admired the IFL for their '*stürmisch*' language.[131] Leese established direct contact with Streicher through 'Professor' Cecil Serocold Skeels, a former missionary and classics teacher, who had suffered a complete nervous breakdown during the First World War.[132] Skeels and the IFL secretary, J.F. Rushbrook, attended a meeting with Streicher in Adolf Hitler Platz, Nuremberg on 30 September 1933.[133] Addressing the 120,000-strong audience, Skeels delivered a message of Nordic solidarity from the 'anti-Jewish Fascists of England' who 'fight with Hitler against the Jews' and for the 'Nordic Race'. After his short speech 'Herr Streicher then grasped Mr. Skeels hand, and the crowd let themselves go. Mr. Skeels then left in Herr Streicher's car amid loud applause and cries of "Hail England".' Leese noted that the IFL was not 'pro-German' but 'we are pro-Hitler, and shall be equally so with regard to any other Hitler who may appear in any country in the world, whose policy is that of Nordic Fascism'.[134] Skeels was expelled from the IFL shortly afterwards, however. He subsequently became active in the Nordic League, a vehemently anti-Semitic coterie notable for its pro-Nazi intriguing. Widely regarded as a Nazi 'spy', Skeels was subsequently jailed for two years during the Second World War.[135]

Streicher was internationally condemned for propagating the 'ritual murder' charge against the Jews in *Der Stürmer* in May 1934. Leese, who had himself been retailing the 'blood libel' charge since September 1932, applauded Streicher's courage, stating that the canard was 'an established fact'.[136] He also obtained twenty-four copies of the offending issue of *Der Stürmer*, selling them for a pound a piece to raise funds for the IFL.[137] Leese may well have obtained these directly from Streicher's son, Lothar, who arrived in London on 8 August 1934, lodging with a female BUF member. Warned against partaking in the activities of British fascist organisations, Lothar was nevertheless alleged to be 'making contacts on behalf of his father' with British pro-Nazi groups before his hurried departure in the following month.[138] In 1937, Streicher's other son, Elmar, also visited London and addressed the IFL – the 'proper' British fascist movement. Leese, he averred, 'was a straight-line anti-Semite, and I wanted to experience it.' There was a fistfight with anti-fascists. 'I finished up in court,' noted Elmar. The Streichers also accommodated a female IFL member at their house, who competed with Unity Mitford, Mosley's sister-in-law, for Julius Streicher's affections. 'She wanted to fight for Germany but at the declaration of war she was bundled out of the country.'[139]

Leese continued to sell Streicher's ritual murder special issue with impunity. Despite concerns being ventilated in the House of Commons in May 1934, the Home Office decided prosecution of those selling the newspaper was not in the public interest.[140] The 'blood libel' accusation was perhaps a niche concern even within anti-Semitic circles. Leese was still hawking the remaining few copies of *Der Stürmer* in 1938, albeit at a greatly reduced price.[141] This consumption of anti-Semitic literature was not one way. *The Fascist* had a small readership in Germany. The Juengersche Buchhandlung in Frankfurt am Main sold it. The IFL also had a 'handful' of German 'associate members' whose 'common purpose' was to render Europe *Judenfrei*.[142]

The IFL did not passively consume Nazi propaganda, however. Reviewing *Hitler*, a pictorial biography of the Führer, published by Berlin's Verlag Tradition, *The Fascist* lamented that whilst the idea was a 'good one ... there is not enough in the book about the Jew Menace for the education of the average English reader.'[143] The IFL was even capable of finding fault with publications like *Der Ewige Jude* (*The Eternal Jew*), an illustrated compilation of portraits of 'Jewish physiognomy'.[144]

An array of personal and political connections with the Third Reich underpinned transnational networking between IFL activists and their German counterparts.[145] Informal efforts to acculturate the membership was facilitated by tours of the 'New Germany' and holidays in the Bavarian Alps ('Aryan Visitors Only').[146] More formal means were provided through officially organised excursions. In September 1935, four IFL activists led by William Bird, the Maidenhead District Leader, attended the Nuremberg rally as 'official guests' of *Der Stürmer*.[147] The visit highlighted the perils of transnational activism. One activist, Benjamin Barrett, a former Liverpool police officer and IFL section leader, recalled the IFL contingent enjoyed 'very cordial' relations with their German counterparts until conversation turned to the question of returning Germany's colonies. IFL policy, unlike that of Mosley's BUF, opposed this. 'Up to that time we had been wearing our blackshirts,' Barrett subsequently recalled, 'but when this information became generally known amongst the Germans who had conversed with us we had an order to take off the blackshirts and travel round Nuremberg in civil attire'. Barrett cut short his trip and returned home.[148] Despite this incident, IFL activists attended the 1936 Nuremberg rally, once more at Streicher's invitation.

Political and personal bonds were also strengthened by the participation of IFL activists in commemorative, memorialising events. For instance, on 6 October 1933, a group of three IFL representatives placed a wreath on the Munich War Memorial. A Nazi functionary officially received them and stated 'English Comrades, you have honoured our dead with the colours of your country which ALSO BEAR THE SWASTIKA, the symbol of our common race. This action we recognise and appreciate to the full. HAIL, GERMANY! HAIL, ENGLAND!'[149] Closer to home, the IFL also signalled their desire to be officially recognised at the ceremony in Potters Bar, Hertfordshire, held to commemorate the German aircrew of two Zeppelin balloons which had been shot down during the First World War, an event which by 1936 had strong Nazi connotations.[150]

Henry Hamilton Beamish remained the pivotal figure, however. In January 1937, Beamish embarked upon a lecture tour of Germany, sanctioned by the Nazi ambassador to London, Joachim von Ribbentrop.[151] Speaking in Bavaria on 20 January, Beamish addressed rumours of 'atrocities' being committed at Dachau concentration camp, which he claimed to have visited. 'It's a good thing *I'm* not commandant at Dachau', he told the audience. He then unfurled a map of Madagascar, decorated with a Star of David, and outlined his plan to deport Europe's Jews to the island *en masse*. Two days later, Beamish spoke in Nuremberg where Streicher introduced him and spoke of 'the blood-relationship between Germany and England and demanded mutual understanding and the reaching out of the hand of friendship'. Reciprocating, Beamish 'took his hat off to Gauleiter Julius Streicher who had dared to defy the whole world in the *Stürmer*'.[152] Having surveyed the *mise en scène*, the British Consulate noted that Beamish 'seems to be quite definitely in Nazi pay'.[153] Returning to England, in April 1937 Beamish delivered a lecture to an IFL audience titled 'National Socialism (Racial Fascism) in Practice in Germany' based on his 'personal observation'.[154]

The IFL also operated within the orbit of transnational Nazi propaganda networks. It was directly involved with the Berlin-based Bund Völkischer Europäer/Alliance Raciste Européene (BVE/ARE), founded in 1928 by Baron Robert de Fabre-Luce, which sought to produce foreign translations of *völkisch* Nazi propaganda. Beamish was its President in 1934.[155] He was not the only IFL activist involved. The British composer Roland Bocquet, an IFL member who in 1936 was appointed Professor of Musical Theory at Dresden Conservatory, sat on the BVE/ARE 'Council' and vetted the quality of its translations.[156] Leese utilised material from the organisation's 'Pan-Aryan' newspaper, *Reichswart*, in *The Fascist*, which he also commended to his own readership.[157]

More importantly, Leese was also involved with the *Welt-Dienst* (*World Service*) network dedicated to 'the resolution of the Jewish question' through *Voll-Zionismus* ('total Zionism'), the enforced migration of Jews to Madagascar. This was also IFL policy. *Welt-Dienst* was run from Erfurt, the capital city of Thuringia, by Colonel Ulrich Fleischhauer. It achieved notoriety after helping organise the defence of a group of Swiss Nazis prosecuted during the 'Berne trials' (1933–1937) for disseminating *The Protocols* which, despite being branded a forgery by the court, did little to discredit the authenticity of the tract in the eyes of its believers.[158] *Welt-Dienst*'s anti-Semitic leaflets, published in several languages and passed hand-to-hand, were part of the 'intellectual armoury of every Aryan' opposed to the malign machinations of the 'Jewish underworld'.[159] The correspondents and disseminators of *Welt-Dienst* represented a veritable 'Who's Who' of the international anti-Semitic milieu. Leese often reprinted its material in *The Fascist* and *Welt-Dienst* itself had an IFL correspondent who used the penname 'Mac-L'.[160] It is with some justification therefore that one contemporary branded the IFL one of several 'subsidiary channels' for Nazi propaganda into Britain.[161] The importance of the Erfurt organisation as a focal point for transnational anti-Semitic agitation can be viewed monochromatically in its absence after 1945. 'With assistance from the Germans it was possible that Leese could formerly claim to be well informed,' stated one post-war MI5 report, 'but now that this assistance was no longer available it was difficult to see that Leese could make the over-confident claims that he did'.[162]

The IFL did not simply passively imbibe Nazi propaganda, however. They actively participated in its production and dissemination. In September 1937, Fleischhauer chaired a three-day anti-Semitic conference in Erfurt. Several British anti-Semites aligned to the IFL attended including Beamish; Margaret Bothamley, a founding IFL activist known within anti-Semitic circles as 'the scourge of the Jews', who later broadcast for the Nazis; Major James Davidson-Houston, a former Kings Messenger; and Brigadier-General R.B.D. Blakeney, who 'went to sleep most of the time,' noted Beamish contemptuously. Leese did not attend. He did, however, contribute an 'excellent paper' recorded Beamish, which was translated into German and French and distributed to the attendees. It was not universally well received. Leese 'put his foot in it badly as he always does,' noted Beamish, by adding at the bottom of his paper that the Englishman's place was not in Erfurt but in England. This took some explanation on my part explaining to delegates many of whom had travelled thousands of miles to attend the Conference!! According to Leese they all should have remained in their own countries![163]

Leese's writings caused rather less controversy when used to buttress the anti-Semitic view of England projected by Nazi propagandists. The Nazi party press agency inserted IFL leaflets into its own official pamphlets, 'presumably to show that a British organisation also preaches the doctrines of Nordic supremacy and anti-Semitism,' noted an observer in 1934.[164] The Nazis also reproduced *Mightier Yet* (1935), the official IFL declaration of policy, as a thirty-page English-language booklet published as Erich Wötzel, *The Imperial Fascist League* (1937).[165] Other Nazi books, including Werner Haas' *Europa Will Leben* (1936) and Heinz Krieger's *England und die Judenfrage in Geschichte und Gegenwart* (1938), made liberal use of IFL propaganda too.[166] Leese's pamphlet *Our Jewish Aristocracy* also informed *Die englisch–jüdische Allianz* (1942) by Wolf Meyer-Christian, a study of the 'Jewification of the English people'.[167] Most important of all, however, was *Das Judentum in England* (1943) by Peter Aldag, who stated of the IFL that they, 'pursue the same program as us in relation to the Jews, and who see in them the greatest danger for England'.[168]

'Peter Aldag' was a pseudonym for the lawyer and SS officer Dr Fritz Krüger. He combined espionage with the dissemination of anti-Semitic propaganda through the Anglo-German Academic Bureau, which organised an exchange programme for German students and teachers as a cover for its Nazi propaganda role.[169] From 1935 onwards, Krüger busied himself with his 'special mission to study the Jewish question' and 'engage in anti-Jewish propaganda among English circles'.[170] Regarded as a Nazi intelligence agent by the British security services, in May 1939 Krüger was refused re-entry into Britain. Interestingly, as he attempted to disembark, the authorities observed that Krüger was in the company of Robert Gair MA, a Scottish anthropologist who had been lecturing on race and ethnology in Germany whilst also pursuing a sideline as a casual MI6 informant on matters pertaining to German academia. Gair, who subsequently altered the spelling of his name to Gayre, went on to play a pivotal role in resurrecting 'racial science' after 1945 through his journal *Mankind Quarterly*.[171]

Beyond these ties to formalised Nazi structures, the development and diffusion of *völkisch* anti-Semitic ideas percolated into IFL through Leese's 'old friend' Capel Pownall, a competitor with the British archery team at the 1908 Olympic Games, who subsequently authored *The Jews, 'News', and Archery* (1928). From his home in Switzerland, Pownall 'indulged in an orgy of anti-British propaganda' during the First World War and was regarded as a 'complete renegade' by MI5. He was expelled from Switzerland in May 1918 but persuaded the authorities to deport him to Germany rather than France enabling him to escape judicial retribution, much to the chagrin of the Foreign Office who regarded him as 'positively pernicious'.[172] Safely ensconced in Konstanz, Pownall translated numerous anti-Semitic articles from Nazi publications like *Völkischer Beobatcher* into English for reprint by *The Fascist*. Pownall returned to live in Woking in the late 1920s, distributing anti-Semitic publications under the guise of 'Hammer Publications'. He soon earned a reputation as a querulous figure; an illuminating portrait of the man provided by the local Conservative Party agent:

> He caused a disturbance at one of our election meetings in Woking; he brought a gang of about six men with him. I had to threaten to turn them all out. Pownall is frequently

in trouble here, he refuses to pay his rates and won't give particulars for the Registers. He was run in for assault recently on a neighbour, and after the election the Post Master in confidence told me he had been caught pasting notices on the pillar boxes: 'You fools to be ruled by Jews'. He used to send me picture postcards of fat Jews smoking big cigars, entitled 'Baby Killers', or with similar idiotic remarks written on them.[173]

Recognising a kindred spirit, Leese hailed Pownall as a 'veritable pioneer' when he died on 8 February 1933.[174] Pownall's lasting contribution to Anglophone anti-Semitism was his translation of *The Riddle of the Jew's Success* (1927), sold by The Britons with whom Pownall had a long association.[175] *The Fascist*'s review of *The Riddle of the Jew's Success* praised its author 'Ferdinand Roderich-Stoltheim' for revealing that the 'absence of social obligation or of shame give him [the Jew] that abnormal code of conduct which is now becoming the rule of business, although quite alien to the Nordic Race'. The Jews' 'abnormal' code of conduct placed more noble Aryan competitors at a considerable disadvantage when confronted with the 'bad ethics of the Jew'. These 'ethics' were deemed genetic and hereditable rather than cultural, underpinning the notion of Jewish incommensurability with European civilisation. Thus, for Leese, 'the entire humanitarian assimilative idea shatters miserably at the first contact with the awful seriousness of racial heredity.'[176]

'Roderich-Stoltheim' was a pseudonym for Theodor Fritsch, a major figure in German anti-Semitic circles from the 1880s onwards, best known for his book *Antisemitenkatechismus* (1887).[177] Fritsch joined the nascent Nazi party, running his own Leipzig-based Hammer-Verlag publishing house and producing *Hammer*, whose articles Pownall often translated for *The Fascist*.[178] A marginal figure for much of his life, Fritsch ended his days as a Reichstag deputy for the Nazi party. Upon his death in September 1933, Leese praised Fritsch as 'the great pioneer' who 'prepared the way for Hitler ... and had the satisfaction of seeing his country saved largely as a result of his 50 years labour against its Jewish pollution'.[179]

The Nordics

The historiography of British fascism has traditionally viewed Leese as the central figure in the development of British racial fascism. Leese was, however, a populariser and vulgariser of *völkisch* racist ideas, many of which percolated into the IFL through John Hooper Harvey, a promising young architectural student who joined the IFL in 1930 and in 1937 would sit on its 'Literary Committee'. In the post-war period, Harvey succeeded in escaping the stigma of his pro-Nazism and anti-Semitism, without having ever publicly recanted either, to become a highly regarded medieval architectural historian. Indeed, his widely read book *The Plantagenets* (1948) gave credence to the 'blood libel' and praised the 'statesmanship' of Edward I for expelling the Jews in 1290.[180]

In January 1933, the same month that *The Fascist* adopted the swastika as its badge of allegiance, Harvey founded The Nordics, a small *völkisch* sect that operated from his home in Little Bookham, Surrey, close to Leese. *The Fascist* heralded it as 'a group of Britons conscious of the ideals of their race, and determined to apply them to the needs of the nation'. The Nordics five-point programme formed 'the foundation of Nordic culture':

1   The sanctity of a given pledge as the keynote of Character.
2   The recognition of Moral Character and Service as the sole criterion of human worth.

3 Marriage and the Family as the basis of National Life.
4 The necessity of Work and Skill for the formation of Character.
5 The inculcation of fitness, moral, mental and physical, and improvement of the Nation's racial standard of health.[181]

Harvey proselytised his racial ideals through a series of lectures to the IFL membership on 'the Nordic Race in History' and wrote a monthly column for *The Fascist* on various aspects of Nordicism.[182] Harvey's small cultic milieu of racial nationalists viewed the British people in millenarian and apocalyptic terms: locked into a terminal spiral of degradation, decay and decline. Only the reawakening and reinvigoration of their waning 'race-consciousness' offered a panacea to the perceived ills of twentieth-century society. Laissez-faire liberalism and the internationalism of both capital and labour were responsible, believed Harvey, for the collapse of traditional values, customs and morals not to mention political authority.

The term 'Nordic', which came into vogue during the 1920s, was generally used interchangeably with 'Aryan'. Synonymous today with Nazi racial theory, 'Aryanism' had a longer indigenous pedigree, however, emerging during the Victorian era as an integral component of the culture of British Empire, 'providing a powerful lens for analysing the pre-colonial past of colonized societies and for the interpretation of the imperial present.' In this respect, IFL racial ideology built upon a conception of 'Aryanism' that had been 'deeply embedded' in Britain's colonial administration of South Asia rather than simply being a Teutonic import.[183]

Indeed, Harvey's beliefs, despite the clear influence of Nazi *völkisch* thought, also derived considerable impetus from the works of Lieutenant-Colonel Lawrence Augustine Waddell, Professor of Tibetan at University College, London who lived at Rothesay on the Isle of Bute, Scotland.[184] Waddell, a former army medical officer who had become an authority on Buddhism whilst in service, was increasingly interested in the 'Aryan' roots of Sumerian and Egyptian civilisations, authoring *The Phoenician Origins of Britons, Scots and Anglo-Saxons* (1924), a confused and confusing work that argued that 'Aryan' blood was concentrated in Britain. Waddell became a staunch IFL supporter.[185] In 1935, he wrote Leese an effusive letter expressing his regret that *The Fascist* 'cannot be read by the vast majority of the British public to put them "Jew wise"'. Leese published the letter in *The Fascist* under the heading 'a testimonial we value'.[186] Following Waddell's death in October 1938, *The Fascist* published a fulsome obituary stating that 'few men have done more than the late Col. Waddell to de-judise British thought by teaching us to know ourselves, and to combat the evil results of the teaching of the Old Testament on the Aryan mind'.[187] Harvey's major work *The Heritage of Britain* (1940), described as 'the story of the coming of civilisation, brought by our Gothic ancestors to Sumeria over five thousand years ago, its history and progress' was a summary of Waddell's researches and was dedicated to him.[188] Leese continued selling *The Heritage of Britain* until 1954 when he sold his remaining stocks to The Britons.[189]

Although Waddell's corpus of work found few converts within mainstream academia, it exerted a pronounced influence upon the racial nationalist tradition in Britain. His book *The Makers of Civilisation in Race and History* (1929) argued that the root of all ancient civilisation sprang from the migration of the 'Sumerian' or original Indo-European or Indo-Aryan peoples, whilst *The British Edda* (1930), a translation of the epic poem, 'served as a constant reminder to the audiences which listened to it, of the fact that the Makers of Civilisation were of the Aryan Race'. Knowledge of the latter, argued Leese, 'gives all Racial

Fascists added confidence in the right of their cause and the certainty of ultimate victory'.[190] Waddell's work showed clearly, 'the vitalizing part played by the blood of the Nordic "Gods" in the whole culture of mankind'.[191] Harvey believed this hidden truth was 'boycotted' because of 'Jewish control' of the media. 'It is impossible to refute his statements', concluded Harvey, 'so he is just ignored, and consequently his books are unheard of by many people'.[192]

Long forgotten by mainstream society, the 'hidden truth' of Waddell's ideas continue to circulate amongst racial nationalist coteries. Colin Jordan, Leese's post-war protégé, proclaimed Waddell's works a 'must' for anyone 'wishing to equip himself or herself as a knowledgeable worker and fighter for the Aryan cause'.[193] John Bean, editor of *Identity*, the British National Party (BNP) journal 'dusted off' his copy of *The Makers of Civilisation in Race and History* in 2004 to argue that European civilisation sprang, not from the Arabs, who were commonly credited with keeping alive the intellectual traditions of ancient Greek civilisation whilst Europe wallowed in the proverbial Dark Ages (an argument that jarred with the anti-Muslim agenda of his party) but from the original Indo-European (or Indo-Aryan) peoples. 'It may all sound rather academic', concluded Bean, 'but I think we need to know where our civilisation sprang from so that we may defend it that much more effectively'.[194]

The Nordics and *ergo* the IFL fervently debated what actually constituted racial identity. Harvey was of the opinion that racial identity was more than mere physical characteristics noting:

> …lots of people in England, Scandinavia and Germany who pat themselves of the back for being 'superior' and 'white men' are lacking in openness, generosity of character etc and are therefore *not* Nordic in the true sense. The real Nordic is certainly not stodgy, but there are plenty of flaxen-haired, blue eyed people who are.[195]

The development of this native 'Nordic' tradition was inevitably influenced by the multitude of *völkisch* nationalist societies that proliferated throughout Germany and Austria before and immediately after the Great War.[196] Harvey developed close ties with the Nazi's leading *völkisch* racial anthropologist Hans F.K. Günther whose book *The Racial Elements of Europe*, published in English in 1927, was swiftly adopted by Leese 'as our textbook on race as the supreme guide to politics'.[197] Günther's work, written amidst a revival of interest in Britain and Germany's shared cultural and linguistic heritage, gained an avid fascist readership who lapped up his claim that, rather than being racially degenerate, Britain comprised between 55 and 60 per cent Nordic stock. At one point, Günther even suggested that Britain and Scandinavia had a higher quotient of Nordic blood than Germany itself. These fantasy findings had no basis in scientific fact. Günther never visited Britain; as a desk-bound Nazi anthropologist, he was reliant upon a racial reading of a handful of artistic portraits, drawings and sculptures for many of his conclusions about Britain's supposed racial composition. Nonetheless, his work had a powerful impact upon the Anglo-German racial imagination not least because its implicit racial internationalism offered fascists an ideological justification for privileging race above nation. 'In the case of Britain', Strobl notes, 'Günther's fundamental "insight" meant that everything could and should be reduced to the alleged racial ties between Britain and Germany'.[198]

'A race,' Günther wrote, 'shows itself in a human group which is marked off from every other human group through its own proper combination of bodily and mental characteristics, and in turn produces only it's like'. His book, which built upon the foundations erected by H.S. Chamberlain and Count Arthur de Gobineau, defined 'race' as being distinct from 'nation' and offered a five-point racial topography of white Europeans: the Nordic, Mediterranean, Dinaric, Alpine and East Baltic. The crude categorisation aside, *The Racial Elements of Europe* offered a stark warning to Europeans. Failure to maintain racial purity, particularly Nordic racial purity, the harbinger of all true culture and human nobility, the seeds of which were carried in the 'blood', would lead inexorably to the real End of History: racial extinction. The book reflected Günther's dread of racial miscegenation and the 'blood chaos' this induced; his fears of the 'Black Peril' were heavily influenced by American eugenicists Lothrop Stoddard, author of *The Rising Tide of Color Against White World-Supremacy* (1920), and Madison Grant, 'the great racialist expert', whose book, *The Passing of the Great Race* (1916) Leese 'thoroughly commended'.[199] Günther's principal concern was the threat 'non-European' Jews, considered to be principally of the Hither Asiatic or Oriental race, posed to white European civilisation. It was the 'Jewish spirit', wrote Günther, coupled with the influence born of 'economic preponderance' that 'brings with it the very greatest danger for the life of the European peoples and of the North American peoples alike.'[200]

The Nordics also introduced *The Fascist*'s readership to Günther's other works including *Rassenkunde des judischen Volkes* (1930), which argued that the root cause of anti-Semitism was 'racial' and was solvable only through the 'complete segregation of the Jewish nation'.[201] Also highlighted was Günther's *Die Verstädterung* (1936), which examined urbanisation from 'a racial standpoint' and which reinforced Leese's belief that 'the poisonous cancer of town life' was responsible for accelerating racial miscegenation. The resulting decline in Nordic racial stock and achievement had to be overcome; 'only then can the Nordic Aryan, noble of the nations, regain his freedom'.[202] *The Fascist* also stressed Nazi 'racial hygiene' books including Arthur Gütt, Ernest Rüdin and Falk Ruttke's *Zur Verhütung erbkranken Nachwuchses. Gesetz und Erläuterungen* (1934), published by J.F. Lehmann Verlag in Munich, the publisher of many of Günther's works.[203]

Whilst *The Fascist* introduced Günther's work into the British racial fascist tradition, it was Harvey rather than Leese who acted as the principal intermediary. Despite being in 'considerable demand', Günther found time to write to Harvey in October 1933, thanking him effusively for the 'friendly note' and copies of *The Fascist* which Harvey had previously sent him and which Günther promised to keep. Their correspondence reveals that Harvey was working on an English translation of *Racial Elements* and that Günther had agreed to authorise his publishers to sanction another English edition once Harvey had found a publisher.[204] Günther also provided Harvey with several new contacts across Europe who had similar if not identical aims to the Nordics.[205] Like the Nazis, the Nordics defined nationalism according to biology rather than geography, allowing them to celebrate and encourage 'friendship with members of foreign nations equally inspired by Nordic ideals.' Honorary membership of the Nordics was open 'to foreigners in sympathy with the objects of the group'.[206]

This attempt to forge a pan-Aryan racial brotherhood was most apparent in Harvey's 'exchange of opinions' with Hans-Rolf Hoffmann, head of the Nazi's Foreign Press Bureau who edited the English-language propaganda sheet *News from Germany* from Starnberg, Bavaria.[207] Hoffmann, whose wife was born in Manchester, regularly visited England, the last time being in February–March 1938 for a 'non-political' lecture tour. MI5 regarded him as 'the chief executive, if not designer, of a propaganda programme in the UK which was carefully thought out and based on a very sound "appreciation of the situation" over here'.[208] Hoffmann was clearly sympathetic to the IFL, contributing several articles to

The Fascist.²⁰⁹ He wrote to Harvey from Munich shortly after the formation of the Nordics praising him for having 'kindled the flame of race consciousness' in England. Hoffmann assured Harvey:

> You can surely rely on our Hitler that he will do all in his power to further the ideals of our Nordic race and to pave the way towards a brighter future. Under Hitler's government it will never happen that we shed precious Nordic blood by going to war with racial-related nations. *Hitler is England's best friend*. The *New* Germany under the swastika banner is well conscious of its high [illegible] and will bring all people of Nordic blood together, as to work hand in hand for the preservation of the old traditions and regeneration of our great race.²¹⁰

Leese also regularly wrote to Hoffmann who in turn frequently contributed articles to *The Fascist*.²¹¹ Hoffmann also forwarded Leese the names of British individuals who had contacted him for material. MI5 noted this transnational traffic. They recorded in 1936 that an IFL 'agent' was functioning from inside the Brown House in Munich.²¹² Leese and Hoffmann were not in complete ideological agreement, however. 'I am with you in everything except the Colonial policy,' wrote Leese who was 'absolutely opposed to any surrender whatsoever'.²¹³

The Nordics was subsumed into the IFL in February 1934, when Harvey went to work with his father in Palestine, though its publishing arm the 'Nordic Press' remained a going concern.²¹⁴ Its influence on Leese's 'Nordic' thinking outlived its demise, however. In March 1934, the IFL changed its badge. The new one consisting of a swastika superimposed upon a Union Jack with a lion crest signalling its further commitment to Nordic racial fascism. 'The change has been felt necessary', wrote Leese, 'since Mussolini has ranged himself with the Jews against Britain's interests in Palestine; we have now to distinguish ourselves from the Kosher Fascist Movements by adopting the racial symbol of Nordic man'.²¹⁵ The badge symbolised a commitment by the wearer: '(1) never to buy from Jews (2) never to employ Jews (3) to do all you can to stop the Jewish invasion of your country'.²¹⁶

For Beamish, the swastika was 'the White Man's Cross' – a symbol of racial salvation as opposed to the Christian Cross, which because it 'includes negroes and all sorts of other people in its fold ... cannot help us'.²¹⁷ Guided by Waddell, Leese historicised and Anglicised the swastika through reference to the supposed ancient Sumer-Aryan linguistic roots of 'The Angled Cross' or 'Fylfot', which meant 'literally a Foot in Fire, symbolic of the moving sun, itself the emblem of the old Aryan's God'. The Angled Cross was a hieroglyph of 'Angle' from which 'English' is derived, claimed the IFL as it struggled to locate the swastika as the ancient *völkisch* symbol of The Briton rather than simply an import from Nazi Germany. Moreover, it was emblematic of Nordic fascist's determination 'to root out the Jewish pestilence from our midst'.²¹⁸

This increasing attempt to historicise Nazism and emphasise its 'British' roots was also reflected in Leese's growing interest in racialised paganism. He had cultivated such ideas through contact with Melbourne solicitor Alexander Rud Mills, an early evangelist for a racialised variant of Odinism, the spiritual backbone of a revitalised 'British race'.²¹⁹ Mills' beliefs led him to Hitler though their meeting was not a success. 'I saw him. Talked to him. He would not discuss my theme', he later lamented.²²⁰ Mills found a more responsive audience in British *völkisch* circles. Visiting England, Mills established his own Nordic society, the Moot of the Anglekin Body, heavily reliant for its mythology upon Waddell's *British*

Edda. Leese's right-hand man, H.H. Lockwood, was secretary.[221] Mills subsequently addressed an IFL meeting on 29 March 1933 on 'The Australian Outlook'. He also donated copies of his book, *And Fear Shall Be in the Way* (1933), written pseudonymously as 'Tasman H. Forth', to the IFL 'to sell for the benefit of the funds'.[222]

Having returned to Australia, Mills set up an IFL branch in Melbourne.[223] Leese advertised Mills' newspaper, *The Angle*, in *The Fascist*.[224] Mills was also a contributor to *The Publicist*, the organ of the Australia First Movement (AFM). W.J. Miles, one of its leading lights, sent Leese copies of *The Publicist* free of charge. Miles wrote to Leese that 'although we are restricted in *The Publicist* we are continuing our anti-Jew propaganda and will use our *Publicist* to attack as soon as we can'. Mills maintained contact with Leese until the outbreak of war, the latter sending him 'instructions and propaganda through a stewardess aboard the ocean liner *Oronsay*'.[225] Mills was subsequently interned.[226] One should not exaggerate Mills' influence, however. 'I haven't the slightest idea what he is talking about!' Leese confessed after reading his book *Coming: A New Religion* in 1953.[227]

The infusion of racialised paganism into the IFL offended the sensibilities of several Christian members. Officially, the IFL regarded its members' religious beliefs as a private affair; its sole concern was 'race', which it invested with a similarly divine quality.[228] However, the embrace of pre-Christian 'Aryan' religions occasioned several resignations and rumours of a secretive 'sub-society' within the IFL 'which is out to smash Christianity'. Leese's hair-splitting response would hardly have mollified his Christian critics: 'That a Society exists which favours the old Aryan code of conduct rather than Christianity, we know full well', wrote Leese, 'some members of it are in the IFL but those who spread the rumour that it is "inside" the IFL are liars, generally, interested liars, and they know it'.[229] Whilst Leese may not have been directly involved in such practices, he had already rejected Christianity, 'as soon as I was old enough to think'. He refuted the suggestion that he was devoid of faith. 'I am however a highly religious man in the real sense of the word religious, believing & trying to practice the ethics of my ancestors who deified Adam-Thor, first King of Sumeria, author of the first known civilization', Leese explained, reflecting just how deeply the influence of Waddell had permeated his thinking.[230]

Anti-Semitism

Leese argued, *pace* Günther, that the Jews were a race not a religion. They were not, however, a pure race but rather a confection of inferior races divided between two separate communities, the Ashkenazim and the Sephardic. For Leese: 'Jewry represents a mongrel conglomeration of Hither Asiatics indigenous to Asia Minor and Armenia, Hamatic and Negroid blood from Egypt, and East Baltic, Inner Asiatic (mongoloid) and Alpine strains from the Khazar Empire.' It was the predominance of the 'Hither Asiatic' bloodline that gave Jews their physical attributes not to mention a unique penchant for sadism, revenge, cruelty, treachery, dishonesty, sexual deviancy or indeed any other malformation of character that Leese cared to project onto them. It did not really matter. 'All Hither Asiatics, whether Jews or Armenians or Afghans or others are foul and should always in my opinion be treated like hereditary madmen', he wrote to the Canadian fascist leader Adrien Arcand.[231] The physical, political and social repulsion that Leese felt towards 'the Jew' was reflected in the visual effusions of F.T. Cooper, *The Fascist* cartoonist, whose dehumanising Jewish stereotypes redolent of those that appeared in *Der Stürmer*, reinforced the textual virulence of Leese's prose.[232]

It was this innate cruelty, argued Leese, that led Jews to positively revel in such retrograde religious rites as circumcision and the ritual slaughter or 'Shechita' of animals. Leese tried in vain to get the Royal Society for the Prevention of Cruelty to Animals (RSPCA) to incorporate a ban into their platform. Leese objected to such meat entering, and in his view contaminating, the Gentile food chain. The invisibility of such pollution made it even more alarming. Leese further believed that, if Gentiles consumed Shechita meat, they were in effect subsidising not just animal cruelty but the propagation of Judaism, which took the fees from the practice and invested them in religious instruction.[233] Leese loved animals, a logical corollary of his veterinary work, and regularly involved them in his political activities. In Guildford, he was known to walk his St Bernard dog through the town centre, with an IFL collection tin strapped to its back.[234] He also had a cat that 'gave the fascist salute for its dinner'.[235]

From claiming that the Jews were capable of such cruelty towards animals, it was not such a great leap for Leese to claim that they were equally capable of ritually murdering Christian children in order to obtain fresh blood to mix in their Passover blood. After all, argued Leese, did not the Jews regard the 'goyim' as 'cattle'?[236] Though groups like The Britons largely abjured from the 'blood libel' accusation, Leese had no such qualms.[237] Leese began publicly accusing the Jews of ritual murder in late 1932 but it was not until 1936 that he and his printer, Walter Whitehead, were arrested and tried for seditious libel and causing a public mischief.[238] The IFL established a 'British Aryan Defence Fund' to raise money for his defence.[239] The proceedings 'caused considerable uneasiness' amongst other fascist and anti-Semitic organisations, which awaited the verdict 'with great interest'.[240] Indeed, when Leese answered the original summons at Bow Street Police Court in August 1936 amongst those present was the BUF propagandist William Joyce, who was 'observed to be taking copious notes of what was taking place'.[241] Leese was eventually acquitted of seditious libel but convicted of the lesser charge of 'conspiring to effect, and of effecting, a public mischief'. He and Whitehead were both fined. Leese characteristically refused to pay and embarked upon six months' imprisonment in September.[242]

Beamish claimed he would petition the King for his release and, if that did not work, he exhorted IFL members to 'do something unusual'. More should be prepared to follow Leese to prison, he commanded.[243] Incarcerated in Wormwood Scrubs, Leese was assaulted by Charlie Goodman, an anti-fascist jailed for his part in the Battle of Cable Street on 4 October.[244] Leese found rather more congenial company in Henry W. Wicks, whom he met whilst working as a machinist in the prison's tailor shop. Wicks was serving twelve months for criminal libel having been found guilty of impugning the reputation of his former employer, Sun Life of Canada.[245] In April 1939, Wicks travelled to Germany. Following a period of internment, the Nazis employed him as a scriptwriter for Radio Metropol, resulting in a four-year jail sentence in 1946 for assisting the enemy.[246] 'I was the first to enlighten Wicks on his real enemies', Leese later boasted.[247] Leese did more than that. He provided Wicks with a letter of introduction to Julius Streicher ahead of his visit to Germany in 1939.[248] 'When I met Arnold Leese in prison,' Wicks wrote to Nazi propagandist Hans-Rolf Hoffmann, 'I became enlightened as to the part played by the Jews, and from then on worked with our Fascist friends for peace and understanding with Germany.'[249]

Released on 17 February 1937, Leese made a 'triumphal' exit to a throng of cheering fascists waiting for him at the prison gates. He was utterly unrepentant, claiming that his criminal conviction was an attempt to discredit him, a plan 'strictly in accordance' with protocol nineteen of the *Protocols of the Elders of Zion*.[250] He immediately sought advice from Major Theodore Rich, a leading member of The Britons who worked in the Army Judge Advocate General's department, as to whether he could get his sentence annulled because he believed the judge was a Freemason.[251] For Leese, this was crucial since 'The danger of Freemasonry consists in the hypnotism of unsuspecting initiates rendering them allergic to anti-Jewishness.'[252] Leese's derogatory remarks at subsequent IFL meetings, impugning the reputation of the 'Masonic Judge' and accusations that prosecuting counsel were in the pay of 'Jewry' led the authorities to contemplate prosecuting him for contempt of court and criminal libel, though ultimately they was decided to ignore him.[253] In April 1938, Leese published *My Irrelevant Defence* (1938), which defiantly repeated, and indeed expanded upon, the charges for which he had been imprisoned. In essence, *My Irrelevant Defence* detailed fifty alleged cases of ritual murder, proof of which he believed to be incontrovertible, not to mention incidents such as the Lindbergh baby case and a child killing in Chorlton, Manchester in 1928, both of which he insinuated were also 'ritual murder'. Ritual murder was the 'dynamite' that led to the Jews expulsion from England in 1290; from Spain in 1420 and, 'in our time' out of Germany too, Leese claimed. The Jew made the Talmud, Leese argued and thus the need for 'human sacrifice' was racial and not religious.[254] This, for Leese, was an important point. The racial basis of Jewry was immutable. 'If Jews all turned Catholic they are still Jews', he asserted.[255]

Leese's particular innovation to the assertion that Jews were motivated by a hatred of Christianity was his claim that ritual murder was part of a secret plan to recover 'Zion' for the Jews. According to his own rationale, ritual murder should 'theoretically' have ceased as a practice with the foundation of the Israel in 1948.[256] Leese was unable, however, to square this assertion with his equally ardent insistence that 'a really juicy Ritual Murder case' had come to light in Bethnal Green in September 1953 after police arrested Zalig Lenchitsky for murdering a five-year-old child, Wendy Ridgwell.[257] Leese was obsessed by an initial news report that suggested 'saliva' had been discovered, conjuring up the image of Jews salivating at the prospect of Christian blood, which excited and nauseated him in equal measure and underlined the importance of the role of fluids in anti-Semitic discourse. Leese attended the trial in person, leading him to animalise the Jews further. 'I had to wait 3/4 of an hour in the street outside the public gallery with the foulest Jews I have ever seen', he remarked to a friend. 'I could not at first understand why their mouths worked backwards and forwards so much more so than ours do. Then I discovered that they had muzzles like animals, wh. [*sic*] gave different muscular attachments.'[258] Echoes of the case reverberate contemporaneously, though it is no longer referred to as an act of 'Ritual Murder'. Instead, Ridgwell featured on the 'fallen list' operated by a BNP supporter, which records the deaths 'of those who have died as a result of multiculturalism'. This again speaks volumes about the position of Jews in the eyes of some BNP members.[259]

Returning to *My Irrelevant Defence*. This publication was far worse than the issue of *The Fascist* for which Leese was originally jailed, 'rivalling in scurrility even the fragrant publications of Nazi Germany,' noted one contemporary observer.[260] Nonetheless, the authorities declined to prosecute Leese, chastened by their previous failure to secure a seditious libel conviction and the pamphlet's limited distribution.[261] Clearly goading prosecution, Leese was outraged by the silence that greeted its publication. Prosecuted or ignored, either way Leese believed the Jews were out to suppress, by any means, the 'hidden truth' he had unearthed. This made the Jews' mysterious and mystical power even more menacing. Indeed, the fact that Jews denied the 'blood libel' made it all the more plausible to

Leese: 'Whom do you believe – the Jews or the English?' Similarly, Gentile repudiation of the canard was likely the result of 'mass hypnotism' inducing 'mental or spiritual subservience to Jewish influence'.[262]

It is hard to overemphasis the physiological power of 'blood' as a motif in Leese's writings. 'Blood means life'. This simple observation helps explain his obsession with its purity, its theft and its cannibal-like consumption by a racial foe. Whilst Leese believed ritual murder to be a 'fact', it was also a cipher for his belief that the Jew was draining not just the wealth but also the literal life-blood out of both nation and Empire, sapping its vitality, degrading its capabilities, and, ultimately, if the transfusion went too far, condemning it to decomposition and death. It was not simply the vampiric removal of blood that concerned him, though this image of Jew, leaching off the spiritual and physical life-force of Nordic nations, remained potent and all pervading.[263] 'It was never in them to create but only to exploit what has been created by the work of others', he claimed.[264] Physically and spiritually parasitic, Leese construed 'Jewry' itself as an act of ritual murder.

Leese was equally fixated by the idea that Jews injected their own blood, itself a corrosive and corrupting contaminant, into the Aryan polity with similarly fatal consequences for the Nordic race itself. Early Aryan civilisations had been 'killed by race mixture' claimed Leese, though he never explained precisely why it was that supposedly superior blood could be so easily overwhelmed and thus imperilled by its mixture with its inferior. Miscegenation polluted the blood, diluted and deteriorated its sublime quality, threatening the 'hereditary memory' of the race that was carried within it, jeopardising the Nordic past, present and future. Such an act of defilement blunted racial instincts and dulled its creative genius, transmitted through the blood to future generations. Pollution of 'noble' physiognomy with the 'ignoble' had an outward cultural corollary in the rise of modernity, materialism and vulgarity.

This fear was writ large in virtually every edition of *The Fascist*. In issue after issue, Leese charted Jewish intermarriage with the British aristocracy, producing genealogical charts to discover the extent of the problem. This 'identity work', designed to root out the flow of Jewish blood, obsessed Leese.[265] He was possessed by the spectre of 'Secret Jews' – the descendants of hard to trace nineteenth-century marriages, lacking 'Jewish physical features' but whose 'fractional origin' was betrayed by their 'actions'. For Leese, the taint of Jewish blood was the only possible explanation for Gentiles embracing 'anti-Aryan causes'.[266] This was quite deliberate. Jews conspired to camouflage their racial origins. It was a 'custom' among certain financially powerful Jews, alleged Leese, 'to farm out their illegitimate children in impoverished but influential Gentile families for spot cash'. To his mind, this accounted for the numerous public figures 'whose features and characters are Jewish' but whose official pedigree appeared as 'unblemished Aryan'.[267] For Leese, the danger lay in the invisibility of 'the Jew'. It also, conveniently, released him from the burden of actual proof. He was determined to prove that Home Secretary David Maxwell-Fyfe was Jewish for instance. 'If he isn't a Jew, I am a Chinaman.' However, although he had no proof whatsoever of Maxwell-Fyfe's supposed Jewish ancestry, Leese remained adamant: Maxwell-Fyfe 'certainly is a Jew'.[268]

His obsession with racial genealogy led Leese to act as a consultant to extreme right activists secretly worried about their own racial lineage. One such was A.E. 'Blackie' Baker, the BUF printer, who became 'very worried about the possibility of his racial purity having been contaminated by Jewish blood,' and so travelled to Guildford in 1945 for an audience with Leese whom he regarded as 'the foremost expert on Semitic research'. His experience was not a happy one. Based on the information presented to him, Leese informed Baker that 'the Portuguese Taxeiras [from whom he was apparently descended] were known to be of so badly polluted stock and in fact could be regarded as more than three quarters Jewish.' As reported by MI5, Leese sympathised with Baker:

> but pointed out that nothing could be done to free him of the horrible taint. Baker asked if there were any hope for him in the Nordic camp and Leese replied that there was a possibility that he may be granted honorary Aryan membership if his record remained good. The effect on Baker was a most unhappy one and he took it all very seriously.[269]

Leese's researches, published at regular intervals, resulted in a schema that supposedly indexed not simply increasing Jewish power but, moreover, the increasing racial defilement of the British polity. The intermingling of blood and the replacement of the Nordic race by a 'khaki-skinned mob' constituted a form of racial and cultural genocide, the first stage of which was achieved through Nordic acceptance of 'the poisonous Jewish Masonic doctrine of Universal Brotherhood'.[270] If a race 'betrays its own standards of values' and allows a lesser race to live amongst it on the basis of 'equality' then it 'will completely disappear, its culture with it,' Leese argued.[271] George Mendel's research offered a glimmer of hope. Nordic blood still accounted for about 65 per cent of the British and German populations, Leese estimated in June 1933. 'Mendel has shown that a Race is never lost through mixture, *provided there is a desire to regain it*'. There was a caveat: this 'desire' for racial resurgence existed only in the Third Reich.[272]

Leese vehemently desired to protect Nordic blood from further degradation. This led him to advocate publicly in March 1931 the extermination of the Jews. For Leese, this was far less abhorrent than assimilation, 'which no decent Nordic man or woman would seriously consider'.[273] In February 1935, Leese declared unequivocally that 'the most certain and permanent way of disposing of the Jews would be to exterminate them by some humane method such as the lethal chamber'. It was 'quite practical', he argued, 'but (some will say unfortunately) in our time it is unlikely that the world will demand the adoption of that drastic procedure'. His interim solution therefore was to follow the historical precedent of his hero Edward I ('an English Mussolini'[274]), who deprived the Jews of their livelihood, required them to wear yellow badges and then expelled them from England altogether in 1290. Leese planned to maroon the Jews on Madagascar, an island in the Indian Ocean, an idea championed by Beamish who had purloined it from French anti-Semite Paul de Lagarde who had first advocated it in 1885.[275] Seemingly outlandish, the Nazis seriously, albeit briefly, entertained the 'Madagascar Plan' as a 'distinct policy option' from 1938 before more radical options presented themselves.[276]

For Leese, Madagascar remained an enticing option, not least because the Jews would be made to pay for their own dispossession, deportation and indeed the cost of purchasing Madagascar from the French. If it were not for sale, 'so much the worse for them, because the other possible island territories are less salubrious'. Following an unspecified length of time, any Jew found outside the island would be executed. Those married to Jews had the option of having their marriages annulled or of moving to Madagascar too. Insofar as offspring were concerned, Leese argued in February 1935:

> Half-caste Jews and quarter Jews constitute a difficult problem, as do half-castes all over the world; we do not think there is any solution to that problem other than sending them away with their Jewish blood-brothers, although they should receive special

assistance. Milder dilutions of Jewish blood can probably be absorbed into our population, but cannot receive full citizenship nor can such be allowed to hold titles or official posts.[277]

This was a harsher definition of who was a Jew than that enshrined in the Nuremberg Laws promulgated in September 1935. In the aftermath of Nuremberg, Leese recognised that a 'watertight' definition of Aryan and Jew was by no means simple but ultimately of little consequence, because 'in *practice*, with the object of purification in view, a hard-and-fast line must be drawn'.[278] In his haste to be rid of the Jew, the quantitative difference between segregation and extermination was similarly imprecise, just as it was for the Nazis. Outlining the 'Madagascar Plan' at a public meeting in Guildford in March 1934, Leese declared 'that he was perfectly prepared to open and shut the door on the lethal chamber all day if he could get rid of the Jews in that way'. Leese then proclaimed that there were 2.5 million Jews in Britain, revealing that he had cogitated on the magnitude of the task ahead of him.[279] Such homicidal fantasies were reflected in his specially made Christmas cards in which he wished his contacts 'peace on earth' – a declaration juxtaposed against a caricature of a Jew hanging from a gallows.[280]

IFL in the East End

Lack of funds was one reason the IFL never became an effective street organisation. Leese's principal activity was therefore the propagation of anti-Semitism. In one sense, the IFL existed as a 'cultural' society for this purpose. To draw attention to their cause, IFL activists engaged in anti-Semitic stunts including running a swastika embroidered Union Jack up the flagpole at the London County Hall in May 1934, to protest the council's employment of Jews, and replacing the plaque adorning Karl Marx's home with an anti-Semitic notice in June 1935.[281] The IFL was also intermittently active in the East End during the 1930s, calling for a boycott against Jewish shops and seeking to convince local traders that a 'Jewish stranglehold' on economic affairs was pushing them towards ruin and unemployment. The solution was characteristically blunt. 'When we get into power', one IFL speaker told his East End audience, 'it will be our duty to clear all the Jews out of the country, and if we cannot accomplish this, we will starve them, as well as murder them'.[282] The IFL claimed there were three million Jews in Britain, 'roughly the same number as there are unemployed Englishmen'. Despite the generally accepted figure being a mere 370,000, Leese's solution was expulsion. This would 'help us kill two birds with one stone,' cure unemployment and 'rid ourselves of three parts of the crime in this land'. With added urgency, IFL literature declared: 'In 1914, you fought for the Jewish Money Power. In 1934, fight for your wives, your children, your very existence.'[283]

This anti-Semitic activism had an impact. Special Branch listed it as one 'contributory cause' to the overall decline of their rivals, Mosley's British Union of Fascists in London during spring 1935; 'many BUF members appear to consider that [in comparison] their movement does not take a sufficiently anti-Jewish line'.[284] The IFL became increasingly active in London's East End, following Leese's release from prison in 1937. The Jewish Defence Committee's London Area Committee observed: 'Evidently funds have reached them from some quarter'.[285] The East London IFL street leader was Phillip J. Ridout, who, having joined the group in May 1933, served as its 'officer in charge of general headquarters and London branches'. Ridout, who was responsible for opening IFL branches in Shoreditch and Hackney, was the sole paid IFL official. He and S.H. Wrigley, leader of

'Imperial Fascist Guard' were Leese's principal assistants during this period.[286] The IFL liked to boast that Ridout's initials – 'P.J.' – were the inspiration for the anti-Semitic greeting 'P.J. – Perish Judah'.[287] Ridout and another of Leese's entourage, Charles W. Gore, ran a 'tough squad' of IFL and BUF members, who cooperated in conducting physical attacks on Jews under the cover of night.[288]

Ridout staged well-attended public meetings in Finsbury Square, Shoreditch, one of which Leese ventured to address on 24 June. It was subject to 'considerable interruption' by Jewish anti-fascists including Charles Emanuel, the Board of Deputies' solicitor.[289] This increase in activity brought the IFL into conflict with the local BUF street leader E.G. 'Mick' Clarke, a tub-thumping anti-Semite, who, having returned to England on 31 July following a fortnight's sojourn in Nazi Germany, was outraged to hear IFL speakers malign the BUF as 'kosher'. Clarke publicly challenged them to bring him concrete evidence of the charges.[290] *The Jewish Chronicle* reported, however, that Clarke was 'rattled' by the extension of IFL activity into Bethnal Green, telling his audience that they had to choose their leader, Mosley or Leese:

> He said the League was worthless, because only one of its members had been arrested during the last year, whereas twenty-six members of the BUF had been arrested. He increased this to twenty-eight a few sentences later. He even trotted out the 'Protocols of Zion', a 'prop' without the aid of which no Fascist actor is complete. He alleged that the League was mentioned in the 'Protocols' as an organization set up by the Jews to distract attention from the real Fascists![291]

By October 1937, IFL activity in East London had declined markedly, largely in response to Clarke's return to activity, which also led to a decline in hostility between the two groups in the area.[292]

There was no concomitant decline in anti-Semitism, however. Following a speech on 11 September 1937 at Tottenham Road, Dalston, Ridout was cautioned by police who also arrested his colleague, George Pownall, the son of Capel Pownall, for shouting 'Perish the Jews' and giving the Nazi salute before 'assaulting police'.[293] Ridout's venom was such that *The Fascist* boasted afterwards that 'a Jew listener had apoplexy and had to be removed feet first. This is a great tribute to our speaker.'[294] On 8 October, he was fined £10 for using insulting words with the intent to provoke a breach of the peace. Ignoring a police caution, Ridout informed his Dalston audience: 'I say again the enemy of the British people is the J-E-W.' The crowd became disorderly. Ridout was arrested. He had acted 'like an unutterable cad', the judge informed him.[295] He was arrested again following a meeting on 28 October in Finsbury Square.[296] His second appearance in court had a more salutary effect. Ridout was, temporarily at least, more circumspect in his 'Jew-baiting'.

Leese directed the show. In May 1938, to reinvigorate his East End organisation Leese posted Ridout to lead the North East London IFL branch using its newly opened premises at 39 Balls Pond Road 'as a centre for intensifying Fascist work in the district and as far afield as he can conveniently work'.[297] Despite this promotion, Special Branch noted that Ridout subsequently led an IFL faction that favoured alliance with the BUF. Ridout himself sought a 'paid position' with Mosley's organisation in exchange for bringing his street activists into the movement, the police observed.[298] For whatever reason, Ridout remained within the IFL, however; his own meetings increasingly the League's sole sign of life, though as war loomed, his audience became 'openly hostile' towards him.[299]

'Leese for Peace'

Leese never wavered in his belief that the impending conflict was a 'Jews war'. In September 1938, at the height of the Munich Crisis, he took it upon himself to write to Adolf Hitler. 'Even although you may not be aware of it, I with the Imperial Fascist League, am your best friend in this country', Leese informed the Führer. 'We know that this talk of war is not German, French, British or Czech, but Jewish. Both of us have been in prison for our knowledge.' Having implored 'the greatest statesmen [sic] in the world' to make peace, Leese stated: 'It is almost inconceivable that there could be war over this affair; the world is not yet quite made. The Jew cannot control the spirit, and no one is interested in the Czechs except the Jew and his touts.' He concluded by asking Hitler 'Can I be of the slightest service? It is only because of the crisis that I forget my normal modesty in asking you.'[300] It is doubtful that Hitler deigned to reply or indeed was even aware of the missive.

Undeterred, Leese turned his attentions to his 'Leese for Peace' campaign, distributing leaflets that declared 'If you want Peace, If you want Prosperity, If you want to see Britain restored to her former greatness, YOU must help Arnold Leese to defeat the International Jew and his ally Democracy!'[301] More crudely, he argued: 'Britain has been shoved into the war by the Jews, as a dirty dog is shoved into a bath.'[302] He intensified his anti-Semitic campaign, engaging in a veritable orgy of anti-Semitic propaganda against Jewish refugees. The IFL leaflet, *A.R.P.: Instructions and Advice* lamented that Britain had become an 'Alien Refugees' Paradise'. Individual IFL members indulged their own initiatives. Benjamin Barrett embarked upon a three-day cycling tour of Kent with a placard strapped to his back proclaiming: 'We've got to be prepared to fight for our Jewish Masters.'[303] Such activities led to a question in Parliament in July 1939 regarding the 'pro-Nazi' activities of the IFL and two other anti-Semitic groups, the Militant Christian Patriots and the Nordic League. They were being 'kept under close observation', the Home Office replied.[304] The IFL 'did all we could' to prevent war, Leese recorded. In his case, the strain became too much. Leese collapsed at one IFL meeting from 'sheer exhaustion'.[305]

As the authorities increased their monitoring of British fascism, commensurately the movement was also becoming increasingly isolated from public sympathy. 'Perhaps the most vital indication of the impotence of the movement in those days', recalled Ronald Jones who had joined a number of extreme right groups after the Munich Crisis, 'lay in the fact that you did not wear a "Flash and Circle" armband in, for instance, Balls Pond Road – you wouldn't dare'.[306] Indeed, when war was declared on 1 September 1939, Leese closed both the Balls Pond Road premises and the IFL headquarters at 30 Craven Street too. The call up of his Staff Officer had also made its continued running an impossibility. Leese also stopped publishing *The Fascist* and prepared to sit out the war in Guildford. 'We intend to continue the existence of the IFL and to open premises again when political and financial circumstances permit', he informed the membership.[307] More conducive circumstances never arose.

Intermittent IFL activity continued, however. The IFL Political Officer A.W. Gittens, a 'food chemist' who led the group's North London branch and Leese's lieutenant Harold Lockwood produced *Weekly Angles* – 'the Anglo-Saxon's weekly newspaper' – which was distributed from the IFL office at 'Troth House' in Crogsland Road, Chalk Farm.[308] *Weekly Angles*, which resembled *Welt-Dienst* stylistically, was limited to 250 copies per issue. Each month, Gittens also produced a special German-language edition that was disseminated by outlets in Nuremberg and Hamburg.[309] In every issue of *Weekly Angles*, Gittens propagated the 'Jews-war' line. In an article published on 3 December 1939, for instance,

Weekly Angles claimed: 'Hitler is the Jews Enemy; he was never the enemy of the British people.... We are fighting the Jews' chief enemy for the Jews.'[310]

To this end, Leese sought to broaden his platform, latching onto other 'peace' initiatives that advocated a negotiated peace with Hitler. Foremost of these was the British Council against European Commitments (BCAEC), which had been established in September 1938. Its founder, Lord Lymington, believed that war with Nazi Germany, 'would benefit no one but the Jews and the International communists'.[311] The BCAEC became a focal point for extreme right and fascist efforts to forestall war. Leese and Ridout attended the inaugural meeting on 16 September but took no active part in the proceedings.[312] Other IFL activists joined the Peace Pledge Union (PPU), a pacifist organisation to which numerous fascist activists flocked.[313]

Leese also stepped up the distribution of IFL 'anti-war' propaganda to Scandinavia and the Low Countries, which were still neutral. There he had fostered contacts with 'true' racial fascist movements in Sweden like Sven Lindholm's Nationalsocialistiska Arbetarpartiet (NSAP – National Socialist Workers' Party), having acting as an agent of sorts for its newspaper, *Den Svenska Nationalsocialisten* since 1934.[314] As war approached, Gordon Woods, the IFL foreign propaganda officer, stepped up the despatch of IFL anti-war propaganda, sometimes translated into Norwegian, to activists in Nasjonal Samlings Ungdomsfylking, the youth wing of Nasjonal Samling (NS – National Unity), the party of Vidkun Quisling whose surname would shortly become a byword for treachery. During the same period, Leese also continued corresponding with the Dutch Nationaal-Socialistische Nederlandsche Arbeiderspartij (NSNAP – National Socialist Dutch Workers' Party) led by Ernst van Rappard. The NSNAP was officially dissolved in 1941 and forcibly incorporated into the much larger Nationaal-Socialistische Beweging in Nederland (NSB – National Socialist Movement in the Netherlands) led by Anton Mussert, which Leese decried as 'another Mosley movement'. Ill-disposed towards the NSB, van Rappard joined the Waffen-SS.[315] MI5 also reported the Nazis were distributing anti-Semitic material under the IFL imprimatur in Norwegian, Spanish and Danish, which, in the latter case, was being distributed to Danish seamen weighing anchor in Hamburg.[316]

Leese propagated a form of anti-Semitic defeatism. Contemplating the prospect of war with Germany, as early as August 1934 Leese had proclaimed that:

> There is one thing that no member of the Imperial Fascist League will do; he will not join the British forces to fight the battle of the Jew against men of his own Nordic race. WE WILL NOT FIGHT FOR THE HOUSE OF ROTHSCHILD![317]

There were some friends and supporters, he claimed, who contemplated joining the German Army to fight 'the white man's battle against the Jewish Power of Britain' and in so doing, would be fighting for the nation's 'true interests'. Leese found the proposition 'unbalanced and unsound' stating instead:

> The Imperial Fascist League will be the rallying point for a new kind of Conscientious Objector, the true patriot. But he will not be a Pacifist. *He will* declare war on the ENEMY – THE JEW, in this country. We shall proceed with strong measures against the Jew living here, beginning, if possible, at the top.... We believe, most sincerely, that such action will bring the war to a speedy end; in fact, it is possible that we might be able to stop this pitiful waste of Nordic blood before the opposing Infantry actually exchange their first shots.[318]

Leese returned to this theme in May 1939 declaring the British Empire could only be defended by waging 'war upon the Jews' which would cleanse and protect it from future attack: 'a clean Aryan British Empire will be invincible'. Service in the Armed Forces 'under the Jew' rendered 'cleansing impossible'. Thus, Leese argued, 'it is hoped that no member already in the forces will either salute a Jew or take orders from one, whatever the consequence may be'.[319] The Director of Public Prosecutions considered the prospect of instituting proceedings against Leese under the Incitement to Disaffection Act (1934) but ultimately declined to take action.[320]

Leese also began preparing for clandestine underground activity. MI5 learned from a source within the group that Leese had given Woods six revolvers and 300 rounds of ammunition. Woods passed them to William Bird, an IFL activist who ran a newsagent in Maidenhead. When the police raided Bird's home on 29 May 1940, they seized a large quantity of fascist literature and two rugs with swastikas sewn into them but only two revolvers.[321] The IFL were stockpiling weapons, Woods later testified, because Leese 'expected them [IFL members] to co-operate with other Fascists and to give what assistance they could to the invaders'.[322]

James van Eusom, an IFL activist from Richmond was tasked with facilitating 'underground work', which included chalking up anti-Semitic slogans, defacing recruitment posters and ARP notices and generally entering into conversation on the subject of 'Jews and the War as much as possible'. Eusom also arranged for two recruits to distribute IFL literature in the Irish Guards.[323] Despite earlier pronouncements, Leese came to see the virtue in having IFL sympathisers in the Armed Forces writing to a Swedish colleague on 11 January 1940 that these activists 'are working hard where perhaps most good can be done'.[324] One such was John Coast, a former employee of the N.M. Rothschild merchant bank, active in a range of extremist groups including the IFL, the Nordic League and Captain Ramsay's Right Club, who bragged of distributing anti-Semitic literature within his regiment, the Coldstream Guards.[325] Similarly, J.F. Rushbrook, the former IFL secretary who had left the group to run the Militant Christian Patriots, also enlisted and became a Lieutenant in the 3rd Dragoon Guards.[326]

Ironically, the Second World War shattered Leese's faith in Hitler. The Nazi–Soviet Pact signed on 23 August 1939 was, Leese wrote to Beamish, 'an ideological blow of the worst description' that he simply could not rationalise. 'Hitler has been a marvel, but he is no longer one ... such a pity.'[327] Hitler's invasion of 'Aryan Scandinavia', regarded as sacrosanct, was almost too much to comprehend.[328] *Weekly Angles* expressed 'regret' for the action demanding that the first condition of peace 'must be the withdrawal of German control from Scandinavia'.[329] Privately, Leese lamented to Beamish that Hitler had 'killed the soul' of the movement.[330] His attitude towards Hitler, misinterpreted by some MI5 officers to be a ruse, caused a genuine breach within the IFL. It alienated the group's more slavishly pro-Nazi faction including Gittens, Elizabeth Berger and her partner H.T.V. 'Bertie' Mills.[331] On 17 April, Gittens challenged Leese at an IFL meeting, arguing that although Hitler had 'thrown over his racial theories' and attacked a Nordic nation, this was no reason for the IFL to become anti-Hitler. Leese expressed his disgust at Hitler's invasion of Norway two days later at another meeting but was given an 'unsympathetic' hearing from his audience who sought to justify Germany's action.[332] That same day, Leese received a letter from John Hooper Harvey, which reflected the general attitude of most IFL members during this period:

> I would not give away secret information to the Germans unless affairs reached the stage they did in Spain, where foreign assistance was our only hope of cleaning out the

pigsty, but in very last resort, I should take up a position of race solidarity before national solidarity … I don't want to be ruled by Germany or any other foreigners but at a pinch even that is preferable to being ground to a pulp under the heel of the Jewish financier and his pimps and proselytes. We should soon regain our independence in such a case, much sooner than at present. Look at the case of Germany herself.[333]

'The position of an English anti-Jewish patriot is awkward just now', Leese lamented to an American correspondent in June 1940, 'and all he can hope for is a stalemate and an early peace'.[334] His disillusionment with Hitler was only temporary, however. Leese was lifted from his funk by the Nazis' invasion of Russia in June 1941. To his wife, Winifred, he wrote:

I feel clearer since Germany declared War on the Bolsheviks … Bolshevism, the last hope of the 'Eskimo' [Leese's code for Jews] will be as dead as mutton by the end of this year everywhere. The situation clarifies the whole Eskimo issue. Hitler has out-twisted the world's greatest twisters.[335]

Though his faith in Hitler as a divine avatar was briefly tarnished, Leese never lost his faith in the 'fact' that the war was a 'Jews war'.

Internment

Seven male and two female IFL activists were arrested and interned under Defence Regulation 18B in May 1940 for 'acts prejudicial to the public safety or the defence of the Realm'.[336] Leese was not one of them. He had already gone into hiding, having previously set-up a series of hideouts and safe houses. A police search of his house in summer 1940 found a series of abusive anti-Semitic letters and notes dotted around the property addressed to 'the Scotland Yard representative of Churchill's Jewish Ogpu'.[337]

Despite the arrests and the disappearance of their leader, a group of IFL activists had continued producing *Weekly Angles*, though this ceased publication on 24 May after police, prompted perhaps by a question about it in Parliament on the previous day, raided the IFL premises in Chalk Farm, north London, seizing papers and propaganda.[338] Despite the raid, the IFL continued operating from the building until June when Gittens and George Yates were arrested following a tussle with police over a parcel. This was subsequently found to contain the army uniform of John W. Lovell, Leese's political secretary who had deserted from the Scots Guards. Both men were sentenced to six months hard labour for offences under the Army Act, which finally snuffed out IFL activity.[339]

Leese remained at large until 9 November when police caught him at his Guildford home. He did not go quietly. He assaulted a police officer whom he discovered searching his house and, as the police tried to arrest him, they were assaulted by his wife and Ann Story, a young woman the couple had virtually adopted as their daughter. Remanded in custody, Leese smashed up his cell receiving a month's imprisonment for his trouble. Mrs Leese and Story were both fined £20 for assault.[340] Mrs Leese, regarded by the authorities as 'a strong headed, bad tempered woman, fully in sympathy with her husband's views', was not interned. She subsequently took over her husband's correspondence. Noting her correspondence with Dr H.J. Boldt, formerly of the Fichte-Bund in Florida, MI5 'desired to ascertain whether this woman is in touch with any other German agents' and had her phone tapped.[341]

Interned in Brixton prison, Leese's chief occupation was the continued study of the 'Jewish question'. He did so with three figures who shared his 'Jew-wise' proclivities: Captain Archibald Ramsay MP, who had run the pro-Nazi Right Club, Captain Robert Gordon-Canning, a wealthy pro-Nazi agitator and Admiral Sir Barry Domvile, a former Director of Naval Intelligence who had run a pro-Nazi organisation called The Link. Ironically, Leese had been hostile to Domvile's endeavour initially. 'We think there must be Jews in the organisation', he had written in *The Fascist*.[342] Leese was a truculent and disruptive prisoner, continually haranguing the authorities about the 'illegality' of his imprisonment. In January 1941, he even returned his military campaign medals to the King stating that 'it did not seem proper to retain medals commemorative of services which had evidently been forgotten'.[343] He declined to plead his case before the Advisory Committee whose authority and indeed legality he refused to recognise. He was scornful of those who lacked similar fortitude:

> I could never understand how people like Ramsay & Domvile ever allowed themselves to plead before the A.C. [Advisory Committee] because I never expected they would ever do so. Mosley, Raven-T[homson], and the like of course they did, they would. There was also a good excuse for men whose wives were suffering. It disappointed me to see [Harold] Lockwood fail the test! I never felt the same to him afterwards....[344]

Leese was transferred to Ascot internment camp on 24 January 1941 for six weeks then moved again to Huyton, Liverpool. On 4 March, he went on a hunger strike ostensibly to prevent his removal to the Isle of Man. The tactic worked. He was returned to Brixton prison but refused to end his hunger strike, prompting the authorities to try force-feeding him. Leese finally capitulated after fifty-five days when Richard Stokes MP publicised his plight in Parliament by asking the Home Secretary if he was aware of his protest. Stokes was assured that Leese had not been detained because of his 'well-known anti-Freemason and anti-Semitic views'.[345] Happy with the publicity, Leese called off his hunger strike.

Leese also received the indefatigable support of fellow internee Captain Ramsay who used parliamentary privilege to table a series of questions from his own prison cell that sought to ascertain when Leese would be released and when his confiscated property would be returned to him.[346] Leese was hospitalised in December 1943 with an inflamed prostate, and subsequently released because of ill health on 2 February 1944. He had spent three years and three months behind bars. MI5 added his name to their 'suspect list' of those to be immediately re-detained in the event of an invasion.[347] The terms of Leese's 'Suspension Order' restricted his movement to within ten miles of his home, a limit he routinely breached.[348] Unlike many fascists who struggled with the stigma of disloyalty that internment imposed upon them, Leese wore his detention as a badge of honour:

> As an ex-18B man myself I am only too glad that as many people as possible should know that I was imprisoned for three years and three months (it would have been longer if I had not evaded arrest for months) for being anti-Jewish and trying to get the war stopped before it destroyed European Civilisation as anyone can see now it has done. Surely it is for those who took part in the war to clear THEIR reputation.[349]

War and internment took their toll on the IFL, however. The group was 'very quiet at the moment and likely to split in post-war years', noted MI5 in October 1943 of the growing rift within the milieu. 'Some members were fanatically devoted to Arnold Leese,' they observed, 'but others regarded him as too soft to lead a post-war movement. A certain coolness appeared to have developed between Gordon Woods and Anthony Gittens, and there was a lot of rumour and suspicion between the various members.'[350]

Post-war

Leese lived by the motto that 'if the Jew does not abuse you today, you must have wasted your time yesterday'.[351] Leese did not waste his time. Doted upon by his wife, Ann Story, and a housekeeper, Leese was in a privileged position compared to many activists after the war. He had the time to devote himself body and soul to his 'Arnold Leese Anti-Jewish Information Bureau' and its new publication, *Gothic Ripples*, 'an occasional report on the Jewish Question'. The word 'Gothic' – derived from his reading of Waddell – was synonymous with 'Aryan'.[352] First published on 22 June 1945, a month after VE Day, Leese explained that he founded the newsletter:

> Because we are convinced that there will never be real peace until the conspiracy of silence on the Jewish Question is broken, 'Gothic Ripples' has been stated to give up-to-date reports on Jews in Public Office and *behind* the news. Hate Propaganda, we believe, only serves Jewish interests in the same way that the War was fought for Jewish survival and not for any Gentile interests. It is our duty, therefore, to oppose the Hate Campaign as we opposed the idea of War between the Aryan Powers.[353]

Distributed globally, *Gothic Ripples* gained 1,500 subscribers, approximately half that of *The Fascist*.[354] Many subscribers hailed from the Dominions, though only one from Australia: 'a very slow continent on the Jew Menace', Leese lamented.[355] *Gothic Ripples* was not for 'the Man-in-the-Street'. It was for those already 'Jew-wise' whom Leese defined as those who 'regard Jews and their descendants as aliens no matter what their legal status may be' and who pursued 'by all lawful means' the task of making Jewish naturalisation 'impossible'. *Gothic Ripples* impressed upon the 'Jew-wise' the extent of 'Jewish interbreeding' with the Aryan peoples and the corrosive effects of this miscegenation upon racial purity.[356]

In its anti-Semitic animus, *Gothic Ripples* differed little from *The Fascist*. Leese continued to accuse Jews of engaging in ritual murder and of subverting race and empire. MI5 regarded the 'Leese Circle' – which it dubbed the 'SS of British fascism' – as fixated upon the propagation of violent anti-Semitism: 'They scarcely have any political ideal beyond the pogrom.'[357] Indeed, the vituperative nature of his 'anti-Semitic libels' led to questions in Parliament about Leese in 1946, though the Attorney-General again declined to institute proceedings against him.[358] Further anti-Semitic activities included publishing *The Jewish War of Survival* (1945). Its foreword, which Leese penned on VE Day, argued that 'this war was Jewish and has never had any other object than the salvation of the Jews from Hitler'.[359] The *Sunday Pictorial* called it 'the most pernicious poison that has ever appeared in the English language'. Leese invoked the review as a testimonial.[360] The book, privately printed, quickly sold out of its initial run of 200 copies.[361] Further editions were hurriedly published in the United States[362] and South Africa,[363] where Leese found several willing collaborators. The book became a 'classic' within extreme right counter-cultures, and is frequently reprinted and disseminated online.

Lacking both energy and enthusiasm, Leese declined to found a new movement after the war, however. 'I am 67 and too old to run an activist movement', he told a correspondent.

'But I am in touch with all sound people of our way of thinking. They are all busy, our aim now being penetration of every other "near" movement to teach the people met in them.'[364] In this respect, the British League of Ex-Servicemen was a particular target for infiltration, the object being to detach its leader, Jeffrey Hamm, from Mosley.[365] This anti-Semitic missionary work was necessary, argued Leese, because the Mosleyite movement had itself been subverted by the Jews. 'If, for instance, you were a Mosleyite, like [Victor] Burgess you wld [sic] have to unlearn everything that the Jew [Alexander] Raven-Thomson taught you,' he claimed.[366] Outside of his immediate circle, even those who admired Leese despaired of his continual disparagement of Mosley, not least because it hindered efforts to reunite the remnants of British fascism.[367]

Leese had more success in infiltrating and influencing the Duke of Bedford's recently resurrected British Peoples Party (BPP), which was regarded as 'sound against the unnecessary war, but will not face the main issue, the Jew Menace'.[368] Though he reviled John Beckett who ran the party as an unprincipled opportunist, Leese nonetheless perceived the BPP to be a useful vehicle for racial nationalism and induced his followers to join it. Almost all did. His trusted pre-war lieutenant, Harold Lockwood, became its research secretary, editing its newspaper *Facts*; Elizabeth Berger and Anthony Gittens sat on the organisation's National Council. Gittens also chaired its Central London branch. The treasurer, Aubrey Lees, was a former Nordic League activist. Former IFL members also founded the East London BPP branch at Leese's behest.[369] However, by 1947, Leese concluded, correctly, that the BPP had run its course.[370] Berger and Lockwood both withdrew from the party. Gittens did likewise in the following year.[371]

The death of Henry Hamilton Beamish, The Britons' founder, in Rhodesia on 27 March 1948 changed the dimensions of the role which Leese was able to play. Beamish bequeathed his friend and erstwhile pupil £3,349 as well as his shares portfolio.[372] This hugely important largesse 'strengthened my position as regards assisting younger men and promising movements, and in many other ways,' Leese recorded of the shift from ideological to financial support.[373] One venture that received 'considerable assistance' was the National Workers Movement (NWM), a group modelled on the NSDAP replete with its own twenty-five-point programme.[374] A.F.X. Baron, an Ipswich insurance clerk in whom Leese had reposed his hopes for a racial nationalist revival, had founded the group on 4 July 1948. Most of its adherents were former IFL activists though Leese, despite being its guiding inspiration, refrained from attending the meeting because Baron 'did not need to be bossed about by someone else and was quite capable of standing on his own feet'.[375]

Leese also backed Baron to take over The Britons. In private, however, he was disparaging of Baron; dismissing him as a 'nonentity' put in place to take responsibility whilst his own 'paid man' – Anthony Gittens, The Britons' secretary – actually ran the Society.[376] Leese was to rue giving Baron even this modest entrée. Baron quickly proved 'temperamentally unfitted' to the role assigned to him. He was soon involved in an acrimonious and damaging feud with The Britons, which ended in the High Court in 1951 and ultimately forced them to vacate their premises.[377] Leese subsequently used a portion of Beamish's legacy to purchase The Britons' new headquarters at no. 74 Princedale Road, Holland Park in 1953, the property becoming a vital resource for a new generation of extreme right-wing activists.[378]

Judgement at Nuremberg

Leese's anti-Semitic opinions were not preserved in aspic. If anything, his asperity became even more vituperative. He applauded reports of renewed pogroms in Poland in November

1945, stating: 'Not withstanding their six years of unadulterated misery and betrayal, the Poles do not lose heart. There has been a wave of terrorism against the Jews at Lodz, with 128 Jews slain.'[379] Despite these genocidal impulses, Leese helped pioneer a seemingly contradictory strand of emerging anti-Semitism: Holocaust denial. He had not immediately denied reports of anti-Semitic atrocities. Instead, Leese had argued that they constituted legitimate retaliation for a war, he claimed, the Jews had started.[380] He soon began to deny the Holocaust entirely, however. In an article titled 'The Six Million Lie' published in January 1953, Leese encompassed the predicament of many post-war fascists:

> The fable of the slaughter of six million Jews by Hitler has never been tackled by *Gothic Ripples* because we take the view that we would have liked Hitler even better if the figure had been larger; we are so 'obsessed by anti-Semitism' that we believe that as long as the destruction was done in a humane manner, it was to be to the advantage of everyone ... if it had been true. However, it wasn't.[381]

Hitler was 'one of the greatest statesmen Europe ever had,' claimed Leese. However, 'he did not deal with the Jews effectively enough'. To succeed where Hitler had failed, 'the first step is to clear the Jews right out,' he averred.[382] For Leese, the Jew was an eternally foreign being: '*Once a Jew, Always a Jew*. It follows that *Once a Jew, Never a Briton*. Also, that the only good Jew is a dead one'.[383] Leese continued to venerate and glorify the Third Reich, which he believed was 'responsible for the finest civilisation Europe has ever known'.[384] 'Europe is dead and gone never to arise again,' Leese argued, 'when the Nordic race merges with the scrub population'.[385] For this reason, 'Racial Fascism' not 'National Socialism' was now 'the only remedy'.[386]

None of this distracted Leese from giving unstinting support to the surviving Nazi leadership on trial for war crimes at Nuremberg. *Gothic Ripples* kept up a running commentary titled 'Notes on Nuremberg', which argued that the trials were a 'purely a Jewish and Masonic affair' and an act of 'revenge' taken against those who sought to free Germany from 'the twin-plagues, Jewry and Freemasonry'.[387] To prove that allegations of Nazi concentration and extermination camps were false and concocted by Jews who conspired to wreak revenge upon those who had opposed International Jewish finance, Leese pointed to the Kol Nidre ('All Vows') prayer. This, he claimed, gave Jews Talmudic sanction to 'assassinate their word' – rendering null and void any inconvenient oath or promise they may have been driven to make with a Gentile. Following the trial of Joseph Kramer, the commandant of Bergen-Belsen and forty-four others, which concluded on 13 December 1945 with the execution of eleven defendants, including Kramer, and lengthy prison sentences for the remainder, Leese invoked the prayer in a letter to *The People's Post*, arguing that 'Jewish evidence at this or any other trial, is thus annulled and void. On such evidence Germans are to hang' because their defence was insufficiently versed in the 'Jewish Question'.[388]

Hoping to ensure that defending counsel was in fact 'Jew-wise', Leese contacted the Foreign Office in December 1945, requesting the address of the International Military Tribunal so that he could send them a copy of *The Jewish War of Survival*. The Foreign Office dutifully supplied him with the address of Brigadier General W.L. Mitchell, General-Secretary to the Tribunal, and asked him to indicate whose counsel it was intended for.[389] Leese replied it was for *Reichsmarchall* Hermann Göring's counsel, which was apparently 'glad to have the use of your book'.[390] Perhaps overestimating their credibility, both Leese and Beamish volunteered 'to give evidence on the Jewish issue in defence of the Nuremberg accused'. The duo received a reply stating that their letter had been passed up to the Tribunal who 'will let you know if your presence or that of Mr Beamish in Nuremberg is required'.[391] It was not. Nor did the 'evidence' contained in *The Jewish War of Survival* prove quite the panacea Leese had hoped. Found guilty, Göring committed suicide in his cell hours before his scheduled execution.[392]

Leese attacked the death sentences handed down at Nuremberg as 'Jewish Lynching's'. The dates connected with the trial were saturated with supposed symbolism. He claimed that, when the Jews failed to 'fix' the date for the execution on the Day of Atonement, thus completing the final aim in the 'Jewish War of Survival', they had settled upon 16 October, the seventh day of the Feast of Booths, a time of rejoicing also known as Hosha'na Rabbah.[393] Julius Streicher, the notorious Jew-baiter once enamoured with Leese, thought likewise. Facing the hangman's noose, Streicher shouted out 'Purim-Fest 1946', a reference to the Jewish festival of Purim commemorating the execution of Haman, an ancient persecutor whose story is found in the Old Testament book of Esther. Streicher's last words signalled that he too believed his execution was ritual murder.[394] He was 'the best man of the lot', lamented Leese 'murdered for doing the same sort of work that I am now doing'.[395]

Leese had also offered to give evidence on the 'Jewish menace' at the trial of William Joyce, the former BUF director of propaganda who had broadcast for the Reich Propaganda Ministry under the moniker 'Lord Haw Haw'. Joyce's trial at the Old Bailey opened on 17 September 1945. Leese viewed the date as portentous because, this being the Day of Atonement, it was clear to him, if nobody else, 'that the Jews were fully in charge.'[396] Joyce was convicted of treason and sentenced to death. Mosley, who had branded Joyce an 'offensive little beast' during his own internment hearing, did not assist his former minion.[397] Other fascist activists rallied round, however. Joyce received public support from *The Patriot* and *The People's Post*, the latter organising a petition of clemency for him.[398] Neither they nor many other British fascists ever forgave Mosley for his criticism of Joyce at the time of the trial.[399] The petition also proved popular in Joyce's native Ireland. There, S.B. Hurley, Leese's Dublin-based associate collected signatures.[400]

Such efforts came to naught. Following the failure of Joyce's appeal to the House of Lords, Leese wrote to the Home Secretary, protesting that the court failed to deal with 'motive' before continuing:

> I only met Joyce once, in 1939, when I had a half-an-hours conversation with him. But for several years I have watched with interest the development of his political education. I have no hesitation in saying that his general political motive was to stop a wholly unnecessary World War, which was, in his (and my) opinion promoted *not* by Hitler but by Churchill, Eden & Duff Cooper and their Jew advisers ... if you allow Joyce to become a war casualty, posterity will class you as an assassin of one whose motive (however misjudged his action was) was to bring Germany and Britain together in the formation of a great European civilisation, and who had no treachery in his heart.[401]

Following his execution on 3 January 1946, Leese proclaimed Joyce a 'hero' – which was diametrically opposed to his February 1940 pronouncement that no man of honour would have done what Joyce had done.[402]

Joyce was not alone in facing judicial retribution, though all fared better than he. Several IFL activists were tried after the war. This included Frances Eckersley, former wife of the chief BBC engineer Peter Eckersley. Eckersley, who had joined the IFL in 1938, was part of Joyce's wider political family, had foreknowledge of his flight, and subsequently used her political contacts to help Joyce establish himself in Berlin. She and her son, James Clarke, were tried for broadcasting for the enemy in November 1945 for which she received just twelve months.[403] In March 1946, it was the turn of sixty-seven-year-old Margaret Bothamley who pled guilty to assisting the enemy having broadcast for Radio Bremen during the war.[404] Thanking Leese for his unqualified support, Bothamley wrote:

> I have never lost hold of my animus for England, though technically I put myself in the wrong, I know actually, that I *must* take the only opportunity I had of warning my own people. It has failed. Now I can only feel better people have suffered more in the great cause.[405]

She too was spared the gallows, sentenced instead to twelve months' imprisonment.[406]

Eckersley and Bothamley were not the only IFL activists to receive lenient sentences. 'Thoroughly disappointed' with the BUF, Scotsman Donald Grant had joined the IFL in September 1938. Grant had formed a small six-man section in Earls Court, Kensington, and, according to some reports, was ADC to Leese himself at one juncture. He was in Germany at the outbreak of war and subsequently became the voice of the Nazis' *faux* Scottish radio station – Radio Caledonia – preparing propaganda for other stations and working as an archivist for the German propaganda service. He was jailed for a mere six months in 1947.[407]

Rat lines

Leese also concerned himself with the 'atrocious treatment' meted out to German POWs and demanded their immediate repatriation.[408] A Prisoners of War Assistance Society (PWAS) was founded to campaign for the early repatriation of POWs and better facilities whilst they were detained. Two female activists, Mary Foss, an IFL supporter whose pro-Nazi mother was detained between 1940 and 1942, and Michele Huntley, herself detained in 1941 for causing disaffection amongst HM Forces by spreading pacifist propaganda, established PWAS.[409] Leese lauded the group as a 'genuine Christian effort'.[410] Leese's own interventions were more direct. He and several former IFL activists helped safehouse two Dutch Waffen-SS soldiers, Gerhard Meijer and Hendrik Tiechen, who were on the run having absconded from a POW camp, and attempted to secure them passage to Argentina. Police arrested Leese and his co-conspirators in 1947, however. The two Dutchmen were also arrested and deported to Holland shortly thereafter.[411]

Evidence presented at Leese's trial made the arrests appear 'accidental' and 'firmly based on evidence of a non-secret nature'.[412] In reality, MI5 had a 'secret source' inside this milieu that they went to great lengths to protect. This source derived from the 'Marita case' – a secret service 'honey trap' established in 1940 to monitor and indeed 'organise' potential traitors and collaborators under the tutelage of 'Jack King' a 'Gestapo agent' operating in Britain. In reality, 'Jack' was MI5 officer Eric Roberts, a former Epsom bank clerk and British Fascisti activist recruited to the service during the 1930s by Charles Maxwell Knight, the agency's chief 'agent runner', who had also been active in the group in the early 1920s. Roberts worked closely with fellow MI5 officers Lord Victor Rothschild and Teresa Clay to subvert and neutralise the potential of these would-be fifth columnists. Roberts' operation successfully identified 500 such individuals during the course of the war.[413]

Roberts' investigations also served to highlight the lethal possibilities of Leese's anti-Semitic genealogical 'research', which was by no means an anodyne activity. During the course of one conversation in May 1943, 'Jack' had asked his chief 'agent' Marita Perigoe, who was blissfully unaware that she was working for MI5 and not the Nazis, whether that 'silly old fool' Leese is 'discreet'. Perigoe conceded that Leese 'sounds pretty hopeless' from all she had been told by one of her own 'sub-agents'. Nonetheless, she valued his research as providing the basis for a murderous pogrom, reporting to 'Jack' that:

> Personally I think the I.F.L. is a better bunch on the whole than the B.U. I haven't much use for them. According to Backer Leese is supposed to collect together a 1 list of the first two thousand names of Jews and converted Jews. (?) that have appeared in the neighbourhood some time or another ... Leese apparently has all these people's life histories and everything written down all their crimes and everything. A good beginning isn't it? The first two thousand of the complete wipe-out. I mean they're not even to be deported, those people [laughs].[414]

MI5 had continued to use the 'Marita network' to quietly monitor Leese's activities throughout the war enabling them to compromise his 'rat line' – such as it was – from the outset.[415] Leese had been adamant it would be 'impossible' for the intelligence services to penetrate his operations after 1945, given the tight-knit nature of his core activists.[416] He had not counted on MI5's patience, however.[417]

Anthony Gittens, the former IFL activist who chaired the Central London BPP branch, was tried with Leese. This was a serious embarrassment for the party, but not for its secretary, John Beckett. He helped to raise £400 to defend Leese.[418] Another supporter, S.F. Darwin-Fox, wrote to *The Spectator*, *Truth* and *The Patriot* arguing that Leese was imprisoned for doing what the American Abolitionists were praised and honoured for doing. Not everyone on the extreme right was as supportive. Mosley's supporters reacted with 'uncompromising hostility' believing that Leese's activities were a 'positive menace' to their own labours to bring about a fascist revival.[419] At the subsequent trial, four of his co-defendants pleaded guilty. Leese, Gittens and another activist did not. Beckett engaged C.B.V. Head, the solicitor who had defended William Joyce, to act for the defence, though Leese chose to defend himself, reflecting his belief that 'to pay a lawyer ... to defend an anti-Jew case is just subsidising betrayal'.[420] It took the jury a mere twenty minutes to find Leese and his co-defendants guilty. All seven were sentenced to twelve months' imprisonment on 31 March. *Gothic Ripples* continued publication under the editorship of John Lovell.[421] MI5 also speculated that Winifred Leese and Ann Story produced the first issues.[422]

Leese's imprisonment also led to a showdown with the Royal College of Veterinary Surgeons whose Council met on 14 April 1948 to decide 'whether it shows that you have been guilty of conduct disgraceful in a professional respect'.[423] Leese declined to present evidence in his defence on the grounds that he was 'to a great extent indifferent' to the Council's deliberations not least because, 'I know that our profession is heavily tainted with Freemasonry and no doubt that goes also for the Committee, in which I have no reason therefore to place much confidence.'[424] Despite the case against him being 'duly proved', Leese was not struck off the Register of Veterinary Surgeons. Chancing his arm, Leese submitted an article on the subject of Jewish and Muslim methods of ritual slaughter for publication in *The Veterinary Record*. It was rejected.[425]

On 12 December 1950, Leese, aged 72, returned to the Old Bailey to answer a charge of criminal libel. He had stated in *Gothic Ripples* that Sir Harold Scott, the Metropolitan

Police Commissioner was 'an obvious Jew' who had instructed his officers in the East End 'to knock off any street corner orator who dares to mention the word Jew in any derogatory sense'. Defending himself, Leese claimed the trial was an attempt to 'silence' him. The judge, Mr Justice Dodson, had previously sentenced Leese to twelve months' imprisonment in 1947. 'He [Leese] seems to think that he is in for a "Nuremburg",' remarked Admiral Sir Barry Domvile who stood surety for him.[426] This time, Leese, however, was luckier; he was acquitted after only nine minutes, which he regarded as 'an outstanding victory for the patriotic anti-Jewish minority'.[427] Leese received congratulatory messages from 'anti-Jewish friends all over the world.' His only regret was that Beamish was no longer alive to share in his 'victory'.[428]

Rebuilding the anti-Semitic international

'Never start talking about "Rights" is a Fascist fundamental,' Leese stated. 'Duties is all we have to worry about, & let us think Racially, not Nationally.'[429] Such internationalised conceptions of 'race' fuelled Leese's re-emergence as an integral part of an informal international network of anti-Semitic propagandists, many of whom regarded him as 'a chief protagonist in the world-wide struggle against Jewry'.[430] Leese quickly re-established contact with Einar Åberg of Norrviken, Sweden, founder of the Sveriges Antijudiska Kampförbund (Swedish Anti-Jewish Action League), a group dedicated to the 'total extinction of Judaism in Sweden'. During February 1947, Åberg deluged Britain with anti-Semitic propaganda, some distributed 'quite openly' by British fascists in London.[431] In one instance, material sourced from Åberg was sent to a British officer in the Middle East who had recently survived a bomb attack by Jewish terrorists in Palestine.[432] Åberg's export of anti-Semitic propaganda into Britain continued unabated into the 1950s, distributed through channels provided by Leese and others.[433] Leese's propaganda was also channelled into the Middle East though the offices of Captain Robert Gordon-Canning, a friend of the Grand Mufti of Jerusalem, who paid for two extra subscriptions of *Gothic Ripples*: one for the Arab League in Cairo and another for the Saudi Arabian Legation in London.[434] Gordon-Canning subsequently fell out with Leese in 1951, denouncing him as a 'mental case'.[435]

In New Zealand, Leese resumed his correspondence with the anti-Semitic conspiracy theorist Arthur Nelson Field with whom he had been in touch since February 1932 and to whom he was distantly related through marriage. He sought to dissuade Field from his nagging belief that Hitler was a tool of the Jews.[436] Leese also renewed his acquaintance with the Canadian fascist leader Adrien Arcand, who had made him an honorary member of his National Unity Party of Canada (NUPC) in 1938.[437] His biographer remarks that though thrilled by Nazism, Arcand 'saved his greatest enthusiasm for the imperial dimensions offered by British fascism,' a fervour that was reflected in the pages of *The Canadian Nationalist*. As the historian Jean-Françoise Nadeau observes, the very existence of Arcand's Parti National Social Chrétien, and its successors, 'was largely a product of the contribution of British fascism as outlined by Lord Sydenham, Sir Oswald Mosley, Henry Hamilton Beamish and Sir Barry Edward Domvile.'[438] Leese should be added to that list of tributaries. Though Arcand imported Nazi literature to augment his own anti-Semitic campaigns, he readily testified in 1938 that 'by far the greater part of our imported propaganda comes from the Imperial Fascist League in London.'[439]

Leese reposed a great deal of faith in the United States for racial salvation. 'The English, German and Scandinavian stock in America is worth all the rest of the rubbish in that continent and I would never be surprised to see Jewish power getting its death blow in the USA,' he mused.[440] It was upon extreme right-wing coteries in the United States that Leese also had perhaps his greatest impact. Not all who imbibed his rabid anti-Semitism were marginal political figures. His writings and those of Harvey, Waddell and Beamish influenced *Adam and Cain: Symposium of Old Bible History, Sumerian Empire, Importance of Blood of Race, etc* (1951) penned by William H. Murray, the former Democratic governor of Oklahoma (1931–1935), who had won his seat on the back of a racist campaign against 'The Three C's – Corporations, Carpetbaggers and Coons'.[441] Leese's rabid anti-Semitism also appealed to the Republican Congressman for Montana (1938–1941) Jacob Thorkelson, denounced by the radio commentator Walter Winchell as the 'mouthpiece of the Nazi movement in Congress'.[442] Thorkelson read *Our Jewish Aristocracy* in its entirety into the *Congressional Record* during August 1940.[443]

Leese became increasingly influential upon American anti-Semites after the war. 'Things are going better in the USA than here,' he remarked in 1953. 'A lot of *Gothic Ripples* go there.'[444] In the following year, he noted that he was on friendly terms with 'good Americans' and 'have got a large connection with them now.'[445] Many of his 'Jew-wise' contacts dated from the inter-war years and had been defendants at The Great Sedition Trial in 1944, which had collapsed after the judge died.[446] Whilst Leese waxed lyrical about his American contacts, in general MI5 recorded that it was 'obvious' his 'great hero' was the anti-Semitic pamphleteer Robert E. Edmondson, an old friend of Beamish who Leese regarded as 'the pre-war No. 1 anti-Jewish worker in America'. Edmondson regularly included material from *Gothic Ripples* in his own publications.[447] In later years, Leese came to regard Robert H. Williams, author of *Know Your Enemy* (1950), as 'The best man now in USA' though, like Edmondson he lamented, 'he does not run a movement; he just dishes out information.'[448]

Leese also corresponded with George W. Armstrong, a wealthy Texan businessman and lawyer, whom he supplied with a range of anti-Semitic pamphlets and periodicals together with a list of publications containing material on 'Jewish ritual murder'. Armstrong sent Leese a donation by return, solicited further anti-Semitic 'facts' from him, and requested he proofread a second edition of his book *The Rothschild Money Trust* (1940) after Leese had critiqued a previous work.[449] Whilst Leese promised to 'do my best'[450] with regards to proofreading the work, privately, he disparaged Armstrong's efforts. He lamented that Armstrong's pamphlet, *World Empire* (1947), was so strewn with inaccuracies regarding the supposed racial antecedents of numerous political figures that, 'even if it were possible to get stocks of this book over here for sale, they wld [sic] not be reliable enough to uphold my own reputation for only selling the best stuff! Which is a pity.'[451] Despite his low opinion of Armstrong's work, Leese continued sending him *gratis* copies of *Gothic Ripples*.[452]

More profitably, Leese also corresponded and exchanged publications with Gerald L.K. Smith, editor of *The Cross and The Flag*, which he described as 'really useful'.[453] For his part, Smith regarded *Gothic Ripples* as a 'pungent little package of fact summary' reproducing its 'Jews in the News' column for his own readers' delectation.[454] Smith also utilised Leese's 'research' on the supposed Jewish control of nuclear weaponry, reproducing it for sale in America.[455] Leese's ideas clearly resonated. *Gothic Ripples*, (reprinted by the Michigan-based 'National Information Service'), was distributed to followers of the 'National Committee to Secure Justice in the Rosenberg case' at a picket in Washington, DC in 1953 supporting the 'atom spies' Ethel and Julius Rosenberg, who were then awaiting execution after betraying nuclear secrets to the Soviet Union.[456] Smith regarded Leese as an authority on the Jews, turning to him for advice about the veracity of *The Protocols*. 'Jewish pressure is moving in on me in the United States in an attempt to brand the distribution of the Protocols as a fraudulent operation', he wrote Leese in June 1955. However, although Smith claimed to have an 'abundance' of evidence establishing their authenticity, 'I would appreciate hearing from you concerning your ability to supply the results of your research on the matter.' Perhaps mindful of the reputational damage such an enquiry might have if it became public, Smith bade Leese 'Please do not publish any reference to this, because I prefer it not to be known.' Before concluding his letter, and in reference to the 1934 Berne trial that had further discredited *The Protocols*, Smith also asked Leese for contacts in Switzerland 'who could bring me up to date on the various legal actions that were undertaken there?'[457]

Another of the so-called 'Seditionists', Mrs Lyrl Clark van Hyning, editor of *Women's Voice*, also distributed Leese's books in the United States.[458] Leese occasionally contributed to *Women's Voice* himself, noting privately that it was an offshoot of 'some of our old friends in Erfurt'.[459] Leese's influence upon van Hyning's anti-Semitic outlook was reflected in the attention she received from the FBI in 1955 after she sent a copy of *Jewish Ritual Murder* to the father of a murdered child in Chicago alleging 'ritual murder' to be the cause.[460] Leese still managed to fall out with her, however, after she published a series of articles about Hitler by 'Leslie Fry' [pseud. Paquita de Shishmareff], author of *Waters Flowing Eastwards* (1931), that Leese believed to be 'poisonous nonsense'. As a result, Leese informed van Hyning, 'I cannot use her stuff over here, and that if that is what she believes about Hitler, she cannot want mine in return.'[461] This proved not to be the case and, unperturbed by the admonishment, van Hyning continued distributing Leese's anti-Semitic books into the 1960s.[462] Leese also corresponded with another of contributor to *Women's Voice*, Eustace Mullins, a protégé of the poet Ezra Pound who had subscribed to *The Fascist* in the 1930s. 'We must defend ourselves and our families from Jewish bloodlust or be wiped off the face of the earth,' Mullins counselled Leese in 1955.[463] Leese's writings also influenced Marilyn R. Allen, an anti-Semitic propagandist based in Salt Lake City, Utah, whose book, *Alien Minorities and Mongrelization* (1949) cited Leese as an authority for its more extreme anti-Semitic pronouncements.[464]

Gothic Ripples increasingly advertised American publications and organisations including the Ku Klux Klan. Leese considered the Klan's campaign of racial terrorism against blacks and Jews to be a 'healthy sign', despite having denounced the group as a 'loathsome secret society' in the 1920s.[465] He corresponded with Jesse B. Stoner, a Georgia-based segregationist whose Christian Anti-Jewish Party was dedicated 'to make being a Jew a crime, punishable by death'.[466] Stoner later founded the National States Rights Party (NSRP), which developed extensive links with newly emergent racial nationalist parties like the British National Party (BNP). The BNP signalled its ideological allegiances by appointing Leese's widow as its honorary vice-president.[467] Dr Edward Fields, editor of the NSRP newspaper *The Thunderbolt* – 'the white man's viewpoint' – also entered into cordial correspondence with IFL veteran P.J. Ridout who became the BNP treasurer in 1963.[468] In a letter to *The Thunderbolt*, Ridout stated, 'we in England are faced with exactly the same state of affairs as yourselves.' He praised Fields for both highlighting the 'real culprits' for the world's trouble and for championing racial purity as paramount in the fight for racial survival because, 'once the White Race has been fouled by nigger or Asiatic blood it can never again produce anything but mongrels'.[469]

Fields also greatly admired Leese; *The Jewish War for Survival* featured on his list of 'approved books'.[470] A quarter of a century after it had first appeared, Fields published his own edition of *Jewish Ritual Murder* (1962), with permission from Leese's widow, embellishing the original with his own 'further research' which, he claimed, included several 'extremely rare pictures of the act of Ritual Murder being carried out, and an actual photograph of a purported victim'.[471] Fields aimed at 'mass distribution' for the booklet, which also entailed a brisk transatlantic trade in copies being sold back to his British counterparts, revitalising their own denuded stocks of such vituperative literature in the process.[472]

Fields' enthusiasm for Leese did not diminish. Almost thirty years later, in 1989, he would publish a paean of praise to Leese in his new newspaper *The Truth at Last* under the by-line 'a patriot for all times'.[473] Fields also continued republishing Leese's pamphlets including *The Legalised Cruelty of Shechita: The Jewish Method of Cattle Slaughter* under his 'Truth At Last' imprint. Fields later visited London where he met with Eric Bass, the sole surviving member of the IFL Guard detachment whom he remembered as 'a very personable gentleman'.[474]

It was through such networks that Leese's disquisitions on ritual murder and the supposed innate evil of Jewry found an avid readership amongst Christian Identity adherents in the United States from the Reverend Gordon Winrod onwards. Klan activist James K. Warner, leader of the New Christian Crusade Church in California, introduced subsequent generations of activists to Leese's works by reprinting the bulk of them under his own 'Sons of Liberty' imprint. George P. Dietz, a former Hitler Youth activist from Kassel, Germany, who settled in the United States in 1957, also republished much of Leese's anti-Semitic oeuvre including *The Jewish War of Survival* (1979) under this 'Liberty Bell Publications' imprint.[475]

Yockey

The United States also disgorged the greatest ideological challenge to the ideological integrity of Leese's racial nationalism: Francis Parker Yockey, a young American lawyer and ardent Nazi sympathiser, who had worked briefly at the Nuremberg trials and had tried to sabotage the prosecutions. Yockey subsequently moved to Ireland where, under the pseudonym 'Ulick Varange', he penned his *magnum opus* titled *Imperium* (1948), dedicated to 'the hero of the Second World War' – Adolf Hitler. The book was deeply critical of the 'materialistic race-thinking of the 19th century', for which Europe had 'paid dearly'. Yockey was briefly associated with Mosley's Union Movement (UM) before founding his own short-lived organisation, the European Liberation Front (ELF).[476]

Yockey had derided Leese's crude 'zoological' thinking, eliciting a response from the latter in July 1950, who attacked Yockey as being 'of unknown mixed races and equally unknown past' and alleged that his patron, Baroness Alice von Pfugel, had 'a Jewish grandfather'. Racially unreliable, Yockey was equally unsound ideologically. For Leese, the Eastern-orientated geopolitics underpinning *Imperium* was 'the Jewish one of a European Superstate', whilst Yockey's intellectual debt to German philosopher Oswald Spengler was vilified as being positively 'anti-racial' on account of Spengler's admiration for Benjamin Disraeli and his animus towards the Nazis.[477] Yockey's 'anti-racial' philosophy, alleged Leese, mirrored that of Professor Trofim Lysenko, Stalin's director of biology who rejected Mendelian genetics. 'That this Lysenkoism should deceive any who understand race or the spelling of the word JEW is tragic,' lamented Leese. '"What does it matter?" say Lysenkoists, "if the Russians overrun Europe since they will absorb Culture?" – Aryan, get your Gun!'[478]

ELF activists were incensed. Anthony Gannon, a Manchester-based fascist who had tried and failed to see if cooperation between the two groups was possible angrily retorted:

> Who does Leese think he is? He is a very old man. This flea-bitten, nasty old buzzard did not know what a Jew was until he was heading for 50 years of age. He is not quick to see the obvious, you will admit. I was fighting Jews at the age of 13 years. I have dedicated my life to this fight – not my retirement like Leese.... He was a complete, political failure before the War, and he is still a failure.[479]

Yockey himself penned a visceral epistle stating that in criticising *Imperium* Leese was disparaging a book he had never read, which Leese had allegedly conceded to him during their correspondence. Thereafter Yockey ridiculed Leese's claim that 'the idea of Europe constituted as one Culture-State-Nation-People-Race is also a Jew idea'. Leese was a slave to 'the lowest kind of prurient Jew obsession', alleged Yockey, which amounted to 'shadow-boxing' with the Jews rather than fighting them politically. Though he alleged Leese had 'mongoloid and negroid ancestry', the real source of his alleged racial contamination was spiritual not biological:

> In truth race is a horizontal classification of men, and not a vertical one, and in this meaning of race, Leese must be classified as a Jew, since his life is devoted to Jewry. He attacks all REAL opponents of the Jew, but never effectively attacks the Jew. It is of little import that he prefers the Frankfurter branch of his Jewish world to the Kaganovich branch, for his world-outlook is exclusively Jewish in either case.[480]

Leese returned to the attack in December 1952 when the *National Renaissance Bulletin*, the organ of James Madole's National Renaissance Party (NRP), published Yockey's article 'What is behind the Hanging of Eleven Jews in Prague?' Yockey argued that the anti-Semitism surrounding the Slánský trial represented 'an unmistakable turning point' in East–West relations. All talk of fighting Bolshevism, proclaimed Yockey, 'belongs now to yesterday' as Russia turned inexorably against the real foe: 'international Jewry'. Leese dismissed as 'rubbish' Yockey's argument that Stalinist Russia was now opposed to 'the Jew'. 'The truth of course', stated Leese, 'is that the Jew fights the Jew behind the Iron Curtain as well as outside it, for he controls everything there as in the USA itself'.[481]

Leese was aghast that the NRP adopted such a stance; his horror probably compounded by having recently praised the group as 'the movement nearer to that of the pre-war Imperial Fascist League than any other we know of'.[482] Indeed, having previously traded publications with Madole who distributed *Gothic Ripples* to 'interested readers', Leese had regarded the NRP as 'a movement based on solid racial principles'.[483] On this basis, he had cultivated contacts with a range of NRP activists including its Brooklyn leader John M. Lundoff, to whom he sold several copies of the old 'Jewish "ritual murder"' edition of *Der Stürmer* after Lundoff's 'good friend' Edward Fields told him to contact Leese directly.[484]

Leese sent Madole an angry rebuke after he published Yockey's article. Stung by Leese's accusation that the NRP 'clearly lacks a real leader', Madole rushed to reassure Leese that 'we have not abandoned our racial or political principles'.[485] Leese also sent a warning to Frederick Polzin, the NRP Pennsylvania branch chairman about Yockey who replied that he had the 'utmost faith in your opinions'.[486] Polzin was either being dishonest or else subsequently evolved towards support for Yockey. 'Polzin Publications' was later responsible for distributing Yockey's essay *The World in Flames* (1961), published by

Frederick C. Weiss, the NRP's chief propagandist with whom Leese also regularly exchanged anti-Semitic publications, and another NRP activist, H. Keith Thompson, the registered agent for Major-General Otto Ernst Remer's Sozialistische Reichspartei (SRP – Social Reich Party) until it was banned in 1952.[487] The NRP activist Mana Truhill who ran the group's 'overseas office' (whilst also informing on the organisation to anti-fascist groups) knew little about Yockey or the ELF. Nonetheless, he was delighted to be in touch with Leese.[488]

These contretemps were ironic given that Kurt Mertig, the New York NRP chairman who edited the *National Renaissance Bulletin,* had been arrested in October 1945 for distributing Leese's *Jewish Ritual Murder* at a party rally in Queens Village, an American edition having been published by Homer Maertz's 'Pioneer News Service'.[489] Sentencing Mertig, Maertz and another activist, Ernest Elmhurst, who had been involved with the Erfurt network and was indicted in the 1944 Great Sedition Trial, the judge described Leese's pamphlet as 'one of the most vicious, venomous' incitements to racial hatred he had ever seen.[490] Reporting on Mertig's arrest the *Daily Worker,* 11 January 1946 (not to be confused with the British *Daily Worker*) had untruthfully alleged that Leese 'was once convicted of rape and sodomy'. Outraged, Leese contacted the US Department of Justice. They informed him that there was no Federal statute under which the newspaper could be prosecuted for libel. The jurisdiction lay with the Attorney-General of the individual states themselves whom he would need to contact. Leese does not appear to have pursued the matter further.[491]

Leese was equally unsuccessful in combating the spread of Yockey's ideas amongst his Canadian contacts including the Canadian fascist leader Adrien Arcand. 'That book *Imperium* is deadly poison and Lysenkoism', Leese had warned him in March 1949. 'The man thinks that environment changes races into other races. I have told the author what I think of it.'[492] For his part, Yockey recalled of their correspondence:

> I might say that Leese – whom I have never met – wrote to me in London some years ago, a long letter against *Imperium,* saying that he read only as far as page 80, Volume 1, and that he could not read further, as it was (sic) 'a wilderness of words'. He interprets *Imperium* as a Jewish book, and says that the Liberation Front is 'all in the Jew plan'.[493]

Arcand clearly found Yockey more convincing, going so far as to comment on and correct an earlier draft of *The Proclamation of London* (1949) issued by Yockey's group.[494] Yockey was delighted to receive Arcand's support, noting of the campaign against him:

> I believe that poor senile Leese is either lying or imaging out of the depths of his suspicion- and persecution mania ... Leese, in case you have not heard the details, is writing private letters about England and elsewhere that I am a Jewish agent, and a Bolshevik agent. Some of his supporters, in order to cover every possibility, are also saying that I am an American agent provocateur.[495]

Leese continued his campaign against Yockey, firing off another angry missive to Arcand upon receiving the August 1950 issue of the ELF newsletter, *Frontfighter,* which announced Arcand's 'support' for the group. Leese demanded to know if this was true.[496] Arcand's diplomatic response rejected Leese's accusation that the ELF programme was 'Jew-inspired' as a 'rather drawn conclusion' (not least, because *The Proclamation* called for the 'immediate expulsion of all Jews and other parasitic aliens from the Soil of Europe'). Furthermore, he told Leese, he had no wish to become embroiled in this 'local affair' concluding: 'I will heartily approve of any book, writing or campaign denouncing the evils of Jewry and striving for ridding any spot in this world of their influence.'[497] Arcand's pretence to be standing aloof from this 'local affair' was untrue. He forwarded his correspondence with Leese and others critical of Yockey, including G.L.K. Smith, editor of *The Cross and The Flag*, to the ELF.[498] Yockey was delighted that Arcand had not been 'duped' by his detractors.[499]

If Leese failed to prevail in his transatlantic struggle to protect racial nationalist orthodoxy against ideological heresy, he had more luck ensuring that his anti-Semitic interpretation of Soviet politics held sway in Britain. His acolyte Colin Jordan internalised and regurgitated Leese's interpretation in *Fraudulent Conversion: The Myth of Moscow's Change of Heart* (1956), arguing that reports of Soviet anti-Semitism were false, since Communism and Judaism were symbiotic and that events behind the Iron Curtain were the result of an internal power struggle between two warring factions of World Jewry.[500] Leese's interaction with the NRP was not entirely fruitless, however. The leader of Madole's uniformed bodyguards, Matt Koehl, later became one of Jordan's closest collaborators.

'Keep Britain White'

Efforts to preserve the ideological purity of racial nationalism continued alongside attempts to ensure its continued transmission. Leese's framework for understanding 'race' remained works like Günther's *Racial Elements* and Waddell's *The Makers of Civilisation in Race and History*, which he continued selling after 1945.[501] Both books were out of print, meaning that important ideological texts were now sorely lacking for educating and engaging younger activists. Foreseeing this development, Leese had previously induced John Hooper Harvey to produce a short summary of Waddell's now 'unobtainable' works, which subsequently appeared as *The Heritage of Britain* (1940). However, because the Blitz had 'wiped out' Paternoster Row, then the centre of London's publishing industry, even this title was now hard to obtain.[502] Printing new material was also problematic. Leese's printer, Walter Whitehead, had handed his business over to his daughter, his appetite for printing 'hot' material declining commensurately as a result. He had lost everything during a German bombing raid in 1944, which probably dented his enthusiasm too.[503] To overcome this ideological lacuna, Leese penned *Racial Inequality in Europe* (1948), a short pamphlet regurgitating Günther's ideas, which concluded: 'In no single case in Europe has a really great civilisation been founded by other than the Nordic people.' Leese also financed the publication *The Five Races of Europe* (1949), a summary of Günther's researches authored by George Pile, The Britons' chairman, which Leese regarded as 'in actuality, a religious book'.[504]

Leese's own thinking on race, always lacking sophistication, became 'even cruder' after the war. He had dubious honour to be amongst the first racist ideologues to popularise the slogan 'Keep Britain White' that he used from July 1952 onwards compared with the Mosleyites who used 'KBW', at least initially, to denote a more localised issue: 'Keep Brixton White', a small but important distinction.[505] From 1946 onwards, Leese had fulminated against the 'black plague' in the pages of *Gothic Ripples*.[506] His anti-black racism perhaps reached its apogee in *Gothic Ripples*' 'Nigger Notes' column, a regular feature from 1953. Of Jomo Kenyatta, one of the leaders of the Mau Mau rebellion in Kenya, Leese stated 'we can see no great difference between his countenance and that of a gorilla', arguing that, 'we suggest that the white man should adopt an attitude towards niggers more considerate to the preservation of civilisation than he has done in the past.' 'We cannot afford to treat the niggers of South Africa who eat nuns or the niggers of Kenya who drink the blood of the people they murder, to live with us without restrictions.'[507]

Mirroring his anti-Semitic solutions, Leese campaigned for complete segregation rather than restriction. He set out his stall in an article titled 'About Niggers', in which argued for the revival of the term 'Nigger'. Leese stated that this racial epithet was not 'a term of contempt' but instead marked 'a great Gulf to be kept well dredged so that it will remain a gulf'. 'I have lived for years surrounded by Niggers: I claim to know something about them. I have learned how greatly they should be appreciated … but as Niggers', he continued. Strict segregation had to be maintained as a prophylactic against miscegenation. 'When white mates with black, the result is permanent', claimed Leese. 'It is a crime for which the offspring are made to suffer the consequences, and there is no cure for its devastating results on Society.' Elsewhere, he demanded that 'interbreeding' should be made 'a penal offence' and encouraging it 'a Hanging Matter'. For Leese, Africans and West Indians 'achieved absolutely nothing by themselves' and thus, whilst they could become 'individually civilised … when the white man withdraws or degenerates by interbreeding into the Nigger himself, he reverts to savagery sooner or later'. The same was true for the Persians and Indians ('Niggers, less black') who, despite being brought civilisation by the Aryan, were unable to keep it up without the 'white man'. He was similarly dismissive of the arguments favouring racial equality that underpinned the movement towards greater colonial freedom, which Leese dubbed the 'back to the gorilla movement'. It was all part of an enormous Jewish plot of course. 'As all Jew-wise people know,' concluded Leese, 'the black-and-tan Jew is using the Equality Lie on a vast scale of propaganda so that the Aryan may be induced to leave the Government of the world to him.'[508]

Legacy

Now an old man, Leese despaired of the future. His efforts to unify the disparate strands of the anti-Semitic hinterland, in disarray by the early 1950s, had come to naught. Movements and publications petered out. The principle vehicle for racial nationalists during this period, the British Empire Party (BEP), run by P.J. Ridout, which held its first public meeting in Trafalgar Square on 5 August 1951, was insignificant.[509] 'Soap-box' meetings, such as the BEP could muster, were regarded by Leese as an ineffective means of communicating the 'Jew-wise' message, particularly given the risks involved, legally and physically, to speakers.[510] Leese preferred lectures to oratory but conceded that his message had failed to resonate. A 'Jew-wise public' was non-existent; the 'Gothic wave' was nowhere in sight. Leese began looking for a kindred spirit, an obdurate anti-Semite who would refuse to moderate their anti-Semitic astringency for the sake of a wider audience or take refuge in 'respectability' counselling 'weak measures' when 'drastic ones' were required.[511] 'In our opinion, the only useful way of opposing the Jews is by attacking them openly, as Hitler and Beamish did', he continued to insist.[512]

Towards the end, Leese was increasingly isolated. Although he continued to fund *Free Britain*, The Britons newsletter, and allowed them to use his premises at no. 74 Princedale Road for their offices, Leese declined invitations to attend their social gatherings. After one such invite, he told Anthony Gittens:

> I haven't spoken for years & I forget words, as you know, & lose continuity & I have nothing to say that is, nothing at a meeting of Jew-wise people; I believe it might be a complete flop & do more harm than good. So count me out ... I did not want to advertise the fact of my disabilities, which include having few teeth to stop the spit flying about.[513]

Not just physical infirmity prevented Leese from addressing such gatherings, however. 'I simply will not be associated in any way with [A.K.] Chesterton,' leader of the League of Empire Loyalists, he told Gittens.[514]

Leese bore Chesterton a good deal of personal animosity. He regarded him as insufficiently anti-Semitic and was equally unable to forgive his past dalliance with Mosley. Leese's personal hopes for the future of 'Jew-wise' politics came to repose in Colin Jordan, a racial nationalist activist then serving as Midland organiser for Chesterton's League, who 'readily absorbed all of his mentor's knowledge and experience'.[515] Leese had first drawn attention to Jordan in *Gothic Ripples* in March 1950, when his young protégé was at the beginning of his political career.[516] Leese did not live to see Jordan's notoriety expand beyond the confines of the 'Jew-wise' milieu, however. He died on 18 January 1956, aged seventy-seven. Following his death, his widow wrote to Gittens, *Gothic Ripples*' new editor, asking him to inform people, and adding 'it was rather sudden at the end, but he has been spared much suffering which I think would have been inevitable had he lived'.[517] Leese was cremated at Brookwood Crematorium near Woking to Wagner's *Tannhäuser Overture* and Elgar's *Chanson de Nuit*. Internationally, his passing was noted by a mere handful of ageing anti-Semites including the Canadian fascist Adrien Arcand, who mourned the passing of 'one of the great specialists of the Jewish problem'.[518] His domestic admirers meanwhile convened a 'Memorial Fund' to publish a joint-life of Leese and Beamish but failed to raise enough money to cover the cost of publication.[519]

As this codicil suggests, Leese was soon forgotten outside the cloistered confines of the extreme right milieu. 'Politically' Leese was never an important figure. Indeed, as one scholar remarked over thirty years ago, more students study Leese's life and ideas for undergraduate degrees every year than were ever members of his party.[520] But herein lay his significance. Leese's vituperative brand of anti-Semitism continues to endure, perpetrators of anti-Semitic acts sometimes explicitly and symbolically invoking his name to invest their own actions with a certain authority.[521] Leese's own writings on the 'blood libel' have assumed their own place in the tradition of folkloric anti-Semitism.[522] *My Irrelevant Defence* and *Jewish Ritual Murder* are periodically reprinted in Britain and abroad and regularly disseminated online, serving as a vital resource for subsequent generations of anti-Semitic activists.[523] Perhaps Leese's greatest contribution, however, was his dogged insistence that 'race' was the 'basis of all politics', which exerted a powerful influence upon a new, younger generation of extreme right-wing activists then emerging onto the political scene, foremost amongst whom was Jordan, who looked to Leese and not Mosley for their intellectual inspiration.

Notes

1 Richard Thurlow, *Fascism in Britain: From Oswald Mosley's Blackshirts to the National Front* (London: I.B. Tauris, 1998), p. 47.
2 Arnold Spencer Leese, *Out of Step: Events in the Two Lives of an Anti-Jewish Camel-Doctor* (Hollywood, CA: Sons of Liberty, n.d.), p. 6.
3 Arnold Leese to A.N. Field, 12 May 1952 in 73.148.081, Arthur Nelson Field papers, Alexander Turnbull Library, Wellington, New Zealand, hereafter Field papers.

4 Leese, *Out of Step*, pp. 1–42.
5 Robert Irwin, *Camel* (London: Reaktion Books, 2010), p. 172. In 'Pages from a Memoir: Computers and Encyclopedias', Richard Bulliet, author of *The Camel and the Wheel* (1990) recalled prophetically:

> I have often reflected upon a lesson of Leese's career that I saw borne out, in lesser degree, in the lives of certain other camel specialists I learned about in my research: *Do not put too much trust in camel scholars when they stray into areas of important human concern.*

6 TNA WO 374/41523.
7 Leese, *Out of Step*, pp. 48–49.
8 A.S. Leese, *Fascism* (London: The National Party [The National Fascisti], 1925).
9 TNA BT 31/32629/198007; TNA J 13/14401 and TNA J 107/115. It was chartered on 27 May 1924 as The British Fascists Limited.
10 James Loughlin, 'Rotha Lintorn-Orman, Ulster and the British Fascists Movement', *Immigrants and Minorities*, vol. 32, no. 1, 2014, pp. 62–89.
11 *The Times*, 13 November 1925. Blakeney became BF president in September 1924. He resigned in April 1926 in protest at Lintorn-Orman's refusal to change the group's name and register it as a non-political organisation as a pre-condition for BF activists being allowed to officially assist the government in countering the 1926 General Strike. Thereafter, Blakeney founded the 'Loyalists', see *The Manchester Guardian*, 28 April 1926.
12 Minute, 28 April 1928 in TNA KV 3/58; and Pierre Dominique [pseud. for Dominique Luccini], *Deux Jours chez Ludendorff* (Paris: Éditions du Siècle, 1924), pp. 104–105.
13 Leese, *Out of Step*, pp. 48–50.
14 *Ibid.*, p. 49.
15 G.C. Webber, 'Intolerance and Discretion: Conservatives and British Fascism, 1918–1926', in Tony Kushner and Kenneth Lunn (eds), *Traditions of Intolerance* (Manchester: Manchester University Press, 1989), p. 163 states the BF 'borrowed the name, but not much else from Italy.'
16 Report no. 10, TNA KV 3/57/49a.
17 Barbara Storm Farr, *The Development and Impact of Right-Wing Politics in Britain, 1903–1932* (New York: Garland, 1987), p. 57.
18 Leese, *Out of Step*, pp. 48–49. For local context, see Steve Woodbridge, 'Local and Vocal: Arnold Leese and British Fascism in Small-Town Politics', *Socialist History*, no. 41, 2012, pp. 43–59.
19 On 16 July 1925, Leese wrote to *The Patriot* deriding the BF as 'non-political', much to the chagrin of his former colleagues, see *The Fascist Bulletin*, vol. 2, no. 9, 29 August 1925.
20 Extract, 11 May 1925 in TNA KV 3/121/1a; 'National Fascisti', 5 November 1924 in TNA KV 3/57; and The National Fascisti, Scotland House report, circa 1925 in TNA KV 3/121//4a. MI5 reported the NF was founded by Colonel Ralph Bingham as an 'off shoot' operating within the BF before it emerged as a separate entity. However, another MI5 report, states Giles E. Eyre, former joint-editor of *British Fascism*, Philip Devereux and Anthony Howard were the founders. Eyre and Howard were 'Jewish', observed the authorities.
21 Extract, 22 August 1933 in TNA KV 3/121/6b. 'Fascism in Great Britain', 27 April 1934 in TNA KV 3/121/6a notes 'several quite reputable people' supported the group financially including Dowager Viscountess Downe, a friend of Queen Mary, until defalcations and minor swindles broke it up.
22 M.K. [Maxwell Knight] to E.B. Stamp, 16 February 1942 in TNA KV 3/121/14a. TNA WO 372/17/230900 lists his rank as 'Major' in the 13th North Staffordshire Regiment, which supports Knight's assessment. *Yorkshire Evening Post*, 30 July 1936 reports that Rippon-Seymour, who subsequently ran the Ex-Service Men's Publicity Bureau, which aimed to find work for former soldiers, was fined £5 in 1936 for falsely claiming he had been awarded the DSO.
23 Rose Collis, *Colonel Barker's Monstrous Regiment* (London: Virago, 2001).
24 Henry Rippon-Seymour to R.D. Blumenfeld, 6 August 1925 in BLU 1/18/RIP1, R.D. Blumenfeld papers, House of Lords Record Office, London.
25 *Fascist Gazette*, 8 November 1926, quoted in Steven Woodbridge, 'The Nature and Development of the Concept of National Synthesis in British Fascist Ideology, 1920–1940' (Unpublished PhD thesis: Kingston University 1998), p. 266.
26 British Fascists organising secretary letter, n.d. in TNA HO 144/19069.

27 Tom Linehan, *British Fascism, 1918–39: Parties, Ideology and Culture* (Manchester: Manchester University Press, 2000), p. 127.
28 Robert Benewick, *The Fascist Movement in Britain*, p. 37.
29 *Ibid.*, pp. 37–38; and Frederic Mullally, *Fascism inside England* (London: Claude Morris, 1946), p. 21.
30 Colin Cross, *The Fascists in Britain* (London: Barrie and Rockliff, 1961), p. 61.
31 *The Times*, 4 November 1925.
32 Major-General Sir Wyndham Childs, *Episodes and Reflections* (London: Cassell, 1930), pp. 215–216.
33 George E.G. Catlin, 'Fascist Stirrings in Britain', *Current History*, vol. 34, 1934, p. 542.
34 Storm Farr, *The Development and Impact of Right-Wing Politics in Britain, 1903–1932*, p. 57; and 'Fascism in Great Britain', 27 April 1934 in TNA KV 3/121/6a.
35 Storm Farr, *The Development and Impact of Right-Wing Politics in Britain, 1903–1932*, pp. 56–57.
36 A.S. Leese, *Fascism* (London: The National Party [The National Fascisti], 1925).
37 Leese, *Out of Step*, p. 48.
38 Woodbridge, 'The Nature and Development of the Concept of National Synthesis in British fascist ideology, 1920–1940', pp. 266–268. He and Simpson held a public BNF meeting in Oakham in October 1926, with Leese denouncing 'international financiers', see *Grantham Journal*, 16 October 1926.
39 Special Branch report, 9 March 1927 in TNA HO 144/19069.
40 *The Times*, 10 March 1927; and *Daily Mail*, 10 March 1927.
41 Simpson was re-elected for a second term.
42 Leese, *Out of Step*, pp. 44–48.
43 Thurlow, *Fascism in Britain*, p. 57; and Leonard Wise, *Arthur Kitson* (London: Holborn Publishing Company, 1934).
44 Sir Richard Paget wrote to *The Times*, 7 October 1937 that Kitson's advice on the subject of monetary reform 'had a real influence on German monetary policy' claiming that Hitler's pronouncement, three days beforehand, that 'money in itself played no role' in Germany's economic recovery and consequent productivity was 'the essence of Kitson's teaching'.
45 Winifred Leese to Arthur Field, 20 May 1956 in 73.148.081, Field papers.
46 Leese, *Out of Step*, pp. 48–49.
47 *The Times*, 16 August 1921, 17 August 1921 and 18 August 1921. For background, see Norman Cohn, *Warrant for Genocide* (London: Serif, 1996).
48 Leese, *Out of Step*, p. 50.
49 Stephen Eric Bronner, *A Rumour about the Jews* (New York: St Martin's Press, 2000). See also Philippe Burin, *Nazi Anti-Semitism* (New York: New Press, 2004).
50 *The Jewish Peril: Protocols of the Elders of Zion* (London: Britons, 1920).
51 Special Branch report, 22 November 1919 in TNA HO 144/21377.
52 Claudia Koonz, *The Nazi Conscience* (Cambridge, MA: Belknap/Harvard, 2003).
53 Leese, *Out of Step*, p. 50.
54 H.H. Beamish, marginalia on Hugh W. White to H.H. Beamish, 30 November 1935, Hyman papers, William Cullen Library, University of Witwatersrand, Johannesburg, South Africa.
55 Arnold Leese to A.N. Field, 20 March 1952 in 73.148.081, Field papers.
56 B.A. Kosmin, 'Colonial Careers for Marginal Fascists: A Portrait of Hamilton Beamish', *Wiener Library Bulletin*, vol. 27, no. 30/31, 1973–1974, pp. 16–23: and also Nick Tozcek, *Haters, Baiters and Would-Be Dictators* (Abingdon: Routledge, 2016), pp. 1–74.
57 Nicholas Goodrick-Clarke, *The Occult Roots of Nazism: Secret Aryan Cults and Their Influence on Nazi Ideology* (London: Tauris Parke, 2009).
58 D. St Clair Gainer to Sir Eric Phipps, 18 December 1936 in TNA FO 371/20739.
59 *The Hidden Hand or Jewry Ueber Alles*, vol. 4, no. 1, February 1923; and *The Times*, 20 January 1923.
60 Special meeting at 40, Great Ormond Street, on 12 July 1923, Britons archive.
61 Minutes of executive meeting held at the offices on Saturday 15 September 1923, Britons archive.
62 Kurt G.W. Ludecke, *I Knew Hitler* (London: Jarrolds, 1938), p. 201.
63 *British Guardian*, vol. 5, no. 7, July–August 1924.

64 *The Fascist*, vol. 1, no. 13, May 1930.
65 Captain A.E.N. Howard, author of *The Beast Marks Russia* (1938), The Britons' agent in China who lived in Shanghai, addressed IFL meetings on 'The Influence of Jewish Finance in the Middle and Far East'. Britons workers W.H. Waller and Richard T. Cooper regularly contributed to *The Fascist* and addressed IFL meetings, see *The Fascist*, no. 35, April 1932, *The Fascist*, no. 51, August 1933 and *The Fascist*, no. 65, October 1934.
66 Harold Lockwood, Advisory Committee hearing, 29 January 1941 in TNA HO 283/46.
67 Minute, 9 October 1928 in TNA KV 3/58/83.
68 Baillie lived in Brighton resigning from the IFL because of 'ill-health' in June 1930. Sherrard lived in nearby Hove but dropped out after the death of his wife in February 1931, see *The Fascist*, no. 18 November 1930 and *The Fascist*, no. 22, March 1931. What became of Brigadier-General D. Erskine Tulloch is unknown though a Denis R.D.S. Erskine-Tulloch filed for bankruptcy in 1930. He may or may not be the same individual.
69 George E.G. Caitlin, 'Fascist Stirrings in Britain', *Current History*, vol. 39, 1934, p. 542. On 17 April 1934, the IFL headquarters relocated to no. 30 Craven Street, see *The Fascist*, no. 59, April 1934.
70 *The Fascist*, no. 34, March 1932; and *The Fascist*, no. 56, January 1934. James Webb, *The Occult Establishment* (LaSalle, IL: Open Court Publishing, 1976), pp. 106 and 126 highlights the influence of the Guild idea in Britain during the early twentieth century, which was by no means confined to the extreme right. Arthur Penty, one of the ideas' modern progenitors, later joined the fascists.
71 *The Fascist*, vol. 1, no. 1, March 1929. *The Fascist*, vol. 1, no. 7, September 1929 notes CINEF's new headquarters.
72 Miranda B. Hickman (ed.), *One Must Not Go Altogether with the Tide: The Letters of Ezra Pound and Stanley Nott* (Montreal: McGill-Queens University Press, 2011), especially pp. 289–295. Pound's correspondence with Leese revealed the poets' 'lack of compunction about reaching out to an anti-Semitic fascist steeped in pseudoscientific theories about the racial inferiority of Jews.' It also paralleled his own shift towards a more racially based form of anti-Semitism than had previously been evident in his writings.
73 Ezra Pound to Graham Seton Hutchinson, 21 Maggio [1936] in YCAL MSS 43, Box 23 f. 1027, Ezra Pound papers, Beinecke Library, Yale University.
74 David Bradshaw and James Smith, 'Ezra Pound, James Strachey Barnes ("The Italian Lord Haw-Haw") and Italian Fascism', *The Review of English Studies*, vol. 64, no. 266, 2013, pp. 672–693.
75 Special Branch report, 9 March 1936 in TNA HO 45/24967.
76 Special Branch report, 9 March 1936 in TNA HO 45/24967; and *The Fascist*, no. 116, January 1939. For comments on African distribution, see *The Fascist*, no 57, February 1934.
77 'The British Union of Fascists' (1941), MI5 memorandum, p. 40 in TNA KV 4/241. IFL activist Bert Wilton estimated 500–600 members, see *Fascism in England: 1928–1940* (London: Final Conflict, 1997), p. 8.
78 Special Branch report, 22 January 1934 in TNA MEPO 2/10646/65c and Harold Lockwood, Advisory Committee hearing, 29 January 1941 in TNA HO 283/46.
79 Special Branch report, 9 March 1936 in TNA HO 45/24967.
80 *The Fascist*, no. 67, December 1934.
81 *Fascism or Democracy?* (London: IFL, n.d.), p. 7.
82 Cross, *The Fascists in Britain*, p. 64.
83 *The Fascist*, no. 47, April 1933.
84 *The Fascist*, no. 67, December 1934. Harold Lockwood, Advisory Committee hearing, 29 January 1941 in TNA HO 283/46.
85 Special Branch report, 9 March 1936 in TNA HO 45/24967.
86 The Imperial Fascist League, MI5 report, 8 March 1942 in TNA HO 45/24967. Lieutenant-Colonel O.A. Harker to W. Oliver, 25 June 1940 in TNA KV 2/1365 describes MacDonald as 'an old man who lives abroad, and is not on active service'. Previously a BUF member, MacDonald's principal interest appears to have been Indian policy, writing on the subject for *The Blackshirt*, 12 October 1934 before moving towards the IFL. *The Fascist*, no. 70, March 1935 sold his pamphlet, *India's Financial Troubles*, a collection of papers 'containing much information suppressed by the Government'. MI5 believed MacDonald was a conduit for

correspondence between Mary Stanford, a Right Club activist and Margaret Bothamley, an old associate of Leese living in Germany, who subsequently broadcast for the Nazis. MacDonald moved to the South of France in 1940, see Mary Stanford, Advisory Committee hearing, 15 May 1941 in TNA KV 2/832.
87 Steven Woodbridge, 'Fraudulent Fascism: The Attitude of Early British Fascists towards Mosley and the New Party', *Contemporary British History*, vol. 23, no. 4, December 2009, pp. 493–507.
88 Robert Skidelsky, *Oswald Mosley* (London: Papermac, 1990), pp. 379–380.
89 Matthew Worley, *Oswald Mosley and the New Party* (London: Palgrave Macmillan, 2010), pp. 159–160.
90 *The Fascist*, no. 41, October 1932.
91 *The Fascist*, no. 42, November 1932.
92 *The Fascist*, no. 36, May 1932.
93 *British Guardian*, vol. 6, no. 10, 13 March 1925.
94 Philip, Viscount Snowdon, *An Autobiography* (London: Ivor Nicolson and Watson, 1934), pp. 876–877, commented on Mosley's 'striking resemblance' to Ferdinand Lassalle, the forefather of the German social democracy. For Leese, this was ample proof that Mosley was Jewish because: 'LASSALLE WAS A JEW'. Ironically, Mosley's future father-in-law, Lord Curzon, former Viceroy of India made a similar observation when Mosley asked for his daughter's hand in marriage in March 1920, noting that Mosley was, 'very young, tall, little black moustache, rather Jewish appearance', see Nigel Jones, *Mosley* (London: Haus, 2004), p. 21.
95 Arnold Leese to Adrien Arcand, 24 May 1950, Adrien Arcand Collection, Library and Archives Canada, Ottawa, Canada, hereafter Arcand papers.
96 Arnold Leese to Major Theodore Rich, 11 December 1955, Leese papers.
97 Mosley's appeal against order of internment, 2 July 1940 in TNA HO 283/13.
98 *The Manchester Guardian*, 3 March 1933.
99 *The Fascist*, no. 54, November 1933. A.N. Field to Sir Herbert Kelliher, 2 April 1935 in 73.148.081, Field papers records that the IFL also abused the BUF as 'Rothschilds Life Guards'.
100 *The Fascist*, no. 95, April 1937.
101 Untitled manuscript, MSS 292/743/12 in Trades Union Congress papers, Modern Records Centre, Warwick University; HO 144/20141/309; and *The Fascist*, no. 55, December 1933. Leese's fellow speakers, J.F. Rushbrook and Brigadier-General Blakeney, were 'seriously injured' during the attack. Blakeney was beaten 'so brutally' that he did not recover until February 1934, see *The Fascist*, no. 57, February 1934. BUF activist, Tony Marino, was bound over for three years and ordered to pay £5 compensation for his part in the fracas, see *The Times*, 27 November 1933 and *The Times*, 4 December 1933. Blakeney later contributed to the BUF publication *Action*, no. 111, 2 April 1938, perhaps having forgiven the assault by its members five years earlier. The IFL may or may not have planned to avenge the insult. G. Flack to Sup. B-CR, 22 February 1934 in TNA HO 144/20158/113 notes that Ian Hope Dundas, BUF chief of staff had contacted police claiming to have information from a former IFL member that the IFL were planning to attack the BUF headquarters that night. Police made the 'necessary arrangements' but nothing appears to have come of such threats, which the police may have regarded as mischief making.
102 'Report on the Fascist Movement in the United Kingdom, excluding Northern Ireland' in TNA KV 3/58.
103 Leese, *Out of Step*, p. 51; and TNA HO 144/20144/229–31.
104 Special Branch report, 12 January 1935 in TNA HO 144/20144.
105 Special Branch report, 26 January 1935 in TNA HO 144/20144; *The Fascist*, no. 74, July 1935; and *The Fascist*, no. 77, October 1935.
106 John Symonds, *The Beast 666: The Life of Aleister Crowley* (London: Pindar Press, 1997) details Fuller's occultism.
107 Stanley J. Passmore to Sir Oswald Mosley, 27 May 1935 in OMN/B/7/4, Oswald Mosley papers, Nicholas Mosley deposit, Birmingham University. This personal antagonism did not prevent Fuller from utilising Leese's pamphlets to support his own contention that Bolshevism was Jewish, see J.F.C. Fuller, *The First of the League Wars: Its Lessons and Omens* (London: Eyre & Spottiswoode, 1936), p. 142.
108 *The Fascist*, no. 77, October 1935; and TNA HO 144/20145/281.

109 Special Branch report, 5 March 1935 in TNA HO 144/20144.
110 *The Fascist*, no. 60, May 1934. Wilson later authored *What is the Purpose of Freemasonry?* (Winchester: Privately printed, 1947).
111 *British Fascism*, May 1934.
112 *The Fascist*, no. 61, June 1934.
113 *British Fascism*, no. 4, new series, June 1934.
114 Special Branch report, 18 July 1934 in TNA HO 144/20142.
115 For the protracted winding up of its financial affairs, see TNA TS 17/284.
116 TNA GFM 34/1282; TNA GFM 33/793 serial no. 441391–3; and James J. Barnes and Patience P. Barnes, *Nazis in Pre-War London, 1930–1939: The Fate and Role of German Party Members and British Sympathisers* (Brighton: Sussex Academic Press, 2005), p. 25.
117 *The Fascist*, no. 74, July 1935.
118 *The Fascist*, no. 16, September 1930.
119 *The Fascist*, no. 17, October 1930.
120 *The Fascist*, no. 49, June 1933.
121 *The Fascist*, no. 44, January 1933; *The Fascist*, no. 58, March 1934; *The Fascist*, no. 59, April 1934; and *The Fascist*, no. 60, May 1934.
122 *The Fascist*, no. 65, October 1934. Leese exempted Don Mario Colonna, Duke of Rignano, a 'Foreign Associate' of the IFL who died in an aeroplane accident on 9 July 1938. 'He had become race-wise and was an active anti-Jewish worker in Italy, the Aryan cause being referred to by him generally as "the solar tradition",' Leese recorded in *The Fascist*, no. 111, August 1938.
123 John Baker White, *The Big Lie* (London: Evans, 1955), pp. 28–29. Baker had himself been a senior BF figure.
124 *The Fascist*, no. 24, May 1931.
125 *The Fascist*, no. 25, June 1931. MI5 made 'discreet inquiries' into the proceedings, see S7, minute, 5 November 1931 in TNA KV 2/952.
126 Barnes and Barnes, *Nazis in Pre-War London, 1930–1939*, p. 7.
127 'The Imperial Fascist League' in TNA HO 45/24967/105.
128 Gerhard L. Weinberg, *Hitler's Foreign Policy, 1933–1939* (New York: Enigma Books, 2010), pp. 28–30 notes Rosenberg's 1933 visit was a fiasco, greatly reducing his chance of playing a leading role in Nazi diplomacy.
129 TNA KV 3/58/151a. Thost had been invited to, though did not attend, an IFL dinner on 29, his place taken by a Commander Glimpf, see *The Fascist*, no. 50, July 1933.
130 *The Times*, 12 November 1935; and *The Times*, 13 November 1935. *The Times*' diplomatic correspondent, aware of Thost's role as a Nazi 'propagandist', recommended his deportation, see Gordon Martel (ed.), *The Times and Appeasement: The Journals of A.L. Kennedy, 1932–1939*, (Cambridge: Royal Historical Society, 2000), pp. 109–110.
131 *Der Stürmer*, no. 2, January 1940.
132 TNA WO 339/15154.
133 E.B. Stamp, MI5 minute, 27 February 1942 in TNA HO 45/25746.
134 *The Fascist*, no. 55, December 1933.
135 Arnd Bauerkämper, *Die 'Radikale Rechte' in Großbritannien: Nationalistische, antisemitische und fascistische Bewegungen vom späten 19. Jahrhundert bis 1945* (Gottingen: Vandenhoek und Ruprecht, 1991), p. 135. E.B. Stamp, MI5 minute, 27 February 1942 in TNA HO 45/25746 observes that Skeels was expelled from the IFL shortly afterwards principally because Leese objected to his joining C.G. Wodehouse-Temple's United Empire Fascist Party (UEFP), subsequently the United British Party (UBP).
136 *The Fascist*, no. 61, June 1934.
137 *The Times*, 6 August 1934; and *The Fascist*, no. 63, August 1934.
138 Special Branch report, 24 August 1934 in TNA FO 371/17730; and *Daily Herald*, 26 September 1934.
139 David Pryce Jones, *Unity Mitford: A Quest* (London: Book Club Associates, 1977), pp. 123–124. Special Branch report, 2 August 1935 in TNA KV 2/882/91a notes Leese had written to Unity Mitford trying to persuade her to sue the *Jewish Chronicle* after it criticised her contribution to *Der Stürmer* in which she branded the Jews as the 'world enemy' – a sentiment that no doubt endeared her to Leese.

140 Hansard, HC Deb., vol. 289, cols 1461–1462 (14 May 1934).
141 *The Fascist*, no. 104, January 1938.
142 *The Fascist*, no. 102, November 1937; *The Fascist*, no. 75, August 1935; *The Fascist*, no. 77, October 1935; and *The Fascist*, no. 101, October 1937. Harold Lockwood Advisory Committee hearing, 29 January 1941 in TNA HO 283/46 notes German members.
143 *The Fascist*, no. 28, September 1931.
144 *The Fascist*, no. 102, November 1937
145 Harold Lockwood, Leese's chief lieutenant had visited Munich during summer 1931 from where he sent back reports as 'special correspondent' for *The Fascist*. Alan Francis Peake, part of the IFL general headquarters staff, was a linguist with a degree from London University previously employed at Vienna University who worked as a 'tutor-translator' in Germany where, he claimed, he had marched with the Brownshirts. Peake visited Hans-Rolf Hoffmann in Munich in 1936 boasting subsequently, noted an MI5 source, 'that he had interviewed Hitler'. Having returned to England, Peake secured employment as technical translator and editor, a job obtained for him by Seton Henry Fox, a fellow IFL member who worked for the Paper Mills Association. In 1942, Peake married Rose Eacott, of Anglo-Spanish descent, who was closely associated with Falangist circles in London. See MI5 report, 16 June 1942 in TNA HO 45/25571. Another member, Major C. Draper, a regular speaker at IFL meetings on subjects like 'the truth about Hitler' had lived in Germany, see *The Fascist*, no. 47, April 1933 and *The Fascist*, no. 49, June 1933.
146 *The Fascist*, no. 75, August 1935.
147 *The Fascist*, no. 77, October 1935.
148 Benjamin Collins Barrett, Advisory Committee hearing, 17 December 1942 in TNA HO 45/23765.
149 *The Fascist*, no. 54, November 1933.
150 'The Imperial Fascist League' in TNA HO 45/25724.
151 Extract from Munich Consular Report for January 1937 in TNA FO 371/20739.
152 *Ibid.*
153 [illegible signature] to C.J. Norton, 16 March 1937 in TNA FO 371/20739.
154 Report of a meeting held by the Imperial Fascist League, 15 April 1937 in TNA HO 262/6. During the course of his homily to Nazi Germany, Beamish attributed Hitler's success to his having 'named the enemy' and noted that it was hoped that Hitler would be able to call an international conference on the 'Jew question' to which he already had his own solution. 'The IFL know of three remedies to rid the world of the Jews', stated Beamish, '(1) kill them; (2) sterilise them (3) segregate them', presumably in order of preference. Responding to questions, Beamish stated that, as a result of the Bolshevik revolution and the destruction of its intelligentsia by 'the Koshers', Russia was in a state of 'decay' inhabited by 'a mass of animal-like people'. With an eerie prescience, Beamish stated that in five years it would be the job of a great leader, 'Hitler for preference' who would be forced 'to march into Russia' and thence 'to place one half of its Russians into the lethal chamber and the other half into the zoo'.
155 Louis Bondy, *Racketeers of Hatred* (London: Newman Wolsey, 1946), p. 133.
156 Martin Finkenberger, '"Die Judenfrage ist der Prüfstein völkischer Gesinnung": Der "Bund Völkischer Europäer" 1933 bis 1936', in Stefanie Schüler-Springorum (ed.), *Jahrbuch für Antisemitismusforschung 26* (Berlin: Metropol Verlag, 2017), pp. 61–89; and Rouven Pons, 'Esoteriker des Klangs. Das Leben des Dresdner Komponisten Roland Bocquet (1878–1945?)', *Neues Archiv für Sächsische Geschichte*, no. 86, 2015, pp. 145–176.
157 *The Fascist*, no. 54, April 1934.
158 Michael Hagemeister, '*The Protocols of the Elders of Zion* in Court: The Bern Trials, 1933–1937', in Esther Webman (ed.), *The Global Impact of 'The Protocols of the Elders of Zion'* (Abingdon: Routledge, 2011), pp. 241–253; and Hanno Plass, '*Der Welt-Dienst*: International Anti-Semitic Propaganda', *The Jewish Quarterly*, vol. 103, no. 4, Fall 2013, pp. 503–522, which highlights that from 1941 onwards *Welt-Dienst* was fully integrated into Alfred Rosenberg's 'Office' and thus an 'official' part of the Nazi propaganda apparatus.
159 *Welt-Dienst*, no. 1, 1 December 1933.
160 *Welt-Dienst*, no. 6, 15 February 1934; *Welt-Dienst*, no. 14, 15 June 1934; and *Welt-Dienst*, vol. 2, no. 10, 15 May 1935, the latter issue proclaiming 'We only wish that we too had a Hitler in this country, who would put the Jews where they belong.'

161 Baker White, *The Big Lie*, p. 32.
162 TNA KV 2/2315/132b.
163 Henry Hamilton Beamish to [no name], 28 September 1937 in ACC/3121/E3/141/1, Board of Deputies of British Jews, London Metropolitan Archives, London, hereafter BDBJ papers.
164 George E.G. Caitlin, 'Fascist Stirrings in Britain', *Current History*, vol. 39, 1934, pp. 542–543. Arnd Bauerkämper, 'The Denigration of British Fascism: Traditional Anti-British Stereotypes and Claims of Superiority in Nazi Germany', in Arnd Bauerkämper and Christiane Eisenberg (eds), *Britain as a Model of Modern Society? German Views* (Augsburg: Wißner-Verlag, 2006), pp. 161–162 notes that the Germany Embassy in London 'eagerly' collected leaflets, pamphlets and other propaganda materials issued by the IFL and The Britons.
165 *The Fascist*, no. 95, April 1937; and Erich Wötzel, *The Imperial Fascist League* (Leipzig: Rohmkopf, 1937). Several regional NSDAP outlets also supported the IFL. *The Fascist*, no. 47, April 1933 recorded *Die Braune Post*, a Düsseldorf-based Nazi weekly, condemned the 'pro-Jewish' policy of the BUF whilst hailing the IFL as 'the vanguard of Fascism in Britain'. Thereafter, stated *The Fascist*, no. 48, May 1933, *Die Braune Post* contained an article on the IFL 'freely quoting from our December number certain words which we wish to be widely known in Germany.' *The Fascist*, no. 101, October 1937 also published a personal telegram of support to Leese from Robert Erben of the Nuremberg Hitlerjugend.
166 Werner Haas, *Europa Will Leben: Die nationalen Erneuerungsbewegungen in Wort und Bild* (Berlin: Batschari Verlag GmbH, 1936), pp. 9 and 120–121; and Heinz Krieger, *England und die Judenfrage in Geschichte und Gegenwart* (Frankfurt am Main: Verlag Moritz Diesterweg, 1938).
167 Wolf Meyer-Christian, *Die englisch–jüdische Allianz: Werden und Wirken der kapitalistischen Weltherrschaft* (Berlin-Leipzig: Nibelungen-Verlag, 1942), pp. 75–76.
168 Peter Aldag, *Das Judentum in England* (Berlin: Nordland Verlag, 1943), p. 437.
169 For details of its activities, see TNA KV 5/7–9.
170 Colin Holmes, *Searching for Lord Haw-Haw: The Political Lives of William Joyce* (Abingdon: Routledge, 2016), p. 149.
171 TNA FO 372/3345; TNA KV 2/2472; and TNA KV 2/2473. Gayre recalls his brief encounter with Krüger, whom he claimed to have rumbled as a 'German intelligence agent', in *Gayre of Gayre and Nigg: An Autobiography* (Edinburgh: Edinburgh Impressions, 1987), pp. 57–59. TNA KV 2/884/7a records Mosley admitting to Special Branch in January 1940 that he too had met Krüger, whose anti-Semitic book he regarded as 'a work of scholarship, and he impressed me as being a serious research worker and not at all the kind of person who would act as an agent.' Mosley later elaborated on his contact with Krüger, which had led to the internment of the former BUF candidate Peter Whinfield in late 1939 due to his alleged contacts with German espionage agents (i.e. Krüger). TNA HO 208/13: 'Yes, Krüger came to see me,' Mosley told his interlocutors.

> He was writing a book and he was introduced to me by the Whinfields [Muriel and her husband Lieutenant-Colonel H.C. Whinfield] as a man who was writing a book on anti-Semitism and had spent years in the National Library looking up his facts, and had certainly produced an amazingly interesting work from a student's point of view. He showed me his work once or twice. Now, I understand it is suggested he was a spy or a military agent. I would eat my hat if that man was a spy. He is [a] little professor whom no Military Intelligence in its senses would ever use, and I do not for one moment believe that. I have only seen the fellow once or twice or at Whinfields but I was told the story how [Peter] Whinfield [their son] had been in Switzerland and saw him and got his mother to write to me for advice.

172 TNA FO 372/1174; TNA FO 372/1051; and 'George Pownall', 4 February 1944 in TNA HO 45/25571.
173 D.A. Gunnell to Reg Cohen, copy included in Reg Cohen to J.M. Rich, 17 December 1931 in ACC/3121/B/04/RI/004, BDBJ papers.
174 *The Fascist*, no. 46, March 1933.
175 The Britons, *A List of Books Published and On Sale by the Britons* (April 1932).
176 *The Fascist*, no. 23, April 1932; and *The Fascist*, no. 46, March 1933.
177 Goodrick-Clarke, *The Occult Roots of Nazism*, pp. 123–128 and 149. Reginald H. Phelps, '"Before Hitler Came": Thule Society and Germanen Orden', *Journal of Modern History*,

vol. 35, no. 3, 1963, p. 247 comments that Fritsch was 'probably the most significant figure of German antisemitism before the Nazis, and the chief instigator of the political and conspiratorial movement from which the Germanen Orden and Thule grew.'
178 *The Fascist*, no. 23, April 1931.
179 *The Fascist*, no. 53, October 1933.
180 Graham Macklin, 'The Two Lives of John Hooper Harvey', *Patterns of Prejudice*, vol. 42, no. 2, 2008, pp. 167–190.
181 *The Fascist*, no. 44, January 1933.
182 *The Fascist*, no. 45, February 1933; *The Fascist*, no. 46, March 1933; *The Fascist*, no. 47, April 1933; *The Fascist*, no. 48, May 1933; *The Fascist*, no. 49, June 1933; *The Fascist*, no. 50, July 1933; *The Fascist*, no. 53, October 1933; *The Fascist*, no. 54, November 1933; and *The Fascist*, no. 55, December 1933.
183 Tony Ballentine, *Orientalism and Race: Aryanism in the British Empire* (London: Palgrave, 2002), pp. 3 and 49.
184 L.A. Waddell to Myra Story, 23 October 1936 and L.A. Waddell to Myra Story, 31 March 1937 in Myra Story papers, Imperial War Museum, London, hereafter Story papers.
185 L.A. Waddell to A.S. Leese, 24 April 1935 [MS Gen 1691/3/80], A.S. Leese to L.A. Waddell, 5 September 1935 [MS Gen 1691/3/78], A.S. Leese to L. A. Waddell, 14 April 1937 [MS Gen 1691/3/79] and 'Fact versus fiction on the Aryan race' incomplete typescript enclosed with previous letter [MS Gen 1691/3/79a] in Laurence Augustine Waddell papers, Special Collections, Glasgow University. Christine Preston, *The Rise of Man in the Gardens of Sumeria: A Biography of L.A. Waddell* (Brighton: Sussex Academic, 2009) does not touch upon his political support for the IFL.
186 *The Fascist*, no. 78, November 1935.
187 *The Fascist*, no. 114, November 1938. *The Fascist*, no. 49, 1933 also pays testimony to the influence of Waddell's work, which constituted a 'vast revolution in historical knowledge'.
188 John Hooper Harvey, *The Heritage of Britain* (London: Right Review, 1940). Harvey continued lauding Waddell's work, see *The Times*, 5 December 1966.
189 Arnold Leese to Anthony Gittens, 1 June 1954, Leese papers.
190 *The Fascist*, no. 98, July 1937. This desire to reconceive the past as an imagined Aryan idyll made such thinkers analogous to 'Eden's Folk' (Webb, *The Occult Establishment*, p. 135): 'They would return to a Garden of Eden.'
191 *The Fascist*, no. 49, June 1933.
192 John Hooper Harvey to A. Frederickson, 3 January 1936, Story papers.
193 *Gothic Ripples*, no. 44, September 2001.
194 *Identity*, no. 42, March 2004. The longevity of Waddell's appeal is attested to by the recent republication of his work by former BNP ideologue Arthur Kemp, see Ostara Publications, http://ostarapublications.com/aryan-origin-alphabet-disclosing-sumero-phoenician-parentage-letters-ancient-modern/ (accessed 28 November 2015). Both Waddell and Günther's books also proved popular with US groups like the National States Rights Party (NSRP), closely associated with the BNP and the NF, see *The Thunderbolt*, no. 208, August 1976.
195 John Hooper Harvey to Delly, 17 March 1933, Story papers.
196 For an extended discussion, see Geoffrey G. Field, 'Nordic Racism', *Journal of the History of Ideas*, vol. 38, no. 3, 1977, pp. 523–540.
197 *The Fascist*, no. 27, August 1931; *The Fascist*, no. 42, November 1932; *The Fascist*, no. 43, December 1932; and *The Fascist*, no. 53, October 1933.
198 Gerwin Strobl, *The Germanic Isle: Nazi Perceptions of Britain* (Cambridge: Cambridge University Press, 2000), p. 53.
199 *The Fascist*, no. 101, October 1937; and *The Fascist*, no. 104, January 1938.
200 Hans F.K. Günther, *The Racial Elements of European History* (London: Methuen, 1927). See also Christopher M. Hutton, *Race and the Third Reich* (Cambridge: Polity, 2005).
201 *The Fascist*, no. 53, October 1933.
202 *The Fascist*, no. 76, September 1935. In *Racial Elements*, p. 239, Günther argued that the industrial age had brought about the decline of racial nobility, deskilling artisans and craftsmen, who mingled and crossbred with the racial inferiors to the detriment of Nordic blood. The industrial age 'opened the way for men of even decidedly inferior hereditary capacity to thrive', argued Günther, finding a use for men, 'to whom the proud individuality of the Nordic was foreign, for men to

whom mass-life, life as one of a herd, was not spiritually repugnant, or was even congenial'. These arguments were commonplace within British 'third positionist' groups during the 1980s.

203 *The Fascist*, no. 61, June 1934. The books Lehmann published, personally inscribed to the Führer by their publisher, formed the 'core collection' of Hitler's personal library states Timothy W. Ryback, *Hitler's Personal Library* (London: Vintage, 2010), pp. 109–113.
204 Harvey envisaged a new English translation. Methuen & Co. of London had previously published an English language edition of the book in 1927 translated by the anthropologist G.C. [Gerald Camden] Wheeler, who drew upon the second German edition of the work.
205 Hans F.K. Günther to John Hooper Harvey, 26 October 1933, Story papers.
206 *The Fascist*, no. 44, January 1933. The Nordics also elicited interest from the Nazi Institute for Border and Foreign Studies, who wrote to Harvey in May 1937 requesting details of its programme. In return for a copy of *The Fascist* forwarded by Harvey, he was received a copy of the first in a series of books on eugenics by the Reich Commissioner for National Health Care.
207 'Case Summary', 10 March 1943 in TNA HO 45/25571/84.
208 TNA KV 3/54/85b. The file records that in July 1937 the British Consul-General informed British intelligence that Hoffmann was also acting as Mosley's 'unofficial representative' in Munich. MI5 also observed his closeness to Admiral Sir Barry Domvile's pro-Nazi organisation The Link noting their suspicion that whether Domvile knew it or not the group 'was largely run from Germany, and by Hoffman[n].'
209 For personal details, see *Sunderland Echo and Shipping Gazette*, 2 March 1938. See *The Fascist*, no. 46, March 1933; *The Fascist*, no. 50, July 1933; and *The Fascist*, no. 56, January 1934.
210 Hans-Rolf Hoffmann to John Hooper Harvey, 10 May 1933, Story papers.
211 *The Fascist*, no. 55, December 1933; and *The Fascist*, no. 56, January 1934.
212 TNA HO 45/24967/105.
213 A.S. Leese to H.R. Hoffmann, 13 March 1939 in TNA KV 2/1365.
214 *The Fascist*, no. 57, February 1934.
215 *The Fascist*, no. 58, March 1934.
216 *The Fascist*, no. 60, May 1934.
217 Extract from Munich Consular Report for January 1937 in TNA FO 371/20739.
218 *The Fascist*, no. 64, September 1934; and *The Swastika Symbol: What it Means* (IFL leaflet).
219 For more on Mills, see A. Asbjørn Jøn, ' "Skeggøld, Skálmöld, Vindöld, Vergöld": Alexander Rud Mills and the Ásatrú Faith in the New Age', *Australian Religion Studies Review*, vol. 12, no. 1, 1999, pp. 77–83.
220 David Bird, *Nazi Dreamtime: Australian Enthusiasts for Hitler's Germany* (London: Anthem Press, 2014), p. 116.
221 Barbara Winter, *The Australia-First Movement and the Publicist, 1936–1942* (Brisbane: GHB, 2005), pp. 40–41 notes Lockwood was secretary of the 'Anglocyn' group. It seems certain it was the same organisation.
222 *The Fascist*, no. 46, March 1933; and *The Fascist*, no. 49, June 1933. *The Fascist*, no. 123, August 1939 subsequently published a favourable review of Mill's *The Odinist Religion: Overcoming Jewish Christianity*.
223 Fascist activities report, no. 12, 1 June 1940 in D1915/SA19070, National Archives of Australia, Adelaide, Australia. Mills was not alone. Andrew Moore, *The Right Road: A History of Right-Wing Politics in Australia* (Melbourne: Oxford University Press, 1995), p. 48 states that 'a few individuals' established 'small groups' of the IFL and BUF in Australia. *The Fascist*, no. 112, September 1938 also recommended the Sydney-based Australian Unity League 'whose Director [E.J. Jones] has a sound knowledge of the Jew Menace.'
224 *The Fascist*, no. 73, June 1935.
225 Winter, *The Australia-First Movement and the Publicist, 1936–1942*, pp. 40 and 88.
226 Bruce Muirden, *The Puzzled Patriots: The Story of the Australia First Movement* (Carlton, VIC: Melbourne University Press, 1968), p. 76 notes Mills was under surveillance 'because of his earlier interest in Germany and his sympathy with English Fascists.' This was the principal reason for his subsequent internment rather than his involvement with the AFM, which was comparatively slight.
227 Arnold Leese to Anthony Gittens, 10 December 1953, Leese papers. Mills pamphlet, *The Call of Our Ancient Nordic Religion* (1957), was subsequently published by the Northern League,

a pan-Aryan cultural group who disseminated it from their Coventry address, the home of Colin Jordan. Jordan remained enamoured of Mills writings on 'our ancient religion' publishing excerpts in *The National Socialist*, no. 10, summer 1966.
228 *The Fascist*, no. 41, October 1932.
229 *The Fascist*, no. 80, January 1936. The resignations to which Leese referred may have included J.F. Rushbrook, founder of Champions of Christ and Crown, which morphed into the Militant Christian Patriots.
230 Arnold Leese to A.N. Field, 26 September 1945 in 73.148.081, Field papers. Leese subsequently expanded upon his religious views, which were also animated by his feelings towards animals, in *Out of Step*, p. 45:

> I always regarded Christianity as a religion alien to white men's instincts, because it takes no note of man's best friends [animals] who share his hearth. It is in the East where dogs are pariahs. I think it is a pity that Christianity has not been adjusted to the spiritual needs of Nordic men, who do not need to be told not to murder and steal; a white man's religion would begin on a higher plane and teach him to be straight-forward, to be kind to animals, to be courageous, loyal and chivalrous.

231 Arnold Leese to Adrien Arcand, 4 January 1949, Arcand papers.
232 Leese published Cooper's contributions in three compendiums, *The Hidden Hand Revealed ... in Black and White* (1934), *More Public Mischief: Our Cartoons 1936–1937* (1938) and *Our Seditious Cartoon Book* (1948).
233 Arnold Leese, *The Legalised Cruelty of Shechita: The Jewish Method of Cattle-Slaughter* (Guildford: The author, 1940). The pamphlet continued to find a readership on the extreme right, *League Review*, no. 22, October 1978.
234 Colin Jordan, 'Notes on Arnold Leese', undated MSS, Leese papers.
235 *The Sunday Times*, 13 April 1947.
236 Colin Holmes, 'The Ritual Murder Accusation in Britain', *Ethnic and Racial Studies*, vol. 4, no. 3, July 1981, pp. 263–288.
237 James Dell to Major Rich, 19 May 1934, The Britons archive.
238 Leese also utilised the services of H.F. Lucas, who printed material for an array of extreme right-wing groups including The Britons and the BUF. He also printed an English edition of *Mit Hitler in die Macht. Persönliche Erlebnisse mit meinem Führer – With Hitler on the Road to Power* (1934) by Nazi publicity agent Otto Dietrich, which was sold in *The Fascist*.
239 *British Aryan Defence Fund: Second Appeal* (IFL leaflet 1936).
240 Special Branch report, 9 September 1936 in TNA HO 144/21379/85.
241 Special Branch report, 14 August 1936 in TNA HO 45/24967. Martin Pugh, *'Hurrah for the Blackshirts': Fascism and Fascists in Britain Between the Wars* (London: Pimlico, 2006), p. 227 notes that Leese's prosecution left Joyce:

> exulting in the thought that the movement had now entered a new phase of government persecution; the more fascists were arrested the more public sympathy they would win. According to Joyce, the fact that the Jews had manoeuvered the government into this tactic 'showed clearly that Britain is today under a hidden dictatorship far harsher than that in Germany and Italy'.

242 Sir Alfred Denning, *Freedom Under the Law* (London: Stevens & Sons, 1949), pp. 42–43.
243 Special Branch report, 9 December 1936 in TNA HO 144/21379/236.
244 Peter Catterall (ed.), 'Witness Seminar: The Battle of Cable Street Revisited', *Contemporary Record*, vol. 8, no. 1, summer 1994, p. 119.
245 H.W. Wicks, *The Prisoner Speaks* (London: Jarrolds, 1938), pp. 196–206; J.R. Spencer, 'Criminal Libel: The Snuffing of Mr Wicks', *Cambridge Law Journal*, vol. 38, 1979, pp. 60–78; Richard Griffiths, 'Anti-Semitic Obsessions: The Case of H.W. Wicks', *Patterns of Prejudice*, vol. 48, no. 1, 2014, pp. 94–113; and also TNA CRIM 1/812.
246 TNA KV 2/418–422 and TNA CRIM 1/1767.
247 Arnold Leese to Major Theodore Rich, 5 September [incomplete date], Leese papers and Arnold Leese to Major Theodore Rich, 25 January 1952, Leese papers.
248 H.W. Wicks to H.R. Hoffmann, 22 June 1939 in TNA CRIM 1/1767.
249 H.W. Wicks to H.R. Hoffmann, 2 September 1939 in TNA KV 2/421.

250 Leese, *Out of Step*, p. 55. Leese claimed that this stated:
> In order to destroy the prestige of heroism for political crime, we shall send it for trial in the category of thieving, murder, and every abominable and filthy crime. Public opinion will then confuse in its conception this category of crime with the disgrace attaching to every other and will brand it with the same contempt.

251 A.S. Leese to Major [Theodore] Rich, 11 February 1937, photocopy in author's possession.
252 Arnold Leese to George Armstrong, 9 July 1946 in Box 150, folder 27, George W. Armstrong papers, AUT Arlington Special Collections, Arlington, Texas, hereafter Armstrong papers.
253 TNA DPP 2/443.
254 Arnold Leese, *My Irrelevant Defence being Meditations Inside Gaol and Out on Jewish Ritual Murder* (London: IFL, 1938). Leese gleaned his knowledge of the Chorlton case from 'information' provided to him from R. Prys-Thomas, John Morice [who had addressed the IFL on 'Political Murders' on 28 February 1934] and Daniel M.S. Nicol, see R. Prys-Thomas to Arnold Leese, 15 September 1936, Leese papers and Daniel M.S. Nicol to Arnold Leese, 20 September 1936, Leese papers.
255 Arnold Leese to Anthony Gittens, 8 December 1953, Leese papers.
256 John Morell, 'Arnold Leese and the Imperial Fascist League: The Impact of Racial Fascism', in Kenneth Lunn and Richard Thurlow (eds), *British Fascism: Essays on the Radical Right in Inter-War Britain* (London: Croon Helm, 1980), p. 62.
257 TNA CRIM 1/2361. Deemed 'feeble minded', Lenchitsky had a mental age of nine though was certified as 'sane' and thus fit to plead and stand trial. Following his conviction, he was detained under Section 8 of the Mental Deficiency Act, 1913.
258 Arnold Leese to Major Theodore Rich, 13 October 1953; Arnold Leese to Major Theodore Rich, 15 October 1953; and Arnold Leese to Major Theodore Rich, 11 December 1953, Leese papers. There was, of course, no evidence of ritual murder. Leese continued to believe otherwise, writing, 'I think Ritual Murder was vaguely in this chap's mind but he probably never began it … except where did the blood come from', see Arnold Leese to Anthony Gittens, 3 December 1953, Leese papers.
259 See 'The Fallen 1905 to 1958', *The Fallen List*, http://thefallenlist.blogspot.com/2005/11/fallen-1905-to-1958.html (accessed 21 December 2011).
260 Louis Golding, *The Jewish Problem* (London: Penguin, 1938), p. 152.
261 TNA DPP 2/530.
262 Leese, *My Irrelevant Defence*, pp. 15 and 55.
263 David Biale, *Blood and Belief: The Circulation of a Symbol* (Berkeley, CA: University of California Press, 2007).
264 *The Fascist*, no. 3, May 1929.
265 Arnold Leese to Major Theodore Rich, 11 February [incomplete date but 1930s], Leese papers.
266 *Gothic Ripples*, no. 65, 21 June 1950.
267 *Gothic Ripples*, no. 70, 20 November 1950.
268 Arnold Leese to Major Theodore Rich, 24 October 1953 and Arnold Leese to Major Theodore Rich, 13 May 1954, Leese papers.
269 MI5, source report, 3 January 1945 in TNA KV 2/2315.
270 Arnold Leese, *Race and Politics* (London: IFL, 1934).
271 *The Fascist*, no. 109, June 1938.
272 *The Fascist*, no. 49, June 1933.
273 *The Fascist*, no. 22, March 1931.
274 *The Fascist*, vol. 1, no. 13, May 1930.
275 *The Fascist*, no. 69, February 1935.
276 Ian Kershaw, *Hitler: Nemesis, 1936–1945* (London: Allen Lane, 2000), pp. 320–325.
277 *The Fascist*, no. 69, February 1935.
278 *The Fascist*, no. 86, July 1936.
279 *Jewish Chronicle*, 20 March 1934.
280 *Christmas Greetings and Best Wishes for a Happy New Year from Arnold Leese* in 73.148.081, Field papers.
281 Special Branch report, 9 March 1936 in TNA HO 45/24967.
282 Austin Hudson MP to the Home Secretary, 12 June 1934 in TNA HO 45/24967.

283 IFL, *A Message to Tradesmen* (IFL leaflet) and *300,000 Jews! What a Lie* (IFL leaflet).
284 Special Branch report, 9 May 1935 in TNA HO 144/20144/46.
285 LAC report for the period 26–29 July 1937 in 1658/3/1B/4, Jewish Defence Committee papers, Wiener Library London, hereafter JDC papers.
286 Special Branch report, 9 March 1936 in TNA HO 45/24967.
287 This seems unlikely, though Ridout did suggest to IFL members at a meeting in 1936 that they use 'P.J.' as a greeting, see Special Branch report, 9 December 1936 in TNA HO 144/21379/237.
288 Thurlow, *Fascism in Britain*, p. 50.
289 TNA HO 144/20243; and TNA HO 144/21380/160.
290 Special Branch report, 31 July 1937 in TNA KV 2/2476; and Special Branch report, 3 August 1937 in TNA HO 144/21380/140.
291 *Jewish Chronicle*, 13 August 1937.
292 New Scotland Yard report, October 1937 in TNA HO 144/21380/183.
293 TNA HO 144/20243/188. George Pownall had so deeply imbibed his father's views, observed MI5, that it was doubted he viewed 'social or political questions with the eyes of a normal British subject'. In July 1937, Professor J. Kraugan wrote to Dr Thost asking him to send Pownall a free copy of *Völkischer Beobatcher* on the grounds that his father had performed a 'great' service 'for the anti-Jewish movement' and that his son and daughter, 'were anxious to carry on his work as much as they could'. Pownall resigned from the IFL and joined the BUF on 30 May 1939 following 'certain differences of opinion'. Pownall was interned from 1940 until 2 November 1943. See 'George Pownall', 4 February 1944 in TNA HO 45/25571. Robert Row, a leading Mosleyite, tried to win Pownall over to the Union Movement (UM) after the war. He was unsuccessful. Pownall 'disagrees strongly with the Movement, mainly on the grounds that we are not devoting enough attention to the Jewish Menace, and appears to want to return to the "Axis Standpoint",' Row wrote to a colleague. 'I am afraid that Arnold Leese seems to have got some influence over him; rather a pity I think. So I am afraid we must cross him out', see Robert Row to Robert Saunders, 8 January 1950, C13 Saunders Papers, Sheffield University. Pownall was indeed reconciled with Leese, see Arnold Leese to Tony [Gittens], 28 December 1954, Leese papers.
294 *The Fascist*, no. 101, October 1937.
295 *The Times*, 8 October 1937.
296 *The Fascist*, no. 103, December 1937.
297 *The Fascist*, no. 108, May 1938.
298 Special Branch report, 1 September 1938 in TNA HO 144/21381/69.
299 TNA HO 144/21381/103; and Henry Solomons to Sidney Salomon, 31 August 1939 in 1658/3/1b/6, folder 4, JDC papers. Leese, *Out of Step*, p. 60 notes that by this time the IFL was able to employ two activists 'on a pittance' during this period. Ridout was almost certainly one of them.
300 Arnold Leese to Adolf Hitler, 'September 1938' in TNA KV 2/1367.
301 IFL, *Leese for Peace* (London: IFL leaflet, 1939).
302 The Imperial Fascist League, MI5 report, 8 March 1942 in TNA HO 45/24967.
303 Special Branch report, 19 July 1940 in TNA HO 45/23765.
304 Hansard, HC Deb., vol. 350, col. 1979W (31 July 1939).
305 Leese, *Out of Step*, p. 60.
306 Ronald W. Jones, 'I was a Blackshirt Menace', *The Spectator*, 5 August 1983, p. 11.
307 Arnold Leese, to members and subscribers, 14 September 1939.
308 Harold Lockwood Advisory Committee hearing, 29 January 1941 in TNA HO 283/46. See also E.W.G. Holderness to Mary Adams, 29 February 1940 in TNA HO 262/6.
309 *The Fascist*, no. 111, August 1938. *Weekly Angles*' meagre circulation was further amplified through replication. Richard Rollins, *I Find Treason: The Story of an American Anti-Nazi Agent* (New York: William Morrow, 1941), p. 154 notes *Blackshirt*, organ of the Fascist League of North America, edited by the Italian-American fascist Paolo 'Paul' Castorina, reproduced content 'word for word' from *Weekly Angles*.
310 TNA KV 2/1365/120b.
311 Richard Griffiths, *What Did You Do During the War? The Last Throes of the British Pro-Nazi Right, 1940–45* (Abingdon: Routledge, 2017), p. 236.
312 TNA HO 144/21381/84.

313 Benjamin Collins Barrett, Advisory Committee hearing, 8 January 1941 in TNA HO 45/23765.
314 *The Fascist*, no. 30, November 1931; *The Fascist*, no. 57, February 1934; and *The Fascist*, no. 78, November 1935. Lindholm reconfigured his group in 1938 as the Svensk Socialistisk Samling (SSS) in an effort to develop a more 'Swedish' form of national socialism. Hans Fredrik Dahl, *Quisling: A Study in Treachery* (Cambridge: Cambridge University Press, 1999), p. 138 notes, however, that Lindholm, subsequently moved closer to Mosley whom he and the Danish fascist Frits Clausen invited to a national convention of Nordic parties in Kolding on 17–18 June 1939. Mosley was unable to attend. Iceland was also singled out for attention as was Finland, albeit to a lesser extent. 'Iceland is almost purely Nordic in population', stated *The Fascist*, no. 16, September 1930, 'And Jews find it too cold. Lucky Iceland.' Within a few years, Leese had established 'useful contact' with a group of Icelandic fascists who, having no Jews to physically fight, had to content themselves with the metaphysical fight against the 'Jewish ideas' of Liberalism and Socialism, see *The Fascist*, no. 52, September 1933.
315 Sentenced to death after the war, his sentence was commuted to life imprisonment. He died in jail in 1953.
316 The Imperial Fascist League, MI5 report, 8 March 1942 in TNA HO 45/24967; and *The Fascist*, no, 98, July 1937. Leese championed a faction within the NSNAP led by Major Cornelis Jacobus Aart Kruyt. 'Being genuine, the latter's movement is naturally poor and struggling', he claimed.
317 *The Fascist*, no. 63, August 1934.
318 *Ibid*.
319 *The Fascist*, no. 120, May 1939.
320 Special Branch report, 19 June 1939 in TNA HO 144/21382.
321 'William Bird', MI5 report in TNA HO 45/25568. Bird joined the IFL in 1933 and The Link, visiting Germany in 1935, 1936 and 1937. The first trip was under the auspices of the IFL. In 1938 and 1939, Bird played host to a visiting Hitler Youth activist. Fiercely anti-Semitic and pro-Nazi, Bird also sponsored an IFL meeting 'which was only open to privileged members' and was attended by Captain Ramsay MP, leader of the Right Club. Bird was detained under DR 18B on 4 June 1940 and held until 11 April 1941.
322 Extract, 9 October 1944 in TNA KV 2/1365.
323 'The Imperial Fascist League' in 1658/10/29, JDC papers. Eusom was subsequently interned.
324 'Extract' MC5 Daily Report, Private Terminal Mail, 15 January 1940 in TNA HO 262/6.
325 'John Coast' in 1658/9/1/3/4 and 'John Coast' in 1658/10/29, JDC papers; Sidney Salomon to Inspector Keeble, 26 February 1940 in 1658/10/29, JDC papers. During the 1930s, Coast was employed as a secretary to the pro-Nazi racial anthropologist George Lane Fox Pitt-Rivers, who hired him on the recommendation of fellow fascist Henry Williamson, author of *Tarka the Otter* (1927). Coast had worked for Williamson on his Norfolk Farm but their relationship was troubled. Similarly, Coast 'did a host of mischief' whilst working for Pitt-Rivers – not least of which was carrying on a romantic liaison with his mistress – and their association was also brief. Pitt-Rivers regarded Coast as a 'Nazi fanatic' and opined his association with a 'mob' that adhered to 'the more vehement and less responsible type of anti-Semitism', see Bradley W. Hart, *George Pitt-Rivers and the Nazis* (London: Bloomsbury, 2015), p. 141. Special Branch report, 4 October 1939 in TNA HO 144/22454 notes Coast's involvement in the Nordic League. Coast also joined the Right Club – he had been to school with one of Captain Ramsay's sons – and was a friend of Anna Wolkoff, supplying her with anti-Semitic 'stickybacks', see Paul Willett's *Rendezvous at the Russia Tea Rooms* (London: Constable, 2015), pp. 152–153. Coast disengaged from extremist politics after the war, however. 'I hear Coast has ratted; was prisoner-of-war in Burma & perhaps that soured him; he chummed up with some Jew & that's that', sneered Leese to Henry Hamilton Beamish, 23 May 1946, Arcand papers. Leese's contempt for Coast did not do justice to the remarkable post war transformation of his pre-war acolyte, on which, see Griffiths, *What Did You Do During the War?*, pp. 264–273. Captured by the Japanese during the fall of Singapore in 1942 – a horrific ordeal he recalled in *The Railroad of Death* (1946) – Coast subsequently worked as a diplomat in the Far East, becoming a supporter of the Indonesian independence movement, before returning to London. Re-emerging as a cultural impresario, Coast managed artistes like Mario Lanza, Luciano Pavarotti, José Carreras, Jon Vickers and Montserrat Caballé, whilst becoming 'the first man to present Bob Dylan in London and take Ravi Shankar to the West'. He also made films on Balinese culture for the

BBC with David Attenborough, see 'Biography of John Coast (1916–1989)', www.johncoast.org/biography.htm (accessed 24 August 2015). Though only 'briefly and very unsuccessfully' employed by Henry Williamson in 1937, Coast would later help finance the film adaptation of *Tarka the Otter*, see *The Henry Williamson Society*, www.henrywilliamson.co.uk/component/content/article/57-uncategorised/150-tara-the-otter-the-film-and-the-opera (accessed 24 August 2015).

326 Like Coast, Rushbrook also disengaged from extreme right politics after the war. He attended Oriel College, Cambridge, and though suggested by Beamish to take over The Britons from James Dell, dropped out of politics, see 'National Front' in VNST II 1/24, Lord Robert Vansittart papers, Churchill College, Cambridge, hereafter Vansittart papers.
327 The Imperial Fascist League, MI5 report, 8 March 1942 in TNA HO 45/24967.
328 *Ibid*.
329 *Weekly Angles*, no. 116, 20 April 1940.
330 The Imperial Fascist League, MI5 report, 8 March 1942 in TNA HO 45/24967.
331 Elizabeth Berger to Richard Findlay, 30 March 1940 in TNA KV 2/1365 states that if Leese adopted this attitude as official policy 'I suppose I should have to resign and I do want to help them as much as I can in the good work they are doing in other directions.'
332 The Imperial Fascist League, MI5 report, 8 March 1942 in TNA HO 45/24967. In *The Fascist*, no. 16, September 1930, titled 'Our Norwegian Kinsmen', Leese had stated '… it is impossible to regard the Norwegian as alien to us; they are of us, and should be with us'. Leese's prioritising of 'Aryan' Scandinavia over and above Hitler's Germany may have stemmed from personal experience. As Leese recorded in *Out of Step*, p. 64, he and his wife had holidayed several times in Norway and Iceland during the inter-war years but, unlike many IFL members, he had 'never set foot in Germany'.
333 John Hooper Harvey to Arnold Leese, 19 April 1940 in TNA HO 45/25571.
334 Arnold Leese to [Dr] Maude S. de Lande, 14 June 1940 in TNA HO 45/25724. DeLand, was a retired psychiatrist at the Topeka State Hospital, Kansas, and was involved with Kurt Mertig's activities.
335 'Arnold Spencer Leese', 15 March 1944 in TNA HO 45/25571.
336 Arnold Leese to H.H. Beamish, 18 June 1944 in 73.148.040, Field papers. It is unclear if Leese's figures include Aldo Balbuce, an Italian IFL activist who escaped from internment, see *Daily Express*, 17 June 1940.
337 TNA HO 45/25724; and TNA KV 2/1365/8a.
338 Hansard, HC Deb., vol. 361, cols 288–292 (23 May 1940); and 'Home Office file no. 840913 for Arnold Spencer Leese' in TNA KV 2/1365/4a. See also *The Observer*, 26 May 1940.
339 *Manchester Guardian*, 3 June 1940; and *Manchester Guardian*, 10 June 1940. Frank Wheatley was remanded under the Emergency Powers (Defence) Act for having in his possession documents containing information that might be directly or indirectly useful to the enemy, though the charges were subsequently dropped. Wheatley was the secretary of the Unity Band, which 'has much in common with the Nordic League' whose meetings he often attended, see note in 1658/9/3/2/1, JDC papers.
340 TNA HO 45/25724; and TNA KV 2/1365/141a.
341 John Redfern, MI5 minute, 9 April 1941 in TNA KV 2/1365. 'The Imperial Fascist League', in TNA HO 45/25724 notes Boldt and another activist, Eugene J. Smith, a member of William Dudley Pelley's Silver Shirt Legion of America, Inc. – both of whom were regarded as 'agents' of the Fichte-Bund – also corresponded with Leese during 1940, sending him copies of the German-American Bund newspaper *Deutscher Weckruf und Beobachter*. Leese had advertised Fichte-Bund publications in *The Fascist*, no. 76, September 1935 and *The Fascist*, no. 106, March 1938. Leese rekindled his contact with Smith after the war, see TNA KV 3/261/15a. Laura Rosenzweig, *Hollywood's Spies: The Undercover Surveillance of Nazis in Los Angeles* (New York University Press: New York, 2017), p. 83 notes Leese's pre-war correspondence with Ingram Hughes, leader of the American Nationalist Party, an organisation closely tied to the Friends of New Germany which later became the German-American Bund.
342 *The Fascist*, no. 107, April 1938.
343 Mrs Winifred Leese to His Majesty the King, 9 January 1941 in TNA HO 45/25724. See also Windsor Castle, Private Secretary to Mrs Leese, 13 January 1941; and Windsor Castle, Private Secretary to Mrs Leese, 5 March 1941, Leese papers.

344 Arnold Leese to Anthony Gittens, 30 October [n.d.], Leese papers.
345 Hansard, HC Deb., vol. 371, cols 171–172 (23 April 1941).
346 Hansard, HC Deb., vol. 396, col. 61W (18 January 1944); and Hansard, HC Deb., vol. 399, col. 2107W (11 May 1944).
347 TNA HO 45/25571.
348 John Beckett to Col. E. Carroll, 27 April 1944 in TNA HO 283/26.
349 *Gothic Ripples*, 10 November 1945. Leese's obdurate stance inspired later generations of activists, notably Alex Davies, founder of National Action, the first British extreme right group to be banned as a 'terrorist' organisation in December 2016, see 'RA Britannia: Under ZOG Interrogation – RA 010818', *Radio Aryan*, 8 January 2018, www.radioaryan.com/2018/01/ra-britannia-under-zog-interrogation-ra.html (accessed 6 March 2018).
350 S.R. Source report, 16 October 1943 in TNA KV 3/282/1923.
351 *Jewish Chronicle*, 28 December 1945.
352 Arnold Leese to Major Theodore Rich, 5 September [incomplete date], Leese papers.
353 *Gothic Ripples*, no. 1, 22 June 1945.
354 Monthly report on Fascist Activities – October 1946 in TNA KV 2/1366/437c.
355 TNA KV 3/264/12. Not that the lack of interest deterred Leese from sending anti-Semitic literature to Australia, which by 1953 was arriving in 'increasing amounts', see Mrs T. Walter to S. Salomon, 23 January 1953 in 1658/10/44, JDC papers. K.D. Gott, *Voices of Hate: A Study of the Australian League of Rights and its Director Eric D. Butler* (Melbourne: Dissent, 1965), pp. 30–31 notes that Melbourne's Heritage Bookshop, run by Eric D. Butler, leader of the Australian League of Rights, distributed Leese's literature.
356 'Witness-Box' in Leese papers; and Arnold Leese, *Rex versus Leese* (London: Carmac Press, 1951), p. 8.
357 'Fascist Activities: April to May 1946', 7 May 1946 in TNA HO 45/25395.
358 Hansard, HC Deb., vol. 431, col. 123W (5 December 1946). See also comments in TNA HO 45/24968.
359 Arnold Leese, *The Jewish War of Survival*, 2nd edn (Guildford: Arnold Leese, 1947), p. v.
360 *Sunday Pictorial*, 10 March 1946.
361 Gladys Fortune, who typed up Leese's handwritten manuscript, was formerly women's district leader of South Paddington BUF and had been engaged to a German *Luftwaffe* officer, who had fought in the Spanish Civil War. In 1939, she had worked as a 'freelance secretary' for the pro-Nazi racial anthropologist George Lane Fox Pitt-Rivers, the extremity of her views even embarrassing him, see Hart, *George Pitt-Rivers and the Nazis*, pp. 141–145. Fortune was detained on 8 October 1940 as a result of her activities, which included regularly attending Nordic League meetings. See 'Gladys Fortune' in TNA HO 45/25568. For foreign editions of the book, see Home Office Monthly Bulletin, March 1947 and Home Office Monthly Bulletin, August 1946, both in TNA KV 3/52.
362 New York-based anti-Semite Conrad K. Grieb published the American edition. During the late 1930s, Grieb had managed the American Review Bookstore, which was owned and operated by Seward Collins, publisher of the *American Review*. Grieb authored *Uncovering the Forces for War* (1947), published by his own 'Examiner Books' imprint.
363 The South African publisher was Ray Kirch Rudman, leader of Die Boernaise, a group which chiefly recruited amongst Germans in and around Pietermaritzburg, Natal. Rudman had been a Greyshirt leader in Natal and from 1938 was active in the Ossewa Brandwag (OB) until his expulsion in 1942, 'probably because of shady financial dealings' recorded MI5 in TNA KV 2/1362/486b. Rudman's expulsion does not seem to have deterred Leese from continuing to supply anti-Semitic information to the OB, see TNA KV 2/355/205a. Rudman's association with Leese came at a cost. Ray K. Rudman to Mrs Coyle, 16 December 1946, Arcand papers, claims the authorities ordered him to cease and desist in his activities as Leese's agent. Fearing re-internment, the visit caused Rudman considerable alarm because he realised the security of their correspondence network – which consisted of five people – had been compromised. Unperturbed, Henry Hamilton Beamish to Ray K. Rudman, 25 December 1946, Arcand papers, instructs Rudman to 'deal with it' and ensure the book was printed. Arnold Leese to Adrien Arcand, 24 May 1950, Arcand papers, calls Rudman 'a blundering muddler, but brim full of enthusiasm' but whose own anti-Semitic effusions gave Leese 'no particular satisfaction'.

364 Arnold Leese to Mr Morey [pseud. Avendis Derounian], 20 March 1946, Avendis Derounian papers, Mardigian Library, National Association for Armenian Studies and Research, Belmont, Massachusetts, hereafter Derounian papers
365 'Extract', 8 August 1945 in TNA KV 6/4/349a. H.T.V. Mills joined the League, see TNA KV 6/4/431c as did Colin Jordan (Chapter 4).
366 Arnold Leese to Mr Morey, 8 December [no year], Derounian papers.
367 G.F. Green to Adrien Arcand, 30 May 1948, Arcand papers.
368 Arnold Leese to [no addressee], 8 December 1948, Derounian papers.
369 Extract, 11 February 1946, TNA KV 6/4/397b.
370 Home Office Monthly Bulletin, January 1947 in TNA KV 3/52.
371 Home Office Monthly Bulletin, August 1947 in TNA KV 3/52. Berger suffered a breakdown two years later. Admiral Sir Barry Domvile noted in his diary, 5 September 1949, DOM 61, Domvile papers, Greenwich Maritime Museum, London: 'Poor Elizabeth Mills [née Berger] has gone potty and stole three kids whom she brought down to see Jean this morning.' Domvile's wife contacted the police after which the children were returned to their parents 'whilst poor Elizabeth went to hospital. Bertie away; he has been very careless'.
372 Midland bank manager to A.S. Leese, 27 October 1949, Leese papers. Arnold Leese to Adrien Arcand, 23 March 1949, Arcand papers notes 'HHB has left me nearer £6000 than the anticipated £1500.' Arnold Leese to Adrien Arcand, 24 May 1950, Arcand papers, highlights that Leese also received £50 from one Otto Kellerman whom he met in London whilst the former was en route to South Africa after being interned in Germany.
373 Leese, *Out of Step*, p. 73.
374 *National Workers Movement: Twenty-Five Points of Policy* (Suffolk: NWM, 1948).
375 A.F.X. Baron to Arnold Leese, 21 May 1948, Britons archive.
376 Arnold Leese to Adrien Arcand, 24 May 1950, Arcand papers.
377 *Gothic Ripples*, no. 73, 20 March 1951. Major R.M. Manson, The Britons representative in Scotland who was involved with the NWM, won a local council seat in 1949, see Morris Beckman, *The 43 Group* (London: Centreprise, 1992), p. 186.
378 Colin Holmes, *Anti-Semitism in British Society, 1876–1939* (London: Edward Arnold, 1979), p. 163.
379 *Gothic Ripples*, no. 7, 30 November 1945. *Jewish Chronicle*, 28 December 1945 noted that Leese regarded renewed pogroms as 'maintaining Polish honour'.
380 Leese, *Jewish War of Survival*, p. 66.
381 *Gothic Ripples*, no. 96, 14 January 1953.
382 *Gothic Ripples*, no. 56, 25 September 1949; and *Gothic Ripples*, no. 121, 2 December 1954.
383 *Gothic Ripples*, no. 109, 10 January 1954.
384 *Gothic Ripples*, no. 22, 15 September 1946.
385 *Gothic Ripples*, no. 14, 11 April 1946.
386 *Gothic Ripples*, no. 108, 12 December 1953.
387 *Gothic Ripples*, no. 6, 11 November 1945.
388 *The People's Post*, vol. 2, no. 12, January 1946.
389 Arnold Leese to the Foreign Office, 17 December 1945; and R.N., Foreign Office minute, 31 December 1945 in TNA FO 371/51006.
390 D. Scott-Fox to Arnold Leese, 12 January 1946 in TNA FO 371/51006 and Captain J.L. Morton to Arnold Leese, 14 February 1946, Leese papers. See also *Gothic Ripples*, no. 15, 10 May 1946.
391 British Secretary, International Military Tribunal, Nuremberg to Arnold Leese, 18 July 1946, Leese papers.
392 Portuguese fascist M. Francisco Dos Santos and Dr Walter Schilling, a German living in Buenos Aires, who had formed a Portuguese support committee for French fascist Maurice Bardèche, recently arrested following publication of *Nuremberg ou la terre promise* (1948), asked Leese to send them a copy of *Jewish War of Survival* for re-direction to Bardèche and requested that Leese print statements of support in *Gothic Ripples*, see M. Francisco Dos Santos to Leese, 31 February 1949, Leese papers. Leese duly highlighted Bardèche's case in *Gothic Ripples*, no. 50, 15 April 1949.
393 *Gothic Ripples*, no. 24, 13 October 1946.
394 See Kingsbury Smith, 'The Execution of Nazi War Criminals', *The Nuremberg Trials: Newspaper Accounts*, 16 October 1946, http://law2.umkc.edu/faculty/projects/ftrials/nuremberg/

NurembergNews10_16_46.html (accessed 13 November 2011). Leese's views on Purim can be found in *My Irrelevant Defence*, p. 7. *Gothic Ripples*, no. 26, 27 October 1946 records Leese's refusal to stock *Failure at Nuremberg* (1946) published by the BPP, 'because the Jewishness of the whole trial is only vaguely hinted at.'

395 *Gothic Ripples*, no. 25, 20 October 1946; and *Gothic Ripples*, no. 88, 12 May 1952.
396 Holmes, *Searching for Lord Haw-Haw*, p. 335.
397 Mosley's appeal against order of internment, 2 July 1940 in TNA HO 283/13.
398 *The People's Post*, vol. 2, no. 11, December 1945.
399 Robert Row to Miss Leonora Westwood, 22 January 1948 in TNA KV 2/1228.
400 'Extract', 19 February 1946 in TNA KV 3/226/1a.
401 A.S. Leese to the Home Secretary, 29 December 1945 in TNA HO 45/22405/543. In *Gothic Ripples*, no. 21, 6 September 1946, Leese stated that: 'Whatever William Joyce did, his motive was to get the war stopped before it destroyed civilisation … which it has now done.'
402 Leese, *Out of Step*, p. 70; and Thurlow, *Fascism in Britain*, p. 139.
403 Holmes, *Searching for Lord Haw-Haw*, pp. 175, 262 and 387.
404 TNA CRIM 1/1763; and Julie Gottlieb, *Feminine Fascism* (London: I.B. Tauris, 2000), p. 286. The Hamburg-based Falken-Verlag published one of her lectures as *What I saw in Germany* (1935), whilst her pamphlet *An English Point of View About National Socialist Germany* (1937) was advertised by the IFL.
405 Margaret Bothamley to Arnold Leese, 21 March 1946, Leese papers.
406 *The Times*, 28 March 1946. Bothamley's close friend Mary Stanford, a schoolteacher obsessed by occultism, surreptitiously destroyed incriminating items left in her flat following Bothamley's departure for Germany in 1939. Introduced to the IFL in 1934, Stanford was known within it as 'Mary Hope'. MI5 regarded her as 'one of the most extreme national socialists known to us'. Today she might have been regarded as a 'fixated threat', since she had first come to the attention of the security services in August 1932 because her infatuation with the Prince of Wales (Edward VIII) meant that she 'dogged his footsteps' at every step until he departed England following his abdication in 1936. Stanford joined the Right Club in February 1940 and, being peripherally involved in the Tyler Kent affair, was interned under 18B in July 1940. Having been released in September Stanford was rearrested in March 1941, suspected of being an accomplice to Nora Briscoe and Gertrude Hiscox, who were both jailed for five years for stealing sensitive documents from the Ministry of Supply. Stanford was released in October 1944 and, having continued to correspond with Bothamley throughout the war, went to live in her London flat. On 9 November 1945 – the anniversary of Hitler's failed Beerhall *putsch* and Kristallnacht, the Nazis' anti-Semitic pogrom – Stanford founded an 'Aryan-British Forum' in which Leese appears to have had some interest though he had 'washed his hands of it' by the following month, see TNA KV 2/832–833. This was probably because of her occultism of which Leese and others disapproved. Stanford attended lectures by the anti-Semitic and pro-Nazi Dutch-Canadian 'spiritualist' Jacobus Johannes van Ryswyk. Regarded as a charlatan and a rogue by the security services, van Ryswyk's 'New (Constitutional) Order' group attracted IFL activists like Seaton Elliot Fox, who briefly served as its propaganda officer as well as H.T.V. Mills and his partner Elizabeth Berger, who became involved after van Ryswyk's group began cooperating with the British Peoples Party, see TNA 2/1523/201a.
407 TNA KV 2/424; and TNA KV 2/425. *The Fascist*, no. 116, January 1939 lists Grant as the Kensington contact point.
408 *Gothic Ripples*, no. 17, 22 June 1945.
409 Home Office Monthly Bulletin, July 1946 in TNA KV 3/52. For Violet Foss, see TNA HO 45/25571/67.
410 *Gothic Ripples*, no. 21, 6 September 1946.
411 Released from prison, Leese established contact with Emilio Gutiérrez Herrero, secretary general of the Unión Cívica Nacionalista, a revolutionary national syndicalist group based in Buenos Aires, exchanging anti-Semitic propaganda with him. The Portuguese fascist Francisco Dos Santos put them in touch, see TNA KV 3/47. Argentinian interest in Leese's ideas was reflected in the posthumous publication of *Gentile Folly: The Rothschilds*, which appeared in Spanish translation as *Los Rothschilds* (Buenos Aires: Editorial Nuevo Orden, 1966). Leese was rather more sanguine about the prospects of rekindling contact with the Brazilian Integralist movement, however, see SR 72 Report, 23 September 1945 in TNA 3/261/1a.

412 Report on Fascist Activities, March–April 1947 in TNA KV 3/50. Leese described the trial in *Gothic Ripples*, no. 32, 31 December 1947. Norman Lucas, *Spycatcher: A Biography of Detective Superintendent George Gordon Smith* (London: W.H. Allen, 1973), pp. 40–46, maintained the façade.
413 J. Curry, *The Security Service, 1908–1945: The Official History* (London: HMSO, 1999), p. 312; Nigel West (ed.), *The Guy Liddell Diaries, Vol. II: 1942–1945* (London: Routledge, 2005), pp. 27, 105, 112, 124, 167 and 219; and Robert Hutton, *Agent Jack: The True Story of MI5's Secret Nazi Hunter* (London: Weidenfeld and Nicolson, 2018).
414 'P.W.', 17 May 1943 in TNA KV 2/3874.
415 The 'Marita network' offered MI5 several windows into Leese's clandestine activities including Hilda Leech who, MI5 officer Guy Liddell recorded in his diary, had been invited to join the 'inner council' of the IFL indicating she enjoyed Leese's confidence. On Leech, see TNA KV 6/119.
416 Extract, 12 June 1945 in TNA KV/1366/256a.
417 MI5 continued to use another of Marita Perigoe's 'agents' – Eileen Gleave, a former BUF officer for its Harrow-Wembley branch – to monitor Leese after his incarceration. 'Notes of a meeting with S.R. [Eric Roberts] on 20 November 1947 on the prospects of the "5th Column" case' in TNA KV 2/3800/115a records that Gleave's 'Gestapo' controllers 'encouraged' her to maintain contact with the Leese-Gittens group 'if this is not completely broken over the P.O.W. case'. The latter reference might also conceivably refer to Gleave's own court case: in July 1947, she too was arrested for harbouring an escaped POW, Joachim Kirmse, with whom she was romantically involved. Kirmse claimed to be a Wehrmacht corporal but, under questioning at the London Cage, MI5's secret interrogation centre in Kensington Palace Gardens, stated that he was actually a former Gestapo agent and SS officer who had adopted the name 'Kirmse' in order to disguise his connection to 'incidents in which he figured prominently'. He also claimed to have taken part in the Nazi's parachute assault on Crete in 1943 and to have been friends with prominent Nazi leaders like Dr Kurt Weissmann, Baldur von Shirach and 'Eichman', who 'was with the Gestapo in the Middle East.' What MI5 made of his claims is remains unrecorded in TNA KV 2/2677/56a.
418 Home Office Monthly Bulletin, March 1947 in TNA KV 3/52. TNA HO 45/24469 notes with satisfaction that Gittens 'is well known to the comparatively respectable fascists and his prosecution may open the eyes of some supporters of the party'.
419 Report on Fascist Activities, March–April 1947 in TNA KV 3/50.
420 *Gothic Ripples*, no. 102, 20 June 1953. For Head, see Beckett, *Fascist in the Family*, p. 313.
421 Lovell became central London organiser for the NWM run by A.F.X. Baron.
422 Home Office Monthly Bulletin, August 1947 in TNA KV 3/52.
423 The Registrar, Royal College of Veterinary Surgeons to Arnold Leese, 5 March 1948, Leese papers.
424 Arnold Leese to the Registrar, Royal College of Veterinary Surgeons, 6 March 1948, Leese papers.
425 W. Brown, editor *The Veterinary Record* to Arnold Leese, 21 May 1948, Leese papers.
426 Admiral Sir Barry Domvile to Adrien Arcand, 10 December 1950, Arcand papers; and Martin Connolly, *Hitler's Munich Man: The Fall of Admiral Sir Barry Domvile* (Barnsley: Pen & Sword, 2017), pp. 116–117.
427 Arnold Leese, *Rex Versus Leese* (London: Carmac Press, 1951).
428 Leese, *Out of Step*, p. 72.
429 Arnold Leese to Adrien Arcand, 18 January 1949, Arcand papers.
430 Report on Fascist Activities, March–April 1947 in TNA KV 3/50.
431 Hansard, HC Deb., vol. 433, col. 216W (20 February 1947); and Sidney Salomon to Vilgot Hammerling, 25 February 1947 in 1658/9/3/3, JDC papers.
432 Home Office Monthly Bulletin, May 1947 in TNA KV 3/52.
433 *Gotesborgs-Tidningen*, 23 March 1947; and *Dagens Nyheter*, 22 July 1947 in 1658/9/3/3, JDC papers.
434 'Captain R.C. Gordon-Canning', 18 April 1947 in TNA KV 2/878/923a; and Graham Macklin, 'A Fascist "Jihad": Captain Robert Gordon-Canning, British Fascist Anti-Semitism and Islam', *Holocaust Studies: A Journal of Culture and History*, vol. 15, nos 1–2, summer/autumn 2009, pp. 78–100.

435 *Gothic Ripples*, no. 82, 17 November 1951. Thereafter, Abdullah Tall of Egypt settled the Arab League account with Leese, see Arnold Leese to Anthony Gittens, 3 July 1954, Leese papers. Their relationship appears to have soured earlier, however. Admiral Sir Barry Domvile recorded in his diary on 27 February 1947, DOM 59, Domvile papers, Greenwich Maritime Museum, London: 'Both Bob [Gordon-Canning] and Jock [Ramsay] were very down on Leese.' His relationship with Ramsay certainly recovered. Ramsay frequently visited Leese at Guildford, calling on Domvile on the way home, see, for instance, diary entries, 5 September 1950 and 28 April 1951, DOM 61, Domvile papers.
436 For the familial link, see A.N. Field to Arnold Leese, 3 May 1952 in 73.148.081, Field papers.
437 *The Fascist*, no. 113, October 1938. See also Martin Robin, *Shades of Right: Nativist and Fascist Politics in Canada, 1920–1940* (Toronto: University of Toronto Press, 1992), pp. 118–120; and Jean-François Nadeau, *The Canadian Führer: The Life of Adrien Arcand* (Toronto: Lorimer, 2010), p. 272. Leese also regarded Ron Gostick's *Canadian Intelligence Review* as 'a good anti-Jewish newspaper', see *Gothic Ripples*, no. 79, 27 August 1951; and *Gothic Ripples*, no. 110, 1 February 1954.
438 Nadeau, *The Canadian Führer*, pp. 310–311.
439 *The Nation*, 26 March 1938. *MacLean's Magazine*, 14 April 1938 notes Arcand's importation of material from Mosley's BUF. Hugues Théorêt, *The Blue Shirts: Adrien Arcand and Fascist Anti-Semitism in Canada* (Ottawa: University of Ottawa Press, 2017) further documents this Anglo-Canadian axis.
440 *Free Britain*, no. 165, February 1956.
441 William H. Murray, *Adam and Cain: Symposium of Old Bible History, Sumerian Empire, Importance of Blood of Race, etc* (Boston, MA: Meador Press, 1951).
442 Neil Gabler, *Winchell: Gossip, Power and the Culture of Celebrity* (London: Vintage, 1995), p. 289.
443 'Steps Toward British Union, a World State, and International Strife: Part V', *Congressional Record*, Proceedings and Debates of the 76th Congress, Third Session, 20 August 1940, pp. 13–18. Republican Senator Rufus C. Holman (Oregon) also read H.T. Mills, *Money, Politics and the Future* (1939) in its entirety into the *Congressional Record* on 8 March 1941.
444 Arnold Leese to Major Theodore Rich, 13 May 1953, Leese papers. 'I have a large mailing list in USA,' Leese boasted to 'Charles L. Morey' on 9 February 1948, Derounian papers.
445 Arnold Leese to Major Theodore Rich, 3 June 1954, Leese papers.
446 O. John Rogge, *The Official German Report* (New York: Thomas Yoseloff, 1961), p. 430 remarks upon the defendants' contacts with Leese and Beamish.
447 'Extract', 13 November 1945 in TNA KV 2/1366/296z; TNA KV 3/261; *Gothic Ripples*, no. 87, 17 April 1952; and *Gothic Ripples*, no. 105, 21 September 1953. Robert Edmondson to Arnold Leese, 10 November 1947, Arcand papers thanks Leese for dedicating *Jewish War of Survival* to him and other patriots. The British edition was dedicated to 18B internees.
448 Arnold Leese to A.N. Field, 20 March 1952 in 73.148.081, Field papers.
449 George Armstrong to Leese, 30 April 1946 and Arnold Leese to George Armstrong, 6 April 1946 in Box 150, folder 27, Armstrong papers. The FBI file 100–11349 highlights that Armstrong was also a 'financial backer' of Conde McGinley's anti-Semitic newspaper, *Common Sense*.
450 Arnold Leese to George Armstrong, 6 May 1946 in Box 150, folder 26, Armstrong papers.
451 Arnold Leese to Adrien Arcand on 13 December 1947, Arcand papers.
452 Arnold Leese to George Armstrong, 22 February 1952 in Box 172, folder 2, Armstrong papers.
453 Arnold Leese to Anthony Gittens, 7 October 1953, Leese papers. See also *Gothic Ripples*, no. 48, 21 February 1949; *Gothic Ripples*, no. 70, 20 November 1950; and *Gothic Ripples*, 77, 28 June 1951.
454 *The Cross and The Flag*, vol. 14, no. 2, May 1955; *The Cross and The Flag*, vol. 13, no. 4, July 1954; *The Cross and The Flag*, vol. 13, no. 7, October 1954; *The Cross and The Flag*, vol. 13, no. 9, December 1954; and *The Cross and The Flag*, vol. 13, no. 10, January 1955.
455 *The Cross and The Flag*, vol. 13, no. 7, October 1954. Smith's publication, *English Journal Reveals ... Jewish Control of A and H Bombs* had been entirely cribbed from *Gothic Ripples*, 29 June 1954 which, Smith claimed,

> revealed in a careful and documented study the fact that the development and control of the Atom and Hydrogen Bombs has been kept within the authority and intellectual control of Jews. We reproduce herewith a photostatic copy of the journal referred to.

456 Kurt Mertig, FBI file 65-20553-146. It was a two-way traffic. *Gothic Ripples*, no. 90, 8 July 1952 sold copies of *Atom Treason* (1951) by Frank Britton, editor of *The American Nationalist*.
457 Gerald L.K. Smith to Arnold Leese, 29 June 1955, copy available at: http://us10.campaign-archive1.com/?u=0021dba1deec21403fbe2e780&id=7630347f21&e=[UNIQID] (accessed 7 April 2016).
458 *Women's Voice*, 24 April 1947; *Women's Voice*, 22 February 1951; and *Women's Voice*, 27 December 1951.
459 MI5, minute, 1 August 1946 in TNA KV 3/261/16a.
460 Mrs Lyrl Clark van Hyning, FBI file 105-456, p. 150.
461 Arnold Leese to Anthony Gittens, 4 October 1953, Leese papers.
462 Van Hyning's FBI file (105-456) highlights her distribution of his material noting (on p. 135) that, in 1957, The Britons had mailed her a package of fifty copies of Leese's pamphlet *Devilry in the Holy Land*, which the US Postal Service destroyed.
463 Eustace Mullins to Arnold Leese, 18 November 1955, original in author's possession.
464 Marilyn R. Allen, *Alien Minorities and Mongrelization* (Boston, MA: Meador, 1949), pp. 54–56, 75, 209–211, 292 and 372. Allen also directed readers to Leese's other publications noting that they could be obtained from 'Examiner Books' in New York, an outfit run by Conrad Grieb. *Gothic Ripples*, no. 90, 8 July 1952 noted, for the benefit of its American readership, that Allen 'turns out a stream of useful anti-Jewish pamphlets of interest chiefly to Americans, who should apply to her for them'.
465 *Gothic Ripples*, no. 17, 22 June 1946; and *Gothic Ripples*, no. 80, 26 September 1951. Leese's belief that racial violence in the United States was a 'healthy sign' (*Gothic Ripples*, no. 77, 28 June 1951) was made in relation to the recent bombing of a Jewish communal centre in Miami, Florida.
466 Jesse B. Stoner to Arnold Leese, 12 November 1954, original in author's possession; and *Washington Post*, 18 April 2005.
467 *BNP Members Bulletin*, no. 6, March 1961, Box 4, Jewish Chronicle Library collection, Wiener Library.
468 Ridout also sat on the BNP National Council, see *Combat*, no. 21, March–April 1963. He was 'a popular speaker' for the party, see *Nation Revisited*, no. 102, April 2003. He retired to Ilfracombe, Devon, working with Tony Gittens, The Britons chairman, another former IFL activist, who lived nearby.
469 *The Thunderbolt*, no. 69, July 1965. The NSRP newspaper was regularly advertised in *Combat*, the BNP newspaper. *The Thunderbolt*, no. 61, September 1964 also carried the following advertisement: 'Going to Britain? Contact: Box KT/4, 201A Newport Road, Leyton, London, England and meet the British Right Wing' indicating the semblance of a more organised network beyond the exchange of publications.
470 James Graham Cook, *The Segregationists* (New York: Appelton-Century-Crofts, 1962), p. 185.
471 *Personal Newsletter – Were Christian Children Secretly Murdered? NSRP Publishing Rare Book* and *Now Republished by Popular Demand – Jewish Ritual Murder by Arnold S. Leese*, copies in H. Keith Thompson papers, Box 10, Hoover Institution Archives, Stanford University, hereafter Thompson papers, the latter indicating its popularity merited a second edition.
472 Edward Fields to Colin Jordan, 26 June 1963, Rockwell papers; and *The Thunderbolt*, no. 51, May 1963. George Lincoln Rockwell's American Nazi Party also bought Leese's books from Colin Jordan's National Socialist Movement, see George Lincoln Rockwell to Martin Webster, 19 January 1964, Rockwell papers. Leese's acolyte Colin Jordan would later help Fields research an article on the idea to banish Jews to Madagascar, a lodestar in this milieu, which was later published in *The Thunderbolt*, no. 328, 10 August 1968.
473 *The Truth at Last*, no. 337, 1989.
474 Dr Edward Fields, letter to the author, 25 April 2002. *Searchlight*, no. 217, July 1993 notes Bass' presence at a 'revisionist seminar' organised by David Irving. Other US organisations also disseminated Leese's writings during this period. *The New Patriot*, a magazine devoted to 'a responsible but penetrating inquiry into every aspect of the Jewish Question', produced by the British expatriate Roger Pearson, offered free copies of Leese's *Gentile Folly: The Rothschilds* with every subscription, see 'The New Patriot. 1965–1967', in The Hall-Hoag Collection, Brown University Library.

475 Susan Cohen, 'In Step with Arnold Leese: The Case of Lady Birdwood', *Patterns of Prejudice*, vol. 28, no. 2, 1994, pp. 61–75; James A. Aho, *The Politics of Righteousness: Idaho Christian Patriotism* (Seattle, WA: University of Washington Press, 1995), p. 280; Martin Durham, *White Rage: The Extreme Right and American Politics* (London: Routledge, 2007), pp. 47–48; and *Liberty Bell*, vol. 12, no. 1, September 1984. Leese's books have been reprinted by 'Sacred Truth Ministries', a Christian Identity group based in Mountain City, Tennessee. This appeal extended beyond Christian Identity circles. House of Representatives, *Nature and Threat of Violent Anti-America Groups in America: Hearing before the Subcommittee on Crime of the Committee on the Judiciary* (Washington, DC: United States Government, 1996), p. 31, highlights *Ritual Murder* being sold in 1995 at weapons and survival training workshops run by Bo Gritz, a former US Green Beret turned paramilitary leader.

476 For the definitive biography, see Kevin Coogan, *Dreamer of the Day: Francis Parker Yockey and the Postwar Fascist International* (New York: Autonomedia, 1999). For a sympathetic 'in-house' biography, see Kerry Bolton, *Yockey: A Fascist Odyssey* (London: Arktos, 2018).

477 His contention that Spengler hated the Nazis was based upon Friedrich Percyval Reck-Malleczewen, *Diary of a Man in Despair* (New York: Macmillan, 1970), p. 12: 'I knew no one who morning, noon and night and in his dreams so hated them (the Nazis) as Oswald Spengler did.'

478 *Gothic Ripples*, no. 66, 15 July 1950. The Britons unsurprisingly sided with Leese, see *Free Britain*, no. 69, 23 July 1950, which denounced 'Varange' in similar terms. Admiral Sir Barry Domvile told the Canadian fascist leader Adrien Arcand on 24 March 1949:

> Varange paid me a visit and honoured me with Vol. 1 of his book. I did not take to either; my wife, who is a Catholic reported very badly on *Imperium*, which I must own [up] I have never read through.

479 *Frontfighter*, no. 4, August 1950. Anthony Gannon to Keith Stimely, 7 September 1980 in Keith Stimely papers, University of Oregon, subsequently recalled, in less intemperate language:

> For Leese, vertical race was everything; for FYP horizontal race was the deciding issue. Perhaps, Leese was too old and rigid in his thinking to ever be expected to grasp such a new approach to race. After all, he was born in the nineteenth century, which for FYP was, almost, a total disqualification for a true understanding of his thinking.... It puzzles me to observe that FYP is now so widely accepted by vertical race merchants and it occurs to me that they have accepted *Imperium* without having read it, and FYP without ever having known him.

480 *Frontfighter*, no. 4, August 1950.
481 *Gothic Ripples*, no. 98, 12 March 1953.
482 *Gothic Ripples*, no. 95, 12 December 1952.
483 *Gothic Ripples*, no. 90, 8 July 1952; *Gothic Ripples*, no. 98, 12 March 1953; James H. Madole to Arnold Leese, 24 June 1952 and James H. Madole to Arnold Leese, 20 January 1953, originals in author's possession.
484 John M. Lundoff to Arnold Leese, 27 May 1952 and John M. Lundoff to Arnold Leese, 16 June 1952, author's possession.
485 James H. Madole to Arnold Leese, 28 February 1953, Leese papers. Madole stated:

> I have never previously heard of *Imperium* or the European Liberation Front. I inquired of the gentleman who presented us with the article concerning Ulick Varange [Yockey] and was informed that this personage was now residing in the Lebanon. Several other complaints concerning the ELF have come in from England and Spain. I am trying to obtain some of their literature but have not so far succeeded. A fellow called [Peter] Huxley-Blythe has written to us but I did not know of his connections, save that he claims to represent AFX Baron of the Natinform outfit in England.

486 Frederick H. Polzin to Arnold Leese, 18 January 1953, Leese papers; and Coogan, *Dreamer of the Day*, p. 51.
487 Coogan, *Dreamer of the Day*, pp. 478 and 486; Keith Stimely interview with Harold Keith Thompson, 13 March 1986 in Thompson papers: Box 18, folder 15a. See also Arnold Forster and Benjamin R. Epstein, *Cross Currents* (New York: Doubleday, 1956), pp. 212 and 252, which notes Leese exchanged publications with Weiss.

488 Mana Truhill to Arnold Leese, 25 February 1954, original in author's possession. Truhill's activities as an informant are discussed in Coogan, *Dreamer of the Day*, pp. 423–425 and 443–445. 'Urgent Memorandum: October 25th, 1954', copy in Thompson papers, Box 15, indicates Truhill's double-dealing was common knowledge within the extreme right by the end of 1954.

489 John Roy Carlson [pseud. Arthur Derounian], *The Plotters* (New York: E.P. Dutton & Co., 1946), pp. 3–8; and John Roy Carlson, *Undercover* (New York: E.P. Dutton & Co., 1943), pp. 30, 148, 192–193 and 205. Maertz was a former Silver Shirt who had been imprisoned on numerous occasions for acts of anti-Semitic vandalism. Arnold Leese to 'Charles L. Morey', 20 March 1946, Derounian papers, expresses sympathy for Maertz's incarceration and expands upon their relationship:

> He was going to print my new book *The Jewish War of Survival* … I hope it is correct when Maertz [sic] says that the Pioneer News Service goes on even if he is 'inside'. I am quite sure my new book is a 'best seller' & Maertz [sic] has a free hand as to sales & price provided he lets me have 750 free copies in batches of 25 over here to sell. No printer here dare touch it.

490 Elmhurst had edited *The Storm*, organ of the National Socialist Workers Party of America during the 1930s, which in its 'Hauptman Extra' on the Lindbergh Baby Affair in 1935 had quoted from *The Fascist*, highlighting his pre-war familiarity with Leese, see *The Storm*, 1935, copy in Florence Mendheim Collection (AR 25441), box 1, folder 10, Leo Baeck Institute, New York. For his part, Leese had published a review of Elmhurst's pamphlet, *The World Hoax* (1938), in *The Fascist*, no. 109, June 1938. Elmhurst was one of three American delegates to attend the 1937 Erfurt congress. Michael Sayers and Albert E. Kahn, *Sabotage! The Secret War Against America* (New York: Harper & Brothers, 1942), pp. 147–148 alleged that Elmhurst's real name was 'Fleischkopf' and that he was 'a Nazi agent active in New York City'. Yockey subsequently accused Elmhurst of working with Leese to denigrate his reputation in the United States, see 'Varange' to Adrien Arcand, 13 November 1950, Arcand papers.

491 Theron L. Caudle to Arnold Leese, 21 March 1946, Leese papers.
492 Arnold Leese to Adrien Arcand, 22 March 1949, Arcand papers.
493 'Varange' to Adrien Arcand, 9 August 1951, Arcand papers.
494 Anthony Gannon to Adrien Arcand, 12 December 1949, Arcand papers.
495 'Varange' to Adrien Arcand, 9 August 1950, Arcand papers.
496 Arnold Leese to Adrien Arcand, 16 August 1950, Arcand papers
497 Adrien Arcand to Arnold Leese, 7 September 1950, Arcand papers.
498 Anthony Gannon to Adrien Arcand, 6 November 1950, Arcand papers. G.L.K. Smith had previously written to Arcand on 25 July warning that: 'A man is roving about who calls himself Ulick Varange. I believe he is either irresponsible or is an agent of the Jew.'
499 'Varange' to Adrien Arcand, 13 November 1950, Arcand papers.
500 Colin Jordan, *Fraudulent Conversion: The Myth of Moscow's Change of Heart* (London: Britons Publishing Company, 1956).
501 *Gothic Ripples*, no. 9, 3 January 1946. Leese also recommended *The Riddle of Prehistoric Britain* (1946) by William Comyns Beaumont, a former staff writer for the *Daily Mail*, which, *Gothic Ripples*, no. 15, 10 May 1946, asserted 'confirms the main researches of the late Prof. L.A. Waddell'. Karl Shaw, *Curing Hiccups with Small Fires* (London: Boxtree, 2009), p. 188 further highlights Beaumont's own peculiar beliefs.
502 Arnold Leese to Henry Hamilton Beamish, 5 July 1945 in 73.148.081, Field papers.
503 Arnold Leese to Henry Hamilton Beamish, 18 June 1944 in 73.148.040, Field papers.
504 *Gothic Ripples*, no. 34, 25 January 1948; and *Gothic Ripples*, no. 45, 9 December 1948.
505 Thurlow, *Fascism in Britain*, p. 227; and *Gothic Ripples*, no. 90, 8 July 1952.
506 *Gothic Ripples*, no. 118, 30 September 1954.
507 *Gothic Ripples*, no. 101, 25 May 1953.
508 *Gothic Ripples*, no. 83, 17 December 1951; *Gothic Ripples*, no. 106, 28 October 1953; *Gothic Ripples*, no. 108, 12 December 1953; and *Gothic Ripples*, no. 116, 29 July 1954. Leese had been making these bridging arguments between anti-black racism and anti-Semitism since the later 1940s, see *Gothic Ripples*, no. 59, 27 December 1949. Whilst admiring South African apartheid, Leese lamented Dr Malan 'knows that the Jew is behind the Nigger agitation', but, 'he is no Hitler to attack the trouble at its root', see *Gothic Ripples*, no. 92, 28 September 1952.

509 *Bridgehead*, no. 1, 1 August 1951. Ridout's post-war career was obscure. 'If you hear rumours about him [Ridout], don't believe them; a deep game is on foot', Leese wrote cryptically to Anthony Gittens on 23 January 1954, Leese papers. Anthony Gittens to A.K. Chesterton, 14 March 1972, Chesterton papers, sheds further light on such activities stating that Ridout (a 'lone wolf' and '…the best infiltrator I know') 'just after the war, single handed he "captured" the whole Tottenham Trades Council and drove out all Communists including the influential [South African Communist] Solly Sachs'. The JDC subsequently discovered that Ridout, 'a well-known member of the Union movement' was working in Hatton Gardens, which had recently experienced a spate of anti-Semitic graffiti, see Sidney Salomon to Chief Superintendent E. Jones, 31 July 1956 in 1658/10/29, JDC papers.
510 *Gothic Ripples*, no. 66, 14 August 1950; and *Gothic Ripples*, no. 76, June 1951.
511 *Gothic Ripples*, no. 90, 8 July 1952.
512 *Gothic Ripples*, no. 115, 29 June 1954.
513 Arnold Leese to Anthony Gittens, 27 May 1954, Leese papers.
514 *Ibid.*
515 George Thayer, *The British Political Fringe: A Profile* (London: Anthony Blond, 1965), p. 16.
516 *Gothic Ripples*, no. 62, 30 March 1950.
517 Winifred Leese to Anthony Gittens, 18 January 1956, Leese papers.
518 *L'Unité Nationale*, vol. 7, nos 3–4, January–February 1956.
519 *Gothic Ripples*, no. 143, 12 March 1957.
520 Michael D. Biddis, 'Migrants, Minorities and Mosleyites', *Ethnic and Racial Studies*, vol. 4, no. 1, January 1981, p. 112.
521 *The Times*, 18 October 1980 reported the distribution of anti-Semitic leaflets under the imprimatur of 'Arnold Leese Information Service'. It was not an isolated occurrence. In 1999, a letter from the Cats Protection League signed by 'Arnold S. Leese' was circulated to veterinary surgeries in North London claiming that, since Jews were prevented from killing Christian children, they 'are now killing our cats, as a substitute for the innocent human blood they crave'. The CPL, a genuine organisation, thoroughly repudiated the letter, see *Jewish Chronicle*, 1 January 1999. For previous instances, see *Jewish Chronicle*, 23 February 1990; and *Jewish Chronicle*, 18 January 1983. A similar echo can be heard in posts to Stormfront on the subject of 'Ritual Slaughter' by someone using the pseudonym 'Gothic Ripples', see www.stormfront.org/forum/t316942/ (accessed 23 January 2017).
522 For similarities in these libels against the Jewish community as well as the reluctance of the authorities to prosecute, see Susan Cohen, 'In Step with Arnold Leese: The Case of Lady Birdwood', *Patterns of Prejudice*, vol. 28, no. 2, 1994, pp. 61–75.
523 In Britain, a number of Leese's works have been reprinted by 'Stevens Books' and the Historical Review Press, a Sussex-based 'revisionist' printing house, including an anthology of his work, *The Leese Collection: A Selection from the Writings of Arnold Spencer Leese* (Uckfield: Historical Review Press, 2007). Numerous US groups have also reprinted his work.

2 Sir Oswald Mosley
From 'Britain First' to 'Europe-a-Nation'

Sir Oswald Mosley, erstwhile leader of the British Union of Fascists (BUF), emerged from his wartime imprisonment unbowed. Determined to re-enter politics, he began circulating his ideas through his *Mosley News Letter* shortly after the war ended. This was followed by *My Answer* (1946), a self-serving apologia appended to a reprint of *Tomorrow We Live* (1938), the cornerstone of BUF philosophy; signalling to his followers that the 'sacred flame' remained alight. Unfortunately, for Mosley, following a Cabinet meeting on 8 April 1946, the Home Secretary, in coordination with the Foreign Office, made a statement to the House of Commons on 6 June, publicly revealing that Mussolini had funnelled £60,403 to the BUF during the 1930s, a substantial financial subvention that underwrote the costs of Mosley's movement.[1] This announcement coincided, deliberately, with the publication of *My Answer*, causing Mosley maximum personal embarrassment and undermining further the nascent fascist revival.[2] Mosley's only option was to lie. He denied the incontrovertible evidence as 'utterly untrue' recognising, perhaps, that forevermore he would be viewed as a puppet not a patriot in the public imagination.[3]

By this juncture, however, Mosley, through dint of his own actions, had already soiled his own early political promise. His inter-war career is well known; thus, a brief narrative overview will suffice.[4] Sir Oswald Ernald Mosley, son of the wealthy Staffordshire baronet, Sir Oswald Mosley, was born on 16 November 1896. From birth, Mosley had considerable financial means at his disposal, which distinguished him from every other British fascist leader since. During the First World War, Mosley served as a Guards' officer and thence in the elite Royal Flying Corps (RFC), providing him with 'a motif fusing dynamism and youthful heroic enterprise in a new and modern age' that would recur in his subsequent political career.[5] A plane crash, whilst showing off his flying skills to his mother, injured his leg, putting an end to his career as an aviator. Invalided out in May 1915, Mosley spent the remainder of the war at the Ministry of Munitions and the Foreign Office. He entered politics after the war, winning Harrow as a Conservative in December 1918. Two years later, he married Cynthia Curzon, daughter of the Foreign Secretary, Lord Curzon. From 1922, he held the seat as an 'Independent' before joining the Labour Party in March 1924. In that year's general election, Mosley nearly unseated the future Prime Minister Neville Chamberlain in Ladywood, Birmingham, returning to the House of Parliament in 1926 as the Labour MP for Smethwick.

A rising star, Mosley became Chancellor of the Duchy of Lancaster in 1929, in which capacity he assisted Labour's Minister of Employment, J.H. Thomas, to alleviate unemployment. Mosley advocated a programme of large-scale public works to solve unemployment. When the Cabinet rejected his radical, Keynesian solution, Mosley resigned, and in December 1930 launched the New Party, which stood against the 'Old Gang' of British politics. When and why Mosley's decided to turn to fascism has been the subject of much scholarly debate.[6] The impact of the Wall Street Crash, his personal frustration with the grinding reality of parliamentary procedures whilst serving as a government minister, combined with his belief that an ossified Labour Party could never 'save' Britain, all served to convince Mosley that parliamentary democracy was 'dead' and had to be overthrown by revolution rather than reformed.[7]

A violent meeting in Glasgow on 20 September 1931, during which he and his supporters brawled with local communists, also propelled Mosley further along the road to fascism in terms of his tactical choices. Later that evening, Mosley's colleague, Harold Nicolson, noted in his diary: 'Tom says this forces us to be fascist and that we need no longer hesitate to create our trained and disciplined force',[8] which suggests, however, that Mosley had been ruminating upon the move for some time already, not to mention cogitating upon the means of crushing his opponents, communist or otherwise. Mosley continued to vacillate, however. Four days later, he was arguing that although Parliament needed urgent reform, he rejected 'Fascist Methods' since he recognised that public opinion, although hostile to 'professional politicians' remained supportive of 'Parliamentary traditions'.[9]

Mosley's New Party failed to win a single seat at the 1931 General Election held on 27 October. Thereafter, with his electoral hopes obliterated and his hope of achieving power never further from his grasp, Mosley's objection to 'Fascist Methods' diminished accordingly. By early December, Mosley was again holding forth to friends about 'the necessity for militant organization against Communism', arguing that 'when the crash came the man who could control the streets would win'. On 30 December, he and Harold Nicolson departed for Rome where Mosley met Mussolini whom he found to be 'affable but unimpressive'.[10] Thereafter, Mosley wholeheartedly embraced both the ideology and 'action' he believed would resurrect his own political career, and, regenerate the nation. Nicolson, who travelled with him, observed that Mosley 'cannot keep his mind off shock troops, the arrest of [Ramsay] MacDonald [the British prime minister] and J.H. Thomas, their internment in the Isle of Wight and the roll of drums around Westminster'.[11] These 'shock troops' – Mosley admitted to Nicolson would 'correspond to the S.S. or *Schultzstaffel* organisation of the Nazis'.[12] Mosley's desire to intern his opponents was particularly ironic in light of his own political fate eight years later.

Believing a revolutionary 'crisis' to be imminent, Mosley was determined to seize the day and on 1 October 1932 founded the British Union of Fascists (BUF), largely comprising members of his New Party and various fascist sects including the British Fascists (BF), whom Mosley had previously denounced as 'the black-shirted, wretched imitators of the ice-cream merchants of another country'.[13] Mosley proselytised his totalitarian fascist vision in the manner of a political religion, expounding his new dogma in three gospels – *The Greater Britain* (1932), *Fascism: 100 Questions Asked and Answered* (1936) and *Tomorrow We Live* (1938) – through which he outlined the momentous nature of the scientific, spiritual and racial revolution that he envisaged would rejuvenate Britain and her empire.[14] Mosley would sweep away British Parliamentary democracy, an obstacle to national rebirth, and, though he denied it, would assume autocratic power.

The British 'roots' of Mosley's fascist politics are well known and so need not detain us here. Instead, the 'imported' and 'foreign' components of Mosley's ideology, and the political decisions that emanated from them, will be the focus since it was Mosley's decision to align the BUF with the 'Axis model' that determined his fate in 1940. Indeed, as the neo-Tory historian Charles Petrie ventured: 'Mosley failed because of his methods, not because of his ends. His continued flirtation with Hitler and Mussolini caused his movement to be regarded as something not far removed from a foreign conspiracy.'[15]

This is not to suggest that domestic and transnational strands of Mosley's ideological inspiration were somehow incompatible. Indeed, Mosley continually emphasised the 'Britishness' of his political project, whilst simultaneously conceiving of the BUF as part of a transnational European-wide 'Fascist' and 'National Socialist' movement. The *British Union Constitution and Rules* defined the party's creed as both. Contemporary observers were also quick to note this duality. 'His British Fascism is Mussolini in policy and Hitlerite in organization', remarked Sir Robert Bruce Lockhart after lunching with Mosley at the Savoy Grill, shortly before he launched his movement.[16] This ideological bifurcation introduced and indeed reproduced within the BUF the tensions that existed at a macro level between Italian Fascism and German National Socialism, posing a challenge for Mosley's leadership that he never fully surmounted.[17]

Initially, Mosley sought to ride on Mussolini's coat-tails, incorporating wholesale the Italian Fasces as its emblem, the Blackshirt, the fascist salute, and the concept of the Corporate State, the central plank of Italian fascist policy, as a panacea to British society's problems. In April 1933, Mosley returned to Rome, accompanied by a ceremonial bodyguard, to meet Il Duce at the Palazzo Venezia. Dictator and disciple were photographed side by side. Mussolini accorded Mosley the honour of a 100,000-strong parade of Blackshirts, who trooped past the rostrum as Mosley gave the fascist salute. 'The Immense Majesty of the Fascist Peace', which appeared in the subsequent issue of *Blackshirt*, declared that there was 'no question of subordination but only a question of a common service to a common cause'. Whilst the BUF retained its 'British independence', at the same time, 'we shall certainly confer with other Fascist movements concerning the advance of universal fascism throughout the world'.[18]

Mosley's Chief of Staff, Ian Hope Dundas, stayed on in Rome to reassure the Italians that the BUF, as Fascism's true embodiment in England, deserved Il Duce's largesse. From 1933 onwards, Mussolini provided Mosley with a stipend of £5,000 a month, his functionaries frequently travelling to Paris and Geneva to collect the money. The party also maintained a 'secret' bank account at the Charing Cross branch of the Westminster Bank, opened by Mosley's confident W.E.D. 'Bill' Allen, the former Ulster MP, which between July 1933 and May 1937 served as a 'conduit pipe' for large sums of foreign currencies into the BUF. In 1934 alone, the account received £77,800. In the following year, £86,000 flowed in, though the sums declined thereafter. When one signatory, Major G.J.H. Tabor, asked Mosley about the source of the money, he became 'very angry' and refused to tell him.[19]

Mosley further obscured the source of BUF finances by filtering them through an interlocking network of private limited companies, which although he was removed from their administration, he still controlled by dint of the fact that spending the money required his sanction. 'Sir Oswald seems to have aimed at making any such investigation impossible', concluded MI5, though they deduced that the £164,000 paid into the Westminster Bank account was suspiciously similar to the £160,500 paid into the BUF Trust Ltd, the party's principle company. This indicated to them that the entire party's funds for the period January 1934 to December 1935 came from foreign currencies secretly channelled into the BUF.[20] Mosley later insisted the monies were simply donations from English supporters living abroad. The Advisory Committee recorded that Mosley's testimony 'was utterly lacking in candour and frankness'.[21]

Whatever its precise source, Mosley used these monies, very little of which derived from actual membership subscriptions, to underwrite the party's running costs – £45,000 a year in 1936.[22] He also used them to finance the organisation's propaganda machine, which built a cult of celebrity around 'The Leader'. Theatrically choreographed fascist events marketed Mosley to the masses as more than a mere political leader. Party propaganda transformed Mosley into the athletic epitome of manhood: a charismatic sex symbol (the 'Rudolph Valentino of Fascism') whose autographed photographs circulated amongst his 'fan club' in the manner of a film star.[23] The BUF initially enjoyed a meteoric rise, fuelled partly by the backing of the *Daily Mail*, owned by Lord Rothermere, who was effusive in his support for both Mussolini and Hitler. Rothermere officially announced his support for Mosley in a *Daily Mail* article titled 'Hurrah for the Blackshirts' on 15 January 1934. He had hoped that Mosley would emphasise the 'British' character of the movement and drop the 'Fascist' appellation. Mosley ignored his advice. 'It is hard to resist the conclusion that the name of Fascists was retained in deference to Mosley's Italian patrons', noted MI5.[24]

Mosley's association with Rothermere was brief. The press baron terminated his support six months later, on 14 July, following the BUF debacle at Olympia. Designed as a spectacle to showcase the majesty of fascism to the great and good, instead the brutal violence meted out to hecklers at the meeting heightened parallels with Nazism and Hitler's recent massacre of his political opponents during the 'Night of the Long Knives' on 30 June. The *Daily Mail*'s 'consistently pro-Nazi' line was undiminished by the purge, however. Rothermere's real objection was that Mosley aimed to overthrow the entire political and economic edifice, rather than simply uniting with the Conservatives 'to defeat Socialism' – an issue on which Rothermere was 'very near to being unbalanced'.[25]

Initially, Olympia appeared as an unmitigated success. 'For the next two days people of different classes queued up from morning until night at the National Headquarters in Chelsea', reported the police.[26] In retrospect, however, Olympia provided a decisive check to Mosley's political ambition. Membership plummeted from 50,000 in August 1934 to 5,000 by October 1935 as conservative fascists (largely 'paper members') left in droves.[27] Thereafter, the movement lost 'momentum' not least, because Mosley had misread the depth of the economic crisis engulfing Britain, inauspiciously founding the BUF as the crisis began to recede. By the autumn, it was increasingly evident to the authorities that 'the conditions which led to the success of the fascist movement in Italy, or of the Nazi movement in Germany, do not exist in England'.[28] The revolutionary moment, upon which Mosley had pinned his career, had stubbornly refused to arrive. Nor was Mosley's legalist strategy any more successful. The party never returned a single Parliamentary candidate and failed to contest the 1935 general election, campaigning instead on the slogan 'Fascism Next Time'. The BUF had failed as a mass movement.

Whilst the impact of Mussolini's money was not immediately obvious, from 1935 onwards it became increasingly evident. During spring 1935, Mosley's stock was reportedly 'very low' in Rome and Mussolini 'did not think he had much future'.[29] Mosley endeavoured to prove him wrong. In August, during the height of Anglo-Italian tensions regarding Abyssinia, Mosley and Ian Hope Dundas travelled to Rome again. Upon Mosley's return on 25 August, MI5 recorded:

> it was apparent, in view of the intense activity immediately commenced in connection with the Italo-Abyssinian dispute, that he had been in touch with high officials of the Italian Fascist Party regarding the attitude to be adopted by the BUF during the crisis.[30]

Mosley's 'National Peace Campaign' gave wholehearted support to the Italian cause, whilst denigrating British government policy and the League of Nations. Twenty thousand posters and 3 million leaflets were distributed. On 4 September, the Italian Foreign Ministry sent secret instructions to London that Mosley was to continue and indeed intensify his campaign. Mussolini got little return upon his investment, however. British opinion remained strongly anti-Italian. Mosley's perceived subservience also fuelled internal dissension. 'It is a pity Rome is now dictating Mosley's policy,' remarked F.M. Box, the BUF Director of Political Organisation. 'It is the old story – the man who pays the piper calls the tune.'[31]

Increasingly, Mosley viewed Nazi Germany as holding the key to the future, though this shift from 'Italophilia' to 'Naziphilia' within the BUF was associated both with Mosley's desire to construct a fascism that was 'better' than the Italian variant, and, on a larger canvas, suggested his broader alienation from Mussolini's growing insistence that fascism was a product of Mediterranean civilisation.[32] Mosley's decision to hitch his coat-tails to Hitler was not a sudden phenomenon since the BUF had long maintained contacts with

Nazi Germany. As early as 24 October 1933, Mosley's Chief of Staff Ian Hope Dundas requested the Army Minister Werner von Blomberg arrange an interview between Hitler and a leading BUF functionary, as Mosley personally began initiating contacts with lower-level Nazi officials. Whilst Mosley lavished praise upon the Nazi regime, the Nazis themselves required convincing and relations were not immediately established. Hitler's Chancellery rejected a proposal to send Mosley a signed photograph of Hitler in November 1933. Hans Heinrich Lammers, *Staatssekretär* in Hitler's Chancellery also counselled a cautious approach with regard to relations with Mosley's BUF – an attitude that prevailed.[33] The Nazis treated Major-General J.F.C. Fuller and Bill Allen in a 'cold' manner when they visited Germany in 1935. Mosley was anxious not to rock the boat, however. When G.A. Pfister, who headed the party's Foreign Relations and Overseas Department, remonstrated with several 'high ranking' Nazi officials about their treatment in March 1935, Mosley suspended him and ultimately closed down his entire department 'in consequence of intrigues with Austrian Nazis'.[34] Julius Streicher, the Nuremberg Gauleiter, was more enthusiastic about Mosley, however, sending him a congratulatory telegram after one speech. Mosley thanked him, replying in May 1935,

> I value your advice greatly in the midst of our hard struggle. The power of Jewish corruption must be destroyed in all countries before peace and justice can be successfully achieved in Europe. Our struggle to this end is hard, but our victory is certain.[35]

Within the BUF, the party's Research Directory, headed by Mosley himself,[36] closely studied Nazi methods of organisation and propaganda. Both *Popolo d'Ital'a* and *Völkischer Beobatcher* were carefully read, with reports from them included in the party's daily bulletin.[37] In January 1935, Mosley dispatched Major-General J.F.C. Fuller to Berlin to study Nazi party organisation. Amidst 'unmistakable signs' that the 'rot' had set in within London BUF branches,[38] Fuller and Box sought to reorganise the party, de-emphasising its paramilitarism in favour of creating an electoral machine. Fuller had previously recommended a range of measures aimed at ensuring the movement's longer term viability since it remained a precarious 'one-man show' – without Mosley, noted Fuller, the BUF 'would not only lose most of its financial support but would rapidly disintegrate'.[39] By March 1936, however, Fuller was reportedly declaring he had 'no time' for the BUF, since fascism would never advance under Mosley.[40]

Seeking to cultivate a personal relationship Mosley had met Hitler at his Berlin flat in April 1935, talking with him for an hour before breaking for lunch with the Nazi elite. Goebbels, Goering, Ribbentrop were all present as were Winifred Wagner, the English-born daughter-in-law of the composer Richard Wagner, and Unity Mitford, the star-struck British Nazi besotted with Hitler with whose sister, Diana, Mosley was having a relationship. Goebbels recorded in his diary that Mosley made

> a good impression. A bit brash, which he tries to conceal behind a forced pushiness. Otherwise acceptable, however. Of course, he's on his best behavior. The Fuhrer has set to work on him. Wonder if he'll ever come to power?[41]

Thereafter, a numerous BUF officials including Alexander Raven Thomson and Robert Gordon-Canning travelled to Germany for conclaves with Nazi officials about funding. One BUF 'collector' later voluntarily testified, on the condition of anonymity, that 'German money came through a financial house in Switzerland to Belfast'.[42]

A shift in emphasis became increasingly evident politically. BUF 'Speakers Notes, no. 11' for June 1935, for instance, instructed party propagandists to emphasise the justice of the German cause. William Joyce, the party's Director of Propaganda, also made clear the party's ideological transition towards Nazism. 'English Fascists must remember that Fascism in England is more closely akin to that of Germany than to that of Italy,' he announced. 'Italy, though struggling to do so, has not entirely thrown off the shackles of International Finance. Germany has succeeded.' BUF propaganda shifted towards a more radical, anti-Semitic anti-capitalist agenda, than Mosley might otherwise have contemplated had the *Daily Mail* fascists remained in the ascendant. Aesthetically too, the BUF was influenced by the Nazi party, adopting in December 1935 the Action Press uniform, similar to that worn by the SS, and its new red armband depicting the 'Flash in the Circle', which replaced the Italian Fasces.[43]

Politically, Mosley increasingly made the case for the Third Reich, proclaiming at a meeting on 22 March 1936 that: 'I want to clear away every argument which is presented against Germany.... If they [the politicians] make an alliance against Germany, then Fascism in power will repudiate it.'[44] In June, Mosley changed the BUF's name to the British Union of Fascists and National Socialists. That the party's 'Marching Song' was sung to the tune of the 'Horst-Wessel-Lied' and indeed appropriated and adapted some of its lyrics provided further testimony to the movement's Nazification.[45] The BUF not only defended Nazism, whitewashing the brutality of the concentration camps for instance, but also acted as a conduit for Nazi propaganda into Britain. *Action* and *Blackshirt*, the party newspapers, frequently featured adverts for Nazi literature from the Fichte-Bund in Hamburg, *Welt-Dienst* in Erfurt and *News from Germany*, the English-language propaganda sheet in Bavaria.[46] Several BUF activists worked directly for these propaganda networks.[47] As well as dispatching official delegations to the annual Nuremberg rally, the BUF also arranged less formalised modes of interaction, German tours ('conducted by German National Socialists') and opportunities for younger members to become pen pals with Hitler Youth activists.[48]

Given the growing parallels with Nazism, the BUF's dependency upon anti-Semitism arguably reflected this growing political synergy. BUF anti-Semitism was not simply a Nazi import, however. Nor was Mosley an 'ideological antisemite' in the sense that hatred of the Jews was the principal engine of his thought and action.

> Rather it was the other way round: his ideology, fascism, compelled him to oppose Jews. Unlike many of his peers, whose visceral antisemitism had driven them towards fascism as a vehicle through which to act out their hatred, Mosley travelled in the opposite direction.[49]

The genesis of Mosley's anti-Semitic campaign reflects this judgement, whilst also refuting Mosley's own long-standing claim that he only attacked Jews after they attacked him. Although anti-Semitism had formed no real part of Mosley's early platform, the signs were there as early as April 1932, when he chaired a meeting of the New Party's youth wing to which Arnold Leese and Henry Hamilton Beamish of the Imperial Fascist League, both die-hard anti-Semites, were invited. Similarly, although *The Greater Britain* was devoid of anti-Semitism, this was thanks to Mosley's colleague, Harold Nicolson, who in June had bade him expunge references to 'Jewish banking houses' that were in the first draft, arguing that the 'Nazi note' would alienate a British audience. Mosley was clearly 'flying a kite' noted his biographer.[50]

He did not abstain for long. Four months later, Mosley's official statement announcing the BUF's formation highlighted Jews' supposed involvement in 'subversive activity', and rebuked them for allegedly holding anti-British aims, 'setting out the precise pattern his party's anti-Semitism would follow'.[51] During 1933, Mosley knowingly appointed a number of voluble anti-Semites to key positions, whilst in November he announced his opposition to Anglo-Jewry in an article titled 'Shall Jews Drag Britain to War?'[52] Mosley barred Jews from joining the BUF in March 1934.[53] He also blamed the loss of the *Daily Mail*'s support in the wake of the Olympia debacle in July on blackmail from Jewish advertisers without providing a scintilla of proof. Mosley's deputy, Dr Robert Forgan, testified in the following month that he was finding it 'impossible' to work with him. He resigned shortly afterwards stating his opposition to Mosley's 'anti-Semitic utterances and the anti-Semitic trend of the Fascist movement'.[54] Rather than being something that was beyond his control as he would later assert, the responsibility for incorporating anti-Semitism into fascist policy was Mosley's alone since, as Leader, he had 'final authority' as the party's ideological arbiter. Mosley set the tone and pace.

Through a constant barrage of anti-Jewish provocations, the BUF's strategy was 'to goad Jews into attacking them [the BUF], with the aim of only fully revealing their antisemitism when it could be presented as a response to Jewish aggression'.[55] This trend was fully evident throughout the autumn when Mosley addressed a series of meetings at Hyde Park, Belle Vue and the Albert Hall. During the latter, in October, Mosley made a vituperative speech, issuing his 'Great Clarion Call' against British Jewry: 'We say to the alien forces that arise against us in our own land of Britain, to rob us of our heritage of patriotism and resolution: "We take up that challenge. They Will It! They shall have it."'[56] In *Fascism: 100 Questions Asked and Answered* (1936), Mosley of course denied that Jews would be persecuted but declared that those who put the interests of Jewry before those of Britain would be expelled; those conducting themselves in an otherwise exemplary fashion, would still be treated as 'foreigners' and deprived of citizenship. He would permit none to serve as MPs or officials.[57] Little wonder then that by that year MI5 had come to regard the BUF's anti-Semitic platform as 'identical' to that of the Nazi party.[58]

Mosley's party was increasingly reliant upon anti-Semitic politicking within East London, which had become the fulcrum of BUF support as wider public interest, particularly in the provinces, evaporated.[59] Whilst Mosley was optimistic regarding his organisation's future prospects, Special Branch reported 'very few tangible signs' of a growth in support.[60] A sustained and intensive propaganda drive in East London over the course of several months culminated on 4 October 1936 in the 'Battle of Cable Street'. Police banned Mosley's attempt to lead a march through the East End, apprehending serious disorder with 100,000 anti-fascist protestors who had gathered to oppose him. Mosley acquiesced to police demands and dispersed his men. Despite denouncing the government for caving into 'Red Terror',[61] Mosley chose not to resist police orders, however, since arrest would have jeopardised his personal plans. On the following day, Mosley flew to Berlin. There he married Diana Guinness, the daughter of Lord Redesdale, at Goebbels' home. Hitler was also present. 'Because he is a friend of mine,' Diana stated.[62] 'It is hardly necessary to point out the significance of this episode as indicating the degree of intimacy which must have existed at that time between Mosley and the Nazi leaders,' recorded MI5.[63] Mosley's best-man, W.E.D. Allen, was more sanguine about its importance, telling MI5 in 1942 that the event was not a success from Mosley's point of view. Mosley was the only member of the group not to speak German 'and he was therefore left very much in the cold.' Hitler did not take to him either, apparently believing that he 'looked

Jewish'.⁶⁴ Mosley succeeded in keeping his marriage a secret, even from his own children, until 26 November 1938, when Diana gave birth to a son, forcing him to make their union public.⁶⁵

In the aftermath of Cable Street, the BUF experienced a temporary surge in recruits, up to 2,000 new members joined amidst a more general increase in anti-Semitic 'hooliganism' in the area. The anti-Semitic asperity of BUF supporters increased accordingly. The BUF organiser E.G. 'Mick' Clarke, for instance, used his platform to declare:

> It is about time the British people of the East End knew that London's pogrom is not very far away now. Mosley is coming every night of the week in future to rid East London and by God there is going to be a pogrom!⁶⁶

However, instead of keeping the situation at 'boiling point', the BUF 'allowed it to subside' possibly as a result of Mosley's incapacity to take advantage of the situation but also perhaps attributable to the announcement of new legislation to deal with these circumstances.⁶⁷ Indeed, the Public Order Act (1936), which came into force on 1 January 1937, banning fascist uniforms, considerably undermined the party's aesthetic allure. Between November 1936 and May 1937, BUF membership continued decreasing.⁶⁸ The London County Council (LCC) elections on 4 March in which the BUF candidates in three East London districts – Bethnal Green, Limehouse and Shoreditch – polled just 7,000 votes out of the total 80,000 cast, provided additional evidence of growing public indifference to Mosley. Working-class support declined further as international antagonism with Germany increased.⁶⁹

Mussolini had lost interest in the BUF as a tool of Italian foreign policy by this point, reducing then ceasing altogether his subsidy, which underwrote the BUF's operating costs. This precipitated a financial crisis within the party, which, only days after the disastrous LCC elections, forced Mosley to retrench. He dismissed numerous leading officials from paid employment, most notably the propagandists William Joyce and John Beckett, ostensibly as a matter of economy but also weighing up other considerations. The crisis compelled Mosley to relocate his offices too, the party's Chelsea headquarters – the 'Black House' – costing between £7,000–8,000 a year to maintain, became an unaffordable luxury.⁷⁰

Mosley's response to this acute crisis was to appeal to the Nazis to shore up his ailing movement. On 19 June, Joseph Goebbels recorded in his diary: 'Mosley needs money ... Wants it from us. Has already had £2000 ... £100,000 necessary. £60,000 promised. Must submit to Fuhrer.' On 23 July, Goebbels again recorded in his diary that Mosley's wife, the principle go-between, was imploring him 'for an infusion of £100,000'. The Nazis were unimpressed, however. 'Mosley must work harder and be less mercenary,' noted Goebbels.⁷¹ When Diana Mosley requested a further sum in February 1937, she encountered strong reservations. 'Goebbels regarded Mosley's case as hopeless and suspected that even the British fascists had been infested by "British" weakness'.⁷² Mosley's close collaborator W.E.D. 'Bill' Allen understood this attitude. Interrogated by MI5 in 1942, Allen stated that 'To do the Germans' sense of reality justice they had no belief in Mosley's prospects of success.'⁷³ Hitler appears to have regarded Mosley more as a thinker than as the man of action, which Mosley believed himself to be, though he did at least credit Mosley with understanding 'the German-European idea' (*die germanisch-europäische Idee*), a comment not without import for understanding the continuity between his inter-war and post-war geopolitics.⁷⁴

Yet, whilst appealing to the Nazis for funds, simultaneously Mosley sought to play down the connection. MI5 had previously learned from an informant that Mosley feared that allegations of Nazi influence could ruin the BUF.[75] In November 1937, in a bid to detoxify the party, Mosley changed its name again, this time to 'British Union'. This did not stop Mosley or Allen from investigating other means of profiting from his wife's Nazi contacts. In 1938, after Diana Mosley had secured Hitler's interest in the project, Mosley began negotiating with the Nazis to build a radio broadcasting station, entirely at their cost, which, once constructed, would benefit its chief shareholders – Mosley and Allen – who planned to use it to sell advertising space to advertisers. Mosley strenuously denied it was anything other than a commercial venture though conceded that his wife's close personal friendship with Hitler 'opened doors' which would otherwise have remained closed. MI5 regarded the whole affair as 'a veiled form of subvention'.[76]

Diana Mosley's Nazi contacts provided a more 'direct means' for Mosley to obtain German funds too. Mosley sought to profit from 'ransoming' Baron Louis Rothschild, who had been arrested and held hostage by the Gestapo after the Anschluss of Austria in March 1938. The Rothschild family in Paris approached Oliver Hoare, brother of the Foreign Secretary Samuel Hoare, to inquire if Mosley might intercede. They would pay Mosley £40,000 for his services. He apparently insisted on £120,000. Allen became involved, contacting a Belgian Rexist financier called Wryns who agreed to oversee the transfer. The Rexists would take 25 per cent commission. Mosley would keep the remainder. Allen suggested an alternative: instead of remitting the money, the Rothschilds could use their influence with King Carol of Romania to secure the release of the imprisoned Iron Guard leader, Corneliu Codreanu. Allen later testified that the suggestion infuriated Mosley, causing him to recuse himself from the negotiation. He later heard, however, as he told MI5, that Diana Mosley visited Reichsführer-SS Heinrich Himmler in Berlin, who subsequently ordered Rothschild's release after the ransom was paid. Allen noted that, coincidentally, Mosley's financial position improved considerably shortly thereafter.[77] Codreanu was not so lucky, 'shot whilst trying to escape' though in reality he was garrotted then shot; then acid poured on his body.

From the Anschluss until the outbreak of war, the BUF used every means at its disposal to influence public opinion in favour of the Third Reich. The anti-war campaign saw membership figures rebound from 16,500 in December 1938 to 22,500 in September 1939, reflective of the membership's changing composition as BUF support expanded beyond its ailing East End redoubt.[78] In the previous month, Mosley had staged a large public meeting at the Earls Court Exhibition Hall, attracting approximately 20,000 people, demanding Germany be unfettered in Eastern Europe and its colonies returned. 'Mind Britain's Business' was Mosley's stock response to Hitler's machinations. In Germany, Goebbels made sure that coverage of the meeting was slight 'so that the democratic press has no locus to depict him [Mosley] as being in the German pay'.[79]

Whilst undoubtedly a triumph for Mosley, the meeting also reflected the gulf between those who sympathised with his views and those who were prepared to become active in the movement. The pro-Nazi campaign continued. When Hitler invaded Czechoslovakia, rather than criticise Hitler, or retract their previous claim that he had no intention of invading the country, *Action* featured a front page article from Mosley titled 'Warmongers Exposed', which began 'The jackals of Jewish finance are again in full cry for war.'[80] After Hitler invaded Poland, on the day before the outbreak of war, Mosley announced 'No War for Jewish Finance'.[81]

In a withering assessment of the *Action*'s content during these years, MI5 disdainfully recorded:

> It is difficult to believe, when reading these back numbers of *Action*, that one is reading a British newspaper and not some organ of the German press. Only in the German press do we find this same slavish adulation of the German Government and completely uncritical approval of every act of the German Fuehrer. Perhaps one reason for the small effect of this propaganda on British public opinion was its exotic character. It bore too clearly the stamp of the Propaganda Ministry in Berlin.[82]

This heady brew of Nazi propaganda and BUF cheerleading posited a cosmic struggle between the supposedly regenerative force of fascism and its degenerative antithesis – Jewish 'Financial Democracy'. It served to pervert patriotism. 'In such a struggle, was it not the manifest duty of every patriotic Englishman to suppose the forces of light, the forces of the new world, against the dark forces of Jewish Capitalism, represented by the British Government?'[83] This was the underlying message of BUF propaganda, assessed MI5. The corrosive impact of this position, which provided a moral justification for wartime treachery, or at least the suspicion of it, was evident from as early as 1935 onwards, when MI5 first detected a 'definitely disloyal element' within the party resulting from its continual denigration of democracy, and the British government, as the puppet of 'alien' Jewish interests. By 1939, it was such that the MI5 Director-General observed 'that it had become impossible to regard the BUF as a loyal body in time of war.'[84]

Mosley continued his efforts to rouse public opinion against the prospect of a war with Nazi Germany, holding a mass rally in East London on 26 August, for instance, during which he railed against 'a war for Jewish interests in Poland'. His wife, meanwhile, in Germany, was met off the train in Nuremberg by Nazi 'Jew-baiter' Julius Streicher and her sister, Unity, and thence onwards to Bayreuth, where she saw Hitler for the final time.[85] In Britain, public meetings tailed off, although Mosley's protracted 'Jews' War' propaganda campaign continued unabated through party publications, anti-Semitic slogans chalked on walls in the dead of night and by word of mouth.

On 1 September, Germany invaded Poland leading Britain and France to declare war two days later. Distressed by the prospect of an Anglo-German war, Mosley's sister-in-law shot herself. Less dramatically, Mosley was compelled to clarify his stance too. Sent to all BUF branches on 1 September, 'Mosley's Message' appeared publicly, in an abridged, modified form, in *Action* on 16 September. 'Mosley's Message' is held up as evidence of Mosley's innate patriotism since in it Mosley implored BUF members 'to do nothing to injure our country, or to help any other Power'. It was in fact disingenuous. The two versions were actually radically different.[86] 'I am not offering to fight in the quarrel of Jewish finance, in a war from which Britain could withdraw at any moment she likes with her Empire intact and her people safe', Mosley declared.[87] The first version, addressing his members, concluded:

> I am now concerned with only two simple facts. This war is no quarrel of the British people; this war is a quarrel of Jewish finance. So to our people I give myself for the winning of peace.[88]

The *public* version, published in *Action*, omitted reference to 'Jewish finance' as well as other anti-Semitic allusions earlier, concluding instead:

It is sufficient to say that a war cannot be fought every twenty years to prevent any remedy of the injustices of the Peace Treaty which concluded the previous war. So to our people I give myself for the winning of the peace.[89]

Far from being a patriotic statement imploring his followers to fight with him for Britain, 'Mosley's Message' enjoined the BUF faithful to follow his lead, and refuse to fight in a 'Jews' War'. Only members *already* in the Armed Services were bade to 'do what the law requires of them'. Mosley urged the remainder 'to take every opportunity in your power to awaken the people and to demand peace'.[90]

On the same day as the party faithful received 'Mosley's message', a small conference took place at BUF headquarters to discuss the possibility of State action against the party. Thereafter, Neil Francis-Hawkins, the BUF Director-General, busied himself with precautions to safeguard the party's records, files and finances; membership lists were also safeguarded either through their destruction or disbursement to lesser officials. Hawkins subsequently instructed all BUF District Leaders to nominate a second in case they 'should cease to be available'. Eight senior officials received a signed document from Mosley announcing that they had his 'complete confidence' to do whatever was in the best interests of the movement in case he too was indisposed by arrest and imprisonment. When the State did not act to repress his party, which in the meantime had kept up a barrage of anti-Semitic propaganda, Mosley took the opportunity to hold public meetings in Dalston on 8 October and at the Stoll Picture Theatre on 15 October, urging a referendum on 'War or Peace' at the latter. In private, at members-only meetings, Mosley was decidedly more militant in his pronouncements.[91]

On the day after the Stoll Theatre meeting, Hawkins issued a circular letter to leading officials stating that: 'Those of us who are now free under the Law to decide the matter for ourselves are not offering our services to fight in this war, *because we do not consider that Britain or her Empire is threatened.*' Accompanying the letter was advice on how to apply to become a Conscientious Objector since the Government 'has deliberately raised the ideological issue by making one of its principal war aims the destruction of the political system of another great nation'.[92] Thereafter, a 'Young Men's Advisory Committee' was founded to aid BUF members raise a 'Fascist' rather than a moral objection to war.[93]

Whilst inducing his activists not to fight a 'Jews' War' – which was at marked variance to his own claims to have 'publicly urged his members to fight once war was declared' – Mosley was scrupulously careful not to do anything illegal that might contravene the Defence Regulations, let alone advocating sabotage or espionage.[94] Nonetheless, the police and MI5 weighed up numerous potentially disloyal statements in the balance during these months, examining them for evidence of Mosley's likely conduct in the event of invasion or aerial bombardment. In January 1940, Mosley issued a new pamphlet, *The British Peace ... and How to Get It*, demanding immediate peace with Hitler.[95] They printed 2,300,000 copies, with a 'considerable number' distributed *gratis*.[96]

The juxtaposition of two phrases encapsulated Mosley's official policy: 'Mosley and Peace' or 'Jewry and War'. This was no coincidence. Captain B.D.E. Donovan, the party's Director of Administration, stated on 30 January that: 'It was the movement's duty to see to it that whenever people thought of peace they connected it with Mosley, and that they always associated the Jew with war and suffering.'[97] To gauge public receptivity to this 'peace' message, the BUF stood two candidates in by-elections in February and March, both revealing a complete dearth of popular support for the party at this point. In Silvertown, London, the BUF polled just 151 votes out of 14,343 cast for the victorious candidate, whilst in North East Leeds its candidate obtained 722 votes out of 23,882 cast, despite, or perhaps because of, Mosley making a speech on his behalf.[98]

Hitler's invasion of Norway did nothing to change the party's attitude; *Action* claimed that the British had violated Norway's neutrality, not the Nazis.[99] Mosley neither criticised Hitler's *blitzkrieg* through the Low Countries, nor modified his policy of non-collaboration with the war effort. When France fell, Mosley positioned himself as the man who could sue for peace at the head of an 'alternative to the present Government', issuing a statement to that effect in *Action* on 23 May.[100] It had no impact. Police arrested Mosley outside his Dolphin Square flat in London that same day, together with numerous other leading figures, the wave of detentions having been triggered by the treasonous activities of Conservative MP Captain Maule Ramsay and his Right Club, a small anti-Semitic coterie.[101] Mosley's association with Ramsay, combined with his unrelenting pro-Nazism, sealed his fate.[102]

Though Mosley and his leading officials had anticipated detention, not least because of the fears fuelled about a largely mythical 'Fifth Column' scare in the newspapers during spring 1940,[103] the movement as a whole was inadequately prepared for the eventuality.[104] Successive waves of internment during the summer crippled the movement completely. The British government proscribed the BUF in July 1940, finishing the movement off as a political force, though not as a source for concern. Police arrested numerous activists for conspiring to assist the enemy and others for minor acts of sabotage, including acts of arson. Other activists, abroad at the time, or subsequently captured, would distinguish themselves as collaborators with the Nazi regime.[105]

Behind bars, Mosley sought to keep a nucleus of the movement alive from his cell in Brixton prison whilst reading key works of German and Greek philosophy. Key figures disbursed throughout a series of internment camps also acted to ensure the party faithful endured. For many, imprisonment served as a deterrent. Previously stalwart fascists deserted the standard after their release, never to return. For others, however, the experience was formative, radicalising and strengthening them in their beliefs. Internment provided these fascist activists with a powerful integrative 'myth' through which they could reinterpret and rationalise the experience, not as defeat, but instead as the darkness before the dawn, through which they had to pass if fascism was to emerge triumphant.[106] The government quietly sanctioned the release of most internees early on in the war. Amidst massive protests, the Home Secretary released Mosley in November 1943, ostensibly for health reasons. He repaired to Crux Easton House near Newbury where he sat out the remainder of the war, biding his time.

Post-war politics

Mosley's sense of destiny was undiminished by internment and military defeat. On 7 July 1947, he declared:

> My life striving in the politics of Britain made known my name and character: my voice can now reach beyond the confines of one country, because it has been heard before. The past has imposed the duty of the future: I must do this thing because no other can.[107]

Now that Hitler and Mussolini 'have been silenced', Mosley proclaimed, he alone could oppose the 'architects of chaos'. Cogitating upon the defeat of fascist ideology, which he still believed 'might have brought the Renaissance of Western Man', Mosley came to believe that 'our creed was brought to dust because the Fascist outlook in each land was too National'.[108] His proposed panacea for Europe's ideological and physical rebirth, outlined in *The Alternative* (1947), was 'Europe-a-Nation'. 'We can only create European Union by getting rid of national alignments,' Mosley argued, to which end he proposed an elected 'European Assembly' voted for by 'Europeans'.[109]

Billed as being 'beyond Fascism and Democracy', for many 'Britain First' fascists Mosley's ideological metamorphosis was simply 'beyond comprehension'. There were numerous resignations over the issue up to 1950. However, Mosley's pan-European philosophy was the ideological cornerstone of the Union Movement (UM), which he founded on 7 February 1948.[110] Although its name was a self-conscious evocation of the pre-war 'British Union', even at its height the UM was never more than a pale imitation of its interwar ancestor, gaining perhaps 1,200 active members and some 2,000 sympathisers. UM membership was open to 'any European or person of European origin'.[111]

The party's electoral impact was negligible. In the 1949 municipal elections, its eight candidates polled only 1,993 votes out of a total 4,097,841 cast. In the aftermath of its electoral drubbing, the party became more violent and more anti-Semitic.[112] By late 1950, however, the UM was all but finished politically, even anti-fascists rarely turned out to confront it. MI5's verdict was dismissive:

> Mosley's movement is at its lowest ebb since the formation of the British Union of Fascists in 1932. Generally, the Party today comprises remnants of the poorest elements of the pre-war organisation, plus a few recently recruited 'natural' fascists of small intelligence. The leadership is poorer than at any time in the past; recruiting is admitted to be at a standstill. Moreover the few remaining adherents of any standing are showing an inclination to break away, while old, loyal supporters of Mosley who have remained on the verge of the Movement since its post-war re-formation are expressing disgust and disappointment at the existing state of the Party.[113]

Even Mosley recognised that the game was up. In 1951, he sold his Wiltshire estate at Crowood, Ramsbury, liquidated many of his assets and reinvested them in South African shares.[114] In March 1951, Mosley and his family took up residence in Clonfert Palace in County Galway, Ireland.[115] Mosley's vocal opposition as a young Conservative MP in 1920 to the atrocities committed by the 'Black and Tan' paramilitaries of the British state still resonated in Ireland, as did his support for a united Ireland albeit within a 'European' framework which probably limited the appeal of his panacea amongst the nationalist community.[116] Mosley had in fact first broached the subject of moving to Ireland in 1946 only to be told by the Dublin authorities that 'the time was perhaps not opportune for him to take up permanent residence and that he might delay his decision for some time until international tempers were quieter'.[117]

Five years later, having convinced Dublin that he would demur from partaking in political activity, which might embarrass the government, Mosley was granted permission to move to Ireland. He publicly announced his decision to leave England's 'island prison' to begin what he claimed was the process of becoming a true 'European'.[118] Mosley's recent defeat in a complicated income tax case also undoubtedly influenced his departure, as did his wife's family ties – her younger sister Deborah, the Duchess of Devonshire, lived at Lismore Castle in County Waterford whilst her older sister, Pamela, lived at Tullamaine Castle in County Tipperary.[119] Mosley's departure, combined with the cessation of anti-fascist activity, which deprived UM of both morale and publicity, led the remnants of

British fascism to shrivel further. When fire destroyed Clonfert Palace in 1954, Mosley bought another house in Fermoy, County Cork, though increasingly he was spending his time living in France proselytising for 'Europe-a-Nation'.

Europe-a-Nation

Mosley's post-war philosophy, which reflected his wide reading in prison, his analysis of the post-war world in which the United States and Soviet Russia had emerged as superpowers, and his interaction with former members of the Waffen-SS, rejected the 'narrow' nationalism of inter-war Fascism and National Socialism. If Europe was to survive and indeed thrive betwixt 'Mob' (Russia) and 'Money' (America), fascist activists required an 'extension of patriotism'. 'National Socialism' gave way to 'European Socialism'. This alone could defeat the 'oriental values' of Communism. How to integrate and rehabilitate Germany and incorporate it into this new 'Europe of the Peoples' was a pressing problem, floundering on the 'Jews' whose 'bitterness' over past suffering, argued Mosley, was 'rooted in those dark, atavistic, memories of the European mind'.[120] Mosley made no mention of the Nazi genocide, which had ceased only three years beforehand, except to voice his scepticism of its reality. *The Alternative* saw him argue that the Jewish 'sepsis of the European spirit' still required excision from Europe. Mosley's post-war settlement meant a *Judenfrei* Europe just as it had in the 1930s. The position of Africa to the development of 'Europe-a-Nation' as geopolitical 'Third Force' was also vital. The continent would, Mosley envisaged, serve as a secure autarkic base for surplus European goods, insulated from the 'coming chaos' of the global economy, which would be exchanged for foodstuffs, raw materials and *Lebensraum*.

Africans themselves would be shunted off to the 'rich and fertile' parts of the continent 'unsuited to white occupation'. Though he claimed the old imperial idea was 'dead', Africa remained for Mosley a 'clean slate' upon which Europe could write its 'plan for the future'. Mosley was resolutely opposed to the end of white rule in Africa, which would mean that the 'Ju-Ju man' would 'fiddle away what the white man has created'. His demand for the continued white 'trusteeship' of the continent was the apex of 'European morality' and 'Creative State Action' rather than the re-imposition of colonialism.[121] Mosley's proposals mirrored those for 'Euro-Afrika', an idea that enjoyed brief intellectual currency in Nazi Germany during summer 1940.[122] For Mosley, the creation of a 'Third Empire' in Africa – following the loss of America in the West and Asia in the East – was paramount. If Europe's remaining colonial powers pooled their resources, energies and imperial possessions then Europeans could 'achieve the final glory of the European Spirit'.[123]

Mosley's solution, originally announced in 1948 as the 'Mosley–Pirow proposals', which he formulated in conjunction with the former South African Minister of Defence and Nazi sympathiser, Oswald Pirow, rejected the 'bogus apartheid' that sought 'to keep the Negro within white territory' ostensibly as a pool of 'sweated labour'. Mosley argued instead for a 'genuine apartheid' separating black and white into 'two nations'. This 'complete division' Mosley hoped could be attained with the 'utmost possible speed'. He denied this plan was either 'racialist' or 'a plan to oppress blacks'. Instead, it represented one of 'the most liberal policies in relation to the negro yet put forward from any quarter' because it would 'help them win the freedom and dignity of nationhood in their own land'. Mosley omitted to mention that his scheme for white settlement would uproot millions from their land. His idea for 'real separation' was 'so liberal' it was unlikely to find much support in South Africa where white supremacy held sway, he claimed. However, no other solution would suffice, he argued. Genuine democracy in Southern Africa could only result in a 'black majority', which, for Mosley, preordained a reversion to 'jungle and savagery' or 'civil war'. The only beneficiaries would be Washington and Moscow. If they did not follow his strictures, the English would 'pass from history' having failed to embrace their destiny.[124]

'The destruction of the beautifully varied tapestry of nature's design had not yet been made an article of faith by those whose deep desire is to make the world as grey as themselves,' Mosley subsequently wrote. However, 'Europe-a-Nation' with its African appendage had been explicitly racial in its initial conception. Mosley rejected left-wing universalism and egalitarianism on the 'practical grounds' that 'it became all too clear that a grotesque medley of skins and cultures could never get anywhere'. For Mosley 'the argument that every savage was the brother and equal of a European just plainly was not true; every sense and every instinct, all history and knowledge, told us that. Those people were obviously and deeply different.' It was a 'dangerous absurdity' to claim otherwise. 'In fact', claimed Mosley, 'they are obviously not equal in intellect, physique, knowledge, achievement, history or tradition'. Mosley's racial and cultural rejection of egalitarianism reflected his belief that any affirmation of equality would destroy 'the higher in the interests of the lower'. This was the ultimate design of Communism and was 'very welcome' to the 'International Money Power' – a euphemism for the Jews – which could manipulate the 'lower' but not 'the values of the higher type' that served as 'natural barriers to corruption and chaos'. The creed of racial egalitarianism thus served as a solvent, corrupting and degrading the spirit of Western civilisation from within like an ideological Trojan horse until it could be conquered materially.[125]

Fascism and National Socialism 'naturally' revolted against this spectacle of racial abasement but lamentably produced 'too narrow a Nationalism' in the process. This was nevertheless entirely understandable, argued Mosley. 'When you are told that you must kiss Harry the Hottentot on both cheeks as a condition of taking a walk down the street you are apt to confine yourself to the close circle of your own family!' To overcome the military defeat of Fascism, argued Mosley, Europeans must follow the 'natural impulse' of uniting with those 'nearest to us in blood, tradition, mind and spirit' embodied in the 'idea of Kinship', which is 'more in accord with fact and nature than any conception which is purely ideological'. This racial brotherhood included the 'kindred of our same kind' in both Americas who, in accordance with the 'deep realities' of the age, 'all Nature impels them in their final test to feel and think as we do'. This global conception of racial interest and indeed racial hierarchy was the 'New Patriotism' that would embrace 'all of like kind' without, however, 'seeking the unnatural mingling of the old Internationalism'. Mosley's newly enunciated 'universalism of like kind' would serve to regenerate 'our ideals' and unite Europe; spiritually and materially, it would rise like a phoenix from the flames, taking up from where fascism left off as the 'Idea of the Future'.[126]

Nation Europa

The Home Office retained Mosley's passport until 1949 when several political figures including his old friend R.J.G. 'Bob' Boothby MP successfully lobbied for its return. Boothby was an active member of the Consultative Assembly of the Council of Europe in Strasbourg and Mosley vaguely hoped to use the connection to his advantage vis-à-vis his German contacts, though Boothby thought this premature since Germany was not yet a member of the Council. Such enquiries aside, there is little reason to believe Mosley successfully exerted even the slightest influence upon nascent European political structures.[127]

His passport returned to him, Mosley embarked upon a period of frenetic transnational networking with the surviving remnants of fascism after 1945. The importance of such contacts was explained by Alexander Raven Thomson, the leading UM ideologue, in a letter to Enzo Erra, a leading figure in the Fasci d'Azione Rivoluzionaria (FAR – Revolutionary Action Fasces), a fascist terrorist group which was produced as evidence in the 1950 trial of its activists. Thomson's letter explained the nature and objectives of the contacts between extreme right-wing elements in Britain and Italy, as well as the role that such seemingly diminutive political grouplets played in a burgeoning transnational fascist network.[128]

Mosley was a vital figure in this network, attending a series of meetings and conferences in Italy that aimed to bring a semblance of organisational coherence to the remnants of European fascism.[129] The upshot of this activity was the Europäische Soziale Bewegung (ESB – European Social Movement), The ESB was founded during a meeting in Malmö, Sweden, on 7–10 April 1951, at the offices of *Vägen Framåt* (*The Way Ahead*), an organ of Nysvenska Rörelsen (The New Swedish Movement) led by veteran fascist activist Per Engdahl. The ESB subsequently adopted Engdahl's book, *Vasterlandets Förnyelse* (1951), as its ideological bedrock.[130] Despite sending an emissary to the initial Malmö meeting, Mosley kept his distance, however, even though his own ideas regarding the defence of European culture and the need to establish a European 'nation' were broadly congruent with those of the ESB.

This first attempt to establish a pan-European organisation was a failure. Problems of weak organisation, despite efforts to develop a common policy, a coordinating mechanism for its national affiliates and a permanent secretariat housed in Italy, confounded the organisation. Ideological tensions, apparent from the outset, compounded the problem, causing a division between a 'reformist' faction and those who favoured a platform based upon biological racism. These tensions played out between Maurice Bardèche, a French intellectual purged from his university position after 1945 who edited the extreme right review *Défense de l'Occident*, and René Binet, a former left-wing militant who cemented his transition to extreme right ideologue by volunteering for the Waffen-SS. Following his release from prison for joining the SS, Binet, who edited *La Sentinelle* (1949–1952) and *Le Nouveau Prométhée* (1950–1951), also penned a racist treatise titled *Théorie du Racisme* (1950). Their disagreements about the direction post-war French fascism should take were symptomatic of broader dissensions within the wider movement. Bardèche dismissed Binet, a dedicated national socialist and revolutionary militant, as 'a fascist of a puritan type who spends his life founding parties and publishing roneo-typed newsletters'.[131]

Having failed to seize control of the French ESB section, Binet and his acolytes left to help found Le Nouvel ordre européen (NOE – New European Order), an overly anti-Semitic and racist umbrella organisation. The Swiss fascist, Gaston-Armand 'Guy' Amaudruz, editor of *Courrier du Continent*, initially the journal of the Volkspartei der Schweiz (VPS – People's Party of Switzerland), administered the group from Lausanne.[132] Amaudruz had been invited to the Malmö meeting, 'but refused to go, judging that the attendees' conception of Europe did not rest solidly enough on a racial foundation'.[133] The NOE grew rapidly, assembling as many of fifty groups across twenty countries, acting from the outset as a rival to the ideological vision of 'Europe' espoused by the ESB and *ergo* Mosley.[134] ESB leaders were alive to this challenge. In the wake of the schism within the French section, Engdahl toured Europe touting a draft manifesto to ESB national affiliates. He submitted it for formal consideration by the organisations' Executive Committee at a meeting in Innsbruck, Austria, in late February 1953. This internal struggle for ideological hegemony within the pan-European fascist movement did little to diminish the group's already negligible influence. Indeed, in the verdict of the CIA, regardless, the ESB 'had little or no impact on the European political scene'.[135]

Declining to become actively engaged in the internal ESB politicking, Mosley focused his efforts instead upon developing his contacts in Italy and Germany as well as on diffusing his ideas into Franco's Spain, the only extreme right-wing regime to survive the Second World War. Despite a concerted effort to build links with the Falange, the Francoist regime held Mosley at arm's length, however, because Franco sought international rehabilitation as an anti-Communist ally rather than remaining an isolated, authoritarian sideshow. Indeed, the Pact of Madrid signed by Franco and the USA and the Concordat with the Vatican, both in 1953, which paved the way for Spain's membership of the United Nations in 1955, ensured that there was little to be gained from officially associating with Mosley. For his part, Mosley did not delude himself that Francoism and fascism were synonymous. Spanish fascism had 'died' in 1936, when the Republicans executed his old friend José Primo de Rivera, Mosley pronounced.[136] Ultimately, Spain afforded holidaying British fascists the opportunity to wear their banned Blackshirts in public – but little more.

The principal focus of Mosley's organisational efforts centred predictably enough upon the remnants of Fascism and Nazism in Italy and Germany. He assiduously fostered close and enduring personal links with numerous leading figures in the Movimento Sociale Italiano (MSI – Italian Social Movement) including 'The Black Prince' – Junio Valerio Borghese, a former naval officer who had commanded Fascist Italy's feared Decima Flottiglia X-MAS squadrons, which had waged unrestricted anti-partisan warfare. Borghese subsequently served faithfully as an under-secretary in Mussolini's Salò Republic, leading Il Duce to refer to him, admiringly, as 'a condottiere of the last hour'. An Italian court sentenced Borghese to twelve years' imprisonment in 1945. Released in February 1949, he became honorary president of the MSI in December 1951. Borghese, who was fiercely anti-Communist, pro-NATO and, like Mosley, viewed Europe as a 'Third Force', reputedly visited England in 1953, 'in order, it was said, to request financial aid for the MSI from the Mosley group'.[137]

Mosley also worked tirelessly to re-establish contact with numerous extreme right-wing parties, publishing houses and people who were struggling into action amidst the wreckage of occupied Germany. The most important point of contact for Mosley was the Deutsche Reichspartei (DRP – German Party of the Right), which had recently gained five seats in the 1949 Bundestag elections. Mosley was in touch with two of these deputies. The first, Dr Fritz Rössler, headed the party's apparatus in its Niedersachsen stronghold. He had contacted UM whilst held as a POW and subsequently served as a conduit for Mosleyite propaganda into Germany. The second was the party's deputy chairman, Adolf von Thadden, son of a Pomeranian nobleman. He and Mosley developed a particularly close relationship. Von Thadden visited London in 1954 and was guest of honour at a UM dinner at which Mosley bade him to convey the best wishes of 'British Union' to the DRP.[138]

Mosley also forged close links with Werner Naumann, former State Secretary in the Propaganda Ministry, whom Hitler had appointed as Josef Goebbels' successor as Minister of Propaganda in his political testament on 29 April 1945. Naumann was with Hitler in his Berlin bunker until 1 May 1945 when he and several others including Artur Axmann, the Hitler Youth leader and Martin Bormann, Hitler's private secretary sought to break out before the Soviets encircled them. After the war, Naumann had become general manager of H.S. Lucht & Co., a firm run by Lea Lucht, a cousin of the exiled Belgian collaborator, SS-Sturmbannführer Léon Degrelle, the most highly decorated of all foreign Waffen-SS members. Degrelle claimed Hitler had once told him 'If I had a son, I would want him to be like you.'[139]

Naumann was a vital point of contact for Mosley. Through him, Mosley met with figures like Hans-Ulrich Rudel, the fanatical and unrepentant one-legged Luftwaffe pilot.[140] Rudel, lauded as the 'Eagle of the Eastern Front' by the Nazis, had flown some 2,530 combat missions and was credited with destroying 519 tanks, 150 gun emplacements, 800 vehicles and three warships. He was the only member of the German armed forces to receive the Golden Oak Leaves with Sword and Diamonds to the Knights' Cross of the Iron Cross, a medal which was invented for him. Following a brief period of imprisonment, Rudel had departed for Argentina but was persuaded to return to Germany by Naumann in 1952 whereupon, despite being banned from public speaking, he stood as a candidate for the overtly Nazi Sozialistische Reichspartei (SRP – Socialist Reich Party). Mosley subsequently published an English translation of Rudel's memoir, *Stuka Pilot* (1952), as part of an ongoing effort to valorise and mythologise Germany's war in the East as a heroic struggle against Bolshevism and in doing so to reframe, repackage, rehabilitate and normalise Nazi anti-Bolshevism within a Cold War context.[141]

Naumann opted for a different strategy to the overtly Nazi politicking of the SRP, banned by the German state in 1952. Instead, the 'Naumann-Kreis', as the milieu that coalesced around him was called, focused its efforts upon infiltrating democratic parties to gain control of them, the Freie Demokratische Partei (FDP – Free Democratic Party) in Nord-Rhine Westphalia, bearing the brunt of their efforts. This subversive strategy led to Naumann's arrest on 14 January 1953 for unconstitutional activity. Ultimately, however, the charges were dropped. Naumann was freed on 29 July. Separate denazification proceedings taken against him forbad his participation in politics but Naumann disobeyed the injunction, becoming the 'directing force' behind the DRP though he did not publicly participate in its affairs.[142] Mosley met Naumann in Germany on multiple occasions, often with his lawyer, as Naumann sought legal redress against the authorities for his arrest. Despite this setback, the Foreign Office reported that:

> Information from our own sources indicates that Sir Oswald Mosley retains his faith in Naumann as the eventual leader of a Nazi revival in Germany. Both Mosley and Naumann are biding their time in the hope that, when Western Germany has regained her full sovereignty and independence, the circumstances will be favourable for the open proclamation of a new European Movement in which the forces of National Socialism will play a predominant role.[143]

Indeed, the two men remained in regular contact thereafter, affording Mosley the opportunity to extend his own networks. One such conclave in Düsseldorf, in September 1954, coincided with the appearance of François Genoud who contacted Mosley upon his arrival. Genoud, a Swiss citizen who had worked for the Abwehr, the German military intelligence organisation during the war, had become Hitler's literary executor and developed a reputation in the post-war period as a shadowy financier of 'neo-Nazi' initiatives.[144]

Mosley also did some financing of his own. From his Irish pile, he successfully lobbied the Department of Finance in Dublin to relax the rules forbidding Irish residents from opening foreign bank accounts, obviating the requirement for official permission that resulted from the imposition of exchange controls in England. The acquiescence of the Irish authorities enabled Mosley to open an account in Paris and in doing so receive funds directly from a 'Swiss publisher' – possibly Genoud. 'In view of the latest developments it cannot be overlooked that the Swiss funds at his disposal during the past two years might have been used by him to aid political friends in Germany', Finance Minister Sean MacEntee told the Dáil in May 1952.[145] In their briefing note to the minister, Irish officials observed that one reason they bent the rules for Mosley was because, 'he is a man of considerable wealth and should be encouraged to retain his Irish domicile'.[146]

Mosley subsequently took legal action against West German Chancellor Konrad Adenauer after he stated that he had been funding the 'Naumann Kriese' – winning an apology from Adenauer. MI5 obtained evidence that Mosley was indeed dispersing funds to Naumann and his contacts, however. UM activists were despatched on the Hamburg ferry posing as 'tourists' and, upon arrival, would convert their traveller's cheques into Deutschmarks, hand the proceeds to their German contacts, and then depart on the next available ferry back to England.[147] Though Naumann's plans to subvert the nascent German democracy came to naught, he continued to regard Mosley as a trusted personal contact. In 1955, Naumann's son and von Ribbentrop's children stayed with Mosley in Ireland as well as being lodged in London with trusted UM families who took in the children of other prominent Nazis too, including Himmler's daughter.[148]

Determined to stamp his intellectual imprimatur upon extreme right-wing ideological discussions regarding 'Europe', Mosley ensured the translation of his own work into several foreign languages although he prioritised the German: *The Alternative* (1947) appeared in German as *Die Alternative* (1949), but was subsequently revised as *Die Europäische Revolution* (1950). It was popular with figures like Karl-Heinz Priester, a former Waffen-SS liaison officer who edited *Die Europäische Nationale* and would go on to establish the Deutsche Soziale Bewegung, the German ESB section.[149] *The Europe Situation: The Third Force* (1950), which outlined the political and military situation as he saw it in light of the Cold War, and *Europe: Faith and Plan* (1958), which recapitulated his pan-European creed as 'in introduction to thinking as an European', were also rendered into German. They appeared as *Die Rettung des Abendlandes: Die dritte Kraft* (1950) and *Ich Glaube an Europa* (1962) respectively, reflecting Mosley's desire to influence the tone and direction of the pan-European debate as it raged within central European circles.[150] He had some success. The DRP newspaper, *Reichsruf* favourably reviewed *Ich Glaube an Europa*.[151]

Perhaps Mosley's most enduring effort to anchor his ideas at the centre of debate within the extreme right-wing milieu was reflected in his role in the establishment of *Nation Europa*, a hugely important focal point for the dissemination of extreme right-wing ideas, which in 2007 had a circulation of 18,000.[152] Arthur Ehrhardt, a former SS major who had been Heinrich Himmler's anti-partisan warfare expert in the Balkans and Russia, founded *Nation Europa* in 1951, publishing and editing it from the Bavarian town of Coburg until his death in 1971. 'Jean' as Mosley was called in the correspondence, acted as a broker on behalf of a consortium of financial backers (referred to as 'Hans interest') that arranged for an investment of 48,000 Deutschmarks to cover the first two years of *Nation Europa*'s overheads. Naumann was also a key player in the venture, meeting with Mosley on several occasions from May 1952 onwards. There were teething troubles and financial wrangles, however. Ehrhardt resented Naumann's treatment of him as a subordinate, leading Mosley to counsel the latter that 'it is clear that you name must disappear from this matter.... But you can so easily deliver your advice through me. I am at a distance but less hated.' Mosley willingly allowed Naumann to use him as his mouthpiece, presenting Naumann's ideas as his own. This ruse diffused tempers, ensuring that Ehrhardt fell into line with their schemes. The appointment Alexander Raven Thomson to the journal's editorial board in 1952 safeguarded Mosley's ideological investment in *Nation Europa*.[153]

112 *Sir Oswald Mosley*

Despite this early friction, Mosley and Ehrhardt developed a close working relationship that enduring for the remainder of their lives. Mosley frequently used *Nation Europa* as a platform for his ideas. Between 1951 and 1973, he contributed at least twenty-six articles to the journal. In May 1950, Mosley had begun describing his regenerative vision for the future industrial organisation of the 'creative state' that would underpin 'Europe-a-Nation' as 'European Socialism', publishing his further thoughts on the matter in *Nation Europa* in June 1951. This new post-fascist creed would enable humanity to transcend its present limits. 'Nothing is beyond the grasp of the united peoples of Europe', Mosley concluded:

> Let us combine the creative energy, organising genius, and deep culture of the Germans – the persistence, adaptability, and skill of the English in relation to many and diverse peoples – the life wisdom of the French and the charm and genius of their civilisation – the fine flower of the Latin imaginative achievement and the rock form character of the Northern peoples. If we can combine these supreme life forces in one great striving of the human spirit beyond and above this experience of division and disaster, we can enter the second Hellas or Schiller's dream. We can and we will.[154]

Less prosaically, Mosley described this transcendent synthesis of ideas, peoples and nations to the UM annual conference in 1955 in the following terms:

> European Socialism is the development by a fully united Europe of European resources in our own Continent, in white Africa, and in South America, for the benefit of all the people of Europe, and of these other European lands, by every energy and incentive that the active leadership of European government can give to private enterprise, workers ownership, or any other method of progress which science and a dynamic system of government finds most effective for the enrichment of all our people and the lifting of European civilization to ever higher forms of life.[155]

Mosley continued to develop his ideas throughout the 1950s, a process aided by his establishment in March 1953 of *The European*, an 'analytical review' dedicated to 'literature, politics, art and the diverse components of culture within the living and developing organism of modern Europe'.[156] *The European*, together with *Nation Europa*, gave Mosley two important platforms from which to debate his ideas with other extreme right-wing ideologues including Maurice Bardèche and Otto Strasser, though he and Strasser found little common ground. By May 1956, however, Mosley was becoming frustrated with the lack of unanimity evident amongst ideologues and the various 'internationals' that had arisen in competition to the ESB, leading him to announce 'we are coming to the point when we must decide whether we are for or against the main principles'.[157]

Mobilising against immigration

Transnational networking coincided domestically with the emergence of 'coloured immigration', which was soon to become the mainstay of extreme right campaigning. In this, the UM were trailblazers. 'We said it all and we said it first', said Jeffrey Hamm, Mosley's devoted political secretary, of the party's position.[158] Mosley set his imprimatur upon a burgeoning grassroots activism demanding to 'Keep Brixton White'. Michael Ryan, the Brixton UM leader, who spearheaded this initiative, had initially found his attempts to organise in South London countered by fierce anti-fascist opposition. Within two months of the foundation of the UM, Ryan's capacity to hold meetings was already 'dropping rapidly'.[159] Casting round for an emotive 'local issue' around which to mobilise, Ryan had alighted upon 'coloured immigration' into Brixton and, in August 1951, a month after immigration was mentioned for the first time in *Union*, the party began campaigning for a 'Colour Bar' to prevent 'black parasites' from 'living on the hardworking white people'.[160] *Union*, the party newspaper, regularly featured lurid and provocative stories regaling readers with tales of a 'Negro invasion' of 'work shy' West Indians living it up on Public Assistance, supplemented by 'dope-peddling' and 'immoral earnings'.[161] The threat, however, was not economic or cultural; it was primarily biological. Racial miscegenation, warned *Union*, threatened to turn all races 'into one coffee coloured, kinky-haired, slit-eyed, mongrel conglomerate'.[162]

The idea of building a campaign around 'coloured immigration' soon drew Mosley's attention. Party activist Michael Quill recalled the discussions between Ryan and Mosley. 'The conclusion was that Mike Ryan was quite correct to tackle the local issue but we would not spread [the] issue nationally because it was not relevant to other parts of the country.'[163] Ryan had failed to keep local momentum going, but Mosley, recognising the importance of the issue, stepped in to lead on it. Mosley announced his 'Decision on the Coloured Question' on 27 February 1952. Forbidding 'offensive abuse of Negroes', Mosley's pronouncement proffered support for racial 'apartheid' and averred that 'we must prevent the residence of Negroes in Britain'. Party ideologue Alexander Raven Thomson attacked the 'corrupt practices' of democratic politics, lambasting Brixton's 'Jewish' MP Marcus Lipton whom, he claimed, was responsible for the district being 'overrun' by immigrants and thus on the verge of becoming 'Harlem' or worse 'little Africa', thereby establishing an early intellectual link between anti-Semitism and racism which was to prove particularly enduring.[164]

Mosley subsequently developed a programme that 'proved' it was economically viable to repatriate 'coloured' immigrants. His audiences failed to grasp the supposed justice of Mosley's 'humanitarian' nostrums. Bethnal Green UM leader Fred Bailey recalled that when party speakers outlined Mosley's carefully costed programme 'we used to get the remark ... well here's three and eight. Send two back!'[165] Another of Mosley's followers, John Bean, who was active in South London, confirmed that the entire platform quickly degenerated into a 'hate the Nigger' campaign.[166] To test the popularity of racist politicking, UM fielded three candidates in the London borough of Lambeth in the 1952 London County Council elections but they polled just 1,654 votes between them.[167] This represented roughly one vote for every immigrant in the borough.[168] Astute observers noted, however, that 'a number of voters, who were prejudiced against coloured people voted not for union, but to show their support for that aspect of its programme'.[169] It was a vote not so much *for* the UM as *against* immigration. It perhaps represented the maximum support the UM could mobilise based upon anti-immigrant prejudice in the district. Many younger activists despaired at the organisation's failure to exploit this 'burning local issue'.[170] 'Any movement not so discredited as Mosley's at the time could have received twenty per cent of the poll on such an issue as this, if they had handled the matter with some tact and logical argument,' remarked John Bean, who left the party soon afterwards.[171]

The centre of gravity for racist anti-immigration campaigning soon moved to East London where Mosley's factotum, Lawrence 'Alf' Flockhart, struggled to revitalise the party's moribund political apparatus. Flockhart, an inter-war activist with a string of criminal convictions, had recently returned to the movement, to the disgust of many older activists. He had served a two-year stint in prison following his conviction for 'assault with intent to commit buggery' in his room above the offices at the UM headquarters, with a seventeen-year-old youth to whom he had offered a bed after the latter had missed his last train home from nearby Victoria Station. Mosley stood by Flockhart. 'His character is extremely manly', Mosley testified at Flockhart's subsequent trial. 'His faults, if he has any, are those of manhood.' Lady Mosley also provided a character reference. 'I have four children, boys, and he knows my children very well', she told the court. 'I have left him with my children on many occasions. Last summer, he travelled across France with the two boys for me. I have the highest regard for his character.'[172] Following Flockhart's conviction on 28 November, Mosley issued a public statement refusing to recognise the verdict:

> I hereby state that I do not agree with, and do not accept, the allegations made against Flockhart, and that I retain complete confidence in him. The case has proved to me nothing except the facts of the system under which we live – and I was aware of them already. These are just some of the things which keep me in the fight.[173]

Whilst the UM continued to publicly insist that Flockhart's conviction had been a 'frame up', MI5 recorded that the movement was internally split, 'with the more observant and intelligent believing him to be guilty'. Furthermore, this was the first occasion on which there had been any 'real disagreement' between Mosley and his followers regarding the party's internal politics. Equally noteworthy, it 'was one of very few occasions that Mosley failed to expel those who made little secret of their disagreement with his opinion'.[174] Mosley recognised the strength of feeling that prevailed against Flockhart within the party but was determined to restore him to his position. Maurice Pacey, the party's national secretary, warned him that if Flockhart returned 'in a challenging and ambitious mood, there is a danger of a considerable split.' He advised Flockhart's return be 'gradual, tactful and as you say, at the right time and place'. Mosley appears to have heeded the advice. Following his release, Flockhart was despatched for a 'holiday in the country', after which a 'private party' was held in March 1952 to officially welcome him back to the fold.[175]

Having returned to the movement, Mosley appointed Flockhart his Central and East London Area UM Organiser, a controversial choice that aggrieved some local activists and occasioned several resignations.[176] Flockhart worked hard to rebuild his reputation, his organisational efforts rewarded by Mosley who gave him a special award for outstanding services to the Movement at the party's annual conference on 3 October 1954. The party conference itself was also notable for its lack of overt anti-Semitism, which prefaced a further shift in UM racial policy. 'Strangely enough only two members present appeared to advocate an extension of anti-Semitic activity,' noted MI5. This was not the result of any principled stance, however. Mosley told those present that 'it is unnecessary to actually print the world "Jew", their names give them away'. The UM relegated anti-Semitism to innuendo rather than policy – in line with Mosley's oft-cited claim that he was not attacking Jews as a race 'but only those individual members who were engaged in criminal activities'.[177] Even so, Flockhart's dogged 'racial line' and the increased resonance of anti-black racism was hard for some of the party's stalwart anti-Semites to stomach, which spilt out at the party's 1955 annual conference.[178]

Nonetheless, Flockhart remained focused upon extending the 'Keep Brixton White' campaign into the East End. He was 'collecting all available information which can be used as adverse publicity against the influx of coloured people into this country and is endeavouring to whip up enthusiasm amongst Union Movement members'.[179] This material was fed into the pages of *East London Blackshirt*, edited by Flockhart, which together with a range of local publications including *East End Worker*, *East End Blackshirt* and *South Hackney Blackshirt*, were saturated with racist invective. 'Flockhart's line of policy is simple,' noted MI5 of his strategy: 'Britain for the Whiteman.' Racial propagandising and the orchestration of racial violence went together. As MI5 observed:

> Flockhart has indicated that he is quite willing to organize violence if he can avoid it personally and if present trends continue the possibility of disturbances in East London next year cannot be discounted, the view is also held that a few fights, arrests and court cases will give the Union Movement the impetus it wants. It is claimed that [racist] slogans against the coloured elements are appearing in increasing numbers, not only in East London but in places such as Bristol.[180]

To focus the campaign and to build its momentum, Flockhart ensured that UM stood candidates on the immigration issue in local elections in the following spring. One such was Harry Jones who stood as an 'East London Blackshirt' pledging to halt the 'Negro invasion'. He received 33 per cent of the vote in a municipal by-election in Moorfields ward in Shoreditch in January 1955. Immigration, noted one anti-fascist observer, 'has given the Blackshirts a very strong platform – they are adding fire to the agitation – and their propaganda is bringing new recruits to their ranks'. It brought a measure of financial stability too. Elated with the result, in the LCC elections shortly afterwards, the UM stood nine 'Blackshirts' across Shoreditch, Bethnal Green and Brixton (where its three candidates stood on the 'vital issue' of immigration pledging to 'stop the negro invasion' and 'Keep Brixton White').[181] More pertinently perhaps, another report observed 'anti-Semitism did not openly appear in their programmes at all'. The combined poll totalled 5,053 votes, less than one-fifth of the vote obtained by the three Labour candidates who all won comfortably.[182]

However, during this ideological and strategic recalibration, the UM was suddenly plunged into crisis. With the death of Mosley's chief lieutenant Alexander Raven Thomson in 1955, Flockhart had become the central figure within the party – 'completely in charge' of UM affairs. Indeed, Mosley gave Flockhart a 'free hand' to act as he saw fit, entrusting him with the party's contacts with the Spanish Falange, which by this juncture had been thoroughly purged of its revolutionary elements leaving it as little more than a pliable tool for Francoism.[183] It was even more embarrassing for Mosley then when Flockhart was arrested again in June 1956; this time for sexually assaulting a twelve-year-old boy in his rooms at the UM headquarters. Flockhart again claimed it was a 'frame-up' but this time most UM activists disowned him.[184] 'We have finished with him', Lady Mosley stated. 'It would only happen again. He was obviously guilty, yet would not take advice and plead guilty so that he might be let off to have medical treatment.' Jeffrey Hamm, the UM Northern organiser replaced Flockhart. He was 'much nicer' remarked Lady Mosley, 'so polite and pleasant on the telephone; he even has cultural interests'.[185]

The prevalence of the 'old guard' now running the movement – former low-ranking BUF functionaries like Jeffrey Hamm and Robert Row – soon gave the UM 'a depressingly familiar look', noted Mosley's biographer Robert Skidelsky, who observed that 'Like the Bourbons, the fascists seemed to have learnt nothing and forgotten nothing.'[186] A series of 'In Memoriam' notices to Mussolini and Hitler, published in *Union* during 1956, highlighted this ideological recidivism.[187] The UM resembled less a political party than a nostalgic cargo cult. When the party newspaper *Union* ceased publication on 7 September 1957, *Action*, the name of the 1930s BUF newspaper, seamlessly replaced it a fortnight later.

Notting Hill

Racist violence exploded in Notting Hill, West London on 29 August 1958. Sporadic violence continued until 3 September. There were 108 arrests: seventy-two white and thirty-six black. Gangs of local white youths, often assumed to be 'Teddy Boys' were largely responsible for perpetrating the violence rather than fascists, though they were well placed to exploit simmering tensions in the aftermath.[188] The UM had actively campaigned in the borough for several years. Indeed, Mosley had chosen Kensington Town Hall in 1956 for his first speech after returning from France to re-engage in domestic politics. Westminster Council was one of the very few local authorities to allow Mosley to use their property. John R. Wood, the local branch leader, regularly sold party newspapers outside Notting Hill Gate tube station whilst Jeffrey Hamm, the UM political secretary, lived at 46 Princedale Road. Colin Jordan's White Defence League operated from number 74. The UM anticipated that it was campaigning on fertile ground. 'Times have changed. The people are waking up. Once against our critics can't take it. But stick close, boys, and hang on tight. There's a lot more coming,' *Action* had declared a month before the riots.[189]

The violence had caught the UM off guard, however. Indeed, on the day before the riots, the *Daily Express* pictured Mosley sunbathing at a Venice Lido, in 'black shorts' of course.[190] The UM youth leader Trevor Grundy remembered being told by a colleague:

> It's like a dream come true and I don't think even the Old Man [Mosley] knew anything about it. I mean, it just sort of happened and now everyone is looking to OM to lead them. You'll really be able to take off with the youth league – there are thousands of kids just waiting to be told what to do. I tell you, it could be bigger than the East End before the war.[191]

The party quickly mobilised to exploit the situation, its activists proselytising in local pubs and they held meetings in the streets during the riots after which portions of the audience 'moved off in an excited state' frequently to go 'nigger hunting'. *Kensington News* reported that one UM meeting on 1 September conducted by Hamm, concluded with a shower of racist leaflets and a cry of 'Get Rid of Them!'

> …A cry exploded as the mob rushed off shouting 'Kill the Niggers'. Women grabbed their small children and followed. Dogs ran in among the crowds barking. Confusion reigned everywhere. Police cars and vans tried to cut off the mob, without success. Within half an hour the crowd, by now over a thousand strong, had broken scores of windows. Women from top floor windows laughed as they called down to the throng 'Go on Boys, get yourselves some blacks'.[192]

On 15 September, nine white youths, arrested just prior to the riots for 'nigger hunting', were jailed for four years apiece. The religion of the judge, Mr Justice Salmon, the first Jewish judge to sit in the Queen's Bench Division since Lord Reading, thirty years previously, did not escape the notice of Mosleyites.[193] 'I knew the families of a number of these lads, and frequently visited their homes,' stated Hamm who campaigned 'relentlessly' but without success on their behalf against the 'savage' sentences.[194]

Following the riots, the UM liberally distributed copies of *The Coloured Invasion* (1958) throughout the borough. The pamphlet blamed the 'coloured invasion' upon successive British governments for signing a 'Black Pact' with Cuba in 1951 and 1953, which replaced West Indian sugar with Cuban produce – to the ruination of the West Indian sugar industry. The subsequent poverty this created, argued the UM, pushed people to emigrate to Britain resulting in 'black belts' in British cities, increasingly blighted by public health issues and drugs – the blame being laid squarely at the door of 'coloured men'. Unscrupulous landlords and racketeers fuelled this social catastrophe, filling properties with immigrants whose 'all-night calypso parties' drove out white tenants; 'often disabled ex-servicemen and solitary old age pensioners', it argued emotively. The consequent increase in unskilled labour undermined white workers' wages, exacerbating racial tensions whilst the 'colour bar' drove frustrated immigrants into the arms of the Communists who 'have no scruples in using them for any dirty work'. Mosley's solution was to invest in the West Indies, rebuild its industries and guarantee 'permanent markets' for their produce so that immigrants 'would then want to go home fast'. Britain should be given Dominion status, demanded *The Coloured Invasion*, enabling it to expel all 'undesirable British subjects of overseas origin' though students would still be tolerated, their presence restricted to a 'limited period' to encourage them to 'go home to improve their countries'.[195]

Mosley's focus upon housing as a wedge issue with regards immigration was especially divisive in the broader context of an already crisis-ridden London housing market caused by pressure on central London land and the liberalisation of rent control in 1957.[196] Having set the ball rolling in North Kensington, Mosley then departed for Johannesburg in February 1959 where, after consultation with 'leading' South Africans, he expanded upon his geopolitical goal of extending apartheid to encompass the entire continent. South Africa, Southern Rhodesia, part of its Northern neighbour, Tanganyika and Kenya should form a 'broad white backbone' that would extend across the Sahara to Algeria, he argued. The first and last countries on this list were the anchors of Mosley's scheme. 'Algeria is the bridge between Europe and Africa, and South Africa is the wide, firm base of the white man's presence in Africa'. On either side of this racial spine, stretching across the high plateau, the larger part of the continent with its warmer climate and rich lands would be black 'Bantustans', free from white interference. This was a 'fair and clear' policy, he argued, giving both black and white the opportunity for a 'full life with the level of civilisation they can reach through their own efforts'. This was Mosley's 'vision splendid' – his scheme to prevent the 'decay' and inevitable sliding from history of European civilisation.[197]

Mosley stayed with Ivor Benson, the *Rand Daily Mail*'s chief assistant editor. Benson's employer had terminated his employment after he penned an editorial praising Mosley as 'a man with exciting political associations', who stood for 'the strong Right wing in political thought'. In an added twist, whilst *Mail* reporters scurried hither and thither trying to elicit a comment from Mosley during his visit, Benson concealed from his colleagues the fact that Mosley was staying with him. Benson subsequently found gainful employment in Ian Smith's Rhodesian regime and became notable as an anti-Semitic writer.[198] Mosley informed the media that he had called on certain Cabinet Ministers for 'purely courteous reasons' and shortly afterwards he received official sanction for *Action* to be sold at state-owned railway bookstalls. Mosley also used the opportunity to publicise the activities of the 'Europe–Africa Association', which had been formed in the previous October by Deryck Alexander, a UM activist residing in South Africa who had formed a 'Friends of

South Africa' group to serve as an 'information service to tell the truth to the people of Britain about the Nationalists in South Africa'. The Afrikaans press were receptive to Mosley, their English-speaking counterparts less so, denouncing this 'undesirable visitor'.[199]

Following his return to England, Mosley announced, at a meeting in Argyll Hall, Kensington on 6 April 1959, that he would stand for Kensington North in the general election, at that time another six months away. Mosley had not stood for Parliament since 1931. He did this, he later claimed, so that history could record that he had given the British people 'a chance to express their opinion on the acute question of coloured immigration'.[200] The announcement re-energised his activist base. 'It will be bigger than the East End', Hamm told a meeting of excited activists.

> Bigger than anything any of us have seen before in Britain. And if we're prepared to dedicate ourselves in a way that we've never dedicated ourselves before, we'll win and in that mighty process we'll win back the soul of Britain.[201]

Seeking to embed himself within the constituency, Mosley opened a 'second headquarters' at 47 Kensington Park Road from whence he and Hamm held weekly surgeries for local people largely on issues relating to housing and race though Special Branch questioned the extent to which local residents availed themselves of such a facility.[202] Seeking to entrench themselves further in the local community, UM activists engaged in low-level community action offering, for instance, to help collect refuse.[203] *North Kensington Leader*, which had first appeared in October 1958, shortly after the riots, appealed to electors through a melange of local issues and racism. It was distributed free of charge to every house in the borough as part of Mosley's saturation strategy. *North Kensington Leader* drew attention to the frightful conditions prevailing in many parts of the constituency, publishing photographs of the destitute conditions in which many residents lived whilst claiming that Mosley's campaign had spurred the local Public Health Inspectors and the Borough Council to action. The dominant message was that the only solution to such destitution was the repatriation of 'coloured' immigrants.[204] Mosley was portrayed as the redoubtable defender of the white working class, ignored and abandoned by the three main parties but especially by the Labour party who, it argued, favoured immigrants over white residents, a theme that has since become central to extreme right-wing campaigning.[205]

Without repatriation, the future for British society was bleak. Mosley's prognosis drew in part upon on his interpretation of the American paradigm. 'The Americans had inherited their problem', he wrote following the Watts Ghetto riots in 1965, 'but British government deliberately created our problem. This seemed to me in long-term policy to be raving insanity.'[206] American correspondents applauded Mosley's stance, one praising him for having the courage to stand against 'the Black cancer growing in the very heart of the British nation, London'.[207]

Not everyone believed that the message was robust enough. One UM activist argued that:

> instead of writing moderate articles in a paper which nobody reads, we should get hold of an immigrant and hang him upside-down from Blackfriars Bridge with a notice round his neck saying, 'Coloured's Go Home. That would give us the publicity we need to kick off the campaign and get Mosley elected.[208]

Mosley reprimanded the man who later recalled 'He shouted at me and said, "Never do that again, Shaw". Then, God's Truth, he looked at me and he winked'.[209] Mosley's appears to have tolerated such activism. He allegedly told one journalist who had questioned the party's racism: 'it takes all kinds to make a political movement. We need these people. In our kind of politics one needs to be as good at a punch up as at talking to a university professor.'[210]

Thus, Mosley actively courted support from local 'Teddy Boys' whom he called 'fine types' who were part of a 'vital' and 'virile' movement 'which is what youth should be'. Theirs were 'the normal, healthy reactions of vigorous young men' rebelling against the 'corrupt and finally destructive values of a rotten society'. This energy Mosley sought to harness. The best place for a 'Teddy Boy', he wrote, was 'in a serious political movement' – UM – that 'obeys the law not to organise as an army, but it has the spirit of an army and not of the mob'.[211] Such overtures won Mosley some support from both the local youth and sections of the Irish community.[212] 'Mosley walked to meetings and was followed by his longtime supporters and often hundreds of Teds,' recalled one former follower, 'who thought it was great to hear this aristocratic figure articulating their fouler thoughts about non-whites. West Indians stood and stared as he walked past; most seemed ignorant of who he was, or quite indifferent.' Two of Mosley's sons, Max and Alexander, also joined the campaign, canvassing for their father. The *Daily Mirror* photographed the two teenagers dressed in 'teddy boy' suits. The tone of Mosley's campaign was perhaps deliberately messianic. 'He is Coming' read campaign posters, soon defaced with predictably lewd innuendo.[213]

On 17 May, as Mosley's campaign gathered momentum, a group of white youths attacked Kelso Cochrane, a young Antiguan carpenter, one of whom stabbed him on the corner of Southam Street and Golbourne Road, a short distance from the epicentre of the previous autumn's riots. Cochrane died shortly afterwards.[214] Two days later Mosley issued a statement, echoing that of the police, which denied the killing had racist motivation whilst disclaiming any responsibility for fuelling the climate in which had led to Cochrane's death with equal vehemence. *Action* blamed the media. 'Saint Kelso was created by them overnight, the victim of "racial hatred", in the hope of turning people against Mosley', it declared whilst asserting that the media ignored incidents of 'race-hatred' from blacks directed towards whites, including what it claimed were racist murders of whites by blacks. 'Saint Kelso' by comparison was a manufactured 'martyr' used to 'smear' Mosley.[215]

Sir Patrick Spens MP for the neighbouring Kensington South constituency stated it was 'absolutely certain' there would be more trouble in Notting Hill if Mosley persisted with racist rhetoric. Mosley denied this, claiming he advocated 'votes not violence'.[216] He failed to convince. Many of those at Cochrane's funeral believed Mosley's campaign had created an atmosphere of license that had enabled the killing. 'Many of them were quite angry during the funeral', recalled one mourner, 'and they were accusing Mosley for it, they were openly shouting that this was a Mosley thing'.[217] These perceptions were only heightened after Peter Dawson, the UM West London organiser boasted to the *Sunday People* that the killer 'was one of the Union mob … a great guy. Did it to teach the nigs a lesson. But none of us in the movement would tell the police a thing'.[218] In response to the accompanying article (titled 'the Biggest Bully in Britain is Unmasked'), Dawson wrote to *The People* stating:

> In Ken Gardner's attack on me … he says rightly that I know the name of Kelso Cochrane's killer. But he is wrong when he calls Cochrane a 'worker'. In fact he was a gangster of the worst possible type – deported from America for criminal activities and

carrying on a profession as a dope peddler when he arrived in Great Britain. The facts are: he pulled a knife on a friend of mine, my friend disarmed him and in the process Cochrane stabbed himself.[219]

Dawson's claims, likely racist fantasy, confirmed many in their belief that UM bore responsibility for Cochrane's killing. Police never solved the case though journalist Mark Olden has since named Patrick Digby, one of the police's initial suspects, as Cochrane's likely killer.[220]

Digby was friends with Peter and Mark Bell, two brothers from an underworld family well known to police.[221] During summer 1959, police charged both men with assaulting a West Indian medical student, Fitzgerald Fraser, and his wife. Police also charged Peter Bell with firing a shotgun at a West Indian painter, Alfonso Nugent.[222] Jeffrey Hamm boasted in his memoirs that he knew many local 'villains' personally 'and am never ashamed to admit that they were my friends'.[223] The Bells were undoubtedly part of this retinue. Their family approached Mosley for help. He and his solicitor were subsequently present throughout the proceedings against the Bell brothers at the Old Bailey. *Action* splashed their acquittal in October 1959 across its front page, proclaiming that 'to have a reputation with the police of not liking Negroes was to wear a ticket which, at the first shadow of opportunity, would land a young man in gaol'.[224]

Barred from holding meetings on council property following Cochrane's killing, Mosley took to the streets. He addressed roughly four street-corner meetings a night for several weeks during July, including one on 21 July on the corner of Golbourne Road and Southam Street, the site of Cochrane's murder only two months previously.[225] His speeches remained inflammatory. Addressing a meeting in Clydesdale Road in August, Mosley spuriously accused West Indians of living off immoral earnings – a charge contradicted by the facts.[226] Mosley also accused immigrants of playing 'juke boxes' all night.

> Our people can't get a wink of sleep. In the past, they have had the neighbourhood turned over to them.… Unless you stop here and now, your children in five years' time will see four coloured men for everyone here today.[227]

To forestall this cultural and demographic displacement, Mosley promised that, if elected, 'everyday' he would table 'dozens' of Parliamentary Questions 'naming brothels, clubs and places where they have these juke boxes', thus embarrassing the police into action. He advocated the establishment of neighbourhood 'watch committees' to highlight the issue and to 'raise such an uproar' that the government would be compelled to act. Interrupted by a car trying to edge its way through the crowd Mosley quipped, upon noticing its driver was a West Indian, 'they'll all be on their way soon'.[228]

Mosley's autobiography made no mention of such incidents, preferring instead to remember that his North Kensington election meetings 'were the largest open-air gatherings I have ever addressed since before the war, and the development of the campaign produced an extraordinary mass enthusiasm'.[229] Police reports concur that Mosley was 'in the main well received' by 'predominantly white' audiences. As polling day approached, Mosley's campaign intensified. Between 18 August and 7 October, Mosley addressed fifty-one outdoor meetings with audiences varying from between 50 to 1,200.[230] The meetings were sometimes rowdy affairs, blighted by violence and arrests. Following one meeting on 9 September, thirty police officers had to be deployed outside UM headquarters after a fifty-strong crowd 'many of them coloured' gathered outside. Someone hurled a brick through the window. 'For a moment we thought a nasty situation was going to develop', stated one UM activist but the police succeeded in dispersing the crowd without further trouble.[231]

Mosley denied that his platform was 'racialist' but it was apparent to nearly everyone that it was. Dan Jacobson recorded an atmospheric account of one of Mosley's outdoor election meetings. 'There was one issue, and one issue only, on which Mosley was fighting the election: the Negroes,' noted Jacobson:

> 'Get them off our backs,' the young man cried; 'Deport them – in a humane British way,' Mosley said more urbanely: but the crowd wasn't fooled for a moment by his urbanity or his humanity. 'Dirty niggers! F – ing Spades! Baboons, baboons, baboons!' they cried in support, and Mosley lifted his hand to acknowledge their fervour. There were no West Indians in the crowd, or if there were, they were at its very outskirts; previously, several had passed through the crowd, without any of them being molested in any way. Interrupters were, however, very promptly silenced by the volume of noise produced by Mosley's supporters, who cried at them 'Jew-boy! Israel! F – ing Jew!'[232]

Jacobson was not alone in experiencing this side of Mosley's Kensington campaign. Paul Barker recalled attending a Mosley meeting in Golbourne Road and experiencing 'that barking voice, those clutching gestures'. When he objected to the 'drip, drip, drip of innuendo', one of Mosley's henchmen informed him 'Go back to Jerusalem, sheenie!'[233]

Insofar as it is possible to ascertain, most black residents of Notting Hill Gate reacted to Mosley's campaign against them with quiet diffidence. The future poet and playwright, E.A. Markham, who had emigrated from Montserrat in 1956 to join his family, recalled a UM rally addressed by Mosley from a podium virtually outside their house in Bevington Road where they were the only black-owned household. His cousin, on leave from the Army, pointedly stood in the crowd wearing his military uniform to show that he fought defending his country and was not on the dole or living off immoral earnings, as the fascists alleged. The gesture also quietly demonstrating that 'here is a black man, a soldier; emerging from his house; you may have targeted this house, you have brought your rabble to this address, but this house, the family in this house, are not a push over'.[234]

In seeking to mobilise racial prejudice, Mosley exhibited once again his characteristic failure of judgement, however. He would deploy base racist rhetoric when addressing audiences comprising the Roman Catholic Church, a reporter from *The Times* and the young novelist Colin Wilson feted for his book *The Outsider* (1956), which had marked him out as a rising literary star, using epithets such as 'Lassie for dogs and Kitty Kat for Wogs'. Yet, when addressing working-class Irish women, he would launch into a lengthy disquisition on the Greek philosophers he had read whilst interned. In the latter case, one woman stood up and stated 'Sir Oswald, I don't know about your Greeks, but I've got niggers in my basement.'[235] Mosley's racist demagoguery alienated some of his more cerebral following for whom, noted his biographer, he became if not an idol with feet of clay, then at the very least a hero 'with feet planted in some pretty unappetising soil'.[236]

Mosley's platform also caused concern amongst those closest to him. His wife sent him a memorandum outlining her belief that the racism saturating party publications was 'so repugnant to intelligent people who might otherwise heed our economic argument: "Fuzzie Wuzzies" "Hottentots" ... do not play into the hands of those who imagine our policy is based on hatred of blacks'.[237] More forthright, Mosley's son, Nicholas, came to see quite acutely, 'that while the right hand dealt with grandiose ideas and glory, the left hand let the rat out of the sewer'.[238] Nicholas wrote to his father asking pointedly why, if were he serious about countering the impression that his movement thrived on racist prejudice, he did not issue:

> Instructions to avoid, in speech and writing and action, all controversial racial issues like the plague: there would be orders, surely, to hold meetings anywhere in London rather than Notting Hill: to keep all sneering references to colour out of *Action*: and when any unfortunate incidents did occur through the stupidity or indiscipline of subordinates, then immediately to take disciplinary steps against the subordinate and to publicise these steps fully, and with apologies to those concerned, in the national press. Failure to take this sort of action seems only to mean that in spite of your words on paper, your intention is not seriously to eradicate from people's minds the impression of your need for racial hatred.[239]

Mosley responded briefly, defying his son to produce any concrete evidence that UM meetings in Notting Hill had resulted in violence. Nicholas' fears were hardly allayed when he attended one of his father's campaign meetings unannounced:

> There was Dad on top of a van again and bellowing; so much older now with his grey hair and grey suit; it was true the crowd around him was quiet and respectful. I had expected that he at least would be putting over the aspect of his case that was reasonable; but instead – I still find it difficult to believe this but other witnesses have confirmed it – there he was roaring on about such things as black men being able to live on tins of cat food, and teenager girls being kept by gangs of blacks in attics. And there were all the clean-faced young men round his van guarding him; and somewhere, I suppose, the fingers of the devotees of the dark god tearing at him.[240]

Nicholas cogitated on such incidences at length to understand what drove his father:

> How on earth was it that the person who had been so serene and unresentful in prison was now once more acting like an insecure racist with a virulent chip of his shoulder? This was his only chance of getting power? But did he now really want or need this sort of power? It seemed that my father was just choosing to do what he was good at, which was standing on top of a loudspeaker-van and bellowing to an adoring crowd. So this was his addiction?[241]

In the immediate aftermath of the meeting, however, his reaction was visceral. Nicholas confronted his father in his office and

> spewed it all out ... my father was not only a racialist but was using racialism to destroy himself; what he was doing was not only wrong it was squalid; he had done this before, he was doing it again, was he do crazy not to know what he was doing?[242]

For good measure, Nicholas threw in that Mosley was a 'lousy father', after which his father declared: 'I will never speak to you again!' Nicholas countered: 'well, I'll always speak to you'.[243] Seven years passed before they spoke again.[244]

Despite costing him his relationship with his son, Mosley continued believing the dividends of his racist campaign were worth the price. Deluding himself that his relations with the white electorate had gone 'from strength to strength', Mosley believed 'The canvass was a winning canvass, if I ever saw one ... it looked all over like a winning fight.'[245] On the eve of poll, householders in North Kensington received Mosley's *Message to Electors*, pledging to end 'coloured immigration' and the 'alien' way of life that British people were being 'forced to accept'. It promised to fight for better housing for local families whose plight he explicitly linked to immigration as a prelude to building a 'new Britain in a world at peace' within the context of the union of Europe. Race was central. 'Remember too', stated Mosley's *Message to Electors*,

> that a vote for any of the other parties will mean FIVE coloured men will be here after ten years for every ONE here today unless you stop it now. This is your last chance to save the Britain we know and love, and the future of our children.[246]

The electorate rejected Mosley's 'last chance'. He polled 2,821 votes (8.1 per cent) out of 34,912 votes cast and lost his deposit. The dismal result was 'one of the chief surprises of my life', Mosley lamented.[247] The shock appears to have been his alone. The *Guardian* commented six days before polling day that although the atmosphere remained 'a bit tense and unreal ... it begins to look as if the storm may not break'.[248] His followers were unprepared for the defeat, however. 'Not only were all our women supporters in tears, but many of the men too wept unashamedly, shocked and stunned by this anti-climax,' recalled Hamm.[249]

Mosley remained unmoved by his failure stating 'in a similar period another movement – similar only in that they stood for great changes – polled 2% in 1928'.[250] Whilst his comparison was telling, Mosley's misreading of history coupled with his own overweening self-belief meant that he was unable to realise that he was 'a spectacle rather than a spokesman' for the white working class of Kensington North.[251] Diana Mosley recognised what her husband did not: though Mosley 'excites his audiences' that 'doesn't necessarily make them vote', though she too struggled to reconcile the enthusiasm with which he was greeted with the meagre vote and low turnout.[252]

Mosley was unable to comprehend that his racist strategy polarised opinion against him and was thus counterproductive. As one astute commentator noted contemporaneously:

> The Mosleyites have the virtue – if that is the word – of putting into blunt, ugly phrases what some people were prepared to think but not say out loud. Perhaps in a curious way, this is a healthy thing. It has removed the temptation for any other candidate to try to curry sly favour with the racialists for the sake of a few votes. You either run with the Mosley pack or you do not. It is as simple as that. There is no use in trying to pad about somewhere in between.[253]

For this reason, Mosley's intervention made no discernible impact upon British immigration policy.[254] Following Mosley's defeat, *Action* reverted to anti-Semitic arguments, claiming that behind the 'black takeover of British homes' stood the 'usury racket'. 'Old Uncle Shylock is still the Tory patron saint,' proclaimed the newspaper, hinting once more that Jews profited from immigration.[255]

Post-mortem

Action's racist rhetoric gave Colin Wilson pause for thought. The young author's fame, accrued following publication of *The Outsider* (1956), which sold 20,000 copies in six months, had 'crashed as quickly as it had grown' and Wilson's literary reputation was already dissipating.[256] He had, however, gathered around himself a small clique of anti-humanist writers that included Stuart Holroyd, author of *Emergence from Chaos* (1957), which greatly influenced Wilson, and Bill Hopkins whose poorly reviewed novel, *The Divine and the Decay* (1957), was dismissed by one critic as 'an adolescent power-fantasy' in 'openly Fascist form'.[257] Holroyd later wrote that the group cohered around shared conception of man 'as a creature with spiritual hunger, a dynamic evolutionary drive' which led them to define themselves as 'religious existentialists' though detractors dismissed them as 'spiritual fascists'. Hopkins, given to breathless pronouncements about the need for fanaticism, founded the Spartacan Society. The name symbolised their revolt. They held discussions and lectures; one staged at the Belgravia home of liberal political hopeful Oliver Moxon. They eventually gained a nucleus of forty to fifty members, and the 'fascist' tag.[258]

Mosley took a keen interest in Wilson's work, his curiosity undoubtedly piqued by the Society's belief in the 'dynamic evolutionary drive', which chimed with his own 'doctrine of higher forms'. *The European* reviewed *The Outsider* in February 1957. 'European' – the pen-name Mosley used – lauded the book. For his part, Wilson sympathised with Mosley's political predicament, egotistically believing they were both men of great ideas unfairly maligned and obscured by lesser men.[259] Perhaps with these parallels in mind, not to mention a desire to associate himself with the 'angry young men' zeitgeist, Mosley invited Wilson, Hopkins and Holroyd for drinks at his son's Chelsea flat in March 1958. Holroyd recorded in his diary that:

> He [Mosley] received us very cordially, and I think was rather playing to impress us with his charm and culture. We sat and drank Scotch and it gradually got quite dark in the room as we talked. He was trying to win us to his political views of European Union, which I find sympathetic because of my sense of cultural affiliation with Europe. But I have doubts about whether a way out of the present international situation would be to create a third power bloc in the world constituting Europe and Not Africa.[260]

In his autobiography, Holroyd, who omitted to mention his own presence at the meeting, stated that Hopkins thought Mosley, 'one of the most able and intelligent men in British politics this century, and an example of how the mediocrities that made up the Establishment ruthlessly put down a man with talent and vision' and that, because of Hitler and the Holocaust, 'European man has been paralysed ever since.' Despite their sympathies, the three men appear to have regarded the visit as a 'social call', accepting Mosley's invitation more out of 'curiosity' than political conviction.[261]

Wilson was historically and politically naïve, however. Having proclaimed Mosley to be a 'rather a decent chap', Wilson's subsequent interview with a journalist revealed that he 'had no knowledge *whatever* of Mosley and the British Union of Fascists, and, even more amazing, nothing but the vaguest notion of the big political issues of the Thirties and Forties.'[262] Wilson's initial attraction to Mosley's philosophical ideas collided with the reality of his racist street politicking in Kensington North. Wilson conducted his own post-mortem into the reasons for Mosley's defeat. Initially, Mosley's decision to stand for Parliament had seemed to Wilson, who approved of his political programme, 'an excellent idea'. Walking through Notting Hill with Hopkins the weekend before the election raised serious questions about Mosley's leadership and strategy, however:

As we turned into Chepstow Road, a loudspeaker van came past, blaring 'Get the niggers out of England. Vote for Mosley. He will free England from niggers.' We were in a bus queue with several Jamaicans in it. They didn't look angry or intimidated; only appallingly embarrassed, as if their privacy had suddenly been invaded. Abruptly, I felt intensely ashamed for my own countrymen.[263]

Mosley had denied to Wilson that he was either 'anti-negro or anti-Jewish'. On the contrary, 'his policy was pro-negro; he hoped to find all these exiled West Indians homes and jobs in their own country'. Wilson was inclined to believe Mosley 'although his account of what went on before the war hardly tallies with that of certain of my Jewish friends.' Furthermore, Wilson considered Mosley's methods betrayed 'a disturbing lack of insight into his own time'. Either Mosley exercised no control over his followers and was thus guilty of 'incompetence', argued Wilson, or, if he was responsible for the strategy, 'then it is the worst kind of incompetence, because it shows a completely false sizing-up of his opponents.' Wilson wrestled to reconcile the duality between Mosley's thought and action. 'I cannot identify myself with him closely enough', he wrote.

> If I imagine myself in his position, with the type of followers he seems to have attracted, I cannot ask myself the question: 'How would *you* deal with the situation?' Because I *wouldn't*. I'd pull out and get back to writing books.[264]

Wilson's critical exculpation drew scathing comment from *Daily Mirror* columnist 'Cassandra'.[265] Wilson complained the article was 'daft' and 'dishonest'. 'Cassandra' retorted 'If you care to have a cautious honeymoon with Mosley and his gang, do so by all means.'[266] Mosley sought to intervene, denying responsibility for the war, its horrors or indeed the speaker van that Wilson had heard. It must have belonged to another organisation 'which had intervened without my consent', he claimed. 'I am not trying to discredit either Sir Oswald or Mr Wilson,' noted 'Cassandra'. 'They do it for themselves with an eloquence and force that I cannot match.' The affair, which highlighted Wilson's sympathy for Mosley, did very little for his already waning literary reputation.[267]

Privately, Mosley had hard words for Wilson too, writing to him to deny many of his claims and challenging him to substantiate others. Wilson's assertions that he lacked control over his own followers incensed Mosley who also bristled at Wilson's fondness for the 'atmosphere' immigration had lent Notting Hill. 'Really, Colin, really – this is the quintessence of the bourgeois attitude – and in you of all people', he remarked.[268] Mosley conceded, however, that *Action* was 'far from satisfactory'. From April 1960, Mosley planned to spend more time in Britain, after which 'I hope to see much more of you.' Indeed, despite their disagreement, Mosley still regarded Wilson as useful to his cause. 'You have now reached the point where you can say what you think', Mosley wrote him,

> and the more original and controversial you are the more the public will buy you. In relation to us, a 'detached, in between position' for you, insisting on 'impartial discussion' is at present ideal. It is a position which most people will understand and appreciate. From our point of view the more everything is discussed and clarified the better.[269]

Mosley's own post-mortem came to a radically different conclusion. He had not lost. Denigrating democracy, Mosley claimed the result was rigged. Citing 'substantial irregularities', Mosley petitioned the High Court to scrutinise the ballot papers on the grounds of alleged fraud. There was no evidence anyone had tampered with the ballot. It was, he later admitted, a 'fishing expedition'. The Royal Courts of Justice heard Mosley's petition on 4 April 1960. The case confirmed, however, that Mosley had misread his canvass returns as concrete assertions of support. A canvass of 739 voters shown in the electoral register as having not voted revealed that 111 had. Mosley was only able to get twenty to agree to testify in court. Even this proved an unreliable cohort. Ten of those summonsed failed to appear.[270] Those that did appear hardly helped Mosley's case. 'One man who had signed something in favour of Sir O. [sic] said "I was wild at being interrupted while watching TV – I'd have signed anything."'[271] Mosley 'hadn't enough evidence for his case, which of course we knew & in the nature of things he couldn't have', admitted Diana Mosley privately.[272] Though the case highlighted minor infractions of electoral law, the court dismissed Mosley's petition, leaving Mosley liable for costs.[273] Kensington North served to reinforce Mosley's belief that the electorate would only respond favourably to his radical, racist panaceas when the 'crisis' arrived.

'The First Reality of Europe'

Skidelsky argues that Mosley viewed 'race' strictly in terms of cultural characteristics, acquired and transmitted through the socially conditioned reflexes of the nation itself. This belief, Skidelsky, argued derived from a combination of the theories of the eighteenth-century French biologist Jean-Baptiste Lamarck and a reading of Bernard Shaw's *Back to Methuselah* (1922).[274] The 'Lamarckian approach' claimed, with little evidence, that organic diversity rested upon the 'power of life' and its propensity towards increased complexity and the confluence of certain environmental circumstances. This belief in the influence of environmental factors in shaping evolution posited that new characteristics could be acquired and then transmitted through hereditary thus fulfilling the larger immutable purpose of 'natural' law.[275]

Mosley's 'neo-Lamarckian' position stated that culture trumped race. For Mosley, 'culture' was the engine of historical change. 'Culture' itself, created by a unique conjunction of heredity, environment and education, became an acquirable characteristic capable of hereditary transmission. Cultural achievement was thus the defining and innate characteristic of a 'race' and the determinant of evolutionary development in and of itself. Thus, the 'differential development' of a 'unique' European culture over the course of millennia stood as a towering achievement. Having fallen behind other, implicitly lesser, races had precluded themselves from further evolutionary development. Mosley's concept of 'Europe-Africa' hinted that the future offered them only the enslavement of 'manual labour' for the greater glory of European civilisation.[276]

This cultural-supremacist interpretation of Lamarckian evolution, which defined culture as the preserve of racial elites, also exuded Oswald Spengler's cultural pessimism. An 'obvious contradiction' existed in this synthesis.[277] Whilst Lamarckian evolution implied an ever-widening base of cultural inspiration, the German philosopher's gloomy prognostications dictated that the absorption of different cultural characteristics was wholly deleterious and could lead only to the 'internal decomposition and decay' of the host culture.[278] This Spenglarian imperative was persuasive to Mosley who sought to protect European civilisation, the pinnacle of white racial achievement, from cultural (and *ergo* biological) debasement through the implementation of apartheid. The contradiction, argues Thurlow, was only fully resolved through reference to Mosley's idea of the 'Thought-Deed Man' and the idea of purposeful evolution towards 'higher forms' which Mosley believed would be his 'main contribution to thought'.[279]

Through a fusion of Lamarck and Spengler, Mosley distanced himself from Nazi racial supremacism. Differing conceptions of 'race' underpinned the ongoing bifurcation of the cultural and biological fascist factions after 1945. Raven Thomson wrote:

> We feel little sympathy for those so called 'Nationalist' circles who seem to take no interest in any other matter than racialism, which, important as it may be in itself, cannot form the sole basis of a constructive policy to meet present world problems, which are mainly economic.[280]

This rejection of Nazi Nordicism was not simply a post-war affectation designed to obscure pre-war enthusiasm for such positions. Raven Thomson had long argued against *völkisch* mysticism because as

> we are men and not mere puppets in the hands of some Nordic Goddess of Fate our answer to the revelations of the great German philosopher [Spengler] is to demand action, and immediate action, to arrest the threatened decay and to end our cultural decline.[281]

Mosley was also particularly scathing that so much time had been 'wasted' in pedantic arguments about Aryan genealogies, judging such obsessions to be one of the infirmities of the 'Teuton mind' which 'brought some discredit' to the supposedly 'plain and observable fact that some races in their present and proved forms, can do certain things and other cannot.' Attacking *völkisch* romanticism, and concomitantly the 'search for a theory which has no practical relevance,' Mosley based his 'functional' interpretation of race upon 'practical science' and 'observable data'. The search for racial origins was fruitless. Mosley was satisfied to observe that the 'special characteristics of our breed' existed as a material fact and that these could function as a basis for 'further development'.[282]

Whilst cultural arguments predominated Mosley's pronouncements against the Jews during the 1930s, he had more ready recourse to biological and eugenic arguments vis-à-vis Commonwealth immigrants in the post-war period.[283] Race, Mosley had declared in 1948, was the 'first reality of European Union'. Deliberately targeting a German audience – his statement was circulated in Germany – Mosley argued that Britons and the Germans shared a common racial 'kinship' and that both peoples were part of an 'inner ring' of 'stock or family' which also included the Northern French and that all creative endeavour was the product of 'race'. The 'entire northern block of Sweden, Norway and Denmark' also possessed 'similar blood'. Outside this 'inner ring' bonded by blood sat the 'related stock' of Spain and Italy 'whose culture has embellished the best volumes of European history'. For Mosley, all creative endeavour was the product of 'race' which was the 'rock foundation' upon which European civilisation had been and would be built again. To deny 'nature' and 'reality' by subjecting Germany to the 'alien occupation' of Russian communism was to 'commit a crime against our own blood'. Mosley denied that his 'functional' interpretation implied racial hierarchy, simply that it recognised different racial endowments and capabilities which affirmed 'the laws of nature'. Illustrating his point, Mosley compared the capabilities of 'the leading physicist of the age' with 'a negro boxing champion', concluding that 'the former is better in the laboratory and the latter in the boxing ring'. One was not superior to the other, he claimed, simply different. It spoke volumes about Mosley's 'functional' view of race that the capacity for intelligence and creation lay with the, presumably white, physicist whilst the 'negro' boxer was suited only for entertainment and physical labour.

Mosley drew upon his knowledge of selective cattle breeding to outline what this entailed in practice: the 'blood line' had to be preserved and the dilution of 'good stock' prevented at all cost. The terminology he employed undermined Mosley's claims that his 'functional' interpretation of race was free of subjective value judgement and therefore characterised by detached scientific objectivity. For there to be a 'good' stock, there had to be a corresponding 'bad' stock, indicating that Mosley (like everyone else) possessed a systematised and inductive conception of value. Mosley was not discussing cattle breeding. He was talking about human ethnicity. Eugenics could intensify and accelerate evolution. 'Good stock' could be breed with 'comparable strains' for the 'highly suitable purpose we require'. To avoid overspecialisation and to induce refinement, 'outcrosses' could be used but this 'should not go outside very similar strains'. His human parallel, as if this had not been what he was discussing from the outset, would be to 'outcross' an Englishman with a French, German or Scandinavian or, for 'special purpose', a Latin type.[284]

A. James Gregor

The European became an important forum for Mosley's efforts to intellectualise racism, ethnocentrism and ethno-plurality. It served as a platform for those deeply critical of Nazi Nordicism, enshrined in the writings of Professor Hans 'Rassen' Günther whose work underpinned the *weltanschauung* of activists like Arnold Leese and Colin Jordan. A. James Gregor, an Italian-American Columbia University graduate, who began contributing to *The European* in July 1954, was a key figure in this process.[285] Gregor was part of a small clique of New York-based activists to whom Mosley and *The European*, available for sale in the city, appealed.[286] Gregor was also likely the *Union*'s 'American correspondent', who earlier that year had penned an article titled 'Syndicalism v. Keynesianism' extolling Mosley's avocation of Syndicalism, which he regarded as 'the final resolution for our time'.[287]

Gregor visited the UM, flying to London in October 1954 to meet with Raven Thomson and Robert Row. He subsequently travelled onwards to Germany, armed with letters of introduction from Mosley and the American Nazi sympathiser H. Keith Thompson, formerly the registered agent in the United States for General Otto Ernst Remer's banned Sozialistische Reichspartei Deutschlands (SRP – Socialist Reich Party), who recalled:

> Gregor, incidentally, was not an easy person to meet. He didn't like to meet people. It was early in his career, and he was very cautious about everything. When Gregor went to Europe I gave him a couple letters of introduction, one to General Remer, who I think he went and met; another to an SS Major friend of mine, Dr. Kurt Gross, who I know he went and met. I tried to facilitate his activities in any way I could, but his interests were largely in Italian Fascism and not in German political movements.[288]

However, shortly before departing to Germany, and whilst his wife translated some German correspondence for 'Alf' Flockhart, Gregor had some luggage stolen from his hotel, including the manuscript of a book he had been working on and a file of correspondence including his letters of introduction from Thompson and Mosley. 'Naturally there is nothing incriminating in the correspondence', he assured Row. Nonetheless, Gregor fretted, there are a great many names of a variety of people on the Continent. In one or two of the letters Keith Thompson speaks of my current trip in rather officious terms which might give the reader the impression that I am here in an official capacity. Then again there are the names of people who might well suffer if anyone should conceive of the possibility that they are somehow active in a network of some sort.[289]

Gregor requested that Row obtain another letter of introduction for him from Mosley 'as quickly as possible since I would like to speak to Dr. [Werner] Naumann concerning the project I had in mind.' These troubles aside, Gregor thanked Row: 'I enjoyed my stay and came away enthused with the efforts you have made.'[290]

Gregor expanded on the nature of the 'project' he wished to speak to Naumann about several days later in a letter to Raven Thomson. He and Keith Thompson planned to publish a monthly magazine in the United States, following the 'format' of *Nation Europa*, which Thompson and another of his confederates, Frederick C. Weiss, would publish. Weiss had pledged $150 a month for the magazine, an estimated 25 per cent of its monthly cost. Gregor informed Thomson:

> In order to start publication we would have to raise at the minimum $2500.00 in order to incorporate the monthly and to insure that it will come out in sufficient number to fulfil all subscription commitments. The immediate consideration upon returning to America will be the raising of such a sum.[291]

Undaunted by the prospect of raising such an amount 'for my little brain-child', Gregor schemed to publish a 'pilot' issue of the journal to ensure its longer-term viability. He would solicit articles from Naumann ('preferably on his confinement, the statements made by him concerning communism etc. etc.') and Remer ('an article on the banning of the S.R.P. – render it a weakening of the anti-communist front, a catering to the July criminals, etc. etc.'). He also hoped to meet Frau Doenitz – with whom Keith Thompson was in contact – with the intention of gaining an article from her too ('perhaps on the conditions under which her husband [Hitler's legal successor, Admiral Karl Doenitz] suffers in Spandau.') He also noted Thompson's contact with Ilse Hess, wife of the imprisoned Nazi war criminal Rudolf Hess ('although I have no idea how approachable she might be.') From Italy, Gregor also planned to solicit further contributions from MSI members 'of sufficient rank to promise me that much support from some of the high level membership that I can count on five a six articles a year from Italy.'[292]

The journal never materialised, but Gregor continued his regular contributions to *The European*.[293] Although Gregor was frequently critical of Mosley's concept 'European Socialism' from a position of orthodox Fascist Corporatism,[294] Diana Mosley, who edited *The European*, 'liked what he wrote'.[295] Mosley's biographer, Robert Skidelsky, has dismissed Gregor's contributions as notable largely 'for their extraordinary proliferation of footnotes'.[296] This aside fails to recognise Gregor's importance to Mosley's ongoing efforts to rescue 'race' as a concept in the wake of the Holocaust. In July 1958, Gregor penned his now seminal attack on Günther's Nordicism for *The European* in an article titled 'National Socialism and Race'. Arguing against the 'popular misconception' that Nazi racial science was a static phenomenon, Gregor asserted that actually it had passed through three distinct stages and, during its third and final 'dynamic phase', had evolved away from the idea of race as a hereditarily immutable factor of life. It had in fact begun to develop a more 'profound' cultural conception of race, which, until the war destroyed its research, was edging towards that of 'an ideal, united in common destiny, nurtured in common environment, the political expression of which is nationhood'. This transition Gregor found both 'scientifically sound and emotionally satisfying'.[297]

In surveying his arguments, one scholar notes that Gregor 'described his material without apparent disapprobation, and indeed seemed to be trying to recover something of value from Nazi racial doctrine that might be usable for a new, intellectually defensible race science.'[298] Gregor went on to enjoy a successful academic career. After completing his doctoral dissertation on the fascist philosopher Giovanni Gentile in 1961, he became a Professor of Political Science at the University of Berkeley, California, in 1967 where he remained until retiring in 2009 having published numerous scholarly works on Italian fascism, notable for their refusal to incorporate Nazism as 'Fascist' because of its biological racism. In *The Search for Neo-Fascism: The Use and Abuse of Social Science* (2006), published by Cambridge University Press, Gregor cryptically thanked both Mosley and Raven Thomson, to whom 'I owe some precious insights into what a neo-fascism could not be'.[299]

Race and modern science

Skidelsky has argued that Mosley 'never delved into ethnological science'. This is incorrect. Mosley was particularly interested in scientific development particularly insofar as race was concerned. Indeed, he reasoned that if the 'facts' of 'modern science' proved his racial and cultural assertions then *ergo* they legitimated his political programme, placing it beyond criticism or moral opprobrium. *Race and Modern Science: A Collection of Essays by Biologists, Anthropologists, Sociologists and Psychologists* (1967), edited by Robert E. Kutter, an associate editor of the racist *Truth Seeker* newspaper, greatly influenced Mosley in this regard. Between 1959 and 1961, *Race and Modern Science* was the 'principal project' of the International Association for the Advancement of Ethnology and Eugenics (IAAEE). The IAAEE's purpose was 'to publish a series of books, monographs, and articles presenting the results of original research and summarising the state of contemporary scientific opinion in the areas of its principal interest,' which was racial science.[300] Put bluntly, however, the IAAEE specialised in the dissemination of 'important discursive weapons' against 'race suicide'.[301] A. James Gregor was one of three signatories to the IAAEE's documents of incorporation on 23 April 1959.[302]

The contributors to *Race and Modern Science* regarded their work as the authoritative scientific statement of the 'anti-egalitarian' position on racial difference and thus a decisive rebuttal to the UNESCO 'Statement on Race' (1950) which the book had been designed to refute.[303] Mosley was particularly enamoured with the chapter authored by Professor Cyril Darlington, an expert in cytology, the branch of biology that deals with the formation and structure of cells.[304] It was Darlington's theory of 'outcrosses' first propounded in *The Facts of Life* (1953) and thence in a revised version, *Genetics and Man* (1964) that provided Mosley with an intellectual underpinning for the 'functional' interpretation of race he had propounded since the publication of *The Alternative* in 1947.[305] Darlington was an admirer of Sir Francis Galton, Charles Darwin's cousin who had pioneered the use of the term 'eugenics'. Darlington propounded a thesis that rested upon the idea of innate genetic racial difference, which determined human civilisation.[306] As Darlington noted in *The Facts of Life*, 'It is absurd to pretend that water and vinegar are equal. Water is better for some purposes, vinegar for others.'[307]

So too with people. For Darlington, the wider racial 'outbreeding' of black and white would led to the irrevocable loss of the 'parental strain'. Mosley invoked such arguments to claim that racial miscegenation would lead to the 'extinction' of the white race. If race was a matter of biology rather than culture then 'race-crossing' was a 'fatal step' because 'you cannot put it right again'. Drawing on his experience of farming in Hampshire and Wiltshire (which had seen him prosecuted in 1945 for causing unnecessary suffering to his livestock[308]), Mosley engaged a string of barnyard analogies to justify his arguments concerning breeding. Mosley objected to 'mixed marriages', which were, he argued, opposed by the 'healthy instinct' of the British, for whom it was 'not normal'. Only 'the trash' seeking 'biological renewal' entered mixed marriages, 'healthy strains' did not. Such anxieties were at root then biological rather than cultural. Lambasting the idea of 'wide outbreeding' which would level humanity to 'one, dull, grey mess', Mosley proposed to stem the impending tide of biological degradation by legislating for mutually exclusive racial development, or apartheid, which alone could preserve 'identity and character' of the white race, whose genetic integrity was under threat from a 'compulsory' mixing of races.[309]

For Mosley, race was paramount and 'a man should be as determined to preserve his own race as to preserve his own family.' Racial science now provided the underpinning for the evolution of Mosley's 'functional' view of race. Races were 'significantly different' from one another, he argued, and claims to the contrary were 'wishful thinking'. Racial equality, which he claimed had only become expedient for 'political reasons' during the Second World War, was simply 'propaganda'. In his defence of the genetic 'integrity' of the white race, Mosley replaced his previous reliance upon 'functional' racial stereotypes with accounts of the 'innate mental differences between races'. He castigated those who claimed racial difference was only skin deep for 'riding the hobby horse of his or her wishes'. Mosley now argued that human development hinged upon heredity, environment and education. The latter two factors allowed for the evolution of culture which 'increases rather than diminishes the difference' between races. The principal factor for evolutionary development, he argued, was 'intelligence' and 'will' – both of which were ascribed genetic qualities. For Mosley, race was thus the product of both heredity and genetics (culture, it was implied, was simply a projection of biology) requiring protection and preservation.[310]

Mosley's concern for the 'diverse threads of humanity' prefigured arguments for 'ethno-plurality' popularised by Nouvelle Droite (ND) ideologue Alain de Benoist during the 1970s, which have since become one of the dominant modes of argumentation in extreme right anti-immigration discourse. De Benoist, who became a pivotal figure in the formation of the Groupment de recherché et d'études pour la civilisation européenne (GRECE – Research and Study Group for European Civilisation) in 1968, the principal conduit for disseminating ND ideology, had previously been active within a group called Europe-Action. Using his pen-name 'Fabrice Laroche', de Benoist was in touch with the UM during this period, perhaps drawn to establish contact with the group precisely because Mosley was making the sorts of arguments he would later pioneer.[311]

However, rather than pursuing cultural arguments for 'ethno-plurality', glimmers of which could be seem in his own writings, Mosley instead turned to 'scientific' explanations of racial difference to prove the case for segregation. He became enamoured with the work of another member of the IAAEE executive committee, Robert Gayre, the Laird of Gayre and Nigg, whom, he wrote, was 'the editor of a periodical which deals with race, and is supported by distinguished scientists from many countries.'[312] The journal in question was *Mankind Quarterly*, the 'house organ' of the IAAEE, which had been established with funding from racist segregationists in the United States in June 1960 to counter the 'strong leaning towards discarding heredity as a valid criterion in the study of man' and to protect ideas that were being 'deliberately suppressed'.[313] *Mankind Quarterly*, founded to provide scientific arguments against desegregation, provided Mosley with another supposedly scientific source to advance his own arguments for racial apartheid against the 'bogus' anthropological ones that propounded or justified 'Black and White crosses'. The extent to which such thinking had penetrated party cadres was revealed in a letter published in *Action* extolling the virtues of *Mankind Quarterly* and those of another publication, *The Biology of the Race Problem* by W.C. George, published by The Britons, whose 'impartially studied facts about race', noted the correspondent, 'are completely consistent with our own proposals'.[314]

The utilisation of *Mankind Quarterly*'s particular brand of ethnographical science – billed as 'the scientific and historical truth about this controversial subject' – highlighted how far Mosley had travelled from his original supposedly Lamarckian position, one that Gayre rejected outright as 'obsolete'.[315] Ironically, by the early 1960s, Mosley's attempts to erect a sophisticated scientific veneer to justify racial segregation drew him closer to the biological determinism of the racial nationalist position than he would have cared to admit.[316] Mosley's willingness to resort to the arguments of both Darlington and Gayre, the latter committed to the principles of hereditary espoused by Mendelian genetics, reinforces the earlier point that Mosley's 'cultural' view of Europe was, at its base, a biological one.[317]

The revival

Mosley's arguments in favour of racial segregation led him to a trenchant defence of apartheid South Africa. The advent of the South Africa Boycott movement, which launched in spring 1960, provided a new impetus for extreme right-wing mobilisation. Mosley led the charge. He and a small group of supporters opposed the official launch of the boycott movement in Trafalgar Square on 27 February 1960. Whilst anti-apartheid supporters listened to speeches from Labour leader Hugh Gaitskell, Liberal leader Jeremy Thorpe and the Reverend Trevor Huddleston, Mosley stood nearby quietly orchestrating the counter-demonstration, his supporters carrying placards proclaiming, 'Beat the Boycott' and 'Support South Africa against the Black Peril and the Red Traitors' whilst several large lorries circled the square, carrying supporters shouting, 'Keep Britain White'. There were violent clashes, including one instance in which seven UM activists set upon a young student. Mosley condemned the violence but argued it was 'understandable if some of my less experienced supporters did lose their tempers after being under consistent abuse for an hour or more'. There were twelve arrests.[318] 'It was alarmingly like the pre-war demonstrations', observed Labour activist Tony Benn.[319]

In its pro-apartheid counter-demonstration, the UM was joined by the week-old British National Party which had been formed from a merger of John Bean's National Labour Party and Colin Jordan's White Defence League. As Bean noted in his autobiography, the two groups were forced into a temporary alliance during the 'fierce fighting' with anti-fascists which continued from Whitehall all the way back to the UM headquarters in Vauxhall Bridge Road. Rather than building on such collaboration, however, Jeffrey Hamm subsequently attacked the BNP, signalling that 'there was to be no co-operation among the radical right as far as they were concerned'.[320] Activists from both groups largely ignored Hamm's injunction, and instead collaborated to disrupt anti-apartheid meetings such as that called by the North and South Paddington Labour Parties in March, at which fascists set off fire alarms, shouted slogans and scuffled with stewards, and another in Portobello Road, North Kensington a few days later.[321]

Debate raged in the South African press as to whether Mosley had been given unofficial 'encouragement' to champion South African interests, the prevailing view being that if he had been induced to intervene then this was an appalling political blunder. British fascists continued to attack anti-apartheid events regardless.[322] Mosley staged two meetings supporting South Africa, both held at Kensington Town Hall to audiences of approximately 600 people, one on 2 March and another on 20 April. There was no disorder. 'In general Mosley has been more moderate than at the time of his election campaign, particularly when he refers to the coloured population,' observed Special Branch, 'whilst his basic policy appears to be the same, he is less derogatory in his references to black races.'[323]

Between Mosley's two meetings, the international situation vis-à-vis South Africa changed dramatically. On 21 March, the South African security services killed sixty-seven protesters in what became known as the Sharpeville massacre though the extreme right referred to it as a 'riot'. There was worldwide uproar, not least in Britain because British-made Saracen tanks were involved. Only days later, on 9 April, Prime Minister Hendrik Verwoerd was shot and wounded by a white farmer at an agricultural show in Johannesburg. Many feared that revolution was at hand. The South African government declared a state of emergency and banned both the African National Congress and the Pan-African Congress. Both went underground. Eric Louw, the South African Minister for External Affairs, who had recently claimed that British foreign policy aimed at handing over South and Central Africa to 'black control', arrived in Britain on 1 May to attend the Commonwealth Prime Ministers' conference. Several dozen UM activists welcomed him at both the airport and his hotel whilst a larger contingent of anti apartheid protesters made their feelings known too.[324]

The deterioration of the situation in the Belgian Congo provided a further spur for UM activity. Riots in the capital Leopoldville in 1959 had led swiftly to independence, sparking chaos in the Congo and prefiguring widespread mobilisation by extreme right groups across Europe. This included a 'most disturbing incident' outside The Ritz Hotel, London, on 23 July 1960. Three UM activists, including Peter Dawson, were demonstrating outside against the presence of the Congolese Prime Minister Patrice Lumumba who was staying there overnight whilst on a flight from Congo to New York, when they attacked the Ghanaian High Commissioner, Sir Edward Asafu-Adjaye, in the mistaken belief he was Lumumba.[325]

Three days after the assault, an assortment of the UM and other extreme right-wing activists shouting 'Keep Britain White' attacked a meeting in Trafalgar Square organised by the Committee of African Organisations leading to a further ten arrests.[326] Dawson continued his campaign of racial violence leading a UM demonstration, which turned into a fracas, outside a Piccadilly restaurant where black singer Sammy Davis Jr was barracked with cries of 'go home nigger' and 'Sammy, back to the trees' as they protested against the announcement of his marriage to white Swedish actress, Mai Britt.[327] Dawson similarly sought to intimidate black entertainer Eartha Kitt sending her an 'open letter' with menacing racist overtones.[328] The adverse publicity generated by these overtly racist actions led Mosley to forbid UM members from taking part in street demonstrations until further notice.[329] Nonetheless, the 'wide publicity' the American media gave the UM's racist heckling of Davis, passed onto them by their American counterparts, clearly pleased senior figures like Robert Row. 'I can assure you that there is a growing feeling regarding the whole black question here in England,' Row wrote excitedly to American national socialist H. Keith Thompson, 'and this is constantly growing as more come in'.[330]

Whilst such attacks, vicious though they were, gave the UM little political traction, Special Branch noted that: 'the present relative calm must not overshadow the fact that current happenings on the African continent may well spark off another wave of racial hatred – a situation which would require close watching'.[331] British fascists were already refocusing their resources and energies around the rise of African nationalism. Whilst South African apartheid provided an admired model, for some in the UM, it was never envisaged as the final stage in South African development.[332] Race, patriotism and identity fused in the exhortation to 'Be White, Be British!'[333] This was more than a matter of benign racial pride, however. It was reflected an international struggle for racial preservation. 'Stand by the White Man: in South Africa, In Rhodesia, In Britain Itself! Support the survival of White Civilisation before it is TOO late', demanded one UM leaflet.[334]

Seeking to explain the 'revolt' in South Africa, 'the rape, murder and chaos' in the Congo, the 'betrayal' of white Kenyans and the 'attempted sell-out' of white Rhodesians, *Action* blamed the Conservative Party. 'Macmillan's "wind of change" speech launched all these atrocities,' it argued. 'None of these things had happened until he released the whirlwind.' Furthermore, Macmillan's rejection of Europe, fracturing of the Commonwealth, exclusion of the white Dominions and encouragement of immigration threatened to turn Britain into 'Mac Mau Mau Island' – 'a little offshore negro island beside the great European civilisation,' claimed *Action*.[335]

Behind the dissolution of white Africa, UM publications hinted at the hidden hand of the Jew. Fusing anti-Semitic and anti-black tropes, *Action* published 'The Apotheosis of the Black Man' – its title redolent of A.K. Chesterton's notorious inter-war article 'The Apotheosis of the Jew' – which argued that the media was pursuing a strategy of 'pan-African indoctrination' through which whites were daily confronted with black cultural production. Black performers and entertainers, though hailed as 'messiahs', they were 'Wall Street puppets'. The media portrayal of blacks as 'a simple, laughing music-loving people' was, the article claimed, designed to push progressive citizens towards demanding that their respective governments liberate their colonial subjects. Such 'propaganda' was 'no accident'. It was designed to 'condition the white mind' into accepting the 'break down' of barriers between black and white, not from any Christian motive, 'but so that the black man can become the white man's supplanter in industrial production'. The African, argued *Action*, was 'credulous and unsophisticated' and therefore a more 'pliant' instrument for 'International Finance' than the 'better-educated and infinitely less gullible' white worker. Black immigration, at the bidding of 'New York bankers' was being deliberately used to break up Europe, neutering its ability to develop Africa *pace* Mosley's plans and enabling the 'money-power' instead to exploit Africa's mineral wealth for its own ends with assistance from local Communist-inspired satraps.[336]

Mosley later denied that the forces ranged against them were exclusively Jewish. 'International financial power', he observed, 'is drawn from almost every race under the sun, and owes allegiance to none' all bound together 'by the sole principle of profit through usury'. Those involved were a 'rootless people' owing loyalty 'to the financial power alone'. They controlled and manipulated British democracy and 'so long as all parliamentary parties are content to work the present system, the real government will be international finance.'[337] Mosley had already undermined his soft peddling strategy, however, through an alleged admission a decade previously that:

> We can still get our point across by playing up 'characteristics' without name calling. We used to talk about international Jewish bankers; now, when we talk about American capitalists our followers know exactly whom we're talking about. We have been identified long enough as fighting Jews for our followers to know what we mean.[338]

Events in Africa also allowed for a further blurring of anti-black and anti-Jewish prejudice. In its attack on the 'black dictators' and their left-wing supporters in Britain who, they claimed, had caused the Congolese famine, *Action* used the tragedy 'to knock down one of the biggest-scale lies of recent history'. The lie in question was the Holocaust. The 'similarity' of photographs showing starving Congolese to photographs of Jews in Belsen and other concentration camps, 'showing people in almost identical conditions', proved, *inter alia*, that 'most' of those who died in German concentration camps had died of starvation and disease, caused by Allied bombing and blockade and not as a result of a programme of systematic mass murder.[339]

Despite denials to the contrary, the prevalence of anti-Semitism was such that UM speakers were issued with instructions in February 1961 not to mention 'Jews' under any circumstances, as this would detract from its attempt to 'defeat the old parties and change the system'. Second, UM speakers were reminded that the UM was *not* a racist party because it did not believe in racial domination. Instead, speakers were to emphasise its stance on racial preservation through the prevention of further immigration and the use of racial science, the 'facts' of which reveal 'that races have different characteristics and that mixture of extremes is detrimental to both races. If our people are given this knowledge, no laws on the subject will be necessary.'[340]

The UM remained a violent, racist party despite such missives, however. South African Prime Minister Hendrik Verwoerd arrived in London in March 1961 for talks to discuss the deteriorating situation between South Africa and Britain, which led ultimately to South Africa holding a 'whites-only' referendum on 31 May, after which the country left the Commonwealth and proclaimed itself a Republic. The UM was on hand to offer Verwoerd their support. 'It is our duty to STAND BY THE WHITES' wrote Jeffrey Hamm to all UM members in London prior to Verwoerd's arrival.[341] The UM subsequently organised a demonstration in support outside the Dorchester Hotel though police pushed them to Trafalgar Square, much to their chagrin.[342] On route to demonstrate their racial solidarity, a dozen UM members travelling in a van driven by Peter Dawson stopped at 200 Gower Street, the headquarters of the Anti-Apartheid Movement (AAM), which subsequently caught fire.[343] Police arrested Dawson and two others, Francis Elliot and Sir Henry David Shiffner.[344] Following an interview with Mosley, police also arrested a fourth, Keith Gibson.[345]

Surprisingly, a court acquitted them. Nonetheless the UM expelled Dawson and suspended Gibson and Elliot, such was the ordure created by the case.[346] Gibson's suspension did him no harm. He became UM political secretary in the following year and subsequently UM organising secretary. Gibson had joined the UM aged seventeen in 1950. He served two years' imprisonment following a speech in 1952, during which he had declared: 'Hitler had the right idea about the Jews. The *Jewish Chronicle* stated that six million Jews were exterminated. That is all lies, but even this figure would not have been enough.'[347] Dawson meanwhile resurfaced nearly fifty years later as a member of the British National Party, his belief in Mosley as a 'great man' undimmed.[348]

Despite instructions to 'maintain order and obey the law whatever provocation is offered to them,'[349] UM activists continued their violent opposition to the activities of the AAM, attacking a meeting in Trafalgar Square on 19 March 1961, held to commemorate the anniversary of the Sharpeville massacre. Police subsequently made twenty-nine arrests including two activists who were circling the square in a UM speaker van bedecked with posters proclaiming, 'Mosley not Mau Mau'.[350] They arrested others for possessing weapons including pickaxe handles and coshes.[351] Denying responsibility for the violence, Mosley blamed the media. At a press conference on 12 May, he stated that, whilst he was committed to stamping out 'gangsterism' within the UM and the nation at large, 'what is true is that the continual suggestion that we like violence is liable to give us some members who like that kind of thing'.[352]

Mosley's son Max was also heavily involved in the party during this period. He had been educated at a southern Bavarian boarding school run by an acquaintance of Mosley's friend Frau Winifred Wagner, the composer's daughter-in-law, to facilitate his learning German.[353] Despite his expulsion from the school, Max Mosley subsequently gained a place to study physics at Oxford in 1958, becoming secretary of the Oxford Union. He combined this role with extramural activity as a UM speaker.[354] In 1961, he was arrested and fined for obstructing a police officer during the UM counter-demonstration against the Sharpeville massacre.[355]

At his father's request, Max also moved to Manchester to become election agent for the UM by-election candidate in Moss Side, Manchester, Walter Hesketh, a former police officer and long-distance runner who had represented England thirty-six times. Earlier that year, he had achieved an athletic first, running 373 miles from Edinburgh to London in eighty-two hours wearing only carpet slippers. Hesketh's leaflets, for which Max Mosley bore responsibility as election agent, proclaimed that 'coloured immigrants brought leprosy, syphilis and TB'. Max's centrality to the campaign was later recalled by Sheffield UM branch chairman, Robert J. Taylor (an associate of Colin Jordan), who remembered:

> Max and I, with other fools, were pushing out leaflets urging the good burghers of Moss Side to vote for the Union Movement candidate, Walter Hesketh, and send the blacks home … Mosley Senior was considering placing Max in Manchester and having him run for the council, as stage one to a big build-up of the Union Movement in the North. In 1961, during the byelection, Sir Oswald told us that he was a bit worried, though, in case the Movement became 'a Mosley family firm'. Believe me, Max was very much a Mosleyite, one of the boys.[356]

Despite gaining plentiful publicity for his candidate by taking the Lord Mayor of Manchester to court for breaching the Representation of the People Act, neither the case nor the campaign were successful.[357] Hesketh came last, polling 1,212 votes (5.2 per cent).[358]

During this period, Max Mosley was also a member of no. 44 Independent Parachute Brigade (T.A.). The Parachute Regiment had a certain glamorous cachet amongst right-wingers because of the role French paratroopers had played in Algeria and with the Organisation Armée Secrète (OAS – Secret Army Organisation), an extreme right-wing terrorist organisation then attempting to assassinate President Charles de Gaulle for his perceived betrayal of French interests in Algeria. Perhaps seeking to emulate his example, three other UM activists joined up, leading to newspaper exposés and an inquiry into their activities in September 1963.[359] TA regulations prohibited members from taking part in political demonstrations.[360] Following an investigation, the TA allowed all four to remain but two, Keith Gibson and Alistair Geldard, resigned in order to devote themselves to UM activism.[361] Max Mosley slowly drifted away from fascist politics, though he remained involved as late as September 1965, accompanying his father to a meeting in the East End at which Mosley gave his last open-air speech.[362] He trained for the Bar and married Joan Taylor, the daughter of a police officer he had met at a UM rally. He later became president of the Fédération Internationale de l'Automobile, the body that oversees Formula 1 racing. There was no great breach. 'He realized I had moved on and never held it against me,' Mosley recalled in his memoir.[363]

The Conference of Venice

Mosley continued to fascinate, and had received regular invites to participate in university debates from as early as 1954 onwards. Ken Clarke, a pro-European Conservative heading the Cambridge University Conservative Association (CUCA), invited Mosley to speak in autumn 1961, 'to add colour to the card for the term' and, more importantly, to raise his own profile ahead of a bid to become Union President. Clarke had seen Mosley give a 'gripping performance' at the Cambridge Union in the previous year. Mosley had spoken for only a few moments when a student 'slapped a custard pie in his face', recalled Clarke.

> This silenced the barracking and produced shocked silence whilst Mosley wiped the custard from his face and the student was removed. He used the incident to capture everyone's attention and thereafter gripped the audience with his commanding delivery of case which did not persuade but was compellingly delivered.[364]

Clarke's friend Michael Howard, the future Conservative Party leader, resigned from the CUCA committee in protest. The Nazis had murdered his grandmother and several cousins. *Varsity*, the student newspaper, published a photograph of him and Clarke sitting together with the caption: 'We used to be friends ... Mosley has broken up another close partnership by splitting Howard and Clarke.' Howard beat Clarke to become secretary and subsequently head of the Cambridge Union.[365] Clarke's debate with Mosley went ahead regardless. He and John Gummer, another future Conservative minister, debated with Mosley. 'It was largely a debate about Mosley's political record', recalled Clarke. 'Mosley was not at his best and I may be a little biased but I think that Gummer and myself got the better of the arguments.'[366]

This was all a sideshow, however, distracting Mosley from the main event – his vision for the rebirth of Europe. Mosley's commitment on this point was unswerving and he continued to traverse Europe seeking to spread his ideals, and increasingly, to organise a concrete political vehicle to drive them forward. Mosley 'has never been so busy – it makes my flesh creep,' his sister-in-law Nancy Mitford wrote in 1960. 'No doubt we shall all be in camps very soon.' Nancy put pen to paper following reports that Mosley was visiting Count Alvise Loredan of the MSI in Venice of whom she noted 'no decent Venetian will speak to him'.[367] Mosley tried later that year to stage a 'European rally' in London on 6 December 1960 but his plans were derailed by the Home Office, which banned his guest speaker, the Luftwaffe ace Hans-Ulrich Rudel from entering the country, and by Marylebone council which rescinded the booking for Seymour Hall.[368] Though it was cold comfort, Count Loredan succeeded in addressing an *Action* dinner on the following evening on the work of the MSI.[369]

Mosley revisited Rome on 20 March 1961 to promote the Italian edition of his book *Europa: Una Fede e un Programme* (1960), which Loredan had translated. 'Hundreds of neo-Fascists had turned out [to meet Mosley at the airport] and roared *viva* with arms raised in salute', according to one account.[370] Thereafter Mosley addressed an MSI meeting arranged by Alberto Mellini Ponce de León, formerly chief of Cabinet to the Under-Secretary of Foreign Affairs at Salò, on the topic 'Europe – Faith and Plan'. The Centro per la Difesa per la dell'Occidente, an MSI youth organisation, sponsored the event. Pino Romualdi MP, deputy secretary of the MSI and a previous vice-president of Mussolini's Partito Fascista Repubblicano (PFR – Republican Fascist Party) shortly before the collapse of the Salò Republic, presided over this organisation.[371] The elderly American poet Ezra

Pound who had broadcast for Fascist Italy right up until April 1945, leading to his confinement to a psychiatric hospital, joined Mosley and Romualdi on the platform.[372] Released in 1958, Pound had returned to live in Italy. Mosley's central thesis enthused Pound who told the attendant media he believed that the day for European unity would come.[373]

Having been twice to Germany and once to Belgium already that year, Mosley returned to Rome in February 1962 for a series of meetings with MSI leaders. This was a prelude to the 'Conference of Venice', which took place over four days on 1–4 March at the luxury Hotel Europa on the Grand Canal. The Venetian section of the MSI organised the event whilst Mosley took responsibility for drafting the discussion documents. Giovanni Nicola Lanfré, a Venetian lawyer, and Count Alvise Loredan, both MSI activists, were key in securing their party's adherence. Official delegates included Mosley, Adolf von Thadden for the Deutsche Reichspartei (DRP – German Reich Party), Alberto Mellini Ponce de León and Count Loredan for the MSI, and Jean-François Thiriart for the Belgian Mouvement d'Action Civique (MAC – Movement for Social Action).[374]

Those officially representing parties were not the only participants. Mosley invited Prince Valerio Borghese, the former naval commando leader, 'who, after my speech in Rome in March last, expressed his warm agreement'. He telephoned Hans-Ulrich Rudel who promised to come, as did former SS commando Otto Skorzeny. Mosley also contacted his old friend Arthur Ehrhardt, *Nation Europa*'s editor, who, unable to attend, recommended either Peter Kleist or Erich Kernmayer, both regular contributors to the magazine, as substitutes. Mosley extended another invitation to Dr Hans-Severus Ziegler, the former superintendent of the Weimar Deutsches Nationaltheater and organiser of the 1938 Entartete Musik (Degenerate Music) show, whom he had met through Frau Winifred Wagner at her Bayreuth salon. 'He became enthusiastic for our idea and very helpful,' Mosley told von Thadden.[375]

A small UM contingent headed by his son Max also joined Mosley and H.G. McKechnie, his political secretary. Max Mosley had driven from London together with UM political secretary Keith Gibson, Barry Ayres and another junior party activist. Walter Hesketh arrived in a second car. On route, Max Mosley's group had stopped at Dachau concentration camp, near Munich. Gibson, who had already been prosecuted for inciting racial hatred as a result of his comments denying the Holocaust wanted to sign 'good try, but not good enough' in the visitors' book but was prevented from doing so by Max. Reflecting subsequently upon the sobering experience, Ayres recalled 'I don't think Max had any illusion at all: he fully accepted the Holocaust.'[376]

The 'Conference of Venice' resulted in the signing of a 'European Declaration' that established 'Europe-a-Nation' as a 'fact' forthwith.[377] The signatories of this grandiose statement included Mosley, von Thadden, Mellini Ponce de León and Alvise Loredan and Thiriart.[378] Mosley had striven for such unity for fifteen years and the conference, with its acceptance of his belief in 'Europe-a-Nation' as an independent 'third power', marked perhaps the apogee of his influence upon extreme right-wing circles in Europe.[379] Mosley, who had drafted the 'European Declaration', believed its reception 'has been very good so far' and he was optimistic of being able to weld the disparate fascist parties attending into a cohesive 'central organisation'. The delegates agreed to constitute a 'bureau de liaison' and to meet six times a year as a precursor to forming a centralised, pan-European political infrastructure.[380] Indeed, having secured agreement for a common political programme, Mosley then turned his face towards the 'urgent and onerous' task of organising its national factions into a National Party of Europe (NPE) under the banner 'Progress – Solidarity – Unity'. 'We are National Europeans', declared the UM after the conference.[381]

Past affiliations counted for nothing in this 'European Front' against Communism. The NPE 'has some members who were previously Nazis,' Mosley told the media but 'we care nothing for the past. We are only concerned with the future.'[382] Disassociating the venture from past politics was a deliberate strategy. 'It will be presented as a perfectly normal occasion to discuss entirely legitimate political opinions,' he told von Thadden a month before the conference took place.[383]

Mosley arranged a follow-up meeting for 1–2 July in Milan to hear reports from the parties involved and gauge their reactions to the decisions made at Venice, which in the case of the MSI had, initially at least, been favourable.[384] However, despite further meetings, notably in Frankfurt later that month, which both Mosley and Thiriart attended, the initiative floundered. Preoccupied with national electoral considerations, neither the DRP nor the MSI would officially commit to the venture. Much to Mosley's chagrin, neither party even published the 'Declaration of Venice'. Without this or indeed the finances to establish its central bureau or a 'practical base' from which to operate, the NPE was never anything more than a grandiose letterhead organisation.[385]

Mosley blamed the failure of the DRP to endorse the NPE upon the Germany's continued 'persecution', which, he claimed, had rekindled 'a sense of old nationalism' that had diluted the party's internationalist impulse.[386] On 28 November 1964, the DRP merged with several other extreme right groups to form the Nationaldemokratische Partei Deutschlands (NPD – National Party of Germany). Mosley wrote enthusiastically to one of its members, Wolfgang Frenz, of his hopes for the party whilst stressing that it is 'of the greatest importance to support the formation of a nationalist party for Europe'.[387] The NPD failed to heed Mosley's entreaties, however. Thereafter, Mosley's followers interpreted the party's lacklustre performance as a vindication of their own pan-European stance. 'The NPD achieved some success by going back on their promises to us at the Conference of Venice in 1962 and becoming very nationalist,' Mosley's political secretary stated. 'We warned them that this would carry them only so far. Now we are being proved right, as their vote goes down.'[388]

Pondering his failure to actualise the 'vision splendid', Mosley agreed, lamenting that the protagonists of Venice 'were then thrown back into nationalism, and in some cases of the lesser groups into a wild futility. This was frustration, but not defeat.'[389] Indeed, Mosley continued to claim the Conference was a 'massive achievement', bordering on the clairvoyant:

> What matters is that we proved it was possible to bring together men from the most diverse standpoints and with the strongest national sentiments in a European policy as complete and wholehearted as Europe a Nation. Crisis and the financial bankruptcy of lesser ideas will bring us back to that position with many new participants drawn from various parties who today lag far behind the advanced idea. We were as usual in action before our time, but we proved that all is possible when time is ripe.[390]

With the NPE stillborn, Mosley forged closer ties with its most enthusiastic exponent besides himself: MAC leader Jean-François Thiriart. Like Mosley, Thiriart, a successful Brussels-based optometrist, had been a socialist in his youth. Drifting rightwards, he had ended up joining the unambiguously named Amis du Grand Reich Allemand (AGRA – Friends of the Great German Reich), a collaborationist group founded in March 1941. The AGRA group considered the espousal of the Nazi cause by Léon Degrelle's Rexist movement, 'to have been too cautious and who advocated the dismantling of the unitary Belgian state in favour of the Walloon race into an expanded German confederation.'[391] Thiriart's experience within AGRA, which prioritised cultural propaganda rather than political activity, 'instilled into him the idea of a supranational European unity but also led to his prosecution after the war for collaboration.'[392] Jailed until 1948, Thiriart returned to politics during the Belgian Congo crisis in 1960 leading to the foundation of the MAC. Actively engaged in trying to forestall African independence, police arrested Thiriart as he stepped from the plane after returning to Belgium from his meeting with Mosley in Venice. They suspected him of aiding the French OAS in its terrorist campaign to stop Algerian independence. Whilst Thiriart was released without charge, several other MAC militants were subsequently jailed.[393]

Thiriart's enthusiasm for pan-Europeanism led him to disband the MAC in September 1962. Jeune Europe (JE – Young Europe) replaced the group and became the network through which Thiriart and Mosley deepened their collaboration. Thiriart provided Mosley with lists of supporters to whom he might send information. Mosley reciprocated, providing Thiriart with 587 names taken from *Action*'s subscription list, though 'some distinguished people who are very good friends of mine' had been extracted from the list lest they be embarrassed by the unsolicited receipt of JE material.[394] The UM bookshop sold *Jeune-Europe* and advertised Thiriart's book *Un Empire de 400 Millions d'hommes: l'Europe – An Empire of Four Million Men: Europe* (1964). The book was glowingly reviewed in the new UM publication, *The National European*, its title mirroring *La Nation Européenne*, a publication Thiriart launched in the following year.[395]

Thiriart's book espoused the concept of a European-wide party, 'imbued with the faith of a religious order and with the discipline of a military order,' which would lead the struggle – 'clandestine' in the East and 'underground' in the West – to forge European unity.[396] Mosley sought to assist Thiriart in realizing this goal, commending to him M.J. Dingley, a supporter studying Russian at Jesus College, Cambridge, who subsequently ran the JE 'information office' in London – one of several such ventures that Thiriart established across Europe in 1963. Dingley was tasked with helping coordinate JE contacts with university students. Mosley also recommended C.W. 'Bill' Dods, 'an old and reliable' Croydon BUF activist who had been the UM 'Accounts Inspector', to Thiriart as someone to entrust JE contacts with East European émigré groups to.[397]

Hitherto, Mosley's had worked through 'official' parties with whom he had long-standing ties, putting any contacts he received in their hands rather than organising with separate groups. However, the failure of the MSI to validate the 'European Protocol' established in Venice changed Mosley's attitude. Lanfré and Loredan, who 'both agree entirely with our Europe a Nation policies and desire for action', shared Mosley's frustration. Loredan's stance was particularly important to Mosley since, as the recently appointed foreign representative of the MSI youth movement, 'his name and personality have considerable influence in Northern Italy.' Mosley proposed Thiriart mobilise his Italian JE affiliate Pierfranco Bruschi, a fascist militant based in Milan who led Giovane Europa, as well as handing over the remainder of Thiriart's Italian contacts to Loredan who 'could do much to pull all these groups together and to energize them'. Because of the disinterest shown by the MSI and the DRP in genuinely internationalising their operations, 'I feel entirely free to make individuals contacts and organise them into groups in both Germany and Italy', Mosley told Thiriart.[398]

Mosley saw no inherent conflict with such a strategy and felt, paradoxically, that working outside the official MSI structure, might induce the party to implement the Venice declaration by exerting an external pressure upon it from its Right flank. Mosley continued to remain on good terms with individual MSI politicians, however. 'You were a great friend of my father's and you were one of the few persons who shared and struggled with him for the same principles and ideas,' Filipo Anfuso's daughter wrote to Mosley in 1963 after the death of this prominent MSI senator who was ambassador to Berlin under Mussolini's Salò Republic.[399] Mosley continued to have dealings with senior MSI politicians for the remainder of his life. In 1972, for instance, Mosley's correspondence reveals his seeking a meeting with MSI leader Giorgio Almirante in Rome, another former Salò Republic functionary, who believed democracy to be an 'infection of the spirit'.[400]

Mosley connected with younger fascist militants through Bruschi, who began organising a conference in Bolzano in the South Tyrol region of northern Italy. This gained an eager response from young MSI militants in the area. 'The sooner we can get this really going the better,' enthused Mosley.[401] Bruschi organised several meetings for the JE network in Italy, including one in 'Red Bologna' in May 1963, chaired by Thiriart, which was attended by sixty activists from various MSI youth groups and the Ordine Nuovo (ON – New Order), the official JE affiliate in Rome.[402]

The ON leader Giuseppe 'Pino' Rauti, a teenage member of Salò's Guardia Nazionale Repubblicana (GNR – National Republican Guard), was notable as an early disciple of Julius Evola and would become a leading exponent of the 'spiritualist-Evolian' current within the MSI. The ON was one of the most militant Italian fascist groups, its activists going on to perpetrate numerous acts of terrorism until the Italian state banned it in 1973. *Action* published a photo of Mosley with Thiriart, Bruschi and Antonio Lombardo, who ran the ON group in Sicily, 'for whom I promised as soon as possible to address a demonstration … it was a chance to meet some new young men of value to the European future'. Lombardo, who edited the ON publication, *Nazione-Europa*, translated and distributed Mosley's work through ON channels.[403] Mosley and Thiriart attended another conference organised by Bruschi in Milan in July 1964. Bruschi meanwhile continued disseminating Mosley's ideas into the Italian fascist firmament.[404] Whilst Mosley's ideas enthused many young Italian militants, his political activities with the ON were indicative, on another level, of his failure to persuade the MSI, the principal engine of post-war Italian fascism, to adopt his own 'European' approach. Mosley was still chasing this chimera in 1967 when even optimistic colleagues like Loredan had begun to lose hope.[405]

There were side benefits. Mosley's networking afforded his activists new opportunities to partake in transnational activism, a powerful mechanism for socialising and acculturating them into fascist militancy. UM political secretary Keith Gibson had led a group of activists to a JE camp held at Bouillon in the Ardennes in 1963, which was attended by Belgian, French, Dutch, German and Italian activists 'and also exiles from the occupied countries of Eastern Europe'.[406] In the following year, Thiriart again invited the UM to join their JE counterparts on a five-country tour – taking in Belgium, Germany, Austria, Switzerland and Italy – beginning on 26 March 1964.[407] He also proposed UM participation in a joint-demonstration of 'European solidarity' – a massive JE-sponsored propaganda drive throughout Europe on 8 May 1965, to coincide with the twentieth anniversary of the 'Soviet–American peace' at which a pamphlet, written in seven languages, was to be distributed 'from Lisbon to Rome and from London to Berlin'.[408] Shortly afterwards, Thiriart attended the 'National European' dinner in London on 3 July, where he and Mosley had the opportunity to 'discuss many things together'.[409]

The continued closeness of this partnership was underlined when the UM printer was jailed for two years, jeopardising *Action*'s continued production. Mosley turned to Thiriart asking him to obtain an estimate from his printer, Maurice Bellen, to produce 65,000 copies of *Action*. Mosley found Bellen's estimate attractive enough to warrant despatching Hamm to Brussels to discuss the matter in person.[410] Thiriart remained in contact with Mosley but by June 1966 domestic priorities were beginning to reassert themselves at the expense of international ones for the UM. Thiriart, too, was experiencing domestic difficulties.[411] Following an internal, ideological split, JE went into sharp decline. Having claimed 5,000 members across Europe in 1965, by the following year, only 300 remained, sixty-six of these located in Belgium. Thiriart dissolved JE, replacing it with the Partie Communautaire Européen, which served as a platform for his left-leaning creed of 'national-communitarianism'. Despite shifting increasingly leftwards – Thiriart began quoting from Che Guevara and Mao in a bid to build 'a global front against US imperialism' – he continued exploring possibilities for pan-European cooperation with Mosley.[412] In 1967, Thiriart proposed to Count Loredan the idea of a 'Club Europa' – a more informal venture that would have a non-political committee in Venice. The MSI accepted the idea, Loredan told Mosley, and inveighed upon him to gain von Thadden's adherence.[413]

Punch-up politics

The publicity surrounding the Conference of Venice had raised Mosley's profile at a moment when, domestically, extreme right-wing activism was again attracting anti-fascist opposition, largely because of the Nazi politicking of Colin Jordan (see Chapter 4). This violent opposition culminated as Mosley sought to stage a meeting in Ridley Road. Marching through Hackney, an anti-fascist demonstrator knocked Mosley to the floor. There were sixty arrests, including Max Mosley. The court subsequently acquitted him of threatening behaviour for fighting with demonstrators who were assaulting his prostrate father. His brother, Nicholas, was also aghast at their father's treatment, though he questioned 'what on earth were the people around him doing wheeling him out like an old Aunt Sally?'[414] Whilst Mosley's supporters grumbled darkly that there was a plot to kill him, the violence renewed his celebrity. 'Mosley … hasn't had it so good since Cable Street,' complained one letter writer to the *Sunday Telegraph*. 'For a quarter of a century nobody has cared whether he lived or died; now, suddenly, Fleet Street leaps out of bed every time he passes […] a duster over his jackboots.'[415]

The violence made it increasingly hard for Mosley to operate, however. The Minister of Public Buildings and Works banned several scheduled meetings in Trafalgar Square which Mosley denounced as an abject surrender to 'red anarchy' having been due to speak from the plinth on 23 September.[416] The Metropolitan Police further curtailed Mosley's room for manoeuvre by obtaining an order banning all political marches for 48 hours on 30 August after Mosley announced his intention to march from Hoxton Square to Victoria Park, Bethnal Green, on 2 September. Mosley staged his meeting in Victoria Park anyway. Police stopped it after only two minutes amidst a general mêlée and forty more arrests.[417] He spoke again in the East End on 9 and 16 September, each time cocooned behind a police cordon as his supporters slugged it out with anti-fascists.[418]

Mosley found a less volatile audience in the United States, which he had not visited since 1926, when he addressed a meeting at the Buffalo University, New York on 25 September. Travelling *incognito* as 'Mr Morley', Mosley addressed the 'Student Forum' on 'Fascism'. The meeting was not without opposition, however, and Mosley curtailed his stay by a day at the request of the university authorities lest his presence prolong the protests.[419] Upon his return, he made another attempt to address a UM meeting in Bethnal

Green on 7 October but the meeting was closed before Mosley even arrived as police made a further thirty arrests during clashes between his supporters and anti-fascists.[420]

The UM attempted to put on a brave face regarding the violence of 1962. 'The Blackshirt Spirit ... still lives, and they will soon know it,' *Action* declared, whilst also claiming that the party was experiencing a 'nation wide' growth as a result.[421] These exaggerated claims did little to ameliorate its immediate predicament, however. Banned from holding a meeting in Trafalgar Square, Mosley attempted to lead a march from Charing Cross Station on 12 May 1963. Police stopped the procession after it had travelled but a few hundred metres amidst fierce fighting and fifteen arrests.[422] Meanwhile, a group of anti-fascists gained entry to the UM offices in Vauxhall Bridge Road through the ruse of wearing UM pin badges. Once inside, they caused £300 worth of damage and seriously assaulted Keith Gibson, the UM political secretary, and Robert Row, the editor of *Action* who they made tear up copies of the newspaper.[423] Six anti-fascists were fined, outraging the UM who, with a nod to both recent history and their own sense of victimhood, argued that the judge, 'evidently did not consider this case as serious as that of the nine Notting Hill youths sentenced to four years' imprisonment each in 1958 for wounding and assaulting coloured men.'[424]

Others had recourse to more militant modes of activity. In the following week, three UM members William Goulding, manager of an Army Surplus Store, and Ernest Palmer, a builder, were charged with possessing plastic explosives and a detonator, whilst a third man, Desmond Curry, a former soldier, was also charged with possessing explosives, after they used army plastic explosives to bomb the offices of the *Daily Worker*. Goulding was jailed for two years, the others for eighteen and fifteen months respectively.[425] Sporadic street violence continued throughout summer 1963, UM activists clashing with members of the North and East London Co-Ordinating Anti-Fascist Committee, who were staging a counter-meeting in the East End.[426]

The UM sought to organise its own violent counter-response. To do so the party turned to its disgraced former organiser 'Alf' Flockhart, who Mosley had quietly readmitted to the UM in July 1963 as an 'associate member' enabling him to act, in an 'advisory capacity', as 'meetings organizer' for the group. One of his tasks, reported Special Branch, 'is to rally effective opposition to anti-fascist element interference at meetings and violence to Union Movement members.' To do so Flockhart collaborated with Denis 'Big Dan' Harmston, a former boxer and self-employed, licensed porter at Smithfield Meat Market, who had joined the UM in 1962.[427] The Special Branch noted:

> The latter claims to be the leader of a group of meat porter colleagues in the Market who are quite prepared to give their services as a 'strong arm' squad at meetings and who would be delighted to indulge in a 'free-for-all' with any opposition – 'just for the kicks!' The outcome of this new arrangement remains to be seen but, as is known, Flockhart is a crafty and capable organizer. There is no doubt that, with reasonable support he will make his presence felt.[428]

One Smithfield porter, Tony Lambrianou, who was involved with East End gangsters Ronnie and Reggie Kray, wrote of his involvement with UM violence, stating that Harmston paid him and his brother 'to create a fracas' whilst Mosley was addressing a meeting in Dalston to gain publicity for his ailing UM. 'We weren't in it for anything other than the money,' Lambrianou claimed. 'On several occasions we were getting £50 a time to be out there Jew-baiting. There's a lot of money in racial issues. Mosley was never short of a bob or two, and he always found money to throw around.'[429] Such activities, which clearly failed to create an ideologically motivated cadre of militants, also failed to reinvigorate the party's ailing fortunes. Its autumn campaign that year was stillborn. The UM applied to over 100 town halls to use rooms for meetings. Westminster Council alone permitted Mosley to use Kensington Town Hall for a meeting.[430]

South Africa

Whilst his supporters clashed with anti-fascists on the streets, Mosley continued forging connections especially in South Africa. In 1962, the publican William Webster, who had previously been active with John Bean's NLP, was despatched to South Africa to prevail upon 'local businessmen' to donate R200,000 (£100,000) to fund the organisation's general election campaign. Webster was granted an audience with J.F.W. Haak, Deputy Minister of Economic Affairs 'who furnished Webster with the names of organisations from which he might obtain information on such South African exporters as were doing business with firms in the United Kingdom.' Thereafter, Webster was introduced to Major-General Sir Francis de Guingand, a former chief of staff to Field-Marshall Montgomery, who chaired the South Africa Foundation, whose function was 'imbued with the ideal of presenting South Africa's case at home and overseas' by countering 'outside pressures' and 'misunderstandings'.[431] Webster also met Afrikaner multimillionaire Anton Rupert who directed him to the headquarters of the ruling Nasionale Party for a donation to the UM coffers. Webster's presence in South Africa became apparent following an injudicious interview with the local media. Embarrassed by the affair, Haak issued a statement claiming that the advice he gave Webster 'certainly cannot be interpreted as in any way associating myself with Mr Webster's political activities.' Mosley also issued a statement denying the Webster's visit was intended to raise funds for the UM.[432]

In January 1964, Mosley arrived in South Africa for a six-week sojourn for the purposes of 'political study combined with business interests'.[433] Diana Mosley did not look forward to visiting the Republic. 'I'm sure S. Africa is ghastly,' she wrote prior to departure. Her mood did not lighten upon arrival. The hotel was 'a complete ivory tower where one is unconscious of what Kit [Mosley] calls question A [apartheid]'.[434] In Johannesburg, Mosley addressed a public meeting on 25 February, which had been organised for him by 'old friends ... most of whom were members of our Movement either pre-war or post-war and have now emigrated to South Africa'.[435] Though *Action* made common cause with the apartheid state, the leadership of the South African Society rebuffed their calls for 'united action', recognising the damage that open association with Mosley would do to their cause.[436] *Cape Times* meanwhile commented: 'the Nationalist Party is getting along very nicely (at least in South Africa) without support from this doubtful quarter, and it would perhaps be a good idea if some eminent Nationalist told Sir Oswald so. Preferably publicly.'[437]

'Every time I visit this country, I am more impressed by its latent power', Mosley remarked to *Die Oosterlig* upon his return in February 1965.[438] Mosley and his wife stayed at the Hotel Schweizerhof, Regent Road, Sea Point. Diana thought it 'ghoulish'.[439] Banned from the airwaves by the BBC, the South African Broadcasting Corporation (SABC) introduced Mosley as a 'leading statesman' and permitted him to deliver a stark message to 'White Africa' warning that although Europe could conceivably survive the loss of Africa it was 'inconceivable that White Africa would survive the loss of Europe'. South Africa, Mosley argued, had to become 'less introverted' and embrace 'Europe-a-Nation'. It was only the UM that offered South Africa unequivocal support, Mosley claimed, hinting rather obviously that donations would be appreciated. South Africa could only be saved from 'one man, one vote negro government', he told listeners by a UM government.[440]

Mosley pursued new avenues for racial apartheid upon his return, staging a press conference on 7 April 1965 to announce that the foundation of an 'Associate Movement' to assist the 'spread our ideas among coloured people'. It was open 'to those coloured people who had expressed their agreement and desire to co-operate with the UM's policy for the return of post-war immigrants to their homelands'.[441] Publicly, it never acknowledged more than three members: Dever Shenbanjo, a Nigerian who had won the Distinguished Flying Cross (DFC) whilst serving with the Royal Air Force (RAF), Denis Mackenzie, an Indian Oxford graduate, and an unnamed doctor.[442] This was the first of many such abortive attempts to forge an alliance with other racial and religious separatists that would again gain traction within the extreme right two decades later.

The 'expert forgetter'

Politically, Mosley's last hurrah was the 1966 general election. He stood for Shoreditch and Finsbury whose constituents he promised better housing and the implementation of 'great policies' through further European union, with the caveat that he would 'keep our island British' by sending immigrants home 'to a fair deal in their homelands'. He polled 1,126 votes (4.59 per cent), losing his deposit again.[443] The party faithful remained unmoved by yet another defeat. 'We went to Shoreditch for the booze-up,' wrote Diana,

> & *they* aren't downhearted a *bit*. Isn't it (in a way) a marvellous miracle – yes a miracle – of *faith* in, I suppose, Kit's STAR, because I've got faith in him as an outstandingly clever person who is about eighty percent right in his ideas – & yet! How can one see a breakthrough for him, ever? (*Between you, me & the gate post.*).[444]

Shortly afterwards, Mosley announced his political retirement after thirty-six years of unsuccessful fascist politicking, though he remained nominal UM leader until 1973. Thereafter, his political secretary, Jeffrey Hamm, re-branded the group as the Action Party. Its activities are of interest only insofar as it was the only far right party to campaign in support of British membership of the European Economic Community during the 1975 Referendum.[445]

Following his political retirement, Mosley turned to the task of rescuing his reputation from the indelible stain left upon it by his ardent pro-Nazism and anti-Semitism, which were the chief, but by no means only, impediments to his rehabilitation. Indeed, his past politics remained a serious obstruction to speaking about the issues that Mosley now desired to discuss. The 'expert forgetter',[446] as one critic dubbed Mosley, now took every opportunity therefore to deny this anti-Semitism, writing, for instance, to *The Observer* in August 1965: 'I have never been an anti-Semite ... I have never attacked any man on account of race or religion.'[447] The following week C.C. Aaronsfeld, of London's Wiener Library, reminded Mosley of several of his anti-Semitic utterances including the assertion of his sister-in-law, Lady Ravensdale, that: 'Mosley's anti-Semitism was most painful and quite terrifying to me ... Mosley's argument was that the Jews as a race put themselves always before their king and country.'[448]

Mosley repudiated the claim outright, stating that he never discussed the Jews 'or any other political subject with her'. This, he asserted to William Frankel, editor of the *Jewish*

Chronicle in June 1966 as proof that he was not, nor had he been, an anti-Semite. *The Observer* correspondence explained the 'reason' for a 'certain quarrel before the war', Mosley lectured Frankel.

> I reiterate that this quarrel is now over. It does not seem to me in accord with the traditional wisdom of your people to turn a past quarrel into a present feud. But that is your business. From my side I have done everything to prevent unnecessary quarrel and bitterness in this country.[449]

Incredulous, Frankel responded:

> Nobody wishes to 'turn a past quarrel into a present feud' but I am sure you will appreciate that Jews cannot be expected to have any great affection for one who is known to have held the opinions to which you gave expression in the past unless it were patent that there had been a sincere change of attitude.[450]

Mosley refused to accept the brush off responding,

> it does not seem to me that a change of attitude enters the question, because I have never been an anti-Semite ... I had before the war a quarrel with some Jews who in my view desired a war between Britain and Germany for the very intelligible reason that Jews were being persecuted in that country.[451]

Mosley evoked moral equivalence between perpetrator and victim to claim, 'both sides in that tragedy suffered terribly.' Mosley's argument chose to ignore the issue of responsibility for the annihilation of European Jewry let alone the outbreak of war. Sidestepping history, Mosley simply argued it was 'surely wrong to divide a country by past bitterness in face of new dangers and problems. That is my attitude which is anyhow clear, and I hope also fair'.[452]

Frankel was unable to reconcile Mosley's denial of anti-Semitism with his assertion that he had clashed with 'some Jews' who wanted war with Hitler when in fact anti-fascism was not, as Mosley implied, a solely Jewish affair. He also easily refuted Mosley's assertion that Jews sought to engineer a war between Britain and Germany because of the persecution of their co-religionists. 'All responsible Jewish opinion tried to arouse the conscience of the world to stop the persecution and to succour the refugees, a humanitarian endeavour in which I do not recall any participation by you at the time.'[453] The correspondence petered out shortly afterwards, Mosley having failed to convince Frankel or indeed anyone else, though periodically thereafter he would write to the *Jewish Chronicle* to deny charges of anti-Semitism.[454]

This agenda motivated Mosley's television appearance on ITV's 'Frost Programme' in November 1967. Questioned by its host, David Frost, Mosley denied anti-Semitism, offering as 'proof' his own denials. He struggled to maintain even this façade when Frost quoted from several of his own speeches, which rather proved the contrary. Mosley's case was further hurt by an audience member who read out Mosley's reply to a congratulatory telegram from Julius Streicher, the notorious editor of *Der Stürmer* 1935. 'I greatly esteem your message in the midst of our hard struggle,' Mosley had replied. 'The forces of Jewish corruption must be overcome in all great countries before the future of Europe can be made secure in justice and peace. Our struggle is hard but our victory certain.' Mosley denied the telegram was true, which was a lie. He denounced the Holocaust as an 'outrageous and vile crime' but was equally adamant the Nuremberg Trials were 'humbug and nonsense'. Frost pressed Mosley, would it have been better if Hitler had never existed? Mosley replied:

> No, certainly better that he should not ever have existed because his existence led to 25 million Europeans being killed. And if I had my way those 25 million would be alive today, including six million Jews who never would have been killed if there hadn't been a war. They certainly made the greatest mistake they ever made when they produced that war.[455]

What Mosley appeared to be asserting was that 'the Jews', whom he still maintained had tried to drag Britain into war with Germany, bore responsibility for the Holocaust. Frost later noted that Mosley 'saw everything through the distorting mirror of his own fantasies, and was irretrievably consumed by them. He would never see himself as others saw him.'[456]

For the Mosleys, the Frost programme was pivotal. 'While it was on, I couldn't stop trembling & my teeth were chattering,' wrote Mosley's wife. The moment it was over Robert Skidelsky, a young Oxford graduate who was then two years into his research for a biography on Mosley, called them to say they'd all watched it at Nuffield College, Oxford. 'He said Kit gave an impression of great force & nothing to use it on.' Skidelsky hoped to get Mosley on a programme about his book on the 1929 government *Politicians and the Slump* (1967) which, 'if he succeeds, that, with the Frost ghoulery, will mean the 30-year boycott is over,' noted Diana. 'Frost alone doesn't mean that & in fact I think it might hinder the Robert Ski [*sic*] programme more than help it. We shall see.'[457]

Mosley's himself was preoccupied with writing his autobiography *My Life* (1968). His position as a former Cabinet Minister, albeit thirty-seven years previously and then only for seven months, led the Cabinet Office to deliberate on the need to view the text prior to publication. Sir Burke Trend, the Cabinet Secretary, observed that, other assorted official reasons aside,

> since the book may be assumed to include a defence of British Fascism it would be better that we should not put ourselves in a position in which it could be said that, by clearing some parts of it, we had implicitly approved the rest.[458]

'I entirely agree,' observed the Prime Minister, Harold Wilson. 'It is outside the 30 years. No barge pole is long enough.'[459]

Not everyone agreed. *My Life* garnered surprisingly positive reviews following its newspaper serialisation, especially from maverick historian A.J.P. Taylor whose own controversial tome, *The Origins of the Second World War* (1961), had been received 'with joy by German Nazis and nationalists', since it served their own revisionist ends.[460] Taylor had a decided tendency to romanticise Mosley as a lost leader – 'a superb political thinker, the best of our age'. He sometimes lunched with Mosley, inviting his former student David Pryce-Jones to join them at The Ritz on one occasion. 'Mosley was even more conceited and unrepentant than Taylor,' Pryce-Jones recalled acerbically years later: 'The more Mosley defended his Hitlerite past, the more Taylor fawned on him. So frustrated was his love of power that if Mosley in 1940 had become Hitler's British Gauleiter, Taylor would have been a natural collaborator.'[461]

Perhaps more importantly the publication of *My Life* coincided with an end of the BBC prohibition on Mosley. The BBC had kept Mosley from the airwaves for thirty-four years.

Mosley belatedly launched a legal action against the broadcaster in February 1966 because it denied him the right of reply to, what he regarded, as the continuous libellous attacks upon him on their programmes. Diana Mosley was doubtful he would succeed. 'I am afraid dear Kit can't win whatever he tries, I wish to goodness he wd [sic] see it. He is really an *outlaw*,' she wrote.[462] Mosley's persistence prevailed, however. He took the BBC to the High Court and then to the European Commission of Human Rights in Strasbourg, ending with victory on 4 October 1968 when, in return for an appearance on the BBC Panorama, Mosley agreed to drop the case.[463]

His appearance on Panorama attracted a record 8.5 million viewers, who heard Mosley confess to his interlocutor, James Mossman: 'In everything I have recommended to the British people for many years past I have been defeated and frustrated, and therefore I have been a failure.' Aged 71, Mosley refused, however, to regard himself 'finally and inevitably as a failure ... I certainly looked into the void, faced depression, sorrow, terrible disappointments and frustrations ... I have never given up and I never shall.'[464] Despite the obligatory denial of anti-Semitism – despite continuing to insist that 'Jews' provoked the war – Mosley delivered a polished performance. Even the *Jewish Chronicle* considered that he looked 'moderate and reasonable'.[465]

Those closest to him, however, reacted with incredulity to his denials, however. 'Have you noted all the carry-on about Sir O?' noted his sister-in-law, 'He says he was never anti-Semitic. Good Gracious! I quite love the old soul now but really!'[466] Mosley also denied that politically he was of the extreme right. 'My position was on the left and is now in the centre of politics,' he declared.[467] Mosley's sympathisers engaged in a coordinated letter-writing campaign aiming to excuse or distort the historical record. 'In the controversy which has been raging we have not of course been able to get in nearly all the replies we wished', noted Mosley, 'but on the whole are satisfied with the outcome. The atmosphere has been changing for some time and seems now to have taken a very considerable turn for the better'.[468] Indeed. Thereafter, Mosley frequently contributed to other television programmes including a debate with *New Statesman* editor Richard Crossman on the BBC's Late Night Line-Up in July 1971. Invites from university debating societies, including Oxford, continued to arrive; the *Sunday Telegraph Magazine* published the occasional uncontroversial article and *Books and Bookmen* allowed him to carve out a niche.[469]

Though he fascinated, few people regarded Mosley as politically relevant, however. The exception perhaps was the press baron Cecil King, nephew of Lord Rothermere, Mosley's erstwhile supporter. King's diaries reveal his numerous meetings with and musings upon Mosley whom he was had become utterly intrigued by.[470] 'There is, perhaps, a magnetic force that draws together in the barren twilight of their lives, in their loneliness and their rejection, the Men of Destiny upon whom inadvertently or wisely destiny did not call,' observed Hugh Cudlipp, King's successor as chairman of the *Daily Mirror* newspaper group.[471]

A case in point was Mosley's relationship with the Duke and Duchess of Windsor, who also lived in self-imposed French exile in nearby Vallée de Chevreuse following the abdication. The Duke liked to discuss with Mosley 'how things would have been had they been respectively king and prime minister', recalled Mosley's son.[472] The Duke was also 'instinctively anti-Semitic'.[473] Mosley confirmed as much to the Royal biographer Kenneth Rose, relating an incident at a dinner party to which the Duke had also invited Sir Walter Monckton, the former Minister of Defence (1955–1956). Mosley recalled that the Duke had turned to Monckton, challenging him: 'Come on, Walter, admit that it was the Jews who brought us into the war.' Monckton naturally refused to agree with the Duke, who then turned to Mosley and repeated the question. Mosley told Rose: 'As I had was interned for three and a half years for maintaining just that, I had had enough and declined to discuss the matter with the Duke.'[474]

Despite lamenting what might have been, Mosley still refused to believe that 'destiny' had irrevocably passed him by, highlighting moreover that he still underestimated the resilience of liberal democracy, just as he had during the 1930s. Indeed, forty years later, W.F. 'Bill' Deedes, the *Daily Telegraph*'s editor, observed following a luncheon with Mosley that 'the spark of hope within him that a call to service might yet come had not been extinguished'.[475] To this end, in 1970, Mosley began publishing *Broadsheet*, ventilating his views on the pressing issues of the day and circulating them to opinion formers and policy makers whom he no doubt hoped would take heed of his panaceas and invite him to 'serve' his country.[476] 'I wanted to be prime minister for very many years', he had conceded to an interviewer in 1968 though it is not clear when, if ever, he finally relinquished this pipedream.[477] He came close, however, to conceding that he may not have possessed the right temperament to succeed politically. 'One of the reasons that I failed in politics', Mosley opined to Kenneth Rose, 'was that I could not resist being rude to people, and naturally they resented it. That is one of the most serious mistakes I have ever made'.[478]

Mosley had travelled privately and without fanfare to address the Washington Center of Foreign Policy Research in February 1970. He returned to the United States in January 1972 to promote the American edition of *My Life*, engaging a Massachusetts public relations firm to promote his interests, stressing to them that he was far more desirous to talk about his post-war ideas than his Cabinet career or other aspects of 'my past'. Mosley also contacted his friend Harry Bruno, an aviator who had flown with the Wright Brothers and who had handled public relations for the pro-Nazi aviator Charles A. Lindbergh, to assist in opening doors for him.[479] During the course of his trip, Mosley gave twenty-nine separate interviews, aired over 304 separate television and 2,432 radio stations.[480] Mosley's followers used the opportunity to connect their Leader to their own US contacts, men like Ralph Townsend, the prominent pro-Japanese isolationist who had been imprisoned during the Second World War and, initially, had been a defendant at the Great Sedition Trial of 1941.[481] Returning to London, in March Mosley recorded an interview for 'Firing Line' with William Buckley, editor of the *National Review*, which enabled him to project a sanitised version of his ideas and actions to an American conservative audience.[482]

Mosley continued to play host to an array of visitors at Temple de la Gloire – his French home – including Liberal Party leader Jeremy Thorpe, whom he had verbally sparred with at the Oxford University Debating Society in 1961, on the question of whether or not South Africa should be expelled from the Commonwealth for upholding apartheid.[483] Thorpe proposed lunching with the Mosleys in September 1971, shortly before his own political career spectacularly imploded.[484] Determined to overcome negative press coverage, in late 1972, Mosley hired a publicist to burnish his image and to ensure that he appeared before the British public more often and that his views appeared more regularly in the press.[485] This broadening of Mosley's public platform was evident that autumn, following the BBC1 broadcast of 'If Britain had Fallen', which cast doubt on the proposition that Mosley would have acted as a collaborator. Mosley of course wholeheartedly agreed, favourably reviewing the programme in *The Listener*, the weekly BBC magazine, which also afforded him the opportunity to put forth a studied defence of his inter-war position, albeit a highly selective one.[486]

Mosley elaborated on his stance in a book authored by the programme's author, Norman Longmate. He would not have collaborated, he claimed, since some 'undercover security agency' would undoubtedly have assassinated him before the question had arisen. Had this not been the case then he would have become a resistance fighter, he averred. 'I had marksman standard in the Army. I would have put on my old Army uniform and fought to a finish and no doubt have been killed, which would have settled the problem.' Had Mosley survived, Longmate probed, would not the Nazis have inevitably offered him 'at the very least some senior position' in a collaborationist government? Mosley remained adamant, however, that whilst a single German soldier was on British soil,

> I would play no part whatsoever, refuse to do anything at all.... When you've withdrawn, if and when you do withdraw from Britain leaving British people, British soil and British Commonwealth intact, then, not before, by commission of the Crown and by election of the people, I will, if I asked to, form a government.[487]

Mosley claimed he would have accepted power on no other terms and would have committed suicide rather than do so. He insisted that ultimately, the Nazis would have recognised him as an uncompromising opponent and he would have found himself back in Brixton 'with German gaolers instead of British ones'.[488]

Though the passing years enabled Mosley to erect such a defence, politically he still made no effort whatsoever to disassociate himself from those who had played an active role in Hitler's regime. Mosley often travelled to meet with 'old friends and new friends' in Germany, where his ideas continued to have purchase in Nazi circles.[489] *My Life* received favourable reviews in Nazi newspapers like *Deutsche Wochen-Zeitung*, whilst *Nation Europa* marked the occasion with a special issue on the theme of 'Europe – Dritte Kraft' ('Europe – Third Force') containing a lead article by Mosley.[490] The German translation of Mosley's autobiography, *Weg und Wagnis: Ein Leben für Europa*, in 1973 revealed much about his ongoing connection with the Nazi hinterland.[491] Mosley's translator was Mabel Narjes, who had been recommended to him a decade earlier by *Nation Europa*'s editor Arthur Ehrhardt after she had translated David Hoggan's *Der Erzwungene Krieg – The Forced War* (1961), a book absolving Hitler of blame for the war and minimising the extent of Nazi anti-Semitism.[492] Narjes later translated portions of Arthur Butz's *The Hoax of the Twentieth Century* (1976), a seminal work of Holocaust denial, into German too.[493]

Druffel-Verlag an extreme right-wing publishing house published Mosley's autobiography. Helmut Sündermann, the former NSDAP Deputy Reich Press Chief, had founded Druffel-Verlag in 1952. Sündermann was close to Mosley, praising him in *The European* using his pen-name 'Heinrich Sanden' as 'a prophetic phenomenon and directing spirit in the otherwise confused thinking of our time'.[494] Sündermann had also played a crucial role running *Nation Europa*, which Mosley helped establish in 1951, and thereafter regularly appraised Mosley of the shifting financial interests behind the journal through which he aimed to 'secure the existence and the [editorial] line of the magazine'.[495] Mosley never lost interest in *Nation Europa*. When its editor, 'my old and valued friend' Arthur Ehrhardt died in 1971, Mosley contacted his successor, NPD functionary Peter Dehoust, asking to be informed of arrangements for the journal's 'future conduct'.[496] Mosley also facilitated Sündermann's contacts in South Africa, introducing him to associates like Martin Spring, the *Financial Mail*'s features editor who had been a 'valuable' UM member before emigrating. Spring subsequently visited Sündermann in Germany.[497]

Mosley was also a valuable contact for Sündermann's stepson, Dr Gert Südholt who combined publishing 'revisionist' materials with chairing the Gesellschaft für freie

Publizistik (GfP – Society for Free Journalism). Sündermann had founded the GfP in 1960 to provide an open forum for national socialist authors and to counter what it regarded as 'untrue descriptions of the causes and backgrounds to both world wars and the defamation of German soldiery'. Mosley addressed a GfP meeting in Frankfurt on 12 October 1973, his speech titled 'Aufbruch nach Europa' ('Departure for Europe').[498] Mosley regarded the meeting as a success and hoped Südholt would be able to arrange further lectures for him.[499] Südholt subsequently became closely associated with figures like David Irving, the now disgraced doyen of Holocaust 'revisionism' who also spoke at GfP events. Südholt was jailed himself in 1993 for publishing extreme right-wing literature.[500]

Mosley's continued involvement with German Nazi networks did not impede his rehabilitation. This received an enormous fillip when Robert Skidelsky's biography, *Oswald Mosley*, appeared in 1975. Mosley was seventy-eight but still believed his time would come, his intent echoed in the biography's epigram from Faust: 'Whoever strives, can be redeemed'.[501] Skidelsky had first encountered Mosley speaking against a motion proposing South Africa be expelled from the Commonwealth at the Oxford University Debating Society in 1961, 'which failed to win the vote, but won for Mosley an ovation'.[502] Skidelsky's research, which began in earnest four years later, initially troubled Diana Mosley who feared its repercussions. 'I can't abide more wounds for Kit (don't tell one soul of which of course – one will have to put on the usual brave face no doubt).'[503] With publication approaching, Diana grew 'curious' as to its reception but still fretted that it contained 'plenty of abuse of Kit which can be picked out by reviewers.'[504]

Though no one questioned the overarching biographical narrative, Skidelsky faced a barrage of criticism for overegging Mosley's economic ideas, the fulcrum of his biography; and for 'whitewashing' the more noxious elements of his political career, including his anti-Semitism, his plaintive excuses for it, and his pro-Nazi foreign policy.[505] It was subjected to a particularly excoriating review by Vernon Bogdanor who asserted that the books' manifest defects resulted from a 'failure of the moral imagination, that is responsible for the desire to rehabilitate Mosley, and to offer such a seriously unbalanced account of his career.'[506] *The Spectator* asked Mosley to review his own biography. Skidelsky's 'rather romantic' depiction puzzled Mosley. It jarred with his own self-conception as 'primarily a very practical person'. He was also irked that Skidelsky did not address his 'vision splendid' – the term invoked to describe Mosley's post-war philosophies – to his satisfaction. This of course was all Mosley wanted to discuss. He no longer wished to be reminded of let alone be held to account for the past, which 'is exasperating to anyone acutely conscious of standing in the face of the greatest moment in history.'[507]

Skidelsky subsequently published several ripostes to critical reviews but conceded in 1980 that his summary of Mosley's anti-Semitism as 'intellectual and moral carelessness' was 'seriously inadequate'. He also downgraded many of his more positive judgements about Mosley. He revised his historical account in other areas as well though, ultimately, he felt no reason to dissent from one of his major conclusions that Mosley, 'erected an anti-Semitic superstructure on the base of a genuine but limited set of issues' and that, however, intellectually and morally inexcusable his response, 'the issues existed'.[508] The underlying reason for its deficiencies were perhaps to be found in the fact that the biography was 'emotionally centred' upon period 1929 and 1931 and Mosley's response as a Labour cabinet minister to the Great Depression, the subject of Skidelsky's doctoral dissertation, published as *Politicians and the Slump* (1967). Having viewed Mosley as Labour's 'lost' leader, as a result Skidelsky was 'loath to admit that he had a dark side'. Mosley's descent into Fascism, Skidelsky viewed as a 'tragic aberration'.[509]

Skidelsky's proximity to his subject, whom he had 'grown to like and respect,' noted the aesthete James Lees-Milne in July 1977, meant that Skidelsky perhaps failed to probe the logical consequences of Mosley's fascist thinking. 'Mosley never hated the Jews,' Skidelsky told Lees-Milne 'merely thought that international Jewry was a bad thing, and that East End Jews ought to be removed. Where to? I asked.' Lee-Milne's diary records no reply.[510] Skidelsky's biographical indulgence of this 'hero' was perhaps also influenced by what he later conceded was his 'calf-like' love of Diana Mosley. He later maintained the book cost him tenure at Johns Hopkins University and indeed Oxford.[511] Diana believed Skidelsky's treatment of her husband's anti-Semitism was 'very unfair' but nonetheless blamed 'the Jews' for confounding his career.[512]

By virtue of the fact that it was Mosley's first biography, the book 'will always remain an essential commentary on Mosley, and an invaluable source for future researchers to tap', observed Jeffrey Hamm. This seemingly throw away aside in fact reflects the underlying revisionist intent invested in Skidelsky's work by Mosley's followers.[513] For Mosley, this benchmark, which failed to grapple with his fascist politics, and detached him and his policies from events in Nazi Germany and Fascist Italy, was its strength, not weakness. Mosley's reaction to David Pryce-Jones' biography of his Hitler-obsessed sister-in-law *Unity Mitford: A Quest* (1976), which highlighted Mosley's own anti-Semitic interactions with figures like Julius Streicher and thus jarred with the image that Mosley now wished to project, underscored this point. Through his lawyers, Marsh & Ferriman, Mosley sought pre-publication redress on several points, which he insisted, were untrue.[514]

'If I did not suppress the book,' Pryce-Jones recalled, 'Mosley and his lawyers threatened, they would not be responsible for the consequences. My lawyer advised me to hire security guards.'[515] Mosley's other sister-in-law, Jessica Mitford, observed that Mosley 'was leading the pack for suppression largely because the book would undermine his recent efforts rehabilitate himself via his self-serving autobiog. [sic] in which he never was really all that anti-Semitic'/[516] Ironically, Mosley's own wife confounded his attempts at impression management. Her opinions, noted Skidelsky, were 'even more chilling than her husbands'. Diana Mosley's autobiography, *A Life of Contrasts* (1977), presented an unrepentant portrayal of her encounters with Hitler, which time had not tempered. 'I was very fond of him. Very, very fond,' she stated in an interview with *Tatler* in 2000.[517]

Mosley spent his summers in Venice and his winters in South Africa or the Bahamas, though he began winding down his international travel as Parkinson's disease took hold. He had continued trying to revise history right up until the end. In what appears to have been his last political act, he penned a letter to *The New Statesman* the week before his death bemoaning an account of the 1934 Olympia meeting. *The New Statesman* published his letter albeit in a box with the introduction: 'Throughout his life he [Mosley] was intent on persuading people that their view of history was mistaken.' Mosley died 3 December 1980 and was cremated shortly afterwards at the Père Lachaise cemetery in Paris. The BBC journalist Hugh Purcell observed:

> Looking at the signatures in the book of those paying their last respects, I noticed Adolf von Thadden, a one-time chairman of the Deutsche Reichspartei, and Giorgio Almirante, the former Italian fascist and leader of the Italian Social Movement (MSI) in its early days.
>
> From the UK came the ever-faithful Jeffrey Hamm, guardian of the Mosley flame, and the Bailey brothers, the acceptable face of East End fascism since the 1930s. If we

had expected a phalanx of old fascists guarding the coffin and communists shouting abuse at the gates, we were mistaken. It was a sombre, low-key funeral.[518]

Attending the funeral with Purcell was the journalist Colin Cross, author of *The Fascists in Britain* (1961), who muttered in a loud voice 'At least he hasn't been strung up by his heels,' an indiscreet reference to the violent fate that befell Mussolini. 'We left by a side entrance,' recorded Purcell.[519]

Following Mosley's death, his widow became the chief defender of his legacy largely because 'no one else is really in a position to do so'.[520] Diana was hopeful she could influence the direction of Nicholas Mosley's family memoirs, *Rules of the Game* (1982) and *Beyond the Pale* (1983), which utilised Mosley's private papers. She was singularly unsuccessful. Having read the proofs, Diana was livid, perceiving it as a betrayal of her late husband's memory. 'The whole tone is VILE.... It is frightful. I completely trusted him,' she wrote to her sister, outraged that he had reproduced Mosley's correspondence with his first wife and cursing herself for the 'awful mistake' of not having vetted the documents first before handing them over.[521] 'I feel I have failed Kit in not having read his private "papers" but I trusted Nicky in a way that one naturally would never have trusted an ordinary biographer,' she lamented.[522] Once published, Diana publicly railed against Nicholas' biography as:

> the degraded work of a very little man.... It's all very well having an Oedipal complex at 19, a second-rate son hating a brilliant father, but it's rather odd at 60. Nicholas wants to get his own back on his father for having had more fun than he's had.[523]

Diana's children felt similarly aggrieved. Max Mosley had been 'very much against' the memoirs from the outset, perceiving them to be 'raking up things that were largely forgotten' when there was 'no need for it, nothing to be gained.' Following their publication, Max circulated a 'dossier' of the most damaging reviews to family members, suggesting, Nicholas felt, that 'I had deliberately set out to destroy our father. He also said, in effect, that I would die dishonoured, [that] no one would be interested in my dismal love affairs or unread novels.' Mosley's other son, Alexander, was similarly unforgiving, believing that 'Nicky has destroyed him [Mosley] as a serious political figure for a generation.' Nicholas Mosley was left to ponder whether such a visceral reaction represented 'a mark of the family's own reluctance to look at any truth about my father?' Whilst Max Mosley refused to speak to his half-brother for decades afterwards, his own autobiography belatedly recognised that Nicholas Mosley's efforts were 'important to historians who want a complete picture of my father and what motivated him.'[524]

Diana Mosley continued her efforts to rehabilitate her late husband undaunted by these egregious blows. She lobbied for the release of government records on Mosley's internment in the mid-1980s in the hope of disproving allegations of treachery (whilst those on the left campaigned for their release precisely because they hoped to discover more about Mosley's presumed malfeasance).[525] A small band of 'true believers' who had remained devoted to the Leader's ideas supported her in this campaign. In 1986, they formed the Friends of Oswald Mosley (FOM), which sought to keep the 'sacred flame' alight and, through their newsletter, *Comrade*, to influence the tone of contemporary historical debate about the 'real' nature of the BUF. Academic historiography aside, *BBC History magazine* voted Mosley the country's 'worst Briton' in 2005, reflecting, anecdotally at least, the failure of this stillborn exercise in public relations.[526]

The BBC caricature notwithstanding, Mosley's legacy for extreme right-wing politics is rather more mixed. His continued activity after 1945 did much to ensure that fascist politics remained a going concern into the post-war period. Whilst his pan-European 'vision splendid' was largely rejected both by the public and indeed most extreme right activists who remained firmly of the 'Britain First' mould, Mosley represented something of a trailblazer for anti-immigration politicking, delineating most of the basic themes and arguments which have since become enshrined within its ideological canon. 'Discredited as he is politically,' Mosley, 'has, I suspect a wider following on the colour question than any of us would dare to admit to ourselves,' Tony Benn noted in 1964.[527]

Benn was only partially correct. Whilst the breadth and depth of feeling on the 'colour question' was undoubtedly probably larger than most Britons would have cared to admit, Mosley was not the principal beneficiary of such sentiment. Despite pioneering many of the techniques and ideas that subsequently became common currency on the extreme right, Mosley and the UM increasingly played second fiddle to groups like the BNP which had recently campaigned in Southall during the 1964 general election, successfully converting its racial nationalist core into a populist anti-immigration platform. Having monitored the BNP's progress since its inception,[528] Mosley began exploring ways to harness the energies of figures like Colin Jordan and John Bean in the hope of reinvigorating his own organisation. Through a former mistress, Mary Taviner, who had been treasurer of the White Defence League (WDL) and who was also involved with West London UM, Mosley approached both men and 'offered to make them his national organisers on a par with his veteran supporter Jeffrey Hamm'.[529]

Jordan rejected the approach outright, later writing that whilst Mosley deserved respect for his 'superb oratory, his commanding personality, his brilliant brain, and his courageous insight in seeking to prevent the catastrophe of World War II' he was nonetheless guilty of 'sophistry' with regards to his position on the 'Jewish Question'. Mosley's publicly professed stance that he judged men on their actions alone appalled Jordan who believed that 'one cannot divorce the man, the racial entity, from his actions.' On these grounds, Jordan pilloried Mosley for maintaining a double standard in his broader stance on racial matters:

> Mosley was far too clever a man not to know full well the fallacies of his presentation. In the matter of coloured immigrants he had no inhibitions in adopting a conflicting racial attitude, calling for coloureds as such to be kept out and sent out of Britain. The ambivalence is to be set down to his desire to move with the times on the then ultrasensitive issue of the Jews. It was part of the renunciatory expediency which led him to make the definitive declaration that he had – after the war and the military defeat of the Axis – gone beyond Fascism and National Socialism, an expediency which in fact worked against him and stands against him as an ultimate major flaw in his character.[530]

Bean's view of Mosley was similarly deleterious, believing that although he was 'right before the war ... now he is a man of the past. We have nothing to do with him because we do not regard his racist views as sufficiently extreme.'[531] Unlike Jordan, he was, however, sufficiently intrigued to meet with Mosley. Despite being 'given the full Mosley hypnosis treatment', Bean who had been a member of the UM in the 1950s, of which Mosley was apparently unaware, declined to re-join. Mosley's failure to persuade either man to join his standard was emblematic of his wider failure to rally the younger generation of racial nationalists to his standard. Their creed was a brand of Nordicist racial nationalism owing more to the politics of Arnold Leese than to Mosley's own 'grand synthesis'.[532]

Another ideological fault line was revealed by Mosley's meeting in 1961 with John Tyndall (Chapter 5), who went on to lead both the National Front and the British National Party, but whose opposing geopolitical outlook precluded any meeting of minds.[533] 'I once met Mosley but cannot claim to have known him,' Tyndall wrote after Mosley's death:

> Our encounter lasted an hour, during which we argued the respective merits of Anglo-Saxon union and the Union of Europe. A devotee of the first, I did battle with perhaps the most formidable advocate of the second. The meeting, which had been arranged by a mutual friend who had hoped we may be able to join forces, was terminated by Mosley abruptly as the hour struck – and rightly, because it was clear that in loyalties we belonged to two different worlds which argument could not bridge. I expect he forgot me quickly after that but I certainly did not forget him. I have long believed that this advanced crisis in our civilisation we can only be saved by exceptional men, and there was no doubted that Mosley was an exceptional man.[534]

Like Jordan, Tyndall dismissed Mosley's attempt to revise the history regarding his inter-war stance on the 'Jewish Question'. 'Much drivel, as he says, has been talked about the Jews, and some of it – sad to say – by himself,' Tyndall adjudged. Mosley's post-war pretence that the 'long and short of the matter' was that he had only opposed certain Jews who wanted 'to start a war in the Jewish interest' was rejected by Tyndall who claimed that Mosley's self-serving exoneration, when measured against the anti-Semitic tenor of his party's own policy pronouncements, was 'glaringly tongue-in-cheek'. Tyndall felt this to have been corroborated during his own conversation with Mosley, 'in which it was evident that his opposition to the Jews was as strong as ever and that public statements he made to the contrary were determined by purely *tactical* considerations.'[535] Despite these objections, however, Tyndall continued to admire both Mosley and his inter-war politics. To commemorate the 100th anniversary of Mosley's birth on 16 November 1896 – declared 'National Mosley Centennial Day' – Tyndall's journal, *Spearhead*, offered facsimiles of BUF propaganda sold by US admirer, Edward Fields, and Stevens Books, an outfit that continues circulating BUF material today.[536]

This new generation of racial nationalist militants had little use for Mosley. His own reputation, irreparably tarnished by the indelible stain of Fascism and Nazism, limited his ability to exploit 'coloured immigration' for political ends and most likely poisoned the well for others too. Indeed, the sudden success of Enoch Powell's populist anti-immigration demagoguery in 1968, which saw him – like Mosley in the 1920s – appealing over the head of his party directly to the electorate, served to highlight the potential salience of the immigration issue when decoupled from overtly fascist politics. In the aftermath of Powell's 'Rivers of Blood' speech, the UM were able to gain a toehold amongst the Smithfield Meat Porters through 'Big Dan' Harmston, a fervent Mosleyite who worked in the market as a porter. His presence was notable during a spontaneous march in support of Powell by the Smithfield porters on 24 April. Harmston did not organise it, however. 'The whole thing just happened. When the lads were all together and blokes were getting up and having their say they got me up there as well,' he recalled.[537] Harmston's message to his fellow porters at a marketplace meeting was clear:

> At last the Englishman has had some guts. This is as important as Dunkirk. We are becoming second-class citizens in our own country. Immigrants have been brought here to undercut our wages in time of crisis. When there is vast unemployment in this country immigrants will compete with you for your jobs.[538]

Six-hundred strong, the porters then marched from Smithfield to Westminster under the banner 'Enoch is Right' – singing songs such as *White Christmas, There'll always be an England* and *Ten Little Niggers*. Having delivered a ninety-two-page petition to Powell supporting him, Harmston again addressed his colleagues. 'This is a colour issue', he told those gathered outside the House of Commons, to loud cheers. 'All immigrants should return home even if it means giving them repatriation grants. They are an embarrassment to our society. We are not racialists – but realists.'[539] Reflecting on the angry but essentially transitory nature of the Smithfield porters march, Harmston later recalled:

> [I]f that day I'd said, 'Pick up your cleavers and knives and decapitate Heath and Wilson', they'd have done it. They really would, but they wouldn't have done it next week. It was just that mood of the moment – like the storming of the Bastille I suppose.[540]

What was also notable about this anti-immigration march, which took place in the full glare of the media, was not so much its racism but the absence of any mention of Mosley whatsoever. Jeffrey Hamm later opined that Harmston marched 'not in support of the views of Enoch Powell, as the Press wrongly reported, but of those of his hero Oswald Mosley'.[541] This might have been true of Harmston but not of the majority. Mosley also sought to distance himself from Powell, who 'is saying nine years later what I have always said,' he sententiously told *The Times*. Powell was simply unworthy of his support. Instead, underlining his frustrated, political impotence, Mosley snobbishly sniped at Powell, deriding him as a 'middle class Alf Garnett', whilst lambasting Powellism as 'the last spasm of Little England'.[542]

To add insult to injury, Mosley and the UM were completely eclipsed by the nascent National Front, led by his former minion A.K. Chesterton, which succeeded, where Mosley had failed, in mobilising the wave of populist anti-immigration sentiment unleashed by Powell. If the public heeded his 'pioneer' anti-immigration campaign in 1959, the issue could have been resolved, Mosley claimed. 'The question now arises what can be done in the existing situation', he wrote in 1977, when the NF was ascendant. 'It is clearly impossible to drag 2,000,000 people – with women and children screaming dissent in face of mankind – into ships for transport to countries which will not receive them,' he continued, thereby implicitly rejecting compulsory repatriation, the NF flagship policy. 'Such policies are as bogus as they are belated.'[543] The new generation of racial nationalists, though they acknowledged Mosley's talents, would repudiate such temporising, together with his 'vision splendid' – the cornerstone of Mosley's post-war philosophy.

Notes

1 Hansard, HC Deb. (series 5), vol. 432, col. 2140 (6 June 1946). Shown the correspondence on 9 August 1945, Guy Liddell, the MI5 counter-subversion chief, observed: 'It made it perfectly clear that Mosley was being subsidised to the tune of £60,000 a year', see Liddell Diaries, 9 August 1945 in TNA KV 4/466.
2 TNA FO 371/60738 includes copies of the correspondence. For MI5's extensive investigation, see TNA KV 3/255–258 and TNA 3/53–55.
3 Mosley Publications 'Press Release', 6 June 1946 in TNA KV 3/54/123a.
4 Mosley is already the subject of two full-scale biographies, Stephen Dorril, *Blackshirt: Sir Oswald Mosley and British Fascism* (London: Penguin, 2006); and Robert Skidelsky, *Oswald Mosley* (London: Papermac, 1975). For the most recent survey, see Martin Pugh, *'Hurrah for the Blackshirts': Fascists and Fascism in Britain between the Wars* (London: Pimlico, 2006).

5 Colin Cook, 'A Fascist Memory: Oswald Mosley and the Myth of the Airman', *European Review of History – revue européenne d'Histoire*, vol. 4, no. 2, 1997, pp. 147–162. For Mosley's military records, see TNA WO 339/15781.
6 Matthew Worley, 'Why Fascism? Sir Oswald Mosley and the Conception of the British Union of Fascists', *History*, vol. 96, no. 1, 2010, pp. 68–83.
7 *Ibid.*
8 Harold Nicolson, *Diaries and Letters: 1930–39, Vol. 1* (London: Collins/Fontana, 1969), p. 91.
9 Kenneth Young (ed.), *The Diaries of Sir Robert Bruce Lockhart, Vol. 1: 1915–1938* (London: Macmillan, 1973), p. 125.
10 *Ibid.*, pp. 194 and 196; and Nicolson, *Diaries and Letters*, p. 107.
11 Harold Nicolson and Nigel Nicolson, *The Harold Nicolson Diaries and Letters 1907–1963* (London: Orion, 2004), p. 79.
12 Nicolson, *Diaries and Letters*, p. 105.
13 *The Times*, 13 December 1926.
14 Thomas Linehan, 'The British Union of Fascists as a Totalitarian Movement and Political Religion', *Totalitarian Movements and Political Religions*, vol. 5, no. 3, 2004, pp. 397–418.
15 Bernhard Dietz, *Neo-Tories: The Revolt of British Conservatives against Democracy and Political Modernity, 1929–1939* (London: Bloomsbury, 2018), p. 123.
16 Young, *The Diaries of Sir Robert Bruce Lockhart, Vol. 1: 1915–1938*, p. 227.
17 Salvatore Garau, 'The Internationalisation of Italian Fascism in the Face of German National Socialism, and its Impact on the British Union of Fascists', *Politics, Religion & Ideology*, vol. 15, no. 1, 2014, pp. 45–63.
18 *Blackshirt*, no. 6, 1 May 1933.
19 TNA HO 283/6; and TNA HO 283/10.
20 'The British Union of Fascists' (1941) in TNA KV 4/241. In their report to the Directors of the BUF Trust, the auditors highlighted 'There was no means of verifying the amounts of subscriptions and donations.'
21 TNA HO 45/24891/49.
22 Special Branch report, 23 March 1936 in TNA HO 144/20147/378.
23 Julie Gottlieb, 'The Marketing of Megalomania: Celebrity, Consumption and the Development of Political Technology in the British Union of Fascists', *Journal of Contemporary History*, vol. 41, no. 1, 2006, pp. 35–55.
24 'The British Union of Fascists' (1941) in TNA KV 4/241.
25 *Daily Mail*, 19 July 1934; and Richard Griffiths, *Fellow Travellers of the Right: British Enthusiasts for Nazi Germany, 1933–39* (Oxford: Oxford University Press, 1983), pp. 163–165.
26 'The Fascist Movement in the United Kingdom, Excluding Northern Ireland – Report no. 2, Developments during June/July 1934' in TNA KV 3/58.
27 G.C. Weber, 'Patterns of Membership and Support for the British Union of Fascists', *Journal of Contemporary History*, vol. 19, no. 4, 1984, p. 577.
28 'The Fascist Movement in the United Kingdom, Excluding Northern Ireland – Report no. 3, Developments during August/September 1934' in TNA KV 3/58.
29 Rome Chancery to Foreign Office, 27 April 1935 in TNA HO 144/20144/55.
30 'The British Union of Fascists' (1941) in TNA KV 4/241.
31 Special Branch report, 4 April 1935 in TNA HO 144/20144/82.
32 Claudia Baloli, 'Anglo-Italian Fascist Solidarity: The Shift from Italophilia to Naziphilia in the BUF', in Julie V. Gottlieb and Thomas P. Linehan (eds), *The Culture of Fascism: Visions of the Far Right in Britain* (London: I.B. Tauris, 2004), pp. 147–161.
33 Arnd Bauerkämper, 'The Denigration of British Fascism: Traditional Anti-British Stereotypes and Claims of Superiority in Nazi Germany', in Arnd Bauerkämper and Christiane Eisenberg (eds), *Britain as a Model of Modern Society? German Views* (Augsburg: Wißner-Verlag, 2006), pp. 156–157.
34 Special Branch report 20 March 1935 in TNA HO 144/20144/109; and 'The Fascist Movement in the United Kingdom, Excluding Northern Ireland – Report no. 3, Developments during August/September 1934' in TNA KV 3/58.
35 'The British Union of Fascists' (1941) in TNA KV 4/241.
36 Special Branch report, 3 June 1935 in TNA HO 144/20145/289. It met every Thursday in the 'Leader's Room'.

37 The Research Directory minutes, 23 May 1935 read: '6. Ceremonial. [Robert] Gordon-Canning to obtain information regarding German procedure at mass meetings. 7. Hitler's speech. [Alexander Raven] Thomson to write an article for *Blackshirt*. Thomson to obtain special authoritative English translation of the speech from the German authorities.'
38 Special Branch report, 9 May 1936 in TNA HO 144/20144/46.
39 Major-General J.F.C. Fuller, 'Report on the Organisation of the BUF', October 1934, Mosley papers, Nicholas Mosley deposit, XOMN/B/7/4, Box 8, Birmingham University.
40 Special Branch report, 27 March 1936 in TNA HO 144/20147/297.
41 Dorril, *Blackshirt*, pp. 341–342.
42 'The British Union of Fascists' (1941) in TNA KV 4/241. In TNA CAB 66/35/48, the Home Secretary conceded that rather than having documentary proof, evidence of Nazi funding for the BUF 'depends on the statements of certain members of the British Union who were in a position to know.' This was hardly surprising given the lengths to which Mosley went to obscure the origins of party funds.
43 Observing this 'striking similarity' between the new BUF armband and that of Nazi formations, MI5 recorded further that 'The emblem of the German S.S. is two flashes in a circle, though it is only fair to say that the "flashes" in the German emblem are in the form of an "S" of German script.'
44 'The British Union of Fascists' (1941) in TNA KV 4/241.
45 For more on this theme, Graham Macklin, '"Onward Blackshirts!" Music and the British Union of Fascists', *Patterns of Prejudice*, vol. 47, nos 4–5, 2013, pp. 430–457.
46 For instance, *Action*, no. 58, 27 March 1937.
47 Figures like Clement Bruning, the Ealing district leader, went to work for *Welt-Dienst*, the anti-Semitic network based in Erfurt, as did another activist, D.C. Wace.
48 *Blackshirt*, no. 194, 9 January 1937 advertises Hitler Jugend pen pals for 'British boys'.
49 Daniel Tilles, *British Fascist Anti-Semitism and Jewish Responses, 1932–40* (London: Bloomsbury, 2015), p. 89.
50 Skidelsky, *Oswald Mosley*, pp. 291 and 378–380.
51 Tilles, *British Fascist Anti-Semitism and Jewish Responses, 1932–40*, p. 78.
52 *Ibid.*, pp. 78–79.
53 *The Fascist Week*, May 1934 announced the exclusion of Jews from the BUF.
54 Geoffrey Alderman, 'Dr. Robert Forgan's Resignation from the British Union of Fascists', *Labour History Review*, vol. 57, no. 1, 1992, pp. 37–41. MI5 recorded, however, that Forgan's embezzlement of a £250 cheque belonging to the BUF had also contributed to his estrangement from Mosley, who had blamed him for the poor financial health of the organisation, observes Dietz, *Neo-Tories*, p. 263.
55 Tilles, *British Fascist Anti-Semitism and Jewish Responses, 1932–40*, p. 80.
56 *Blackshirt*, no. 80, 2 November 1934. Several Dutch fascists including Anton Mussert attended the meeting.
57 Oswald Mosley, *Fascism: 100 Questions Asked and Answered* (London: BUF Publications, 1936), questions 95–98.
58 'The British Union of Fascists' (1941) in TNA KV 4/241.
59 Thomas P. Linehan, *East London for Mosley: The British Union of Fascists in East London and South-West Essex 1933–1940* (London: Frank Cass, 1996).
60 Special Branch report, 23 March 1936 in TNA HO 144/20147/382.
61 *Action*, no. 34, 10 October 1936.
62 TNA KV 2/1363/68a.
63 'The British Union of Fascists' (1941) in TNA KV 4/241.
64 F.B. Aikin-Sneath, 'Interrogation of W.E.D. Allen', 28 February 1942 in TNA KV 3/53/8b.
65 Dorril, *Blackshirt*, p. 445.
66 Martin Pugh, *'Hurrah for the Blackshirts': Fascism and Fascists in Britain Between the Wars* (London: Pimlico, 2006), pp. 227–228.
67 'The Fascist Movement in the United Kingdom, Excluding Northern Ireland – Report no. 4, Developments from August 1936 to November 1936' in TNA KV 3/59.
68 'The Fascist Movement in the United Kingdom, Excluding Northern Ireland – Report no. 5, Developments from November 1936 to May 1937' in TNA KV 3/59. This does not necessarily contradict the figures presented in TNA HO 144/21062/403–407 and TNA HO 144/21281/112–114 that record a *rise* from 15,500 to 16,500 members between November 1936 and December 1938.

69 Dorril, *Blackshirt*, p. 443.
70 Special Branch report, 4 April 1935 in TNA HO 144/20144/82.
71 Dorril, *Blackshirt*, pp. 376–377 and 381.
72 Bauerkämper, 'The Denigration of British Fascism', p. 163.
73 Interview by Mr. Stamp and Mr. Noakes of MI5, 8 April 1942 in TNA KV 3/53.
74 H. von Kotze (ed.), *Heeresadjutant bei Hitler, 1938–1943. Aufzeichnungen des Majors Engel. Schritenreihe der Vierteljahrshefte fur Zeitgeschichte*, no. 29 (Stuttgart 1974), pp. 82 (diary entry, 14 June 1940) and 85 (diary entry, 15 July 1940). Engel was one of Hitler's adjutants.
75 'The British Union of Fascists' (1941) in TNA KV 4/241.
76 'Lady Diana Mosley', 26 June 1940 in TNA KV 2/884/48a.
77 'Interrogation of W.E.D. Allen', 27 February 1942 in TNA KV 3/53/8b. TNA KV 2/1363/20a records:

> At the time when he [Hoare] tried to arrange matters he was told that it was too soon, and before he got into the business again Mosley nipped in and pinched the reward, not that Oliver Hoare of course wanted any money!

TNA HO 45/23741 indicates that Peter Pendleton Eckersley, the former BBC radio engineer involved in the commercial broadcasting scheme, was also aware of the Rothschild negotiations.
78 Weber, 'Patterns of Membership and Support for the British Union of Fascists', p. 577. TNA KV 4/241 gives the considerably lower estimate of 6,600 members in December 1938 rising to 10,922 in August 1939.
79 Dorril, *Blackshirt*, p. 457.
80 *Action*, no. 161, 25 March 1939.
81 'The British Union of Fascists' (1941) in TNA KV 4/241.
82 *Ibid.*
83 *Ibid.*
84 *Ibid.*
85 TNA KV 2/1363/68a.
86 For an illuminating discussion, see Richard Griffiths, 'A Note on Mosley, the "Jewish War" and Conscientious Objection', *Journal of Contemporary History*, vol. 40, no. 4, 2005, pp. 675–688.
87 *Ibid.*; and 'The British Union of Fascists' (1941) in TNA KV 4/241.
88 *Ibid.*
89 *Ibid.*
90 *Ibid.*
91 'The British Union of Fascists' (1941) in TNA KV 4/241.
92 TNA HO 144/21429/102–3.
93 'British Union: Memorandum by the Home Secretary', 14 April 1943 in TNA CAB 66/35/48.
94 Griffiths, 'A Note on Mosley, the "Jewish War" and Conscientious Objection', p. 679.
95 Oswald Mosley, *The British Peace ... and How to Get It* (London: Greater Britain Publications, 1940).
96 TNA KV 2/884/36e.
97 TNA HO 45/24895/3 quoted in Griffiths, 'A Note on Mosley, the "Jewish War" and Conscientious Objection', p. 683.
98 TNA KV 2/884/21a.
99 *Action*, no. 214, 11 April 1940.
100 *Action*, no. 220, 23 May 1940.
101 For studies of this subversive anti-Semitic coterie, see Richard Griffiths, *Patriotism Perverted: Captain Ramsay, the Right Club and British Anti-Semitism, 1939–40* (London: Constable, 1998); and Paul Willetts, *Rendezvous at the Russia Tea Rooms* (London: Constable, 2016).
102 A.W. Brian Simpson, *In the Highest Degree Odious: Detention without Trial in Wartime Britain* (Oxford: Oxford University Press, 1994) remains the best study on internment.
103 Richard Thurlow, 'The Evolution of the Mythical British Fifth Column, 1939–46', *Twentieth Century British History*, vol. 10, no. 4, 1999, pp. 477–498. Tim Tate, *Hitler's British Traitors: The Secret History of Spies, Sabateurs and Fifth Columnists* (London: Icon, 2018) offers an alternative interpretation.
104 TNA KV 2/884/36a notes Mosley held an 'exclusive' meeting for NHQ staff on 13 May to discuss plans for carrying on the movement in the event of 'strong Government action'.

105 For an overview, see Adrien Weale, *Renegades: Hitler's Englishmen* (London: Warner Books, 1995); and Sean Murphy, *Letting the Side Down: British Traitors of the Second World War* (Stroud: Sutton, 2003).
106 Graham Macklin, '"Hail Mosley and F' Em All": Martyrdom, Transcendence and the "Myth" of Internment', *Totalitarian Movements and Political Religions*, vol. 7, no. 1, 2006, pp. 1–23.
107 Oswald Mosley, *The Alternative*, p. 9.
108 Oswald Mosley, *Union of Europe* (Ramsbury: Mosley Publications, 1947).
109 *Europe-a-Nation: Mosley's Speech in East London, 16 October 1948 on The Election of a European Assembly – Let the People Vote* (Ramsbury: Sanctuary Press, 1948).
110 For a detailed history, see Graham Macklin, *Very Deeply Dyed in Black: Sir Oswald Mosley and the Resurrection of British Fascism after 1945* (London: I.B. Tauris, 2007). See also Luke LeCras, ' "Europe A Nation" or "Common Market Suicide"? Fascism, European Entanglement and the Ideology of Britain's Extreme Right, 1945–75', *Australian Journal of Politics and History*, vol. 64, no. 3, 2018, pp. 436–449.
111 *Constitution of Union Movement and Guide to Organisation* (1948), p. 5. Section 1(4)(a) of the *British Union Constitution and Rules* (1938) states:

> any Briton at the age of not less than 18 years from whom the Union shall receive an application for membership in such form as may from time to time be provided, signed by him and accompanied by such sum as he shall therein undertake to pay by way of monthly subscription, shall be eligible for membership.

It provided no further indication as to who or what constituted a 'Briton'.
112 See the legal discussion relating to *American Jews Threaten Britain* (Ramsbury: Sanctuary Press, 1949) in TNA LO 2/232, for instance.
113 'Fascism – November 1950' in TNA HO 45/25401.
114 B.G. Atkinson to G.N. Jackson, 29 March 1951 in TNA HO 45/25401.
115 James Loughlin, *Fascism and Constitutional Conflict: The British Extreme-Right and Ulster in the Twentieth Century* (Liverpool: Liverpool University Press, 2019) provides a thorough analysis of Mosley's stance towards Ireland.
116 Oswald Mosley, *Ireland's Right to Unite when Entering European Union* (London: Sanctuary Press: 1948). Mosley had met the Irish nationalist MP Cahir Healey (South Fermanagh), a founding member of Sinn Féin, in Brixton prison in July 1941 where the latter was interned for fear he sought to collaborate with the Nazis in order to advance the anti-partition cause. Healey and Mosley enjoyed an 'especially close relationship' after 1945, see Christopher Norton, 'The Internment of Cahir Healey MP, Brixton Prison July 1941–December 1942', *Twentieth Century British History*, vol. 18, no. 2, 2007, pp. 170–193. Healey was an occasional contributor to Mosley's post-war journal *The European*, for instance, *The European*, no. 36, February 1956, pp. 21–25 and *The European*, vol. 8, no. 5, January 1957, pp. 282–285.
117 For an overview of this period, see Maurice Walsh, 'Mosley in Ireland', *Dublin Review*, no. 26, spring 2007, http://thedublinreview.com/mosley-in-ireland/ (accessed 6 January 2016).
118 *Union*, no. 158, 10 March 1951.
119 Maurice Walsh, 'Mosley in Ireland'; and TNA IR 59/466 and TNA IR 59/467.
120 Mosley, *The Alternative*, p. 212.
121 *Mosley: Policy and Debate – From the European* (Southend: Euphorion Books, 1954), p. 37.
122 Mark Mazower, *Hitler's Europe: Nazi Rule in Occupied Europe* (London: Penguin, 2008), pp. 116–117.
123 *Europe-a-Nation – Africa: Empire of Europe. Text of Mosley's Speech at Kensington Town Hall, on 18 October 1949* (Ramsbury: Sanctuary Press, 1949).
124 *Mosley: Policy and Debate*, pp. 37–46; and Oswald Mosley, *My Life* (London: Nelson, 1968), pp. 483–485.
125 Oswald Mosley, *Union of Europe* (Ramsbury: Mosley Publications, 1947).
126 *Ibid.*
127 Bob Boothby MP to Oswald Mosley, 23 November 1949 in TNA KV 2/4096/179a.
128 Quoted in Matteo Albanese and Pablo del Hierro, 'A Transnational Network: The Contact between Fascist Elements in Spain and Italy, 1945–1968', *Politics, Religion & Ideology*, vol. 15, no. 1, 2014, p. 89.
129 Macklin, *Very Deeply Dyed in Black*, pp. 77–117 deals with these organisational efforts at length.

130 CIA report, 'Meeting of European Neo-Fascist Parties to be Held in Sweden', 10 April 1951, www.cia.gov/library/readingroom/docs/CIA-RDP82-00457R007400040008-2.pdf (accessed 23 January 2020).
131 Phillip Rees, *Biographical Dictionary of the Extreme Right since 1890* (New York: Simon & Schuster, 1990), p. 36.
132 Damir Skenderovic, *The Radical Right in Switzerland: Continuity & Change, 1945–2000* (New York: Berghahn, 2009), pp. 279–280.
133 Jean Yves-Camus and Nicolas Lebourg, *Far-Right Politics in Europe* (Cambridge, MA: Belknap, 2016), p. 73.
134 Damir Skenderovic, *The Radical Right in Switzerland*, pp. 279–280.
135 CIA report, 'Relations with Spain: Appendix' (n.d.), www.cia.gov/library/readingroom/docs/CIA-RDP78-00915R000400120005-9.pdf (accessed 23 January 2020).
136 William Buckley Interview, Oswald Mosley: Briton, Fascist, European, www.oswaldmosley.com/william-buckley-interview/ (accessed 4 April 2018).
137 CIA report, '(Prince) Junio Valerio Borghese', 5 June 1963, www.cia.gov/library/readingroom/docs/BORGHESE%2C%20JUNIO%20VALERIO_0022.pdf (accessed 23 January 2020); and Jack Greene and Alessandro Massignani, *The Black Prince and the Sea Devils: The Story of Valerio Borghese and the Elite Units of the Decima MAS* (New York: De Capo, 2008).
138 TNA KV 2/2997/54a.
139 'Obituaries: Leon Degrelle Fascist Leader in Belgium, 87', *New York Times*, 2 April 1994, www.nytimes.com/1994/04/02/obituaries/leon-degrelle-fascist-leader-in-belgium-87.html (accessed 4 April 2017).
140 Mosley established contact with Johannes Bernhardt, a former SS officer and intelligence agent who had been managing director of SOFINDUS, a Nazi-controlled concern established during the Spanish Civil War to supply Franco with war *matériel*. TNA KV 2/2949/8a notes that Raven Thomson's interview with Bernhardt in May 1949, which 'although cordial proved negative'. D. Stewart to Miss K.N. Coates, 5 July 1954 in TNA KV 2/3997 notes that five years later Alf Flockhart, the UM national organiser, visited Spain and met with former SS officer Otto Skorzeny, which was perhaps more fruitful. Skorzeny applied for a visa to meet UM leaders in England. MI5 blocked it. Not everyone trusted Skorzeny either. Falangist officials told Per Engdahl, the Swedish ESB leader, who visited Spain in 1952, that Skorzeny 'was no longer invited to important Fascist gatherings.' This was because they believed him to be 'in close contact with French and American intelligence officers or military attaches, to whom he reports every bit of information on Fascist activities.' See CIA report, 'Otto Skorzeny', 7 November 1952, www.cia.gov/library/readingroom/docs/SKORZENY%2C%20OTTO%20%20VOL.%202_0058.pdf (accessed 23 January 2020). For more on Mosley's dealings with Skorzeny, see Guy Walters, *Hunting Evil* (London: Bantam, 2009), pp. 280–282.
141 Hans-Ulrich Rudel, *Stuka Pilot* (London: Euphorion, 1952). Plesse Verlag founded by former SS officer Waldemar Schütz, whose chief political purpose was to rehabilitate the SS, previously published the book as *Trotzdem* (1951). Schütz was prominent in the DRP, later becoming a senior NPD figure.
142 TNA KV 2/4023/278.
143 PUSD to 'R', 12 July 1954 in TNA KV 2/3997/68.
144 TNA 2/3798/89. Mosley and Genoud were in regular contact. Pierre Pean, *L'Extremiste: François Genoud, de Hitler à Carlos* (Paris: Fayard, 1996) notes that they exchanged ninety-three letters between 1950 and 1957.
145 Dorril, *Blackshirt*, p. 603.
146 Walsh, 'Mosley in Ireland'.
147 TNA KV 2/9997/43a.
148 TNA KV 2/4000/126d.
149 *Die Europäische Nationale*, no. 15, 15 January 1951.
150 For an extended discussion, see Kurt P. Tauber, 'German Nationalists and European Union', *Political Science Quarterly*, vol. 74, no. 4, 1959, pp. 564–589. Activists also distributed thousands of copies of *Die Rettung des Abendlandes: Die dritte Kraft* to Germans attending the England–Germany football match in 1955, see *Feinde der Demokratie [Enemies of Democracy]*, vol. 5, no. 3, December 1955–January 1956, p. 35.

151 *Reichsruf*, no. 17, 28 April 1962. Nouvelle Editions Latines later published it in French as *La Nation Europe* (1962).
152 Gerard Braunthal, *Right-Wing Extremism in Contemporary Germany* (London: Palgrave, 2009), p. 118.
153 For further details, see Macklin, *Very Deeply Dyed in Black*, pp. 111–114.
154 Oswald Mosley, *European Socialism* (London: Sanctuary Press, 1951).
155 Oswald Mosley to Alexander Raven Thomson, 25 July 1955 in OMN/B/2/4, Oswald Mosley papers, Nicholas Mosley deposit, Birmingham University. *Six Points of European Socialism* (London: Sanctuary Press, c.1957) distilled Mosley's main ideas for public consumption.
156 *The European*, no. 1, March 1953.
157 Oswald Mosley, *European Socialism: A Summary of the Policy and A Reply to Comment and Criticism from Britain, Germany, Italy and America* (London: Sanctuary Press, 1956) and *Mosley: Policy and Debate*, pp. 14–21 and 77–88.
158 John Charnley, *Blackshirts and Roses: An Autobiography* (London: Brockingday Publications, 1990), p. 221.
159 Jewish Defence Committee (JDC) South West London District Committee, minutes, 13 April 1948 in 1658/3/2/14, Jewish Defence Committee papers, Wiener Library, hereafter JDC papers. The UM gained little traction in Brixton early years. Special Branch reports to be found in TNA HO 45/25401 reveal that UM speakers at speaking pitches in Rushcroft Road and Electric Avenue in Brixton during 1949 and 1950 rarely raised an audience in double figures and on one occasion on 6 January 'failed to attract an audience' at all.
160 Report on Meeting in Rushcroft Road, 31 August 1951 in 1658/10/4/4, JDC papers; and *South London Press*, 4 September 1951. Joe Mulhall, 'The Unbroken Thread: British Fascism, its Ideologues and Ideologies, 1939–1969' (Royal Holloway, University of London, PhD thesis, 2016), p. 212.
161 *Union*, no. 195, 8 December 1951; and *Union*, no. 200, 19 January 1952. The UM characterised 'Jewish' crime in a markedly similar manner. *Union*, no. 196, 15 December 1951 claimed that Jews were 'liable to have a very different moral standard towards crimes such as smuggling' because, although they did no harm to an individual, they were to the detriment of the nation to which 'they may feel no strong sense of loyalty towards.' Thus, *Union* argued, all such 'alien races' should be denied British citizenship.
162 *Union*, no. 196, 15 December 1951.
163 Michael Quill, letter to the author, January 2000.
164 *Union*, no. 208, 15 March 1952; and 'Chairman's statement – July 1954', Provincial Liaison Committee, JDC papers, which observes another attack on Lipton and his 'coreligionists'.
165 Fred Bailey, interview with the author, 21 April 1999.
166 John Bean, *Many Shades of Black: Inside Britain's Far Right* (London: Millennium, 1999), p. 83.
167 Lewisham Branch leader Pat Dunigan received 758 votes, Frederick Lewis, a former Bombay Police Officer, received 523 votes, and Michael Ryan 373 votes. 'Chairman's report – April 1952' in Provincial Liaison Committee, minutes, 1952–1959, 1658/1/3/3, JDC papers notes Lewis' own son undermined his campaign, writing to the local press to denounce his father's racist views as 'obnoxious and nonsensical'.
168 There were only 414 West Indians, 55 Pakistanis, 776 Indians and 102 West Africans resident throughout the entire Borough of Lambeth according to the 1951 census, see Shelia Patterson, *Newcomers: The West Indians in London* (London: Centre for Urban Studies and George Allen & Unwin, 1960), p. 53.
169 Jewish Defence Committee, minutes, 10 June 1952 in 1658/1/1/3, JDC papers.
170 *Union*, no. 212, 19 April 1952.
171 Bean, *Many Shades of Black*, pp. 83–84.
172 Special Branch report, 29 November 1950 in TNA KV 2/4017.
173 *Union*, 2 December 1950.
174 MI5, 'Extract', 20 November 1951 in TNA KV 2/4017/433z.
175 MI5, 'Extract', 11 February 1952 in TNA KV 2/4017; and *Union*, 1 March 1952.
176 TNA KV 2/4017/448a.
177 TV KV 2/4018/502b.

178 Trevor Grundy, *Memoir of a Fascist Childhood: A Boy in Mosley's Britain* (London: Heinemann, 1998), p. 96 recalls his father's performance at the 1955 party conference:

> Members had said that too many West Indians were coming into Britain and that there'd be trouble. My father rose and said that the problem wasn't the blacks it was the Jews. Red-faced and with great passion he'd screamed, 'And if you're looking for the first man in Britain to turn on the gas taps, I'm here!' He hit his chest with a clenched fist and waited for applause. It did not come. He sat down, looked around several times and then looked at Mosley. I watched the Leader's face. For a few moments he stared at my father and then Jeffrey Hamm went to him with a bit of paper and announced we'd have a short break. As we moved from our seats, a few old members slapped my father on the back. One said 'Suppose you shouldn't have said that, Sid, but I would too'.

179 Special Branch report, 24 May 1954 in TNA KV 2/4018/485a.
180 TNA KV 2/4018/503a.
181 *This is the Vital Issue – London County Council Elections – Thursday, 31 March 1955* (UM handbill).
182 'Chairman's Statement – April 1955', in 1658/1/3/3, Provincial Liaison Committee, JDC papers.
183 Report 'Thomson and Flockhart', 16 June 1955 in TNA KV 2/4019.
184 Grundy, *Memoir of a Fascist Childhood*, pp. 112–113 notes that a group of East End activists informed Mosley that if Flockhart was ever seen again at UM headquarters, or allowed to join the movement, 'they would all resign'.
185 MI5, 'Extract', 28 June 1957 in TNA KV 2/4019/564a. Mosley remained loyal to his disgraced activist despite the nature of his offences, however. Despite barring him from re-joining UM after his release in October 1958, Mosley granted him several private interviews and assisted him in finding employment.
186 Row was a veteran fascist, active in the BUF from 1934. Interned in 1940, from 1955 onwards he edited *Union* and subsequently *Action*, the latter until November 1992.
187 *Union*, 28 April 1956 and the following issue.
188 The precise role played by fascist activists in the riots remains hard to ascertain because the germane records remain classified. The Board of Deputies of British Jews (BDBJ) noted that UM and other fascist groups used the riots 'to intensify prejudice and ill feeling', which, they feared, could be 'channelled into anti-Semitism'. The BDBJ otherwise had little intelligence on the actual mechanics of fascist activism in the late 1950s because the Jewish Defence Committee had not been functioning 'for some considerable time'. In the wake of the riots, the BDBJ reconstituted its intelligence gathering apparatus, see R. Lieberman to Dr H.J. Stern, 27 November 1958 in 1658/3/3/8, JDC papers.
189 Quoted in Edward Pilkington, *Beyond the Mother Country: West Indians and the Notting Hill White Riots* (London: I.B. Tauris, 1988), p. 100.
190 *Daily Express*, 28 August 1958, quoted in Mulhall, 'The Unbroken Thread', p. 221.
191 Grundy, *Memoir of a Fascist Childhood*, p. 172.
192 *Kensington News*, 5 September 1958, quoted in Edward Pilkington, *Beyond the Mother Country*, p. 118.
193 Special Branch report, 28 May 1959 in TNA HO 344/34. For a report of their trial, see Dan Jacobson, 'After Notting Hill', *Encounter*, vol. 40, no. 6, December 1958, pp. 3–10.
194 *Kensington News*, 10 October 1958 and 24 October 1958; and Hamm, *Action Replay* (London: Howard Baker, 1983), pp. 178–179.
195 *The Coloured Invasion* (London: Sanctuary Press, 1958).
196 John Davis, 'Rents and Race in 1960s London: New Light on Rachmanism', *Twentieth Century British History*, vol. 12, no. 1, 2001, pp. 69–92.
197 *Action*, 31 October 1959; and *Action*, no. 72, 15 March 1961.
198 Benjamin Pogrund, *War of Words: Memoir of a South African Journalist* (New York: Seven Stories Press, 2000), pp. 53 and 58.
199 *Wiener Library Bulletin*, vol. 13, nos 1–2, 1959.
200 Mosley, *My Life*, p. 448.
201 Grundy, *Memoir of a Fascist Childhood*, p. 175.
202 Special Branch report, 17 June 1959 in TNA HO 344/34.
203 *West London Observer*, 16 October 1959; and *Kensington News*, 16 October 1959.

204 *North Kensington Leader*, no. 3, December 1958; *North Kensington Leader*, no. 9, July–August 1959; and *North Kensington Leader Supplement*, September 1959.
205 *What the Papers Say – Labour Loves London Blacks* (UM election flyer c.1961) declared a subsequent election flyer, whilst *Action*, no. 142, 29 November 1963 simply declared 'Let's Go Black with Labour'.
206 Mosley, *My Life*, pp. 448–450.
207 R.E. Cavendish to Sir Oswald Mosley, 3 October 1959, Oswald Mosley papers/Nicholas Mosley deposit, Box 7, Birmingham University.
208 Grundy, *Memoir of a Fascist Childhood*, p. 176. Nicholas Mosley in *Beyond the Pale*, p. 304 indicates further evidence of Mosley's ambivalent attitude towards violence by his followers.
209 *Ibid*.
210 *Daily Herald*, 21 November 1962.
211 'European' [Oswald Mosley], 'Analysis', *The European*, no. 68, vol. 12, no. 2, October 1958, pp. 67–71.
212 Loughlin, *Fascism and Constitutional Conflict*, pp. 180–181.
213 Grundy, *Memoir of a Fascist Childhood*, p. 177.
214 Mark Olden, *Murder in Notting Hill* (Aylesford: Zero Books, 2011) provides the definitive account of Cochrane's murder. Police files relating to his murder – MEPO 2/9894 – remain closed until 2041.
215 *Action*, 17 October 1959 and *Comrade*, no. 52, November–December 1999, journal of the Friends of Oswald Mosley (FOM), continues to hold the line arguing that 'every cause needs a martyr to exploit and in the murder of the West Indian Kelso Cochrane, in May 1959 an icon was manufactured.' It goes on to state that 'the knife that killed him was probably his own, he liked to carry one.'
216 *The Observer*, 26 April 1959; and *The Observer*, 31 May 1959.
217 Mike Phillips and Trevor Phillips, *Windrush: The Irresistible Rise of Multi-Racial Britain* (London: Harper Collins, 1999), p. 187.
218 *Sunday People*, 24 September 1961.
219 *The People*, 1 October 1961, quoted in Olden, *Murder in Notting Hill,*, p. 72.
220 Olden, *Murder in Notting Hill*, pp. 115–126 and 140–142.
221 *Ibid.*, pp. 53 and 100 notes Bell's reference to Digby and another suspect as 'our mates'.
222 *The Times*, 25 and 27 August 1959; and Hamm, *Action Replay*, pp. 178–179. See also *North Kensington Leader*, no. 8, June 1959; and Jewish Defence Committee, *Current Notes*, August 1959 in 1658/1/1/3, JDC papers.
223 Hamm, *Action Replay*, p. 179.
224 *Action*, no. 56, 24 October 1959. TNA DPP 2/3099 for the trial of Peter Bell and his father, who, together with members of another crime family, were later tried (though acquitted) for the killing of another local gangster in 1960.
225 *Kensington News*, 17 July 1959.
226 D.E. Webb to J.M. Ross, 19 November 1959 in TNA HO 325/9 notes that there were 120 prosecutions for such offences between 1 January and 30 September 1959: 70 were of 'foreign' origin; of which 27 were 'coloured'. The Maltese accounted for 35.
227 *Kensington News*, 28 August 1959.
228 *Ibid.*
229 Mosley, *My Life*, pp. 448–450.
230 Special Branch report, no. 4, 10 November 1959 in TNA HO 325/9.
231 The *Guardian*, 10 September 1959.
232 Dan Jacobson, *The Time of Arrival and Other Essays* (London: Weidenfeld and Nicolson, 1962), pp. 64–68.
233 David Kynaston, *Modernity Britain: 1957–1962* (New York: Bloomsbury, 2014), p. 350.
234 E.A. Markham, *Against the Grain: A 1950s Memoir* (Leeds: Peepal Tree Press, 2008)
235 Grundy, *Memoir of a Fascist Childhood*, pp. 180 and 189–190. Grundy, a UM youth leader who greatly admired Wilson recalled that Wilson's 'face reflected the horror he felt,' as Mosley uttered the phrase. 'I cringed'.
236 Skidelsky, *Oswald Mosley*, p. 511.
237 Nicholas Mosley, *Beyond the Pale* (London: Secker and Warburg, 1983), p. 303; and Nicholas Mosley, *Efforts at Truth: An Autobiography* (London: Secker and Warburg, 1994), p. 123.

238 The *Guardian*, 29 June 1971. Mosley's journal, *The National European*, no. 1 July 1964, reflected this dichotomy, discussing his grandiose ideas whilst simultaneously advertising *The Thunderbolt*, newspaper of the National States Rights Party (NSRP), a violent racist organisation whose members committed numerous acts of terrorism. *The Thunderbolt*, no. 60, July–August reciprocated, advertising *The National European* alongside ones for *The Protocols of the Elders of Zion* and other racist publications. *The National European*, no. 4, September 1964 abruptly terminated this relationship, which, the FBI observed, had existed since 1958, see the memo dated 10 October 1958 in Federal Bureau of Investigations file: 100–268487. Thirty years later, former NSRP leader Edward Fields was guest speaker at the 1995 Friends of Oswald Mosley (FOM) dinner. Fields publishes facsimiles of inter-war BUF publications (as well as those of Arnold Leese), *The Truth at Last*, no. 357, n.d.
239 Mosley, *Beyond the Pale*, pp. 306–307.
240 *Ibid.*, p. 307.
241 Nicholas Mosley, *Paradoxes of Peace* (London: Dalkey Archive Press, 2009), p. 68.
242 Mosley, *Beyond the Pale*, p. 308.
243 *Ibid.*
244 The *Guardian Weekend*, 24 January 1998.
245 Mosley, *My Life*, p. 451.
246 *Mosley – Message to Electors* (London: Highgate Press, 1959).
247 Mosley, *My Life*, p. 451.
248 The *Guardian*, 3 October 1959
249 Jeffrey Hamm, *Action Replay*, p. 184.
250 'Notes by O.M. on C.W.'s article in the "Twentieth Century" and letter to him, with much more to follow if Toynbee comes up to scratch' in MS124/1/28, Jeffrey Hamm papers, University of Birmingham, hereafter Hamm papers.
251 Keith Kyle, 'North Kensington', in D.E. Butler and Richard Rose, *The British General Election of 1959* (London: Macmillan, 1960), p. 181.
252 Diana Mosley to Deborah Mitford, 9 October 1959 in Charlotte Mosley (ed.), *The Mitfords: Letters Between Six Sisters* (London: Fourth Estate, 2007), p. 318.
253 The *Guardian*, 5 October 1959.
254 Ian R.G. Spencer, *British Immigration Policy since 1939* (London: Routledge, 1997), p. 120.
255 *Action*, no. 55, 17 October 1959.
256 Nicholas Tredell, *The Novels of Colin Wilson* (London: Vision Press, 1982), p. 19.
257 Graham Hough, 'New Novels', *Encounter*, vol. 10, no. 2, February 1958, p. 86.
258 Stuart Holroyd, *Contraries: A Personal Progression* (London: Bodley Head, 1975), pp. 16, 71–73 and 79. The novel *Awake for Mourning* (1958) by Bernard Kops, the East End son of Dutch Jewish immigrants, satirised the group and its elitist philosophy contemporaneously as a prolegomenon to fascism, on which, see 'Teddy Boy Riots & Right-Wing Angry Young Men', *Stewart Home*, www.stewarthomesociety.org/sex/kops.htm (accessed 26 March 2015).
259 Colin Wilson to Oswald Mosley, 2 February 1958 in OMN/B/2/4, Mosley papers.
260 Stuart Holroyd, Diary entry for 10 March 1958, quoted in Craig Fowlie, 'Bill Hopkins – From Angry Young Man to Cultured Thug' (forthcoming).
261 Holroyd, *Contraries*, pp. 144–145.
262 Kenneth Allsop, *The Angry Decade: A Survey of the Cultural Revolt of the Nineteen-Fifties* (Wendover: John Goodchild, 1985), pp. 22 and 148–194.
263 Colin Wilson, 'The Month', *The Twentieth Century*, vol. 166, no. 994, December 1959, pp. 492–498.
264 *Ibid.*
265 *Daily Mirror*, 10 December 1959.
266 *Daily Mirror*, 15 December 1959.
267 *Daily Mirror*, 21 December 1959.
268 Manuscript titled 'Notes by O.M. on C.W.'s article in the "Twentieth Century" and letter to him, with much more to follow if Toynbee comes up to scratch' in MS 124/1/28, Hamm papers.
269 'Notes by O.M. on C.W's further letter of 31/12/1959' in MS 124/1/28, Hamm papers. Wilson and Mosley remained in contact. Having seen Mosley on television in 1971, Wilson wrote to him, full of praise for his performance, asking Mosley to bear in mind 'that I'd always be willing to say nice things about you in similar programmes – if, as I hope, you begin to get more

TV time.' See Colin Wilson to Oswald Mosley, 28 July 1971, OMN/B/2/4, Mosley papers. Deborah Lipstadt, *Denying the Holocaust: The Growing Assault on Truth and Memory* (London: Penguin, 1994), pp. 119–121 notes Wilson endorsed *Did Six Million Really Die?* (1974) in a review in *Books and Bookmen*. From 1985 onwards, Wilson often contributed to *Lodestar*, a journal edited by Jeffrey Hamm, Mosley's former political secretary.
270 For the minutiae of the case, see TNA LCO 6/3310.
271 Nancy Mitford to Deborah Mitford, 6 April 1960 in Mosley, *The Mitfords*, p. 355.
272 Diana Mosley to Deborah Mitford, 6 April 1960 in Mosley, *The Mitfords*, p. 336.
273 *The Times*, 6 April 1960.
274 Skidelsky, *Oswald Mosley*, p. 476.
275 Richard W. Bukardt jr, *The Spirit of the System: Lamarck and Evolutionary Biology* (Cambridge, MA: Harvard University Press, 1977), pp. 143–185.
276 Oswald Mosley, *The Alternative* (Ramsbury: Mosley Publications, 1947), p. 259.
277 Thurlow, *Fascism in Britain*, p. 225.
278 Skidelsky, *Oswald Mosley*, p. 555.
279 Thurlow, *Fascism in Britain*, p. 225.
280 Alexander Raven Thomson to Austin J. App, 6 January 1950 in The Austin J. App Collection, Box 5, American Heritage Centre, University of Wyoming. App was a German-American national socialist and Holocaust denier who occasionally contributed to *Union*.
281 *The Fascist Week*, 9–15 February 1934.
282 Mosley, *The Alternative*, pp. 256–257.
283 David Redvaldsen, '"Science must be the Basis": Sir Oswald Mosley's Political Parties and their Policies on Health, Science and Scientific Racism 1931–1974', *Contemporary British History*, vol. 30, no. 3, 2016, pp. 368–388.
284 Mosley, *The Alternative*, pp. 257–258. Mosley had had recourse to eugenic arguments during the 1930s arguing in *Fascism: 100 Questions Asked and Answered* (1936) that Fascism offered the 'unfit' the choice between voluntary sterilisation and segregation 'sufficient to prevent the production of unfit children.'
285 A. James Gregor, 'Eisenhower: A Study in American Economy', *The European*, no. 17, July 1954, pp. 7–13.
286 H. Keith Thompson, 'I am an American Fascist – Part Four', *Expose*, December 1954 in 100–370871, H. Keith Thompson FBI file. Thompson stated: 'The officials of Union Movement are honest, hard working organizers, and the movement is steadily gaining supporters in the United States due to its keen insight.'
287 *Union*, no. 331, 1 May 1954.
288 Keith Stimely interview with H. Keith Thompson, 13 March 1986 in H. Keith Thompson papers: Box 18, Hoover Institute, Stanford University, California.
289 A. James Gregor to Robert Row, 13 October 1954 in TNA KV 2/3998.
290 *Ibid.*
291 A. James Gregor to Alexander Raven Thomson, 23 October 1954 in TNA KV 2/3998.
292 *Ibid.* It is unclear if the two men actually met. In 'Copy of letter SF 709/USA/E1/ARTS of 20 October 1954' in TNA KV 2/3999/96a, MI5 note Gregor wrote to Naumann on 19 October 'but received no reply'. He tried again on 8 November: 'In this letter, he merely says that he is shortly leaving for South Germany and has a recommendation from friends in England who are of the opinion that a meeting between Naumann and himself would be of mutual interest.' Alexander Raven Thomson to A. James Gregor, 15 January 1955 in TNA KV 2/3999 records:

> I am glad to hear from you again and to have your present address, so that we can keep in touch with you. I have little to report, except that I have had a letter from Keith Thompson and also from Dr. Naumann, who does not however refer to your visit, presumably for security reasons.

293 Gregor's contributions included: 'Some Problems of Race', *The European*, no. 24, February 1955, pp. 19–25; 'Capitalism and the Law of Markets', *The European*, no. 28, June 1955, pp. 13–26; 'An American Considers European Socialism', *The European*, no. 33, November 1955, pp. 17–24; 'Syndicalism: A Critical History', *The European*, no. 38, April 1956, pp. 10–20; 'Marxism as Philosophy', *The European*, no. 42, August 1956, pp. 11–26; and 'Marxism as a Theory of History', *The European*, no. 45, November 1956, pp. 146–162.

294 A. James Gregor, 'European Socialism' [Letter], *The European*, no. 17, July 1954, pp. 60–62; Oswald Mosley, 'European Socialism' [Letter], *The European*, no. 18, August 1954, pp. 58–59; and A. James Gregor, 'An American Considers European Socialism', *The European*, no. 33, November 1955, pp. 17–24.
295 Diana Mosley letter to the author, 12 January 2001.
296 Skidelsky, *Oswald Mosley*, pp. 493–494.
297 A. James Gregor, 'National Socialism and Race', *The European*, no. 67, July 1958, pp. 273–291. For another attack, see A. James Gregor, 'Nordicism Revisited', *Phylon*, vol. 22, no. 4, 1961, pp. 351–360, which singles out *Northern World*, journal of the Northern League, for its exultation of Günther's 'philosophy of despair' which no longer had any purchase in 'serious' circles.
298 A. James Gregor, Biographies, *Institute for the Study of Academic Racism*, www.ferris.edu/htmls/othersrv/isar/bibliography/gregrbib.htm (accessed 21 August 2018).
299 A. James Gregor, *The Search for Neofascism: The Use and Abuse of Social Science* (Cambridge: Cambridge University Press, 2006), p. xi. A. James Gregor, 'Once Again on Roger Griffin and the Study of "Fascism"', in Roger Griffin, Werner Loh and Andreas Umland (eds), *Fascism, Past and Present, East and West: An International Debate on Concepts and Cases in the Comparative Study of the Extreme Right* (Stuttgart: ibidem-Verlag, 2006), p. 318 highlights his minority view that: 'Long study of the literature of Oswald Mosley's British Union of Fascists and National Socialists, together with extensive conversations with some of its principal ideologues, convinced me that there was very little Fascism or National Socialism in the BUF.'
300 Idus A. Newby, *Challenge to the Court: Social Scientists and the Defence of Segregation, 1954–1966* (Baton Rouge, LA: Louisiana University Press, 1967), p. 134.
301 *Eugenics Review*, no. 3, October 1960. Despite this announcement, it took another six years for the book to appear. Andrew S. Winston, 'Science in the Service of the Far Right: Henry E. Garrett, the IAAEE, and the Liberty Lobby', *Journal of Social Issues*, vol. 54, no. 1, 1998, p. 205.
302 John P. Jackson, Jr, *Science for Segregation: Race, Law, and the Case against Brown v. Board of Education* (New York: New York University Press, 2005), pp. 64–65 and 106–110 notes that prior to helping found the IAAEE in February 1958, Gregor became secretary of the Association for the Preservation of the Freedom of Choice (APFC). This organisation was dedicated to maintaining racially pure neighbourhoods in New York by championing a landlord's right to discriminate against tenants based on ethnicity.
303 *National European*, no. 15, September 1965 featured adverts for *Truth Seeker*.
304 Oren Solomon Harman, *The Man Who Invented the Chromosome: A Life of Cyril Darlington* (Cambridge, MA: Harvard University Press, 2004), pp. 246–247 states that despite agreeing to join its executive committee and later becoming head of the organisation, Darlington was 'uncharacteristically cautious' about his association with the IAAEE. He fretted about its political aims though his concerns were 'quelled' by another member, Corrado Gini, Mussolini's demographer. Friends and family thought he was being 'naïve' whilst professional colleagues steered clear of the group.
305 Skidelsky, *Oswald Mosley*, p. 555.
306 Robert S. Moore, 'Racism in Science', *Patterns of Prejudice*, vol. 9, no. 6, November–December 1975, p. 5.
307 Oswald Mosley, *Mosley: Right or Wrong?* (London: Lion Books, 1961), p. 120. In a similar vein, Diana Mosley observed in *National European*, no. 15, September 1965 that:

> A famous gardener told me recently that in the melon growing district of France a local law forbids the cultivation of cucumbers. No offence meant to cucumbers, which are excellent in their own way, but these plants can cross-pollinate, and in the process the quality of both is lost.

308 TNA HO 144/22846. The case against Mosley, which was heard in November 1945, was dismissed with the caveat that although

> The Bench do not consider that the prosecution has proved the case. They do, however, consider that you should have been further aware of the state in which the pigs were and should have taken earlier steps to see that they were properly fed and better housed.

Mosley's efforts to have the Magistrates publicly retract the remark failed.
309 Mosley, *Mosley – Right or Wrong?*, pp. 118–121.

310 *Ibid.*
311 'Laroche' sent them a (undated) postcard stating: 'Happy New Year for yourself and the Union Movement! – with best regards, Fabrice Laroche.' E.J. Hamm to Fabrice Laroche, 10 June 1966, Hamm papers thanked 'Laroche' for sending copies of *Europe-Action* and requested copies of other publications such as *Cahiers Universitaires*. *National European*, no. 5, October 1964 advertised *Europe-Action*.
312 Mosley, *Mosley – Right or Wrong?*, p. 123. Gayre had changed the spelling of his name from Gair.
313 Gavin Schaffer, *Racial Science and British Society, 1930–1962* (London: Palgrave, 2008), p. 142.
314 *Action*, no. 112, 5 April 1963.
315 I.A. Newby, *Challenge to the Court*, p. 323.
316 Richard Thurlow, 'Racial Populism in England', *Patterns of Prejudice*, vol. 10, no. 4, July–August 1976, p. 31.
317 UM pamphlets like *Colour: The Immigration Crisis – Union Movement Policy Pamphlet no. 4* (London: Venture Press, n.d.) further highlight the use of racial science to lend authority to party policy pronouncements.
318 *Manchester Guardian*, 29 February 1960; *The Times*, 1 March 1960, 24 March 1960 and 9 April 1960. The arrests included West London UM organiser Peter Dawson, who was fined £20 for insulting words and behaviour. Police suspected Dawson of committing several anti-Semitic actions. These included sending a series of abusive letters and late-night phone calls to Jewish MPs and painting 'Juden Raus' ('Jews Get Out') together with five swastikas on the wall of the Notting Hill Gate synagogue (on which, see *Kensington Post*, 8 January 1960). Police also suspected Dawson was responsible for planting a small home-made bomb outside his own headquarters on 10 January 1960 then daubing a Star of David on a nearby wall to incriminate the Association of Jewish Ex-Servicemen (AJEX) who were guarding the synagogue he had allegedly recently defaced. Jewish Defence Committee, *Current Notes*, November–December 1959–January 1960 in 1658/3/2/4, JDC papers; and [illegible signature] to Sidney Salomon, 26 January 1959 and Sidney Salomon to Commander E. Jones in 1658/10/29, JDC papers. For more background, see *The Times*, 11 January 1960; The *Sunday People*, 24 September 1961; and 'Who Killed my Brother?', *Steve Silver*, May 2006, http://stevesilver.org.uk/who-killed-my-brother/ (accessed 18 October 2011). Carol Ann Lee, *The Hidden Life of Otto Frank* (London: Viking, 2002), p. 256 notes that 'Peter Dawson' sent anti-Semitic letters to Otto Frank, the father of Anne Frank, who was told his murdered daughter's 'stinking diary is a fake and a phoney'. Though Frank's biographer states this was not the antagonists' real name, it would certainly fit his *modus operandi*.
319 Ruth Winstone (ed.), *Tony Benn: Years of Hope, Diaries, Papers, Letters, 1940–1962* (London: Arrow, 1994), p. 325.
320 Bean, *Many Shades of Black*, pp. 142–143.
321 *The Times*, 14 March 1960; and *Kensington Post*, 18 March 1960.
322 *Manchester Guardian*, 29 February 1960. For instance, on 13 March, Dawson led six UM activists to overturn the platform at a meeting in Queensway Hall, leading to his arrest. When the South African boycott campaign culminated with a rally in Trafalgar Square on 27 March, approximately forty UM and BNP activists clashed with its supporters whilst over 500 boycott supporters converged upon the UM headquarters 'but these were eventually dispersed by police without any serious disorder'.
323 Special Branch, report no. 5, 18 May 1960 in TNA HO 325/9.
324 *Ibid.*; and *Manchester Guardian*, 9 February 1960.
325 Special Branch, report no. 6, 19 December 1960 in TNA HO 325/9.
326 *The Times*, 27 July 1960.
327 *The Times*, 8 June 1960; *Oldham Evening Chronicle*, 10 June 1960; and Sammy Davis Jr, *Yes I Can* (London: Cassell, 1965), pp. 534–537.
328 Peter Dawson … an Open Letter to Eartha Kitt, in 1658/3/2/7, JDC papers. The full text of the letter read:

> We Europeans are opposed mixed marriages [sic], whether they be 'White and Black' or 'Black and White'. We can only look on your recent marriage with disgust. When your male counterpart, Sammy Davis Junior, (the one-eyed-Jewish-negro) insulted the British People by coming to Britain to announce his engagement for an (already married) White woman I

organised a protest. It was a complete success ... he cut short his stay ... and has since been 'picketed' many times back in the States by other patriotic groups. In view of the reports in our press that you have [sic] are 'over here to appear in a London show' I feel that is [sic] my duty to warn you that we of the Notting Hill Branch of Mosley's UM will not permit you to perform in Britain without making some form of practical protest. Mosley for a clean show-business.

329 Union Movement to Press Association, 12 August 1960, MS124/1/18, Hamm papers.
330 Robert Row to H. Keith Thompson, 16 September 1960 in H. Keith Thompson papers, Box 16, Hoover Institution Archives, Stanford University.
331 Special Branch, report no. 6, 19 December 1960 in TNA HO 325/9.
332 Robert Row, a leading UM activist, optimistically observed that the discovery of uranium in Bechuanaland would stimulate a 'Second Klondike'. The lure of higher wages would cause black Africans to migrate from South Africa, thereby precluding the use of 'Fascist methods' needed to facilitate a racially pure South African state which appeared to be his preferred preference, see Robert Row, *Proposals for Bechuanaland*, in Oswald Mosley papers, Diana Mosley deposit: Box 18, the University of Birmingham.
333 *Action*, no. 66, November 1960.
334 *Stand by the White Man* (UM leaflet). *Action*, the UM newspaper, carried advertisements during this period for the *South African Observer* – 'the truth about the white man in this great country' – as well as proclaiming: 'Stand by South Africa! Buy South African fruit, tinned goods and wines. South African goods are the very best!'
335 *Action*, no. 72, 15 March 1961.
336 *Ibid*. This conspiratorial view included sports too. *Action*, no. 143, 6 December 1963 featured a letter asking 'Is the sending of West Indian cricket teams and West Indian cricketers to Australia a move to condition the Australian people to receive coloured immigrants?'
337 *Action*, no. 138, 1 November 1963.
338 *The ADL Bulletin*, March 1954.
339 *Action*, no. 68, January 1961.
340 *Action*, no. 70, 15 February 1961.
341 Jeffrey Hamm to all members and supporters of Union Movement in London area, 2 March 1961, copy in authors' possession.
342 *Action*, no. 72, 15 March 1961.
343 *The Times*, 8 March 1961; and *The Times*, 9 May 1961.
344 *The Times*, 15 March 1961; and *The Times*, 22 March 1961.
345 *The Times*, 29 March 1961; and *The Times*, 7 April 1961.
346 *The Times*, 10 May 1961; and *The Times*, 11 May 1961. The judge had previously ruled that Shiffner had no case to answer. *Action*, no. 76, 15 May 1961 notes the expulsions.
347 *Comrade*, no. 46, August–October 1995; and *Jewish Chronicle*, 7 October 1952.
348 Olden, *Murder in Notting Hill*, pp. 73–74.
349 Jeffrey Hamm to all members of the Union Movement in the London area, 14 March 1961, copy in authors' possession.
350 George Doolette who described himself as 'a personal assistant to Sir Oswald Mosley' and William Webster, the former NLP candidate were both sentenced to two months' imprisonment though later freed on appeal, see *The Times*, 16 August 1961.
351 *Action*, no. 76, 15 May 1961 notes the expulsion of P. Bingham as a result.
352 Jewish Defence Committee, *Current Notes*, March–May 1961 in 1658 /1/1/4, JDC papers.
353 Max Mosley, *Formula One and Beyond: The Autobiography* (London: Simon & Schuster, 2015), p. 7.
354 *Action*, no. 78, 1 July 1961.
355 *Daily Mail*, 2 April 2008.
356 The *Guardian*, 26 November 1997; and *Sunday Telegraph*, 26 August 1962.
357 Mosley, *Formula One and Beyond*, pp. 19–20.
358 *The Times*, 5 January 1961; and *The Times*, 26 September 1961.
359 Mosley, *Formula One and Beyond*, pp. 21–23. *Daily Herald*, 19 November 1962 had previously reported that a North Kensington UM activist had joined the TA to become proficient in the use of weapons ready for a right-wing revolution.

360 *The Times*, 23 September 1963; and *Action*, no. 136, 18 October 1963. Diana Mosley to Deborah Mitford, 8 January 1964 in Mosley, *The Mitfords*, p. 408, claimed:

> a man who said he was in 'intelligence' during the war made friends with Max & tried to persuade him to take some ammunition from the TA, purpose not specified; this man told Max that he had been in the paras, & rather impressed him for a time with his boastful stories. The suggestion about ammunition opened Max's eyes and he had no more to do with him. Imagine if Max had been stupid or gullible enough to agree. The man posed as a great friend, asked them to dinner & so on, never off the telephone. Heaven knows who he was working for … Kit did not go for Max's person because the TA officers have been very good to Max & he loves the paras – in any case it wd [sic] be his word against the man's.

361 *Daily Express*, 10 October 1963. Geldard, the UM Surrey organiser who had run the UM bookshop committed suicide shortly afterwards, see *The National European*, no. 2, August 1964; and The *People*, 21 June 1964.
362 Sam Greenhill and Bill Akass, 'Oops! Another Memory Lapse for Max Mosley', The *Daily Mail*, 8 March 2018, www.dailymail.co.uk/news/article-5479785/amp/What-Max-Mosley-doing-vile-anti-Semitic-rally-1965.htm (accessed 13 March 2018).
363 Mosley, *Formula One and Beyond*, p. 23.
364 Ken Clarke, *Kind of Blue: A Political Memoir* (London: Macmillan, 2016), pp. 25–26. Clarke was not the only future Conservative politician studying at Cambridge to be impressed by Mosley. Peter Temple-Morris, *Across the Floor: A Life in Dissenting Politics* (London: I.B. Tauris, 2015), pp. 16–17 recalled of Mosley's previous address to the CUCA in 1960 that Mosley 'retained his gentlemanly ways' after a student threw jelly in his face as he spoke.

> There was no plate, but it was still not very pleasant. It hit Mosley and carried on in small pieces to drench the secretary, sitting behind him. Dabbing his face with his handkerchief Mosley carried on speaking as if nothing had happened. He came to tea with us after the meeting, and discussed personalities and issues as the establishment figure he was and as if he had never left mainstream politics. A formidable performance by any account.

365 Michael Crick, *In Search of Michael Howard* (London: Simon & Schuster, 2005), pp. 71–74.
366 Clarke, *Kind of Blue*, p. 26.
367 Nancy Mitford to Violet Hammersley, 22 August 1960 in Charlotte Mosley (ed.), *Love From Nancy: The Letters of Nancy Mitford* (London: Hodder and Stoughton, 1993) p. 387.
368 *Action*, no. 67, December 1960. Mosley was to have chaired this meeting of the 'vital forces' of Europe which would have included Filipo Anfuso, Mussolini's former Foreign Minister who was on the executive of the MSI; Giorgio Almirante, another MSI executive member; Pino Romualdi, vice-president of the MSI; Giorgio Lanfré, a member of the MSI central committee and Count Alvise Loridan. There were to be other speakers from Austria and 'leading' European countries.
369 *Action*, no. 68, January 1961.
370 Archie Henderson, 'Pound, Sweden, and the Nobel Prize: An Introduction', in Richard Taylor and Claus Melchior (eds), *Ezra Pound and Europe* (Atlanta, GA: Rodopi, 1993), p. 164.
371 *Action*, no. 73, 1 April 1961.
372 For a photograph of the three men, see http://pinoromualdi.blogspot.co.uk/ (accessed 4 November 2017).
373 Henderson, 'Pound, Sweden, and the Nobel Prize', p. 164.
374 Oswald Mosley to Robert Saunders, 7 February 1962, Robert Saunders papers, Sheffield University, hereafter Saunders papers.
375 Oswald Mosley to Adolf von Thadden, 9 February 1962, Adolf von Thadden papers, Niedersächsisches Landesarchiv, Hannover, Germany, hereafter von Thadden papers. Terence O'Reilly, *Hitler's Irishmen* (Cork: Mercier Press, 2008), p. 296 cites an Irish G2 intelligence report dated July 1961 stating that Mosley had reportedly met Skorzeny in the past few months.
376 Richard Pendlebury and Bill Akass, 'No Regrets, Max?', *The Daily Mail*, 28 February 2018, www.dailymail.co.uk/news/article-5446991/No-regrets-Max-trip-Dachau.html (accessed 2 March 2018).
377 *Action*, no. 91, 15 March 1962. The conference also issued a statement regarding the situation in the South Tyrol, a divisive issue for Austrian and Italian fascists who both laid claim to the

region. Oswald Mosley to Arthur Ehrhardt, 6 February 1962 in MS124/1/5, Hamm papers notes that the Belgian MAC representatives were bringing several Austrian delegates 'who are already prepared to make a declaration that when Europe is made the Tyrol question will no longer exist'. Mosley had told Rudel 'to bring Austrians if he wished'. The conference also issued an oblique notice stating that they had not invited any French delegates because 'we do not intervene in the internal affairs of France, where two parties clash who are both opposed to communism'. This referred to the activities of the OAS. The impetus most probably came from Mosley, who domiciled in France, was anxious not to give the French authorities any excuse to deport him. That said, this stance did not stop Mosley from consorting with MAC leader Jean Thiriart, a notable OAS supporter. Mosley's own activists also breached the injunction. On 18 September 1963, Georges Parisy, an OAS activist on the run from the French authorities was arrested in London with a loaded pistol at the home of a UM activist who was safe-housing him, see *The Times*, 27 September 1963.

378 Oswald Mosley to Robert Saunders, 7 February 1962, Saunders papers.
379 *Ibid.* Mosley was especially keen that foreign translations of his work should appear, believing that they provided a 'sharp and definite' alternative to the European model propounded by figures like Macmillan and Adenauer, see Oswald Mosley to Arthur Ehrhardt, 27 April 1960 in MS124/1/5, Hamm papers.
380 *Action*, no. 148, 1 May 1964.
381 *Action*, no. 92, 15 April 1962.
382 *Daily Mail*, 24 July 1962.
383 Oswald Mosley to Adolf von Thadden, 9 February 1962, von Thadden papers.
384 Oswald Mosley to Jean Thiriart, 26 June 1962 in MS124/1/24, Hamm papers notes that Giovanni Nicola Lanfré had informed Mosley, following an MSI Executive Committee meeting in Rome, that its secretary Arturo Michelini and other leaders 'agreed with all the decisions taken in Venice except the change of name; a point on which accommodation might be reached without difficulty.'
385 Oswald Mosley to Jean Thiriart, 21 July 1962 in MS124/1/24, Hamm papers mentions a forthcoming meeting at the end of the month in Frankfurt with Thiriart and Adolf von Thadden. Mosley conceded that the NPE had come to naught in *Action*, no. 148, 1 May 1964.
386 Mosley, *My Life*, pp. 438–439.
387 *National Vanguard*, no. 117, March–April 1997 quotes the letter.
388 E.J. Hamm to David Clausen, 6 April 1971 in MS124/1/3, Hamm papers.
389 Mosley, *My Life*, p. 440.
390 *Ibid.*, p. 441.
391 Martin Conway, *Collaboration in Belgium: Léon Degrelle and the Rexist Movement* (New Haven, CT: Yale University Press, 1993), p. 72.
392 Rees, *Biographical Dictionary of the Extreme Right since 1890*, p. 388.
393 Kevin Coogan, *Dreamer of the Day: Francis Parker Yockey and the Postwar Fascist International* (New York: Autonomedia, 1999), pp. 541–542; for more details, see Jeffrey M. Bale, *The Darkest Sides of Politics, Vol. 1: Postwar Fascism, Covert Operations and Terrorism* (Abingdon: Routledge, 2018), pp. 94–105.
394 Oswald Mosley to Jean Thiriart, 27 November 1962 and 28 November 1962 in MS124/1/24, Hamm papers.
395 *The National European*, no. 2, August 1964. Glaswegian activist W.G. Eaton subsequently translated the book into English as *Europe, an Empire of 400 Million People* (1964). Returning from a JE camping trip in Italy, Eaton wrote to Mosley from Brussels, where he was staying with Thiriart: 'During the trip we had excellent press conferences in Ferrara, Parma and Rome. The enthusiasm of the Italian members is very exciting and hopeful.'
396 Camus and Lebourg, *Far-Right Politics in Europe*, p. 81.
397 *Action*, no. 90, 1 March 1962; and *Action*, no. 144, 13 December 1963. See also Jean Thiriart to Oswald Mosley, 9 May 1963 and Oswald Mosley to Jean Thiriart, 13 May 1963 in MS124/1/24, Hamm papers. *Action*, no. 78, 1 July 1961 notes Dingley 'became interested in politics after seeing an Aldermaston march'. He was a CND 'camp-follower' for two years before hearing Mosley speak in Trafalgar Square in 1960 after which he joined the UM.
398 Oswald Mosley to Jean Thiriart, 1 December 1962 in MS124/1/24, Hamm papers. Thiriart's Italian affiliates included Stefano Mangiante (Genoa), Emilio Gay (Torino), Paolo Molin

(Venezia), Piero Biraghi (Firenze), Andrea Arpaja (Napoli) and the Ordine Nuovo (Rome). Jean Thiriart to Oswald Mosley, 3 December 1962, Hamm papers communicated the addresses of Rutilio Sermonti (Rome) and Dr Carlo Maria Maggi (Milan) though asked that Loredan to deal directly with Bruschi. Patrice Chairoff, *Dossier Neo-Nazisme* (Paris: Éditions Ramsay, 1977), pp. 112–113 notes that Thiriart had rebuked Bruschi for his anti-Semitic activism.
399 Carmelina Anfuso to Oswald Mosley, 23 March 1964 in MS124/1/1, Hamm papers.
400 Giovanni Nicola Lanfré to Oswald Mosley, 6 June 1972 in MS124/1/12, Hamm papers. For Almirante, see Rees, *Biographical Dictionary of the Extreme Right since 1890*, p. 8. Mosley's ideas also found favour with Italian fascist intellectuals like Mario Tedeschi, the editor of *Il Borghese*, who published an Italian translation of his *Il Fascismo Inglese* (1973).
401 Oswald Mosley to Jean Thiriart, 22 February 1963 in MS124/1/24, Hamm papers. Mosley and Thiriart met in Brussels on 13–14 July with Adolf von Thadden and Arthur Ehrhardt. This coincided with a JE network meeting attended by Antonio Mendez Garcia (Madrid), Pierfranco Bruschi (Milan) Joaquin Duarte (Lisbon) and Kurt Kohl (Hannover). Thiriart also intimated that the heads of the Swiss and Dutch JE sections would be there – Tijmon Balk (Groningen) and Roland Gueissaz (Lausanne). This gave Mosley the opportunity to meet the leading figures in Thiriart's network, see Jean Thiriart to Oswald Mosley, 15 June 1963 in MS124/1/24, Hamm papers. Thiriart hosted a second meeting in Brussels on 24–25 August 1963 at which several Italian and German militants joined him and Mosley. 'So the participants will be the same as the conference of Venice,' notes E.J. Hamm to Jean Thiriart, 29 July 1963 in MS124/1/24, Hamm papers. Oswald Mosley to Jean Thiriart, 1 September 1963 in MS124/1/24, Hamm papers highlights that both men met again in Madrid between 12 and 16 September.
402 *Wiener Library Bulletin*, vol. 17, no. 3, July 1963 reported participation from the following MSI youth groups: Raggruppamento Giovanile Studenti e Lavoratoni (Youth Group of Students and Works); Fronte universitario d'azione nazionale (FUAN); Formazioni Nazionale Giovanile (FNG – National Youth Formations); and Associazione Studentesca di Avanguardia Nazionale – Giovane Italia (Student Association of the National Vanguard – Young Italy). Fred Borth, a former Werwolf paramilitary who led the Austrian JE section was also there as were several observers from Per Engdahl's 'National Left'. *Action*, no. 126, 26 July 1963 features Mosley's summary of policy written for Italian and South American university students.
403 *Action*, no. 117, 17 May 1963; *Action*, no. 119, 31 May 1963; *Action*, no. 122, 28 June 1963; and Antonio Lombardo to Oswald Mosley, 12 July 1964 in MS124/1/12, Hamm papers. Andrea Mammone, *Transnational Fascism in France and Italy* (Cambridge: Cambridge University Press, 2015), pp. 90–91 highlights that Lombardo became the 'key element' between ON and the French 'Europe-Action' group. He founded the Centro Nazione Europa (Center Nation Europe) in 1966 with which one young Europe-Action militant, Alain de Benoist, 'was about to collaborate', according to its own files. The Centre had hoped to organise a conference in 1968 to which they intended to invite Adolf von Thadden and Mosley.
404 *Action*, no. 148, 1 May 1964. Thiriart and Bruschi had proposed a meeting in Milan in March 1964 but Mosley was unable to attend, see E.J. Hamm to Pierfranco Bruschi, 24 February 1964 in MS 124/1/2, Hamm papers. Bruschi subsequently provided Mosley with a list of 450 names to which the UM sent materials. He also translated and disseminated *The National European* articles to further dissemination Mosley's ideas through the Italian fascist firmament, see E.J. Hamm to Pierfranco Bruschi, 16 June 1964 and Pierfranco Bruschi to E.J. Hamm, 23 June 1964 in MS 124/1/2, Hamm papers. Oswald Mosley to Ernesto Massi, 4 July 1964 in MS124/1/13, Hamm papers highlights the fact that Mosley sought to harvest addresses of sympathetic Italian business and trade union leaders from Massi.
405 Oswald Mosley to Count Alvise Loredan, 9 February 1967 in MS124/1/12, Hamm papers.
406 *Action*, no. 114, 26 April 1963 and *Action*, no. 130, 6 September 1963, the latter featuring a photograph of Thiriart with a group of European militants in which a UM banner is clearly visible.
407 Jean Thiriart to E.J. Hamm, 5 February 1964 in MS124/1/24, Hamm papers issues the invite for the road trip. Jean Thiriart to Oswald Mosley, 21 June 1965 in MS124/1/24, Hamm papers again invites young UM activists to join another Belgian JE trip on 18 July 1965 from Brussels to Naples. Such activities were a regular feature of fascist militancy. Mosley himself arranged with Arthur Ehrhardt, *Nation Europa*'s editor, for several young UM activists to attend a 'European' camp run by Dr Norbert Scharnagl in Villach, southern Austria during summer 1960, see

Oswald Mosley to Arthur Ehrhardt, 16 June 1960 and Arthur Ehrhardt to Oswald Mosley, 20 June 1960 in MS124/1/5, Hamm papers.
408 Jean Thiriart to Oswald Mosley, 13 April 1965 in MS124/1/24, Hamm papers.
409 Oswald Mosley to Jean Thiriart, 13 June 1965 in MS124/1/24, Hamm papers.
410 Oswald Mosley to Jean Thiriart, 7 May 1965 in MS124/1/24, Hamm papers. As Mosley explained on 13 June 1965:

> We have had a very unfortunate experience in our own printing [...] it is a very expert matter in which even the most enthusiastic amateur has difficulty. We only had one real printing expert in our party, and he went to jail for 2 years shortly after we had purchased the expensive machinery for him to supervise.

411 [No signature] to Jean Thiriart, 8 July 1966 in MS124/1/24, Hamm papers.
412 Camus and Lebourg, *Far-Right Politics in Europe*, pp. 87–89.
413 Count Alvise Loredan to Oswald Mosley, 11 January 1967 in MS124/1/12, Hamm papers.
414 Mosley, *Beyond the Pale*, p. 309.
415 *Sunday Telegraph*, 20 August 1962.
416 *Manchester Guardian*, 15 August 1962.
417 *The Times*, 31 August 1962; and *The Times*, 1 September 1962. For footage of the UM meeting, see British Pathé, www.britishpathe.com/record.php?id=42474 (accessed 25 October 2011).
418 The *Guardian*, 10 September 1962; and the *Guardian*, 17 September 1962.
419 Federal Bureau of Investigations (FBI) file: 100–268487.
420 *The Times*, 8 October 1962; and the *Guardian*, 8 October 1962. During the course of the disturbances, fascists smashed the window of the Bethnal Green Labour Party office.
421 *Action*, no. 99, 1 October 1962; and *Action*, no. 115, May 1963. The *Guardian*, 7 January 1963 reported the UM claiming to have seen a large increase in its 'unrevealed membership' including 'businessmen and professional people' and 'non-members who are supporters'. *Action*, no. 116, 10 May 1963 meanwhile reported that the party had expanded from 120 'points of organisation' in November 1960 to 217 in May 1963.
422 *Daily Herald*, 13 May 1963.
423 *The Times*, 13 May 1963; the *Guardian*, 5 June 1963; and *The Times*, 5 June 1963. For an anti-fascist account of this incident, see Unite, *Tony Hall: Trade Unionist, Anti-Racist and Radical Cartoonist* (London: Unite, 2015), pp. 11–17.
424 *Action*, no. 127, 2 August 1963.
425 TNA CRIM 1/4142. Asked if he had anything to add after being charged, Goulding stated: 'Not really. The Labour party are traitors and corrupt.' Goulding had joined the UM after being introduced to a female member, Dorothy Boyd, by Palmer who was also a UM activist as was Curry. Goulding was an associate of Fredrick J. Sheppard, the Shoreditch UM organiser who was a 'cab washer' at the taxi firm the trio used to travel to the *Daily Worker* offices and who held a bag for Goulding, which, whether he knew it or not, contained additional explosives, whilst they bombed the *Daily Worker* offices. Though Palmer claimed to have 'lost interest' in the UM by March 1963, he and Curry attended a UM meeting on Highbury Corner the day after the attack. Later that evening, Palmer met with Sheppard and Frederick Kemp, the north London organiser at the 'European Books' premises at 6 Fieldway Crescent, near Holloway Road, both of whom, according to his subsequent testimony, coached him to deny having seen Goulding or indeed Curry. In his subsequent police statement, Sheppard denied having seen Curry.
426 The *Guardian*, 8 July 1963.
427 For a profile of Harmston, see *Action*, no. 131, 13 September 1963.
428 Special Branch report, 3 July 1963 in TNA KV 2/4020. Flockhart's behind-the-scenes role, aggravated tensions with Jeffrey Hamm, the latter fearing it jeopardised his own position with Mosley. 'In spite of strong feeling by some members against Flockhart's return, many other members would seem to prefer his organizing ability to Hamm's ineptitude,' records and Special Branch report, 24 April 1964 in TNA KV 2/4020.
429 Tony Lambrianou, *Inside the Firm: The Untold Story of the Kray's Reign of Terror* (London: Pan, 2003), p. 46. Lambrianou and his brother served fifteen years apiece for their involvement in the Kray twins' brutal murder of Jack 'The Hat' McVitie in 1967. John Pearson, *The Profession of Violence: The Rise and Fall of the Kray Twins* (London: Bloomsbury, 2013), p. 249 claims that 'Ronnie [Kray] was offered money to assassinate the Fascist leader, Colin Jordan'

though when and by whom it is not stated. This intersection between the criminal *demi-monde* and extremist politics is underexplored. Lillian Pizzichini, *Dead Man's Wages* (London: Picador, 1992) highlights the interest paid to the UM campaign by her grandfather – 'a long-firm conman and fraudster' – who had been briefly active with the BUF in Harlesden during the 1930s. *East End Underworld: Chapters in the Life of Arthur Harding* (London: Routledge, Kegan Paul, 1981), the autobiography of an East End crook who graduated from pick-pocketing and 'shoot-flying' to armed robbery and 'protection' and was involved with the race course gang wars in Brighton during the 1930s, was also involved after 1945 with the Mosleyites in Dalston.

430 *Action*, no. 140, 15 November 1963.
431 Ron Nixon, *South Africa's Global Propaganda War* (London: Pluto, 2016), pp. 17–18.
432 *Sunday Express*, 26 January 1962; *South African Sunday Times*, 29 July 1962; *Wiener Library Bulletin*, vol. 18, no. 2, April 1964; Dennis Eisenberg, *The Re-Emergence of Fascism* (London: MacGibbon & Kee, 1967), pp. 307–308; and Brian Bunting, *The Rise of the South African Reich* (Harmondsworth: Penguin, 1969), p. 71.
433 *Jewish Chronicle*, 7 February 1964.
434 Diana Mosley to Deborah Mitford, 2 January 1964 in Mosley, *The Mitfords*, pp. 406, 413 and 428.
435 *Action*, no. 147, 13 March 1964.
436 *Action*, no. 145, 20 December 1963; and *Jewish Chronicle*, 7 February 1964.
437 *Wiener Library Bulletin*, vol. 18, no. 2, April 1964.
438 *Wiener Library Bulletin*, vol. 19, no. 2, April 1965. Mosley met with John Wilkinson, a former BUF district leader who lived in Natal, see *National European*, March 1965. The internal UM publication *Social Justice*, no. 1, May–June 1967 notes that another activist, Frank Mooney, was actively trying to form branches of the organisation in South Africa, particularly in Cape Town.
439 Diana Mosley to Deborah Mitford, 11 February 1965 in Mosley, *The Mitfords*, p. 428.
440 'Sir Oswald Mosley: South African Broadcast' in C377/16 Eric Stoneman collection, British Library Sound Archive.
441 Union Movement press release, 9 April 1965, copy in authors' possession.
442 The *Guardian*, 9 April 1965; and *National European*, May 1965.
443 *Make Mosley Your Man* (UM election handbill, 1966). Mosley had taken time out of his own campaign to support that of Jeffrey Hamm in Handsworth. Hamm polled a mere 1,337 votes (4.1 per cent), on which, see John D. Brewer, *Mosley's Men: The British Union of Fascists in the West Midlands* (Aldershot: Gower, 1984), pp. 133–147.
444 Diana to Deborah, 5 April 1966 in Mosley, *The Mitfords*, pp. 455–456.
445 *Action*, no. 190, 1 March 1975. The Action Party contested several seats in the 1977 Greater London Council (GLC) elections before it too abandoned electoral politics. In 1978, it became the Action Society, concentrating upon publishing. It ceased existence when Hamm died in 1992. In the United States, an American admirer, Hamilton Barrett, founded an 'Action Society' in San Francisco to propagate Mosley's ideals across the Atlantic, see *League Review*, no. 38, June 1982.
446 C. Welch, 'The White Hope in the Black Shirt', *Daily Telegraph*, 2 April 1975, quoted in Thurlow, *Fascism in Britain*, p. 89.
447 The *Observer*, 8 August 1965.
448 The *Observer*, 15 August 1965. Oswald Mosley to Mr Abrahamson, 2 April 1966 in MS124/1/1, Hamm papers records 'the book written by Lady Ravensdale ceased further publication on representation from my solicitors. The statement in question was untrue and my solicitors have so informed the Wiener Library.'
449 Oswald Mosley to William Frankel, 8 June 1966 in MS124/1/6, Hamm papers.
450 William Frankel to Sir Oswald Mosley, 10 June 1966 in MS124/1/6, Hamm papers.
451 Oswald Mosley to William Frankel, 7 July 1966 in MS124/1/6, Hamm papers.
452 *Ibid.*
453 William Frankel to Oswald Mosley, 13 July 1966 in MS124/1/6, Hamm papers.
454 William Frankel to Oswald Mosley, 24 August 1966 in MS124/1/6, Hamm papers; and *Jewish Chronicle*, 21 February 1969.
455 'The Frost Programme: Interview with Oswald Mosley on 15 November 1967', YouTube, www.youtube.com/watch?v=7j5jJ-VYSps (accessed 23 January 2020).
456 Dorril, *Blackshirt*, 637.
457 Diana Mosley to Deborah Mitford, 17 November 1967, in Mosley, *The Mitfords*, p. 501

458 Sir Burke Trend to the Prime Minister, 27 February 1968 in TNA CAB 164/335.
459 [Illegible signature] to D. Gruffydd Jones, 6 March 1968 in TNA PREM 13/2146.
460 Kurt P. Tauber, *Beyond Eagle and Swastika: German Nationalism since 1945, Vol. 1* (Middletown, CT: Wesleyan University Press, 1967), p. 619.
461 Patrick Skene Catling, 'David Pryce-Jones Settles Old Scores', *the Spectator*, 2 January 2016, www.spectator.co.uk/2016/01/david-pryce-jones-settles-old-scores/ (accessed 5 January 2016).
462 Diana to Deborah, 18 February 1966, in Mosley, *The Mitfords*, p. 451.
463 TNA FCO 41/101.
464 *The Listener*, 31 October 1968, pp. 576–578.
465 Dorril, *Blackshirt*, p. 638.
466 Mosley, *Love From Nancy*, p. 478.
467 *The Times*, 26 April 1968.
468 Oswald Mosley to Robert Innes-Smith, 13 November 1968 in MS124/1/9, Hamm papers.
469 Gyles Brandreth to Oswald Mosley, 8 July 1969 in MS124/1/2, Hamm papers, for instance. Gyles Brandreth, *Something Sensational to Read on the Train: The Diary of a Lifetime* (London: John Murray, 2009), p. 201 notes Mosley declined the invitation.
470 Cecil King, *The Cecil King Diary: 1965–1970* (London: Jonathan Cape, 1972); and Cecil King, *The Cecil King Diary: 1970–1974* (London: Jonathan Cape, 1975).
471 Hugh Cudlipp, *Walking on the Water* (London: Bodley Head, 1976), p. 395.
472 Mosley, *Formula One and Beyond*, p. 24.
473 Andrew Motion, *17 Carnations: The Windsors, the Nazis and the Cover-Up* (London: Michael O'Mara, 2015), p. 59.
474 D.R. Thorpe (ed.), *Who's In. Who's Out. The Journals of Kenneth Rose* (London: Weidenfeld & Nicolson, 2018), p. 466. Other members of the Royal Family were less agreeably disposed to Mosley than the Duke. When Rose met with the Queen Mother at Clarence House on 24 April 1979 to discuss King George V, he told her that he never accepted Mosley's claim not to have encouraged either violence or anti-Semitism, 'she taps the table and agrees with considerable vehemence: "He did, he did."' (p. 577).
475 W.F. Deedes, *Brief Lives* (London: Pan, 2004), p. 158.
476 For excerpts, see Oswald Mosley, *Last Words: Broadsheets, 1970–1980* (London: Black House Publishing, 2012).
477 *The Listener*, 31 October 1968, p. 576. Angus McIntyre, 'The Aging Narcissistic Leader: The Case of Sir Oswald Mosley at Mid-Life', *Political Psychology*, vol. 4, no. 3, 1983, pp. 483–499, for instance, speculates that Mosley was driven by a 'narcissistic personality' observable since middle age, leading him to break with democratic politics, but which, as Deedes and others observed, persisted for the remainder of his life.
478 Thorpe, *Who's In. Who's Out*, p. 385.
479 Oswald Mosley to T. Cassidy, 16 November 1971 in MS124/1/3, Hamm papers.
480 Oswald Mosley to Professor David Calleo, 2 March 1972 in MS124/1/3, Hamm papers.
481 Dick Bellamy to the Secretary, The Mosley Secretariat, 1 January 1972 in MS124/1/2, Hamm papers.
482 William F. Buckley Jr. to Oswald Mosley, 7 March 1972 in MS124/1/2, Hamm papers; and *Historical Reprint Series: Firing Line – Buckley/Mosley* (London: Stevens Books, 1976).
483 Skidelsky, *Oswald Mosley*, p. 15 notes the impact that watching Mosley debate Thorpe at Oxford University had upon him personally: 'My interest in him was born at this point.'
484 Oswald Mosley to Jeremy Thorpe, 11 May 1972 and Jeremy Thorpe to Oswald Mosley, 15 May 1972, Hamm papers. Thorpe's personal assistant told *The Times*, 1 October 1971 that 'He [Thorpe] is quite a friend of Sir Oswald personally' but that he would decline an invitation to debate on the same side as him at the Oxford Union later that year on the merits of Common Market membership.
485 *Daily Mail*, 11 October 1972.
486 *The Listener*, 21 September 1972. The contemporaneous view of Mosley's likely role was somewhat different to his own post-war re-imagining. Having lunching with Marshal Pétain, Vice-President of the Council of Ministers, on 4 June 1940, William Bullitt, the US Ambassador to France, recorded Pétain's belief that the British would desert France. Then, 'after a very brief resistance or even without resistance would make a peace of compromise with Hitler, which might even involve a British Government under a British Fascist leader,' see William Bullitt to

the Secretary of State, *Office of the Historian*, 4 June 1940, https://history.state.gov/historical-documents/frus1940v01/d202 (accessed 16 December 2017). On the following day, the French Prime Minister Paul Reynaud told Bullitt 'the British intend to conserve their fleet and air force and their army, and, either before a German attack on England or shortly afterwards, to install eight Fascist[s] trained under Oswald Mosley and accept vassalage to Hitler.' See William Bullitt to the Secretary of State, *Office of the Historian*, 5 June 1940, https://history.state.gov/historicaldocuments/frus1940v01/d203 (accessed 16 December 2017). Seeking to allay such fears, on 10 June, Winston Churchill, the British prime minister, tried reassuring Joseph Kennedy, the US Ambassador to Britain that 'as long as he lived the British Fleet will not be handed over to the Germans.' Kennedy noted, however, 'it is possible some other government, the Moseley [sic] government for instance, might turn over anything that Hitler wanted in order to save England from destruction,' see Joseph Kennedy to the Secretary of State, *Office of the Historian*, 10 June 1940, https://history.state.gov/historicaldocuments/frus1940v03/d29 (accessed 16 December 2017).
487 Norman Longmate, *If Britain Had Fallen* (London: BBC, 1975), p. 116.
488 *Ibid.*
489 Mosley regularly travelled to Germany. TNA 2/3400/131a highlights Mosley's September 1955 visit to meet Werner Naumann. He also attended a soirée including Frau von Ribbentrop, wife of the former Nazi Foreign Minister, hanged at Nuremberg as a war criminal; Ribbentrop's adjutant, former SS Obersturmbannfürher Richard Schulze; Karl Heinz Peter, a former Hitler Youth Leader and librarian at the Hitler Youth headquarters; and Professor Benno von Arent who became publicity head of the UFA in 1933. His stepson, Jonathan Guinness, was also there. Such contacts persisted. Oswald Mosley to Arthur Ehrhardt, 21 October 1963 in MS124/1/5, Hamm papers notes a visit to Munich in 1963 and requests that Ehrhardt provide him with:

> a list of other people whom you think it important I should see during that period. At some time I shall go up from Munich to Bonn for the night and can see people if necessary in the Rhineland. But I think most of the people I should see are not very far from Munich. I might possibly go down to Austria as well.

490 Arthur Ehrhardt to Oswald Mosley, 4 December 1968 in MS124/1/5, Hamm papers; and *Nation Europa*, vol. 19, no. 2, February 1969. UM activists also sought to publicise German Nazi efforts. *Action*, no. 139, 8 November 1963 contains the following lament from E.W.P. Veale:

> I myself have been trying to 'place' a book by a former member of the SS who spent the war on the Eastern front in the Northern sector, but so far without success. The book has been published privately in Germany, but banned publicly. Apparently the only part of the Wehrmacht that has any right to self-satisfaction is the Afrika Corps, which can hold a re-union without let or hindrance, whereas a proposed Waffen-SS re-union at Hamelin had to be cancelled.

491 Oswald Mosley, *Weg und Wagnis: Ein Leben für Europa* (Leoni Am Starnberger See: Druffel-Verlag, 1973).
492 Arthur Ehrhardt to Oswald Mosley, 11 December 1962 in MS 124/1/5, Hamm papers.
493 Mark Weber, 'In Memoriam: Mabel Elsabe Narjes', Institute for Historical Review, 12 September 1981, www.ihr.org/jhr/v02/v02p289_Weber.html (accessed 5 November 2014).
494 *The European*, no. 19, September 1954. TNA KV 2/3999/119a and 117a notes Sündermann's sojourn in Britain between 28 April and 9 May 1955. Sündermann stated his intention to visit The Britons Publishing House and the British Museum but before doing so stayed in Eye, Suffolk with Ronald Creasy an avidly pro-Nazi former BUF activist. Creasy introduced Sündermann to Mosley at a 'Friends of Union' dinner in London on 30 April. Ronald Creasy to Alexander Raven Thomson, 2 July 1955 in TNA KV 2/4023 notes Sündermann used his visit as research for *Alter Feind – Was Nun? Wiederbegegnung mit England und Engländern/Old Enemy – What Now? Re-Encounter with England and Englishmen* (1956), which explored whether 'after two world wars it is possible to overcome the Anglo-German hostility.'
495 Helmut Sündermann to Oswald Mosley, 27 September 1965 in MS124/1/21, Hamm papers.
496 Oswald Mosley to Peter Dehoust, 24 March 1972 in MS124/1/4, Hamm papers.
497 Helmut Sündermann to Oswald Mosley, 27 September 1965 in MS124/1/21, Hamm papers; and Oswald Mosley to Shaun Mosley, 19 September 1965 in MS124/1/15, Hamm papers. During

1955, Spring had worked as a courier for the Spanish Travel Bureau, see TNA KV 2/4019/522z. Mosley remained a point of contact for German Nazis interested in South Africa. In December 1963, Mosley had met with Peter Dehoust in Coburg. Hartmut Fröschle, a young *Nation Europa* employee subsequently visited Mosley in Orsay. He later chaired Das Hilfskomitee Südliches Afrika e.V., an initiative in which Dehoust was also active. See Peter Dehoust to Oswald Mosley, 23 March 1964 in MS124/1/4 and Hartmut Fröschle to Oswald Mosley, 23 March 1964 in MS124/1/6, Hamm papers.

498 See the two invitation cards in OMD5/7/7, Oswald Mosley papers, Diana Mosley deposit, Birmingham University. The former Nazi jurist, Dr Erich Stolleis, who sympathised with Mosley's ideals but was unable to attend the meeting, sent Mosley his best wishes and recollections of meeting Unity Mitford in Munich during the 1930s, see Dr Erich Stolleis to Oswald Mosley, 12 October 1973 in MS124/1/21, Hamm papers.

499 Oswald Mosley to Dr Gert Südholt, 17 October 1973 in MS124/1/21, Hamm papers. Patrick Moreau, 'Germany', in Jean-Yves Camus (ed.), *Extremism from the Atlantic to the Urals* (La Tour-d'Aigues: Éditions de l'aube/CERA, 1996), p. 122 notes that instead the GfP went into 'slow and steady decline' after 1975.

500 'Irving's Earlier Activities in Germany, 1978–1981', *The Nizkor Project*, http://nizkor.com/hweb/people/f/funke-hajo/Irving-03.01.shtml (accessed 23 January 2020).

501 Skidelsky, *Oswald Mosley*, p. 520. For an early attempt to understand Mosley, see also Robert Skidelsky, 'The Problem of Mosley – Why a Fascist Failed', *Encounter*, vol. 33, no. 3, September 1969, pp. 77–88.

502 Skidelsky, *Oswald Mosley*, p. 15.

503 Diana Mosley to Deborah Mitford, 8 April 1965 in Mosley, *The Mitfords*, p. 430.

504 Diana Mosley to Deborah Mitford, 31 March 1975 in Mosley, *The Mitfords*, p. 611.

505 For a review of the reviews, see Richard Thurlow, 'The Black Knight: Reactions to a Mosley Biography', *Patterns of Prejudice*, vol. 9, May–June 1975, pp. 15–19.

506 Vernon Bogdanor, 'A Deeply Flawed Hero', *Encounter*, vol. 44, no. 6, 1975, pp. 69–77.

507 *The Spectator*, 4 April 1975, p. 14.

508 Robert Skidelsky, 'Reflections on Mosley and British Fascism', in Kenneth Lunn and Richard C. Thurlow (eds), *British Fascism: Essays on the Radical Right in Inter-War Britain* (London: Croon Helm, 1980), pp. 78–99.

509 Robert Skidelsky, *Interests and Obsessions: Historical Essays* (London: Macmillan, 1993), p. xi.

510 James Lees-Milne, *Through Wood and Dale: Diaries, 1975–1978* (London: John Murray, 1998), p. 172

511 *Financial Times*, 28 August 2009.

512 Diana Mosley to Deborah Mitford, 4 June 1975 in Mosley, *The Mitfords*, p. 612.

513 Hamm, *Action Replay*, p. 213.

514 Marsh & Ferriman to Weidenfeld and Nicolson, 22 June 1976 in MS124/1/18, Hamm papers.

515 *The Spectator*, 6 May 2006, p. 24.

516 Jessica to Deborah, 19 November 1975 in Mosley, *The Mitfords*, pp. 634–635.

517 Skidelsky, *Interests and Obsessions*, p. 217; and Diana Mosley to Deborah Mitford, 18 August 2000 in Mosley, *The Mitfords*, p. 802.

518 Hugh Purcell, 'Oswald Mosley: Memories of an Unrepentant Fascist', *New Statesman*, 22 August 2013, www.newstatesman.com/archive/2013/08/oswald-mosley-memories-unrepentant-fascist (accessed 24 July 2017).

519 *Ibid.*

520 Diana Mosley to Deborah Mitford, 26 November 1981 in Mosley, *The Mitfords*, p. 678.

521 Diana Mosley to Deborah Mitford, 16 March 1982 in Mosley, *The Mitfords*, p. 686.

522 Diana Mosley to Deborah Mitford, 27 March 1982 in Mosley, *The Mitfords*, pp. 697–699.

523 Melissa Benn, 'You're Wicked, You're Insane', the *Guardian*, 4 July 2009, www.theguardian.com/lifeandstyle/2009/jul/04/nicholas-moseley-max-moseley (accessed 4 March 2017).

524 Max Mosley, *Formula One and Beyond*, p. 15; and Diana Mosley to Deborah Mitford, 27 March 1982 in Mosley, *The Mitfords*, pp. 697–699; and Benn, 'You're Wicked, You're Insane'.

525 Richard Thurlow, 'The "Mosley" Papers and the Secret History of British Fascism, 1939–1940', in Tony Kushner and Kenneth Lunn (eds), *Traditions of Intolerance: Historical Perspectives on Fascism and Race Discourse in Britain* (Manchester: Manchester University Press, 1989), pp. 173–195.

526 '"Worst" Historical Britons List', BBC News, 27 December 2005, http://news.bbc.co.uk/1/hi/uk/4561624.stm (accessed 31 October 2014).
527 The *Guardian*, 5 June 1964.
528 'Alf' [Flockhart] to Sir Oswald Mosley, 23 April 1961 in TNA KV 2/4020 highlights that Flockhart, the disgraced UM organiser, privately monitored public racial nationalist meetings for Mosley. Having observed their sales drives in Ladbroke Grove, Flockhart proposed attending the BNP 1961 meeting in Trafalgar Square, 'and will let you have my comments upon speeches, audience and any UM people who may be attending and possibly taking some active part.'
529 Martin Walker, *The National Front* (London: Fontana/Collins, 1977), p. 44.
530 *National Review*, no. 44, winter 1985.
531 *Daily Herald*, 16 June 1959.
532 Bean, *Many Shades of Black*, pp. 163–164.
533 Whilst Tyndall became markedly more sympathetic to Mosley during the course of his career, quite possibly because he believed himself to be a man of similar stature, contemporaneously he was more disparaging. Reviewing Mosley's autobiography, *My Life*, in *Spearhead*, no. 21, November–December 1968, Tyndall averred that in world affairs 'he is an internationalist, favouring an even more total integration with Europe than the Government at this stage dares to espouse' whilst on the question of 'race' his views 'are no stronger than those of many Tories.' Furthermore, insofar as his recent views made 'any sense at all' to Tyndall, he believed that they placed Mosley 'a good deal near to the Left than to ourselves. That anyone who has read his latest book should consider him some kind of "ally" of ours is quite fantastic.' He subsequently dismissed Mosley 'who addresses massed rallies of swans from the balcony of his Temple of Glory chateau' in *Spearhead*, no. 45, August 1971 on the grounds that the Common Market was 'not a "White Man's Club"'. 'Whatever the "extremism" of Mosley's past,' *Spearhead*, no. 68 September 1973 stated, 'today he stands for a policy that is definitely "in" with the controllers of the media, while the NF policy of British nationalism is equally "out".'
534 *Spearhead*, no. 147, January 1981.
535 *Spearhead*, no. 191, September 1984.
536 *Spearhead*, no. 33, November 1996. Fields also produced and disseminated a 'Special Commemorative Edition' of Mosley's inter-war newspaper, *Action*, see *Spearhead*, no. 294, August 1993.
537 Walker, *The National Front*, p. 110. The authorities concluded the same thing. A security service report in TNA PREM 13/2315 for the events of 24–25 April notes that 'with the exception of Harmston's participation there does not appear to have been any organized political action behind the demonstration.'
538 Camilia Schofield, *Enoch Powell and the Making of Postcolonial Britain* (Cambridge: Cambridge University Press, 2013), p. 244.
539 Schofield, *Enoch Powell and the Making of Postcolonial Britain*, pp. 244–245; and Simon Heffer, *Like the Roman: The Life of Enoch Powell* (London: Weidenfeld and Nicolson, 1999), p. 463.
540 Robert Sheppard, *Enoch Powell: A Biography* (London: Hutchinson, 1996), p. 355.
541 Hamm, *Action Replay*, p. 180. *Spearhead*, no. 72, October 1972 highlights the prominent role Harmston subsequently played in the anti-immigration agitation at Smithfield Meat Market in August and September 1972 against the Ugandan Asians in which he spoke alongside Martin Webster of the National Front. Again, Mosley went unmentioned.
542 *The Times*, 24 April 1968; and Dorril, *Blackshirt*, p. 639.
543 *The Times*, 24 May 1977.

3 A.K. Chesterton
From 'Fascist Revolutionary' to 'Jew-wise' conspiracy theorist

Mosley's new pan-European philosophy alienated many extreme right-wing activists. None more so than A.K. Chesterton, formerly one of his leading propagandists and author of the fawning hagiography, *Oswald Mosley: Portrait of a Leader* (1936). Chesterton had already severed his connection with the BUF in 1938. Having burned his bridges, he only saw Mosley again a handful of times after 1945 – 'on each occasion socially and not politically'.[1] On the first, in July 1946, the two men had a 'long talk' at Mosley's flat, during which Chesterton told Mosley that, although he still considered BUF policy to be 'worthy of serious consideration', he disagreed with his pan-European creed and declined therefore to offer his services.[2] Chesterton's doubts regarding Mosley's personal authority were confirmed with the publication of his post-war apologia, *My Answer* (1946), which appeared shortly afterwards. 'Sir Oswald speaks hopefully of the future referring to prison as the classic road to greatness,' Chesterton wrote.

> It is unlikely, however, that he himself will now achieve that final objective. What inhibits him is something more restricting than Brixton, the stone wall of his own egocentric temperament, combined ... with too long a training in that worst of schools – the party game.[3]

This ideological rift was cemented in the following year when Mosley published *The Alternative* (1947) in which he fully outlined his idea of 'Europe-a-Nation'. Chesterton was flabbergasted:

> How thoroughly in keeping with the hapless Mosley temperament it is that he should seek to return to political life without the least hope of ever being able to escape the odium, whether deserved or undeserved, of his Fascist past, and yet having divested his political stock in trade of the one part of the Fascist argument which was demonstrably true![4]

For Chesterton, National Socialism's only 'sane' contention was that 'internationalism must always be a racket run by the worlds' only international people [i.e. the Jews]'. Mosley's advocacy of 'European Socialism' struck at the very heart of Chesterton's worldview. The gulf became irreconcilable. Mosley's hagiographer became his most trenchant critic as the two men travelled in diametrically opposing ideological directions. When Mosley announced his decision to leave England's 'island prison' to become a true 'European' in 1951, Chesterton mocked: 'If only Europe knew what blessings must accrue from Sir Oswald's removal of himself to Ireland its flags would no doubt be fluttering joyously at their mastheads. As it is Europe remains strangely calm. It cannot know.'[5]

Whilst Mosley became an evangelist for 'Europe-a-Nation', Chesterton remained committed to the 'Britain First' autarkic nationalism of inter-war fascism, dedicating himself to defending Britain and its Empire against the malign machinations of the 'International Money Power'. For keeping faith with its original ideological remit, post-war Mosley publications abused Chesterton, ironically, as a 'die hard fascist'.[6] But he was more important than this. It was Chesterton's 'extremely doubtful privilege' observed his biographer, 'to go down in modern history as the man most responsible for keeping alive, spreading, and developing, the British tradition of conspiratorial thinking.'[7] He did so through his journal, *Candour*, and his seminal book *The New Unhappy Lords* (1965), which had a significant impact upon the ideological framework of successive generations of extreme right-wing activists who looked to Chesterton, not Mosley, for intellectual inspiration.

Early life

Arthur Kenneth Chesterton was born in South Africa in 1899 on the cusp of the British Empire's imperial apogee. That he was born in South Africa rather than England did nothing to diminish his patriotic ardour, as he insisted:

> Judging from my name my family would appear to go back to Roman times in Britain so that the fact that I happen to have been born in South Africa because my parents were living there at the time does nothing to destroy my Englishness.[8]

'I live in England because this is where I feel I belong,' he noted subsequently.[9] Chesterton grew up in awe of his second cousins, the renowned Catholic journalists Gilbert and Cecil

Chesterton. The adolescent Chesterton held Cecil as his 'exemplar'.[10] Both men, together with their colleague Hilaire Belloc, had played a pivotal role in exposing government corruption in the sale of shares in the Marconi wireless company in 1912 – the so-called 'Marconi Scandal' – which developed markedly anti-Semitic overtones as a result of the involvement of several prominent Jewish businessmen in what was essentially insider trading.[11] This family connection created something of 'shadow' which followed Chesterton throughout his life, explaining too the affinity of a certain Catholic milieu to his own cause in subsequent years.

Too young to enlist when the First World War broke out in 1914, Chesterton joined the 5th South African Light Infantry in the following year after his family returned to South Africa, falsifying his age in order to do so. It was almost the death of him. Campaigning against Germany in East Africa, he became too ill to continue marching and was left at the roadside to die. 'What I got out of my soldiering in German East Africa,' he remembered, 'was three bob a day, malignant tertiary malaria and amoebic dysentery.'[12] Rescued and cared for, ironically, by a group of Africans, Chesterton transferred to fight with the British army in Europe following his recuperation. He reported for duty on 12 September 1918 with the 2/2 Battalion, City of London Regiment, Royal Fusiliers, taking part in the Battle of Épehy six days later. During their assault on German positions near Peizeres, Chesterton's platoon was engaged in eight hours of 'strenuous fighting in which every inch of ground had been vigorously contested.'[13] Aged nineteen, Chesterton was awarded a Military Cross for 'conspicuous gallantry' during which, under heavy fire, 'he personally led bombing parties and finally succeeded in capturing Poplar trench killing the machine-gun detachment that barred his way.'[14]

His personal bravery aside, the manifest horror of trench warfare left an indelible mark upon Chesterton. 'I have fought with my fellow-Britons in two World Wars and know their quality,' he remembered. 'Their blood often enough has gushed over me and the brains of my best friend were blown into my face.'[15] Chesterton's experience of a world turned into 'one vast necropolis' haunted him for the rest of his life.[16] 'For years after the first war it had been my recurring nightmare to walk over a carpet of dead bodies stretching to infinity.'[17] Like many young veterans, Chesterton sought oblivion in alcohol. 'It is not for me to pass judgement on the subject of excessive drinking,' he later wrote. 'Emerging from the last war with taunt-strung nerves and a system shaken by dysentery and malaria I became an addict, and a long and fearful struggle took place before I got the better of it.'[18]

Chesterton returned to South Africa in 1919, working as a journalist for the *Johannesburg Star*. Covering the 'Red Revolt' in Witwatersrand in March 1922 for the newspaper, Chesterton also took an active part in the South African government's brutal suppression of white Afrikaans miners whose strike was simultaneously an anti-capitalist uprising and 'a deliberate, violent assault on the political organisation of their African working-class peers'.[19] The episode also succeeded in arousing 'a vicious and visceral blend of anti-Bolshevism and antialienism' culminating in calls for restrictions to be placed on Jewish immigration.[20] Whilst the conflict was more militantly racist than socialist, something which Chesterton certainly sympathised with, the event exerted a powerful influence upon his subsequent analysis of the 'Red Methods' used by Fascism's opponents in Europe.[21]

In 1924, Chesterton returned to England, carving out a career for himself as a renowned and respected Shakespearean drama critic under the tutelage of his friend, the Shakespearean scholar Professor G. Wilson Knight. He worked as a journalist and festival critic for the *Stratford Herald* then as a public relations officer at the Shakespeare Memorial Theatre in Stratford-upon-Avon, a town he christened 'The Immortal Shrine'.[22] During

1928, Chesterton edited the *Shakespeare Review*, a short-lived monthly that served as a laboratory for the development of his ideas on cultural decay, a theme that underpinned his later writings for the fascist press. Indeed, his evolving ideas on the pressing need for spiritual rebirth, based on a model of English nationhood, 'crystallised around the metaphysics of Shakespearean drama'.[23] As the *Manchester Guardian* observed, the journal's chief purpose,

> would seem to be to use Shakespeare for stopping the dry rot which has set in, and is rapidly sapping our national sanity and virility, since the evil day when a group of men discovered how profitable a game it is to exploit the masses by providing them with cheap pornography.[24]

It was a prophetic comment.[25]

British Union of Fascists

Between 1929 and 1931, Chesterton continued honing his journalistic skills as editor-in-chief of the *Torquay Times* and as chairman of the south Devon branch of the National Union of Journalists. Two years later, however, he discovered a political movement dedicated to stopping this 'dry rot' – the British Union of Fascists (BUF). In August 1933, Rex Tremlett, a former Johannesburg miner and journalist who edited the BUF newspapers *Fascist Week* and *Blackshirt* began seeking 'a few young and keen free-lance men whose work is at present too virile and advanced to sell. I can then give them our ideas, and train them into being Fascist-minded in their writings.'[26] He perhaps had Chesterton in mind. Recruited by Tremlett, who would soon resign denouncing his fellow fascists as 'cads, thieves and swine',[27] Chesterton joined the BUF in November whilst still employed by the Shakespeare Memorial Theatre, 'believing that no other party had anything to offer'.[28]

Chesterton was attracted to the BUF through a combination of culture despair and its idealisation of the classless comradeship and martial spirit he had felt in the trenches, a theme he frequently eulogised in the pages of the fascist press: 'British Union was born in War', he proclaimed. 'Dead Battalions March In Spirit with Us.'[29] Thus began an extreme right-wing career spanning four decades. Within six months of joining, Chesterton was appointed BUF officer-in-charge of Warwickshire and Staffordshire and in April 1934 became 'officer-in-charge' of the Midlands Area.[30] Chesterton's deep devotion to his new cause was reflected in an article for *Fascist Week* written by his wife Doris titled 'Fascist Widows'.[31]

Chesterton commanded the 'central tiers' at the BUF Olympia meeting on 7 June, which famously descended into violence as fascist stewards brutally ejected anti-fascist hecklers – 'Red ape-men' armed with 'the weapons of the Ghetto' in Chesterton's parlance – from an event that was supposed to showcase British Fascism to the great and good.[32] The violence caused Lord Rothermere, owner of the *Daily Mail* whose front page had recently declared 'Hurrah for the Blackshirts!' to withdraw his patronage – due to Jewish pressure, Chesterton alleged.[33] The negative publicity surrounding Olympia caused a slump in BUF support, though recent revisionist accounts of the violence suggest this has been overstated.[34] Publicly, Chesterton lauded Olympia as 'the symbol of our Fascist victory', though privately, according to his widow, he was appalled by the fascist violence.[35]

Following Olympia, Chesterton claimed Mosley was 'genuinely puzzled' by Jewish hostility towards the BUF and 'ordered a thorough research into the Jewish question, especially into the financial and political activities which the movement attacked'. Chesterton, who was transferred to National Headquarters later that month, appointed London deputy administrative officer and elevated to the party's Policy Directorate, was selected for the task. The result was a forgone conclusion. Chesterton was already 'hopelessly prejudiced against the Jews' and Mosley's decision to commission him to undertake the work presumably gave him the study he wanted, given that Mosley was already, as Daniel Tilles convincingly argues, a convinced anti-Semite himself.[36] However, in Chesterton's telling, it was after reading his 'investigation' that Mosley 'discovered' not just that the 'whole capitalist racket' was 'dominated by the Jew' or indeed that the British press and cinema was 'Jew-ridden' but, more importantly, that 'every vitiating and demoralising factor in our national life was Jew-influenced where it was not Jew-controlled. Mosley thereupon took up the challenge...'[37] In a line of argument repeated *ad nauseam* by Mosley's admirers, 'the Jew' was to blame for anti-Semitism. For Chesterton too, whatever the rights and wrongs of Mosley's subsequent platform, he was 'driven into a racial policy by the very people who had most to lose from the implementing of that policy'.[38]

Chesterton's anti-Semitism did not germinate in a vacuum nor was it mono-causal. Whilst his background and familial exposure to the Chesterton-Belloc circle certainly acculturated him to anti-Semitism, as his biographer has pointed out, what is often ignored is

> the degree to which he gained his more extreme anti-Semitism from within the movement – as a result of a concentrated exposure to fascist beliefs.... This process of socialisation must have been important as there is little evidence of such extreme or systematic anti-Semitism in his pre-fascist writings.[39]

Whatever the cause, shortly after conducting this 'research', Chesterton's anti-Semitism became increasingly voluble. He penned a series of articles for *The Blackshirt*, published between August and October 1934, and subsequently reprinted as *Creed of a Fascist Revolutionary*, demanding the abrogation of individual rights and freedoms to the Fascist Corporate State through which, he argued, only true 'freedom' could be obtained. 'If we appear to destroy liberty,' Chesterton railed, 'it should be remembered that the particular liberty we destroy is that which is destroying the race.' Blackshirts must be Spartan, self-sacrificial and single-minded in their pursuit of the fascist 'revolution' during these 'putrescent days of democracy's life-in-death.' If not, Chesterton argued, the fascist millennium would not be attained. Led by Mosley, however, Blackshirts 'fear no more for the future of our race,' Chesterton reassured readers. Mosley reciprocated the praise, lauding Chesterton as a 'brilliant and incisive writer', who captured the 'resurgent soul' of the war generation, 'who could find no home but Fascism.'[40]

Mosley further utilised Chesterton's writing talents by appointing him as Director of Press Propaganda, a subsection of the BUF Propaganda Department on a salary of £250 per annum, a less lavish salary than that enjoyed by some of his BUF contemporaries. 'Press Propaganda' was less imposing than it sounded. Chesterton's colleague, J.A. McNab, the son of a prominent Harley Street surgeon who edited *Fascist Quarterly* and penned the 'Jolly Judah' column for *Blackshirt*, noted wryly that it 'was simply him and me and the typewriter, that is all'.[41]

Chesterton's principal contribution was *Fascism and the Press*, an anti-Semitic assault upon the British media (the Rothermere Press exempted), 'as one of the most corrupt, unscrupulous and degraded vested interests of our time', not least because it systematically misrepresented Fascism and Nazism, 'the great movements of liberation'. Chesterton's remedy was to integrate the media into the Corporate State so that it functioned for the good of the nation instead of feeding it the 'slop and slush of the world's spiritual disorders'. Emergency laws would be enacted to stop publications endangering 'international relationships' (i.e. criticising Fascism); owners would be forced to share responsibility with editors; defaming the 'nation' would become subject to libel action; undesirable journalists, editors and owners would be weeded out; and any publication 'directly or indirectly' owned by 'Jews' would have to record that fact in its title.[42]

The BUF operated as something of a diarchy during this period: split between the organisational and administrative-organisation group led by F.M. Box, the Director of Political Organisation, and its political-propaganda faction, whose leading lights included Chesterton, William Joyce, the Director of Propaganda, and John Beckett, the Director of Publicity. The Olympia debacle had caused serious financial problems for the BUF as a result of which, at Mosley's behest, Box and the famed mechanised warfare strategist, Major-General J.F.C. Fuller, recommended a series of austerity measures aimed at forging the movement into a more orthodox electoral machine, including toning down that party's radicalism. Chesterton intrigued to have Box removed, possibly because he also opposed 'Jew-baiting'.[43]

Despite scheming against Box, Chesterton was still despatched as an Inspector to oversee these reforms in his former Midlands fiefdom. Touring the area in January 1935, he was appalled to discover that the local organisation he had left behind but a year beforehand had failed utterly to live up to his own exacting revolutionary idealism. Many branches were scarcely more than social clubs with no regard for the ideology he revered. In Coventry, Chesterton found the local branch had separate bars marked 'Officers' and 'Blackshirts' with their names embossed on lines of tankards. He could discern no political activity. Chesterton closed the club and expelled the branch leader. Stoke-on-Trent, the biggest BUF branch in the country, presented a similarly dismal scenario, having gained a 'sinister reputation' locally as 'part thieves kitchen and part bawdy house'. Disgusted, Chesterton expelled 300 members on the spot, the largest purge in the organisation's history.[44]

Chesterton's draconian approach did not hinder his ascent within the organisation, which continued unabated. In March 1935, Mosley appointed him to the BUF 'Research Directory', the party's 'inner circle' of policy makers and strategists.[45] During spring 1935, he had, however, started drinking again and 'frequently' arrived at BUF headquarters 'in a drunken state'. There were calls for his expulsion, quite possibly from his colleague William Joyce, who sought to have him certified insane during this period, according to a BUF medical officer.[46] Mosley, who regarded Chesterton as 'one of his ablest propagandists', refused to countenance such suggestions, however, 'and said that it did not matter in what condition Chesterton arrived at headquarters as long as he put in an appearance and did his work.'[47] His condition worsened. In July, *Blackshirt* reported diplomatically that, 'consequent on terrific overwork in the spring' Chesterton 'is having a well-deserved rest, on the strict orders of his doctor. We are all hoping that soon he will be back with us'.[48]

Having convalesced at Beckenham's Bethlem Royal Hospital, Chesterton returned wholeheartedly to promulgating the fascist creed. 'Metaphorically speaking,' recorded the official BUF history, Chesterton 'preferred writing in vitriol to ink.'[49] His stock as a propagandist was never higher. Mosley entrusted him to write his officially sanctioned biography, *Oswald Mosley: Portrait of a Leader* (1936), a sycophantic paean of praise, lauding Mosley as 'an outstanding leader of men' – a notion that was soon to desert its author.[50] The Nazis published a German edition in 1937. Chesterton's new foreword stated that:

'Nobody knows better than Mosley that only after the power of the Jews has been broken by common action, can humanity be rid of the most insupportable of all tyrannies; the dictatorship of money which now enslaves the World'.[51] Impressed, Mosley appointed Chesterton editor of *Action*, the party newspaper, where his fulminations were widely admired. 'This splendid writer has for many months given distinguished service to Fascism, but in our view he is now writing at the height of his form', noted *Blackshirt*.[52] Many readers felt likewise.[53]

But Chesterton's alcoholism remained a serious problem. He was frequently too inebriated to work and would go missing for days at a time. Beckett would invariably find him 'drunk and filthy in some dive' before 'returning him to his wife to be cleaned up'.[54] This time Mosley paid for Chesterton to be treated in a specialist clinic in Germany. During his enforced absence – Chesterton returned to Britain in April 1937 – the BUF underwent a severe financial retrenchment, which saw a 70 per cent reduction in its expenditure and a fundamental restructuring of its political apparatus. The crisis was precipitated by Mussolini's withdrawal of his subsidy from the movement, which plummeted from £86,000 in 1935 to only £7,630 by 1937.[55]

Employed at the BUF headquarters in Great Smith Street as secretary to Chesterton's colleague J.A. McNab, Margaret Bowie, wife of the BUF cartoonist Alexander Bowie, arrived for work on the morning of 11 March to find 'everyone was muttering'.[56] She had just missed Mosley's statement dismissing Beckett and Joyce together with the bulk of the Policy Propaganda Department. The decision also represented the culmination of an internal power struggle for control over the party's political machinery waged between the propagandists and Neil Francis Hawkins, Director-General of Organisation who, having won, emerged as one of the most powerful figures in the movement after Mosley as a result.[57] Wilfred Risdon, the Deputy Director-General, considered his superior to have 'no political knowledge whatsoever' having been promoted by Mosley over and above his abilities to the detriment of others who were shunted out of the BUF. Hawkins' victory did not augur well for Chesterton either. Despite regarding Chesterton as 'a brilliant and honest man', Risdon noted that his vanity was 'a weakness upon which they played'.[58] Thereafter, Chesterton was regularly 'in trouble' with Hawkins' clique, largely as a result of clashing personalities.[59]

Despite the mounting acrimony and the departure of his political friends, Chesterton remained *in situ*, his enthusiasm for National Socialism undimmed. Following his sojourn in Germany, he penned a series of articles for *Blackshirt* titled 'Aspects of the German Revolution', which heaped exorbitant praise upon the Third Reich.[60] And yet, as Chesterton later recounted, it was his personal encounter with Nazism that sowed the seeds of his subsequent disillusionment. He had attended a Nazi meeting at Berlin's Deutscher Halle addressed by Joseph Goebbels, the Third Reich's propaganda minister, then campaigning against the Catholic Church:

> Although not a Catholic myself what he said seemed to me to be so monstrously tendentious and unfair that I wrote an attack on it for *Action* when I returned. O.M. insisted that it be deleted saying 'We don't want to offend the Germans at the present time, Chesterton.' This was the first sign I had that the movement was becoming more German than the Germans.[61]

Contemporaneously, however, Chesterton kept such concerns to himself. There is no record of him objecting to Mosley's decision to re-brand the BUF as the British Union of

Fascists and National Socialists in June 1936 or baulking at the adoption of the 'Action Press' uniform reminiscent of that worn by Hitler's *Schutzstaffel* (SS), which, in a rare display of perspicacity, even Mosley would later concede was 'a considerable mistake'.[62] Likewise, Mosley continued to repose complete confidence in Chesterton, promoting him in June 1937 to 'Director of Publicity and Propaganda' with responsibility for 'creating new propaganda and publicity and acting in a general advisory capacity to the leader on these subjects'.[63] In August, Chesterton added the editorship of *Blackshirt* to his roster of official duties, appointing Philip Spranklin, a young BUF activist working in the Munich Foreign Press Office, as the newspaper's 'official correspondent' in Germany, indicating again that some of his qualms developed *post facto*.[64]

Chesterton's appointment saw BUF anti-Semitism entering a new phase, shifting from its East End crusade against the 'small' Jew to a more conspiratorial interpretation of those controlling Britain's 'financial democracy' – a 'gang of greasy gesticulating Jews', Chesterton railed.[65] His anti-Semitism reached its apogee during this period. *The Apotheosis of the Jew: From the Ghetto to Park Lane* (1937) saw Chesterton arguing that no matter what lofty heights 'the "English" Jew' ascended to in British society, his predilection for the 'debasement of culture' to the lowest common denominator remained. Cultural and physical pollution were intertwined. 'To go to a swimming pool anywhere near London or the large cities,' Chesterton wrote, 'is as efficacious as baptism in the Jordan; one becomes positively anointed with Semitic grease.'[66]

Conspiratorial anti-Semitism was not a new concern for the BUF. *Blackshirt* had advertised to readers that *The Protocols* could be acquired from The Britons from as early as February 1935.[67] The Britons' secretary, J.D. Dell, was delighted, rhapsodising that:

> Sir Oswald Mosley's British Union of Fascists seems to be coming out more openly on the Jew question. Their paper *The Blackshirt* mentioned the Protocols a few months ago and they have put in a couple of advts. of the book (paid for) and have bought two or three dozen copies so far.[68]

With Chesterton in the editorial chair, however, *Blackshirt* began pushing *The Protocols* with greater verve, proclaiming it to be 'the most astounding book ever published', in September 1937. Having previously refrained from openly utilising such propaganda, under Chesterton's editorship, short extracts from *The Protocols* appeared in *Blackshirt*; the book was now touted as one 'every fascist should read … it's terrific' – 'read it, loan it to friends, it will convince'.[69] There is no record of Mosley objecting to Chesterton's utilisation of *The Protocols* or indeed of his decrying its sale in the BUF bookshop.[70]

Though his anti-Semitic ardour was undimmed, Chesterton began experiencing a personal loss of faith in 'The Leader' – whom he and Beckett had always irreverently referred to as 'The Bleeder'. 'Mosley's leadership was at first very good', Chesterton recalled, 'but the adulation he received warped his temperament and after the middle of 1937 I lost all confidence in him'.[71] What finally caused the scales to fall from his eyes remains unclear but Chesterton appears to have come to see Mosley as a political dilettante, insufficiently committed to the fascist revolution. Perhaps the roots lay in an anecdote Chesterton later recounted concerning Mosley's intentions after he had achieved power. Chesterton lamented:

> The answer is, I am afraid, that he would not have known what to do with it. One day he said to me with the air of a man making a momentous announcement: 'When we

come to power, Chesterton, we will sack a senior Civil Servant. That will shake them!' It certainly shook me![72]

Chesterton had already penned his resignation when he learned that Mosley had been knocked unconscious with a brick whilst addressing a BUF meeting in Liverpool. He tore up his resignation and instead submitted a defiant front page for *Blackshirt* declaring that 'nothing can prevent our victory'.[73] Three months later, however, on 18 March 1938, Chesterton tendered his resignation to Sanctuary Press, his nominal employer, assuring them that the BUF could 'rely upon my complete professional integrity' as he worked out his notice. *Action* announced his resignation in the following week without fanfare.[74] The Mosley machine immediately set in motion its internal propaganda mechanisms to airbrush Chesterton from its historical memory. The process was immediate, irrevocable and persists to this day. Two days after Chesterton had resigned, the BUF held its annual dinner for the London administration at the Victoria Grill restaurant, an invitation only event confined to the hundred or so senior party officers, many of who defiantly wore the banned blackshirt at the gathering. Following Mosley's peroration, Hawkins paid tribute to all the senior officers of the London organisation by name, though pointedly omitted Chesterton.[75] The Hawkins clique subsequently reviled Chesterton as a 'traitor'.[76]

In 1940, Mosley told his Advisory Committee hearing that Chesterton was 'bitterly against me' and that their relations were 'of the worst'. He also blamed Chesterton and Joyce for 'rumours' of foreign finance, which were of course true.[77] Yet despite Mosley's antipathy, Chesterton held no animosity towards his Leader in the immediate aftermath of his departure. When Mosley 'decides he is fed up with the rats around him and sends for me again, I will come back,' Chesterton stated.[78] Much of Chesterton's venom was directed instead at the BUF ideologue Alexander Raven Thomson (a 'worm' and a 'Yid'), whom he regarded as a rank hypocrite for preaching 'Britain for the British' in the East End whilst his wife ran an 'Anglo German Domestic Agency', which brought German, Austrian, Czech and Hungarian servant girls into the country to work as 'reliable foreign maids' in English households.[79] Chesterton's real fury was reserved for Francis Hawkins, however, whom he accused of denuding the movement of its revolutionary impetus. Chesterton cited conversations with Mosley who, he claimed, would agree to one idea or another but, as soon as his back was turned, 'Mosley would press the desk-button to summon Francis Hawkins. The suggestion would then be rejected or cut down until it was useless.' Chesterton changed his mind soon afterwards, sending Mosley a second letter conceding he had been mistaken. Francis Hawkins was not to blame. He was only doing Mosley's 'dirty work' so he did not have to bear the responsibility.[80] Mosley was unmoved. 'Poor old Chesterton has gone a little in the head', he was noted to have said, as if mental illness was the only reason anyone would desert his standard.[81]

Chesterton revisited his reasons for resigning thirty years later after reading Mosley's autobiography, *My Life* (1968), in which Mosley shifted his personal accountability for the rampant anti-Semitism that saturated BUF publications onto others. Mosley claimed, unconvincingly, that 'party journals were in other hands, because I was often absent from London, and I do not accept responsibility without effective authority'.[82] Chesterton was astonished, writing to Mosley to remind him that the content of BUF newspapers was decided at the weekly policy directorate meeting,

> over which you presided for the express purpose of reading the page proofs of *Action* and *Blackshirt* and indeed it was my refusal to print *de jeune* articles by some women

writers which you wished me to publish which finally led me to conclude that denial to me of full responsibilities over the papers I edited made my position untenable. There was never the slightest disagreement between us about Jewish policy.[83]

The BUF officers A.G. Findlay, the Deputy Chief of Staff, and Wilfred Risdon, the Assistant Director-General, 'would find their recollections nearer to mine than to yours', Chesterton testily told Mosley.[84] Indeed, as Chesterton's biographer rightly observes, with regard to *The Apotheosis of the Jew*, Chesterton's most noxious piece of anti-Semitic invective, this would never have been published without Mosley's express authorisation. Indeed, having previously appeared in the April–June 1937 issue of *British Union Quarterly*, one can only assume that Mosley not only approved of the article but also believed it merited wider circulation in pamphlet form.

Days after his resignation, Chesterton was invited to attend a meeting of the National Socialist League (NSL), the small pro-Nazi *groupuscule* William Joyce ran with John Beckett. Shortly afterwards, the duo issued a statement citing Chesterton's departure from the BUF as further evidence of Mosley's continued denigration of 'pure National Socialism'.[85] Chesterton told Beckett that if Francis Hawkins did not stop his 'campaign of calumny' against him, he would 'take immediate action to expose his traducers, and he believed he could, if he wished, "cut the BUF in half".'[86] He attempted to make good this threat in his parting shot, *Why I Left Mosley* (1938), published by the NSL, which excoriated the BUF as a perverse 'parody' of National Socialism and a 'projection of Mosley's ego'. It represented his rage against the God that had failed him.[87]

Chesterton was 'guest of honour' at an NSL meeting in April 1938 and lectured its members later that month, greeting his audience as 'my fellow National Socialists'. He never joined the NSL, however, and when Beckett left the group in October, he was glad not to have done so because, as he wrote Joyce, it preserved him from 'the unpleasant business of choosing between two friendships'. That aside, Chesterton told Joyce he remained willing to do all he could, beyond joining, to advance 'the main idea'.[88] The *post facto* reason Chesterton gave for not joining the NSL was Joyce's unabashed pro-Nazism. Indeed, at one such NSL conclave, Chesterton expressed his concern at imminence of war. 'Joyce arose vehemently to dispute my contention. "There will be no war," he thundered. "I trust Adolf Hitler to see to that". Something had happened to Joyce's clarity of vision…'[89] This might be so but there was certainly no diminution in Chesterton's own commitment to the National Socialist cause.

The Fascist fringe

With war looming, many British fascists channelled their energies into the anti-war campaign, not against war per se but against war with Nazi Germany. Chesterton became involved with the British Council against European Commitments (BCAEC), a short-lived coalition of fascists, national socialists and anti-Semites, organised by Beckett, Ben Greene and Lord Lymington, which had coalesced during the 'Munich crisis' in 1938. Chesterton also addressed the 'Economic Road to Peace' conference in January 1939, which brought together economists, monetary reformers, pacifists and businessmen who believed a permanent post-Munich peace would be achieved only if democracy adopted Fascist economic ideals which, it argued, were based upon 'barter' and not 'debt'.[90] Chesterton spoke on 'The Imperial Problem: Development or Exploitation', calling for the British Empire to be freed from the control of international finance which would secure 'the only true democracy, which is economic democracy'. 'The basis of civilisation must be rebuilt upon the soil,' he demanded. The proceedings were hardly harmonious. The final session 'nearly ended in a brawl' when one speaker, Emil Ludwig, a German journalist and biographer, violently denounced the Nazi's 'warrior dream'. Chesterton and Greene, who were sharing the platform, both excoriated him. 'Large sections of the audience shouted loud approval of the attitude of the Greene-Chesterton axis.'[91]

Chesterton's demand that civilisation had to be 'rebuilt upon the soil' saw him participate in another of Beckett and Lymington's ventures, the New Pioneer Group which was founded in December 1938. Chesterton contributed several articles per issue to its journal, *New Pioneer*, regarding 'the nature and motives of the forces for war', venting his spleen against those he believed to be inciting war, particularly President Roosevelt but also Hitler after he invaded Czechoslovakia. German radio stations broadcast his attack on Roosevelt though naturally not the one condemning Hitler.[92] Chesterton's final contributions to *New Pioneer* were dropped when war was but two months away and he retained a suspicion that certain members of Lord Lymington's circle 'were seriously perturbed by my forthrightness. They thought, no doubt, that when the warmongers triumphed, I was [a] designated victim for vengeance and they had no desire to share it with me'.[93]

The New Pioneer Group had evolved from the pro-Nazi English Array, which Lymington had created in 1937 after a split in the English Mistery, a *völkisch* sect espousing a racist 'blood and soil' philosophy. This Mistery itself had originally been formed in 1930 by a disaffected freemason and IFL member called William Sanderson, author of *Statecraft* (1927).[94] Chesterton's own ideas chimed with the group's core concerns, having previously written in *Blackshirt* that a people,

> unless they know, mystically, that beneath the concrete lies the earth which has nourished their race for a thousand years and ... that it is their own earth from which their blood is shed and renewed, then they are a lost people and easy prey for those who had lacked roots for many centuries [i.e. the Jews].[95]

Despite his own views, Chesterton mocked the Mistery for its somewhat 'precious' nature, recalling irreverently of its meetings:

> Its members sat in assembly each with hands placed firmly upon knees, that being believed to be the traditional attitude of the yeomen of Old England. A chair at the head of the table was always reserved for the Sovereign, who appears never to have been aware that his royal presence was expected.[96]

Chesterton remained peripherally involved after the war, his anti-Semitic musings on the 'money power' meeting 'general approval' within the group, but he resigned in July 1946 believing that it was insufficiently active in challenging the system. He was temporarily mollified with the promise of a more activist agenda but the organisation dissolved soon afterwards.[97]

Though Chesterton did not plunge headlong into 'muck and mysticism', the same could not be said of his complete immersion in the anti-Semitic *demi-monde*. Indeed, during the fourteen months between his leaving the BUF and the outbreak of war, Chesterton served as a roving propagandist and speaker for a plethora of anti-Semitic and racial fascist *groupuscules*. Foremost was the Nordic League, a pro-Nazi sect most of whose leading members were interned in 1940 with several narrowly escaping prosecution under the

Treachery Act.[98] In one address to the group on 23 May 1939, Chesterton suggested utilising the nation's lamp-posts as 'the only way to deal with the Jew. In that way alone should be find peace and salvation'. His speech received a resounding round of applause. Shortly afterwards, Chesterton joined the Nordic League Council 'to advise on propaganda'.[99] Chesterton also joined the Right Club, a small anti-Semitic coterie run by Conservative MP Captain A.M.H. Ramsay, whose own treasonous activities served as the trigger for the internment of British fascists in the following year.[100] In June 1939, Chesterton even formed his own anti-Semitic grouplet, the British Vigil with the assistance of John Clarke-Goldthorpe, a medical student and former NSL activist who acted as the group's secretary. The British Vigil was, in Chesterton's words, 'a political companionship of patriots bound together by ties of loyalty' whose object was 'to resist alien or cosmopolitan inroads into the cultural and social traditions of the British people.' It had petered out by January 1940.[101]

Given the range of his activism, it is hardly surprising that from summer 1939 onwards the security services took a 'great interest' in Chesterton. 'A little man was placed beneath our window at Hampton Court, where we then lived', he recalled,

> and there he stayed for months, keeping us in sight when we went for walks, and even on one occasion catching the bus in which my wife travelled every day and following her as far as the school in which she taught. Sometimes as he passed up and down he would carry an oar on his shoulder (our flat was within a stone's throw of the Thames) no doubt feeling that this served to conceal his purpose.[102]

On one occasion, when a torrential downpour soaked his Special Branch watcher to the skin, Chesterton cordially invited him to come in and maintain his vigil out of the rain. 'His only response was a sickly grin.'[103]

For Chesterton, the relative calm of the 'Phoney War' was rudely interrupted when he turned on the wireless one evening in September 1939 only to recognise William Joyce proclaim 'Jairmany Calling! Jairmany Calling!' He and his wife 'stiffened in our chairs and exchanged horrified glances', Chesterton later recalled.

> My wife who is not given to invective, made a comment more bitter than I have ever heard from her. My own anger, although mixed with bewilderment, was not less intense than hers, for I had been associated with William Joyce in a cause which never for a moment had I supposed could produce a situation such as this.... What could have induced the man to do this appalling thing?[104]

Ultimately, Chesterton excused his friend's universalised conception of Fascism, as an 'intellectual aberration' wherein his 'political passion' for National Socialism had overruled his love of his country: 'It was as though a man were to proclaim himself an exponent of the principle "my country, right or wrong" and then go in search of a country which he considered to be right'.[105]

Whilst one might quibble with Chesterton's analysis, his own prioritisation of 'nation' over supranational ideology placed him on a very different path to Joyce. Surprisingly, Chesterton was one of the very few leading fascists to avoid internment in May 1940. The oft-repeated story is that he escaped the dragnet because British intelligence intercepted a job offer from the Nazis to come and work – as Joyce had done – as a propagandist in Berlin, which he angrily refused.[106] This may or may not be true. There is no reference to it in his otherwise voluminous MI5 files. It also jars with Chesterton's professed position vis-à-vis Nazism. He later claimed to have 'consistently and publicly' opposed 'Germany's policy' (he was no more specific) since the invasion of Prague in March 1939:

> when it seemed to him – and events have not proved him wrong – that Hitler was playing into the enemy's hands. That enemy, however, was not – as the publicists proclaim – 'outraged humanity', but finance-capitalists of New York, whose international racket was placed in mortal danger by the principles and practices of the National Socialist system of honest barter.[107]

Whilst Chesterton clearly retained his core sympathy for national socialism and anti-Semitism, MI5 regarded him as a 'patriot'.[108] Indeed, privately, Chesterton raged against those former BUF members who took the attitude that they could 'pick and choose' the wars in which they would support their country. In doing so, they were guilty, he asserted, 'of fantastically perverting our original ideas'.[109] This is important only insofar as equally strident professions of patriotism by former colleagues failed to save them from the ignominy of internment. Free, Chesterton joined the British Army, serving in Kenya and Somaliland where he again started drinking, only to be nursed back to health, ironically, by a Jewish doctor. That he was allowed to enlist stunned former colleagues. Geoffrey Dorman, who took over editing *Blackshirt* and *Action* until he too was given notice to quit in April 1939, was gobsmacked to see his predecessor – 'just back from the Middle East' – interviewed by Movietone news whilst frequenting a local cinema because he had been interned and then prevented from signing up.[110]

Truth

Having relinquished his commission on grounds of ill health in spring 1943, Chesterton struggled to find work. MI5 intervened to ensure that the BBC did not employ him though, given his animus towards the Corporation, it is rather surprising that he applied in the first place.[111] His career as a freelance journalist encountered similar stumbling blocks. Symptomatic was a letter from Grenville Poke, editor of *Everybody's Weekly* declining to publish his article 'Britain Reborn'. Returning Chesterton's article, Poke replied:

> It is a pity, because if you will allow me to say so, you can write and you have courage; but we cannot do it. Lamentations are useless. Your arguments are known and deplored. You are right, but what is the use of grousing now when the country, with Churchill, is doing so well.[112]

Chesterton finally found employment sub-editing the *Sheffield Evening Telegraph*, though a bout of malaria forced him to resign after which worked on the *Southport Guardian* and the Liverpool *Evening Express*.[113] He supplemented this precarious living by freelancing for a range of publications including *Weekly Review* (previously *G.K's Weekly*), which had proclaimed that its principal task was 'a consistent struggle against a political clique of cosmopolitan Jewry'.[114] *Weekly Review* was edited by two right-wing Catholics, Reginald 'Rex' Jebb, Hilaire Belloc's son-in-law, and H.D.C. Pepler, printer, poet and leading exponent of mime, who had served as the paper's managing director since G.K. Chesterton's death in 1936.[115] The assistant editor was Rex Tremlett, who had brought Chesterton into the BUF a decade earlier.[116]

Chesterton struggled to escape his past. In August 1943, *Daily Worker* journalist Douglas Hyde exposed his connection to the *Weekly Review* and highlighted his past association with William Joyce, by now widely known as the Nazi broadcaster 'Lord Haw Haw'. The article impugned Chesterton's patriotism and implied he too was guilty of treachery.[117] Outraged, Chesterton issued a writ against Hyde and the *Daily Worker* and subsequently against the *Jewish Chronicle* too after it repeated the libel.[118] Chesterton approached Mosley's solicitors, Marsh and Ferriman, for assistance but his libel case was eventually dropped for lack of funds, though he did succeed in eliciting an apology.[119] Mosley himself had been reluctant to finance Chesterton in case he lost and was unable to repay him but, moreover, was unwilling to become embroiled in a case which would only remind the public of his own link to Joyce.[120] Though he never denied his past, Chesterton successfully fought fourteen libel actions against those who defamed his reputation, many of them utilising lawyers from Oswald Hickson, Collier & Co., a firm favoured by right-wing politicos including Mosley.

His *Weekly Review* contributions also illuminated Chesterton's views on the 'anti-fascist' war. Chesterton objected to a review in *The Observer* of Douglas Reed's *Lest We Regret* (1943), written by George Orwell, that highlighted Reed's virulent anti-Semitism and his admiration of Otto Strasser, the anti-capitalist Nazi ideologue who had fled Germany in 1933 after Hitler had his brother Gregor murdered during the 'Night of the Long Knives'. Pondering the parallels between Reed's pronouncements and Mosley's propaganda, with his strident call for a British victory, Orwell asked 'if Britain is the Jew-haunted plutocracy that Mr Reed believes, what is it that makes him wish to see Britain victorious?'[121] Chesterton responded tartly: '"My country – right or wrong" is a maxim which apparently has no place in Mr Orwell's philosophy.' 'We want Britain to win,' he lectured Orwell, 'because she belongs to us and we belong to her; our lives derive from her soil and our spiritual roots lie deep in her tradition.' For Chesterton, the real struggle would commence *after* the war. It would be 'a fight to the death between the soul of Britain and cosmopolitan finance, which is determined that the fruits of victory shall be nothing less than the nations of the world in pawn to international usury and control.'[122] In the meantime, however, Chesterton continued using the *Weekly Review* as a platform through which to subtly propagate fascist and anti-Semitic themes and ideas. As he noted to a colleague:

> The great secret of writing for such a journal, I find, is always to remember that they [the readership] only come a part of the way with people like you and me.... This means that one has to keep within fairly narrow limits, besides toning down everything one writes, but it is worth it. By dint of being judicious I have managed to get various aspects of policy across such diverse periodicals as *Empire Review*, *Blackfriars*, *National Review*, *Nineteenth Century*, *Truth*, *British Weekly* and *Everybodys*.[123]

In September 1944, Chesterton's personal fortunes turned a corner. He was appointed deputy editor of *Truth*, an extreme right-wing conservative periodical edited by Collin Brooks, once described as 'almost the last remaining home of the declining art of invective,' which had included, since 1878, a marked antipathy to Jews and Judaism.[124] During the inter-war years, *Truth* was regarded as the nearest thing the Conservative Party had 'to a dependable organ' by its chairman Sir Thomas Dugdale.[125] *Truth* had been secretly controlled by Sir Joseph Ball, a former MI5 officer employed by Conservative Central Office who used the journal as a plausibly deniable front through which to denigrate those within the Conservative Party who were opposed to Neville Chamberlain's appeasement of Nazi Germany.[126]

Chesterton had been friendly with *Truth*'s then editor Henry Newnham, a former a 'chief advisor' to the press magnate Lord Kemsley, whose wife had been interned.[127] He developed an even closer relationship with Brooks in his capacity as *Truth*'s chief leader writer, chief contributor and its political commentator under the pen-name 'Entre Nous', a position he held for nine years. Chesterton soon exerted 'considerable influence' on the journal's policy with anti-Semitism becoming 'more pronounced' as a result, observed MI5.[128] *Truth* afforded Chesterton a measure of financial stability and political influence that other former fascists could only marvel at. It was also a position from which he could help others like Susan Hilton, a former BUF activist, who had been released in 1947 after serving an eighteen-month sentence for 'assisting the enemy'. Hilton had broadcast for *Irland-Redaktion*, the Nazi's Irish radio propaganda station and joined an undercover SS unit whose purpose was to spy on Americans and Germans resident in Vienna, who were suspected of giving succour to the Allies. Chesterton engaged her as a secretary.[129] Hilary Cotter, a former naval officer turned anti-Semitic activist observed that Chesterton 'is always willing to see young nationalists at *Truth* offices'.[130]

Chesterton repudiated 'Fascism' after the war, resolutely denying that he was pursuing a 'neo-Fascist' agenda. Whether Fascism had been a good idea or not 'it would now be profitless to argue,' he wrote nearly a decade after Fascism's defeat. 'The regimes which espoused them [fascist ideas], turning criminally insane in their final amok-run, left as their memorials the foulness of Ravensbrück, the gas-ovens, and the vile doing to death of British airmen.' Addressing the stigma now attached to his own inter-war associations, Chesterton claimed that:

> nobody recoiled with more horror from such outrages than those of us who had been advocates of the Corporate state, nobody gained a clearer perception then we did of the danger of vesting unbridled power in any one man or set of men ... I have renounced those beliefs which, honourably held though they were, have been outdated by events.[131]

He was also genuinely dismissive of the impulse towards ideological universalism that had taken 'traitors to Fascism' like his old colleague William Joyce to Berlin and thence to the gallows. Returning to the subject in 1955, Chesterton recorded:

> Whatever was good in the Fascist idea may live again at some time in the distant future, despite the hideous dishonour which some of its exemplars in one country brought upon it. The wreck now lies for the most part in the gutters of history, and for my part I have neither the means nor the desire to pick up any part of it and try to piece it together again. For one thing, I have learnt that good ideas are not enough. Inadequately safeguarded, even the best idea can become an evil weapon in the employment of a man who has gone off his head. I do not think there will be a revival of Fascism in my time: if there is, I shall be no party to it. I said good-bye to it nearly twenty years ago. My disenchantment has increased, not faded, with the years.[132]

Yet Chesterton still regarded himself to be engaged in a 'bitter, more intangible war' than the one he had fought wearing the blackshirt. In essence, this 'intangible war' remained the same struggle, 'between the spirit and the destroyers of spirit'.[133] Disabused of Fascism's revolutionary panaceas, Chesterton now accepted democracy, albeit a democracy purified of Jewish influence and regenerated in the 'national interest'. This stance indicated how little his world-view had changed in its fundamentals. 'I am not, as you think, committed to collectivism in any shape or form,' he replied to one detractor.

> What I endeavour to do is to fight the process whereby democracy is completely ruled by national and international plutocrats. In other words, I see no acceptable alternative to representative Government, but I am very much concerned that the Government should function on behalf of the national interest and not on behalf of an international financial cabal which is what is happening today.[134]

His acceptance of democracy retained some traces of his inter-war commitment to Corporatism too. Elsewhere, Chesterton wrote that 'although I am not sure that representation solely on a geographical basis is enough to meet the needs of our times. It could be supplemented by an occupational franchise which would conceivably bring more peace into industry.'[135]

Chesterton's solution to the international insecurity wrought by globalisation also remained within the inter-war mould. This was evident in his opposition to the 1944 Bretton Woods agreement, which remade the international financial architecture in the United States' favour, granting it the dominant position in the world's economy, which it retained until the 1970s. Bretton Woods, which saw the foundation of the International Monetary Fund and the World Bank (which the United States effectively controlled), was part of a broader process that also inaugurated supranational bodies like the United Nations, a development Chesterton abhorred. This loathing was manifest in *The Menace of the Money Power* (1946) and *Britain's Alternative* (1946), two of Chesterton's earliest post-war pamphlets, which rejected neo-liberalism and argued for a return to nationalist, autarkic economics.[136]

Truth became a focal point for right-wing opposition to Bretton Woods as well as agitation against the Labour government's nationalisation programme. *Truth*'s offices also housed Aims of Industry, a free-market think-tank founded in 1942. Brooks, who was present at its inaugural meeting, edited most of its early propaganda. Aims of Industry, which had close links to the Conservative Party, rose to national prominence in 1949 with its 'Mr Cube' campaign. Sponsored by Tate and Lyle, as part of a coordinated effort to oppose the Labour government's plans to nationalise the sugar industry, Aims of Industry played a 'very important role' thereafter as 'almost the only pressure group' working on behalf of free-enterprise industrialists.[137]

In November 1944, shortly after joining *Truth*, Chesterton was informed by Brooks that several 'big industrialists' were 'anxious to support a strong nationalist movement with the object of opposing the spread of socialism and communism'. Brooks asked Chesterton to help supplement his efforts. This he duly did, assembling a group of right-wing activists for a meeting on 24 November of the 'National Front After Victory' group. The Conservative Party were also alarmed by the prospect of a socialist administration and had long sought an effective response to the Labour Party's platform. In 1941, the Conservative Party chairman, Douglas Hacking, seeking to reinvigorate what many regarded as the limpid propaganda emanating from Conservative Central Office, appointed a liaison committee through which it would 'work closely' with the backbench 1922 Committee whose secretary was Finchley MP Captain J.F.E. Crowder.[138] Crowder attended the initial meeting of the National Front for Victory, perhaps as a scoping mission to see if the group were a fitting vehicle through which to oppose Labour's plans to nationalise the coal, steel and sugar industries. It would seem that they were not. Crowder never returned.[139]

Indeed, whilst the National Front after Victory served briefly as a rallying point for extreme right-wing activists, many of whom were also active in the Constitutional Research Association, an anti-Semitic, pro-Nazi luncheon group, it soon fizzled out. Chesterton's overt anti-Semitism alarmed several participants whilst revelations in the House of Lords in 1945 that the group was to merge with John Beckett's recently re-founded British Peoples Party (BPP) engendered paranoia, distrust and disharmony since it revealed the group had been infiltrated. It atrophied rapidly thereafter though Chesterton only finally washed his hands of it on 7 August 1946.[140]

Despite their occasionally fraught friendship, Chesterton became involved with Beckett's BPP – though not publicly. Using the pen-name 'Philip Faulconbridge' (the illegitimate son of Richard the Lionheart in Shakespeare's *King John*), he contributed to its newspaper the *People's Post* and penned the anonymous foreword to *Failure at Nuremberg* (1946), which gained the attention of the French fascist and 'revisionist' writer Maurice Bardèche, whose brother-in-law, the collaborationist journalist Robert Brassilach, had been executed.[141] MI5 also suspected that Chesterton was the anonymous author of 'I Marched with Mosley' that appeared in the *People's Post* in January 1948, occasioning 'a good deal of angry comment' within the fascist fringe.[142] Chesterton only publicly associated himself with the BPP in October 1950, when it was announced he had joined its 'research department' shortly before the party imploded.[143] As 'Alexander Keith', Chesterton was also an occasional contributor to Beckett's private newsletter, *Fleet Street Review*, a non-fascist publication which offered news 'unobtainable through ordinary channels'.[144]

Other literary endeavours

Truth enabled Chesterton to continue his freelance activities, which included turning his hand to fiction. He penned a play, *Leopard Valley* (1943), set prophetically against the backdrop of a native insurgency against white rule, which enjoyed a two-week run at a Southport theatre in the following year. Utilising another Shakespearean *nom de plume*, 'Caius Marcius Coriolanus' (from the tragedy *Coriolanus*), Chesterton penned a short anti-Labour satire titled *No Shelter for Morrison* (1945), published by Dorothy Crisp, a right-wing writer and publisher prominent in the British Housewives' League.[145] As 'Philip Faulconbridge', Chesterton also wrote *Commissars Over Britain* (1947) which satirised social democracy as the midwife for Communism through a fictional depiction of Britain under Soviet domination until freed by a 'British Resistance Movement'.[146] *Commissars Over Britain* had been serialised in *London Tidings*, a newsletter edited by Douglas Reed, the former Central European correspondent for *The Times* and bestselling author of *Insanity Fair* (1938). Though anti-Nazi, Reed was also a voluble anti-Semite. Chesterton took over as *London Tidings*' editor in April 1947 as Reed became increasingly invested in the lobbying campaign to allow Otto Strasser to return to Germany from his Canadian exile.[147]

During this period, Chesterton also published a novella, *Juma the Great* (1947), which portrayed the trials and tribulations of Juma, a tragi-comic Baganda tribesman recruited in Uganda to fight for the British Army in Abyssinia (as Chesterton had done) during the Second World War. 'Juma was like most Africans,' wrote Chesterton, 'the more towering their virtues the more staggering their defects and the more inexplicable the occasions on which those defects were manifested'. A good-natured indolent drug user with a propensity for drink, rash action and tall stories who, despite himself, wins a gallantry medal, Juma conformed to most racial paternalistic stereotypes and provided ample, if unconscious, testimony to Chesterton's belief in the virtues of imperial government.[148]

Chesterton's views on the Chinese and South East Asians were markedly less favourable. 'I have always had for the Chinese some of [Thomas] de Quincey's horror,' he recounted.[149] Such views would no doubt have disappointed Hing Shung Mok, Chesterton's childhood friend.[150]

'The Jews' remained Chesterton's central preoccupation, however. He never denied his past allegiance to Mosley or that he had written articles 'praising the pre-war Nazi movement as I knew it during the six months I spent in Germany in 1937', with the caveat that this was 'six years before Hitler or the regime or both went clean off their heads and became engaged in criminal lunatic activities on a vast scale'.[151] Chesterton's own accounting was not strictly accurate. The articles he penned for *Blackshirt* following his return from Germany had included denying these self-same 'criminal lunatic activities'. 'Nobody in Germany has been punished because of his opinions – that is since Hitler came to power,' he had written whilst dismissing the concerns of 'gullible' Britons regarding Nazi concentration camps.[152] Indeed, even as war raged, Chesterton could accuse Hitler and Mussolini of committing many 'foul' crimes whilst also proclaiming that 'these men did at least perform one signal service for their peoples – they delivered them from the menace of the foreign money-lender [i.e. the Jews]'.[153]

Post-war revelations of 'gas chambers and crematoria' at Auschwitz Chesterton did not dispute, unlike Leese or indeed Mosley. 'The unutterable abomination of Buchenwald and elsewhere completely knocked me flat and filled me with such horror that I began to doubt whether human affairs were not too far gone in depravity for anybody to do anything about them,' he wrote in 1948.[154] Moreover, Chesterton made no effort to claim, as subsequent 'revisionists' like David Irving would do, that Hitler knew nothing of the Holocaust. For Chesterton, to shift the blame onto Hitler's satraps was 'to miss the whole significance of the crime, which is that the order to exterminate Jews was made in the twentieth century by the Government of a Central European country ... Hitler should not be crowded off his pedestal.'[155]

If Chesterton acknowledged the reality of the Holocaust, he was, however, profoundly unmoved by the fate of its victims. Couldn't the Jews 'pipe down a little?' he enquired. The 'hideous persecutions' they suffered 'must be constantly on their minds', he conceded, but they should remember, 'that those persecutions did not occur because they kept quiet, but for quite the opposite reason'.[156] In a similar vein, thirteen years later, Chesterton would decry the 'blatantly bogus trial' of Adolf Eichmann and insist that the Jews 'should cease to prosecute the world' and 'comport themselves in a more decorous fashion. That would be the only acceptable "final solution" to the Jewish question'.[157]

Though he later applauded Otto Strasser's 'exposure of the lie about six million Jews being done to death in gas chambers', Chesterton's general line was to minimise rather than deny the Holocaust.[158] That he felt compelled to do so stemmed from the 'great overmastering sincerity' he still imputed to National Socialism, and indeed to those in the dock at Nuremberg. He refused to accept that Nazism represented a 'criminal' enterprise. Nazism's project for 'national regeneration' met with 'Jewish opposition and intrigue' but physical violence against Jews was not part of 'official policy' nor were 'pogroms' – refuting Kristallnacht's categorisation as such as 'a flagrant misuse of the word'. It was war that unleashed the 'deplorable frenzy' that led to the 'final abomination' of mass killing. But in this the Nazis were not alone, he argued. No 'devilry' committed under Nazism matched Soviet atrocities, Britain's firebombing of Dresden, or America's atomic attacks upon Japan. Nuremberg represented the 'crowning horror' of the war – 'a regression into barbarism and night' – which had been fashioned in part by 'Jewish brains', a theme which echoed Leese's arguments regarding the Trial being part of a Jewish war of 'revenge'.[159] Indeed, Chesterton would subsequently claim that Nuremberg was 'more deadly than the death camps' because it had the form 'though nothing whatever of the substance' of legality. The trials, he opined, were a 'parody' of Europe's most cherished virtues and one that 'could never have been incubated in a European mind, although myopic Europeans enthusiastically carried co-operated in carrying it out.'[160]

Chesterton's preoccupation with conspiratorial anti-Semitism was such that in 1947, MI5 noted that he was considering embarking upon a book about *The Protocols of the Elders of Zion*. Brooks was 'enthusiastic about the project'. More measured opinion prevailed, however. The book never appeared.[161] Chesterton subsequently enquired of Robert Lynd, literary editor of the *News Chronicle*, about writing a book on the Jews. 'As regards books about the Jews,' Lynd replied, 'I think that there is so much danger in the spread of anti-Semitism that arguments about Jewry are better discouraged.'[162] Chesterton was not discouraged. He co-authored *The Tragedy of Anti-Semitism* (1948) with Joseph Leftwich, a Jewish literary scholar noted for his translations of Yiddish literature whom he had known since the 1930s.[163] Chesterton was at pains to deny he was an 'ideological' anti-Semite, insisting instead 'Jews should face the fact that they, and only they, are the creators of anti-Semitism.'[164]

The poorly structured, disjointed and rambling book, meant that Leftwich never gained the initiative, failing to grapple with the numerous unsupported assertions and misquotations contained in the nuances of Chesterton's phraseology.[165] Chesterton had been inspired to write the book by his wartime conversations with Israel 'Izzy' Somen, a Jewish army officer who later settled in Kenya where he became President of the Board of Kenya Jewry and Mayor of Nairobi. Chesterton was dismayed by contemporary reviews of the book. 'The reaction to this in Jewish quarters', Chesterton wrote to Somen,

> has been much more violent than I hoped it would be, as my intention in writing it was not to stir up passions but, rather, to try and find a way whereby those passions might be abated. It seems I have not succeeded.[166]

Where Chesterton did succeed was in carving out a niche for himself as a commentator on international affairs. In 1946, using his pen-name 'Caius Marcius Coriolanus', Chesterton penned a 'world commentary' column for the short-lived, quarterly periodical, *Sovereignty – The Voice of National Britain*. By November 1950, however, he was writing a semi-regular column on 'The International Situation' under his own name for the respected *Royal United Services Institution Journal*, which continued for most of the decade. Edging further towards the mainstream, Chesterton had also applied for a job at the *Daily Express* earlier that year but was rejected by editor Arthur Christiansen, who lamented that 'although I admire your writings in *Truth* and agree with much of the opinion they express', he was unable to offer him employment at that time.[167]

In 1953, Brooks, struggling against the ravages of Alzheimer's disease, resigned as *Truth*'s editor and sold his shares in the journal triggering its sale. In a parting message to Chesterton, Brooks recorded:

> my great appreciation of your devotion and industry as my senior colleague over the past ten or twelve years … your unusual knowledge of foreign and imperial affairs, your wide general culture and your forceful prose style, have been of inestimable value to me, as editor.[168]

Much to Chesterton's horror, *Truth* was sold to the Staples Press whose owners appointed the liberal journalist George Scott editor. Scott immediately began fumigating *Truth*'s reputation for noxious anti-Semitism by appointing Jewish journalists like Bernard Levin to its staff. Indeed, when Scott's secretary showed him Levin's application, he was delighted by the Jewish name and stated: 'Show him in, he's got a job.'[169] Chesterton was aghast. His response was a visceral diatribe titled *Truth Has Been Murdered*, distributed *gratis* with copies of *Free Britain*, newsletter of The Britons.[170]

Leaving *Truth*, Chesterton became Information and Public Relations Officer to the London Committee of the United Central Africa Association (UCAA).[171] In this capacity, he penned its brochure *Birth of a Nation: The British Purpose in Central Africa* (1953), a paean of praise to Britain's past imperial achievements in Africa which, in making the case for Central African Federation, argued, 'it is the inescapable duty of the European to make all major policy decisions on matters which lie outside the purview of his African wards'. Leopold Amery, the former Cabinet minister whose son, John, an ardent Nazi sympathiser, had been hung for treachery in 1945, contributed a foreword.[172] Chesterton sent three dozen copies of the booklet to the Colonial Office, who forwarded them to its secretariats in Northern Rhodesia and Nyasaland with a note that they 'may be of some use to you'.[173]

Chesterton's employment was short-lived, ending later that year when the organisation wound up. During this period, Chesterton also applied for a job with the 'Truth about Kenya' campaign chaired by the Earl of Portsmouth (formerly Lord Lymington), who was 'horrified' to learn of the sale of *Truth*, 'which has been a power of sanity in so many ways including East African Affairs'.[174] Launched on 23 January 1953, the Truth about Kenya's publicity campaign aimed to counter 'malicious slander, misrepresentation and downright lies' about the achievements of 'the British way of life' in the Colony and to promote confidence in its future.[175] Chesterton bought into its dream and was on the cusp of emigrating to Kenya when, in April, the media mogul Lord Beaverbrook, responded to a letter from him seeking employment, offering him a job as a journalist writing for the *Daily Express*, *Sunday Express* and the *Evening Standard*.[176] Chesterton accepted, quickly becoming Beaverbrook's 'literary advisor' and ghost-writer of *Don't Trust to Luck* (1954), the 'Beaver's' autobiography.

In November 1945, shortly before his execution, William Joyce had remarked that Chesterton's own sympathies were 'entirely with us'. Those sympathies evidently persisted. Indeed, no sooner had he joined the *Sunday Express*, than Chesterton penned a sympathetic portrait of Joyce, pondering how his old friend had come to commit treason before concluding that it was because Joyce was an 'idolator' – first of Mosley and then Hitler: 'Hence his plunge into the abyss.'[177] Chesterton presented Joyce's hanging as an illegal killing based on a technicality. Though a fuller study was spiked by the *Sunday Express*, Chesterton's revisionist account provided a counterpoint to *The Meaning of Treason* (1952) by Rebecca West, which had supported Joyce's execution. Chesterton's article was also important for helping to frame the subsequent historical record, as Joyce's friends and admirers had hoped. Chesterton's counter-attack 'introduced arguments and details from Margaret [Joyce] and [J.A.] McNab which have seeped uncritically into subsequent biographies,' notes Joyce's biographer Colin Holmes.[178]

Candour

His employment with Beaverbrook could have served as a bridgehead for Chesterton's further rehabilitation and re-integration into the mainstream Right. But it was not to be. His tirade against *Truth*'s new management brought him to the attention of Robert K. Jeffrey, an eccentric expatriate millionaire living in Chile who had made his fortune in the nitrate industry. Jeffrey subsisted on porridge and walnuts, keeping a bathtub full of the latter in case of a world shortage. He squirrelled away part of his fortune in gold bars, which at one point he stashed in a cupboard under the stairs together with stacks of £5 notes, each of which he had individually signed.[179] Jeffrey offered Chesterton £1,000 to set up his own 'white weekly' to replace *Truth*, with the proviso that he advocated a return to the gold standard. Chesterton declined to do so, not least because he believed that currency should be based on productive power not on gold salted away in the vaults of the Bank of England. Persuaded, Jeffrey dropped the stipulation.[180] Thus, on 30 May 1953, seventeen people gathered to hear Chesterton outline his plans for the foundation of a 'really vigorous patriotic publication'.[181]

Chesterton initially intended to establish a limited company in order to support the venture.[182] Upon reflection, however, he decided to retain 'absolute editorial control' over the endeavour and instead invited those still willing to help to form an editorial advisory committee.[183] This editorial council, announced in January 1954, comprised Chesterton (chairman); Leslie Greene (secretary); Lieutenant-Colonel John 'Jock' Creagh Scott, author of the nakedly anti-Semitic tract, *Hidden Government* (1954) published by The Britons; Commander W.S. Cox RN; Lady Elizabeth Freeman, widow of Air Chief Marshall Sir Wilfrid Freeman; and barrister Alice Raven who had authored *Motive Forces of the Mind* (1928) and *The Psychology of the Murderer* (1931), which were 'fairly well-known in medico-psychological circles' and who had been involved in pro-Nazi circles before the war.[184] Without the support of these three 'patriotic' ladies, but especially Lady Freeman, Chesterton would have returned Jeffrey's cheque leaving the initiative 'still born'.[185]

The first edition of *Candour* – 'the British Views Letter' – duly appeared on 30 October 1953 under the editorship of 'Philip Faulconbridge' its purpose being, as indicated by the title of its first article, to 'Sound the Alarm' at the decline of British Imperial power. Chesterton was particularly keen to gain an African readership and from March 1954 onwards *Candour* appeared with a by-line declaring that its avowed role was 'to serve as a link between Britons all over the world in protest against the surrender of their world heritage'.[186] *Candour* was printed by The Clair Press, a firm operated by Tony Gittens, a former IFL section leader who ran The Britons. Many of Chesterton's leading associates were intimately involved with The Britons and Chesterton not only contributed to its newsletter, *Free Britain*, but occasionally disbursed funds to the group.[187]

Jeffrey's backing also gave Chesterton the financial clout to offer a paid weekly column in *Candour* to Douglas Reed, whose most recent book *Far and Wide* (1951) had declared 'no proof can be given that six million Jews "perished"', whereas 'proof can be adduced that so many could *not* have perished'.[188] Reed had also become convinced that Hitler was part of the Jewish conspiracy. The latter assertion held no appeal for Chesterton. 'I can think of only one piece of closed territory so far as we are concerned – that is your view of the adherence of Hitler to the modern conspiracy,' Chesterton stated in offering Reed the job. 'Otherwise, all the world is your oyster and we should consider ourselves greatly privileged to have the formidable assistance of your skill and name.'[189] Reed declined on financial grounds to which Chesterton, whilst sympathetic, countered that:

> from the point of view of the patron and from my own point of view, the battle is ideological and service to the common cause matters very much more than any personal benefit, apart from the satisfaction that doing this work yields.[190]

Despite declining, Reed occasionally contributed anonymously to *Candour*.

Chesterton later claimed that when Beaverbrook learned of *Candour*'s existence, he dismissed him on the spot. In fact, his contact had already expired in January 1954 and was not being renewed. Chesterton had had a difficult relationship with the newspapers' editors and they had decided against re-employing him. Whilst Beaverbrook declined to intercede on his behalf, he did offer to use his 'influence' to secure alternative employment for Chesterton, who evidently decided not to take him up on the offer.[191] Whilst the archival evidence contradicts Chesterton's own version of events, Chesterton certainly bore the newspaper magnate no malice. Despite using a pseudonym to 'avoid embarrassing my employer ... it was too much to expect that this venture would be tolerated. I make no complaint.' Chesterton retained an affectionate admiration for Beaverbrook,

> ... based on the conviction that according to his own lights he has done his best – not a very effective best – to preserve the British Empire. I admire him in particular for having allowed me, in one of his own newspapers, to attack him as a political impotent.[192]

Chesterton could afford to be magnanimous. The regular cheques arriving from Chile gave him that latitude, affording Chesterton a stable living and enabling him to contemplate how he could best use Beaverbrook's lacklustre efforts to maintain Britain's Empire.[193]

League of Empire Loyalists

Chesterton viewed the ongoing disintegration of Empire with absolute horror, though he never really reflected upon the fact that fascist and Japanese militarism were partly responsible for prising open a space for indigenous anti-colonial nationalisms that accelerated the dissolution of the British Empire.[194] He reserved his wrath for the 'Money Power' instead. Chesterton continued to believe that:

> A strong British Empire is the only protection of hundreds of millions of people against the wholesale putrefaction of their social organisms, the only possible guarantee, indeed, that the world will not become a sort of global brothel run by savages for the benefit of High Finance.[195]

Simply editing *Candour* was no longer enough. In March 1954, Chesterton wrote:

> There should be brought rapidly into being an organisation of British patriots which would raise such a hornet's nest under any public man who dared to speak or act against British sovereignty as to put him in fear of his political career.[196]

To this end, Chesterton founded the League of Empire Loyalists (LEL) on 16 October, its principal aims encapsulated in the titles of three pamphlets he published between August and October – *Sound the Alarm*, *Stand by the Empire* and *Beware the Money Power* – each 'a warning to the British nations'.[197] The League, which from 1955 onwards operated from offices at 11 Palace Chambers, Bridge Street, opposite Parliament, filled the political vacuum left by the implosion of the BPP after the Duke of Bedford's apparent suicide in the previous October. *Candour* had received a considerable fillip from John Beckett, who passed on to Chesterton the *People's Post* subscription list, after its final issue in February 1954 had proclaimed that Britain went to war because 'Hitler had offered a challenge to the

International Money Power' and thus 'the Jews wanted revenge on the nation which was the principal obstacle to their ambition of dominating the world.'[198] Beckett declined to join the League, however. Enraged, Chesterton terminated their friendship, returning Beckett's letter with the word 'FUCK' scrawled angrily across it.[199]

If old friends fell by the wayside, new ones emerged to help Chesterton spearhead the LEL's activities, which he controlled and directed.[200] His 'organising secretary' was Margaret 'Leslie' Greene, the daughter of his old friend Ben Greene, who had recently converted to Catholicism, much to the chagrin of her father. A classics graduate (St Andrews), Greene had known Chesterton since 1938, when he visited her parent's home with John Beckett. 'I sat devotedly at your feet the whole day imbibing your conversation,' she recalled.[201] Greene was also one of Chesterton's pupils at Marlborough Gate Secretarial College, where he taught journalism until the 1960s.[202] Leslie Greene was also a cousin of the novelist Graham Greene and BBC Director-General, Sir Hugh Carlton Greene. 'With all due respect to Leslie', Chesterton later observed, 'the Greenes are nothing if not an extremely eccentric family and in the case of dear Hugh the eccentricity would appear to verge on madness'.[203]

From the *Yorkshire Post*, Chesterton recruited Austen Brooks, the son of *Truth*'s former editor, to become *Candour*'s deputy editor, campaigns director and honorary treasurer of the LEL, the latter posting an appointment with unforeseen future ramifications. Chesterton's director of public relations was Aidan Mackey, headmaster of St Tarcisus School in Camberley, Surrey, who edited *The Defendant*, a Catholic distributist journal opposed to 'World Government' which meant 'the death of all that we understand by the word Christendom' and which could not 'of its nature, be anything other than a Communist state',[204] Another trusted confidant was Frank Clifford, a former BUF activist.[205] Agnostic himself, Chesterton remarked of the preponderance of Catholics in his inner circle, 'that our main supporters through the years do happen to have been Catholics whose staunchness and continuity of purpose in the face of many vicissitudes have been equalled by few Protestants and excelled by none'.[206]

The League's imperial credentials were enhanced by the endorsement of a number of military and colonial figures like Field Marshal Lord Ironside, General Sir Hubert Gough, Sir Richard Palmer, Lieutenant-General Sir Balfour Hutchison and Major-General P.J. Mackesy, not to mention a range of lesser figures, who joined its 'National Council'. Later attempts to induce such quintessentially British figures as Scout leader Robert Baden-Powell and fighter ace Group Captain Douglas Bader (an outspoken defender of white minority rule in Africa) to lend their prestige to the League proved unsuccessful, however.[207] Chesterton believed such 'Blimpish' grandees gave the League cachet but in reality they fuelled popular impressions that the group was anachronistic and reactionary, led by an imperial Canute who viewed Empire's end and the rise of American-led globalism with an uncomprehending, ducal disdain.[208] This characterisation of Chesterton is unfair. He certainly understood himself to be living in an era of 'almost total change' but interpreted the motor of this revolutionary upheaval through a conspiratorial, anti-Semitic lens.[209]

Chesterton also sought to mobilise residual youthful enthusiasm for Britain's past imperial glories through school meetings and essay competitions on subjects like 'the case against the scuttle' which in one case was disseminated to schools and youth clubs by a local educational authority.[210] Those youngsters who did join were largely ineffectual, however, a fact verily attested to by the misadventures of Auberon Waugh, son of the novelist Evelyn Waugh, who later achieved fame for his venomous journalism.[211] His famously imperious father was unimpressed. 'I trust your Empire League is not under the auspices of Sir Oswald Mosley?' Waugh wrote his son. 'If it is you will end in prison like my old friend Diana Mitford.'[212] Though the stigma coupled with its 'Blimpish' image undoubtedly detracted from its broader appeal to young people, in a period in which racial nationalist parties were in abeyance, the League's noisy, public activism against internationalism and immigration, usually led by Greene or Brooks, did indeed attract a coterie of highly committed young activists. Some, like Colin Jordan, Chesterton's Midlands organiser, and John Bean, his Northern organiser, already had a track record of right-wing extremism, whilst others, like John Tyndall and Martin Webster, were beginning to build one and would subsequently shape the future trajectory of the British extreme right in their own image.

Beyond its trenchant defence of Britain's diminishing imperial interests, Chesterton's League continued the tradition of 'third way' thought readily recognisable in the anti-capitalist and anti-communist components of British fascist ideology during the inter-war period. This was particularly evident with regards to Chesterton's encounter with Otto Strasser who had begun sending Chesterton information for inclusion in *Truth* in 1949 and thereafter became an early contributor to *Candour*.[213] Exiled from Germany for twenty-two years, Strasser returned to Europe in February 1955 and hoped to meet Chesterton on his stopover in London, 'for the purpose of discussing with me the fight against International Finance and International Communism in which we are both engaged.' Strasser was refused permission to disembark, which Chesterton blamed upon the machinations of 'Financial Jewry'.[214] Chesterton subsequently travelled to Dublin to meet Strasser on 22 March, the latter having stated that the only purpose was to pay a visit to the Order of the Divine Word at Donamon Castle, Co. Roscommon. The superior of the Order denied the visit had any political significance.[215] True or not, Strasser's visit had some significance for Chesterton. Reflecting on the symmetry of their ideological positions, Chesterton remarked: 'May his cause prosper, because in essentials it is our own.'[216] Strasser subsequently gave an exclusive interview to *Candour* in the following year.[217] Chesterton's personal links with Strasser were subsequently strengthened when Leslie Greene married a member of Strasser's extended entourage.[218]

The LEL is often mischaracterised as a Tory 'ginger group'. Chesterton's radical, anti-Semitic 'third way' stance invalidates this supposition. Though he initially sought to influence Conservative imperial policy, Chesterton's relationship with the party became increasingly adversarial as the pace of decolonisation accelerated. The Conservatives, he argued, formed, together with the Labour and Liberal parties, a 'united front to denigrate patriotism'.[219] Chesterton was also profoundly at odds with the prevailing Conservative economic ethos which, to him, represented the abject surrender of Britain's imperial destiny to the 'Dollar Empire'. Indeed, Chesterton had once lunched with Peter Thorneycroft, Chancellor of the Exchequer (1957–1958), who told him, 'I have the greatest contempt for you people who think that Britain can solve her economic difficulties within a British world context.' Chesterton retorted: 'and I have the greatest contempt for those of you who think that Britain can only survive by becoming the handmaiden of American financed capitalism.' The lunch was not a success.[220]

Chesterton's vehement opposition to the abrogation of national sovereignty was writ large in his reaction to the signing of the Treaty of Rome in 1957 and the creation of the European Economic Community, which he regarded as 'Britain's Graveyard'.[221] Chesterton was contemptuous of Conservative Prime Minister Harold Macmillan, whom he believed supported Federal Union as a staging post to 'World Government'. 'I am unable to discern any essential difference between their crime and the crime of William Joyce:

indeed, as they are indubitably British subjects the case against them is to my mind clearer-cut than was the case against Joyce,' Chesterton wrote.²²²

> As William Joyce was hanged, so should these men ... also be tried and hanged. Their only hope of reprieve should lie in their reversal, before it is too late of policies which, because they require the surrender of national independence, are acts of constructive treason.²²³

Mobilising around this position, the LEL found a niche for themselves on the margins of the wider anti-EEC campaign during the early 1960s.²²⁴

Chesterton's staunch support of Empire won the League support from many grassroots Conservatives. Supporters with dual membership, particularly those overseas, were urged to further LEL objectives by joining bodies like the Conservative Commonwealth Council to increase the League's breadth of contacts and to gather information.²²⁵ But the League was no 'entryist' body. Chesterton regarded 'infiltrating' the Conservative party as 'about as useful as to take cover under a sieve during a rainstorm.'²²⁶

For its part, Conservative Central Office (CCO) was, broadly speaking, only interested in the League insofar as it might act as a drain upon party funds. It rarely condemned its politics per se though the Conservative Party chairman did issue a statement attacking the League as 'anti-Semitic' and 'semi-fascist' in 1955.²²⁷ But such forthright condemnation could backfire. Pandemonium ensued at one Conservative Party meeting when Geoffrey Stevens MP rebuked LEL hecklers for following a former fascist only to be embarrassingly reminded by them that the chairman of his own meeting, Sir Jocelyn Lucas MP, was former chairman of the BUF Appeals Board.²²⁸ Conservative strategy in dealing with the League was emollient and accommodatory, CCO counselling one MP concerned by its incursions into his membership:

> It is a fact that many sincere Conservatives are members of the LEL because of their belief in Empire ... I am quite sure that the Conservative members of the League will not allow any disagreement between the League and our Organisation to interfere with their efforts to return Conservative Members of Parliament in this major struggle.... We have not questioned the League's sincerity and we believe that its members will adhere to its objects. Since the League is strictly non-party, those who speak and work for the Conservative Candidate should do so as Conservatives and not as members of the League.²²⁹

Whilst CCO did not prohibit dual membership to avoid alienating such supporters – most senior League figures were also active Conservatives²³⁰ – Area Chairmen did apply discreet pressure to remind them 'they cannot serve two bodies whose purposes are apart.' The League's 'bad manners and hooliganism' increasingly irritated the Conservatives but ultimately the group failed to gain a significant foothold amongst its grassroots membership.²³¹ If the Conservative party was ambivalent, Chesterton was actively hostile. 'They Will Betray You Yet, These True Blues', he proclaimed albeit at the risk of alienating precisely those dual members whom the Conservative Party had been at pains not to offend. Chesterton was adamant that the British Empire, far from 'growing up, not breaking up' in official Conservative parlance, was in fact being destroyed by 'deliberate, flagrant treason' conducted at the behest of the forces of Jewish 'supranational finance'.²³²

Chesterton's anti-Semitic interpretation of imperial decline sounded shrill in comparison to the 'muted, mild and tepid' reaction that Britain's waning world power elicited from the electorate for whom the end of empire never became a salient domestic issue; largely, it has been argued, due to an array of institutional factors that inhibited or otherwise restricted its importance and a unique confluence of international circumstances that further deadened rather than amplified its potential domestic impact.[233] Chesterton's analysis was insulated from this reality. His staunch defence of Empire during the 1956 Suez Crisis brought the League a short-lived dividend, though it was not one that exerted any influence upon the arc of history. For Chesterton, Suez was 'catastrophic' – British credibility as a global power had been dangerously denuded as a result and the nation's prestige demeaned and traduced by their supposed ally, the United States. Following Britain's humiliating withdrawal, League activists burned effigies of the Egyptian President Gamel Abdel Nasser and the Israeli Prime Minister David Ben-Gurion in Trafalgar Square on Guy Fawkes Night, whilst in the following week, the LEL attempted to present an effigy of the Foreign Secretary Anthony Eden as a 'gift' to the Israeli Embassy in London.[234] Eden became the scapegoat for the loss of imperial prestige and power symbolised by Suez. The League's attacks upon him continued unabated into his own premiership, crystallising at a Conservative Party fete in 1956, when John Bean presented Eden with a coal scuttle – a humiliating symbol of his role in the 'scuttle' of Britain's Empire. This was simply one in a plethora of audacious, well-publicised, stunts through which the League thrust its case into the media spotlight and which also included, that autumn, gestures such as taking down the UN flag at an official ceremony and trampling it underfoot.[235]

Chesterton's adamant refusal to countenance Britain's withdrawal from Suez had converged with the position of the Conservative Suez Group which in turn won the League support from Lady Rhondda's *Time and Tide* magazine.[236] Chesterton developed 'unofficial' contact with two members of the 'Suez Group': Sir Harry Legge-Bourke MP (Ely) and Captain Henry 'Bob' Kerby MP (Arundel and Shoreham). Legge-Bourke, a Tory nationalist for whom 'internationalism' was an anathema, subscribed to both *The Patriot* and *Truth*. Lamenting the demise of *Truth*, Legge-Bourke wrote to Chesterton that 'if it is any comfort to you, please rest assured that I will endeavour to hold fast to those principles and beliefs that inspired you and those who, with you, gave heart to all who loved their Land.'[237] When Legge-Bourke refused the Conservative whip over the Suez 'scuttle', Chesterton sent him a congratulatory telegram 'which I now regret,' he wrote in 1957, 'having wryly observed the completeness of his return to the Central Office womb.'[238] When Legge-Bourke urged a second group of Suez rebels to return to the fold later that year, Chesterton despaired: 'to think some of us once regarded Harry Legge-Bourke as the White Hope of a resurgent Britain'.[239]

Kerby meanwhile greatly admired Chesterton's anti-Semitic conspiracy theories, becoming 'a very staunch supporter of *Candour*'.[240] Kerby was associated with Mosley during the late 1940s though Mosley, despite thinking highly of him, believed he was working for MI5 'and was reserving judgement upon him until he was tested under pressure'.[241] Shortly after becoming an MP, Kerby assisted Chesterton in July 1954 by asking the Home Office why Otto Strasser had been refused leave to enter the country.[242] Kerby subsequently used his parliamentary privilege to table a series of Parliamentary Questions based on articles from *Candour*, which impinged upon the LEL's racial antennae.[243] Ultimately, however, Chesterton felt betrayed by him too.[244]

The League's obdurate imperialism was such that during the height of the Suez Crisis, Sir Reginald Dorman-Smith, a former governor of Burma who had also been an English Mistery member, was powerless to intervene as the LEL 'raped my young Conservative branch'.[245] Rosine de Bounevialle, secretary of the Liss Conservative Association and vice-president of the Liss Young Conservatives led the defections. A former air hostess and Catholic Traditionalist, de Bounevialle became perhaps Chesterton's closest collaborator. She had worked as an Admiralty signals clerk during the war but 'could never stomach the deal with atheist Russia'.[246]

The League were also capable of causing serious internal ructions within rightward leaning Conservative Associations, as Nigel Nicolson MP (Bournemouth East) found out to his cost. In 1955, Chesterton had devised a lobbying campaign, sending questionnaires to every single Conservative MP demanding their assurance that under 'no circumstances' would they support any revision in the Charter of the United Nations that would involve 'further surrender of National Sovereignty' to the forces of 'World Government'.[247] Only six replied, including Nicolson.[248] His support for 'eventual world government' outraged Chesterton whose League distributed his response to the questionnaire as a leaflet titled *Conservatives! Do You Repudiate Nigel Nicolson?*[249]

Nicolson was hardly more popular with his own Conservative Association which took the unprecedented step of deselecting him in 1957 whilst he was the sitting MP following his public opposition to the government's Suez policy.[250] His Association, which was on the right-wing of the party, found a far more amenable replacement in Major J.A. 'Chummy' Friend, a reassuringly ardent right-winger.[251] It transpired, however, that Friend had solicited the League's assistance in his own campaign to despatch Nicolson, addressing the inaugural meeting of its Bournemouth branch in the hope of enrolling new members to support his campaign with the full knowledge of his constituency chairman.[252] When the incongruity of soliciting support from a body which openly reviled the prime minister as a traitor was publicly commented upon, Friend publicly disassociated himself from the League and denied cooperating with it.[253] Infuriated, Chesterton passed on his correspondence with Friend to *Reynolds News*. Confronted by the Central Office about its authenticity, Friend was forced to admit his duplicity and withdraw his candidacy – association with the LEL having become the political kiss of death after the 1958 Conservative conference.[254]

These revelations galvanised Lord Hailsham, the Conservative Party chairman, to bring this festering issue to a conclusion at a frosty meeting brokered with Nicolson and his local party on 24 January 1959. It was agreed to put the issue to the vote whilst League activists were left 'chanting their ludicrous slogans out in the street'. Nicolson lost the ensuing poll on 26 February by a narrow margin of ninety-one votes, earning him the dubious distinction of being the first Conservative MP to be ejected from the House of Commons by his own Association rather than the electorate.[255] Though there were fears during this period that the Conservatives were being 'outflanked' by the Right, the League never posed a particularly grave threat to the party, ostensibly because – its vociferous and seemingly omnipresent protests aside – it lacked concrete support 'in the suburbs and shires' of the Tory heartlands.[256]

Outside the Conservative Party, the LEL made common cause with other right-wing campaign groups including the British Housewives' League led by Joyce Mew, who sat on the LEL executive council.[257] League activists were also involved with the National Council for the Reduction of Taxation (NCRT), a middle-class pressure group founded in 1954 by Oliver Smedley, a former Liberal Party activist.[258] Smedley pitched his campaign towards native 'Poujadist' sentiment prevalent amongst small shopkeepers and ratepayers, which he sought to canalise into opposition to the Government's Re-Evaluation Act. The NCRT acted as an umbrella for similar pressure groups who, at a 'packed meeting' in Caxton Hall on 8 January 1957, chaired by Edward Martell, leader of the anti-trade union People's League for the Defence of Freedom (PLDF), pledged their support for Leslie

Greene who was standing as an 'Independent Loyalist' candidate in the forthcoming North Lewisham by-election.[259]

This election, in a Conservative marginal, was fiercely contested by the League. Greene polled only 1,487 votes (4 per cent) but the victorious Labour candidate won the seat by 1,110 votes, leading some commentators to conclude that the League's intervention had cost the Conservatives the seat. Thereafter, Greene continued her involvement with the NCRT, speaking regularly from its platforms and joining its Council Committee in the following year. The League became one of its 'supporting bodies'.[260] The Conservative Party became concerned that the NCRT 'could prove a very serious danger to both the Party and the country', not least because its speakers attacked the government and poured vitriol upon Home Secretary R.A. 'Rab' Butler who was accused of being 'semi-socialist'.[261] Conservative anxiety proved misplaced. The NCRT had a 'pathetically small' membership and despite their impressive publications 'didn't cut very much ice'. Its activities subsequently dovetailed into those of the newly formed Institute of Economic Affairs, the free-market think-tank that provided the intellectual impetus for the emergence of 'Thatcherism', which operated from the same building.[262]

Anti-Immigration

In common with every other extreme right-wing group, the LEL was resolutely opposed to mass immigration. In 'In Defence of the Colour Bar', published in 1957, Chesterton argued that without such a mechanism 'White civilisation will be drowned in the flood' as calls for 'multi-racialism' would inevitably be superseded by 'mono-racialism'.[263] 'We must discriminate or die', Chesterton urged his readers, because 'Financial Jewry' was deliberately leveraging the 'coloured invasion' in order to dilute the nation's racial fibre as a consequence of which 'there will die in the Gentile spirit that survival sense which might otherwise resist Jewish world domination.'[264]

Nonetheless, anti-immigration politicking did not become the *defining* feature of the League. Chesterton's personal fixation with 'financial Jews' rather than 'race' fuelled Arnold Leese's enmity. Leese disparaged Chesterton and tried to derail his publishing activities, counselling Tony Gittens, proprietor of The Britons, against any involvement with him for fear that Chesterton's 'moderation' would dilute their own purpose and resolve. Leese never forgave Chesterton his Mosley hagiography. Reviewing *Why I Left Mosley*, Leese disparaged Chesterton in the following terms: 'Typical BUF mentality. Having backed the wrong horse, Chesterton blames the horse, announcing himself a poor judge of horseflesh.'[265] 'To hell with him,' Leese raged after the war.[266] He was equally scathing of *Candour*, which he regarded as 'not anti-Jewish'[267] and 'about 25 years behind us'.[268] Thus, Leese exhorted Gittens, who printed *Candour*:

> Make them pay thro. [sic] the nose for everything. Can we keep the Britons address out of it. Otherwise we shall be told that the Britons are running away from the Jews. I have nothing but contempt for AKC. How are sale of anti-Jewish literature going on? *That* is all that interests me. I don't like the idea of this evasive *Candour*, but you have got to live. Don't let *Candour* live on the Britons, whatever you do![269]

Chesterton's racial vision differed from the *völkisch* racism of Leese and Jordan and indeed Mosley's supposedly 'neo-Lamarkian' position. Rejecting the Nazi Nordicism of Alfred Rosenberg, Chesterton commented sardonically: 'My definition of the Nordic man, not an original one, is that he is blond – like Hitler, tall – like Goebbels, slender – like Goering, and a great lover of women – like Roehm'.[270] The boundaries of racial ideology were porous, however. *Candour* reprinted articles from *Northern World*, journal of the Northern League, a pan-Aryan Nordicist cultural group run by Roger Pearson, with whom Chesterton maintained a friendly correspondence.[271] Chesterton also became a 'contributing editor' to *Western Destiny*, a successor to *Northern World*, which Pearson edited at one point.[272]

Though he mocked those mystic, racial evangelists who proclaimed the discovery of a 'race soul',[273] Chesterton's own writings were underpinned by an unshakable belief in the racial predestination of the 'British'. He believed in a 'British destiny'. Empire was an indissoluble part of Britain's 'earthly duty'. The stability, he believed, imperial governance brought to world affairs was 'completely beyond the American genius'. This was underpinned by the 'British spirit' which, vaguely defined, encompassed notions such as 'playing the game', and 'leadership based on bold initiative but without arrogance', which, though perhaps antiquated, 'still seem to me to hold good in life as in sport'.[274]

Chesterton denied 'antipathy' towards other races but was forthright in his abhorrence of interracial relationships,

> not because I hold a White skin to be a virtue, but because the White races have made a unique contribution to the sum of human life on this planet, and I believe they have made that contribution because of their distinctive racial characteristics.[275]

Mixing such traits did not produce a 'bred of better men' but a 'breed of men less able to maintain white standards.'[276] Thus, for Chesterton, the conspiracy to 'poison the bloodstream' through immigration had to be resisted, 'because no recovery of Britain's greatness could be expected from a mulatto nation.'[277] His belief that 'miscegenation' was 'sheer human tragedy' stemmed from his view that African tribes – the Zulu, the Basuto and the Afrikaner – all had a strong sense of 'belonging'. The progeny of mixed race relationships, Chesterton asserted, lacked this sense of 'communal identity' that in turn deprived them of a 'corporate identity' and thus a 'corporate conscience' leading to a further fragmentation of 'race relations'.[278]

His views were given a 'scientific' veneer through the utilisation of studies emanating from the United States including Audrey Shuey's *The Testing of Negro Intelligence* (1958) and Bela Hubbard's *The Hybrid Race Doctrine* (1959). Another source was *Mankind Quarterly*, the journal edited by Robert Gayre, who was being bankrolled by segregationists to 'prove' the biological and intellectual inferiority of blacks to whites which provided a further intellectual backstop to racial prejudice.[279] To this end, Chesterton distributed copies of *Race, Hereditary and Civilisation* (1961) by Professor W.C. George, Professor of Histology and Embryology at the School of Medicine at the University of North Carolina, free of charge to all *Candour* subscribers, as 'a reasoned and convincing answer to the advocates of race-mixture'.[280] Though such works gave a semblance of disinterested scientific validation to racist views, cruder expressions of such beliefs continued to circulate amongst League supporters. Ahead of the 1958 *Candour* dinner, Chesterton was anxious that those attending be 'rationally dressed and sworn not to talk about Niggers and Jews and the Ku Klux Klan.'[281]

Kenya

Resolutely opposed to immigration at home, Chesterton was equally trenchant in his defence of white supremacy abroad. He considered those favouring de-colonisation or worse, those who actively supported national liberation struggles, to be 'racial renegades' and 'traitors'.[282] A particular target for his wrath was Fenner Brockway MP, chairman of the Movement for Colonial Freedom (MCF) whom Chesterton regarded as a 'pestilential renegade and scab'.[283] The MCF was attempting to accelerate the pace of de-colonialisation with as much brio as the League exerted in trying to prevent it and LEL activists regularly disrupted its meetings.[284] In response to such developments, Chesterton began organising his overseas supporters through a worldwide network of 'Candour Leagues', which stretched from Africa to the antipodes.[285]

In April 1957, a Central African Branch of the League was founded under Lieutenant-Colonel E.V.M. Cresswell-George with Betty Wemyss as his secretary and treasurer.[286] Shortly afterwards, in July, Southern Rhodesian 'Loyalists' paid for Chesterton and Greene to embark upon a two-month tour of Africa, which aimed to mobilise the white settler community in defence of their perceived racial self-interest.[287] In Salisbury, Chesterton publicly debated with Colonel David Stirling, founder of the Special Air Service (SAS), who had established the Capricorn Africa Society (CAS), a multi-racial society, which presented itself as 'the hope in Africa for racial harmony and togetherness'. Stirling believed 'one patriotism' and not the 'barren doctrine' of racial nationalism would protect the Empire and indeed democracy from Communism, to which end he advocated a federal union of East and Central Africa – 'Capricorn Africa' – that would also stand against African nationalism, South African republicanism and Asian immigration.[288] Needless to say, both the idea and the CAS were an anathema to Chesterton who defeated Stirling on the motion: 'The ideas of the Capricorn Africa Society, if adopted, would be the ruination of the British Empire.' Chesterton won by 278 votes to 191, a feat frequently heralded thereafter as proof of the League's rectitude in African affairs.[289]

From Rhodesia, Chesterton and Greene then travelled to Nairobi, the Kenyan capital, to continue their proselytising which, despite concerns, local authorities could see no grounds to prevent.[290] 'We believe that if White leadership is to continue in Africa the time has come for a movement which will adopt an attitude of no further compromise in any circumstances,' Chesterton told the local media. 'We have come to Kenya to rally the British people. Unless the British world coheres, it will be broken between the American and Soviet blocs.'[291]

There were a series of meetings which led to the foundation of a Kenyan LEL branch under Major B.P. Roberts, leader of the Federal Independence Party. The initial burst of enthusiasm for the League, which saw the establishment of eight League branches and the adherence of 167 members throughout the colony, soon dissipated. By the end of the year, its influence was judged 'negligible' by local intelligence sources.[292] Chesterton's disappointment was palpable. '[N]o sooner had we left than everything flopped,' he lamented.[293] When Roberts subsequently resigned, Chesterton lambasted him for having the temerity to accept the opening of the White Highlands to Africans. Had the Kenyan LEL leadership not 'ratted', Chesterton believed the League 'could have saved that country'.[294]

Such perceived backsliding led Chesterton to a visceral breach with his former patron, the Earl of Portsmouth who had emigrated to Kenya and voted in the Kenyan Legislative Council in 1959 to throw open the exclusively white enclave to African farmers. Chesterton was incandescent with rage. He wrote:

Not only have I placed my health, for what it is worth, in grave jeopardy fighting for the preservation of Kenya in two harsh campaigns, but you can trace the graves of my friends and comrades-in-arms all the way from Salaita Hill to Songea, and all the way from the Juba River to Gondar in the North. They did not die in the belief that the stamping of delighted African feet would one day make a holiday in the Earl of Portsmouth's heart.... Unfortunately, Portsmouth, the law will allow me to go no further than that in telling you what I think.[295]

The two never met or spoke again.

Consequent upon such betrayals, Chesterton's prognosis for Kenya was bleak. 'I do not think that any one in Kenya today is putting up a fight worthy of the name,' he lamented.[296] However, the brutality of the Mau Mau insurgency offered Chesterton's League new opportunities for mobilisation as Kenya began its transition towards independence. This process was initiated in 1960 at the Kenyan constitutional conference at Lancaster House outside of which two League activists dressed as 'witchdoctors' waved placards stating 'Witchdoctors Demand Home Rule for Mau Mau'.[297] *Candour* claimed to be the first publication, extreme right or otherwise, to publish details of the Mau Mau oathing ceremonies, a feat Chesterton was particularly proud of.[298] Chesterton published this 'obscene document', allegedly obtained from official sources, as a *Candour* supplement subsequently circulating it as a warning to white colonies beyond Kenya as *Mau Mau Oathing Ceremonies* (1960).[299] Elaborating on the source of his information, Chesterton stated:

What I published was material collected by the Kenya Police and submitted to Government House in Nairobi, which handed over the documents to its Information Department. However, the Information Department was only able to get it into the hands of a few members of Legco before Government House changed its mind and forbade further distribution. One highly placed member of the Administration was so hopping wild that he took it into his own hands to see that I was furnished with a copy. The police definitely considered prosecuting me, as the *Daily Telegraph*'s Scotland Yard reporter whispered in our ear, but desisted when they found that our publication repeated word for word an official document which had on it the stamp of the Information Department of the Kenya Government.[300]

'Mau Mau' served to ingrain the idea of the African peoples' essential barbarism at the heart of extreme right-wing propaganda on race and immigration. They frequently used 'atrocity' photos to both engage and enrage activists.[301] 'The full facts about Mau Mau are not for the squeamish to read,' wrote Martin Webster, a former League activist, imprisoned in 1964 for assaulting Jomo Kenyatta, a leader of the insurgency who became Kenya's first Prime Minister after independence:

The induction ceremonies it practised were nightmares from a bottomless pit of depravity – that bottomless pit being the mind of Jomo Kenyatta. Sipping blood from the severed heads of little boys. Chewing the brains of old men. Performing perverted sexual acts with both live and dead animals and human beings. Eating 'stews' concocted of human and animal genital organs and body secretions. The pledging of souls to the Devil by means of the practice of every form of obscene barbarism.[302]

The League continued agitating against Kenyan independence throughout 1961. Activists daubed the Colonial Office with 'Mau Mau HQ' and 'Hang Kenyatta' and dumped a bag of goat's entrails on the doorstep of Colonial Secretary, an act evocative of the Mau Mau oathing ceremony.[303] When Kenyatta visited London in the following November, activists paraded an effigy of him outside his hotel before burning it at the site of Tyburn Tree, where public executions had historically taken place. During a press conference, Wing-Commander Leonard Young threw a bag of sheep's entrails at him whilst at a subsequent event, Avril Walters slapped him across the face. Outside, another activist, Derek Johnson hit Kenyatta with an egg. In court, Johnson pleaded guilty 'with provocation' stating that as League members 'we feel it is impossible to insult Jomo Kenyatta'.[304] Seeking to keep the issue in the public eye, in 1962, League activists showered MPs with copies of the aforementioned *Candour* supplement from Parliament's public gallery.[305]

Decline

But whilst decolonisation offered opportunities for activism, this masked the fact that from 1958 onwards the League had begun to atrophy. Chesterton lost two long-standing collaborators at the beginning of the year, Nettie Bonnar, *Candour*'s business manager, and Leslie Greene, who resigned as the League's organising secretary in order to work full time for the Institute of Economic Affairs though she remained LEL 'Director of Research'.[306] Greene's replacement was Major W.J. 'Bill' Harrison, a recently retired soldier fresh from fighting the counter-insurgency campaign against Malayan communists. Harrison became 'Director of Organisation' but was almost immediately expelled for advocating clandestine paramilitary action and betraying 'confidential information'.[307] Further defections soon occurred. Colin Jordan had previously resigned in 1957 to found the White Defence League whilst Chesterton expelled John Bean, the League's Honorary Director of Special Campaigns, and John Tyndall for soliciting support within the LEL for a separate movement.[308] They subsequently founded the National Labour Party. Major-General Richard Hilton also resigned at the AGM that year, subsequently establishing the short-lived 'True Tory' movement, its inaugural meeting heckled by League activists who comprised half the audience.[309]

But despite these losses, the League's constant heckling and interjections at political meetings retained the capacity to embarrass leading Conservatives. The League 'may not be much of a factor to reckon with politically,' observed the *Manchester Guardian*, 'but it is becoming a real hazard to politicians who find that an unexpected interruption can throw them off their stride in the course of a public speech.'[310] League activists found increasingly innovative ways to 'sound the alarm' too which included interrupting BBC broadcasts using a pirate transmitter.[311] In terms of publicity, however, the League's most high profile action involved activist Philip Burbidge slapping Lord Altrincham across the face in 1957 for an article the LEL perceived as dishonouring the Queen. Burbidge described his fine as 'the best investment ever I made'.[312]

The set piece of League activism in 1958 was its plan to disrupt the Conservative Party conference in Blackpool in October. Prime Minister Harold Macmillan recalled that, as a result of the League's interjections, the conference was 'more militant' than usual that year.[313] This was something of an understatement. LEL activists who infiltrated the conference were seized and brutally manhandled by Conservative stewards, in full view of the press corps, as they tried to heckle.[314] It signalled the abrupt end to Conservative's benign tolerance of League activities. Ironically, having previously insisted that BUF stewards had the absolute right to maintain order at their own meetings,[315] Chesterton now took legal action against the Conservative Party, which failed, much to his chagrin. However, the 'downright illegal methods' used by the League to gain entry to the conference caused its chairman, Commander D.S. Fraser-Harris, a former police officer, to resign in protest.[316] League membership waned following Blackpool, though not necessarily solely on account of it.[317] The decline impacted upon the League's financial situation which, Chesterton confided, was already so dire that, without a significant financial injection, 'we shall soon peter out.'[318]

Despite such setbacks, Chesterton declined to change strategy or tactics; refusing to countenance standing 'Independent Loyalist' candidates in the 1959 general election, which, it had been suggested, would reinvigorate the League and present an alternative to the party politicians they constantly inveighed against.[319] More ominously for Chesterton personally were the successive bouts of bronchitis which afflicted him and which subsequently developed into emphysema. On doctor's orders, he began to spend roughly three months a year wintering in South Africa. Thereafter, his prolonged absences placed the burden of maintaining the movement's continued 'dynamism' upon his close colleagues.[320]

The advent of the Campaign for Nuclear Disarmament (CND), whose opposition to the acquisition and retention of an independent nuclear deterrent, regarded by Chesterton as imperative to Britain's retention of her status as a world power, was a complete anathema. League activists harassed CND marches to the Atomic Weapons Research Establishment at Aldermaston from its inaugural protest march in 1958 onwards. The Oxford biologist and barrister Kennedy McWhirter, together with his younger brother Norris (who founded *The Guinness Book of Records* with his twin brother Ross), drove a speaker car past the Aldermaston demonstration proclaiming through a loudhailer:

> Marchers, every one of you is guilty of increasing the risk or war.... You are voting with your feet for Soviet imperialist domination. That means bringing Budapest to England. The people of Britain are determined to resist Communist aggression. Most of you have been bamboozled into supporting Communist aggression and butchery.[321]

A number of marchers trapped the car in a field, causing it superficial damage.[322] Kennedy McWhirter told the press that the demonstration 'was planned and carried out entirely by ourselves and there is no sort of organisation political, or otherwise, behind it'.[323] Rosine de Bounevialle disputed this, asserting that the episode was a League stunt and that the McWhirters were *Candour* subscribers.[324] When not harassing CND marches, Chesterton revelled in humiliating its activists – whom he dismissed as 'bi-sexual pantaloons' – when they found themselves in court. When the Reverend Michael Scott refused to pay a £1 fine for involvement in a sit-down protest organised by the Committee of 100, the League chipped in 'to prevent his enjoying a second spell of martyrdom.'[325] League counter-protesters often ended in violence as its activists fought with CND demonstrators not all of whom it transpired were pacifists.[326]

'In all that pertains to sovereignty we are being wiped, like a dirty mark, out of history', Chesterton lamented in 1961 as he surveyed the situation at the 'twelfth hour'. The 'Money Power' was not solely responsible; the British people had become decadent. 'There is scarcely a single manifestation of their present-day spirit which does not stink of decay.' Such beliefs reflected how little Chesterton's world-view had changed since the inter-war years. Indeed, his fundamental vision still remained one of expiation and salvation. A revival of the 'British spirit' would 'reclaim the West and save the world'. His efforts to 'sound the alarm' and acquaint people with the 'facts' had not been enough, however, and Chesterton finally felt compelled to outline his 'practical alternative to shipwreck'.

Chesterton's 'positive' programme for national regeneration, published as *Tomorrow – A Plan for the British Future* (1961), urged the rejection of international institutions and treaty organisations coupled with a recognition that the United States was an 'enemy' as much as Moscow. Controversially for his membership, Chesterton also urged the rejection of the British Commonwealth, which he believed now functioned as an agent for the 'dissolution of the British world system'. Instead, Chesterton envisaged a 'resurgent world system' based upon mutually beneficial 'alliances' with other European states and the 'White Dominions', including Republican South Africa, upon which could be built 'a sense of identity, a sense of common danger and a sense of common purpose'.[327]

The Jeffrey largesse

Chesterton lamented, however, that many of his own followers had become habituated to the *status quo* – only 7 per cent of his membership answered his appeal for funds that year. This would not have mattered had not the cheques stopped arriving from his principal benefactor R.K. Jeffrey, who had donated approximately £70,000 to Chesterton since 1953.[328] Chesterton despatched Mackey to Chile in July 1961 to find out what had happened. Mackey reported dreadful news. Jeffrey was dead, having passed away on 22 April from gangrene of the intestines 'after making his own medicine to cure acute constipation.'[329] Named as Jeffrey's sole heir in 1958, Chesterton had expected to inherit a sizeable sum of money but Mackey brought worse tidings than news of his benefactor's death: Jeffrey had changed his will hours before his death in favour of a woman claiming to be his 'daughter'. He promptly engaged lawyers in Santiago to contest the will. The case dragged on for a decade before Chesterton's last legal recourse was finally dismissed in 1971. The League's political future had been staked upon the Jeffrey largesse and without it, the movement was plunged into crisis, its immediacy hastened by the £2,500 Chesterton spent on legal fees contesting the will. His appeal to the membership for funds failed to raise enough to save *Candour*, which ceased its weekly publication in March 1962, replaced by a rather less substantial *Candour Interim Report*, which appeared bi-monthly thereafter. It only returned to being a monthly publication in May 1965. In the interim, Chesterton spent £600 of his own money keeping the LEL afloat and, rather than appeal to members for further funds, negotiated a loan against a £3,000 inheritance he was expecting from an octogenarian aunt.[330]

Chesterton viewed the defence of Britain's imperial inheritance as a 'British responsibility' but the depths of the League's financial crisis compelled him to look across the Atlantic to those engaged in a similar 'revolt against Wall Street's Communist conspiracy'.[331] He wrote to Lieutenant-General Pedro Augusto del Valle, leader of the Defenders of the American Constitution (DAC), with whom he had a long-standing relationship, requesting the names of wealthy 'American patriots' he could approach for funds. Del Valle readily acquiesced sending his own small donation to its coffers.[332] Chesterton primed Austen Brooks with this information, despatching him upon a three-month fund-raising tour of North America in April 1963 'to discuss with American and Canadian patriots how they and British patriots could co-operate with each other' in their fight against 'the same enemies'. Chesterton's 'Million Dollar Appeal' highlighted his expectations for the tour which was organised with the support of Gerald L.K. Smith, leader of the Christian Nationalist Crusade (CNC) and editor of *The Cross and the Flag* in Los Angeles.[333] Smith had been introduced to Chesterton's work in the late 1950s by Ron Gostick, editor of the *Canadian Intelligence Service*, who thought Chesterton a 'brilliant journalist' and regularly reprinted articles from

Candour (and previously *Truth*) in his own newsletter.[334] Brooks made a 'fine impression' upon Smith. He gave him a list of his own subscribers who might appreciate receiving *Candour*. Smith also arranged for Brooks to meet Benjamin H. Freedman, an 'anti-Zionist' Jew who had converted to Catholicism and was noted for his financing of Conde McGinley's anti-Semitic newspaper, *Common Sense*, which also occasionally reprinted *Candour* articles.[335] Despite Smith's fulsome support for the League, Chesterton privately maligned him as a vainglorious and self-important man who 'rather sickened' him.[336]

In Southern California, Brooks addressed meetings staged by the local branch of the Keep America Committee, Thomas Serpico's Omni Publications and another organised by C. Leon de Aryan's *Sun-Workshop* in San Diego not to mention a Republican Women's Club and a Baptist Church meeting. His attacks on the 'International Money Power' were greeted with 'wave after wave of applause'. In Glendale, Arizona, Brooks addressed a meeting organised by Edith Essig, a former organiser for the isolationist America First Committee who was a long-term supporter of *Candour*.[337] Travelling on to Texas, Brooks met Senator Frank Owens, recent sponsor of a Bill in the State Senate that prohibited the flying of the UN flag from any state-owned property. Giles Miller, proprietor of *Park Cities – North Dallas News*, who owned a string of Dallas radio stations invited Brooks on air, 'which enabled me to put the League's case against Communism and internationalism to millions of people in the United States and Canada.'[338]

Miller also arranged for Brooks to speak with Howard 'Dan' Smoot, a former FBI agent (1942–1951) turned ultraconservative activist and broadcaster for the Texan oil millionaire H.L. Hunt. Smoot also edited the *Dan Smoot Report* and had authored *Invisible Government* (1962), in which he revealed the supposed plans of the Council of Foreign Relations 'for a Socialist America in a Socialist World!'[339] After several more media appearances, Brooks called upon General Edwin A. Walker, a highly decorated soldier who had faced a military tribunal for distributing John Birch Society literature to his troops and making derogatory remarks about Harry Truman being 'definitely pink' which had led, ultimately, to his resignation. Walker had recently gained notoriety for helping incite a riot at the University of Mississippi during the campaign to prevent its desegregation in the course of which two people were killed and 375 injured.[340]

Travelling to Washington, DC, Brooks met Senators James Eastland (Mississippi), Spessard Holland (Florida), Herman Talmadge (Georgia) and Strom Thurmond (South Carolina), all noted for their staunch opposition to civil rights. He also met Congressmen Donald Bruce (Indiana) and James Utt (California). Utt was also a vociferous opponent of the UN and Chesterton often reprinted his speeches in *Candour*. Brooks' tour continued with meetings in Missouri, Ohio and Illinois, where he addressed Andrew McAllister's Pro-American Forum in Chicago. Thereafter, Brooks travelled to Canada addressing a string of meetings set up for him by the local Candour League.[341] Important in terms of transatlantic networking, the trip was not financially remunerative. 'The more money people have the less ready they are to give any significant help to those fighting to save Western civilisation', lamented Brooks.[342]

Rhodesia

Chesterton viewed native Africans as having little appetite for democracy, development or indeed self-determination, concepts which meant 'as little to their minds as does the Quantum Theory to the minds of monkeys'.[343] He was therefore incredulous at Harold Macmillan's 'Winds of Change' speech in 1960 which, to his mind, offered nothing but 'decay and death'. Macmillan, Chesterton asserted, was guilty 'of wrecking the British world system, of handing Kenya over to Mau Mau diabolism and Northern Rhodesia and Nyasaland to internecine gang warfare and general rioting and terror'.[344]

Chesterton was by no means the only extreme right ideologue to lament the loss of Empire though he felt its loss more keenly than figures like Mosley who saw Britain's future in Europe. The decline of Europe's Empires was a global phenomenon. The end of 'Algérie Française' and with it the demise of France's Fourth Republic, elicited a ferocious and bloody response from the country's extreme right, Algerian *pied-noirs*, and sections of the nation's military which, from January 1961, began waging a protracted terrorist campaign targeting Algerians, the French state and President Charles de Gaulle. It resulted in 553 deaths and left an indelible mark upon French politics.[345] In Belgium, which ceded independence to the Congo during the same period, there was also an overspill of violence into domestic affairs though nothing like on the same levels.[346]

Despite the passions it aroused, the situation with regard to Ian Smith's white supremacist regime in Southern Rhodesia, which in November 1965 made its Unilateral Declaration of Independence (UDI) was muted in comparison. Chesterton hailed Smith as having 'rescued from the abyss of cancerous political degeneracy the heroic thing which is the soul of the British peoples' and proclaimed UDI, 'a beacon to reawaken in Briton's everywhere their historic will to greatness'.[347] Chesterton had extensive contacts throughout Rhodesia, where a deeply ingrained belief that African nationalism was a front for communist insurgency, combined with a belief that Rhodesians were the indomitable inheritors of an imperial mandate Britain itself had relinquished, conferred upon his ideas a respectability they otherwise lacked in Britain.[348] Chesterton's supporters were generally to be found within the right-wing Dominion Party and its successor the Rhodesian Front (RF). British Prime Minister Harold Wilson stated that Smith had been pushed towards UDI by certain colleagues and 'the unreasoning extremists of the Rhodesian Front'.[349] Chesterton subsequently asserted that his supporters formed a 'hard core' of RF support.[350] Rallying his followers, Chesterton helped reorganise the remnants of the old LEL Central Africa Branch into the Candour League of Rhodesia (CLR), which Chesterton claimed had 3,000 members.[351] It was run by Dr Ian Anderson and Betty Wemyss who published *Rhodesia and World Report*. Chesterton quickly fell out with Anderson following a perceived slight, though their relations were subsequently restored. The CLR later became a component of the World Anti-Communist League (WACL).[352]

In spring 1966, Chesterton conducted a 3,000-mile speaking tour of South Africa and Rhodesia. In Salisbury, the Rhodesian capital, his meeting was attended by five Rhodesian MPs whilst another meeting in Umtali was attended by Colonel Alan MacLeod MP and Brigadier Andrew Skeen MP, Rhodesia's High Commissioner in London, himself an Empire Loyalist,[353] who had been expelled following UDI. Chesterton was granted an interview with Ian Smith. The two men had an 'amicable' though 'frank' exchange of views.[354] Chesterton's contacts on the right-wing of the RF included pronounced anti-communists like William Harper, Rhodesia's Minister for Internal Affairs; Lord Graham, the Duke of Montrose, Minister of Defence and External Affairs who, like Chesterton, had been involved with Captain Ramsay's pro-Nazi Right Club and had attended the Nuremberg Rally; and Harvey Ward, director of Rhodesia's television and radio services, all of whom he conversed with during his visit. Chesterton also developed a close working relationship with Ivor Benson, Rhodesia's chief information officer who, as well as having 'a complete understanding of the international conspiracy' had worked as a speech writer and public relations manager for Smith.[355]

Benson, who contributed to *Candour*, was also a member of Chesterton's CLR but accusations of extremism were dismissed out of hand by the Rhodesian Minister of Information, Pieter Kenyon 'PK' van der Byl – noted by *The Times* as 'a man calculated to give offence'.[356] Indeed van der Byl responded to Benson's detractors with anti-Semitic innuendo. This was perhaps unsurprising since he too was reputedly 'close' to the CLR. Ten other members of Parliament were also believed to have been members. Behind the scenes, Benson and van der Byl directed the 'psychological warfare' effort against the European political opponents of the RF, especially those in the media whom the Smith regime sought to intimidate by the tapping of journalists' phones, opening of their correspondence, raiding their offices and having them followed by Special Branch. Those not cowed by such tactics were arrested and deported, and newspapers shut down. The majority, however, acquiesced and engaged in 'self-imposed censorship' to such an extent that, even before the official imposition of press censorship, Benson and van der Byl had already considerably diminished the independence of the Rhodesian press. These punitive measures were, in van der Byl's words, designed to protect 'the true interests' of Rhodesia – white minority rule.[357]

The British government's imposition of sanctions upon Smith's renegade regime, which aimed to isolate Rhodesia internationally, energised those eager to defend white supremacy. Together with J.M. Gray and Moyna Traill-Smith, respectively the chairman and secretary of the Candour League of South Africa, Chesterton helped organise three well-publicised, sanction-busting petrol convoys, financed by British supporters, which were channelled through the CLR to the Rhodesian government.[358] In February 1966, Chesterton watched one such truck depart from Stellenbosch in the company of John Gaunt, Rhodesia's representative in South Africa, and the Mayor of Stellenbosch.[359] Each consignment was officially received by a Rhodesian government minister, providing Smith's beleaguered government with approximately 10,000 gallons of petrol.[360] Little more than a symbolic gesture of defiant racial solidarity, nevertheless the League played its own small part in the humiliation of Labour sanctions against Rhodesia which, the government admitted in October 1967, had 'no immediate prospect' of success 'while South Africa continues to support the Rhodesian economy'.[361]

Yet despite myriad personal and political connections developed within Southern Rhodesia, extreme right-wing support for the country in Britain did not generate the levels of violence seen in France. That the response of the League, which was no less pungent than that of continental extreme right-wing groups, failed to resonant with wider society or crystallise into a broader political counter-mobilisation either at home or abroad was perhaps to be found in the very different historical position of British colonies as opposed to those belonging to France. Algeria, for instance, was held to be an intrinsic part of France, whereas Rhodesia never assumed the same status in Britain's national imagination. The extreme right's failure to galvanise wider public support over Rhodesia was also a product of its ideological and organisational bifurcation during this period, split as it was between Mosley's pro-European stance and Chesterton's Empire loyalism; given that both viewed Africa as a geopolitical pivot, this division should not be overemphasised though it undoubtedly hindered broader, coordinated mobilisation.

Perhaps another reason was to be found in the figure of Smith himself, who was perceived to be courting 'moderate opinion' at the expense of the right-wing, which Chesterton believed had become an embarrassment to him. As early as April 1966, Chesterton indicated he had no doubt that Smith would 'sell out' Rhodesia as de Gaulle had 'sold out' Algeria.[362] Chesterton later recalled:

It so happens that the last time I talked to Ian Smith I sought confirmation of my feeling that all was not well with the Right-Wing of the Rhodesian Front, which showed what to me were obvious signs of disquiet. The Prime Minister disagreed. He told me that the next task was to woo the Centre, whereupon I said I thought the elections showed that the Centre had not only been wooed but won. 'Is it possible, sir, that when you speak of wooing the Centre what is really involved is the wooing of the Financial Left?' On the instant his private secretary sprang up to say: 'I hate to remind you, Prime Minister, but you are ten minutes late for your next appointment.' That, I think, gave me my answer.[363]

He subsequently attacked Smith's image as a 'hero' of the Right as 'completely false'. If anything, he was 'left of centre'. Furthermore, Chesterton argued, it was an 'absolute fact' that had it not been for objections from within his own Cabinet, Smith would have 'fallen in' with the wishes of the British government as outlined in the joint memorandum issued after the Tiger talks with Labour Prime Minister, Harold Wilson. Worse, Smith 'accepted multiracialism' and accepted the concept of 'parity' despite being fully aware that, north of the Zambezi, this promised 'black political domination'.[364]

South Africa

Disheartened by Smith, Chesterton's hope was already reposed in apartheid South Africa, which in October 1960 had held an all-white referendum triggering the process whereby it became a Republic and departed from the Commonwealth in March 1961. Thereafter, South Africa's geopolitical isolation increased, heightened by the growing opprobrium directed towards the country's racist system of apartheid. South Africa's intelligence apparatus had effectively smashed internal opposition to apartheid through a combination of brutal policing, draconian legislation and severe sentencing. London quickly became a central hub for anti-apartheid activity where activists from banned organisations like the African National Congress (ANC), the South African Communist Party (SACP) or the Pan-Africanist Congress (PAC) were not only free from detention, banning and censorship, and indeed other measures aimed at them by the South African state, but were supported by groups like the International Defence and Aid Fund (IDAF) and the Anti-Apartheid Movement (AAM), which engaged the British public in broad-based opposition to apartheid. South Africa's security apparatus was well aware of this development and actively sought to counter it. In this, Chesterton and the League had a role to play.[365]

Chesterton punched above his weight politically in South Africa too where he counted parliamentarians and ministers amongst his friends. Prime Minister Hendrik Verwoerd sent him a Christmas card every year until his assassination in September 1966.[366] Through his contacts in the South African Parliament, in April 1964, Chesterton secured a meeting with Henning Klopper, Speaker of the House; J.H. Conradie, the former speaker; Hilgard Muller, Minister for Foreign Affairs; and A.E. Trollip, Minister for Labour and Immigration. Chesterton complained about the lack of official help the LEL had received from the South African Embassy in London, whilst recounting 'the many ways in which our movement had endeavoured in London and elsewhere to help the White communities in Africa.' At the end of the meeting, Klopper told Chesterton: 'Of course I am outside politics but I will do everything in my power to help. In my view nothing but good can come of this meeting.' Conradie was similarly enthusiastic and, as Chesterton was leaving, seized his hand and urged him 'to carry on your excellent work'.[367]

Chesterton regarded the meeting as a breakthrough in his relationship with the South African government, writing excitedly that 'it may well prove that at long last we have secured from South Africa the co-operation which, in my view, we so richly deserve'.[368] As a quid pro quo for their aid, Chesterton promised these members of the South African Government that his League would do everything in its power to disrupt the latest phase of the drive to boycott of South African goods which was due to culminate on 17 April 1964. The boycott itself, which had been going since 1959, received a huge fillip following the Sharpeville massacre on 21 March 1961, creating a moral backlash against the apartheid state and generating a groundswell of support for its opponents. Disrupting anti-apartheid meetings, particularly those organised by the AAM, was something of a staple diet for the League which by 1964 had been harassing, harrying and heckling anti-apartheid activists as 'renegades' and 'traitors' for almost a decade.[369]

League and other extreme right-wing activists regularly confronted anti-apartheid activists demonstrating outside the South African High Commission in Trafalgar Square (subsequently its Embassy after becoming a Republic), which were contributing to the increasing ordure in which the apartheid regime was viewed. Perhaps most notoriously, in 1963, League activists raised a banner proclaiming 'Remember Cato Manor, where the police were hacked to pieces,' at an AAM rally in Trafalgar Square designed to embarrass and discredit the marchers.[370] Such demonstrations of racial solidarity garnered headlines in the South African press whilst the South African Broadcasting Corporation also aired them.[371] The concerted attacks on the AAM boycott campaign during spring 1964 differed from those that the LEL had previously engaged in, however, because this was the first time that group was deliberately destabilising the AAM at the behest of members of the South African government. For Chesterton, it was imperative that they do so, 'as success could crown my own efforts in Cape Town to compel the Government to recognise its obligations'.[372] With Chesterton's reputation on the line, his activists ensured that the 1964 boycott rally endured a certain amount of disarray.

Chesterton also utilised the Candour Leagues – his Commonwealth-wide network of supporters – to provide him with information on 'communist' subversion, particularly in Southern Africa which he then fed to Republican Intelligence (RI), South Africa's internal security police which was created in 1963.[373] Chesterton enjoyed a particularly close relationship with its head Brigadier Hendrik van den Bergh, who had been interned in 1942, as had the South African Prime Minister Balthazar 'John' Vorster, for his membership of the pro-Nazi Ossewabrandwag (OB – Oxwagon Sentinel). Van den Bergh had already proven himself an extremely effective opponent of the African National Congress (ANC), which included the arrest of its leader, Nelson Mandela. 'What Mandela conspired to do,' Chesterton remarked after his imprisonment, 'was in effect to remove the restraints imposed by the White Man so as to return the continent to unchallenged barbarism and insensate cruelty'.[374]

Through his personal correspondence with van den Bergh, Chesterton passed RI information on the activities of exiled anti-apartheid activists in Britain, on British firms believed to be aiding the anti-apartheid cause; and of 'communist' subversion along the South African borders, particularly in the British Protectorate of Swaziland, where he also reported on the activities of British military intelligence amongst the white settler community. Chesterton gleaned this information from Candour League supporters, which he hoped could be used to shore up support for South Africa in the region. Chesterton also communicated his thoughts to van den Bergh on figures he regarded as internal subversives like Petrus Johannes 'Piet' Cillie, editor-in-chief of *Die Burger*, whom Chesterton felt was guilty of peddling 'corrosive liberalism' which made him 'a far greater menace to the long-term security of South Africa than any known agitator'.[375] He also fed van den Bergh a range of documents relating to Sir Robert Birley, the former headmaster of Eton who, following his retirement, became visiting Professor of Education at Witwatersrand University, South Africa.[376] Birley's activities were of undoubtedly of interest to van den Bergh because of his continued friendship with Mandela.[377]

It is unlikely that Chesterton was ever formally 'recruited' by van den Bergh, their relationship simply being based upon a shared support for apartheid. Yet the value of the morsels of information Chesterton fed to South Africa's security services ought not to be underestimated. Van den Bergh clearly believed them important enough to supply Chesterton with an introduction to Petrus 'Piet' Schoeman, First Secretary of the South African Embassy, through whom Chesterton could pass scraps of information to the security services.[378] 'You will like him', van den Bergh told Chesterton. 'He has turned out to be quite a diplomat. But don't misjudge him because of this. Deep down he remains my man.'[379] Schoeman was in fact 'the head of South Africa's intelligence network in Britain,' according to one of van den Bergh's former agents.[380]

White South Africa was not without its faults for Chesterton, however. He became increasingly exasperated by the lack of unity within the South African extreme right, lamenting that English-speaking South African's were 'not welcome' within the predominantly Afrikaans Nasionale Party (National Party), which had pushed out both S.E.D. Brown, editor of the *South African Observer*, and Ivor Benson who had returned to South Africa from Rhodesia and begun editing his own anti-Semitic news-sheet, *Behind the News*.[381] This lack of unity was symptomatic of a greater and more dangerous malaise, Chesterton believed. 'The changed factor', he wrote was not the activities of black Africans but 'the White man's amazing loss of nerve and verve and instinct to survive'. The collapse of white morale and with it white rule, resulting from 'brain-washing', represented a far greater problem for Britain's imperial pretensions than African 'demands'.[382] Chesterton was increasingly perturbed that this rot had spread to the bastions of white civilisation, South Africa and Rhodesia, particularly as both were, to his mind, moving ever closer to accepting the prospect of African's exercising some form self-rule. He was buoyed up, however, by the belief that it was 'very much easier to secure a hearing and an acceptance of one's views' in those countries:

> because the danger to White survival there is so very much more apparent than it is in Great Britain. As long as people over here have their jobs and their washing machines and their television sets they display no desire to delve beneath the surface to ascertain on what a flimsy basis their 'prosperity' rests.[383]

As the sun set on Empire, Chesterton looked to the white Commonwealth countries to provide the geopolitical model that would restore Britain's position as a world power. 'Our own solution still seems to me to be a practical one given only enough guts in a British government', he wrote:

> If Great Britain, Canada, Australia, New Zealand, Rhodesia and even South Africa were to form an association for economic and strategical purposes I believe the balance would be restored to the world and, because of our unrivalled strategical advantages in the geographical sense, we could again become the dominant force. Like you I am all

for quality, and I believe that the British quality, psychologically as well as scientifically, could still lead the world once the Wall Street stranglehold was broken. At any rate, I for one see no other hope for mankind.[384]

Distilled to its essence, it was in South Africa, the country in which Chesterton was born, that salvation for 'European civilisation' lay.[385]

The New Unhappy Lords

In July 1965, Chesterton published *The New Unhappy Lords: An Exposure of Power Politics*.[386] The book took its title from the poem 'The Secret People' by his cousin G.K. Chesterton, which also served as an allusion to its contents. Mainstream media reviews were universally damning. *The Times Literary Supplement* wrote scathingly that 'it is pathetic and yet disturbing that this can still be written ... the belief in political witchcraft dies hard even in this country'.[387] Written as Chesterton convalesced in South Africa and financed by a wealthy Cape Town supporter, *The New Unhappy Lords* instantly became an underground bestseller.[388] By June 1969, it had sold over 17,000 copies.[389] A third enlarged edition was published in the following month and a fourth revised edition in 1972. Written specifically with a South African and American audience in mind, *The New Unhappy Lords* became extremely influential in the United States. Lieutenant-General Pedro Augusto del Valle assisted in the publication of the American edition. The book had a huge impact upon those anti Semites who coalesced around Willis Carto's Liberty Lobby, an extreme right umbrella organisation founded in 1955 to combat 'international socialists' which also absorbed many of Chesterton's contacts in the DAC including del Valle. Carto reputedly considered Chesterton 'the best writer on our side'.[390] Revilo P. Oliver, a professor of classical philosophy at the University of Illinois, associated with a range of extreme right-wing causes, held Chesterton in similarly high esteem.[391]

Though it is difficult to distil individual elements from the conspiratorial tradition from Nesta Webster onwards that steeped Chesterton's own thinking, perhaps the greatest self-confessed personal influence upon his thought was New Zealander Arthur Nelson Field, a monetary reformer and anti-Semitic conspiracy theorist whose most famous work, *The Truth about the Slump* (1931), went through numerous editions and also exerted a powerful influence upon Kitson and Leese.[392] Chesterton recommended Field's work 'without mental reservation' – a rare accolade.[393] 'In some ways my book [*The New Unhappy Lords*] may be said to take over from where A.N. Field left off', he remarked to a friend.[394] Despite harbouring an initially deleterious opinion of Chesterton, fuelled by correspondents like Leese and Admiral Sir Barry Domvile, Field's own attitude softened after Chesterton visited him as part of his Australasian tour in February 1960.[395] Chesterton failed, however, in his quest to induce Field to lend the prestige of his name to the League.[396]

The New Unhappy Lords reflected Chesterton's belief that 'the proper study of political mankind is the study of power elites, without which nothing that happens can be understood'.[397] This materialist focus upon 'power elites' remained at root, however, an elegantly written anti-Semitic assault upon the subversive and occult conspiracy which was supposedly seeking to replace the British Empire, and subjugate Western civilisation in general, to a 'One World' Jewish super-state. Distinct from other anti-Semitic screeds, *The New Unhappy Lords* distilled Chesterton's long-running anti-Semitic commentary upon, and critique of, America's rise to globalism and the commensurate decline of British imperial prowess into one volume. Chesterton's consistent animus to American hegemony, at a time when many right-wingers were committed to the North Atlantic Alliance as the only effective bulwark against Communism, was such that one correspondent accused him and his supporters in 1953 of being 'a dangerous bunch of crypto-communists'. This was perhaps a not altogether surprising assertion given contemporary left-wing anti-Americanism, manifest in publications such as *The American Threat to British Culture* (1952).[398]

Where *The New Unhappy Lords* also parted company with many contemporary anti-Semitic and anti-Communist diatribes was in its location of the engine of a vast subversive conspiracy in New York not Moscow. For Chesterton, the transfer of financial power from London to New York in the aftermath of the First World War cemented the primacy of the 'New York Money Power', which had wrested control of monetary policy from the American government through the creation of the Federal Reserve in 1913. This gave them the power to make or break nations, including the United States, with the aim of dragooning all nations into a 'One World Government'. Whilst *The New Unhappy Lords* articulated the thesis that the 'Money Power' was taking control of the world through the banks and the banking system, the book itself betrays a lack of any real understanding of banks, their role or influence in world affairs. Chesterton's interest was piqued solely by the role he perceived Jews to be playing within these institutions, information which was misinterpreted and misconstrued perhaps even before it was filtered through his anti-Semitic analytical apparatus.

The book argued that once Nazi Germany had been destroyed for its 'revolt against the Money Power', the only remaining impediment to the implementation of 'One World Government' was the British Empire and the Commonwealth with its system of Imperial preference. This was being liquidated by the financial architecture of free-market capitalism, which flowed from Lend-Lease agreements designed to ensure Britain's financial dependency on New York's financial houses, Chesterton concluded. *The New Unhappy Lords* highlighted the role of a range of international 'front' groups including the World Bank, IMF, Common Market, NATO and the United Nations through which the 'Dollar Emperors' worked for the dissolution of national sovereignty and the 'enslavement of mankind'. The 'Money Power' aimed first to erode the spiritual fibre of the nation by promoting internationalism over nationalism and mass immigration and racial 'mongrelisation' at home with the aim of 'softening' up Europe's racial fibre, thereby reducing the continent to a suitably servile consumer plantation.[399]

Importantly, insofar as the tradition of anti-Semitic literature is concerned, *The New Unhappy Lords* also highlighted the role played in the 'conspiratorial bureaucracy' by transatlantic think-tanks like the Council for Foreign Relations and the Royal Institute for International Affairs (Chatham House), which was consequently picked up by American conspiracy theorists.[400] Chesterton was also in the vanguard of those who alighted upon the Bilderberg Group as one of the principal movers in this global subterranean conspiracy – though he was not the first author to do so.[401] Chesterton identified Denis Healey, the Secretary of State for Defence and subsequently Chancellor of the Exchequer, 'as subverter-in-chief in the United Kingdom'.[402] Ironically, Chesterton credited himself with playing a part in the formation of the Bilderberg Group believing that the 'remorseless light' he had shone on Chatham House whilst working for *Truth*, 'may have led to its manipulators seeking new facades behind which to work'.[403] Chesterton's researches on the Bilderberg Group influenced US conspiracists like Willis Carto whose Liberty Lobby recycled them in their own publications.[404]

For Chesterton, anti-'Communism' was a form of false consciousness. Capitalist and Communist internationalism served the same master, a fact evinced for Chesterton by the actions of Kuhn, Loeb & Co who, he believed, funded the 1917 Bolshevik revolution. Chesterton dismissed the 'cold war' as an 'entirely fraudulent' dichotomy perpetuated by 'the same power instrument', which periodically staged 'alarms and excursions' such as Korea and Cuba in order to obscure the fact that mankind was being corralled 'into two nominally antagonistic sheep-pens, as a prelude to merging the pens to form the all-embracing empire over which World Government intends to rule'.[405] For Chesterton, this conspiracy was indubitably the product of the Jewish mind 'which is preoccupied with the drive towards monopoly, above all a world monopoly of political power.' The ultimate consummation of 'Zionism', he argued, was not the foundation of the state of Israel but 'World Government'.[406]

Chesterton was unable to do more than unmask the supposed agencies of the conspiracy, however. The 'conspirators' themselves remained in the dark with the exception of the financier and presidential advisor Bernard Baruch whom Chesterton branded 'the effective head of the Money Power'. Baruch's passing temporarily deprived Chesterton of his figurehead, though he subsequently identified Sidney J. Weinberg, a Wall Street banker, as his supposed successor in *American Mercury*.[407] The others, world leaders and other sundry statesmen were either 'dupes' or 'agents' of the 'Money Power'. The conspiracy was not monolithic which made detection harder. It was, argued Chesterton, a complex and ever-shifting alliance of amorphous financial interests internal rivalries, both Jewish and Gentile, all of which were, however, working towards the same end.[408]

The impact of *The New Unhappy Lords* extended far beyond the extreme right. One particularly enthusiastic South African reader was Major-General Hendrik J. van den Bergh, the titular head of Republican Intelligence (RI), who also subscribed to *Candour*, though his details were removed from the 'official list' for security reasons.[409] Van den Bergh declared that he owed a debt of gratitude to those, like Chesterton, who shared his struggle: 'What a pleasure to have been associated with them and to have shared with them the honour of upholding white civilisation in South Africa'.[410] He received a specially autographed edition of *The New Unhappy Lords* from Chesterton. Its central thesis was clearly persuasive. 'I think it was a good day, the day we met,' he wrote to Chesterton.

> No, I know it was a good day. I have since re-read your Unhappy Lords. I wish we could take men like [Robert] Kennedy – I am sorry – I mean adolescents like Kennedy and push it down their throats. Will they ever read it?[411]

How van den Bergh interpreted 'subversion' was evident in his address to the International Symposium on Communism, held in Pretoria on 30 September 1966 convened by the National Council to Combat Communism, which was organised by the Inter-Church Anti-Communist Action Committee of the Dutch Reformed Church with the aim of preserving South Africa's 'Christian heritage' against Communism.[412] In his speech, van den Bergh attacked the recent campaign of 'sabotage' in South Africa, which, as head of the Security Police, his fiercely repressive methods had succeeded in smashing. Far more dangerous, however, was the 'psychological sabotage' used by the Communists to undermine white South Africa's morale, argued van den Bergh. The leaders of this conspiracy were, he claimed, a cabal of 'white so-called intellectuals'.[413] In response to a question regarding the supposed preponderance of Jews within the anti-apartheid movement, van den Bergh replied that Jews 'tend to be involved' because 'Communism was the highest form of capitalism'.[414] Privately, he told Chesterton: 'I had to give my tremendous and wonderful audience some background against which they had to judge what I had to say!'[415]

Chesterton believed wholeheartedly in a Jewish conspiracy bent on establishing 'One World' government. Though he acknowledged the role of impersonal factors in shaping the world and emphasised that there were 'various bodies', 'pragmatic in their methods' utilising 'diverse approaches' to achieve its objectives, Chesterton believed unerringly in a single, unified conspiracy behind which stood the Jews.[416] *The New Unhappy Lords* bore few outward similarities, however, to the guttural invective produced by obdurate anti-Semites like Arnold Leese. Chesterton was not prepared to believe and regurgitate any old canard about the Jews. Regarding the 'blood libel', Chesterton recalled being contacted by a man from Leeds during the 1930s, who telephoned

> [T]o tell me that he had the positive knowledge of a ritual murder in the next street to one in which he was living. I suggested that instead of ringing me he should make a report to the nearest police station, whereupon he rang off in anger. I have invariably encountered the same thing when asking for proof.[417]

On another occasion he remembered, 'somebody wrote to me of the sinister doings of the "Illuminati" ... I caused much wrath by requesting their names and addresses'.[418] Nor was Chesterton's anti-Semitism rooted in antipathy towards Jewish religious scripture. 'The Talmud interests me scarcely at all', he told Joseph Leftwich in 1948,

> the Protocols still less. I do not think there is an occult conspiracy on the part of the Jewish leadership, handed down from one generation to another. Even if it were, I would not imagine that anybody was privy to it outside a small circle.[419]

Though Chesterton affected disinterest in *The Protocols* (which he had promoted whilst editor of *Blackshirt*), his response to Leftwich was disingenuous. Only a year beforehand, he had remarked:

> My refusal to hitherto quote from this source has been due to an unwillingness to be drawn into an argument about its authenticity.... Whatever the explanation, the policy revealed in the Protocols is today being implemented in the most amazing and terrifying fashion.[420]

Chesterton's anti-Semitism was defined by this duality, acknowledging *The Protocols*' fraudulent provenance whilst simultaneously affirming their arguments. When the BBC broadcast 'Always Tell a Big Lie: A Study of the Protocols of the Elders of Zion' in May 1961 debunking the anti-Semitic forgery, Chesterton penned *Learned Elders and the BBC* (1961) in response. 'I have never based any part of *Candour*'s case on the Protocols,' he asserted,

> for the simple reasons that I know nothing of their origin and care less.... The Protocols may be a fake, a fabrication, call them what you will. But they are not, as the BBC presented them, mad, in the sense of being divorced from the realities of subversion and revolution. Lacking though they be in authority, they yet march in step with the unfolding conspiracy of which they are a prophetic utterance ... Jewish power is real.[421]

He returned to *The Protocols* only weeks before his death, writing to a follower:

> The work of Professor Nilus is not satisfactory and it is improbable that the documents in question were produced for the benefit of the Zionist Conference in Basle. Most of them can be traced to a work by M. Joli [*sic*] written in the reign of Napoleon III. That they are a masterly analysis of the weaknesses of Gentile society cannot be doubted, but any competent Jewish writer can make a nonsense of attempts to prove their authenticity.[422]

As a result, *The Protocols*, by necessity, formed part of the esoteric rather than exoteric ideology of the extreme right. 'Even if the Protocols are a genuine document,' noted Chesterton, 'their integrity is certainly not accepted by those we seek to warn.'[423]

For this very reason, Chesterton was fiercely critical of anti-Semites like Eustace Mullins, a devotee of the pro-Fascist poet Ezra Pound who utilised *The Protocols* openly and without qualification. In doing so, Chesterton believed, Mullins traduced the credibility of the researches undertaken by others like himself opposed to the 'Money Power'. Chesterton was absolutely appalled by Mullin's book, *Mullins' New History of the Jews* (1968), which he derided as full of 'monumental errors', 'obvious fakes', 'falsehoods' and 'old canards', complaining that for anti-Semites like Mullins, 'any stick is good enough to beat the Jewish dog with.' The use of such crude anti-Semitism, in Chesterton's eyes, rendered authors like Mullins 'a liability and a menace' to the nationalist movement.[424] In September 1970, Chesterton launched a scathing public attack on Mullins under the heading 'this man is dangerous'.[425] Chesterton poured particular scorn on Mullins' use of a fake quote taken from an equally fake book titled *A Racial Programme for the Twentieth Century* (1912) 'by one Israel Cohen, a Communist', which purported to show how Jewish Communists were using 'racial tension' to destroy white civilisation though, ironically, *Candour* had quoted from the same forgery in 1957, which rather undermined Chesterton's case.[426]

Though Chesterton attempted to raise his own work onto a higher intellectual plane – *The New Unhappy Lords* made no specific reference to *The Protocols* – its pages resonated with its principal argument that the course of world events was 'deliberately contrived' by 'hidden hands' to the furtherance of its nefarious ends. Chesterton's writings often spoke in eschatological terms of the struggle between the white race and the 'Devil'.[427] It should not be assumed a priori that Chesterton was speaking metaphorically. The demonisation of the 'Jew' as devil, sorcerer and ritual murderer, as the literal and figurative embodiment of evil incarnate, has a historical lineage stretching back to the Middle Ages.[428] Though he denied to Leftwich that he believed in an 'occult conspiracy', in the last years of his life, Chesterton alluded to such anti-Semitic traditions, believing himself to be getting closer to the heart of the plot whose influences, he confided in a friend, 'are definitely evil, emanating from a circle which practices black magic.'[429]

National Front

During the late 1960s, it became increasingly obvious to Chesterton that the LEL had run its course. None of its three candidates in the 1964 general election retained their deposits leaving Chesterton 'terribly disappointed', even though he had opposed contesting elections in the first place.[430] By autumn 1965, running the LEL was putting a strain on Chesterton's health, worsened by the fact that he wrote the majority of *Candour* by himself.[431] League finances also suffered as a result of competition from Edward Martell's organisation and the Conservative Monday Club, formed in 1961 in reaction to Macmillan's 'Winds of Change' speech.[432] League membership had slumped from 3,000 in 1958 to 337 in 1966. Rodney Legg, who joined the group in 1962, was the 'last activist' to enroll.[433] With the League struggling organisationally, Chesterton began to seriously entertain treaties from other extreme right-wing *groupuscules* to pool resources during the course of 1966. Chesterton coveted the activist base of John Bean's British National Party (BNP) whilst, for its part, the BNP looked to the LEL and its national council, replete with right-wing grandees, for funds and comparative respectability. Though Chesterton publicly disabused them of the idea of 'marrying money', he failed to tell the BNP that his own organisation's finances were 'so dismal that we are beginning to act on the assumption that we have almost reached the end of the road.'[434]

The consequence of numerous meetings, discussions and correspondence, the National Front (NF) was founded on 15 December 1966 by merging the LEL, the BNP and the Racial Preservation Society (RPS).[435] Its inaugural conference was attended by 175 people, some of whom clashed with anti-fascist activists outside resulting in eleven arrests.[436] Chesterton became chairman whilst Andrew Fountaine, the BNP President, was appointed Executive Director. The two men were not destined to enjoy a profitable working relationship. Fountaine was a wealthy Norfolk landowner who had driven ambulances for the Abyssinians when Mussolini attacked them in 1935 – 'Though I now see I was on the wrong side,' he later remarked.[437] He had atoned for his erroneous behaviour by fighting for Franco for 'several months' during the Spanish Civil War. Fountaine followed his father – Admiral Charles Fountaine – into the Royal Navy, rising to become a Lieutenant-Commander before being wounded in a Japanese kamikaze attack on HMS *Indefatigable* in April 1945. He witnessed the flash of the atomic bomb dropped on Nagasaki and was present at the ceremony marking the Japanese surrender.[438]

Fountaine subsequently pursued a political career but blotted his copy book at the 1948 Conservative Party conference after lambasting the Labour government as 'that group of national traitors, that hierarchy of semi-alien mongrels and hermaphrodite Communists that have the impudence to call themselves that which they are not – a British Government'. His view of trade unionists was equally pungent. 'If we have a military war with Russia', he stated, 'a large percentage will actively fight on the other side'.[439] His views were 'at complete variance' with those of the Conservatives who removed Fountaine from its official list of party candidates.[440] Undeterred, Fountaine stood in the 1950s general election in Chorley, Lancashire, where, without official party support, he polled 22,872 votes (46.9 per cent). Thereafter, he founded a short-lived 'National Front Movement', leading him to claim, much to Chesterton's irritation, that he was the progenitor of the idea behind the organisation.

The NF was publicly launched on 7 February 1967 at a meeting in Caxton Hall, London. Its aim was 'to preserve our British native stock, to prevent inter-racial strife ... and to eradicate race-hatred, by terminating non-white immigration, with humane and orderly repatriation of non-white immigrants (and their dependents) who have entered since ... 1948'.[441] Internally, each component part had differing ideological interpretations as to what this platform entailed for the nascent racial nationalist movement. Bean instructed BNP members to regard the NF not as a new movement 'but rather as a continuation of the BNP with added strength and increased ability and potential as a result of the merger.'[442] That not everyone felt likewise was highlighted when one over-zealous BNP official proclaimed that NF membership itself was restricted to those of 'National British/European descent'. For Chesterton, whose League had several members of Scandinavian, German and Hungarian descent, not to mention others, this was an unacceptable attempt to introduce 'discredited Rosenberg nonsense' into the bargain and would have led to the League's withdrawal from the merger had not senior BNP leaders interceded.[443]

League activists were not particularly impressed with their new partners. 'Really, all that we can say for the National Front is that it exists and a certain amount of money seems to be coming into it', de Bounevialle told Chesterton, voicing her concern that the BNP activists needed a 'strong hand'. She believed that the party had few activists outside Southall, its former stronghold, 'and few ideas above those that bought the BNP to ask for a merger in the first place'.[444] Chesterton did not despair quite so quickly, determining 'that a rabble outfit shall become a disciplined political instrument'.[445] He toiled tirelessly in its cause working, he estimated, eight hours days, sometimes as many as eighteen, during which he made on average twenty-seven telephone calls a day and dictated 100 letters a week.[446] It was the nucleus of LEL activists within the NF leadership who, during its early days, kept the fledgling movement afloat:

> Although we have not been able to halt the main advance of the enemy we have at least kept alive the vital spark of resistance, and for its first year we have provided the National Front free of charge with an office in the heart of London, the services of a full-time secretary, most of the time of my own part-time secretary, and for what they are worth, about twelve working hours a day of my own services for which I do not get paid and for which I do not seek payment. In addition we have met the major costs of the new movement.[447]

This came at considerable personal cost to LEL veterans. In January 1967, Chesterton's deputy Austen Brooks, who had become NF joint-secretary, suffered a nervous breakdown and attempted suicide.[448] He subsequently confessed to Chesterton that he had been embezzling funds from him since 1958.[449] Chesterton hushed the matter up. Astonishingly, despite this betrayal, Chesterton not only published several fulsome tributes to Brooks in *Candour* but kept him on the payroll until August when he 'retired' permanently from politics.[450] Brooks later sub-edited the *Bournemouth Evening Echo*.[451] *Candour* observed that subsequently 'if Austin caught sight of any of his former friends he crossed the road to avoid contact'.[452] His job was taken by an NF activist called Ken Foster, noted for always carrying a large holdall. 'Once it was opened in a pub and a guinea pig climbed out'.[453]

In addition to the burdens of the NF chairmanship, Chesterton also became head of the Policy Directorate whose self-imposed duties included acting as 'watchdog' against undesirable or irresponsible elements infiltrating the party.[454] Chesterton personally paved the way, however, for a notable number of Nazi activists to ascend to the party's upper echelons almost from the outset. Aidan Mackey, the NF deputy chairman, was supported in his role by former NSM activists Denis Pirie and Martin Webster, who, Chesterton assured Mackey, 'will do most of the work'.[455] Having initially refused to countenance it, Chesterton also became increasingly amenable to the inclusion of John Tyndall (Chapter 5) who, after resigning from the League in 1958, had plunged headlong into the national socialist *demi-monde*. Having disbanded his Greater Britain Movement (GBM) in 1966, Tyndall had been a leading advocate for unity within the extreme right milieu and now hovered on the fringes of the NF seeking entrée. Against considerable internal resistance, Chesterton forced through Tyndall's membership in May 1968 and subsequently secured his election to the National Directorate in 1969. Colin Jordan (Chapter 4) remained beyond the pale, however.[456]

Chesterton's attitude was paradoxical. Whilst he facilitated the elevation of Nazi activists to the highest echelons of the NF, when it came to their counterparts abroad, he sought distance. In April 1968, Chesterton's old colleague, former BUF NHQ speaker Derek Talbot Baines, contacted him after returning from Hannover where he had visited the Nationaldemokratische Partei Deutschlands (NPD – National Democratic Party of Germany). The NPD were 'very friendly' towards the NF, Baines reported.[457] Chesterton, whilst interested, baulked at open association because 'our opponents are all too eager to bespatter us quite falsely with a pro-Germanic smear and we must avoid giving them any legitimate occasion for doing so'.[458]

There was another more fundamental ideological tension enshrined at the heart of the NF leadership. Racial nationalists like John Bean believed that 'race is the basis of politics' whilst Chesterton asserted that restoring 'national sovereignty' represented the *sine qua non* for the preservation of 'racial identity'.[459] This tension remained unresolved. The NF's racial nationalist propagandists, Chesterton lamented, were often 'incapable to considering any of the other perils which beset our national path ... these perils do exist and would still exist if every immigrant here were to be returned overnight to his country of origin'.[460]

New legislation further complicated racist activism. The party's formation coincided with the passing of the Race Relations Act (1968) and the subsequent arrest of five RPS activists in East Grinstead, Sussex for inciting racial hatred. The Act had sent a warning shot across the bows of the extreme right. Both Chesterton and Robert Gayre, *Mankind Quarterly*'s editor were well aware that their respective publications would now warrant closer scrutiny from the authorities.[461] The RPS newspaper, *Southern News*, and indeed the group's narrative throughout the subsequent trial was designed to court sympathy rather than be nakedly offensive. In considering the preferment of charges against the RPS, the legal advisor to the Director of Public Prosecutions observed: 'I have no doubt that a good deal of care was put into the construction of this newspaper with a view to a possible prosecution and a contemplated Defence.'[462]

The RPS prosecution gave the extreme right the opportunity to mount this challenge. Chesterton founded the Free Speech Defence Committee to raise funds for their legal defence and arranged for Gayre to testify at their trial. The five RPS activists were acquitted in March 1968.[463] It was a successful challenge to a piece of legislation that Chesterton believed was another component of the Jewish conspiracy ranged against the white race. 'You may be right in thinking that Sigmund Warburg is the driving force behind the Race Relations legislation, but he is certainly not alone', he wrote to one correspondent. 'I would say that the entire tribe has been involved, perhaps with the intention of diverting public attention from their own activities, by concentrating it upon the coloured immigrants.'[464]

Enoch Powell

The party's first electoral foray was the candidature of its executive director Andrew Fountaine in the March 1968 Acton by-election. During the course of the campaign, Fountaine railed against 'coloured Bolshevism rolling up the last outposts of civilisation' whilst branding the constituency's non-white electors as 'alien immigrants living one third off prostitution, one third off National Assistance and one third off Red gold'.[465] Chesterton felt Fountaine brought the NF into disrepute, however, when he declared that:

> it isn't a colour problem we have in this country, it's a renegade white problem.... If anything Macmillan is worse than Wilson; at least he had some upbringing and should have known better. But frankly I'd put them both in the gas chamber.[466]

Fountaine polled 1,400 (5.6 per cent), coming fourth, which, although lower than expected, helped cement the nascent organisation.

The result was deemed promising but paled into insignificance compared to the fillip the NF received from Enoch Powell's 'Rivers of Blood' speech on 20 April, which catapulted immigration to the forefront of British politics. Edward Heath, the Conservative Prime Minister, sacked Powell from the Shadow Cabinet for his remarks, ending his ministerial career. Public support for Powell was widespread, however. Seventy-four per cent of people agreed with him and only 15 per cent disagreed, one poll recorded. In the four days after Powell's speech, approximately twenty strikes took place involving 10,000–12,000 workers. The largest involved 6,000–7,000 London dock workers, constituting about a third of the overall workforce. The number of workers who actively marched on Westminster was much smaller, however, and also included the Smithfield meat porters who were noticeably vociferous in their support for Powell.[467] Within five days of the speech, Powell received 30,000 letters of support which by early May had reached 43,000 letters of which only 800 disagreed with him. His speech certainly appears to have impacted upon public attitudes towards immigration. Prior to his speech, 75 per cent of people surveyed felt that immigration controls were not tight enough. After his speech, this rose to 83 per cent.[468]

In this respect, Powell was preaching to the converted – reflecting rather than leading public opinion on immigration which had strongly endorsed the passage of the Commonwealth Immigration Act (1968) which had a significant impact upon migration.[469] Between 1968 and 1972, successive opinion polls found widespread support for the idea advocated by Powell in his speech, of voluntary repatriation, though not the compulsory variant endorsed by the NF. The 'Powell Effect' upon British attitudes to immigration was comparatively short-lived, however. The basic, stable divisions in public opinion on the subject soon reasserted themselves. Tellingly, even at its height, the month Powell delivered his speech, public support for anti-immigration activism (as opposed to legislation) was more shallow than was commonly presumed. One poll taken that month found that 76 per cent of respondents thought that the dock workers had been wrong to strike in support of Powell. In retrospect, this should perhaps have been a sign.[470] Failure to take cognisance of this led the NF to mistake the level of support they might ultimately derive from identifying solely with the immigration issue.

'What Mr Powell has said does not vary at all from our views,' Chesterton told *The Times* in the aftermath of his speech.[471] *Private Eye* satirised the similarity with an article titled 'League of Empire Powellites'.[472] In reality, however, Chesterton's response to Powell was more critical, largely because of his de facto support for immigration whilst in Macmillan's government. Thus, Chesterton argued vehemently against

> placing too much reliance on a knight errant who arrives at the thirteenth hour, gives momentary battle only now and then before vanishing from sight to turn up at the most unexpected places, such as a Bilderberg conference in Canada.[473]

Indeed, it was Powell's attendance at this Bilderberg meeting, within a week of his speech, more so than his refusal to countenance 'compulsory' repatriation, that really grated.[474]

For Chesterton, the outpouring of popular support for Powell raised another serious question. Was the NF a distinct political movement,

> or simply a leaderless rabble trying to hitch our wagon to an ambitious Tory lone wolf who speaks out on coloured immigration about once every seven months, and for the

rest supports the Wilson-Warburg combine in our withdrawal from Suez, is a Manchester School free-trader, a Little Englander and now a proponent of Rhodesian republicanism, which in everything would be a complete red-herring except in as far as it would further diminish the British world.[475]

Chesterton refuted the idea from subordinates that the NF could use Powell to help to cut the Tories in two over the immigration issue as 'a complete pipe-dream'.[476]

His stance was unpopular within the party, particularly amongst younger activists who, Chesterton noted, 'are having to be restrained from parading with banners demanding Enoch Powell for Prime Minister!'[477] This was 'most unwise' he felt since 'shouting "Enoch, Enoch, Enoch" every time the man's name is mentioned would suggest that we are supporters of a contender in the leadership stakes of the Conservative party'.[478] This, in effect, meant they were chanting 'Blessed be the name of the Devil!!'[479] Chesterton's aversion to Powell – which precipitated the bulk of Portsmouth NF to resign in November 1969 – held little sway within the upper echelons of the party either.[480] His deputy, Aidan Mackey, struggled to impose Chesterton's will on the Directorate, warning them at a meeting that month not to become 'obsessed' with Powell since this could become 'a diversion of our energies, whether into working for him or against him' and would 'detract from our principal work and from our effectiveness'.[481]

In the short term, however, Chesterton struggled to assert his views within the NF and was drowned out in the groundswell of support for Powell which had created a space to the right of the Conservative Party for popular mobilisation against immigration. 'The speech has finally lifted a weight off people's minds', noted Denis Pirie of its psychological impact. 'They no longer feel guilty for their beliefs'.[482] The NF benefited directly from this cognitive opening, becoming a vicarious repository for those who supported Powell's stance after he himself had refused to form a political party. 'Powell's speeches gave our membership and morale a tremendous boost,' claimed the NF. 'Before Powell spoke we were getting only cranks and perverts. After his speeches we started to attract, in a secret sort of way, the right-wing members of the Tory organisations.'[483] *Spearhead* claimed membership 'trebled' but declined to print an exact figure.[484] Not all this influx was of the desired calibre, however. In June 1969, Chesterton had to issue instructions that 'the movement must not get involved in confrontations with coloured immigrants as such, but with the political forces which brought them to Britain and encourage them to stay here'.[485] Powell's resolute refusal to endorse the NF, however, curtailed its ability to ever truly expand beyond its anti-immigration niche. His speech also served, ultimately, to strengthen voter identification with the Conservatives as the party tough on immigration. Chesterton, who remained highly critical of the 'Enoch cult' within the NF, perceived early on that the Conservatives would be the only real beneficiaries.[486] Powell, he argued conspiratorially, was a 'safety valve'.[487]

Fountaine

Despite the increasingly favourable external climate in which it was operating, internally the NF was already experiencing the first of many waves of internal factionalism which would dog its progress throughout its existence. Chesterton and Fountaine were perennially at odds with one another, a tension that was exacerbated by the NF constitution which saw the party governed by a policy directorate, overseeing the party's ideological and tactical approach and an executive directorate, concerned with administration and propaganda – the former ruled by Chesterton and the latter by Fountaine. In May 1968, shortly after Powell's speech, Fountaine responded to news of student insurrection in Paris by circularising the party's organisers to prepare for civil war and report to the nearest police station with their activists in the event that trouble spread across the channel. Chesterton immediately countermanded the order, which he regarded as 'juvenile hysteria', but was aghast that Fountaine would circulate such a 'clownish document' against his express wishes in the first place.[488]

Matters came to a head at the NF Directorate meeting on 7 June to which Fountaine submitted an organisational scheme, seeking to give it 'active' leadership by bringing provincial and area organisers directly into the party's governing body. His scheme was rejected and his office of Executive Officer was abolished by the Directorate. In response, Fountaine circularised all branch and regional officers, railing against the 'incompetence' of Chesterton's inert 'drawing room circle' who led the movement by 'remote control'.[489] Privately, Chesterton reviled Fountaine as 'a mentally retarded meglomanic'.[490] Fountaine's appeal to the membership, over and above Chesterton's leadership, secured his dismissal on 19 June.[491] Fountaine subsequently secured a legal victory over Chesterton in the High Court, who ruled his dismissal unconstitutional but his attempt to usurp Chesterton's leadership at the NF AGM later that year ended in complete failure. He was defeated by a resounding 316 votes to 20.[492]

Secure in his position, Chesterton's peroration to the assembled members at the AGM addressed the betrayal of British interests abroad and at home leading to the emigration of 'our finest types' and their replacement with 'coloured gentlemen who simply cannot make the grade where our British way of life is concerned, and are hundreds of millions of years away from our ancient culture and traditions.'[493] Chesterton despaired, however, that unless the NF 'is able to move quickly the end result will be the total depravity of the British nation.'[494]

In an effort to 'move away from hooliganism', the NF began raising money for an election fund.[495] The 1970 general election would be a key test for the party's political progress. Public concern about immigration, stoked by further dire warnings from Enoch Powell who demanded a halt to immigration, a new citizenship law and voluntary repatriation, peaked in 1970 at 77 per cent, though remained at high levels thereafter. Powell's public popularity and the resonance of his message played their part in the election of a new Conservative government.[496] The NF stood ten candidates in the general election who collectively polled 10,902 votes, averaging 3.6 per cent of the vote, which, in light of the support for anti-immigration politics that 'Powellism' had highlighted, was undoubtedly disappointing. Financially, it put the fledgling movement 'back to square one'.[497] Only in hindsight could this been seen as something of a highpoint. Whilst the number of NF candidates and votes rose, year in, year out, the vote per candidate dwindled in each of the four successive general elections the NF contested during the 1970s.

Disillusionment and death

Throughout its early years, there remained a 'difference in outlook' between old League members and 'the more youthful and impetuous' activists with whom they had aligned themselves which caused Chesterton the 'greatest unease'.[498] Hoping to mould the NF into a 'serious' political organisation, Chesterton issued a 'code of conduct' stating imperiously that 'young members frequently think that they know better than their leaders. Before they can be of maximum use to the movement they must be prepared to learn.' For the NF to become a real political contender, argued Chesterton, its activists had to marshal their energies to counter the policies of the established parties rather than 'seeking opportunities for a clash with the fringe elements of the Left'.[499] His edict was generally ignored.

Chesterton was increasingly out of step with the radicalism of a younger generation of activists who comprised the organisation. Poor election results further fuelled their discontent with his leadership. Tyndall had proposed a successful motion to re-elect Chesterton as National Director for 1971 at the NF AGM on 5 September 1970, which was seconded by the NF elections officer 'Gordon Brown' who had been Tyndall's principal benefactor in the GBM and whose real name was Gordon Marshall.[500] No sooner had Chesterton left for South Africa, however, than 'Brown' began intriguing for his removal. An 'Action Committee' was formed, its activities culminating in the sending of a letter to Chesterton on 6 October, which was highly critical of his leadership.[501] Disgusted and disillusioned, Chesterton, who was convalescing in South Africa, determined to resign:

> The job has caused me endless worry and expense, and while it was possible for me to ignore the distaste which NF types have always aroused in me, I am now filled with such loathing and disgust, to say nothing of a mounting sense of futility, that it would be unpardonable of me to feign an optimism to which I can no longer even pretend.[502]

He penned a scathing attack upon Brown in *Candour* called 'Portrait of a Wrecker' before resigning on 19 November 1970.[503] 'As things are', he wrote, 'the idea of continuing to work with declared antagonists and their appeasers makes me want to vomit'.[504] He seethed at the perceived betrayal.

> Thus the fifty years or so which I have devoted to playing a part in trying to restore to Britain her lost soul have ended in derision because of the action of Brown and his confederate rats. Honestly, it would be easier to bring about the resurgence of our people at the head of a posse of lavatory attendants than by leading these leprous little traitors.... There is no sense in thinking of keeping the NF in being. The sooner it busts up the better.[505]

Several activists including John Bean implored Chesterton to rescind his resignation. 'The three years during which I have presided over the NF have been so filled with stupidity, deceit and traitorous activity that only an archangel might be prepared to do what you now ask of me', Chesterton replied.[506] G.K. Rylands, chairman of the NF National Council also resigned, as did the majority of former League activists.[507] To Tyndall's dismay, so too did Aidan Mackey. Tyndall appealed to Mackey to stay in order 'to ensure that the gutter does not take over'.[508] Mackey was persuaded to sit on a hastily convened, six-man steering committee formed to prevent the NF from disintegrating.[509] Keen to prevent a split, Tyndall published a critique of those supporting Chesterton's ouster, 'without a moment's thought for what was to follow him'. 'He still has an enormous amount to give the British cause', Tyndall declared. 'We would be mad if we rejected it.'[510] John O'Brien, *Candour*'s business manager, was elected as Chesterton's successor at an Extraordinary General Meeting held on 20 February 1971. Tyndall took the opportunity to again express his resolve to seek a reconciliation with Chesterton so that he could served as 'an ally and advisor' to the NF.[511] This was despite Chesterton having already made it 'quite clear that under no circumstances will I come back',[512] He did not completely break with the NF, however. He continued supplying the NF with publications whilst the Candour Publishing Company continued paying half the rates for the NF premises in Fleet Street until April 1971.[513]

From South Africa, Chesterton founded the Candour League in January 1971 to focus exclusively upon studying 'the highly intricate means ... whereby the master-internationalists are endeavouring to turn the earth into one vast human ant-heap'. Its aim was to serve as 'a loosely-knit fellowship working on the intellectual plane to do for the patriotic Right what the Fabian Society did in the nineties for the international Left – change the climate of opinion'.[514] Chesterton sought a 'qualitative' rather than 'quantitative' membership for the endeavour gathering round him his old League acolytes Aidan Mackey (chairman), Rosine de Bouneviale (treasurer), Ben Biggs (organising secretary), Lady Elizabeth Freeman (president), Leslie von Goetz, G.K. Rylands and Casimir Marmaduke de Bounevialle DFC (vice-presidents).[515] By this juncture, however, Chesterton was no longer a well man. His health was deteriorating rapidly and in South Africa that year he was forced to seek the attention of a top lung specialist.[516]

Chesterton remained in regular touch with John Tyndall who advertised *Candour* to the NF membership through *Spearhead*, over and above the objections of his colleagues after Chesterton had published a series of acidic articles regarding the NF in its pages.[517] Chesterton also rekindled his relationship with Colin Jordan who had founded the British Movement (BM). Chesterton thought Jordan's pamphlet *White Power in Britain* (1971) was 'excellent' and agreed to advertise it *Candour*. 'I will try and think of a way round the objections of my readership which still link you with neo-Nazi proclivities and fail to take into account that you now preach a straightforward doctrine of British patriotism'.[518] This peculiarly naïve interpretation of Jordan's ideological repositioning led Chesterton to accept an invitation to address a BM St George's Day rally in Wolverhampton on 23 April 1972, though ultimately he was unable to attend, sending a message of support to the conclave instead.[519] Chesterton subsequently sought to arrange publicity for another Jordan publication, *Britain Awake*, praising it as 'one of the best short statements' on 'coloured immigration ... the first successful invasion of the country since the Norman conquest'.[520] *Candour* readers did indeed complain but Chesterton assured them 'that the link [with Jordan], if maintained, would be a very tenuous one'.[521]

This was all quite ironic given that Chesterton had proscribed the BM in 1969.[522] This ban had been more honoured in the breach than in the observance, even amongst his own inner circle. Ben Biggs, the former Reading NF organiser and the Candour League's organising secretary had joined the BM after resigning from the NF in December 1970. Chesterton counselled him 'to minimise the knowledge of your recent and unexpected step' but did not demand he resign.[523] Chesterton himself also occasionally acted as an arbitrator during periodic disputes within the BM, interceding on Jordan's behalf in the growing row between him and the Liverpool BM organiser Michael McLaughlin in 1973.[524] In the end, personalities outweighed politics. 'I do indeed like C.J.', Chesterton stated 'and admire his courage, while being fully conscious of his defects'.[525]

Tyndall's assumption of the NF chairmanship in 1972 led to a more pronounced 'reconciliation' with Chesterton who, despite refusing to re-join the party offered 'constructive criticism' to his former protégé.[526] This included trying to persuade Tyndall to moderate his centralising attitude towards other extreme right grouplets. Chesterton observed:

> I have an idea that he feels the NF to be going ahead so well that all other groups should at once pack up their identity and merge with it. This would be an ideal situation but it is simply 'not on'.[527]

In June 1973, Tyndall led efforts to anoint Chesterton as NF President though Martin Webster, previously reviled by Chesterton as 'the Fat (and Fatuous) Boy of Peckham', opposed the move.⁵²⁸ Webster was 'inspired by an almost pathological personal hate', Tyndall informed him.⁵²⁹ The matter was to be voted upon at the NF AGM in October. Tyndall's plans remained unrealized, however. Chesterton was diagnosed with terminal cancer in July 1973 but had already come to agree with Jonathan Guinness, chairman of the Conservative Monday Club, that the NF was 'irredeemably second-rate'.⁵³⁰

As news of his impending demise spread, tributes and testimonials from across the world flooded in.⁵³¹ Symptomatic was a letter from his friend Revilo P. Oliver:

> Your noble courage, your lucid thought, your brilliant style, and your unwavering loyalty have for decade given heart and hope to all men who still dare to desire a future for our unhappy race and once great civilisation. Your influence has been felt far more widely and strongly than you suspect, and will never be forgotten so long as there are Aryans who retain a memory of their heritage, but I cannot imagine what the prospect will be when the files of *Candour* are closed. I feel as though an age of the world were coming to an end. So long as I shall love, I shall be proud – very proud – that you numbered me among your friends and thought me worthy of a great man's Roman valediction. It is with profound sorrow that I bid you farewell: *ave atque vale*.⁵³²

Oliver was not completely bereft of hope and consulted an eminent pathologist 'who knows your work and met you some years ago' and whom recommended that Chesterton be treated with the drug Laëtrile 'which has often been officious in extreme cases and can do no harm.' Banned in the United States, Laëtrile, which was legal in England, was believed to have little effect in treating cancer.⁵³³ Such treatments, effective or not, came too late for Chesterton. He was admitted to St Christopher's Hospice in August 1973. There he continued his correspondence from his bed whilst writing his final leaders for *Candour*, and putting the finishing touches to 'a couple of new books which are likely to be published in the near future'.⁵³⁴ He worked until 13 August before suffering a haemorrhage and lapsing into a coma. He died three days later on 16 August.⁵³⁵ His final book, titled *Facing the Abyss*, a sequel to *The New Unhappy Lords*, was published posthumously in 1976.

Legacy

In his speech to the very first NF AGM on 7 October 1967, Chesterton had intoned: 'The man who thinks that this is a war that can be won by mouthing slogans about "dirty Jews" and "filthy niggers" is a maniac whose place should not be in the National Front but a mental hospital.'⁵³⁶ As one former activist lamented 'his advice was ignored but his books are remembered.'⁵³⁷ And herein lies Chesterton's legacy, one which he grappled to perpetuate even as he lay dying. Having invested twenty years of his life in *Candour*, Chesterton's principal concern was to ensure its survival beyond his passing. 'It would considerably distress me if I thought that everything I had tried to do ended with my own end', he wrote.⁵³⁸ He need not have worried. His loyal acolyte Rosine de Bouneviale continued publishing *Candour* until her own death in 1999, after which the torch passed to Colin Todd, a former NF activist, who continues to publish it today.⁵³⁹

In 2018, *Candour* celebrated its sixty-fifth year of continuous publication, making it Britain's longest running extreme right-wing journal. *Candour* was not simply Chesterton's personal legacy but an important discursive weapon in its own right, serving as a journal of record for the anti-Semitic *demi-monde*. 'Where but in these pages', *Candour* had once asked, were the careers of those deemed to have betrayed their country to the Jewish-led conspiracy, 'marked and their courses plotted, and the ammunition wherewith to resist treachery provided?'[540] Providing an explanatory rather than predictive narrative, *Candour*'s characterisation of the threat ranged against humanity represented a form of 'rolling prophecy' – a perpetually unfolding, liminal conspiracy, according to which humanity was heading inexorably towards, though never quite arriving at, its enslavement by the 'hidden hand'.[541]

The intellectual framework that *Candour* and *The New Unhappy Lords* provided left an indelible mark upon successive generations of extreme right-wing leaders. John Tyndall, twice chairman of the NF and founder of the British National Party (BNP) declared 'without hesitation, what understanding of political affairs I have I owe much more to A.K. than to any other person.'[542] Tyndall continued recommending Chesterton's writings right up until his death in July 2005, writing in the final issue of his journal, *Spearhead*: 'A.K. Chesterton's clear exposition of the malignant malaise affecting Britain, and the solutions required to correct the situation, can be regarded as the seminal and guiding influence in the National Front, and later the BNP.'[543] Similarly, Martin Webster, the former NF National Activities organiser viewed *Candour*'s narrative as 'very important' because 'it tied together the threads of what is happening, why and who's doing it … it had a tremendous impact'.[544]

Not everyone agreed. *National Democrat*, an important voice for 'New Right' ideas in Britain during the 1980s (which became *The Scorpion* in 1983), argued in its review of *The New Unhappy Lords*, that Chesterton made himself 'ridiculous' by stating that a singular, unified conspiracy existed. 'Life isn't quite that simple', declared its reviewer, 'which is not to say that a lot of what Mr Chesterton wrote wasn't true or relevant'.[545] Most discussion of his work, however, was less critical. The book was lauded by the NF and subsequently its 'political soldier' faction to which the future BNP chairman Nick Griffin belonged.[546] Even after Griffin became BNP chairman in 1999 and launched his 'modernisation' strategy which aimed to expunge the party's extremist associations and make it electable, party publications continued to recommend *The New Unhappy Lords* as 'an exposure of the financial power that seeks to dragoon mankind into a global police state'.[547] *Identity*, the BNP journal edited by John Bean, formerly a League organiser, favourably reviewed its sequel, *Facing the Abyss*, as being 'as fresh and apposite today as when it was written, which to my mind [is] the mark of any important political or philosophical work'.[548] Meanwhile *British Nationalist*, the internal BNP members bulletin, lauded the work as 'a graphic portrayal of our political and social life by one of the out-standing figures of post-war Nationalism'.[549]

Whilst such overt references to such anti-Semitic publications were gradually phased out of BNP literature, the January 2005 issue of *Identity* featured an article that paid homage to Chesterton and another anti-Semitic author, S.E.D. Brown, editor of the *South African Observer*, for revealing that the Bilderberg Group 'are without doubt the sinister black heart of western "democracy".' The article, titled 'The Hidden Hand' – a traditional euphemism for Jews – was scrupulously careful not to mention the Jews but in case readers were left in any doubt as to who lay behind the Bilderberg Group a picture of Chesterton, the 'Jew-wise' British patriot, was juxtaposed against one of his racial nemesis, Henry Kissinger.[550] Many BNP members and voters would no doubt have understood such coded anti-Semitism. Polling data from 2009 suggested that 33 per cent of BNP voters subscribed to the central tenet of Chesterton's work, whether they are aware of it or not, by agreeing completely or in part, with the proposition that there exists a major international Jewish/Communist conspiracy to undermine the traditional Christian values of Britain and other Western countries.[551]

Nick Griffin's own thinking about global geopolitics also owes a debt to Chesterton's conspiratorial opus. Writing in September 2001, Griffin stated:

> We will either have a nationalist government that recognises the duty of government to protect those things that have no direct economic value – the poor, the sick, the environment, our heritage, our identity and the patrimony of generations yet unborn – or we will become the wage slaves of the new privatised fascism of the global elite, Chesterton's 'New Unhappy Lords'.[552]

Chesterton's influence endures to this day. The 'A.K. Chesterton Trust' published new editions of *The New Unhappy Lords* (2013) and *Facing the Abyss* (2014), each featuring a foreword by the former BNP MEP Andrew Brons. Echoing the *National Democrat* twenty years beforehand, Brons felt Chesterton had been 'ill-advised' to use the term conspiracy 'so frequently and to use it in the singular' because its pejorative overtones invited ridicule. Nonetheless 'Even those of us who are sceptical of much theorising about conspiracies, must take account of extremely incongruous facts that AK brought to our attention.'[553] Whilst his foreword reflected the longevity of the tradition of conspiratorial anti-Semitism embodied by Chesterton, Brons' contribution to *Facing the Abyss*, one of his last duties as an MEP, took issue with Chesterton's views on immigration, noting that 'he seemed to address the issue as though it were merely a symptom of a greater ill'. In a reversal of Chesterton's own position vis-à-vis the BNP in 1967, racial nationalists like Brons now argued that whilst Chesterton viewed immigration as being a tool of the 'international power elites', perceiving their defeat as the necessary corollary to solving the problem, 'the removal of all of the instruments of the power elite tomorrow would still leave a vast problem for us to solve.'[554] Brons comments reflected the extent to which the ideological re-prioritisation of race, immigration and overt anti-Semitism would continue to evolve after Chesterton's death in 1973.

Notes

1. A.K. Chesterton to *Rand Daily Mail*, 17 June 1965, Chesterton papers. Chesterton hoped to meet Mosley in South Africa in March 1966, see A.K. Chesterton to Oswald Mosley, 11 January 1966, Chesterton papers and A.K. Chesterton to Oswald Mosley, 11 January 1966, Hamm papers. He met Mosley again in 1968–1969 shortly after becoming National Front chairman, see A.K. Chesterton to Oswald Mosley, 9 December 1968, Chesterton papers.
2. Special Branch report, 16 July 1946 in TNA KV 2/1349/339a and 322a. Prior to this meeting, Chesterton expressed his utter indifference to Mosley: 'I mean I am quite willing to meet OM and I am quite willing to do what I can to help with the general idea, which can or cannot include him. I don't care a damn.'
3. *Sovereignty*, no. 3, November–December 1946.
4. *London Tidings*, November 1947.
5. *Truth*, 30 March 1951.
6. *Union*, no. 194, 1 December 1951. Mosley's political secretary regarded Chesterton's views as 'an absurdity in a period when there was no longer an Empire,' see E.J. Hamm to H. Ashton, 22 May 1975, Hamm papers. This was ironic given Hamm had sought out Chesterton in 1945 when running the League of British Ex-Servicemen, a development that 'greatly interested' Mosley, see TNA KV 2/890/480dx.
7. David Baker, *Ideology of Obsession: A.K. Chesterton and British Fascism* (London: I.B. Tauris, 2018), p. 198. For a broader survey of Chesterton's life, see Luke LeCras, 'A.K. Chesterton and the Problem of British Fascism, 1915–1973' (Unpublished PhD: Murdoch University, 2017).
8. A.K. Chesterton to Harry Crossley, 21 June 1966, Chesterton papers.

9. A.K. Chesterton to Harry Crossley, 2 June 1967, Chesterton papers.
10. Baker, *Ideology of Obsession*, p. 88.
11. Colin Holmes, *Anti-Semitism in British Society, 1876–1939* (London: Arnold, 1979), pp. 70–79.
12. A.K. Chesterton to Harry Crossley, 2 June 1967, Chesterton papers.
13. 2/2 Battalion London Regiment 'War Diary' in TNA WO 95/3001. Major W.E. Grey, *The 2nd City of London Regiment (Royal Fusiliers) in the Great War (1914–19)* (London: Regimental Headquarters, 1929), p. 378 records Chesterton's platoon 'came speedily into action, and did splendid work.'
14. *London Gazette*, 30 July 1919; and also TNA WO 372/4/810907.
15. A.K. Chesterton to Harry Crossley, 19 May 1967, Chesterton papers.
16. Lieutenant A.K. Chesterton MC, *How the British Army Marched to Victory* (Stratford-on-Avon: Henley-in-Arden Branch of the British Legion, 1925), p. 1.
17. A.K. Chesterton, *Blame Not My Lute*, unpublished MSS, Chesterton papers.
18. David Baker, 'The Making of a British Fascist: The Case of A.K. Chesterton' (University of Sheffield, unpublished PhD thesis, 1982), p. 55.
19. Keith Breckenridge, 'Fighting for a White South Africa: White Working-Class Racism and the 1922 Rand Revolt', *South African History Journal*, vol. 57, no. 1, 2007, pp. 228–243. Chesterton's role is noted in Norman Herd, *1922: The Revolt on the Rand* (Johannesburg: Blue Crane Books, 1966), pp. 144, 155 and 157.
20. Milton Shain, *The Roots of Antisemitism in South Africa* (Charlottesville, VA: University of Virginia Press, 1994), pp. 92–92.
21. Luke LeCras, 'A.K. Chesterton and the Problem of British Fascism, 1915–1973', pp. 107–108 records Chesterton writing in *Action*, 3 September 1936: 'The same Red types who bathed the Rand in blood are to be found in Britain. They throng Blackshirt meetings to try to break them up, knowing that on no condition will Fascist power tolerate their foulness.'
22. A.K. Chesterton, *The Immortal Shrine* (London: Stratford-upon-Avon Town Council, n.d.).
23. For a detailed discussion of this theme, see G.D. White, 'Shakespearean Fascist: A.K. Chesterton and the Politics of Cultural Despair', in Angel-Luis Pujante and Ton Hoenselaars (eds), *Four Hundred Years of Shakespeare in Europe* (Newark, DE: University of Delaware Press, 2003), pp. 89–97.
24. The *Manchester Guardian*, 29 May 1928.
25. Chesterton imbibed the cultural pessimism of German philosopher Oswald Spengler only after joining the BUF, developing his philosophy of cultural nationalism. Chesterton revised this, believing that the British Empire not 'Faustian' culture to be the imperilled geopolitical unit. Unlike Spengler, Chesterton ranked culture in terms of significance with 'Europe' at its zenith.
26. Rex Tremlett to [W.E.D.] Allen, 8 August 1933 in OMN/B/7/2, Oswald Mosley papers, Nicholas Mosley deposit, Birmingham University.
27. 'The Fascist Movement in the United Kingdom, Excluding Northern Ireland', Report no. III, Developments during August/September 1934 in TNA KV 3/58.
28. A.K. Chesterton to Alex Smith, 10 March 1970, Chesterton papers.
29. See *Action*, no. 91, 13 November 1937; and *The Blackshirt*, 7 August 1937, for instance.
30. *The Blackshirt*, no. 50, 6–12 April 1934.
31. *The Fascist Week*, no. 27, 11–17 May 1934.
32. A.K. Chesterton to Sir Oswald Mosley, 29 December 1965, Chesterton papers; and A.K. Chesterton, *Oswald Mosley: Portrait of a Leader* (London: Action Press, 1936), p. 125.
33. 'I am unable to disclose some private information in my possession about Lord Rothermere's dropping of the Blackshirts,' Chesterton wrote after the war, 'but I do not think you will deny the significance of the fact that, on the day the announcement was made, both the *Daily Mail* and the *Evening News* appeared with leading articles full of fulsome praise of Jewry,' see A.K. Chesterton and Joseph Leftwich, *The Tragedy of Anti-Semitism* (London: Robert Anscombe, 1948), p. 235.
34. Martin Pugh, 'The British Union of Fascists and the Olympia Debate', *The Historical Journal*, vol. 41, no. 2, June 1998, pp. 529–542; Jon Lawrence, 'Fascist Violence and the Politics of Public Order in Inter-War Britain: The Olympia Debate Revisited', *Historical Research*, vol. 76, no. 192, May 2003, pp. 238–237; and Martin Pugh, 'The National Government, the British Union of Fascists and the Olympia Debate', *Historical Research*, vol. 78, no. 200, May 2005, pp. 253–262.

35 Baker, *Ideology of Obsession*, p. 128; and *The Blackshirt*, no. 60, 15 June 1934.
36 Daniel Tilles, *British Fascist Antisemitism and Jewish Responses, 1932–1940* (London: Bloomsbury, 2014).
37 Chesterton, *Oswald Mosley*, p. 126.
38 Chesterton and Leftwich, *The Tragedy of Anti-Semitism*, pp. 65–66.
39 Baker, *Ideology of Obsession*, p. 127.
40 A.K. Chesterton, *Creed of a Fascist Revolutionary* (London: BUF Publications, n.d.). Though Chesterton's own revolutionary ardour dissipated, his booklet continued to inspire future generations. Frequently reprinted, most recently it was turned into an audio book by 'Radio Aryan', see www.radioaryan.com/2016/01/aryan-narrations-creed-of-fascist.html (accessed 2 May 2018).
41 TNA KV 2/2474/91a.
42 A.K. Chesterton, *Fascism and the Press* (London: BUF Publications, n.d.).
43 Special Branch report, 17 January 1935 in TNA HO 144/20144; and Thomas P. Linehan, *East London for Mosley* (London: Cass. 1996), p. 6.
44 Colin Cross, *Fascists in Britain* (London: Barrie Rockliff, 1961), pp. 137–138. BUF publications made no mention of the purge. *Blackshirt*, no. 92, 23 January 1935 featured an article from Chesterton emphasising Fascism's disciplined martial spirit and devoted service which stated:

> There is in Fascism no place for the grumbler, the double-crosser, the non-co-operator ... Only the man who works in harmony with his unit is the true Fascist, and it is through his devoted service that the Fascist cause shall triumph.

It was followed in the next week by an article arguing that Blackshirts were 'The Samurai of the Modern World' (*Blackshirt*, no. 93, 1 February 1935). The 'reorganisation' of the Leicester branch was noted in *Blackshirt*, no. 94, 8 February 1935.
45 Special Branch report, 11 March 1935 in TNA HO 144/20144.
46 'William Joyce' entry for 3 April 1935 in TNA KV 2/245/1a.
47 Special Branch report, 4 April 1935 in TNA HO 144/20144.
48 *The Blackshirt*, no. 116, 12 July 1935.
49 Richard Reynell Bellamy, *We Marched with Mosley: The Authorised History of the British Union of Fascists* (London: Black House Publishing, 2013), p. 85.
50 Chesterton, *Oswald Mosley*, pp. 164–168. For more on the theme, see Andrew Mitchell, 'Mosley, British Fascism and Religious Imagery: Fascist Hagiography and Political Myth Making', in Clyde Binfield (ed.), *Sainthood Revisioned: Studies in Hagiography and Biography* (Sheffield: Sheffield Academic Press, 1995), pp. 107–122.
51 A.K. Chesterton, *Mosley, Geschichte und Program des Britischen Fascismus* (Leipzig: Verlag E.A. Seeman, 1937), quoted in Louis Bondy, *Racketeers of Hatred* (London: Newman Wolsey, 1946), p. 144. Mosley claimed that Chesterton personally sold the rights to the biography in Germany, noting that it 'was attractively produced and I gather some 30 copies, or something, were sold in our shop' primarily to German customers, see Mosley's Advisory Committee papers, notes of re-hearing, 22 July 1940 in TNA HO 283/16/71.
52 *The Blackshirt*, no. 145, 31 January 1936.
53 *Action*, no. 91, 13 November 1937; and *Action*, no. 95, 9 December 1937.
54 Francis Beckett, *The Rebel Who Lost His Cause the Tragedy of John Beckett, MP* (London: London House, 1999), p. 136.
55 TNA HO 45/25393/33–34.
56 Margaret Bowie, interview with the author, 31 January 2005.
57 Thomas Linehan, *British Fascism 1918–1939: Parties, Ideology and Culture* (Manchester: Manchester University Press, 2000), pp. 110–111.
58 J.L. Risdon, *Blackshirt and Smoking Beagles* (Scarborough: Wilfred Books, 2013), pp. 638–639.
59 KV 2/2145/216/28a details Chesterton's clash with Captain U.A. Hick, senior administrator of the London area, and B.D.E. Donovan, the Assistant Director-General, in October 1938 which required Mosley's arbitration as Hick threatened to resign, accusing Chesterton of intriguing against him.
60 The series ran (irregularly) from *Blackshirt*, no. 207, 10 April 1937 to *Blackshirt*, no. 220, 17 July 1937.
61 A.K. Chesterton to J.A.L. Hancock, 17 January 1972, Chesterton papers.

62 Oswald Mosley, *My Life* (London: Thomas Nelson, 1968), p. 302.
63 *Blackshirt*, no. 219, 10 July 1937.
64 A.K. Chesterton to Philip Spranklin, 24 November 1937 in TNA KV 2/621. Spranklin was a close friend of Unity Mitford and wore 'Heinrich Himmler's SS badge for privileged Nazi sympathisers abroad.' Ernest R. Pope, Reuters' Munich correspondent, used Spranklin as a source.

> In return for lucre or liquor, Spranklin would lift the veil of Unity's love life with Hitler, or other goings-on within the walls of inaccessible Nazidom. Young and boastful, Phillip enjoyed proving how close he stood to the Nazi leaders,

Pope recalled in *Munich Playground* (London: W.H. Allen, 1942). Spranklin, who returned from Germany in October 1940, was killed in June 1944 during a German bombing raid together with Denyss Chamberlaine Wace, a former BUF and IFL activist who had worked as a broadcaster for Nazi radio before his repatriation, see *Daily Telegraph*, 30 June 1944; and T.M. Shelford, 6 February 1944 in TNA KV 2/185/1891a.
65 Tilles, *British Fascist Antisemitism and Jewish Responses, 1932–1940*, pp. 46–51.
66 A.K. Chesterton, *The Apotheosis of the Jew: From Ghetto to Park Lane* (London: Abbey Supplies, 1937).
67 *Blackshirt*, no. 94, 8 February 1935.
68 J.D. Dell to A.N. Field, 30 September 1935 in 73.148.055, Field papers.
69 *Blackshirt*, no. 230, 25 September 1937; *Blackshirt*, no. 235, 30 October 1937; and *Blackshirt*, no. 243, 24 December 1937.
70 *Blackshirt*, no. 232, 9 October 1937 ran an advert proclaiming:

> Don't read it at Night. Don't read it if you have a weak heart. *The Protocols of the Learned Elders of Zion*. In many countries every copy was secretly purchased and destroyed. By whom and why? Read it – and see. 1/3 from the Blackshirt Bookshop.

71 A.K. Chesterton to Alex Smith, 10 March 1970, Chesterton papers.
72 A.K. Chesterton to Revilo P. Oliver, 24 August 1970, Chesterton papers.
73 *Blackshirt*, no. 233, 16 October 1937. D.R. Thorpe, *Selwyn Lloyd* (London: Jonathan Cape, 1989), p. 54 notes that Lloyd and Sidney Silverman defended the man charged with causing Mosley GBH at Manchester Assizes on 7 December 1937.

> Our defence, putting it crudely, was that the brick which our client admittedly threw, was not the one which hit Mosley. It was not a very easy argument to make convincing but we procured a disagreement in the jury at Manchester Assizes, and the prosecution did not pursue the case.

74 A.K. Chesterton to A.G. Findlay, 18 March 1938 in TNA KV 2/1345; and *Action*, no. 110, 26 March 1938.
75 Special Branch report, 24 March 1938 in TNA KV 2/1335/24x.
76 Special Branch report, 24 March 1938 in TNA HO 144/21381/34.
77 Mosley's advisory committee papers, notes of hearing, first day, 2 July 1940 in TNA HO 283/13/65.
78 Special Branch report, 24 March 1938 in TNA HO 144/21281/34. For further details, see Peter Pugh, 'A Political Biography of Alexander Raven Thomson' (Unpublished PhD thesis: University of Sheffield, 2002), pp. 174–175.
79 TNA KV 2/1345/28a and TNA KV 2/1348/287a.
80 Special Branch report, 7 April 1938 in TNA HO 144/21381/59.
81 F3/483 report, 3 September 1943 in TNA KV 2/1245/42a.
82 Mosley, *My Life*, p. 342.
83 A.K. Chesterton to Sir Oswald Mosley, 21 November 1968, Chesterton papers.
84 *Ibid.*
85 William Joyce and John Beckett, circular letter, 30 March 1938 in 1658/9/1/3/2, Jewish Defence Committee papers, Wiener Library.
86 Special Branch report, 7 April 1938 in TNA HO 144/21381/59.
87 A.K. Chesterton, *Why I Left Mosley* (London: National Socialist League, 1938). Count Potocki of Montalk, a pretender to the Polish throne, printed the pamphlet under the imprint of his 'Right Review' press.

88 'Arthur K. Chesterton' in TNA KV 2/1346/183a.
89 Baker, *Ideology of Obsession*, pp. 137–138.
90 *Catholic Herald*, 16 December 1938; and *Catholic Herald*, 13 January 1939. Speakers included Sigmund Metz, author of *New Money for New Men* (1938), on Financial Reform under a New Order; C. Howard Jones and Sir Daniel Hall, on Agricultural Production; Dr G.T. Wrench, author of *The Causes of War and Peace* (1926), on Agriculture and the Problem of Nutrition; Anthony M. Ludovici and Odon Per, on the Financing of National Development in Italy (though illness prevented Per from speaking); and T. Balogh, of London University on German Economic Experiments. Glyn Thomas, a Yorkshire-based manufacturer, John Scalon and Ben Greene also took part in the conference which was organised by Theodore Faithfull, an ancestor of the rock singer, Marianne Faithfull.
91 *Catholic Herald*, 3 February 1939.
92 A.K. Chesterton, *Blame Not My Lute*, Chapter 16, p. 1. Bernhard Dietz, *Neo-Tories: The Revolt of British Conservatives against Democracy and Political Modernity, 1929–1939* (London: Bloomsbury, 2018), p. 198 notes that Lymington was acutely aware that Hitler's invasion of Czechoslovakia had 'put the [British] friends of Germany into an impossible position.'
93 *Candour*, vol. 11, no. 321, 18 December 1959.
94 Dan Stone, 'The English Mistery, the BUF, and the Dilemmas of British Fascism', *The Journal of Modern History*, vol. 75, no. 2, June 2003, pp. 336–358.
95 Dorril, *Blackshirt*, p. 417.
96 *Candour*, vol. 11, no. 321, 18 December 1959 records that despite his mockery of the group, Chesterton's attempts to awaken the 'Jew consciousness' amongst its membership had some resonance. Chesterton was persuaded by Collin Brooks, editor of *Truth* and a member of the Mistery, to speak on the 'Final Act of Bretton Woods' at one meeting. Chesterton recorded it was a roaring success. John Greene, subsequently head of the BBC talks department, congratulated Chesterton with the words 'we must do something about this' whilst Roger Gresham Cooke, the Recorder of the Mistery and later a Conservative MP called his speech 'superb'. However, as Chesterton noted sardonically in 1959, if both men were still fighting international finance, 'they manage to keep the noise of the encounter beyond the range of the human ear.'
97 'Extract, 11 April 1946' in TNA KV 2/1349/314 and 337c.
98 The two activists in question were David Esmé Vaughan, 'a degraded and corrupt young man' (E.B. Stamp, MI5 minute, 27 February 1942 in TNA HO 45/25746) who had joined Joyce's NSL and 'Professor' Cecil Serocold Skeels, a Charterhouse schoolmaster, private tutor and IFL activist, regarded as mentally unbalanced if not insane by the authorities. The two men, both of whom had joined Mosley's BU at the outbreak of war, had sought to communicate with Joyce in Berlin. The Nordic League 'was in closer touch with Germany than we imagined,' noted MI5 spymaster Guy Liddell in his diary. He consulted with the Director of Public Prosecutions who felt that 'there should be a case under the Treachery Act.' In the event, however, Skeels was sentenced to two years' imprisonment and interned thereafter whilst Vaughan was committed to a mental hospital, see 14 January 1941 and 19 February 1941, Guy Liddell diaries, vol. 3 in TNA KV 4/187.
99 TNA HO 144/21379/292–3. Publicly hanging Jews was a recurrent motif in the Fascist vernacular. *Blackshirt*, no. 96, 22 February 1935, recorded Chesterton being asked:

> The Nazis once said that Germany would never do any good until they had strung a Jews to everything telegraph pole. Is that your policy in England? He replied (to laughter): 'Certainly not; we have too much respect for the amenities or our countryside.'

100 Richard Griffiths, *Patriotism Perverted: Captain Ramsay, The Right Club and British Anti-Semitism* (London: Constable, 1998), p. 137. For more on this milieu, see Paul Willetts, *Rendezvous at the Russian Tea Rooms* (London: Constable, 2015). Robin Saikia (ed.), *The Red Book: The Membership List of the Right Club – 1939* (London: Foxley, 2010), pp. 88–93, a facsimile of the group's membership ledger, lists Chesterton several times under the categories 'speakers', 'writers' and 'FS' which, Saikia speculates, 'may represent an initial attempt to assemble Staff along military lines.'
101 *British Vigil* (handbill) and 'Arthur Kenneth Chesterton', 14 October 1943 in TNA KV 2/1345/581.
102 A.K. Chesterton, *Blame Not My Lute*, unpublished MSS, Chesterton papers.

103 *Ibid.* Chesterton believed his own mail was scrutinised by the authorities but was equally sanguine about the prospect.

> It is quite impossible to discover whether or not letters have been opened in the post, because the technique is to slit open the bottom of the envelope and re-seal by dipping in a solution. The process was exhibited to me some years ago by a friend of mine in the Secret Service.

A.K. Chesterton to Harold Falconer, 15 June 1973, Chesterton papers.
104 *Candour*, vol. 34, no. 6, June 1982.
105 *Ibid.*
106 Cross, *Fascists in Britain*, pp. 184–185.
107 [John Beckett and Harold Lockwood], *Failure at Nuremberg: An Analysis of Trial, Evidence and Verdict* (London: BPP, 1946), p. 14.
108 G.S. for P.M. Burke, note, 8 July 1943 in TNA KV 2/1345/28a.
109 A.K. Chesterton to W.A. Cathles, 6 March 1944 in TNA KV 2/1346/150c.
110 Geoffrey Dorman to Lord Sempill, 21 November 1941 in TNA KV 2/1335/77a. Special Branch report, 5 April 1940 in TNA KV 2/1335/43a states Dorman was 'rather fond of drink, and further, is strongly suspected of having sadistic tendencies.' After the war, he worked for the *Croydon Times* and later the *Croydon Advertiser* and the *Clapham and Balham Times*.
111 P.M. Burke, MI5 minute, 27 March 1943 in TNA KV 2/1345.
112 Greville Poke to A.K. Chesterton, 14 July 1943, Chesterton papers.
113 A.K. Chesterton to Harry Crossley, 2 June 1967, Chesterton papers; and TNA KV 2/1347/221a.
114 Andrew Sharf, *The British Press and Jews Under Nazi Rule* (London: Oxford University Press, 1964), p. 202. Defending the newspaper from accusations that it was sympathetic to Fascism, Lewis Filewood, '"Fascism" and the Weekly Review: A Response to Gregory Macdonald and Jay P. Corin', *The Chesterton Review*, vol. 3, no. 1 – fall/winter 1976–1977, pp. 21–31 argued that Chesterton 'was not an especially frequent contributor, nor was he representative of the views of the paper. He was merely noticeable because of his name.'
115 *The Times*, 22 September 1951; and *The Times*, 19 April 1977. Pepler was later noted to have addressed the Hampstead Literary Society, which was a front for Mosley's North London activists, see *Hampstead and Highgate Express*, 25 July 1947. In 1947, *Weekly Review* was sold to Kenneth de Courcy, editor of the *Review of World Affairs*, who wanted its paper ration. The two journals promptly merged to become *Review of World Affairs and Weekly Review*, see Home Office Monthly Bulletin, July 1947 in TNA KV 2/52. Following the demise of *Weekly Review*, Pepler and Jebb published another Distributist newsletter, *The Register*, until 1951. Thereafter, the Distributist tradition was upheld by Aidan Mackey who launched his own journal, *The Defendant*, in January 1953, see Aidan Mackey, 'A Distributist Remembers', in Tobias J. Lanz (ed.), *Beyond Capitalism and Socialism: A New Statement of an Old Ideal* (Norfolk, VA: IHS Press, 2008), p. 6. Mackey later numbered amongst A.K. Chesterton's most trusted confidants.
116 TNA KV 2/1347/176a.
117 TNA KV 2/1348/216z notes Joyce later used one of Chesterton's *Weekly Review* articles in his broadcasts.
118 *Daily Worker*, 20 August 1943; *Jewish Chronicle*, 27 August 1943; and also TNA KV 2/1346/92a.
119 [Illegible signature] to Oswald Mosley, 3 February 1945 in OMN/B/2/3 – 5, Oswald Mosley papers/Nicholas Mosley deposit, Birmingham University. TNA KV 2/1345/54b for the apology.
120 M.E. Roberts, MI5 minute, 13 February 1945 in TNA KV 2/889/43a. Former colleagues also declined to get involved. Chesterton's former British Vigil colleague John Clarke-Goldthorpe replied:

> To do as you request would be to take a 90% chance of smashing something I have built up; and would ruin, perhaps irretrievably, my own future and that of my wife & children & I would require a mighty cause indeed for me to risk that. I cannot therefore in any way, undertake to do as you ask,

see John Clarke-Goldthorpe to A.K. Chesterton, 25 September 1943 in TNA KV 2/1345/50a.
121 Peter Davison (ed.), *George Orwell: Two Wasted Years 1943* (London: Secker & Warburg, 1998), pp. 303–304.

122 *Weekly Review*, 9 December 1943. In *The Tribune*, 24 December 1943 Orwell retorted:

> The operative phrase is *any other war*. There are plenty of us who would defend our country, under no matter what government, if it seemed that we were in danger of actual invasion and conquest. But 'any war' is a different matter. How about the Boer War, for instance? There is a neat little bit of historical irony here. Mr AK Chesterton is the nephew of GK Chesterton, who courageously opposed the Boer War, and once remarked that 'My country, right or wrong' was on the same moral level as 'My mother, drunk or sober'.

123 A.K. Chesterton to W.A. Cathles, 6 March 1944 in TNA KV 2/1346/150c.
124 Claire Hirschfield, 'Labouchere, Truth and the Uses of Antisemitism', *Victorian Periodicals Review*, vol. 26, no. 3, fall 1993, pp. 134–142; and Claire Hirschfield, 'The Tenacity of a Tradition: *Truth* and the Jews 1877–1957', *Patterns of Prejudice*, vol. 28, Nos. 3 and 4, 1994, pp. 67–85. For Brooks's own views, see N.J. Crowson (ed.), *Fleet Street, Press Barons and Politics: The Journals of Collin Brooks, 1932–1940* (London: The Royal Historical Society, 1999). Brooks was attuned to *Truth*'s inter-war agenda having authored *Can Chamberlain Save Britain? The Lesson of Munich* (London: Eyre and Spottiswoode, 1938).
125 Stephen Koss, *The Rise and Fall on the Political Press in Britain. Vol. 2: The Twentieth Century* (London: Hamish Hamilton, 1984), p. 611.
126 Richard Cockett, 'Ball, Chamberlain and *Truth*', *The Historical Journal*, vol. 33, no. 1, 1990, pp. 131–142.
127 A.K. Chesterton to Mary Howarth, 19 July 1968, Chesterton papers.
128 TNA KV 2/1347/235a.
129 'Extract', 7 August 1947 in TNA KV 2/1249/40Ja and KV 2/423. See also David O'Donoghue, *Hitler's Irish Voices: The Story of German Radio's Wartime Irish Service* (Belfast: Beyond the Pale, 1998), pp. 194–206.
130 *Rogues Gallery* in BDBJ C6/9/3/2, JDC papers.
131 *Candour*, vol. 2, no. 5, 26 November 1954.
132 *Candour*, vol. 3, no. 109, 25 November 1955.
133 Hugh McNeile and Rob Black, *The History of the League of Empire Loyalists and Candour* (London: A.K. Chesterton Trust, 2014), p. 16.
134 A.K. Chesterton to C.R.S. Mill, 17 May 1973, Chesterton papers.
135 A.K. Chesterton to Air Vice-Marshall D.C.T. Bennett, 11 April 1973, Chesterton papers.
136 A.K. Chesterton, *Menace of the Money Power: An Analysis of World Government by Finance* (Bristol: Yeoman Press, 1946); and A.K. Chesterton, *Britain's Alternative* (Bristol: Yeoman Press: 1946).
137 Richard Cockett, *Thinking the Unthinkable: Think-Tanks and the Economic Counter-Revolution, 1931–1983* (London: Fontana, 1995), p. 73.
138 Philip Goodhart with Ursula Branston, *The 1922: The Story of the Conservative Backbenchers' Parliamentary Committee* (London: Macmillan, 1973), pp. 105–106; and 'Gracchus', *Your MP* (London: Victor Gollanz, 1944), p. 31.
139 'The National Front: Its Formation and Progress', 6 July 1945, Ivan Greenberg papers, 110/5, Mocatta Library, University College London.
140 TNA KV 2/1349/347a.
141 Joe Mulhall, 'The Unbroken Thread: British Fascism, its Ideologues and Ideologies, 1939–1960' (Unpublished PhD thesis: Royal Holloway, 2016), pp. 109–110.
142 Home Office Monthly Bulletin, January 1948 in KV 3/52.
143 *People's Post*, vol. 6, no. 11, October 1950.
144 Home Office Monthly Bulletin, April 1948 in KV 3/52; and Beckett, *The Rebel Who Lost His Cause the Tragedy of John Beckett, MP*, p. 191. Published by Beckett, *Fleet Street Preview* was edited by John Davenport, who wrote under the pseudonym 'John Agard' until replaced by Henry Newnham, *Truth*'s former editor, who wrote under the pseudonym 'Henry Alexander'.
145 Caius Marcius Coriolanus [pseud. A.K. Chesterton], *No Shelter for Morrison* (London: Dorothy Crisp, 1945).
146 Philip Faulconbridge [pseud. A.K. Chesterton], *Commissars Over Britain* (London: Beaufort Press, 1947).
147 *London Tidings* was published by Beaufort Press – which published *Commissars*. This firm was run by Archibald G. Findlay, former deputy to the BUF Chief-of-Staff Ian Hope Dundas and

Francis B. Lillis, see B.A. Hill to J.A. Drew, 25 September 1947 in TNA KV 2/1349/407a. Chesterton's assumption of the editorial chair coincided with Reed's dissolution of his business partnership with Lillis (*The London Gazette*, 23 May 1947), under which *Tidings: Weekly News-and-Views-Letter*, as it was originally called, began publication in April 1946. For Reed, see Richard Thurlow, 'Anti-Nazi Antisemite: The Case of Douglas Reed', *Patterns of Prejudice*, vol. 19, no. 1, 1984, pp. 23–24.
148 A.K. Chesterton, *Juma The Great* (London: Carroll & Nicholson, 1947), p. 61.
149 A.K. Chesterton to H.B. Isherwood, 12 October 1961, Chesterton papers. In *Confessions of an English Opium Eater* (Oxford: Oxford University Press, 1821, 1996), p. 73, Thomas de Quincey noted his drug induced nightmares of 'unimaginable horror' full of 'oriental imagery' as a result of which 'I could sooner live with lunatics, or brute animals,' than Chinese.
150 Hing Shung Mok to A.K. Chesterton, 8 July 1955, Chesterton papers.
151 A.K. Chesterton to John Tyndall, 21 September 1966 in Chesterton papers.
152 *Blackshirt*, 1 May and 26 June 1937, quoted in Baker, *Ideology of Obsession*, p. 146.
153 *The Patriot*, 17 August 1944.
154 Chesterton and Leftwich, *The Tragedy of Anti-Semitism*, p. 150.
155 A.K. Chesterton, 'Belsen and Auschwitz', *Truth*, 11 March 1949.
156 Chesterton and Leftwich, *The Tragedy of Anti-Semitism*, pp. 250–251.
157 *Candour*, vol. 14, no. 391, 21 April 1961.
158 *Candour*, vol. 4, no. 138, 15 June 1956.
159 *Failure at Nuremberg*, p. 15.
160 *Candour*, no. 19, 5 March 1954.
161 'AKC, 3 November 1947' in TNA KV 2/1349/408a.
162 Robert Lynd to A.K. Chesterton, 15 September 1948, Chesterton papers. In a handwritten note attached to the letter, Lynd noted: 'I don't think I dictated that sentence but my secretary has typed it so!'
163 Chesterton regarded Leftwich as 'a man of fearless and independent mind' and had reviewed his book *What Will Happen to the Jews?* (1936) – as 'A.C.' – for *Action*, 30 July 1936.
164 Chesterton and Leftwich, *The Tragedy of Anti-Semitism*, p. 253.
165 James Parkes, 'The Tragedy of Antisemitism', *International Affairs*, vol. 24, no. 4, October 1948, p. 627 made similar criticisms.
166 A.K. Chesterton to Colonel Israel Somen, 11 December 1948 and A.K. Chesterton to Colonel Israel Somen, 5 February 1949 in uncatalogued BDBJ file, JDC papers. Chesterton's friendship was such that he lent Somen his prized Rigby 12-bore shotgun 'as a mark of gratitude and esteem'. This did not prevent Chesterton from savaging Somen in an article in *Truth*, however.
167 Arthur Christiansen to A.K. Chesterton, 26 June 1950, Chesterton papers.
168 Collin Brooks to A.K. Chesterton, 23 February 1953, Chesterton papers.
169 The *Guardian*, 10 August 2004.
170 *Truth Has Been Murdered: An Open Letter to Ronald Staples*: Supplement to *Free Britain*, 8 March 1953.
171 *World Press News*, 27 February 1953.
172 *Birth of a Nation: The British Purpose in Central Africa* (London: London Committee of the United Central Africa Association, 1953), p. 22.
173 Douglas Williams [Colonial Office] to R.P. Bush [Secretariat of Northern Rhodesia], 24 April 1953 in TNA CO 1015/152/48; and Douglas Williams to V. Fox-Strangways [Secretariat of Nyasaland], 24 April 1953 in TNA CO 1015/152/49. Information from Chesterton, in his capacity as the Information Officer to the London Committee, was also included in the Colonial Office Press Intelligence Summary, see TNA CO 1015/152/42; CO 1015/152/46; and CO 1015/152/51.
174 Earl of Portsmouth to A.K. Chesterton, 19 February 1953, Chesterton papers.
175 *The Times*, 23 January 1953, and *The Times*, 18 March 1953.
176 A.K. Chesterton to Sir Oswald Mosley, 17 July 1953, Chesterton papers. A.G. Millar to A.K. Chesterton, 29 April in BBK/B/462, Lord Beaverbrook papers, House of Lords Record Office, hereafter Beaverbrook papers, records Chesterton was contracted from May 1953 until January 1954, employed to 'engage in such work as [Beaverbrook] may designate for you.'
177 *Candour*, vol. 34, no. 6, June 1982.
178 Colin Holmes, *Searching for Lord Haw-Haw: The Political Lives of Williams Joyce* (Abingdon: Routledge, 2015), pp. 347–349. Mosley's organising secretary Alf Flockhart, who sent the story

to McNab in Spain alleging that Chesterton had been 'dismissed' from *Truth*, was 'finding it very hard of obtain a living,' and thus his article on Joyce 'is a help to him at the expense of William.' McNab forwarded the letter to Chesterton who wrote to Mosley on 17 July 1953 (TNA KV 2/1350/446a) dismissing Flockhart's 'professionally damaging' remarks. 'Perhaps you could restrain this sweet boy as I do not think he would be a particularly bright ornament in a witness box.'

179 *Sunday Times*, 30 March 1969. Living in Jersey in 1940, Jeffrey was required, very much against his will, to surrender his gold to the Treasury under the Defence (Finance) Regulations, demanding reimbursement in £5 notes, see TNA TS 231/1304.

180 *Candour*, vol. 24, no. 534, June 1973.

181 They were: T.V. Holmes, Mrs Mary Clarkson, Miss Alice Raven, Mrs M.A. Jones, Mr and Mrs Marfleet, Mr and Mrs Cuthbert Reavely, Dr Basil Steele, L.R. Padgett, Mr and Mrs Horsfall-Ertz, Lady Elizabeth Freeman, Anthony Gittens, G.G. Gordon, Henry Devereux Gordon and Miss M.G. 'Leslie' Greene.

182 Lady Elizabeth Freeman, Dr Eugene R. Horsfall-Ertz and his wife, Ethel, and Leslie Greene were to sit on the Board of Directors. Chesterton's choice of Horsfall-Ertz, a private tutor, was interesting. Horsfall-Ertz had been detained from 29 June 1940 to 8 December 1944 on account of his association with several German intelligence agents, see TNA HO 283/35 and TNA HO 45/25730. MI5 were particularly interested in his connection to Mrs Mathilde Krafft, the German intelligence paymaster for the MI5 'double agent' SNOW, see Nigel West (ed.), *The Guy Liddell Diaries, Vol. 1: 1939–1942* (London: Routledge, 2005), pp. 65 and 158; and Nigel West, *The Guy Liddell Diaries, Vol. 2: 1942–1945* (London: Routledge, 2005), pp. 6 and 112.

183 'Circular letter RE new "News and Views Letter" sent to all who guaranteed finance, 1 July 1953'; 'News letter project report of a private (preliminary) meeting which was held at St. Ermin's Hotel, Caxton Street, SW1 on 30 July 1953' and 'Copy of letter sent to all donors to Candour' all in Chesterton papers.

184 Raven joined the LEL National Council and published several articles in *Candour* before her death in 1956. She had been one of several pro-Nazi 'enthusiasts' who formed 'The Anglo-German Group' in 1935. This group was connected with the Golden Eagle Publishing Company founded by pro-Nazi journalist George Knight whose output included *In Defence of Germany* (1933). Knight, a member of the Anglo-German Fellowship, also contributed to *Germany in the Third Reich* (1939) published by Verlag Moritz Diesterweg. 'The official representatives of the [Nazi] Party here do not treat this group of enthusiasts seriously and state the Party has no need of such dilettante support, in its propaganda or aims,' observed Special Branch. Knight had previously published a single-issue newsletter titled *European Affairs*, distributed 'freely and gratis' in German political circles in Britain by the Nazi's London *Ortsgruppe* as well as being sent to Leese's IFL, see Special Branch report, 17 January 1935 and Special Branch report, 24 April 1935 in TNA FO 371/18868.

185 *Candour*, vol. 18, no. 471, December 1967. Lady Freeman, who compiled the *Traditionalists Anthology*, became an early member of the British National Party Glasgow branch, see *Spearhead*, no. 211, May 1986.

186 *Candour*, no. 20, 12 March 1954. The number of *Candour* subscribers is unclear. The last number featuring on a list of paid-up subscribers for 1955/1956 attached to the minutes of the League Executive Committee meeting, 21 August 1957, Chesterton papers is 7,256. There are by no means that many names on the list, however, and the figure could equally denote a membership number unrelated to its circulation.

187 A.K. Chesterton to H.M. Chief Inspector of Taxes, 8 September 1964, Chesterton papers. See, for instance, Britons, receipt for £100 donation from A.K. Chesterton, 4 June 1954; Britons, receipt for £250 loan from A.K. Chesterton, 4 June 1954, Britons archive; and *Free Britain*, no. 140, January 1954; and *Free Britain*, no. 141, February 1954.

188 Douglas Reed, *Far and Wide* (London: The Non-Fiction Book Club, 1951), p. 308.

189 A.K. Chesterton to Douglas Reed, 25 October 1954, Chesterton papers.

190 Douglas Reed to A.K. Chesterton, 27 November 1954, Chesterton papers; and A.K. Chesterton to Douglas Reed, 2 December 1954, Chesterton papers.

191 Lord Beaverbrook to A.K. Chesterton, 8 December 1953 in BBK/B/462, Beaverbrook papers.

192 *Candour*, no. 10, 1 January 1954. The incident Chesterton alludes to took place after Beaverbrook pointedly asked Chesterton whether he thought him a political success or failure. Without

hesitation, Chesterton replied that Beaverbrook was a 'political failure'. After listening to his reasons, Beaverbrook insisted he write an article on the subject. 'It will be an attack,' warned Chesterton. 'Of course it will be an attack,' replied Beaverbrook. 'Get on and write it.' The article in the *Evening Standard*, 14 September 1953, lambasted Beaverbrook as a 'failure' not because he lacked sincerity, but because his protest was 'feeble', lacking the clarity, conviction and capacity for ruthless invective. Ironically, Mosley complained, writing to Beaverbrook attacking Chesterton as 'one of the few remaining die-hard fascists'. Beaverbrook rebuked Mosley, stating that Chesterton's comments were 'perfectly fair and entirely within the limits of reasonable controversy,' see correspondence in BBK C/254, Beaverbrook papers. Chesterton apparently once asked Beaverbrook why his personal views were not emblazoned across his newspapers for all to read. Beaverbrook answered that '*They* can tear the flesh from off your bones'. Chesterton drew the inference that '*they*' were the Jews. Chesterton parted company with Beaverbrook on far more amicable terms than he had done with Mosley. 'Of the three authentic men of genius I have known, Beaverbrook was one,' he later recorded in *Blame Not My Lute* unpublished MSS, p. 7.

193 A.K. Chesterton to H.M. Chief Inspector of Taxes, 8 September 1964, Chesterton papers.
194 David Motadel, 'The Global Authoritarian Moment and the Revolt against Empire', *American Historical Review*, 2019, pp. 843–877.
195 Luke LeCras, 'A.K. Chesterton and the Problem of British Fascism, 1915–1973', p. 202.
196 *Candour*, no. 21, 19 March 1954.
197 A.K. Chesterton, *Sound the Alarm!* (London: Candour, 1954); A.K. Chesterton, *Stand by the Empire* (London: Candour, 1954); and A.K. Chesterton, *Beware the Money Power* (London: Candour, 1954).
198 Quoted in *Wiener Library Bulletin*, vol. 8, nos 5–6, September–December 1954.
199 John Beckett circular to *People's Post* subscribers, 2 November 1953; *People's Post*, November 1953; *People's Post*, February 1954; and Beckett, *The Rebel Who Lost His Cause the Tragedy of John Beckett, MP*, p. 193.
200 For an 'in-house' account of its activities, see McNeile and Black, *The History of the League of Empire Loyalists and Candour*.
201 Leslie Greene to A.K. Chesterton, 15 July 1944 in TNA KV 2/1347/200a.
202 *Candour*, vol. 70, nos 2 and 3, February–March 1997.
203 A.K. Chesterton to Anthony Gittens, 25 February 1972, Chesterton papers. Graham and Hugh Greene's brother, Herbert, also contributed doggerel verse to *Candour*, notes Francis Beckett, *Fascist in the Family: The Tragedy of John Beckett MP* (Abingdon: Routledge, 2017), pp. 329–330. For more on the family, see Jeremy Lewis, *Shades of Greene: One Generation of an English Family* (London: Jonathan Cape, 2010).
204 *The Defendant*, vol. 3, no. 7, July 1955. Mackey also contributed to The Britons newsletter, that is, *Free Britain*, no. 157, June 1955. He left the League's paid employ after a year but remained an activist and trusted confidant.
205 Clifford became the 'senior' NF representative for Southern England and deputy chairman of the NF directorate. He authored *Alternative to the Common Market* (1970) and died in May 1974 aged 84, see *Candour*, vol. 25, no. 534, May 1974; *Spearhead*, no. 77, July 1974; and A.K. Chesterton to Frank Clifford, 24 April 1967, Chesterton papers. Another BUF member who joined the League's National Council was W.K.A.J. Chambers-Hunter on whom, see Liz Kibblewhite and Andy Rigby, *Fascism in Aberdeen: Street Politics in the 1930s* (Aberdeen: Aberdeen People's Press, 1978).
206 *Candour*, vol. 23, no. 522, May 1972. Stuart Rawnsley 'The Membership of the British Union of Fascists', in Kenneth Lunn and Richard Thurlow (eds), *British Fascism* (London: Croon Helm, 1980), pp. 150–164 observes 'there is much evidence to suggest that the percentage of Catholics in the BUF was higher than in the population as a whole.' For broader discussion, see Tom Villis, *British Catholics & Fascism* (London: Palgrave, 2013).
207 Robert Baden-Powell to Austen Brooks, 12 December 1960; Robert Baden-Powell to Austen Brooks, 19 December 1960; and Austen Brooks to Robert Baden-Powell, 21 December 1960; Austen Brooks to Douglas Bader, 17 April 1961 and Douglas Bader to Austen Brooks, 19 April 1961, Chesterton papers.
208 The League was contemporaneously satirised in film and literature including Alan Boulding's film *I'm Alright Jack* (1959) and Graham Greene's novel *Travels With My Aunt* (1969).

209 *Candour*, vol. 14, nos 388 and 389, 31 March and 7 April 1961.
210 *Candour*, vol. 2, no. 21, 18 March 1955; *The Times Education Supplement*, 10 August 1956; *Reynolds News*, 19 August 1956; *Candour*, vol. 6, no. 167, 4 January 1957; and Hansard, HC Deb. (series 5) vol. 557, col. 1579 (2 August 1956).
211 Auberon Waugh, *Will This Do? The First Fifty Years of Auberon Waugh, an Autobiography* (London: Century, 1991), pp. 54–57; and Alexander Waugh, *Fathers and Sons: The Autobiography of a Family* (London: Headline, 2004), pp. 320–322. Waugh contributed to *Candour*, vol. 2, nos 31 and 32, 27 May and 3 June 1955. His subsequent claims that his LEL membership was confined to his schooldays is slightly confounded by *Candour*, vol. 8, no. 243, 20 June 1958, which printed a glowing tribute to Waugh, after he was seriously wounded on national service in Cyprus, stating that he 'has been since his schooldays a member of the League of Empire Loyalists.'
212 Evelyn Waugh to Auberon Waugh, 14 June 1955 in Mark Emory (ed.), *The Letters of Evelyn Waugh* (London: Phoenix, 1995), p. 442.
213 'Extract, 12 October 1949', in TNA KV 2/1350/438a.
214 *Candour*, vol. 2, no. 18, 25 February 1955.
215 Daniel Leach, *Fugitive Ireland: European Minority Nationalists and Irish Political Asylum, 1937–2008* (Dublin: Four Courts Press, 2009), p. 183.
216 *Candour*, vol. 2, no. 22, 25 March 1955.
217 *Candour*, vol. 4, no. 125, 16 March 1956; *Candour*, vol. 4, no. 126, 23 March 1956; and *Candour*, vol. 4, nos 127 and 128, 30 March and 6 April 1956.
218 In January 1963, Greene married Richard von Goetz, a young American LEL supporter whom she had met in Germany in the previous year when visiting Otto Strasser, see *Candour Interim Report*, March 1963. Von Goetz was part of Strasser's circle and his sister, Cecile, another *Candour* contributor, was the Washington correspondent for *Deutsche Arbeit*, an extreme right-wing journal published by Strasser's lawyer, Rudolf Aschenaur. Richard von Goetz had another sister, Barbara, who served as the secretary (and mistress) to George Lincoln Rockwell, leader of the American Nazi Party from 1961 until his death in 1967. Barbara von Goetz had volunteered for the LEL during a visit to London in 1956, see Barbara von Goetz to Colin Jordan, 22 May 1964, George Lincoln Rockwell papers.
219 McNeile and Black, *The History of the League of Empire Loyalists and Candour*, p. 26.
220 A.K. Chesterton to Wing-Commander Michael Young, 15 June 1973, Chesterton papers.
221 A.K. Chesterton, *Britain's Graveyard: Dangers of the Common Market* (London: Candour, 1957).
222 *Candour*, vol. 8, no. 225, 14 February 1957.
223 *Ibid.*
224 Robert F. Dewey Jr, *British National Identity and Opposition to Membership of Europe, 1961–63: The Anti-Marketeers* (Manchester: Manchester University Press, 2009), p. 117 highlights that Lord Beaverbrook refused an invitation to speak by the Anti-Common Market Union, which held a series of rallies in the Albert Hall during 1962, because an LEL speaker had also been invited.
225 *League of Empire Loyalists Bulletin*, no. 4, 16 September 1955.
226 A.K. Chesterton to The Editor, *Daily Telegraph*, 5 September 1967, Chesterton papers.
227 *Candour*, vol. 2, no. 18, 25 February 1955. CCO 3/5/88 and CCO 3/5/89, Conservative Central Office papers, Bodleian Library, Oxford, hereafter CCO papers. For more on the Conservative response, see Mark Pitchford, *The Conservative Party and the Extreme Right, 1945–1975* (Manchester: Manchester University Press, 2011), pp. 56–63 and 78–83.
228 *Candour*, Vol. 34, nos 7 and 8, July–August 1983.
229 Mr Adamson to Sir Fergus Graham, 11 May 1955 in CCO 3/4/75, CCO papers.
230 CCO 3/5/89, CCO papers, highlights the following League members who held dual membership of the Conservative Party: The Earl of Buchan who 'has been a supporter of the MP, Sir Lionel Heald, in the past'; Lady Elizabeth Freeman supported Chichester Conservative Association; Air-Commodore G.S. Oddie, supported Midlothian Conservative Association; Sir Richard Palmer, the former governor of Cyprus was a 'large financial benefactor' to the Keswick Conservative Association whilst his wife was a supporter of the City of Westminster Conservative Association; Lord Ironside was a member of the Central Norfolk Conservative Party Executive Committee; Sir Balfour Hutchison made modest financial contributions to the Eye Conservatives in Suffolk; Joyce Mew, leader of the British Housewives' League (BHL) and an

LEL member, was a member of the Tunbridge Conservative Association; D.S. Fraser-Harris, the LEL Chairman, was a member of the Falmouth Conservative Association and Councillor Joseph Holden, another LEL member, was the vice-president of the Preston Conservative Association; Major-General Richard Hilton was Vice-Chairman of one of the branch committees of the Stratford-upon-Avon Association and, it was noted, 'works hard for the Association and is regarded by the agent as one of his most valued workers.'

231 Confidential memo from Conservative Central Office to Chairman, 5 July 1957 in CCO 3/5/88, CCO papers.
232 *Candour*, vol. 16, no. 436, 2 March 1962.
233 J.G. Darwin, 'The Fear of Falling: British Politics and Imperial Decline Since 1900', *Transactions of the Royal Historical Society*, vol. 36, 1986, pp. 27–43.
234 *Candour*, vol. 5, no. 159, 9 November 1956; and *Candour*, vol. 5, no. 160, 16 November 1956.
235 *Candour*, vol. 4, no. 140, 29 June 1956.
236 John Ramsden, *An Appetite for Power: A History of the Conservative Party Since 1830* (London: Harper Collins, 1998), p. 332.
237 Harry Legge-Bourke MP to A.K. Chesterton, 17 March 1953, Chesterton papers.
238 *Candour*, vol. 6, no. 186, 17 May 1957.
239 *Candour*, vol. 6, no. 187, 24 May 1957.
240 A.K. Chesterton to Douglas Reed, 4 June 1954; and Nettie Bonnar to Henry Kerby MP, 2 April 1957, Chesterton papers.
241 TNA HO 45/25400. Peter Wright, *Spycatcher* (New York: Viking, 1987), pp. 67–70 concurs with Mosley.
242 Hansard, HC Deb., vol. 529, cols 2326–2327 (8 July 1954). When Strasser was refused leave to disembark in 1955, Kerby tabled another question, see Hansard, HC Deb., vol. 537, col. 2222 (3 March 1955), raising the matter again in January 1957, see Hansard, HC Deb., vol. 563, cols 92–93W (25 January 1957). In 1957, the Home Office also refused permission for Gottfried Griesmayer, a former member of Martin Bormann's staff who had written speeches for Hitler and his companion Kurt Schenke, to enter the country and visit Chesterton. Chesterton again turned to Kerby, see A.K. Chesterton to Henry Kerby MP, 6 June 1957; Henry Kerby MP to A.K. Chesterton, 12 August 1957; and A.K. Chesterton to Henry Kerby MP, 14 August 1957, Chesterton papers.
243 Brian H. Robertson to Henry Kerby MP, 20 March 1957; Ministry of Health to Henry Kerby MP, 2 April 1957; and A.K. Chesterton to Henry Kerby MP, 14 August 1957, Chesterton papers. Kerby also tabled parliamentary questions to the Ministry of Health relating to sickle-cell anaemia fed to him by another of his constituents, the racial propagandist H.B. Isherwood, see H.B. Isherwood to A.K. Chesterton, 3 June 1969, Chesterton papers. Chesterton's impressions of a meeting with Kerby in the House of Commons are recorded in *Spearhead*, no. 73, February 1973. Chesterton also thought Kerby to be working for British intelligence.
244 A.K. Chesterton to Henry Kerby MP, 5 January 1962, Chesterton papers records Chesterton's anger that, though Kerby would not become a member of the LEL, he had join Edward Martell's National Fellowship.
245 Reginald Dorman-Smith to Sir Stephen Pierssene, 25 October 1956 in CCO 3/5/88, CCO papers; and *Candour*, vol. 5, no. 153, 28 September 1956.
246 The *Guardian*, 18 February 1981.
247 *League of Empire Loyalists Bulletin*, no. 5, 14 October 1955.
248 *General Election, 26 May 1955: Questions for Candidates* in BDBJ C6/2/1/5, JDC papers.
249 *Conservatives! Do You Repudiate Nigel Nicolson?* (LEL handbill, 1955).
250 For the broader context, see Lawrence W. Martin, 'The Bournemouth Affair: Britain's First Primary Election', *The Journal of Politics*, vol. 22, no. 4, 1960, pp. 654–681.
251 *Daily Mail*, 12 February 1957. BDBJ C6/7/2/4, folder 3, JDC papers, lists Friend as having 'extreme views' when a prospective parliamentary candidate for Newcastle-under-Lyme in 1950. His obituary records that he was a 'strong sympathiser' with South Africa and Rhodesia, see *Daily Telegraph*, 12 April 1988.
252 *The Times*, 15 December 1958.
253 *The Times*, 17 December 1958.
254 The *Independent*, 8 December 1990. Friend subsequently became a sponsor of the Conservative Monday Club's Action Fund run by former deputy MI6 director George Kennedy Young.

255 Nigel Nicolson, *Long Life: Memoirs* (London: Weidenfeld and Nicolson, 1997), pp. 168–176; and Geoffrey Lewis, *Lord Hailsham: A Life* (London: Jonathan Cape, 1997), pp. 174–175.
256 John Ramsden, *The Age of Churchill and Eden, 1940–1957* (London: Longman, 1995), pp. 297–298.
257 *Candour*, vol. 13, nos 366 and 367, 28 October and 4 November 1960.
258 Cockett, *Thinking the Unthinkable*, p. 126.
259 CCO 3/5/58, CCO papers. Chesterton noted in *Candour*, vol. 17, no. 446, October 1965 that 'several scores' of LEL members joined Martell's organisation 'with a view to swinging it over to the anti-Common Market cause!' The Minutes of LEL Executive Committee meeting, 21 August 1957, Chesterton papers, records the decision that 'it would be a good idea to try and get an LEL person on the Peoples League Ctte. And felt that Miss Greene would be suitable.'
260 For instances of Greene's NCRT activity, see *Candour*, vol. 6, no. 167, 4 January 1957; *Candour*, vol. 6, nos 172 and 173, 8 and 15 February 1957; *Candour*, vol. 6, no. 180, 8 April 1957; *Candour*, vol. 9, no. 267, 5 December 1958; *Candour*, vol. 8, no. 225, 14 February 1958; and *Candour*, vol. 8, no. 226, 21 February 1958.
261 CCO 3/5/58, CCO papers.
262 Leslie von Goetz, interview with the author, 24 January 2000.
263 *Candour*, vol. 6, no. 191, 21 June 1957.
264 *Candour*, vol. 14, no. 377, 13 January 1961.
265 *The Fascist*, no. 110, July 1938.
266 Arnold Leese to Anthony Gittens, 3 July [n.d.], Leese papers.
267 Arnold Leese to Anthony Gittens, 9 October [n.d.], Leese papers.
268 Arnold Leese to Anthony Gittens, 4 January 1955, Leese papers.
269 Arnold Leese to Anthony Gittens, 9 October [n.d.], Leese papers.
270 A.K. Chesterton to The Editor, *The Rhodesia Herald*, 24 September 1965, Chesterton papers.
271 *Candour*, vol. 7, no. 200, 23 August 1957.
272 *Western Destiny*, vol. 10, no. 5, May 1965 published Chesterton's article 'the trend of decadence', whilst *Western Destiny*, vol. 10, no. 8, October 1965 contains a favourable review of his book *The New Unhappy Lords*. A decade beforehand, in 1958, Chesterton had attended an Edinburgh dinner party with Alistair Harper and Thomas Leonard, two leading Northern League activists, together with the Laird of Muck ('a grand old fellow' who had supported the BUF), Air-Commodore G.S. Oddie (a former BPP activist and Christian Identity adherent), and Dr and Mrs Murray ('pleasant but not a lot of use'). A.K. Chesterton to Rosine de Bouneville, 22 May 1958, Chesterton papers notes:

> Harper and Leonard (very decent Northern League leaders whom we are trying to win over. We beat them hands down in argument, as they admitted, but did not win them from their mystique. However, I think we shall – even if we have to send you up to shock them into surrender!).

273 A.K. Chesterton to John Bean, 21 November 1967, Chesterton papers.
274 *Spearhead*, no. 25, September 1969.
275 *Candour*, vol. 13, nos 353 and 354, 29 July and 5 August 1960.
276 *Ibid.*
277 *Candour*, vol. 9, no. 254, 5 September 1958.
278 *Spearhead*, no. 25, September 1969.
279 *Candour*, vol. 13, no. 365, 21 October 1960; and *Candour*, vol. 16, no. 439, 23 March 1962.
280 *Candour*, vol. 14, no. 391, 21 April 1961.
281 A.K. Chesterton to Rosine de Bouneviaille, 23 September 1958, Chesterton papers.
282 *Candour Interim Report*, April–May 1964.
283 *Candour*, vol. 4, no. 139, 22 June 1956.
284 Keith Robbins, *The Eclipse of a Great Power: Modern Britain, 1870–1992* (London: Longman, 1994), p. 271.
285 *Candour*, vol. 13, nos 353 and 354, 29 July and 5 August 1960 notes that in India the League gained support from Captain K.K. Lalkala MBE.
286 *Candour*, vol. 6, no. 180, 5 April 1957.
287 TNA FCO 141/6622.

288 I.R. Hancock, 'The Capricorn Africa Society in Southern Rhodesia', *Rhodesian History*, vol. 9, 1978, pp. 41–62. For a wider reaction, see Richard Hughes, *Capricorn: David Stirling's Second African Campaign* (London: Radcliffe Press, 2003), pp. 162–163.
289 A.K. Chesterton Trust, *A.K. in Rhodesia – In Defence of the British Empire* (London: CD, n.d.).
290 TNA FCO 411/6622.
291 *The East African Standard*, 13 July 1957.
292 Director of Security and Intelligence to Chief Secretary, Nairobi, 22 November 1957 in TNA FCO 411/6622.
293 A.K. Chesterton to Robin Beauclair, 3 November 1967, Chesterton papers.
294 *Ibid*.
295 *Candour*, vol. 11, no. 321, 18 December 1959.
296 A.K. Chesterton to Colonel G. Wright, 27 December 1959, Chesterton papers.
297 *Candour*, vol. 12, no. 326, 22 January 1960.
298 A.K. Chesterton to H.B. Isherwood, 29 April 1971, Chesterton papers.
299 A.K. Chesterton to H.B. Isherwood, 6 May 1971, Chesterton papers.
300 *Ibid*. The document continues to circulate in extreme right-wing circles fifty years later, reprinted in 2012 in a response to the High Court's decision to allow former Mau Mau detainees who had been tortured to sue the British government, see *Candour*, www.candour.org.uk/#/9-mau-mau-oaths/4550760289 (accessed 19 October 2012).
301 See, for instance, the images in Immigration Studies, *The has not happened here, it happened in Africa in 1960* (handbill, 1960), which also graced the cover of *Spearhead*, no. 32, April 1970.
302 *Spearhead*, no. 28, December 1969. A previous article on Mau Mau in *Spearhead*, no. 26, October 1969 had ended with the simple exhortation 'Britain: Melting Pot or Cooking Pot?'
303 *Candour*, vol. 15, no. 409, 8 and 25 August 1961.
304 *Candour*, vol. 15, no. 422, 17 November 1961; and *The Guardian*, 10 November 1961.
305 *Candour*, vol. 16, no. 435, 22 February 1962.
306 *League of Empire Loyalists Bulletin*, no. 20, 13 March 1958; and Leslie von Goetz, interview with the author, 24 January 2000. Greene subsequently worked as a schoolteacher before retiring in 1984. Thereafter, she and her husband became prominent campaigners for the legalisation of cannabis which sufferers of MS and arthritis state relieves their symptoms. She stood in the 2001 general election for the Legalise Cannabis Alliance in North-East Fife, a decision that would have bemused Chesterton. Until her death in April 2005, she was a 'firm supporter' of the BNP, see *The Scotsman*, 14 May 2001; and *Identity*, no. 55, June 2005.
307 Rosine de Bouneviallle to A.K. Chesterton, n.d., Chesterton papers. For a profile, see *Candour*, vol. 3, no. 227, 28 February 1958.
308 *League of Empire Loyalists Bulletin*, no. 21, 11 August 1958, Chesterton papers.
309 *Candour*, vol. 8, no. 236, 2 May 1958; and *Candour*, vol. 14, no. 378, 20 January 1961. Another departure was that of Roger C. Gleaves whom Chesterton expelled. Gleaves subsequently founded the 'Greater Britain Campaign' whose sole activity was a largely ignored meeting in Trafalgar Square staged in order to prevent CND from being able to use the site on that date, *The Times*, 24 April 1962. Gleaves subsequently achieved infamy as a paedophile, see Hansard, HC Deb., vol. 896, cols 2359–2390 (31 July 1975).
310 *Manchester Guardian*, 12 December 1957.
311 The *Guardian*, 26 June 1958.
312 'Peer Raises a Storm', Pathé Newsreel, 12 August 1957, British Pathé, www.britishpathe.com/video/peer-raises-a-storm/query/Symon (accessed 4 September 2013).
313 Harold Macmillan, *Riding the Storm, 1956–1959* (London: Macmillan, 1971), p. 725.
314 A.K. Chesterton to Rosine de Bouneviallle, 2 October 1958, Chesterton papers. Chesterton sought redress for activists Donald Griffin and Stanley Hulka, a former Young Communist League member. Griffin, regarded as particularly promising, subsequently left the LEL and sold his story to *The People*, 29 January 1961, much to Chesterton's annoyance.
315 Luke LeCras, 'A.K. Chesterton and the Problem of British Fascism, 1915–1973', p. 207.
316 D.S. Fraser-Harris to A.K. Chesterton, 20 May 1959, Chesterton papers; and *Candour Interim Report*, November 1963. He later reprised the role.
317 *Candour*, vol. 10, no. 275, 30 January 1959 alludes to this development.
318 A.K. Chesterton to Rosine de Bouneviallle, 2 January 1958, Chesterton papers. Chesterton despatched de Bouneviallle to try and gain a £20,000 donation from Lord Nuffield who had funded

the BUF. There is no evidence to suggest she was successful, see Rosine de Bounevialle to A.K. Chesterton, 15 November 1957 and A.K. Chesterton to Rosine de Bounevialle, 20 December 1957, Chesterton papers.
319 Rosine de Bounevialle to A.K. Chesterton, 15 September 1959, Chesterton papers.
320 A.K. Chesterton to Rosine de Bounevialle, 10 December 1959, Chesterton papers.
321 *The Times*, 8 April 1958.
322 TNA HO 325/149; and *The Times*, 8 April 1958.
323 *Daily Telegraph*, 8 April 1958.
324 *Lobster*, no. 19, p. 11.
325 *The Times*, 5 May 1961.
326 *The Times*, 24 April 1962; and *The Times*, 20 July 1962.
327 A.K. Chesterton, *Tomorrow: A Plan for the British Future* (Croydon: Candour, 1961).
328 *Candour*, vol. 34, no. 9, September 1983.
329 Aidan Mackey to A.K. Chesterton, 1 August 1961, Chesterton papers.
330 'Statement for senior members of the Candour/League movement', Chesterton papers. Aside from Jeffrey, Charles Hill, a wealthy Norfolk-based backer of extreme right causes, and Lady Elizabeth Freeman were the two next largest financial benefactors, see A.K. Chesterton to Lady Elizabeth Freeman, 2 February 1966, Chesterton papers. Reader's subscriptions covered *Candour*'s running costs but Chesterton estimated staffing and overheads were an additional £2,500 a year, see A.K. Chesterton to Robert Bread, 19 January 1970, Chesterton papers.
331 'Special Statement by A.K. Chesterton', Chesterton papers.
332 A.K. Chesterton to Pedro del Valle, 26 April 1962 and A.K. Chesterton to Pedro del Valle, 9 May 1962, Pedro del Valle papers, Special Collections and University Archives, Knight Library, University of Oregon, hereafter del Valle papers. The LEL and the DAC were ideologically symbiotic, on which, see Kevin Coogan, 'The Defenders of the American Constitution and the League of Empire Loyalists: The First Postwar Anglo-American Revolts against the "One World Order"', https://socialhistory.org/sites/default/files/docs/coogan.doc (accessed 15 September 2018).
333 *Million Dollar Appeal to Help British Patriots Fight Communism throughout the World* (LEL handbill, 1963), copy in G.L.K. Smith papers, Bentley Historical Library, University of Michigan, hereafter, Smith papers. For details of the tour, see *Candour Interim Report*, July 1963.
334 *The Cross and The Flag*, vol. 14, no. 11, February 1956 reprinted 'The New Kuhn, Loeb International', from *Canadian Intelligence Service*, vol. 5, no. 12, December 1955, which in turn was republishing it from *Candour*. Another Canadian author who utilised Chesterton's work was William Guy Carr, a Lancashire-born Canadian naval officer who authored the conspiratorial classics *Pawns in the Game* (1955) and *Red Fog Over America* (1955). Carr presided over the 'Federation of Christian Laymen' in Toronto, which published its own version of Chesterton's *The Menace of World Government*.
335 Gerald L.K. Smith to A.K. Chesterton, 1 May 1963; Gerald L.K. Smith to Austen Brooks, 18 June 1963 and Austen Brooks to G.L.K. Smith, 23 June 1963, Smith papers. For *Candour*, see *Common Sense*, no. 344, 1 June 1960 and *Common Sense*, no. 382, 1 April 1962. Brooks sought out Conde McGinley for a meeting. He was in poor health, however, and it is not clear that the meeting took place. Brooks also tried to arrange a meeting in New York with an unnamed multimillionaire supporter whom Smith believed could be cultivated by the League. Contact between Smith and the LEL endured. They entertained Smith's nephew during a visit to England in 1963 and his secretary, Renata Legant, in the following year.
336 A.K. Chesterton to O.G. Allanson-Winn, 2 May 1973, Chesterton papers.
337 Essig, a close associate of G.L.K. Smith, had been active in the America First Committee and contributed to *Candour*. John Tyndall also favoured her work, see *Spearhead*, no. 3, February 1965.
338 *Austen Brooks: American Mission 1963* (CD – The A.K. Chesterton Trust, 2015) features one such speech, though there are no sleeve notes to reveal where and when on the tour it was recorded.
339 Sean P. Cunningham, 'The Paranoid Style and its Limits: The Power, Influence, and Failure of the Postwar Texas Right', in David O'Donald Cullen and Kyle G. Wilkison (eds), *The Texas Right: The Radical Roots of Lone Star Conservatism* (College Station, TX: Texas A&M University Press, 2014), p. 108; and *The Dan Smoot Report*, vol. 10, no. 28, 13 July 1964. Dan Smoot,

People Along the Way ... The Autobiography of Dan Smoot (Tyler, TX: Tyler Press, 1996), pp. 254–256 records his visit to London in 1964 but gives no details of any political assignations.

340 For Walker, see Clive Webb, *Rabble Rousers: The American Far Right in the Civil Rights Era* (Athens, GA: University of Georgia Press, 2010), pp. 134–153. Brooks also met General Clyde Watts, the attorney and DAC member who had secured Walker's release from psychiatric hospital, to which he had been committed following the riot, though charges against him were eventually dropped. Robert Welch, leader of the John Birch Society (JBS), had declined to assist Brooks whilst he was touring the United States, 'despite the fact that members of the JBS who arrived with letters of introduction to me were courteously received and entertained,' A.K. Chesterton to Revilo P. Oliver, 6 January 1966, Chesterton papers, recorded testily.

341 In Winnipeg, Brooks stayed with D.J. Mackenzie and Percy Haywood, a friend of Ron Gostick; in Yorkton, Saskatchewan, with L.L. Ball and in Ontario with A.T. Klassen, see Austen Brooks to Gerald L.K. Smith, 2 June 1963 and Austen Brooks to Gerald L.K. Smith, 15 June 1963, Smith papers. Philip de L.D. Passy to Adrien Arcand, 9 February 1963, Arcand papers, appeals to Arcand to introduce Brooks to 'influential citizens' though no further information has come to light regarding his involvement in this leg of Brooks tour.

342 *Candour Interim Report*, July 1963.

343 *Candour*, vol. 34, no. 6, June 1983.

344 A.K. Chesterton to Rosine de Bounevialle, 23 July 1963, Chesterton papers.

345 Alistair Horne, *A Savage War for Peace: Algeria 1954–1962* (New York: New York Review of Books: 2006); Hugo Frey and Christopher Flood, 'Questions of Decolonization and Post-Colonialism in the Ideology of the French Extreme Right', *Journal of European Studies*, vol. 28, no. 1, 1998, pp. 69–88; and Hugo Frey and Christopher Flood, 'Defending the Empire in Retrospect: The Viewpoint of the Extreme Right', in Tony Chafer and a Sackur (eds), *Promoting the Colonial Idea: Propaganda and Visions of Empire in France* (Palgrave: Basingstoke, 2002), pp. 195–211.

346 Guy Vanthemsche, *Belgium and the Congo, 1885–1980* (Cambridge: Cambridge University Press, 2012), p. 95.

347 *Candour*, vol. 17, no. 447, November 1965.

348 Donal Lowry, 'The Impact of Anti-Communism on White Rhodesian Political Culture, ca. 1920–1980', *Cold War History*, vol. 7, no. 2, May 2007, pp. 169–194.

349 Hansard, HC Deb., vol. 720, cols 349–364 (11 November 1965).

350 A.K. Chesterton to Robin Beauclair, 3 November 1967; and A.K. Chesterton to Robin Beauclair, 21 January 1968, Chesterton papers.

351 McNeile and Black, *The History of the League of Empire Loyalists and Candour*, p. 101.

352 A.K. Chesterton to Dr Ian Anderson, 25 July 1967, Chesterton papers.

353 *Candour*, vol. 8, no. 241, 6 June 1958.

354 In *Spearhead* no. 54, July 1972.

355 *Candour*, vol. 17, no. 452, April 1966. A.K. Chesterton to Philip Burbidge, 14 April 1973, Chesterton papers, notes Chesterton had interviewed Smith on the eve of his becoming prime minister, which was 'cordial without being excessively friendly'.

356 *The Times*, 4 November 1976.

357 Elaine Windrich, 'Rhodesian Censorship: The Role of the Media in the Making of a One-Party State', *African Affairs*, vol. 78, no. 313, October 1979, pp. 523–534; and Gerald Horne, *From the Barrel of a Gun: The United States and the War Against Zimbabwe* (Chapel Hill, NC: University of North Carolina, 2001), p. 112.

358 Horne, *From the Barrel of a Gun*, p. 104 notes the role of the CLR in connecting and coordinating a plethora of pro-Rhodesian groups across the world.

359 A.K. Chesterton to Rosine de Bounevialle, 10 February 1966, Chesterton papers. Eric D. Butler, National Director of the Australian League of Rights, who was for a period the LEL contact in Australia, also organised the delivery to Rhodesia from South Africa of a 3,000-gallon tanker, driven by his son Philip, which was officially accepted by the Duke of Montrose in June 1966, see 'The Anzacs Are Here!', *On Target*, vol. 2, no. 22, June 1966, *The Australian League of Rights*, https://alor.org/Storage/OnTarget/Volume2/Vol2No22.htm (accessed 27 January 2004).

360 Rosine de Bounevialle to A.K. Chesterton, 29 November 1965; A.K. Chesterton to Rosine de Bounevialle, 10 February 1966; A.K. Chesterton to Rosine de Bounevialle, 17 February 1966;

A.K. Chesterton to Rosine de Bounevialle, 20 February 1966; A.K. Chesterton to Rosine de Bounevialle, 23 February 1966; *Candour*, vol. 17, no. 455, June 1966; and *Candour*, vol. 17, no. 452, April 1966.
361 TNA CAB 129 (67) 162, 20 October 1967.
362 A.K. Chesterton to Philip Burbidge, 14 April 1966, Chesterton papers.
363 In *Spearhead*, no. 54, July 1972.
364 *Spearhead*, no. 25, September 1969.
365 For further details, see Graham Macklin, 'The British Far Right's South African Connection: A.K. Chesterton, Hendrik van den Bergh, and the South African Intelligence Services', *Intelligence and National Security*, vol. 25, no. 6, 2010, pp. 823–842.
366 A.K. Chesterton to Norreen Collyer, 14 December 1965, Chesterton papers.
367 A.K. Chesterton to Lieutenant-Commander G.K. Rylands, 27 May 1964, Chesterton papers. On the following day, Chesterton spoke at a *Volkskongres* (People's Congress) in Pretoria, sponsored by the Inter-Church Anti-Communist Action Committee of the Dutch Reformed Church and presided over by Dr J.D. Vorster, brother of the prime minister, which aimed to rally the forces of Afrikaner nationalism against 'liberalism'. Chesterton hoped to name the real enemy (i.e. 'the Jew') at the gathering. The main speaker was Major Edgar Bundy of the Anti-Communist Church League of America. Two years later, on 17 March 1966, Chesterton was feted with an invitation to address the University of the Witwatersrand Conservative Club. Chairman Carl Albrecht assured Chesterton, who was anxious that his name was not associated with a brawl, that there would be no violence at the meeting, not least because John Vorster 'has weeded all the realy [sic] dangerous elements out of the campus.' To assuage Chesterton's misgivings, Albrecht offered to invite several plainclothes security men as a precaution, see Carl Albrecht to A.K. Chesterton, 16 February 1966 and A.K. Chesterton to Carl Albrecht, 18 February 1966, Chesterton papers.
368 A.K. Chesterton to Austen Brooks, 30 March 1964 and A.K. Chesterton to Frank Clifford, 20 April 1964, Chesterton papers.
369 Martin Walker, *The National Front* (London: Fontana/Collins, 1977), p. 35.
370 *Candour Interim Report*, November 1963.
371 *Candour*, vol. 17, no. 443, July 1965.
372 A.K. Chesterton to Austen Brooks, 30 March 1964, Chesterton papers.
373 For a full account, see Graham Macklin, 'The British Far Right's South African Connection', pp. 823–842.
374 *Candour Interim Report*, no. 14, June–July 1964.
375 A.K. Chesterton to Brigadier Hendrik van den Bergh, 6 July 1965, Chesterton papers.
376 Anthony Gittens to A.K. Chesterton, 22 July 1965, Chesterton papers.
377 Birley paid the fees for two of Mandela's children to attend boarding school whilst he was incarcerated on Robben Island, see T. Lodge, *Mandela: A Critical Life* (Oxford: Oxford University Press, 2006), p. 142.
378 A.K. Chesterton to Major-General Hendrik van den Bergh, 27 May 1966, Chesterton papers.
379 Major-General Hendrik van den Bergh to A.K. Chesterton, 14 June 1966, Chesterton papers.
380 Gordon Winter, *Inside BOSS: South Africa's Secret Police* (London: Allen Lane, 1981), p. 163.
381 A.K. Chesterton to Robin Beauclair, 8 December 1967, Chesterton papers.
382 *Candour*, vol. 16, no. 439, 23 March 1962.
383 A.K. Chesterton to Charles Hill, 30 May 1961, Chesterton papers.
384 A.K. Chesterton to Commander W.I.L. MacEwen, 25 August 1965, Chesterton papers.
385 *Spearhead*, no. 25, September 1969.
386 *Candour*, vol. 184, no. 184, 3 May 1957 indicates Chesterton was working on such a book as early as 1957.
387 *The Times Literary Supplement*, 23 September 1965.
388 A.K. Chesterton to Harry Crossley, 24 April 1967, Chesterton papers made the claim that 'so far from making a penny piece out of the book I am at the present moment £1,100 the poorer because of it.'
389 A.K. Chesterton to H.B. Isherwood, 6 June 1969, Chesterton papers.
390 For a full discussion of the transnational impact of Chesterton's ideas, see Graham Macklin, 'Transatlantic Connections and Conspiracies: A.K. Chesterton and *The New Unhappy Lords*', *Journal of Contemporary History*, vol. 47, no. 2, 2012, pp. 270–290. Chesterton also received

Carto's publications. His name features on the mailing list for Liberty Lobby's *Washington Observer*, see Group Research papers, Box 202, Liberty Lobby Confidential file (Horne Collection), Butler Library, Columbia University, New York.
391 Revilo P. Oliver to A.K. Chesterton, 6 November 1971, Chesterton papers.
392 Marinus F. La Rooji, 'From Colonial Conservative to International Anti-Semite: The Life and Work of Arthur Nelson Field', *Journal of Contemporary History*, vol. 37, no. 2, 2002, pp. 223–239.
393 A.K. Chesterton, *The New Unhappy Lords* (Liss: Candour Publishing Co., 1972), p. 247.
394 A.K. Chesterton to H.L. Fendall, 22 April 1965, Chesterton papers.
395 A.N. Field to A.K. Chesterton, 29 February 1960 in 73.148.049, Field papers.
396 A.K. Chesterton to A.N. Field, 20 December 1960 in 73.148.049, Field papers.
397 Chesterton, *The New Unhappy Lords*, p. 197.
398 *Candour*, no. 1, 30 October 1953.
399 Chesterton, *The New Unhappy Lords*, p. 171.
400 For example, James Perloff, *The Shadows of Power: The Council on Foreign Relations and the American Decline* (Appleton, WI: Western Islands, 1989), pp. 72–73 and 254, which refers to Chesterton as 'the distinguished British author'. Earlier works stressing its importance include Dan Smoot's *Invisible Government* (Dallas, TX: Dan Smoot Report, 1962), which claimed the objective of the CLR was 'to convert America into a socialist state and then make it a unit in a one-world socialist system.'
401 Chip Berlet and Matthew N. Lyons, *Right-Wing Populism in America: Too Close for Comfort* (New York: Guilford Press, 2000), 202. *The New Unhappy Lords* was not the first book to make such claims about the Bilderberg Group. Phyllis Schlafly, *A Choice, Not an Echo* (1964), posited that the Republican Party was secretly controlled by an elite cabal dominated by Bilderberg members who sought to pave the way for global communist conquest, a theory that differed from Chesterton's insofar as he believed Communism and Capitalism served the same Jewish master.
402 A.K. Chesterton to Anthony Gittens, 25 February 1972, Chesterton papers.
403 Chesterton, *The New Unhappy Lords*, p. 201.
404 Liberty Lobby, *Spotlight on the Bilderbergers: Irresponsible Power: Documents from the Archives of the Liberty Lobby* (Washington, DC: Liberty Lobby, n.d.), pp. 4–5, for instance.
405 Chesterton, *The New Unhappy Lords*, p. 53.
406 *Ibid.*, pp. 211–217.
407 A.K. Chesterton, 'Weinberg Replaces Baruch', *American Mercury*, May 1959, pp. 132–137.
408 Chesterton, *The New Unhappy Lords*, p. 156.
409 Brigadier H. van den Bergh to Miss Moyna Traill-Smith, 18 May 1965; and A.K. Chesterton to Brigadier H. van den Bergh, 2 June 1965, Chesterton papers.
410 Major-General Hendrik van den Bergh to A.K. Chesterton, 14 June 1966, Chesterton papers.
411 *Ibid.*
412 *Ibid.*; and Brian Bunting, *The Rise of the South African Reich* (Harmondsworth: Penguin Books: 1969) pp. 74–75.
413 Major-General H.J. van den Bergh, 'Sabotage in South Africa', in *Battle for the Mind: Papers Read at the International Symposium on Communism, September 1966, Pretoria* (Potchefstroom: NCCC, 1967), pp. 21–45.
414 *Rand Daily Mail*, 30 September 1966; and *Die Transvaller*, 30 September 1966.
415 Major-General Hendrik van den Bergh to A.K. Chesterton, 9 November 1966, Chesterton papers. Van den Bergh held Chesterton in such high regard that when the latter returned to South Africa in winter 1966, he tried to arrange an appointment for him with South Africa's new Prime Minister, John Vorster. 'I know he would appreciate a chat with you,' he stated. It was not to be, however. Van den Bergh proved too busy to arrange a meeting and Chesterton returned to England in February 1967, though not without van den Bergh's profuse apologies, see Major-General Hendrik van den Bergh to A.K. Chesterton, 2 March 1967, Chesterton papers.
416 *Spearhead*, no. 25, September 1969.
417 A.K. Chesterton to Colonel Philip de L.D. Passy, 9 November 1965, Chesterton papers.
418 *Candour*, vol. 12, no. 348, 24 June 1960.
419 Chesterton and Leftwich, *The Tragedy of Anti-Semitism*, p. 242.

420 *London Tidings*, 6 September 1947.
421 *A.K. Chesterton, Learned Elders and the BBC* (London: BPS, 1961). The pamphlet was published by The Britons for whom publishing and re-publishing *The Protocols* was their bread and butter. 'Read The Learned The Protocols of the Learned Elders of Zion And Judge For Yourself' enjoined the back page of pamphlet.
422 A.K. Chesterton to J.F. Noble, 13 July 1973 and 25 July 1973, Chesterton papers.
423 *Candour*, vol. 7, no. 195, 19 July 1957.
424 A.K. Chesterton to Professor Revilo P. Oliver, 24 August 1970, Chesterton papers. The Britons expressed their concerns about Mullins' reliability as early as 1958, see Anthony Gittens to A.K. Chesterton, 29 September 1958, Britons archive.
425 *Candour*, vol. 21, no. 503, September 1970. Mullins never received a copy of *The New Unhappy Lords* though he remembers it 'was well received here', see Eustace Mullins, letter to the author, 30 May 2008. He felt aggrieved by Chesterton's attack largely because

> a few weeks later Chesterton writes to me asking me to do anything I could to help him collect royalties from [Thomas] Serpico [their shared publisher] ... I thought it was *chutzpah* on his part, first he denounces me, then he asks for my help,

quoted in Alexander Baron, *Eustace Clarence Mullins: Anti-Semitic Propagandist or Iconoclast* (London: Infotext, 1993), p. 22.
426 *Candour*, vol. 7, no. 195, 19 July 1957. For the genealogy of the canard, see 'Israel Cohen, A Communist – and his Book that Never Was', *Wiener Library Bulletin*, vol. 19, no. 3, July 1965. *Candour* has continued to quote from the fogery, see *Candour*, vol. 70, no. 8, August 1997.
427 *Candour*, vol. 17, no. 448, December 1965.
428 Joshua Trachtenberg, *The Devil and the Jews: The Medieval Conception of the Jew and Its Relation to Modern Anti-Semitism* (Philadelphia, PA: Jewish Publication Society of America, 1983).
429 A.K. Chesterton to Professor Revilo P. Oliver, 20 April 1971, Chesterton papers.
430 A.K. Chesterton to Frank Clifford, 16 October 1964, Chesterton papers. Standing as 'Independent Loyalist' candidates Brooks polled 497 votes (1.3 per cent) in Wandsworth, Streatham; de Bounevialle polled 391 votes (0.7 per cent) in Petersfield, whilst Greene polled 629 votes (0.7 per cent) in East Fife.
431 A.K. Chesterton to Frank Clifford, 24 September 1965, Chesterton papers.
432 A.K. Chesterton to Frank Clifford, 7 October 1965, Chesterton papers.
433 Rodney Legg, *Legg Over Dorset* (Wellington: Halsgrove, 2011), pp. 17 and 30.
434 A.K. Chesterton to M.F. Bellasis, 10 May 1966, Chesterton papers; and *Candour*, vol. 17, no. 452, April 1966. One supporter subsequently sent Chesterton 'small packages of uncut gems' as a contribution to funds, see A.K. Chesterton to Aidan Mackey, 13 June 1968, Chesterton papers.
435 Importantly, despite the merger, Chesterton never formally disbanded the League for financial reasons. This became apparent when a supporter, one Edward Gonzalez-Moreno, died bequeathing £1,000 to the LEL and £1,000 to Spanish dictator General Franco, see the *Observer*, 17 November 1968. Chesterton had ensured the League remained a legal entity for just such an eventuality. The NF had expected Gonzalez-Moreno's money to come to them. Chesterton felt, however, that the NF had 'a long way to go before it wins my confidence' and was 'quite determined' it would gain neither this inheritance nor the £3,000 the League still had in its own accounts. The NF was not a 'successor movement,' Chesterton argued, because 'the LEL has never been wound up and I do not propose that it shall be ever wound up,' see A.K. Chesterton to Aidan Mackey, 19 December 1968, Chesterton papers. This fact was raised again in a letter to the *Sunday Times*, 20 April 1969.
436 'National Front Party' in TNA HO 325/8.
437 *Daily Telegraph*, 20 July 2005.
438 John Bean, *Many Shades of Black: Inside Britain's Far Right* (Bloomington, IN: Ostara, 2013), p. 123; and Andrew Fountaine, *The Meaning of an Enemy: Collected Writings from 'Combat' Magazine, 1960 to 1965* (Marston Gate: Ostara, 2012).
439 The *Guardian*, 9 October 1948.
440 The *Guardian*, 17 December 1949.
441 National Front, *NF Objectives*, quoted in *Tribune*, 28 March 1969.
442 'The National Front', signed J.E. Bean to BNP members, 1967.

443 *Candour*, vol. 18, no. 461, February 1967.
444 Rosine de Bounevialle to A.K. Chesterton, 20 March 1967, Chesterton papers.
445 A.K. Chesterton to Rosine de Bounevialle, 3 July 1967, Chesterton papers.
446 *Candour*, no. 478, July 1968.
447 A.K. Chesterton to Robin Beauclair, 3 November 1967, Chesterton papers.
448 A.K. Chesterton to Harry Crossley, 24 April 1967, Chesterton papers notes Brooks confessed to stealing £1,500 'but this is certainly an under-estimate.' A.K. Chesterton to Rosine de Bounevialle, 17 March 1967, Chesterton papers noted that £730 was 'unaccounted for' between September and December 1966 alone.
449 A.K. Chesterton to Harry Crossley, 24 April 1967, Chesterton papers.
450 A.K. Chesterton to W.A. Brooks, 30 August 1967, Chesterton papers.
451 Bill Bryson, *Notes from a Small Island* (London: Black Swan, 1996), p. 92. Bryson was an early journalistic colleague.
452 *Candour*, vol. 36, no. 10, October 1986.
453 Walker, *The National Front*, p. 74.
454 McNeile and Black, *The History of the League of Empire Loyalists and Candour*, pp. 108–109.
455 A.K. Chesterton to Aidan Mackey, 23 September 1968, Chesterton papers.
456 Avril Walters to A.K. Chesterton, 6 January 1967 and A.K. Chesterton to Avril Walters, 10 January 1968, Chesterton papers. Chesterton kept himself apprised of events within Nazi *groupuscules* through Avril Walters, a member of his inner circle who fed him information from inside groups like the NSM. 'BNP, GBM and NSM members are highly interchangeable units,' she noted, 'one often belonging secretly to one or two units other than the one to which he officially belongs.' Avril Walter's husband was reportedly a member of the German NPD which was a step too far for Chesterton who regarded it as an 'absurdity' that an Englishman should belong to a foreign party. G.K. Rylands, the League chairman, felt it explained why Walters was 'starry eyed' about National Socialism, see A.K. Chesterton to G.K. Rylands, 7 June 1968 and G.K. Rylands to A.K. Chesterton, 8 June 1968, Chesterton papers.
457 Derek Talbot Baines to A.K. Chesterton, 26 April 1968, Chesterton papers. Baines also visited the NPD in Munich in October 1967.
458 A.K. Chesterton to Derek Talbot Baines, 2 May 1968, Chesterton papers.
459 *Candour*, vol. 18, no. 469, October 1967.
460 *Candour*, vol. 20, no. 485, February 1969.
461 A.K. Chesterton to Lieutenant-Colonel Robert Gayre, 15 May 1967, Chesterton papers.
462 Legal advice on *Southern News* in TNA DPP 2/4378.
463 For Chesterton's account of the case, see *Not Guilty: An Account of the Historic Race Relations Trial at Lewes Assizes in March 1968* (Chulmleigh: Britons, 1968).
464 A.K. Chesterton to F. Ratcliffe, 17 May 1973, Chesterton papers.
465 *The Times*, 22 September 1997.
466 The *Sunday Times*, 25 February 1968.
467 Fred Lindop, 'Racism and the Working Class: Strikes in Support of Enoch Powell in 1968', *Labour History Review*, vol. 66, no. 1, 2001, pp. 79–100.
468 Simon Heffer, *Like the Roman: The Life of Enoch Powell* (London: Faber & Faber, 2008), pp. 462–467. The notable feature of such letters, notes Amy Whipple, 'Revisiting the "Rivers of Blood" Controversy: Letters to Enoch Powell', *Journal of British Studies*, vol. 48, no. 3, 2009, p. 720, was that 'supporters envisioned Powell as the politician they wanted, not the politician that he was' and as such he became a 'blank screen' onto which they projected their own image of 'the leader they wanted, the man they believed that Britain needed.'
469 Stan Taylor, *The National Front in English Politics* (London: Macmillan, 1989), p. 20 notes that migration declined from 60,000 in 1967 to 44,000 in 1969.
470 Donley T. Studlar, 'British Public Opinion, Colour Issues and Enoch Powell: A Longitudinal Analysis', *British Journal of Political Science*, vol. 4, no. 3, July 1974, pp. 371–381.
471 *The Times*, 24 April 1968.
472 *Private Eye*, 31 January 1969.
473 *Candour*, vol. 19, no. 476, May 1968.
474 Heffer, *Like the Roman*, p. 465.
475 A.K. Chesterton to Denis Pirie, 9 December 1968, Chesterton papers.
476 *Ibid*.

477 A.K. Chesterton to H.B. Isherwood, 19 May 1969, Chesterton papers. The NF Sub-Directorate for Student Affairs to Enoch Powell, 7 December 1968, Chesterton papers, further indicates the support Powell's anti-immigration stance had amongst younger NF activists.
478 A.K. Chesterton to H.B. Isherwood, 29 May 1969, Chesterton papers.
479 A.K. Chesterton to H.B. Isherwood, 6 June 1969, Chesterton papers.
480 G.R. Hutson to A.K. Chesterton, 9 November 1969, Chesterton papers.
481 Aidan Mackey to A.K. Chesterton, 9 November 1969, Chesterton papers.
482 *The Times*, 24 April 1968.
483 Taylor, *The National Front in English Politics*, p. 21.
484 *Spearhead*, no. 21, November–December 1968.
485 NF National Directorate Minutes, 26 June 1969, Chesterton papers.
486 A.K. Chesterton to H.B. Isherwood, 11 September 1969, Chesterton papers.
487 A.K. Chesterton to Dr Lance Taylor, 13 June 1973, Chesterton papers.
488 A.K. Chesterton to Andrew Fountaine, 29 May 1968; and A.K. Chesterton to G.K. Rylands, 7 June 1968, Chesterton papers.
489 Andrew Fountaine to Area and Branch Organisers, June 1968, Chesterton papers.
490 A.K. Chesterton to Frank Clifford, 15 July 1968, Chesterton papers.
491 A.K. Chesterton to Andrew Fountaine, 19 June 1968, Chesterton papers.
492 *Candour*, no. 481, October 1968.
493 *Spearhead*, no. 21, November–December 1968.
494 *Candour*, vol. 22, no. 492, September 1969.
495 'Fascist and Pro-Fascist Organisations' in TNA HO 325/8.
496 Matthew Goodwin, *New British Fascism: Rise of the British National Party* (Abingdon: Routledge, 2011), p. 28; and Heffer, *Like the Roman*, pp. 553–565.
497 *Candour*, vol. 21, no. 553, September 1970.
498 A.K. Chesterton to Rosine de Bounevialle, 11 March 1969, Chesterton papers. Martin Walker, *The National Front*, pp. 88–89 highlighted Chesterton's growing approbation at the rowdy tactics employed by some activists after the founding of the party.
499 *National Front Code of Conduct by The National Director* (London: Albion Press, 1969).
500 *Candour*, vol. 21, no. 553, September 1970. *Spearhead*, no. 18, February–March 1968 notes Brown led the newly formed Croydon NF branch.
501 Chesterton was already in receipt of regular reports of the Action Committee's incessant intriguing, for instance, 'Report of NF Sabotage to A.K.C. from Several Sources', Chesterton papers.
502 A.K. Chesterton to Aidan Mackey on 23 October 1970, Chesterton papers.
503 *Candour*, vol. 21, no. 504, November 1970. A.K. Chesterton to Rosine de Bounevialle, 19 November 1970, Chesterton papers for date of resignation.
504 A.K. Chesterton to Rosine de Bounevialle, 20 October 1970 (a), Chesterton papers.
505 *Ibid*.
506 A.K. Chesterton to John Bean, 7 December 1970 and A.K. Chesterton to John O'Brien, 7 December 1970, Chesterton papers.
507 G.K. Rylands to Martin Webster, 12 January 1971, Chesterton papers.
508 John Tyndall to Aidan Mackey, 11 December 1970, Chesterton papers. *Electronic Loose Cannon*, no. 21, 11 October 2007, alleged that Mackey was later suspended from his job as headmaster of a Bedfordshire primary school after *The Sunday People*, 18 January 1976, 'ran a front page story in which he [Mackey] admitted playing "trouser-dropping games" with eleven-year-old boy pupils in the school's changing rooms.' Mackey denied any imputation of 'indecency'. He subsequently established a name for himself as a leading authority on G.K. Chesterton.
509 Aidan Mackey to A.K. Chesterton, 13 December 1970, Chesterton papers.
510 *Spearhead*, no. 39, January 1971.
511 *Spearhead*, no. 41, March 1971.
512 A.K. Chesterton to Aidan Mackey, 15 January 1971, Chesterton papers.
513 *Candour*, vol. 22, no. 509, April 1971; and A.K. Chesterton to John O'Brien, 2 August 1971, Chesterton papers.
514 *Candour*, vol. 22, no. 506, January 1971.
515 *Candour*, vol. 22, no. 511, June 1971.
516 A.K. Chesterton to Rosine de Bounevialle, 19 February 1971, Chesterton papers.

517 *Spearhead*, no. 43, June 1971.
518 A.K. Chesterton to Colin Jordan, 27 August 1971, Chesterton papers.
519 Paul Jackson, *Colin Jordan and Britain's Neo-Nazi Movement: Hitler's Echo* (London: Bloomsbury, 2017), pp. 169–170.
520 *Candour*, vol. 24, no. 530, February 1973.
521 A.K. Chesterton to A.J. Dickerson, 11 April 1973, Chesterton papers.
522 'Members' Bulletin – From the National Director to all Members', 26 September 1969, Chesterton papers.
523 A.K. Chesterton to Ben Biggs, 25 June 1973, Chesterton papers.
524 A.K. Chesterton to Michael McLaughlin, 2 July 1973, Chesterton papers. Rosine de Bounevialle continued cooperating with Jordan following Chesterton's death, see *Candour*, vol. 25, no. 546, September 1974.
525 A.K. Chesterton to Ben Biggs, 9 July 1973, Chesterton papers.
526 *Spearhead*, no. 103, March 1977.
527 A.K. Chesterton to Frank Clifford, 11 April 1973, Chesterton papers.
528 *Candour*, vol. 22, no. 509, April 1971.
529 John Tyndall to A.K. Chesterton, 6 June 1973 and A.K. Chesterton to John Tyndall, 13 June 1973, Chesterton papers.
530 A.K. Chesterton to Martin Webster, 11 May 1973, Chesterton papers.
531 Many were collected in *Arthur Kenneth Chesterton, MC* (*c*.1973) as a tribute by friends and colleagues.
532 Revilo P. Oliver to A.K. Chesterton, 2 August 1973, Chesterton papers.
533 Revilo P. Oliver to A.K. Chesterton, 8 August 1973, Chesterton papers. 'The main support for dangerous nostrums like Laetrile comes from far-right groups to whose politics of paranoia the fantasy of a miracle cure makes a serviceable addition, along with a belief in UFOs,' noted the writer Susan Sontag who also noted incidentally that the John Birch Society, to which Oliver had once belonged, had distributed a 45-minute film called, '*World Without Cancer* … like a world without subversives', see Susan Sontag, *Illness as Metaphor and AIDS and its Metaphors* (London: Penguin, 2002), p. 70.
534 A.K. Chesterton to Eric Butler, 9 August 1973, Chesterton papers.
535 Unsigned letter to H.B. Isherwood, 29 August 1973, Chesterton papers.
536 *Candour*, vol. 18, no. 469, October 1967.
537 Bill Baillie, 'European Outlook #12, December 2014: Populist Parties', *European Outlook*, 30 November 2014, http://europeanoutlook.blogspot.co.uk/2014/11/european-outlook-12-december-2014.html (accessed 14 January 2015).
538 A.K. Chesterton to Ben Biggs, 25 July 1973, Chesterton papers. Chesterton began training Kevan Bleach, 'who is very well-versed in our general case and highly intelligent,' to take over from him when he died, see A.K. Chesterton to Ivor and Joan Benson, 18 July 1973, Chesterton papers.
539 'De Bounevialle used the cellars at Forest House to store the A.K. Chesterton archives, which have become required reading for today's far-right activists,' noted her obituary in *The Sunday Times*, 16 July 2000.
540 *Candour*, vol. 16, no. 436, 2 March 1962. A.K. Chesterton to D.C. Nesbit, 23 April 1973, Chesterton papers notes:

> Unfortunately this country is in a much sorrier position than it was in 1953 but we can at least claim that there is no single development which we did not foresee and against which we failed to issue warnings. One such warned from the very first was the swamping of our country with peoples of unassimilable stock, while *Candour* was the first journal in the world to point to the dangers of our adherence to the EEC.

541 David G. Robertson, '(Always) Living in the End-Times: The "Rolling Conspiracy" of the Conspiracy Milieu', in Sarah Harvey and Suzanne Newcombe (eds), *Prophecy in the New Millennium: When Prophecies Persist* (Farnham: Ashgate/Inform, 2013), pp. 207–219.
542 *Spearhead*, no. 39, January 1971.
543 *Spearhead*, no. 438, August 2005.
544 Martin Webster interview with the author, 21 July 2009.
545 *Candour*, vol. 34, no. 6, June 1983.

546 *National Front News*, no. 23, June 1980; *New Nation*, no. 1, summer 1980; and *Nationalism Today*, no. 9.
547 British National Party, Books, www.bnp.org.uk/books.html (accessed 30 September 2001).
548 *Identity*, no. 5, January 2001.
549 *British Nationalist*, February 2003.
550 *Identity*, no. 51, January 2005.
551 'YouGov Poll', Channel 4, June 2009, www.channel4.com/news/media/2009/06/day08/yougov poll_080609.pdf (accessed 19 March 2019). For a more recent survey indicating the prevalence of conspiracy theories within British society, see 'Conspiracy Theories', YouGov: Cambridge Centre, https://d25d2506sfb94s.cloudfront.net/cumulus_uploads/document/5j57dtwlc0/YGC%20Conspiracy%20Theories%20(GB).pdf (accessed 19 March 2019).
552 *Identity*, no. 13, September 2001. Eleven years later glimmers of Chesterton's influence upon Griffin can still be observed, see @NickGriffinBU, Twitter, 12 April 2012, http://twitter.com/nickgriffinmep/statuses/190332973311213568 (accessed 11 April 2012).
553 A.K. Chesterton, *The New Unhappy Lords* (London: A.K. Chesterton Trust, 2013), pp. 13–14.
554 A.K. Chesterton, *Facing the Abyss* (London: A.K. Chesterton Trust, 2014), p. 13.

4 Colin Jordan
Dreaming of the Nazi 'Vanguard'

In May 1937, aged fourteen, Colin Jordan and his aunt spent a fortnight in Cologne under the aegis of the Anglo-Continental Family Centre, an organisation based in London Bridge, who had billeted them with a Germany family in the city's Hohenzollern Ring Strasse. The trip provided a 'political awakening' for the teenager. 'I appreciated the atmosphere, which was most remarkable, and in my experience unprecedented, that euphoria which was general in the population over there,' he later remembered. 'I couldn't have failed to be impressed by the feeling of well-being and confidence in the future that was manifest everywhere in Germany, there was a joyfulness, a joy in living that I have never come across anywhere else.'[1] Jordan retained his euphoria for the Third Reich for the rest of his life. In this experience were the seeds of Jordan's subsequent political development that saw him become the 'godfather' of the post-war British 'neo-Nazi' movement and its most vocal proponent of violent, direct action.[2]

Born in Birmingham on 19 June 1923 to Percy Jordan, a college lecturer and his wife, Bertha (*née* Beecham), the headmistress of a Warwickshire school, John Colin Campbell Jordan grew up in rural Leek Wootton. His parents provided a formative political influence. Particularly pivotal was his father's belief in the 'kinship' between Germany and Britain, likely a product of his experiences in the First World War, which 'helped form Colin's political mindset of race before nationality, leading him to become a National Socialist with a pan-European outlook rather than a plain British Nationalist.'[3] Growing up in a rural environment also influenced his future 'blood and soil' trajectory. 'As a young man the exhileration [sic] of being in the woods, feeling in tune with Nature. From this came my politics,' Jordan, a keen Boy Scout, later recalled.[4]

It was whilst attending the prestigious Warwick School, possibly the world's oldest boy's school, from 1934 to 1941, that Jordan encountered 'politics' in a concrete form after obtaining a copy of *Action*, the newspaper of Mosley's BUF, from a fellow pupil. Thereafter, Jordan gained a place at Sidney Sussex College, Cambridge but the Second World War interrupted his education. Having been an active member of his school's army cadet corps, Jordan volunteered for the Fleet Air Arm, qualifying in December 1942. He proved 'unsuitable' for flight duty, however, and, after ten months as a naval airman, was transferred to the Royal Air Force before being allowed to defer his service, having previously requested to be transferred to a non-combatant role because of his belief in a negotiated peace.[5] This stance put Jordan very much in the minority. By the end of the war, only 0.2 per cent of conscripts claimed conscientious objector status.[6] Following a brief spell working as a teacher in Solihull, Jordan transferred to the Army in November 1943, where a military psychiatrist determined his conscientious objection quite genuine, 'although his reasons are those of an immature intellect.'[7]

Unfit for a combat unit, the Army posted Private Jordan to the Royal Army Medical Corps (RAMC) at the Royal Herbert Hospital, South East London. Jordan found life in the RAMC debilitating, physically and mentally. Whilst not being formally registered as a conscientious objector, the Army treated Jordan as such, confining him to duties as a nursing orderly. He was 'a very round peg in a square hole', noted the military authorities whilst pondering why he did not pursue his discharge from the Army on the grounds of conscientious objection. 'However, it is not for us to suggest this to him.'[8] Another report described Jordan as an 'introspective lad' who 'cannot adjust himself to the barrack room life'. An Army doctor prescribed him sedatives. Jordan's political stance, noted the report, was viewed a symptom of his failure to adjust to Army life and, because he is well educated and an only child, 'both factors make his Army life singularly difficult.'[9] MI5 noted that Jordan's career in the Forces 'was not a happy one; it is clear that he is a neurotic subject who takes himself too seriously'.[10] Nonetheless, Jordan persevered, his menial existence probably enlivened by the political contacts he was cultivating. Indeed, during this period, one of Jordan's commanding officers observed, presciently, that although Jordan was impressive in many ways 'if he felt so inclined could very easily establish himself as "quite a little Fuehrer" amongst those with whom he came into contact'.[11]

Jordan first came to the attention of the Security Services in October 1941 after contacting the Daily Worker Defence League, though thereafter all his contacts were on the extreme right. In December 1942, he joined the British National Party (BNP), a minute *groupuscule* run by Edward Godfrey, owner of a chain of fish and chip shops in Middlesex, who had served in the Navy with Admiral Sir Barry Domvile, founder of the pro-Nazi Link group. The BNP, with its platform of monetary reform and anti-Semitism, emerged from discussions between numerous former BUF members and sundry anti-Semitic activists associated with the Duke of Bedford, who provided Godfrey with a guiding hand. Following its implosion in April 1943, Jordan joined its successor, the English Nationalist Association, which quickly dissolved without achieving anything of note.[12]

MI5 also noted that during 1944 Jordan was gathering information about the anarchist movement and, in early 1945, observed him frequenting the offices of the International Friendship League, an organisation founded in 1932 for 'the promotion of a spirit of friendliness and mutual toleration amongst the peoples of the world'. The group had recently focused its resources 'on being kind to Refugees', which was somewhat ironic given Jordan's subsequent political trajectory.[13] When the war ended, Jordan applied to transfer from the RAMC to the Army Educational Corps, though his political views made the military authorities wary of assenting to the request.[14] Jordan was still serving in the RAMC when he began associating himself with the Mosleyite revival, attending the December 1945 meeting at the Royal Hotel in central London at which Mosley and other detainees met publicly for the first time since 1940.[15] In March 1946, he joined Jeffrey Hamm's British League of Ex-Servicemen, a front for Mosley's political resurrection, taking part in several of its increasingly violent meetings in Ridley Road, East London.[16]

These political dalliances palled in comparison to the importance of his encounter with Arnold Leese, erstwhile leader of the Imperial Fascist League (IFL), who became his political mentor. Jordan first encountered Leese sometime prior to 1941. It was not until five years later, however, that his interest was seriously piqued after reading an article in *The Sunday Pictorial* on 10 March 1946.[17] Impressed by Leese's obdurate refusal to apologise for his Nazi past, Jordan wrote him on 31 August: 'Dear Sir, I would be glad to have information on the policy and standpoint of your organisation, and its relations to other organisations, if any.'[18]

> The result was a characteristically brief and blunt Arnold Leese reply which I most vividly recall as saying that his ideas were just the same as before the war, and that if he was not the age he then was, he would have just the same organisation as before. There followed three crisp sentences forever engraved on my mind: 'The Jews are our misfortune! Democracy is death! Fascism is the only solution!'[19]

Shortly afterwards, Jordan was handed a copy of *Gothic Ripples* by one of Leese's followers at a meeting. Jordan later recalled:

> I must admit that there and then some of its contents relating to the war were such strong meat as to be hard for me then to digest. However, before long nothing less meaty satisfied me, and I have become an Arnold Leese disciple for life.[20]

Despite his lifelong allegiance, Jordan only ever met Leese once, though he corresponded with him until his death in 1956, which he regarded as 'an irreplaceable loss to the nationalist cause in Britain.'[21] 'In his character coupled with his convictions Arnold Leese was for me one of the most impressive persons I have ever known in politics,' noted Jordan. 'Certainly he had the greatest formative effect on my own politics and thereby my life through the enlightenment provided by his guiding principle that "Race is the basis of politics"'.[22]

Discharged in August 1946, in the same month he had contacted Leese, Jordan took up his place at Cambridge, studying for a history degree (and later a master's degree too). In the same month, he also joined a group in which Leese's influence was writ large. Founded in April 1939, the British People's Party (BPP) had campaigned against 'usury' and against war with Nazi Germany. Ben Greene and John Beckett, its founders, were both former Labour activists. In 1925, Beckett had become the Labour Party's youngest MP (Peckham) as well as secretary and election agent to Clement Attlee the future Labour prime minister, before drifting into the Independent Labour Party. Shortly after losing his seat in 1931, Beckett joined Mosley's BUF, rising to become one of its chief propagandists, editing both its newspapers, before acrimoniously departing from the party in 1937. Thereafter, he formed the National Socialist League with William Joyce whose path to Fascism led to treachery and in 1946 to the gallows.[23] 'Next to Arnold Leese, my prime political mentor, I rate John Beckett the most impressive political figure I then met', Jordan subsequently recalled.[24]

The BPP President was the Duke of Bedford, who combined a mania for arachnids with monetary reform and an admiration for Hitler. The Duke had never wavered in his opposition to the war, which, he argued in 1942, 'represents an attempt by the money-lending financiers, currency speculators and big business monopolists to destroy the relatively sane financial system of the Axis Powers'.[25] The Duke was quick to deny the extent of Nazi atrocities against the Jews as 'greatly exaggerated by propaganda' whilst asking rhetorically whether Hitler's prejudice against the Jews was understandable? 'Yes, very,' replied the Duke to his own question.[26] Leese regarded the Duke with mixed emotions, viewing him as 'never more than halfway on the road to Fascism'. He also harboured a sneaking suspicion that the Duke escaped internment in 1940 because of Jewish ancestry.[27] Sidney Salomon of the Jewish Defence Committee (JDC) remarked of the Duke:

> He is a character which it is quite impossible to analyse, who would not live long in Nazi Germany and yet he is to all intents and purposes one of the most insidious influences on Nazi ideology in this country.[28]

MI5 harboured no such ambivalence, declaring in 1941 that, should the Duke fall into enemy hands, 'he would be likely to be set up as a gauleiter or the head of a puppet British government'.[29]

Unlike the Duke, both Beckett and Greene were interned. The BPP disbanded as a result but reformed in July 1945 with Beckett as general secretary and the Duke as president. Leese regarded Beckett as an unprincipled opportunist but overcame his antipathy and instructed his followers to join the party. He soon lost faith in the organisation's ability to achieve any tangible results, however.[30] Jordan did not. The BPP, he argued 'is neither of the orthodox Left nor Right, but is concerned with the propagation of a middle way of national reform'.[31] The future parameters of Jordan's political philosophy were visible in outline through his contributions to the *People's Post*, the party newspaper, in which he argued for a 'genuine and permanent Anglo-German unity' based on common 'racial affinity' whilst also railing against 'alien' immigration albeit not in the crude racist terms with which he would become synonymous.[32] His anti-Semitic proclivities were more apparent from his operation of a 'literary stall' on Cambridge marketplace from which he hawked copies of *The Protocols of the Elders of Zion*.[33] The *People's Post* regularly feted Jordan's efforts, highlighting his emergence as the party's most dynamic recruit, though given the BPP had shrunk to fifty members by 1948, this was not perhaps an outstanding achievement.[34] In February 1948, Jordan joined the BPP National Council.[35]

Jordan was politically active on the university quad too, joining the university debating society and contributing to *Varsity*, the student newspaper of which he became 'circulation manager'.[36] During May 1947, he argued in *Varsity* with anti-fascist journalist Frederic

Mullally following his assertion that the BPP had 'pronounced Fascist tendencies'. Mindful of the stigma attached to the word, Jordan claimed the word was simply a 'sobriquet of the Left' and a 'hysterical device' used to close down debate.[37] In their replies, Mullally and the University Labour Club made 'quite a good case', noted MI5 wryly.[38] Whilst at Cambridge, Jordan founded his own Social Action Movement, issuing two newsletters *New Approach* and *England Arise!* These set out a policy wholly derivative of the BPP. Jordan's Social Action Movement morphed into the Nationalist Reform Club and thence into the Cambridge University Nationalist Club (CUNC), which he established with Harry Rogerson – the only other BPP activist in Cambridge.[39] The CUNC advocated a 'democratic alternative' to Capitalism and Communism, 'reconciling individual liberty with social justice and national welfare'.[40] It gained brief notoriety after inviting Labour MP H.N. Smith (Nottingham South), an ardent anti-Zionist and monetary reformer, to speak, most likely because he had recently declared in Parliament that 'the State of Israel is obnoxious and odious to most British working men'.[41] Despite pressure, Smith refused to decline the invitation, though ultimately the meeting fell through anyway.[42]

This episode aside, despite disrupting a few local events, the CUNC generated precious little public interest on its own merits.[43] When the Duke of Bedford addressed a meeting in October 1948, only thirty people attended, including ten elderly women 'who appeared to have attended the meeting out of idle curiosity to see the Duke of Bedford.'[44] By early 1950, the BPP was in terminal decline. Heckled at public meetings with cries of 'go back to Germany', even the otherworldly Duke realised that 'there was no headway to be made against established public opinion'.[45] Struggling to staunch its haemorrhaging membership, it adopted a more 'elastic' form of organisation and re-branded itself as the National Freedom Rally.[46] It disappeared virtually overnight on 11 October 1953, when the Duke died in a shooting 'accident' whilst out hunting on his estate.

Jordan had already moved on by this juncture. Graduating with a second-class degree in history in 1949, he moved to Leeds to take up a teaching post whilst running his own 'Nationalist Book Service' and a 'Nationalist News Service'. He soon relocated to Birmingham, however, working alongside his father as a private tutor at a local correspondence college whilst running the Birmingham Nationalist Club (BNC), which functioned 'to bring together a variety of people, simple nationalists, racial nationalists and national socialists.'[47] The group's aims were non-sectarian and it operated an open-door policy regarding membership though the majority of those associated with the group came from the Midlands' branches of Mosley's Union Movement (UM) including Peter Ling who became a long-term political collaborator.[48] The 'majority' of these activists broke away from the UM 'because they did not consider Mosley's organization adopted a sufficiently strong attitude against the Jews', observed MI5.[49]

In January 1950, Jordan began producing *Defence – Against Alien Infiltration and Control*, which served as a mouthpiece for his campaign against immigration. 'Amongst other things we are endeavouring to take up the coloured issue in this city,' Jordan wrote to the Canadian fascist leader Adrien Arcand, 'for Birmingham now has no less than 4,000 coloured persons living in its bounds – a surprising state of affairs for a city situated not in Africa, but in the very heart of England'. The local and the global fused in Jordan's mind and the best riposte to 'world government protagonists … is assuredly the alliance of nationalists in Europe and the Americas'. To this end, Jordan had already initiated contact with G.L.K. Smith and his Christian Nationalist Crusade, advertising his publication, *The Cross and The Flag*, in *Defence*. Jordan also imported anti-Semitic literature from Sweden's Einar Åberg and from Canada, selling copies of Arcand's *The Key to the Mystery* through his book service. Such international contact was psychologically important for activists in small impecunious *groupuscules* like the BNC. 'We shall be glad at any time to receive news of the progress of the nationalist cause overseas; and to supply news from England in return', Jordan wrote to Arcand. 'It interests our members and makes them feel part of something much bigger when we can put little bits in *Defence* about kindred movements abroad',[50]

Ahead of the 1950 general election, Jordan and the BNC mounted an anti-Semitic campaign against the Labour MP Julius Silverman (Erdington), proclaiming 'Silverman for Israel' and inaugurating 'Operation Dial', a telephone canvassing initiative enjoining electors to 'Vote British' though the tenor of the campaign was often less subtle.[51] Having received a financial subvention from Leese, Jordan felt duty bound to apprise him of this anti-Semitic campaign, sending the ageing IFL leader press clippings from Birmingham's *Evening Dispatch* reporting on an anti-Semitic daubing campaign in 'Julius the Jew's constituency' which, Jordan confessed, he was responsible for.[52] Proudly recalling the campaign, Jordan stated that Silverman had

> had a fit when a group got to work in his constituency, attending his meetings and raising the Jewish Question, selling nationalist literature outside his meetings, even putting up nationalist slogans in white lead paint and letters 3 ft. high a half a dozen points in the area.[53]

The *Birmingham Journal* noted that local fascists were extremely active in support of his rival, Conservative candidate Air-Commodore J.A. Cecil Wright, whom Silverman had displaced in 1945.[54] Soon afterwards, Birmingham's Chief Constable highlighted that, whilst small, the BNC represented the 'principal source' of anti-Semitic propaganda in the City.[55]

Jordan's activities brought him to the attention of Oswald Mosley's followers. Geopolitically, Jordan's advocacy of a 'British Block'[56] in world politics put him at odds with Mosley's European politics. 'Truly Sir Oswald's mind had passed far beyond Fascism, Democracy, or anything he had previously stood for', Jordan had lamented. Indeed, in championing European union Mosley,

> had graduated to the cosmopolitan front ... his new ideas, whatever fresh support they may attract, are nicely calculated to rid him sooner or later of all sincere nationalists, and to reduce his old following to those who adhere to the dictum: 'The Leader is always right'.[57]

Despite this stance, UM activists continued to woo Jordan, hoping he might be converted to their cause.[58] Conscious that the party was haemorrhaging support in the region, Jeffrey Hamm, the UM Northern organiser, was despatched to address the BNC in January 1951. The UM hoped that 'as a result of this meeting, several of the BNC will have advanced beyond their nationalism to the new conception of European Union'.[59] The BNC ignored Hamm's overtures though *Union*, the UM newspaper, and continued to find utility in advertising Jordan's 'Nationalist Book Service' to its readership.[60] Indeed, Alexander Raven Thomson, *Union*'s editor, regularly availed himself of Jordan's literary service but lamented: 'It is such a pity that he is obsessional on the Jewish problem'.[61]

Out on a limb, geographically speaking, in the West Midlands, Jordan's contacts increased exponentially during this period through his involvement with a profusion of largely London-based racial nationalist *groupuscules* orbiting The Britons, the anti-Semitic publishing house.

Jordan had attended its meetings since his demobilisation, bringing him into contact with many veterans of Britain's pre-war racial nationalist movement.[62] Jordan became increasingly involved with the group, folding *Defence* into *Free Britain*, The Britons' news-sheet in December 1951. Thereafter, he penned a weekly news digest column for *Free Britain* titled 'Newsview' together with innumerable articles attacking immigration.[63] Jordan had previously participated in a Britons' conference in February 1950 aimed at unifying the fissiparous 'Jew-wise' *groupuscules* that dotted the political hinterland.[64] Embracing the idea, he addressed the 'May Day rally of Free Britons' in April, which was organised by the Tottenham Nationalist Party, an amalgam of former IFL activists and former UM activists and, after that, groups like the Nationalist and Empire Unity Party and Edwin Bassett Horton's Bath and West Nationalist Rally. The Special Branch officer observing Jordan speaking at the latter event regarded his speech as a 'more or less polished effort'.[65]

League of Empire Loyalists

In 1953, having gained an MA degree, Jordan temporarily abandoned teaching to take up employment as a sales representative for the Inverness-based soap manufacturer Thomas Headley & Sons, causing him to wind down the BNC. The group revived two years later as a vehicle for the increasingly vehement anti-immigration campaign then taking place in Birmingham.[66] The BNC, Jordan declared, was the 'one and only Midlands movement prepared to go out into the streets and fight the menace. All power to its fist!'[67] Jordan combined this militant anti-immigration activism with his membership of the League of Empire Loyalists (LEL), founded the previous year by A.K. Chesterton to 'sound the alarm' at the decline of the British Empire. Jordan joined the League in June 1955 because 'I believe that Mr. Chesterton deserves the support of all shades of nationalist opinion for the lead he is giving on fundamental nationalist issues.'[68] Chesterton, impressed by Jordan's potential, sent him a £50 donation.[69] Jordan's initial contribution to the LEL was to compile a list of people he knew to be 'solidly rightwing' though not yet 'within the nationalist camp' from whom the LEL could solicit support.[70] Less than a month after he joined, Chesterton appointed Jordan to the LEL Executive Committee and thereafter as his Midlands organiser.[71] Explaining his rapid elevation, Leslie Greene, the LEL organising secretary, informed Jordan that Chesterton 'has the greatest respect for your part in the movement particularly with regard to future leadership'.[72] At the LEL AGM on 29 October, Jordan obtained election to the group's Executive Committee.[73]

In January 1956, Jordan returned to live with his recently widowed mother in Birmingham.[74] That same month, his mentor, Arnold Leese, also passed away. Jordan led the tributes in *Free Britain*:

> The death of Mr Arnold Leese is an irreplaceable loss to the nationalist cause in Britain ... In a political field in which there were many comings and goings, he stood his ground from the day he entered it until the day he died. So it seems to me of comparatively minor importance whether you or I agreed or disagreed with some of his views. Transcending that is the tribute we owe him for his heroic fight for the freedom of our country from Jewish occupation and control. Let us salute a great Englishman and a grand old warrior.[75]

Leese's enduring influence upon Jordan's world-view was evident in his first book, *The Fraudulent Conversion: The Myth of Moscow's Change of Heart* (1956) published later that year. Leese had financed its publication with monies from the Beamish largesse. The Britons published it.[76] *The Fraudulent Conversion* was part of Leese's ideological rearguard action against the influence of the mercurial American anti-Semite Francis Parker Yockey and his Eastern-orientated geopolitical approach. Like Leese, Jordan believed that Yockey was talking twaddle. For Jordan, it was axiomatic that Communism and Judaism were synonymous, reflected in the early working title of the book, *Communism is Jewish*, which distilled its central ideological message.[77] Jordan felt likewise. *The Fraudulent Conversion* argued *pace* Leese, that reports of Soviet 'anti-Semitism' were false and could not be otherwise. Soviet 'anti-Semitism' was nothing more than a reflection of an internal power struggle between two factions of 'World Jewry'.[78] *Candour*, the League journal, recommended the book as 'an ideal introduction to those who know nothing but the *Daily Worker* level of Communism'.[79] Reviews from outside the extreme right were less generous. 'The most fanatical attack on the Jewish race that one has read since the Nazis were at the height of their frenzy,' was how one of the few newspapers to give it the time of day described it.[80]

Returning to teaching after his sojourn as a soap sales representative, Jordan taught English and mathematics at Stoke Secondary Modern Boys School in Coventry. Chesterton championed Jordan's political career but was aware from the outset that the extremity of his racial views threatened to push him beyond the pale. Writing to him in February 1956, Chesterton stated that although Jordan's desire to deport Blacks and Jews from England was one 'which many people in their hearts no doubt share', it was not 'practical politics' and to propagate such a view, particularly with regard to Jews, would ensure he was not taken 'seriously'. Anything beyond attempting to 'subordinate Jewish power and influence' to 'British power and influence' was 'sheerly Utopian'. Indeed, 'the work upon which we are engaged', wrote Chesterton, 'is sufficiently quixotic without having to charge impossible windmills'.[81] Chesterton's letter revealed an increasing gulf between his own 'research'-based activities aimed at highlighting the machinations of the 'Money Power' and Jordan's own activist-based anti-Semitism which favoured a 'final solution of the Jewish problem based on apartheid'.[82] Despite the increasing tension between the two approaches, Chesterton did not see fit to remove Jordan as an LEL officer.

Jordan was heavily involved in organising the League's protests at the State visit of Marshal Nicolai Bulganin and Soviet Premier Nikita Khrushchev to Britain in April 1956 through which he met John Bean, the League's Northern organiser. Jordan distrusted Bean initially because of his past involvement with Mosley.[83] During the prolonged protest, Jordan contacted some 'tough' members of the staunchly anti-Communist Ukrainian émigré community in Coventry, some of whom had collaborated with the Nazis, their puppet government and the *Einsatzgruppen* death squads.[84] Throughout the visit, the LEL sought to cause the British government the maximum amount of embarrassment. A rigorous policing operation was mounted to prevent the LEL from disturbing the diplomatic equilibrium and, whilst there was 'a certain amount of minor horseplay' from the League, 'who demonstrated angrily, displayed and distributed anti-Russian leaflets wherever the Communist leaders passed', the 'meticulous work' of Special Branch and the 'efficient organisation' of the Metropolitan Police ensured 'nothing unseemly occurred'.[85]

The League did indeed distribute thousands of leaflets during its campaign, produced with the assistance of J.F. Stewart, chairman of the Scottish League for European Freedom (which also operated as a 'front' for MI6 operations against Soviet Russia), which highlighted the invidious record of the two Soviet leaders. League activists also delivered a tenfoot spoon to Downing Street as a reminder of the adage that he who sups with the Devil should have a long spoon.[86] The protests climaxed as Anthony Eden greeted the Soviet leaders at Victoria Station. As he did so, Leslie Greene shouted, 'Sir Anthony Eden has just shaken hands with a murderer'. Police arrested her and Jordan.[87] Chesterton was delighted and 'proud' to number them amongst his friends, though the publicity cost him his chairman, Martin Burdett-Coutts, scion of the famous banking family, who resigned, so *Candour* claimed, due to pressure from his family.[88] Later that year, Jordan contributed a critique of the Soviet strategy of coexistence to the German Nazi journal *Nation Europa*, a major forum for extreme right thought in the post-war period.[89]

White Defence Force

Increasingly, however, it was opposition to 'coloured immigration' not anti-Communism that inspired Jordan's activism. His visceral racism was closer in many respects to that espoused by the racist organisations of the American Segregationist South, whose 'kindred fight' he was keen the LEL should support. Jordan kept abreast of events through a plethora of American journals. These included *Arkansas Faith*, organ of the White Citizens' Council of Arkansas ('a prominent force in the South's fight against the desegregation dictates of the race mixers'); numerous publications from the Association of Citizens' Councils of Mississippi ('which is a very big element in the fight'); and *The Virginian* ('another factor among many more in the great Southern alliance in defence of white civilisation'). 'It is good to see that in the South the people who are inspiring and leading the white man's fight are almost all of good Aryan stock and, moreover, mostly of British ancestry', wrote Jordan. 'We are dealing with real Americans here, folk who can think the same way as we do', he told Greene, 'not the rabble of toad-like Hebrews and half-breeds infesting the big cities of the north east'.[90] Jordan was equally eager to support those 'fellow fighters for white civilisation' – white South Africans – to the point of supporting their cessation from the Empire, if it meant the preservation of a 'white' South Africa.[91]

Influenced by the racist politics of the Deep South and apartheid South Africa, Jordan lobbied the LEL to 'Keep Britain White'. In *Free Britain*, Jordan argued that given the government's 'intolerable irresponsibility' over immigration, he would not be surprised to learn of the emergence of 'Vigilante groups on the lines of the American Ku Klux Klan' to counter the problem directly.[92] Privately, he was on the cusp of forming such a group himself. In the following month, he wrote Leslie Greene, the LEL organising secretary, that if resources were directed towards whipping up 'a mass movement on the Colour issue' then 'any good mob orator with a sound truck and plenty of colour and noise could set that part of town where the local Harlem is situated on fire.'[93] The menacing undertone of violence in Jordan's letter horrified her. 'We are not at all attracted to the idea of setting your local Harlem on fire', scolded Greene.[94]

Jordan's choice of political associates also appalled Chesterton who baulked at Peter Ling and Dick Tynan, two UM/BNC activists who were also active with the LEL in the Midlands. Jordan badgered Chesterton to give Ling paid employment. Chesterton refused after learning that Ling had been involved in a 'little enterprise' against the local offices of the Communist Party in Birmingham. Nor was Chesterton amused to learn that Ling was associated with Peter Greenslade, an extreme right-wing activist who, 'spoke with the utmost abandon of collecting guns and acquiring a van which, among other things, would run by accident into groups of coloured people in Brixton and elsewhere'. He personally admonished Ling and invited Jordan to do likewise, unaware of the latter's own connection to Greenslade.[95]

Jordan knew neither man would ever be acceptable to Chesterton but valued the political and physical muscle they afforded him. Jordan decided therefore to found a White Defence Force (WDF), enabling UM and LEL members to combine outside their respective organisations for more militant action against political opponents than their parent organisations would be willing to countenance.[96] WDF members frequently travelled down to London from the Midlands in order to attack opponents' political meetings and it is clear that Jordan envisaged them as the nucleus of a paramilitary force. Fresh from violently disrupting a Movement for Colonial Freedom (MCF) meeting at Conway Hall, London, Jordan wrote:

> Roll on the day when we can blow a whistle, as it were, and fast cars converge from all over the country to hit the enemy with the impact of a thunderbolt. This is definitely the new conception in political organisation: the small, trained, disciplined, specialist, elite-force, mechanised, permanently alert: the introduction of the blitzkrieg principles into politics.[97]

Chesterton was horrified to learn of the activities of the WDF and issued Jordan a stinging rebuke stating he wanted no part in 'brawls' or any other 'general stupidity' that would bring the LEL into disrepute.[98]

Tensions reached a head at the LEL AGM in October 1956. Jordan proposed a resolution demanding the LEL restrict membership to Britons excluding Jews and other minorities. 'If you do not want to exclude them', he wrote to Greene, 'then you must want to include them'. A perceived lack of progress towards fulfilling a resolution adopted at the previous year's AGM to 'stop coloured immigration' further exacerbated Jordan's agitation. His own resolution represented a challenge to Chesterton to pick up the gauntlet and 'stop the rot'.[99] It failed and Jordan petulantly resigned from the Executive Council accusing Chesterton of being 'kosher'. He remained an LEL member until April 1957, when he resigned to concentrate on his role as British 'agent' for *Northern World*, journal of the Northern League, a pan-European 'cultural' society dedicated to spreading the Nordic racial philosophy of National Socialism.[100] Chesterton lamented Jordan's decision to adopt the 'millstone' of National Socialism, writing to him:

> It is a very great grief to me that a man of your calibre should vitiate his usefulness because of what seems to me a complete incapacity to differentiate between the strategy which the enemy fears and the strategy which the enemy welcomes. However, I now despair of getting you to see that it is you who is playing the kosher game.[101]

Undeterred by Chesterton's caustic rebuke, Jordan, with Peter Greenslade as his London deputy, continued their activities as before, though now calling themselves a 'Frei Korps'. The groups' actions were, noted the police, 'directed towards terrorizing Jews, Negroes and communists and the establishment of a National Socialist dictatorship' though most of their 'wildcat' schemes were ultimately 'harmless and ridiculous' since they lacked the funds to enact any of them. In September 1957, however, the group secretly travelled down to Brighton to daub six-foot high anti-Semitic and pro-Fascist slogans on a local monument. When Special Branch visited Greenslade on 27 September to caution him about this incident, the 'Frei Korps' collapsed amidst paranoia, aware that their supposed security had been breached. For a moment at least, police intervention caused Jordan to reign in his activities as he contemplated emigrating to South Africa.[102]

White Defence League

Jordan did migrate eventually, but only from the West Midlands to London. He quartered himself at 74 Princedale Road, Holland Park, the home of the Britons Publishing Society, chaired by former IFL activist Anthony Gittens. That Jordan was able to relocate there was due to Leese, his recently deceased mentor, having owned the property. When Leese died in January 1956, he had bequeathed an estate worth £18,378 to his widow. This considerably augmenting the Beamish largesse that Leese in his turn had inherited from his mentor in 1948, and which was still funding racial nationalist activities a decade later. This entire estate, now controlled by Winifred Leese, included the Princedale Road property. Mrs Leese permitted Jordan to use the top two floors of the building.[103] Largely dormant during the week, the property came alive at the weekends when Jordan travelled down from Coventry to meet fellow activists who likewise converged upon it.[104]

Relations between Jordan and The Britons were initially cordial. The Britons had published *The Fraudulent Conversion* whilst Jordan regularly contributed to, and at one point even edited, their newspaper *Free Britain*.[105] Jordan had also recently joined The Britons executive committee in February 1957 to inject some political dynamism into the organisation's moribund affairs.[106] The Britons also published Jordan's overtly racist tabloid, *Black and White News*, copies of which appeared during the course of July 1958.[107] *Black and White News* was replete with lurid headlines such as 'Blacks Invade Britain', 'Blacks Seek White Women' and 'Colour Influx Worsens Housing Problems'. Tellingly, the newspaper also contained adverts for a host of American racist publications including *The Citizens Council*, *The White Sentinel* and *The Virginian*, to connect Notting Hill to the Deep South.[108] This was not a development confined to the extreme right fringe. Indeed, it was indicative of broader debates about 'multi-racial' Britain taking place contemporaneously.[109] *Black and White News* had a reciprocal resonance in the United States. Willis Carto, founder of the influential Liberty Lobby, imported and sold copies of the tabloid stating that it 'gives many shocking facts about the invasion of some 500,000 coloured undesirables into Britain, once a white nation.'[110] Only one issue of *Black and White News* ever appeared, however. In a portent of things to come, racist activists sold such literature outside the grounds of Queens Park Rangers and West Ham football clubs.[111]

The timing of Jordan's relocation to London was fortuitous. Shortly after establishing himself at Princedale Road, 'race riots' erupted in neighbouring Notting Hill on 31 August 1958. Whilst not directly involved in the violence, Jordan wasted no time stoking the resultant racial tension. He rushed to disseminate the remaining copies of *Black and White News*, whilst ordering a further print run of 10,000 copies from The Britons.[112] In September, Jordan formed a new organisation to capitalise on the violence, the White Defence League (WDL), its name a reflection of Jordan's grievance narrative.[113] Its membership was restricted to those of 'Northern European ancestry' drawn from 'the five races of Europe' (the Nordic, Mediterranean, Alpine, Dinaric and East Baltic), a racial categorisation defined by Nazi racial scientist Hans F.K. Günther.[114]

Jordan's increasingly public racist activism led to a commensurate decline in his relations with The Britons. Gittens had no objection to Jordan's politics but he was resistant to Jordan's desire to convert the building into the WDL headquarters, fearing that this would endanger The Britons own activities. In return, Jordan mocked Gittens, writing to him:

> I am sorry indeed if the emergence, at last, of an active political movement to implement the ideas propagated by the literature handled by your Society is to be viewed by

your Society as an unwelcome intrusion when housed in a distinct portion of the same building. Surely books are useless unless they lead to action?[115]

Although her late husband had kept The Britons afloat financially, Mrs Leese now backed Jordan during the ensuing struggle for control of the property, resulting in The Britons being ejected from the premises in January 1959. Their departure was acrimonious. WDL activists, impatient to use the building, assaulted The Britons' President, Commander Frank Graves, and two other Committee members as they left. 'It was precisely this type of enthusiastic youngster that we feared to be associated with', Gittens lamented.[116] Thereafter, Mrs Leese gave Jordan free reign of the Princedale Road property, rent-free. He moved in on 28 March, and promptly re-christened the property 'Arnold Leese House'. It served as his base of operations for over a decade until he relocated to the Midlands in 1968.[117]

Whilst Leese's money and property played a crucial part in preserving and perpetuating the 'Jew-wise' tradition, it is important not to understate the agency of his widow, Winifred Leese, who loyally supported Jordan 'in my efforts in continuation of her husband's work'.[118] Indeed, whilst Jordan only met his political mentor in person once – at a Britons dinner in 1955 – he regularly visited Leese's widow from 1956 onwards. Jordan's contact with her only ceased when Mrs Leese went into a care home in around 1970. Thereafter, Ann Story, their 'adopted' daughter, wrote to Jordan

> and requested that I did not seek to visit Mrs Leese because I could be identified at the place and my 'political notoriety' could cause the staff to react unfavourably to Mrs Leese. I conformed to the request with regret at ceasing to visit Mrs Leese, after seeing quite a lot of her over quite a number of years … I never saw Mrs Leese again.[119]

Her unequivocal support proved pivotal for Jordan's future activities. When she died on 3 August 1974, Mrs Leese bequeathed the bulk of her monies to Ann Story but left Jordan the Princedale Road property, duty free, which remained his most tangible asset.[120] Mrs Leese was not Jordan's only link to the IFL. He frequently consorted with other former members including Eric Bass, a former IFL Guard Detachment activist, who led Jordan and Peter Ling in secretive Nazi rituals in the New Forest.[121] The 1993 BNP Annual Rally feted Bass as the last surviving IFL member. He and party chairman John Tyndall were photographed together at the event.[122]

By 1959, an estimated 60,000 immigrants had arrived in Britain, touching 100,000 in the following year. Such numbers affirmed to Jordan the rectitude of his campaign. 'The Blacks are Coming', proclaimed WDL literature. It railed against the 'black policy' of the 'old gang' politicians (a term borrowed from Mosley) claiming that 'they' planned 'to let the coloured invasion continue indefinitely so that (at the present rate) there will be 6 million in 20 years' time, and to spread them all over the country so that ultimate intermarriage will produce a half-breed Britain.'[123] Jordan did not distinguish between Jews and Blacks. 'As far as we are concerned,' he told the press, 'a Jew is a black man. Both of them should be deported from this country, and they should certainly not be allowed to marry with our gentle Nordic women.' Those who ignored this injunction were 'racial perverts'; their progeny derided as 'coffee-coloured monstrosities'.[124]

Jordan's WDL was a direct-action group with paramilitary pretensions. He scoffed at the 'democratic obsession' exhibited by John Bean and another young LEL renegade, John Tyndall, who had founded the National Labour Party (NLP) in May 1958.[125] His fingers burned by the Frei Korps episode, Jordan had declined Bean's invitation to join the NLP, preferring to wait and see whether it 'got a good start' or not.[126] The two organisations cooperated closely, however. Having no newspaper of their own, NLP activists distributed *Black and White News*.[127] The two groups also undertook joint political actions, one of the first being to attack an MCF meeting at Central Hall, Westminster, addressed by Kanyama Chiume, publicity secretary of the banned Nyasaland African National Congress, who was then living in exile in London. As he rose to speak, banners were unfurled reading 'Hang Chiume for sedition' and 'Keep Britain White'. Chiume had fireworks thrown at him as 'stewards forced several interrupters out of the hall after fist battles ... Mr. Jordan was thrown to the floor in a tussle with stewards.'[128] On another occasion, Jordan barracked Grantley Adams, prime minister of the short-lived Federation of the West Indies, during a press conference, accusing him of using Britain as a 'dumping ground' for West Indian immigrants.[129]

On 17 May 1959, Kelso Cochrane was murdered in Notting Hill (Chapter 2). On the following weekend, the WDL and NLP a staged a joint 'White Defence' meeting in Trafalgar Square under the banner 'Keep Britain White' having spent the previous week distributing pamphlets throughout Notting Hill protesting against 'the nation being mongrelised'.[130] Bean and Jordan addressed the meeting, as did NLP president Andrew Fountaine, a wealthy Norfolk landowner whose definition of 'coloured' encompassed 'all non-Europeans' including Americans and who inveighed against a 'huge coloured army invading the western world' with West Indian immigrants acting as 'a Trojan horse for the hordes of Asia.'[131] In the following month, Special Branch noted that Jordan had begun distributing an inflammatory leaflet titled *Who Killed Kelso Cochrane?* This claimed that Cochrane's death was being used to 'Smear the White folk of Notting Hill,' '*Frame* white resistance organizations in the district,' and 'Demand new laws to stifle and punish resistance' – 'Was Cochrane's killing arranged for this foul purpose?' The WDL used his murder to announce, once more, that 'We stand for the white people of Notting Hill Against the coloured invasion.'[132] In the week when Cochrane was laid to rest, the WDL began distributing a 'One Way Ticket from Britain' available to 'all Coloured people' courtesy of 'The White Britain Steamship Company'.[133] Jordan subsequently distributed another news-sheet, *Notting Hill News*, to reinforce this message.[134]

The government contemplated prosecuting Jordan for distributing such material but concluded that an unsuccessful prosecution would do more harm than good.[135] Unchecked, Jordan's public pronouncements became increasingly forthright. 'I loathe the blacks,' he told *Reynolds News*, 'we are fighting a war to clear them out of Britain'. 'If a Fascist is a person who wants to keep Britain White,' he told the *Daily Herald*, 'then I am a Fascist and proud of it'.[136] His uncompromising stance meant that Jordan quickly became 'the white extremist spokesman to whom the national press turned for an instant quote on the racial problems in Notting Hill'.[137] This had already included an interview with BBC's current affairs programme *Panorama* on 13 March 1959.

Edged out of the racist spotlight by Mosley's general election campaign in North Kensington, both the WDL and the NLP turned their attentions to North London. Whilst the NLP focused upon St Pancras North where it stood a candidate, Jordan concentrated upon Hampstead where the West Indian-born Labour candidate Dr David Pitt was barracked at public meetings, had his committee rooms vandalised with racist epithets and received death threats.[138] At one such meeting, Pitt struggled to make himself heard above shouts of 'Keep Britain white' and 'We don't want England a dumping ground for niggers' as the assembly descended into a general mêlée between WDL activists and Labour Party stewards.[139] Responding to a letter in *The Times* from the joint chairman of the British Caribbean Association deploring his activities as prejudicial to race relations, Jordan made no apology for seeking 'to preserve Britain as a white man's country' stating that 'better race relations … is thus a euphemism for racial treason'.[140]

Jordan's vehement racist platform had already brought him to the notice of white supremacists in the United States. The *Citizen's Council* newspaper began praising him as part of their broader efforts to internationalise the struggle to maintain racial segregation.[141] Jordan duly immersed himself in this burgeoning transatlantic nexus. In January 1957, he contributed an article to *The Virginian*, the racist, pro-segregationist periodical edited by William Stephenson bemoaning the impact of the 'coloured invasion' on Britain. His article drew plaudits from veteran US white supremacist Colonel Earnest Sevier Cox (noted for his friendship with the Black separatist Marcus Garvey during the 1920s) who sent Jordan a copy of his book *White America* (1937).[142] Jordan derived 'great satisfaction' from the knowledge that his article made 'some tiny contribution to promoting a feeling of solidarity among the defenders of white civilisation and opponents of miscegenation throughout the world' writing to Cox that 'the great fight that our American friends are putting up against the common enemy is a great example and encouragement to us over here'.[143]

Cox and Stephenson were both involved with the Northern League, a transnational 'pan-Nordic' cultural society originally based in Scotland before moving to the Netherlands behind which stood figures like Willis Carto and Roger Pearson. Jordan was the agent for its journal, *Northern World*, but relinquished the role in October 1958 to concentrate on the WDL, whereupon The Britons stepped in to manage its affairs.[144] Nonetheless, Jordan remained intimately involved with the League. In January 1959, the WDL and the NLP both affiliated to the organisation. In July, Jordan attended its 'Teutoburger Moot' in Detmold, Germany, meeting with a range of groups and individuals, including both Cox and Stephenson, who had gathered to celebrate the 1950th anniversary of the defeat of three Roman legions by Teutonic tribal chieftain Arminus whose victory they held to have heralded the preservation of North European cultural and racial heritage.[145]

British National Party

Despite the reams of publicity Jordan had generated for the WDL, even before he departed for Detmold, Special Branch recorded that he appeared to be losing interest in it. The WDL had held no public meetings in the vicinity 'and very little local interest has been shown in the premises', they noted.[146] Indeed, stimulated by his involvement in the Northern League,[147] Jordan appeared less interested in staunching the flow of WDL supporters to the rival NLP than he was in transnational initiatives. In December 1959, he began editing *The Nationalist*, the self-declared 'voice of Northern European Racial Nationalism', which reflected his 'pan-Nordic' conception of race based upon the peoples of North Western Europe, North America and the Dominions. During this period, Jordan's overt Nazism came to the fore. He was involved in the 'swastika epidemic' that exploded following the desecration of a Cologne synagogue on Christmas Day 1959. This rash of anti-Semitic vandalism only petered out in March 1960 after generating hundreds if not thousands of similar incidences across thirty-four countries.[148]

England was no exception. Synagogues across the country were covered with anti-Semitic graffiti; the offices of the *Jewish Chronicle* had 'Juden Raus' scrawled on them and Woburn House, which housed the Board of Deputies of British Jews, had its windows smashed, fireworks thrown inside and swastikas and SS signs daubed on its walls.[149] Despite lacking 'conclusive proof', Special Branch had included Jordan on a list of individuals 'most likely' to have engaged in this wave of anti-Semitic vandalism. They questioned him about his involvement, which he thoroughly denied.[150] In later years, however, Jordan all but admitted his participation, intimating that NLP activist John Tyndall had also engaged in such acts.[151] In January, police also had cause to question Jordan following a series of menacing letters and anonymous telephone calls made in the name of the 'British Nazi Movement' to Jewish personalities. Jordan denied he was the perpetrator, though another fascist activist had already inadvertently confirmed his identity to police as the caller.[152]

Like the WDL, the NLP was also having trouble. Mired in debt, losing several key activists and lacking a headquarters as a focal point for activism, John Bean, the NLP leader, sought to overcome the denouement by reaching out to Jordan. Though Bean's concept of racial preservation was wider than Jordan's – extending to all 'European cultures' – there was enough common ground between the two to facilitate the merger of their respective *groupuscules* to form the British National Party (BNP) on 24 February 1960. Jordan had initially favoured calling the organisation the 'British Racial Nationalist Party' but yielded to the NLP faction who favoured more anodyne nomenclature. The group's initial membership numbered approximately 300 individuals, 240 coming from the NLP and roughly fifty from the WDL.[153]

The influence of pan-Nordic ideology was evident in the BNP constitution which demanded 'the preservation of our Northern European folk – predominantly Nordic in race – and thereby the preservation of Northern European civilisation and the heritage of Britain.' Utilising the Nordic sunwheel as its symbol, BNP membership was exclusively for those 'of purely Northern European racial ancestry'. The BNP fought to free Britain 'from Jewish domination and the coloured influx' and to restrict nationality 'to our Northern European folk'. It would terminate all non-European immigration 'inclusive of Jews' forthwith and begin, 'the gradual and humane transfer of all such racial aliens already here to lands of their own.' Standing for 'racial solidarity and defence against Communism and International Finance', the BNP sought to replace the 'multi-racial' Commonwealth and United Nations with 'a close confederation of all the Northern European peoples' at the root of which stood Britain and its Dominions and the cooperation of this federation with 'other sections of the White world community for security and prosperity'.[154]

Highlighting his evolution away from the imperial ideology of the LEL, Jordan mused that it had been in fact been a 'racial mistake' to acquire the empire since through it the country had also acquired a 'colossal Coloured population', which meant Britain was 'in constant danger of racial mixture'.[155] Jordan mapped out the finer details of BNP ideology in a series of articles for *Combat*, the BNP newspaper, though, echoing Leese, the starting point was that 'Race is the basis of all history'.[156] Indeed, for the BNP, race and immigration were the most important issues of the twentieth century. 'Civilisation *may* die *if* there is a nuclear war,' declared its propaganda. 'Civilisation *will* die if European man is bred out of existence'.[157]

Jordan became the group's national organiser whilst Bean served as his deputy. Andrew Fountaine became president; Winifred Leese served as vice-president. The BNP quickly established itself through violent attacks on meetings of the South African boycott movement including one held in Trafalgar Square on 28 February, only four days after its inception.[158] During one such action, South African communist Guy Routh knocked Jordan unconscious outside Hampstead Town Hall.[159] Sporting two black eyes and a deep gash in his forehead, Jordan continued undaunted, stating to a reporter: 'I'm not anti-Semitic – I am just 100 per cent anti-Jew'.[160] This much was evident at a BNP rally in Trafalgar Square on 29 May during in which Jordan denounced

> the folly of Britain being driven into war in 1939 with the only country in Europe which drove the Jews out of public life ... how much more sensible if we had joined hands with Germany and fought the Jews.[161]

The BNP continued its 'Keep Britain White' campaign too; pursuing those regarded as racial renegades even more ruthlessly. Leslie Plummer MP (Deptford), whose Racial and Religious Insults Bill had recently failed to gain a second reading in the House of Commons, received death threats leading to a police guard on his house during April and May 1960. Jordan had also formed a special corps of activists to take the BNP message to the provinces during this period. In the wake of one such foray to Leeds in July, the group left anti-Semitic literature in local telephone boxes. When Charles Pannell MP (Leeds West) raised objections to the dissemination of such works in Parliament, Jordan targeted him.[162] He wrote to Pannell menacing him, 'that in the resurgent Britain of tomorrow it may well be that you and your fellow racial renegades who face trial for your complicity in the coloured invasion and Jewish control of our land.' Judged a threat and therefore a *prima facie* breach of Parliamentary Privilege, Jordan's letter was referred to the Committee of Privileges, which, despite finding him guilty, declined to take further action.[163]

BNP activists targeted the points of arrival for immigrants, descending upon Waterloo railway station to barrack those newly arrived with cries of 'Send the Blacks Home'.[164] The also targeted areas with a settled migrant population including Smethwick in the West Midlands where police observed Jordan distributing the BNP newspaper, *Combat*. One of his associates, Birmingham BNP member, Roy Davidson, followed suit but came to favour more direct action.[165] In the following year, police arrested Davidson carrying a home-made bomb on his way to attack immigrants at random. 'I thought that putting bombs in their cars would scare them into going home', he told the court.[166] BNP activists continued targeted Jews too, demonstrating against the investiture of a Jewish Lord Mayor, Sir Bernard Waley-Cohen, leading to four arrests. During a screening of the film *Exodus* – a popular target for extreme right-wing activists – BNP members released rats into the auditorium.[167]

Within the BNP, Jordan prioritised running its 'External Department', which focused upon fostering 'white world solidarity'. To this end, he and Peter Ling organised the Northern European Ring (NER), which aimed to weld together racial nationalist and national socialist groups from across the world in a 'circle of friendship and co-operation'.[168] To facilitate such international 'pan-Nordic' fraternity, Jordan re-branded *The Nationalist* as *The Northern European*, which became simply 'the voice of Nordic racial nationalism' and served as an international point of contact for its various affiliates. To facilitate international cooperation, Jordan departed on a month-long continental tour in April 1960, during which he visited Denmark, Sweden and Germany to consolidate this burgeoning network.[169]

Jordan held a 'Nord-Europa' camp in the North Downs, near Wrotham, Kent, on 29 July–2 August, affording those present 'the opportunity to get away from the cosmopolitanism of the cities, and to live in the manner of our forefolk amidst the beauty of our own Northland, England'. Those attending made a pilgrimage to an iron-age burial tomb near Pilgrim's Way. 'None will forget the comradeship around the campfire on those summer nights, with song of our race and nation upon our lips, and tankards of English ale in our hands.'[170] From the camp flagpole flew 'the sunwheel flag of Nordic racial nationalism' whilst in a nearby clearing 'a giant sunwheel – constructed by campers from branches bound with foliage, and mounted on a tall pole – made an impressive sight'. The date too was significant, the first day of August being the sun festival day of Lammas, named after the Celtic sun God, Lugh, which they celebrated with a special campfire meeting.[171] The guest of honour was Paul van Tienen, a former Nationaal-Socialistische Beweging (NSB – National Socialist Movement) activist who had served five years of an eight-year sentence imposed after 1945 as punishment for collaborating with the Nazis; he had fought on the Eastern Front with the Waffen-SS winning the Iron Cross.[172] In December, SS commando Otto Skorzeny, a legendary figure famed for his daredevil rescue of Mussolini, wrote to Jordan intimating that he was 'hoping to be helpful to you'. Skorzeny's endorsement enhanced Jordan's standing within these transnational networks whilst opening doors for him in Germany and Austria as well as amongst Nazi expatriates in South America and South Africa.[173]

The largest cooperative set-piece staged by Jordan's NER network took place over ten days from 8 December 1961 when its members, including the BNP, coordinated their resources for a 'world campaign' on behalf of the 'Freiheit für Rudolf Hess' campaign initiated by the wife and son of Rudolf Hess.[174] Hitler's deputy flew to Scotland on 19 May 1941 on an unofficial mission to negotiate peace with the Duke of Hamilton but was instead imprisoned, found guilty of war crimes at Nuremberg, and sentenced to life imprisonment in Spandau prison where he died in 1987. British fascists were quick to publicise his plight, proclaiming him a martyr. The Britons were amongst the first, publishing an English translation of Ilse Hess' *England – Nurnberg – Spandau: Ein Schicksal in Briefen* (1952) as *Rudolf Hess: Prisoner of Peace* (1954).[175]

Hess' flight itself was a pivotal moment in Jordan's life:

> Sharp in my memory is that day in 1941 when my father came hurrying to my bedroom to impart the early morning news on the radio that Rudolf Hess had flown to Britain. His face, as he told me his startling news, was bright with gladsome anticipation, for, in his naïveté, he thought that this meant that the crazy conflict between the brother-nations of Britain and Germany would be ended. Those were the days when an African was a curiosity in our country, and when the combination of the British Navy and German Army could have kept the peace of the world, and guaranteed a glorious, Jew-free future for the white man.[176]

Jordan visited Ilse Hess in 1960 and again during summer 1961, staying at her Bavarian guesthouse for a week, where he was permitted to inspect her husband's private library and other family artefacts.[177] Having made such personal connections, Jordan corresponded with her and her son, Wolf Rüdiger Hess (Hitler's godson), for more than thirty years.[178] Jordan subsequently penned an article for *Combat* titled 'Rudolf Hess: Prisoner of Peace, 1941–1961' to mark the twentieth anniversary of his incarceration in Spandau prison.[179] Tyndall and Denis Pirie had accompanied Jordan on this trip, the wider purpose of which was to build up the NER network in which Jordan intended the BNP would play a major role. They travelled on to Munich, meeting Gudrun Himmler, daughter of Reichsführer-SS Heinrich Himmler, architect of the Nazi genocide, who introduced them to some of her father's former friends and colleagues. Such meetings indicated that Jordan's stock within the international national socialist milieu was growing, particularly amongst the *alte kämpfer* (old fighters).[180]

Jordan never wavered in his instrumentalisation of Hess as the living embodiment of National Socialist heroism and self-sacrifice. He was a role model to be emulated.[181] Jordan's efforts to communicate his personal solidarity to Hess met with less success. The Spandau prison authorities confiscated his Christmas card to Hess as part of a broader effort to stop the imprisoned Nazi war criminal from becoming a rallying point for a younger generation of activists.[182] Undeterred by his failure to establish personal contact, Jordan's idealisation of Hess reached its apogee in an article titled 'Hess: Prisoner of Vengeance' published in 1986 in the BNP journal *Spearhead*. Jordan proclaimed Hess the victim of 'Jewish' revenge who 'made more sacrifices for world peace than the rest of mankind put together.... No-one deserves the Nobel Peace Prize more than this man.'[183] Jordan's campaign also led him to inveigh upon Terry Waite, special envoy to the Archbishop of Canterbury, to intercede on Hess' behalf.[184] Such efforts came to naught, however, not least because Hess committed suicide in August 1987. Jordan claimed he had been 'murdered' by the SAS, a conspiracy theory probably derived from his son, author of *Who Murdered My Father, Rudolf Hess?* (1989).[185] Documents released in 2007 revealed that the British authorities had in fact long been working for his release on humanitarian grounds.[186]

Following Hess' death, Michael Kühnen, a prominent West German Nazi activist, approached Jordan to become president of 'The International Rudolf Hess Memorial Fund', which would operate as an English-speaking subsidiary of the Volksbund Rudolf Hess organisation. Although Jordan had supported Michael Kühnen following his incarceration in 1979,[187] this time, he declined to assist. The ongoing furore surrounding Kühnen's 1986 admission that he was homosexual (he died of an AIDS-related illness in 1991) undoubtedly influenced Jordan's refusal.[188] Instead, Jordan focused upon his own campaign to rehabilitate Hess posthumously. This culminated in November 1993 with the erection of a memorial to his hero in a field 15 miles from Glasgow, on the spot Hess had landed.[189] Anti-fascists promptly obliterated it, though not before Wolf Rüdiger Hess, in the company of several German and American activists, had paid homage there.[190] Outraged, Jordan offered £50, later increased to £300, for personal information about Aamer Anwar, the 'impudent Asian' he blamed for destroying the monument.[191] Anwar featured on a 'Nazi hit list', the police informed him. 'He was forced to move flat and change his name, before arrests were made a year later.'[192] Jordan's outrage remained palpable, impotently fantasising about Anwar's brutal physical disablement in his fiction.[193]

Hess was not the only figure for whom Jordan sought to build international support. The BNP also ran a campaign in support of Adolf Eichmann, a pivotal figure in the annihilation of European Jewry. Mossad, the Israeli secret service, had located Eichmann and abducted him from his Argentinean bolt-hole in May 1960. Eichmann went on trial in Israel on 11 April 1961. Found guilty, Eichmann was executed on 1 June 1962. The trial was the catalyst for a wave of anti-Semitic acts across Britain. Anticipating the upsurge, Special Branch maintained the 'closest contact' with its informants inside the movement. The Metropolitan Police stepped up their protection of the Israeli Embassy in London and the private residence of its Ambassador, having learned that a group of British fascists plotted to kidnap him and hold him hostage for the duration of the trial.[194]

To offset accusations that the BNP supported gassing Jews through its support for Eichmann, Jordan ramped up his 'anti-Zionist' propaganda, arguing that the Israeli Prime Minister Menachem Begin should also be in the dock.[195] During the height of 'Operation Counterblast', Jordan and Bean drove across central London carrying posters proclaiming: 'Eichmann trial – Jews caused World War II' and 'Punish atrocities by Jews'. They stopped outside the Princes Theatre, High Holborn, where a Jewish meeting to commemorate the Warsaw ghetto was taking place. Police arrested all eight occupants, including Jordan and Bean who were fined for insulting behaviour.[196] *Combat*, the BNP newspaper edited by Bean, issued a special 'Jewish atrocity' supplement to coincide with the trial, written by Jordan and Ling, which claimed that the trial was 'a Jewish propaganda stunt' designed 'to smear and discredit ... any and every form of criticism to their world power.' *Combat* claimed the supplement had a 'worldwide' circulation though only the National States Rights Party (NSRP), itself part of the NER network, saw fit to reproduce it in their newspaper, *The Thunderbolt*.[197]

Combat claimed Eichmann was a 'fabricated monster' and branded the Holocaust 'palpable balderdash'.[198] It also accused Jews of faking concentration camp photographs and included an article titled 'the great lie of the six million', which denied the existence of Nazi gas chambers.[199] Jordan's own Holocaust denial coupled with his support of Eichmann drew him deeper into international 'revisionist' networks. Arthur Ehrhardt, editor of *Nation Europa*, invited Jordan to participate in a conference in Coburg, Germany, in 1961.[200] This visit introduced Jordan to *Nation Europa's* core contributors. Also present was F.J.P. Veale, a Brighton solicitor and Mosley supporter whose 'revisionist' classic *Advance to Barbarism* (1948) was translated into German in 1954. Veale's book was important. It provided German Nazis with:

> the kind of psychic satisfactions which only an Anglo-Saxon author can provide who pretends to have discovered the advance of barbarism less in the genocide apparatus of the Third Reich than in the Allied postwar trials of Nazi criminals and who locates the historical sources of barbarism in the distant past, but principally in the activities of ancient Hebrews.[201]

Veale's second book, an indictment of the war-crimes trials titled *Crimes Discreetly Veiled* (1958), published in Germany in 1959, though less well read, also 'found a safe place among the standard literature of German revisionism'.[202]

Such acts of racial solidarity and the increased international networking that accompanied them fed Jordan's desire to globalise the racial struggle. Under Jordan's aegis, the BNP staged an international rally in the grounds of Fountaine's Norfolk estate on 20–26 May 1961 'to celebrate the racial holiday and study Race with fellow Whitemen from all over Europe.'[203] The Home Office barred at least twenty foreign delegates from entering Britain but fourteen slipped through the net.[204] Guards armed with sticks and wearing sunwheel insignia armbands patrolled the perimeter. The camp opened with a torchlight procession and the ceremonial burning of a giant wooden sunwheel, the symbol of Arminus, victor of the Battle of the Teutoburger Wald in AD 9, whose defeat of the Rome's Legions 'kept Europe clean from the taint of Roman corruption'.[205] Cultural excursions to Castle Acre, Grimes Graves and the Norfolk coast were laid on for the delegates as were physical activities including games, sports, hiking and 'storming the Red platform'. During the evenings, they sang songs, like the BNP anthem 'Unfurl our Banner' and several 'Southern Rebel' songs taught to them by the NSRP delegates.[206]

The rally also served an educational purpose with delegates listening to a series of lectures including one on 'The message of Adolf Hitler' delivered by Savitri Devi, a Greco-French esoteric Hitlerite. Though her contemporary influence in post-war Nazi networks is overplayed, Savitri Devi was important for propagating a quasi-religious view of Nazism, reflected in her seminal book, *The Lighting and the Sun* (1958), completed during a visit to

Mosley's friend, Hans-Ulrich Rudel, which deified the dead Führer as an avatar of the Hindu God Vishnu. Her ideas, a mélange of Aryan supremacism, anti-Semitism, Hinduism, animal rights and ecology, served as the basis for her post-war redefinition of Nazism as a 'religion of nature'.[207]

She greatly influenced Jordan who struck up a lifelong friendship with her.[208] It was partially because of Savitri Devi's influence that Jordan began to move beyond political fetishism to begin extolling the virtues of Nazism as a *Lebensphilosopie* ('religion of life') rather than as a 'cult of death' and racial extermination, which most people outside its own cloistered intellectual confines understand it to be.[209] 'We are concerned to be, as our title suggests, not merely a political party but something much wider and deeper, and a movement regarding National Socialism as a way of life, and accordingly interested in all aspects of life,' wrote Jordan.[210] His conception of Nazism as a living, transcendent creed would underpin Jordan's subsequent outright rejection of Fascism. Because it denied race, Jordan averred that Fascism, 'belonged to the old order, being in line with its non-racial notion of nationality, a notion which now naturally extends to encompass that of a global community devoid of racial distinction, which is now being pressed upon us'.[211]

Spearhead

On 5 March 1961, Jordan founded 'The Spearhead' with express permission from the BNP national council. Bean became his second-in-command. Jordan conceived of Spearhead as the party's elite cadre, a 'vanguard of active workers' each of whom would work 'as a fighter for, and servant of, the cause of Racial Nationalism'. Its membership comprised largely the BNP 'Special Active Service' unit led by Tyndall. Those selected to join Jordan's embryonic paramilitary formation were subject to two forms of training: functional, consisting of 'marching drill, physical culture, endurance, and unarmed combat'; and ideological, consisting of compulsory ideological training seminars, summer camps as well as 'exchange visits' with foreign counterparts. Spearhead members wore uniforms consisting of a grey drill shirt, and black trousers, black tie and a red, white and blue sunwheel armband, though party documents warned that wearing political uniforms outside 'private functions' was in breach of the Public Order Act (1936). Indeed, Jordan expressly warned that 'the legal existence, and thereby the success of Spearhead depends on the careful avoidance of any *noticeable* contravention of this Act within whose shadow we have to operate'.[212]

Potential recruits were expected to be of 'predominantly Nordic type' but despite its membership form asking searching questions about previous military experience, Spearhead's aims were not solely paramilitary.[213] The 'role of the SP man' was to act as the 'bodyguard of ideology' and for those activists 'eager to be mobilised in mind and spirit to *live* as a Racial Nationalist (or National Socialist); who wants to make our revolution now in himself; who wants to represent now, in himself, our new order of the future.' Participating in the 'action group' and providing security for BNP activities 'in the spirit of the National Socialist Revolution' would facilitate this sense of transcendence. The principles of race and nation had to be upheld, 'if needs be to the last man and the last breath'.[214] The police observed Spearhead members drilling in the grounds of a derelict school in Culverstone, Kent, on 4 August 1961. When a police officer approached the BNP sentry on the gate and asked what the drilling was for, a BNP activist informed him it was, 'to get rid of the blacks'.[215] Shortly afterwards, on 2 November, Jordan led fifteen Spearhead members in an attack upon an MCF meeting in St Pancras Town Hall which ended in 'fierce fighting' with the 'communist' stewards.[216]

Jordan's paramilitarism and his increasingly overt veneration of the Third Reich alarmed the ostensibly racial nationalist faction within the party. Jordan's 'personal statement of policy' won the backing of fifty-eight of the sixty-nine delegates present at the BNP AGM on 27 January 1962. Jordan had given what Special Branch described as a 'party-splitting' speech, railing against the group's 'watered down' ideological platform. Now was the time, Jordan declared, to rally around Spearhead 'to secure the real aims of the party.' Indicating the impact of his NER networking, Jordan informed those present that British 'national socialism' had to be replaced by 'world-wide national socialism'. Moreover, he wanted the BNP to transcend its origins as 'a ragged bunch, fighting coloured immigration' to become a militant power modelled on the original Nazi party. He was also enthused by the 'more demonstrative' activities of the French OAS 'and declared that the time was near when the British Nationalists would join with these partisans.' At this point, P.J. Ridout, the former IFL activist who served as the group's treasurer, interrupted Jordan to ask if the Nazi party had taken over the BNP. Jordan replied 'Yes it has, but this time we will not fail.' Roughly twenty delegates, including all the Spearhead members, applauded Jordan's statement. He also claimed that the BNP should celebrate Hitler's birthday – 'the greatest nationalist of the century'. Jordan then demanded a vote of confidence or he would resign as National Organiser. When numerous leading figures, including Bean, dissented, Jordan tendered his resignation. Tyndall announced that if they did not reverse the decision, Spearhead would break away.

> After a few minutes discussion, Bean and his supporters agreed to allow Jordan to continue as national organizer on the grounds of 'party unity'. Tempers having been aroused by this 'blackmail' on Jordan's part, the meeting adjourned for about fifteen minutes.[217]

Whilst Jordan carried the day at the BNP AGM, its National Council meeting a fortnight later was an altogether more acrimonious affair. Bean submitted a motion attacking Jordan for his 'wrongful direction of tactics in placing an increasing emphasis on directly associating ourselves with the *pre-war* era of National Socialist Germany to the neglect of Britain, Europe and the White World struggle *today and the future*.' Fountaine assailed Spearhead with similar vehemence, arguing that the BNP was not a 'corpse raiser' and those,

> who cannot maintain their dedication and fanaticism to the cause without resort to extrovert political exhibitionism in the spurious imitation of what they fondly imagine to have been the nexus of the NSDAP merely insult the past and destroy the future.[218]

Jordan refused to disband Spearhead. Fountaine accused him of 'political masturbation' and expelled him.[219] Thereafter, the BNP dropped the sunwheel as their political symbol and adopting the Celtic cross to differentiate themselves from Jordan and to foster the idea of a 'Northern European' heritage.[220]

Jordan initially refused to accept his expulsion or indeed the 'debasing policy' he believed Bean and Fountaine were pursuing which denied the fact 'that with a racialist policy, revolutionary spirit and militant methods we are a National Socialist movement'. Soft-peddling anti-Semitism, Jordan exclaimed, would 'reduce our creed to the level of back-street grumbles against negroes whose presence here is only one aspect of the Jewish democratic system'. His subsequent attempt to rally Spearhead members to crush Bean's 'breakaway' movement failed, leaving Jordan without a political home.[221] Spearhead provided Jordan with the nucleus of a new political organisation, however. The dozen or so activists who remained loyal to Spearhead continued their paramilitary training. On 18 April 1962, Jordan led the group in 'military field exercises' on Leith Hill in Broadmoor near Dorking. Wearing their uniforms under their jackets, Spearhead members split into two groups, taking turns to storm and defend a derelict tower. Unbeknownst to the group, the police were observing them. They had also monitored Spearhead performing similar manoeuvres on 6 May.[222] Spearhead was also watched from within. Unwisely, they allowed themselves to be photographed by fellow 'activist' John Nicols, a former paratrooper enlisted to help train Spearhead. He was actually a private investigator appalled by Fascism. Nicols subsequently passed the photographs and other materials purloined from NSM headquarters to *The People*, who duly published them. These photos would be used in Jordan's subsequent prosecution.[223]

National Socialist Movement

Two days after these 'military field exercises', Jordan founded the National Socialist Movement (NSM) on 20 April – the anniversary of Hitler's birthday. Those gathered for its inauguration at 'Arnold Leese House' listened to speeches and sang songs whilst consuming a buffet graced with a swastika shaped cake. Jordan implored those present to 'keep faith' with 'the great years and the great creed and the great Leader' Adolf Hitler and to 'strive by our propaganda or word and deed to make in Britain a beacon of the National Socialist faith, whose light will bring new hope and courage to our comrades everywhere'. The evening culminated with a transatlantic telephone call to George Lincoln Rockwell, a former US navy commander who led the American Nazi Party (ANP), at his headquarters in Arlington, Virginia, 'ending with the Atlantic ether punctuated by three hearty "Sieg Heils"'. The NSM would not succumb to the 'folly' of 'ideological looseness' or the 'democratic constitutional character' of the BNP. Jordan had complete dictatorial control. The foundation of the NSM underlined a development in Jordan's thinking, which moved beyond Arnold Leese's 'Jew-wise' Nordicism towards pan-Aryan Nazism underpinned by a cosmological religion of race. Indeed, Jordan would later claim that although he was not a Christian, he was religious. 'National Socialism is itself a faith'.[224] Justifying his decision to launch an explicitly National Socialist organisation, Jordan argued that 'the tactics of disguise' emasculated ideological purity and were thus 'morally wrong and spiritually debilitating. If the creed was right before its military defeat, it is no less right since that defeat'.[225]

'Democracy, the harm it has done and the harm that it is doing to Britain,' was what had made him a National Socialist, Jordan claimed. It was responsible for the threat to racial purity at home and abroad, which, he argued, was eroded by a 'cosmopolitan' (i.e. Jewish) concept of racial equality that was 'inimical to the security of the White people of Britain and elsewhere'. The resulting change in cultural mores exacerbated racial miscegenation and the weakened the 'White, Anglo-Saxon stock'. This was no accident but the culmination of a malign conspiracy, aiming to soften up the nation, ready for 'alien takeover'. For Jordan, democracy was the harbinger of racial ruination. This motivated his own lasting 'revolt against democracy' and underpinned his assertion that:

> if there is anything worth fighting for, it is to preserve my own race in possession and control of my homeland, and to see that our resources of all kinds are used to the full for the betterment of our own nation.[226]

No. 74 Princedale Road housed the 'Phoenix Bookshop' through which the NSM distributed Nazi materials and a small library, stocking titles like *Mein Kampf* and *The Protocols*. It also housed two mail-order music companies 'Westapes Recordings' and 'Viking Records' through which they disseminated gramophone and audiotape recordings of Hitler's speeches and the music of the Third Reich. This was not incidental. 'The strident sounds of martial music, the lusty singing, the sound of marching men, take the mind back to those days of National Socialist greatness, and give us an insight into the spirit of the age', noted the party newspaper. This pronouncement highlighted the importance of music for socialising, integrating and radicalising listeners through the construction of 'collectives of emotion' and common identities.[227] NSM members were also expected to attend bi-weekly lectures or 'combat training' in the building's cellar, which had been converted into a gymnasium. Imitating the Nazis, it also doubled as an impromptu beer hall.[228] John Tyndall, who became Jordan's deputy, reminded members that the NSM was not a social club but 'the militant task-force of political revolution'. Underpinning this sentiment, Spearhead was reorganised. He imposed harsher discipline with a view to 'strengthening of the National Socialist spirit'. The Nazi salute became the mandatory greeting between party members.[229] Mosley's secretary, Jeffrey Hamm, who also lived on Princedale Road claimed, 'My peace late at night would be disturbed by the sound of heavy footsteps, as the trio [Jordan, Tyndall and Webster] marched past beneath my window, whistling the Horst Wessel anthem'.[230]

The NSM was always small. It attracted roughly eighty members in its first few months. Throughout its entire history, the group gained only 187 members, according to one police estimate, though *Searchlight* claims that it had 680 members at its peak in 1962 with approximately 1,200 people associating with it over the course of its lifespan.[231] The police were scathing, stating that the group comprised of 'converted fanatics' whose only recourse was violence and 'illiterate dupes' who were 'fed visions of power and influence through the medium of violence and race hatred'.[232] Even Tyndall conceded many of its members were 'oddballs' and 'freaks'.[233] By 1966, only thirty-five remained. In addition to its 187 members, the NSM had 271 'supporters' (who paid a lower subscription rate) over the course of its existence, though by 1966 only seventy-seven were active. There were 105 Book Club members and 114 subscribers to its newspaper, *The National Socialist*.[234]

On 1 July, the NSM held a meeting in Trafalgar Square under the banner 'Free Britain from Jewish Control'.[235] Despite representations calling for the banning of the meeting, the Cabinet were unable to find any legal grounds on which to do so.[236] The meeting duly went ahead. The first speaker, Denis Pirie, read a message of support from Rockwell.[237] Tyndall followed him, fulminating that 'in our democratic society, the Jew is like a poisonous maggot feeding off a body in an advanced state of decay'. From the rostrum, Jordan then declared:

> More and more people every day are opening their eyes and coming to see that Hitler was right. They are coming to see that our real enemies, the people we should have fought, were not Hitler and National Socialists of Germany but world Jewry and it associates in this country.[238]

Jordan was heckled throughout 'and pelted with pennies, tomatoes and rotten eggs, by and overwhelmingly hostile crowd of some 2,000'. Jordan had demanded a show of strength. NSM members were expected to form 'a solid cordon of support at the front'.[239] 'The few people who did raise their hands in an earnest Nazi salute looked distinctly nervous', reported *The Times*. Twice the crowd broke through the police cordon forcing the police to stop the meeting to allow tempers to cool. As the meeting ended, the speakers, under heavy police guard, left the rostrum for their Land Rover, parked behind Nelson's Column. 'Within seconds', noted *The Times*, 'the crowd had burst the cordon, smashed the van's windscreen and set fire to the party's banner.' Pirie was 'severely manhandled'. The crowd then turned its attention to Jordan who was still on the plinth. A 'strong police escort' was required to protect him from harm. Police made twenty arrests.[240] It was probably the highpoint of Jordan's political career.

Mosley was less than impressed. He had addressed seven meetings in Trafalgar Square between 1959 and 1962. Press and public alike had ignored them all.[241] Now, in the wake of Jordan's antics, Mosley's activities drew violent opposition. A large, hostile crowd attended his meeting on 22 July which was stopped after fifteen minutes amidst fifty-five arrests after which anti-fascists marched on the UM headquarters. Mosley's march in Manchester in the following week was accompanied by more disorder and thirty-nine arrests. Anti-fascists knocked Mosley down three times and harried the march along its route to a meeting, which the police then cancelled.[242] Having attempted to march in Hackney on 31 July, Mosley abandoned his meeting amidst a hail of coins, tomatoes and invective. Mosley was knocked down again, and his son was arrested as he sought to defend him. Recognising the baleful impact of Jordan's activities, Mosley issued a public statement on 14 August stating that Jordan belonged to the 'idiot fringe' and his ideas were 'completely alien to us'.[243] With ducal disdain, Mosley later proclaimed that 'there is always something tragically comic in the spectacle of live dwarves posturing in the clothes of dead giants'.[244] A.K. Chesterton was no less dismissive: 'Colin Jordan, so far from being a menace to Jewish interests, makes himself by virtue of his puerilities the answer to the Jewish prayer.'[245]

If other extreme right leaders excoriated Jordan's activities, the authorities viewed his conduct even more dimly. Three days after the Trafalgar Square meeting, the Home Secretary informed the House that he was considering prosecution of the speakers under Section 5 of the Public Order Act (1936). Jordan and Tyndall received summonses on 19 July requiring them to appear at Bow Street Magistrates Court on 20 August.[246] The publicity surrounding his speech also threw his employment as a schoolteacher into sharp relief.[247] Although Jordan emphatically denied his politics entered the classroom, the school governors, appalled by his political activities, suspended him on 4 July following a 'deluge' of parental complaints. 'I shall not alter my principles in any way and this will only confirm my beliefs. We want to make Britain white and the Jews have a country of their own and should be confined to it', Jordan told reporters.[248] Jordan was 'certain' that 'the Jews' were responsible for what he regarded as his 'martyrdom'.[249] The school governors subsequently recommended that Jordan's suspension continue and that his employment should terminate at the end of the Christmas term.[250] They formally dismissed him on 29 August. Jordan never taught again, becoming instead a full-time worker for the cause of National Socialism.

The furore surrounding the Trafalgar Square meeting had yet to abate when Jordan issued the NSM manifesto. *Britain Reborn: The Will and Purpose of the National Socialist Movement* (1962) stated that Britain could only escape Jewish domination and be 'reborn' if it adopted 'the revolutionary new-life force of National Socialism' and in doing so recognised the 'epic triumph' of German Nazism in 1933, after which 'an era of human grandeur unsurpassed in the annals of mankind followed'. The introduction of a 'British form' of National Socialism 'suited to the circumstances of our time and the character of our own country' was the only way to save Britain, though there was little in the document to suggest anything other than a slavish imitation of Nazism.[251]

On 14 July, the day after publishing the manifesto, Jordan and Tyndall had a ninety minute meeting with Colonel Saad Mohamed El-Husseiny El-Shazly, the newly appointed military attaché for the United Arab Republic, to discuss potential financing for the NSM.[252] Through such 'secret' and 'clandestine' channels, Jordan hoped to forge links with anti-Semitic Arabs and therefore 'constructively co-operate in fighting the organised forces of Zionism and World Jewry, who threaten the interests mutual to both'. El-Shazly requested concrete proposals. Tyndall duly delivered them, together with a request for £15,000 to underwrite the costs of four salaries, anti-Semitic research and the production and dissemination of anti-Semitic materials, including *The Protocols of the Elders of Zion*. To demonstrate the materials he hoped to produce, Jordan furnished El-Shazly with copies of Leese's *Devilry in the Holy Land* and the *Combat* supplement on the Eichmann trial. He earmarked £11,000 to subsidise a Pirate radio station, which would broadcast anti-Semitic propaganda from outside the three mile limit in the Thames Estuary reaching, Jordan estimated, fifteen million people. As a quid pro quo, Jordan proposed that his Phoenix Bookshop would stock, 'a large number of books putting the Arab case with respect to Middle Eastern questions.' He also stated that 'we understand that the Arab League have published a great volume of literature dealing with these questions, and we are prepared to help in every way we can in distributing this literature into influential channels.'[253]

Nothing came of the proposal but El-Shazly was sympathetic to their anti-Semitism. Shortly before the Yom Kippur war with Israel in 1973, in which he served as Chief of the Egyptian general staff, El-Shazly issued a pamphlet *Our Faith Our Way*, in which he stated:

> The Jews have overstepped their bounds in injustice and conceit. And we sons of Egypt have determined to set them back on their heels, and to pry round their positions, killing and destroying, so as to wash away the shame of the 1967 defeat and to restore our honour and pride. Kill them wherever you find them (see Qur'an 2.192, 4.91) and take heed that they do not deceive you, for they are a treacherous people. They may feign surrender in order to gain power over you, and kill you vilely.[254]

El-Shazly was appointed Egyptian ambassador to Britain in 1974 despite a flood of complaints protesting his appointment, though he was moved to Portugal in the following year.[255]

During this period, Jordan also launched the NSM youth-wing, the British National Youth (BNY) led by Brendan Wilmer, a seventeen-year-old Leicestershire teenager, which had its own news-sheet, *The Bugler*.[256] Through such mechanisms, the NSM hoped to permeate youth clubs, sports clubs, educational establishments and military cadet units. Those showing signs of receptivity should be 'carefully cultivated'.[257] Jordan held Wilmer in high regard, believing that he was doing an 'absolutely wonderful job'.[258] He was a 'definite prodigy, and [is] certainly going to be one of the big names in National Socialism in the future,' predicted Jordan, who viewed the BNY as functioning as a 'preparatory body for us' – its members groomed as future NSM cadres. Though, as he confided in Rockwell:

> For the BNY to do this kind of valuable work successfully, however, it is really essential that as far as the public appearance is concerned the NSM and the BNY are quite separate and the BNY is not explicitly National Socialist.[259]

Major-General Richard Hilton, a former LEL member who ran his own True Tory Party, became Honorary President of the group whilst Admiral Sir Barry Domvile was a 'sponsor'. 'I am in demand as a youth leader: comic, ain't it?' mused Domvile who was then approaching ninety.[260] A.K. Chesterton did not share their enthusiasm, dismissing such initiatives as attractive only to 'defrocked scoutmasters and other pederasts'.[261]

From the outset, the BNY was networked with extreme right-wing youth groups in Germany and Austria. These included the Bund Heimattreuer Jugend (BHJ); Junge Kameradschaft (JK); the youth section of the Deutsches Reichspartei (DRP – German Reich Party); the Kameradschaftsring Nationaler Jugendverbände (KNJ – Fellowship Ring of National Youth Association); the Wiking Jugend (WJ – Viking Youth); and the White Youth Corps (WYC), a short-lived adjunct of the ANP set up to recruit high school students. *The Bugler*'s first issue contained a contribution from Konrad Windisch, editor of the KNJ newspaper, *Der Trommler* (*The Drummer*).[262]

Ultimately, Wilmer was to disappoint Jordan, splitting from the NSM in 1965. Appalled by the betrayal, Jordan enjoined BNY activists, 'who really consider themselves National Socialists to sever their connection with the renegade Mr Wilmer, and instead help the NSM to create in the near future its own youth division, entirely and thoroughly National Socialist.'[263] In December 1965, Wilmer changed his organisation's name to the National Youth League (NYL) 'to make clear that we are an independent patriotic youth association, unconnected with any other group or movement.'[264] The NYL subsequently aligned itself with A.K. Chesterton's LEL, which became its 'parent body' but it fizzled out soon afterwards.[265]

This setback was in the future, however. Following the foundation of the NSM, Jordan's principal concern was competing with the BNP for activists, resources and attention. When Fountaine announced a second BNP rally to be held on his Norfolk estate, Jordan sought to upstage it with his own international conference titled 'National Socialism: The World Movement for the White Man' on same August weekend.[266] About forty people attended the camp including several foreign delegates like Savitri Devi and former SS Lieutenant Friedrich Borth, an Austrian extreme right-wing activist who led the Legion Europa, a splinter from Jean Thiriart's Jeune Europe network, who was involved in the pro-German terrorist campaign in the South Tyrol region of Italy.[267] The guest of honour was ANP leader George Lincoln Rockwell whose presence ensured the eclipse of the BNP event.[268] The Home Secretary barred Rockwell from entering the country. Rockwell sidestepped the ban through the simple subterfuge of flying, not to Britain, but to Ireland's Shannon airport. Jordan and Tyndall met Rockwell there and escorted him on to England taking in several 'short meetings' with 'key individuals' on the extreme right en route to the conference.[269] It was a serious embarrassment for the British government whose decision to ban Rockwell was well publicised and because it exposed a gaping hole in British immigration controls vis-à-vis Ireland.[270]

The conference itself took place in a small private wood near the hamlet of Guiting Power, Gloucestershire, rented especially for the occasion. NSM members patrolled the perimeter armed with heavy sticks. Police units watching the camp observed men dressed in German forage caps, singing the Horst Wessel song and shouting 'Sieg Heil'. Speeches containing 'antagonistic references towards the Jews and the negroes' were overheard by police who also observed 'what appeared to be a type of field exercise in a small wooded area surrounding the camp.'[271] Although Jordan was happy to speak to journalists, offering photos of Rockwell to the highest bidder, those seeking their own exclusives were unwelcome. A female *Daily Mail* photographer seeking an unsolicited picture was shot with an air rifle.[272]

The principal achievement of the weekend was the launch of the World Union of National Socialists (WUNS). Rockwell has been characterised as the 'moving force' behind WUNS, dominating the more 'submissive' Jordan.[273] Whilst there is some truth in this characterisation, it neglects the fact that WUNS grew out of Jordan's NER network, which Rockwell's ANP had joined in 1961.[274] It also ignores the fact that it was Jordan who became 'world Führer' at the meeting with Rockwell as his second-in-command. 'The Cotswold Agreement' set out WUNS purpose:

1. To form a monolithic, combat-efficient, international political apparatus to combat and utterly destroy the international Jew-Communist and Zionist apparatus of treason and subversion.
2. To protect and promote the Aryan race and its Western Civilisation wherever its members may be on the globe, and whatever their nationality may be.
3. To protect private property and free enterprise from Communist class warfare.

Those wishing to partake in the establishment of a 'world order' based on 'race' had to acknowledge the 'spiritual leadership' of Adolf Hitler and in doing so agree 'to find and accomplish on a world-wide scale a just and final settlement of the Jewish problem.'[275] The establishment of WUNS had an important symbolic value of its participants. 'For me it has meant the assertion of the essential principle of National Socialist resurgence of today and tomorrow. Race and Faith above Nationality,' Jordan reflected.[276] Rockwell was similarly enthusiastic, his publication declaring 'A White Man's Internationale at Last.'[277] The British media were less reverent. 'The New "World Fuhrer" – Elected by 27 Idiots!', declared the *People*.[278]

The camp ended amidst scuffles with irate local villagers who invaded the campsite. During the mêlée, a shot was fired through the swastika flag flying above the campsite, which the villagers the captured. The police moved in forcing Jordan to close the camp. An NSM activist, Beryl Cheetham, Peter Ling's partner, smuggled Rockwell out of the camp.[279] On the following day, as Jordan tried to negotiate an interview with the *Daily Mail* for Rockwell, with the proceeds going to the NSM, police apprehended the ANP leader in central London. He was deported shortly thereafter.[280] Rockwell was nonetheless ecstatic with the publicity gained. 'I am sure it is unnecessary to say,' he wrote to Jordan, 'that my visit to Britain was a walloping success all round, and the Jews here are almost literally screaming in rage at the FBI for letting me "slip out".'[281]

Jordan had little opportunity to reflect upon his success. Police searched the NSM headquarters on 10 August whilst simultaneously another unit visited Jordan's Coventry home, where he lived with his widowed mother. Police also raided the homes of three other leading members.[282] Whilst searching the NSM headquarters, the police also encountered two German Nazis one of whom, Gerd Zimmerman, had a pistol and blank cartridges on his person.[283] They also seized a plethora of items including several knives, wooden coshes, two air pistols, Nazi flags, recordings of Nazi marching songs, portraits of Hitler, Julius Streicher and his British counterpart Arnold Leese, photos of Rudolf Hess and a broken German wireless transmitter. Ominously, there were also several tins of sodium chlorate, a weed killer which, when mixed with sugar formed an explosive, a fact that all those questioned by police conceded they knew.[284] The words 'Jew killer' were scrawled on one tin with the instruction, 'place a few crystals in a sealed room full of Jews'.[285] 'How could we explain that away? We hadn't even got a window box,' quipped NSM activist Martin Webster, a teenager who had recently joined the group from the LEL.[286]

Special Branch also recovered several documents and tape recordings, which laid bare Jordan's intentions. In one lecture, titled 'Soldiers of the Ring', Jordan stated, 'our first task is to embody, to study and to master, the basic operational routine' of the paramilitary *Freikorps* formations 'and as such are largely differentiated from the concept of an organised political party'. The reason for such 'systematised training' was to enable Spearhead to 'be in a position to assert ourselves in the field of overt political struggle' and thus be ready for 'national emergency, for uprising and chaos'. Underlining the importance of military training, Jordan stated that Hitler's 'national revolution against the strangling power of the Jew' was only possible because of the paramilitary underpinnings of the *Freikorps* who had 'the fanaticism, the hardness and the resolution to drown a communist insurrection in the welter of its own blood ... Britain too needs a vanguard'.[287]

Tactically, Jordan drew inspiration from 'Hitler's commando' Otto Skorzeny, whose innovations including the use of special units, consisting of English-speaking troops wearing Allied uniforms, who infiltrated American lines during the Ardennes offensive in 1944 and the organisation of 'stay behind' networks to fight a guerrilla war against Allied occupation.[288] For Jordan,

> our aim is the revolutionary application to present political warfare of Skorzeny's revolutionary military principle of the future. Our aim is therefore to strike at the enemy with the greatest effect that our strength allows through operations employing small bodies of highly trained personnel in surprising ways.[289]

Such initiatives would put Jordan and his colleagues in the dock.

Jordan and Tyndall appeared at Bow Street Magistrates Court on 20 August to face trial for their Trafalgar Square speeches. Jordan argued that his remarks were a statement of fact and fair comment whilst Tyndall stated that his reference to the Jews was an expression of opinion. Stating that the pair had used 'words as bad as anybody could imagine', the magistrate sentenced Jordan and Tyndall to two months and six weeks' imprisonment, respectively. They both appealed their sentences and received bail. The London Sessions Appeals Committee allowed Jordan's appeal. They dismissed Tyndall's because the Committee considered his speech 'much more vitriolic'. They substituted Tyndall's prison sentence with a £10 fine, however.[290]

Released on bail, Jordan and Tyndall, together with Denis Pirie and Ian Roland Kerr-Ritchie, were charged on that same day with belonging to a group 'organised and equipped for the purpose of enabling them to be employed for the use or display of physical force in promoting a political object' in contravention of Section 2(1)(b) of the Public Order Act (1936).[291] The trial, which began at the Old Bailey on 2 October and lasted for thirteen days, focused on Spearhead's paramilitary pretentions. Central to this was the discovery of the weed killer, some of which, it transpired, Tyndall had purchased from a nearby hardware store.[292] The principal scientific officer of Woolwich Arsenal testified that not only was it 'one of the least difficult explosives to use' but that twelve pounds of such mixture, roughly the quantity seized, would have the same explosive effect as 100 Mills hand grenades. Cross-examining the witness, Tyndall asked what quantities were required to destroy the Communist Party headquarters, a question the scientific officer, at the behest of the judge, declined to answer. The judge also bade him to refuse to answer all questions on the best mixtures for explosives.[293]

Tyndall also subpoenaed Bean, himself a former Spearhead member, to testify. It did him little good. In court, Bean testified that he broke away from Spearhead 'because he was opposed to the brain-washing of a group of young men, many of whom did not have much brain to wash, including some of those in the dock'.[294] The jury took less than two hours to find all four men guilty. The judge sentenced Jordan to nine months' imprisonment, Tyndall six months. The others received three months apiece. Martin Webster issued a bulletin urging that 'The Fight Must Go On!' whilst an 'emergency committee' was convened to run the NSM in Jordan's absence.[295] Jordan had already arranged for Peter Ling to take over as NSM chairman. Rockwell would become 'world Führer', a title he retained until his murder in 1967.[296] Rockwell's assumption of the title was also a decision taken in deference to the Foreign Agents Registration Act; he feared that if he took a 'single order' from a 'foreign principal' (i.e. Jordan) then he risked prosecution and imprisonment.[297] Rockwell was delighted that Jordan readily acquiesced to his request, believing it reflected their personal subordination to the 'Holy Cause'.[298] Rockwell, who saw himself as St Paul to Hitler's Aryan Jesus 'who took the whip to the kikes' subsequently sought to elaborate a strategic 'Christian' front in his discourse which was something that Jordan, who shared Rockwell's belief in national socialism as a divine cause, baulked at, not sharing the former's moral flexibility.[299]

To protest Jordan's prison sentence, Rockwell's ANP demonstrated outside the British Embassy in Washington, DC.[300] Jordan continued communicating with Rockwell during his incarceration. The ANP journal, *The Stormtrooper*, reproduced some of his correspondence, in which Jordan thanked the group for its support, whilst proclaiming that WUNS would be the instrument through which 'we shall smash the Jewish World Front and establish the National Socialist New Order of the White Man. Sieg Heil!'[301] Jordan's mother served as an intermediary for such letters but he also kept in 'direct personal touch' with Rockwell through Michael Slatter, the Eton-educated son of the late Air Marshall Sir Leonard Slatter, who worked as an executive with a firm of timber merchants. Slatter, who briefly ran the NSM from October until December 1962, when Pirie and Roland Kerr-Ritchie were released, had previously been active with a small Nazi 'cell' in New Orleans and had visited Rockwell's headquarters in Arlington, Virginia in 1961, which no doubt explains why Jordan had selected him for this task.[302]

Whilst Jordan languished in prison, the Home Secretary, Henry Brooke, began discussing with his Cabinet colleagues measures to strengthen the Public Order Act (1936) and the Public Meeting Act (1908).[303] Ultimately, Brooke did not consider an amendment to the law necessary, beyond strengthening the penalties courts were able to impose.[304] This did not mean the NSM were free to organise, however, something they discovered after making numerous applications on Jordan's behalf to the Ministry of Works for permission to hold another Trafalgar Square meeting under the title 'National Socialism for Britain' to celebrate his impending release.[305] Hastily convened Ministerial meetings discussed the grounds upon which they could deny the use of the Square to fascist organisations without contravening free speech. Exasperated, Prime Minister Harold Macmillan declared 'I don't care on what *grounds* these meetings are banned as long as they *are* banned. They are uncivilised.'[306] Jordan's application was refused, as was every subsequent one.[307]

Jordan was released from prison on 31 May. Tyndall and his new fiancée, a young French woman called Françoise Dior, met him outside the prison gates together with a group of supporters he had ordered to 'report for duty'. Tyndall had met Dior in Paris whilst attending to WUNS business on Jordan's behalf. The two men went straight from prison to the Foreign Office to deliver a petition calling for the release of Rudolf Hess.[308] That same day a new issue of *The National Socialist* hit the streets featuring a front-page photograph of Hitler with the caption 'His spirit lives on'. The accompanying article, titled 'From Jail to Victory', declared that prosecution and privation were vital for generating 'a new type of man ... the REVOLUTIONARY FRONTFIGHTER'.[309]

Jordan had languished first in Wormwood Scrubs and then Spring Hill open prison in Buckinghamshire, whiling away the hours sewing mailbags and producing television aerials for a local firm whilst musing about 'defence' preparations for a reinvigorated NSM. Whilst in Wormwood Scrubs, Jordan claimed that he had 'talked daily' with John Vassall, an assistant private secretary to an Admiralty junior minister, who was serving eighteen years for espionage on behalf of the KGB and from whom Jordan learned 'quite a lot about a ring of queers in the highest circles' with possible links to the 'Profumo affair'. This was reference to the revelation that the Defence Minister John Profumo shared a mistress with a Soviet naval attaché but lied about it to Parliament before admitting the truth and resigning; the farrago hastened the demise of Macmillan's government.[310]

Following his release, Jordan wrote to Macmillan on 13 June 1963, sending a copy simultaneously to the Press Association to ensure maximum publicity, claiming to have new information that had never come before the Radcliffe Tribunal that had investigated Vassall's case.[311] Two days later, MI5 interviewed Jordan but did not set great store in his claims. 'Jordan told my officer that the notes made by Vassall were recorded on lavatory paper,' noted MI5 Director-General Roger Hollis. 'This seems appropriate.'[312] Questioned in Parliament on 9 July, Macmillan denied Jordan's information added anything of substance to Lord Denning's inquiry into the Profumo affair but forwarded his statement to Denning anyway to guard against accusations that his allegations had been ignored or made light of because of their source.[313]

Homosexuality remained a criminal offence and Jordan subsequently published his version as 'Behind the Democratic Curtain – Homosexual Network Endangers National Security' in *The National Socialist* which, though scrupulously careful not to name names, claimed that the Soviets were blackmailing a group of prominent homosexuals with whom Vassall was acquainted in order to further their spying.[314] MI5 dismissed Jordan as a 'tainted source' who had probably 'embroidered' what information he claimed Vassall had given him. Nonetheless they were obliged to investigate his allegations further, in particular his charge that:

> An acquaintance of Vassall who kept a establishment catering for sexual perversions at an address in London, W8, numbered among his distinguished clients one of our most frequently televised peers, who used to go there to procure 'chickens' (the homosexual term for boys).[315]

Without commenting on the veracity of the allegations, MI5 identified 'one of our most frequently televised peers' as Sir Robert Boothby, Mosley's old friend. MI5 subsequently re-interviewed Vassall on 17 September who, despite refusing to talk about the allegations he had made to Jordan, did read *The National Socialist* article, commenting that 'it was all true except for one statement about "a distinguished member of the Joint War Staff" which Vassall agreed was [redacted]'.[316]

Though he was now a free man, Jordan had emerged from prison to find that the NSM had fallen into considerable disarray in his absence. The brief tenure of Kerr-Ritchie, who ran the NSM for a short period following his own release from prison, only exacerbated matters. He had employed as a part-time office assistant 'Peter Compton', whom it subsequently transpired had infiltrated the NSM for the anti-fascist 62 Group whom he supplied with photographs, documents and membership lists.[317] Kerr-Ritchie had also expelled Martin Webster from the NSM though Tyndall reinstated him after his own release having determined him to be a 'scapegoat' for the 'serious errors of others'.[318] More seriously,

Tyndall learned, Kerr-Ritchie had 'misused a very substantial amount of money'. Upon further investigation, Kerr-Ritchie became disruptive, created 'factions' and went so far as to inform the *Daily Telegraph* he had no confidence in Tyndall's leadership and would abstain from political activity until Jordan returned.[319]

Some of the monies Kerr-Ritchie allegedly embezzled, he had funnelled to Peter Ling to finance his own 'underground' group.[320] The nature of its activities can perhaps be gainsaid from newspaper reports that appeared whilst Jordan and Tyndall were imprisoned, detailing several explosions in the dense pine forests between Bere Regis and Wareham in Dorset caused by a group of nine NSM activists. The police subsequently linked these tests to a small explosion outside a Jewish-owned firm in Newcastle a fortnight beforehand. Asked for comment by the media, Ling denied involvement but added 'I am not surprised this has happened'.[321] Returning to the leadership, Jordan expelled Kerr-Ritchie. Ling departed with him.[322]

On 20 June, shortly after his release, Jordan embarked upon a holiday with his mother. Visiting Brussels, Jordan used the opportunity to meet Jean-Robert Debbault, a former Walloon SS officer who edited *L'Europe Réele* (*Real Europe*) to whom he was introduced by the Swiss fascist Gaston-Armand Amaudruz, leader of Le Nouvel ordre européen (NOE – New European Order). Presumably unaware of the NSM's internal contretemps, Amaudruz had recently appointed Kerr-Ritchie as his English correspondent.[323] Debbault agreed to head the WUNS Belgian section.[324] Using the pseudonym 'James Wilson', Jordan travelled on to Bavaria in West Germany where he painted 'Hitler was Right' below Hitler's former residence in Berchtesgaden, generating worldwide headlines. Though he was not known to have been the culprit at the time, a photograph subsequently appeared in *The Stormtrooper* which provided a clue. Jordan also met with contacts in Freiburg and Munich and had planned to meet with Bruno Ludtke, the man entrusted with the clandestine distribution of WUNS literature in West Germany.[325] However, Jordan arrived in Frankfurt to find that the police had already arrested Ludtke on 9 July in response to this propaganda drive, which had seen the dissemination of thousands of German-language NSM leaflets declaring 'Hitler was Right'.[326] German police also issued an arrest warrant for Jordan on a charge of sedition in connection with the distribution of these leaflets but were unable to execute it.[327] In solidarity, the NSM picketed the West German embassy in London on 27 July calling for the release of 'political prisoners' whilst Jordan and Tyndall presented a petition to officials. They also raised funds for Ludtke's family, as did the ANP.[328]

Françoise Dior

Jordan's initially abortive attempts to extend the WUNS network into France were transformed by a young French Nazi, Marie Françoise Suzanne Dior, whose relocation to Britain in September 1963 would ultimately precipitate a serious split within the NSM. Born in Paris on 7 April 1932, Françoise Dior was the daughter of Madeline Leblanc and Raymond Dior, a left-wing journalist and brother of legendary French *couturier*, Christian Dior, though her biological father was, allegedly, Valentin de Balla, a Hungarian nobleman. Dior, who was bisexual, married Comte Robert-Henri Aynard de Caumont La Force, a descendent of Prince Honoré III of Monaco in 1955 with whom she had a daughter. The couple soon separated, however, as Dior drifted away from ardent monarchism towards Nazism. Dior's family disowned her as a result.[329] Her mother publicly stated 'I would not allow that man Colin Jordan into my home' and distanced the family from this 'sad affair'.[330] Similarly, her aunt, Catherine Dior, a former French resistance fighter imprisoned in Ravensbrück concentration camp, pleaded in vain with journalists not to mention her brother's name whilst reporting on her niece's Nazi antics.[331]

Awestruck by Jordan's headline grabbing antics, Dior had visited him shortly after the 1962 Trafalgar Square meeting and again in prison in December.[332] Jordan was also suitably impressed and tasked her with helping to establish WUNS in France, making her rapturously happy. 'I am so glad he choosed [sic] me to obey *all* his orders', she wrote to Rockwell. 'I think I am the happiest woman in the world, to be able to help, a little, such a great leader.'[333] Together with monies supplied by Savitri Devi amongst others, Dior began her organisational efforts by recruiting Claude Janne, a former Waffen-SS veteran to lead the French section. In September 1963, Jordan attended a conference in Paris at which the WUNS French section became the Féderation Ouest Européen (FOE). Yves Jeanne, the former Algerian contact for the BNP newspaper *Combat*, who had served with the SS Brigade 'Frankreich', soon gained control of the group and attempted to use it as a platform to seize control of the entire WUNS-Europe network from Jordan, splitting the French movement in the process. Jeanne's attempts to place all French-speaking national socialists under one command, regardless of geographical boundaries, quickly alienated Belgium's J.R. Debbault who resigned from WUNS when Rockwell acquiesced to Jeanne's request. His replacement, Rudiger van Sande, lacked the requisite abilities and within months, what had been the group's showcase, such as it was, was in disarray.[334]

Dior's presence proved internally corrosive upon the NSM too. She had originally struck up a relationship with Tyndall who declared his intention to marry her in May 1963.[335] However, within a matter of weeks, she had transferred her affections to Jordan who proposed to her on a flight from France to England.[336] 'All I want is a little Nazi baby', Dior told reporters shortly after announcing she would wed Jordan and not Tyndall.[337] The marriage took place on 5 October in Coventry, a town levelled by the Luftwaffe and therefore pregnant with symbolism for anti-fascists. The ceremony attracted 500 protesters and worldwide press coverage.[338] Having dispensed with the legal formalities, a suitably Nordic wedding ceremony – 'plighting the troth' – took place at NSM headquarters on the following day. Standing behind a candlelit table, bedecked with a swastika flag, Jordan and Dior declared they were 'of Aryan descent and racial fitness' over an SS dagger before each making a small incision in their ring fingers which were held together to symbolise the mingling of blood. A drop of this mingled blood was then allowed to fall on the blank fore page of *Mein Kampf*. Each in turn then placed a swastika engraved ring on the finger of the other, after which they declared the marriage enacted. The attendees then gave the fascist salute, sang the *Horst Wessel Lied* and toasted one another with Mead, 'the ancient drink of the Nordic peoples'. Tyndall was not present.[339]

For all the ceremony's solemn ritualisation of Nazi paganism, Jordan and Dior cut an incongruous couple, their juxtaposition captured thus by one reporter:

> Hip and Square. Erotic leather and tweedy tweeds. Like two strangers sheltering from the rain. The elegant top model and the balding scout master. She with a little English. He with less French. She with a bold taste for whisky. He with a taste for a little shandy. She a chain smoker. He a non-smoker. Improbably, unpromising – an unblessed marriage under the crooked cross. Britain's top Nazis. They are at the very bottom.[340]

Their marriage immediately encountered difficulties not least because Dior's fanaticism soon collided with reality.[341] When the couple honeymooned in the Scottish Highlands,

Jordan brought his mother with them. Bertha Jordan and Dior did not get on and she came to dislike her son's wife 'intensely'.[342] In November, the couple went house hunting in Yorkshire. Jordan's desire to retreat to 'an isolated house in the countryside' mortified Dior who was still reeling from her discovery that Jordan wanted her to become a 'housewife' which, she opined, 'is contrary to my aspirations, my education and the social class [to which] I belong'. Having left Coventry and returned to Paris, on 13 December Dior admonished Jordan:

> ALL my respect, my admiration and my adoration are for the ETERNAL Fuhrer and His glorious followers of the Third Reich – I did, for the *actual* rebirth of N.S., all I could, but for now, what I can do, when the Leader, himself, is *only* concerned by his *personal* life?! But I am sure, perhaps after our death, far later, in spite of your defection, a REAL MAN, the genuine successor, will come![343]

Their disintegrating relationship unfurled in excruciating detail before the tabloid media. 'It's odd to me,' Jordan mused to a journalist, 'she knows I am a good Nazi'.[344] He told another: 'I can't believe that I didn't measure up to her ideological standards. Mark you, she was always a bit of a hero-worshipper. But I gathered I came up to her standards, in that direction.'[345] Evidently, he did not. 'I thought I was marrying a leader and a hero', she railed. 'Instead, I found I had married a middle-class nobody.'[346] 'I believe that my husband, chief of British National Socialism, is not up to this role', Dior told the *Daily Mail*. 'He can say and do anything he likes – I want a divorce. And after an interval for reflection I will once again take care of the white race.'[347]

Jordan flew to Paris on 9 January 1964 in a bid to reconcile with his errant wife, and to rebuild his political relationship with the FOE, which had disassociated itself from WUNS following Dior's accusations. Jordan's cross-channel journey healed the breach, at least temporarily. Having conferred with Savitri Devi, Dior wrote 'There is hope for you and me, BUT YOU MUST accept my first concern is for the Fuhrer and his glory. It is the *condition* of a reconciliation.'[348] Having agreed to return to London, Dior stated 'I was *wrong* when I did not want to be firstly your wife, you were wrong not to be firstly the leader – I am sure it would be the Fuhrer's opinion.'[349] Dior later claimed she had left Jordan, 'to shock him into being a good leader'.[350] To demonstrate to Dior that he was indeed the Leader, Jordan suspended his wife from the NSM for two months and then compelled her to apologise for her actions in *The National Socialist*.[351]

Privately, Jordan blamed this embarrassing farce upon a Parisian occultist and clairvoyant called Jean-Louis Bernard Klingel-Schmidt, 'an evil character' who claimed, 'to possess and exercise magical powers!' This individual, Jordan claimed, was 'linked with the Jews and other enemy quarters' and had used his 'semi-hypnotic influence' to lure Dior away from him.[352] Dior had been introduced to Klingel-Schmidt through Savitri Devi who 'knew him fairly well', remembered former NSM activist Terry Cooper who regarded him as a con artist. One of Dior's contacts had warned her that Klingel-Schmidt was a 'psychic vampire' who could extract the 'life force' of anyone he met. 'From what I understood the only thing Bernard was capable of extracting from people was money', observed Cooper. 'He must have cried his eyes out the day when Françoise left Paris for England.'[353]

This whole farrago had also led Jordan to neglect the NSM, fuelling internal dissent regarding his leadership, or lack thereof, which was exacerbated when he threatened to pull out of the group and confine himself to WUNS work.[354] In January 1964, Jordan conceded to Tyndall that the 'ridicule' he had been subjected to because of his marriage was a 'handicap' he was unable to surmount but Tyndall continued to back his leadership.[355] However, within three months Jordan's political partnership with Tyndall had imploded too. After months of festering tensions, Tyndall wrote to Jordan on 21 April that he was no longer willing to accept his leadership, demanding that he step aside.[356] Jordan claimed that was Tyndall 'very bitter' that he had replaced him in Dior's affections. He also pointed to ideological tensions between Tyndall's 'narrow old-fashioned nationalist spirit' and his own 'new and vital spirit of Aryan unity' embodied in WUNS as another source of the rift.[357] Tyndall attempted to blackmail Jordan, stating that if he did not step aside he would issue a bulletin to all NSM members and WUNS leaders covering 'every aspect' of his conduct, including some things which 'morally speaking' should have been exposed already but which he had withheld 'in the hope of saving the name of the National Socialist Movement'.[358]

Irreconcilable, in May 1964, both men rather farcically expelled one another from the NSM. 'I once thought Colin was weak', Dior approvingly told the press. 'Now, by firing Tyndall, he has proved his strength and I love him for it.'[359] Jordan issued a special internal bulletin stating that he had expelled Tyndall for 'gross mismanagement, misconduct and disloyalty'. A second bulletin titled 'The Eradication of a Troublemaker – The Expulsion of J. Tyndall' alleged that he was motivated by personal 'spite' vis-à-vis Dior.[360] Though entertained that Jordan had expelled him from his 'Ruritanian' political movement, Jordan's belittling of him in the media angered Tyndall. 'Even in the days of my greatest disgust at your lack of political leadership, I never thought that you would descend so low as to use these kind of tactics.' His parting shot was a withering critique of Jordan's leadership:

> The plain fact is, Mr Jordan, that you, who have never been in politics out of any really sincere dedication to a selfless ideal, but only in service to the whims of your own overdeveloped ego, cannot bear to accept that you are no longer wanted at the top. Rather than play some useful part in a successful movement, you would prefer to be the lord over a futile back-street rabble ... I now assume the leadership of that body of National Socialists who have rejected you. I do so, not in any gleeful anticipation of the vanities of supreme rank, but only with a grave awareness of the burdens of such a job – which only future events will tell whether I am fit to bear ... I hope that this is the last occasion on which it is necessary to be in any kind of correspondence with you.[361]

Both Rockwell and Savitri Devi wrote numerous letters to both men imploring them to settle their differences, something they adamantly refused to do. 'Disillusioned and disgusted' with Rockwell's perceived indulgence of his rival, Jordan resigned from WUNS.[362] Surprised by the whole episode, which he first read of in the newspapers, a horrified Rockwell refused to accept his resignation. He sent out an official bulletin denouncing Tyndall as a 'mutineer' and stated that in a National Socialist world he would put Tyndall on trial for 'mutiny' and then 'hang him personally' if he was found guilty.[363] In December, Tyndall, evidently still trying to wrest control of WUNS from Jordan, sent Rockwell a large 'dossier' outlining Jordan's alleged misdeeds. Rockwell forwarded it to Jordan.[364] Tyndall also wrote to Mrs Leese in a fruitless effort to persuade her to rescind her support for Jordan and transfer control of Princedale Road to him.[365]

Savitri Devi was furious to learn from this that Tyndall had invoked her name in support of his feud with Jordan without consulting her.[366] Jordan also had harsh words for her, writing an 'amiable but firm' rebuke expressing his anger that despite affecting a 'neutral' position, Savitri Devi had communicated 'confidential' information to Tyndall in line with her 'foolish notion' that reconciliation could be achieved. 'I say you have in fact acted contrary to the high principles of National Socialism which you have so eloquently expounded in your books. You have not practised what you preached,' Jordan chided.[367]

Eventually, after nine months of temporising with Tyndall, Rockwell gave up on trying to reconcile the pair and, invoking clause ten of the Cotswolds Agreement, ordered all genuine Nazis to 'report for duty' with Jordan.[368] It was a pyrrhic victory for Jordan. Tyndall's departure and the formation of his own Greater Britain Movement (GBM) left Jordan with approximately twenty followers 'of which a mere handful are active.'[369] It was a salutary lesson for the 'World Führer' as to the limits of his authority. Thereafter, GBM activists continued to harass Jordan, distributing leaflets in Notting Hill Gate declaring 'Jordan is Jewish' and daubing 'Jordan is a Ponce' on the NSM headquarters; a humiliating reference to Jordan's financial reliance upon his wife. Dior was not as wealthy as some imagined, however. Her family had disinherited her leaving her with an income, derived from property rents, of £140 a month.[370] GBM activists also made menacing late-night telephone calls to Jordan's mother and wife, which, Jordan claimed to Rockwell, caused Dior so much distress that she had a miscarriage.[371] Both sides sought to undermine the other by passing information to the anti-fascist 62 Group.[372]

Leyton

Following Tyndall's departure, the NSM sought to reinvigorate its greatly diminished activist base through a series of placard protests. The first involved picketing a Jewish-owned firm in Regent Street, central London.[373] The second entailed a demonstration outside the French embassy protesting the arrest of Yves Jeanne and eight other FOE activists, which added to Jordan's woes.[374] Jeanne lost his job and Dior sold some jewellery in order to help him.[375] What really re-energised the NSM, however, was the racist campaign waged against Patrick Gordon Walker, Labour's shadow Foreign Secretary during the October 1964 general election in the West Midlands constituency of Smethwick.[376] The Conservative Party candidate, Peter Griffiths, ran an openly racist campaign against Walker, an opponent of immigration control, remembered for the slogan 'if you want a nigger neighbour, vote labour'. Griffiths denied personally using the slogan, deploring those who adopted it as a 'political rallying call' but refused to condemn and 'certainly will not criticise those who use it to express their protest against politicians who preach morality they are not called upon, by choice or circumstances, to practice'. Jordan used the slogan on stickers which Griffiths argued was 'the sum total of Right-wing intervention' whilst claiming that 'many people are still under the completely mistaken impression that the election in Smethwick was marked by massive race-hate publicity. Nothing is further from the truth'.[377]

Griffiths unseated Walker. Westminster viewed his campaign with distaste, however. During the debate on the Queen's Speech on 3 November 1964, Harold Wilson, the Labour prime minister, furiously denounced Griffiths' 'utterly squalid' campaign, famously branding him a 'parliamentary leper'.[378] There was uproar at Wilson's remarks. Twenty Conservative MPs walked out in protest and it was ten minutes before order was restored – 'the most chaotic scene in the House since Suez,' noted Griffiths' obituary.[379] Privately, however, many Conservatives were extremely uneasy about his election. Edward Heath recalled in his memoirs that 'Griffiths was a severe embarrassment to us and he was rightly shunned in Parliament when he arrived'.[380] From the nearby constituency of Wolverhampton South West, there was, however, what would appear to be, with the benefit of hindsight, a prescient warning from its local MP, Enoch Powell. 'I was shocked by the sounds of self-righteous criticism which arose after the defeat of Gordon Walker at Smethwick', he wrote. 'Immigration was, and is, an issue. In my constituency it has for years been number one.' Whilst Powell scented a new political issue, for Labour the 'Smethwick factor' signalled that immigration was, as Richard Crossman noted in his diary, 'the greatest potential vote loser for the Labour party'. Thus, Labour did not repeal the 1962 Commonwealth Immigration Act upon entering office, having already accepted the need for tighter controls, though it did introduce improved race relations machinery and commit to criminalising racial incitement, much to the chagrin of the extreme right.[381]

Though Jordan played little active part in the Smethwick campaign, he still regarded it as a 'limited victory' for the racial nationalist cause.[382] Having understood Smethwick's potential, Jordan campaigned actively against Walker, who, despite not being an MP, Wilson had appointed Foreign Secretary on the assumption that he would win the Leyton by-election in North East London in January 1965. Jordan was not alone in seeking Walker's defeat. Both the UM and the BNP withdrew their candidates so as not to split the anti-immigration vote which, they calculated, could again humiliate Walker.[383]

Jordan harried the Foreign Secretary from beginning to end, denouncing him as a 'disgusting race traitor' at his own press conference on 4 January. The NSM disrupted his first public meeting at Leyton Town Hall three days later. As Walker was introduced, Hugh Llewellyn Hughes, a serving soldier, blew a whistle. At this prearranged signal, Jordan emerged from his hiding place to barrack Walker. Denis Healey, Labour's Defence Minister, prompted knocked him off the platform. Meanwhile, Hughes and his colleagues, shouting racial epithets and throwing bags of flour, turned the meeting into a mass brawl.[384] On nomination day, an NSM activist, his face blacked up, arrived at Leyton Town Hall holding a placard stating that he was Gordon Walker 'the race-mixing candidate' whose policy was 'to make Britain black'. Having had his nomination rejected, he and Dior flanked Jordan on the Town Hall steps where Jordan gave a short speech to the assembled media. Walker's torment did not end there. On 16 January, two NSM members, Gordon Lawman and Michael Trowbridge, arrived at his committee rooms dressed in monkey suits carrying placards that proclaimed, 'we immigrants are voting for Gordon Walker'. Lawman was sentenced to three months for his 'political joke'.[385]

The NSM harried Walker right up to his eve of poll meeting at Leyton Baths on 20 January, with one activist Robert Relf, throwing a thunder flash onto the platform as he tried to speak. Jordan also sought to disrupt the meeting but was beaten-up and ejected from the meeting following a violent fracas with members of the anti-fascist 62 Group who were stewarding the meeting.[386] Defying expectation, Walker lost a safe Labour seat. Harold Wilson could do little more than offer his condolences and look for a new Foreign Secretary.[387] To celebrate their part in Walker's downfall, Jordan and Dior went to the National Film Theatre, which was screening three performances of Leni Riefenstahl's *Triumph of the Will*. 'My wife and I went to all of them,' boasted Jordan.[388] Walker's defeat was only temporary; he became MP for Leyton in the 1966 general election.

Synagogue arsons

The NSM continued its campaign of anti-Semitic daubing and desecration aimed at Jewish communal property after Leyton.[389] Dior remained a cathartic presence for such incidents.

During the Leyton by-election campaign, she had become involved in an altercation with a Jewish taxi driver called Wolfe Bussell who, having recognised her, refused her fare. 'Well, if you are a Jew, what are you doing out of the ovens,' retorted Dior. In the ensuing argument, the taxi driver tore off her swastika pendent. Police arrested him.[390] In retaliation, two NSM members firebombed his home precipitating his subsequent emigration to Israel.[391] Britain was 'too hot' for him, quipped *The National Socialist*, which proclaimed that 'with Bussell the Second Expulsion of the Jews has already begun'.[392] In retaliation, 'persons unknown' set fire to the NSM headquarters on the following evening.[393]

The bulk of NSM activity was divided between Friday evenings and Saturday afternoons, according to a former activist. 'Friday evening was Francoise's occupation, organising secretarial work, ranging from counting leaflets and stickers into bundles of twenty-five, preparing mail for distant members and typing.' Jordan, however, would return to London on Saturday to lead its occasional paper sales in Notting Hill 'and protest marches along a deserted Whitehall'.[394] Dior was an attractive woman and many of the younger male activists who joined her on a Friday night were in her thrall, forming a worshipful coterie around her. Between May and July 1965, four of these young NSM activists committed ten arson attacks on synagogues in London.[395] A second NSM arson gang attempted to set fire to two more synagogues. Hugh Hughes, the group's leader, tried to destroy one using a home-made bomb on 31 July.[396] Police apprehended Hughes' group in October after one member, Paul Dukes, was 'turned' by Harry Bidney of the 62 Group and confessed. The trial, which ended with guilty verdicts for all six activists, had commenced in February 1966 as workmen laboured to remove a dozen two-foot swastikas that supporters had daubed on the Old Bailey overnight.[397] In delivering his verdict, the Judge stated:

> I have no doubt that in doing these acts you have been led into this by the indoctrination you received in this pernicious movement. I am quite satisfied that the people in charge of his movement inculcated not only hatred of the Jews and coloured people but encouraged active steps against them.[398]

Whilst the judge held him morally responsible for the attacks, Jordan emphatically denied accusations that he had prior knowledge of them, though he had been quite happy to pose with the accused outside court for a photograph in which they all gave the Nazi salute. There were a further nineteen cases of arson or malicious damage against synagogues and Jewish communal property reported within the Metropolitan Police district in 1966 and a further nine in 1967 though the NSM, was not deemed responsible having declined by then to 'a very small band'.[399] Indeed, after the arrests, NSM membership 'dropped to zero overnight', recalled activist Terry Cooper. 'As far as I knew I was the only remaining member.'[400]

During this period, the NSM newspaper, *The National Socialist*, was printed by one of the more colourful characters to adorn the extreme right: Count Geoffrey Potocki de Montalk, a former New Zealand milkman, poet, pagan and sun worshipper. Potocki also claimed to be the rightful King of Poland, Hungary and Bohemia, Grand Duke of Lithuania, Silesia and the Ukraine, Hospodar of Moldavia and High Priest of the Sun. Potocki had gained a certain amount of notoriety during the inter-war period after being twice convicted of indecency as a result of his poetry. He was a familiar figure in the West End where, noted a police report, 'he may sometimes be seen, parading bare-headed with hair falling down almost to his shoulders, and wearing a flowing red velvet cloak and sandals.' Police regarded him as a 'sexual pervert' and suspected him of 'procuration'. He served as a printer for several of fascist organisations both during the 1930s, including William Joyce's National Socialist League. When Hitler invaded Poland in September 1939, precipitating the Second World War, Potocki sensed an opportunity for royal restoration, requesting leave from the British government to travel to Poland 'to pull things together'. They ignored his entreaties and in the following month, facing eviction from his flat for the unkingly offence of unpaid rent, Potocki vented his feelings to the judge by declaring 'I sincerely hope that Hitler will win the war, your honor.' He was removed from court. Potocki continued printing fascist material throughout the war, from his home in Little Bookham, Surrey, where he lodged with John Hooper Harvey, the *völkisch* IFL ideologue, who served as his 'royal' genealogist and etymologist and 'honorary treasurer' for Potocki's Polish Royalist Association. Potocki's publishing activities became a serious concern to the authorities when he published literature that (rightly) blamed Stalin for the Katyn massacre in 1943, which was embarrassing for British relations with their Soviet ally.[401]

Jordan's involvement with Potocki was perhaps curious given that his mentor, Arnold Leese, had despised him as 'that greasy scaly-necked Pole'. Savitri Devi had introduced Jordan to Potocki, whom she had met by chance in a London street shortly after the end of the war, Potocki in his royal garb and she in Hindu dress. The reimaging of their conversation by NSM activist Terry Cooper – 'Who are you? I'm the King of Poland, who are you? I'm a Hindu princess' – was perhaps not too far from the truth. Shortly after their meeting, Potocki printed 1,200 swastika emblazoned leaflets and posters for Savitri Devi, which she took with her to distribute in Germany in 1948, leading to her imprisonment in the following year.[402]

Potocki's role as the NSM printer quickly became another casualty of Jordan's volatile marriage, however. Jordan and Dior sometimes stayed with Potocki and his daughter until spring 1965 when, following another row with her husband, Dior sought sanctuary with them, alone. 'There was a great deal of excellent unpleasantness,' recalled Potocki's daughter. Whilst they all locked themselves inside,

> Jordan rampaged round the outside offering to break windows, which he probably never intended, as that would have put him on the wrong side of the law. And at another time he parked himself in his car outside the gate and even the law didn't seem able to make him go away.[403]

Jordan and Potocki acrimoniously parted company soon afterwards. Thereafter, Potocki began claiming to any one who would listen that Jordan was 'MI5'.[404]

Following this rupture, Jordan had NSM material printed by Berence Press, a firm based in Willesden, North West London, which also printed *Candour* as well as orders for Savitri Devi and The Britons. *Searchlight*, the anti-fascist magazine, asserted that Berence Press represented a business 'partnership' between Jordan and Roy Walter Purdy, a former BUF member who had joined the British Free Corps during the war for which he was given a death sentence in 1945, subsequently commuted to life imprisonment. He was released in 1954.[405] Jordan denied the story.[406]

Jordan's woes increased during summer 1965, when a group of Midlands-based NSM activists including George Newey, Patrick Webb and Robert Relf, who police 'strongly suspected' were responsible for 'numerous' racist incidents in Leamington Spa, formed a Ku Klux Klan (KKK). Its inaugural meeting on 12 June at the Chapel Tavern, Birmingham, attended by several journalists, was shambolic and immediately invited schism.[407]

It might have been coincidence, but three days later, the Home Secretary, Sir Frank Soskice, announced that Robert Shelton, Imperial Wizard of the United Klans of America, was to be denied entry to Britain.[408] Relf was undeterred. In the following week, he led twelve racists in a cross-burning ceremony at Long Lawford, Warwickshire, where one of its participants proclaimed that the group's aims were 'to rid Britain of the Jews, Roman Catholics and coloureds … by every possible means including violence'. Relf and two others were sentenced to three months' imprisonment, the remainder received fines. Their prosecution, under Section 1(1) of the Public Order Act (1936) was the first of its kind in Britain for wearing Klan uniforms.[409] Jordan issued a statement disassociating him from this 'ridiculous society of hooded men' whose antics, he claimed, were 'thoroughly damaging to the cause of serious political opposition to the coloured invasion of Britain' – a charge that could equally have been levelled at him.[410]

Jordan also engaged in a series of racist stunts including gate crashing a meeting organised by the West Indian National Association shouting at Jamaican politician Norman Manley to 'Go back to Jamaica'.[411] Notably, Jordan and Dior both disrupted the Conservative Party conference in Brighton in October 1965. Dior was escorted from the building, amidst laughter and applause, after shouting 'Keep Britain White' though a megaphone.[412] Jordan was ejected having mounted the rostrum and shouted 'The National Socialist Movement says stand by Rhodesia'.[413] On 1 November, he was sentenced to three months for using insulting words and behaviour likely to cause a breach of the peace after appearing in Downing Street during a visit by Rhodesian Prime Minister Ian Smith waving a placard stating: 'To Harold Wilson – Award for Treachery – For Betrayal of our White Kinsfolk in Rhodesia'. His sentence was reduced to a fine upon appeal though an attempt to get the conviction quashed failed.[414] In the following week, Jordan was 'savagely beaten' in Birmingham by unknown assailants who stole his briefcase.[415] Undeterred, in the following week, he was removed from the Strangers' Gallery in the House of Commons having interrupted the debate on the Second Reading of the Southern Rhodesia Bill.[416]

By spring 1966, Jordan's marriage was over. Following the arrest of the two NSM arson gangs, he spent most his time in Coventry, whilst Dior resided in London. Although only the NSM 'secretary', Special Branch noted that in reality there was 'no doubt' that Dior was 'presiding over its London activities'.[417] The net was closing in on Dior regarding her suspected role in previous years' arson spree, however. After the police interviewed her, she and Terry Cooper promptly departed to France, on 15 March. When he discovered Dior had eloped with Cooper, Jordan followed her to Paris informing the police there that his wife had disappeared with Cooper who he described as a 'homosexual who would get her drugs.'[418] By post, Dior again demanded a divorce, adding that: 'You need not think that after the divorce I shall maintain you. In ten years you have killed any possibility of the growth of National Socialism in England. You tried too much to make it a Nationalist Movement.'[419]

His marriage over, Jordan's only recourse was to expel the unfaithful pair from the NSM, citing Cooper in the subsequent divorce proceedings.[420] 'Without engaging in the unpalatable practice of apportioning blame, I would say that, with the wisdom of hindsight, I would have been wiser to have avoided marriage,' Jordan later lamented.[421]

Dior and Cooper continued their French travails, travelling on to Nice where they stayed with Denis Travers, an NSM sympathiser who introduced them to a range of Nazi contacts on the Côte d'Azur, including André Trochu through whose ministrations Dior became interested in the mystical, esoteric side of Nazism. Savitri Devi also visited them. Cooper disliked her intensely, commenting disparagingly, 'she looked like a refugee from a gypsy camp, complete with the typical gypsy odour'. In October, however, French police arrested Dior and she was compelled to serve the four-month sentence which had been imposed *in absentia* after being found guilty of daubing a swastika on the British Embassy in Paris in 1962. Following her release, she and Cooper travelled, at Savitri Devi's suggestion, to Vienna. There they met a former Luftwaffe pilot involved in one of Savitri Devi's schemes, and then onto Munich where they met several leading figures associated with the National-demokratische Partei Deutschlands (NPD – National Democratic Party of Germany) including former SS lieutenant Walter Brandner, a party deputy in the Bavarian Landtag.[422]

Upon her return from France, British police arrested Dior at Cooper's Dagenham home for her part in the 1965 synagogue arson campaign. Unrepentant, on the eve of her trial in September 1967, Dior told the *Daily Telegraph*, 'I would like to make an Act of Parliament to burn down all synagogues by law.'[423] Found guilty of conspiring with others to commit arson, though not of inciting them to do so, Dior was sentenced to eighteen months' imprisonment. Her marriage to Jordan prevented the British authorities from deporting her after she had served her sentence.[424] 'There wasn't a flicker of emotion on that beautiful face,' noted Inspector Bert Wickstead, the arresting officer. 'True to her code, she clicked her heels together and shouted defiantly "Heil Hitler!"'[425]

Seeking to restore his reputation after the Dior debacle, Jordan turned himself towards the task of making Nazism relevant to the modern world. To this end, he authored his now seminal article 'National Socialism: A Philosophical Appraisal', which appeared in the inaugural issue of *National Socialist World*, the quarterly WUNS magazine edited by Dr William Pierce, a physicist who had previously lectured at Oregon State University.[426] Rockwell regarded Jordan's contribution as 'a genuine historical classic – on a level with Martin Luther's Declaration and other such great documents'.[427] Jordan's biographer, Paul Jackson, describes it as his 'definitional statement' of political philosophy, written for an international audience.[428]

Jordan's essay, which appeared alongside an eighty-page distillation of Savitri Devi's *Lighting and the Sun*, argued that National Socialism's survival across the chasm of military defeat and the subsequent decades of 'vilification' proved its immutable beauty and 'indestructible' nature. National Socialism, he claimed, represented a transcendent, holistic political philosophy, which, properly understood, was much more than a theory for the political organisation of the state. It was a truly universal creed harnessing the organic 'blood feelings' of the Aryan 'folk' for the 'rebirth' of Western civilisation from the morass of decadency and degeneracy into which the 'modern' world had sunk following the passing of the 'old medieval order'. In its totalising conception of thought and action, life and death, Jordan theorised that National Socialism was an eternal cosmological creed through which man, reduced to a biological component of the 'racial community', achieves 'immortality' because of the endless cycle of rebirth and renewal. Reasserting the primacy of race in the modern world, Jordan espoused a pan-Aryan vision that transcended the vagaries of national boundaries and indeed the nation state itself, which was rendered 'integrally subordinate to a nationalism of the whole race.' For Jordan, '*thinking with the blood* on all questions' represented the 'basic value' of National Socialism which, through eugenics, could provide 'the breeding of better human beings' whose destiny would be realized through the will to achievement of a hierarchical racial state under a 'supreme leader' operating under the dictum 'all for the folk and the folk for all'.[429]

British Movement

Police arrested Jordan again on 15 November 1966 for sending numerous pieces of anti-Semitic ephemera to a teenage NSM activist, Peter Pollard, who had daubed 'Jews get out' on the door of a Plymouth synagogue together with several swastikas. Jordan had sent the material to Pollard congratulating him on distributing a 'mass of material which will certainly make an impact' – though not perhaps in the manner he had envisaged. Found guilty of conspiracy to contravene Section 6 of the Race Relations Act (1965), and of inciting others to do so, Jordan became one of the first individuals convicted of such an offence, and was jailed for eighteen months on 25 January 1967. Pollard received three years on probation.[430]

The Court of Appeal dismissed Jordan's subsequent appeal against his conviction. Undeterred, Jordan made representations to his local MP, Richard Crossman, about the supposed illegality of his arrest.[431] This was somewhat ironic. 'Years ago', Crossman recalled, 'Mr. Jordan came to see me, sat down opposite me in my office in Coventry, accused me of being pro-Jewish and the proceeded to lecture me mercilessly at length.'[432] Now, however, Jordan appealed to him for assistance. Crossman dutifully presented Jordan's case to the Home Secretary, Roy Jenkins, who declined to refer the case back to the Court of Appeal and rejected Jordan's numerous allegations against the police and judge. Jenkin's did consent, however, to move Jordan to an open prison closer to his home to ease the burden on his eighty-one-year-old mother, left to fend for herself because of her son's antics.[433] His visceral hatred of the Labour Party aside, Jordan was most grateful to Crossman for easing his personal predicament.[434]

Whilst languishing in prison, Jordan's political fortunes deteriorated further. In February 1967, the National Front was launched; its populist anti-immigration platform quickly became the principal vehicle for racial nationalist politics, relegating Jordan's influence to the margins of the extreme right milieu. Jordan's avowed Nazism precluded him from ever being allowed to join the NF as did his personal history of rancorous relations with its leading figures, A.K. Chesterton, Andrew Fountaine and John Bean. Jordan also suffered a grievous personal loss in August: George Lincoln Rockwell was gunned down and killed by a disgruntled party member, John Patler, former editor of *The Stormtrooper*, expelled from the ANP, according to Matt Koehl, for his 'Bolshevik leanings'. Rockwell's death deprived Jordan of a friend, ally and inspiration, causing him to feel a 'crushing sorrow'.[435] Rockwell's death coincided with the collapse of the NSM, which came to a 'standstill' in the following month, after Jordan sacked his underling, J.D.F. Knight, who had been overseeing its operations for him.[436]

There was one bright spot, however. Whilst Jordan languished in prison, Tyndall had developed an emollient attitude towards him, signing a petition calling for his release and defending Jordan's right to free speech in *Spearhead*.[437] Tyndall also wrote to Jordan in prison expressing his sympathy for his predicament and offering his assistance vis-à-vis his elderly mother. Following Jordan's release, the two men met on 24 January 1968. Tyndall, despite his own past, had been allowed to join the NF. He held out the possibility of Jordan's own 'elevation', if he were prepared to be patient but despite cordial correspondence and further private meetings it soon became clear to Jordan he would never be allowed to join.[438]

On 8 May, Jordan founded the British Movement (BM), which operated from his Coventry home. Through his internal newsletter, *British Tidings*, Jordan sought to inculcate its membership with a 'British' form of National Socialism, adopting the Celtic cross in place of the swastika – an act he had criticised Tyndall for only four years previously. Otherwise, the BM was largely indistinguishable from the NSM. Indeed, the longer-term ideological continuity of the BM with the British Nazi tradition was evident in Jordan's sale of old copies of Leese's newspaper, *The Fascist*.[439] Another change, which discombobulated many of his international associates, including William Pierce, was Jordan's decision to disaffiliate himself from WUNS, which Matt Koehl had led since Rockwell's assassination the previous year. He did retain, however, an informal cooperation with the organisation and individual BM activists became associate members.[440] Jordan's nascent group suffered an initial blow, however, when anti-fascists disrupted an early BM meeting and made off with membership cards and other documents.[441]

Despite founding a rival organisation, Jordan retained a cordial correspondence with NF chairman, A.K. Chesterton, though his fraternisation with NF members soon created problems. On 6 September 1968, Jordan met with several Sheffield NF activists, a development about which Chesterton was remarkably sanguine. Subsequently, however, four men, including Joe Short, the NF student organiser, set fire to a Sheffield synagogue.[442] Though Jordan denied foreknowledge of the attack, the judge viewed his presence as a catalyst. He informed the defendants:

> You came away roaring like paper tigers going to strike a blow for something – and I am not quite sure what – and allowed yourself to be carried away by drink and a feeling of elation, perhaps because you had spent the evening in the company of a man who had achieved a considerable degree of notoriety.[443]

Within the NF, Martin Webster used the arson attack to marginalise Jordan further. Jordan in turn protested to Chesterton that Webster was deliberately linking him to the arson attack in order to discredit him.[444] Chesterton lamented the 'futile vendetta' between the former colleagues but was powerless to put a stop to it.[445] Nevertheless, he and Jordan came to a 'gentlemen's agreement' that their respective organisations would not officially attack one another.[446]

The aura of violence continued to dog Jordan. In the following month, two brothers, Robert and John Oliffe, appeared in court charged with numerous offences under the Firearms Act (1967) for possessing illegal weapons. Police had arrested them in August with a cache of weapons including submachine guns, rifles, pistols and hundreds of rounds of ammunition. Police also unearthed a range of material during a search of their home indicating an 'intense interest in matters concerning the Nazi regime.'[447] One brother was an NSM member.[448]

Jordan's decision to remove the overt trappings of Nazism motivated a small cadre of former NSM activists led by David J. Courtney, the former Greenwich NSM organiser, to found the National Socialist Group (NSG).[449] Courtney had replaced J.D.F. Knight as Jordan's right-hand man, after his dismissal, helping Jordan's mother to run what was left of the NSM prior to Jordan's release.[450] The NSG, it was argued, represented an attempt to form a covert parallel paramilitary structure to the BM, a valid suspicion given that Courtney appears to have joined the BM too.[451] Styling itself as a 'cultural' organisation, the NSG was a secretive underground group, which, by its own recognisance, existed 'to provide a framework wherein its members can strive towards a mental, physical and spiritual goal within the bounds of National Socialism.' NSG members donated their 'political allegiance' to Jordan, though he claimed this loyalty was unsolicited. Questions surrounding Jordan's relationship with the NSG surfaced in May 1969 when Chesterton received several documents regarding the NSG 'claiming that your present movement was only a blind and that you were one of its leading spirits'.[452] Jordan countered that this was 'completely untrue'. His only political interaction with the NSG, he stated, was to pass on international contacts to the group after it superseded the BM as the British section of WUNS.[453] The NSG subsequently collapsed when police arrested several members on firearms charges and the group itself 'lost' all its files following an anti-fascist action.[454]

The argument, that Jordan was really pursuing a twin-track strategy, gained some credence after he announced that the BM would simultaneously contest elections for the first time, partly because he believed that it would be harder for the State to target a group engaged in democratic politics. In pursuit of this new strategy, and looking askance at Hitler's early breakthrough, Jordan closed no. 74 Princedale Road and relocated the base of his operations believing that 'our Munich is most likely to lie in the Midlands'.[455] Enoch Powell's 'Rivers of Blood' speech, delivered in Wolverhampton on 22 April 1968, which highlighted the potential of immigration as an electoral issue, served to influence Jordan's decision. 'What Enoch Powell said in his speech constitutes what I said in a pamphlet – for which I got 18 months under the Race Relations Act', Jordan told the press.[456] Seeking to capitalise upon what he believed was their common message, Jordan staged a noisy counter-demonstration at a Conservative Party rally in Dudley five days later, heckling Edward Heath, the Conservative prime minister, for sacking Powell. Thrown out of the meeting, Jordan gave an impromptu speech on the steps of Dudley Town Hall to cries of 'eighteen months for telling the truth' from his supporters. BM activists regularly demonstrated their support of Powell thereafter distributing *Powell was Right* leaflets outside his meeting at Wulfrun Hall, Wolverhampton, on 9 June 1969, for instance.[457] Jordan also continued to harass Heath, trying and failing to obtain a warrant for his arrest under the Treason and Felony Act (1848) from Bow Street Magistrates Court because of his efforts to take Britain into the Common Market.[458]

The electoral potential of anti-immigrant politicking highlighted by Powell stimulated Jordan to consider elections as a viable alternative for the first time in his career. In June 1969, he stood as a candidate in a Parliamentary by-election in Ladywood, Birmingham, demanding a halt to all immigration, compulsory repatriation for those already here and the revision of British citizenship 'rightly preserving its privileges for white citizens'.[459] His election agent, Leicester BM organiser Ray Hill, later recalled: 'we ran a predicable campaign, election addresses and leaflets which blamed everything on blacks and Jews and unashamedly proclaimed our devotion to National Socialism' in order to provoke violent opposition and in doing so to raise the political temperature.[460] Jordan gained 282 votes (3 per cent), viewing the result as a vindication for 'open' Nazism given that the NF candidate polled only marginally better results.[461] His electoral strategy, accompanied by a *Wolverhampton Newsletter* targeting local NF members, sought to forestall the BM becoming 'some society on the side' because of the NF's dominance on the extreme right.[462]

The publicity that Jordan's electoral exertions generated masked the fact that the BM itself languishing 'in the doldrums'. In August, Jordan allegedly began 'contemplating' a merger with John O'Brien's British Defence League in a bid to 'break new ground' in the West Midlands. Indeed, despite 'strenuous efforts', the BM's organisational capacity remained confined to two branches: London and Liverpool.[463] By the end of the year, Jordan was appealing for 'national solidarity' between 'patriotic organisations' because the 1970s 'will be the decade of decision' in which extreme right-wing politics either rose to the challenge and confronted the nation's 'destruction' or 'will probably lose its last opportunity to do so'.[464] The response to Jordan's 'Unity' agenda was 'worse then disappointing'.[465] Few paid the call any heed, particularly when they learned that Jordan was behind the initiative.[466] Chesterton rebuffed Jordan, highlighting that 'prevailing opinion' within the NF was such that he could not think of a single Directorate member who would be amenable to 'any kind of association' which Jordan 'may advocate or in which you may be thought to participate, so that a movement towards union on those lines would, in fact, be a move towards disunity'. His exclusion from the NF still wrangled with Jordan, particularly because Tyndall, Webster and Pirie had been admitted to the party. Chesterton held out an olive branch. Were Jordan to develop a 'British nationalist policy', counselled Chesterton, then at some distant date cooperation with him might become politically viable but, for the moment, this was 'impossible'.[467] Jordan was extremely disappointed, issuing a leaflet, *Frankly Now*, in January 1971 lambasting most nationalists as 'gutless and bone idle politically' whilst, pointedly, lamenting the inability of their leaders to work together.[468]

Grassroots NF activists ignored the injunction not to cooperate with Jordan. In the West Midlands, the BM maintained 'friendly relations' with local NF branches, despite the national organisation having proscribed them. Likewise, Jordan would re-establish correspondence with Tyndall, which, if nothing else, at least kept the channels of communication open between the two men.[469] During the 1970 general election, Jordan refrained from contesting the more fertile constituency of Wolverhampton North East in favour of Aston, Birmingham, where, on a fairly anodyne anti-immigration platform, he polled 704 votes (2.5 per cent) after reaching an 'agreement' with the local NF not to compete against it.[470]

During summer 1972, John Tyndall again held out the prospect of Jordan joining the NF. 'He made it clear that I could run the Midlands for the NF if I would join him', recalled Jordan who claimed he was non-committal. Webster remained implacably opposed to Jordan, however, warning him that he might face 'elements I cannot control', if he continued to encroach upon what he regarded as NF territory.[471] Indeed, Jordan's efforts to retain relevancy, which often involved insinuating himself onto NF demonstrations and then hijacking the resultant publicity, angered Webster who wrote to him that if Jordan thought his actions were endearing himself to the NF 'I can assure you that your bumptious vanity is deluding you'.[472] Tyndall also became more hostile to Jordan though not to the BM to whom he held out an olive branch. In the following year, he wrote:

> There is nothing at all to prevent a coming together of the people in British Movement with those in the National Front other than the question of Mr. Jordan himself. If he did not insist on a place for himself in the NF but accepted instead a non-party political role, the membership of BM could be merged into the NF without trouble.[473]

Thereafter, the two groups stood against one another in the February 1974 general election. Standing in Wolverhampton North East, Jordan polled 711 votes (1.5 per cent) compared to the 2,548 votes (5.3 per cent) polled by the NF candidate.

Largely unnoticed contemporaneously, during the early 1970s, Jordan's racial rhetoric underwent a subtle shift. On 15 May 1971, as the centrepiece of 'White Power Day', Jordan delivered a speech in Wolverhampton titled 'White Power for Britain'. During the speech, Jordan lamented that in less than thirty years 'racial renegades' had transformed 'a white man's country' through mass immigration, which he regarded as 'the greatest betrayal in our history'. This threatened the white race with biological 'obliteration' as it faced a metaphoric and literal 'darkness' in the shape of 'a largely Afro-Asian Britain of the future'. The solution? 'White Power!' The phrase acted as a counterpoint to calls for

'Black Power' whilst also serving as shorthand for the BM policy of compulsory repatriation. 'The paramount question of today, raised by the present mass immigration, amounts to this,' stated Jordan, who offered his listeners a racially polarised choice:

> are we going to keep our country for our own people or not? Which is it to be: Britain for anyone and everyone, or Britain for the British? Which do you want: to make Britain multi-racial, or to keep Britain white? Black Power or White Power?[474]

Although Jordan's clarion call for 'White Power' failed to resonate more widely, it injected into the British extreme right a concept coined by George Lincoln Rockwell who had begun using the slogan during his campaign for governor of Virginia in 1965. Rockwell's views gained their fullest exposition in his racist tome *White Power* (1967), in which he specifically appealed to 'white Europeans' to 'stand up and fight' Jews and Blacks alongside 'men who share your blood'.[475] Rockwell's all-encompassing definition of 'white' created doctrinal problems for the National Socialist faithful, obsessed as they were with ideas of 'Nordic' purity, but his new theoretical framework for 'pan white' unity aimed to encourage whites to think of themselves as 'white' with their own specific racial interests. Rockwell sought to use this platform to broaden his appeal amongst those racists who would not ordinarily support a National Socialist group. The creation of a racially charged electorate, it was believed, would also 'mainstream' National Socialist ideas. To reinforce his new direction, on 1 January 1967, Rockwell renamed the American Nazi Party, the National Socialist White Peoples' Party (NSWPP).[476] It is not a coincidence that Jordan re-branded the NSM as the BM in the following year in a similar attempt to broaden the ideological appeal of Nazism.

During the course of July 1974, Jordan sought to deepen his organisation's international connections, arranging for a small BM contingent to take part in the Flemish nationalist festival at Diksmuide, Belgium, at which his activists could wear political uniforms without fear of prosecution.[477] However, the burden of caring for his elderly mother caused Jordan to wind down his involvement as BM leader, one of his last public activities being to lead approximately thirty activists in a 'Smash the IRA' march through Liverpool on 30 November 1974.[478] In February 1975, he officially stepped down as National Chairman of the group.[479] Jordan's retirement from active politics was hastened following his arrest in March 1974, and subsequent conviction in May 1975, for shoplifting several pairs of red women's knickers and a box of chocolates from Tesco. Jordan claimed he was the victim of a 'Jewish plot'. He was unable to explain, however, why he was in a 'Jewish-owned' store in the first place. As the *Sun* gleefully pointed out, 'Pantie Thief' Jordan's credibility had been grievously damaged for the sake of £1.94.[480] When Bertha Jordan died in November 1975, the BM paid tribute to her, noting her efforts to keep both the NSM and the BM going whilst her son was imprisoned. Over eighty, she had played a key role in keeping correspondence going, preparing stickers and flyers for distribution, not to mention cleaning the NSM offices. 'Few members did as much donkey work of this kind as she did over the years,' they recorded.[481]

Jordan's successor was Michael McLaughlin, the Merseyside BM leader who had previously been active in the NF but had resigned in 1971, allegedly because the organisation 'failed to recognize the spiritual leadership of Adolf Hitler'.[482] Ideologically, McLaughlin appeared the perfect successor to Jordan though his personal antecedents meant that, on the face of it at least, he was a rather unlikely heir. A former merchant seaman now working as a milkman, McLaughlin was the son of staunch Irish Republican parents; the family home being the 'virtual headquarters not only of the Liverpool Communist Party', he later grandiosely claimed, 'but the Irish Republican cause too'. Both his parents had been involved with the IRA in their native Ireland during the 1920s. His father, Patrick, subsequently emigrated to New York where he joined the Communist Party of the United States of America and fought with the Abraham Lincoln Brigade during the Spanish Civil War. McLaughlin's mother, Kathleen, 'a former nun turned gun-running revolutionary', had corresponded with the Spanish Communist firebrand 'La Pasionaria' – Dolores Ibárruri.[483]

There was no doubting the nature of his racist commitment, however. Prior to taking over the BM, McLaughlin had been convicted under Section 63(1) of the Representation of the People Act (1949), for which he was fined £50, and under Section 6 of the Race Relations Act (1965), for which he was fined £100 plus costs, after being found guilty of interfering with an election and inciting racial hatred. These convictions stemmed from his distribution of anti-Semitic stickers during the October 1974 election targeting Jewish MP Michael Fidler (Bury and Radcliffe), which read 'The Jews have Israel – Let the British have Britain'.[484] The BM subsequently claimed that the total cost of the case (£345) had almost bankrupted the organisation, which spoke volumes about its financially impecunious nature.[485]

Though Jordan was no longer leader, he remained active within the BM, allowing the group to host camps on his Yorkshire property in 1975 and 1976. He was also outspoken in his support for Robert Relf, a former NSM activist, Klansman and self-styled 'race martyr' who was jailed in May 1976 for contempt of court after he refused to remove a sign outside his house stating that it was 'for sale to an English family'. After his release, Relf, an unemployed bus driver, refused to surrender to the 'white renegades' of the Race Relations Board and was returned to jail for 'gross, deliberate and wanton contempt of court'.[486] He promptly went on hunger strike. Whilst Relf's obdurate stance had garnered a modicum of public support, this rapidly dissipated after his political antecedents were revealed. The BM demonstration outside the court led to Jordan and McLaughlin's arrest. A judge fined Jordan £50 and bound him over to keep the peace. Undeterred, Jordan continued supporting Relf throughout his one-man campaign against the Race Relations Act and indeed the periodic bouts of imprisonment that resulted from it, publicising his legal travails through American white supremacist publications like *Liberty Bell* and *White Power Report* in an effort to internationalise support for his case.[487]

Jordan and McLaughlin were increasingly at odds with one another, however. Jordan publicly 'terminated' his support for his designated successor in 1978.[488] Thereafter, Jordan engaged in a steady stream of invective against 'the mad milkman of Merseyside'.[489] The dispute left an indelible mark. Indeed, McLaughlin insinuated in his memoirs, published in 2016, that Jordan was a Soviet spy and a cross-dressing pervert motivated only by avarice, claims that were angrily dismissed by former BM activists.[490] This festering personal animosity aside, there were, however, genuine political and strategic differences between the two men. McLaughlin had endeavoured to expand the BM activist base by recruiting skinheads and football hooligans. Jordan viewed the resulting plebeian composition of McLaughlin's BM with increasing distaste. Its 'Hollywood-style pop-perversion of National Socialism' traduced Jordan's elitist vision of spiritual racial idealism, usurped by a 'crude, raucous racial hatred' and bellicose anti-Communism, lacking both depth and vision. Jordan was equally dismissive of McLaughlin's involvement with the burgeoning white power music scene, arguing that degenerate 'monkey-music' was just an excuse for acts of violent, drunken nihilism 'and other forms of blindly rebellious, anti-social self-assertion'. Such noise 'would not have been tolerated for 10 minutes in NS Germany', he asserted. It was 'the sound of Aryan downfall'. Believing it impossible to combat degeneracy with degeneracy, Jordan had nothing but contempt for the young skinheads who swelled the BM ranks whom he regarded as 'a product of its [society's] sickness; not an agency for its rejuvenation, and a vanguard of the future.'[491]

Jordan was hardly more complimentary about Tyndall's NF, periodically denouncing it as a 'kosher front' and a 'side tracking fake' – mirroring Leese's denunciation of Mosley's 'Jewnion of Fascists' fifty years beforehand.[492] There was no denying its popularity, however, and Jordan readily conceded that the NF Leicester branch, 'probably has more members than the whole of the BM'.[493] Although the BM remained small compared to the NF, it quickly gained a well-deserved reputation for racial violence. So much so that by 1981 – a year in which there were twenty-six racist murders – the Home Secretary, Willie Whitelaw, noted that the group had 'replaced' the NF as the principal engine for racial violence and harassment.[494]

Searchlight, the anti-fascist magazine, eagerly exploited Jordan's bitter clash with McLaughlin. Their 'mole' inside the BM, Ray Hill, exacerbated the resulting tensions to destabilise the BM by having Hill legally challenge McLaughlin for its leadership. Facing bankruptcy because of the case, McLaughlin disbanded the organisation in 1983.[495] McLaughlin continues to hold Jordan responsible for his ouster as BM leader.[496] There is certainly some truth in the charge. Whilst seeking to obfuscate the extent to which Jordan, like most other extreme right-wing leaders were taken in by Hill, his biographer claims Jordan 'restricted his input into making scathing remarks about the current BM leader and offered "pointers" to Ray Hill regarding legal representation and possible tactics'.[497]

Party time is over

Prior to the split with McLaughlin, in 1974, Jordan had repaired to Coldstone Fold, a house in Greenhow near Pateley Bridge, an ancient Norse community in the Yorkshire Dales, which he promptly renamed 'Thorgarth'.[498] Though Jordan never again belonged to a political organisation, this is not to suggest that he ceased political activity. In December 1979, he founded a new anti-Semitic newsletter, *Gothic Ripples*, its title paying homage to Arnold Leese's own occasional 'anti-Jewish' newsletter. Jordan composed each issue on Leese's writing desk, bequeathed to him by Leese's widow in 1956, together with her husband's bookcase, many of his books and newspaper clippings, and the shirt from the IFL uniform he had worn until political uniforms were banned in 1936.[499] *Gothic Ripples* gave Jordan a pulpit from which to pontificate on the supposed machinations of Jews in contemporary affairs.[500] His imprisonment under the 'evil' Race Relations Act in 1967 had made Jordan more cautious though. Those wishing to receive his new publication had to enrol as 'life members' of the 'Gothic Ripples Supporters Club' enabling Jordan to take advantage of an exemption in the Act applying to publications circulated only to members of an involved society.[501]

Increasingly, however, Jordan sought to establish himself as a theoretician. In the aftermath of the NF's defeat in the 1979 general election, Jordan penned a pamphlet reflecting on the state of the extreme right as it entered a new decade, titled, *Which Way Now?* The collapse of the NF simply confirmed to Jordan that, far from advancing the cause, electoral participation sapped ideological vitality, and therefore, ironically, reinforced of the democratic status quo ante. The chimera of democracy was not the only problem facing the extreme right, he argued. The movement itself had to be purged of religion, monarchism, skinheads and, most of all, from 'the box, booze, bingo, and the ball'. These 'twilight days' following the destruction of the Third Reich required a complete 'mental revolution'. The starting point for this process of self-purification was:

> The perception that the purpose of life is the struggle for the fulfilment of one's potentialities, which are racial, as part of the struggle of the Folk for survival and advancement in harmony with the organic pattern of Nature; and that courage and strength and consequent achievement in this are the greatest virtues. What helps is right and good, and what harms this is bad and evil.[502]

In Jordan's view, 'radical racialism' had to break free from the 'spiritual sickness' of Christianity and become 'its own religion for politics'. This life and death struggle for race, nothing short of a racial holy war – a phrase that would later enter the common lexicon of the extreme right – signalled a no holds barred fight:

> In this the ends of racial survival and revival are to be seen as justifying all means consistent with them, unfettered by any other ethics, and requiring a relentless fixity of purpose intolerant of the contrary. Standing in thought and spirit outside the old order, we have to renounce allegiance to its state, recognise no obligation to its authority, and regard its laws which stand in our way as but the impediments of illicit force without any moral sanction whatsoever.[503]

Jordan regarded his enunciation of 'revolutionary folkism' as 'National Socialism developed to its ultimate implications'. The vehicle was to be the revolutionary vanguard based upon a secret cellular structure for 'militant and unorthodox action' to be kept 'strictly separate' from overt political forms, as well as a network for 'infiltrating positions of power and influence'. He had deviated little from the paramilitary fantasies that had led to his incarceration in 1962, which, ironically, Hitler had had the sense to jettison following his ill-fated *putsch* in 1923 in favour of building a mass base. There was one small innovation, however. Jordan now perceived his racial task force as forming the nucleus of a 'survival service' that would ensure the cream of the white race survived 'atomic conflict'.[504]

Jordan not only repudiated electioneering, he also continued decrying the 'old, narrow nationalism' espoused by Tyndall and the NF, which he held responsible for the 'catastrophe' of 1939 and the eventual destruction of National Socialism:

> What is required now [wrote Jordan] if there is to be any hope at all for Aryan mankind, is not a reversion to a revival of geographical nationalism, as embodied in such as the NF, which in the ultimate analysis puts each country above the others as a supreme entity, and thus aligned to conflict with them at some or any time; but a realisation and development of the racial implications of National Socialism whereby loyalty to race and the ideology based on it transcends the boundaries of existing nation-states, and becomes the supreme allegiance ... the cause and community must be no less than White Folk of the World![505]

His next pamphlet, *National Socialism: World Creed for the 1980s* (1981), reflected Jordan's concern to prevent the religious luminosity of National Socialism from becoming 'a barren exercise in nostalgia', made a mockery by 'Hollywood Nazis' or having its eternal principles castrated by compromise with external exigency.[506] The booklet enhanced Jordan's standing within the transnational milieu. *Nordisk Kamp*, journal of Sweden's

Nordiska rikspartei (NRP), favourably reviewed it,[507] whilst Χρυσή αυγή, the theoretical magazine Golden Dawn, also began to republish his writings for a Greek audience.[508] Indeed, Jordan continued to believe Nazism was 'a living creed, not some antique' for the remainder of his life. The 'pioneering achievement' of the Third Reich had to be recognised and respected though, he conceded,

> it can be permissive at some time in some circumstances to be reticent regarding Hitler, but never of course to echo the democrats in disparagement of Hitler. To do so would be disgracefully to show yourself unfit for the fight, and disqualify you from calling yourself a National Socialist.[509]

If nothing else such sentiments signalled that Jordan, like Leese before him, would 'keep troth' with Nazism's original vision. Veteran national socialist leaders like Hans-Ulrich Rudel recognised this fact, sending Jordan fraternal greetings shortly before he died in 1982. So too did Belgian SS General Leon Degrelle, the contemporary figure Jordan admired most. The package of books Degrelle sent Jordan in 1965, 'inscribed with his complements, have a much-valued place in my library'.[510] The idea of keeping 'troth' or 'true' was an important concept. It served, like 'Meine Ehre heißt Treue' ('Loyalty be My Honour'), the motto emblazoned on the belt buckle of every SS member, as an oath of fidelity, reflecting personal devotion to the Führer, who for post-war Nazis like Jordan could only be a representative and mythic figure rather than a literal one. It also signified an act of 'blood loyalty' to the *Volksgemeinschaft* (Peoples' Community) to which 'supreme moral value' was attached.[511] Jordan's trenchant restatement of national socialist first principles, considered by many 'to be his most important work to date',[512] went together with a series of further disquisitions on 'building the vanguard' organisation capable of toppling a State he regarded as universally 'degenerate'. Jordan's Nazi Leninism counselled that, organisationally, six 'elite' activists represented the ideal number, 'offering the highest prospect of security, while providing a suitable size of operational unit; and with the maximum autonomy consistent with unified purpose and concerted action'.[513]

Amidst this revolutionary theorising, Jordan's personal life remained beset by elements of farce. In 1981, he sued the former tenants of a Leeds bungalow he owned for £346 in unpaid rent and damage to two apple trees, claiming they had breached a verbal agreement to repair and maintain the property building in exchange for reduced rent. They countered that he had banned them from inviting Jews and blacks to the house. His constant intrusions into their life to check on the status of the repairs had made their lives a misery, they claimed. Jordan appealed to the judge to award him the maximum damages allowed by law. The judge granted him £60.72 and costs informing him that he was acting 'like Shylock in the Merchant of Venice'. Jordan leapt to his feet: 'In view of my background sir, please not Shylock.'[514]

The re-election of Margaret Thatcher in 1983 – regarded by Jordan as the 'Kosher Queen' of international Jewry – effectively closed the door on any chance of an extreme right-wing resurgence. The sixty NF candidates polled just 1.1 per cent, less than it had polled during its fateful performance in the 1979 general election. Tyndall's BNP fared worse. Jordan was convinced this was a permanent reality, not least because the extreme right itself was in utter disarray.[515] A radical shift in strategy was required, he argued:

> Racial survival and national resurgence constitute a law higher than the rules of democracy they justify absolutely any and every means consistent with them. Only failure is

condemnable. The one and only road to power for all real fighters for race and nation lies in furthering the breakdown of the present system ruinous to both, for only through this breakdown can emerge the time of chance for the attainment of victory. All else is illusion.[516]

Debating the point with him in *Spearhead*, Tyndall acknowledged that as 'a statement of the morality of our position' he agreed. However, Tyndall differed with Jordan 'tactically'. The time was not yet ripe to wage an armed racial struggle against the state, not least because, 'where the will exists the capability is totally lacking; where the capability exists, there is no will'. Instead of 'the twin futilities of the ballot and bullet', Tyndall endorsed a third strategy: a return to *groupuscular* politics and the construction of a 'network' of activists who would build 'an alternative mass media' through which to engage in a counter-cultural war against the establishment which, Tyndall argued, was the future for 'nationalist' politics.[517]

Jordan was not convinced. His belief that 'our cause is vitiated by the dead end politics of the party, a proven failure as an instrument of struggle' led to the publication of his seminal essay 'Party Time Has Ended', published in April 1986 in *National Review*, the journal of the League of St George, a national socialist umbrella group with international reach. Here Jordan reiterated his belief that the only mode of action now open was to found an elite 'task force' or 'spearhead' – 'a microcosm of the New Order' – which, in the manner of Skorzeny's special units, would perform 'dramatizing deeds of propaganda' [terrorism] as part of a 'total war' against the establishment.[518] The article, whilst seminal, signalled how little Jordan's thinking had changed since the 1960s. Nor was it hollow rhetoric. Simultaneously, Jordan sold copies of the *Improvised Munitions Handbook* and *Unconventional Warfare Devices*, detailing how to make munitions, weapons and incendiaries.[519]

Tyndall published a riposte, again arguing that armed struggle was a 'complete non-starter'. Tyndall, perhaps chastened by his experience of Spearhead, did not dismiss Jordan's idea out of hand. He did argue, however, that:

> the small scale activity – which obviously Mr Jordan has in mind when he speaks of the role of the *elite* task force – must therefore be seen as supplementary to the large political campaign, not a substitute for it – a useful 'tactical' extra which at no huge sacrifice can help the campaign a little further on its way but never a practice capable of winning power on its own.[520]

Whilst Tyndall counselled a twin-track strategy, Jordan remained single-minded in his belief that racially inspired terrorism against 'the system' remained the only path to victory. Racist militants far beyond British shores devoured Jordan's article. Republished in *Liberty Bell*, it also received a response from Harold Covington, former leader of the National Socialist Party of America (NSPA), a group that achieved notoriety in 1979 when its activists and a group of local Klansmen shot dead five anti-Klan demonstrators in Greensboro, North Carolina.[521] Covington also disagreed with Jordan. 'The political party will continue to be the basic building block of the White Resistance movement whether Colin Jordan approves or not', he argued.[522]

Strategic and tactical debates aside, increasingly, Jordan assumed the mantle of elder statesman within the Nazi counter-cultures, particularly in the United States. Typical of this deference was the stance of Matt Koehl, who had assumed leadership of the NSWPP following George Lincoln Rockwell's murder in 1967. Koehl, who changed the organisation's name to the New Order in 1983, had recently taken possession of the mortal remains of Savitri Devi after her death in October 1982. He interred them, purportedly next to those of George Lincoln Rockwell, in the New Order's Nazi 'hall of honour' in Milwaukee, Wisconsin. Jordan had helped to arrange the funeral, cremation and shipping of her ashes through a wealthy young supporter, Tony Williams.[523] As well as writing for New Order's publications, Jordan also supported them 'with generous financial donations'.[524] Ideologically, Jordan was particularly enthused by Koehl's idea of racial communities, as well as similar initiatives enunciated by other figures.[525]

Koehl toured Europe four years later visiting with surviving luminaries of the Third Reich including Florrie Rost van Tonningen, the widow of a senior NSB figure; Major General Otto Ernst Remer, who played a pivotal role in the suppression of the 20 July 1944 bomb plot; and Hans Baur, Hitler's pilot. He evidently believed that such contact perpetuated the 'living link' with the Third Reich and thereby bestowed upon himself an unassailable authority as leader of '*the* Movement of Adolf Hitler'.[526] Koehl viewed Jordan in a similar light. During a visit to Jordan's Harrogate home in March 1986, Koehl awarded him the 'Loyalty Badge' of the New Order group, making him an 'honorary member'.[527]

The desire to establish a 'living link' with Hitler's disciples, and *ergo* with the Führer himself, also fuelled celebrations of the centenary of Hitler's birth in 1989. For Jordan, it was a devotional experience. His own celebratory essay, titled 'Adolf Hitler: The Man Against Time', saw Jordan attack Jesus as 'the counterfeit Christ of the Christians'. Hitler was the real 'messiah' and 'saviour' – a seer and priest who brought a 'message of salvation'. 'The crucifixion of his creed was by the spears of baleful war alone, devoid of higher sanction from any worthier creed. His was the spiritual victory', proclaimed Jordan, who forecast Hitler's ultimate 'resurrection' as 'the spiritual conqueror of the future'.[528] Jordan's stature in the transatlantic national socialist nexus was such that excerpts from his seminal essay 'National Socialism: A Philosophical Appraisal' featured in *Liberty Bell*'s special issue celebrating the centenary of Hitler's birth.[529]

Jordan's deification of Hitler coincided with his increased efforts to disseminate his ideological message through fiction, which, in the spirit of 'leaderless resistance', further facilitated self-selecting radicalisation and action.[530] His first effort, *A Train of Thought* (1989), charted the evolution of a fictional young activist away from democratically constituted racial nationalist organisations and towards racist terrorism.[531] The booklet employed a simple, yet important, narrative device: character development, often missing from extreme right-wing fiction (whose 'heroes' frequently appear fully conscious ideologically), in order to heighten the readers identification with the protagonists' ideological journey and thus to educate and acculturate new activists.[532] Jordan's second novella, *Merrie England – 2,000* (1993), offered readers a crude Orwellian-style parody that envisaged a country governed by an omnipresent and omniscient 'Ministry of Harmony', which enforced integration, miscegenation and homosexuality as 'the final solution for the elimination of folk feeling in Whites'. Those guilty of the thought-crime of 'racism' – predominantly the bigoted elderly – are arrested by the 'Harmony Force' and subjected to 're-education' in the 'House of Harmony', whilst the remainder of the population willingly prostrated themselves through daily acts of racial atonement in the shadow of a newly erected statue of Nelson Mandela which had replaced Nelson's column in Trafalgar Square. The book's dystopian vision served as a stark warning of the fate awaiting the white race, if its readers failed to act now.[533]

Jordan was completing the first draft when, on 4 June 1991, the 'thought police' raided his house. Gerald Kaufman MP (Manchester Gorton) had complained to police about the distribution of *The Ballad of Gerald Kaufman the Jew* in which Jordan urged the electorate not to vote for Kaufman because his allegiance was to Israel not Britain: 'He wants to make it a new Commandment here: "Not a soul shall criticise the Chosen Ones for fear."' During the raid, Jordan noticed that the date on the search warrant was incorrect and thus invalid. It was a costly error. A series of legal challenges ensued. These ended in November 1992, when the authorities dropped the case against him on the eve of a Judicial Review.[534] Jordan was subsequently awarded £10,000 in damages from North Yorkshire police and £4,000 costs.[535] When *Merrie England – 2,000* finally appeared, in March 1993, it featured a sarcastic dedication to Kaufman.[536] Its appearance coincided with the publication of *National Socialism: Vanguard of the Future – Selected Writings of Colin Jordan* (1993), which collected many of Jordan's hard to find writings on the past, present and future of Nazism into one volume.[537] Despite his own travails, Jordan supported and financially assisted others in conflict with the legal system during this period including Canadian-based Holocaust denier Ernst Zündel, author of several books including *UFOs – Nazi Secret Weapons?* and *The Hitler We Loved and Why*, whose ideological evolution had also been facilitated through his encounter Savitri Devi.[538]

Between 1994 and 1999, Jordan serialised in *Gothic Ripples* 'The Way Ahead – A Primer for the N-S Vanguard', often perceived as being his most important disquisition.[539] Veteran militants like Tyndall praised Jordan's thesis, which inspired younger Nazi activists too, particularly within the US Nazi milieu.[540] Jordan was 'particularly gratified' when *Liberty Bell* began reprinting it.[541] The 'Vanguard' series contained little Jordan had not advocated for years, however. Nor had his formula for seeking to operationalise his ideas changed substantially either. He again turned to 'literature', publishing a sequel to *Merrie England – 2000* titled in *The Uprising* (2004), a fictionalised account of race war in Britain in which a 'British Freedom Force' of racial revolutionaries overthrow the 'anti-white' system and replace it with a resurgent, New Order.[542]

Jordan had originally intended that *The Uprising* be published in 1998 but on 4 August of that year, the police raided his home again, seizing the manuscript and 8,831 other items. This included the leaflet *The Two Sides of Jack Straw's Jewish Justice*, alleging the Home Secretary Jack Straw was a tool of Jewish interests.[543] Jordan was particularly perturbed that his VHS copy of George Eliot's *Middlemarch* and several audiotapes of Wagner's Ring Cycle went missing during the search.[544] Jordan faced eleven charges brought under the Public Order Act (1986) for publishing and distributing material intended or likely to stir up racial hatred. Arrested again in April 1999 (the police were looking for the *Gothic Ripples* subscription list, alleges Jordan's hagiographer), the case against Jordan was subsequently postponed indefinitely in November 2001 after the judge ruled that his 'disabling heart condition' rendered Jordan 'unfit' to stand trial.[545] Physically but not ideologically frail, Jordan subsequently had the book published by NS Publications in Milwaukee, Wisconsin, in 2004, their services procured via an American subscriber to *Gothic Ripples*.[546] The Historical Review Press, a major purveyor of Holocaust denial material run by Anthony Hancock, distributed it in Britain.[547]

In its ideological intent and indeed content, *The Uprising* was essentially derivative of *The Turner Diaries* (1978), written by William Pierce, leader of the National Alliance. Jordan had regularly corresponded with Pierce, whom he considered 'a great luminary of Aryan National Socialism'.[548] *The Turner Diaries*, written under the pseudonym 'Andrew MacDonald' represented a fictionalised account of a race war in the United States in which the 'Organisation' led by Earl Turner embarks upon a 'Great Revolution' against the anti-white 'System' – a race war that culminates in the extermination of blacks, Jews and those guilty of miscegenation. This racist revolution is successful in 1999 'according to the chronology of the Old Era – just 110 years after the birth of the Great One'. Adolf Hitler, born in 1889, is clearly the unnamed 'Great One'.[549]

The influence of *The Turner Diaries* has been immense. Its reputation as a 'blue print' for terrorism was cemented after Timothy McVeigh, a militia movement activist who read, sold and admired the book, particularly its defence of gun rights, killed 168 people and injured 800 more in a bomb attack on a Federal building in Oklahoma in 1995. Prior to 9/11, this was the deadliest terrorist attack on American soil.[550] 'I wouldn't have chosen to do what he did,' Pierce later stated. Nonetheless, he praised McVeigh as 'a man of principle', who was 'willing to accept the consequences' of his actions. McVeigh's terrorist attack led some militants to drop out, but it galvanised others. 'Probably, on the whole, it was helpful,' claimed Pierce.[551] It certainly raised the profile of his writings. '*Every* nationalist has heard about *The Turner Diaries*', Pierce subsequently remarked.[552] In 2000, it was estimated that the book, an underground bestseller, had sold 500,000 copies.[553]

The Turner Diaries also served to inspire the foundation of the Brüders Schweigen (the Silent Brotherhood), more commonly known as The Order in July 1983. Led by Robert J. Matthews, a member of Pierce's National Alliance, The Order sought the overthrow of the US government, which, it argued, was little more than a puppet for 'ZOG' ('Zionist Occupation Government'). During its short lifespan, Matthew's group staged a series of arsons, bombings and armed robberies, netting, in one instance, $3.6 million, to fund its revolutionary activities and those of several 'above ground' extreme right-wing groups too. Its trail of destruction left four dead. Matthews died during an armed stand-off with the FBI on 8 December 1984 and his colleagues were arrested and imprisoned.[554]

Jordan claimed never to have read *The Turner Diaries* or its sequel, *Hunter* (1984) before writing *The Uprising* but he had sold it through *Gothic Ripples*.[555] *The Scorpion*, a 'New Right' magazine edited by Michael Walker, which espoused a 'cultural' strategy in contrast to Jordan's own violent panaceas, commented sardonically that *The Uprising* 'indicates a change of heart about terrorism':

> Racial nationalists have persistently denounced the terrorists of the IRA for their bombings, not only for the politics be it noted but for the method too. I trust that Colin Jordan and others who admire Bob Matthews will no longer denounce the tactics of the IRA or Muslim fundamentalists. That would be highly disingenuous now that we have this gleefully depicted scenario of increasing terrorism leading to the overthrow of the hated alien multi-racial regime.[556]

Jordan did indeed admire Matthews, sending regular sums of money to his widow to help her and her children rebuild their lives.[557] Furthermore, he dedicated *The Uprising* to Matthews and his colleagues Richard Scutari and David Lane, who were serving prison sentences of 60 and 190 years respectively. All three men are totemic figures for the extreme right. Jordan promoted Scutari and Lane as 'POWs' in *Gothic Ripples*, publicising their prison addresses, and those of other activists, so readers could send letters of support.[558] *Gothic Ripples* also reprinted an article on The Order by Scutari, the last member of the group to be captured, describing its evolution, not to simply to glorify its history, but in order that the movement could learn from its failures and successes, 'so others will have the courage to take the next step and succeed'.[559] Scutari's conception of the successful 'next step' emerged through his prison correspondence with Jordan. 'I am a firm believer in Colin Jordan's Vanguard approach,' he wrote. 'The methods used by Hitler to bring

National Socialism can be effective and win today through the Vanguard method laid out by Colin Jordan ... I am all for it.' In another letter, Scutari advised: 'The Vanguard is the only way to victory. Each of us must follow the pattern as laid out by Colin Jordan and adapt it to fit our individual nations'.[560]

Jordan's relationship with David Lane – 'prisoner of the US regime of genocide' – was equally important.[561] A founding member of The Order, Lane had taken part in the killing of radio talk show host Alan Berg on 18 June 1984. Behind bars, Lane's stature grew as extreme right counter-cultures the world-over lionised him for the ideological imperative embodied in his dictum: 'We must secure the existence of our people and a future for White children'.[562] For its adherents, the '14 Words' encapsulate the essence of the racial nationalist cause. Jordan believed Lane's clarion call for racial struggle was 'an *oath* for revolutionary national socialists and racial nationalists'.[563] Lane and Jordan recognised in one another kindred pan-Aryan spirits whose revolutionary strategies for the overthrow of 'the system' were symmetrical. In his newsletter, *Focus Fourteen*, Lane stated he was 'proud and honoured' to introduce a contribution from Jordan, heralding him as 'long admired here for his relentless passion and dedication to a Victory for the 14 Words!'[564] Lane's website also reproduced selections from Jordan's collected works.[565] Jordan's introduction to *Deceived, Damned and Defiant: The Revolutionary Writings of David Lane* (1999) reflected this mutual respect. Jordan praised Lane as 'someone extraordinary in both thought and deed'. He also eulogised The Order, the 'heroic' death of its leader, Bob Matthews, and 'the sacrificial steadfastness of his imprisoned comrades' as 'the most outstanding instance of a revolt of our race since World War II' and therefore 'a unique lantern of luminosity for all who remain wholeheartedly loyal to our race'.[566]

Jordan's promotion of Lane's writings highlighted the tension between racial revolutionaries like himself and those occupied with the practical realities of political organisation like Tyndall. In praising the revolutionary road taken by Lane and Matthews, Jordan's simultaneous disparagement of the BNP for deceiving its activists with the 'fruitless fantasy' that a legal, electoral route could ever deliver power, elicited a retort from Tyndall in 2000 that:

> Mr. Jordan, in his juxtaposition of these two items, seems to have missed the irony of the comparison. Far be it for us to depreciate David Lane, who is a courageous patriot, but if Mr. Jordan is speaking of 'futility', we can only ask: what greater futility can there be for such a man to be languishing in a jail all that time rather than being out free working for his race and nation. Like David Lane, Colin Jordan is much to be admired for his courage. However, since he seems unable to resist denigrating the efforts of the BNP, we have to ask: just what has *he* achieved in his own lifetime that comes anywhere near what our party has achieved?[567]

Legacy

Jordan had previously owned a croft in Wester Alligin in the North-West Highlands which he had first visited in 1949 and, following this second raid on his home, he purchased a second one which he named 'Thor Nook' after the Norse God of Thunder in the tiny hamlet of Diabaig in Wester Ross. Even in this remote location, which he visited for 'relaxation', Jordan's mono-racial tranquillity was disrupted. Several residents proposed constructing a multi-faith centre in 2002 to which he objected vociferously.[568] His health failing, Jordan ceased publishing *Gothic Ripples* in October 2004 after forty-eight issues, ostensibly to concentrate upon writing his autobiography. The centrepiece of the final issue was an article titled 'Democracy is Death' – Arnold Leese's favourite slogan.[569] Despite his frailty, Jordan still travelled to Budapest, Hungary, in 2008 to attend a rally of the Magyar Gárda, the paramilitary wing of the Jobbik party, which was banned in the following year.[570]

Jordan suffered a massive stroke and died on 9 April 2009, aged eighty-five. His funeral took place at a Harrogate crematorium, fittingly enough, on 20 April, Hitler's birthday, whilst Wagner's *Tannhauser Overture* played, as it had for Leese.[571] His ashes were scattered at 'Thorgarth'. His estate, worth close to £1 million, he bequeathed to his Hungarian-born second wife, Julia Safrany (whom he had married in 2007) and stepdaughter.[572] For the duration of his life, he had been a marginal political figure. Like his mentor, Arnold Leese, he was always been profoundly 'out of step' with wider developments in the fascist firmament. His reaction to the rise of the BNP after 2001 exemplified this. Jordan had enjoyed a correspondence during the mid-1990s with Nick Griffin, the future BNP chairman who had evinced enthusiasm for his 'vanguard' ideal (Chapter 6). Jordan lauded Griffin's anti-Semitic publication, *Who Are the Mindbenders?* as 'a new and truly outstanding booklet' and supported the young militant when he stood trial for inciting racial hatred in 1998, publicising the PO Box for donations.[573] He rapidly became disillusioned with Griffin once he became BNP leader in the following year, however. Griffin had taken Tyndall's 'genuine article' and replaced it with a 'kosher product', Jordan proclaimed, which was, ironically, a charge he had levelled at Tyndall during the 1970s.[574] Reflecting the international authority of William Pierce, Jordan took his campaign to the letter pages of *National Vanguard*, accusing BNP 'modernisers' of 'trimming' core ideals.[575] Jordan and Tyndall had rekindled their friendship in later life and the latter's death in 2005 was a 'personal blow' to Jordan, who claimed thereafter that 'a pat on the back for Griffin is a knife in the back of JT's memory'.[576]

Whilst the BNP publicly repudiated Jordan's revolutionary strategies, their influence on sections of the violent *groupuscular demi-monde* remains discernible. Jordan, like Leese before him, remained the torch-bearer for the 'no surrender' brand of Nazism in Britain, impervious to change or compromise. His personal and political intransigence constituted both a strength and a weakness. Jordan conceded as much, admitting that:

> my constant aversion to enfeebling compromise can cause me at times to be immediately and excessively, impatiently and irritably intolerant of its advocates and practitioners, unwilling to listen to them. This I recognise can be a failing just as much as succumbing to any substantial extent to their message where it amounts in cause and effect to the voice of feebleness.[577]

The BM, the organisation Jordan had founded in 1968, became an important vehicle for preserving, and projecting, his political legacy. McLaughlin had abruptly shut the organisation down in 1983, though a group of leading activists resurrected it shortly thereafter as the British National Socialist Movement (BNSM), 'a return to the use of the old NSM's title while retaining the movement's traditional campaign name'.[578] Though Jordan never re-joined the group, he remained in touch, subscribing to its publications and 'occasionally provided direct financial support for some specific BM projects'.[579] Jordan's example inspired its new leader, Stephen Frost, a former Yorkshire BM organiser, who had been one of those determined to continue the group's work after McLaughlin disbanded it. Following Jordan's death, Frost became the principal person propagating his legacy, publishing a photo-book glorifying his life and work in 2009. A full-scale hagiography, *'Twas a Good Fight* (2014), followed five years later which valorised Jordan in order to inspire further commitment to the cause from its activists. Indeed, their late founder continues to be venerated at party 'moots' held to commemorate the memory 'of the National Socialist leaders of the past; Adolf Hitler, Rudolf Hess and Colin Jordan'.[580]

Jordan also inspired those Nazi militants running the Blood and Honour (B&H) music network. Though Jordan disparaged the 'scene' and reviled its musical output, this did not stop B&H revering him. They publicised Jordan's writings and offered him their unqualified support during his legal travails.[581] 'Our struggle is for me the meaning and purpose of life', Jordan told *Blood & Honour*.

> Never give in ... for in the very act of struggling on, regardless of the outcome otherwise, you are achieving a victory of the spirit which alone truly makes life worth living, and the achievement of which ennobles you in the assertion of your being.[582]

Following his death, *Blood & Honour* proclaimed Jordan an 'inspiration to all'.[583] This was ironic given that as late as 1990 Jordan was still attacking 'Rock against Communism' as 'Rock against Race Revival'. He also had harsh words for the organisation's founder, Ian Stuart Donaldson, the lead singer of the Nazi rock band Skrewdriver, deriding him and his colleagues as 'white niggers' who Hitler himself would have placed in Dachau concentration camp, alongside other 'anti-social elements'.[584]

Through his writings, Jordan remained an ambient influence upon Britain's national socialist underground throughout the early 1990s. His standing was paramount amongst militant networks grouped around the BM in Yorkshire where he also lived which enabled him to keep abreast of the latest developments.[585] Like Tyndall's BNP, the BM were increasingly at odds with the violent Nazi *groupuscule* Combat 18 (C18), which had come to dominate the activist milieu. As clusters of its activists in West Yorkshire and the West Midlands began leaving to join C18, the BM issued a scathing indictment of C18, which drove a wedge between the two organisations.[586] Jordan's supporters were located on both sides of the divide.

Jordan's writings were disseminated more widely throughout the movement during this period by a series of book clubs including Life Rune Books (LRB) run by Paul Jeffries, described as one of Jordan's 'few trusted associates'. Jeffries ran LRB with John Cato, a former BM activist who had previously been active in the anarcho-punk scene who wrote, designed and distributed the C18 publications, *Putsch* and *Lebensraum*.[587] Cato also edited a magazine titled *The Oak*, which served as the British mouthpiece of William Pierce's National Alliance. C18 considered *The Oak* to be 'the best' national socialist publication in Britain.[588] Jordan was similarly impressed, sending Cato words of encouragement. 'It is good to hear that, despite all the harassment you have experienced, you are undeterred, and that *The Oak* is continuing and with a new issue ahead', he wrote.[589]

> That you thus remain stalwart is much to your credit indeed for the going is tough in our line of business and many fall by the wayside. However, as the Great One [Adolf Hitler] remarked, adversity only serves to toughen and temper the real fighters. Congratulations on proving them wrong.[590]

Cato reciprocated, praising Jordan as 'the greatest modern thinker and post-war NS ideologist, almost certainly in the United Kingdom'.[591]

Jordan's direct influence upon C18 itself is rather more difficult to discern, however. C18 leader Steve Sargent rated Jordan as the 'most respected movement member' in 1994.[592] For the most part, however, C18-aligned publications barely mentioned Jordan at all. Instead, they propounded a visceral racism and crude Nazism whose only clear points of reference were the 'leaderless resistance' strategy propounded since 1983 by Klansman Louis Beam and the inspiration provided by Robert J. Matthews rather than the transcendental, pan-Aryan National Socialism enunciated by Jordan.[593] That said, the National Socialist Alliance (NSA), the C18's political arm, staged a meeting in Wolverhampton in May 1995, addressed by the convicted NSM arsonist Hugh Hughes, highlighting the historical continuity within this militant milieu.[594] The salience of Jordan's 'excellent' writings was also observable in the pages of *The National Socialist*, organ of the NSA.[595] *Europe Awake*, a West Midlands C18 publication that had defected from the BM, similarly urged its readership to absorb Jordan's writings, whilst also featuring Arnold Leese on its cover for good measure.[596] *Blood & Honour* magazine, controlled by C18 supporters, boasted meanwhile that within their group, 'a cadre or vanguard has been created as outlined by Colin Jordan several years ago'.[597]

There were multiple and diffuse patterns of transatlantic influence too. The prominent American national socialist Harold A. Covington publicly mourned Jordan's death.[598] Covington had previously operated the US postal address for the C18 publication *Redwatch* and his book, *The March Up Country* (1987), a practical and ideological instruction manual for racial revolutionaries fighting against the 'extinction' of the white race, was 'required reading' for Cato and other C18 leaders.[599] Tom Metzger, leader of White Aryan Resistance (WAR), whose website publicises Jordan's writings alongside those of others including David Lane, also paid tribute to him.[600]

Jordan's impact was more evident upon a smaller group of former C18 activists who, in 1997, formed another National Socialist Movement (NSM). The group was led by David Myatt, a former BM activist, and Tony Williams who had been entrusted with Savitri Devi's ashes following her death in 1982. Myatt had been a bodyguard to Jordan in the early 1970s. Jordan had invited Myatt to join the BM 'inner council' but he had refused. Nonetheless, Jordan had been a formative influence upon Myatt's political development, recommending he read the works of Savitri Devi, lending him books and discussing ideas with him, as well as introducing him to German Nazis.[601] In time, Myatt came to perform a similar role for the NSM. Steve Sargent, whose older brother Charlie, the former C18 leader, was recently jailed for murder, became a leading figure. NSM activists were introduced to Jordan's thought through *Column 88*, the quarterly magazine Williams edited, which featured an interview with Jordan proclaiming: 'His sincerity, his commitment, his devotion to National-Socialism, his determined fighting spirit, is a model which shall inspire comrades in our struggle for generations to come.' Jordan had a message for the NSM:

> Never give in, however hopeless things seem, for in the very act of struggling on, regardless of the outcome otherwise, you are achieving a victory of the spirit which alone truly makes life worth living, and the achievement of which ennobles you in an assertion of your being.[602]

For his part, Jordan promoted C18/NSM publications like *Strikeforce* in *Gothic Ripples* but they were not quite to his taste. Indeed, having recommended the magazine, he immediately took its editors to task for its 'foul language. The cause is too noble for this.'[603]

The NSM hurriedly disbanded in May 1999 after one of its members, David Copeland, a former BNP activist, who had joined the group in the previous April, detonated three nail bombs in central London, leaving three dead, including a mother and her unborn child and injuring hundreds.[604] As the extreme right rushed to distance itself from Copeland's actions, Jordan's denunciation of his 'misdirected mayhem' represented a critique of Copeland's strategy and targeting rather than his methods:

> Had Copeland directed his attention to some culprits of the system of genocide and repression, and focussed his punishment on them alone one could certainly have felt that they had brought it upon themselves by their wickedness against our race and nation, and in what amounts to a war waged by them against us had been fairly and properly punished. As it has been with this misdirected mayhem, prime culprits have gone unscathed, and we have been damaged along with Copeland's victims. Altogether a bad business.[605]

Even after the NSM dissolved it continued to attract the attention of individuals who would go on to commit acts of terrorism. On 22 July 1999, 'a young militant nationalist' – Maxime Brunerie – wrote to the NSM from France expressing his interest after reading an interview with them in *Race et Nation*.[606] Brunerie, who was active in Unité Radicale, subsequently attempted to assassinate the French President Jacques Chirac on 14 July 2002, after posting a message on the C18 Guestbook on the previous night, stating: 'Watch the TV this Saturday. I will be the star. Death to ZOG, 88!'[607]

Jordan's ghost continues to pervade such violent milieus. Following his death, Mark Atkinson, formerly a leading C18 activist, paid homage to Jordan's personal support. Jordan had contacted Atkinson in 1997 whilst he and another C18 activist, Robin Gray, were serving a twenty-one-month sentence for publishing the C18 magazine *Stormer*.[608] 'His support helped me through my incarceration', recalled Atkinson who subsequently founded the Racial Volunteer Force (RVF) to perpetuate the ideals of C18. Jailed for five years in November 2005 for publishing another magazine called *Stormer*, and operating the RVF website with the intention of inciting racial hatred, Atkinson again took comfort from Jordan's encouragement. 'Mr Jordan was a true soldier till the end', observed Atkinson, 'and we at the RVF will never forget the support he gave Volunteers when others forgot. We salute you, see you in Valhalla brother, RIP comrade'.[609]

The RVF was not alone in viewing Jordan as a 'guiding light'.[610] The British People's Party (BPP), a violent Nazi *groupuscule* whose membership contained several individuals subsequently convicted of offences under the Prevention of Terrorism Act, proclaimed Jordan their 'spiritual leader' after his death, quietly removing John Tyndall from the masthead of their website from whence he had previously been heralded as their inspiration. The group's 'firm and militant racial nationalist policy', which rejected the populist 'ethnonationalist' platform of the BNP, had impressed Jordan.[611] The BPP actively courted his support but age, infirmity and his own non-partisan stance precluded Jordan's active involvement, though *Searchlight* alleges that he disbursed monies to the group.[612] Extending its commitment to the historical continuity of Jordan's ideals, the BPP subsequently joined a re-incarnated version of WUNS, reconvened on 6 September 2006 under the aegis of Jeff Schoep's National Socialist Movement (NSM), a further nod towards the continued influence of Jordan's 'universal' brand of Nazism.[613] 'Your word is alive,' wrote another Nazi militant, Michael Heaton, on the extreme right-wing VNN Internet forum shortly after Jordan's death. Heaton was imprisoned for thirty months in June 2010 for inciting racial hatred against Jews whilst active with a small *groupuscule* called the Aryan Strike Force (ASF).[614] In the previous month, another leading ASF activist and his son were jailed for ten years and two years, respectively, for producing a chemical weapon, ricin, preparing for 'acts of terrorism' and possessing terror handbooks.[615]

Jordan's influence continues. The Historical Review Press republished his two 'classic' treatises, *National Socialism: Vanguard of the Future* (2011) and *The National Vanguard: The Way Forward* (2011), perhaps hoping to inspire a new generation of revolutionary racist activists. Both books are freely available on Amazon ensuring that Jordan continues to find readers from beyond the grave. Several individuals associated with National Action, banned as a 'terrorist' group in 2016, appear to have been influenced by his life and ideas.[616] Jordan's ideas will undoubtedly continue to permeate such milieu. However, in seeking to locate Jordan's historical importance within the British fascist tradition, his strategic theorising and preoccupation with the 'vanguard' is perhaps of secondary importance to the negative consequences his actions have had for its wider political progress. 'Colin Jordan appears to me emblematic of so many Nazis since the war', noted the US racial nationalist journal *Instauration*, ruefully. 'They have a sort of death wish. Even their publications give the impression that they are trying to prove something to themselves rather than to be effective.'[617] Though Jordan poured scorn on 'Hollywood Nazis', his own activities had a similarly debilitating effect on public perceptions of the extreme right. They left an indelible stain upon the political career of John Tyndall and the political parties which he led: The National Front and the British National Party.

Notes

1 *British Movement Interviews Colin Jordan* (BM: DVD 2005).
2 *Searchlight*, no. 151, January 1988 profiled Jordan as 'The Godfather'. For a full biography, see Paul Jackson, *Colin Jordan and Britain's Neo-Nazi Movement: Hitler's Echo* (London, Bloomsbury, 2017).
3 Stephen Frost, *'Twaz a Good Fight!': The Life of Colin Jordan* (Heckmondwike: N.S. Press, 2014), pp. 10–11.
4 *Ibid.*, p. 9.
5 *Ibid.*, p. 23.
6 Martin Ceadel, *Pacifism in Britain, 1914–1945: The Defining of a Faith* (Oxford: Clarendon Press, 1980), p. 301.
7 Major W.M. McLellan, 17 November 1944 in TNA KV 2/4386.
8 Miss M.E. Roberts to Captain B.T. Synge, 25 April 1945 in TNA KV 2/4386.
9 Lt. Col. G.M. Konrower, 16 May 1945 in TNA KV 2/4386.
10 Sir Percy Sillitoe to Commander E.R.B. Kemble, 25 September 1946 in TNA KV 2/4386.
11 Captain T. Ronald to Miss Roberts, 17 December 1944 in TNA KV 2/4386.
12 For more details, see Richard Griffiths, *What Did You Do During the War? The Last Throes of the British Pro-Nazi Right, 1940–1945* (Abingdon: Routledge, 2017), pp. 113–121.
13 M.E. Roberts, note, 8 March 1945 in TNA KV 2/4386.
14 MI5 to Major R.H. Evans, War Office, June 1946 in TNA KV 2/4386/109a.
15 Frost, *'Twaz a Good Fight!'*, p. 24.
16 TNA KV 6/4/389a; and Frost, *'Twaz a Good Fight!'*, pp. 25 and 27.
17 The article was Douglas Warth, 'New Fascist Gang is Probed by Yard Men', *Sunday Pictorial*, 10 March 1946.
18 Colin Jordan to Arnold Leese, 31 August 1946 in TNA KV 2/4386.
19 Colin Jordan, 'Notes on Arnold Leese', undated MSS, Leese papers.
20 *Ibid.*
21 *Free Britain*, no. 165, February 1956.
22 Colin Jordan, 'Notes on Arnold Leese', undated MSS, Leese papers.

23 Stephen Frost notes that through the BPP Jordan met and conversed with Joyce's brother, Quentin, at a gathering at the home of BPP supporter Lady Claire Annesley, see *'Twaz a Good Fight!'*, p. 33.
24 Francis Beckett, *Fascist in the Family: The Tragedy of John Beckett MP* (Abingdon: Routledge, 2017), pp. 302–303.
25 Hansard, HL Deb., vol. 123, cols 1–68 (2 June 1942).
26 The Duke of Bedford, *Propaganda for Proper Geese* (Glasgow: Strickland Press, 1942), pp. 16–17.
27 *Gothic Ripples*, no. 107, 12 November 1953.
28 Sidney Salomon to the Reverend James Parkes, 28 May 1943, MS 60/15/86, Reverend James Parkes papers, University of Southampton.
29 MI5 report, 7 December 1941 in TNA HO 45/25570/88.
30 Extract, 11 February 1946, TNA KV 6/4/397b.
31 *Leamington Spa Courier*, 4 July 1947.
32 *People's Post*, October 1948.
33 BDBJ C6/9/3/4, Jewish Defence Committee papers, London, hereafter JDC papers.
34 'Fascist Organisations in the United Kingdom' in TNA KV 3/51; and *People's Post*, vol. 3, no. 6, August 1946.
35 *People's Post*, vol. 5, no. 2, February 1948; and *People's Post*, vol. 5, no. 16, April 1949. Jackson, *Colin Jordan and Britain's Neo-Nazi Movement*, pp. 47 and 50 notes Jordan became secretary of a local Distributist Society that month.
36 Jackson, *Colin Jordan and Britain's Neo-Nazi Movement*, p. 50.
37 *Ibid.*, p. 42.
38 Marjorie Roberts, 27 January 1948 in TNA KV 2/4386.
39 For Rogerson, see *People's Post*, vol. 5, no. 15, March 1949.
40 Sir Percy Sillitoe to Commander E.R.B. Kemble, 23 October 1947 in TNA KV 2/4387.
41 Hansard, HC Deb. (series 5), vol. 459, cols 8–10 (6 December 1948).
42 *Jewish Chronicle*, Collection, Box 4, Wiener Library, London, details the episode.
43 *People's Post*, vol. 5, no. 17, May–June 1949. See also B.G. Atkinson to S.H.E. Burley, 3 August 1949 in TNA HO 45/25401.
44 TNA KV 2/4388/176a.
45 John, Duke of Bedford, *A Silver-Plated Spoon* (London: Reprint Society, 1959), p. 167.
46 *People's Post*, vol. 6, no. 8, May 1950.
47 *British Movement Interviews Colin Jordan* (BM: DVD 2005).
48 Ling, records *Coventry Evening Telegraph*, 13 April 1961, had served a seven-year prison sentence for armed robbery. The *Birmingham Post*, 11 July 1956 notes police had arrested Ling on 3 June for daubing 'Export Jews, not Cars' on a local bridge, an incident in which his housemate, Irishman Richard 'Dick' Tynan, the UM Coventry branch organiser, was also involved. Tynan was imprisoned on 24 April 1957 for false pretences regarding the sale of a car and again in 1958 for cattle rustling (*Birmingham Daily Post*, 9 July 1958). Both men had been prominent 'in demanding that a stronger anti-Semitic line be taken by the Union Movement' at its 1955 party conference, see 'Chairman's Statement – October 1956' and Provincial Liaison Committee, minutes, 14 April 1957, in 1658/1/3/3, JDC papers, Wiener Library.
49 Percy Sillitoe (MI5) to J. Barnett (Chief Constable of Leeds), 12 February 1951 in TNA KV 2/4388.
50 Colin Jordan to Adrien Arcand, 6 May 1950, Arcand papers. Domvile had given Jordan Arcand's address. He was a subscriber to *Defence*, see diary entry, 26 April 1950, DOM 61, Domvile papers, Greenwich Maritime Museum, London.
51 *Birmingham Daily Gazette*, 18 February 1950; and *Labour Israel*, 21 April 1950.
52 Colin Jordan to Arnold Leese, 10 June 1950 in TNA KV 2/4388.
53 Colin Jordan to Mr Sarnd, 10 October 1951 in BDBJ C6/9/3/4, JDC papers.
54 *Rogues Gallery* BDBJ C6/9/3/2, JDC papers. Thankful of the support, Wright apparently expressed his agreement with the principles of the BNC.
55 Birmingham Chief Constable to Sir Percy Sillitoe, 5 December 1950 in TNA KV 2/4388.
56 *People's Post*, vol. 5, no. 7, July 1948.
57 *People's Post*, vol. 5, no. 13, January 1949. Jordan had previously squabbled with Mosleyite Jeffrey Hamm in the pages of *Varsity* after his own CUNC meeting had fallen through, notes Paul Jackson, *Colin Jordan and Britain's Neo-Nazi Movement*, p. 48.

58 TNA KV 2/4388/256b. UM activist Brian Richardson who corresponded with Jordan reported to Lawrence 'Alf' Flockhart, the UM Assistant Secretary, on 9 July 1950, that Jordan's only objection to the UM 'seemed to be a racial one; no mention of "bread and butter" was made.' UM activist Owen 'Jock' Holliwell had previously urged Richardson to accept an invitation to talk to the BNC believing that there was a 'very good chance' that they could win Jordan and his friends over to the Birmingham UM.
59 *Union*, no. 152, 27 January 1951.
60 *Union*, no. 263, 9 May 1953.
61 TNA KV 2/4388/216a.
62 Frost, *'Twaz a Good Fight!'*, p. 38 claims Jordan met Henry Hamilton Beamish at one such event, though this is the sole reference the author has seen to Beamish returning to England after 1945.
63 *Free Britain*, no. 119, 2 December 1951; and *Free Britain*, no. 120, 9 December 1951.
64 Britons Publishing Society, minutes of meeting, 11 February 1950, Britons papers. The Britons also advertised BNC activities in *Free Britain*, no. 162, November 1956.
65 TNA KV 1353/374z; Chief Constable H.P. Hind to Home Office, 28 June 1950 in TNA HO 45/24968. Whilst Horton vanished shortly thereafter he re-emerged in 1968, sending an 'offensive' letter to the Chief Rabbi, see Jewish Defence Committee, Minutes, 3 March 1969 in ACC/3121/C6/1/6, Board of Deputies of British Jews papers, London Metropolitan Archives.
66 *Free Britain*, no. 152, January 1955; and *Free Britain*, no. 156, May 1955, which announced the BNC was opening an office imminently.
67 *Free Britain*, no. 163, December 1955. BNC activists had handed out racist leaflets in support of a bus workers strike in West Bromwich striking against the advent of 'Coloured labour', notes *Free Britain*, no. 154, March 1955. BNC secretary, Donald Tennant, was also the Birmingham UM election agent. He arranged for Oswald Mosley to address a small fifty-strong, invitation only, BNC meeting on 18 January 1956, Mosley's first meeting in Birmingham since the Second World War (*Birmingham Daily Gazette*, 19 January 1956). A local Labour councillor who protested the meeting received an anonymous telephone call condemning him to death on behalf of the 'Nordic Peoples' League' shortly thereafter (*Birmingham Daily Gazette*, 20 January 1956). Mosley was billed to address another BNC meeting two months later (*Birmingham Daily Gazette*, 13 March 1956) ahead of an official UM meeting at Birmingham Town Hall on 28 October 1956. Prior to the event, local BNC activists began a campaign of racist harassment using anonymous telephone calls and anti-black leaflets (*Birmingham Daily Gazette*, 2 October 1956).
68 Colin Jordan to Leslie Greene, 6 June 1955, Chesterton papers. Then, Jordan's own opinions were co-terminus with Chesterton's platform. 'Today, even more so than then, it is the Empire which holds the key to Britain's future,' he had written in *People's Post*, vol. 5, no. 7, July 1948.
69 R.A.J., Birmingham Nationalist Club receipt for £50 from A.K. Chesterton, 21 June 1955, Britons papers.
70 Colin Jordan to Leslie Greene, 12 August 1955, Chesterton papers.
71 Leslie Greene to Colin Jordan, 13 July 1955, Chesterton papers.
72 Leslie Greene to Colin Jordan, 28 September 1955, Chesterton papers.
73 *LEL Bulletin*, no. 6, December 1955.
74 Leslie Greene to Colin Jordan, 11 January 1956, Chesterton papers.
75 *Free Britain*, no. 165, February 1956.
76 Britons Publishing Society to Arnold Leese, 8 September 1954; and Arnold Leese to Anthony Gittens, 23 September 1954, Leese papers.
77 Arnold Leese to Anthony Gittens, 23 September 1954, Leese papers.
78 Colin Jordan, *Fraudulent Conversion: The Myth of Moscow's Change of Heart* (London: Britons Publishing Company, 1956). In the USA, far right activists opposed to Yockey (and some who were not) also sold the book. G.L.K. Smith, leader of the Christian Nationalist Crusade, for instance, cited it as a source in his pamphlet *Jews Change Names*. Edith Essig also advertised it in *Keeping the Record Straight*, 27 January 1956.
79 *Candour*, vol. 3, no. 113 and no. 114, 23 and 30 December 1955.
80 *Oldham Evening Chronicle and Standard*, 28 October 1955. The book proved particularly popular in the United States. Frank L. Britton, a Californian journalist who edited *The American*

Nationalist, told his readership 'you can't afford to miss this sensational new book.... Definitely the best book to come out this year.' Seeking to disseminate this 'fine book' as widely as possible, Britton offered copies to his readership for $3, see Frank L. Britton, *December [1955] – A Crucial Month for the American Nationalist*, copy in H. Keith Thompson papers, Box 10, Hoover Institution Archives, Stanford University. American Jewish Committee, *Anti-Semitic Activity in the United States: A Report and Appraisal* (New York: AJC, 1954), p. 8 reported suspicions that Britton could distribute expensive pamphlets and books at cut-price because he was 'covertly backed'.

81 A.K. Chesterton to Colin Jordan, 23 February 1956, Chesterton papers.
82 Colin Jordan to Leslie Greene, 1 June 1956, Chesterton papers.
83 Colin Jordan to Leslie Greene, 23 February 1956; Colin Jordan to Leslie Greene, 8 April 1956; and Leslie Greene to Colin Jordan, 10 April 1956, Chesterton papers.
84 John Bean, *Many Shades of Black: Inside Britain's Far Right* (London: New Millennium, 1999), p. 101 recalls addressing a meeting of Coventry's Ukrainian National Committee, an apocryphal choice of name given its use by Ukrainian collaborators in Galicia, who subsequently founded the 14th Waffen-SS Volunteer Division Galizien in April 1943. Bean had not appreciated the nationalist tensions within the Ukrainian community and 'my audience almost came to blows among themselves when I praised the Russian people who had suffered so much under the Communist yoke.' See John Bean's Nationalist Notebooks, 'Ukraine is Not All That it Seems', British National Party, 16 December 2004, www.bnp.org.uk/columnists/notebook2.php?jbId=5 (accessed 21 January 2006). *Daily Telegraph*, 9 April 1956 notes Bean's participation in a march and wreath laying ceremony organised by the Coventry branches of Anglo-Ukrainian Society and the Polish Ex-Service Combatants' Association, and addressed by Malcolm Muggeridge, editor of *Punch*, and the Dowager Lady Hesketh, president of the Anglo-Ukrainian Society and chairwoman of the Daventry Conservative Association. It was after this event that Bean and Jordan met for the first time. Fedir Kowalenko subsequently approached the LEL for financial assistance for a bilingual news-sheet the Ukrainian community produced. Bean contributed an article but little more resulted from the collaboration.
85 Leonard Burt, *Commander Burt of Scotland Yard* (London: Pan Books, 1959), pp. 101–102.
86 *Candour*, vol. 4, no. 131, 27 April 1956; and *Don't Shake Hands with Murder!* (LEL handbill, 1956). Stewart was an early contributor to *Candour* who believed that 'there has never been an equal to the British Empire for good to the whole world.' He also regarded Nesta Webster as 'the greatest authority' on subversion, see *Candour*, vol. 3, nos 92 and 93, 29 July and 5 August 1955. Stewart was formerly a forestry engineer in the Baltic having spent most of his early working life managing an import trading company on the Gold Coast. John F. Stewart to Sir V. Tewson, 2 February 1952, MSS 292/770.2/3, Trades Union Congress papers, Warwick Modern Records Centre, Warwick University, states he was in the 'closest contact' with members of what he termed the 'Ukrainian Resistance and Independence Movement'. For the use of the SLEF by MI6 to recruit the more 'extreme' Ukrainians for its clandestine war with Soviet Russia, see Tom Bower, *The Red Web: MI6 and the KGB Master Coup* (London: Aurum Press, 1989).
87 *Daily Telegraph*, 20 April 1956.
88 *Candour*, vol. 4, no. 130, 20 April 1956; and *Candour*, vol. 4, no. 131, 27 April 1956.
89 Colin Jordan, 'Die Strategie der "Koexistenz"', *Nation Europa*, vol. 6, no. 11, November 1956, pp. 21–23.
90 Colin Jordan to Leslie Greene, 5 May 1956, Chesterton papers. Jordan was also a regular recipient of *The Cross and The Flag*, *Women's Voice*, *Williams Intelligence Summary*, *Closer Up*, *Don Bell Reports*, *American Nationalist*, *Keeping the Record Straight* and *Point*, 'plus odd issues of others'.
91 Colin Jordan to Leslie Greene, 5 May 1956, Chesterton papers.
92 *Free Britain*, no. 166, March 1956.
93 Colin Jordan to Leslie Greene, 8 April 1956, Chesterton papers.
94 Leslie Greene to Colin Jordan, 10 April 1956, Chesterton papers. From their correspondence, it appears that Jordan was amorously pursuing Greene, noting after one meeting 'it is hard if not utterly impossible to like some of your views but very easy to like their advocate,' see Colin Jordan to Leslie Greene, 25 May 1956, Chesterton papers. Jordan was particularly disturbed to

learn that Greene had had Jewish friends, however. He was perhaps only half joking when he wrote,

> if only our dear organising secretary had had six months at a Berlin racial institute pre-war ... how much better everything should be, and I should not now be having to cope with the gruelling proposition of liking someone while hating their ideas like poison ... anyway I hope we'll still keep good friends even if your Jewish friends want to shoot me and I want to shoot them.

see Colin Jordan to Leslie Greene, 1 June 1956, Chesterton papers. Greene was less than amused by the undertone of anti-Semitic violence implicit in Jordan's letter stating that 'it made me feel positively sick', see Leslie Greene to Colin Jordan, n.d., Chesterton papers.

95 A.K. Chesterton to Colin Jordan, 7 November 1955; Colin Jordan to Leslie Greene, 8 April 1956; and A.K. Chesterton to Colin Jordan, 4 May 1956, Chesterton papers. Known also as 'Peter Green', Greenslade had rechristened his Croydon home 'William Joyce House' from whence he ran an outfit called the 'British Pan German Movement'. 'We cannot find anything on him here,' Sidney Salomon of the JDC recorded, 'but I am told that they are getting quite active in Germany', see Sidney Salomon to Chief Superintendent E. Jones, 11 February 1957 in 1658/10/29, JDC papers, Wiener Library. Greenslade also associated with 'Wolf Cleveland', a pseudonym for Maurice Woolford, whose efforts to provoke racist violence, Chesterton believed, could only discredit the cause of racial nationalism. Woolford was a member of the minute British National Socialist Party (BNSP) founded by former LEL member Peter Erwood, which aimed to foment racial strife in Brixton through posters stating, 'Nigger Labour is Scab Labour'. He was also noted to be hatching plans for arson attacks against Jewish and West Indian property. Woolford formed his own short-lived KKK before continuing to play his 'lone hand' against blacks and Jews, see Christopher Cowling, 'Report on Fascist Organisations', in DCL 42/10, National Council for Civil Liberties papers, Hull University, hereafter NCCL papers. Jordan noted that the dominant feature of Cleveland's organisations 'was its display of whips and interest in flagellation', see *Gothic Ripples Supplement*, no. 9, September 1982.
96 Colin Jordan to Leslie Greene, 25 May 1956, Chesterton papers.
97 Colin Jordan to Leslie Greene, 28 June 1956, Chesterton papers.
98 A.K. Chesterton to Colin Jordan, 7 September 1956, Chesterton papers.
99 Colin Jordan to Leslie Greene, 17 October 1956, Chesterton papers.
100 Colin Jordan to Leslie Greene, 9 March 1957, Chesterton papers. Jordan is listed as the agent for *Northern World* in Willis Carto's *Right*, no. 24, September 1957 and then subsequently in *First National Directory of 'Rightist' Groups, Publications and Some Individuals in the United States (and Some Foreign Countries)*, 3rd edn (San Francisco, CA: Liberty and Property, 1957), p. 27.
101 A.K. Chesterton to Colin Jordan, 31 October 1956, Chesterton papers.
102 Special Branch report, 17 December 1957 in TNA KV 2/4389; and Special Branch reports, 5 September 1960 and 3 August 1963 in TNA KV 2/4390. The latter report notes that after the collapse of the Frei Korps, Jordan was 'rarely seen' in London again until 28 March 1959.
103 Arnold Spencer Leese, Last Will and Testament, 21 December 1949.
104 Special Branch report, 28 May 1959 in TNA HO 344/34.
105 Frost, *'Twaz a Good Fight!'*, p. 39 makes the claim of editorship. He contributed to it until its demise in 1957
106 Britons Publishing Society, minutes of meeting, 16 February 1957, Britons papers.
107 TNA KV 2/4389/255a. The Britons later printed another racist provocation, 'Thomas Johns', *Unfair to Apes* (London: SSPPP, 1961), albeit officially published by a non-existent 'Scientific Socialist Progressive Party' which operated from behind a Notting Hill PO Box. The pamphlet, an act of racist mischief making, enjoined 'negroes' to overcome racial prejudice by procreating 'only' with 'white girls' to create, 'as fast as you can', as many 'coffee-coloured babies' as possible outside the 'out-of-date' concepts of marriage and family. This injunction was bound to be deeply provocative to local white youths who were derided as 'smaller and weaker than you'.
108 There was a mutual recognition. *The White Sentinel*, vol. 7, no. 4, April 1957, mouthpiece of the National Citizens' Protective Association, quoted from an article written by Jordan for *Free Britain*.

109 For a broader context, see Elizabeth Buettner, '"This is Staffordshire not Alabama": Racial Geographies of Commonwealth Immigration in Early 1960s Britain', *The Journal of Imperial and Commonwealth History*, vol. 42, no. 4, 2014, pp. 710–740.
110 *Right*, no. 38, November 1958.
111 *Fighting Talk*, no. 9.
112 *Black and White News*, no. 1, 1958; and *The Times*, 10 September 1998.
113 Special Branch report, 5 September 1960 in TNA KV 2/4390 intimates that Jordan was already operating as the 'White Defence Bureau', whilst living in Coventry and that he changed its name once he moved to London on 28 March 1959.
114 *The Five Races of Europe* (1949), authored by George Pile, a leading figure in both The Britons and the LEL, regurgitated Günther's central thesis putting his ideas back into circulation at a time with English translations of his inter-war works were increasingly hard to come by.
115 Colin Jordan to Anthony Gittens, 14 October 1958, Leese papers.
116 Britons Publishing Society to Mrs Leese, 22 January 1959, Leese papers; and Anthony Gittens to Mr Pakenham-Walsh, 22 June 1959, Britons papers.
117 Colin Jordan to Mrs Leese, 4 March 1968, Leese papers.
118 Colin Jordan, 'Notes on Arnold Leese', unpublished MSS, Leese papers.
119 Colin Jordan, letters to the author, 1 November 2001, 22 November 2001 and 12 December 2001.
120 May Winifred Leese, Last Will and Testament, 31 August 1960.
121 *Colin Jordan: A National Socialist Life* (Heckmondwike: Sunwheel Publications, 2009), p. 4.
122 *Gothic Ripples*, nos 33–34, March 1996 notes Bass died in November 1995.
123 *The Blacks are Coming* (WDL handbill, 1959).
124 *West London Observer*, 10 April 1959.
125 Bean, *Many Shades of Black*, pp. 126–127.
126 Extract, 29 May 1958 in TNA KV 2/4389/254.
127 *Daily Mail*, 23 May 1959.
128 *The Times*, 21 March 1959; and Kanyama Chiume, *Autobiography of Kanyama Chiume* (London: Panaf, 1982), p. 120.
129 *Coventry Evening Telegraph*, 24 April 1959.
130 *Daily Mail*, 23 May 1959.
131 *The Times*, 25 May 1959; and *Combat*, no. 4, autumn 1959.
132 *Who Killed Kelso Cochrane?* (WDL handbill, 1959), copy in Jewish Chronicle Library Collection, Box 6, Wiener Library, London.
133 *One Way Ticket from Britain* (WDL handbill, 1959); and *Kensington Post*, 12 June 1959.
134 Jackson, *Colin Jordan and Britain's Neo-Nazi Movement*, pp. 88–89.
135 'Draft', no date, in TNA HO 325/9
136 *Reynolds News*, 4 June 1959; and *Daily Herald*, 15 June 1959.
137 Martin Walker, *The National Front* (London: Fontana/Collins, 1977), p. 34.
138 *The Times*, 21 September 1959.
139 David Kynaston, *Modernity Britain: 1957–1962* (New York: Bloomsbury, 2014), p. 358.
140 *The Times*, 6 October; and *The Times*, 21 October 1959.
141 *Citizens' Council*, vol. 1, no. 5, 1956, quoted in Mulhall, 'The Unbroken Thread: British Fascism, its Ideologues and Ideologies, 1939–1960', p. 242.
142 Earnest Sevier Cox to William Stephenson, 10 January 1957; and William Stephenson to Colin Jordan, 15 February 1957, Box 12, Ernest Sevier Cox papers, Duke University, hereafter Cox papers.
143 Colin Jordan to Colonel Cox, 7 April 1957, Box 12, Cox papers.
144 The Northern League, Circular letter no. 4, January 1959; *The Northlander*, vol. 2, no. 1, March 1959; and *The Nationalist*, no. 4, March 1960.
145 Frost, *'Twaz a Good Fight!'*, pp. 55 and 58–60. Earnest Sevier Cox to Colin Jordan, n.d. [1959], Box 13, Cox papers, notes Cox's visit to England and desire to meet with Jordan.
146 Special Branch report, 17 June 1959 in TNA HO 344/34.
147 Jordan remained involved with the Northern League. The *Jewish Chronicle*, 3 December 1971 reported his presence at a meeting of the group in Brighton in 1971, during which its three German guests, Fred Ehlert, Horst Bongers and a Mr Braun, were injured in a mêlée with anti-fascists who attacked the meeting.

148 Howard J. Ehrlich, 'The Swastika Epidemic of 1959–1960: Anti-Semitism and Community Characteristics', *Social Problems*, vol. 9, no. 3, winter 1962, pp. 264–272 examines such incidences in the United States. John Barron, *KGB: The Secret Work of Soviet Secret Agents* (London: Hodder and Stoughton, 1974), pp. 173–174 and 319 claims KBG General Ivan Agayants arranged for 'faked' swastikas to appear on Jewish property in the Federal Republic to discredit West Germany, though the supposition he 'conceived' the entire 'swastika operation' is overblown. Oleg Kalugin, *Spymaster: My Thirty-Two Years in Intelligence and Espionage against the West* (New York: Basic Books, 2008), p. 54 also notes the KGB's 'active measures campaign' to foment racial hatred in the USA during the 1960s to discredit democracy.
149 *Jewish Chronicle*, 8 January 1960.
150 Special Branch report, 5 September 1960 in TNA KV 2/4390.
151 Frost, *'Twaz a Good Fight!'*, pp. 47–48.
152 Extract, 17 January 1960 in TNA KV 2/4389/273.
153 Special Branch report, 20 January 1960 in TNA KV 2/4389. Police estimated total WDL membership at 100 but recorded that this figure included 'lapsed members and members who have transferred to other right wing organisations, including the N.L.P.'
154 Constitution of the British National Party (1960) and 'British National Party – For Race and Nation' in TNA DPP 2/3331.
155 Jackson, *Colin Jordan and Britain's Neo-Nazi Movement*, p. 96.
156 *Combat*, no. 13, August–October 1961. For analysis of these articles, see Jackson, *Colin Jordan and Britain's Neo-Nazi Movement*, pp. 92–95.
157 *Your Child's Future: Civilisation or Jungle Law?* (BNP leaflet, n.d.)
158 Special Branch report, 28 February 1960 released following FOI request.
159 Special Branch report, no. 5, 18 May 1960 in TNA HO 325/9.
160 *Sunday Mercury*, 20 March 1960; and *Daily Herald*, 30 May 1960.
161 *The Times*, 30 May 1960.
162 Hansard, HC Deb., vol. 626, cols 1184–1194 (12 July 1960).
163 *The Times*, 13 July 1960; and *The Times*, 30 July 1960.
164 *The Times*, 2 September 1960. The next BNP action was an attack on a CND meeting in London during which activists threw fireworks at the speakers including Labour MP Arthur Greenwood, see *The Times*, 1 November 1960.
165 Assistant Chief Constable of Staffordshire to MI5, 12 December 1961 in TNA KV 2/4390 highlights Jordan's association with Davidson and his younger brother.
166 The *Observer*, 1 July 1962.
167 Frost, *'Twaz a Good Fight!'*, p. 71.
168 *The Northern European*, no. 3, October–November 1960.
169 Special Branch report, 13 April 1960 in TNA KV 2/4390. In Denmark, Jordan maintained contact with Sven Salicath, leader of the Danmarks Nationalsocialistiske Arbejderparti (DNSAP – Danish National Socialist Workers Party). In Sweden, he met with veteran Swedish fascist Per Engdahl, maintaining a 'general liaison' with the remnants of his ESB network thereafter, see Colin Jordan to Bengt Olov Ljunberg, 6 May 1960 in Per Engdahl papers, National Archives, Stockholm. In *Gothic Ripples*, no. 43, May 2001 Jordan highlights his meeting with Göran A. Oredsson, leader of the Nordiska Rikspartei (NRP – Nordic Reich Party) who became a key contact. His German contacts during this period are unknown though Jordan visited Hannover following his Scandinavian sojourn. Le Nouvel ordre européen invited him to their conference in Karlsruhe scheduled for mid-April. It is unknown if he attended.
170 *BNP: The First Year 1960* (BNP: Combat Press, 1960), p. 5.
171 *The Northern European*, no. 3, October–November 1960.
172 *The Northern European*, no. 2, August–September 1960. Van Tienen had joined the SS in 1940, aged eighteen, winning the Iron Cross (First Class) and distinguishing himself as one of the few 'volunteer officers who were allowed to command German units'. Shortly after his release, having served five years, van Tienen founded the Boekhandel Europa bookshop. In 1952, he became leader of the Dutch section of the ESB contributing to its journal *Nation Europa*. The authorities promptly banned the Dutch ESB and van Tienen with fellow leader Dr Jan Wolthius were imprisoned, though their sentences were later quashed. Thereafter, van Tienen concentrated on the publishing activities of the Boekhandel Europa and his newsletter *Social Weekblad*.

173 Frost, *'Twaz a Good Fight!'*, p. 61.
174 *The Northern European*, no. 9, November–December 1961.
175 George Pile, a Britons activist, edited the book, which featured an introduction from Air Commodore G.S. Oddie, a Christian Identity adherent who had been involved with the British People's Party (BPP).
176 *Gothic Ripples*, no. 11, July 1984. A.V. Schaerffenberg, *Nazi Questions and Answers* (2008) available at: www.nazi-lauck-nsdapao.com/nazi.htm (accessed 17 February 2014) intimates that Hess was one of the reasons for Jordan's subsequent conscientious objection:

> The plight of Rudolf Hess stirred deep reconsideration in the soul of Colin Jordan, so much so the young RAF man told his superiors that he could no longer support Churchill's war in good faith and agreed with Hess that hostilities should be brought to a swift end through a negotiated settlement.

177 Frost, *'Twaz a Good Fight!'*, pp. 61–62 and 82–83.
178 *Liberty Bell*, June 1979; and *Gothic Ripples*, no. 42, March 2002.
179 *Combat*, no. 14, November–December 1961.
180 Frost, *'Twaz a Good Fight!'*, p. 61.
181 Thomas Dörfler and Andreas Kläner, 'Rudolf Hess as a "Martyr for Germany": The Reinterpretation of Historical Figures in Nationalist Discourse', in Jan Herman Brinks, Stella Rock and Edward Timms (eds), *Nationalist Myths and Modern Media: Contested Identities in the Age of Globalisation* (London: Tauris Academic Studies, 2006), pp. 139–153. For an evocation in contemporary Nazi subcultures, see Ryan Shaffer, 'From Outcast to Martyr: The Memory of Rudolf Hess in Skinhead Culture', *JEX: Journal EXIT-Deutschland*, no. 3, 2014, pp. 111–124. New generations of activists have used his experience to re-imagine their own tribulations. 'I am now the closest to the treatment Rudolf Hess, my hero and role model, got,' wrote jailed Holocaust denier Ernst Zündel, *Setting the Record Straight: Letters from Cell #7* (Pigeon Forge, TN: Soaring Eagles Gallery, 2004), p. 36.
182 A.H. Le Tissier, 'Spandau Allied Prison – Card from Colin Jordan', 22 December 1983 in TNA FCO 161/3.
183 *Spearhead*, no. 213, July 1986. *Liberty Bell*, vol. 13, no. 12, August 1986; and *The New Order*, no. 67, March–April 1987 reprinted it for an American audience. Martin Webster argued in *Spearhead*, no. 114, February 1978 that Hess and the NF faced the same adversary.

> Let us remember that the same forces which sought to hang Hess, which secured his imprisonment, and which now rejoice in his perpetual torture – the forces of Communism and Zionism – are the same forces which have brought about the Race Relations Laws whose sole purpose is to put into jails those who dare to speak out against their wickedness.

184 Jackson, *Colin Jordan and Britain's Neo-Nazi Movement*, p. 200.
185 *New Gothic Ripples*, 15 May 2013, http://newgothicripples.wordpress.com/2013/05/15/justice-liberty-interview/ (accessed 21 March 2014).
186 TNA FCO 50/16–22; and Dominic Casciani, 'British Sympathy for Jailed Nazi', BBC News, 28 September 2007, http://news.bbc.co.uk/1/hi/uk/7017191.stm (accessed 21 March 2014).
187 *Gothic Ripples*, no. 2, March 1980.
188 Frost, *'Twaz a Good Fight!'*, pp. 288–289. Jordan almost certainly knew of Kühnen's illness. Rumours had circulated within the milieu 'as early as his prison term that ended in 1988,' states Michael Schmidt, *The New Reich: Penetrating the Secrets of Today's Neo-Nazi Networks* (London: Hutchinson, 1993), p. 19.
189 The *Independent*, 20 November 1993; and *Sunday Sun*, 21 November 1993. Two BNP members, Bill Owen and Thomas Graham, made possible the memorial. Owen, who died in 1993, bequeathing the BNP £20,000, provided the finances. Graham arranged for its physical construction. Graham was an old consort of both Jordan and Leese who had praised his 'thorough knowledge of race' in *Gothic Ripples*, no. 36, 20 March 1948. Graham was deported from Canada in 1948 following a conviction for seditious libel having circulated a document titled 'Canadians Awake – Boycott All Jews – Down with Jewmocracy'. Thereafter, Graham was active in A.F.X. Baron's NWM. In 1960, he was again distributing literature that regurgitated the 'blood libel' myth. See *Wiener Library Bulletin*, no. 4, May 1948; 'Fascist Activities: May–June 1948' in TNA KV 3/51; and BDBJ C6/10/5, JDC papers.

190 *The Times*, 19 November 1993; and *Gothic Ripples*, no. 45, March 2002.
191 Frost, *'Twaz a Good Fight!'*, p. 301. Jordan later published and circulated his personal information, see *Communist Capitalists – Blood Brothers in Crime* (Harrogate: Gothic Ripples, 1993); and *Rudolf Hess Memorial at Eaglesham – Levelling the Livingston Lie* (Harrogate: Gothic Ripples, 1993). *Combat 18*, no. 3, [c.1993] also circulated Anwar's personal details, which appeared after several pages of bomb-making instructions and exhortations to kill.
192 Rachel McCallion, 'Who is Aamer Anwar, the Human Rights Lawyer Running for Glasgow Rector?', *The Tab – Glasgow*, 15 March 2017, http://thetab.com/uk/glasgow/2017/03/15/aamer-anwar-human-rights-lawyer-running-glasgow-rector-15069 (accessed 21 March 2017).
193 Colin Jordan, *The Uprising* (Milwaukee, WI: NS Publications, 2004), p. 47 contains the following passage:

> The cocky Asian, who had got away with his despicable desecration to the acclaim of *Stoplight* [*Searchlight*], was discovered one morning in a grievous condition at the base of a disused warehouse near to Glasgow. Apparently he had taken off at a high level without the benefit of a parachute, adorned with a placard reading 'Remember Rudolf Hess!' Though he survived as a permanent cripple, he certainly never forgot the message and the circumstances of his wingless flight, his permanently disordered brain causing him at intervals to exclaim mournfully 'Remember Rudolf Hess!'

194 Special Branch report, 28 March 1961 in TNA MEPO 2/10139. The instigator was one Frank Bennett, a fascist activist who held 'Third Reich' parties at his flat in Onslow Gardens, South Kensington, which regularly attracted groups of approximately twenty fascists. Those involved in the kidnapping 'would consist of volunteers who have proved their mettle by desecrating Jewish synagogues'. Bennett had fallen out with fellow fascist Sidney Proud who informed the authorities of the plot. The film-makers Kevin Brownlow and Andrew Mollo had attended an earlier party held in October 1960. They subsequently cast Bennett as a Nazi ideologue in their film *It Happened Here* (1964) giving him and two others the opportunity to expound their philosophy in a discussion with the lead actors to give the scene the ring of authenticity. The controversial scene was cut due to pressure and only restored when the film was re-released in 2006, see Kevin Brownlow, *How It Happened Here* (Portishead: UKAPress, 2005), pp. 122–124, 153–154 and 164.
195 Bean, *Many Shades of Black*, p. 150.
196 *The Times*, 18 April 1961; and *The Times*, 2 May 1961.
197 *The Northern European*, no. 3, October–November 1960.
198 *Combat*, no. 11, March–April 1961; and *Combat*, no. 12, May–July 1961.
199 *The Eichmann Trial – 'Combat' Supplement*.
200 On 8–9 July 1961, Jordan also attended a 2,000-strong 'European Youth Meeting' in Lippoldsberg, Germany, staged in connection with the 19th Dichtertreffen ('Meeting of Poets'), organised by *völkisch* author Hans Grimm, see 'Extract from MI6 report re an international Fascist Meeting in Germany', 14 September 1961 in TNA KV 2/4390/298a.
201 Frost, *'Twaz a Good Fight!'*, pp. 61 and 78; and Kurt P. Tauber, *Beyond Eagle and Swastika: German Nationalism Since 1945, Vol. 1* (Middletown, CT: Wesleyan University Press, 1967), p. 621. UM ideologue Alexander Raven Thomson had originally published Veale's first book pseudonymously as 'A Jurist', *Advance to Barbarism* (London: Thomson and Smith, 1948).
202 Tauber, *Beyond Eagle and Swastika*, p. 621. F.J.P. Veale, *Verschleierte Kriegsverbrechen* (Wiesbaden: Verlag Karl Heinz Priester, 1959). Karl Heinz Priester, the publisher was a leading figure in the European Social Movement and was involved with Mosley. He subsequently published a second edition of Veale's first book as *Der Barbarei entgegen* (Wiesbaden: Verlag Karl Heinz Priester, 1962) too.
203 *The Thunderbolt*, no. 25, January 1961.
204 These were Hans Rehnvaal and Kurt Ake Zakrisson (Nordiska Rikspartiet), Tenerani Franco (Avanguardia Nazionale Giovanile), Erik Johnson (Danmarks National-Socialistiske Arbejder Parti), Robert Ketels (Belgian NER member), Ingo Mengel and Wolfgang Seil (Bund Vaterladischer Jugend), Savitri Devi (French NER member), Horst Nolte (Arbeitsgemeinschaft Nationaler Kreise), Gerhard Raisin (German NER member), Winifred Schneider (New European Order – Germany) and Horst Strauss (Kameradschaftsring Nationaler Jungendverbande), Robert Lyons and A.C. Hayden (National States Rights Party). The transnational solidarity such

events were designed to inoculate was evident in the NSRP delegates. Lyons, NSRP Pennsylvania branch chairman, returned:

> with the knowledge that we his comrades in Britain in Europe are spiritually with the American people in their struggle against the enforcement of integration with American Negroes just as much as we are with our kinsmen in South Africa and Rhodesia,

proclaimed *Combat*, no. 12, May–July 1961.
205 *The Times*, 26 May 1961.
206 TNA CRIM 1/3973.
207 Nicholas Goodrick-Clarke, *Hitler's Priestess: Savitri Devi, the Hindu-Aryan Myth and Neo-Nazism* (New York: New York University Press, 1998). See also Arthur Versluis, 'Savitri Devi, Miguel Serrano, and the Global Phenomenon of Esoteric Hitlerism', in Henrik Bogdan and Gordan Djurdjevic (eds), *Occultism in a Global Perspective* (Durham: Acumen, 2013), pp. 121–134.
208 Jordan sold Savitri Devi's works through *The Northern European*, no. 5, January–February 1961. *Combat*, no. 13, August–October 1961, the BNP newspaper, also sold *Defiance* (1951), *Gold in the Furnace* (1952), *Pilgrimage* (1958) and *The Lightning and the Sun* (1958), listing them under 'National Socialism'.
209 Robert A. Pois, *National Socialism and the Religion of Nature* (Beckenham: Croon Helm, 1986).
210 *NSM Bulletin*, February 1966.
211 *Gothic Ripples*, no. 41, August 2000.
212 'The Role of the SP Man' in TNA CRIM 1/3973; BNP *Member's Bulletin*, no. 6, March 1961; and Frost, *'Twaz a Good Fight!'*, p. 87.
213 'Spearhead membership application form' and 'The Spearhead of the British National Party: Provisional Basic Structure' in TNA CRIM 1/3973. To be eligible to join Spearhead BNP members had to fulfil the following criterion:

> (i) Age 16–45 (ii) Predominantly Nordic type (iii) tolerably good appearance (iv) sensible (v) keen (vi) able-bodied and reasonably robust (vii) basic understanding of racial nationalism (viii) an active member of the BNP for not less than 3 months, satisfactorily (ix) accepted by the Commander of the Spearhead by personal interview.

They were expected to devote 12 hours a week to the making the formation 'a vanguard of idealism and core of strength in the service of the Party.'
214 'The Role of the SP Man' in TNA CRIM 1/3973.
215 DC Thomas, police statement in TNA CRIM 1/3973.
216 *Combat*, no. 14, November–December 1961. Also present in the hall 'were one young lady from the League of Empire Loyalists and six Union Movement members who also put up a courageous fight against the Communist stewards.'
217 'Extract from Special Branch report re Annual General Meeting of the British National Party (Fascist Org), 1 February 1962 in TNA KV 2/4390.
218 *Combat*, no. 16, March–April 1962.
219 'Statement by Andrew Fountaine, BNP president' in Searchlight papers, Southampton University; and Frost, *'Twaz a Good Fight!'*, p. 93. Though Fountaine and Bean objected to Jordan's Nazi proclivities, the BNP still harboured many activists whose political sympathies were similarly inclined. The BNP Ilford and West Essex organiser was the lorry driver and former military policeman Ron W. Tear who, presumably with Bean's sanction, sold inter-war IFL literature to *Combat*'s readership through its 'BNP Readers Service' – copy in author's possession. Furthermore, Tear, who was married to a German woman, kept a 'Nazi shrine' in his Ilford home where he entertained the German Nazi leader Wolfgang Kerstein, see Walker, *The National Front*, pp. 121–122. Tear became a leading light in the NF during its early years.
220 French groups like Jeune Nation had also adopted the Celtic Cross as a symbol during the 1950s, see Jacques Delarue, 'The Radical Right in France', *Wiener Library Bulletin*, vol. 21, no. 2, spring 1967. For a broader discussion, see Andrew Fergus Wilson, 'From Apocalyptic Paranoia to the Mythic Nation: Political Extremity and Myths of Origin in the Neo-Fascist Milieu', in Marion Gibson, Shelley Trower and Garry Tregidga (eds), *Mysticism, Myth and Celtic Identity* (Abingdon: Routledge, 2013), pp. 199–215.

221 *BNP Special Members' Bulletin – From the National Organiser*, 15 February 1962.
222 DC Dennis Courtman, police statement and DC Alexander Tilling, police statement in TNA CRIM 1/3973.
223 Frost, *'Twaz a Good Fight!'*, p. 142. *The People*, 18 November 1962 subsequently ran an exposé after the trial naming Nicols as their source. Nicols revealed encountering puerile political stunts like their 'I Love Bacon' week, which entailed inviting the Board of Deputies to a 'Jewish Bacon BBQ' at Princedale Road, or simply mailing of rashers of bacon to prominent Jewish MP's like Sidney Silverman and Sir Barnett Janner (i.e. *National Jewish Bacon Week* [NSM handbill] in BDBJ C6/9/2/1, JDC papers). To ingratiate himself, Nicols volunteered to plant a dummy bomb at the Astoria Cinema, Charing Cross, prior to the premier of the film *Exodus* though he tipped off the manager. Despite the plot's failure, his credibility increased, enabling him to gain greater access to its activities. Nicols' recalled helping train the Spearhead group: 'It was the most satisfying job I had in Jordan's service. I used it as an excuse to plant my boot or fist on every member of the gang.' Jordan subsequently entrusted Nicols with the 'security' for George Lincoln Rockwell's visit to the NSM camp.
224 Jackson, *Colin Jordan and Britain's Neo-Nazi Movement*, p. 135.
225 *The National Socialist*, no. 1, June 1962.
226 Colin Jordan, *Why I am a National Socialist ... And Why You Should Be Too* (NSM handbill, 1962).
227 *The National Socialist*, no. 7, 1964. Jordan himself was, unsurprisingly, a Wagner devotee. In 1977, Frau Winifred Wagner gave an interview during which she stated 'If Adolf Hitler came through that door today, I would be just as pleased as ever to see him.' Jordan wrote to congratulate her. 'Among my treasured possessions is the reply she sent me to my message of congratulations on that occasion,' he recalled in *Gothic Ripples*, no. 3, June 1980. Frost, *'Twaz a Good Fight!'*, p. 278 records that her reply read: 'It was very kind of you to understand my loyal sentiments for Adolf Hitler – and I thank you very much indeed for expressing your attitude towards my documentation of our friendship!'
228 Lawrence Hanley, police statement in TNA CRIM 1/3973.
229 Spearhead circular, 28 May 1962 in TNA CRIM 1/3973.
230 Jeffrey Hamm, *The Evil Good Men Do: A Study in Decline* (London: Sanctuary Press, 1988), p. 184.
231 Thurlow, *Fascism in Britain*, p. 240.
232 Detective Inspector Bert Wickstead to [no name], 12 November 1965 in TNA MEPO 2/10502.
233 John Tyndall, *The Eleventh Hour: A Call for British Rebirth* (London: Albion Press, 1988), p. 188.
234 Detective-Inspector William Edward Sullivan, witness statement, p. 23 in TNA ASSI 26/416. 'Brief for Tuesday', 22 November 1966 in TNA KV 2/4392/465a gives a slightly different figure of 235 NSM members and 250 subscribers to its magazine and book club.
235 Jordan originally applied to the Ministry of Works for permission to hold a meeting in Trafalgar Square on 4 April, giving 17 or 24 June as his preferred dates. Neither date was available. The Ministry of Works consulted the Metropolitan Police who raised no objection (though they later admitted they did not know the anti-Semitic nature of the demonstration). They therefore granted 1 July to the NSM; see Colin Jordan to Ministry of Works, 4 April 1962; and L.J. Greenaway to John Tyndall, 18 April 1962 in TNA WORK 20/357.
236 CC (62) 39, 31 May 1962 in TNA CAB 128/36/39. The Attorney-General found no legal reason to ban the meeting, a stance supported by the Home Office. 'If you disallow this mtg.,' noted Home Secretary Rab Butler, 'you will have to launch a general policy for suppressing anti-Semitic speeches etc,' records CC. 39 (62) in TNA CAB 195/21/5.
237 Colin Jordan to George Lincoln Rockwell, 8 July 1962, George Lincoln Rockwell papers, private collection. These papers have since been deposited at the University of Kansas.
238 Transcript of speeches of Colin Jordan and John Tyndall, NSM rally, 1 July 1962 in NCCL papers.
239 *The National Socialist*, no. 1, June 1962.
240 *The Times*, 2 July 1962. Martin Webster, a nineteen-year-old LEL member, was photographed helping the NSM in defending the plinth, leading to his expulsion from the League. 'In a sense, therefore, that expulsion left me with no political home to go to, so I became involved with the National Socialist Movement,' he recalled in *Spearhead*, no. 114, February 1978.

241 Between 1959 and 1961, there were twenty-four fascist meetings in Trafalgar Square, see *Current Anti-Semitic Activities Abroad*, p. 5, http://collections.americanjewisharchives.org/ms/ms0603/ms0603.049.003.pdf (accessed 12 August 2017).
242 The *Guardian*, 30 July 1962.
243 Statement issued to the press by Sir Oswald Mosley, 14 August 1962, Hamm papers. This row spilt out into international networks. Jean Thiriart, a Belgian fascist closely associated with Mosley during this period (see Chapter 2) counselled an urgent response to the conflation by the European media of Mosley and Jordan's politics, see Jean Thiriart to Union Movement, 9 August 1962, Hamm papers.
244 *National European*, August 1965.
245 *Candour Interim Report*, October 1962.
246 *The Times*, 19 July 1962.
247 *The Times*, 3 July 1962.
248 The *Guardian*, 5 July 1962; and *The Times*, 5 July 1962. Jordan had previously commented on educational matters in *Combat*, writing that 'Racial nationalists will replace democrats as teachers. Authority and discipline will replace the present laxity which fosters widespread juvenile delinquency.'
249 See Media Archive for Central England, www.macearchive.org/Media.html?Title=4 (accessed 8 October 2007).
250 *The Times*, 19 July 1962.
251 Colin Jordan, *Britain Reborn: The Will and Purpose of the National Socialist Movement* (1962).
252 This was not a new development. 'Extract', 17 July 1962 in TNA KV 2/4390/318a highlights Jordan was previously in touch with a UAR Consul called Izzat on the same subject. He had also previously met the UAR representative in Amsterdam in November 1961. 'They agreed to co-operate. The possibility of the sending of an agent to Israel was discussed,' noted MI5. This was not the first time Jordan's anti-Semitism had led him to try and forge alliances with the Muslim world. In January 1956, Jordan accompanied Peter Ling and Austen Brooks who spoke from the platform of the Conference of the Palestine Day Committee of the Arab Student League in Holborn Hall. See Colin Jordan to Leslie Greene, 13 January 1956, Chesterton papers. Jordan's campaign on behalf of Adolf Eichmann in 1961 had also won him plaudits from figures such as Cevat Rifat Atilhan, a Turkish anti-Semite who had introduced *The Protocols* into Turkey in 1934 and who was an old contact of The Britons, see Frost, *'Twaz a Good Fight!'*, p. 73. Later in the decade, Jordan was also in contact with Ibrahim Abaza who sold copies of *The Protocols* outside Regents Park Mosque, see *Searchlight*, no. 121, July 1985.
253 John Tyndall to Col. Shazly, 20 July 1962; and 'Proposals for Co-Operation with the United Arab Republic' in TNA CRIM 1/3973. In August 1962, MI5 noted (TNA KV2/4390/232y and 232z) that John Muhammad Webster (the former British fascist John Alban Webster who had converted to Islam) had stated that Jordan had support in Cairo 'indirectly and also directly' and that he had seen 'Jordan's papers' in the possession of 'Muhammad Ali', the Director of Information.
254 Quoted in Lord Janner to James Callaghan, 1 April 1974 in TNA FCO 93/414.
255 TNA FCO 93/411 to 414.
256 *The Bugler*, no. 1, July–August 1962. The BNY initially had two units, one in Leicestershire led by Wilmer and another in Glasgow led by Arthur Smith. This had expanded to six in the following year, see *The Bugler*, no. 3, November 1962–February 1963. The BNY subsequently relocated its headquarters from Syston, Leicestershire to Wallasey, Cheshire, see *The Bugler*, no. 5, November 1963.
257 *Sunday Telegraph*, 25 November 1962.
258 Colin Jordan to George Lincoln Rockwell, 10 June 1963, Rockwell papers.
259 Colin Jordan to George Lincoln Rockwell, 3 August 1963, Rockwell papers.
260 Admiral Sir Barry Domvile to Anthony Gittens, 19 April 1965, Britons archive.
261 A.K. Chesterton to Revilo P. Oliver, Chesterton papers.
262 *The Bugler*, no. 1, July–August 1962; and no. 4, March–May 1963. FBI file 105–12114–1A records contact between the BNY and the WYC.
263 NSM *Member's Bulletin*, October 1965, Rockwell papers; and *Sunday Telegraph*, 30 May 1965.

264 *Wiener Library Bulletin*, vol. 20, no. 1, winter 1965–1966. The BNP youth wing founded in 1962 was also called the National Youth League. Lance Stewart led it, see BNP *Members' Bulletin*, no. 9, July 1962. He later ran the 'Intelligence Unit' for Nick Griffin's BNP, see *Searchlight*, no. 391, January 2008.

265 *Candour*, vol. 17, no. 456, August 1966. Wilmer subsequently founded the Leicester NF branch before relocating to South Africa in 1969, where he continued to fund-raise for the group, see Ray Hill with Andrew Bell, *The Other Face of Terror: Inside Europe's Neo-Nazi Network* (London: Grafton Books, 1988), pp. 36 and 256. He became national director of the 'Save Rhodesia Campaign' (*Spearhead*, no. 110, October 1977) and subsequently the 'little-known' South Africa First Campaign, which allied itself to Dr Andries Treurnicht after his expulsion from the ruling National Party, see *The Times*, 22 March 1982. Wilmer's activities led to his deportation in 1983, see the *Guardian*, 17 April 1983. He returned in 1989, leading the Natal Freedom Campaign against the 'Communist' African National Congress, see *The Independent*, 2 November 1993.

266 *The Times*, 2 August 1962. Groups that had previously collaborated with Jordan's NER such as the NSRP remained aligned to the BNP. The NSRP newspaper, *The Thunderbolt*, no. 48, January 1963 told its readers that the BNP was 'similar' to the NSRP 'in many ways and is the closest political movement overseas that resembles the NSRP.' Furthermore, although the NSRP, 'firmly believes in no alliances with foreign organisations because we are American Nationalists … we must compliment these men on the fine job they are doing in England for the White Race.' *The Thunderbolt*, no. 63, December–January 1965 went further stating the BNP was 'our sister organisation' and that 'their views on race are the same as ours'. *The Thunderbolt*, no. 69, July 1965 meanwhile featured an endorsement from P.J. Ridout, the BNP treasurer. The NSRP also had links to the Northern League network, see FBI file 62–105/97-X.

267 Angelo del Boca and Mario Giovana, *Fascism Today: A World Survey* (London: Heinemann, 1970), pp. 87–89 and 208–209. For Savitri Devi's recollections, see R.G. Fowler (ed.), *And Time Rolls On. The Savitri Devi Interviews* (San Francisco, CA: Counter Currents, 2012), pp. 96–103.

268 Rockwell had previously explored the possibility of coming to England in 1961. A.G. Lake to T.C. Baker, 17 August 1962 in TNA FCO 168/869 notes his approach to the British Consul in New York about applying for a visa. He was informed that, as an American citizen, he did not require one but that the right of leave to land was vested in the Immigration Officer. Realising that this would not be granted Rockwell (temporarily) abandoned his plans.

269 Frost, *'Twaz a Good Fight!'*, p. 110.

270 *The Times*, 2 August 1962. For Rockwell's account of the meeting, see *The Stormtrooper*, no. 3, November 1962.

271 DI Herbert Trull, police statement in TNA CRIM 1/3973.

272 *The Times*, 7 August 1962.

273 Frederick J. Simonelli, 'The World Union of National Socialists and Postwar Transatlantic Nazi Revival', in Jeffrey Kaplan and Tore Bjørgo (eds), *Nation and Race: The Developing Euro-American Racist Subculture* (Boston, MA: Northeastern University Press, 1998), p. 36.

274 Jack Baker to A.D. Massel, 18 December 1961 in 1658/9/3/1, JDC papers, observes ANP activists distributing 'Liberate Hess' flyers in Washington, DC as part of a coordinated NER activity.

275 *The Cotswold Agreements* (Arlington, VA: WUNS, 1962).

276 Colin Jordan to George Lincoln Rockwell, 29 July 1964, Rockwell papers. Jeffrey Kaplan and Leonard Weinberg, *The Emergence of a Euro-American Radical Right* (New Brunswick, NJ: Rutgers, 1998), p. 43 highlights some of the transnational tensions within the milieu. Notably, NRP leader Göran A. Oredsson, who had worked closely with Jordan in the NER network refused to join WUNS because he was unable to accept that the United States should be its headquarters. Not everyone felt likewise. *The Stormtrooper*, vol. 3, no. 2, March–August 1964 announced that Adolf Eichmann's son, Horst, had joined the network through its Argentina affiliate.

277 *The Rockwell Report*, no. 21, 15 August 1962.

278 The *People*, 12 August 1962.

279 'Obituary: Beryl Cheetham', *NS Outlook*, July 2015, www.bmsunwheel.blogspot.co.uk/2015/07/into-july-2015.html (accessed 27 July 2015). A former Merseyside UM activist, Cheetham moved to Germany when her relationship with Ling broke down, living with a German extreme

right-wing activist. There, she continued her political activities 'alongside veteran German NS activists'. She maintained contact with Jordan and 'established a network of political contacts across Europe and in the USA.' She was a close friend of Savitri Devi.
280 *The Times*, 9 August 1962.
281 George Lincoln Rockwell to Colin Jordan, 15 August 1962, Rockwell papers.
282 Three Special Branch teams simultaneously raided the homes of Denis and Eric Pirie in South London where they lived with their grandmother, Ian Roland Kerr-Ritchie who lived with his mother, and the YMCA hostel where Tyndall lived with his father. *Searchlight*, no. 398, August 2008, alleges sympathetic police sources forewarned Peter Ling and Pat Webb, giving them time to bury an NSM arms cache prior to being raided.
283 'World Union of National Socialists (W.U.N.S.)', MI6 memo, 5 November 1963 in TNA KV 2/4390/378a notes that German police also searched Zimmerman's home, and that of the other activist who had been at the NSM headquarters, a man called 'Kirchstein'. This was quite possibly Wolfgang Kirchstein of Bamberg, Germany, who founded an 'International Viking Movement' in the following year which was aligned to WUNS, see 'Nationalist Youth', *Wiener Library Bulletin*, vol. 20, no. 1, winter 1965–1966, p. 32.
284 Walker, *The National Front*, p. 40.
285 *Daily Telegraph and Morning Post*, 28 August 1962.
286 Walker, *The National Front*, p. 73. Bertha Jordan to George Lincoln Rockwell, 22 December 1962, Rockwell papers, blamed the anti-fascist infiltrator John Nicols for the weedkiller – an assertion at odds with Webster's admission. The NSM expelled Nicols in August following a 'court martial'. Police subsequently arrested him leaving the NSM headquarters with a sheaf of stolen documents, which he confessed he intended to photograph and offer to a newspaper before returning them to the NSM by registered post. He was also carrying an air pistol, which he claimed to have retrieved from the building. The jury believed Nicols that he was going to return the documents, acquitting him of larceny, and also that he had retrieved the pistol *from* the property, rather than taking it *with* him, thereby acquitting him of 'having an offensive weapon in a public place'. For further details of the case, see The *Birmingham Post*, 6 March 1963; and *The Birmingham Post*, 7 March 1963.
287 'Soldiers of the Ring' in TNA CRIM 1/3973.
288 Glen B. Infield, *Skorzeny: Hitler's Commando* (New York: St Martin's Press, 1981); Otto Skorzeny, *Skorzeny's Special Missions* (Aylesbury: Panther, 1959); and Charles Whiting, *Skorzeny: The Most Dangerous Man in Europe* (London: Leo Cooper, 1998).
289 'Strategic methods to be adopted by Special Service Personnel of the Ring during Operations' in TNA CRIM 1/3973.
290 *The Times*, 21 August 1962; and *The Times*, 5 September 1962.
291 'Statement of offence' in TNA CRIM 1/3973. The word 'equipped' was later removed from the indictment.
292 Montague Wimborne, police statement in TNA CRIM 1/3973.
293 Vernon Clancey, police statement in TNA CRIM 1/3973; and *The Times*, 29 August 1962.
294 *The Times*, 12 October 1962.
295 NSM, *Emergency Bulletin from HQ*, 17 October 1962.
296 Colin Jordan to George Lincoln Rockwell, 1 September 1962; and George Lincoln Rockwell to Colin Jordan, 3 September 1962, Rockwell papers.
297 George Lincoln Rockwell to Bruno Ludtke, 26 September 1962, Rockwell papers.
298 *Ibid*.
299 Frederick J. Simonelli, *American Fuerher: George Lincoln Rockwell and the American Nazi Party* (Chicago, IL: University of Illinois Press, 1999), pp. 118–120.
300 *The Stormtrooper*, vol. 2, no. 1, January–February 1963.
301 *The Stormtrooper*, vol. 2, no. 2, March–April 1963.
302 Colin Jordan to George Lincoln Rockwell, 25 August 1962, Rockwell papers. For Slatter, see *The People*, 10 February 1963; and A.M. Rosenthal and Arthur Gelb, *One More Victim: The Life and Death of a Jewish Nazi* (New York: New American Library, 1967), p. 140. Slatter was almost certainly the clandestine channel through which Jordan arranged Rockwell's presence at the August 1962 NSM camp. Colin Jordan to George Lincoln Rockwell, 18 July 1962, Rockwell papers, states 'I would like to say that I hope very much that the project concerning yourself which has been discussed with you through M.S. in London will prove possible.' Ironically,

given his Nazi politics, Slatter was a jazz aficionado, helping to record sessions for jazz trumpeter Kid Thomas Valentine amongst others. In his memoir, Mick Burns (ed.), *Walking with Legends: Barry Martyn's New Orleans Jazz Odyssey* (Baton Rouge, LA: Louisiana State University Press, 2007), pp. 23–24, the English jazz drummer Barry Martyn recalled meeting Slatter in New Orleans noting that:

> In later years I visited him in Chelsea London, and he had pictures of Adolf Hitler on the walls. In fact, he even answered the door dressed as a storm trooper – black riding pants, boots, and all that. It was weird: you'd be talking about Kid Thomas, and he'd suddenly switch the conversation to solving the Jewish problem. It seems impossible that you could like a man who held views like that, but he was really a very nice guy. Strangely, in music he was absolutely not a racist, and all the New Orleans musicians really liked him … Eventually Mike Slatter had to leave England because of his fascist connections, and I think he moved to Spain.

303 For the discussions, see C. (62) 156, 18 October 1962 in TNA CAB 129/111.
304 For the decisions, see C. (63) 70, 26 April 1963 in TNA CAB 129/113.
305 For correspondence, see TNA WORK 20/358.
306 Harold Macmillan, minute, 2 May 1963 in TNA PREM 11/4287.
307 Subsequent requests for meetings on 29 September and 27 October 1963 were also turned down on grounds of 'public inconvenience'. Furious, Jordan wrote to the Ministry of Works that the decision was 'due not so much to your Government's concern for "public inconvenience" as its fear of the National Socialist exposure of the present democratic system with its Jewish control and Coloured immigration,' see Colin Jordan to The Minister of Public Buildings and Works, 1 October 1963 in TNA WORK 20/359. TNA HO 325/61, a currently closed file, indicates that this ban persisted with the BM being refused permission to hold a meeting in Trafalgar Square in September 1971 'on basis of group leader's previous abuse of political speech'.
308 Colin Jordan to George Lincoln Rockwell, 10 June 1963, Rockwell papers; and Frost, *'Twaz a Good Fight!'*, p. 151.
309 Special Branch report, 3 August 1963 in TNA KV 2/4390; and *National Socialist*, no. 4, May 1963.
310 Denis Pirie to George Lincoln Rockwell, n.d., Rockwell papers.
311 Colin Jordan to Harold Macmillan, 13 June 1963 in TNA PREM 11/4462.
312 Roger Hollis to T.J. Bligh, 17 June 1963 in TNA PREM 11/4462.
313 TNA PREM 11/4462; and Hansard, HC Deb., vol. 680, col. 1045 (9 July 1963).
314 *The National Socialist*, vol. 1, no. 5, August 1963.
315 C.1., 'Note for File', 31 October 1963 in TNA KV 2/4097/225a. The MI5 files on Boothby (e.g. TNA KV 2/4097) give credence to some of Vassall's claims.
316 *Ibid.*
317 Frost, *'Twaz a Good Fight!'*, p. 131; and Walker, *The National Front*, p. 172.
318 John Tyndall to George Lincoln Rockwell, 11 March 1962; Bertha Jordan to George Lincoln Rockwell, 22 December 1962; John Tyndall to George Lincoln Rockwell, 23 April 1963; John Tyndall to George Lincoln Rockwell, 30 March 1963; Colin Jordan to George Lincoln Rockwell, 10 June 1963 and Colin Jordan to George Lincoln Rockwell, 18 June 1963 and Colin Jordan to Martin Webster, 2 January 1965, Rockwell papers.
319 Denis Pirie to George Lincoln Rockwell, 25 March 1963; Colin Jordan to George Lincoln Rockwell, 10 June 1963; Colin Jordan to George Lincoln Rockwell, 28 June 1963; Colin Jordan to George Lincoln Rockwell, 24 July 1963; George Lincoln Rockwell to Colin Jordan, 29 July 1963, Rockwell papers. Roland Ritchie had form. In May 1954, police arrested him and his father for stealing £400 worth of books and oil paintings from Shelia MacDonald Lochhead, daughter of former Labour Prime Minister Ramsay McDonald. He was sentenced to two years' imprisonment. Declared bankrupt whilst imprisoned, he began using the surname 'Kerr-Ritchie' in 1956. He joined Jordan's WDL and then the BNP for whom he acted as 'research officer'. John Bean (*Many Shades of Black*, pp. 155–156) derided Kerr-Ritchie's contribution to 'the cause', which consisted of a huge tome titled *Facts the Jews Fear*.

> It had no chapters, less than twenty paragraphs, and the average length of a sentence was 500 words. I don't think the Jewish Board of Deputies lost much sleep worrying over its impact. I never met anybody who had progressed beyond page three: It was unreadable.

This did not stop Bean from advertising his three pamphlets 'Evil is their End: The Jews in Our Midst', 'The Jewish Peril: White Resurgence in Germany, 1933–1939' and 'The Jewish War of Revenge, 1939–1945' in the pages of *Combat*.

320 Colin Jordan to George Lincoln Rockwell, 24 July 1963, Rockwell papers.

321 *Daily Mail*, 26 March 1963; *Poole and Dorset Herald*, 27 March 1963; *Western Mail*, 26 March 1963; *Daily Mail*, 25 March 1963; *Bournemouth Evening Echo*, 25 March 1963; and *Newcastle Evening Journal*, 26 March 1963. Prior to these reports, on 21 March, the offices of the *Jewish Chronicle* newspaper in Holborn, central London, were also bombed. 'The blast shattered glass doors, smashed holes in the marble facing on the walls and roof of the entrance walls, as well as windows of cars in the street nearby,' see 'London's "Jewish Chronicle" Building Bombed: Police Investigating', *Jewish Telegraphic Agency*, 22 March 1963, www.jta.org/1963/03/22/archive/londons-jewish-chronicle-building-bombed-police-investigating (accessed 21 February 2014).

322 Colin Jordan to George Lincoln Rockwell, n.d., Rockwell papers. *Searchlight*, no. 318, December 2001 states that Ling was later caught in bed with a twelve-year-old girl at the Diksmuide festival in Belgium. *Gothic Ripples*, no. 19, February 1988 notes that Ling, 'a life-long National Socialist', died on 16 October 1987.

323 G-A. Amaudruz to Roger Cowley, 16 July 1963 in SCH/01/Res/BRI/20/003, Searchlight archive, University of Northampton. Kerr-Ritchie, who later married an Egyptian woman, subsequently took an 'active role' in the 're-founding' of a WUNS affiliate in the United Kingdom prior to his death in November 1982, see *NS Bulletin*, no. 292, December 1982.

324 Debbault had broken with WUNS by July 1965 having argued with its French representative, Yves Jeanne regarding the FOE and the extension of its 'authority' over Belgium's French-speaking Walloon region over which the Belgian section had hitherto had control, see Colin Jordan to Rudiger van Sande, 29 July 1965, Rockwell papers. In 1966, Jeanne founded the Cercle National et Socialiste Européen (CNSE) and disassociated from WUNS, see Colin Jordan to Yves Jeanne, 1 August 1966, Rockwell papers. The French authorities banned the CNSE in October 1966, see Joseph Algarzy, *L'extrême-droite en France de 1965 à 1984* (Paris: Éditions L'Harmattan, 1989), pp. 39–41. *WUNS Bulletin*, no. 5, 3rd Quarter 1966 notes CNSE was independent of WUNS 'but friendly disposed towards it'.

325 Frost, *'Twaz a Good Fight!'*, pp. 63 and 150. For the photograph, see *The Stormtrooper*, vol. 2, no. 4, July–August 1963. *Jewish Telegraphic Agency*, 31 July 1963 recorded the arrest of three West German Nazis noting furthermore that 'there may be a connection between the three and an unidentified British subject believed responsible for the distribution of Nazi posters in Frankfurt, Munich and Freiburg during the latter part of June and all of July.' This was undoubtedly Jordan.

326 *The Times*, 10 July 1963 reported that these leaflets fixed to Jewish buildings in Berlin and Frankfurt.

327 L. Thompson to MI5, 11 July 1963 in TNA KV 2/4390. When Jordan returned, police searched his car and found *Der Mythus der 20 Jahrhunderts* by Alfred Rosenberg; *Unser Liederbruch Leder – der Hitler Jugend*; *Pilgrimage* and two copies of *Gold in the Furnace* by Savitri Devi; *Mein Kampf*; and two packets each containing 200 leaflets in German published by the NSM.

328 Colin Jordan to George Lincoln Rockwell, 19 June [sic] 1963; Colin Jordan to George Lincoln Rockwell, 20 July 1963; Colin Jordan to George Lincoln Rockwell, 24 July 1963; Colin Jordan to George Lincoln Rockwell, 27 August 1963, Rockwell papers; *The National Socialist*, no. 6, 1963; and *The National Socialist*, no. 7, 1964. ANP literature also circulated in Britain. In one instance, someone posted it to a nine-year old girl who had advertised in the *Jewish Chronicle* for a pen friend. Clearly contravening Section 6 of the Race Relations Act, the Director of Public Prosecutions was unable to prosecute, the sender being unidentifiable, see TNA LO 2/418.

329 Terry Cooper, *Death by Dior* (London: Dynasty Press, 2013), pp. 118–132 alleges Dior was introduced to Nazism by a former lover, Swedish diplomat Ragnar Kumlin.

330 *Daily Express*, 4 October 1963.

331 *Birmingham Evening Mail*, 5 October 1963; and *Daily Telegraph*, 4 October 1963.

332 Colin Jordan to George Lincoln Rockwell, 23 September 1962; and Bertha Jordan to George Lincoln Rockwell, 22 December 1962, Rockwell papers.

333 Françoise Dior to George Lincoln Rockwell, 29 August 1963, Rockwell papers.

334 Colin Jordan to Captain Koehl, 22 June 1964, Rockwell papers. See also Simonelli, *American Fuehrer*, pp. 93–94. Jordan's initial attempts to organise in France had a 'false start' after he tried working with Jean-Claude Monet, editor of *Le Viking* who ran the French Organisation of the Swastika. In *National Socialist*, no. 7, 1964 Jordan later denounced Monet's Parti Prolétarian National-Socialiste (Proletarian National Socialist Party), which was attempting to found its own 'World Assembly of National Socialists' as a 'political perversion'. For the wider political context, see Jean-Yves Camus, 'Nostalgia and Political Impotence: Neo-Nazi and Extreme Right Movements in France, 1944–64', in E.J. Arnold (ed.), *The Development of the Radical Right in France* (London: Macmillan, 2000), pp. 195–216.
335 John Tyndall to George Lincoln Rockwell, 13 May 1963, Rockwell papers.
336 Cooper, *Death by Dior*, pp. 80–81 notes 'the first thing she [Dior] did after their marriage was to apply for, and obtain, British nationality which she kept for the rest of her life.'
337 *Sunday Mirror*, 29 September 1963.
338 Rockwell was outraged by the protests, complaining to The Queen, see George Lincoln Rockwell to The Queen, 6 October 1963, copy in Jewish Chronicle Library Collection, Wiener Library, London.
339 *Ancient Viking Blood Rite Revived: The Colin Jordan Wedding* (Stormtrooper brochure, 1962). A photograph of their wedding adorned the front cover of *The Stormtrooper*, vol. 2, no. 5, September–November 1963.
340 *Daily Sketch*, 8 October 1963.
341 Savitri Devi, *And Time Rolls On*, p. 104, observed that Dior found it difficult 'to live up to the austerity of a real National Socialist.… She tries to live up to it. At least she tried.' Savitri Devi told Rockwell that Dior's 'religious approach' to Nazism made her by far the more ideologically committed than Jordan!

> Her husband is a sincere, efficient, and valuable fighter no doubt, but *she* has the religious approach (if I am not mistaken) and she is the one who, far from wishing to be loved first, *wants* her husband to put the Idea before her – and who herself puts the idea before him, by all means. That ideological one-pointedness (*in spite of* a personal life entirely *different* from mine) is precisely what I like in her.

See 'Savitri Devi's Correspondence with George Lincoln Rockwell, Part 4', edited by R.G. Fowler, *The Savitri Devi Archive*, www.savitridevi.org/rockwell_correspondence_4.html (accessed 13 January 2011). Jordan also observed this trait, albeit filtered through a misogynistic lens. 'My wife is a wonderful woman in many ways, and politically a great personality,' he wrote to Rockwell on 31 October 1964,

> but the great trouble is that she is in fact far too political to seem to want to and be able to – so far – provide a real home. Her tremendous keenness – in some ways too intense – rather blinds her to the personal life of marriage.

342 Frost, *'Twaz a Good Fight!'*, p. 153.
343 Françoise Dior to Colin Jordan, 25 December 1963 in TNA KV 2/4391. Dior told the *Daily Telegraph*, 8 January 1964, 'I reproach him [Jordan] notably with wanting to withdraw to the countryside in Yorkshire from where he claims he can direct his movement which I deny, as London is the arena of British political battles.'
344 *Daily Express*, 7 January 1964.
345 *Daily Mirror*, 8 January 1964.
346 *Daily Mirror*, 23 January 1964.
347 *Daily Mail*, 9 January 1964.
348 Françoise Dior to Colin Jordan, 12 January 1964 in TNA KV 2/4391.
349 Françoise Dior to Colin Jordan, 14 January 1964 in TNA KV 2/4391.
350 George Thayer, *The British Political Fringe* (London: Anthony Blond, 1965), p. 27.
351 *The National Socialist*, no. 7, 1964.
352 Colin Jordan to George Lincoln Rockwell, 9 March 1964, Rockwell papers.
353 Cooper, *Death by Dior*, p. 160.
354 Martin Webster to Colin Jordan, 'Friday' [November–December 1963] in TNA KV 2/4391.
355 Jackson, *Colin Jordan and Britain's Neo-Nazi Movement*, p. 126.
356 John Tyndall to Colin Jordan, 21 April 1964 in TNA KV 2/4391.

357 Colin Jordan to George Lincoln Rockwell, 27 April 1964; and Colin Jordan to George Lincoln Rockwell, 29 July 1964, Rockwell papers.
358 John Tyndall to Colin Jordan, 30 April 1964 in TNA KV 2/4391.
359 *Daily Mirror*, 13 May 1964, quoted in Walker, *The National Front*, p. 47.
360 Special Branch report, 22 May 1964 in TNA KV 2/4392. Jordan alleged that the plot against him was hatched at the home of Dr William J. Mitchell, a former BUF activist cashiered from the Army in 1943 for his indiscreetly proclaimed fascist sympathies. When Dior left England, she gave her British address as William's surgery in New Cross, south London, see Special Branch report, 29 April 1966 in TNA KV 2/4392/456a. Mitchell later became active in the National Front, as did his son.
361 John Tyndall to Colin Jordan, 13 May 1964 in TNA KV 2/4391. Tyndall sent a copy to Mrs Leese too.
362 Colin Jordan to George Lincoln Rockwell, 29 July 1964, Rockwell papers.
363 George Lincoln Rockwell to Colin Jordan, 3 August 1964, Rockwell papers.
364 George Lincoln Rockwell to Colin Jordan, 1 January 1965, Rockwell papers. The dossier – subsequently stolen from Jordan by the 62 Group – is located in SCH/01/Res/BRI/20/005, Searchlight archive.
365 Frost, *'Twaz a Good Fight!'*, p. 160.
366 Savitri Devi to John Tyndall, 6 February 1965, Rockwell papers.
367 Colin Jordan to Savitri Devi, 26 February 1965, Rockwell papers.
368 George Lincoln Rockwell to All National Commanders and All National Socialists, 9 January 1965, Rockwell papers. He later apologised to Jordan for his prevarication, see George Lincoln Rockwell to Colin Jordan, 17 July 1965, Rockwell papers.
369 Special Branch report, 23 November 1964 in TNA KV 2/4391. Jackson, *Colin Jordan and Britain's Neo-Nazi Movement*, p. 128 notes that only the Coventry NSM branch followed Jordan.
370 Colin Jordan to George Lincoln Rockwell, 18 December 1964, Rockwell papers.
371 Colin Jordan to George Lincoln Rockwell, 7 July 1964; Colin Jordan to George Lincoln Rockwell, 26 December 1964; and Colin Jordan to George Lincoln Rockwell, 26 December 1964, Rockwell papers.
372 Frost, *'Twaz a Good Fight!'*, p. 132. Jordan believed that outside actors were manipulating the split. He claimed to have 'growing evidence that this whole affair was fostered by a certain element in the background, acting in conjunction with a man in their midst who definitely appears to be a spy and agent provocateur.' He accused Diana Hughes, a former member who had sided with Tyndall, of tipping off both the press and the 62 Group about his ongoing contretemps with Dior.
373 Special Branch report, 5 August 1964 in TNA KV 2/4392; and *The National Socialist*, no. 8, January–March 1965. Three NSM activists, Gordon Callow, Keith Polley and Gerald Lawman, staged an anti-Semitic picket outside the Regent Street Headquarters of Rolls Razor Ltd, which had manufactured washing machine components until going into receivership, singling out the firm because its owner, John Bloom, was Jewish. Parading outside the building wearing swastika armbands and holding aloft banners – both supplied by Jordan – which proclaimed 'Boycott Bloom and Jewish Business' the trio were arrested following a confrontation with 'a gang of Jews'. Oswald Mosley owned £790 of deferred shares in Rolls Razor, which would hardly have diminished Jordan's antipathy towards him, had he known, see Oswald Mosley papers, Nicholas Mosley deposit, Box 12.
374 *Sunday Telegraph*, 9 August 1964 notes that during the police raid several letters from Jordan to the Jeanne and another defendant were uncovered together with 'anti-Semitic pamphlets thought to have been inspired from Britain but printed in France.' Whilst the French police were largely dismissive of Jeanne's group, a Sûreté official stated that the Ministry of the Interior were considering permanently banning Jordan from entering the country as a result. In Rheims, the police discovered two pistols and a quantity of plastic explosives built up by Jesus Monsegur, a Spanish Nazi involved with the group who 'admitted under questioning that he intended using them in raids on cafes and other meeting places of coloured people in Rheims.' Whilst Jordan had nothing to do with this, the police noted Dior's role as an intermediary with the group.
375 Colin Jordan to George Lincoln Rockwell, 18 December 1964, Rockwell papers.
376 Michael Hartley-Brewer, 'Smethwick', in Nicholas Deakin (ed.), *Colour and the British Electorate 1964: Six Case Studies* (London: Pall Mall Press, 1965), pp. 77–105; and Paul Foot, *Immigration and Race in British Politics* (London: Penguin, 1965).

377 Peter Griffiths, *A Question of Colour* (London: Leslie Frewin, 1966), pp. 171–172.
378 Hansard, HC Deb., vol. 701, col. 71 (3 November 1964).
379 *Daily Telegraph*, 27 November 2013.
380 Edward Heath, *The Course of My Life: The Autobiography of Edward Heath* (London: Hodder and Stoughton, 1998), p. 455.
381 Dennis Dean, 'The Race Relations Policy of the First Wilson Government', *Twentieth Century British History*, vol. 11, no. 3, 2000, pp. 259–283.
382 *The Coventry Express*, 23 October 1964.
383 *Stratford Express*, 4 December 1964; and *The National European*, no. 8, February 1965. See also Bean, *Many Shades of Black*, pp. 172–173; and *Combat*, no. 30, February 1965.
384 Denis Healey, *The Time of My Life* (London: Michael Joseph, 1989), p. 297. The Army subsequently dismissed Hughes, see Hansard, HC Deb., vol. 706, col. 826 (15 February 1965).
385 *Leyton Express*, 8 January 1965; and *The National Socialist*, no. 9, April–June 1965.
386 *Birmingham Evening Mail and Despatch*, 22 January 1965.
387 Harold Wilson to Patrick Gordon Walker, 25 January 1965 in GNWR I 1/26, Patrick Gordon Walker papers, Churchill College, Cambridge.
388 Colin Jordan to George Lincoln Rockwell, 19 February 1965, Rockwell papers.
389 Hansard, HC Deb., vol. 712, cols 1652–1654 (20 May 1965) records that, whilst police proceeded against eighteen fascists in 1964, they prosecuted twelve in the first quarter of 1965 alone. Further information on the activities of such individuals are in TNA MEPO 2/9729. This contains a dossier of letters obtained from NSM activist Gordon Williams whose home was burgled, police suspected, by a 62 Group activist who then sent the incriminating documents, anonymously, to Reginald Freeson MP (Willesden, East), who edited the newspaper *Searchlight*, a forerunner of the anti-fascist magazine of the same name, which was founded in 1975.
390 *Birmingham Evening Mail and Despatch*, 8 January 1965.
391 *Daily Worker*, 18 January 1965. Kenneth Spivey, a 62 Group activist who infiltrated the NSM in January 1965 identified the arsonists as Hugh Hughes and Michael Trowbridge, acting at Dior's behest, a belief with which the Metropolitan Police concurred, though they did not have enough evidence to charge either man. The 62 Group relayed this information to the Labour MP Reginald Freeson who kept the pressure up by asking a question in the House of Commons. Acting on Spivey's information, the police questioned all those believed to have been involved in the arson attack including Jordan, though they failed to come to any definite conclusion. In fact, the police believed that Jordan had rumbled Spivey 'and that he gave him enough scope to know what he was doing, and then told him to leave.' See TNA MEPO 2/9727.
392 *The National Socialist*, no. 9, April–June 1965.
393 The *Guardian*, 18 January 1965.
394 Cooper, *Death by Dior*, p. 68.
395 *Evening Standard*, 16 August 1967; and *Evening Standard*, 7 September 1967. Police believed that a fire at a Talmudical College in Stoke Newington on 10 November 1964, which resulting in the death of a young Jewish student, was unconnected finding 'no evidence of incendiarism'. The coroner returned a verdict of 'accidental death', see Det. Ch. Supt. W. Brereton to Mr Holden, 19 July 1965 in TNA MEPO 2/9729. The four synagogue arsonists were Williams Evans, Raymond Hemsworth, Colin Rainbird and David Thorne, the latter subsequently resurfacing as the 'overseas liaison officer' for the League of St George, see *League Review*, no. 38, June 1982. Their actions appear to have been an open secret within the NSM. Cooper, *Death by Dior*, p. 68 notes Thorne and Evans attached newspaper clippings of the fire that destroyed Brondesbury synagogue to the walls of the NSM offices 'I had taken no notice at the time and in any case the clippings were gone the following week.'
396 On 9 July 1965, police arrested Aubrey Cadogan after he broke into the Palmers Green and Southgate District Synagogue. He was unconnected to the NSM arson gangs but at his home, police discovered 'considerable quantities' of Nazi literature, including a book titled 'Hitler Was Right'. Cadogan, the former managing director of a Jewish-owned tailoring firm, reportedly told police that his mother was Jewish. He was jailed for five years. See TNA CRIM 1/4419. DPP 2/4012 remains closed.
397 The *Guardian*, 9 February 1966. For full details of the trial, see TNA CRIM 1/4469 and TNA DPP 2/4078–4080. The six arsonists, Paul Dukes, Graham Chant, Colin Rainbird (again), Hugh Hughes, Malcolm Sparks and Alex Gordon were all sentenced to between three and five years'

imprisonment. Dukes received six months, presumably a quid pro quo for cooperating. Following his release from prison, Sparks joined the 4th Battalion, Green Jackets, Territorial and Army Volunteer Reserve (TAVR). However, having failed to disclose his previous convictions, he was dismissed, see Hansard, HC Deb. (series 5), vol. 793, col. 214 (10 December 1966).
398 *The Times*, 16 February 1966.
399 Hansard, HC Deb., vol. 756, cols 615–616 (14 December 1967).
400 Cooper, *Death by Dior*, p. 86.
401 Graham Macklin and Craig Fowlie, 'The Fascist who would be King: Count Geoffrey Potocki of Montalk', *Patterns of Prejudice*, vol. 53, no. 2, 2019, pp. 152–177.
402 *Ibid.*
403 *Ibid.*
404 *Ibid.*
405 Adrian Weale, *Renegades: Hitler's Englishmen* (London: Warner, 1994); and *Searchlight*, no. 313, July 2001.
406 *Searchlight*, no. 256, October 1996; *Searchlight*, no. 313, July 2001; and Frost, *'Twaz a Good Fight!'*, pp. 299–300. The Press Complaints Commission dismissed Jordan's subsequent complaint because he filed it outside the permissible time limit, Independent Press Standards Organisation, email to author, 10 June 2015.
407 *Sunday Mirror*, 20 June 1965. Newey, the Birmingham NSM leader, was a former BNP activist who had unsuccessfully stood for a seat on its national council in 1962, see *Combat*, no. 21, March–April 1963.
408 Hansard, HC Deb., vol. 714, cols 240–247 (15 June 1965).
409 TNA DPP 2/4009; and *Sunday Express*, 21 June 1965. NSM activists Patrick and Michael Webb were the two most notable members. Patrick Webb, the Coventry NSM leader had a string of criminal convictions for breaking and entering, theft, disorderly conduct, and larceny and affray for a gang fight in Coventry in July 1961 during which a youth had been stabbed. He and his brother both received twelve months' imprisonment. Only weeks before the cross burning, on 24 March 1965, he was fined for using threatening, abusive and insulting words or behaviour likely to cause a breach of the peace and for malicious damage. In 1949, aged sixteen, he had been arraigned before Rugby Juvenile Court 'as being beyond parental control following an assault on his mother with a knife.' The police also had 'reliable information' that the brothers were dabbling with the use of explosives in their racist campaign. Bernado O'Reilly, *Undertones: Anti-Fascism and the Far-Right in Ireland 1945–2012* (Dublin: AFA Ireland, 2012), pp. 15–16 notes Webb's subsequent involvement with the National Socialist Irish Workers Party. *Searchlight*, no. 398, August 2008 states that Webb killed a black youth in a bomb attack in the 1970s. Another member, William Duncan, had three convictions for indecently assaulting children, in 1955 and 1957. He was imprisoned for three months for a third assault in 1960. Prior to this, on 20 April 1945, he served three months 'for larceny in a dwelling house and for unlawful possession of a firearm'.
410 The *Guardian*, 19 June 1965.
411 Special Branch report, 22 September 1965 in TNA KV 2/4392.
412 *Brighton and Hove Gazette*, 15 October 1965.
413 *Evening Standard*, 16 October 1965.
414 *The Times*, 26 November 1965.
415 The *Guardian*, 11 November 1965.
416 *Daily Telegraph*, 16 November 1965.
417 TNA 2/4392/452b.
418 Special Branch report, 29 April 1966 in TNA KV 2/4392/456a.
419 Françoise Dior to Colin Jordan, n.d. but 1966 in TNA KV 2/4392.
420 *The Times*, 28 October 1967.
421 *Blood & Honour*, no. 30.
422 Cooper, *Death by Dior*, pp. 96–98. Patrice Chairoff, *Dossier Neo-Nazisme* (Paris: Éditions Ramsay, 1977), p. 31 describes 'André Tochou' as Dior's 'ex-secrétaire très particulier'. Whilst Dior was no longer involved with NSM, WUNS' *Eastern Hemisphere Bulletin*, no. 8, January 1967 records the group protesting her arrest, and sending a letter to President Charles De Gaulle demanding her release.
423 Walker, *The National Front*, p. 46.

424 TNA CRIM 1/4749.
425 Bert Wickstead, *Gangbuster: Tales of the Old Grey Fox* (London: Futura, 1985), p. 61. Three months later, two men, posing as police officers, kidnapped Cooper and interrogated him for two days about the fascist movement. Enquires by the Dagenham police revealed that Cooper's house had been under surveillance for several days prior to the kidnapping by members of the 62 Group. Scotland Yard questioned several activists but released them without charge because Cooper failed to identify them as his kidnappers, see Special Branch report, 25 March 1969 in TNA HO 325/55. On 10 April 1968, Cooper was arrested on the Strand bearing a letter of introduction to the military attachés of Rhodesia House, South Africa House, the Portuguese Consulate and the Spanish Embassy, which stated:

> May I introduce myself as the private secretary to Madame Françoise Jordan of the National Socialist Movement, England. In this letter I am representing the West African Travel Agency Ltd. Within the next two or three weeks the directors of this company expect to be in possession of various documents taken from an African Embassy [the Democratic Republic of the Congo] which may be of importance to you concerning your state.

Police found Cooper in possession of documents, as well as a rubber truncheon and faked identity cards. These revealed his own involvement in a conspiracy to kidnap the Congolese Ambassador by men disguised as police detectives. His motive, Cooper told the court, was that the Congolese Embassy in London 'is the headquarters for organising most of the Communist funds for the activities in the Congo'. In a statement to police, Cooper claimed 'a man he met in a public house in Belgravia' promised him £5,000 if he stole papers from the Embassy. Cooper received a two-year suspended sentence after being found guilty on all five counts, see *Evening Standard*, 1 August 1968; and *The Times*, 2 August 1968. *Searchlight*, no. 120, June 1985 alleged Cooper had offered his services to the British Mercenary Force run by the self-styled 'Major' Douglas Lord, a former sergeant major active in the Congo who had acted as a bodyguard to former Premier Moïse Tshombe. Following her release, Dior and Cooper briefly relocated to Jersey (where she attempted suicide) and thence to Normandy, where Savitri Devi visited them again – 'my heart sank into my boots' recalled Cooper. On a subsequent visit, she stayed for six months until finally persuaded to visit Yves Jeanne in Nantes. The couple separated after a decade. In his autobiography, Cooper alleged that Dior later developed a taste for Satanism and began a lesbian affair with her own daughter whom she later induced to commit suicide! She was financially ruined following a bad investment in a Parisian nightclub before marrying her third husband, Count Hubert de Mirleau. Cooper also claimed (pp. 135–264) that he occasionally performed 'little jobs' for the Renseignements généraux (RG – General Intelligence), the intelligence service of the French police. He was also involved with the Front de Libération de la Bretagne (FLB – Breton Liberation Front), a militant Breton separatist group engaged in a terrorist campaign against the French state and the more cerebral Mouvement Normand (MN – Norman Movement). In June 1981, Cooper was arrested and tried for possessing a firearm and explosives – 'which I had made for the FLB' – receiving a two-year suspended sentence, subsequently avoiding jail for a multimillion-franc bank fraud after his sentence was rendered inapplicable due to a legal technicality. He was also an associate of Claude Cornilleau, leader of the extreme right-wing Parti nationaliste français et européen (PNFE – French European National Party), which developed links with John Tyndall's BNP. Dior also remained involved with extreme right-wing politics, subsequently helping to bankroll Martin Webster's short-lived 'One Nation' group, which was founded on the premise of racial nationalism, 'the idea that a nation is based on heredity.' Another former NSM member involved in One Nation was Denis Pirie then employed as an export market research advisor for the Department of Trade and Industry (DTI). The DTI subsequently conducted an enquiry though Pirie – who dismissed his Nazi past as 'a bit silly' – was cleared and allowed to keep his job, *The Times*, 16 April 1985; and *The Times*, 17 April 1985. Dior was also a member of the Paris Association of the Conservative Party, see *The Times*, 20 February 1984.
426 For Pierce's contribution to physics, see E. Brun, J.J. Kraushaar, W.L. Pierce and Wm. J. Veigele, 'Nuclear Magnetic Dipole Moment of Ca41', *Physical Review Letters*, vol. 9, no. 4, 1962; and E. Brun, R.J. Mahler, H. Mahon and W.L. Pierce, 'Electrically Induced Nuclear Quadrupole Spin Transitions in a GaAs', *Physical Review*, vol. 129, no. 5, 1963.

427 George Lincoln Rockwell to Colin Jordan, 19 January 1964, Rockwell papers. *The Stormtrooper*, vol. 2, no. 5, September–October 1964 announced the forthcoming publication of *National Socialist World* but it took a further two years to appear.
428 Jackson, *Colin Jordan and Britain's Neo-Nazi Movement*, p. 146.
429 *National Socialist World*, no. 1, spring 1966.
430 TNA ASSI 26/416; and TNA LCO 2/411. Jordan was not alone in falling foul of the new legislation. NSM member Vincent Morris followed him behind bars in July 1967. Another teenage NSM activist, Malcolm Lowes, protested Jordan's conviction by setting fire to a timber yard in Poole, Dorset, on 4 February 1967 for which he was jailed for three years. He had been released from prison for another offence on the previous day.
431 J.C.C. Jordan to R.H.S. Crossman, 9 May 1967 in MSS.154/3/COV/1/163, Richard Crossman papers, Modern Records Centre, Warwick University, hereafter Crossman papers.
432 R.H.S. Crossman, 'International Commentary', 4 July 1962 in MSS.154/4/BR/9/163, Crossman papers.
433 Roy Jenkins to R.H.S. Crossman, 17 July 1967; and R.H.S. Crossman to J.C.C. Jordan, 31 July 1967 in MSS.154/3/COV/1/161 and 165, Crossman papers.
434 Bertha Jordan to R.H.S. Crossman, 16 August 1967 in MSS.154/3/COV/1/160, Crossman papers.
435 William H. Schmaltz, *Hate: George Lincoln Rockwell and the American Nazi Party* (Washington, DC: Brassey's, 1999), p. 325.
436 F.I.A., 22 September 1967 in TNA KV 2/4392.
437 Chief Superintendent A. Cunningham to MI5, 4 August 1967 in TNA KV 2/4392; and Jackson, *Colin Jordan and Britain's Neo-Nazi Movement*, p. 141.
438 Walker, *The National Front*, p. 77; and Frost, *'Twaz a Good Fight!'*, pp. 217–218.
439 *British Patriot*, no. 39, November 1975. The BM subsequently published its own edition of Leese's *Jewish Ritual Murder: My Irrelevant Defence – Meditations Inside Gaol and Out* (Clwyd: BP Publications, 1980) as well as its own edition of *The Protocols of the Meetings of the Learned Elders of Zion* (Shotton: BP Publications, 1978).
440 Colin Jordan to William Pierce, 14 July 1968 in SCH/01/Res/BRI/23/002, Searchlight archive.
441 Dave Hann, *Physical Resistance: Or, One Hundred Years of Anti-Fascism* (London: Zero Books, 2012), p. 231.
442 Short, a student at Queen's College, Cambridge, received a suspended sentence and was expelled from the NF in June 1969. *Combat* [no date] indicates Short subsequently became branch secretary of London BM. He subsequently left the BM to join the National Democratic Freedom Movement run by the BM's former Leeds organiser, Eddy Morrison, after he split from the group in 1973. In the following year, Short infiltrated the Croydon North West Branch of the Liberal Party, becoming an executive committee member. He was present for the meeting at which the party voted to become the SDP Liberal Alliance, voting for the name change. He stood as its candidate for Rylands Ward, Croydon. *Daily Mirror*, 30 April 1982 and the *Guardian*, 30 April 1982 exposed him, forcing his resignation. Short was also an occultist. Jordan derided his claim that he possessed the gift of 'automatic writing' whereby occult forces would guide his hand in revelation.

> Joseph Short's thesis is that the fountain-head of National Socialism was occult power, a concoction he has in common with the paper-back portrayers of Hitler and his early circle as a bunch of star-gazing devil worshippers. Such playboys of the bizarre we can well do without,

Jordan argued in *Gothic Ripples*, no. 9, September 1982.
443 *Current Notes*, December 1969 in ACC/3121/C6/1/2, London Metropolitan Archives, London.
444 Colin Jordan to A.K. Chesterton, 10 July 1968; A.K. Chesterton to Colin Jordan, 15 July 1969; and Colin Jordan to A.K. Chesterton, 16 July 1969, Chesterton papers.
445 A.K. Chesterton to Colin Jordan, 5 August 1969, Chesterton papers.
446 A.K. Chesterton to Colin Jordan, 30 September 1969, Chesterton papers. When Alan Marney, Tunbridge Wells NF organiser, breached this agreement by publicly expelling a member for fraternising with the 'pro-Nazi' BM, Chesterton admonished him. He also apologised to Jordan for this 'unfortunate' incident, stating that the individual in question was expelled for an entirely different reason, see A.K. Chesterton to Colin Jordan, 7 September 1970, Chesterton papers.

447 For their trial, see TNA CRIM 1/4996. They were both jailed for six months, suspended for eighteen months
448 JDC, Minutes, 30 September 1968 in ACC/3121/C6/1/1, LMA papers, London.
449 Daniel Jones and Paul Jackson, 'The National Socialist Group: A Case Study in the *Groupuscular* Right', in Nigel Copsey and Matthew Worley (eds), *'Tomorrow Belongs to Us': The British Far Right since 1967* (Abingdon: Routledge, 2018), pp. 27–47.
450 *WUNS Bulletin*, no. 10, 4th Quarter 1967 notes Courtney had assumed management of the NSM offices.
451 Colin Jordan to David Courtney, 22 June 1968 in SCH/01/Res/BRI/23/001, Searchlight archive records: 'I am glad that you will shortly join British Movement yourself, and your group – which of course has my sympathy and agreement – will have the best possible relations with us.'
452 A.K. Chesterton to Colin Jordan, 5 May 1969, Chesterton papers. Colin Jordan to Martin Webster, 30 May 1969, Chesterton papers concedes that he did attend two 'private' meetings in London in September 1968 and February 1969 at which NSG members were present. Jordan told Chesterton that that the NSG was 'entirely apart' from the BM and that he had 'no part whatsoever' in its foundation of direction, see Colin Jordan to A.K. Chesterton, 14 December 1968, Chesterton papers. Concerned by its activities, Chesterton arranged for Webster to have the group infiltrated and, on his instruction, to meet its leaders. NF activists Desmond Smith and Donald Mudie, who had joined the NSG, were suspended. Webster reported the NSG to the police in April 1969, see *Searchlight*, no. 88, October 1982. Tyndall's supposed membership of the NSG was raised at the NF Directorate meeting on 9 May but the 'proof' – a membership card – was a forgery circulated to cause dissention by either rivals or anti-fascists. Indeed, *Spearhead*, no. 23, April–May 1969 had already reported that Tyndall's passport stolen together with other documents during a break-in at the 'Nationalist Centre'.
453 *WUNS Bulletin*, no. 13, 3rd Quarter 1968. Colin Jordan to A.K. Chesterton, 17 May 1969; Colin Jordan to Martin Webster, 17 May 1969; and Colin Jordan to A.K. Chesterton, 29 May 1969, Chesterton papers.
454 *Searchlight*, no. 35, May 1978; *Searchlight*, no. 69, March 1981; and *Searchlight*, no. 78, December 1981.
455 Frost, *'Twaz a Good Fight!'*, pp. 221 and 226–227.
456 *The Times*, 24 April 1968.
457 *British Tidings*, no. 10, May/June/July 1969; and *Powell was Right* (BM leaflet, 1969).
458 *The Times*, 23 December 1971.
459 *Ladywood Parliamentary By-Election – British Movement Candidate Colin Jordan* (BM election leaflet, 1969). R.A. Duffen stood as a BM candidate in Ladywood ward in the May 1969 local elections to test the water.
460 Ray Hill with Andrew Bell, *The Other Face of Terror: Inside Europe's Neo-Nazi Network* (London: Grafton Books, 1988), p. 39.
461 The BM subsequently stood several candidates in the May 1970 local elections, including Arthur Shorthouse (Aston, Birmingham) and Thomas Tatlow (St Michael's, Coventry).
462 *British Tidings*, no. 10, May/June/July 1969; and Frost, *'Twaz a Good Fight!'*, p. 233.
463 'Fascists', 8 August 1969 in TNA HO 325/8.
464 *Nationalist Solidarity in '70* (BM leaflet, 1970).
465 Frost, *'Twaz a Good Fight!'*, p. 232.
466 A.K. Chesterton to Colin Jordan, 30 April 1970, Chesterton papers.
467 A.K. Chesterton to Colin Jordan, 23 May 1970, Chesterton papers. John Tyndall, *The Eleventh Hour*, p. 204 notes that Jordan and the BM 'had to be left out of the reckoning for the time being'.
468 Jackson, *Colin Jordan and Britain's Neo-Nazi Movement*, p. 164.
469 Frost, *'Twaz a Good Fight!'*, p. 251.
470 Colin Jordan to A.K. Chesterton, 23 June 1970, Chesterton papers; and *Colin Jordan – British Movement Candidate for Aston* (BM 1970) in SCH/01/Res/BRI/20/005, Searchlight archive.
471 Walker, *The National Front*, p. 134.
472 Frost, *'Twaz a Good Fight!'*, pp. 246–247.
473 John Tyndall to *The Liverpool Newsletter*, 5 March 1973, copy in author's possession.
474 Colin Jordan, *White Power for Britain* (Coventry: British Movement, 1971). For the launch of the 'White Power' campaign, see *British News*, no. 1, April 1971; and *British News*, no. 2, May 1971. See also Jackson, *Colin Jordan and Britain's Neo-Nazi Movement*, p. 164.

475 George Lincoln Rockwell, *White Power* (n.p., 1983), especially pp. 462–466.
476 Simonelli, *American Fuehrer*, pp. 96–106.
477 Frost, *'Twaz a Good Fight!'*, p. 252.
478 *Liverpool Daily Post*, 2 December 1974.
479 *British Tidings*, February 1975 announced Jordan's resignation as National Chairman and his cessation of political activity.
480 The *Sun*, 17 May 1975.
481 *British Patriot*, no. 39, November 1975.
482 Labour Research Department, *The National Front Investigated* (London: LRD, 1978), p. 26.
483 Mike Walsh McLaughlin, *The Rise of the Sunwheel* (Createspace: 2016), pp. 3–6. See also 'Patrick McLaughlin', *ALBA!, Abraham Lincoln Brigade Archives*, www.alba-valb.org/volunteers/patrick-mclaughlin (accessed 7 June 2016).
484 TNA DPP 2/6179 notes the Director of Public Prosecutions considered preferring further charges against McLaughlin for inciting racial hatred in July 1976.
485 Jackson, *Colin Jordan and Britain's Neo-Nazi Movement*, p. 178.
486 *The Times*, 8 June 1976; and *The Times*, 16 June 1976.
487 The *Guardian*, 16 June 1976; Frost, *'Twaz a Good Fight!'*, pp. 274–275 and 279; *White Power Report*, February 1978; and *Liberty Bell*, June 1979.
488 'British Movement: Support for Michael McLaughlin Terminated', in James N. Mason papers, Box 14, folder 33, Kenneth Spencer Research Library, University of Kansas, hereafter Mason papers, and also Colin Jordan, 'More Mendacity from Michael McLaughlin – The Big Lie in "British Tidings"', 1 March 1979 in SCH/01/Res/BRI/23/001, Searchlight archive. The split between Jordan and McLaughlin also affected international networks. The American Nazi propagandist Gerhard Lauck, head of the NSDAP-AO, sided with McLaughlin leading Jordan to demand he be stricken from Lauck's mailing list. Jordan was also critical of NSRP leader Edward Fields and British anti-Semite Lady Jane Birdwood, reported *The Liberty Bell*, June 1979.
489 *Gothic Ripples*, no. 2, March 1980.
490 For an array of accusations against Jordan, see Mike Walsh McLaughlin, *The Rise of the Sunwheel*, pp. 19–29. For a rebuttal by former Yorkshire BM organiser Eddy Morrison, see *Heritage and Destiny*, no. 77, March–April 2017.
491 *Gothic Ripples*, no. 6, June 1981; and *Gothic Ripples*, no. 9, September 1982.
492 *The Liberty Bell*, January 1979. The BM proscribed the NF in September 1976 as 'an affront to real nationalism', though it made little difference in practice, see *British Tidings*, no. 55, September 1976.
493 Colin Jordan, 'A Case of Indecent Exposure by the Mini-Messiah from Merseyside – Colin Jordan Skewers Michael McLaughlin's Package of Lies', 1 March 1979.
494 TNA CAB 128/70, CC (81), 5th Conclusions, 5 February 1981. Keith Tompson, *Under Siege: Racial Violence in Britain Today* (London: Penguin, 1988), p. 171.
495 Ray Hill, *The Other Face of Terror*, pp. 116–147. Gerry Gable, the editor of *Searchlight*, subsequently claimed in *Jewish Chronicle*, 22 April 2009:

> Many years later I had a long phone conversation with him [Jordan] about the way he had been forced out of British Movement by his rival Michael McLaughlin. Despite all the threats over the years and our work in getting him and his followers sent to prison, he was prepared to talk to me about a 'common enemy'.

496 Mike Walsh McLaughlin, *The Rise of the Sunwheel*, p. 67.
497 Frost, *'Twaz a Good Fight!'*, p. 263.
498 'Patheley Brige' was first mentioned in 1130, see 'Pateley Bridge', *The Yorkshire Dales*, www.yorkshire-dales.com/pateley-bridge.html (accessed 9 October 2007).
499 Colin Jordan, 'Notes on Arnold Leese', undated MSS, Leese papers.
500 *Gothic Ripples*, no. 1, December 1979.
501 *Liberty Bell*, vol. 7, no. 5, 1980.
502 *Gothic Ripples*, no. 4, October 1980. NS Publications of Cicero, Illinois, published an extended version in *The National Socialist*, no. 3, n.d.
503 *Ibid.*
504 *Ibid.*
505 *League Review*, vol. 1, no. 25, n.d.

506 Colin Jordan, *National Socialism: World Creed for the 1980s* (Thorgarth: Gothic Ripples, 1981), which had originally appeared in the *WUNS Journal*, winter 1981 as 'National Socialism: Our World Creed in the 1980s'.
507 *Gothic Ripples*, no. 9, September 1982.
508 *Χρυσή αυγή*, May–June 1981.
509 *Gothic Ripples*, no. 46, December 2002.
510 Frost, *'Twaz a Good Fight!'*, pp. 127 and 281; *Gothic Ripples*, no. 3, June 1980; and http://members.odinsrage.com/ravenfjord/CJ.htm (accessed 6 January 2004).
511 For an extended discussion of this idea, see Raphael Gross, '"Loyalty" in National Socialism: A Contribution to the Moral History of the National Socialist Period', *History of European Ideas*, vol. 33, 2007, pp. 488–503.
512 Colin Jordan, *National Socialism: Vanguard of the Future – Selected Writings of Colin Jordan* (Aalborg: Nordland Forlag, 1993) pp. 75–101.
513 *Gothic Ripples*, November 1981.
514 The *Guardian*, 12 August 1981; and *Yorkshire Post*, 1 May 2009.
515 *Spearhead*, no. 176, June 1983. Peterborough BM organiser, Peter Gallagher, had attempted to stand in the 1983 general election as 'Labour' but his nomination papers were invalid, see detailed 1983 election list in 'England Boroughs', www.election.demon.co.uk/1983EB2.html (accessed 12 February 2014).
516 *Spearhead*, no. 177, July 1983
517 *Spearhead*, no. 178, August 1983.
518 *National Review*, no. 45, April 1986.
519 Gothic Ripples Booklist, February 1986, Mason papers, Box 14, folder 35.
520 *National Review*, no. 47, 1987.
521 Elizabeth Wheaton, *Codename Greenkill: The 1979 Greensboro Killings* (Athens, GA: University of Georgia Press, 1987) covers Covington's role.
522 *Liberty Bell*, vol. 14, no. 5, January 1987; and *Liberty Bell*, vol. 14, no. 7, March 1987 reprinted Covington's 'Circular Letter No. B-5 – 15 January 1987' in which his critique had originally appeared. *Liberty Bell*, vol. 15, no. 1, September 1987 featured a further response from Covington in which he elaborated upon his own criticisms.

> I think I might better have said the *formal, open party* is dead as an option, and in this I agree with Colin Jordan, although I disagree with him about the necessity of working with (I say working *on*) the White population as a whole. What is needed is a vehicle that *functions* like an organization, yet is *not* an organization, by which I mean a group that works politically to bring about actual change, and yet has nothing for the enemy infiltrators to worm their way into…

523 Goodrick-Clarke, *Hitler's Priestess*, p. 224.
524 Frost, *'Twaz a Good Fight!'*, p. 329.
525 Jackson, *Colin Jordan and Britain's Neo-Nazi Movement*, p. 206.
526 'Our Commander Koehl: A Living Link', *The New Order* www.theneworder.org/commentary/alivinglink.htm (accessed 6 July 2012). Florentine S. Rost van Tonningen exemplified the idea of this 'living link' with the past. Her unrepentant autobiography, *Triumph and Tragedy: Some Personal Remembrances of Dutch and European History in the 20th Century* (Netherlands: Consortium De Levensboom, 2000), p. 217 ended with the following message:

> Finally, from the bottom of my heart I would like to thank our *Führer*, his followers and the German people for having fought on to the bitter end, despite all the suffering they had to endure at the hands of the enemy. And to our younger generation I would like to wish both courage and faith in our people, helping them to tie together the torn thread and strengthen it for a sound and healthy Europe and Aryan world.

Broadsword, no. 13 [no date] highlighted the British Movement's own links with 'the "Grand Old Lady" of Dutch and European National Socialism' who 'has visited Britain to attend British Movement events and BM activists have visited her home and campaign office in Holland.'
527 *NS Bulletin: Official Newsletter of the New Order*, no. 333, May–August 1986. See also 'In Memoriam: John Colin Campbell Jordan', *The New Order*, www.theneworder.org/news/heroism/090410jordan.htm (accessed 6 July 2012).

528 *NS Bulletin: Official Newsletter of the New Order – Special Centennial Issue*, 1989.
529 Having already sold copies of the article through the pages of *White Power Report*, vol. 1, no. 7, 20 April 1977, *Liberty Bell*, vol. 16, no. 8, 20 April 1989 republished it in its entirety. Jordan was delighted. His effusive letter, thanking its editor, George Dietz, for this 'superb' collection, featured in *Liberty Bell*, no. 12, August 1989. Jordan believed this issue was 'something to treasure permanently as a magnificent commemoration' regarding it as:

> an additional personal pleasure to discover that you had found my old article 'National Socialism: A Philosophical Appraisal' worthy of inclusion in this monumental issue ... It was kind of you to preface the reproduction in the centenary issue with the too complimentary remarks concerning myself, and the wording of one of my centenary stickers.

Dietz was clearly enamoured with Jordan's article. He reprinted it again in *Liberty Bell*, vol. 21, no. 10 June 1994. Having been unable to include it in the April 1989 centenary edition, Dietz also reprinted Jordan's essay 'Hitler was Right' in *Liberty Bell*, vol. 17, no. 8, April 1990. Matt Koehl's magazine, *The New Order*, no. 81, January–August 1989 also disseminated Jordan's writings. They were also recycled by, for instance, *The Torch: The National Voice of Christian Identity*, no. 120, January 1984, mouthpiece of The Church of Jesus Christ in Bass, Arkansas, and *Aryan Workers Front*, vol. 1, no. 1, c.1989–1990 operating from DeKalb, Texas (which published excerpts from Jordan's 'A Great Idea National Socialism Then and Now').
530 For a broader analysis, see George Michael, 'Blueprints and Fantasies: A Review and Analysis of Extremist Fiction', *Studies in Conflict and Terrorism*, no. 33, 2010, pp. 149–170.
531 Colin Jordan, *A Train of Thought* (Thorgarth: Gothic Ripples, 1989).
532 George Michael, *Confronting Right-Wing Extremism and Terrorism in the USA* (Abingdon: Routledge, 2003), pp. 117–118 notes William Pierce employed the same technique in *The Hunter*.
533 Colin Jordan, *Merrie England – 2,000* (Thorgarth: Gothic Ripples, 1993). See also Paul Jackson, 'British Neo-Nazi Fiction: Colin Jordan's *Merrie England – 2000* and *The Uprising*', in Nigel Copsey and John E. Richardson (eds), *Cultures of Post-War British Fascism* (Abingdon: Routledge, 2015), pp. 86–108. *Merrie England – 2000* was, surprisingly, reviewed and sold in the 'New Right' journal *The Scorpion*, no. 17, spring 1995 whose editor, Michael Walker, lamented that Jordan's admiration of Hitler 'puts him beyond the pale for many who would do well to listen to what he has to say here regardless of what they think of the late German chancellor.' Walker's stance alarmed the French Nouvelle Droite ideologue Alain de Benoist who chided:

> The question of knowing to what extent a platform should be offered to extreme individuals or groups is *not* a matter of respectability, but rather, as I see it, a question of knowing what positions one wishes to affirm. If you decide to publish Mr. (Colin) Jordan elucubrations that is up to you but it should be done on condition that you clearly distance yourself from him or you run the risk of not being taken seriously as a platform for debate...

(Correspondence reproduced in *Liberty Bell*, vol. 22, no. 7, March 1995). The row rumbled on. 'Third Way' leader Patrick Harrington wrote criticising Walker's (unapologetic) promotion of Jordan in *The Scorpion*, no. 18, spring 1997, eliciting a reply from Jordan in *The Scorpion*, no. 19, spring 1998 castigating his 'exoneration' of Jewry, which 'results either from an ignorance of the realities of power and influence in the present world or else a contemptible cowardice. Personally I diagnose his [Harrington's] affliction as chronic cold feet.'
534 *Jewish Telegraph*, 10 April 1993.
535 The *Guardian*, 24 March 1994; and *Yorkshire Post*, 12 August 1998.
536 The initial print run was 5,000, see *Northern Echo*, 29 March 1993. To facilitate further sales, *Merrie England – 2000* also appeared on the Internet, then still a relatively new means of communication, see *Gothic Ripples*, no. 35, December 1996. *Liberty Bell*, vol. 24, no. 7, March 1997 advertised the URL for an American audience.
537 Colin Jordan, *National Socialism: Vanguard of the Future – Selected Writings of Colin Jordan* (Aalborg: Nordland Forlag, 1993). See also *Gothic Ripples*, http://gothicripples.wordpress.com/ (accessed 13 November 2011).
538 Frost, *'Twaz a Good Fight!'*, p. 293; and *NS Worldview*, no. 2, summer 1995, p. 106. *Spearhead*, no. 217, March 1987 notes that Jordan regularly kept the BNP apprised of Zündel's legal travails.

539 The series began in *Gothic Ripples*, no. 27, September 1994 and ended in *Gothic Ripples*, no. 39, April 1999.
540 For example, Richard Butler, leader of Aryan Nations, began reprinting excerpts of 'The Way Ahead' in *Aryan Nations Newsletter*, no. 84.
541 *Liberty Bell*, vol. 22, no. 9, January 1995. George Dietz reprinted the series in full in *Liberty Bell*, that is, *Liberty Bell*, vol. 22, no. 9, May 1995; *Liberty Bell*, vol. 24, no. 7, March 1997; and *Liberty Bell*, vol. 25, no. 9, May 1998.
542 Colin Jordan, *The Uprising* (Milwaukee, WI: NS Publications, 2004).
543 *Gothic Ripples*, no. 42, January 2001 outlines Jordan's failed effort to have Straw charged under the Genocide Act (1969)
544 'Colin Jordan, 'The Two Sides of Jack Straw's Jewish Justice', *Skrewdriver.org*, www.skrewdriver.org/jordan.html (accessed 13 November 2011); and Frost, *'Twaz a Good Fight!'*, p. 306. In 2009, Jordan issued a summons under the Police (Property) Act 1897 against the Chief Constable of Yorkshire for the return of 8,831 items which he alleged had not been returned to him following the collapse of the case against him in 2001. He was also in the process of taking legal action against the anti-fascist magazine *Searchlight* for defamation when he died. For further details, see *Heritage and Destiny*, no. 35, January–March 2009.
545 Frost, *'Twaz a Good Fight!'*, p. 307. Jordan's printer, Anthony Hancock, was acquitted of two charges of aiding and abetting Jordan to publish or distribute material which was threatening, abusive or insulting and intended or likely to stir up racial hatred in September 2002. Though BNP chairman Nick Griffin was silent on Jordan's prosecution, which irked Jordan considerably, he did defend Hancock in *Identity*, no. 56, July 2005 noting that his prosecution was an attempt 'to intimidate not just him but every other printer in the country, into refusing to handle Politically incorrect material.'
546 Wallace Wears, an International Third Position activist who had worked on its 'French farming project' financed its publication. Wears died on 10 September 1997 having been baptised into the Catholic faith at Rosine de Bounevialle's Hampshire home during the previous summer, see *Final Conflict*, no. 16, autumn 1997; and *Candour*, vol. 70, nos 9, 10 and 11, September, October and November 1997.
547 *Heritage and Destiny*, no. 18, October–December 2004 reviewed and advertised *The Uprising*. Jordan wrote to *Heritage and Destiny*, no. 20, April–June 2005 praising the magazine for fulfilling 'a vital function in sustaining the supremacy of racial loyalty above party politics and petty manoeuvres.'
548 *Gothic Ripples*, no. 46, December 2002. Frost, *'Twaz a Good Fight!'*, p. 315 notes that Pierce's National Alliance made Jordan an honorary member in 2006.
549 'Andrew MacDonald', *The Turner Diaries* (Hillsboro, WV: National Vanguard Books, 1978). For further analysis, see Renee Brodie, 'The Aryan New Era: Apocalyptic Realizations in the Turner Diaries', *Journal of American Culture*, vol. 21, no. 3, fall 1998, pp. 13–22; and Brad Whitsel, 'The Turner Diaries and Cosmotheism: William Pierce's Theology of Revolution', *Novo Religio*, vol. 1, no. 2, April 1998, pp. 183–197. For an analysis of the book's ongoing influence, see J.M. Berger, *The Turner Legacy: The Storied Origins and Enduring Impact of White Nationalism's Deadly Bible* (ICCT Research Paper – September 2016), https://icct.nl/wp-content/uploads/2016/09/ICCT-Berger-The-Turner-Legacy-September2016–2.pdf (accessed 1 October 2016).
550 Lou Michel and Dan Herbeck, *American Terrorist: Timothy McVeigh and the Oklahoma City Bombing* (New York: Harper Collins, 2001), pp. 39, 88, 167 and 228–229. *The Turner Diaries* profoundly influenced McVeigh. He had originally considered bombing the J. Edgar Hoover FBI Building in Washington, DC like Earl Turner, the eponymous hero of *The Turner Diaries*. In the days before the bombing, McVeigh also left several cryptic messages for Richard Coffman, a National Alliance activist, in the hope the group might help him secure refuge in the aftermath of his impending attack. In the event, McVeigh failed to connect with the NA, however.
551 Jo Thomas, 'Behind a Book that Inspired McVeigh', *New York Times*, 9 June 2001, www.nytimes.com/2001/06/09/us/behind-a-book-that-inspired-mcveigh.html (accessed 9 December 2016).
552 *National Alliance Bulletin*, October 1998.
553 The *Guardian*, 3 April 2000.
554 Kevin Flynn and Gary Gerhardt, *The Silent Brotherhood: Inside America's Racist Underground* (New York: Free Press, 1989); Thomas Martinez and John Guinther, *Brotherhood of Murder*

(New York: Pocket Books, 1990); and Stephen Singular, *Talked to Death: The Murder of Alan Berg and the Rise of the Neo-Nazis* (New York: Berkley Books, 1989). More recently, see Kathleen Belew, *Bring the War Home: The White Power Movement and Paramilitary America* (Cambridge, MA: Harvard University Press, 2018). For the broader context, see James William Gibson, *Warrior Dreams: Paramilitary Culture in Post-Vietnam America* (New York: Hill & Wang, 1994).

555 *Heritage and Destiny*, no. 18, October–December 2004. Jordan denied reading Pierce's novels though 'Gothic Ripples Booklist, February 1986', Box 14, folder 33, Mason papers, highlights he had stocked and sold copies.
556 *The Scorpion*, no. 24, spring 2005.
557 Frost, *'Twaz a Good Fight!'*, pp. 285–86. *Gothic Ripples*, nos 22–23, April 1990 solicited donations for Matthews' widow.
558 *Gothic Ripples*, no. 24, December 1990 urged readers to send cards to the following members of The Order: Gary Yarborough, David Lane, Bruce Pierce, Richard Scutari, Randy Duey and Richard Kemp. 'Their fight was yours! Show Solidarity!'
559 *Gothic Ripples*, no. 41, August 2000.
560 Magnus Söderman and Henrik Holappa, *Unbroken Warrior: The Richard Scutari Letters* (Stockholm: Nationellt Motstand Förlag, 2011), pp. 29, 31 and 34.
561 *Gothic Ripples*, no. 41, August 2000.
562 George Michael, 'David Lane and the Fourteen Words', *Totalitarian Movements and Political Religions*, vol. 10, no. 1, March 2009, pp. 43–61.
563 *Gothic Ripples*, no. 41, August 2000.
564 *Focus Fourteen*, no. 709; and see Colin Jordan, 'Smashing the Peace Stone', *W.o.t.a.n*, www.allfatherwotan.org/smashingthepeacestone.html (accessed 13 November 2011).
565 See Colin Jordan, 'Dealers in Flotsam and Jetsam', *W.o.t.a.n*, http://allfatherwotan.org/dealersfj.html (accessed 13 November 2011). For Jordan's influence on Lane's thinking, see *W.o.t.a.n*, http://allfatherwotan.org/strategy.html (accessed 13 November 2011).
566 *Deceived, Damned and Defiant: The Revolutionary Writings of David Lane* (St Maries, ID: Fourteen Words Press, 1999), pp. xvii–xxii. His introduction also appeared online at *W.o.t.a.n*, http://allfatherwotan.org/jordanintro.html (accessed 13 November 2011). Jordan is also mentioned in passing in Ron McVan's *Voice of our Forefathers – An Aryan Manifesto* (No publishing details: 2010), p. 2. McVan worked with Katja Lane, David Lane's wife, on the 14 Words Press and Wotansvolk, a politico-religious grouping espousing a brand of Aryan pagan mysticism.
567 *Spearhead*, no. 372, February 2000.
568 Colin Jordan, '"The Demon of Diabaig" writes from Thor Nook', *Heretical.com*, www.heretical.com/British/diabaig.html (accessed 13 November 2011). See also *Aberdeen Press and Journal*, 13 March 2002. Jordan satirised and fictionalised this experience for *Spearhead*, no. 401, July 2002.
569 *Gothic Ripples*, no. 48, October 2004.
570 Jackson, *Colin Jordan and Britain's Neo-Nazi Movement*, p. 239. Jordan had previously been in contact with Albert Szabó who in April 1993 had co-founded the 'Hungarist Movement' – the name an obvious reference to the Arrow Cross – after returning to Hungary, following a seven-year sojourn in Australia.
571 Frost, *'Twaz a Good Fight!'*, pp. 333–334.
572 John Colin Campbell Jordan, Last Will and Testament, 11 March 2008. *Gothic Ripples – Yuletide Supplement*, 2005 notes she fled Hungary in 1956 with her first husband whom had been active in the anti-Soviet uprising.
573 *Liberty Bell*, vol. 24, no. 9, May 1997; *Gothic Ripples*, no. 26, March 1997; and *Gothic Ripples*, no. 38, March 1998.
574 *Gothic Ripples – Yuletide Supplement*, 2005. Nor did Jordan tire of expressing his disgust to senior BNP officials. 'Amongst my postbag was a scathing letter from Colin Jordon [sic],' recorded deputy BNP chairman Simon Darby in January 2008.

> According to him I am a sell out for stating that we have Jewish members in the BNP. At first I am a little wounded but then accept that criticism from someone with a sixty-year track record of abject failure is not such a bad thing,

see Simon Darby blog, http://simondarby.blogspot.com/ (accessed 17 January 2008).

575 *National Vanguard*, no. 118, September–October 2002; *National Vanguard*, no. 119, January–February 2003; and *National Vanguard*, no. 120, May–June 2003. Tyndall was not immune from criticism on this score. Jordan had previously attacked the BNP in *Liberty Bell*, vol. 24, no. 9, May 1997 for their claim that they only opposed Jews 'on grounds of what they do' and not because of their 'Jewishness', which echoed Mosley. Jordan was appalled. 'This is a rejection of the racial standpoint basic to National Socialism which holds that it is because of what they are that Jews do what they do, being by nature injurious to our race and nation.'
576 Frost, *'Twaz a Good Fight!'*, p. 325.
577 See http://members.odinsrage.com/ravenfjord/CJ.htm (accessed 6 January 2004).
578 See 'The Great Idea: National Socialism, Part 1', *Northland Forum*, 9 March 2015, http://northlandforum.blogspot.co.uk/2015/03/the-great-idea-national-socialism-part-1.html (accessed 22 April 2017).
579 Frost, *'Twaz a Good Fight!'*, p. 265. *Broadsword*, no. 8 features a letter from Jordan congratulating the BM on their new journal. 'It is obvious that this represents an upgrading of your output of literature which I applaud.'
580 *Colin Jordan: A National Socialist Life* (Heckmondwike: Sunwheel Publications, 2009). See also *British Movement: 40 Years of National Socialist Struggle, 1968–2008* (Heckmondwike: Sunwheel Publications, 2008). For contact, see *Broadsword*, no. 27, 2004; and *Broadsword*, no. 28, n.d. The BM also produced a DVD interview *British Movement Interviews Colin Jordan* (2005). See also Colin Jordan, *Defiant and Unrepentant* (Mad Dogs and Englishmen: CD, 2009); and *National Socialism in Britain: A History* (Mad Dogs and Englishmen: DVD, 2009), the latter dedicated to Jordan's memory. For Jordan's continued veneration at party functions, see 'British Movement News and Views Round-Up', April 2015, http://bmsunwheel.blogspot.co.uk/2015/05/april-2015-ns-struggle-continues.html (accessed 22 July 2015); and 'British Movement News and Views Round-Up', July 2014, http://bmsunwheel.blogspot.co.uk/2014/08/july-2014-british-movement-news-and.html (accessed 22 July 2015).
581 *Blood & Honour*, no. 14 highlighted his arrests in 1998–1999. *Blood & Honour*, no. 15 encouraged activists to buy 'thought crime' stickers from Jordan. *Blood & Honour*, no. 16 urged activists to send donations. *Blood & Honour*, no. 31 reviewed *The Uprising* and urged readers to 'Support Colin Jordan' Britain's 'leading NS activist'. *Blood & Honour*, no. 36 revered Jordan as a 'Veteran National Socialist, Patriarch of post-war resistance in Britain'.
582 *Blood & Honour*, no. 30.
583 *Blood & Honour*, no. 42.
584 *Gothic Ripples*, nos 22–23, April 1990.
585 Nicholas Goodrick-Clarke, *Black Sun: Aryan Cults, Esoteric Nazism and the Politics of Identity* (New York: New York University Press, 2002), p. 42 makes this observation.
586 *Sunwheel: British Movement National Members Bulletin*, no. 35, spring 1995; and British Movement – *A Message to the West Midlands from Sunwheel*, n.d. See also *A statement regarding the split between the British National Socialist Movement and its former Bradford Group*, n.d.
587 *Searchlight*, no. 223, January 1994; *Searchlight*, no. 231, September 1994; and *Searchlight*, no. 274, April 1998. See also *Life Rune Books – Catalogue no. 10*, April 1998 advertised Jordan's *Vanguard of the Future* alongside other Nazi and 'neo-Nazi' works, particularly those emanating from the National Alliance, and the US Army manual, *Hand-To-Hand Combat FM21–150*, which was described as 'essential reading'. Ian Glaser, *The Day the Country Died: A History of Anarcho-Punk, 1980–1984* (London: Cherry Red Books, 2006), pp. 120–127 contains a long interview with Cato who maintains he had remained racist throughout his anarcho-punk period. For more on Cato, see Morbid Symptoms, 'Admit You're Shit', *Who Makes the Nazis*, 30 October 2010, www.whomakesthenazis.com/2010/10/admit-youre-shit.html (accessed 19 March 2019).
588 *The Order*, no. 7, autumn 1993.
589 *The Oak*, no. 7, autumn 1993.
590 *Ibid*.
591 *Ibid*.
592 *Thor-Would*, no. 4, December 1994. *The Order*, no. 11, 1995 argued that personal revolution was a prerequisite of racial revolution. Therefore,

> we ask each and every nationalist to in the words of Colin Jordan, purge his mind of all attachment to the existing state and system and society abstracting himself to the utmost from the group of this alien world so as to be in total rebellion against its decadence.

593 *The Order*, no. 4, circa October 1993, for example. Nick Lowles, *White Riot: The Violent Story of Combat 18* (Bury: Milo, 2001), pp. 45–46 further highlights these influences.
594 *Europe Awake*, no. 10.
595 *The National Socialist*, no. 2, 1996.
596 *Europe Awake*, no. 4, July–August 1994; *Europe Awake*, no. 5; and *Europe Awake*, no. 7, January–February 1995.
597 *Blood and Honour Magazine*, 1996.
598 See Covington's obituary for Jordan, http://downwithjugears.blogspot.co.uk/2009/04/in-memoriam-colin-jordan-1923-2009.html (accessed 12 February 2014). Covington had helped found the National Socialist White People's Party of America whose journal, *Plexus*, regularly referenced Jordan's writings. For instance, *Plexus*, no. 13, January 1994 advertised Jordan's *National Socialism: Vanguard of the Future* alongside James Mason's *Siege*. *Plexus*, no. 25, February 1995 published 'Some Thoughts from Colin Jordan' taken from *National Socialism World Creed for the 1990s*.
599 Harold A. Covington, *The March Up Country* (Reedy, WV: Liberty Bell, 1987), p. vi; and Lowles, *White Riot*, pp. 27–35 for the book's influence, which is also evident in *Spearhead*, no. 236, October 1988. Covington had visited Tyndall at his home in 1981. 'I certainly found him to be intelligent, though there was something about the man's personality that told me I should be on my guard,' Tyndall recalled in *Spearhead*, no. 319, December 1995. Covington had a small British audience. *Liberty Bell*, vol. 14, no. 7, March 1987 notes Covington's mailing list had 400 addresses though only four were in the United Kingdom. During early 1987, Covington informed subscribers that mail would reach him at 'Box 123, Douglas, Isle of Man, British Isles'.
600 See Colin Jordan, 'The Way Ahead', www.resist.com/ColinJordan/Jordan-TheWayAhead-0.html (accessed 12 February 2014). Martin Kerr, a former ANP activist who edited *White Power* also mourned Jordan's passing, recounting, as part of his tribute, a visit he had paid to Jordan in 2003, see *Heritage and Destiny*, no. 37, July–September 2009.
601 David Myatt, *Myngath: Some Recollections of a Wyrdful and Extremist Life* (May 2013), http://davidmyatt.files.wordpress.com/2013/04/david-myatt-myngath.pdf (accessed 21 May 2013). *Memoirs of a Street Soldier* by Eddy Morrison, who founded Leeds BM in October 1970, also touches upon Myatt's political activism during this era, see http://memoirsofastreetsoldier.blogspot.co.uk/ (accessed 21 May 2013). Morrison later claimed to have expelled Myatt because of his 'black magic rantings', see *Nationalist Week*, no. 19 – online bulletin of the Spearhead Group, www.bpp.org.uk/nw19.html (accessed 30 June 2016).
602 See http://members.odinsrage.com/ravenfjord/CJ.htm (accessed 6 January 2004). *Gothic Ripples*, no 38, March 1998 had previously advertised *Column 88*.
603 *Gothic Ripples*, no. 37, December 1997.
604 Graeme McLagan and Nick Lowles, *Mr Evil: The Secret Life of Racist Bomber and Killer David Copeland* (London: Blake Publishing, 2000).
605 *Gothic Ripples*, no. 41, August 2000.
606 Maxime Brunerie to the NSM, 22 July 1999 in SCH/01/Res/BRI/21/01, Searchlight archive.
607 *Searchlight*, no. 326, August 2002. Seeking to take credit for Brunerie's actions, C18 put out a mischievous statement claiming that 14 July was:

> a reminder that C18 and its supporters are willing and able to act in any European country. We do not target people because of their racial origins but we will continue to target the Global Capitalists and their allies who use the race issue for their own ends. Our enemies are on both the left and right of the political spectrum. We have nothing further to say on this matter – actions speak louder than words.

See www.skrewdriver.net/indexb.html (accessed 13 November 2011).
608 *Gothic Ripples*, no. 37, December 1997.
609 See www.rvfonline.com/articlefiles2/colinjordanmemory.htm (accessed 13 November 2011).
610 See www.bpp.org.uk/colinjordanrip.html (accessed 13 November 2011).
611 See www.bpp.org.uk/colinjordan.html (accessed 13 November 2011).
612 *Searchlight*, no. 396, June 2008; and The *Guardian*, 13 April 2009. Jordan sent a message of support to the BPP 'Senior White Nationalists Forum' on 24 March 2007, see www.bpp.org.uk/cj.html (accessed 13 November 2011).

613 See http://nationalsocialist.net/ (accessed 13 November 2011). The BPP reprinted the original Cotswolds Declaration as part of this initiative, see www.bpp.org.uk/cots.html (accessed 13 November 2011).
614 'Sad News – Colin Jordan Died!', *VNN Forum*, 10 April 2009, www.vnnforum.com/showthread.php?t=92153 (accessed 4 October 2012).
615 'County Durham Terror Plot Father and Son are Jailed', BBC News, 14 May 2010, http://news.bbc.co.uk/1/hi/england/wear/8682132.stm (accessed 4 October 2012).
616 Colin Jordan, *The National Vanguard: The Way Forward* (Uckfield: HRP, 2011); and Colin Jordan, *National Socialism: Vanguard of the Future* (Uckfield: HRP, 2011). Seeking to propagate Jordan's legacy, BM leader Stephen Frost, addressed National Action (NA) on the imperatives of National Socialism and the '14 words' at a meeting on 9 August 2014, see YouTube, www.youtube.com/watch?v=7SFXnWyL2fI (accessed 11 December 2016). Ben Raymond, one of NA's founders, has publicly attested to Jordan's influence and praised his 'enormous courage', see http://national-action.info/wp-content/uploads/2015/03/Resistance-Interview.pdf (accessed 23 March 2015). Jordan's book, *National Socialism: Vanguard of the Future* was 'essential reading' for London NA activists, see https://nationalactionlondon.files.wordpress.com/2015/06/colin-jordan-national-socialism-vanguard-of-the-future.pdf (accessed 11 December 2016). Radio Aryan, aligned with NA, has also turned *The Uprising* into an audio book, see 'Aryan Narrations: The Uprising by Colin Jordan', *Radio Albion*, March 2016, www.radioaryan.com/2016/03/aryan-narrations-uprising-by-colin.html (accessed 26 March 2016). Jordan's novel, *The Uprising*, was also available from the Siege Culture website which promoted the work of James Mason, a former activist in Rockwell's ANP who went on to exert a pivotal influence on a violent US *groupuscule* called Atomwaffen Division, which was closely allied with National Action. Highlighting the continuity and durability of this transatlantic extreme right milieu, Jordan and Mason had been in contact with one another since at least 1977. In *Siege*, August 1983, Mason had praised Jordan's work as that of 'Old Fighter' which, whilst considered 'old style and contradictory' compared to *Siege*, was nonetheless, 'important enough to merit this mention'. Colin Jordan to James Mason, 12 October 1983, Box 35, folder 33, Mason papers, thanked Mason for sending him a copy of *Siege* 'and for the kind mention made it of myself and my booklet.' The BM blogsite subsequently reproduced material from Mason's website (siegeculture.com) for a new generation of activists, see 'NSM: The Cotswold Camp 1962', *Northland Forum*, 22 November 2017, http://northlandforum.blogspot.no/2017/11/nsm-cotswold-camp-colour-archive-images.html (accessed 22 November 2017).
617 *Instauration*, vol. 3, no. 5, April 1978.

5 John Tyndall
In pursuit of the 'Anglo-Saxon Reich'

John Tyndall died at his home in Hove, West Sussex, on 19 July 2005, shortly after his seventy-first birthday. Jailed three times already during his life, he was again facing prison after the Crown Prosecution Service had once more charged him with inciting racial hatred. The BBC had secretly filmed him making a speech at a British National Party (BNP) meeting in Burnley, Lancashire, in the preceding March. 'The only thing the Africans have given us,' Tyndall had proclaimed to his audience, 'is voodoo, witchcraft and Aids.'[1] He had faced trial alongside Nick Griffin, the BNP chairman and Mark Collett, the party's director of publicity, from whom he was estranged. Griffin had expelled Tyndall from the BNP, the party he had founded, for a second time, earlier that year. Tyndall had launched a civil action against Griffin in the High Court to challenge the legality of his expulsion, but was increasingly isolated politically. He had appeared at the preliminary hearings at Leeds Crown Court in April buoyed by supporters from the Nationalist Alliance, a miniscule Nazi *groupuscule* proscribed by the BNP.

Tyndall's career finished much as it had begun – adrift in the Nazi hinterland. During the 1970s, however, Tyndall was *the* pre-eminent figure on Britain's extreme right.

He chaired the National Front (NF), the largest extreme right-wing street movement in Europe, from 1972 to 1974 and again between 1976 and 1979. At its peak, NF membership reached approximately 17,500, though to put this figure in perspective, it was still less than half that of Mosley's BUF in 1934.[2] That said NF membership was 'like a bath with both taps running and the plughole empty'.[3] Between 1967 and 1979, an estimated 64,000 people passed through its ranks.[4] Electorally, however, the NF never gained national or local political representation despite some impressive electoral outings, including, at the peak of its popular support, the 119,060 votes it polled in the Greater London Council elections in May 1977.

The party's success, such as it was, served as a beacon for like-minded activists across Europe and the United States. It served as a model for the French Front National (FN). Indeed, in its heyday the NF was 'greatly admired and envied' by young FN militants who regularly traversed the Channel 'to visit British fellow patriots and sometimes to take part in their activities'. Tyndall entertained many of them in his home, basking in the 'respect' they paid his party. The NF 'was worthy of that respect, for then it set the pace for its French ally,' Tyndall recorded.[5] The halo of success did not last. The NF imploded following its poor performance in the 1979 general election and Tyndall resigned amidst considerable acrimony with his colleagues shortly thereafter.

In 1982, Tyndall founded the BNP, which enjoyed far greater electoral success than the NF ever had before poor election results and internal intriguing stymied its progress. Tyndall played no part in its short-lived though unprecedented progress, which occurred only after he was ousted as chairman in 1999. This is not to dismiss Tyndall's importance for the BNP. He was, as one former colleague remarked, 'both its greatest asset and its greatest drawback'.[6] Whilst the taint of Nazism clung indelibly to Tyndall like the proverbial Mark of Cain, simultaneously, his longevity was a singular achievement. Within the fractious extreme right-wing *demi-monde*, Tyndall exhibited a metronomic consistency, both ideologically and organisationally, which kept intact a large portion of the extreme right during a period when its fortunes – under Thatcher and her successors – were very much in abeyance.

Early activism

John Hutchyns Tyndall was born in Exeter on 14 July 1934, of Anglo-Irish parentage. Tyndall's father, a former police officer, was the warden of St George's House, a YMCA hostel in Southwark where he grew up. Educated at Beckenham Grammar School, Tyndall was 'more involved in sports than in any scholastic achievements'.[7] He represented his school at cricket and had trials for Kent. Tyndall was a descendant of William Tydale (1494–1536), who had dedicated his life to printing and disseminating an affordable English-language translation of the Bible, the first of which rolled off the presses in 1526. As one historian noted:

> He was an immediately recognizable historical type – austere, unswerving, a little fanatical, but tireless in pursuit of his mission, which was easily stated: 'It was not possible to establish the lay people in any truth except [that] the scriptures were so plainly laid before their eyes in their mother tongue.'[8]

Such traits were, *in extremis*, recognisable in Tydale's descendant, who held a similarly intransigent belief that, if presented with racial 'truth' in a language it understood, the public would acknowledge the divine writ of white racial supremacy. Through the Irish branch of Tyndale's descendants, Tyndall was a relation of his namesake – the physicist, natural philosopher and part-time mountaineer, John Tyndall (1820–1893). The Irish connection loomed large. Tyndall's grandfather was a District Inspector in the Royal Irish Constabulary, spending much of his life fighting 'the rebels' in both North and South. His uncle Charles became Bishop of Kilmore, Elphin and Ardagh in 1956 and, two years later, Bishop of Derry and Raphoe, a position he held until 1969.[9]

Having left school in 1951, Tyndall worked as a bank clerk and at New Zealand House before being called up for National Service and posted to Germany. He served with the Royal Artillery as a gunner, subsequently promoted to lance bombardier. Describing himself as 'something of a loner', Tyndall demurred from drinking and 'whoring' with his fellow recruits. 'I kept to myself, read a lot of books, went on country walks and meditated' leading to the development of his 'national conscientious'. National Service proved pivotal for Tyndall. 'If you haven't been beyond the borders of your own country your horizons are limited and you don't think of your own country in relation to the rest of the world,' he later observed.[10] Demobilised on 17 October 1954, Tyndall's conduct was described as 'very good'. Fresh from National Service, Tyndall started to 'grope my way in the political fog sensing instinctively that there were forces afoot that were wilfully destroying Britain but not really knowing what they were or how to deal with them.'[11]

Regarding himself as 'a socialist in the sense that I believed in the community rather than the individual', Tyndall was unable to reconcile himself to a Labour Party, which, he believed, was unprepared 'to stand up for the interest of this country'.[12] Nonetheless, in 1957, aged twenty-three, Tyndall answered an advertisement in a sporting magazine offering reduced rates to attend a 'world youth festival' in Moscow. Describing himself as a 'political innocent', Tyndall was apparently naïve enough to be surprised that the majority of those attending were committed left-wingers.[13] Political rivals later claimed, unconvincingly, that this suggested Tyndall was a secret communist.[14] Having returned, Tyndall drifted towards the extreme right. He was initially attracted to Mosley's UM but, already rigidly Anglo-centric in his world-view, was 'immediately put off' by its 'Europe-a-Nation' platform, which he regarded as 'wholly undesirable and not remotely possible'.[15] Mosley's pan-European dream was a 'monumental non-starter' for Tyndall.[16]

An 'ardent imperialist' since childhood who deeply resented the 'orchestrated onslaught against national pride',[17] it was perhaps inevitable that Tyndall would visit the offices of the League of Empire Loyalists (LEL) led by A.K. Chesterton. 'As I entered the room', he later recalled, 'I took a step that was to have profound consequences for my life.' Following an initial meeting with Austen Brooks, Tyndall became acquainted with *Candour* and with it the 'conspiracy theory' of politics. Seeking further illumination, Tyndall conducted his own 'comprehensive examination' of the available literature, which he obtained from 'the small patriotic groups with which I had become involved or acquainted, one of which was The Britons Publishing Company'.[18] By his own account, Tyndall was not particularly anti-Semitic before joining the League, imbibing such prejudices once radicalised and socialised within the movement. 'I well remember my own induction into Jewish issues,' he wrote shortly before his death in 2005:

> It occurred when, as a young man in the late 1950s, I first became involved in British Nationalism. Essentially, I wanted to do something to lift up my own country and people; I had no wish whatever to become engaged in fights with Jews. I recall, with some embarrassment today, the rather pompous and precocious lectures I gave to

others that they should steer well clear of any mention of Jews in an unflattering context lest this bring down upon us the charge of 'anti-Semitism' or, even worse, 'Nazism'. I once wrote a letter to my then chief and mentor A.K. Chesterton containing some strictures of this kind. His reply stung me a little at the time, though when I think about it now it seems a masterpiece of diplomacy. Here was this upstart – a virtual know-nothing – presuming to tell him what was what on a subject on which he had been a world-acclaimed authority for at least 20 years![19]

Chesterton carefully nurtured and encouraged Tyndall's 'enlightenment', writing enthusiastically of his delight that the younger man was 'in substantial agreement with the views of our little periodical'. He invited Tyndall to contribute to *Candour*. The theme, Chesterton suggested, 'should be the cultural attack from across the Atlantic and its deplorable effect upon impressionable young British minds'.[20] Tyndall's subsequent article assailed the steady diet of glamorised 'cultural garbage' emanating from America and lamented its deleterious effect upon the 'cultural heritage' and 'national spirit' of British youth, which had 'deadened' their pride and thus had brought low the nation. It proved just the tonic for Chesterton.[21] One should not exaggerate Tyndall's contribution to the League. He only penned two more articles for *Candour*, one of which displayed his Manichean mindset ('on the one side stands Christendom and patriotism. On the other – The Devil') and, aside from soliciting contacts for a South London branch, Tyndall played only a minor role in a handful of League actions.[22]

Significantly, Chesterton placed Tyndall in the care of his Northern organiser, John Bean, a former UM activist employed as a works manager for a Hull-based paint manufacturers. After departing from Mosley's orbit, Bean had briefly operated his own *groupuscule*, which he merged into the League in November 1955 before returning to London to work part-time for Chesterton in July 1956.[23] 'Choose your people with care', Chesterton told Bean. 'Give the crooks and maniacs a wide berth. Quality in this movement is immeasurably more important than quantity.' In his autobiography, Bean, who had already joined a violent action in Birmingham staged by Jordan's White Defence Force, lamented 'it was a pity that I did not make full note of Chesterton's caution'. Chesterton would later accuse Bean of having a penchant for associating with people 'of markedly eccentric views whose membership of any movement would infallibly damn it'. However, as Bean wryly observed, 'Chesterton ignored the fact that I had met most of the eccentrics on League activities where he too had tried to use them.'[24]

Bean first met Tyndall in February 1957 during Leslie Greene's by-election campaign in North Lewisham.[25] Bean became Tyndall's 'mentor' and – one might speculate – it was under his tutelage that Tyndall's 'cultural' concerns became more explicitly biological.[26] Tyndall came to feel 'great subsequent shame and regret' regarding his subsequent decision to abandon the LEL with Bean and nine other London-based League activists to form a new political party. The action was 'wholly wrong', Tyndall later lamented.[27] Chesterton was furious, attacking their 'Fascist-type break-away movement' and raging that their efforts to recruit another League activist were 'Nazi in tone and substance. There was talk of "Strength through Joy"'. Even more indicative was the statement: "Of course we shall not be such fools as to go in waving swastikas – not yet, anyway"'. Chesterton felt Bean's betrayal most keenly. Not just because he had recently lent him the money towards a deposit on a house but also because he had had 'sufficient faith' in Bean to admit him 'to our inner councils'. Chesterton expelled both men. 'The movement is the more wholesome for their going.'[28]

Though his personal relationship with Bean never recovered, Chesterton was more forgiving of Tyndall. 'I always had a personal liking for you and always regarded you as one of our members showing the most promise', Chesterton subsequently wrote to him.[29] Chesterton's influence upon Tyndall was profound (Chapter 3). 'I have always felt ideologically akin to the League and to yourself, and would, where principles are concerned, regard you as an essential stream of Rightist thought in this country', Tyndall replied.[30] Tyndall would later claim Chesterton's mantle, using it to buttress his own claims to political leadership within extreme right-wing circles. Indeed, in 1982, Tyndall stated that although the League no longer existed, 'its work is being carried on today by the British National Party'.[31]

National Labour Party

The National Labour Party (NLP) – 'National because we love our country; Labour because we love our people' – was founded by Bean and Tyndall on 24 March 1958 (Empire Day). Tellingly, Tyndall had favoured calling it the 'National Socialist Party'. Whilst the LEL attracted right-wingers of a 'Tory bent', the NLP positioned itself to appeal to racist, working-class Labour Party supporters blending its nationalism with 'a kind of popular socialism, shorn of left-wing ideology'.[32] NLP activities centred upon Bethnal Green.[33] 'Audiences were nothing spectacular and I cannot recall us gaining more than two new members,' Bean recalled. Whilst most recruits were 'salt of the earth' others were directly involved in criminality, one supporter being connected to Sid Bullen, a minor East End gangster connected to the more formidable 'Italian' Albert Dimes, who offered Bean protection against 'the reds and the Jews' in exchange for the support of his own 'pugilistic supporters' when Dimes required. Bean wisely declined.[34]

The NLP enabled Tyndall to begin building his activist credentials. He participated in an attack upon a Movement for Colonial Freedom (MCF) meeting on 11 December 1958, during which a fellow activist hurled a dummy bomb on stage amidst cries of 'Keep Britain White' and 'Britain for the British'.[35] Police arrested Tyndall and Bean in March 1959 as they attempted to daub slogans on the home of Labour MP, John Stonehouse. Both pleaded guilty but the charges were later dropped.[36] During this period, Bean began courting the mercurial Norfolk landowner and forester Andrew Fountaine who was standing as a 'National' candidate in the South-West Norfolk by-election.[37] Fountaine's campaign was controversial locally. His deceased father had been chairman and president of the local Conservative Association leading his mother to denounce her son publicly for 'letting the nation down by opposing a Conservative.'[38] Fountaine polled just 785 votes (2.61 per cent), having run on a platform to restore British national sovereignty and oppose 'American rocket bases' in East Anglia, which 'not only fail to guarantee our protection; they make us a legitimate target for Russian rockets'.[39] Fountaine became the NLP President shortly afterwards. 'Tyndall's bull headedness and well known inability to compromise meant that the two did not take to each other', remarked Bean.[40]

The NLP newspaper, *Combat*, became an important mouthpiece for racial nationalist politics. Tyndall's early contributions set the tone for what turned out to be a lifelong career as an extreme right-wing agitator. 'The Jew in Art' saw Tyndall arguing that:

> If the European soul is to be recovered in our Country and throughout Europe, it can only be done by the elimination of this cancerous microbe in our midst. Let us remember this eternal truth – that Culture is Race, Race is Culture, and only by the purification of its culture can our race and nation rise to its highest ennoblement.[41]

The NLP also afforded Tyndall the opportunity to hone his oratorical skills. His first foray, at an NLP meeting in Trafalgar Square on 25 May 1959, was not a startling success. Fountaine, the main speaker, declared that European civilisation was facing 'the greatest peril since the sack of Rome' and that this was all the fault of the Jews. Tyndall, chairing the meeting, echoed these words 'until a failure of the public address system reduced his harangue to a silent pantomime.'[42] His second venture, on 6 September, at an NLP meeting staged to commemorate the twentieth anniversary of an 'unnecessary war', was more successful. Bean recalled Tyndall had become 'quite a forceful, though rather strident speaker'.[43] Anti-fascist observers also rated Tyndall 'a more effective orator, with better vocabulary, greater fluency, but more excitable' than his NLP colleagues, though 'I doubt if many of the [800] people were impressed.' The content of Tyndall's speech was notable for its crude anti-Semitic attacks upon 'the so-called victims of Belsen and Buchenwald' whom, he claimed,

> came to this country and bought it up lock, stock and barrel. Hitler liberated Germany from the tyranny of the Synagogue ... the same people who drove us into war in 1939 ... international Jewish finance. These are the real criminals, these are the real enemy.[44]

Though overshadowed by Mosley's 1959 general election campaign in Kensington North, the NLP carried out its own violent, racist campaign in North St Pancras. Their candidate, William 'Bill' Webster, was a former boxer turned publican who had previously campaigned as an 'independent' against 'Black parasites' and 'Cypriot thugs' in local council elections.[45] The advent of multi-racial society was 'biological sacrilege', Webster told reporters. The solution: deportation. 'It is a matter of racial survival and I can see in this a lowering of standards. The Negro is on a lower evolutionary plane as far as I can see.'[46] The NLP campaign culminated on 28 September in an attack upon an MCF meeting in St Pancras Hall by a group of thirty NLP activists, including Tyndall, shouting 'keep Britain white' and 'down with the niggers'. Police arrested Bean – Webster's election agent – and ten other NLP activists, including the candidate and his son during the general mêlée that followed. Bean and another activist were jailed for one month. Both pronounced themselves 'political prisoners'.[47] The group's violent reputation was such that, having testified against Bean, one local Labour Party activist observed: 'I suspect that I may be a candidate for a hiding so I carry a police-whistle and a good stout stick.'[48] *The Times* argued that Webster 'will receive the votes only of the disgruntled and of those who do not normally vote at local elections, but these may turn out to be a considerable number'.[49] He polled 1,685 votes (4 per cent).[50]

British National Party

Whilst languishing in prison, Bean concluded that if the NLP were to 'further progress' it should combine with Colin Jordan's White Defence League (WDL), giving it access to Jordan's principal political asset: 74 Princedale Road. However, during the subsequent merger negotiations Tyndall suddenly resigned from the NLP, indicting Bean not just for his failure to deliver firm leadership – which Bean conceded was his 'principal weakness' – but for his 'Liberal tendencies'. This criticism underscored Tyndall's rejection of democratic politics, even within a racial nationalist grouplet, and his inexorable move towards overt Nazism.[51] Of Tyndall's resignation, Bean subsequently recorded:

> But it would appear that it has taken him [Tyndall] his forty years of political struggle since then to appreciate that, if you are trying to seek political influence you must have a democratic movement that tolerates and unites all types of people. It would appear to me that his present British National Party is not that dissimilar in its approach to the National Labour Party of 1960.[52]

Though Bean acknowledged Tyndall had many personal attributes that made him a valuable activist, his 'openly expressed support for aspects of Nazi Germany' had begun to outweigh these traits. Bean's deletion of such references from Tyndall's *Combat* contributions had fuelled arguments. Tyndall's departure was politically advantageous to Bean. He calculated he could more easily control Jordan if he deprived him of an 'extremist' confederate within the new group, thus tipping the balance of power towards the racial nationalist faction. 'This was without doubt the biggest political mistake I made,' Bean conceded.[53]

The NLP and WDL merged to form the British National Party (BNP) on 24 February 1960. Tyndall joined the group three months later, allying himself, as Bean had feared, with Jordan's national socialist faction. There was internal resistance to Tyndall's membership due to 'his arrogance, his overbearing personal manner, and the way he brought the authoritarianism of his politics into his personal life'. Nevertheless, once permitted to join, Tyndall quickly became one of the group's leading ideologues. He regularly spoke from a pitch in Earls Court where meetings frequently degenerated into violence amidst sustained barracking from left-wing opponents.[54] Following one such meeting in July 1961, Tyndall was fined 40 shillings for assaulting a police officer and for using threatening behaviour, the first in a string of criminal convictions but the one he regretted most, given his oft enunciated zeal for 'law and order'.[55]

In October 1961, *The Authoritarian State* appeared, Tyndall's turgid, anti-Semitic indictment of 'democracy ... the modern Jew inspired illusion of "freedom"'. Quoting approvingly from *The Protocols of the Elders of Zion*, Tyndall argued that, in his quest to vanquish Britain and establish a totalitarian Communist state, the 'diabolically clever' Jew had launched a twin-pronged assault on the spiritual and racial health of the nation. Whilst 'comic papers, sex films and rock 'n' roll' undermined the former, immigration played an integral part destroying the latter, claimed Tyndall:

> As Democracy tamely allows droves of dark-skinned, sub-racials into our country, the Jew cleverly takes advantage of their presence to propagate the lie of racial equality, thus gradually encouraging their acceptance into European society, with the ultimate results of inter-marriage and race-degeneration that he knows will follow.[56]

Tyndall's racially regenerative panacea was the 'Authoritarian State', a rigidly hierarchical corporate state based on 'occupational franchise' rather than popular democracy and governed in accordance with 'the leadership principle'. This was the only route through which the nation's 'inner vitality' be resurrected, argued Tyndall. Rigorously applying 'state discipline' would create 'a society moulded upon the best traditions of ancient Greece, with the Spartan qualities of courage and virility blended with the Athenian qualities of purity of mind and culture.' To create this racially purified warrior caste, young people would be 'legally compelled' to undergo 'compulsory national service'. The aim was to produce obedient, dutiful and racially fertile citizens out of which would arise 'a national community in which that natural Nordic birthright of freedom is not something to be taken for granted by the dregs of society, but something earned by labour, loyalty and sacrifice'.[57]

This was the bedrock of Tyndall's political philosophy. He and Jordan became ever-closer political allies within the BNP, leading them to found Spearhead, the party's would-be paramilitary arm, though which the 'Authoritarian State' would be realized. Tyndall was appointed 'London Group Leader' and edited the solitary issue of its journal, *Greyshirt*, which recognised that no political movement dedicated to the 'dynamic regeneration' of society could hope to succeed unless driven by 'a fanatical core of hardened men, trained and disciplined in the struggle' and united in 'spirit of comradeship'. Spearhead was this body. Membership demanded 'a markedly higher conception of service than is normally asked of the average party adherent.'[58] Tyndall used its internal bulletin to offer members a portrait of the infamous Nazi Jew-baiter Julius Streicher – described as a 'must for your drawing room wall'.[59]

Such behaviour made Tyndall both sinister and comical in equal measure. During summer 1961, Tyndall accompanied Jordan on a pilgrimage to Germany to meet numerous former Nazi functionaries and to build up the 'Northern European Ring' network (Chapter 4) but behind his back Tyndall's comrades mocked his 'Prussianism' and his penchant for 'always wearing jackboots'. Jordan later recalled that:

> as soon as we got across the frontier into Germany Tyndall made us look for a shoe shop. Then he kept us waiting for an hour while he tramped up and down the shop in his first pair of genuine German jackboots. He was something of a figure of fun, but he upset people.[60]

'He was always trying to persuade me to do away with the [BNP] national council', stated Jordan. 'He wanted a much more authoritarian structure. At least Spearhead got him out of the way at weekends.'[61]

'The SS state is now our aim!'

In 1962, the BNP split. Bean's racial nationalist faction engaged in what Tyndall denounced as a 'sly little plot' to expel the Nazi faction of which he and Jordan were the principals.[62] Tyndall and Jordan founded a new group, the National Socialist Movement (NSM) of which Tyndall became 'national secretary'. As he told the *Guardian*:

> We who followed Colin Jordan believe in orthodox National Socialism. We are concerned only with the five percent – the best. We are organising ourselves on the system in Germany between 1933 and 1945. The average man is today indifferent to politics, but this will change. In the meantime we are recruiting the best types to be trained as leaders. We are not after an elusive mass following. That will come later.[63]

He expanded upon this stance in *The National Socialist*, the NSM newspaper for which he penned the 'news comment' and 'principles of national socialist ideology' columns. He also acted as its 'business manager'. Tyndall eulogised the SS for their 'high moral order, the aesthetic self-discipline, the courteous and kindly bearing, the honour and loyalty to one's race, the self-less devotion to duty, and the supreme consciousness of the SS mission.' Denying the Holocaust as a 'Jewish invention', Tyndall claimed the SS were an aristocratic 'antidote to human decadence'. Its history carried important lessons for Britain, he believed. Only the 'super-humanity' of the SS could win out against the 'sub-humanity', which, through 'interbreeding' with lower strains and 'the injection of Jewish blood', was systematically eliminating 'the British racial type'. Only by re-establishing an elite racial order could the 'Jewish machine of world power' be defeated and past glories restored, he argued. 'The SS man has been our model,' declared Tyndall. 'The SS state is now our aim!'[64]

In the meantime, however, Tyndall had to contend with 1960s counter-culture. He registered his disgust in an article for *The National Socialist* titled 'Beatlemania: A Study in Degeneracy', in which he lambasted the Beatles' 'nigger symphony' that fell a long way short of the 'proud martial airs of their European fatherland'. For Tyndall, whose predictable preference was for Wagner, British youth faced a stark choice, either to accept the Beatles as role models or 'the virile splendour of a new British and Nordic young manhood under National Socialism!'[65] British youth opted for the Beatles.

Tyndall's forthright Nazism soon brought him into conflict with the law. He was the penultimate speaker at Jordan's notorious 'Hitler was Right' NSM rally in Trafalgar Square in July 1962, railing from the plinth that Jews were 'maggots' feeding off the body politic. He was subsequently jailed for six weeks, reduced to a £10 fine on appeal.[66] Simultaneously, Tyndall found himself back in court because of his role in organising Spearhead, which contravened the Public Order Act (1936). Speaking in his own defence at the trial, Tyndall denied, as was stated in court, that he had bought the weed killer found at the NSM headquarters, which, other witnesses testified, when mixed with sugar could be used to manufacture explosives. He accused the shop owner, who had identified him as its purchaser, of perjury. The judge admonished him for this baseless accusation. Tyndall explained to the court how he became a 'National Socialist' stating:

> I read *Mein Kampf* and realised every word of it was true. I realised the conditions to which Hitler referred in Germany, which he saw as a young man, were the conditions which I, and so many of my colleagues in this movement, have seen and still recognise in this country today.[67]

In cross-examining Lawrence Manifold, news editor of *The People*, to discover his source for several hard-hitting exposés of the NSM (which emanated from anti-fascist infiltrator John Nicols), Tyndall appeared more interested in establishing the existence of a Jewish conspiracy against the group than in conducting a vigorous defence. He failed to convince the jury of his innocence. The judge jailed him for six months. Following his conviction, Tyndall objected to media reports that he was unemployed, single and living with his parents, stressing instead that since November 1961 he had in fact been living at NSM headquarters, a habitué far more befitting an aspirant Nazi leader.[68]

Tyndall was undaunted by prison, writing to George Lincoln Rockwell, the ANP leader to tell him how much he had enjoyed the experience, except for two occasions 'when I was assaulted by a Kike and a Coon'. He regaled Rockwell with stories of how he had won over the other prisoners, despite a campaign of persecution by 'the Kikes'. He told Rockwell:

> I outline all this just to show how, if one plays one's cards the right way, one can get the Hebes enough rope to hang themselves – just by their own uncontrollable way of behaving when in the presence of the swastika and the light of truth it radiates.[69]

Whilst Jordan sewed mailbags, Tyndall was employed chopping wood in a nearby forest. 'It was all good Arbeitsfront stuff', he boasted.[70]

Whilst incarcerated, Tyndall was also a defendant in a libel case brought by Sir Leslie Plummer MP (Deptford), a hangover from his role as election agent for three BNP candidates on 13 April 1961. Tyndall had been responsible for their election address, *Your Pro-Black MP*, which accused Plummer of stifling opposition to 'coloured' immigration and supporting 'coloured spivs and their vice dens as opposed to the white people of Deptford.' The quartet lost the case. Plummer received £2,000 in damages.[71] Tyndall – who did not appear – was represented in court by Brighton solicitor F.J.P. Veale, an important figure in the early 'revisionist' milieu.[72] His most recent book, *Crimes Discreetly Veiled* (1958), Tyndall regarded as 'the best book so far on Allied war crimes against Germany and Japan during World War Two' including the 'barbarous bombing' of Dresden and the 'perverted justice' of the Nuremberg Trials. 'Those who have been reared on "atrocity" stories about Fascism should be made to read this book.'[73]

Released on 8 March 1963, his NSM colleagues treated Tyndall to a 'bumper party'. Their 'wonderful demonstration' of support quite overawed him.[74] He immediately set about reactivating the group, turning its headquarters into a hive of activity. NSM activist Denis Pirie boasted to Rockwell that, 'we have been working at such a pressure not seen since Aushwitz [sic] 1944.'[75] In the following week, Tyndall wrote to George Lincoln Rockwell announcing his intention to marry Françoise Dior. 'She is a beautiful Nordic blonde, of French aristocratic background, and a fanatical Nazi. I am a very lucky fellow.'[76] Rockwell congratulated him.[77] Tyndall maintained a long correspondence with Rockwell in which he unburdened himself on the difficulties of running the NSM in Jordan's absence. He always signed off his letters 'Heil Hitler'. On Hitler's birthday, Tyndall telephoned the ANP to celebrate but, unfortunately, Rockwell was not in to receive the call.[78] Tyndall sought an increasingly close relationship with the ANP commander, suggesting to Rockwell that they combine *The National Socialist* with *Stormtrooper*, though Rockwell felt the NSM newspaper too 'strong' for an American audience.[79]

Tyndall's relationship with Dior was short-lived. She left him for Jordan shortly after his release from prison. Tyndall's relationship with Jordan deteriorated. Tyndall did not attend their wedding in October and he stepped down as NSM national secretary shortly afterwards citing 'domestic reasons'. He had returned to his post by December. Whilst Jordan and Dior honeymooned, Tyndall granted an interview to American journalist George Thayer who observed of him:

> He was a composite of all the characteristics I had vaguely associated with Nazis in Hitler's Germany: he had cold, evasive eyes, was blond and balding, and had not the slightest spark of humour. He was suspicious, nervous and excitable, and moved with all the stiffness of a Prussian in Court.[80]

Thayer found Tyndall more impressive than Jordan in his own way. 'Tyndall, unlike Jordan, is willing to fight for what he believes and, if necessary, to go to gaol in pursuit of his ideals,' Thayer remarked. 'Of the two men, for instance, he alone wears with pride the "martyrdom" of his previous convictions.'[81] Tyndall relished this period of personal and political *kampfzeit* since it confirmed him in his belief of ultimate success. As he wrote to Rockwell in January 1964:

> ... We've had it before. The Fuhrer had it. It will always lurk there. These trouble [sic] are just part of the rocky road to victory. The victory would be nothing worth having were it not achieved through the supreme trial and struggle, hardship and sacrifice.

Were we not to know the depths of despair, as well as the heights of triumph, we would ultimately be unfitted for the role we have taken upon ourselves. That I believe with all my heart. And it is why I believe that your trials, and ours will not break us, but will only strengthen our will to fight through and win. If this task was easy – I think I would become uneasy, as I always tend to do when gains suddenly appear to drop from heaven, as it were, without tears and blood being spent in attaining them. When troubles come, I feel they are just part of the pain Nietzsche said leads to purity.[82]

One quasi-religious text encapsulated this 'purity' – '*Mein Kampf* is my doctrine', Tyndall told the press.[83]

Tyndall's commitment to the *Führerprinzip* was waning, however. Within months, he had deserted Jordan. Each man farcically expelled the other from the NSM, both claiming its mantle. Jordan blamed Tyndall for the split and alleged that his behaviour made the atmosphere in headquarters 'unpleasant', the result being he spent most of his time residing in Coventry whilst Tyndall remained in charge of the NSM office in London. When the split came, Jordan claimed Tyndall had taken advantage of this situation to remove NSM records, money and 'other property' including the NSM subscriber index cards. Jordan and a colleague subsequently raided Tyndall's basement office in Battersea to retrieve the items. Tyndall responded by returning to Princedale Road with his own accomplice removing yet more 'property' and, so Jordan alleged, £40. Jordan reported the matter to the police. Tyndall was summoned to appear in court on a charge of larceny on 17 July, though the case was subsequently dismissed.[84]

Jordan was furious, accusing Tyndall of rendering 'a singular service to the Jews'. Tyndall and his followers were traducing Nazism, Jordan complained to Rockwell by:

> living like tramps, playing German marches night and day at full volume to the discomfort of all neighbours, swaggering about with sticks and cudgels, shouting silly insults at individual Coloured folk who pass by, and chalking childish slogans on peoples [sic] doors.[85]

He derided his former colleague Martin Webster who had left the NSM with Tyndall as a 'white nigger'. More importantly, Jordan charged that Tyndall had 'dropped the swastika and reverted to a purblind narrow nationalism.' It was only a matter of time before Tyndall's claim to be a National Socialist would be 'discarded' too, Jordan claimed.[86] Whilst Tyndall's brand of national socialism was certainly beginning to diverge from Jordan's, he was, by his own admission, 'adhering to the essential principles of Fascism and Nazism, but presenting them in a manner which Britons could identify with the cause of their own country, as Germans and Italians did a generation before.'[87]

Reflecting upon his expulsion, Tyndall later claimed he had briefly contemplated hanging up his jackboots. Tyndall concluded, however, that his 'principles' were not wrong, only the 'methods, organisation, strategy and tactics' through which he had pursued them. The NSM was a 'mistake' only insofar as its outward trappings had left him 'isolated' even on the fascist fringe. This was a pivotal period in Tyndall's life. During this phase, he developed 'a set of absolutely cast-iron and unshakable beliefs as to the necessary programme for the salvation and rebuilding of Britain.' Herein were the ideological roots of the modern BNP. Tyndall saw no need to deviate from core principles, commenting over twenty years later: 'I find that I have no reason to change any of these beliefs, except in the minutest detail.'[88]

Greater Britain Movement

In July 1964, Tyndall founded the Greater Britain Movement (GBM), which was 'the same movement in every respect' as the NSM aside from its leader and name. Instead of a swastika, however, the GBM adopted a Sunwheel, surrounded by a wreath and topped with a lion, as its emblem, symbolising the fusion of 'the Nordic folkish heritage of our people' with the 'modern British nation' and 'the imperial role that destiny has allotted to her.'[89] The nation's slide into 'degeneracy and sloth, vice and perversion' could be arrested, Tyndall maintained, only through the imposition of the authoritarian state with citizenship based upon 'Aryan racial blood'. Minorities, whose presence polluted the biological and cultural well-being, would be expelled. The removal of the Jews from Britain 'must be a cardinal aim of the new order'. To protect 'British blood' from pollution or dilution racial laws would be enacted

> forbidding marriage between Britons and non-Aryans. Medical measures will be taken to prevent procreation on the part of those who have hereditary defects, either racial, mental or physical. A pure, strong, and healthy British race will be regarded as the principle guarantee of Britain's future.[90]

The establishment of the GBM coincided with the foundation of *Spearhead*, the self-declared 'organ of National Socialist opinion in Britain', which Tyndall began publishing in August 1964, its name an obvious homage to the paramilitary group for which he had been jailed only two years previously. It served as his personal mouthpiece until his death in 2005, providing a ready-made platform for anti-Semitic invective.[91] Writing under the pseudonym 'Julius' – a reference to the notorious Nazi 'Jew-baiter' Julius Streicher – in *Spearhead*'s 'Gleanings from the Ghetto' column, Tyndall informed his readership that the Jews were 'a race of unheroic, greasy, shifty-eyed, sickly moneylenders, rent-racketeers, pornographers, and big-business wide-boys'.[92] In a later issue, Tyndall proclaimed that: '[I]f Britain were to become Jew-clean she would have no "nigger neighbours" to worry about ... It is the Jews who are our misfortune: T-h-e J-e-w-s. Do you hear me? THE JEWS!'[93] Confronted with these quotes over thirty years later, Tyndall conceded only that his remarks were, 'too much of a generalisation ... that's not the way I would put it now.'[94] Contemporaneously, however, *Spearhead* did not mince its words:

> With the numbers of these murdering asocials and perverts on the increase, as a direct result of our sick democratic society, there will be an unanswerable case, when the day for the great clean-up comes, to implement the final solution against these sub-human elements by means of the gas chamber system.[95]

Tyndall appointed Martin Webster who left the NSM with him as *Spearhead*'s assistant editor. Webster spelled out his own hard-line views unequivocally in an article for *The National Socialist* titled 'Why I am a Nazi'. Webster authored *Spearhead*'s 'trouble-shooting' column as well as funding its first three issues.[96] *Spearhead* provided Tyndall with a financial lifeline. GBM activists were expected to buy a copy, 'which gave him a basic minimum wage for the time being,' noted Terry Cooper, a young militant who had flirted with the GBM before throwing his lot in with the NSM instead. Tyndall's 'meagre revenues' were boosted by *Spearhead* sales drives, observed Cooper for whom Tyndall resembled 'a life-sized replica of Mosley'. Tyndall never assisted his activists, Cooper opined, 'and I never saw him once at any of the protest meetings,' most which failed to materialise leaving members to repair to the nearest pub.[97] For Cooper, Tyndall was on a quasi-religious mission:

> As far as he was concerned he was in exactly the same position as Moses with the Israelites, Mohammed on the Hijra, or Joseph Smith and his Mormons on their way to Salt Lake City; he had received a divine mission and was leading his faithful across a temporary desert, in preparation for the day when he would become the leader of a mighty party, with Mosley as his deity.[98]

Whilst Tyndall would not have appreciated Cooper's mockery, his writings in *Spearhead* mirrored Cooper's essential point. *Spearhead*, as Tyndall noted, slowly 'extended the influence of my ideas beyond the tiny circle of my immediate friends and colleagues.'[99] He later credited *Spearhead*, with only some exaggeration, with fostering the 'climate of opinion' within the extreme right that made possible the foundation of the NF in 1966.[100]

The GBM initially operated from 39 Eckstein Road, Battersea, the home of activist Daniel Bartram who had left the NSM with Tyndall. In September 1964, the GBM relocated to Winchmore Hill, north London, where another supporter, Maude Coggins, allowed Tyndall to use a room in her house.[101] GBM activists also favoured *The Phoenix* pub in Victoria for their 'National Forum' discussion group, booked surreptitiously as the 'Westminster Wine Club'.[102] In February 1965, the GBM fraudulently obtained the lease of the commercial premises at 106 Norwood High Street for Tyndall's two business ventures: 'Viking Books', which sold Nazi literature; and 'Albion Press', which published *Spearhead*. The building also doubled as the party headquarters. Tyndall lived upstairs. The premises became a magnet for demonstrations, fights and the late-night singing of Nazi songs to the horror of local traders, residents and indeed the owner who applied to the courts to prevent the GBM using the building for political purposes.[103] Facing eviction, Tyndall appealed to Mrs Leese, acknowledging that although she had always reposed her faith in Jordan, this had yielded little by way of 'practical results' and that political activity at Princedale Road had 'completely ceased'. That being the case, Tyndall argued, she should make a gift of the building to the GBM.[104] Rebuffed by Leese's widow, in July 1966, Tyndall and his colleagues moved to new premises in Tulse Hill, acquired with assistance from Gordon Brown, a wealthy supporter who subsidised the purchase.[105] Tyndall's 'Nationalist Centre' served as a venue for members of 'kindred patriotic groups' to socialise with GBM activists and to build up a rapport with them. The Nationalist Centre gave the GBM a secure base of operations. It also enhanced Tyndall's standing within the milieu.[106]

Tyndall envisaged the GBM as a 'stop-gap measure' designed to keep his small band of followers politically active whilst they worked for their return to the 'mainstream' extreme right, which was beginning to show signs of realignment. It gained 138 members and lasted a mere four years. It entered public consciousness with its first public foray in July 1964 when Webster physically assaulted Jomo Kenyatta, Kenya's prime minister, as he left his hotel to attend the Commonwealth Prime Ministers conference. Tyndall heckled Kenyatta through a megaphone from across the street. Webster claimed he had only intended to give Kenyatta a leaflet but confessed to police 'when I saw the black bastard I had to hit him'. Webster was jailed for two months. Tyndall was fined £25.[107] The assault reverberated internationally.[108] It also earned the GBM £400, a fee Webster had negotiated with a news agency for getting the 'scoop' on the story. Webster had become disillusioned with

Tyndall's 'lack of flair', however, and temporarily withdrew from politics, opening the 'Yeoman Bookshop' in St Albans, Hertfordshire.[109]

Violence enveloped subsequent GBM activities. One meeting in Kerbela Street, Bethnal Green, on 4 October 1964, ended amidst considerable disorder and twenty-two arrests as GBM activists fought with anti-fascist activists from the 62 Group.[110] In the following August, Tyndall was working in his office when six shots were fired into the building, one of the bullets narrowly missing him, another grazing a portrait of Hitler that graced the mantelpiece.[111] 'Living on my own as well as working in the building in question, I decided to acquire a firearm for my future protection,' Tyndall later recorded of a decision that would subsequently send him to jail.[112] The GBM continued to be embroiled in violent disorder with anti-fascists. Its second public foray, to Ridley Road, Dalston, led to seventeen arrests with further violence later that afternoon as anti-fascists 'ambushed' Tyndall and his men when they returned to their headquarters.[113] Relishing the opportunity for further confrontation, on 22 November the GBM provided an unofficial 'body of helpers' to steward an Anglo-Rhodesian Society meeting, 'at which there is a possibility of trouble from left-wing elements.'[114]

Tyndall's development of a more 'secular' form of politics compared to the 'esoteric' and religious vision of a pan-Aryan Nazism Jordan was cultivating was becoming increasingly apparent.[115] Noting this shift, American journalist George Thayer observed what he regarded as Tyndall's 'dual personality' which

> on the one side are the traits of the scar-faced Nazi, with all that that entails, and on the other side of his personality are the characteristics of John Bull – proud of his Britishness and fiercely patriotic in his own way.[116]

Tyndall's own model for remoulding National Socialism along 'British' lines was the 'Britain First' stance of Sir Oswald Mosley during the inter-war period. Indeed, the chosen name for his new *groupuscule* consciously evoked Mosley's seminal work *The Greater Britain* (1932). It was on these grounds that Tyndall explicitly appealed to former BUF activists 'who probably brought their sons up in the right way' and who 'will now be in the age group we wish to recruit.'[117] Tyndall's political vision, a mélange of Anglo-Saxon racial supremacy, imperialism and Nazism, might have rejected Mosley's pan-European philosophy but it had espoused its own equally grandiose confederation. Tyndall advocated a 'British imperium' of white dominions based upon 'a vast world-wide community of British blood' that would be forged into 'a *volksgemeinschaft* of the Anglo-Saxons – within an Anglo-Saxon "Reich"' thereby forming a rival power bloc to Russia and the United States.[118]

Whilst Tyndall passed caustic commentary upon Mosley's post-war pretence that he had never been anti-Semitic (Chapter 2), his own brand of conspiratorial anti-Semitism clearly owed its intellectual debt to Arnold Leese. That said, Tyndall tempered his admiration with the recognition that Leese tended to 'over-state' his case 'at times, to the point of absurdity.' By way of example, Tyndall highlighted Leese's insistence that Chinese communism was 'Jewish' because 'Jews were behind the opium trade which was one of the factors giving rise to the revolutionary conditions in China which led to the Maoist victory in 1949!'[119] Tyndall was perhaps being wise after the fact. During the 1960s, he was photographed in full paramilitary regalia, replete with swastika armband, in front of a portrait of Leese. For over twenty years, he openly sold Leese's books.[120] *Spearhead* itself was a magnet for ageing IFL activists.[121]

Tyndall continued to be engaged in violent activity. Following a *Spearhead* sales drive on 19 March 1966, Tyndall and seven activists were arrested in Ladbroke Grove after the lorry in which they were travelling was stopped and searched. Police uncovered an array of offensive weapons including thirty wooden coshes and six metal bars. Tyndall pleaded self-defence but was refused bail and remanded in custody on the advice of the police who saw his detention as a means of lowering the political temperature.[122] He was fined £20.[123] Tyndall was back in court on 27 October. Having illegally acquired a gun two years earlier, Tyndall was convicted of possessing a firearm without a certificate and sentenced to two three-month terms of imprisonment to run concurrently. He appealed. Much to his consternation, however, the Inner London Sessions Appeals Committee doubled Tyndall's sentence, commenting that:

> he was very lucky not to have been charged with being in possession of a firearm with intent to endanger life. These cases of having firearms are always serious and one cannot help remembering what happened in Germany when the Nazis came to power.[124]

National Front

When the BNP and LEL merged with the RPS and several other anti-immigration groups in December 1966 to form the National Front (Chapter 3), they excluded Tyndall from the union. His firearms conviction projected precisely the image its founders wished to avoid. A.K. Chesterton, its founding chairman, regarded Tyndall's notoriety as a serious 'stumbling block' to his admission to the nascent party. Indeed, as Chesterton noted to a colleague, 'if we were to become associated with him we should do great damage to our own image.'[125] Whilst the aura of violence that clung to Tyndall meant that the NF held him at arms-length, Chesterton was personally more sympathetic to Tyndall than this rebuff suggested. Only three years earlier Chesterton had written to Tyndall lamenting his jail sentence in 1962 as a 'monstrous miscarriage of justice' whilst noting that 'I am afraid that the cold feet of my lawyers rather impeded my attempt to help.'[126]

Tyndall had been at the forefront of calls for 'nationalist' unity as the disparate extreme right firmament began to cohere during summer 1966. His essay 'Where is the Right?' in the July issue of *Spearhead* was widely read.[127] Not everyone appreciated his intervention, however. Chesterton damned the article in *Candour*, occasioning a flurry of correspondence between the two men. Tyndall remonstrated with Chesterton for publicly denigrating his efforts. Chesterton mocked the pomposity of Tyndall's epistle, which argued that the divisive behaviour of the 'right' was letting the country down. Tyndall's railing against 'factionalism' was, to Chesterton, akin to 'Satan rebuking Sin'.[128]

The correspondence continued into the autumn but Tyndall failed to convince Chesterton that anything positive would come from collaborating with him.[129] Tyndall's greatest mistake, admonished Chesterton, was to have 'publicly linked yourself with the putrescent Nazi corpse, to my own great regret as I had not hitherto suspected you of such unsoundness of judgement.' Chesterton was at pains to emphasise that he harboured no personal antipathy towards Tyndall, intimating that his exclusion from the merger was not necessarily permanent as 'these things can to a certain extent be lived down, although perhaps never completely as your own reference to my pre-war Mosley activities helps to demonstrate.'[130] The speed with which Chesterton chose to forgive and forget was to be rather quicker than expected, however.

Bean was more sympathetic, though he believed that Tyndall should wait on the 'sidelines' until a suitable time had elapsed though his objections appeared tactical rather than ideological.[131] His collusion with Tyndall led to the resignation of the BNP Southall leader, Ron Cuddon who departed decrying that 'a neo-Nazi plot was afoot'.[132] Cuddon's suspicions were correct. Shortly after his release from prison, Tyndall had reassured William Pierce, editor of *National Socialist World*: 'Our faction – the National Socialist faction – will have the key strategic advantage and will therefore put us in a position to thwart any moves towards a takeover by liberal elements.' He conceded, however, that:

> To be frank, I do not believe that a movement with an open Nazi label has a hope of winning national power either in Britain or the UK in the foreseeable future. I have therefore sought to modify the form of our programme though not of course the essence of our ideology.[133]

This pragmatism was similarly evident in a letter Tyndall wrote during the same period to NSM leader Colin Jordan as he languished in Exeter jail. Characterising their breach four years earlier as a 'plain straightforward political disagreement', Tyndall added the following caveat:

> I stress the word 'political' rather than 'ideological', and hope that you will appreciate the difference. My sentiments have remained where they always were, but practical experience – allied with sober reflection – has convinced me that things in this country and in this era must be done in a very different way from that which we adopted before together.[134]

Tyndall's strategy of sublimating ideological essentials successfully 'closed the gap' between the national socialist and racial nationalist factions, opening the possibility of unification. Conceding that he 'may have to take a step down in rank' to help facilitate unification, Tyndall noted that he intended to concentrate on publishing. He recognised, however, that:

> the possession of these resources, and of the vital premises, will give our faction – the NS faction – the key strategic advantage in any merger, and will therefore put us in a position to thwart any moves towards a take-over by any liberal elements. Our strategy is to use the moderate elements, to work behind them for as long as is necessary, but to effectively control them.[135]

Tyndall could put this plan into action because he was quick to perceive a crucial flaw in the fledgling NF. It had been formed without a 'unanimous concept of what sort of movement it was intended to be' beyond a shared racial nationalist ideology and an imperative to rally people to the banner of 'patriotic resistance'. There was 'no strategy but only a set of principles and a desire for action – any action.'[136] Tyndall suffered no such lack of clarity, however. He clearly perceived that this new entity could become a 'revolutionary' force for the nation's racial rebirth. Committed GBM cadres thus insinuated themselves, alongside BNP activists, into every key NF post available, all with the knowledge and tacit approval of its chairman A.K. Chesterton himself.[137] When one former LEL activist complained, Chesterton told him bluntly that, 'those who had already joined had done more work for the cause in a few weeks than he had done in years.'[138]

Waiting on the margins, Tyndall also tempered his ideological outpourings. He reframed them in such a way as to impress figures like Chesterton who, despite his earlier reticence, had become increasingly amenable to Tyndall's own inclusion in the NF. Tyndall's pamphlet *Six Principles of British Nationalism* (1967), which exuded the 'Britain First' fascism to which he had earlier adhered, particularly impressed Chesterton. Tyndall's aspiration in writing it was to provide an ideological focal point for the extreme right to cohere around, 'even if they may differ over small details'. Tyndall assailed the 'madness' of 'liberalism and internationalism' that had impoverished the political, economic and moral health of the nation. Britain's political class, possessed of a 'will to die', had plunged the nation into the 'darkest crisis'. His panacea was a 'dynamic new political faith' – a resurgent British Nationalism – which rejected the 'fairyland' of international 'interdependence' that had transformed Britain into 'a second class colony of the Dollar Empire' and in doing so would create a 'Greater Britain'. Through strong 'national' government and economy, freed from the trammels of 'International Finance', Britain would harness the material might of the Commonwealth to ensure the British peoples, including their kith and kin in Africa, 'a glorious future' which would enshrine their racial preservation at its heart. It highlighted how little Tyndall had changed from his fundamental desire for an 'Anglo-Saxon "Reich"'.[139]

Though *Six Principles* raised Tyndall's profile within the extreme right, he remained excluded from the NF. However, in furtherance of the strategy he had outlined to Pierce, Tyndall disbanded his GBM in September 1967, pledging *Spearhead*'s 'whole hearted support' to the nascent NF.[140] Chesterton was delighted with his decision, writing to Tyndall from South Africa on 29 October that, subject to the approval of Andrew Fountaine, the deputy chairman, 'I am happy to regard you as a fully-fledged member of the National Front and on my return in the Spring I will ensure that you take your rightful place in the leadership.'[141] Fountaine's consent was not forthcoming, however. Therefore, whilst GBM activists quietly joined the NF, Tyndall was prevented from doing so. The party did allow him to attend its first AGM, however. Publicly, John Bean commended Tyndall and applauded his 'utmost selflessness' in not seeking a position for himself.[142] Bean later credited Tyndall with playing a 'significant' role in the formation of the NF.[143]

Bean himself played a largely unsung role in both the ideological trajectory of the NF and in Tyndall's own personal development. He made a 'major contribution' to the development of immigration and race as a 'central plank' because of his BNP activism. 'He more than anyone at that time, perceived the importance of this issue in the coming struggle,' noted *Spearhead*. Bean also played an important role in developing the more esoteric aspects of extreme right-wing *völkisch* ideology, whilst his ability to combine this with 'populist' racial campaigns had a 'great influence' upon Tyndall. Indeed, Bean's strategy of emphasising the 'bread-and-butter' ramifications of immigration served as 'an example of the technique of popular propaganda' that became central to NF racial politicking.[144]

Fountaine, who had collaborated closely with Bean for decades, proved less forgiving of Tyndall's past misdemeanours and remained implacably opposed to his admission. Tyndall contributed an article to *Combat* following the merger. Fountaine ordered local branches not to sell the offending issue. Most ignored the injunction.[145] Chesterton meanwhile was determined to admit Tyndall to membership over and above Fountaine's objections and indeed those of two other Directorate members, Gerald Kemp and Rodney Legg, a former League activist who worked for the *Basildon Standard*. Chesterton presented them with an ultimatum. 'It was the one thing I was prepared to make a stand on,' remembered Legg. Chesterton 'stood at the door, wearing a dirty raincoat, and demanded we approved his actions. Andrew walked out and Gerald Kemp and I followed him.'[146] Such was the odium in which some extreme right activists held Tyndall that Chesterton's determination to admit him cost the NF £1,500 in lost donations and membership dues.[147] It also cost the BNP Ron Cuddon their Southall organiser who, after being persuaded to re-join the party, resigned again, together with half his branch and the party's national youth leader.[148]

Tyndall was not overwhelmingly impressed with the calibre of many of those who had joined the NF. 'Nothing is more depressing than meeting, as one often does these days, people whose outlook starts and finishes with an embittered sourness towards immigrants. No serious movement in politics can ever function on a sentiment such as this,' he lamented.[149] Seeking to transform racist recruits into racial revolutionaries, Tyndall began running 'Leadership Training Seminars' for NF branch officers and group organisers at his Nationalist Centre, teaching them the rudiments of public speaking, organisation and propaganda. Such activities became integral. By February 1969, the NF was subsidising three-quarters of the running costs of the Nationalist Centre, which 'is in constant use by the NF'.[150] Forty local organisers attended another course Tyndall organised later that year.[151] Through *Combat*, Tyndall also offered packets of British, South African, Rhodesian and American right-wing literature during this period. This attracted the attention of the Director of Public Prosecutions, though ultimately insufficient evidence of widespread distribution existed to prosecute.[152] Tyndall also began pushing for larger NF set pieces including a public meeting in Porchester Hall. The party's National Directorate worried it could provoke violence but Tyndall was adamant that 'it is a bad thing for us to have our decisions influenced by the violent actions of aliens and Jews.'[153]

In the event, the meeting was cancelled but Tyndall was making his mark upon the party. At the NF AGM on 13 September 1969, Tyndall and Webster were both awarded 'badges of honour' by Chesterton as reward for their activism.[154] Chesterton desired Tyndall be co-opted onto the National Directorate asking de Bounevialle to propose it at the next meeting because he 'has done an immense amount of work for the NF since its formation and done it quite selflessly, not making a claim for any position.' As Chesterton was aware, however, 'there is, I know, considerable prejudice against him but I am sure that his promotion to a recognised status would have far more advantages than disadvantages.'[155] Tyndall was duly elected.[156] With Chesterton recuperating in South Africa for the winter and his deputy, Aidan Mackey, likewise unwell, Tyndall was given a 'supervisory role over the movement, being responsible for its cohesion and discipline, reporting direct to me' from January to April 1970.[157]

Though Chesterton was keen to distance the NF from crude anti-Semitism, racism and Nazism this proved hard to enforce, particularly where Tyndall was concerned. Indeed, Tyndall maintained an array of openly Nazi and racist contacts, especially abroad. Following the split with Jordan and his failure to secure Rockwell's backing, Tyndall had developed a close political relationship with Dr Edward Fields, editor of *The Thunderbolt*, the vehemently racist and anti-Semitic mouthpiece of the National States Rights Party (NSRP), an organisation that 'consistently and emphatically' advocated a policy of violence in support of racial segregation. Fields viewed Rockwell as a 'scoundrel' and a 'publicity seeker' and, noted the FBI, 'had no use for him'.[158] Tyndall had been acquainted with the NSRP since 1961 when several of its activists attended the first BNP international gathering. The NSRP actively encouraged its activists to contact the British extreme right,[159] and from February 1965 onwards, *Spearhead* began advertising *Thunderbolt* to its readership in an effort to forge an alternate Anglo-American alliance to Jordan's WUNS network.[160] The NSRP took an active interest in British politics stating that England, 'a land that was all white only a few years ago,' was now the subject of 'a peaceful invasion by negro immigrants' which 'is about to destroy the ancestral home of so many of our readers.' It concluded with the fervent exhortation, 'that our brothers in England will soon rise up and drive these modern day Moors from their country.'[161]

Tyndall played a pivotal role in this transatlantic network. Following the assassination of civil rights leader Dr Martin Luther King Jr on 4 April 1968, *Spearhead* suggested that 'in all probability King was killed by the very people who had promoted him in the Civil Rights movement.'[162] The propagation of crude conspiracy theories went hand-in-hand with more practical measures to assist King's actual killer, James Earl Ray, who read *The Thunderbolt*.[163] Fields organised a 'Patriot Legal Fund' to assist Ray who was then fighting extradition from London, where he had fled to following the killing. Fields offered to defend Ray, free of charge, and pay all his legal costs. Fields made the offer to Ray through Tyndall, the British representative of the Fund.[164] Ray subsequently appointed Jesse B. Stoner, the NSRP chairman (and an old contact of Arnold Leese) as his defence attorney. In December 1969, Stoner visited a range of right-wing extremists throughout Europe, purportedly on behalf of the killer, though the FBI singled out his contact with 'NF officials' for special mention.[165]

Tyndall retained his links with both men. Fields traversed the Atlantic to meet with the NF in 1975.[166] Stoner followed suit in the next year.[167] Stoner was belatedly jailed for ten years in 1980 for his role in the 1958 bombing of the Bethel Baptist Church in Birmingham, Alabama. Police suspected him of involvement in many more such acts of racist terrorism.[168] Indeed, Herbert Jenkins, the Atlanta, Georgia, police chief had remarked in 1964 that Stoner has 'probably been involved in more bombings than any one individual in the South ... Invariably the bastard is in the general area when a bomb goes off.'[169]

Tyndall also continued corresponding with openly Hitlerite figures in Europe too, including Savitri Devi who had previously detected in Tyndall a 'religious approach' to National Socialism, which she lamented she saw in too few others.[170] Tyndall's contact with Savitri Devi had survived the split with Jordan and, in September 1968, he journeyed to Munich to meet her – she was banned from Britain – and several other Nazi sympathisers including Mosley's friend Hans-Ulrich Rudel and his wife Uschi. Thereafter, Tyndall travelled with Savitri Devi and others to the Austrian border for a meeting with Fred Borth, leader of Legion Europa, recently expelled from Jean Thiriart's Jeune Europe network for his support for the separatist terror campaign raging in the South Tyrol. Police were seeking him in this regard too.[171]

Chairman

For Tyndall, the 'Swinging Sixties' were a catastrophe: a miserable, low decade in which British and European civilisation reached 'rock bottom' politically, morally and physically, as they retreated before communism. 'The Western nations seem to be in the grip of a kind of mass madness,' *Spearhead* recorded:

> One by one, the bastions of ordered society have been allowed to crumble. Everywhere the fumes of decadence pollute the air. In the Western World in general, and in Britain in particular, it is going to require nothing less than a revolution to bring things to order: a revolution in our political structure; a revolution in the hearts and minds of men. As we enter the seventies, let us not deceive ourselves that anything less than this will do. And let us dedicate ourselves with revolutionary zeal to the task ahead.[172]

The dawn of a new decade provided a conjunction of personal and political opportunity that would enable Tyndall to combine his own 'revolutionary zeal' for racial purification with the leadership of what would soon become a mass political movement. Tyndall rejected the equation of 'racialism' with Nazism. 'If racialism has on occasions been applied in a brutal way,' he retorted, 'that is the fault of individual racialists and not of racialism as such.' Though he praised the 'humane' application of racialist principles in apartheid South Africa, Tyndall's preferred solution remained the only one to preserve racial homogeneity: repatriation.[173]

Tyndall perceived that Enoch Powell's speech in 1968 had fuelled public appetite for such policies. Powell's speech also reinforced his own belief in the inevitability of 'race war' whilst highlighting that 'we may as well start preparing ourselves for an era of racial strife that will make Little Rock and Sharpeville look like mild skirmishes after closing time.'[174] More soberly, Tyndall reflected upon the potential political gains occasioned by Powell's transformation of the immigration debate. 'The workers will never go Tory despite their respect for Powell,' Tyndall argued. He also recognised, however, that Labour's condemnation of Powell put them at odds with a large swathe of working-class voters.[175] Tyndall observed further potential for NF growth on the Right of British politics following the election of Edward Heath as prime minister in June 1970, which also closed the door on Powell returning to front-bench politics. 'There will not be a successful Powellite revolution in the Tory Party in the foreseeable future,' Tyndall asserted. The frustration of Powell's political promise would simply accelerate the 'natural downward evolution of old guard politics'.[176] Tyndall feared, however, that Powell himself would become 'a source of monumental disappointment and disillusionment'.[177] And for the NF, so he was.

Whilst Tyndall surveyed the increasingly favourable political conditions for the NF, his own personal prospects also brightened following Chesterton's resignation as party chair in November 1970. Whilst the intriguing against his political mentor appalled Tyndall, he was more than happy to conspire to usurp Chesterton's successor. John O'Brien, the NF office manager and *Candour*'s business manager was a relatively recent convert to racial nationalism. A Shropshire fruit farmer, O'Brien had left the Conservative Party in 1968, launching his own British Defence League to campaign to elect Enoch Powell as prime minister.[178] He had then joined Colin Jordan's British Movement.[179] O'Brien was the best man for the job of NF chairman 'in as far as he was the only one willing to accept it,' Chesterton observed sardonically.[180] Indeed, it was much to his own 'surprise and consternation', that O'Brien was elected chairman at an NF Emergency General Meeting. He only reluctantly accepted what 'seems to me just about the most thankless task in the United Kingdom.' Indeed, O'Brien privately accepted that he had 'insufficient contact with the Movement at large to present a figure of credibility' and was a compromise candidate elected to ensure the party's short-term stability.[181]

A seasoned political operator like Tyndall would have no problem despatching the new incumbent. O'Brien's inability to arrest the electoral decline of the NF in towns like Huddersfield, West Yorkshire, where it had shown early promise, favoured Tyndall.[182] O'Brien's efforts to govern the NF itself had been hamstrung by 'an excess of reaction against personal rule' in the wake of the coup against Chesterton's own autocratic style.[183] The party adopted a new constitution in 1971 that enabled would-be leaders to appeal directly to the membership for election to the party's Directorate at the AGM rather than the NF chairman appointing them. This new selection process led to 'a particularly faction-ridden and eccentric Directorate … a peculiar amalgam of the talented, the vastly over-promoted, and the plain cranky,' recalled O'Brien.[184] O'Brien's move towards collective leadership dismayed Tyndall. He began conspiring to remove him not least because he believed that with the exception of himself – Tyndall harboured a self-belief in himself as a man of destiny every bit as strong as that which had afflicted Mosley – the NF lacked 'strong-minded individuals' equipped with a 'philosophy for a long struggle'.[185]

Elevated by the Directorate as O'Brien's deputy, Tyndall was ideally situated to execute his plan. In the following year, Tyndall was appointed chairman of the Directorate's Policy Department, which gave him considerable power to shape the future ideological direction of the NF, and cemented his personal position further. Importantly, Tyndall had also retained personal control of *Spearhead*, which he had been unwilling to turn over to the party because, he later recalled, 'I have always been wary that the NF might get into the wrong hands and be diverted from the original aims of its founders.'[186] *Spearhead*, combined with his new position, gave Tyndall an unprecedented opportunity to proselytise his hard-line beliefs to every party member. 'Every branch should possess a good range of *Spearhead* back issues,' Tyndall instructed, 'for the expositions of policy in the magazines never dates and are therefore important educational aids.'[187] Tyndall's effort to develop the party's ideological base through pamphlets such as *The Case for Economic Nationalism* (1972), which demanded economic autarky, remained rooted in articles like '"Laissez Faire" or National Socialism?', which he had penned for the inaugural issues of *Spearhead*, however.[188]

Flaunting his credentials as a racial revolutionary, Tyndall embraced the appellation 'extremist' as a badge of honour. 'What is an extremist?' he asked rhetorically:

> Whatever he may have been in the past, in our times he is the man who poses a serious challenge to the internationalist liberal establishment – the power wielders. If he is not labelled an extremist, one can usually reckon that he poses no such challenge. I think therefore that today any sincere patriot should regard the "extremist" tag as it is applied by those power-wielders as a recommendation rather than the reverse.[189]

Increasingly perturbed by such sentiment, O'Brien despaired of 'a small caucus' within the party 'attracted by the trappings and ideologies of foreign nationalisms from the past. These persons see Britain's future best served by her becoming a rigidly administered, authoritarian police state.' It disturbed O'Brien that leading activists 'were going over to Germany, seeing ex-Nazis and ex-members of the SS and taking part in reunions.' His concerns were compounded by receipt of the October 1971 issue of *Das Reich*, a German Nazi magazine, which boasted of its contacts with Tyndall whom it referred to as the NF 'Führer' – even though O'Brien was chairman.[190]

Unwilling to play the role of 'docile puppet', O'Brien tried and failed to marginalise Tyndall and Webster. He was no match for their experience of infighting and intrigue.[191] Indeed, on 3 June 1972, Tyndall drove up to Leicestershire for an NF march and meeting after which he met with Colin Jordan, the BM leader. 'He was very amiable,' Jordan recalled, 'and sounded me out on the possibility of my joining the NF.' Jordan was 'non-committal' and it soon became evident that Tyndall was looking for information that he could use to damage O'Brien based on his past association with Jordan.[192] Tyndall judged O'Brien's tenure as party chairman to have been an 'absolute disaster'. 'In less than two years he had reduced the NF to a divided, demoralised and dispirited shambles, near to financial bankruptcy,' Tyndall lamented.[193]

The Ugandan Asians

Tyndall became the NF's third chairman in July 1972. Regarding the party leadership as a poisoned chalice, A.K. Chesterton offered his former protégé the following embittered advice:

> He will find that the organisation he has taken over can only be run on a tight rein, and that every time the curb is used the atmosphere around him will become toxic with the resentment of essentially small people with hugely inflated egos. As two men can now attest, it is not a pleasant job.[194]

When Tyndall took over as chairman, NF membership had slumped to below 2,000, he later claimed. However, over the next two years, Tyndall found himself in control of a rapidly growing mass movement, its membership quadrupling.[195] This was largely due to happenstance rather than any innate genius for leadership on Tyndall's part. Public concerns about 'coloured' immigration, which never dropped below 70 per cent between 1964 and 1979, reached their zenith in 1970 at 77 per cent shortly before the passage of the Immigration Act (1971) to stop 'large-scale permanent immigration'.[196]

Despite Tyndall's dismissal of such immigration 'control' as largely meaningless – he believed that the nation still faced 'racial catastrophe' because of high immigrant birth rates – the Immigration Act served to undercut the NF's fragile electoral appeal.[197] Its fortunes had changed literally overnight, however. On 7 August 1972, the Ugandan dictator Idi Amin gave the 50,000-strong Asian populace, whom he characterised as 'bloodsuckers' and accused of 'milking Uganda's money', ninety days to leave the country as part of his intention to 'Africanize' his country's economy. Thirty thousand of these expellees had British passports. Ironically, Amin espoused a similarly anti-Semitic world-view to Tyndall, regularly quoting from *The Protocols of the Elders of Zion*. He had also written to UN Secretary-General Kurt Waldheim claiming that: 'Hitler was right about the Jews, because the Israelis are not working in the interest of the people of the world, and that is why they burned the Israelis alive with gas in the soil of Germany.'[198] His actions even engendered a certain respect amongst some NF activists. 'What we need in this country is a white Amin,' one member told the press.[199]

The subsequent entry of approximately 27,000 Ugandan Asians into Britain – which occurred before the 1971 Immigration Act entered the statute books on 1 January 1973 – occasioned widespread dissatisfaction with Conservative Prime Minister Edward Heath. Increasingly, Heath was perceived not simply as 'liberal' but as dangerously weak on the issue of immigration. The NF were the political beneficiaries, experiencing a surge in popular support. Idi Amin 'was the best recruiting officer the NF ever had,' commented *Guardian* journalist Martin Walker.[200] The advent of the 'Ugandan Asians' was also fortuitous for Tyndall since it enabled him to quickly gloss over his schism with O'Brien, the resignation of half the Directorate, and a series of disappointing local election results.[201]

The NF mobilised quickly to take advantage of this 'conspiracy' to 'flood Britain'. Nationwide demonstrations to 'Stop the Asian Invasion' were hastily arranged, beginning with a picket of Downing Street on 18 August. Tyndall delivering a petition to the 'Whitehall traitors' in Number 10 before leading a 200-strong march to the Ugandan Embassy to support Joy Page of the Immigration Control Association. The NF also mobilised behind the Smithfield meat porters, previously prominent in their support for Powell, whose opposition to the 'Asian Invasion' begat marches on both the Home Office and the respective headquarters of the Labour and Conservative parties. New arrivals at Heathrow airport were barracked by three 300 NF activists chanting: 'If they're Black – Send them Back' whilst scuffling with airport security, resulting in ten arrests. The widespread publicity they received was marred, however, by the 'uninvited intrusion' of Colin Jordan, who both the *Daily Mail* and the *Daily Mirror* reported as being 'leader of the National Front'. Webster subsequently wrote to Jordan warning him that he might face 'elements I cannot control', if he continued trying to hijack NF activities.[202]

The NF staged similar demonstrations weekly at Manchester airport too.[203] The NF *Urgent Activities Bulletin* instructed activists to view the 'Keep the Asians Out' campaign as an 'Election Campaign' and to mobilise all possible resources behind it:

> A time of great opportunity has come upon our movement.... The Government, Press and the Left Wing is reeling with the shock of the reaction against the Asian Invasion which we to a large extent have organised. Large numbers of people are frightened and are looking to us for leadership. We must not let them down.[204]

In 1972–1973, the NF disseminated an estimated four million leaflets – most attacking the Ugandan Asians titled 'The Fight for Survival Is On'.[205] The campaign brought the NF a great deal of popular support. 'During the last month or so, the NF has experienced the most rapid growth in its five year history', recorded *Spearhead*, which noted that after 'quiet but unspectacular progress' recruitment 'has suddenly started to shoot ahead at a tremendous pace'.[206] *Searchlight*, the anti-fascist magazine, claimed NF membership peaked at 17,500 during the course of the year.[207] To cope with the burden placed on the NF by this influx of new members, Tyndall sought to develop the administrative capabilities of the party. He launched a development fund to raise £20,000 which he anticipated would allow him to hire full-time regional organisers for the South, the Midlands and the North of England, as well as an elections officer and two secretarial staff, who would relieve pressure on a beleaguered Webster who, as National Activities organiser, risked being 'overloaded' by the party's rapid expansion.[208]

The campaign paid electoral dividends. In May 1973, Webster, standing in a parliamentary by-election in West Bromwich, polled 4,789 votes (16.1 per cent), saving his deposit in the process, and coming third behind the Conservative candidate David Bell whose vote collapsed by 19.4 per cent. Enoch Powell's public refusal to endorse Bell because his views on immigration and the EEC had a 'malign effect' upon his vote, argues his biographer. Webster claimed that this amounted to a direct endorsement of his candidature. With Webster finishing less than 3,000 votes behind Bell, other West Midlands Conservatives 'were quick to spot the portents for the next general election'.[209] But Webster had also worked the constituency assiduously. 'For the NF, West Bromwich was a saturation attack', notes Walker. 'It was the NF's most professional campaign'.[210] In local and national elections on 7 June, the NF vote surged in Leicestershire, Blackburn and West London, all areas associated with the arrival of the Ugandan Asians. The results were encouraging elsewhere too.[211]

The Monday Club

Whilst the Ugandan Asians had facilitated a rapid growth in NF support, the party was still unable to claim 'ownership' of the immigration issue which was still held by the Conservatives. However, many Conservatives had become disillusioned with their party's commitment to tackling immigration personified by Enoch Powell who openly criticised his party's record and, by 1974, was urging his supporters to vote Labour. Powell never countenanced supporting the NF, however. Indeed, in the following year, someone asked Powell if he felt the NF was the only party that could save Britain. 'We should not abandon democracy in the hope of finding something better in the gutter', Powell replied, much to the party's chagrin.[212]

However, for those voters who remained concerned about immigration but unconvinced that either party would satisfactorily deal with the issue 'there appeared few obvious homes for their vote'.[213] In seeking to capitalise upon this burgeoning political space, Tyndall faced a significant impediment to building further support on the Right in the form of the Monday Club (MC), a 'Radical Right' grassroots ginger group that desired to regenerate the Conservative Party and lead it back to 'true conservatism'. If the Conservative Party was untroubled by the NF which it regarded as 'too discredited to prove a real threat to us', even as it noted that 'some of our extreme right-wing members' were attracted to it, the MC was an altogether different proposition. With its respectable membership, vehement anti-immigration politicking and attacks upon the 'liberal establishment', the MC 'threatened to identify society's divisions explicitly with those of the Conservative Party.' The problem only grew after the 1970 general election when twenty-nine Club members were elected to Parliament. Six more joined shortly afterwards.[214]

The MC had been founded on 1 January 1961, its name commemorating 'Black Monday' when Harold Macmillan made his 'Winds of Change' speech. Though its initial efforts focused unsuccessfully upon forestalling the 'surrender of responsibility' in Africa, particularly in Rhodesia, the Club's founders were more generally alarmed by the 'pink miasma' they perceived enveloping Conservative policy. Increasingly defined by its campaign for 'stringent' immigration control and the repeal of the Race Relations Act, there was 'considerable' support within the MC for Enoch Powell whose 'remedies' and 'diagnosis' in this sphere they accepted wholeheartedly. Powell refused to join, however. Their advocacy of repatriation was enshrined in *Who Goes Home?* (1969), a pamphlet authored by leading activist G.K. Young, a former merchant banker and MI6 officer, who chaired the Society for Individual Freedom.[215]

Whilst Tyndall applauded the Club's anti-immigration stance, believing that it served 'a useful purpose as a rallying point for people of patriotic inclinations,' he lamented that it evinced 'no scientific understanding of the machinations of international politics', (i.e. conspiracy theory). 'We know very well that the MC has to play a careful game,' *Spearhead* observed.

> The many good friends we have among its rank-and-file and junior officials are continually pointing out to us this fact.... At least the gentlemen of the Monday Club are learning. And for those who are prepared to learn there is always hope.[216]

Where Tyndall parted company with the MC was concerning its 'internationalist' ethos. 'We cannot regard ourselves as the friends and allies of people who support, or even compromise with, internationalism, and this a large part of the leadership of the Monday has done,' he chastised. 'We are neither of the Left or the Right. We are Nationalists and we reject Internationalism.' Tyndall was also fundamentally at odds with the Club's mission to revitalise the Conservative Party, which he viewed as a defence of sectional class interest. 'The Right will always be weak so long as it is based predominantly on white collar support,' he lamented. Indeed, if the working classes and their trade unions were left to the 'educated weaklings, eunuchs and pansies' of the Labour Party, there could be no true national reawakening. Only the NF, Tyndall argued, could genuinely reconcile class divisions, and 'synthesise the best of conservatism and radicalism and unite every section of the community in the process.'[217]

'No – we are not Tories,' Tyndall proclaimed bluntly. However, if the MC could 'weed out the fakes and jettison their policies', then *Spearhead* would 'support them to the hilt'. However, in March 1971, instead of weeding out 'fakes' the MC expelled several leading members of the Sussex Monday Club including Tony Hancock and John Ormowe after the latter praised Hitler in an interview.[218] There were indications, however, that the MC's anti-immigration stance was hardening. The *Daily Telegraph* reported attempts to remove the 'moderating influence' of John Biggs-Davidson and Patrick Wall, two MPs who sat on the MC's executive, to adopt policies advocating 'compulsory repatriation'.[219] The MC chairman, George Pole, certainly recognised the NF's appeal for those on the Right: 'We don't give these people enough red meat. But the National Front must not be turned aside as of no account; they have people who are motivated by the highest ideals.'[220]

In November 1971, the MC founded a sub-committee on immigration which, it was reported, 'will follow a strongly Powellite line.'[221] This certainly appealed to NF members who flocked to its events. When the MC held a large 'Halt Immigration Now' rally at Central Hall in September 1972 at the height of the agitation surrounding the arrival of the Ugandan Asians, there were 2,000 attendees. This included 400 NF activists. The meeting passed a resolution demanding Heath immediately halt immigration, repeal of the Race Relations Act, and commence repatriation.[222] A group of MC MPs handed a petition to Downing Street following a march festooned with NF banners. 'This was the first time Conservative MPs joined what was in effect a National Front organised march through London,' crowed *Spearhead*.[223] The prime minister rejected their demands.[224] The MC was undeterred. Its 'Halt Immigration Now Campaign' was an integral part of its political strategy. As such it was to receive 'absolute top priority' and 'nothing whatever must be allowed to impede its progress,' counselled one internal report. 'It is the issue which, probably more than any other, will not merely bring support and gratitude from a great many people, but will also cause severe inroads to be made into the heretofore traditional Labour support.'[225]

Its anti-immigration agitation helped transform the MC into a national organisation with a membership of 2,000, including thirty-four MPs. However, whilst several of its branches leaned sympathetically towards the NF, the Club's leadership notably did not. Jonathan Guinness, the stepson of Sir Oswald Mosley, elected MC Chairman in June 1972, sought to dispel any association with 'an outfit as parochial, as irredeemably second-rate, as the National Front.'[226] Elements within the MC openly colluding with the NF found themselves on borrowed time. Guinness had a meeting with the Conservative Party Chairman on 14 January 1973 who raised his concerns about NF infiltration of the Club. Guinness shared these concerns but was 'somewhat reluctant' to be seen 'hounding' members out of the Club. 'The Chairman said that if anybody was to take the responsibility for removing extremists from the Monday Club then it had to be Mr. Guinness.'[227] The first shot was fired later that month when the West Middlesex MC branch was disbanded, an inevitability given its defiant public support for the NF candidate in the recent Uxbridge by-election against the official 'Heath-ite nonentity' put forward by their own party.[228] The West Middlesex branch, it was reported, disagreed with the NF only on the matter of whether to send Asians 'back by boat or in boxes'.[229]

Increasingly bitter internal divisions within the MC regarding immigration (and to a lesser extent economic philosophies), which saw the group haemorrhaging support, culminated in G.K. Young challenging Guinness for its leadership.[230] Young was regarded, even by the man who seconded his candidature, as being 'really dangerous' for the Club's future due to his 'obsession over immigration'.[231] His victory, reported *The Sunday Telegraph*, 'would mean the resignation of most of the twenty or so Tory MPs who are still Monday Club members.'[232] Young's support for compulsory repatriation also represented an ideological red line for Guinness who declared: 'If in the last resort it's a choice between a white Britain which is a police state and a multi-racial Britain that is not a police state, then I would be for a multi-racial Britain.'[233] Guinness feared that if Young won, 'it could be considered a move in the National Front direction'.[234] The NF dismissed claims of collusion, however. 'Just about the only point of agreement between Young and ourselves is compulsory repatriation,' stated Martin Webster. 'For the rest, he is a merchant banker and we are a working class organisation.'[235] Fears that the MC was moving towards the NF were magnified further during the leadership contest when it emerged that the organisation's membership lists had been vetted for NF members. They discovered only twelve names amongst 2,000 members, according to reports. Those identified 'were all perfectly harmless, obscure members,' stated Guinness. 'If they were "sleepers", they were still asleep.'[236]

On 30 April 1973, Guinness comfortably beat Young by 625 votes to 455, though the fractious and increasingly polarised contest diminished the Club's wider salience.[237] Young promptly resigned.[238] On 15 May, Len Lambert, chair of the Essex MC was expelled, a consequence of his refusal to rescind an invitation to Tyndall who had addressed his branch on 16 March. This had generated much adverse publicity for the MC ahead of the Lincoln by-election in which Guinness had been the candidate. Tyndall mischievously revelled in the embarrassment his direct involvement caused the Conservatives. 'An altogether better impression of the Monday Club is gained by meeting its members at grass roots level than by examining the words and actions of its hierarchy,' he stated afterwards.[239] Lambert was similarly impressed. 'This was the sort of meeting which does more good than harm,' he told the press.[240] Aghast, Guinness moved to staunch the porous boundaries that existed at a grassroots level between the NF and the MC. He disbanded the entire Essex branch on 19 June, though he only won the vote by a narrow margin.[241] Amidst further attempts to unseat him, Guinness purged another fifty activists in the following month, reflecting his promise to expel, 'people who have deliberately stirred up controversy and trouble over the past year'.[242]

As faction fighting continued, Webster proclaimed that the MC 'is like a tree laden with over-ripe fruit which does not need to be picked. The defection of rank and file members of the Club into the NF is inevitable.'[243] Ironically, this 'over-ripe fruit' quickly gave Tyndall indigestion. Those who defected included John Kingsley Read, a prominent figure within the Blackburn Conservative Party who had joined the NF in October 1972, and Roy Painter, an MC activist selected to contest Tottenham South for the party who joined in July 1973. Both men would upset Tyndall's political equilibrium: Read by challenging him for the party's leadership.[244]

Whilst this interlude highlighted not so much the strength of such 'Powellite' opinion within the Conservative Party but rather the party's ability to effectively marginalise it, NF policies now lurched 'sharply' to the Left.[245] To this end, the NF sought to wean young student radicals from Trotskyist politics by establishing the NF Students Association in September 1972.[246] Through its newspaper, *Spark*, Tyndall sought to convince young readers that the real 'radicals' were those arguing for 'fundamental challenge to the basis of money power'.[247] In tandem with this, the NF stepped up its efforts to appeal to the white working class using 'race' as a wedge issue. The NF Trades Unions Association, founded in July 1974, sought to exploit racial tensions within the workplace and thereby establish a toehold within working-class organisations.[248] The catalyst was the Ulster Workers Council strike in the previous May, which the NF hoped to emulate.[249] The NF had more success on the industrial front, however, through its interventions in the already racially charged industrial disputes at Mansfield Hosiery (1973) and Imperial Typewriters (1974). For the NF, the Imperial Typewriters strike in Leicestershire was nothing less than a 'racial struggle' pitting white workers 'against the forces of communism and international capitalism which seek to destroy the British nation and which use as their tool the immigrant minorities placed by them in our midst'.[250] 'In the six months after the defeat of their allies in the Monday Club, the NF had moved not only to the Left, but towards a coherent populist programme. It was a key change', argued Walker.[251]

'March and grow'

Despite some encouraging electoral results, including Webster's vote in West Bromwich, Tyndall demurred from fighting further parliamentary by-elections. The NF contested only one of the following seven by-elections. The institution of a 'National Elections Department' did little to alleviate the party's organisational weakness in this regard. Instead of building an effective electoral machine, Tyndall pursued the strategy of 'march and grow'. He denied that the strategy of marching through areas with high concentrations of ethnic minority residents amounted to a provocation, blaming the oft-resulting disorder and reputational damage the NF suffered upon political opponents and tendentious media reporting. Whilst arguing, with some truth, that marching 'was one of the very few forms by which we could manifest our presence in Britain and publicise our aims' because of local councils refusing to let public property to the NF for meetings, Tyndall was also temperamentally unsuited to electioneering. Indeed, justifying his subsequent decision to prioritise street activity over and above the mundanity of electoral activity, Tyndall claimed that door-to-door leafleting and paper sales, whilst fine, 'do not give any impression of a movement of substantial strength and, in the case of leafleting, are wholly impersonal'.[252]

Marches, on the other hand, served several important political and personal functions for Tyndall. First, the marches themselves asserted the 'right' of the NF to those localities, emphasising their symbolic control of its streets. For Tyndall – whom the journalist Martin Walker believed to be 'a subtle political psychologist' – the 'colour and pageantry' that accompanied this performative aspect of NF activism was 'as important as speeches and articles'.[253] Marches also allowed Tyndall to project political power. The intention was to impress or intimidate the local populace, depending on the ethnic composition of their audience. Internally, the marches themselves served as an important integrative mechanism through which the 'collectives of emotion' were generated between NF activists and through which they were integrated into the party.[254] What Tyndall wanted was not so much recruits who agreed with the party platform but those who would work for it 'and if necessary, to *fight* for us'.[255]

The task of implementing this street-based strategy fell to Webster, the National Activities organiser, who had famously distilled this strategy as a means through which the NF would 'kick our way into the headlines'.[256] Webster subsequently stated that he was misquoted and the actual phrase he had used was 'crashing our way into the headlines'.[257] Nevertheless, the result was the same. Whilst there 'wasn't much love lost' between Tyndall and Webster personally, politically their dynamic worked, recalled one of

Tyndall's close colleagues. Tyndall was 'the ideologue, the driving force, but Webster was the man who made it all happen.'²⁵⁸ Under his organisational impetus, teams of NF activists were soon making front page news through 'riot, mayhem, outrage' as they combined the persistent disruption of left-wing and 'progressive' meetings with high-profile stunts such as the tarring and feathering of Karl Marx's bust in Highgate Cemetery. Public figures deemed 'traitors' were also to experience 'the horrific bedlam of National Front disapproval'.²⁵⁹ Gradually, however, NF tactics evolved, as a subsequent government analysis of the group's strategy recognised:

> Since that time [the early 1970s] the NF has sought publicity not by attacking its opponents but by staging well-disciplined demonstrations and marches in areas of high immigration, designed to provoke the coloured population and the extreme left. Its aim now is to remain just within the law while encouraging its opponents to step outside it. So far the NF has always co-operated with the police over demonstrations. In this way it tries both to secure protection for its members and to present itself as a party of law and order.²⁶⁰

NF performance in the February 1974 general election only served to confirm Tyndall in his opinion regarding the ephemerality of electoral activity when weighed in the balance against his predilection for marches and demonstrations. The election, the first fought with Tyndall at the helm, cost the NF over £25,000. It fielded fifty-four candidates, largely to assuage Tyndall's desire for a party-political broadcast and thus a nationwide audience. In total, the NF polled 76,865 votes, an average of 3.2 per cent per candidate, slightly lower than that polled by ten candidates in the 1970 general election. Whilst constituency boundary changes which took place between the two elections hamper direct comparison, it was nonetheless symbolic of the extent to which the passions stirred by the Ugandan Asian had receded from the public imagination that the NF vote in Leicester slumped from 9.1 per cent in to 3.6 per cent.²⁶¹ Even in the newly created West Bromwich East constituency, Webster polled only 2,907 votes (7 per cent) compared to the 4,789 votes (16 per cent) he had achieved in the old West Bromwich seat.²⁶² If popular support was proving more transient than had perhaps been expected, and indeed appeared to be declining, the NF could take some solace from a parliamentary by-election in Newham South in May, which took place between the two general elections that year, in which its candidate polled 11.5 per cent, nearly 5 per cent more than in the general election only weeks earlier.²⁶³

The death of Kevin Gately, killed by police as they attempted to disburse anti-fascists trying to close an NF meeting in Red Lion Square, London, in June 1974 overshadowed this result. Whilst Gately's death was important for the Left, it mattered to the NF too. As one leading militant later recalled, Gately's death signalled that 'the tempo was changing. Red Lion Square went down in Nationalist mythology – the election result in Newham South was forgotten.' Instead of highlighting the party's electoral advances in Leicestershire, *Spearhead* gave what some activists perceived, in retrospect, to be undue prominence to the violence. 'Despite rapid electoral progress and despite the rapidly expanding membership there was still a belief in the theory that nationalism could only triumph in a situation of major internal disorder,' the same activist lamented. 'Red Lion Square was the only real example that theorists could use at this stage, and so it was looked back on with considerable nostalgia.'²⁶⁴ This was hardly surprising. Elections, demonstrations and violence during summer 1974 had made the NF a 'household name ... canvassers reported that voters no longer looked blank when asked if they would vote for the NF. The movement was nationally recognised.'[265] There was another surge in membership with approximately 20,000 people passing through the party that year, per one estimate.[266]

Notwithstanding his dismissive attitude towards electioneering, Tyndall nonetheless backed the party in fielding ninety candidates in the October 1974 general election. The party polled 113,843 votes with an average of 3.1 per cent per candidate, slightly lower than its percentage in February's poll. Its increase in votes, a consequence of standing more candidates, masked to an extent a downward trajectory in the party's electoral performance. Only two of its combined 144 candidates, standing in Hackney South and Shoreditch and Haringey, Tottenham, respectively, polled higher than either the 9 per cent polled by John Bean in Southall in 1964 or the 8.1 per cent polled by Sir Oswald Mosley in North Kensington in 1959.[267] The NF also failed to benefit from Enoch Powell's disillusionment with Conservative immigration policy. He had urged his supporters to vote Labour instead. Webster was unperturbed at losing ninety deposits, weighing them in the balance against the value of obtaining a second party political broadcast. 'We are laughing all the way to the bank,' he told the *Guardian*. 'Where else can you get simultaneous five minute broadcasts on the BBC and ITV for thirteen and a half grand?'[268]

The 'populist' challenge

Tyndall was also pleased with the performance. Others, however, their expectations raised and then dashed, not so much. Simmering tensions between the national socialists who led the party and the 'racial populist' faction who desired to, began to boil over. This influential characterisation of split had its roots in the reporting of *Guardian* journalist Martin Walker.[269] Tyndall conspiratorially claimed Walker's articles deliberately 'promoted' his rivals.[270] For Tyndall, 'populism' meant simply the watering down of core racial nationalist principles, which was unacceptable. The ideological struggle between the two factions, which mirrored the fissure in the party highlighted by Tyndall's struggle with O'Brien, was fought out in party publications throughout the course of 1974. Pretending to value ideological plurality, Tyndall published Roy Painter's article 'Let's make Nationalism Popular' but appended his own critique dismissing it as 'claptrap, sheer unadulterated claptrap'.[271] For their part, the 'populist' clique grouped around the NF newspaper, *Britain First*, edited by Richard Lawson, disparaged Hitler, claiming 'that the Nazis were closely and specifically connected with Wall Street and other cosmopolitan banking interests'.[272]

For the 'populists', Tyndall was a liability whose presence retarded further progress, not least because photographs of him in Nazi regalia damaged the party's electoral fortunes.[273] In preparation for the impending showdown, the struggle for control of the Directorate became key over the course of the summer. Tyndall himself saw no need to be emollient, openly disparaging the principle of parliamentary democracy in *Spearhead*'s September issue, which only inflamed tensions further.[274] Tyndall's personal stock took a further tumble on 5 September with the screening of a television exposé of the NF on 'This Week', a current affairs programme, during which Tyndall's hard-line views were laid bare for an eight-million-strong primetime audience. Thus, on 21 October 1974, at the first Directorate meeting after the general election, Tyndall was voted out of office, replaced by the Blackburn NF chair, John Kingsley Read, a thirty-eight-year-old textile agent.[275] Tyndall's ouster was made easier by a 1971 constitutional change whereby the Directorate not the membership elected the chair and his deputy. Tyndall and Kingsley Read had each received ten votes. The Directorate's acting chair, Tony Reed-Herbert, a Leicestershire solicitor and former Conservative Party activist, cast the deciding vote in

Kingsley Read's favour. Tyndall again tied with Roy Painter in the vote to appoint a new deputy NF chairman. This time the vote went in his favour, though he seethed at his demotion.[276]

In a further repudiation of Tyndall's politics, the December 1974 issue of *Britain First* not only equated Fascism with Communism but also further affirmed both its complete commitment to 'democratic' nationalism and its total rejection of 'all forms of authoritarianism'.[277] Webster countered in the following issue of *Spearhead*, attacking the danger of 'OPPORTUNISM and IDEOLOGICAL PRAGMATISM', whilst warning that 'if this party is to survive, each and every member, humble or exalted, has the continuing duty to defend the Idea'.[278]

Tyndall's standing with some 'populist' NF members was such that they jeered 'Nazi, Nazi' at him during his party's own AGM held on 4 January 1975.[279] Insofar as there was any discernible difference between the two competing factions with regards to the staples of NF ideology – race and immigration – 'the crux of the dispute' hinged not upon the definition of 'nationalism' but rather on the place of 'race' within its public presentation. Speaking in favour of a resolution to expel all those of mixed race, non-European or 'coloured' ancestry, Webster upheld the principal of Britain's 'ethnic homogeneity'. Other speakers, 'closer to the mood of the meeting', were more forthright, stating 'we know that these people come from primitive people in the jungle and that these tendencies come back to them after a while'. The resolution's proposer argued 'we have to be 100% racialist in the National Front. If people who are half or quarter coloured are allowed in, it will kill everything.' Though the strength of such pronouncements indicated little cause for concern, Tyndall and Webster both feared the party was being inundated with ideologically uneducated 'populists' who could turn their party into Tory ginger-group. The 'populists' meanwhile, no less committed to the premise of racial nationalism, argued that to advance further 'Nazis' like Tyndall had to go.[280]

1976 split

Kingsley Read, the new NF chairman, was eminently more charismatic than Tyndall. Read had gained notoriety during summer 1974, after distributing 2,000 letters to Blackburn residents urging them not to sell their homes to 'coloured immigrants'.[281] The *Guardian*'s Martin Walker rated his polished performance in the party's October 1974 party political broadcast highly.

> Bearing a close physical resemblance to the American [segregationist] politician George Wallace, he gave the same impression of being a plain-spoken, common man, speaking for the people against the intellectuals and the planners and the arrogant politicians who could be blamed for the nation's problems.[282]

Nonetheless, Read proved unable to stop the rot. NF membership stagnated, candidate rosters for municipal elections dropped, and morale declined commensurately. Left-wing groups were also increasingly disrupting NF activities, the party 'reaping the whirlwind of organized opposition that had been sown at Red Lion Square.' The NF became increasingly isolated politically too. Disbarred from the National Referendum Campaign which agitated for a 'No' vote against joining the European Economic Community, meaning that its own campaign 'failed to get off the ground', the NF turned in on itself, increasingly consumed by its own internal troubles.[283]

Despite being deposed as chairman, Tyndall never wavered in his 'absolute conviction' that only under his 'leadership and control' could the NF hope to progress or survive. He determined to seize back control of the party from its present incumbents, 'not one single one' of whom 'was fit for the power they had inherited.' Believing himself to be in a 'bloody war' of attrition, Tyndall battled with the 'populists' for control of the party.[284] He proposed a series of constitutional reforms that would have transformed the NF into an 'elective dictatorship'.[285] The Directorate decried his propositions as 'authoritarian' and rejected them entirely when Tyndall subsequently tried to have them discussed at the party AGM later that year.[286]

The Directorate was further infuriated that Tyndall had chosen to publish his proposals in *Spearhead* first, effectively appealing over their heads directly to the membership. This episode, together with a widely circulated *ad hominem* attack upon the 'populists' which many attributed to him, saw Tyndall summoned to a Directorate meeting on 14 May. The result was a vote of no confidence. Walker characterised it as Tyndall's 'weakest moment'. Fortunately for Tyndall, Read failed to seek his expulsion. Walker speculates that Read may have been seeking to play Tyndall off against Roy Painter, because Read, 'feared that his own control of the Party would not long survive the eclipse of either. Both had to go, or neither.' Whatever his motive, Read's vacillation ensured that the intriguing and backbiting continued throughout the year, undermining the party's efficacy further.[287]

His political career in the balance, Tyndall reasserted his hard-line credentials in successive issues of *Spearhead*. Webster kept a foot in both camps, Walker argues.[288] He proscribed the League of St George – a 'neo-Nazi' organisation that had grown out of the Mosley movement – enabling him to burnish his credentials amongst the 'populists'.[289] In September 1975, Tyndall was re-elected to the NF Directorate with 1,028 votes, though Webster topped the poll with 1,201.[290] Tyndall, who was also elected as chairman of the NF policy department,[291] immediately returned to excoriating *Britain First*, whose 'downgrading' of the concept of 'leadership' represented 'a left-wing Marxist concept' based on the 'fallacy' of egalitarianism. Of *Beacon*, another 'populist' publication edited by former NSM activist Denis Pirie, Tyndall proclaimed 'we can do without this muck'.[292]

Responding, Richard Lawson, *Britain First*'s editor, claimed Tyndall only implied his newspaper was communist, 'because it does not share *Spearhead*'s obsession with blindly following the alien "Leader" cult, but takes pride in encouraging the native British trait of thinking for oneself.'[293] The same issue featured a 'Personal Letter to the Editor' from Read, which attacked Tyndall and his supporters 'as autocratic minded with very little real understanding of British Nationalism and the political philosophy behind it.' It also issued a challenge: 'If you want a pressure group organization led on a one-man basis, then you should get out of the National Front and form one.'[294] Tyndall did not intend to go anywhere. NF activists were the 'Trustees of an Idea' – 'Racial Nationalism' – whose purity had to be safeguarded against the 'perennial heresy' of 'Marxism in the guise of Nationalism'.[295]

Following weeks of invective and intriguing, Read finally moved against Tyndall and his Directorate supporters. On 10 November, the locks on the NF Head Office were changed. When Martin Webster tried to gain access, he was confronted by NF activist Steve Brady, 'who waved a cosh and then a canister of C.S. gas at me and told me I was suspended'. Tyndall and his colleagues were formally suspended on 16 November but Mr Justice Goulding overturned Read's precipitous action in the High Court on 20 December.[296] Read promptly resigned and two days later established the National Party (NP). Tyndall and Webster quickly outmanoeuvred him, however. They reoccupied the NF Head

Office and obtained a court order requiring the 'populists' to hand back the party's membership lists, depriving Read of the means of communicating with the membership. Having bankrolled the legal action that precipitated Read's resignation, Andrew Fountaine was appointed 'Acting Chairman' until a Directorate meeting reaffirmed Tyndall's tenure on 6 February 1976.[297] Webster later claimed that Fountaine believed he had 'purchased' the right to be Chairman, his ouster magnifying his enmity towards Tyndall.[298]

The split took a toll on the NF. Twenty-nine branches departed with the NP faction, leaving the NF with two-thirds of its party's membership and 101 branches.[299] Tyndall denied reports the NF was verging upon disintegration, announcing triumphantly to a London NF rally on 14 January: 'This party will live forever!' Moving onto the ideological offensive, he attacked those who had deserted the NF as either biologically inferior – invoking Lothrop Stoddard's concept of the 'Under-Man' to prove his case – or psychologically weak, 'utterly unfitted to political activity which involves *struggle* and demands combativeness of spirit and a determination to conquer adversity.' In short, they suffered a 'lack of will'.[300] Webster meanwhile attacked Read for ideological duplicity, retelling an incident in which Read had boasted privately, 'I am a bigger Nazi than JT ever was.' For good measure, Webster added that Painter had also told him, 'What you don't realise is that I am a National Socialist at heart. Only I am careful!'[301] Read retorted in kind. 'John Tyndall has told me that his plans are to use the immigration issue to gain power and then to get rid of the race he hates most, the Jews,' he remarked to *The Times*.[302]

The NP appeared to be off to a credible start when Read and a colleague were elected as NP councillors in Blackburn, Lancashire, in May 1976 – something the NF never achieved. Read's fellow NP councillor, John Frankman, a self-employed builder, resigned two months later, however. He was ineligible to sit as a councillor since he was under a suspended sentence at the time of his election.[303] Read claimed his NP offered 'harder' immigration policies than the NF. His base racist overtures quickly proved Read was no moderate.[304] 'I have been told that I cannot refer to coloured immigrants,' he told an East End NP meeting in June, 'so you will forgive me if I refer to niggers, wogs and coons…' He then directly referenced Gurdip Singh Chaggar's murder in Southall on the weekend before: 'That was terribly unfortunate. One down, a million to go.' Prosecuted for inciting racial hatred, Read was subsequently acquitted.[305]

There were concerted calls for 'nationalist unity' on both sides of the split but by September, Tyndall felt sufficiently secure to ignore them. Indeed, Fountaine, the deputy chairman, argued that anyone 'stupid enough' to join the NP in the first place should be prevented from re-joining the NF unless possessed of a 'particular virtue'.[306] Read and colleagues evinced a similar disdain; rejecting the prospect of 'shackling the NP to the rotting corpse of the remnant "National" Front, poisoned as it is with unprincipled egotism, opportunism, hypocrisy and deceit.' Nor did they regret the split. 'The only thing to be regretted', stated *Britain First*, 'is that the Front still enjoys some sort of existence. The Front cannot be regarded as simply a "rival gang" of Nationalists. *The Front are political opponents standing in the way of the British Nationalist cause.*'[307] Despite its defiant stance, however, the NP, having clearly failed to live up to its 'populist' promise, faded into obscurity.[308]

Having resumed leadership, Tyndall immediately ended the party's 'extreme' experiment with democratisation, reinstituting a more 'personalised' leadership.[309] Tyndall's utter repudiation of the 'populist' strategy was communicated to the membership by his symbolic appointment of Richard Verrall as *Spearhead*'s editor, enabling him to devote more time to party matters.[310] Verrall was an anti-Semite who had pseudonymously authored the seminal Holocaust denial text, *Did Six Million Really Die?* (1974) under the pen-name 'Richard Harwood'.³¹¹ Ideologically intransigent, Verrall declared that the NF:

> shall never give up until we have won back our country *and seen to it that every single coloured immigrant is repatriated from Britain*. There are no qualms or difficulties about it. That is our policy – because it is essential to our national survival.³¹²

No longer restrained by a wider coalition of ideological interest, Tyndall penned his own disquisition on the place of anti-Semitism, invoking *The Protocols* to support his contention that 'The Jewish Question' was 'a central issue in the struggle for the salvation of British nationhood.'³¹³

With hard-edged ideological positions reasserting themselves, Tyndall cautioned against appeal of *faux* 'militancy' and the seduction of 'political leaders of a bygone age'. Rejecting the posturing he had once embraced, Tyndall dismissed 'fringe' criticism. 'In all due humility, I do not think that I require any lessons from anyone on the matter of militant commitment to one's political ideals,' he asserted. 'I have more than once lost my freedom through such commitment and much more besides.'³¹⁴ Tyndall turned his attention instead to ideologically overhauling party publications as a means of building a mass organisation. *Britain First*, deemed to have descended into ideological obscurantism appealing only to 'a pseudo-Leftist, politically neurotic self-styled elite', was replaced by *National Front News*, a mass distribution broadsheet which contained instead 'lots of short, snappy articles with plenty of illustrations, dealing in a direct and simple way with issues important to ordinary folk who might VOTE NATIONAL FRONT'.³¹⁵

The reorientation away from ideological abstraction proved timely for the NF. Tyndall's resumption of the NF leadership again coincided with increased public concerns regarding immigration, revived this time following President Banda's expulsion of the Malawi Asians, which rekindled fears, stoked by the tabloid press, that as British passport holders, they too would settle in Britain. NF activists again picketed Heathrow airport to protest their arrival. Following hard on the heels of their arrival, the NF stood 176 candidates in the local elections in May. The party polled strongly in the Midlands and its environs, notably in Leicester where forty-eight NF candidates polled 43,733 votes, an average of 18.5 per cent, as well as in Wolverhampton and Bradford 'with its support fading outside these areas with substantial Asian populations'.³¹⁶ Increasingly, the spatial distribution of NF support was relegated to, and only exhibited any buoyancy within, decaying ('inner city') areas including London's East End, where sections of the urban working class, sustained by a long and ingrained history of racist hostility to immigration, perceived migrants as a distinct threat to local cultural traditions and identities.³¹⁷

Proving once more that NF membership was 'highly responsive' to racial issues and the reporting of them, the party experienced another surge during summer 1976.³¹⁸ Internal party figures stated that 2,096 members had joined since January; 611 had joined in June alone. Previously, the largest single monthly increase was 400 in the aftermath of the October 1974 general election campaign.³¹⁹ Tyndall later asserted that 4,500 new members had joined between March and December 1976, whilst the party also established forty-one new branches and upgraded twenty 'groups' to branch status.³²⁰ By 1977, NF membership had reached 12,000–13,000 members.³²¹ By 1979, it stood at between 12,000 and 15,000.³²² Rising membership mirrored the rising circulation of party publications. *Spearhead* also enjoyed its peak circulation between 1977 and 1979, whilst *NF News* had a print run of 50,000 compared to the 17,000 reached by *Britain First* at its peak.³²³

The passage of the Race Relations Act (1976), which made inciting racial hatred an indictable criminal offence, received royal assent on 22 November. The new legislation presented the NF with new challenges. Initially, the party went on the offensive. Roy Jenkins, the Home Secretary who had introduced the Bill was an object of wrath, turned into a 'temporary snowman' at one public meeting after being hit with bags of flour, soot and manure thrown by a group of female NF activists.[324] Brons and Webster passed a motion exhorting NF members to act in 'deliberate defiance' of the new laws at the party's 1976 AGM.[325] *Britain First*, meanwhile, had already reassured its readership that the party 'will escalate the fight to save Britain from being reduced to a multi-racial slag heap,' quoting Webster that 'with the worsening racial situation there may come a time when people will decide that "they no longer need a political party – they need an army!"'[326] In the longer term, however, the NF was pushed on the defensive, forming a Legal Department of the NF Directorate to help defend the growing number of its activists facing legal action.[327]

Whilst Tyndall continued raging against the 'race traitors' and 'race perverts' he blamed for the nation's disintegration, he also offered his own grandiose vision for the restoration of national greatness. Tyndall's boyhood admiration for the British Empire, he acknowledged, had shaped his geopolitical vision. 'I have had this ideal since I was a small boy and it has motivated all that I have ever done in the way of political work,' he wrote:

> I believe the British are a remarkable race with a scale of achievement second to no other. I believe that such a race deserves a leading position in the world, a place of the highest honour and respect among nations. In earlier times I would have been an extreme imperialist; today I believe in an updated form of imperial idea which seeks to link the British race worldwide in a mighty union which can guarantee its independence from either of the two major power blocs of today.[328]

In this sense, Tyndall's nostalgic 'vision' was not backward looking. It was the future. Imbued with a deep sense of racial predestination, Tyndall viewed the NF as a 'Phoenix Rising', a cipher for the nation's racial rebirth, heralding the country's restoration as 'a race striding the world like the colossus it once was – and stamping its power and its genius on the future pages of history'.[329]

Lewisham

To realize such goals, Tyndall told the party's 1976 AGM, the NF must become 'the instrument of steel needed to cut forward through all the chaos and conflict and grasp the reins of power – real power'.[330] The first step towards 'real power' was to 'control the streets' – 'our great marches, with drums and flags and banners, have a hypnotic effect in solidifying the allegiance of our followers so that their enthusiasm can be sustained'. Implicitly, these marches were also calculated to provoke and intimidate, often being routed through, or on the borders of, areas with large immigrant populations. The Trotskyist Socialist Worker's Party (SWP) responded by physically confronting such marches. As one SWP activist later quipped of Tyndall's stratagem, 'marches are nowhere near as hypnotic and solidifying if everyone taking part has to run behind a bus shelter, using the drums to protect themselves from a shower of rubble'.[331]

In tandem with its street mobilisations, Tyndall also sought to professionalise the party's electoral campaigning. In February 1977, he oversaw the founding of a new NF National

Elections Department. Its immediate task was to maximise the party's presence in the Greater London Council (GLC) elections.[332] In the event, the NF contested all but one of the ninety-two seats available, polling 119,000 votes, more than 5 per cent of the vote. In Hackney South, the NF polled 19 per cent. The party's 400 candidates also collectively garnered 235,000 votes in the May 1977 County Council elections. Beyond such headline figures, however, academic studies of the NF vote highlighted an overall decline with the party failing to maintain, consolidate or increase its support since the 1976 District Council elections.[333] In the aftermath of the election, Webster warned against complacency, fretting that the party's 'long struggle' mentality was waning. 'I think that this is a serious lapse in our membership education which must be rectified,' he warned, mindful of the harm that creating false expectations would cause if the party faltered.[334] His prescient warning went unheeded.

Low-level political violence between the NF and its opponents was 'endemic' and 'woven into the very fabric of life for active members of the NF.'[335] However, this violence was 'magnified manifold' through the Tyndall's 'march and grow' strategy, which increased resistance from local communities and indeed anti-fascist activists. The announcement that the NF would hold a march through Lewisham, South London, on 13 August 1977 to 'Clear the muggers off the streets' – part of the NF's ongoing strategy to racialise crime – was the culmination of several months of escalating tension and hostility between the extreme right and their anti-fascist opponents.[336] In the event, the march ended in a general mêlée with protestors, during which 110 people, including fifty-six police officers, were injured; 210 arrests were made. In the aftermath, Tyndall wrote to the prime minister, James Callaghan, warning him not to ban future NF demonstrations. Vehemently denying that the NF had marched through south-east London to provoke 'immigrants' or violence but rather to appeal to its own supporters, Tyndall suggested for good measure that the Labour Party should proscribe marches organised by the SWP, whom he blamed for the violence, and implement an 'immediate' ban on the Notting Hill Carnival.[337]

The NF leadership had anticipated that the Lewisham 'do' would give the party more publicity than that which it had accrued from the LCC election results.[338] They were not wrong. For the following three weeks, the NF Publicity Department conducted 'one continuous press conference', whilst Webster believed 'we have had a staggering impact on the minds of the public'.[339] In the longer term, however, violence adversely effected the social and political composition of the NF. In the late 1960s, NF marches had attracted 'old men with the Union Jack around their shoulders and mothers pushing prams'.[340] After Lewisham, however, the 'state of siege' under which the party operated 'had the effect of driving out of positions of responsibility the predominantly middle-aged and middle class people who comprised what one might call the first generation of the NF's middle management.'[341] In their absence, the NF mutated into 'a younger, aggressive organisation of young thugs.'[342] NF activities became subject to the law of diminishing returns. Reduced to a 'physical and political hardcore' on the streets, the NF increasingly resembled less a political party than a 'skinhead cult.' This, in turn, accelerated its further decline.[343] Tyndall's speech to the party's 1977 Annual Conference highlighted his belief that rising opposition to the NF meant that the party's public impact was, 'greater than at any time in our 10-year history.'[344] Twenty years later, BNP 'modernisers' seeking to oust Tyndall recognised that Lewisham was indeed a 'watershed' – for all the wrong reasons.

To overcome the increasingly hostile environment within which the NF now operated, Webster engineered a publicity stunt, 'to demonstrate a simple but important point to the press, the police and the public – that National Front activities themselves, do not generate public disorder.' When an NF march through Hyde, Greater Manchester in October 1977 was banned, Webster, having overcome internal opposition from Fountaine to the idea, staged his own 'solo' march along the proposed route under the banner 'Defend British Free Speech from Red Terrorism'.[345] Simultaneously, another secretly organised NF march set off from nearby Levenshulme, ensuring that the party marched without opposition.[346] It was not the hoped-for publicity coup. The NF Directorate regarded most of the media coverage as 'poisonously unfair' to the party.[347] Nonetheless, Webster intimated his desire to the party's Directorate to switch from being Activities Organiser to concentrate upon publicity and journalism as a long-term goal, which chimed with his belief that the party was becoming more press relations orientated.[348]

Increasingly besieged politically, the year ended on a happier personal note for Tyndall. In November, he married Valerie Parker, a Brighton NF activist from a family of 'dedicated' party members.[349] Tyndall and his wife relocated to Hove, Sussex. For the previous eight years, he had lived with his mother in south London.[350] Tyndall's personal respite was brief. In February 1978, the Home Office applied a two-month ban on all demonstrations in the Metropolitan Police district in response to a proposed march through Ilford, north London, the first time such measures had been implemented in fifteen years.[351] Whilst anti-fascist opposition continued unabated – there were thirty-four arrests following a clash at an NF meeting in Brixton in April,[352] – the NF now added 'police harassment' to its litany of complaints.[353] Indeed, believing that the 'Establishment' was using the police as a 'bludgeon' against the NF, the Directorate voted to cease its practice of ending its meetings with 'three cheers for the police'.[354] 'The name of the game is not Politics; it is Total War,' Tyndall railed. 'They can never complain if the rules they have adopted for the conduct of Total War are one day used against them.'[355]

This increasingly militarised language also reflected the growing pressure brought to bear upon Tyndall by local NF branches, concerned by the ongoing impact of Labour's 'character assassination' and anxious to know 'When are we going to hit back?'[356] The party's growing political marginalisation during the course of 1978 fuelled Tyndall's own belligerent characterisation of the NF as 'a guerrilla army in an occupied country'.[357] Ironically, the militancy which Tyndall's own pronouncements and strategies had helped foster, forced him to address the party's unruly skinhead contingent which had increasingly characterised party support since Lewisham. Ever the martinet, Tyndall backed the idea of a 'Special Active Unit', which he insisted represented an elite cadre of super-activists, 'not as a braces and boots group'. Tyndall envisaged that a disciplined assemblage would alter the party's internal dynamic insofar as 'the keen youngster would emulate the behavior of the men in the special unit rather than the yobbish behaviour which tends to be prevalent at the moment'. The combination of 'brain and body', noted fellow Directorate member Paul Kavanagh, would create 'whole men' – a variant perhaps of the Fascist 'new man'.[358]

Tyndall also felt his leadership compromised by an 'absurd and destructive feud' with Webster, 'which has poisoned relationships between us over the last year or so which has hampered liaison and therefore running efficiency in the party and which has distressed and perplexed our colleagues'.[359] One cause of disagreement appears to have been Webster's clash with Tyndall's father-in-law regarding an anti-homosexual campaign he was running in Sussex, which had Tyndall's backing. Webster, who was homosexual, denied undermining the campaign, claiming instead that he simply sought to establish that 'the lawful moral conduct of private individuals is a matter where the party is not required, or does not wish, to take an official policy stance.' He nonetheless resigned as chairman of the NF Publicity Department, which Tyndall accepted.[360] Tyndall also had to reckon with increasingly strained relations across the party's National Directorate, which was manifest in bad behaviour, interruptions and a refusal to recognise the authority of the chair.[361] Nor did Tyndall's relationship with Webster recover entirely. When Webster arrived late to a Directorate meeting in February 1979, Tyndall admonished him, leading to an exchange of words between the two men.[362]

The 1979 general election

The general election held on 3 May 1979 was a disaster. Three hundred and three NF candidates polled 191,719 votes (0.6 per cent), compared to 114,415 votes (0.4 per cent) in October 1974, despite contesting three times as many seats. To make matters worse, each candidate averaged only 1.3 per cent compared with 3.1 per cent in 1974. The highest vote was Tyndall's own in Hackney South and Shoreditch – 1,958 votes (7.6 per cent) – and even this represented a decline from the 2,544 votes (9.4 per cent) the NF had polled in the previous election. The downward trend occurred in other strongholds too.[363] In retrospect, the NF 'over-estimated' what it could achieve, Tyndall conceded.[364] He also made the hollow claim that winning votes was 'never the main object', it was to use elections to attract 'the greatest possible nationwide publicity' thus triggering a 'big wave' of recruitment. If anything, it had the opposite effect.

Tyndall appeared content to accept that the party had simply overstretched itself rather than probing more deeply into the cultural and political factors that had led to his party being outflanked. There were 'three specific reasons' for the party's failure. First, the NF insisted upon provocative, confrontational marches, which 'advertised its extremism' and commensurately brought it young, violence prone recruits who regularly indulged their proclivities. Second, Tyndall and his colleagues not only failed to overcome the 'Nazi' appellation but also reinforced it, solidifying further political resistance from mainstream parties and trade unions. Third, from 1977 onwards, the Conservative hierarchy deliberately set out to court the NF vote by talking tough on immigration, which undercut the party's already waning appeal.[365] Less sensationalised media reporting also belatedly helped to neuter some of the party's appeal.[366]

Tyndall had recognised that 'race' was pivotal strategically as well as ideologically since it was a 'trendy' issue for liberal journalists whose reports publicised the NF on this basis. There were political tensions within the Directorate, however, as figures like Fountaine wanted to emphasise a broader raft of policies, which he felt, were of 'equal importance' to race.[367] Ironically, this wrangling about the party's ideological parameters rendered obsolete by a profound challenge to the party's core appeal. In January 1978, the Conservative Party leader, Margaret Thatcher, made a pitch for NF supporters, expressing her empathy with voters who 'are really rather afraid' that the country 'might be rather swamped by people with a different culture' leading her to hold out 'the prospect of an end to immigration' under Conservative rule.[368] The speech had an immediate effect. 'We had been averaging 500–700 letters a week when, discussing immigration in a TV interview, Mrs Thatcher used the word "swamped",' her clerk recalled. 'In the following week she received about 5,000 letters, almost all in support, almost all reacting to that interview. I had to read them. We were swamped indeed: swamped by racist bilge.'[369] Thatcher never repudiated her statement. Indeed, on the eve of the election, she reiterated it. Consequently, voters felt she was 'on their side' concerning immigration, even if ultimately her 'tough' stance prefaced no substantive shift in Conservative Party policy. If Powell had opened the door to the NF's expansion in 1968, Thatcher slammed it shut in 1978. The vote in

Thatcher's own constituency was symptomatic. Whilst she polled 20,918 votes (52.5 per cent), the NF candidate who opposed her polled a paltry 534 votes (1.3 per cent), coming a distant fourth out of five candidates.[370]

Prior to the election, Tyndall had made the unconsciously prescient comment that, more important than the result of the general election itself, was 'the quality and strength of the party with which, after the election, we resume the fight'.[371] Following its electoral annihilation, the 'quality and strength' of the NF was tested and found wanting. In response to their defeat, the NF leadership began debating future strategy, which highlighted a growing tactical tension between Tyndall and Webster. Webster understood that the general election had cost the NF 'almost all' of its 'populist' recruits who had returned to the Conservative Party. The NF poll reflected the party's 'hard core' vote, gained from 'the desperate and the dispossessed among the White Working Class'. To 'secure our social base', the NF 'must develop and stress policies which meet the needs and aspirations of those who, so far, have remained loyal to us'. The NF 'won't be built on middle class foundations', he concluded firmly.[372] Tyndall disliked the idea of advocating an overtly 'working class' line, however, believing that it contravened NF appeals to 'national unity'. Tyndall also dismissed Webster's plea for further 'ideological development', which he felt distracted from the prime task of 'building a machine for winning political power', thereby threatening to transform a 'disciplined active movement' into an ideologically fractious 'debating society'.[373] Tellingly, Tyndall returned to advocating developing a revolutionary elite since mass electoral activity had proven incapable of delivering 'national regeneration'.[374]

Transatlantic travails

With his party languishing in the doldrums, Tyndall departed for the United States to undertake a speaking tour organised for him by Edward Fields, editor of NSRP newspaper, *The Thunderbolt*.[375] Ironically, when Tyndall revealed his invitation to the NF National Directorate, they all agreed that he should not address meetings of either the NSRP or the NA since to so would 'represent a link' that could damage the NF's image. Whether by design or default, Tyndall failed to honour this undertaking.[376] As Tyndall was aware, the NF was an inspiration for US racial nationalists. 'To us here in the America the National Party and the National Front are not only symbols of hope, but a living lesson in practical politics', noted *Instauration*, a popular racial nationalist journal edited by the reclusive Wilmot Robertson (Humphrey Ireland), author of *The Dispossessed Majority*.[377] *Instauration* had suggested on several occasions that Tyndall 'come over here and set up and American National Front. We need one more desperately than any other English speaking nation'.[378] Following his experiences with WUNS, Tyndall declined to:

> help build or get involved with elaborate paper organisations throughout the world. We don't think that is really very practical. But to meet each other and swap experiences and talk about tactical organizational and political problems, that's all very stimulating.[379]

Arriving in Marietta, Georgia, Tyndall stayed with Fields for three days who introduced him to Sam G. Dickson, an extreme right-wing attorney who had run for Lieutenant Governor of Georgia in 1978 on a segregationist ticket, polling 11 per cent. Together the two men travelled onwards to North Carolina to visit Wilmot Robertson, who interviewed Tyndall for *Instauration*. Tyndall assured Robertson's readership that beyond the NF commitment to compulsory repatriation, if elected, he was prepared to take 'whatever harsh measures' necessary 'to safeguard our racial future.' Dismissing the Nazi 'smear', Tyndall paradoxically stated that Nazi Germany 'wasn't as bad as we have been told'. Continuing in this vein, Tyndall argued that: 'We know there will come a time when the world will look on Hitler in a different perspective and history will treat him rather more generously than it has so far.' The NF did not slavishly follow Hitler, Tyndall claimed. 'We must adopt whatever is most appropriate to our traditions, customs and racial psychology' and acknowledge that Britain's democratic traditions set it apart from Nazi Germany. 'What I am trying to say', stated Tyndall, 'is we must neither copy the Nazis nor try to be absolutely different from them. We must take the middle way'. *Instauration* lamented, 'would that we have a Tyndall in the United States'.[380]

Tyndall flew on to Memphis, Tennessee, where he addressed a meeting of the local Citizens' Council hosted by Elmore D. Greaves, 'a very ardent Southerner and one of those who believe in the cause of Southern independence', which he promoted as editor of *Southern Review*. Greaves, a Klansman, with whom Tyndall stayed overnight, had chaired the White Christian Protective and Legal Defence Fund, a front-group for the White Knights of the KKK whose most infamous member was Byron De La Beckwith, murderer of civil rights activist Medgar Evers.[381] Tyndall's concluding remarks were reported in *The Citizens Informer*, mouthpiece of the Citizens' Council, in capital letters to emphasis his point, that: 'the white man will once again march victoriously through the jungles and deserts of the world and stamp his will and his genius on every corner of the globe.'[382] Tyndall also met with several of Greaves colleagues including Robert E. Lee McCampbell, leader of the neo-Confederate Southern National Party, and Ronnie Kennedy who gave him a guided tour of the Vicksburg civil war battlefield.[383] In Jackson, Mississippi, Tyndall gave an address to the Governors Patriotic Advisory Committee before flying to Washington, DC for an interview with Liberty Lobby radio whose affiliated newspaper, *The Spotlight*, had previously reprinted his speeches.[384] Tyndall clearly made an impression. 'He's most impressive and is obviously more capable than any of the racist leaders in this country', wrote one white nationalist following his visit.[385]

'Perhaps the most radical of all the political groups with which I came into contact', wrote Tyndall, was the National Alliance led by Dr William Pierce, author of *The Turner Diaries* with whom he had 'a number of useful conversations' at his office and at his home 'where I was most hospitably received'.[386] Pierce's journal, *National Vanguard*, published a profile of Tyndall prior to his arrival but the relationship between the two men dated back nearly fifteen years. Whilst political rivals like Jordan venerated Pierce from afar, Tyndall met and built a close personal relationship with him. Pierce described them as being 'keen friends'.[387] Importantly, Tyndall's visit also opened the door to the wider circulation of Pierce's revolutionary Nazism within British extreme right-wing cadres, principally through the sale of *National Vanguard*, whose subscription base outside the United States had hitherto been 'quite incidental'. Thereafter, Buckinghamshire schoolteacher Steve Brady, a British NA activist, led a 'major campaign' to sell *National Vanguard* in England.[388]

The visit reinforced Tyndall's vision of Britain's racially dystopian future. The Southern States populated by 'Anglo-Celtic types' were a breath of fresh air. 'I did not see one single mulatto in the area' which, Tyndall postulated, 'no doubt has something to do with the old Southern tradition by which Blacks sexually accosting White girls one night were liable to end up hanging from some magnolia tree the next'. In comparison to the South where 'the White Man is in control', Tyndall lamented that whites were 'cowed' and 'depressed' in

Washington, DC which led him to believe that 'any Briton who can walk these streets and then go back home thinking that the multi-racial experiment can succeed is an imbecile'.[389]

Tyndall's Southern sojourn influenced his geopolitical thought. He subsequently told an American correspondent, M.W. Bonds, editor of the *Western Guardian*, that 'I have always been basically a pan-Anglo-Saxonist' and 'deeply regretted' the divergence between Britain and America following the war of Independence (1775–1783). Tyndall had always advocated the idea of a 'white Commonwealth' but started to modify this concept 'when I became aware of the existence of a large number of outstanding thinkers in the US', who sought the restoration of America's 'Anglo-Saxon destiny' and offered 'practical proposals' for its achievement. Reflecting upon the burgeoning transatlantic exchange of ideals, Tyndall wrote that his visit 'greatly helped this process', particularly as

> I spent most of the time in the Southern States, in which of course the Anglo-Saxon element is much more in predominance than elsewhere in the country. This was the first time that I had been anywhere outside the British Isles and not felt a foreigner.[390]

Tyndall reflected that an 'Anglo-Saxon Commonwealth' – a repackaged variant of his 'Anglo-Saxon Reich' – would enable America to 'wield considerable influence and enjoy great power' though correspondingly Britain, 'would probably lay the strongest cultural stamp on such a community'.[391]

Resignation

Tyndall's leadership now came under intense pressure. In his absence, Fountaine, in his capacity as NF regulatory officer expelled Martin Webster in July, the catalyst for which was a complaint about his alleged conduct but behind which numerous other issues festered.[392] Tyndall 'refused to consider the allegations', reinstated Webster, and suspended Fountaine, who had proven as much a thorn in Tyndall's side as he had been to Chesterton.[393] Fountaine responded by challenging Tyndall for the leadership at the NF AGM in October. He lost. Tyndall polled 1,480 votes to 883 for Fountaine. The result was immaterial. Fountaine, already facing a series of disciplinary charges, had been expelled from the party on 17 September, before the election had taken place.[394] Fountaine's colleague, Paul Kavanagh, was expelled on 14 November having admitted to photographing NF membership lists. Harrogate NF organiser Andrew Brons, a former NSM activist, who lectured on politics and government at Harrogate College, and who had chaired the Disciplinary Tribunal, which expelled Kavanagh, replaced Fountaine as deputy chair.[395]

This power struggle engulfed NF Properties Ltd, the entity that owned 'Excalibur House' – a Hackney warehouse, which since September 1978 had doubled as the party's headquarters. Fountaine and Kavanagh used their control of the company to further undermine Tyndall's leadership.[396] Kavanagh served the NF Publicity Department, the party's propaganda arm, which nominally rented the premises from its parent company, with an eviction notice on 22 December. Administrative chaos ensued. In a five page members' bulletin supplement, Tyndall ruminated darkly about the supposed 'conspiracy' to destroy the NF.[397] Ironically, this fractious squabbling dovetailed with a planning enquiry, concluding in April 1980, which prohibited the NF from using the building for political purposes.[398] Michael Walker, the central London NF organiser, recognised that losing Excalibur House was an egregious blow. The NF didn't just lose office space but a vital 'social venue' where members 'would meet for a drink or to play billiards'. The fact that others could not understand the importance of this, 'suggests to me that they do not understand the importance of social cohesion, association, and solidarity as a prerequisite of any political advance or influence'.[399]

Though Tyndall had survived Fountaine's leadership challenge, it set in motion a train of events that precipitated his own departure from the NF. 'There's only the hard way, the way of struggle,' Tyndall told the party faithful at the NF AGM in Great Yarmouth that year. Analysing the party's setback in its fight against 'Shylockracy', Tyndall warned that the party – 'a crusading army' – would only win back the anti-immigration vote from Thatcher, 'if we don't destroy ourselves in the meantime'.[400] Tyndall despised the 'liberal principle of decision by mere head-counting'.[401] This applied as much to the party's own internal democratic structures as it did to parliamentary democracy. His remedy, following this bruising electoral defeat, which had called into question his own leadership, was to propose two 'Constitutional Amendment' resolutions, which essentially invested full power in the party chairman ... John Tyndall. The National Directorate, led by Webster, baulked at endorsing Tyndall's demand for dictatorial control. Furious, Tyndall turned his wrath upon Webster, whose behaviour, he claimed, had become increasingly divisive. Suddenly, Tyndall alighted upon Webster's homosexuality as grounds for proposing his expulsion.[402] 'The man had known me since 1962,' commented Webster acidly.[403]

The National Directorate rejected Tyndall's motion eighteen votes to two. They also rejected Tyndall's demand that they convene an EGM so that he could seek the requisite power to remove the 'homosexual element'.[404] Tyndall resigned as NF chairman on 31 January 1980, declaring that the Directorate had failed to grant him the necessary powers to expunge 'the taint of homosexuality from the party's leadership'.[405] He immediately severed *Spearhead*'s connection to the NF and sacked Verrall as editor whilst announcing that 'due to instructions' from the magazine's owner, the editor would no longer be publishing articles from Webster. Since Tyndall was both owner and editor, the statement was as childish as it was ridiculous.[406] *Spearhead* had 'thrived' because of its linkage to the NF. Cutting the umbilical cord occasioned a 'severe setback' in the magazine's circulation, which plummeted to less than a third of its peak in the late 1970s.[407]

Evaluating Tyndall's tenure as NF chairman, *The Times* judged him to have been 'a quieter and less charismatic leader of British fascism than either Sir Oswald Mosley or Mr. Colin Jordan.' Whilst 'remarkably consistent' in his beliefs, in their verdict Tyndall 'has not become a household name in the way that Mosley and Jordan did to earlier generations.' Damning him with faint praise, *The Times* profile did concede, however, that 'through a combination of rabble-rousing oratory and cool organisation' Tyndall had succeeded in propelling the NF 'into the headlines even if he has never managed to make it look like a respectable political party'.[408] Making the NF the 'brand name' of British fascism was perhaps Tyndall's most significant achievement at this point.

British National Party

The extreme right splintered into factions following the general election. In November, Fountaine and Kavanagh launched the National Front Constitutional Movement (NFCM), gaining roughly 2,000 members,[409] who presumably agreed with Fountaine that Tyndall and Webster, 'are hanging like putrefying albatrosses round the party's neck'.[410] The large Leicester NF branch, led by solicitor Anthony Reed-Herbert, also broke away to become the British People's Party, changing its name to the British Democratic Party shortly thereafter.[411]

Tyndall initially counselled that the party's problems could 'only be remedied by people staying in the NF' and remedying its wrongs 'within the constitutional framework'.[412] When this strategy failed to yield results, he founded the New National Front (NNF) on 22 June 1980 as a 'reform' movement to regenerate the existing party by purging it of the 'notorious homosexual' within its ranks, after which Tyndall promised a 'complete reunification' with the NF.[413] US racial nationalists applauded his stance. 'Hitler put up with his homosexual contingent for more than a decade until that famous Night of the Long Knives in 1934 when he liquidated Ernst Roehm and others of similar sexual persuasion. Tyndall had less patience', congratulated *Instauration*.[414] Tyndall also retrofitted the NNF with the *Führerprinzip* constitution denied him by his former colleagues, which 'has made party work a pleasure once again'.[415] Webster, who mocked Tyndall as a 'pompous mini-*Duce*', also unkindly quipped that the NNF constitution invested Tyndall with 'leadership power in inverse proportion to his powers of leadership'.[416]

Tyndall received a measure of financial backing for his new venture from his father-in-law, Charles Parker, as well as reigniting old partnerships.[417] Surprisingly, John O'Brien, the former NF chair who Tyndall had acrimoniously usurped in 1972, re-emerged to endorse Tyndall's politics as 'entirely sound'.[418] It quickly became clear to Tyndall that his goal of recapturing the NF would not occur anytime soon, however.

Tyndall no doubt experienced a certain déjà vu. Mass support already a distant memory, Tyndall returned to the vanguardist politics of the GBM, adumbrating a strategy for long-term political development, like his American counterpart, William Pierce. 'Our function in this first phase', Tyndall argued, 'is going to be less that of a party and more that of a combination of educational body and business'.[419] Lacking the material wherewithal to transform such stratagems into reality, Tyndall imagined instead that he was cultivating a racial elite. 'It is your duty to think and behave as befits a member of an aristocracy – that is a true aristocracy of *blood*', Tyndall advised his followers.[420] As exemplars of 'Race and Nation', young activists were to be disciplined and dedicated, intellectually and physically, no doubt emulating the Hitler Youth who Tyndall regarded as 'strong, fit, proud – a formidable generation'.[421] Advocating 'a disciplined programme of regular bodily exercise,' Tyndall led by example with *Spearhead* featuring photographs of him out jogging. The racial imperative overrode personal choice, argued Tyndall and extended to 'choosing a mate' based upon eugenics. 'Do not waste your own genetic inheritance by marrying someone below your standard racially', Tyndall stated, 'whatever the momentary sexual or romantic attraction'.[422] In pursuit of the elite cadre, Tyndall invited young, physically fit activists to join the Special Tactical Activities Group (STAG) for 'special duties', which included providing 'personal security' for the leader, marches and meetings, whilst also forming activist 'detachments' to 'break new ground' in areas the party had no history of activity.[423]

Tyndall's preoccupation with SS-style aristocracies of 'Aryan blood' stemmed from his Spenglarian interpretation of Britain's ongoing racial decline, combined with a Nietzschean repudiation of liberal-humanist morality vis-à-vis (racial) weakness. Tyndall's interpretation of Nietzsche was informed by a reading of *Which Way, Western Man?* (1978) by William Gayley Simpson, an NA member, whom he felt, had provided an expert updating of Nietzsche's thought for 'our current Western predicament'.[424] Tyndall believed:

> Decadence is the loss of the will of a race to have a future.... Decadence is that perversion which induces us to pour out bounty to subside the breeding of other races while taking every step within the bounds of modern medical science to limit our own.[425]

Democracy offered no solution. Only a 'New Caesarism' – as Spengler and Yockey had both called it – could arrest the decay and bring about a racial 'renaissance'. Such leadership would emerge, Tyndall proclaimed, 'from the titanic struggle soon to come for the survival or death of Western Man.'[426]

Tyndall's attempts to strike an accord with other groups were ignored. Only representatives of the League of St George and the British Movement, both proscribed whilst Tyndall was NF leader, addressed a 'unity' rally on 15 July 1981.[427] The breach with the NF irrevocable, on 7 April 1982, Tyndall rechristened the NNF as the British National Party (BNP). It was the fifth party in the history of British fascism to bear the name, reflective perhaps of Tyndall's alienation from the 'class warfare' politics of the 'Gay NF', which had abandoned any pretence of being a 'national' party.[428] For Tyndall, racial nationalism was 'immutable' and the 'radical ideological line' advocated by the NF represented a personal and political affront.[429] To validate his argument, Tyndall turned to history. Nazism's rise to power was only possible, he remarked, when Hitler 'rejected the demands of those within his own party who agitated for a more socialistic programme'.[430] Ideologically divorced from the NF, Tyndall still struggled to extricate himself from beneath its political wreckage. In July, he declared bankruptcy because of legal actions he had been embroiled in whilst NF chairman. Tyndall fumed that the Directorate had 'reneged' upon its 'duty' to pay his costs.[431]

When he founded the BNP, Tyndall had declared 'I do not envisage that any substantial resources will be devoted to the fighting of elections.'[432] Nonetheless, despite downgrading both elections and marches, which also reflected his lack of resources, the BNP still stood fifty-three candidates in the 1983 general election – only six fewer than the NF – qualifying it for a party-political broadcast. The BNP polled just 14,621 votes. Tyndall's bankruptcy disbarred him from standing. His wife stood in his stead in the Hackney South and Shoreditch constituency, where Tyndall had previously polled 1,958 votes (7.6 per cent) in 1979. Valerie Tyndall polled a mere 374 votes (1 per cent). The NF candidate beat her, probably one of the party's few satisfactions considering its own lacklustre performance.[433]

The result confirmed to Tyndall that Thatcher who, like Jordan, he maligned as the 'Kosher Queen',[434] represented the death knell for 'nationalism' until the country was engulfed by a 'total' systemic crisis. France, meanwhile, offered a stark contrast. The breakthrough of the Jean-Marie Le Pen's FN in Dreux in September 1983, after a decade 'crossing the desert', put British activists 'to shame' but also provided 'food for deep thought' and, equally importantly, hope.[435] Plotting his own route across the wasteland, Tyndall debated potential strategy with Jordan (see Chapter 3). Tyndall had already republished Jordan's views on building a 'vanguard' prior to the election, reflecting his ongoing disenchantment with mass political organisation after 1979.[436] Chastened by experience, however, Tyndall, unlike Jordan, eschewed 'direct action' and counselled 'legality' instead. 'It is not an easy way, I know, but all other ways lead in one direction: jail.'[437]

Tyndall's disagreement with Jordan 'on certain fundamentals' regarding their respective racial philosophies was 'basic to our natures and will never be resolved.' By inclination, Tyndall was 'an Anglo-Saxon nationalist' stating that:

> I feel a bond with fellow members of that race that is stronger than any bond I feel with Germans, Swedes etc. That is not to say that I exclude the desirability of some kind of wider alliance and agreement between all White nations for common preservation – only that within that wider alliance I feel that the grounds for close association with fellow Anglo-Saxons are especially strong.[438]

'What matters to me is the ethnic tie', Tyndall continued, 'and this totally transcends any momentary status of citizenship that a person may have by reasons of living in a particular territory and under a particular political dispensation'. A racially pure Britain, linked to kindred peoples across the globe, would 'guarantee prosperity and expansion for at least the next 1,000 years'[439] – Tyndall's own version of Hitler's Thousand-Year Reich.

Whilst completely sympathetic to Jordan's own pan-Aryan philosophy which gave the white race 'ultimate priority' over and above 'purely national ambitions', Tyndall differed insofar as he believed that during the 'current phase of history' – wherein the white race was organised into nations – 'immediate political requirements' had to be national *not* transnational. 'I can only profoundly regret that this difference of opinion has been allowed to cause division between people whose cause is, basically, the same,' he lamented. Whilst his purpose was to proselytise for a 'unified movement for racial resurgence,' Tyndall sincerely believed that this ideological bifurcation need not fragment the movement 'as we can simply regard the two schools of thought as representing two wings, among others, in a single political and ideological movement – for which we must strive for an acceptable synthesis'.[440]

Though he rejected Jordan's revolutionary fulminations, Tyndall's came to similar conclusions about immediate prospects for racial nationalist politics. 'For us to view the ballot box as anything more than a sometimes useful facility for publicity is to dwell in the clouds,' Tyndall wrote in *Spearhead*.[441] Surveying the fissiparous state of the extreme right, then at its lowest ebb in decades, Tyndall still rejected the need for unity. 'We do not believe that there is room for more than one Nationalist political party in Britain,' he stated. Those who maintained otherwise were 'an enemy of the Nationalist movement whom we shall oppose and fight with the same determination as we oppose and fight our external enemies.'[442]

However, Tyndall became emollient following Webster's expulsion from the NF in 1983 (Chapter 6), emphasising that 'divisive people' not 'ideological division' had 'manufactured [a] pretext for keeping the separate factions apart'.[443] His entreaties again rebuffed, Tyndall dug in for a decade-long struggle for 'the soul of racial nationalism'. There were some teething problems, however.[444] In March 1984, Ray Hill, the former BNP publicity officer, came out as a 'mole' for the anti-fascist *Searchlight* magazine. Hill's defection was embarrassing for Tyndall, though more so for others, since he had publicly defended Hill against his detractors.[445] *Post facto* Tyndall claimed, unconvincingly, that Hill was 'liked but never completely trusted'.[446]

The Eleventh Hour

On 8 July 1986, Tyndall and John Morse appeared in Southwark Crown Court. They were charged with conspiring together to contravene Section 5a of the Public Order Act, after publishing a series of articles in *British Nationalist*, the BNP newspaper, which Morse edited, between 1 March 1984 and 31 August 1985, as a result of which 'hatred was likely to be stirred up against black people, Asians and Jews in Great Britain'.[447] Tyndall was charged with a further set of offences relating to the publication of BNP material between 1 May 1983 and 31 August 1985.[448] Found guilty on both counts, Tyndall was sentenced to twelve months apiece. He appealed. The sentences were found to be 'marginally too severe' and Tyndall's two sentences were made concurrent, effectively halving his term of imprisonment, the remainder being suspended.[449]

Tyndall believed that his conviction was part of a Jewish conspiracy, aided and abetted by white liberal jurors who were 'so flabby of mind' that they preferred 'racial death' rather than risk offending another ethnic group. To 'prove' his assertion, he quoted approvingly from *The Protocols of the Elders of Zion*. Tyndall published a post-mortem aimed at keeping other racial 'publicists' from prosecution by outlining the legally acceptable parameters of debate, as he saw them, in the light of his own conviction. Although *Spearhead* ceased publication between August and December, having turned their shared cell into a 'nationalist "regime" in miniature', Tyndall compensated for this by using his imprisonment, much as Hitler had done in 1923, to produce his political testament-cum-memoir.[450]

The result was *The Eleventh Hour: A Call for British Rebirth* (1988), which *Spearhead* confidently proclaimed 'will duly penetrate the fog of censorship and become established reading, just as did the English Bible before it.'[451] It did no such thing. What it did provide, however, was Tyndall's most comprehensive exposition on the racial nationalist position and an ideological cornerstone for the BNP. It also proved popular in the United States. *Instauration* called the book an 'encyclôpedic blueprint for 21st-century Britain [which] deserves study and meditation'. Reflecting both Tyndall's own innate authoritarianism and his orthodox racial nationalist beliefs, *The Eleventh Hour* also highlighted the depths of his antipathy towards Liberal democracy. *The Times* had once asked Tyndall to diagnose the nation's ills. 'If you want me to encapsulate this in one word, it is liberalism', he had replied without hesitation. If liberalism represented the negation of strong leadership – and everything that he believed flowed from it – paradoxically, Tyndall had to look beyond the West for role models, praising figures like the Shah of Iran and Lee Kwan Yew, the Singaporean prime minister, and the Chilean military junta. 'I have to admit that as a white racialist, the few political leaders I have any admiration for are not white', Tyndall had previously conceded.[452]

Tyndall's loathing of 'liberalism' went beyond the political. For Tyndall, liberalism was a biological pathology. He argued that there was a 'liberal gene', which was not a normal gene, but rather a 'mutant' or 'deformed' gene analogous to a 'cancer' requiring rapid surgical excision. That Tyndall should employ such a metaphor is unsurprising. 'Cancer,' wrote Susan Sontag 'is a metaphor for what is most ferociously energetic; and these energies constitute the ultimate insult to natural order.'[453] Tyndall viewed 'liberalism' and the 'liberal state' as the antithesis of this 'natural order', which his own political project for racial rebirth sought to reconstitute. Tyndall interpreted its commitment to racial equality as an attempt to transcend blood and thus as an affront to biology. This aberration was a biological dysfunction. For Tyndall, 'liberals' were psychologically disfigured and physically deracinated, cancerous and corrosive: their behaviours were the product of genetic malformation that enabled their categorisation as a distinct 'biological type'. This thesis was born out by Tyndall's own crude anthropological observation that:

> Liberals, generally speaking, constitute the most unimpressive specimens of the white race – and, interestingly enough, it is almost only among the white race that real liberals (as distinct from those who just chant liberal slogans for tactical reasons) are to be found.[454]

The internal 'predictability' of this 'liberal character', argued Tyndall, 'permits us to regard liberals as a distinct species – perhaps even genetically determined'.[455] Liberalism was thus as much a racial problem as it was a political one. Indeed, 'at root' Liberalism reflected a deep-seated sense of racial inadequacy. Tyndall wrote:

> The Liberal has a sense that he is a poor specimen of his own race, and in the company of his co-racials this is acutely felt. In a 'raceless' world, on the other hand, the liberal

feels entirely at home ... surrounded on all sides by the 'oppressed' and the 'disadvantaged', he feels a proper little aristocrat by comparison with his position in the natural order of things among his own people.[456]

For Tyndall, 'liberalism' was act of racial treachery, promoted by inferior genes, and thus, as his American colleague Revilo P. Oliver had argued in *Conspiracy or Degeneracy?* (1967), it was the Achilles heel of the white race: the enemy within.[457]

Tyndall's mélange of anti-liberalism and social Darwinian elitism had a long lineage traceable to Nietzsche. Tyndall imbibed much of this Nietzschean antipathy towards Liberalism from more contemporary sources, however. S.E.D. Brown, editor of *The South African Observer*, had a good deal of influence in this regard. Tyndall had regularly reprinted his articles, including serialising his coruscating attack – 'The Anatomy of Liberalism' – in *Spearhead* in 1983.[458] For his part, Brown's own views had been influenced *The Specious Origins of Liberalism: The Genesis of a Delusion* (1967) by Anthony M. Ludovici, a former private secretary to the French sculptor Rodin and an ardent devotee of Nietzsche from whose work Tyndall also quoted liberally.[459]

Francis Parker Yockey was another influence upon Tyndall's visceral anti-liberalism. Tyndall reprinted a chapter from Yockey's magnum opus *Imperium* (1948) titled 'Liberalism: The Sickness of the West', in which he had derided Liberalism as feminine and thus weak, together with his own commentary, in *Spearhead* in 1993.[460] Tyndall hailed Yockey, whom he often cited, as 'a prophet who one day will be honoured' but he 'never subscribed' to Yockey's geopolitical belief that the United States represented a greater danger to the white race than the Soviet Union.[461] Tyndall's particularly astringent 'anti-liberal' vision had an enduring impact upon BNP cadres, inculcating them against democracy. If the 'populist' radical right parties that have emerged across Europe since generally adhere to a form of 'illiberal liberalism' that embraces democratic norms, the BNP most certainly did not. This was certainly one reason the party exerted so little crossover appeal under Tyndall.[462]

The BNP lost none of its racist militancy whilst Tyndall languished in jail. In November 1986, Tony Lecomber, the Redbridge BNP organiser, was jailed for three years after a home-made bomb accidentally detonated in his car. Lecomber had parked close to the Workers Revolutionary Party, though the jury rejected the prosecution's contention that he had intended to use the device for 'political' purposes.[463] In the following February, it was the turn of Richard Edmonds, Tyndall's National Activities organiser, who, together with two other activists, received a six-month suspended sentence for defacing the memorial on London's South Bank to 'red terrorist' Nelson Mandela.[464] That same month, the BNP contested the Greenwich parliamentary by-election polling a derisory 116 votes (0.3 per cent). The result was significant only insofar as it was the first time that the BNP had outpolled the NF whose candidate, Joe Pearce, got 103 votes (0.3 per cent). In retrospect, it subtly signalled the shifting balance of power within the extreme right.[465] This was relative, of course. Tyndall judged the BNP to be too weak to contest the 1987 general election, though two activists disagreed, standing without his blessing only to receive a derisory vote and a brief expulsion for their troubles.[466] Seeking to bolster the BNP, Tyndall consented to the formation of a 'liaison committee' to discuss a merging with one of the two NF factions though the talks led nowhere.[467] Three years later, however, the BNP was sufficiently strong for Tyndall to refuse to consider such an amalgamation.[468]

Throughout the 1980s, overtly Nazi politicking moved to the forefront of BNP propaganda, perhaps reaching its apogee in 1989, the centenary of Hitler's birth, upon which

Tyndall editorialised: 'Born 100 years ago, was he as bad as made out? In an allegedly "free" society, we are surely entitled to hear a balanced debate and make up our own minds.'[469] Tyndall needed no convincing. Whilst leading the NF, he had cultivated close contact with German attorney Manfred Roeder, who insisted that Grand Admiral Karl Dönitz, Hitler's successor, had appointed him *Reichsverweser* (Custodian of the Reich). Roeder had illegally entered Britain in August 1979 to meet with Tyndall. In the following year, he founded the Deutsche Aktionsgruppen (DAG – German Action Group), which committed five bomb attacks and several arson attacks on asylum hostels, including one in Hamburg that killed two Vietnamese refugees whom Roeder derided as 'half-apes'. Roeder was jailed for thirteen years in 1982 for founding and leading a terrorist organisation. Tyndall and the BNP gave him their unrelenting support throughout his incarceration, declaring him a 'Hero of our time'. Following Roeder's release in 1990, Tyndall invited him to address the BNP annual rally. The Home Office banned Roeder from entering the country. *Spearhead*'s report on the rally, at which a Nationaldemokratische Partei Deutschlands (NPD – German National Democratic Party) official spoke in Roeder's stead, was titled 'Triumph of the Will'.[470]

Holocaust denial, already an article of faith for Tyndall, was also increasingly to the fore thanks in part to Richard Edmonds, the BNP National Activities organiser. Edmonds, who had a 'religious faith' in Tyndall as 'the divine führer-designate of Britain', derided the Holocaust as 'scientifically provable as a load of rubbish. All that Hitler (a great man) tried to do was to take away the power of the Jews, and that's no bad thing.'[471] For Edmonds, the Holocaust was a 'lie' which 'serves the purpose of denigrating all Whites who wish to stand up for their own race, irrespective of nationality.'[472] To proselytise this view beyond the confines of the BNP, Edmonds helped disseminate *'Holocaust' News*, edited by 'Richard Harwood', which declared the Holocaust an 'evil hoax'.[473] Thirty thousand copies were distributed, many of them to Jewish homes.[474] This was perhaps its peak. 'Holocaust Revisionism' was discussed at a BNP leadership conference circa 1990 at which Tyndall decided simply to 'give it less prominence and devote less attention to it than previously' because 'it was a matter of historical debate that fell outside the proper range of issues with which the BNP should be connected.'[475]

Tyndall and Islam

Tyndall was slow to appreciate the extent to which the evolving nature of 'multiculturalism' would change the face of extreme right-wing politics. The most obvious sign of this shift was to be found in the visceral reaction to the publication of *The Satanic Verses* (1988) by Salman Rushdie, which sparked global protests, book burnings, several killings and a 'fatwa' for the author himself issued by Iran's Ayatollah Khomeini. Tyndall viewed this agitation as the work of 'zealous' Muslims. He was slow to perceive, however, that religion and religiosity was assuming an increasingly important role for many British Muslims, who no longer defining themselves as 'Asian' and less still 'Black', which was a defining characteristic of anti-racial struggle and solidarity during the 1970s.[476]

Betraying scant understanding of this shifting dynamic, Tyndall grumbled instead that his own book, *The Eleventh Hour* (1988), which had been published in the same year as *The Satanic Verses*, was simply ignored behind which Tyndall scented a conspiracy of 'other interests and lobbies'.[477] 'I am almost certainly some kind of relative of William Tyndale, and his problems in getting the first English Bible printed and distributed were a foreshadow of mine,' he wrote pompously. 'I hope, however, that the historical parallel ends there!'[478]

Through the 'Rushdie affair', which acted as a 'catalyst'[479] for the BNP and others to ratchet up racial tensions, the future contours of extreme right campaigning were gradually coming into focus. In August 1989, the BNP staged a 'Rights for Whites' march in Dewsbury, West Yorkshire, in support of local white parents who had withdrawn their children from school in the predominantly Muslim area of Savile Town.[480] BNP supporters chanting 'Rushdie, Rushdie' clashed with Muslim youths as the event ended in a riot. 'This event proved impossible to follow up,' stated one BNP organiser, 'partly due to the instability of the local BNP organisation, and partly because the authorities quickly got wise to the BNP's attempts to put on repeat performances, and used the Police to squash out anything similar.'[481] Indeed, Tyndall's attempt to hold rallies in Bradford and York later that year were banned.[482]

Such occurrences remained incidental rather than integral to Tyndall, who remained the intellectual prisoner of older anti-Semitic paradigms. His conspiratorial interpretation of history distorted his interpretation of contemporary events. This was evident in his reaction to the first Gulf War (1990–1991) and with it George Bush's enunciation of a 'New World Order'. In keeping with the anti-Semitic prism through which he viewed the world, Tyndall perceived this as further evidence of the advance of the 'invisible government', which, having prevailed over the Western World since 1945, was now set to encompass the globe. *British Nationalist* had featured a perfunctory front page titled 'Gulf War: Moslem Threat' in February 1991.[483] However, Tyndall believed that because Islam disavowed 'usury' – the perceived mainstay through which 'international finance' exercised control over national economic life, and controlled vast oil reserves – it posed a significant threat to the forces of 'world-revolution' through its direct challenge to Israel and 'Zionism'.[484]

1991 visit to USA

Shortly after the end of the Gulf War, Tyndall embarked upon a speaking tour of the United States. He had previously been invited to speak at the Populist Party's annual committee meeting to be held in Winston-Salem, North Carolina on 25–27 May 1990 together with figures like Kirk Lyons, a Houston-based attorney prominent in defending extreme right-wing figures through his 'Patriot's Defence Foundation'. Tom McIntyre, the Populist Party national chair, stated that 'Mr Tyndall is well-known both here and in Europe, and we're honoured to have him speak to us.'[485] However, upon his arrival at Charlotte, North Carolina, the authorities immediately deported Tyndall because of his previous convictions.[486]

He had rather more luck in the following May, flying into Atlanta, Georgia, for a nineteen-day speaking tour aimed at building transatlantic racial solidarity.[487] Edward Fields, the former NSRP leader and Sam G. Dickson, an attorney who acted as the US distributor for *The Eleventh Hour*, organised Tyndall's tour. In the verdict of one observer, Tyndall's visit 'turned into one of the movement's largest cross-organisation collaborative efforts' between white nationalist groups. His visit was important because it revealed:

> many of the cross organisational bonds that created a movement out of what looked like a series of un-coordinated single enterprises. It was also an early manifestation of the increased level of transatlantic interchange by white supremacists in the years that followed the collapse of the Soviet bloc.[488]

Tyndall again spent 'many delightful hours' in the company of Wilmot Robertson, author of *The Dispossessed Majority*, whom he had first met in 1979. Following a meeting in Atlanta organised by Dickson, Tyndall was chaperoned by Fields to a meeting in North

Carolina organised by the Populist Party. Here he finally met Kirk Lyons, who had recently defended Holocaust denier Fred Leuchter. Tyndall also met other movement 'veterans' including Emory Burke,[489] a leading light in The Columbians Inc., a racist terrorist group active in Atlanta, Georgia during the 1940s, and DeWest Hooker, who had been instrumental in persuading George Lincoln Rockwell to adopt a more open 'Nazi' strategy.[490]

Travelling on to Washington, DC, Tyndall met for the first time with Willis Carto, head of the Liberty Lobby and publisher of *The Spotlight* before addressing a Populist Party meeting in Lanham, Maryland, a short distance from the capitol later that evening. Having visited New York (which he abhorred for its racial degeneration), Tyndall addressed a meeting in New Jersey chaired by Chester Grabowski, editor of the Polish-American *Post Eagle* and chairman of the local Populist Party. Thereafter, Tyndall flew to Los Angeles, addressing more meetings on 'historical revisionism', which, he told his audience 'was a matter of common sense'. On the following day, he visited the offices of the Institute for Historical Review (IHR) by now infamous as the engine of Holocaust denial in the Western world, where he met with its director Tom Marcellus as well as Mark Weber and Ted O'Keefe, both of whom he had met in 1979. He also met Jean Scott, the IHR's executive secretary, originally from Preston, Lancashire, whose husband Michael Scott had been an NF member. 'This encounter was just like old times,' enthused Tyndall.[491]

Tyndall then travelled to Urbana, Illinois, for the highlight of his trip, a meeting with Revilo P. Oliver, a Professor of Classics with a long history of involvement in extreme right-wing politics, with whom he spent 'several days'. Tyndall later recounted that, 'this meeting followed several years during which Professor Oliver had written regularly to me with helpful ideas.' Oliver had subscribed to *Spearhead* for twenty-six years, spoke generously of it, and frequently quoted from it.[492] Travelling onwards to Chicago, Tyndall addressed a meeting alongside Fields and Matt Koehl, leader of the New Order with whom he later had a 'stimulating talk'. Koehl, who had taken over the National Socialist White Peoples' Party after George Lincoln Rockwell's murder, was an openly Nazi activist close to Colin Jordan. Tyndall was clearly enthused by the 'cross-fertilisation' of ideas he had participated in during his tour and flew home firmly believing in the benefit of transnational activism.[493] Tyndall's transnational message of racial solidarity was important. 'Separatism in some nations is one route to racial salvation but mutual assistance at the genetic level is equally important,' proclaimed *Instauration*. 'Tyndall's rousing words ... tells us that we are not alone in this darkening, disintegrating world and that our ideas and aspirations transcend national boundaries'.[494] 'He should emigrate', enthused *Instauration* in a later edition. 'We need leaders like John.'[495] Indeed, US white supremacists were increasingly envious of the BNP and hoped it would 'inspire the formation of a similar party in the US'.[496]

Tyndall also looked across the channel to France for potential allies. He had cultivated contacts with the French extreme right for years though increasingly Jean-Marie Le Pen's FN exerted a limited appeal. Instead, Tyndall forged connections with Claude Cornilleau's Parti Nationaliste Française et Européen (PNFE – French European National Party), a small, violent Nazi *groupuscule* aligned with the BNP through the 'Euro-Ring' network coordinated by his Leicestershire organiser, John Peacock.[497] Cornilleau addressed the BNP party rally in 1992 whilst Tyndall returned the favour in the following year, delivering a 'brief message in French' at its party congress after speeches from its leading militants Eric Sausett, Michel Faci and Cedric Begin. Thereafter, attendees took part in a torchlight parade with German and Swiss delegates to round off the event. Tyndall was impressed, perceiving the PNFE as a 'militant organisation with a programme designed to select and educate the best of its youth as future leaders in the fight to rescue France.'[498]

'Rights for Whites'

Though the BNP remained at the margins, party activism was gradually connecting with local political concerns in the London borough of Tower Hamlets.[499] Local activists – rather than Tyndall per se – had begun to internalise the idea that to make progress: 'We must stop talking just about what we like to talk about and start talking about the things local people are crying out to hear.'[500] The party's 'community' politicking combined with a recalibration of the party's supremacist ideology. Local party strategists like Eddy Butler had begun organising under an old NF slogan – 'Rights for Whites' – which evoked narratives of 'grievance' and 'unfairness' that resonated with some socially and economically marginalised white residents in the borough who did indeed perceive themselves to be an 'ethnic minority'. Subsequent election results were heartening for the party. In May 1990, a BNP candidate standing in the Holy Trinity ward of Tower Hamlets (Globe Town) polled 290 votes (9.71 per cent) which, given the party's historically poor performances in the local area was encouraging. The same candidate gained 8.4 per cent of the vote in a local by-election (Park ward) two months later. BNP electoral strategy began focusing heavily upon the area.

The 'Rights for Whites' campaign took place amidst an upsurge in violent activity by party activists who attacked a public meeting by American civil rights campaigner, the Reverend Al Sharpton, in April and organised a violent assault on an anti-racist march staged by the National Black Caucus in Bermondsey in August. The BNP denied responsibility for the violence, claiming to advocate 'lawful political action' as the 'correct method' of opposing the 'evils' of the multi-racial society created by successive British governments. It added, however, that 'as long as those rulers do not respond to the peoples' wishes by bringing their hideous experiment to an end the kind of street warfare we saw in Bermondsey on this day is inevitable.' Privately, however, the BNP leadership were ecstatic. 'Welcome to Nuremberg, Bethnal Green-style,' Edmonds announced as he greeted activists arriving for the party rally that October. Tyndall's speech to those assembled was reportedly punctuated with cries of 'Fuhrer' whilst at the climax of his speech he declared:

> that all the race traitors would be in need of protection when – not if – he came to power. The audience was in a state of frenzy and gave their leader a three-minute standing ovation while the B&H skinhead contingent stood at one side giving straight arm salutes.[501]

In the 1992 general election, Tyndall concentrated upon two constituencies: Bow and Poplar; and Bethnal Green and Stepney. Tyndall stood in the former gaining 1,107 votes (3 per cent) whilst Richard Edmonds, polled 1,310 votes (3.6 per cent) in the latter. Whilst the votes were 'unremarkable' in themselves, they still signalled a rise for the BNP, a view given further credence when its candidate polled 657 votes (20 per cent) in a local by-election in Millwall ward in October 1992. Reaping the benefits of long-term socio-economic neglect and local political failure, which included the legitimisation of 'racist' campaigning by the local Liberal Democrats and Labour's own 'talking up' BNP chances of success, Butler's campaign carved out the political space for the BNP to pose as the legitimate defender of white interests in Tower Hamlets. It paid dividends. On 7 September 1993, the BNP candidate Derek Beackon, the party's Chief Steward, polled 1,480 votes (34 per cent) in Millwall ward, only seven more than his Labour rival, but enough to become the first ever BNP councillor.[502]

Tyndall proclaimed the result 'a moment in history ... the most tremendous step forward the party has ever made.' If the party could win in Tower Hamlets, Tyndall believed, then 'it can begin to do so elsewhere in London – and far beyond.' More modestly, however, he hoped the victory would enthuse BNP activists 'to persevere and redouble their efforts.'[503] The party received over 500 enquires from members of the public in the following days and, whilst few joined, 'this represented the greatest single influx of interest in the organisation's history.'[504]

Beackon's rhetoric following his election highlighted what 'Rights for Whites' meant for many activists. In February 1993, Richard Edmonds declared that 'we [the BNP] are 100% racist, yes.'[505] Councillor Beackon did nothing to disabuse people of this notion. 'I am only going to represent the white people [in Millwall ward],' he told the press. 'I will not represent Asians. I will not do anything for them. They have no right to be in my great country.'[506] 'I don't care what the Bengalis think,' Beackon stated. 'We are here for the white people. They are the ones being racially attacked.'[507] Asked about rubbish collection on the Isle of Dogs, he retorted ominously: 'The Asians are rubbish and that is what we are going to clear from the streets'.[508]

Whilst Beackon claimed to deplore violence, his first official duty as councillor was to attend Thames Magistrates court in East London to support Edmonds and four other party activists, who had been charged with 'violent disorder' following a 'savage' attack on a black man who, together with his white girlfriend, had walked past the pub in which they were drinking. Police had made thirty-three arrests that day following a violent clash between BNP activists and anti-fascists in Brick Lane.[509] *British Nationalist*'s editor, John Morse, was also charged (though later acquitted) alongside the 'Brick Lane Four'.[510] Tyndall regarded the prosecution as a 'conspiracy' designed to cause the party's 'immobilisation'.[511] Remanded in custody, the BNP proclaimed Edmonds a 'political prisoner'. He received a three-month jail sentence in June 1994 but was released due to time spent on remand.[512] 'There is no doubt from what I have heard in this case that people in the BNP respect you and look up to you,' the judge told Edmonds. 'It is, however, a dangerous animal and when it is loose on the streets you must restrain it and not goad it.' Tyndall issued a trenchant defence of his colleague, declaring Edmonds 'totally innocent'.[513]

Beackon's victory was universally condemned. Prime Minister John Major publicly lamented the 'unfortunate result' and said 'I hope it won't be repeated.'[514] Opposition was widespread, vocal and occasionally violent. Tyndall launched a 'Security Fund' shortly afterwards claiming that a firebomb had been thrown at his house.[515] More seriously, Tyndall also had to contend with a large-scale anti-fascist mobilisation. On 16 October, thousands marched on the BNP bookshop in Welling, south-east London which had opened in April 1989. Anti-racism campaigners linked the presence of the BNP 'bunker' to a rise of racist violence – there had been four racist murders in the area and a 210 per cent increase in racist attacks.[516] The protest descended into a riot after police charged protestors resulting in thirty-one arrests.[517]

Beackon's victory enthused transatlantic extreme right-networks, enhancing Tyndall's standing within them. The influential US journal *Instauration* declared Tyndall a 'latter-day Robert Bruce'.[518] Seven hundred people reportedly flocked to the party's annual rally held on 6 November. The BNP had advertised David Irving, the prominent 'revisionist' historian, as a speaker but he did not appear on the final programme.[519] The foreign guests who did attend included Claude Cornilleau and Michel Faci of the PNFE,[520] Günther Deckert, the NPD chairman from Germany, and Kirk Lyons, the white supremacist lawyer, who flew in from the United States. John Morse introduced the newly minted 'councillor'

Derek Beackon to the audience. 'The standing ovation went on for several minutes,' noted *British Nationalist*, adding, fancifully, that, 'it was generally agreed by the foreign guests who attended that Britain would probably be the first European nation to achieve a nationalist government.' Concluding its coverage, the newspaper invoked an old Nazi slogan, '*Tomorrow belongs to us!*'[521]

Beackon's election signalled to Tyndall that the BNP had 'to cease to be a street gang and to become a serious political party.' Those who could not shed the 'street gang mentality' he warned risked becoming 'redundant'.[522] The BNP planning conference on 29 January 1994 now stressed that electioneering 'would take precedence over all other activity' and Tyndall disbursed extra funding to Tower Hamlets BNP believing that further gains in the impending local elections were a 'distinct possibility'.[523] Electoral activity was a means to establishing 'credibility'. It would only succeed, however, if accompanied by a tactical reorientation.[524] To this end, the BNP held a press conference on 15 March at which Lecomber declared 'the days of street warfare are over.' There would be 'No more marches, meetings, punch-ups.'[525] Tyndall's new modus operandi took some time to filter down to BNP cadres, but his efforts to operate the BNP as a conventional political party would eventually succeed in removing militant anti-fascism from the equation.[526]

Beackon lost his council seat in May 1994, which Tyndall, in applying to the returning officer for a judicial inquiry, blamed upon Labour's mobilisation of the 'Asian' vote and electoral 'malpractice'.[527] It would be another seven years before the party won another council seat. Yet, Beackon's defeat belied an upward trend in support for the BNP. Despite losing, Beackon increased his vote by 561 to 2,041, then 'the highest total for any BNP candidate so far, in any sort of election.' Elsewhere, across East London, BNP candidates also benefited from the 'Millwall Effect'.[528] Later that summer, on 9 June, having hoped to piggyback upon further electoral gains in Tower Hamlets, Tyndall stood in a parliamentary by-election in Dagenham, outer East London, uncontested by an extreme right party in the last three general elections. He polled 1,511 votes (7 per cent), becoming the first BNP candidate to save his deposit and only the second 'nationalist' candidate to do so since Webster's victory in West Bromwich in 1973. It was an early signal of the constituency's potential for the BNP.[529]

Despite their defeats, the BNP were emboldened by these results. Tyndall endorsed an education and training programme for activists. The party produced an *Activists Handbook* (1994) to facilitate the party's professionalisation. They marketed it alongside the *Membership Handbook* (1993) of William Pierce's 'admirable' NA, billed as an 'extremely valuable guide to the best ways of promoting nationalism and organizing a nationalist movement.'[530] Party strategists meanwhile kept the BNP's public focus upon the white 'grievance' narrative and community-based electioneering.[531] Thereafter, BNP propaganda focused largely upon the 'vicious hypocrisy of "anti-racism"', which they claimed, ignored racial attacks against whites.[532] Indeed, *British Nationalist* was saturated with reports of 'anti-white' racism juxtaposed against graphic reports of Black and Asian criminality under headlines such as 'Asian Gang Violence' and 'Race-Hate Crimes Against Whites – A Growing Trend'.[533]

Combat 18

Ironically, whilst local BNP strategists struggled to make the party electable, Tyndall steered the party further towards the ideological margins. This was partly a consequence of the political pressure he was under to counter the challenge posed by the rise of Combat 18

(C18), a violent *groupuscule* whose ideological leanings could be gainsaid from its numerology which represented the first and eight letters of the alphabet – 'A' and 'H' – 'Adolf Hitler'. Ironically, C18 had begun life as a BNP stewards group, formed in the run-up to the 1992 general election to harass, violently, political opponents and to provide security for BNP events. Tyndall clearly endorsed its activities. In July 1992, he was 'personally chaperoned' to a BNP meeting in Walsall by C18 leader, Paul 'Charlie' Sargent.[534]

Enthused and infused by visions of revolutionary violence, C18 quickly broke free of its original moorings. They denied, however, that they were trying to split the BNP, stating that they supported Tyndall '100%' – though not his close colleague Dave Bruce 'a half-Jew and has no place in the leadership of a Nationalist Movement.'[535] Despite this pledge, as early as spring 1993, the C18 magazine, *The Order*, had begun berating the BNP leadership for their continued reliance upon 'the failed tactics of the 1970s – rally's [sic] and elections – to win support.'[536] Other C18 publications like *Thor-Would* simply denigrated Tyndall personally.[537] C18 quickly came to dominate the militant milieu, taking over the lucrative Blood and Honour (B&H) music network after the death of its founder Ian Stuart Donaldson in a car crash in September 1993. Personally, Tyndall abhorred Ian Stuart's music but recognised his standing: *Spearhead*'s obituary hailed him as a 'martyr'.[538] The C18 takeover of B&H created immediate division amidst claims that leading figures were pocketing the proceeds for themselves whilst bootlegging records to provide further funds. The British Hammerskins decried C18's approach as 'nothing more than blatant capitalism!'[539]

C18 rejected the BNP's electoral strategy as a 'complete and utter failure' – something even Beackon's recent election could not detract from – issuing a more direct challenge to Tyndall's authority by advocating the establishment of 'cells' inside the BNP 'with the aim of taking over the BNP from within' to ensure that 'National Socialists' were in control.[540] Tyndall proscribed C18 as a 'hostile organisation' shortly afterwards in December 1993.[541] Sargent was incensed, declaring: 'I now regard Tyndall and anyone who is connected to this bulletin as enemies of the Aryan struggle.'[542] Despite these recriminations, Tyndall proved reluctant to expel members even with proven links to C18, however.[543] He had to tread a fine line between denouncing the group and recognising that his opposition to C18 was 'resented' by many BNP activists, several of whom resigned in consequence.[544] Tyndall had to convince these militants that in proscribing C18 he had not gone 'soft' whilst simultaneously attempting to diminish the political threat they posed the BNP.

This was reflected in Tyndall's correspondence in January 1994 with John Cato, editor of *The Oak*, the mouthpiece of the National Alliance UK, who was close to C18. Cato indicated his opposition stemmed from the fact their respective ideologies were opposed to one another. 'I do not know what you mean when you speak of our ideologies being opposed,' Tyndall responded, emphasising his personal relationship with William Pierce, the NA leader. He then itemised a plethora of NA publications he had read. 'I agree with practically all that has been written in these publications,' he informed Cato. Tyndall conceded that he disagreed with Pierce over 'tactical matters' but this was simply a matter of national context. 'That is to say that were I in Dr. Pierce's shoes I may well favour doing exactly what he is doing,' Tyndall wrote. 'I have a very great respect for him and admiration for his work. I certainly know of no-one who is doing better work in the USA.' Where Tyndall disagreed with Cato was whether a British branch of NA was necessary. Tyndall claimed that his objection was not because the BNP 'has now obtained a foothold – albeit a small one – in local government.' Rather, he believed that 'our cause' would be better off 'if everyone were to concentrate all efforts in helping build up the BNP.' Thus, Cato's initiative would 'just syphon off support that might otherwise go to those who thus far have proved themselves the most effective and successful.'[545]

Whilst Tyndall sought to mollify figures like Cato, his proscription of C18 only poured fuel on the fire. Sargent responded:

> [T]hose involved in the struggle now have a straight choice between the failed policeys [sic] of tory rightwingism or the ideology of Adolf Hitler as National socialist revolutionaries, the two groups cannot work together, one must be crushed one must triumph as we enter the 2nd era of nationalist politics.[546]

Tyndall responded by pouring scorn on C18's lack of 'mettle' in spring 1994 when three BNP officials were seriously attacked by anti-fascists. 'In the event, their response was pathetic – *in*action was the order of the day.'[547] 'Why should a group he [Tyndall] had "fucked off" continue to do his dirty work?,' C18 responded.[548] Increasingly, however, Tyndall was concerned less by C18's passivity than by its actions against his own officials. After talks between the C18 leadership and Richard Edmonds failed to rekindle their relationship, C18 took it upon itself to administer 'punishment' beatings to several internal opponents, including BNP organisers Peter Rushton, Eddy Butler and Tony Lecomber.[549]

Increasingly militant, C18 rejected the BNP as a 'pressure valve' and ridiculed Tyndall's entire strategy. 'We at C18 reject democracy. It is jewish and no White should take part in it. The only realistic way to power is a White Revolution.'[550] Tyndall was not adverse to the politics of the revolutionary vanguard group per se. Indeed, in the midst of his contretemps with C18, Colin Jordan published 'The Way Ahead – A Primer for the N-S Vanguard'. Tyndall wrote him a long appraisal of the concept, stating that although their ideas differed:

> Where I feel is the greatest coincidence of views is in the final part of your document, heading 'Starting the revolution – in you.' In this section, there is scarcely a single word with which I can disagree, and I would like to say that this is a topic which could be greatly expanded in its scope. A book could be written about it, and perhaps one day may be.[551]

What Tyndall objected to were both the inroads C18 was making into the BNP activist base and its questioning of his authority. In September 1995, he issued a five-page broadside against C18 titled 'Doing the Enemy's Work', which censured the group for its 'lazy-minded' appeals to violence and terrorism which attracted only the 'thrill-seeker' who lacked the discipline for 'real politics'. Tyndall's analysis of its strategy confused political expediency with genuine 'modernisation', leading him to write that:

> when a movement has no hope of an appeal beyond the fringes, it can afford the indulgence of pandering almost solely to fringe opinion – and it is indeed to some extent forced to do so if it is to keep its nucleus intact.[552]

However, '[w]hen on the other hand, it sees open the door to support among the mainstream, it has to adjust both its targets and its approaches.' Certainly, in the present circumstances, the violent strategy C18 advocated represented 'the easy way out' and led in one direction – 'to the criminal court and the jail cell.' Tyndall also interpreted the C18 appeal as part of conspiracy to destroy the BNP:

I believe that what we are dealing with today is a strategy employed by the establishment to divide the nationalist movement, and therefore neutralise it, in exactly the same way that was done in the 1970s. The tactics to some degree differ – in those days they attacked my supporters and me for being 'too extreme', while this time we are being attacked for being 'not extreme enough' – but the end being pursued is identical in all essentials. Meanwhile the time-honoured methods of lie, smear and malicious rumour are alive and kicking. I know these kind of people, and I know their game.[553]

C18, Tyndall concluded, were a 'cancerous growth that has battened like a parasite on our rear.'[554] Nonetheless, following a slew of phone calls and letters, Tyndall was forced to clarify his position stating that his quarrel was not with the group's membership; 'it is with a tiny few at the centre of Combat 18 who are responsible for the group's actions and policies.'[555] Indeed, Tyndall's attack had cost the BNP its Liverpool, Derby and Dundee branches, who defected to the C18's political-wing, the National Socialist Alliance (NSA). C18 also claimed a new NSA unit had started in South Wales, 'taking most of the BNP membership with them'. Furthermore, they boasted, after Tyndall's broadside, 'over one hundred letters have arrived from BNP members (mostly the younger element of the party) pledging support.'[556]

To outmanoeuvre C18, Tyndall invited the NA leader William Pierce to be guest-speaker at the BNP Annual Rally, which took place on 11 November. For many BNP activists, Pierce was a legend, greatly admired for 'his single-minded dedication to the cause of his race.'[557] Given his profile and standing within the Anglo-American militant subcultures, Pierce's presence at the BNP event represented a tacit endorsement of Tyndall's leadership. Lowles credits it with 'reversing' BNP fortunes in its struggle against C18.[558] BNP publications highlighted that a small contingent of C18 activists 'lubricated by drink' had displayed a distinct lack of 'respect' for Pierce 'by behaving in a general silly manner during most of the event.'[559]

Tyndall's association with Pierce made a mockery of his critique of C18 strategy, an irony that was not lost on C18 itself.[560] Earlier in the year, Pierce's racist fantasy, *The Turner Diaries* had been widely proclaimed as a 'blue print' for the bombing of the Alfred P. Murrah Building in Oklahoma City on 19 April, in which 168 people had been killed. Tyndall himself was quick to insinuate that the atrocity was the work of the Federal Government itself.[561] Whilst Tyndall was 'most grateful' to Pierce for addressing the BNP rally, he did not automatically endorse his own stratagems. Mirroring his debates with Colin Jordan, Tyndall felt the NA offered only limited lessons for the BNP, principally because it eschewed electoral activity. Pierce believed that a 'political breakthrough' hinged upon the construction of an 'elite force', leading Tyndall to lament that how this group would actually attain power was 'a little ambiguous', particularly since Pierce 'often spoke as if he couldn't see it coming except by armed insurgence.'[562] In this respect, Tyndall regarded both *The Turner Diaries* and *Hunter* as 'the products of moments when personal frustration got the better of the writer's pre-eminent virtue as ideologist and political strategist.'[563] Pierce disagreed with Tyndall too. 'The BNP has got the best programme in Britain,' he argued, albeit with the caveat that its platform 'is a little bit restrained. I would express things differently – if anything, the BNP is a little too conservative.'[564] The Home Secretary promptly banned Pierce from returning to Britain.[565] Tyndall's admiration of Pierce remained undiminished. When Pierce died in 2002, Tyndall praised him as 'an example to us all'.[566]

The threat C18 posed to Tyndall's leadership of the extreme right ultimately proved transient. Their controversial control of B&H helped poison the well. Influential music magazines like *Resistance* (USA) and *Nordland* (Sweden) turned against them. David Lane, a leading figure in The Order, a group idolised by C18, issued a statement from prison stating that:

> the leadership of C18 are obviously Zionist agents or they are so ignorant and dangerous that they might as well be. It can no longer be tolerated. At the appropriate time the enemy amongst us will face a night of the long knives.[567]

In February 1996, C18 began disintegrating into murderous acrimony. Its leader, Charlie Sargent and former Skrewdriver drummer Martin Cross, murdered Chris Castle a friend of Sargent's factional rival Will Browning, leading, ultimately, to C18's demise.[568] C18's waning control over the lucrative 'white power' music scene re-opened the door to the BNP. *Spearhead* observed that whilst the music was not to everyone's taste – which was to put it mildly given Tyndall's preference for Elgar, Purcell and Wagner – 'such major gatherings of people "on our wavelength" are too good an opportunity to miss,' and urged all party units to seize the opportunity to 'boost sales and spread the word.'[569]

Tyndall successfully staved off the C18 challenge but his decision to appoint a young, hard-line militant called Nick Griffin (Chapter 6) as *Spearhead*'s editor, as part of the same effort to prove he had not gone 'soft', proved politically terminal. Tyndall denied that he had ever seen Griffin as a potential successor. 'From the very start there was something about him that inspired doubt,' he later claimed. Nonetheless, he forgave Griffin's history of factionalism as 'the immaturity of youth', despite warnings to the contrary from his wife and close colleagues. Tyndall subsequently admitted he had taken a 'gamble' upon Griffin. It did not pay off. 'I later realised too late that he had not changed a jot,' Tyndall lamented.[570]

By Tyndall's own admission, the internecine struggle with C18 had caused 'tremendous internal harm' to the BNP though party membership received a boost as 'the best returned to the fold' once C18 became moribund.[571] Unfortunately, for Tyndall, his success in stabilising the BNP did little to mitigate the fact that the 'Millwall Effect' had waned, confirmed by a string of disappointing local election results and lacklustre recruitment.[572] Political reversal incubated internal discontent with Tyndall's leadership which from spring 1997 onwards coalesced around *The Patriot*, a journal edited by Tony Lecomber which became the focal point for those frustrated by the party's stalled 'modernisation' and lack of progress. Tyndall found little within its pages with which he disagreed ideologically and concluded that *The Patriot* was simply concocting an 'imaginary conflict' between 'modernisers' and those allegedly resisting 'modernisation' to unseat him.[573] Rallying the party faithful, Tyndall made the 1997 general election campaign the centrepiece of BNP efforts, which 'helped us out of what might have become a debilitating rut.'[574]

The party platform during the election, Tyndall's last as party leader, was explicitly racial.[575] 'We're appealing to the white British voter,' Tyndall told the audience at the party's annual rally. 'We're not crawling for the Black and Asian vote.'[576] The BNP election broadcast opened with Tyndall standing, symbolically, in front of the white cliffs of Dover.[577] The party's fifty-six candidates polled a meagre 35,832 votes between them. Tyndall's vote of 2,849 (7.3 per cent) in the strategically chosen Poplar and Canning Town constituency was one of the few highlights.[578] Nonetheless, the BNP claimed to have received between 2,500–3,000 enquiries because of the election, which resulted in a landslide for 'New Labour' – a development Tyndall believed offered 'quite unprecedented possibilities for advancement'.[579] Though prescient, Tyndall's analysis presumed he would be at the helm to oversee this advance. Prior to the election, Tyndall had taken personal charge of the BNP propaganda drive, declaring: 'if that propaganda turns out to be a flop the flop will be mine and members will be entitled to hold me to blame.'[580] Increasingly, Tyndall personified the 'flop'.[581]

Despite his unrelenting commitment to the cause of racial nationalism, it was becoming increasingly obvious to many BNP activists that Tyndall was no longer the man to lead the party into the new millennium. Weakened politically by the death of two leading lieutenants, Dave Bruce and John Peacock, who both died in 1998, Tyndall faced a concerted campaign against him from a curious union of its 'modernising' and 'hard-line' wings of the BNP against the 'old guard' surrounding Tyndall.[582] Their candidate, Nick Griffin, who Tyndall had by now come to deeply regret admitting into the BNP, launched his leadership challenge as the party geared up for the 1999 European election campaign, its first foray into this electoral arena. To fund the European election campaign, Tyndall relied in part upon the B&H network whose East Midlands activists, many of whom were also BNP members, staged a series of fund-raising 'White Pride' concerts.[583] The BNP eventually raised £89,000 for the campaign, though Griffin subsequently accused Tyndall of spending approximately £50,000 of this to fund the day-to-day running of the BNP, though he conceded that a legacy bequeathed to the party allowed Tyndall to make up the shortfall.[584]

The European elections on 10 June 1999 saw the BNP poll 102,647 votes (1.1 per cent) giving further weight to arguments for Tyndall's ouster, which only accelerated over the course of the summer.[585] The increasingly acrimonious election campaign saw Griffin's supporters responding with a scurrilous website – 'Tyndall Exposed' – that, amongst other things, accused him of being a closet homosexual and secret communist who had feathered his own nest with embezzled party funds. It also attacked Tyndall for allowing Jews and 'race-mixers' into the party, in a bid to pre-empt Tyndall's own criticisms of Griffin's 'modernisation' strategy.[586]

Tyndall was overwhelmingly defeated in the leadership election, winning only 38 per cent of the vote. The result was a 'watershed' in extreme right politics. Tyndall had been the dominant force for thirty-five years. He would not be again. Tyndall urged his supporters to continue to support the party but many were unable to reconcile themselves to the change. Those who tendered their resignations included Richard Edmonds who *British Nationalist* conceded 'will be sorely missed'.[587] Edmonds was 'so angry' he moved to Russia for three years. 'I couldn't bear to live in Britain. A Britain, which had Nick Griffin as the chairman of the British National Party,' he recalled.[588] Thereafter, Edmonds spent time working as a deputy head teacher with the 'Schulverein zur Förderung der Rußlanddeutschen in Ostpreußen' (School Association for the Promotion of Russian-Germans in East Prussia). This initiative, run by Henning Pless, formerly active in the banned Bund Heimattreuer Jugend, sought to renew the German presence in what had been East Prussia before 1945.[589]

Following his defeat, *Spearhead* announced that Tyndall was 'stepping down' as leader, a curious elision of the truth, but would remain a member and support the party.[590] Tyndall found it hard to let go, however. Opponents alleged that he sought to frustrate the succession by refusing to hand over party accounts to the new leadership for five months and accused him of embezzling party funds, an allegation Tyndall placed in the hands of his solicitors.[591] Tyndall's immediate problem was to keep *Spearhead* solvent. Griffin had launched a new party journal, *Identity*, which led to a dramatic reduction in *Spearhead*'s sales to BNP branches. Tyndall formed the 'Friends of Spearhead' to raise capital from supporters but after three months, only thirty-one people had registered.[592]

In March 2001, following several months nursing his wounds, Tyndall announced that he would challenge Griffin for the party leadership and that his official nomination would be submitted in June.[593] Tyndall dropped this challenge following Griffin's strong performance in the 2001 general election. Whilst Griffin polled 6,552 votes (16.4 per cent) in Oldham West and Royton, Tyndall, standing in Mitcham and Morden, had mustered a mere 642 votes (1.7 per cent), hardly a compelling argument to reinstall him as party leader. Simultaneously, Tyndall sought to take credit for Griffin's success claiming that it was under his leadership that the BNP evolved 'from a mere street gang involved in demonstrations into a mature election-orientated political machine.' Internal critics assailed Tyndall's claims. 'He is quite right when he says that the modernisation programme began when he was party Chairman,' they stated, 'but that is not the same thing as saying that it began under his "leadership".'[594]

End game

Unsurprisingly, Tyndall proved unable to accept Griffin's leadership, personally or politically. Griffin's public admission 'that a whites-only Britain was no longer possible' incensed him. So too did Griffin's claim that the BNP simply wished 'to make the best of a bad job out of the multi-cultural society.'[595] For his part, Griffin began to isolate Tyndall, suspending activists and de-registering party units that invited him to speak.[596] In January 2003, Griffin banned *Spearhead* from distribution within the BNP because it was a source of 'demoralisation'.[597] Responding directly to Tyndall's constant grousing, Griffin denounced him as a 'Hollywood Nazi' whose 'totalitarian' politics were rooted in 'the sub-Mosleyite whackiness of Arnold Leese's Imperial Fascist League and the Big Government mania of the 1930s' and thus completely out of step with 'modern' nationalism.[598]

Matters culminated on 3 August when a disciplinary tribunal found Tyndall guilty of having personally 'slandered' Griffin and of collectively slandering the BNP leadership, leading to his expulsion from the party.[599] Prior to the proceedings, the party's internal membership bulletin had accused Tyndall of instigating a campaign of 'subversion' within the party whilst a four-page 'tirade' against him in *Identity*, written by Griffin, 'was no doubt intended to prime members to accept my kicking out of the party.'[600] There was little doubt that Tyndall was guilty of course. The first charge related to an email Tyndall had sent to the former NPD chairman Günther Deckert in which he had asserted, amongst other things, that Griffin was 'a classic psychopath' with a 'streak of insanity'. Tyndall also speculated that Griffin might be a 'government agent' – he calculated the probability at a ratio of 65:35 – but was certain that he had been leveraged into the party leadership by those who certainly were government agents, leading to the second charge of 'collective slander of leadership' being preferred against him.[601]

Tyndall's expulsion was rationalised to the membership as a matter of political pragmatism. Recalling the first time he had heard Tyndall speak, Martin Wingfield, editor of the BNP newspaper, *Voice of Freedom*, stated: 'It was a life changing moment for me. It seemed as though John had switched on a light in a darkened room, and the solutions to all those political imponderables suddenly became crystal clear.' Tyndall's uncompromising message was 'pertinent and feasible' in 1975, argued Wingfield. A quarter of a century later, however, it was not only impossible but an 'embarrassment' to the party. Tyndall's expulsion was also symbolic, signalling publicly 'that the BNP is not stuck in the past and that his kind of racism has no place in the British National Party'.[602]

Tyndall responded to his expulsion with a lengthy article titled 'The Problem is Mr. Griffin', urging BNP members to 'get rid of the wrecker-in-chief'.[603] He engaged solicitors, though Griffin pre-empted him by settling out-of-court, quashing Tyndall's expulsion and reinstating him as a member. The debacle allegedly cost the BNP around £12,000.[604] Despite this setback, Griffin remained committed to removing Tyndall. During the 2004 local elections, Griffin forbade him to speak at a BNP meeting. 'The many photographs of you in neo-nazi uniform ... are a public relations handicap for the party,' Tyndall was informed.[605]

Pushed to the margins, Tyndall flew to the United States to address the International European-American Unity and Rights (EURO) Leadership Conference held in New Orleans, Louisiana, on 28–30 May 2004. Founded in 2000, EURO projected itself as a 'white civil rights' organisation for 'European and Americans wherever they may live'. The conference itself celebrated the release of its founder, former Ku Klux Klan 'Grand Wizard' David Duke who they hailed as a 'political prisoner' despite his incarceration for mail and tax fraud. Duke spoke of his 'tremendous respect' for Tyndall, later stating he was 'far more than a friend, he was a leader from whom I learned much when I was younger. He stood as an example of both intellect and courage and he influenced my life greatly.'[606]

Tyndall's speech denounced the 'tragic illusion' of moderation and compromise. Racial truths such as those once prevailing in the segregationist South were immutable, he proclaimed. Only the perception of 'truth' changed. 'Racial equality', once a marginal and 'extreme' view was now mainstream thanks to 'Jewish media', claimed Tyndall. Ideological repackaging diverted efforts away from the one thing that would genuinely alter perception: the acquisition of 'complete power ... activity geared towards anything else is a waste of time.'[607] The conference culminated with delegates signing the 'New Orleans Protocol', which Tyndall helped frame, pledging them to maintain a 'pan-European outlook'. Whilst the conference was a small-scale affair, 67,000 people from around the world later listened to the speeches online.[608]

Following the conference, Tyndall flew to Atlanta, Georgia, with Sam Dickson to address a small gathering where he met with Joshua Buckley, co-editor of *Tyr*, a journal specialising in the pagan folklore of pre-Christian Northern Europe. He travelled on to Washington, DC to meet former *Washington Times* journalist Samuel Francis who had become a prominent racial nationalist ideologue, responsible for framing the constitution of the Conservative Council of Citizens, a successor to the White Citizens' Councils of the 1950s. Thereafter, Tyndall stayed with Jared Taylor, editor of *American Renaissance*, before addressing a meeting in Arlington, Virginia, chaired by Francis. Reporting his impressions of the United States since he last visited in 1991, Tyndall opined that 'the ethnic minority presence is absolutely overpowering. Americans are simply losing their country. So, of course, are we but the process over there is much further advanced.'[609]

Tyndall loyalists formed the Spearhead Support Group (SSG) as a platform from which to oppose 'any liberalising or "watering down" tendencies in the nationalist movement' to which end it produced *The Griffin File*, a booklet documenting Griffin's record of reneging upon the 'core principles'.[610] The SSG also tried (and failed) to create 'an effective campaign machine for Mr Tyndall's bid to take back and reform the BNP.'[611] The BNP responded – with some justification – that the same 'neo-Nazi' elements that he had condemned in 1995 as a 'lazy-minded' 'cancerous growth' on the 'nationalist scene' were now Tyndall's principal backers.[612] Tyndall continued his campaign against Griffin undaunted, challenging him for the BNP leadership on 12 July 2004. His supporters hyperbolically declared that this 'will go down in the annals of Nationalist history as the day the rot was stopped and the great change around back to White Nationalist principles as the bedrock of the BNP began!'[613]

Tyndall soon had other concerns, however. Three days later, the BBC aired 'The Secret Agent', a documentary filmed in conjunction with a disillusioned Bradford BNP organiser whose cooperation with the anti-fascist magazine *Searchlight* provided an undercover BBC reporter entrée to the party. Its consequences for the BNP, not all of them negative, would reverberate for several years. Eight days after the documentary screened, police arrested Tyndall on suspicion of inciting racial hatred in Blackburn after he had attended the Christmas social of the SSG and *Heritage & Destiny*.[614]

Griffin disrupted Tyndall's leadership challenge by issuing an edict banning him and Edmonds from addressing any officially constituted meetings, a gambit Tyndall declared illegitimate after taking legal advice.[615] Undeterred, Tyndall set out his stall for the leadership challenge in *Spearhead*'s September issue. It highlighted the depths of Tyndall's ideological alienation from the BNP's publicly professed anti-Muslim platform. 'I personally do not see Islam as any threat to Britain,' Tyndall wrote, 'as long as the ethnic groups bringing it here are excluded from this country. In other words, the threat is racial, not religious.' His anti-Semitic animus was such that even after 9/11 Tyndall had pondered potential 'collaboration' with Islamists against US-led globalisation and 'Zionism', though he demanded 'strict lines of demarcation' between 'the white and Islamic Worlds: we stay out of their lands and they stay out of ours.' His considered view was that 'Islam need not be a threat but neither should it be considered an ally.'[616] This put him at odds with Griffin whom he attacked for 'singling out' Islam. 'Mr Griffin claims that we are menaced by a militant Islamic imperialism,' Tyndall asserted. 'I contend that by far the greatest menace is the imperialism of Zionism'. Promising to re-orientate the BNP accordingly if re-elected, 'I intend in the future the BNP will focus its attention on this menace much more and on Islam much less,' he declared.[617]

Tyndall never had a chance to put his view to the BNP membership. He was suspended on 25 September. Prior to this, the party's constitution had undergone a subtle change to prevent Tyndall appealing a 'guilty' verdict, which was, of course, a foregone conclusion.[618] Tyndall faced thirteen disciplinary offences at disciplinary tribunal chaired by Tony Lecomber, the BNP group development officer, who was notably hostile towards him. Found 'guilty' of seven of these charges, Griffin duly expelled Tyndall from the party for the second time in sixteen months.[619] In May 2005, the BNP went further. Griffin proscribed Tyndall – 'a former BNP member in Hove'.[620] Tyndall's wife was 'amused' to read in the internal members' bulletin, 'that as a BNP member she was required to shun all contact with the proscribed individual!'[621]

Though Tyndall again reached for legal redress, his exclusion was complete. He and his followers traversed the country addressing numerous 'Save the BNP' meetings but Tyndall found it difficult to energise his support base. His declaration that there was 'no time limit' on his bid to take back control undermined any momentum his campaign might have built. Some concluded that the task of ousting Griffin was 'hopeless'.[622] Others unsuccessfully pressured Tyndall to form a new party, something he dismissed as a 'non-starter'.[623]

Tyndall's followers continued to push for action. The Spearhead group reconstituted itself as the Nationalist Alliance (NA) on 20 March 2005, with the avowed aim of uniting and channelling the activities of various racial nationalist *groupuscules* but quickly disintegrated following a series of splits. The group's key task was to provide Tyndall with 'moral' support following his arrest and arraignment for inciting racial hatred. Though Tyndall declined to join the organisation, its support was 'most welcome'.[624] Overshadowed by larger BNP demonstrations outside Leeds Crown Court for Griffin and Mark Collett, the NA held their own protest against 'the oppressive ZOG regime' attempting to have Tyndall imprisoned.[625] Tyndall's last political act was to address an NA meeting held in Brighton on 9 July.[626] He died at home ten days later. Tyndall had been due to return to court on 21 July. In his absence, the NA held a symbolic memorial demonstration, a group of activists wearing black armbands, dipping their flags in salute during a two-minute silence to Tyndall's memory.[627] 'Many rank-and-file BNP members came over to the NA and expressed their sorrow at their former Leader's sudden passing,' the group claimed.[628]

Tyndall's death dealt a terminal blow to the political aspirations of those within the BNP opposed to Griffin, personally, politically and strategically. It left them with little long-term future in the party. *Spearhead*, which Tyndall had published continuously for forty years, died with him. There was a halting effort to keep the venture alive but this ceased in the absence of support from Tyndall's widow. In retrospect, *Spearhead*'s closure was a political mistake. It denied Griffin's opponents a centre of gravity to rally around.[629] The magazine's overarching importance to the milieu can be surmised from *Heritage & Destiny*'s obituary of Tyndall titled 'Death of a Leader – End of an Era':

> *Spearhead* was a shining beacon of truth lighting the way for many British and other English speaking racial nationalists through four often dark decades. It is difficult to credit that the voice of John Tyndall's *Spearhead* will not be heard with its pungent commentary on the next stages of our struggle.[630]

The new BNP leadership did not mourn Tyndall's passing. He represented the antithesis of the 'modern' extreme right that Griffin wanted to project. They quickly purged Tyndall from the party's public memory. The BNP published a critical obituary of its founder on the party website highlighting his 'Nazi' connections and 'authoritarian' leadership.[631] *Identity*, the BNP journal, also published a brief obituary but got Tyndall's date of birth wrong.[632] When a short appreciation appeared two months later, it was titled 'End of an Era' – meant literally and figuratively – acknowledging simply that without Tyndall 'there would be no British National Party today.'[633] Simultaneously, however, the BNP hoped to make political capital from his death, claiming that the Labour Party and the Crown Prosecution Service 'have hounded a pensioner to death for the "crime" of speaking his mind.'[634]

This was not the prevailing sentiment outside Griffin's BNP, however. Tyndall's longtime colleague Colin Jordan blamed Tyndall's death squarely upon 'the treacherous treatment' he had received from Griffin, 'a disgusting, time-serving, compromiser,' which 'probably contributed to the heart attack which killed Britain's top nationalist.' Jordan's obituary revealed his ongoing personal antipathy:

> There is absolutely no way whatsoever to render honest and sincere tribute to John Tyndall without expressing clear and complete rejection of Griffin and his kosher organisation who have rejected and opposed what John Tyndall stood for, and thereby have made themselves part of the enemy, his enemy and mine, and must be treated as such, unless we are to dishonour his memory and ourselves in the process.[635]

Despite Tyndall's personal disdain for 'white power music' *Blood & Honour*, mouthpiece of the international music network, revered him as an 'inspirational figure' who 'gave his life to the land and ideals he knew were right.' His contribution to extreme right politics was, they argued, 'immeasurable, his influence far reaching, his passion drive and ambition to achieve our goals something we all must find within us if we are to have a chance of survival.'[636] Tyndall was respectfully mourned internationally too. *National Vanguard*, the NA magazine, 'dips its standards to the passing of a giant of our race',[637] whilst the German national socialist magazine, *Nation Europa*, published a generous tribute describing Tyndall as 'ein bekennender Freund der Deutschen' ('an avowed friend of the Germans'), a euphemistic description of his politics.[638] Even the anti-fascist magazine *Searchlight* would pay Tyndall a backhanded compliment:

> We are not sad to see his passing. But we do recognise that, however nasty he was, he had at least some consistency and scruples. Unlike Nick Griffin, who has cut and trimmed to make the BNP appear more acceptable, Tyndall stayed true to his principles of wanting an all-white Britain. He was a true Nazi.[639]

Legacy

Tyndall's widow derided Griffin as a 'pip squeak' but believed that the best means of preserving her husband's legacy and *ergo* the cause of racial nationalism was for his supporters to remain within the BNP and to 'rescue' it from Griffin.[640] Internal opposition to Griffin's control of the BNP culminated in August 2007 with the first of several challenges to his leadership. Griffin detected Tyndall's ghost behind those pushing for his usurpation. 'I respect their loyalty to their old friend,' Griffin wrote,

> but he's been dead several years now, the party he founded has never been stronger, and they must now either accept the status quo fully and get on board fully and constructively, or they must leave. If they sincerely believe that the old Tyndall tactics and attitudes would be more successful than the way things have been done in recent years, then the proper home for them now is in the National Front.[641]

In an effort to prove that the BNP itself was still a hard-line racial nationalist organisation, Griffin co-opted Richard Edmonds, Tyndall's loyal lieutenant, onto the BNP Advisory Council. Edmonds' opinions had not changed one iota, praising Griffin's internal opponents for acting 'as a brake on liberalising tendencies.'[642] Edmonds subsequently swung his weight behind Eddy Butler's leadership challenge.[643] This led to Edmonds removal from the Advisory Council in 2010, 'because he used information provided to him in confidence at an AC meeting and twisted it into a falsehood. He then spread this outright lie at numerous leadership challenge meetings,' alleged the BNP.[644] Following the party's poor performance in the May 2011 local elections and the death of Valerie Tyndall in June,[645] Edmonds issued his own challenge to Griffin's leadership.[646] His ultimately abortive challenge precipitated Edmonds own defection from the BNP to the NF in October 2011, ending any residual hopes Tyndall's supporters harboured of recapturing the party.[647]

By this point, there was arguably little to salvage, however. The BNP rose and fell after Tyndall's death. Today it is utterly moribund, leaving Tyndall little organisational legacy. Ideologically, however, Tyndall, like Jordan and Mosley, has become a totemic figure. For over a decade now, racial nationalists have gathered annually at a 'John Tyndall Memorial Meeting', an event currently organised by Mark Cotterill, editor of *Heritage and Destiny*. These meetings, held in Preston, Lancashire, highlight the 'broad church'[648] approach taken by *groupuscular* racial nationalist groups to their comparative organisational isolation. Regardless of their differing ideological and tactical approaches, a shared alienation from Nick Griffin's BNP, a party they no longer recognised as their own, united this milieu.

Activists from almost every group outside the BNP gathered to commemorate and memorialise Tyndall's life, and those of other recently deceased activists.[649] In the spirit of 'unity', old adversaries now delivered homilies. Andrew Brons, the BNP MEP, eulogised Tyndall at one such meeting, having previously denounced 'Conservative "Nationalists"' like Tyndall as 'political illiterates'.[650] As well as glossing over old divides, these 'John Tyndall Memorial Meetings' afford veteran racial nationalists, many of whom knew Tyndall personally, the opportunity to meet with the leaders of newer youth-orientated 'street' organisations like National Action, a small but vociferous national socialist group banned as a 'terrorist' organisation in December 2016. 'John Tyndall's political legacy lives on even in a generation that was still at primary school when he died,' noted the organisers.[651] In this sense, Tyndall – idealised and beatified – has transmogrified into a cipher for the continued persistence of an increasingly marginalised political tradition. Speaking at one such event, Peter Rushton, assistant editor of *Heritage & Destiny*, asserted that: 'the future belonged to radical nationalism, because our ideas are based on nature, while liberalism is anti-nature … We nationalists following in the tradition of John Tyndall assert our racially based, nature-based alternative to the establishments [sic] melting-pot dystopia.'[652]

Notes

1 The *Guardian*, 20 July 2005.
2 Richard Thurlow, *Fascism in Britain: From Oswald Mosley's Blackshirts to the National Front* (London: I.B. Tauris, 1998), p. 259.
3 Martin Walker, *The National Front* (London: Fontana/Collins, 1977), p. 9 estimated that the party's stable membership was roughly 12,000.
4 Kate Taylor, 'The Rise of the 1970s National Front', *Searchlight*, no. 314, August 2001, p. 19.
5 *Spearhead*, no. 189, July 1984. The writings of François Duprat, one of the founding members of the Front National in 1972, reflect contemporary French interest, see 'La percée politique du Nationalisme en Grande-Bretagne', *Défence de l'Occident*, vol. 149, 1977, pp. 57–65. Duprat's own journal, *Cahiers européens*, provided French militants with regular updates on the NF.
6 John Bean, *Many Shades of Black: Inside Britain's Far Right* (Bloomington, IN: Ostara, 2013), p. 238.
7 Nigel Fielding, *The National Front* (London: Routledge & Kegan Paul, 1981), p. 22.
8 Simon Schama, *A History of Britain* (London: Bodley Head, 2009), p. 240.
9 John Tyndall, *The Eleventh Hour: A Call for British Rebirth* (London: Albion Press, 1988), pp. 7–8.
10 Douglas R. Holmes, *Integral Europe: Fast-Capitalism, Multiculturalism, Neofascism* (Princeton, NJ: Princeton University Press, 2000), p. 150.
11 *Spearhead*, no. 39, January 1971.
12 Holmes, *Integral Europe*, p. 150.
13 *Spearhead*, no. 43, June 1971.
14 'Tyndall the Communist?', www.tyndallexposed.com/commie.htm (accessed 20 March 2005).
15 Tyndall, *The Eleventh Hour*, pp. 48–49.
16 *Spearhead*, no. 350, April 1998.
17 Tyndall, *The Eleventh Hour*, p. 16.
18 *Ibid.*, pp. 49–50 and 96.
19 John Tyndall, 'Do We Need Jewish Candidates: John Tyndall Addresses a Vexed Issue', *Spearhead*, www.spearhead.co.uk/0405-jt4.html (accessed 5 June 2015).
20 A.K. Chesterton to John Tyndall, 5 April 1957, Chesterton papers. In *Spearhead*, no. 39, January 1971, Tyndall recorded that he and Chesterton had first met in 1956.
21 *Candour*, vol. 6, nos 189 and 190, 7 and 14 June 1957.
22 *Candour*, vol. 7, no. 196, 26 July 1957; *Candour*, vol. 8, no. 229, 14 March 1958; *Candour*, vol. 8, no. 231, 28 March 1958; and *Candour*, vol. 8, nos 232 and 233, 4 and 11 April 1958.
23 *Candour*, vol. 3, no. 109, 25 November 1955.

24 Bean, *Many Shades of Black*, pp. 100, 105 and 119. The League is viewed as a 'training ground' for a post-war generation of militants with the implicit assumption that this is where they met. However, Colin Jordan had left the League in October 1956, resigning finally in April 1957, whilst Martin Webster only joined in 1960. Tyndall never mentioned meeting either man whilst he was active in the League, though he may have.
25 Bean, *Many Shades of Black*, p. 116.
26 *Identity*, no. 57, August 2005.
27 *Spearhead*, no. 417, November 2003; and *Identity*, no. 57, August 2005.
28 *Candour Supplement*, 25 April 1958; and Bean, *Many Shades of Black*, p. 108.
29 A.K. Chesterton to John Tyndall, 2 September 1966, Chesterton papers. O.G. Allanson-Winn, a South African friend of Chesterton's subsequently told Tyndall 'he said you were the best he had met,' see *Spearhead*, no. 146, December 1980.
30 John Tyndall to A.K. Chesterton, 5 September 1966, Chesterton papers. Tyndall was also greatly influenced by another of Chesterton's colleagues, Ivor Benson, the South African author of numerous anti-Semitic works including *The Zionist Factor*, of whom Tyndall wrote in *Spearhead*, no. 289, March 1993: 'I would say that after the death of A.K. Chesterton, who he knew well, Ivor Benson provided more guidance to me in the quest for enlightenment on national and international issues than any other single person.' Benson was not the only former Rhodesian official with whom Tyndall was acquainted. *Spearhead* regularly published articles by Noel Hunt (*Spearhead*, no. 309, November 1994), who had retired from the Rhodesian government in 1975 with the rank of Deputy Secretary at the Ministry of Internal Affairs.
31 *Spearhead*, no. 168, October 1982. Canterbury BNP leader Derek Whiting was a former LEL activist.
32 Tyndall, *The Eleventh Hour*, p. 182.
33 *East End Advertiser*, 30 May 1958. Its local branch was run by Joe Warren, who operated out of the Carpenter's Arms on Cheshire Street, Bethnal Green, holding meetings in the street as well as in nearby St Matthews Row.
34 Bean, *Many Shades of Black*, p. 122 and 125–126.
35 *The Times*, 12 December 1958.
36 *The Times*, 7 March 1959.
37 The *Guardian*, 27 September 1997 states that Tyndall was his election agent.
38 *The Times*, 22 September 1997.
39 The *Guardian*, 9 March 1959; and the *Guardian*, 11 March 1959.
40 Bean, *Many Shades of Black*, p. 124.
41 *Combat*, no. 3, April–June 1959.
42 *The Manchester Guardian*, 25 May 1959.
43 Bean, *Many Shades of Black*, p. 128.
44 'Report of NLP meeting, Trafalgar Square, 6 September 1959' in 1658/9/2/2, Jewish Defence Committee (JDC) papers, Wiener Library, London, hereafter JDC papers.
45 *North St. Pancras Election News – Webster Says 'Britons First'* (London: Clair Press, 1959).
46 *The Times*, 18 September 1958.
47 *The Times*, 30 September 1959; *The Times*, 16 October 1959; *Combat*, no. 5, January–March 1960; and Bean, *Many Shades of Black*, p. 136.
48 Thomas Wright to 'Dear Sir', 3 November 1959 in Labour Research Department archive, Box 2/D/2, London Metropolitan University, London.
49 *The Times*, 25 September 1958.
50 Webster's campaign was such that his brewery gave him notice to quit his pub during the campaign. He later defected to Mosley's UM, see *The Times*, 23 September 1958.
51 Bean, *Many Shades of Black*, pp. 138 and 140–141.
52 *Ibid.*, p. 141
53 *Ibid.*
54 Tyndall, *The Eleventh Hour*, pp. 181–182; and Bean, *Many Shades of Black*, pp. 143–144.
55 Tyndall, *The Eleventh Hour*, pp. 183–194.
56 John Tyndall, *The Authoritarian State: It's Meaning and Function* (London: British National Party, 1961). Gary Rex Lauck, leader of the NSDAP-AO published an American edition under the imprint of his 'Westrope Social Alliance Press' in 1973. *NS Report*, no. 62, July–August 1985, the NSDAP-AO publication, was still selling copies.

57 Tyndall, *The Authoritarian State*.
58 *Greyshirt*, no. 1, January 1962.
59 Spearhead circular, 4 December 1961 in TNA CRIM 1/3973.
60 Walker, *The National Front*, p. 35.
61 *Ibid.*
62 Tyndall, *The Eleventh Hour*, p. 185.
63 The *Guardian*, 19 June 1962.
64 *The National Socialist*, vol. 1, no. 5, August 1963.
65 *The National Socialist*, no. 7, 1964.
66 *Daily Express*, 5 September 1962.
67 Spearhead Trial, The Press Association Special Reporting Service, 2 October to 15 October 1962, copy in Wiener Library London.
68 *Ibid.*
69 John Tyndall to George Lincoln Rockwell, 11 March 1962, Rockwell papers.
70 *Ibid.*
71 *The Times*, 25 October 1962.
72 *Daily Worker*, 24 October 1962. Veale had also acted for the NSM, see F.J.P. Veale to Martin Webster, 14 November 1962 in SCH/01/Res/BRI/20/002, Searchlight archive.
73 *Viking Books: Literature for Patriots of all Nations – Catalogue, 1964*.
74 John Tyndall to George Lincoln Rockwell, 11 March 1962, Rockwell papers.
75 Denis Pirie to George Lincoln Rockwell, 25 March 1963, Rockwell papers. His younger brother, Eric, was also an NSM activist, see *Nation Revisited*, July 2013, http://nationrevisited.blogspot.co.uk/2013/07/nation-revisited-106.html.
76 John Tyndall to George Lincoln Rockwell, 13 May 1963, Rockwell papers.
77 George Lincoln Rockwell to John Tyndall, 31 May 1963, Rockwell papers.
78 George Lincoln Rockwell to John Tyndall, 28 April 1963, Rockwell papers.
79 George Lincoln Rockwell to Colin Jordan, 2 May 1964, Rockwell papers.
80 George Thayer, *The British Political Fringe: A Profile* (London: Anthony Blond, 1965), p. 28.
81 *Ibid.*, p. 31.
82 John Tyndall to George Lincoln Rockwell, 8 January, 1964, Rockwell papers
83 The *Guardian*, 8 February 1964; and The *Guardian*, 22 October 1974.
84 *Daily Express*, 16 September 1964.
85 Colin Jordan to George Lincoln Rockwell, 25 May 1964; Colin Jordan to George Lincoln Rockwell, 1 June 1964; Colin Jordan to George Lincoln Rockwell, 7 July 1964; Colin Jordan to George Lincoln Rockwell, 26 December 1964; and Colin Jordan to Martin Webster, 2 January 1965, Rockwell papers.
86 *Ibid.*
87 *Searchlight*, no. 38, August 1978, quoting Tyndall's correspondence with Karl Allen, a former ANP activist.
88 Tyndall, *The Eleventh Hour*, p. 198.
89 *Spearhead*, December 1964.
90 *Official Programme of the Greater Britain Movement* (London: GBM, n.d.).
91 *Spearhead*, no. 1, August–September 1964.
92 *Spearhead*, no. 2, December 1964.
93 *Spearhead*, no. 4, February 1965.
94 BBC, *Lost Race* (1999).
95 *Spearhead*, no. 4, February 1965.
96 Martin Webster, CV.
97 Terry Cooper, *Death by Dior* (London: Dynasty Press, 2013), pp. 51 and 61.
98 *Ibid.*, p. 51.
99 Tyndall, *The Eleventh Hour*, pp. 198–202.
100 Walker, *The National Front*, p. 47.
101 Colin Jordan to George Lincoln Rockwell, 25 May 1964; and Colin Jordan to George Lincoln Rockwell, 26 December 1964, Rockwell papers. See also *Spearhead*, April 1965.
102 *Morning Advertiser*, 17 December 1964.
103 *The Times*, 15 July 1966. The action was taken against the individual who took out the lease, GBM activist Paul Trevelyan, a former Swaziland police inspector and former LEL activist,

John Tyndall 411

whose wife, Valerie, worked with Tyndall producing *Spearhead*, see *Sunday Telegraph*, 16 May 1965.
104 John Tyndall to Mrs Winifred Leese, 30 April 1966 in SCH/01/Res/BRI/23/002, Searchlight archive.
105 Walker, *The National Front*, p. 72.
106 *Spearhead*, no. 13, November–December 1966.
107 TNA MEPO 2/10633; and *Spearhead*, December 1964.
108 Kenyatta's Nation Union party issued an angry statement demanding an apology from Foreign and Commonwealth secretary Duncan Sandys whilst Martin Shikuku, general secretary of the opposition Democratic Union, demanded the expulsion of Sir Geoffrey de Freitas, the British High Commissioner. Irate African students stormed the British Embassy in Bulgaria, whilst in Kenya itself angry crowds gathered outside the British High Commission in Nairobi. In Bomet, 200 miles from the capital 'Kipsigis tribesmen blew war horns and yelled their hatred of the League of Empire Loyalists' at a meeting called by Daniel Moi MP in the mistaken belief that the LEL was again responsible for the outrage. The meeting subsequently passed a resolution,

> calling on the Government to check all Europeans in Kenya to uncover any supporters of the League. Unless this was done, Mr Moi said, 'every white skin' would be assumed to be a support of the league and thus an enemy of the country.

The Kenya Plantation and Agricultural Workers' Union warned British farmers in Kenya to 'pack up and go'. Anger only abated when Kenyatta returned to Kenya and, addressing a mass rally in Nairobi, asked that the incident be forgotten. See *The Times*, 17 July 1964; *The Times*, 21 July 1964; and *The Times*, 27 July 1964.
109 TNA MEPO 2/10633; *Spearhead*, no. 2, December 1964; and Martin Webster, CV. Jordan told George Lincoln Rockwell that Webster was considering moving to South Africa, see Colin Jordan to George Lincoln Rockwell, 26 December 1964, George Lincoln Rockwell papers.
110 *The Times*, 5 October 1964.
111 *Daily Express*, 14 August 1965.
112 *Spearhead*, no. 302, April 1994.
113 *The Times*, 25 October 1965; and *Daily Express*, 25 October 1965.
114 *The Spectator*, 24 December 1965.
115 Brad Whitsel, 'Ideological Mutation and Millennial Belief in the American Neo-Nazi Movement', *Studies in Conflict and Terrorism*, vol. 24, no. 2, 2001, pp. 89–106 notes similar developments in North America.
116 Thayer, *The British Political Fringe*, p. 31.
117 *Stratford Express*, 20 August 1965; and *Ilford Pictorial*, 19 August 1965.
118 *Spearhead*, no. 8, July 1965.
119 Tyndall, *The Eleventh Hour*, p. 112.
120 *Viking Books – Literature for Patriots of All Nations* (London: Albion Press, November 1964).
121 Frequent *Spearhead* contributors included Peter Peel, a prominent 'revisionist' living in Reseda, California, who had joined the IFL as a teenager, and Oliver Gilbert, who also active in the Nordic League. Interned during the Second World War, MI5 suspected Gilbert was in the pay of German intelligence. The IFL continued to fascinate. *Spearhead*, no. 262, December 1990 contained the following advert: 'Are there any surviving pre-war members of the old IFL still around? Contact would be welcomed. State branch and branch leader's name when replying, and give your telephone number. Reply to Box 88, Spearhead'.
122 *The Times*, 22 March 1966; *The Times*, 30 March 1966; and *The Times*, 14 April 1966. His co-accused included Ralph Richardson, Leslie Hylands, Gordon Brown, John Hammond, Carole Dunnett, Paul Trevelyan and David Rowley.
123 *The Times*, 30 June 1966. The case against two defendants was dismissed whilst another, Ralph Richardson, claimed in court to have only joined the GBM to gather evidence for the police.
124 *The Times*, 18 November 1966.
125 A.K. Chesterton to Avril Walters, 12 June 1966, Chesterton papers.
126 A.K. Chesterton to John Tyndall, 2 May 1963 in SCH/01/Res/BRI/20/001, Searchlight archive.
127 *Spearhead*, no. 12, July 1966.
128 John Tyndall to A.K. Chesterton, 29 August 1966; and A.K. Chesterton to John Tyndall, 2 September 1966, Chesterton papers.

129 John Tyndall to A.K. Chesterton, 5 September 1966; A.K. Chesterton to John Tyndall, 7 September 1966; John Tyndall to A.K. Chesterton, 11 September 1966; A.K. Chesterton to John Tyndall, 13 September 1966; and John Tyndall to A.K. Chesterton, 17 September 1966, Chesterton papers.
130 A.K. Chesterton to John Tyndall, 21 September 1966, Chesterton papers.
131 John Bean, *Many Shades of Black*, pp. 183–184 and 205. Bean and Tyndall were soon exchanging articles for each other's publications, over and above the objections of Andrew Fountaine. Bean subsequently moved *Combat*'s publishing offices into 'The Nationalist Centre', which also housed *Spearhead*.
132 Bean, *Many Shades of Black*, p. 184
133 *Searchlight*, no. 38, August 1978, quoting Tyndall's correspondence with William Pierce. When the letters emerged during a *World in Action* documentary broadcast in July, Tyndall was dismissive of their veracity. 'I do not keep files of all correspondence going back that far nor is my memory so good that I can recall it,' he wrote in *Spearhead*, no. 120, August 1978. 'I therefore do not know whether the letters were forged or just stolen … However, if the idea was to point out that this was the way I was thinking in the 1960s, my reply is: so what?' Sidestepping the question of intent indicated by his letter to Pierce, Tyndall claimed simply that the letters were irrelevant because he had changed his opinion.
134 Tyndall to Jordan, 20 March 1967 in SCH/01/Res/BRI/23/002, Searchlight archive.
135 *Searchlight*, no. 38, August 1978, quoting Tyndall's correspondence with William Pierce.
136 *Spearhead*, no. 139, May 1980.
137 A.K. Chesterton to Denis Pirie, 24 November 1967; and A.K. Chesterton to Denis Pirie, 27 November 1967, Chesterton papers. The NF Director of Information Michael Passmore was a case in point. Passmore, a former GBM activist, had been making an annual pilgrimage to Germany since 1958 and had established contact with the Bund Heimattreuer Jugend (BHJ) to whom he had disseminated illegal propaganda materials, including stickers bearing a portrait of Hitler with the words 'He was right'. Passmore also visited Gudrun Burwitz, Himmler's daughter, in Munich before his arrest by the German authorities, which led to him being jailed for a year in August 1965, see *The Times*, 30 March 1965; *The Times*, 9 August 1965; and *Der Spiegel*, 34, 1965. Tyndall claimed Passmore's 'demeanour' at the trial 'was a credit to the movement', see *Spearhead*, no. 9, February–March 1966.
138 A.K. Chesterton to John Bean, 29 October 1967, Chesterton papers.
139 John Tyndall, *Six Principles of British Nationalism* (London: Nationalist Centre, 1967), pp. 1–29.
140 *Candour*, vol. 28, no. 467, August 1967; and *Spearhead*, no. 16, September 1967.
141 A.K. Chesterton to John Tyndall, 29 October 1967, Chesterton papers.
142 *Combat*, no. 42, November–December 1967.
143 Bean, *Many Shades of Black*, pp. 183–184.
144 *Spearhead*, no. 103, March 1977.
145 Bean, *Many Shades of Black*, pp. 203–204.
146 Walker, *The National Front*, p. 87. Thereafter, Legg immersed himself in the campaign to return the 'lost' Dorset hamlet of Tyneham, see Patrick Wright, *The Village That Died for England* (London: Faber & Faber, 2002), pp. 304–310.
147 A.K. Chesterton to Colin Jordan, 23 May 1970, Chesterton papers.
148 Bean, *Many Shades of Black*, p. 189.
149 *Spearhead*, January 1969, quoted in Walker, *The National Front*, p. 116.
150 Meeting of the Leadership Council of the National Front, Minutes, 27 February 1969, Chesterton papers.
151 Walker, *The National Front*, pp. 115–116.
152 TNA LO 2/470.
153 NF Directorate meeting, Minutes, 12 April 1969, Chesterton papers.
154 *Candour*, vol. 20, no. 492, September 1969.
155 A.K. Chesterton to Rosine de Bounevialle, 6 September 1969, Chesterton papers.
156 'Members' Bulletin – From the National Director to all Members', 26 September 1969, Chesterton papers.
157 A.K. Chesterton to Martin Webster, 1970, Chesterton papers.
158 FBI file, 'White Extremist Organisations: Part II National States Rights Party'.

159 *The Thunderbolt*, no. 61, September 1964.

160 *The Thunderbolt*, September 1961; and *Spearhead*, no. 4, February 1965.

161 *The Thunderbolt*, no. 93, September 1967.

162 *Spearhead*, no. 25, September 1969.

163 Hampton Sides, *Hellhound on his Trail* (London: Penguin, 2011), p. 418. Following the killing, Ray's brother, Jerry, a 'personal bodyguard' to NSRP leader J.B. Stoner, was 'guest of honour' at its convention in Jacksonville, Florida, on 7–8 June 1969. 'All three Ray brothers are true conservative patriots and your editors willingly vouch for them,' stated *The Thunderbolt*, no. 116, August 1969. Jerry contributed an article to *The Thunderbolt*, no. 157, February 1973 titled 'Ray Brothers Persecuted Over Martin Luther King Case'. He was also 'guest of honour' at the 1973 NSRP Chicago rally, see *The Thunderbolt*, no. 161, June 1973.

164 *New York Times*, 28 June 1968; and *Spartanburg Herald*, 28 June 1968. Tyndall was not the only British activist involved in this nexus. Sidney Carthew, a merchant seaman involved with Liverpool BNP during the 1960s, also became involved in the campaign to have King's killer acquitted, though he did not come forward until 1995. Ray's defence hinged upon his claim to have been set up by a mysterious arms dealer called 'Raoul/Raul' who was never traced. Ray's defence lawyer, William Pepper, drew upon Carthew's testimony that he too had met 'Raoul/Raul' in Montreal's Neptune bar, frequented by British sailors, in a bid to corroborate his client's claims that he was an innocent 'patsy', see William F. Pepper, *An Act of State* (London: Verso, 2008); *Orders to Kill* (New York: Carroll & Graf, 1995); and *The Plot to Kill King* (New York: Skyhorse, 2016). The Department of Justice were dismissive of Carthew's testimony, see 'Footnotes', U.S. Department of Justice, 6 August 2015, www.justice.gov/crt/footnotes (accessed 7 August 2016). Carthew later joined Tyndall's BNP, becoming his Yorkshire Regional Organiser, and standing as a regular election candidate in Halifax. Five years after his death in 2003, Halifax BNP instituted an annual trophy for activism in the name of their 'venerated colleague', see 'Richard Edmonds tells Yorkshire Meeting of BNP London's Success', *BNP News*, 14 November 2008, http://bnp.org.uk/2008/11/richard-edmonds-tells-yorkshire-meeting-of-bnp-london's-success/ (accessed 9 March 2009).

165 FBI file, 'White Extremist Organisations: Part II National States Rights Party'; and *The Thunderbolt*, no. 122, February 1970. Jerry Pope, the NSRP Kentucky organiser had already visited the NF, see *The Thunderbolt*, no. 116, March 1969.

166 *The Thunderbolt*, no. 192, July 1975; and *The Thunderbolt*, no. 219, July 1977. Fields and his San Francisco organiser Ray Reimer visited the NF again in July 1977. 'The NF people showed their deep appreciation for the support the NSRP has given them,' recorded Fields. 'We simply recognise that the NF has the leadership that has enabled a new movement to capture the spirit of a nation.' Tyndall granted Reimer a filmed interview, described as 'an inspiring message to the American people'. Fields hoped to provide screenings of the interview to readers of *The Thunderbolt*, 'and let this movie give you the real feeling of the new wave of White Racism which is sweeping England and may well save that nation in this its [sic] truly darkest hour.'

167 *The Thunderbolt*, no. 208, August 1976.

168 *New York Times*, 29 April 2005. Stoner was released in 1986 having served a mere one-third of his sentence.

169 Dan T. Carter, *The Politics of Rage* (Baton Rouge, LA: Louisiana State University Press, 2000), p. 165.

170 See 'Savitri Devi's Correspondence with George Lincoln Rockwell, Part 4', edited by R.G. Fowler, *The Savitri Devi Archive*, www.savitridevi.org/rockwell_correspondence_4.html (accessed 13 January 2011).

171 *Spearhead*, no. 20, September–October 1968; and Nicholas Goodrick-Clarke, *Hitler's Priestess: Savitri, the Hindu-Aryan Myth, and Neo-Nazism* (New York: New York University Press, 1998), p. 208.

172 *Spearhead*, no. 28, December 1969.

173 *Spearhead*, no. 29, January 1970.

174 *The Times*, 24 April 1968.

175 *Spearhead*, no. 19, May–June 1968.

176 Walker, *The National Front*, p. 121.

177 *Spearhead*, no. 35, August 1970.

178 *Tribune*, 28 March 1969 reported that the BDL was 'closely linked' with the Midlands section of the Racial Preservation Society (RPS) with whom it issued a 'joint news-letter', which was sent to Conservative MPs and activists, urging them to withhold donations from the Conservative Party until Powell was reinstated to the Shadow Cabinet. O'Brien also served as an Executive Committee member of the National Democratic Party (NDP), a small right-wing party led by David Brown, who was also prominent in the RPS.
179 *British Tidings*, no. 32, April–May 1972; and *Combat*, no. 13, July 1972.
180 *Candour*, vol. 12, no. 509, April 1971.
181 John O'Brien to Aidan Mackey, 12 December 1970, Chesterton papers.
182 Stan Taylor, *The National Front in English Politics* (London: Macmillan, 1989), pp. 22–23. See also Paul Ward with Graham Hellawell and Sally Lloyd, 'Witness Seminar: Anti-Fascism in 1970s Huddersfield', *Contemporary British History*, vol. 20, no. 1, March 2006, pp. 119–133.
183 John O'Brien to Frank Clifford, 5 November 1971, Chesterton papers.
184 *Spearhead*, no. 135, January 1980.
185 *Spearhead*, no. 38, December 1970.
186 *Spearhead*, no. 89, November 1975.
187 *Spearhead*, no. 47, October 1971.
188 *Spearhead*, December 1964.
189 *Spearhead*, no. 40, February 1971.
190 *The Listener*, 28 December 1972.
191 Bean, *Many Shades of Black*, p. 213.
192 Walker, *The National Front*, p. 134; and Frost, *'Twaz a Good Fight!'*, p. 244.
193 *Spearhead*, no. 89, November 1975. O'Brien departed with approximately fifty NF members, noted Nigel Fielding, *The National Front*, p. 25. He formed his own National Independence Party but it soon faded from view, as did he for the remainder of the decade.
194 *Spearhead*, no. 89, November 1975.
195 *Spearhead*, no. 183, January 1984.
196 For opinion poll figures, see Goodwin, *New British Fascism*, p. 28.
197 *Spearhead*, no. 49, January–February 1972.
198 Francis Wheen, *Strange Days Indeed: The Golden Age of Paranoia* (London: Fourth Estate, 2010), p. 233.
199 *Daily Mail*, 13 September 1975.
200 Walker, *The National Front*, p. 134.
201 *Ibid.*, p. 133.
202 *Ibid.*, p. 134.
203 *Spearhead*, no. 57, October 1972.
204 *NF Urgent Activities Bulletin*, 4 September 1972.
205 *Spearhead*, no. 56, September 1972; and Walker, *The National Front*, pp. 135–136 and 166 for the figures.
206 *Spearhead*, no. 57, October 1972 claimed its Head Office received 100 enquiries a day, peaking at 150 in one day alone. Even on 'slack days', the NF claimed enquiries numbered at least fifty. 'These enquiries are being largely converted into enlisted members as fast as literature can be sent out and branches can contact the enquirers concerned.' By 20 September, the NF claimed to have enrolled 250 new members. Walker, *The National Front*, pp. 135–136, 139 reports that the NF had gained 800 new recruits in the last four months of 1972.
207 Kate Taylor, 'The Rise of the 1970s National Front', *Searchlight*, no. 314, August 2001, p. 19; and Stan Taylor, *The National Front in English Politics*, p. 24 gives a slightly lower figure of 14,000 members by 1973.
208 Walker, *The National Front*, p. 140 observed:

> A permanent staff of this size involved a minimum annual expenditure of £10,000 on salaries alone, without counting the costs of three regional offices. Since Tyndall and Webster were already receiving a small income from *Spearhead* (which still depended on annual appeals for its solvency), the £20,000 for which Tyndall appealed was clearly going to have to be an annual subsidy.

209 Simon Heffer, *Like the Roman: The Life of Enoch Powell* (London: Faber & Faber, 2008), pp. 667–668.

210 Walker, *The National Front*, p. 142.
211 Stan Taylor, *The National Front in English Politics*, p. 25.
212 *Britain First*, no. 32, September 1975.
213 Goodwin, *New British Fascism*, pp. 28–29.
214 Mark Pitchford, *The Conservative Party and the Extreme Right, 1945–1975* (Manchester: Manchester University Press, 2011), pp. 148 and 216.
215 Robert Copping, *The Story of the Monday Club: The First Decade* (London: The Monday Club, 1971).
216 *Spearhead*, no. 31, March 1970. In *Spearhead*, no. 46, September 1971, Martin Webster argued that this 'internationalist' stance resulted from the conspiratorial machinations of Conservative Central Office. 'The brief of the infiltrators was simple: water down the Club's policies; prevent genuine patriots from rocking the Tory Party boat; turn the Monday Club into a harmless safety-valve for the Tory Right Wing.'
217 *Spearhead*, no. 40, February 1971. Martin Webster elaborated upon these differences in a letter to the *Sunday Telegraph*, 1 April 1973.

> While we are able to absorb ex-Monday Club members who come to accept our policies on economics and finance we have no wish to endanger the unity of our movement by taking in people whose 19th century views on free enterprise oblige them to condone 20th century monopoly capitalism and international usury.

218 *Evening Argus*, 16 March 1971. Hancock was a leading RPS activist who had attended the Brighton Northern League meeting in 1971. He was active in the 'Sussex Forum', which had several NF activists on its committee. Hancock became a major publisher of racist and anti-Semitic literature.
219 *Daily Telegraph*, 10 March 1971.
220 *Daily Mirror*, 15 March 1971.
221 *The Times*, 6 November 1971. Geoffrey Barber, a Kensington councillor, chaired it. There were three MPs on the committee – Ronald Bell, John Stokes and Harold Soref ('all have reputations as hard-liners on immigration') – who were joined by G.K. Young, Richard Ritchie, an LSE student, and Gerald Howarth whose mother, Mary, was a prominent anti-immigration campaigner and NF member (on which, see *Searchlight*, no. 31, January 1978; and *Searchlight*, no. s397, July 2008).
222 Walker, *The National Front*, p. 127.
223 The *Sunday Times*, 10 December 1972.
224 Text of a letter from the Prime Minister to the Chairman of the Monday Club Mr. Jonathan Guinness, 20 September 1972 in CCO 20/43/6, Conservative Central Office papers, Bodleian Library, Oxford University, hereafter CCO papers.
225 'Report by A Sub-Committee of the Executive Council set up to Enquire into: The Organisation and Structure of the Monday Club and to make Recommendations', February 1973, p. 7 in DPW/40/13, Sir Patrick Wall papers, Brynmor Jones Library, Hull University, hereafter Wall papers.
226 *Daily Telegraph*, 31 May 1973. Opponents sometimes used Guinness' familial ties and pro-European views to defame him as a 'Mosleyite'. Few went quite so far as Sir Wolstan Dixie, however. A prominent Monday Club member in the Market Bosworth Conservative Association – which Guinness chaired. Dixie was asked to resign after publicly maligning Guinness as 'a henchman of Sir Oswald Mosley', see *Leicester Mercury*, 21 April 1970.
227 'Note of a meeting with Jonathan Guinness', 14 January 1973 in CCO 20/43/6, CCO papers.
228 *Spearhead*, no. 60, January 1973; and Monday Club, 'Minutes of the meeting of the Executive Council held on Monday', 29 January 1973 in DPW/40/13, Wall papers. The membership of the branch secretary, Mrs Gillian Gould, was terminated on 6 February 1973. She subsequently stood as an NF candidate (Norwich North) in the February 1974 general election.
229 Pitchford, *The Conservative Party and the Extreme Right, 1945–1975*, p. 204.
230 *The Spectator*, 31 March 1973, for instance, speculated that the Club's intense and increasingly myopic focus on immigration would prove its 'undoing' as it detracted from its economic philosophy and other policy platforms.
231 Sam Swerling to Patrick Wall MP, 10 August 1973 in DPW/40/13, Wall papers. Swerling was a member of the Monday Club Executive Council who edited *Monday News* (1972–1973) and was Vice-Chairman of the St Marylebone Conservative Association (1971–1973).

232 *Sunday Telegraph*, 29 April 1973. *The Times*, 30 April 1973 recorded that there were thirty-five MPs in June 1970; reduced to twenty-two over the 'last few months'.
233 *Sunday Telegraph*, 29 April 1973.
234 *Daily Telegraph*, 27 March 1973.
235 The *Sunday Times*, 22 April 1973.
236 Leslie Wooler, a former activist in Oswald Mosley's Union Movement (UM) was responsible for vetting the files. Wooler had joined the UM in 1960, having served in the Merchant Navy and a Royal Air Force regiment. He quickly rose to become the party's Woolwich organiser and served as a 'bodyguard' to Mosley. Wooler was also involved in Mosley's international activities. *Action*, no. 134, 4 October 1963 listed him as the UM contact for 'enquires on Spain', whilst [Unsigned] to Jean Thiriart, 9 February 1963 in MS124/1/24, Hamm papers, recommended Wooler as a potential contact for Belgian fascist Jean Thiriart who was then looking to organise a London office for his Jeune Europe group. 'Wooler is a good man,' noted the letter.

> He has for some time past been an efficient branch leader and has now been promoted to be area leader [South East London]. He is a very good worker for our Movement, and you many have full confidence in him.

Wooler apparently left the UM in spring 1964. During his time in the UM, Wooler had also gathered intelligence for the anti-fascist 62 Group. Thereafter, he was briefly associated with the League of Empire Loyalists, see, *Candour Interim Report*, September 1964. The identity of the MC official who authorised the vetting of the membership list is unknown. Guinness, his predecessor and Lieutenant-Commander Michael Woolrych, the Club's Director, all denied any knowledge. *Britain First*, no. 34, November–December 1975 later named Ian Greig, the Club's membership secretary until 1969, as the individual responsible. Martin Webster, who had identified Wooler as a 62 Group source in *Spearhead*, no. 56, September 1972, speculated in *Spearhead*, no. 64, May 1973 that Wooler had drawn upon NF files stolen from the party's Head Office three years previously, cross-referencing these with the Monday Club membership list, to identify NF members within the Club. If Webster's assertion is correct – that outdated information was being utilised – this could explain why so few NF members were identified. Also, Wooler may not have had access to branch membership files. These were not vetted by the MC head office and following the 'Wooler Affair', the Essex MC, a group noted for its NF sympathies, refused to tender their membership lists to head office, see *Daily Telegraph*, 21 May 1973. *Spearhead*, no. 95, June–July 1976 subsequently alleged that Wooler was a source of some of the 'gossip' appearing in the anonymously authored pamphlet, *The Monday Club – A Danger to Democracy*. Wooler's authorship of *Guide to Extremism in Britain* (1973), which appeared under the imprimatur of the 'Circle for Democratic Studies' and which he co-wrote with Julian Radcliffe, is rather more certain. Wooler was later involved in a range of other 'anti-communist' concerns, including the pro-Saigon Vietnamese Ad Hoc Committee, which he ran from his home. *CounterSpy*, vol. 3, no. 2, December 1976 subsequently claimed that Wooler, 'who 'infiltrated pro-Palestinian organisations in the sixties', was recruited by the former Chilean Embassy press attaché Jorge Navarrete to gather intelligence on the Chile Solidarity offices which opposed the Chilean Junta.
237 *Daily Telegraph*, 30 April 1973.
238 *Daily Telegraph*, 2 May 1973. Thereafter, Young addressed the remnants of the dissolved West Middlesex Monday Club. Fewer than twenty people attended the meeting during which Young accused Guinness of 'obtuseness' with regards immigration and warned that 'the unwarranted and unwanted intrusion of incompatible races and cultures' was 'now threatening to tear apart the very fabric of our society as it has evolved over a thousand years.' Shortly afterwards, Young was named as 'honorary president' of the West Midlands Action Group. 'The group was annoyed they were called NF supporters, so they formed this group,' Young told the press. 'They're a rather decent crowd', see the *Guardian*, 12 June 1973; and *Willesden and Brent Chronicle*, 22 June 1973. Young subsequently stood as the Conservative Candidate in Brent East in the February 1974 general election, polling 13,441 votes (31.5 per cent). His election agent was David Lazarus, a London businessman who chaired the Brent Conservative Association, who the *New Statesman*, 6 April 1973, reported had 'emerged as the front man for a group of millionaires backing Enoch Powell.' Lazarus had been an LEL activist before joining the NF in 1968, see *Candour*, vol. 17, no. 448, December 1965. Young later formed Tory Action.

239 *Spearhead*, no. 62, March 1973.
240 *New Statesman*, 2 March 1973.
241 The *Observer*, 24 June 1973 highlights the vote was eleven to eight.
242 *Daily Telegraph*, 2 May 1973. One of Guinness' opponents on Executive Committee was Beryl 'Bee' Carthew, the Meetings Secretary who was also Secretary of the Monday Club Immigration Group and was active in the HINC. She was expelled in July. Carthew simultaneously ran the Powellite Association, which 'set the seal on Powell's personality cult within the Conservative Party, and acted, with his arm's-length co-operation, as a guerrilla movement among Conservative activists for Powell's ideas.' The group faltered, however, after Carthew's flat was burgled in October 1972 with members' details being stolen. 'Some of the material was published later in the anti-fascist magazine *Searchlight*, and Powellite's organisers drew their own conclusions about who had been responsible,' observed Simon Heffer, *Like the Roman*, pp. 652–653. Carthew subsequently became the Kingston and Richmond NF organiser, see *The Times*, 8 July 1976.
243 *Spearhead*, no. 64, May 1973. Less hyperbolically, Webster cogitated, in *Spearhead*, no. 67, August 1973, upon the necessity of recruiting disillusioned Conservative activists whose skillsets could enhance their forthcoming general election campaign.
244 Painter was active in the Monday Club, speaking at its HINC meetings, but resigned from the Conservative Party in early July because he 'could no longer defend Tory policy on immigration.' His decision was also influenced by Enoch Powell's refusal to endorse the official Conservative Candidate at West Bromwich, see the *Guardian*, 9 July 1973; and *Daily Telegraph*, 11 July 1973.
245 Walker, *The National Front*, p. 146.
246 *Spearhead*, no. 57, October 1972 states former NSM activist Denis Pirie led the NFSA initially.
247 *Spark*, no. 1, Summer Term 1973.
248 *Spearhead*, no. 75, May 1974 argued that the NF work through existing trade unions, 'to promote NF doctrines, seek the election of NF members to office and combat the left.' This strategy built on the 1972 NF AGM which voted down a proposal to found a distinct NF trade union 'but strongly supported plans for an NF trade union group which would be active within existing unions,' see *Spearhead*, no. 58, November 1972.
249 Walker, *The National Front*, p. 159 notes that the NF tried and failed to negotiate 'official working alliances' with the Ulster Defence Association (UDA) in the wake of the strike. Indeed, an NF 'anti-IRA' march in September 1974 paid testimony to NF frustration in this regard. The Ulster Loyalist Albert Bridge Accordion Band accompanied the march. The subsequent rally was addressed by Bob Marno, leader of the Orange Volunteers who was also active in the Loyalist Association of Workers; George Green, head of the B-Specials Association; and Councillor Brooks of Castlereagh City Council; whilst Webster read out a letter of solidarity from the Rev. Robert Bradford, a prominent Unionist politician who supported the NF (and was murdered by the IRA in 1981). Coverage of the event in *British First*, no. 24, October 1974 highlighted tension with the UDA, which had declined to support the activity. The NF claimed the UDA was a 'Communist infiltrated' organisation controlled by 'Andrew Terry' [sic – Tyrie] 'who has been praised as a "radical" in *Socialist Worker*, the paper of the International Socialists.' Simultaneously, Tyndall, who had met Tyrie during a visit to Belfast earlier that year (*The Times*, 3 August 1974), issued an edict published in *NF Members' Bulletin*, October–November 1974 forbidding involvement with Loyalist paramilitary organisations, 'no matter how patriotic its intentions may be', under pain of expulsion. For their part, the UDA disparaged the NF as a 'neo-Nazi movement' and prohibited its own members from attending NF marches. Jim Cusack and Henry McDonald, *UVF* (Dublin: Poolbeg, 1997), p. 217 note that the Ulster Volunteer Force publication, *Combat*, had shown greater sympathy towards the NF earlier in that year.
250 *Spearhead*, September–October 1974, cited in Walker, *The National Front*, p. 155.
251 Walker, *The National Front*, p. 148.
252 Tyndall, *The Eleventh Hour*, p. 224.
253 Walker, *The National Front*, pp. 144–145. 'What is it that touches off a chord in the instincts of the people to whom we seek to appeal?' Tyndall had mused.

> It can often be the most simple and primitive thing. Rather than a speech or article, it may just be a flag; it may be a marching column; it may be the sound of a drum; it may be a

> banner or it may be just the impression on the crowd. None of these things contain in themselves one single argument, one single piece of logic ... They are recognised as being among the things that appeal to the hidden forces of the human soul.

254 Thomas Linehan, 'Cultures of Space: Spatialising the National Front', in Nigel Copsey and John E. Richardson (eds), *Cultures of Post-War British Fascism* (Abingdon: Routledge, 2015), pp. 49–67; and Fabian Virchow, 'Performance, Emotion, and Ideology: On the Creation of "Collectives of Emotion" and Worldview in the Contemporary German Far Right', *Journal of Contemporary Ethnography*, vol. 36, no. 2, 2007, pp. 147–164.
255 Walker, *The National Front*, p. 145.
256 *The Listener*, 28 December 1972.
257 *Spearhead*, no. 103, March 1977.
258 'Interview with Richard Edmonds', *Counter-Currents*, Radio Podcast No. 125, April 2015, www.counter-currents.com/2015/04/interview-with-richard-edmonds/ (accessed 7 May 2015).
259 *Spearhead*, no. 103, March 1977.
260 'National Front', 7 February 1978 in PREM 16/2084.
261 Stan Taylor, *The National Front in English Politics*, p. 29.
262 The old West Bromwich constituency was divided into West Bromwich East and West Bromwich West. In the latter, the NF candidate polled 3107 votes (7.8 per cent).
263 Stan Taylor, *The National Front in English Politics*, p. 31.
264 *The Patriot*, no. 1, winter 1997.
265 Walker, *The National Front*, p. 163.
266 *Ibid.*, p. 9.
267 M.J. Le Lohne, 'The National Front and the General Elections of 1974', *New Community*, vol. 5, no. 3, autumn 1976, pp. 292–301; and for an analysis of the vote, see C.T. Husbands, 'The National Front: A Response to Crisis?' *New Society*, 15 May 1975, pp. 403–405.
268 The *Guardian*, 12 October 1974.
269 Walker, *The National Front*, p. 149. Whilst portrayed as primarily an ideological split, Richard Thurlow, 'Authoritarians and Populists on the English Far Right', *Patterns of Prejudice*, vol. 10, no. 2, March–April 1976, p. 19 highlights numerous other social, cultural and political cleavages, latent within many local groups. These included divisions between 'middle class intellectuals' and 'working class workers' and 'between the political and social functions of the movement' all of which were exacerbated by 'regional differences' in the movement's class structure and the attendant 'personal loyalties' emanating from them.
270 *National Front Members' Bulletin*, January–February 1976.
271 Walker, *The National Front*, p. 151.
272 *Britain First*, no. 27, March–April 1975.
273 Ironically, despite their complaining about Tyndall's ideological antecedents, the 'populist' faction would include NSM activist Peter Holland and GBM backer Gordon Brown, who both subsequently backed the *putsch* against Tyndall. Walker, *The National Front*, p. 177 also intimates tactical disagreements fuelled the split, particularly over the formation of 'defence groups' to counter anti-fascist violence which, by the November 1974 Remembrance Day parade, had coalesced into an 'Honour Guard'. Webster's contention that the time was ripe 'to turn and smash our enemies into a pulp' apparently helped confirm the 'populists' in their belief that they needed to be rid of Tyndall and Webster altogether.
274 *Spearhead*, no. 74, September–October 1974 stated:

> [T]his journal is not a doctrinaire supporter of parliamentary government as an end in itself; it is a supporter of good government that operates in the national interest ... The survival, and the national recovery, of Britain stands as top priority over all. We will support whatever political methods are necessary to attain that end, although we admit to a marked preference to democratic methods so long as such methods can be found which will work.

275 For biographical details, see *John Kingsley Read: A Profile of the National Front's Latest Chairman – November 1974* (Birmingham: A.F. and R. Publications, 1974); and *Britain First*, no. 25, December 1974.
276 *NF Members' Bulletin*, October–November 1974; and Walker, *The National Front*, p. 176.
277 *Britain First*, no. 25, December 1974.

278 Quoted in *Private Eye*, 7 January 1975.
279 Walker, *The National Front*, p. 179.
280 *Private Eye*, 7 January 1975.
281 *NF Members' Bulletin*, March 1975; and *Britain First*, no. 25, December 1974.
282 Walker, *The National Front*, p. 177.
283 *Ibid.*, pp. 180–181. *Spearhead*, no. 125, January 1979 outlines Tyndall's case against even participating in the European Parliament elections: 'We are in business to fight the collaborators, not to join them; to wage war on Treason, not to enter into the chambers of Treason,' Tyndall declared.
284 Tyndall, *The Eleventh Hour*, pp. 221–223.
285 Stan Taylor, *The National Front in English Politics*, p. 83.
286 *Spearhead*, no. 84, May 1975 contains Tyndall's constitutional critique.
287 Walker, *The National Front*, p. 183.
288 *Ibid.*, pp. 185–186.
289 *Britain First*, no. 32, September 1975; and *Britain First*, no. 33, October 1975, which also announced the proscription of Column 88, another overtly Nazi grouplet. *Spearhead*, no. 132, October 1979 explained the League's proscription resulted from its 'clear desire to infiltrate and take over the NF.' Trevor Malcolm Smith was forced to resign from the NF Directorate and its Executive Committee following an article in *Searchlight*, no. 35, May 1978 exposing his attendance at a League meeting on 21 April. Former US Klan organiser James Warner had been the main speaker, see NF Directorate meeting, Minutes, 27 May 1978 in MS 321/1, Patrick Harrington papers, Modern Records Centre, Warwick University, hereafter Harrington papers.
290 *Spearhead*, no. 87, September 1975.
291 *Britain First*, no. 34, November–December 1975.
292 *Spearhead*, no. 89, November 1975.
293 *Britain First*, no. 34, November–December 1975. Ironically, *Britain First* had earlier been criticised by some NF activists not for its 'left-wing' content but because it was perceived to bear an (unwanted) visual similarity to *Socialist Worker*, newspaper of the International Socialists, see *Britain First*, no. 26, February–March 1975.
294 *Britain First*, no. 34, November–December 1975.
295 *Spearhead*, no. 90, December 1975–January 1976.
296 For the Tyndall faction's version of events, see *Spearhead*, no. 90, December 1975–January 1976.
297 *Spearhead*, no. 92, March 1976.
298 *Spearhead*, no. 132, October 1979.
299 Walker, *The National Front*, pp. 191. Other sources give a lesser figure. Stan Taylor, *The National Front in English Politics*, pp. 44 and 102 states that the NP took 2,000 members, one-fifth of the total membership, leaving the NF with approximately 7,000 members. Nigel Fielding, *The National Front*, p. 39 similarly affirms the NP had 2,000 members but puts 'hardcore' NF membership at 4,000 as of September 1976. This was not necessarily representative of its 'activist' base, however. Martin Webster claimed that only 187 people attended the NP Inaugural AGM, see *Spearhead*, no. 92, March 1976.
300 *Spearhead*, no. 91, February 1976.
301 *Ibid.*
302 *The Times*, 2 July 1976.
303 *Britain First*, no. 38, June 1976; and *Britain First*, no. 42, November 1976. Read was elected in St Thomas' ward with 1,106 votes (41.6 per cent) whilst Frankham was elected in St Jude's ward with 1588 votes (39.7 per cent). Their colleague, Robert Horman, chairman of Blackburn NP, missed out being elected by twelve votes having received 1,435 votes (36 per cent). In the ensuing by-election on 16 September 1976, Horman failed to reclaim the seat, gaining 767 votes (21.5 per cent), which signalled a significant drop in the party's support.
304 *The Times*, 2 July 1976. The NP contained numerous hard-line figures whose politics hardly differed from Tyndall's. Robin Beauclaire, an RPS activist was a leading figure in the Holocaust denial milieu. He was also one of Read's 'personal financial patrons'. Read too was involved in publishing such literature. Ray Hill with Andrew Bell, *The Other Face of Terror: Inside Europe's Neo-Nazi Network* (London: Grafton, 1988), p. 235 claims Read designed the cover art for the British edition of *The Hoax of the Twentieth Century* by Arthur Butz, a leading

American Holocaust denier. David McCalden, the NP 'Activities Organiser' subsequently emigrated to the United States where he became one of the founders of the Institute for Historical Review.
305 TNA DPP 2/6168–69.
306 *NF Members' Bulletin*, September 1976; and NF Directorate minutes, 27 February 1977, MSS 321/1, Modern Records Centre, Warwick University, hereafter, MRC papers. See also *Spearhead*, no. 100, December 1976.
307 *Britain First*, no. 41, October 1976.
308 *Britain First*, no. 42, November 1976 records Roy Painter's heart attack, which surely undermined some of the party's momentum.
309 *Spearhead*, no. 103, March 1977.
310 *Spearhead*, no. 91, February 1976. Described by Tyndall as 'one of the most outstandingly talented younger men to emerge in the party in recent years,' Verrall remained editor of *Spearhead* until January 1980. Verrall was a London University graduate and from 1976 onwards the NF administration officer. He sat on its National Directorate and Executive Council. From 1980, he was Acting Deputy Chairman. Like many within the NF, Verrall owed his 'fullest understanding' of politics to A.K. Chesterton.
311 The response to such literature was not uniform. Ironically, despite receiving a favourable review in *Spearhead*, no. 95, June–July 1976, the NF officially refused to stock Arthur Butz's, *The Hoax of the Twentieth Century* after Martin Webster objected that the party was not set up to defend 'German nationalism', see NF Directorate meeting, Minutes, 30 July 1976, Harrington papers.
312 *Spearhead*, no. 97, September 1976. Emphasis in the original.
313 *Spearhead*, no. 92, March 1976.
314 *Spearhead*, no. 94, May 1976.
315 *National Front Members' Bulletin*, April–May 1976.
316 Stan Taylor, *The National Front in English Politics*, p. 47. NF Directorate meeting, Minutes, 26 February 1976, Harrington papers, highlights that the NF had its administrative headquarters in Leicester, the largest branch outside London, a fact that it deliberately obscured, pointedly referring to its Teddington offices as its 'headquarters'.
317 For an account of this phenomenon, see Christopher T. Husbands, *Racial Exclusionism and the City: The Urban Support of the National Front* (London: George Allen & Unwin, 1983). For a longitudinal analysis, see Christopher T. Husbands, 'East End Racism, 1900–1980: Geographical Continuities in Vigilantist and Extreme Right-Wing Political Behavior', *The London Journal*, vol. 8, no. 2, 1982, pp. 88–104.
318 *Spearhead*, no. 96, August 1976. Nigel Fielding, *The National Front*, p. 39 states membership stood at 12,500 in July 1976.
319 *NF Members' Bulletin*, July–August 1976.
320 *Spearhead*, no. 103, March 1977. These branches and groups were controlled by a series of twenty-one regional councils who reported vertically to the National Directorate as well as horizontally to NF regional election agents and *ergo* its National Elections Department.
321 Tyndall, *The Eleventh Hour*, p. 224.
322 *Spearhead*, no. 183, January 1984. Based on a newspaper report, Nigel Fielding, *The National Front*, p. 39 gives a dramatically lower figure of 5500 members 'in late 1979'.
323 *NF Members' Bulletin*, February 1977; and *Spearhead*, no. 194, December 1984. *Spearhead*, no. 98, October 1976 noted that of the 33,000 copies of issue four of the newspaper 4,000 were sold in the East End whilst a further 6,000 were sold 'door-to-door' by Leicester NF activists.
324 Roy Jenkins, *A Life at the Centre* (London: Macmillan, 1991), p. 429.
325 *NF Organiser's Bulletin*, 20 September 1976.
326 *Britain First*, no. 34, November–December 1975.
327 Stan Taylor, *The National Front in English Politics*, p. 93.
328 *Spearhead*, no. 106, June 1977. Tyndall's grandiose aim was to 'reform the present multiracial Commonwealth into an exclusive, closely-knit association of White States' which could 'maintain close and friendly relations with White South Africa.' Highlighting the party's 'world-wide impact', many racial nationalist grouplets began identifying themselves with its growing profile. Tyndall appears to have genuinely believed that such groups would form the nucleus for 'the full establishment of the National Front over that part of the world which previously formed the

British Empire and today remains under the control of White, mainly Anglo-Celtic peoples.' To this end, he was 'closely involved' (*Spearhead*, no. 113, January 1978) in negotiations to form a network of 'affiliate' branches from 1977 onwards. The New Zealand NF was (re)-formed in March 1977 under the chairmanship of David Crawford, a group having originally been founded from the remnants of the New Zealand League of Empire Loyalists a decade earlier. *Spearhead*, no. 111, November 1977 highlighted the formation of the 'National Front of Canada' under Ontario's Hal Thompson. Slower progress was made in Africa. Tyndall announced in *Spearhead*, no. 94, May 1976 that he had been invited to visit NF supporters in South Africa and Rhodesia in 1976, though this visit never materialised, on which, see TNA FO 371/188128; and FCO 45/2406. *Britain First*, no. 20, May–June 1974 reported the formation of an NF group in Johannesburg by Michael Childs, whilst *Britain First*, no. 30, July 1975 noted the formation of a South African group under Dave Habbitts. It was not until mid-1978, however, that the 'National Front Association of South Africa', chaired by Jack Noble, was officially formed (*Spearhead*, no. 118, June 1978). Tyndall was refused a visa to South Africa to address the NFSA, which had jointly organised meetings with the Herstigte Nasionale Party (*Spearhead*, no. 127, March 1979). The National Front of Australia was also formed in June 1978, chaired initially by Rosemary Sisson, on which, see Evan Smith, 'Exporting Fascism across the Commonwealth: The Case of the National Front of Australia', in Nigel Copsey and Matthew Worley (eds),*'Tomorrow Belongs to Us': The British Far Right since 1967* (Abingdon: Routledge, 2018), pp. 69–89.
329 *Spearhead*, no. 111, November 1977.
330 The *Sunday Times*, 17 October 1976.
331 Mark Steel, *Reasons to be Cheerful: From Punk to New Labour through the Eyes of a Dedicated Troublemaker* (London: Schribner, 2002), p. 36.
332 *Spearhead*, no. 102, February 1977.
333 Christopher T. Husbands, 'The National Front Becalmed?', *Wiener Library Bulletin*, vol. 30, NS nos 43/44, 1977, pp. 74–79.
334 *Spearhead*, no. 106, June 1977.
335 Joseph Pearce, *Race with the Devil: My Journey from Racial Hatred to Rational Love* (Charlotte, NC: Saint Benedict Press, 2013), pp. 54–55.
336 Paul Gilroy, *There Ain't No Black in the Union Jack* (London, 1991), p. 120 also highlights this evolving tactic.
337 John Tyndall to James Callaghan, 18 August 1977 in TNA PREM 16/2084.
338 NF Directorate Meeting, Minutes, 29 July 1977, Harrington papers.
339 NF Directorate Meeting, Minutes, 28 August 1978, Harrington papers.
340 Regarding an NF march in June 1968, see Ricky Tomlinson, *Ricky* (London: Time Warner, 2003), p. 86.
341 *Spearhead*, no. 129, July 1979.
342 Pearce, *Race with the Devil*, p. 59.
343 Sean Birchall, *Beating the Fascists: The Untold Story of Anti-Fascist Action* (London: Freedom Books, 2010), p. 40.
344 *Spearhead*, no. 111, November 1977.
345 For the internal discussion, see NF Directorate Meeting, Minutes, 24 September 1977, Harrington papers.
346 *Spearhead*, no. 110, October 1977.
347 NF Directorate Meeting, Minutes, 9 October 1977, Harrington papers.
348 NF Directorate Meeting, Minutes, 30 October 1977, Harrington papers.
349 *Spearhead*, no. 111, November 1977. Her father, Charles Parker, a former soldier who lost an arm in service, was the Surrey and Sussex NF regional organiser. He was a regular NF election candidate. *Spearhead*, no. 98, October 1976 applauded the 'sterling work' he and his wife, Violet, had done on behalf of the party in both the Midlands and the South of England.
350 *Spearhead*, no. 118, June 1978.
351 Sir David McNee, *McNee's Law* (London: Collins, 1983), p. 99. These events had future ramifications for the policing of marches. Discussing the Public Order Act in 1985, Merlyn Rees MP told the House of Commons: 'In 1978, in a small way, we began to reassess the public order legislation in the light of the marches problem at the time,' see Hansard, HC Deb., vol. 79, cols 506–521 (16 May 1985).

352 *The Times*, 17 April 1978. Martin Webster was arrested and charged with obstruction. He was found guilty and fined £60 with costs and order to pay £30 towards his legal aid, see *The Times*, 29 June 1978.
353 *Spearhead*, no. 117, May 1978.
354 NF Directorate meeting, Minutes, 14 May 1978, Harrington papers.
355 *Spearhead*, no. 117, May 1978.
356 NF Directorate Meeting, Minutes, 29 July 1978, Harrington papers.
357 *Spearhead*, no. 126, February 1979. Such pronouncements were ironic given NF Directorate concerns about NF members turning up to party activities wearing combat fatigues, see NF Directorate Meeting, Minutes, 3 December 1977, Harrington papers.
358 NF National Directorate Meeting, Minutes, 28 October 1978, Harrington papers.
359 John Tyndall to Martin Webster, 31 July 1978, quoted in *Searchlight*, no. 50, August 1979.
360 NF Directorate Meeting, Minutes, 28 January 1978, Harrington papers.
361 NF Directorate Meeting, Minutes, 30 December 1978, Harrington papers.
362 NF Directorate Meeting, Minutes, 24 February 1979, Harrington papers.
363 Christopher T. Husbands, 'The Decline of the National Front: The Elections of 3 May 1979', *Wiener Library Bulletin*, vol. 32, new series, nos 49–50, 1979, pp. 60–66.
364 *Spearhead*, no. 139, May 1980.
365 Roger Eatwell, 'The Extreme Right in Britain: The Long Road to "Modernisation"', in Roger Eatwell and Cas Mudde (eds), *Western Democracies and the New Extreme Right Challenge* (London: Routledge, 2004), p. 64.
366 Barry Troyna, 'The Media and the Electoral Decline of the National Front', *Patterns of Prejudice*, vol. 14, no. 3, July 1980, pp. 25–31; and Barry Troyna, 'Reporting the National Front: British Values Observed', in Charles Husband (ed.), *'Race' in Britain: Continuity and Change* (London: Hutchinson, 1982), pp. 259–278.
367 NF National Directorate Meeting, Minutes, 14–15 January 1978, Harrington papers.
368 Granada TV transcript, 27 January 1978 [embargoed until 30 January 1978], Thatcher archive, Churchill Archive Centre, Churchill College, Cambridge.
369 *The Times*, 29 October 2014. Nick Griffin, Tyndall's successor as BNP chairman later dismissed the Thatcher effect as a 'myth' claiming instead, in *Identity*, no. 21, June 2002, that the NF was defeated simply because it lacked 'a politically mature strategy, organisation and image.'
370 John Campbell, *Margaret Thatcher: Vol. 1, The Grocer's Daughter* (London: Jonathan Cape, 2000), pp. 400–445.
371 *Spearhead*, no. 126, February 1979.
372 *Spearhead*, no. 128 May–June 1979.
373 *Spearhead*, no. 126, February 1979; *Spearhead*, no. 128 May–June 1979; and *Spearhead*, no. 129, July 1979 for Webster's further response.
374 *Spearhead*, no. 139, May 1980.
375 *The Thunderbolt*, no. 243, July 1979; and *Spearhead*, no. 130, August 1979. *Spearhead*, no. 161, March 1982 notes that Fields tried to visit Britain in 1981 but was banned by the Home Office.
376 NF Directorate meeting, Minutes, 25 March 1978, Harrington papers. The FBI monitored Tyndall but deemed his visit irrelevant to 'current domestic security interests. Accordingly, no active investigation is to be conducted based on information set forth in the enclosed [redacted],' see FBI file DocID: 32683822, released in response to FOIA enquiry, 4 November 2016.
377 *Instauration*, vol. 2, no. 6, May 1977.
378 *Instauration*, vol. 3, no. 11, October 1978.
379 *Instauration*, vol. 4, no. 4, April 1979.
380 *Ibid.*
381 Reed Massengill, *Portrait of a Racist* (New York: St Martin's Press, 1994), p. 234.
382 *Citizens Informer*, vol. 11, no. 4, July–August 1979.
383 The Southern National Party also republished Tyndall's Memphis speech, selling cassette tapes of it in *The Southern National Newsletter*, vol. 2, no. 1, fall 1979; Leonard Zeskind, *Blood and Politics: The History of the White Nationalist Movement from the Margins to the Mainstream* (New York: Farrar, Straus and Giroux, 2009), p. 419.
384 *The Spotlight*, 19 June 1978.
385 *Instauration*, vol. 4, no. 11, October 1979.

386 *Spearhead*, no. 130, August 1979.
387 *Independent on Sunday*, 2 March 1997.
388 *National Vanguard*, March 1979; and *National Alliance Bulletin*, July 1979. For a photo of Brady selling the newspaper, see *National Vanguard*, no. 73, December 1979. Brady contributed an article on the 'red' takeover of British schools shortly after his own dismissal as a teacher to *National Vanguard*, no. 76, May 1980.
389 *Spearhead*, no. 130, August 1979.
390 The *Western Guardian*, vol. 1, no. 2, May–June 1980.
391 *Ibid.*
392 There was also an ambient ideological imperative. John Bean, *Many Shades of Black*, p. 221 lamented that *National Front News*, which Webster edited, 'seemed to concentrate on racialist abuse of coloured immigrants.' The authorities were also concerned. Webster was prosecuted on two counts of inciting racial hatred in November 1979, receiving a fine and two concurrent six-month jail sentences, see *Spearhead*, no. 131, September 1979; and *Spearhead*, no. 133, November 1979. Webster's case file – TNA DPP 2/6674 – remains closed until 2064.
393 NF Directorate Meeting, Minutes, 29 July 1979, Harrington papers notes the Executive Council voted to suspend Fountaine by five votes to one for committing an 'act prejudicial to the security of the NF', namely, 'communicating such matters outside the party' with regards Webster's 'unratified' suspension.
394 *Spearhead*, no. 132, October 1979.
395 *Spearhead*, no. 134, December 1979. Kavanagh was the Islington NF treasurer and sat on the NF Finance Committee, see *Spearhead*, no. 102, February 1977. Webster objected to Kavanagh's 'populism' in cavilling from mentioning 'Zionist Jewry' lest it bring further opposition, see *Spearhead*, no. 131, September 1979.
396 *Spearhead*, no. 122, October 1978. *Daily Mail*, 20 August 1977 notes the closure of the NF's previous premises in Teddington headquarters in 1977 for breaching planning laws. Their eviction was not entirely unconnected with the violence in Lewisham earlier in that month.
397 *National Front Members' Bulletin – Supplement*, January–February 1980.
398 *Time Out*, 11–17 January 1980 provides a snapshot of the ongoing intrigue during the planning inquiry, which the Fountaine-Kavanagh faction evidently hoped, would dislodge Tyndall for them. The inquiry also heard graphic evidence about NF activities from Simon Read, an anarchist infiltrator, from August 1978 onwards. *New Society*, 3 January 1980 records Read telling the inquiry:

> The ground floor [of Excalibur House] consists of a 'security box', which is a tiny room by the front door…. Stacked in the corner, under the window, there was a pile of weapons, including wooden clubs and iron bars. A wooden pickaxe handle had something written on it in ballpoint pen. I think it said 'Jew beater'.

399 See *American Renaissance*, vol. 19, no. 8, August 2008, www.amren.com/ar/2008/08/index.html (accessed 21 April 2015). Thereafter, the NF moved into a building in Streatham, South London.
400 *Spearhead*, no. 133, November 1979.
401 *Spearhead*, no. 136, February 1980.
402 Tyndall stated in *Spearhead*, no. 140, June 1980 that Webster's sexuality was not the sole issue. 'On the public level, Tyndall recorded,

> I was compelled repeatedly to choke with shame and embarrassment at the humiliation brought upon the party by his filthy language, bizarre gestures and frequently total loss of personal control. Internally, his presence became more and more intolerable – undermining discipline, reducing working relationships to a shambles and creating an atmosphere of rancor and poison through the nationwide network of regions, branches and departments.

403 Martin Webster, CV.
404 *Spearhead*, no. 140, June 1980.
405 *Spearhead*, no. 135, January 1980; *Spearhead*, no. 136, February 1980; and *The Times*, 1 March 1980.
406 *Spearhead*, no. 135, January 1980.
407 *Spearhead*, no. 300, February 1994.

408 *The Times*, 22 January 1980.
409 *Spearhead*, no. 134, December 1979 claimed NFCM support was concentrated in Hertfordshire and Bedfordshire but was scant elsewhere. Tyndall took to deriding the group simply as the 'Con-Movement'. *Spearhead*, no. 159, January 1982 states that Fountaine resigned from his own movement in late 1981 after failing to convince members to changed its name to the 'National Conservative Party'.
410 *The Times*, 7 December 1979. Beyond clashing personalities, Fountaine also disagreed with Tyndall on policies and tactics. The NFCM journal, *Excalibur*, no. 5, May 1980, argued that 'the cruder forms of racism must be publicly eschewed', whilst Fountaine also accused Tyndall of transforming the NF into 'a street organisation fighting Pakistanis and communists', when instead 'we should have stopped marching two and a half years ago.' Fountaine was not, however, averse to marching but simply believed 'you should only march when you are able to put 10,000 well-dressed troops on the streets, conducting themselves like Englishmen.'
411 Stan Taylor, *The National Front in English Politics*, p. 91.
412 *Spearhead*, no. 135, January 1980; *Spearhead*, no. 136, February 1980; and *The Times*, 1 March 1980.
413 *Spearhead*, no. 140, June 1980; and *Spearhead*, no. 141, July 1980.
414 *Instauration*, vol. 6, no. 5, April 1981.
415 *Spearhead*, no. 144, October 1980.
416 *Nationalism Today*, no. 17, 1983; and *Loose Cannon*, no. 1, September 1999.
417 *Spearhead*, no. 145, November 1980 notes Parker was appointed NNF branch liaison officer to rebuild Tyndall's network of support, especially in the West Midlands where he had political links. *New Frontier*, no. 4, May 1981 highlights Parker's role as NNF national organiser.
418 *Spearhead*, no. 135, January 1980; and *Spearhead*, no. 141, July 1980. O'Brien regularly contributed to *Candour* until his death on 21 September 1982, see *Candour*, vol. 33, nos 11 and 12, November–December 1982; and *Spearhead*, no. 171, January 1983.
419 *Spearhead*, no. 164, June 1982.
420 *Spearhead*, no. 151, May 1981.
421 *Spearhead*, no. 171, January 1983. This stance gained support from a professional Judo instructor in Norfolk called Eric Pleasants, a former BUF activist who had conducted PT exercises for the British Free Corps (BFC), a Waffen-SS unit comprised of British renegades. He witnessed the firebombing of Dresden and been captured and imprisoned in a Soviet labour camp in the Arctic Circle for seven years before being repatriated to England in 1953. See Eddie Chapman, *I Killed to Live: The Story of Eric Pleasants Professional Strong-Man* (London: Cassell, 1957) and his posthumous autobiography, Eric Pleasants, *Hitler's Bastard Through Hell and Back in Hitler's Germany and Stalin's Russia* (Edinburgh: Mainstream, 2003).
422 *Spearhead*, no. 151, May 1981.
423 *Spearhead*, no. 154, August 1981. Tyndall also founded a youth group – the 'Young Nationalists' – which was headed by Kevin Randall, one of the few YNF activists to follow Tyndall out of the NF, see *New Frontier*, no. 1, January–February 1981; and *Spearhead*, no. 149, March 1981. Randall became deputy editor of the NNF newspaper, *New Frontier*. In August 1984, Tyndall announced that the new editor of its newspaper, *Young Nationalist* would be 'Tony Wells' – Tony Lecomber.
424 *Spearhead*, no. 135, January 1980. Tyndall's diagnosis of Britain's industrial decline lent heavily upon 'The Pride and Fall' tetralogy by economic historian Corelli Barnett. Longer term, Tyndall's Spenglerian pessimism was also informed by a (racial) reading of summary of Edward Gibbon's *Decline and Fall of the Roman Empire*. 'I could not help being struck by the similarities between this great writer's descriptions of that long past tragedy and the evidence I saw with my own eyes all around me,' see Tyndall, *The Eleventh Hour*, p. 42.
425 *Spearhead*, no. 197, March 1985.
426 *Ibid.*
427 *Spearhead*, no. 154, August 1981. Many League activists subsequently supported Tyndall's BNP, see *Spearhead*, no. 167, September 1982. League publications, *League Review* and *National Review*, were regularly advertised in *Spearhead* thereafter.
428 *Spearhead* no. 146, December 1980; and *Spearhead*, no. 151, May 1981.
429 *Spearhead*, no. 153, July 1981.
430 *Spearhead*, no. 157, November 1981.

431 *Spearhead*, no. 367, September 1999. *Spearhead*, no. 145, November 1980 records that Tyndall was more successful in legal action taken against the magazine's typesetters who were aligned with Fountaine/Kavanagh.
432 *Spearhead*, no. 164, June 1982.
433 Tyndall's in-laws also stood as BNP candidates. Charles Parker gained 632 votes (1.3 per cent) in Walsall South, his wife, Violet, polling 295 votes (0.6 per cent) in Wakefield.
434 *Spearhead*, no. 200, June 1985.
435 *Spearhead*, no. 189, July 1984; and *Spearhead*, no. 190, August 1984.
436 *Spearhead*, no. 159, January 1982, which also advertised *National Socialism: World Creed for the 1980s*.
437 *Spearhead*, no. 188, June 1984.
438 Frost, *'Twaz a Good Fight!'*, p. 281.
439 *Spearhead*, no. 149, March 1981.
440 *National Review*, no. 41, June 1983.
441 *Spearhead*, no. 178, August 1983.
442 *Spearhead*, no. 177, July 1983. Tyndall dismissed Brons' claims that he was impeding 'unity' in *Spearhead*, no. 200, June 1985 stating that Brons and his colleagues:

> worked with me in the 1970s in a united movement and not only he but most of the others failed to raise any of the issues of 'ideological' disagreement that they now erect as barriers to the necessary and the inevitable.

443 *Spearhead*, no. 183, January 1984.
444 For a full overview of these years, see Nigel Copsey, *Contemporary British Fascism: The British National Party and the Quest of Legitimacy* (London: Palgrave 2008), pp. 28–49.
445 Ray Hill with Andrew Bell, *The Other Face of Terror*, pp. 286–290.
446 *Spearhead*, no. 186, April 1984. Curiously, Hill wrote to Tyndall (*Spearhead*, no. 188, June 1984), objecting to being called a 'traitor' and disputing he had committed 'treason'. He also added 'that I was not disloyal to you – and you know it! I made no attempt to embarrass you, either politically or personally.' Needless to say, Tyndall took an alternate view.
447 John Morse and John Tyndall, 'Indictment', released in response to an FOI request. Three case files – TNA DPP 2/9340–42 – remain closed until 2062. Three issues of *British Nationalist* were involved, namely, its October 1984, May 1985 and July–August 1985 editions. By Tyndall's own admission, 'certain races were referred to in terms of superiority and inferiority' in the editorial of the May 1985 edition, which, he surmised, was the principal reason for Morse's prosecution, see *Spearhead*, no. 214, December 1986.
448 John Tyndall 'Indictment', released in response to an FOI request. The charges that Tyndall faced separately related to three issues of *Spearhead*: a Special Supplement to *British Nationalist*, and three BNP leaflets *If Only We Were Black*, *Middle Class Awakenings* and *Maternity Wing*. He and Morse were not alone; nine other BNP activists were charged at around this time with offences relating to the incitement of racial hatred, see *Spearhead*, no. 208, February 1986.
449 Transcript of Appeal Court Judgement, heard at the Royal Courts of Justice, 20 October 1986, released in response to FOI request.
450 *Spearhead*, no. 214, December 1986.
451 *Spearhead*, no. 236, October 1988.
452 *The Times*, 30 August 1977.
453 Susan Sontag, *Illness as Metaphor and AIDS and its Metaphors* (London: Penguin, 2002), p. 69.
454 Tyndall, *The Eleventh Hour*, p. 131.
455 *Ibid.*, p. 140.
456 *Ibid.*, p. 139.
457 *Ibid.*, pp. 132–137. Oliver had been a member of the 'Advisory Board' of William Pierce's National Youth Alliance. Oliver regularly wrote for *Liberty Bell*, an extreme right-wing publication edited by George P. Dietz who regularly reprinted articles from *Spearhead*. Possibly Oliver had put Tyndall in touch with Dietz. *Liberty Bell*, vol. 11, no. 3, December 1983 featured a letter from Tyndall informing Dietz of his recent receipt of a copy of *Liberty Bell* from a friend, 'and am much impressed by its contents.'
458 The serialisation began in *Spearhead*, no. 179, September 1983. *Spearhead*, no. 270, August 1991 pays tribute to Brown's influence upon Tyndall.

459 On Ludovici, see Dan Stone, *Breeding Superman: Nietzsche, Race and Eugenics in Edwardian and Interwar Britain* (Liverpool: Liverpool University Press, 2001), pp. 33–61. *Spearhead*, no. 321, November 1995 reprinted Ludovici's article 'On Feminine Influence in Politics'. *The Specious Origins of Liberalism* (1967) was originally published by The Britons, the anti-Semitic publishing house. It comprised a collection of articles that Ludovici had originally contributed to Brown's newspaper, *The South African Observer*, between March 1961 and January 1963 with additions from a series titled 'The Importance of Racial Integrity', published in the journal some years earlier, see www.anthonymludovici.com/so_pre.htm (accessed 1 April 2010).
460 Yockey had also loomed large in Tyndall's article 'Away from Liberalism – Towards Leadership', *Spearhead*, no. 103, March 1977.
461 *Spearhead*, no. 295, September 1995. Nor, incidentally, did Tyndall agree with Yockey's supra-national conceptualisation of 'Europe'. Instead, Tyndall argued that if geography were the basis for replacing 'national' loyalty then surely transcending this with a 'greater loyalty' to the 'White Race', whose territory was no longer synonymous with 'Europe', was more appropriate, see *Spearhead*, no. 166, August 1982.
462 Hans-Georg Betz and Carol Johnson, 'Against the Current – Stemming the Tide: The Nostalgic Ideology of the Contemporary Radical Populist Right', *Journal of Political Ideologies*, vol. 9, no. 3, 2004, pp. 311–327 makes a similar point.
463 The *Guardian*, 28 November 1986. Lecomber was convicted of making ten grenades, seven detonators, two petrol bombs and a bomb in a biscuit tin.
464 *Daily Telegraph*, 3 February 1987; and *Spearhead*, no. 330, August 1996. Edmonds was a schoolteacher at Tulse Hill School, Lambeth, where over half of the 1,700 pupils were black, when he joined the NF and stood as a candidate in the 1974 general election. There were calls for his dismissal, though the local authority declined to intervene, see *The Times*, 30 August 1974; and *The Times*, 31 August 1974. Edmonds resigned his post in 1975, subsequently penning an article for *Spearhead*, no. 85, July 1975 titled 'Anarchy at Tulse Hill'. Edmonds became Lambeth NF chairman and was elected to the party's National Directorate, see *Spearhead*, no. 87, September 1975. When Tyndall resigned in 1980, so did Edmonds, initially taking on the role as Lewisham BNP organiser, see *Spearhead*, no. 173, March 1983.
465 *Heritage and Destiny*, no. 36, April–June 2009.
466 The two candidates were Alf Waite who polled 184 votes (0.4 per cent) in Ravensbourne, and Mike Easter, who polled 369 votes (0.6 per cent) in Tonbridge and Malling.
467 *Spearhead*, no. 222, August 1987. *Spearhead*, no. 179, September 1983 notes that failure of a previous endeavour to persuade the NF and BM to amalgamate with the BNP.
468 *Spearhead*, no. 352, February 1990.
469 *Spearhead*, no. 242, April 1989.
470 For a fuller exploration of this theme, see Graham Macklin, 'Transnational Networking on the Far Right: The Case of Britain and Germany', *West European Politics*, vol. 36, no. 1, 2013, pp. 176–198.
471 *Time Out*, 23–29 January 1986.
472 *Spearhead*, no. 224, October 1987. The same issue contained an advertisement for titles like *The Hoax of the Twentieth Century*, *Did Six Million Really Die?*, *The Six Million Reconsidered* and *The Zundel Trial and Free Speech*
473 *'Holocaust' News*, no. 1, 1982.
474 *Spearhead*, no. 230, April 1988; and *Sunday Times*, 6 March 1988. The Centre for Historical Review (CHR), which printed and published *'Holocaust' News* had been formed in 1982 by 'Richard Harwood' according to *National Front News*, no. 40, May 1982, but now appeared to exist in name only. Edmonds refused to disclose the source of the publications' funding, stating only that the CHR 'had Palestinian sympathisers' as well as links to the Institute of Historical Review in California, which had received money from Saudi Arabian supporters. Edmonds lost his job at Cable & Wireless Ltd following the *Sunday Times*' exposé. TNA DPP 2/7808 highlights the Director of Public Prosecution declined to prosecute the publication in 1982.
475 *Spearhead*, no. 402, August 2002.
476 Kenan Malik, *From Fatwa to Jihad: The Rushdie Affair and its Legacy* (London: Atlantic Books, 2009).
477 *Spearhead*, no. 242, April 1989.
478 *Instauration*, vol. 14, no. 2, January 1989.

479 Glyn Ford [Rapporteur], *Report drawn up on behalf of the Committee of Inquiry in Racism and Xenophobia* (Luxembourg: Office for Official Publications of the European Communities, 1991), p. 39.
480 Fred Naylor, *Dewsbury: The School Above the Pub* (London: Claridge Press, 1989).
481 *Patriot*, no. 2, winter 1997.
482 *Spearhead*, no. 249, November 1989; and *Spearhead*, no. 250, December 1989.
483 *Britain Nationalist*, no. 107, February 1991.
484 *Spearhead*, no. 265, March 1991; and *Spearhead*, no. 266, April 1991.
485 *The Populist Observer*, no. 52, May 1990.
486 *The Populist Observer*, no. 53–54, June–July 1990; and *Spearhead*, no. 257, July 1990.
487 For speaking engagements, see *Spearhead*, no. 267, May 1991. *Forward*, 7 June 1991, states Liberty Lobby activists had lobbied the US government for the past year to get Tyndall's travel ban overturned.
488 Leonard Zeskind, *Blood and Politics*, pp. 252–257 provides an account of the tour.
489 Prior to the meeting, Tyndall published a letter from Burke in *Spearhead*, no. 252, February 1990 stating 'I have been a subscriber to *Spearhead* for many years, and have read some of the most powerful articles ever published at any time or place in our English speech...'
490 Frederick J. Simonelli, *American Fuehrer: George Lincoln Rockwell and the American Nazi Party* (Urbana, IL: University of Illinois Press, 1999), p. 26.
491 *Spearhead*, no. 269, July 1991; and *Truth at Last*, no. 350, 1991.
492 *Spearhead*, no. 307, September 1994.
493 *Spearhead*, no. 269, July 1991. Tyndall's US tour begat a reciprocal visit from four American extreme right-wing lawyers in 1992. Kirk Lyons, David Holloway, Sam Dickson and Martin O'Toole as part of a European-wide tour to promote CAUSE – billed as 'America's only pro-White law firm' – but which was simply Lyon's 'Patriot's Defence Foundation' under a new name. Lyons addressed a Glasgow BNP meeting on 27 June and another in West Yorkshire on the following day. He and Dickson were both billed to address a BNP meeting in London on 4 July organised by 'an *ad-hoc* committee of British historical revisionists, which the BNP will be supporting'. Both men were clearly impressed with the BNP. Dickson returned to England on 24 October 1992 as guest of honour at its annual party rally whilst Lyons was feted with the honour in the following year, see *Spearhead*, no. 281, July 1992. For Lyons, see 'In the Lyons Den', *Intelligence Report*, no. 99, summer 2000.
494 *Instauration*, vol. 16, no. 9, August 1991.
495 *Instauration*, vol. 16, no 10, September 1991.
496 *Instauration*, vol. 18, no. 1, December 1992. *Instauration*, vol. 17, no. 11, October 1992 had previously lamented that whilst Europe had figures like Jean-Marie Le Pen, Jorg Haider and Tyndall, 'we are represented by a variety of Hollywood Nazis, hooded Joe Sixpacks and other well-meaning, but frankly uninspiring "spokesmen".'
497 *British Nationalist*, no. 138, December 1993.
498 *Spearhead*, no. 291, May 1993.
499 *Spearhead*, no. 245, July 1989 highlighted beginnings of the BNP campaign.
500 *Spearhead*, no. 281, July 1992, p. 9.
501 Nick Lowles, *White Riot: The Violent Story of Combat 18* (London: Milo, 2014), p. 13.
502 Nigel Copsey, 'Contemporary Fascism in the Local Arena: The British National Party and "Rights for Whites"', in Mike Cronin (ed.), *The Failure of British Fascism: The Far Right and the Fight for Political Recognition* (Basingstoke: Macmillan, 1996), pp. 118–140.
503 *Spearhead*, no. 296, October 1993.
504 Lowles, *White Riot*, p. 37.
505 *Guardian*, 20 February 1993.
506 The *Evening Standard*, 17 September 1993.
507 The *Observer*, 19 September 1993.
508 The *Mirror*, 18 September 1993.
509 The *Guardian*, 21 September 1993. *Searchlight*, no. 219, September 1993 records Edmonds' appointment as British representative of the Le Nouvel ordre européen (NOE – New European Order), a transnational national socialist group operated from Lausanne, Switzerland, by Gaston-Armand 'Guy' Amaudruz, which had had its heyday in the early 1950s but which was, by this juncture, reportedly largely moribund.

510 *Spearhead*, no. 300, February 1994.
511 *Spearhead*, no. 298, December 1993.
512 The *Guardian*, 18 June 1994. Whilst on remand, Edmonds and Tyndall were fined £100 apiece for displaying racist recruitment posters, see *Independent*, 6 October 1993.
513 *Spearhead*, no. 305, July 1994.
514 'Mr Major's Joint Doorstep Interview with Prime Minister Keating', 17 September 1993, www.johnmajor.co.uk/page1090.html (accessed 4 May 2015).
515 *Spearhead*, no. 296, October 1993. It raised £3,547, records *Spearhead*, no. 300, February 1994.
516 'The Police have a Poor Record in the Fight Against Fascism', The *Guardian*, 21 March 2010, www.theguardian.com/theobserver/libertycentral/2010/mar/21/police-demonstrations-fascism-racism (accessed 8 September 2018).
517 For an anti-fascist critique, see Colin B. West [pseud.], *Ready Welling and Able: Reflections on the Events at Welling (16.10.93)* (London: Pentagon Press, 1994). For a view from a former undercover police officer, see Rob Evans and Paul Lewis, *Undercover: The True Story of Britain's Secret Police* (London: Guardian/Faber & Faber, 2013). *Spearhead*, no. 330, August 1996 notes the eventual closure of the bookshop.
518 *Instauration*, vol. 18, no. 12, November 1993.
519 Three years later, Irving denied any knowledge whatsoever of the BNP: 'I am not familiar with their programme or policies, so cannot judge if they are "Nazi" or not,' though he conceded that Focal Point Publications had supplied them with books. That said, Irving clearly knew who Tyndall was, since he stated 'I hold this gentleman at arm's length.' Irving also noted that:

> When *Churchill's War vol. 1* was presented at a press conference aboard HMS Belfast in November 1987, Mr Tyndall was observed to be present: he had not been invited, and I conducted an internal inquiry as to how he came to be there.

(It turned out that one of the guests had invited him, without my authorisation), see David Irving, 'About the Author: A Biographical Letter', 11 August 1996, www.fpp.co.uk/docs/Irving/Julius110896.html (accessed 20 September 2017).
520 Faci told *The Order*, no. 3, n.d. that he had been an NF member in 1976.
521 *British Nationalist*, no. 138, December 1993.
522 *Spearhead*, no. 299, January 1994.
523 *Spearhead*, no. 300, February 1994; and *Spearhead*, no. 301, March 1994.
524 *Spearhead*, no. 311, January 1995.
525 Birchall, *Beating the Fascists*, p. 355.
526 Sean Birchall, *Beating the Fascists*, p. 355. See also Nigel Copsey, 'From Direct Action to Community Action: The Changing Dynamics of Anti-Fascist Opposition', in Nigel Copsey and Graham Macklin (eds), *British National Party: Contemporary Perspectives* (Abingdon: Routledge, 2011), pp. 123–141.
527 *Spearhead*, no. 304, June 1994.
528 *Spearhead*, no. 305, July 1994.
529 *Spearhead*, no. 302, April 1994.
530 *Spearhead*, no. 310, December 1994.
531 Goodwin, *New British Fascism*, p. 47.
532 *British Nationalist*, no. 147, September 1994. The murder of fifteen-year-old Richard Everitt in an unprovoked attack by a Bangladeshi gang in Somers Town, King's Cross, on 13 August 1994 was a case in point. The BNP attempted to exploit his killing for political gain contemporaneously and continue to do so. Twenty years later, however, the BNP refers to his killers not as 'Asian' but 'Muslim' to fit the requirements of its virulent anti-Islam platform, see 'Remembering Richard Everitt', *Civil Liberty*, 11 December 2011, www.civilliberty.org.uk/2011/12/10/remembering-richard-everitt/ (accessed 23 January 2020).
533 *British Nationalist*, no. 160, September 1995; *British Nationalist*, no. 172, October 1996; and *British Nationalist*, no. 174, December 1996.
534 Lowles, *White Riot*, p. 25.
535 *The Order*, no. 1, n.d.
536 *The Order*, no. 2, n.d.
537 *Thor-Would*, no. 8, n.d. *British Oi*, no. 27 stated *Thor-Would* was 'the best zine if you want a laugh a John Tyndalls [sic] expense.'

538 *Spearhead*, no. 299, January 1994.
539 Quoted in *Fighting Talk*, no. 16, March 1997.
540 *The Order*, no. 4, circa October 1993.
541 *BNP Organisers' Bulletin*, 14 December 1993.
542 *Putsch*, no. 7, circa December 1993.
543 Lowles, *White Riot*, p. 151.
544 *Spearhead*, no. 351, May 1998.
545 John Tyndall to John Cato, 31 January 1994 in SCH/01/Res/BRI/TMP/010, Searchlight archive, University of Northampton.
546 *The Order*, no number or date ['Hail Victory' cover].
547 *Spearhead*, no. 311, January 1995.
548 *Putsch*, no. 30, November 1995.
549 *Putsch*, no. 4, August 1993; *Putsch*, no date/number circa January 1995; and *Putsch*, no. 30, November 1995.
550 *International Redwatch*, issue 1.
551 Frost, *'Twaz a Good Fight!'*, pp. 296–297.
552 John Tyndall, 'Doing the Enemy's Work', *Spearhead*, no. 319, September 1995.
553 *Ibid*.
554 *Ibid.*
555 *Spearhead*, no. 320, October 1995.
556 *The Order,* November 1995.
557 *Spearhead* had regularly reprinted Pierce's articles as well as advertising his publications *Attack* and *National Vanguard*. Tyndall also advertised *Lincoln Rockwell: A National Socialist Life*, an homage written by Pierce, see *Spearhead*, no. 259, September 1990. 'Life Rune Books' advertisements in *Spearhead*, no. 270, August 1991 and *Spearhead*, no. 272, October 1991 offered for sale *The Turner Diaries, Hunter* and *Serpent's Walk*, by Randolph D. Calverhall, a racist science fiction novel published by NA, as well as Michael Hoffman's *A Candidate for the Order*, which had a similar pedigree. The admiration was mutual. *Spearhead*, no. 246, August 1989 contained a letter from Kevin Strom, a leading NA activist, stating that *Spearhead* was 'one of the best' magazines he read. Throughout its history, *Spearhead* also featured advertisements for a range of other US publications including *Instauration, The Nationalist, Calling Our Nation, American Renaissance* and *The Truth at Last*, edited by Tyndall's friend Edward Fields, which was listed as an 'allied publication'. When Fields retired from active politics in 2008, he handed *The Truth at Last* subscription lists to *The David Duke Report*, mouthpiece of former Ku Klux Klan leader, David Duke, see *Intelligence Report*, no. 132, winter 2008. Fields later joined the National Alliance, see www.nationalvanguard.org:80/story.php?id=668 (accessed 11 October 2003).
558 Lowles, *White Riot*, p. 353.
559 *British Nationalist*, no. 162, December 1995; and *Spearhead*, no. 322, December 1995. *The Order*, no. 14 blamed BNP members for the lack of respect. Mark Cotterill, 'Heritage and Destiny Interviews Will Williams', *National Vanguard*, 30 December 2014, http://nationalvanguard.org/2014/12/heritage-and-destiny-interviews-will-williams/ (accessed 21 June 2016) states that BNP activist Peter Rushton and the NA's future leader Will Williams facilitated the visit.
560 For C18's bemused reaction, see *Putsch*, no. 31, December 1995.
561 *Spearhead*, no. 315, May 1995.
562 'A Great Man Passes On: Buckley and Tyndall pay Tribute to Dr. W.L. Pierce', *Spearhead*, www.spearhead.com/0209-ib.html (accessed 24 January 2012).
563 *Spearhead*, www.spearhead.co.uk/0507-jt3.html (accessed 22 September 2016).
564 The *Independent*, 2 March 1997.
565 *National Alliance Bulletin*, March 1996 reproduces the letter.
566 'A Great Man Passes On', *Spearhead*.
567 Quoted in *Fighting Talk*, no. 16, March 1997.
568 Sargent was jailed for life in January 1998.
569 *Spearhead*, no. 33, December 1996. Music at BNP meetings was 'not to "entertain" those present; it is to induce in them a mood most conducive to emotional receptiveness to the party's message,' stated *Spreading the Word: British National Party Handbook on Propaganda* (Welling: BNP, n.d.), p. 57. Thus, whilst personally discomforted by 'white resistance' music, Tyndall allowed BNP publications to advertise events by B&H, many of which were organised

in conjunction with local BNP units. Some of Tyndall's disdain for skinhead aficionados of white power music was misogynistic. *Spearhead*, no. 194, December 1984 featured a photo of female NF skinheads. 'That party, it seems, is as proud of its unfeminine women as it is of its unmasculine "males". What need have the media to portray nationalists as ill-behaved and repulsive freaks when some nationalist propagandists do it for them?'

570 John Tyndall, 'The Problem is Mr Griffin: It is Not Policies Which Divide the BNP, Says John Tyndall', *Spearhead*, www.spearhead.co.uk/0310-jt2.html (accessed 30 June 2016).
571 *Spearhead*, no. 335, January 1997.
572 *Spearhead*, no. 323, January 1996.
573 *Spearhead*, no. 366, August 1999. It is often forgotten that the 'modernising' faction were equally 'hard-line'. During 1997, Lecomber attempted to recruit Terry Blackham, the former NF National Activities organiser, then recently released from prison after being caught with several guns and a grenade launcher in his car that he had attempted to convey to Loyalist paramilitaries in Northern Ireland. Tony Lecomber to Terry Blackham, 11 October 1997 in MSS 412/BNP/3/1, Wayne Ashcroft papers, written with Tyndall's sanction, dismissed his serious criminal conviction stating:

> As you know both our party leader John Tyndall and myself have got criminal records sustained in the course of pursuing (or on the fringes of) political action. Neither of us can cast any stones in that direction! I can tell you Terry that your political record is well known in BNP circles. You are a good activist. You are loyal, brave, committed and a credit to your family and your race. If you should ever decide that you wanted to cross to the BNP, there would be no problem with that, and that goes for anyone else too. You would make a welcome addition to our list of Organisers, and you could also make a useful contribution to our stewarding group, maybe even as a senior steward. Also, you may know that we have a good London instant response activity team…

574 *Spearhead*, no. 335, January 1997.
575 *Britain Reborn: A Programme for a New Century: Election Manifesto, May 1997* (Welling: BNP, 1997), pp. 42–46.
576 *Spearhead*, no. 336, February 1997.
577 'BNP Election Broadcast 1997', YouTube, www.youtube.com/watch?v=bsSCCUIE0rQ (accessed 25 August 2016).
578 Poplar and Canning Town was a new constituency formed in part of the old Bow and Popular constituency where Tyndall had stood previously in 1992. Due to a combination of demographic churn and boundary changes, the BNP's three 'best wards' Beckton, Millwall and Custom House and Silver (based on BNP performance in the 1994 metropolitan council elections when its candidates polled 33, 28 and 27 per cent respectively) were now grouped into one parliamentary constituency, see *British Nationalist*, no. 178, April 1997 for the BNP analysis.
579 *Spearhead*, no. 340, June 1997.
580 *Spearhead*, no. 335, January 1997.
581 This was relative of course. Jeff Wilkerson of the American First Party, Inc. looked to the BNP being able to stand fifty-four candidates as 'proof of what can be done if one and all take this work seriously and put their shoulder to the wheel,' see *America First Party Newsletter*, vol. 2, no. 17, 1997.
582 It was perhaps no coincidence that Tyndall released a new edition of his autobiography, *The Eleventh Hour* (Welling: Albion Press, 1998) in which he thanked both Griffin and Lecomber 'who have rendered invaluable help to me in the preparation of this book.' By the time it was advertised to the BNP membership (*Spearhead*, no. 363, May 1999), Tyndall probably had a less generous attitude towards both men.
583 *Spearhead*, no. 351, May 1998.
584 *Identity*, no. 27, December 2002.
585 Tyndall set out his stall in *We've Come a Long Way – Don't Let's Ruin It!* and *Lies from Griffin & Co.*, 17 September 1999.
586 www.tyndallexposed.com (accessed 29 March 2005). The website highlighted the case of Ken Francis, the Newham BNP organiser whose partner was an Ecuadorian.
587 *British Nationalist*, no. 207, October 1999. Those who resigned included Richard Edmonds (National Organiser and South East London Regional Organiser); Iain Wilson (Dewsbury

Organiser); Keith Axon (West Birmingham Organiser); John Morse (Mid-South Regional Organiser and editor of *British Nationalist* until June 1998) and Ian Dell (Chief Steward). *British Nationalist* was dismissive, stating that in the case of Axon, Morse and Wilson 'their performances were so poor that it is felt that they have jumped before they were pushed'. *Searchlight*, no. 292, October 1999 notes Paul Ballard, Griffin's 1998 co-defendant, supported Tyndall.

588 'Interview with Richard Edmonds', *Counter-Currents*.
589 *Spearhead*, no. 411, May 2003; and Stephan Braun and Daniel Hörsch (eds), *Rechte Netzwerk: eine Gefahr* (Wiesbaden: VS-Verlag, 2004), pp. 110–111. *Preußische Allgemeine Zeitung*, 29 July 2002 reported that Edmonds viewed his work as 'Wiedergutmachung' ('reparation') for the Allied bombing of Germany during the Second World War.
590 *Spearhead*, no. 368, October 1999.
591 See www.tyndallexposed.com/sink.htm (accessed 14 March 2005); and *Spearhead*, no. 372, February 2000. The claims related to a behest left personally to Tyndall to promote the party and/or *Spearhead* by a member called John Lawson who died in 1991.
592 *Spearhead*, no. 373, March 2000.
593 *Spearhead*, no. 385, March 2001.
594 'Tyndall and "Modernisation"', www.tyndallexposed.com/modern.htm (accessed 14 March 2005).
595 *Spearhead*, no. 392, October 2001.
596 Branches in Clitheroe, Lancashire and Hillingdon, West London were a case in point.
597 *Spearhead*, no. 407, January 2003.
598 *Identity*, no. 34, July 2003.
599 'Sacked!', *Spearhead*, www.spearhead.co.uk/0309-jt2.html (accessed 30 June 2016).
600 *British Nationalist: British National Party Members' Bulletin*, July 2003; and Tyndall, 'The Problem is Mr Griffin'.
601 'Tyndall's 2003 Expulsion', www.tyndallexposed.com/expel2003.htm (accessed 14 March 2005) reproduces the correspondence.
602 *Voice of Freedom*, no. 42, September 2003.
603 Tyndall, 'The Problem is Mr Griffin'.
604 'Onslaught of the BNP Wreckers', *Spearhead*, www.spearhead.com/0412-jt2.html (accessed 30 June 2016).
605 The *Guardian*, 20 July 2005.
606 'A Salute to John Tyndall 14/7/1934–18/7/200, 19 July 2005:, https://davidduke.com/john-tyndall-1471934-1872005/ (accessed 24 January 2012). Tyndall had a long association with Duke. He had offered videotapes of Duke's Louisiana Senate campaign (*Spearhead*, no. 269, July 1991), publishing reports of its progress (*Spearhead*, no. 245, July 1989) written by his old friend, Edward Fields. *Spearhead*, no. 276, February 1992 highlights Tyndall accepted £500 from a Duke supporter towards the BNP 1992 general election campaign. Ironically, however, Tyndall's NF had ignored Duke when he visited Britain in March 1978, due to the Klan's deleterious image rather than its racism. 'Had Mr. Duke come to Britain as the representative of an American equivalent of the National Front ... then I am sure I and other NF officials would have been interested to meet him,' stated Martin Webster in *Spearhead*, no. 115, March 1978. 'But the KKK connection made that quite impossible.' *Spearhead*, no. 116, April 1978 was even more forthright in dismissing the KKK as 'another foreign import we can do without'. Duke whatever his 'sincerity' has 'nothing at all to contribute to the cause of the White Man in Britain and he would have done better not to come.' Not all NF activists felt so constrained. David Duke, *My Awakening: A Path to Racial Understanding* (Covington, LA: Free Speech Press, 2000), pp. 591–597 notes that he was honoured by a cross-burning ceremony at the Warwickshire farm of NF/RPS activist Robin Beauclaire. Duke was deported shortly afterwards and refused leave to re-enter Britain, see Hansard, HC Deb., vol. 946, cols 108–110W (14 March 1978); and Hansard, HC Deb., vol. 947, col. 470W (13 April 1978). Nor was Duke alone. In the following month, William Wilkinson, Imperial Wizard of the Invisible Empire of the Knights of the Ku Klux Klan, despite having been banned from entering Britain by the Home Secretary in February, also succeeded in illegally entering Britain but was deported upon arrival, see Hansard, HC Deb., vol. 947, cols 156–156W (6 April 1978).
607 *International European American Unity and Leadership Conference, 2004: Disk 2* (Mandeville, LA: David Duke Report, 2004). Fellow speakers included David Duke, Sam Dickson, Edward

Fields, Kevin Strom, Bob Whitaker, Germar Rudolf, Paul Fromm, Don Black, Willis Carto, Edgar Steele, David Pringle, Howie Farrell and Kenny Knight.
608 'Hear the Historic and Inspiring 2004 EURO Conference MP3s!', 15 September 2008, https://davidduke.com/hear-the-historic-and-inspiring-2004-euro-conference-mp3s-scroll-down/ (accessed 24 January 2012).
609 'Tyndall in America', *Spearhead*, www.spearhead.com/0407-jt2.html (accessed 24 January 2012).
610 *Heritage and Destiny*, no. 18, January–March 2005.
611 *Heritage and Destiny*, no. 22, October–December 2005.
612 'Tyndall and Combat 18', www.tyndallexposed.com/c18.htm (accessed 27 February 2005). One of the SSG's organisers was Leeds activist Eddy Morrison whom Tyndall had denounced as an 'inveterate disrupter' in an article titled 'The Wanderings and Posturings of the Pathetic Mr Morrison', *Spearhead*, no. 174, April 1983. Tyndall announced Morrison's re-admittance to the BNP in *Spearhead*, no. 243, May 1989.
613 Nationalist Week, no. 7, 12 July 2004, www.bpp.org.uk/nw7.html (accessed 30 June 2016).
614 'New Labour's Soviet Republic', *Spearhead*, www.spearhead.com/0501-jt2.html (accessed 24 January 2012).
615 Nationalist Week, no. 14, 29 August 2004, www.bpp.org.uk/nw14.html (accessed 30 June 2016).
616 George Michael, *The Enemy of My Enemy: The Alarming Convergence of Militant Islam and the Extreme Right* (Lawrence, KS: University of Kansas Press, 2006), p. 276.
617 *Spearhead*, no. 427, September 2004.
618 Shortly before Tyndall's hearing, *British Nationalist: British National Party Members' Bulletin*, November 2004 informed the membership of an alteration in the party constitution. Section 6, titled 'Discipline', had a new subsection inserted reading:

> Once the constitutionally defined internal disciplinary mechanisms of the party as outlined in this Section are exhausted in regard to the disciplinary procedures and proceedings, then the decision of the disciplinary tribunal is final and binding on the member concerned. As such, members (including those who have been disciplined or expelled) *legally affirm and agree that they will not seek any external legal (or non-legal) review of any disciplinary tribunal decision or its procedures* [author's emphasis]. They also agree and affirm that they will accept the decision of any disciplinary tribunal as final and binding.

Tyndall, rightly, interpreted this as a 'blatantly obvious' attempt to prevent him from seeking legal redress if the December disciplinary hearing ended in his expulsion, see 'Onslaught of the BNP Wreckers', *Spearhead*, www.spearhead.com/0412-jt2.html (accessed 30 June 2016).
619 'Expelled: Yet Again!', *Spearhead*, www.spearhead.co.uk/0501-jt1.html (accessed 26 August 2016). One such charge was that Tyndall had published advertisements for *The Turner Diaries* by William Pierce and *The Uprising* by Colin Jordan in the February 2004 issue of *Spearhead*, thereby 'causing the BNP to be associated with "Nazism" and "terrorism".' This was not an isolated instance, of course. Tyndall had reprinted articles from *Gothic Ripples* in *Spearhead* and often carried advertisements for cassettes of Jordan's speeches and books throughout the intervening decades, see, for example, *Spearhead*, no. 182, December 1983; *Spearhead*, no. 192, October 1984; and *Spearhead*, no. 303, May 1994. He had also rekindled his personal relationship with his former colleague. 'Whenever the opportunity arose, Colin and John Tyndall would meet socially, usually over a meal whenever 'JT' was travelling to meetings in Yorkshire,' records Frost, *'Twaz a Good Fight!'*, p. 299. Tyndall found the accusation of associating the party with terrorism 'utterly comic' since Lecomber himself had been jailed in 1986 following the accidental detonation of a home-made bomb whilst he sat in his car, see www.rwb.org.uk/JTrepsonse.html (accessed 8 February 2005). Tyndall might also have highlighted that *Spearhead* had advertised *Gothic Ripples* and *National Socialism: Vanguard of the Future* whilst Griffin himself was assistant editor, see *Spearhead*, no. 331, September 1996 and *Spearhead*, 334, December 1996. Lecomber's objectivity was further questioned when Tyndall received an email Lecomber had originally sent to Martin Webster outlining his 'personal loathing and contempt' for Tyndall whom, he believed, 'has cost us 20–25 years', see 'Expelled: Yet Again!', *Spearhead*, www.spearhead.com/0501-jt1.html (accessed 24 January 2012). For Tyndall's statement on his expulsion, see Nationalist Week, no. 27, 5 December 2004, www.bpp.org.uk/nw27.html (accessed 30 June 2016).

620 *British Nationalist: British National Party Members' Bulletin*, May 2005.
621 'Death of Valerie Tyndall', 25 June 2011, http://efp.org.uk/death-of-valerie-tyndall/ (accessed 30 June 2016).
622 Nationalist Week, no. 21, 18 October 2004, www.bpp.org.uk/nw21.html (accessed 30 June 2016); and *Heritage and Destiny*, no. 22, October–December 2005.
623 *Spearhead*, no. 434, April 2005.
624 *Spearhead*, no. 436, June 2005.
625 *Heritage and Destiny*, no. 22, October–December 2005.
626 *Spearhead*, no. 438, August 2005.
627 Nationalist Week, no. 58, 25 July 2005, www.bpp.org.uk/nw58.html (accessed 30 June 2016).
628 See www.nationalist.net/memorialdemo.html (accessed 1 August 2005).
629 Supporters maintain an online archive of Tyndall's key writings at *Spearhead*, www.spearhead.co.uk/index.html#directory (accessed 30 June 2016).
630 *Heritage & Destiny*, no. 22, October–December 2005.
631 'Obituary: John Tyndall', 19 July 2005, www.bnp.org.uk/news_detail.php?newsId=402 (accessed 20 July 2005).
632 *Identity*, no. 57, August 2005. *Voice of Freedom*, no. 63, August 2005 was more generous but still criticised his brand of racial nationalism as outmoded; what might have appealed politically during the 1970s had, by the time of his death, become 'a very personal philosophy to John Tyndall'.
633 *Identity*, no. 59, October 2005.
634 'Obituary: John Tyndall, 19 July 2005', www.bnp.org.uk/news_detail.php?newsId=402 (accessed 20 July 2005). They reiterated this claim on the first anniversary of his death, see British National Party, www.bnp.org.uk/news_detail-3481.php (accessed 18 July 2006).
635 *Gothic Ripples: Yuletide Supplement*, 2005.
636 *Blood & Honour*, no. 32.
637 *National Vanguard*, September–October 2005.
638 *Nation Europa*, vol. 55, no. 9, September 2005.
639 *The Times*, 20 July 2005.
640 'Death of Valerie Tyndall', 25 June 2011, http://efp.org.uk/death-of-valerie-tyndall/ (accessed 16 May 2012).
641 See 'Nick Griffin, "Catching Up"', *Chairman's blog*, 11 August 2007, http://chairmans-column.blogspot.co.uk/2007/08/first-my-sincere-apologies-for-long-gap.html (accessed 12 August 2007).
642 'Friends of JT Memorial Meeting', *Spearhead*, www.spearhead.com/0906meeting.html (accessed 30 August 2016). Edmonds own views had not moderated. On 1 March 2010, he was part of a group of British activists waiting outside Mannheim prison to greet Canadian-German Holocaust denier Ernst Zündel, who was released after serving a seven-year sentence.
643 See Eddy Butler's blog, July 2010, http://eddybutler.blogspot.com/2010/07/statement-from-richard-edmonds.html (accessed 1 August 2010).
644 See www.democracyforum.co.uk/bnp/80513-organisers-bulletin-disciplinary-procedures-2.html (accessed 20 August 2010).
645 See 'Obituary: Valerie Tyndall', www.bnp.org.uk/news/obituary--valerie-tyndall (accessed 30 June 2016). Valerie Tyndall died shortly before she was due to address the newly reformed Brighton and Hove BNP branch. She was afforded a more generous tribute on the party website than that afforded to her late husband. Ironically, it was penned by Griffin.
646 See www.bnpreform2011.co.uk/?p=1960 (accessed 1 December 2011).
647 Edmonds subsequently supported Andrew Brons' initiatives to forge 'unity' between various disparate groups now outside the BNP, see 'Nationalist Veteran Richard Edmonds Endorses Unity Drive', 6 January 2012, http://bnpideas.com/?p=3507 (accessed 1 December 2011).
648 See http://efp.org.uk/category/events-news/ (accessed 30 August 2016).
649 *Tenth Annual John Tyndall Memorial Meeting* (Heritage and Destiny: Preston 2015 – DVD). Groups attending in recent years include A.K. Chesterton Trust, Blood & Honour, British Movement, British Democratic Party, British National Party, Church of the Creator, Heretical Press, National Action, National Front, New British Union, Northern Patriotic Front and Telling Films.
650 *The Chairman's Bulletin*, no. 1, spring 1984. Similarly, other groups have organised their own events that elide real personal and political tensions within their movement's history. Since

2011, Yorkshire British Movement has held its own annual 'Colin Jordan & John Tyndall Memorial Meeting' to honour their respective memories. See http://bmsunwheel.blogspot.co.uk/2013/07/remembering-colin-jordan-and-john.html (accessed 30 August 2016); and http://bmsunwheel.blogspot.co.uk/2015/09/into-september-new-month-with-new.html (accessed 30 August 2016) for example.

651 'Record Attendance at John Tyndall Memorial Meeting', http://efp.org.uk/record-attendance-at-john-tyndall-memorial/ (accessed 30 August 2016).

652 See http://efp.org.uk/category/events-news/ (accessed 30 August 2016).

6   Nick Griffin

From the 'Third Position' to anti-Muslim 'populism'… and back again

Looking out from the platform in Manchester Town Hall shortly after 2 am on 8 June 2009, the BNP leader Nick Griffin was jubilant. The Returning Officer had just declared his election as the eighth and final Member of the European Parliament for the North-West region with 132,094 votes (8 per cent). Heading to Brussels with Griffin was fellow BNP activist Andrew Brons, elected to represent Yorkshire and Humberside. Altogether, the BNP had polled 943,598 votes (6.2 per cent), an unprecedented figure in the annals of British extreme right-wing electoral history. Griffin's election was met with anger and indignation; rival candidates promptly and pointedly left the platform amidst shouts and catcalls from BNP activists. The press now encircled Griffin. Rounding on his opponents as an 'out of touch, liberal elite', Griffin claimed his election breached the 'dam of lies', so that now 'the waters of truth and justice and freedom are once again flowing over this country. It's a great victory we go on from here.'[1]

Griffin had grounds for optimism. Having wrested control of the BNP from its founder, John Tyndall in 1999, he had transformed the party from an 'unelectable joke'[2] into a political machine that boasted fifty-six local councillors, three county councillors, one member of the Greater London Assembly and now, two MEPs.[3] It was a pyrrhic victory, however. Within five years, the BNP had imploded, losing all but a solitary local councillor by 2015. Griffin lost his seat in the 2014 European elections, polling a mere 32,826 (1.87 per cent). Brons was defeated too, though by this juncture he had already left the BNP after falling out with Griffin. Nationally, the BNP vote plunged to 1.14 per cent amidst a surge in support for the United Kingdom Independence Party (UKIP), a right-wing Eurosceptic and anti-immigration party that carried none of the BNP's historical baggage.[4]

Whilst the BNP havered on the verge of political extinction, Griffin's personal prospects appeared equally bleak. Following a brief interlude as Honorary President, the BNP expelled him in October 2014 for leaking 'damaging and defamatory allegations'[5] about party officials and finances onto the Internet in an effort to destabilise the new leadership and regain his tarnished crown. 'What makes the fall of Griffin and the BNP so intriguing,' commented Matthew Goodwin, 'is that they were given everything they could ever hope for – a global financial crisis, recession, rising inequality, immigration, an expenses scandal, Islamist terrorism and fiscal austerity, much of which hit their favoured territory in northern England.'[6] If Griffin led the most successful extreme right-wing party in British history, paradoxically many activists now held him responsible for squandering its greatest chance of success, driving the BNP into the ground in the process.

Early years

Nicholas John Griffin was born in Barnet, north London, on 1 March 1959. His father, Edgar, served in the Home Guard during the Second World War servicing barrage balloons, before joining the Royal Air Force. He worked as ground crew servicing Spitfire radios including a two-year stint in India. 'I was in charge of a group of around 20 young Indian aircraft mechanics, and I got on very well with them,' he recalled.[7] Returning to run an electrical business in St John's Wood, Edgar joined the Hendon South Young Conservatives in 1948 where he met Jean Thomas as they both heckled a Communist Party meeting. They married in December 1950.[8] The family's Barnet home was large and spacious. Griffin recalled living in genteel poverty, 'eating sugar sandwiches for dinner', but nonetheless enjoyed a 'great childhood'. During the 1964 general election, Griffin pedalled up and down the street outside his house with Conservative posters, supporting Reginald Maudling, Barnet's right-wing Conservative MP, affixed to his tricycle.[9] Both parents were bitterly disappointed when Labour again emerged triumphant in 1966. Griffin remembered being woken the next morning by his mother, who exclaimed: ' "It was a terrible night, we lost everything" – so even at seven I knew that the family were intensely political and was interested as well.'[10] Aged eight, Griffin's family moved to Southwold, Suffolk, after his father's electrical business failed. Griffin would later portray this as an early example of 'white flight'.

Griffin's induction into extreme right-wing politics came through his parents rather than formal party structures, highlighting the importance of family for the transmission of racist and 'neo-fascist' 'frames' regarding history, society and politics.[11] Edgar Griffin, having retrained as an accountant, became a Conservative district councillor in Suffolk. He ensured his son was well versed in 'the politics of race'. A member of the right-wing Monday Club who greatly admired Enoch Powell, Edgar was appalled when Edward Health sacked Powell following his 1968 'Rivers of Blood' speech. Other familial influences also weighed on Griffin's ideological development. His initial acquaintance with the 'Jewish Question' – aged twelve – came from reading books and pamphlets published by Mosley's BUF owned by his grandfather (who later became 'completely pro-National Front').[12]

'At 13, I read *Mein Kampf*, making notes in the margins,' Griffin recalled in a politically damaging interview whose veracity he subsequently disputed. 'I remember thinking, are the Jews really that bad? The chapter I most enjoyed was the one on propaganda and organization there are some really useful ideas there.'[13] Griffin learned to identify Jewish boys at school, his favourite childhood game, 'counting black people on the streets from the car window when my parents drove through London.'[14] After attending Woodbridge School, Suffolk, Griffin won a scholarship to St Felix in Southwold, an all-girls sixth form. He was one of only a few boys to attend. Staff soon noticed his views. 'I'm a socialist – a national socialist,' he told the school librarian who had challenged him.[15]

Young National Front

Familial socialisation and acculturation made Griffin a 'British nationalist' as a matter of 'gut instinct'. Hearing about the National Front (NF), 'something inside just clicked,' he wrote. 'Here was a party that was strongly patriotic and unashamedly pro-white. I said to myself this is the party for me.'[16] He was formally 'introduced' to extreme right-wing politics by William 'Bill' Fitt, the Norwich NF organiser who had been active in Jordan's WDL.[17] 'Bill was the first nationalist I ever met,' Griffin stated. 'It was due to a letter he had published in a local newspaper that I first became interested in nationalist politics.'[18] Fitt helped Griffin cement his thinking by lending him a copy of Frank Britton's anti-Semitic tract *Behind Communism* (1952), which, together with a subscription to *Spearhead*, introduced Griffin – in 'theoretical terms' – to the 'Jewish Question'.[19] This anti-Semitic acculturation coincided with Griffin's actual induction into the NF. Invited by a fellow Conservative county councillor, Edgar Griffin decided to attend an NF meeting at Norwich's Cavalier Hotel in 1975. 'Nicholas was a Young Conservative at the time and asked to come along,' recalled Edgar, 'so I took him. To my surprise, he seemed quite impressed, much more impressed than I was.'[20] Following the meeting, the speaker, Martin Webster, the NF National Activities organiser recalled being approached by Edgar who enquired whether his son should 'serve the cause' by joining the NF or the Conservative Party, working from within. Webster recommended he join the NF and 'fight the battle openly'.[21]

Aged fifteen, Griffin joined the Ipswich NF branch shortly afterwards, quickly becoming branch secretary. NF activism was a family affair. His sister, Susan, stood for the NF in Ipswich (Rushmere) in the May 1977 county council elections polling 79 votes (2.5 per cent) and was purportedly engaged to Tony Williams, the Ipswich NF organiser.[22] Meanwhile, Griffin's father continued attending NF meetings in East Anglia, defending the party in the regional press from 'the media's ceaseless anti-NF smear campaign'. *Spearhead* praised him as one of a 'tiny handful of genuine patriots who have held out' against 'the sickly creed of modern internationalist and multi-racialist Toryism.'[23] The Conservative Party would expel Edgar Griffin over his extreme right links, though not until 2001.[24]

Initially, the NF failed to impress Griffin. He 'came close' to letting his membership lapse, 'because I felt that a [membership] card and two bulletins in the previous year wasn't much of a return for my hard-earned money.'[25] His perseverance was repaid, however, as the party began focusing upon 'youth' as central to party recruitment and mobilisation. 'Large sections of British youth, deprived of leadership, are drifting to drugs, dirt and the worship of weird alien jungle rhythms,' *Spearhead* opined. 'The NF aims to restore in youth the virtues of discipline, fitness, smartness and national pride.'[26] This opened the door to young militants within the party including Derek Holland, a Huntingdon-based activist who was agitating for the establishment of a youth wing, independent of older figures who 'did not understand the nature and aims of this wing – seeing it as a personal vehicle or in the nature of politicised Boy Scouts.'[27]

Tyndall remained unconvinced by the merits of a separate youth organisation, believing that young activists who were politically mature enough should simply join the main party.[28] The subsequent formation of the Young National Front (YNF) in July 1977 represented a compromise therefore since it aimed to pro-actively integrate young militants into 'mature and serious' political work at branch level.[29] Contrary to Holland's wishes, the YNF was presided over by NF vice-chairman Andrew Fountaine, highlighting its singular lack of autonomy from party structures. Griffin, who had recently been part of the NF 'colour party' during its march through Lewisham, which was accompanied by widespread public disorder,[30] immersed himself in a range of YNF initiatives designed to instil a 'positive' sense of racial 'identity', 'worth' and 'pride' into its new recruits.[31] This activism caught the attention of the NF Directorate, who singled him out at a meeting on 3 December as someone who 'might form part of the nucleus of the [YNF] Secretariat.'[32] Thereafter, Griffin was ordained 'regional representative' at the inaugural YNF meeting, held at the Leicester NF headquarters.[33]

Importantly, it was at this meeting that Griffin met Joe Pearce, the YNF National Activities organiser, for the first time. The two subsequently became 'best of friends'. Pearce, a sixteen-year-old working-class YNF activist from Dagenham, east London, edited *Bulldog*, a racist tabloid, which had first appeared in September 1977, published on his own initiative. Embraced by the party, it became the official YNF newspaper with a print run in the thousands. The NF rewarded Pearce for his labours in January 1978 with a full-time, paid position.[34] Griffin also assumed an increasingly prominent role, addressing the first YNF rally in Birmingham on 18 February 1978.[35]

Bulldog was 'proud to be racialist and we are not afraid to say it, illegal or not.' Griffin contributed to this editorial philosophy with a letter published under the heading 'Black behaved like an animal'.[36] *Bulldog* targeted white working-class youths, railing against teachers and the police, whilst eulogising the skinhead revival which was 'rougher, more aggressive' than its initial incarnation.[37] Indeed, many youthful adherents of this increasingly politicised skinhead resurgence adopted 'neo-Nazi style' constituting 'an ugly subculture in many depressed inner cities, with their swastika and NF/BM badges.'[38] *Bulldog* also embraced football hooliganism; actively encouraging reader's 'to send in reports of racist abuse and racist chants at soccer games.' Pearce collated these into *Bulldog*'s 'Racist League' column. 'Fans of rival teams sought to outdo each other and become top of the league,' he recalled.[39] It proved remarkably popular. 'Plenty of Chelsea fans purchased the paper,' football hooligan Chris 'Chubby' Henderson remarked,

> not because they were interested in politics, but for the league table of louts on the back page. Chelsea, Leeds and West Ham were regularly in the top three. Fans would purchase it just to be able to tell their mates they'd read it first.[40]

Bulldog also played a key role in the YNF classroom campaign against 'Marxist indoctrination'. The party published *How to Combat Red Teachers* (1978) and disseminated *How to Spot a Red Teacher* leaflets, encouraging the disruption of 'politically correct' classes. 'The Anti-Nazi League did not really help matters by asking teachers, of all people, to speak out against the Front,' noted one observer. 'What further encouragement did you need to fork out ten pence for a copy of *Bulldog*?' Pearce upped the ante, publishing a 'Black List' in *Bulldog* comprising of the names and addresses of 'red teachers' and other opponents, many contributed by its teenage readership. By issue 40, *Bulldog* had published the details of 133 'anti-British Reds' – an average of three per issue.[41] Opposed to 'race-mix brainwashing', the YNF also campaigned to inoculate pupils against the idea 'that multiracialism and inter-racial sex are normal and desirable.'[42]

The YNF generated 'huge publicity' for its parent party. Indeed, for Webster, its success reflected his belief that the NF was manifesting itself as a 'cultural movement'.[43] However, the depth of its penetration in the cultural lives of young people is open to question. Its own protests were sparsely attended – only fifty youths showed up to protest sex education films being shown by the Inner London Education Authority, for instance, highlighting its failure to engage the great mass of young people. Undoubtedly, however, the headlines it generated gave the NF an immeasurable boost, putting pressure on local authorities. The YNF also helped its parent party spread its racial doctrines amongst those its own propaganda may never have reached.[44] YNF activity certainly reflected the party's increasingly youthful demographic. Contemporaneous academic studies recorded that 20 per cent of NF supporters were aged between fifteen and twenty years, whilst a further 16 per cent were aged between twenty-one and twenty-four. The 'model' NF supporter was 'a young, urban working-class male' likely to have left school at sixteen with minimal qualifications.[45]

Griffin followed the YNF template in his own locality with gusto. He helped to produce a magazine called *Combat*, edited by Nick Wakeling, a Norwich YNF activist, urging supporters to contact them for 'operation NF', which would take the YNF campaign against the 'stranglehold' of Marxist thinking into local schools, colleges and youth clubs. 'Send us news about race-mixing and communism at your college,' enjoined *Combat*. They also advertised YNF activities including 'the first RACIALIST disco ever held in Norwich … whites only.'[46] Wakeling also edited *Anglian News*, which agitated to 'Keep Norwich White'. It regularly reported upon Ipswich NF activity involving Griffin and Tony Williams.[47] This rural campaign was psychologically important, argued *Anglian News*, because it reaffirmed that:

> it's no good trying to move out of towns and cities with coloured populations … there is nowhere else to move to. Then, when they realise this, the British people will have no alternative but to stand their ground and start to fight back.[48]

Driving home this message, *Anglian News* featured lurid reports on the 'Negro menace in Ipswich' to support its supposition that 'the Race War is spreading!' The 'tyrannical' Race Relations Act (1976) was treated with contempt: 'we fight on in the knowledge that there is only one law above all laws – and that is the *Law of Survival*.'[49]

Nationally, the YNF also sought to energise white youth through sporting activities and social events as a means of attracting young members.[50] It held several youth camps as a means of integrating new joiners into party activity, one on Bodmin Moor in Cornwall was organised by Ipswich NF leader Tony Williams. In his capacity as Ipswich NF secretary, Griffin let Williams use his Suffolk home as the contact point.[51] The group also conducted seminars to teach fledgling activists rudimentary political skills like 'silk screen poster printing' and 'producing a local NF newsletter'. A party rally and social event usually followed, addressed by senior NF leaders and rising young stars. At one such event, Griffin delivered a lecture on strategies to promote the NF in colleges before the commencement of a disco.[52]

The NF also sought to channel those militants displaying the greatest aptitude into a series of educational seminars, designed to countermand the 'Marxist mind-bending' of the school curriculum. These colloquia provided a vital 'training mechanism' for the broader political socialisation of youthful recruits; they were intended to induct attendees into the fundaments of racial nationalist ideology thus nurturing them for future leadership roles.[53] Reflecting the importance invested in such activities, senior NF leaders including Tyndall, Webster, Brons and Verrall addressed them.[54] At one event, Verrall, author of *Did Six Million Really Die?* (1974), sought to move his young charges beyond simple racist positions by apprising them of the importance of dismantling the Holocaust 'hoax' which he deemed, 'the main weapon in the armoury of anti-racialists'.[55] Testifying to Billig's theorisation of the exoteric and esoteric nature of NF ideology, Pearce recalled that 'one could not graduate to the inner sanctum of the cognoscenti within the Party without tacitly accepting Nazi ideology and without secretly regretting the defeat of Hitler and the Third Reich.'[56]

Despite the pivotal role it fulfilled for the acculturation of young militants, Griffin later disparaged the NF training programme. He claimed that between joining the party and the early 1980s the party held, excluding lectures on fighting elections, 'three day-long training seminars – not per year, or in one region, but over the whole of Britain, in something like eight years.'[57] In 1978, the period in which the NF intensified its youth training programme, Griffin began studying history at Downing College, Cambridge, undertaking an intensive law course in his final year. Finding an anti-apartheid leaflet in his pigeonhole protesting Barclays Bank's investment in white South Africa, Griffin strolled down to the bank and opened a bank account in solidarity.[58] He made 'no secret' of his political views whilst at university. During a debate on whether the NF should be banned or not, 'he bravely stood up in a Red infested hall and argued the NF point of view,' claimed *Bulldog*, the defeat of the motion being 'a humiliating defeat for the extremists'.[59]

Griffin's life increasingly revolved around politics, however. He apparently expressed a desire to drop out of university to work full time for the party on several occasions. Nevertheless, Griffin spent his weekends either providing 'security' at 'Excalibur House', the newly opened NF headquarters at 73 Great Eastern Street, Shoreditch, or, on Sunday mornings, selling the party newspaper from the nearby pitch at the top of Brick Lane, the heart of Britain's Bangladeshi community.[60] The NF had celebrated the opening of their new headquarters with a 1,600-strong march through Shoreditch on 24 September 1978. Police re-routed the march at the last moment to avoid Brick Lane, which, during the summer, had become the loci for clashes with anti-fascists and the local Bengali youth. NF triumphalism was especially provocative in an area that had already witnessed several racist murders and the 'Brick Lane rampage' of 11 June during which 150 white youths ran down the street shouting racist abuse, assaulting passers-by and smashing property.[61] In November, Griffin addressed a 'stirring patriotic rally' on the South Bank after the NF Remembrance Day parade alongside John Tyndall and other NF leaders.[62]

Griffin also sought to bring NF activism onto campus. At the NF AGM in January 1979, he proposed a YNF Students' Organisation to 'nurture the future leadership of the party'.[63] Acceptance of the motion formalised Griffin's work as YNF Student Liaison Officer and editor of *Front Page*, the YNF publication targeting students that had begun in the previous summer.[64] Griffin's role entailed passing on the details of YNF activists at university to local NF organisers to ensure they remained involved in party activities whilst also avoiding duplication between local units and national structures 'as happened with the old NF Student Association'.[65] Griffin was 'optimistic about the future for NF students,' recorded *Bulldog*, a sentiment later tempered by experience.[66] In July, during the summer holidays, Griffin succeeded in getting a tirade against the SWP/ANL published in his local newspaper, the *East Anglian Daily Times*. He won 'Letter of the Month' and a £1 'Nationalist Books voucher' when *Spearhead* reprinted it, raising his profile within the movement.[67]

Ideological recalibration

Griffin envisaged himself in the vanguard of 'the development of the racial-nationalist intellectual movement which Wilmot Robertson, in *Ventilations*, stresses as an important step towards the White man's regaining control over his destiny.'[68] Highlighting the ongoing importance of transnational extreme right networks, Robertson's magazine *Instauration* was widely read on the British extreme right. The NF leader, John Tyndall, who visited Robertson in June 1979, gained many 'valuable ideas' from its pages.[69] Evidently, so did Griffin. *Ventilations* (1974), which contained a chapter on undergraduate student activism, represented an important disquisition on 'stigma transformation'. Robertson prescribed overcoming the 'stigma' of white supremacy by making it more 'digestible'. He sought to do so by intellectualising its arguments, repackaging and recalibrating 'old ideas' in such a way as to dis-identify them from the negative appellations of 'racist' or 'violent', situating them instead within the normative framework of mainstream society. Robertson attempted to disarm anti-racist opponents by appealing to scientific 'objectivity' in matters of race – 'letting the facts speak for themselves' – whilst employing rhetorical frames that positioned 'liberals and minorities' as the real oppressors, intent upon dispossessing the 'majority'. Racial separatism and support for apartheid was re-framed as a form of universalistic egalitarianism championing the self-determination of *all* races, enabling extreme right-wing activists to pose as white 'civil rights' activists. Subsequently popularised by Klan leader David Duke and the 'ethno-pluralist' arguments of the French Nouvelle Droite, Robertson was a progenitor of such 'impression management' strategies, the lessons of which Griffin would also seek to implement.[70]

The NF imploded amidst factional strife following its catastrophic 1979 general election result. Tyndall came under significant internal pressure because of the defeat, though not from Griffin who signed a declaration of support.[71] However, when Tyndall stormed off in high dudgeon in the following year, Griffin declined to follow him. Andrew Brons, the NF deputy chair replaced Tyndall on 3 February 1980. A long-standing extreme right activist, Brons was an equally hard-line choice for leader.[72] Having joined Colin Jordan's NSM as a teenager, Brons had sounded out contacts for the group in West Yorkshire. Reporting back to Françoise Dior on an 'enthusiastic nationalist' in Leeds she had introduced him to, Brons recorded that this individual had mentioned 'bombing synagogues', on which 'I have a dual view, in that although I realise he is well-intentioned, I feel that our public image may suffer considerable damage as a result of these activities. I am however open to correction on this point.'[73]

Despite the party's implosion, Brons believed the 1980s offered the NF 'very big opportunities'.[74] He tried 're-activating' the group with a 1,700-strong 'anti-mugging' march through south London, which was designed as a show to strength following the split with Fountaine's NFCM. Political mobilisation ran in parallel with ideological development. Brons believed the party had faltered because it lacked the 'fully articulated system of beliefs' necessary to sustain personal commitment and motivate 'sacrifice' from its activists which would preclude 'compromise, betrayal and surrender'.[75] In July 1980, Brons outlined his 'Five Year Plan' with the objective of giving the NF a clear political direction, thereby preventing it from being 'tossed around like a cork in a sea of events over which it has no control.'[76] Its key ingredients – membership education, public dissemination of party policies, embedding branches at a local level and maintaining financial stability – were also prerequisites of 'organising for the collapse', which *Nationalism Today* argued was the party's only chance for assuming power.[77]

Brons was an altogether more radical thinker than Tyndall. Under his tutelage, NF publications began exploring the social and political thought of textile designer and socialist William Morris (1834–1836); artist and social thinker John Ruskin (1819–1900); patriotic socialist Robert Blatchford (1851–1943), rural writer Richard Jeffries (1848–1887); social reformer Robert Owen (1771–1858); and the pamphleteer William Cobbett (1763–1835). Brons regarded the latter as 'probably the most unambiguous precursor of Racial Nationalism'.[78] The NF transposed the horror these nineteenth-century thinkers felt for the consequences of the Industrial Revolution, together with their yearning for a return to a pastoral idyll, onto their own anti-Semitic, anti-capitalist framework. This expansion of the NF ideological pantheon aimed to establish an indigenous lineage for British *völkisch* nationalism, one distinct from Nazism.

Brons' principal philosophical innovation was to make 'Distributism' central to the party's ideological cannon.[79] Inspired by Pope Pius X's Encyclical *Rerum Novarum* ('Of New Things'), which mapped out a Catholic alternative to Capitalism and Communism, and the writings of Edwardian Catholic authors Hilaire Belloc (1870–1953) and G.K. Chesterton (1874–1936), Distributism envisaged private property and the widespread distribution of the means of production as a counterweight to state centralisation and economic exploitation. Simultaneously, it also subordinated economic activity and *ergo* materialism to the needs of a healthy, organic society.[80] Though the NF appropriated both Belloc and Chesterton, despite their anti-Semitism and admiration of Mussolini, neither were unequivocally 'pro-fascist' figures.[81]

Despite gaining greater prominence under Brons, Distributism was not a new feature of extreme right-wing ideology, a 'direct link' having long existed between its exponents and the League of Empire Loyalists (see Chapter 4).[82] Its appeal to young activists seeking a radical 'third way' was palpable, whilst older militants like Webster also used it buttress pre-existing ideological positions arguing consequently that 'we most definitely are not against the ancient Nordic idea of private enterprise.'[83] The extent to which Distributist thought disseminated downwards from ideologically motivated NF cadres to the membership was not obvious, however. Blunt, racist messaging remained paramount. *We Are the National Front* (1981), a photo-book celebrating the party, copiously illustrated with pictures of young skinheads, distilled NF economic policy into the slogan: 'We want jobs, not more wogs!'[84]

Griffin embraced such thinking, later authoring 'Nationalism's Radical Alternative: An Introduction to Distributism' (1990), which, he claimed, 'has done more than any other work on this subject to spread support for this Catholic-originated set of ideas in Catholic Eastern Europe.' Griffin continued to believe that Distribution 'is a concept which will grow in importance to us as we work out how to rebuild the shattered, dispossessed communities and exhausted land left by capitalist agriculture.'[85] Under Griffin's leadership, BNP economic policy also became 'strongly influenced' by Distributism.[86]

Brons sought to implement this ideological overhaul by establishing *New Nation* in June 1980, as a 'political and ideological forum ... independent of private or factional interests.'[87] Edited by Verrall and Webster, *New Nation* lauded an array of ideas and ideologues, including Henry Hamilton Beamish, founder of The Britons and publisher of *The Protocols*, as a 'Great British Racialist'.[88] The journal also invoked socio-biological research particularly Richard Dawkin's *The Selfish Gene* (1976), which they interpreted as providing a scientifically neutral and *ergo* 'irrefutable' justification for their own policies on race, racial selection and racial segregation.[89] *New Nation* also endorsed the work of psychologists Arthur Jensen and Hans Eysenck whose book, *Race, Intelligence and Education* (1971), was considered, 'compulsory reading for any young racist wishing to understand the intellectual basis of his beliefs, supplying what was considered irrefutable evidence of genetically determined differences in the inherent intelligence between races.'[90]

Griffin's contribution to *New Nation* was of a more traditional racist vintage, however. Writing on the imperative of white racial survival, Griffin did not dwell upon the biological or psychological 'failings' and 'shortcomings' of 'Coloured races', though he argued that public education was required regarding 'inherited racial characteristics'. Instead, he lavished praise upon 'the genius, vision and creativity of the Indo-European', going so far as to claim that it was an 'eternal fact' that 'the White race is civilisation'. This achievement was endangered, he claimed, because now the 'entire White race, not merely a segment of it as before' was in the process of 'committing suicide' through 'miscegenation and downbreeding'. The 'central aim' of the political struggle had therefore to be 'the preservation of the White man and his unrivalled capacity to tame nature and to create order, prosperity and beauty'.[91]

Nationalism Today

Brons' ideological programme aimed to transform the NF into 'a cult among young White youth'.[92] The rabid racism of the NF 'street' epitomised by *Bulldog* and the racial religiosity propagated by *New Nation* coalesced into an emerging radical ideological tendency within the party, which together pushed militants even further in this direction. Griffin and Pearce met in his rooms at Downing College to discuss starting a new publication. 'The meeting was secret,' recalled Pearce, 'because of the internecine disputes that were dividing the nationalist movement at the time.'[93] In March 1980, *Nationalism Today*, a 'radical nationalist' magazine, was launched, produced from Griffin's home in Halesworth, Suffolk. Pearce was editor, assisted by Griffin and Nick Wakeling, *Bulldog*'s assistant editor.[94] Pearce subsequently resigned as YNF National Organiser to concentrate on publishing, which caused the YNF to atrophy.[95]

Nationalism Today, which rejected 'negative personality cults', followed the trajectory outlined by Brons. It opened its pages to 'all those who feel that they have some constructive ideas to offer towards strategy, organisation and tactics which will benefit British

Nationalism.' For Pearce, it was a matter of urgency: 'If the Party does not make substantial progress during the 1980s, the whole future of our racial and nationalist ideology will be jeopardised, if not totally destroyed.'[96] *Nationalism Today* became an 'official' NF publication after five issues reflected its editor's 'confidence' in the current leadership after 'reactionary elements' (i.e. Tyndall) had been expelled or left the party.[97]

The adoption of the old Nazi slogan 'Neither Red Front or Reaction' encapsulated NF opposition to Communism *and* Capitalism. This was replaced by the marginally more sophisticated 'Neither Capitalism nor Communism but the Third Position'.[98] Yet, the anti-Semitic master frame remained the same. Griffin attacked the de-spiritualised, ahistorical economic materialism of both ideologies, arguing that they were handmaidens of a Jewish conspiracy to destroy race and nation. Drawing parallels with the Russian Revolution, he claimed that the contemporary Left used immigrants as the 'shock troops' in the same way the Bolsheviks used 'Asiatic Mongols ... to crush the White Russians'. Communism was Jewish, Griffin stated emphatically:

> over 80 per cent of the Bolshevik leaders were of alien origin and the proportion is similar in Britain today. These people, nursing an ancient hatred of White Civilisation and a messianic desire for power, are just as dangerous and ruthless as they were in 1917.[99]

The NF had become a truly revolutionary movement, Griffin proclaimed. It aimed 'not to tidy up and de-niggerise the present System' but to destroy it completely, overthrowing the 'Old Gang' politicians – a phrase he lifted straight from Mosley – as a precursor to 'the utter destruction of its parasitical system' and the removal of 'alien populations'.[100] Broader right-wing 'unity' with 'a band of tactical and ideological cripples' was rejected as being 'of no use to us'. 'We have different aims and a different vision.'[101] Griffin attacked Tyndall as a reactionary conservative who was 'happy to see working class "skins" fighting the Blacks and Reds' only to reward them 'by crushing their trade unions, restricting their freedom and birthrates and selling off their council houses to grasping landlords with the right of immediate eviction.'[102]

Griffin's effusions reflected increased efforts by the NF to cultivate working-class appeal by trumpeting radical, anti-capitalist positions. Webster had helped fuel this shift, arguing in 1979 that the NF 'will not be built on Middle-Class foundations.'[103] Now he declared that: 'The Salvation of Capitalism is NOT a NF objective.'[104] This evolving 'leftist' stance set the tone for *Nationalism Today*, which its opponents branded 'Strasserite'. Griffin and his colleagues certainly admired the ideas of the Gregor and Otto Strasser, leaders of the northern wing of the Nazi party, declaring them 'as relevant today as they were in the 1930s.'[105] Summarising his own position, Griffin subsequently stated:

> Personally, I have no time for Hitler. His 1933 decision to mothball many of the most revolutionary of the 25 Points and to side with the Prussian aristocracy and military-industrial complex, instead of with the German peasantry, together with his outdated, chauvinistic contempt for the Slavs, were two of the most important factors which led to our peoples facing replacement in their own homelands today.[106]

Mischaracterised as 'socialist' or 'left wing', the Strasser brothers' ideas were never as revolutionary as the NF imagined them to be, constituting instead a melange of racist chauvinism and petty bourgeois anti-capitalism.[107] *Nationalism Today* was never simply a

'Strasserite' publication, either, drawing as it did upon Britain's long-standing indigenous tradition of anti-Semitic, anti-capitalism, espoused by figures like A.K. Chesterton and elements of Mosley's BUF.[108] Indeed, this broader ideological influence was epitomised by *Yesterday & Tomorrow – Roots of the National-Revolution* (1983), an amalgam of texts by early Nazi, British socialist, Catholic distributist and syndicalist authors intended to convey the party's new intellectual underpinning.[109]

Such nuance was lost during the ill-tempered debate that *Nationalism Today*'s emerging ideological position engendered. Tyndall reviled 'Strasserism' as ideological heresy, branding Griffin and his colleagues 'National Trotskyites'. Their ideas were 'crypto-Marxist claptrap parading as "Nationalism".'[110] *Nationalism Today* responded by denouncing Tyndall's 'National Capitalism' whilst declaring 'only muppets join the BNP'. To illustrate the point, they mocked Tyndall by publishing a cartoon of Fozzy Bear juxtaposed against a photo of him in Nazi uniform stating: 'Fozzy say: The man is fu-n-n-y.'[111] Tyndall swallowed this lack of deference and, during summer 1983, began seeking 'nationalist' unity with his detractors by downplaying the division between 'radicals' and 'reactionaries' as being 'probably more over choice of emphasis than over fundamentals of ideology.'[112] Rebuffed, his contempt for the 'radicals' resurfaced. *Spearhead*'s front cover featured a cartoon of Trotsky astride a British lion.[113] Ideological feuding would continue unabated. *Spearhead* took particular exception to Derek Holland's statement that Hitler had 'betrayed' the revolution and that Nazi Germany was 'Capitalism with jackboots'.[114] *Spearhead* retorted that Strasser was a 'loser' whose political outlook 'decreed that he could never be anything else.'[115] Colin Jordan was equally scathing, denouncing Strasserism as 'Bolshevism in a Brown Shirt'.[116] Jordan's outrage mirrored that of his 'mentor' Arnold Leese who had attacked Strasser contemporaneously as 'a sloppy socialist with no race knowledge' who had 'no real reason' for hating Hitler – aside from the latter murdering his brother! For good measure, Leese accused Strasser of collaborating with the Jews against the Nazis.[117] 'William Joyce was hanged for a much less serious crime than that,' Leese stated.[118]

Unperturbed, Griffin continued his efforts to engage socialists, anarchists and Greens in discussion, though this proved singularly unsuccessful. He appeared particularly keen to engage with anarchists whose 'arguments for self-sufficiency and decentralization, the anti-Statist socialism ... [are] not so far removed from the Distributism of Chesterton and Belloc.' 'It is time that such ideas were rescued from obscurity and integrated into the programme of the Nationalist movement.' *Black Flag*, the anarchist newspaper, rejected Griffin's entreaties with two words: 'FUCK OFF'.[119]

Continuing to prioritise this 'left-wing' platform, Griffin became 'acting organizer' for the NF Trade Unionists Association. He also penned the 'Industrial Front' column in *Nationalism Today*, which emphasised industrial organisation and trade union activity. This 'leftist' stance saw the NF voicing support for the 1984 Miners' Strike, though not the National Union of Mineworkers and its leader, 'national traitor' Arthur Scargill.[120] This position caused some internal dissension. Tower Hamlets NF activists, for instance, were outraged when *Nationalism Today* compared David Jones, a miner killed picketing Ollerton colliery, Nottinghamshire, to Albert Marriner, an elderly NF activist who had died several days after being struck by a brick at an NF meeting, describing it as 'an insult to his memory'.[121] For their part, the miners ignored or rejected NF support, unsurprising given their proud tradition of militant anti-fascism. *Nationalism Today* continued trying to make the NF more attractive to workers. It apologised for 'union-bashing on a grand scale' during the 1970s, which had included Tyndall calling for the Army to be used against striking workers: 'Fortunately for us, the people responsible for that have long since disappeared from our movement.'[122]

International capitalism had reduced Britain 'to a mere outpost of Wall Street Coca Cola imperialism,' Griffin argued. His own redemptive panacea was a 'Racial Nationalist state' underpinned by a 'Social Nationalist' economy comprising nationalised industries, producer's cooperatives, prioritising individual enterprise and family businesses. It contained a distinct dose of neo-Medievalism too: Griffin advocated reinstituting the values of 'craftsmanship and durability' and recreating 'a modern form of the old craft guilds', an idea whose admirers stretched back to Arnold Leese.[123] Ideological succour was also gained from the Basque co-ops in Mondragon (on which the NF screened films at training seminars) and E.F. Schumacher's economic critique *Small is Beautiful: A Study of Economics as if People Mattered* (1973), copies of which were disseminated to members.[124]

For Griffin, the traditional NF platform of 'British Jobs for British Workers', which entailed 'blaming the Blacks', might have been 'vital in the short-term' but, ultimately, national regeneration required a 'back-to the-land' ruralism which represented 'an integral part of our Nationalist tradition.' Harking back to the ideas of Cobbett, Jeffries, Morris and Blatchford, Griffin's pre-industrial pastoralism contrasted 'the stability and permanence of the eternal life of the Soil with the transient materialism of the city.' 'The materialists may worship the Urban Machine, but we stand by the values of Blood and Soil,' Griffin declared in classic Nazi parlance. This pure, healthy rural idyll stood in contradistinction to the 'cancerous influence of the Metropolis'.[125]

Nationalism Today paraded purity of the Land as 'the sacred inheritance of the Race, to be husbanded with care, loved, cherished and if need be died for.'[126] For Griffin, one of the 'first priorities' for an NF government would be the replacement of 'highly mechanized Capitalist agriculture' with 'small, privately owned and labour intensive farms' enabling the nation to enjoy the benefits of industrialised society 'without its evils of waste and exploitation'.[127] Additional food and employment opportunities, Griffin maintained, would flow from urban regeneration and the creation of 'city smallholdings' set up within 'urban villages' created by clearing Brixton, Southall and Stamford Hill – symbolic areas of Black, Asian and Jewish settlement.[128]

Political soldiers

Griffin's encounter with a group of fugitive Italian fascists including Roberto Fiore, Massimo Morsello, his wife Marinella, Stefano Tiraboschi and Marcello de Angelis, radically transformed his politics.[129] Fiore's group had fled Italy where the authorities wanted to question them about the Bologna bombing on 2 August 1980, which killed eighty-five people, including two young Britons inter-railing together after their graduation. Two hundred people were injured, many horrifically. Visiting Bologna's morgue following the explosion, one reporter recorded seeing 'the cadavers of many small children clad in short pants, brightly coloured shorts, and beach sandals.'[130] The group responsible – to which both Fiore and Morsello belonged – was the Nuclei Armati Rivoluzionari (NAR – Armed Revolutionary Nuclei), which in the opinion of the CIA 'is now the most dangerous rightist terrorist group in Italy.'[131] NAR leaders, Giuseppe Valerio Fioravanti, a former child actor and Francesca Mambro, a police officer's daughter, were jailed for the attack, though both denied their guilt. NAR had emerged from Terza Posizione (TP – Third Position), a fascist *groupuscule* co-founded by Fiore and several other militants which, ideologically, had more in common 'with Argentinian Peronism and the Iranian Revolution than with the MSI,' which Fiore dismissed as 'conservative'.[132]

Arriving in Britain, Fiore sought out the NF, an organisation he was aware of thanks to the 'massive coverage' it had received in Italy. Early one morning, Fiore knocked on the door of NF activist Steve Brady, who was also overseas officer for the League of St George, who lived in Brighton. Brady recalled:

> This ragged-looking dishevelled Italian [Fiore], who didn't speak any amount of English said 'Refugees, we are persecuted Italian state. We have hunger, no food, no money, help'. He took me down to Brighton bus station and there were loads more, heaps of rubbish suddenly started to move and I realised they were people, a couple of dozen at least. They only stayed in my house for one night, and then made contact with people in London.[133]

'I was eventually introduced by friends to Nick Griffin,' Fiore recalled.[134] Griffin had recently graduated from Cambridge with a second-class Law degree and moved to London where he was elected to the NF's National Directorate whilst also becoming secretary of the Croydon NF branch.[135] 'Roberto was certainly a charismatic figure,' Griffin remembered. 'A very magnetic personality with, at the time, a great deal more experience of political organisation.'[136] Pearce likewise observed that the Italian group

> added a certain sophistication to the Nationalist cause in England, or so it seemed at the time. Whereas the NF's membership was becoming more proletarian, comprising largely of young and disaffected skinheads, our Italian confreres were clearly better educated and more cultured.[137]

The Italians noted this gulf too. Morsello commented upon the distance between his own 'radical background' and that of the NF militants – though this would soon change.[138]

In September 1981, British police arrested Fiore. He spent 5 months on remand in Brixton but was released after the Italian authorities failed to secure his extradition.[139] An Italian court subsequently convicted Fiore *in absentia* for 'political conspiracy' and involvement with an 'armed gang' and sentenced him to nine years, reduced to five-and-a-half on appeal. He only returned to Italy in April 1999, when the country's statute of limitations had expired.[140] Meanwhile, Fiore propagated the conspiracy theory that Bologna was a State-sponsored 'pretext' to crush the TP.[141] His response was indicative of a wider politics of 'non-reconciliation' amongst Italian fascist groups, who portray themselves as 'victims' of state violence rather than acknowledging their own roles as perpetrators.[142] Griffin parroted Fiore's conspiratorial critique, claiming the Italian security services used this and other bombings 'to stir up public opinion against Italian Nationalists.'[143]

Attuned to the 'suffering' of the TP, Derek Holland believed it 'proves that from the blood of martyrs there will always spring others ready to continue the combat. The National Front has much to learn and much to do.'[144] Whilst applauding the inspiring sanguinary sacrifice of TP activists, Holland nonetheless attacked Martin Webster for implying that terrorism might be legitimate under certain circumstances. 'The repressive actions of the State have proven the shallowness of this approach: now is the time for serious analysis and reflection, not veiled hints at terrorism,' he chided.[145] He returned to the theme in an article titled 'Terrorism: An Enemy of Nationalism'.[146]

Fiore viewed political conflict in religious, eschatological terms, regaling the NF with his belief that the global 'struggle' took place on 'higher levels' than Earth. He claimed that 'we are a race come from the heavens' and that a 'final conflict' was now taking place that would usher in 'a new and spiritual conception of life' – or lead to its annihilation:

> In my opinion we are coming to the final struggle, a battle predicted in a number of religious documents. We are now living through that period, although the majority of people are oblivious to it. Our militants, however, must understand it if they are to succeed. I would also add that even if these are not the Last Times predicted, we should act as if they were.[147]

Fiore's sacralised, millennial beliefs inspired young militants like Griffin who sought to emulate TP ('a highly motivated spiritual movement') and, in so doing, transform the NF into a 'national revolutionary' group. This vanguard of activists (the 'new nobility') would proceed with the 'purification' of nationalist ideology in order to bring about a genuine 'spiritual revolution'.[148]

Ideological inspirations

The Italian clique also hastened the party's ideological metamorphosis by introducing NF militants to the thought of Julius Evola, an elitist Italian meta-political and Traditionalist philosopher frequently accused of inspiring 'black' terrorism. Whilst Evola had admired fascism's totalitarian character, it was 'too little' for him, not least because of his imperious disdain for its 'plebeian' character. Evola had desired 'a fascism which is more radical, more intrepid, a fascism that is truly absolute, made of pure force, unavailable for any compromise' – a 'super-fascism'. His 'natural environment' was Nazi Germany. He greatly admired its attempt 'to create a kind of new political-military Order with precise qualifications of race.' Evola loathed Jews viscerally, harbouring a 'horror' of the 'corrosive irony' he perceived in Jewish culture. Following fascism's defeat in 1945, Evola came to the pessimistic conclusion that humanity now languished in the final stages of the *Kali-Yuga* or Dark Age. His post-war entreaties addressed those militants 'rising above the ruins' whom, he hoped, would spearhead a physical and spiritual revolution against the profanity of liberal democracy.[149]

Evola's influence saturated *Rising*, a small ideological journal founded in 1982 by Fiore and Holland, who edited it as 'Richard Murphy'. *Rising*, heralded as 'a booklet for the political soldier', sought to generate 'a revolutionary elite able to stand above the world of ruins.'[150] The phrase self-consciously invoked Evola's seminal book *Men among the Ruins* (1953). The *Rising* group imbibed Evola's ideas, though his professed elitism sat ill at ease with the party's broader 'Strasserite' position. They declared themselves to be 'traditional revolutionaries, defenders of historical reality, a dynamic force obeying principles from on high.' Tradition, *Rising* averred, 'is not only the past – Above all it represents permanence in development, permanence in continuity.'[151] Having already printed a synopsis of its arguments, the *Rising* group appealed for funds to publish an English translation of Evola's *The Aryan Doctrine of Fight and Victory* (1941) though it never appeared.[152]

It is important not to overplay the breadth of Evola's influence upon Griffin or indeed the political soldiers more generally. One former 'political soldier' maintains that Evola's genuine influence was actually 'very slight' – the bulk of his writings untranslated into English at this point whilst those that were, were arguably 'misunderstood' by his adherents.¹⁵³ Others argued that Evola's ideas were transmitted to the *Rising* group secondhand through *La disintegrazione del sistema – The Disintegration of the System* (1969), a tract authored by one of his disciples, Franco Freda. Though Freda was a major populariser of Evola's work, he rejected his mentor's apoliteia approach, favouring militant action instead. He was jailed in 1981 (though subsequently acquitted) for the 1969 Piazza Fontana bombing, which killed sixteen people and injured eighty-eight.¹⁵⁴ This atrocity had inaugurated the 'strategy of tension' – a protracted fascist terrorist campaign aimed at preventing Italy from sliding leftwards. *Rising* praised Freda as a 'martyr to our cause', whilst *Nationalism Today* published his photograph on the front page with the caption: 'In an unjust society, the only place for a just person is in prison.'¹⁵⁵

Rising also provided Holland with a platform for developing a spiritualised dimension to NF activism. Integral to this was the 'awe-inspiring' example of 'Captain' Corneliu Codreanu, leader of the Romanian Iron Guard (also known as the Legion of the Archangel Michael), who had been 'martyred' by the Romanian authorities in 1938.¹⁵⁶ Codreanu's autobiography, *Pentru Legionari – For My Legionaries* (1936), translated into English in 1976, inspired Holland.¹⁵⁷ Blending intense nationalism with Romanian Christian Orthodoxy, the Iron Guard sacralised politics.¹⁵⁸ The charismatic Codreanu, who stressed the virtues of sacrifice, martyrdom and expiation, would arrive in Romanian villages on a white horse; kneel and pray with his entourage, proclaim before God the sacred nature of his struggle; and in turn be acclaimed as the reincarnation of the Archangel Michael. A political evangelist, Codreanu saw political programmes as secondary to the creation of the 'new' man who would regenerate the nation.¹⁵⁹ 'Let him of boundless faith come join us,' he wrote. 'Let him who doubts stay out.' Such messianic movements were 'closer to cargo cults than they are to fascism,' observed Eugen Weber.¹⁶⁰ The 'political soldiers' internalised the Iron Guard's spiritual zeal and its *mistica dei morti*, embodied in the slogan 'Long Live Death' – an identical phrase to '¡*Viva la Muerte!*' motto of the pro-Franco Legionary José Millán-Astray, which also finds a contemporary echo in Jihadist millenarianism.¹⁶¹ Its meaning was also captured the pro-Fascist poet Ezra Pound's aphorism, which often graced *Rising*: 'If a man is not prepared to die for his ideas, either he or his ideas are useless.'¹⁶²

Codreanu's ideas on political organisation also directly influenced the group's structural development as they had Fiore's TP, which used the *cuib* or 'nest' – the Iron Guard's cell structure – as its basic unit of organisation.¹⁶³ To this end, the NF published its own edition of *Carticica Sefului de Cuib – The Nest Leader's Manual* under the title *Legion* with a foreword by 'Bob Eccles' and Michael Walker, editor of *The Scorpion* eulogising the Iron Guard – who stood 'between earth and sky' – as a 'spiritual and political point of reference' that 'helps us to endure and persist'. For Eccles and Walker, the 'revolutionary task' of the political soldiers 'can only be fulfilled by the legionary ideal reborn. The martyrs of the Iron Guard have shown succeeding generations that repression may postpone our revolution but it cannot destroy it.'¹⁶⁴

The official Legionary group in Spain denounced the NF booklet as 'unauthorised and fraudulent'.¹⁶⁵ Undeterred, the NF marketed their edition as 'a valuable work for those seeking to become real Political Soldiers'. They sold it alongside photographs of Codreanu 'produced by Legionary emigres'. Griffin, *New Nation*'s editor, subsequently published an interview with Jianu Dianieleau, a former Legionnaire, valorising the group's 'spiritual revolution' and its leading figures martyrdom for 'Christ and Christian civilisation'.¹⁶⁶ The Iron Guard was an ironic inspiration for an organisation seeking to ditch its violent image. Murderously anti-Semitic, during the disintegration of the short-lived 'National Legionary

State' in January 1941, its activists engaged in a three-day pogrom, murdering dozens of Jews whose bodies were suspended on meat hooks in a Bucharest abattoir in a parody of kosher slaughter.[167] The Iron Guard also mistreated British citizens, a fact the NF ignored.[168]

Outside inspirations were synthesised with elements of Britain's native fascist tradition. Holland was 'heavily involved' in founding the 'A.K. Chesterton Academy' together with Rosine de Bounevialle, *Candour*'s editor and the guardian of Chesterton's legacy. De Bounevialle's large Hampshire home was the venue for a series of seminars that were 'invaluable to the creation of Political Soldiers.'[169] 'I was privileged to be invited to give a lecture in a personal capacity,' recalled Griffin. He saw them as a 'successful model' the wider NF should emulate forthwith.[170] Older activists imparted their knowledge and skills to younger activists at these seminars: 'It was felt that there are valuable lessons still to be learnt from the experiences of the League of Empire Loyalists', noted one report.[171] De Bounevialle's open house also helped to politicise and socialise 'countless patriots', who were initiated into 'the Cause' through 'discussions in the drawing room over a bottle or three of wine, or in private talks in the woods, or in heated, almost furious exchanges whilst washing the dishes'.[172] Fiore and the Italian clique also used the secluded estate for 'quasi-military' training exercises. Their mastery of martial arts 'duly impressed' younger NF militants, remembered Pearce.[173]

The other major ideological innovation in the extreme right firmament during this period was an increasing awareness of meta-politics and cultural struggle. In spring 1980, Richard Lawson, former editor of *Britain First* founded a new magazine, *Heritage and Destiny*, to 'promote interest in the historical achievements and culture of our nation and race'. This would 'instil a proper understanding of and positive price in our ethnic identity'.[174] Lawson's venture was short-lived and he soon passed his mailing lists to Michael Walker, the central London NF organiser who edited his own publication, *National Democrat*. Believing that its name conveyed the wrong impression – one reader noted that *National Democrat* was in fact 'international' and 'anti-Democratic' – Walker changed its name to *The Scorpion* in 1983, detaching it from party politics in order to promote 'cultural independence and regeneration, outside the political arena'.[175]

Walker's key insight was to understand that the Left had won the cultural struggle against the NF in the 1970s. The old slogan 'Have you half a mind to join the National Front? That's all you need' summed up for Walker 'what nearly everybody believed about the British right and with reason.' Having encountered their ideas through *League Review*, mouthpiece of the League of St George (LSG), Walker drew intellectual sustenance from French Nouvelle Droite intellectuals like Alain de Benoist who rejected the intellectual 'baggage' of the 'old right' in France which he found to be 'shrill, monotonous and wholly predictable … an insult to the intelligence'.[176] Following de Benoist's example, *The Scorpion* similarly internalised the ideas of Italian Marxist Antonio Gramsci, who had argued that the 'cultural hegemony' was the precursor to political power.[177]

The Scorpion's own politics never quite aligned with those of the French Nouvelle Droite, however. 'The NR has never really penetrated the Anglo-Saxon world', de Benoist once observed. 'A journal like *The Scorpion*, to which I am very sympathetic, has never been completely part of our movement.'[178] This was largely because the magazine remained 'impregnated' with overt, racial nationalism and Holocaust 'revisionism' – absent from de Benoist's arguments – which impeded further collaboration between the two ideologues.[179] Reflecting Walker's proximity to the *Rising* group, *The Scorpion* described Evola as 'the champion of a European spiritual and national revival against the liberal, multiracial quagmire of the United States'.[180] Even within its own limited sphere, *The Scorpion*, which at its peak only had 600–700 subscribers, had a 'negligible' impact upon the extreme right, when weighed in the balance against other contemporary factors influencing its ideological development.[181] Indeed, in the intervening years, Griffin would come to dismiss the Gramscian strategy as 'useless' since the 'long march through the institutions' presupposed the 'luxury' of time, which his own gloomy racial prognosis denied.[182]

During this period, Griffin and Fiore worked with Walker on 'Heritage Tours' offering 'chauffeur-driven, personal guided tours of historic Britain'. Fiore worked as a tour guide.[183] Whilst the struggle for cultural hegemony failed to resonate more widely, committed NF activists immersed themselves in the cultural activities of the NF 'Heritage Group', which organised 'cultural' visits to museums and exhibitions.[184] Griffin embraced such developments wholeheartedly. He joined The Sealed Knot, the historical association dedicated to re-enacting battles from the English Civil War. 'From such gatherings, he had learned many English folk songs, which he and I and our comrades would sing around camp fires, especially during gatherings at his parents' home', recalled Joe Pearce.[185]

Further ideological and tactical influences derived from the United States. The ideas of William Pierce, leader of the National Alliance (NA), percolated into the NF through *Attack* and *National Vanguard*, circulated within the party by Steve Brady.[186] Brady, who operated as both the LSG International Liaison Officer and the London NA organiser, believed that NF chair Andrew Brons looked 'favourably' upon his activities because they dovetailed with his own strategy for the NF's ideological development.[187] Griffin also played a role in disseminating Pierce's seminal race war novel, *The Turner Diaries* (1978). In October 1980, *Nationalism Today*'s editors purchased a caseload of books from Pierce, following its reprint in the previous month.[188] These they sold from *Nationalism Today*'s editorial offices: Griffin's Suffolk home.[189] *Nationalism Today* acclaimed *The Turner Diaries* as a 'shockingly honest portrayal of a White Revolution in America.' They highlighted its militant message by quoting following passage: 'Today it finally began! After all these years of talking – and nothing but talking – we have finally taken our first action. We are at war with the System, and it is no longer a war of words.'[190]

Rising star

This ideological effervescence coincided with Griffin's political ascent. Elected to the NF Directorate on 27 September 1980,[191] by the following year, he was heading up the NF Elections Department. The NF selected him as their candidate for the Croydon North West by-election on 22 October 1981.[192] Griffin implied to the *Croydon Borough News* that the NF chose this constituency because 'rising racial tension' – reflected in two 'racist' murders – 'show that the multi-racial experiment has failed.' His solution was to repatriate 'all Afro-Asian and other non-Whites.'[193] Griffin's constituency newsletter, *The Croydon Patriot*, edited by Margaret Ballard, highlighted his 'special political interests' including 'youth unemployment and the difficulties facing young White couples in finding a home.'[194] The NF claimed to have delivered 25,000 copies of the newsletter and urged members to support Griffin's campaign. This was to have culminated in a 'British Jobs for British Workers!' march through the constituency on 17 October until the authorities banned it. The NF hastily arranged a new route, skirting the constituency's borders, but it proved 'no substitute'. Election hustings was also fraught. One event saw all three of the main party candidates leave the meeting together with 'half the audience' in protest at Griffin's presence.[195]

During the campaign, Griffin participated in a 'Defend Rights for Whites!' rally in Fulham on 20 August during which Martin Webster told those present: 'If you love your Race, Nation and Family – You must hate, hate, hate those who would destroy them.'[196] The NF deliberated scheduled the rally to coincide with the 'multi-racial bedlam' of the nearby Notting Hill Carnival.[197] It did little to boost Griffin's electoral fortunes. He polled 429 votes (1.2 per cent), markedly less than the 1,049 votes (2.8 per cent) polled in October 1974 when the NF last contested the constituency. He was no more successful thereafter. In 1982, Griffin stood in Croydon's Whitehorse Manor ward polling just 50 votes. Standing again in Croydon North West during the 1983 general election, Griffin's vote decreased further to 336 votes (0.9 per cent).[198]

Earlier that year, Griffin had lost an important political collaborator. Following three separate trials, a judge jailed Joe Pearce for 6 months in January 1982 for inciting racial hatred in the pages of *Bulldog*. Defiant, Pearce told the judge: 'you are an enemy of the British people and one day you will face their judgement.'[199] 'Although I would deny the charges in court, it would be true to say that *Bulldog*'s ultimate purpose was to incite racial hatred,' Pearce later admitted, 'to stir up enmity and hatred between black and white youths, thereby making multiracialism untenable and a race war inevitable.'[200] NF leader Andrew Brons encouraged his members to 'follow Joe's example and defy the Race Traitors and their Zionist-Jew overlords.'[201]

Griffin replaced Pearce as editor of *Nationalism Today*, its front cover declaring 'Joe Pearce: Political Prisoner'.[202] The NF also staged numerous demonstrations in solidarity. Pearce's wife and another female activist chained themselves to the railings of no. 10 Downing Street, 'a stunt which got us a stack of publicity.'[203] Whilst languishing in jail, Pearce penned *Fight for Freedom* (1984), which advocated a 'mono-racial society'. All other freedoms – financial, industrial, social and national – were 'pointless' without it, he argued. 'The choice before the British people is a simple one; either they must accept enslavement, or they must fight for freedom.' Griffin contributed a glowing introduction, claiming that Pearce was jailed 'simply for telling the truth' about the 'horrors' of 'mass Coloured immigration'. *Fight for Freedom* he described as 'one of the most important documents to emerge from the British Nationalist movement for at least a decade.'[204] After his release, Pearce resumed editing *Nationalism Today*. Griffin reverted to 'assistant editor' promising 'to contribute articles to the magazine on a regular basis.'[205]

The continuing fermentation of NF ideology included a repackaging of its anti-Semitic animus as 'anti-Zionism'. This moved to centre stage after the 1982 Israeli invasion of Lebanon. The NF AGM passed a resolution affirming that the party 'would, by whatever means necessary, assist the Palestinians in their struggle.'[206] The Jews 'have no racial, historical or moral right to the territory called Israel,' Holland declared. Linking the Palestinian struggle to that of the NF, he concluded 'Britain for the British! Palestine for the Palestinians!'[207] Holland also authored a supplement to *Nationalism Today* titled 'Victory to Palestine! Israel – The Hate State', which, it concluded, 'must be destroyed'.[208] In seeking to undermine Israel's legitimacy, which it understood simplistically as being rooted only in the Holocaust, the NF promoted *'Holocaust' News*, a publication which 'shows convincingly that the accounts of "mass gassings" are scientifically impossible.' The *'real* Holocaust,' it claimed, was 'the massacre of Palestinian villagers and the theft of their land.'[209] The Sabra and Shatilla massacre provided further grist to the mill. *Nationalism Today* featured a front cover of Israel's leader, Menachem Begin, in Nazi uniform over the caption 'Israel über Alles'. He and Ariel Sharon, the military leader ultimately responsible for the massacre, 'are wicked, evil tyrants ruling over a wicked, evil people,' it declared.[210]

Webster's removal

Brons appointed Griffin to the NF Policy Department where he assisted writing the party's 1983 general election manifesto, *Let Britain Live* – 'the most radical National Front Manifesto ever' – which declared 'usury is the root cause of all the other evils of capitalism.'[211] Racism was at its core. Prior to the compulsory repatriation of all non-Whites, regardless of whether they were born in Britain or not, *Let Britain Live* advocated segregating them into 'separate facilities' covering housing, education and welfare, in effect transforming Britain into a full-scale apartheid State and thence a white ethno-state.[212] Its hard-line racist message received little support at the ballot box. The Falklands War provided the Conservative Party with a surge in support, pushing the NF even further to the political margins. Sixty NF candidates polled an average of 1.1 per cent, marginally less than 1.3 per cent average its 303 candidates polled in 1979.[213] That they outpolled Tyndall's rival BNP was cold comfort.[214]

Following this electoral debacle, Griffin and his allies staged a coup against Martin Webster, the NF National Activities organiser since 1969. Webster had begun to express serious misgivings about the direction of the party. He complained to Brons in September 1983 that the media's depiction of the party as a haven for 'delinquents, criminal thugs and anti-social cranks' ensured that this became a self-fulfilling prophecy.[215] Moreover, although he too contributed to *Nationalism Today*, authoring its 'trouble shooting' column from issue eight onwards, Webster was increasingly perturbed by Fiore's influence upon the 'political soldiers'. Following a series of intrigues, Griffin's faction moved against Webster in November 1983. He and Pearce resigned from the NF leadership and circulated a four-page statement attacking Webster's conduct. This triggered a chain of events that resulted in his removal from office. From the margins, Tyndall crowed that Webster's removal represented a 'total vindication' of his position four years previously.[216] Following Webster's dismissal, the NF leadership instituted several administrative changes to 'increase the effectiveness' of the party.[217] These measures were not conspicuously successful. NF membership slumped to 3,148 by October 1984.[218] It had declined further, to approximately 2,500 by the following August.[219]

Refusing to accept his fate, Webster took his case to the High Court who reinstated him. Events had moved on, however, and he remained out in the cold.[220] Thereafter, Webster lamented that the 'Italian group' had taken over the NF 'and Fiore is the major influence.'[221] This was not the sole reason for Webster's fall from grace. Indeed, he had found himself increasingly at odds with the party's wider ideological metamorphosis.

> They feel that if they can ditch and indeed attack the likes of Hitler, Mussolini, Franco and sundry other people who've contributed to national socialist or nationalist thinking and claim Hilaire Belloc ... everybody loves Belloc, and also Chesterton, with his *Father Brown* stories ... they think they can clothe themselves in the nice beery jollity and even religiosity of these people.[222]

Webster stated:

> This, they assume, would reflect on themselves as a far more respectable image than they would otherwise enjoy if they were true to *all* their ideological mentors. The development they are involved in is not ideological at all by psychological. They are feeling besieged, unloved and worn down by ardent hostility. And they haven't the moral courage to stand up for the fundamental ideas they believe in and lift two fingers to whoever disagrees with them. They want to be loved.[223]

Webster's expulsion was the wider context in which Holland's musings on the 'political soldier' moved to centre stage from the pages of *Rising* to *Nationalism Today* in January 1984, thereby introducing the concept to the wider membership. Shortly thereafter, *The Political Soldier* (1984) appeared, a booklet setting out the 'radical roots' of a new 'radical Nationalist ideology' that would purify the individual activist, the movement and the nation. Purification was personally important to Holland. Prior to Webster's removal he had become profoundly disillusioned with the NF, opining that it was 'just so low grade ... If you are a degenerate, you cannot regenerate a society. It's as simple as that. Death does not give life.' Holland recalled that he wrote his original treatise 'in about an hour and a half' and claimed to be 'very surprised' when *Nationalism Today* published it.[224] Nonetheless, it quickly gained cult status, reprinted first by American national socialist magazines.[225]

The crux of Holland's argument was that the NF had made 'fundamental errors' during the 1970s. Echoing Codreanu, he argued that new politics, doctrines and activities were superfluous. What they required was 'a new type of Man who will live the Nationalist way of life each and every day of his life.' Unquestioning devotion to the 'cause' would provide a 'beacon' to others.

> The political soldier is the Man driven by an Eternal Ideal, a burning Faith, who will act positively in any and all situations in defence of what is Right, Good and True ... The Political Soldier is all that now stands between Death and the Reawakening.[226]

wrote Holland, highlighting the transcendent nature of political soldier ideology – from 'Being' to 'Becoming'.[227] To enthuse its readers, *Nationalism Today* regaled them with historical examples of such martial valour: the Spartans; the Roman Legionnaires; the Christian Crusaders; the 'warrior ethic' of the Samurai;[228] and even 'Men like the Islamic Revolutionaries today'.[229] Holland's concept was especially redolent of the Waffen-SS, however. 'We were without a doubt political soldiers,' SS veteran Otto Skorzeny had declared, 'we defended an ideology which superseded politics and parties.'[230]

Reich 'n' Roll

Having administered a *coup de grâce* to Webster's political career, Griffin remained committed to his strategy of appealing to the white working class, albeit a rather narrower subsection of it. 'Above all, we are now gaining the vast majority of our recruits from a section of the population which is not so afraid of violence – the White working class youth,' he had proclaimed. Such recruits proved vital in re-energising the party's activist base, following the collapse of its electoral support, particularly as British society appeared increasingly riven by racial strife. In January 1981, thirteen black youths died in a fire in Deptford, a tragedy many believed was an act of racially motivated arson. The NF had tried to exacerbate racial tensions by marching past the house under the emotive banner 'Don't blame whites for the New Cross fire' but were banned from doing so.[231] 'The Brixton riots, which came only days after the ban ended would have paled into insignificance against the disorders that such a march would have attracted had it been allowed to go ahead,' remarked the Metropolitan Police Commissioner.[232]

Whilst prevented from fomenting major disorder after Deptford, the 'race riots' which exploded in Brixton in April, followed by further large-scale disorder in other cities in July, offered the NF further opportunities. In this racially charged climate, Griffin staked the future of the NF – 'the instrument of White Revolution in Britain' – on racist skinheads. 'If our party is to continue to function, we must be able to defend our meetings and activists. That means we must recruit members who are prepared to stand up to violence and fight back.'[233] He excused reports of racist skinhead violence as simply 'the inevitable Racial Defence by young White people who were seeing Blacks get their jobs, Blacks get their homes, and Blacks getting their country.'[234] *Nationalism Today*, meanwhile, eulogised skinheads as 'warriors of the White Race', who would provide the NF with a 'mass base' and 'a ready made army'.[235]

Politically engaging young skinheads actually proved problematic, structurally speaking. The YNF had stagnated after Pearce's resignation in 1980. Emphasis on youth activity had 'faded somewhat' as a consequence. The YNF Secretariat also ceased to exist. Thereafter, 'all activity in which the Party involved itself became generated from "the top".'[236] Griffin and his colleagues hoped that aligning themselves with skinhead and 'punk' culture would make the NF a more enticing proposition for white youth. This tentative shift in NF strategy towards 'culture' as a site of political struggle was not an overriding success. The party had a superficial understanding of 'punk' and 'Oi' music as a cultural manifestation, believing it simply to be the soundtrack of 'white rebellion'. Its efforts to establish its 'ownership' of various bands, venues and localities, in which this youth culture was expressed failed to resonate more widely with diverse, competing and often overlapping youth identities and subcultures.[237]

Having failed to successfully 'contest' or 'colonise' these musical subcultures, the NF moved to 'construct' their own, a strategy resulting, ironically, in the nullification of its broader cultural engagement programme.[238] Few understood this at the time, however. Towards the end of 1982, the NF re-established the YNF Secretariat and reformed Rock against Communism (RAC), conceived as a counterpoint to the Anti-Nazi League's Rock against Racism.[239] The focal point for RAC quickly became Skrewdriver, an unabashed 'white power' band fronted by Blackpool NF activist Ian Stuart Donaldson. 'At last – there is a band with guts!' declared *Bulldog* in May 1983.[240] The NF fixation with Skrewdriver, perhaps understandable given the paucity of other musicians willing to declare an allegiance to the NF, also highlighted the narrowing of the party's cultural horizon. Whilst Skrewdriver emerged from punk culture, its increasingly racialised musical variant was marginal to the wider 'scene'. If embracing 'white power' music paid dividends for the NF in the short term, it came at the expense of a deeper, more meaningful engagement with broader punk music culture and, in the longer term, was particularly detrimental to the popular image of extreme right politics.

Contemporaneously, the NF harboured no doubts about their strategy, however. Eager to harness the perceived potential of racist rock, Pearce and Patrick Harrington, another young London-based activist, founded 'White Noise Records' in 1983, ostensibly so they could release Skrewdriver's *White Power E.P.*[241] *Bulldog* reported that the release was 'selling by the thousands', with copies selling in Germany, Holland, Sweden and the United States.[242] Skrewdriver's subsequent record, *Voice of Britain* (1984), contained lyrics markedly sympathetic to the Third Reich, though Donaldson changed these in order to align the band with the NF.[243] In spring 1984, 'Nationalist Books' the party's merchandising outfit, began exporting Skrewdriver records to West Germany. The party signed an exclusive distribution deal with Rock-O-Rama records in the following year, which helped build Skrewdriver's European audience.[244]

Griffin also played an important role in building the white power music scene. During summer 1984, he renovated the dilapidated outbuildings of his father's Suffolk farmhouse to create a 'rural community training centre' for party development. The brickwork floor of one barn incorporated a sunwheel into its design.[245] The property subsequently served as a venue for several 'white noise' festivals staged under the RAC banner. The first took place on 29 September. Skrewdriver were the headline act. They opened their set with 'White Power' to the evident delight of the 400 or so skinheads present who gave Nazi salutes throughout the performance whilst chanting 'Nigger, Nigger, Nigger! Out! Out! Out!'[246] Ian Stuart appreciated Griffin's support, thanking him and his parents on the sleeve notes to his third studio album, *Blood & Honour* (1985).[247] Ian Stuart also thanked 'Nick and Jackie Griffen [sic]' in the first issue of *White Noise*, the NF music fanzine.[248]

'No to Cruise, No to CND'

During summer 1984, Griffin, in his capacity as West Suffolk NF chairman, became increasingly exercised by the presence of American cruise missiles on British soil, an issue first campaigned upon by fellow East Anglian NF activist Andrew Fountaine in 1959. His opposition was based on anti-Semitism, namely, that their presence increased Britain's likelihood of being dragged into 'a stage-managed quarrel' between two superpowers 'controlled by alien Asiatics'.[249] Notably, Griffin organised a 'No to Cruise, No to CND' demonstration outside USAF Lakenheath, the American airbase near Bury St Edmonds.[250] It was not just the infringement of Britain's national sovereignty he objected to, but also the permeation of American culture. This concern pervaded a piece of doggerel verse Griffin penned for *The Scorpion* titled '53rd State Blues':

> Our biggest new McDonald's has an old and famous dome.
> We've painted it with Stars and Stripes to make you feel at home.
> It used to be St. Paul's and if you want the proof –
> An angel with a hamburger we've stuck upon the roof.[251]

In November, Andrew Brons stepped down as NF chair after nearly five years at the helm. Brons had previously been fined £50 following an incident at an NF paper sale in Leeds in October 1983, during which he and the Leeds NF organiser were reportedly heard shouting 'white power' and 'death to Jews'. When asked to disperse by a police officer of Malaysian heritage, the pair racially abused him leading to their arrest.[252] The court rejected his appeal against conviction. Although Brons stood down, according to Griffin, he continued to play 'a very active role in deciding our strategy and tactics.'[253] Griffin continued assisting Brons with *New Nation* until 1985 when he assumed editorial control.[254] Brons' departure was significant insofar as it marked the last time that militants who had cut their political teeth in the Nazi sects of the 1960s controlled the NF. A younger generation now assumed control. Ian Anderson, NF Newham branch chair who had read zoology and then agriculture at Pembroke College, Oxford (but failed to graduate), picked up the mantle. Griffin became his deputy. *The Times* portrayed the duo as presenting a new 'intellectual' image for the NF.[255]

Though Griffin opposed the American military presence in Britain, he was not antagonistic to the United States as a racial entity. 'We look upon America as the largest repository of white genes in the world,' Griffin told an America interlocutor. 'It is therefore of supreme importance that the white race in your country survive.'[256] He paid tribute to Robert Matthews, leader of The Order, killed in a shoot-out with the FBI in December 1984. Griffin argued that whilst no-one can dispute the bravery of Robert Matthews, whose poetry and last letters display great sensitivity, intelligence and dedication, the tragedy is that such a man should die in an act of isolated defiance in a country where the potential for intelligence *political* action is immense.[257]

Thereafter, he penned a two-page survey of the American 'scene' titled 'The Deadly Trap', which counselled against terrorism as a 'dead-end road'.[258] Reflecting his fundamental ambivalence towards political violence, Griffin continued hailing Matthews as a 'martyr'.[259]

Griffin's familiarity with events Stateside stemmed from a 'very successful' visit to the United States in February 1985, during which he interviewed Tom Metzger, a former Klansman who led the White Aryan Resistance (WAR), for *Nationalism Today*.[260] Metzger ran a telephone hotline supporters could call to hear a string of pre-recorded racist messages, a service admired by British activists.[261] During his visit, Griffin stayed with Robert Hoy, a professional photographer he had met when the latter visited England to take photographs of the NF, several of which subsequently appeared in *New Nation* and *The Scorpion*.[262] Griffin addressed several groups, including the Washington-Baltimore unit of William Pierce's NA, which was then in mourning for Matthews. He regaled the meeting with news of the recent changes with the NF and the tactics it had adopted to offset 'rapidly mounting repression in Britain'.[263]

In Washington, Griffin met Gary Gallo, a West Point graduate and former NA activist who led the National Democratic Front (NDF), a small revolutionary nationalist *groupuscule* committed to 'White Revolution – The only solution'.[264] Griffin apparently spent the last two weeks of his trip writing a book, as yet unpublished, titled *Power*, in Gallo's spare room.[265] Gallo and his colleagues subsequently formed a 'small group' in Alexandria, Virginia, 'with a view to raising funds [for the NF] in exchange for newsletters, information and subscriptions to our numerous publications.'[266] Later that year, Gallo arrived in Britain. During his three-month visit, he contributed to *Nationalism Today*, using the pseudonym 'Gary Rossi' and spoke alongside Griffin at the 1985 YNF Whitsun camp on 'The USA: Coca-Cola or White Revolution'.[267] Transnational networking operated in both directions. Joe Pearce contributed to Gallo's journal, *The Nationalist*, whilst Matt Malone, his assistant editor would subsequently publish *Ideas for the Movement* (1987), which lauded Holland's *Political Soldier* as 'inspirational', after his own visit to the United Kingdom two years later.[268]

Griffin developed ties with other American 'white nationalists' too including Wilmot Robertson, editor of *Instauration*. Mindful that Robertson was a political associate of John Tyndall, however, Griffin was conciliatory. He told Robertson that although 'irreconcilable differences' separated their two parties, he hoped Tyndall might transform *Spearhead* into a:

> non-party political mouthpiece, leaving organisational work to us and taking a position similar to that of A.K. Chesterton in the early 1970s, who was a sort of elder statesman of the patriotic movement in Britain, a grandmaster of pro-British ideology.[269]

After returning from the United States, Griffin married fellow NF activist Jacqueline Cook whom he had met in 1978.[270] Joe Pearce was best man.[271] Roberto Fiore served as an usher.[272] The newly-weds honeymooned in France where they visited Robert Faurisson, a former professor of French literature at University of Lyons II recently suspended from his post for Holocaust denial.[273] The NF was already promoting Faurisson's writings.

New Nation, edited by fellow Holocaust denier Richard Verrall, had published Faurisson's speech 'Gassing – The How and Why It Never Happened' in its inaugural issue.[274] Faurisson had recently been a defence witness and head of the research team in the Toronto trial of Ernst Zündel, author of *The Hitler We Loved and Why*, who was prosecuted for disseminating Verrall's pamphlet, *Did Six Million Really Die?* The NF took a keen interest in Zündel's trial. *Nationalism Today* published an article by Harrington and Tom Acton, the party auditor, arguing the 'Holocaust Myth' had been 'a millstone around the necks of racial Nationalists everywhere for forty years' but since the Zündel case, 'we can confidently predict its eventual demise, and sooner than we had previously thought.'[275]

Racist militancy was beginning to impact upon the NF, however. During the first half of 1985, eight activists, including three of the six NF Executive Council members, faced prosecution for offences under the Race Relations Act.[276] Railing against this 'repression', the NF defiantly declared at its EGM on 22 June that they would 'refuse to recognise the validity of any such proceedings' brought against its' activists. Griffin, recently elevated to deputy NF chairman, denounced the Act as 'tyrannical' but also claimed that the legislation had had a 'beneficial effect' for the party: it had reduced the amount of negative 'lunatic fringe propaganda' that 'helped discredit our own more sensible and more moderate racial preservation messages.'[277]

Griffin remained implacably hostile to British democracy, railing against the rise of the 'Police State' and drawing upon the historical precedent of Mosley's internment to highlight 'how far the British State will go against its opponents if provided with a suitable excuse.'[278] The experience of his Italian contemporaries provided Griffin with a further 'frightening insight' into how democracy supressed 'dissident groups'. Preparing to resist such an assault, Griffin became secretary of the Militant Patriots Legal Defence and Aid Fund; formed in 1981 to raise funds for NF activists who 'in the service of their Race and Nation, fall foul of the repressive race laws and other anti-British legislation.'[279] Four years later, it was reorganised as The Nationalist Welfare Association 'to help those people who are fighting for you and who are prepared to go to jail in the struggle to help our country.'[280] The organisation fulsomely supported the party's new National Activities organiser, Martin Wingfield, a Sussex bookmaker who edited *National Front News*, hailing him as a 'political prisoner' when he was jailed for three months in April 1985 for refusing to pay a £1,500 fine levied following his conviction for inciting racial hatred.[281]

Despite Griffin's insistence upon a 'unifying central leadership',[282] it was felt that decentralising the party's administration, files and assets, presumably to frustrate their seizure, would safeguard the NF from further 'repression'. The resultant restructuring saw key assets, including the NF printing operation, relocated Griffin's East Anglian property.[283] Whilst Tyndall's BNP operated in accordance with the *Führerprinzip*, a new NF constitution was also propagated, purportedly protecting the party from itself, bringing an end to the 'monopolisation' of key positions by certain individuals within the leadership whilst preventing splits caused by 'egotistical squabbles'.[284] The reality was rather different. Indeed, within less than a year, the NF had irrevocably split. Whilst failing in its principal goal, the new constitution did facilitate the introduction of a 'voting member' system aimed at restricting the right to participate in the party's future political development to active members only, the first step towards the NF becoming 'a revolutionary cadre Party'.[285] When combined with its advocacy of the right to bear arms,[286] it was perhaps unsurprising that one scholar advanced the view that its ideological radicalisation was such that the NF might be considered a 'subversive organisation … it has become effectively a proto-terrorist organisation.'[287]

The 'race riots' that engulfed Brixton and Tottenham during September and October 1985 had temporarily overshadowed internal party development, however. Griffin excitedly penned 'An Open Letter to Blacks in Britain' reflecting his Manichean belief that the country faced two alternatives – race war or compulsory repatriation, the latter billed as 'Our Only Choice'. The 'multi-racial experiment' would soon collapse in 'riot, blood and fire', he argued. Griffin's 'plan for peace' indeed 'the only hope of peace for Britain's cities' was a 'simple, feasible and humane' plan to deport Britain's five million-strong immigrant communities at a rate of 1,500 people a day, 100,000 families a year (approximately 500,000 individuals) over ten years, each of whom would be given a £3,000 'resettlement grant'.[288]

In the wake of the riots, the NF began revising its racial ideology, shifting slowly from 'racism' towards 'racialism'. The decision to ditch *Bulldog*, the YNF newspaper, in October 1985 in favour of 'more moderate racial preservation messages' was part of this process, albeit one also connected to Pearce's ongoing legal travails which culminated in his incarceration again two month later.[289] *Bulldog* epitomised the party's image problem. Though Pearce was offered unqualified support, *Nationalism Today* subsequently rounded upon *Bulldog* for 'encouraging a mindless hatred of other peoples ... encouraging our young supporters to engage in violent aggression.'[290] Though it reflected the party's new 'positive' racial policy, this scathing critique, penned two years later, was also a post hoc attack upon Pearce who by this point had deserted the 'political soldiers' for a rival faction. The attack was also somewhat ironic given that Griffin had helped edit *Bulldog* when Pearce was jailed.[291] Nor was *Bulldog*'s replacement, *New Dawn* – 'revolutionary voice of British Youth' – so very different. Issued to coincide with (another) relaunch of the YNF, *New Dawn*, which lasted for only a few issues, stuck to *Bulldog*'s tried and tested formula of 'white noise' and racism.[292]

Whilst *New Dawn* indicated the party's continued desire to channel the potential of racist rock, its key protagonist, Ian Stuart Donaldson, Skrewdriver's lead singer who also now served as the NF London organiser, was absent. Donaldson was jailed for twelve months in December 1985, the day before Pearce, after being convicted of racist assault.[293] From his cell, Donaldson penned an article titled 'Faith in the Struggle' for *Nationalism Today*, concluding in apocalyptic terms that 'we must have faith in this, our battle to the death.'[294] Following their release, Donaldson and Pearce co-authored *Skrewdriver: The First Ten Years* (1987), a paean of praise to the band, and began publishing *White Noise*, a fanzine for the burgeoning 'white power' music scene.[295]

Ulster

Griffin meanwhile had become fixated with Ulster. The NF stepped up its agitation after Margaret Thatcher and Irish Taoiseach Garret FitzGerald signed the Anglo-Irish Agreement in November 1985, which affirmed the Irish Republic's right to be consulted on policy within Northern Ireland. The event was 'deeply traumatising' for Ulster Unionists.[296] Griffin believed that the agreement had brought Ulster 'to the brink of an open uprising'.[297] The NF had traditionally struggled to make inroads into Ulster's Loyalist community, failing to convince it that the struggle against Irish republicanism and immigration were 'one and the same fight, waged against one and the same enemy. Blacks and Republicans know that – so should Loyalists and Racial Nationalists.'[298] Thus links between the extreme right and Loyalism were 'very slight', 'usually initiated by the racist right', and 'fail to endure'.[299] MI5 held a similar view, recording that although the London Ulster Defence

Association (UDA) 'attracted members of the skinhead movement of the extreme right', no formal links existed because 'at leadership level there is mutual suspicion.'[300] The NF were certainly enthused by the activities of Loyalist paramilitaries, gloating over the fate of their victims. In 1984, *Bulldog*, the YNF newspaper, had named Jim Campbell, northern editor of the *Sunday World*, in a 'Bulldog blacklist'. When Campbell narrowly survived an assassination attempt by the Ulster Volunteer Force (UVF) shortly afterwards, the following issue boasted provocatively 'beware the curse of Bulldog'.[301]

There was never a simple synergy of interest between militant Loyalism and the extreme right, however. In part, this was because of their differing political identities. Loyalism encompassed a spectrum of political views. Most wanted union not independence, which the NF advocated. Similarly, the militant defence of Protestant identity, central to Loyalism, was never a cornerstone of extreme right-wing identity.[302] Griffin inadvertently underscored this mismatch in his speech to the NF Remembrance Day parade later that year whilst explaining 'how whites were duped into fighting other whites' and 'that the real victors of World War Two have been the Capitalists, Communists, and Zionists.'[303] The political memory of most Ulster Loyalists meanwhile was irrevocably bound to the pride felt nationally in defeating Fascism.

The increased militancy by the 'revolutionaries' within the NF surrounding Ulster also fuelled internal ideological and tactical tensions, pushing the party further towards schism. Figures like Wingfield and Anderson, so Griffin later argued, opposed the 'Independence for Ulster' motion at the party's AGM. The increasingly confrontational stance adopted by Griffin's faction also alarmed them. This tension was palpable when 500 NF activists protested the 'pro-IRA' Bloody Sunday march in London on 2 February 1986, resulting in fifteen arrests after a contingent of activists tried to break through the police cordon. The NF counter-demonstration culminated in the hanging of an effigy of an IRA man from gallows in Hyde Park.[304] Griffin claimed that his faction 'and most of the activists' had wanted to break-up the march. Wingfield, Anderson and 'just under half of the Directorate' meanwhile were content with 'a noisy but symbolic counter-demo' they had negotiated with the police. Afterwards Griffin reiterated his commitment to physically opposing Republican marches at an NF rally. 'When we spoke of physical opposition we were not even hinting of bombs or guns,' he stated, 'but we were prepared to use "the traditional British methods – the brick, the fist and the boot."' Wingfield, seated next to Griffin on the platform, 'buried his head in his hands.' These militant pronouncements, once publicised, provided 'a well-timed boost to our drive to become properly established in Ulster,' Griffin claimed.[305]

In Ulster, unionist mobilisation against the Anglo-Irish Agreement culminated with a 'Day of Action' on 3 March, which shut down most industry and commerce in Northern Ireland. Rioting later that evening injured forty-seven RUC officers, with hundreds of attacks occurring intermittently thereafter.[306] That months' issue of *Nationalism Today* featured the Red Hand of Ulster on the cover with the slogan 'Ulster Must Fight'.[307] In this febrile atmosphere, police arrested Andy McLorie, the NF Belfast organiser under the Prevention of Terrorism Act. Jailed for two years, McLorie had conspired to firebomb the home of an RUC officer, part of a broader Loyalist strategy to make the accord unenforceable. McLorie's arrest was significant. He was one of four activists arrested in Larne and Belfast whom Griffin characterised as 'the kingpins of the massive sales rounds in Belfast.' It was a 'devastating blow' for the NF's ability to spread its message, and its reputation.[308] *New Dawn* declared the RUC to be 'the enemy' whilst soliciting financial support for McLorie as a 'P.O.W.'.[309] McLorie was not alone. In the previous month, a court jailed several NF and UVF sympathisers in Glasgow for conspiring to procure explosives for Loyalists paramilitaries.[310]

Griffin travelled to Northern Ireland. The *Today* newspaper claimed that he and John Field, a Welsh NF activist who later became the Ulster organiser, had flanked the Reverend Ian Paisley, leader of the Democratic Unionist Party (DUP) as he led 4,000 Unionists to occupy Hillsborough, where the Anglo-Irish Agreement had been signed on 10 July 1986. Griffin alleged that Paisley knowingly and deliberately co-opted them to march with him because he 'knew the value of the NF's hard-line image and fast growing reputation for concrete proposals for political resistance.' He also alleged that, as Paisley arranged the photo opportunity, 'he would naturally have taken steps to ensure that the press were told who we were.'[311]

Griffin supported Ulster's independence as the 'only way' to maintain the provinces freedom and identity 'as part of the British family of Nations'. He denied advocating the break-up of Britain, claiming instead to support 'the first liberated zone of our future Britain.' Ulster represented 'the best opportunity for a genuine National Revolution anywhere in Europe. History beckons us, we must not turn our backs.' Loyalists prioritised the military over the political situation, Griffin argued, envisaging the NF could provide the 'ideological backbone' and 'to help provide the blue-print for the social and economic structure of the new nation.' Many European extreme right-wing groups were pro-Republican and, Griffin claimed, 'the NF's widely acknowledged position as one of the most respected Racial Nationalist movements in the world also places us in a unique position from which to influence foreign Nationalist groups and swing them behind the Ulster cause.'[312]

During the tumult, the NF platform occasioned a short-lived flurry of interest. *National Front News*, with a print run of 14,000, allegedly sold 4,000 copies in Ulster. The 'Hang IRA Scum' issue of the newspaper proved predictably popular, reputedly selling 3,000 copies. The NF also produced *British Ulsterman*, paid for by its 'Step up the Propaganda War' appeal, which was initially distributed as an insert to *National Front News*. The group also produced a more bespoke local publication, *Ulster Nation*. 'Given the size of the loyalist population, this made us an important voice, and ours was the only one which offered a coherent strategy whereby rank-and-file loyalists could do something positive to strengthen their position,' Griffin claimed. 'The paramilitaries only asked for financial support and for support for their operations; Ian Paisley could only march his men to the top of Hillsborough high street and march them down again.'[313] The failure of the Loyalist leadership to derail the Anglo-Irish Agreement meant that 'the potential for the NF is unlimited,' Griffin enthused.[314]

Griffin misread the political temperature, however. Loyalist outrage gradually dissipated during the following year, precipitating a commensurate decline of interest in NF. Though the NF opened a bookshop in east Belfast in November 1986, the initiative soon faltered, closing in June 1989, allegedly at the insistence of an increasingly hostile UDA, which had moved away from the independence line even before the NF began advocating it. More mundanely, one leading Ulster NF activist claimed they relinquished the lease voluntarily because the venture was 'losing money'.[315] There were, however, clearly tensions between the NF and Ulster loyalist organisations. When NF activist John Field criticised Gusty Spence, a leading figure in the UVF-linked Progressive Unionist Party (PUP) after he derided the NF as Nazis who 'must be stopped', paramilitary pressure reportedly forced Field out of Belfast.[316] By this juncture, however, the 'revolutionary' moment, which Griffin and the political soldiers had perceived in the wake of the Anglo-Irish Agreement, had passed, if indeed it ever really existed, 'though they failed to realise it'.[317]

'Europe of a hundred flags'

NF support for an independent Ulster (and other regional nationalisms) was the logical corollary of its evolving pan-European philosophy. Griffin's faction rejected Mosley's statist 'Europe-a-Nation' concept in favour of 'A Europe of the Peoples', a free federation of ethnic-based nation states which offered a panacea to the cultural and racial homogenisation held to be implicit in the EU project.[318] Support for 'Europe of a hundred flags' – as it was alternatively known – had been popularised by the Breton nationalist ideologue Yann Fouéré whose book, *L'Europe aux Cents Drapeaux* (1968), was translated into English in 1980.[319] It was influential upon *The Scorpion*'s editor, Michael Walker, and Richard Lawson who now ran Iona, a cultural society 'devoted to the study, revival, promotion, development and enjoyment of the islands of the North Atlantic.'[320] In turn, the NF adopted such ideas. Walker and Lawson successfully proposed a motion to the 1984 NF AGM: 'Recognising the cultural diversity of the native peoples of the British Isles the NF supports and will encourage the preservation of the Celtic languages and English dialects.'[321]

This development chimed with a burgeoning interest in regional ethno-nationalism, especially Welsh nationalism with which the NF sought to align themselves. They hailed Welsh nationalist Saunders Lewis as 'a brother in nationalism' – a characterisation that wilfully ignored his rejection of Fascism – whilst the NF Welsh language publication, *Y Ddraig Goch* (*The Red Dragon*), echoed that of the inter-war Plaid Cymru publication.[322] The NF began offering rhetorical support to more radical manifestations of Welsh nationalism including Meibion Glyndwr (Sons of Glendower), a militant group engaged in an arson campaign against estate agents selling Welsh properties as holiday homes to English buyers. Engaged in an NF picket outside one such estate agent in Ross-on-Wye, Herefordshire, Griffin refused to condemn, 'people who are taking the only road which they see to stand by their country.' He did criticise Meibion Glyndwr, however, for taking the 'wrong road' when 'they should be organising politically to mobilise the entire Welsh people in defence of their culture and language.'[323]

Griffin certainly identified personally with this aspect NF ideology, relocating to a smallholding in rural Wales where, like Mosley before him, he began rearing pigs. He also ensured his children learned Welsh. This revived interest in regional cultures, customs and ethnicities not only supposed that cultural roots were 'found more readily at the local level', it also assumed that they represented a deeper, more authentic form of white ethnic identity, resistant to 'multiracialism' and *ergo* any redefinition of citizenship determined by the nation state that infringed upon it.[324] Griffin's 2009 claim that there 'is no such thing as a black Welshman' encapsulated such argumentation. 'You can have a black Briton; you can't have a black Welshman. Welsh is about people who lived in Wales since the end of the last ice age,' he argued.[325]

Whilst the NF remained a 'unionist' party, its downgrading of 'British' identity fuelled ideological internal tensions between the 'political soldiers' and the orthodox 'British nationalist' faction. It offended the wider fascist firmament too. BNP chair John Tyndall was primarily a 'British Nationalist' (or, as he alternatively described himself, 'a nationalist of the British Race') for whom 'Anglo-Saxon' *not* 'Celtic' heritage was paramount. Tyndall rejected regionalism as a bulwark against the EU. Quite the opposite. He dismissed 'mini-nationalism' as hastening national disintegration, aiding only those plotting to mongrelise the white race.[326] If that was not enough, it also affronted Tyndall's belief in a centralised and centralising State.[327]

The 1986 split

Faltering attempts to outmanoeuvre Tyndall's BNP combined with and exacerbated already simmering tensions within the NF which boiled over in the following year. In January 1986, Martin Wingfield became NF leader, replacing Ian Anderson. Recently released from prison, Wingfield represented a party faction more attuned to its old guard racial nationalism. The clash was not long coming. Indeed, Griffin's opponents were increasingly exasperated by the 'political soldiers' – their desire to change the party's structure, their racial stance, their interminable ideological abstraction, and, not least, a series of exposés regarding Fiore and his Italian confreres, which exacerbated tensions within the NF Directorate.[328] 'Three weeks ago the NF bulletin said I was a martyr for going to prison in defiance of the Race Relations Act,' opined Wingfield. 'Now they claim I'm in the pay of the Jewish Board of Deputies.'[329]

Matters came to a head at a Directorate meeting on 3 May 1986 as the two factions clashed, ostensibly over Anderson's alleged financial malfeasance, leading to an open breach. By the time of a second meeting two days later, Griffin's faction, which controlled the 'Executive Council', had obtained enough votes to suspend Wingfield, Anderson, Brons and others. The political soldiers began removing records from the Norwich headquarters in a bid to extend their control, whilst Wingfield's group sought a High Court injunction to freeze party funds in response to their expulsion.[330] In a section of the *NF Organisers' Bulletin* titled 'A Kosher NF' issued on 9 May, Griffin accused his opponents of wanting:

> [T]o drop all revisionist history material from NF publications and also from the bookshop. They want us to weaken our opposition to the bandit state of Israel on the grounds that 'the Arabs are just as bad as the Jews.' Either they know nothing about reality in Britain today, or they are looking to the Board of Deputies for funds.[331]

The National Directorate held a further meeting shortly afterwards. 'Going into that meeting I had been the chairman of the National Front and Andrew [Brons] a member of the directorate,' recalled Wingfield. 'Coming out of that meeting 40 minutes later neither of us were even members of the Party and Nick was the new NF chairman!'[332] Both groups continued to court Pearce whilst he languished in prison. Much to Griffin's chagrin, Pearce subsequently threw in his lot with Wingfields' faction after his release on 12 June.[333]

Adding fuel to the fire, in August, Griffin published *Attempted Murder: The State/Reactionary Plot against the NF* (1986), a vituperative pamphlet publicly attacking Anderson as an incompetent and Wingfield as a 'reactionary Tory racist' unable to grasp the finer points of the evolving NF doctrine.[334] Attacking the 'racist' position of his former colleagues, Griffin singled out Ted Budden, a former BUF activist – Wingfield's 'political mentor' – as a particularly egregious example of the base racist bigotry infecting NF publications.[335] Pearce was simply astounded. 'The "facts" published in this booklet were so poisonous that I found it hard to believe that my friend could have been capable of such gutter-scrapping mendacity,' he recalled.[336] Griffin's opponents responded by circularising NF branch officials with *'Attempted Murder': Absolute Insanity*, a bulletin dissecting the 'paranoia, malice, gossip and insufferable self-righteousness' saturating Griffin's missive.[337]

Beyond reconciliation, both factions claimed the name, a farcical situation that endured for several years. The 'official' NF led by Griffin, Holland and Harrington retained control of *Nationalism Today* and *National Front News* whilst Wingfield, Anderson and Brons formally constituted themselves as the NF Support Group (NFSG) in January 1987. The NFSG, alternatively known as the 'Flag Group' because its newspaper, *The Flag*, symbolically restored the Union Jack to pride of place on the masthead, which reflected its continued commitment to orthodox 'British' racial nationalism. *Vanguard*, the NFSG journal, portrayed 'Race' as central to the schism, claiming that Griffin's faction had 'banned all mention of the scientific basis of racial differences from the theoretical journal of Britain's foremost racialist party' and now wanted race 'soft-pedalled, or softened altogether.' Reasserting 'Race' as the 'foundation of our radical faith', the NFSG espoused a 'radical populism' based upon racial purity, national freedom and social justice, which represented the three branches of the Life Rune – a symbol popularised by Himmler's SS – 'whose stem and well-spring and root is the survival and advancement of the Race, our ultimate purpose in life.'[338]

Vanguard also mocked the political soldiers' esoteric ideology, their pretence to have 'become the embodiment of the idea' and their tendency to smother concrete policy 'beneath reams of pseudo-revolutionary subspartan ramblings.' This, *Vanguard* suggested, emanated from the 'class prejudices and arrogance' of middle-class activists like Griffin 'who came from what can only be described as Conservative backgrounds.'[339] *Vanguard* was particularly derisive of their obsession with 'Captain Codfish' branding it 'Legionnaires Disease', whilst assailing the 'cliquish cultism' that lead 'away from the people … to irrelevance and oblivion.'[340]

Tower Hamlets NF organiser Eddy Butler was similarly scornful of their 'pseudo-revolutionary cant and posturing' and their vision for 'a European imperium, a new Christendom of rural statelets'. Whilst ruralism had much to recommend it, argued Butler, advocates like Griffin had taken it to 'ridiculous extremes' by 'seeking to destroy the cities and reduce Britain to a pastoral existence. Now ask yourself: who is the radical and who is reactionary.'[341] Dismayed, Butler departed for Tyndall's BNP.[342] Butler was part of a larger exodus from the party, which played a 'major part' in the BNP becoming 'the main force in urban racist politics – a virtually inconceivable development at the turn of the decade when Tyndall formed the BNP after breaking with the NF.'[343] Illustrative of the extreme right's personal and political fragmentation was a curious *mise en scène* several months later when Griffin, Butler and Wingfield each found themselves at Brick Lane market, 'leaning against the wall just a few yards apart' selling rival 'nationalist' newspapers: *National Front News*, *British Nationalist* and *The Flag*.[344] It would have been hard to foresee that twenty years later the three activists would be reunited, albeit temporarily, under Griffin's leadership.

Griffin's faction were untroubled by the NF haemorrhaging members. Believing that they constituted a 'Redeemed Few', they proceeded to further purify what remained of the organisation they had captured. The NF AGM in November 1986, billed as 'probably the most important gathering ever in the history of the Movement', announced fundamental structural changes. This included the realization of the 'cadre' system, supposedly transforming the party, through intensive ideological training, into an elite, revolutionary movement. 'The days when the NF tolerated drunks, sexual perverts and crooks in the leadership *are at an end*,' it announced:

> The days when strategy and tactics were constructed to please the membership, rather than promote the *true* interests of the NF *are at an end*. The days when just anybody could join our ranks *are at an end*. The new National Front is now *unreservedly* a movement committed to National Revolution.[345]

These changes, including a large increase in membership dues intended to drive out ideologically uncommitted members and to prepare the NF for the long haul. Like Mosley, Griffin saw no hope of political success until the 'crisis'. 'We must understand,' he wrote, 'that our chances of carrying out a national revolution are non-existent in stable economic and social conditions.'[346]

Their decision to retreat from street activism was not simply the result of an abstract strategy, but also one which was forced upon them by anti-fascist opposition. Earlier that year, on 5 July, the day after American Independence Day, the NF staged a march in Bury St Edmunds, Suffolk, celebrating 'British Independence Day'. 'Yanks Out Now! End the foreign military occupation of Britain and Europe', declared the front page of *National Front News*. Griffin was pictured at the demonstration standing next to a banner with a skull and crossbones reading 'US death bases out now', whilst NF activists burned the Stars and Stripes amidst chants of 'Superpowers out of Europe' and 'Death to America'.[347] The subsequent march was less successful. Attacked by Anti-Fascist Action, it degenerated into 'pandemonium'.[348] Anti-fascists observed Griffin 'holding his hands in the air, as if appealing for divine intervention.'[349]

Overwhelmed by physical opposition, the political soldiers staged a handful of sparsely attended marches before retreating from street activity altogether, which took its own cumulatively deleterious toll upon their faction's fortunes. A further self-inflicted humiliation came when they attempted to usurp the annual NF Remembrance Day parade to The Cenotaph on 8 November 1988. The police refused permission for two marches. The political soldiers had to march 'one coach load apart' from the official NF march. NF organisers claimed 500 people joined their parade compared to the fifty the political soldiers mustered.[350]

The political soldiers also downgraded, and then rejected, electoral activity. With the NF in disarray following the split, Griffin's faction failed to contest the 1987 general election at all, citing the increase in the deposit required from £150 to £500 as the reason. Instead, Griffin stated, 'we are running an active campaign to persuade people not to vote at all.'[351] It was not a success: 32.5 million people voted in the 1987 general election. Only 839 cast their vote for the three extreme right candidates who stood.[352] The political soldier's one and only foray into parliamentary politics came in June 1989, when Patrick Harrington stood in the Vauxhall by-election in south London, 'merely as an attempt to spread its racial separatist message among Blacks in a constituency that included Brixton.'[353] Harrington polled 127 votes, whilst Ted Budden, who stood against him as an NFSG candidate, polled eighty-three. The rival factions exchanged blows at the count.[354]

The departure of the Flag Group, whose activists had favoured both street and electoral activity, loosened internal constraints upon the political soldiers. As part of their vision of becoming a 'movement' rather than a 'party', *Nationalism Today* ceased attributing articles to named authors because: 'It is not *who* believes, but *what* is believed that counts above all else. After all the National Revolution is an *idea* not a person or a clique.'[355] Spurred on by their elitist ideals, the political soldiers now sought to discover 'the Few' who would be 'indispensable to our operations'. Emphasising quality over quantity, *Nationalism Today* spoke of the 'ideal thousand', which if composed of sufficiently 'zealous, tenacious and ideological cadres,' represented the party's best chance of 'reaching out to the multitude and of continuing to have a beneficial, decisive and lasting influence over them.' Viewed as 'obsolete', the traditional branch structure underwent a 'phased conversion' to the 'Circle' – special interest groups, modelled partly on the structure of the Apristas, the American Popular Revolutionary Alliance, a populist, anti-democratic Peruvian movement whose founders had admired Nazism. These 'circles' would concentrate on distinct components of the ideological struggle such as abortion, ecology or the Palestinian struggle.[356]

Revolutionary elitism coexisted with Griffin's continued desire to develop a 'counter power' through, amongst other things, 'white power' music. In August 1986, he had staged a second 'white noise' gig again headlined by Skrewdriver – Ian Stuart's first gig since his release from prison. Reflecting the increasing transnational nature of the scene, 650 people attended including nearly 100 'drawn from various European nations'.[357] Ian Stuart once noted that 'A pamphlet is read only once, but a song is learnt by heart and repeated a thousand times.' The NF understood this too, noting that 'for many youngsters White Noise is their first introduction, at a low level, to Nationalist politics.'[358] Their desire to orchestrate and manipulate this milieu for their own political ends received ample testimony in a vivid account of Griffin's involvement a 'NF disco' in Bury St Edmunds that same year. Griffin was observed to be 'managing' the evening's activities, acting as conductor, signalling the moment at which 'white power' music could be played and then watching as the skinheads whipped themselves into a frenzy. Intermittently, he intervened to urge the volume to be increased. Griffin and his friends then retreated to the periphery where they 'stood transfixed, studying the group' taking its measure. 'They understood something about the workings of the crowd; they respected it. They knew that its potential – its raw, raw, uncontrollable power – was in all of us, even if it was so persistently elusive.'[359]

To harness this potential, in 1986, Holland and Harrington had founded the White Noise Club (WNC), which sold records and merchandise to an increasingly global audience fuelled by Skrewdriver's popularity. The WNC also promoted concerts. It was under this banner that Griffin hosted the 'White Noise Summer Festival' at his parents' property on 25 April 1987, again headlined by Skrewdriver and including Legion 88 from France, the first foreign band to be involved.[360] It was now an international event with 'dozens' of skinheads from France, Belgium, Germany and Austria attending.[361] The event was filmed by Michael Hoffman II, an American 'revisionist', who passed the videotapes to the WAR leader Tom Metzger who then sold them in the United States, cementing his reputation as a leading figure in the burgeoning American skinhead scene.[362]

Shortly after this gig, however, Donaldson fell out with the NF over money.[363] Instead of reinvesting the proceeds of White Noise back into the music scene, the party's leadership, Donaldson claimed, 'just pocketed all the money', using it instead to subsidise their 'political' activities including the production of *NF News* and *Nationalism Today*.[364] Having handed his resignation to *White Noise* and the NF, Donaldson founded Blood & Honour (B&H), which quickly blossomed into an international Nazi music network that persists to this day.[365] It was not an amicable divorce. *Blood & Honour* singled out Holland, Harrington and Andrews as 'vermin' and proclaimed unequivocally: 'We will follow the example of the one uncorruptible ideal: – National Socialism, and its great martyr Adolf Hitler. Victory will be ours.'[366] The political soldiers quickly proscribed B&H citing Donaldson's 'lies' and 'reactionary Nazi views', which they had turned a blind eye to whilst he was making money for them.[367] *Blood & Honour* responded by extending its sanction to the whole 'Nutty Fairy Party', advising activists to back rival extreme right factions instead.[368] B&H had effectively marginalised the NF by 1988, though local branches continued to sell 'nazi' merchandise. *Welsh Leak*, the Cardiff NF fanzine, claimed that: 'all units of the NF and WN [White Noise] have been told to clear all stock bearing the name of the nazi band "Skrewdriver". So, all the T-shirts are being "sold off" for just £3.50.'[369]

Hostility softened over time. Griffin remains a Skrewdriver fan – 'some of the early stuff was good.'[370] Griffin was, he stated on the twenty-fifth anniversary of Donaldson's death, 'honoured to have known him. Always remembered.'[371]

'The New Alliance'

Continuing to evolve its racial ideology, the NF launched their 'Race Campaign' on 25 July 1987. Racial hatred had been the 'dominant tone' of NF propaganda for the past fifteen years, Holland conceded, confining the party to an 'ideological ghetto'. Consequently, he lamented, 'we appeared as mind-less, nihilistic, race-hating individuals with nothing constructive to say.' By allowing 'race' to enjoy a 'fallow period' in its publications, the NF believed the public would to see the party and its socio-economic policies in a 'new light', thereby removing the 'last major impediment to rapid growth'. Henceforth, the NF would replace crude 'race hatred' with the promotion of racial segregation as a solution to 'multiracialism' because 'the bulk of White people have their counterparts in the Black community who want to keep themselves apart.'[372]

Pursing this stratagem, the NF sought dialogue with Black separatists. Griffin had pioneered this approach in the aftermath of the Brixton riots through his 'Open Letter to Blacks in Britain', which urged a recognition that 'our destinies differ' and they should 'go our separate ways in peace'.[373] *Nationalism Today* alighted upon Louis Farrakhan, leader of the separatist Nation of Islam (NOI) as a potential partner. 'White Nationalists everywhere wish him well,' they stated, 'for we share a common struggle for the same ends. Racial Separation and Racial Freedom.'[374] When the British government banned Farrakhan from Britain in 1986, *Nationalism Today*, which sold tapes of him speaking, responded that 'the thought of anybody – Black or White – exposing Jewish power and demanding racial separation and racial freedom is a horrific challenge to the "Powers that Be".'[375]

Promoting racial separatism above racial supremacy was not especially novel. Mosley had formed an 'Associate Movement' for funnelling such sentiment, whilst Tyndall had also praised Black Muslim separatists.[376] Where the 'political soldiers' differed was in their efforts to establish a concrete alliance. In 1986, *Nationalism Today* published an NOI 'photo essay' authored by Abdul Wali Muhammed, editor-in-chief of its newspaper, *Final Call* (copies of which the NF later advertised for sale). The accompanying editorial declared that Black Power and White Power 'are allies in the struggle to resist and defeat the race and nation destroying Capitalism that is engulfing the globe.'[377] In May 1988, Croydon NF activist Chris Marchant visited an NOI 'anti-dope' project in Washington, DC, the excursion facilitated by the NF's American colleagues Matt Malone and Robert Hoy. Pursuing an identical strategy, Malone held 'in depth' discussions with Black separatist Robert Brock, head of the Self-Determination Committee, who *Nationalism Today* had profiled. Hoy, who was billed as 'a representative of the NF in America' and spokesman for 'White Americans', appeared alongside Brock on television on 23 February 1989 with the latter 'denouncing integrationists and demanding reparations'.[378]

Griffin also brokered a relationship with the Florida-based Pan-African International Movement (PAIN), which espoused a more radically separatist platform than NOI, which only advocated relocating to Black Separatist States *within* America. PAIN favoured the 'Back-to-Africa' policy pioneered by Marcus Garvey in the 1920s. Led by Osiris Akkebala, PAIN sought to establish a Pan-African Federal Republic as the embodiment of their belief in the 'sacredness' of racial separatism.[379] To underline this burgeoning link, *National Front News* featured a front-page photograph of its American correspondent,

Matt Anger, reading and discussing NF literature with Akkebala under the headline 'Top Blacks back NF Plan'.[380]

These dalliances were not universally popular and occasioned several resignations.[381] The political soldiers insisted on the political utility of such alliances, arguing that they insulated the group from accusations of 'racism', whilst also giving their own advocacy of racial segregation a 'moral' underpinning it had hitherto lacked. The polarisation of 'racial and cultural identity' implicit in such a strategy was also deemed to strengthen opposition to multiracialism and miscegenation, 'which is, of course, racial destruction ... of not one but two races'. They believed that rejecting the 'racial negativism' would make the NF more palatable 'to the wider white population who've never wanted multi-racialism, but at heart are a fair, tolerant people who need to be given a rational and moral justification for their desire to maintain Britain as a White European country.' Justifying this strategy, Holland claimed, unconvincingly, that 'racial hatred' was actually alien to the extreme right – 'injected into nationalism' in the 1970s by the Conservatives – by which rationale the NF was actually 'purifying' rather than 'compromising' its principles 'and eliminating from our creed something which has no right to be there in the first place.'[382] *National Front News* took the next step of announcing in August 1987 that racial science, a cornerstone of extreme right argumentation, was 'utterly irrelevant'. What concerned the 'political soldiers' was not 'superiority' but 'difference' highlighting the influence of arguments for 'ethno-plurality' championed by the French Nouvelle Droite.[383]

The NF also regarded the Muslim world as a potential ally, particularly Iran. This was somewhat ironic given that only a few years previously, in August 1980, Griffin and Joe Pearce had led a march through Tunbridge Wells, Kent, 'in protest at the way this lovely town is being spoiled by an influx of Iranian "students".'[384] Embracing their new position, however, *Nationalism Today* began praising Iran's 'National Revolution', which had overthrown the US-backed Shah in 1979, on the following basis: 'We have mutual enemies, if somewhat divergent aims. Anti-imperialists and anti-Zionists must stand together' to bring about 'National Freedom for the enslaved nations of the world.'[385] Holland argued that it was in the interests of the Middle East to assist the 'national revolutionary' struggle in Europe through a 'Euro-Arab alliance' to defeat 'Zionism'.[386] A shared anti-Semitism undoubtedly helped the NF imagine itself a part of a wider 'anti-Zionist' axis. *Nationalism Today* applauded Iran's reprinting of *The Protocols of the Elders of Zion*, which had appeared with a commentary in *Iman*, an English-language Iranian publication distributed by the Iranian Embassy in London.[387] It also reproduced an *Iman* article, which expressed 'the official view of the Islamic Republic of Iran and demonstrates that nation's resolute opposition to Zionism.'[388]

Increasingly, the political soldiers also identified with Iran's Revolutionary Guard, lavishing praise upon them in party publications:

> Their belief in the cause is so strong that they will run through mine fields unarmed to attack enemy positions; their ideals are so all-consuming that they will drive truck bombs into enemy camps knowing full well that death is inevitable.... This power, this contempt for death, is the stuff of which victories are made.[389]

The language of Iranian publications made it easier for the NF to draw such parallels. *Kayhan International* editorialised 'The Birth of a "New Man"' in terms markedly similar to *National Front News*.[390] NF publications began advertising *Islam and Revolution* by the

Iranian Ayatollah Khomeini; *Roots of the Islamic Revolution* by Hamid Alger; and *CIA: America Supports the Usurpers of Palestine* by the Iranian Ministry of Islamic Guidance. It also promoted titles like *One People Too Many* by Afif Safieh, a pro-Palestinian tract written by the PLO representative to The Hague; and Gaddafi's *Green Book* – 'Read the ideas which the Zionists and Capitalists want to suppress'.[391]

This ideological transition found visual confirmation in the first issue of *Nationalism Today* to appear after the 1986 split. It ceased being the 'radical voice of British Nationalism' with its masthead instead issuing 'a call to arms, a call to sacrifice'.[392] More profoundly, the Union Jack – the 'old flag of centralised Westminster' which symbolised 'City of London imperialism' – was replaced with a Celtic cross (the 'symbol of our past, symbol of our future'), which 'has now become *the* design of National Revolutionaries in Europe as a symbol of our common determination to avoid another tragic Brothers War.'[393] Ditching the Red, White and Blue, and replacing it with the Black, Red and Green prefigured a more profound ideological realignment. This became apparent in March 1988 when *National Front News* pronounced 'The New Alliance' on its front page alongside photographs of Farrakhan, Khomeini and Libyan dictator Colonel Gaddafi (see below) who, regardless of their many differences, all supported the 'Third Way'.[394]

In the following month, in a further reflection of this trajectory, the NF inaugurated a Campaign for Palestinian Rights, picketing the Association of British Travel Agents, after it announced its annual conference in Israel that year. The London PLO office and the Palestine Solidarity Campaign both rebuffed NF approaches, despite which Harrington and another activist still joined the annual pro-Iranian Quds Day march in London in May 1988, handing out their 'Terror Tours' leaflets and chatting to the organisers.[395] Former NF chairman John Tyndall looked on in horror as the party he once led was transformed 'from a full-blooded British nationalist movement … to a party that shares much more in common with the radical left than it does with nationalism in this country.'[396]

Libya

NF ideological development underwent further transformation through its synthesis of the ideas of the Libyan dictator Colonel Muammar Gaddafi, who had seized control of the North African state in a military coup in 1969. There were 'strong rumours' that Libyan largesse had paid for the 'Israel – The Hate State' *Nationalism Today* supplement.[397] Martin Webster certainly intimated that a financial relationship existed between his usurpers and the Libyan People's Bureau.[398] This relationship, whatever its precise parameters, was complicated when WPC Yvonne Fletcher was shot dead outside the Libyan Embassy in London on 17 April 1984 by a gunman inside the building who opened fire upon anti-Gaddafi demonstrators. Her killing precipitated an eleven-day siege and the rupture of diplomatic relations between Britain and Libya.[399]

Whilst direct dealings with Libya became impossible as a result, Gaddafi's *The Green Book* (1975) helped the NF evolve their rejection of parliamentary liberal democracy. In *The Green Book*, Gaddafi espoused his Third International Theory,

> to indicate that there is a new path for all those who reject both materialist capitalism and atheist Communism. The path is for all the people of the world who abhor the dangerous confrontation between the Warsaw and North Atlantic military alliances. It is for all those who believe that all nations of the world are brothers under the aegis of the rule of God.[400]

The NF found an obvious synergy with their own vision. They were particularly enthused by Gaddafi's formulation of 'popular' direct democracy, a utopian mirage masking the reality of the Libyan despot's repressive rule.[401]

Nationalism Today hailed Gaddafi as 'one of today's greatest minds'. No genuine revolutionary should be without *The Green Book*, they proclaimed, 'its knowledge and its thoughts, for by its very words is the Revolution in essence defined.'[402] *National Front News* evinced similar enthusiasm, it stated:

> Libya is a Third Position nation and the National Front has become, independently, a Third Position movement. Our common ideology is the great, and indeed the only, threat to global Capitalism in the next century. That is why Libya, like the National Front, is subjected to a continuous barrage of groundless smears and hatred.[403]

Holland advocated giving weapons 'free of charge to every adult citizen' transforming them into 'active partisans' and defenders of the 'National Revolution'.[404]

On 5 April 1986, a bomb planted in West Berlin's La Belle discothèque killed two American servicemen and a Turkish woman, injuring 250. The United States blamed Libya, responding ten days later with air strikes on Tripoli and Benghazi that targeted Gaddafi's office and private residence. Gaddafi survived but the raid killed his eighteen-month-old adopted daughter and approximately ten others. The NF was incensed that Thatcher had allowed the USA to use airbases in East Anglia for the airstrike, vehemently denying that Libya was a sponsor of terrorism. Gaddafi was really attacked, they claimed, because he

> is the most powerful champion of the Third Position – the only ideology capable of breaking down the global stranglehold of US dollar imperialism ... the real aim was to make the world safe for General Motors, IBM and Wall Street.[405]

The bombings elicited a wave of extreme right sympathy for Gaddafi. Despite ridiculing Griffin and his colleagues as the 'Gaddafi Front', Tyndall also believed he was attacked 'because he was labelled as an enemy of Israel and because America's Jews demanded that he be destroyed and their White House marionette obediently jumped to the crack of their whip.'[406] Despite NF denials, Libya was indeed responsible for the Berlin bombing. Four people, Libyan secret service agents and workers at its embassy in East Berlin, were convicted and jailed in November 2001 – though the judge stopped short of blaming Gaddafi directly for the atrocity.[407]

On 17 September 1988, Griffin, Harrington and Holland (three of the NF's five-man leadership) flew into Libya on a four-day 'fact-finding' trip at the behest of the 'Libyan Peace Committee', an organisation aiming 'to spread awareness of the injustices and horror of the US bombing of Libya.' This was no 'junket', claimed *Nationalism Today*, but an opportunity for detailed study of how Gaddafi's 'Third Universal Theory' worked in practice. In their 'extensive tour' of Tripoli, the trio visited bombsites, a supermarket and a factory – the Libyan Bus and Truck Company.[408] 'They were at all times free to go where they wanted,' declared *National Front News*, a common claim from fellow travellers visiting a dictatorship. 'They were free to talk to anyone they wished and, in spite of obvious language difficulties, found the people there, friendly sincere and contented.' A highlight of the trip was a visit to the bombed wreck of Gaddafi's former residence, where they left a sympathetic message in the visitors' book attacking Thatcher and Reagan as 'war criminals' which ended: 'We thank God that this attempt to murder a leading Arab statesman failed.'[409] 'Libya is *not* paradise on earth, but there is a lot our people could learn from it,' concluded *Nationalism Today*. 'And the first lesson is: *Don't believe the calculating lies of the Zionist and Capitalist media!*'[410] *National Front News* subsequently featured a photograph of Griffin and Holland posing under a giant billboard of Gaddafi's visage, the same issue trumpeting their pledge to 'continue our work to show that Libya is the victim, not the perpetrator of State Terrorism.'[411] Two months later, Libyan intelligence agents bombed Pan Am Flight 103 killing 270 people in Lockerbie, Scotland.[412]

The overarching purpose of this NF expedition was to gain money from the Libyan dictator. Ironically, Gaddafi had been channelling money and weapons to the IRA since the 1970s, a fact the political soldiers would have been perfectly aware of following the 1987 seizure of the *M.V. Eksund* en route to Northern Ireland laden with approximately 1,000 AK-47 machine guns, over fifty ground-to-air missiles and 3 tons of Semtex.[413] Such dalliances mortified other extreme right groups. Gaddafi 'may be a genuine anti-Zionist,' noted the NF Flag Group, 'but he still supplies the bullets which end up in the back of Loyalists in Ulster.'[414] The political soldiers had no such scruples. Had Gaddafi offered funding, Griffin recalled, 'we'd have been very pleased to take it, and we hoped that we would be.'[415] In the event, the trio returned empty-handed save for a 'big crate' of *The Green Book*, 'which promptly disappeared in customs,' Griffin lamented, 'so we didn't actually get any.'[416]

Ironically, whilst Griffin was busy trumpeting his 'New Alliance', the rival 'Flag Group' intuited that the racial nationalist future lay not in aligning oneself with radical Islamists, Black Separatists or North African despots, but in opposing 'The Third Enemy' of the white race – Islam. 'Islam was the mortal enemy of Europe before ever Capitalism of Communism was born,' declared *Vanguard* in 1987. 'Islam will still be the mortal enemy of Europe after Capitalism and Communism are dead. Only when the last mullah, as well as the last banker and the last Bolshevik has faded into history will our Race be safe.'[417] They also rejected the political soldiers' 'Victory to Palestine' platform, which *Vanguard* argued meant '*more* Jews in Europe and America', which contravened *its* policy of 'repatriating' Jews to Israel whose right to exist they supported for this very purpose.[418] Griffin was behind the curve concerning the first rumblings of this emergent *zeitgeist*. It was another fourteen years before he embraced 'populist' anti-Muslim campaigning as a core campaign strategy.

International Third Position

Like latter-day Jacobins, Griffin's faction pursued ideological purity at the expense of all else. As a result, the NF became 'a splintered laughing stock'. It was not so much its descent into ideological obscurity that had condemned it, Griffin subsequently reasoned, but rather the result of 'hasty change' implemented by 'a small group who have "seen the light"' and 'set out to impose their new way of doing things on an organisation of volunteers.'[419] Such wisdom came with the benefit of hindsight. In 1989, the NF split again, wrecked by 'ideological indigestion … indiscipline and inexperience'.[420] Personalities, politics and anti-Semitism all played a role. In July, Rabbi Mayer Schiller, an orthodox Talmudic lecturer at Yeshiva University High School in Washington Heights, who was sympathetic to the core ideas of the 'third position' visited the NF. Though he objected to the plethora of anti-Semitic sentiments ingrained within NF publications, Schiller nonetheless found the party's broader platform 'very attractive'. He stated that it combined 'the best of the anti-capitalist, anti-multi-racial continental European right with the humanism and communalism of the New Left.'[421] Harrington was particularly pleased with such dialogue, arguing that evolution of NF Jewish policy was the logical conclusion of the party's racial separatist platform. Griffin and Holland disagreed.[422]

Spurred on by such disputes, in September 1989, Griffin and Holland announced to Harrington their plans to relocate to the Normandy village of Falaise to establish a rural commune based upon Distributist principles – an idea first mooted in *Rising* in 1985.[423] Holland had initially scoffed at the plan to move to France 'to be in closer contact with the soil,' suggesting sententiously 'it surely had to be our soil!' He also allegedly doubted Griffin's claim he could train activists in France since he was only doing the 'absolute minimum' in England because of his house renovation projects. Furthermore, Holland argued, it could be difficult and embarrassing to explain to other NF activists that Griffin had departed to France 'to further improve your financial well-being' when 'in terms of assets you were probably the wealthiest cadre in the movement.'[424]

Having apparently resolved these contradictions, Griffin and Holland both resigned from the NF Directorate at the beginning of October. Shortly afterwards, the *Jewish Chronicle* published a letter from Harrington apologising to the Jewish community, and declaring 'that anti-Semites will be expelled and Jews are welcome to join the National Front,' attesting to the impact of his interaction with Rabbi Schiller.[425] Griffin subsequently charged that Harrington had sent the letter without Directorate approval and, 'that as much as the message was unacceptable. I personally at the time felt that that was going too far.'[426] Harrington blamed Fiore for Holland's refusal to countenance a rapprochement. According to Harrington, Fiore 'seemed to identify Jews with being followers of the Anti-Christ'. Griffin, recorded another activist, criticised 'Pat's appalling attitude on the Yids.'[427] Following this second split, in January 1990, Harrington wound up what remained of the NF, re-configuring it as 'Third Way', which whilst remaining a 'separatist' organisation, also advocated 'voluntary' repatriation, setting it apart from other groups.

Griffin and Holland sought to poach the remaining NF cadres for their own initiatives, circulating a video titled *Revolution in Action* together with a document called 'A Future for the North'. Harrington 'proscribed' them both. It mattered little. Thereafter, Griffin and Holland together with Fiore and several others co-founded the International Third Position (ITP), its name a homage to Fiore's former TP group. Religion and politics, discipline and devotion, fused in their continued quest for the 'new man'. As Griffin explained in *Revolution in Action*, 'absolute values' are at the 'heart of our struggle'. Those in the vanguard of this 'new network' were Catholics, other Christians and figures like himself who were 'eco-pagans'. They were united, Griffin argued, not by sectarianism, but by their belief that there had to be a 'religiosity at the base or apex of our struggle … what is needed is an understanding that spirituality is crucial to our struggle.' To emphasise the non-sectarian nature of the political soldier's creed, Griffin stated that 'we intend to work with the Muslims' – an ironic statement given his position a decade later. Racialised 'religiosity' and the 'spiritual perspective' to their 'struggle' remained an integral to his politics. Griffin rejected any notion it deviated from the cause. 'We just don't accept that at all,' he intoned, 'as far as we're concerned this has always been central to the third position and to our struggle.'[428]

The ITP remained committed to the 'new alliance' strategy. Liberation, a small ITP-aligned *groupuscule*, sought out links with Saddam Hussein's Baathist regime.[429] Prior to the first Gulf War, Holland and Colin Todd (*Candour*'s current editor), spent eight days in Baghdad in November 1990, as guests of Iraq's Ministry of Religious Affairs, apparently following an invitation from the Palestinian Liberation Organization (PLO). They went with Malik Afzal of the Union of European Muslims in the hope of obtaining funds from the Baath party. Staying at the Al Rasheed Hotel, which was also hosting FN leader Jean-Marie Le Pen (who met with Hussein before returning home with fifty-five foreign hostages), Holland and Todd took a three-day trip to Jordan, visiting a Palestinian refugee camp near Amman too.[430] Despite returning empty-handed, the ITP positioned itself as 'the lone voice of the pro-Iraqi counter-media'.[431] Todd expounded to the 'Zionist capitalist press' that Hussein was an 'extremely able leader' leading an 'ideologically motivated force', who would prevail against the 'mercenary armed forces' amassing against him in the Gulf. He also praised the 'religious freedom' he had seen in Iraq, 'during a visit which had included meetings with the Speaker of the parliament, the Deputy Minister of Information, and the Minister for Religious Affairs.' Harrington, who had split with Griffin in the previous year, claimed that the 'political soldiers' sought such an alliance because 'they hate the Jews so much that anyone who attacks Israel is their friend.'[432]

The ITP was an experiment in 'pure' ideology and thus a complete retreat from practical politics in which its activists evinced an ever-decreasing interest. During its heyday, the NF, from which the ITP sprang, was an 'urban' phenomenon.[433] Withdrawing to the countryside was therefore little more than a revolutionary conceit. For the ITP, however, the 'French project' represented idealism in action, though reality never quite lived up to expectation. Griffin's belief in a reinvigorating rural Arcadia reinforced his enduring idea that 'cities are parasites' – the seat of corruption, decadence and racial ruination.[434] The quest for spiritual purity, supposedly found in the authenticity of rural living, had a long-standing lineage within the British fascist tradition. Alexander Raven Thomson, Mosley's leading ideologue, had proclaimed:

> [T]he medieval peoples who lived in hovels and built cathedrals were nearer to a realisation of the divine purpose than we are today.... It will be in recovering the 'age of faith' of Christendom and the vital energy of Tudor England that we may realise in part the great future of our nation.[435]

Similar impulses fired Griffin's imagination. Asked to describe his ideal polity in 2002, he replied: 'In some ways middle mediaeval England, at a time when serfdom had given away to huge numbers of people owning their own plot of land and having access to the village commons.'[436] Griffin's historical yearnings were flooded with fantasy, quite literally in the case of his interpretation of J.R.R. Tolkien's *Lord of the Rings* as racial allegory. 'The hobbit's Shire is still, as it always was, a symbolic representation of the quintessential decency and tolerance of the folk-communities of all Anglo Celts,' he asserted.[437]

Griffin claimed that the ITP was originally intended to operate as a 'resource centre' that would allow him and his colleagues to 'build some contacts, carry out some organizational experimentation, and then build something truly effective.' However, Holland's austere quasi-monastic Catholicism, which saturated the second volume of *The Political Soldier. Thoughts on Sacrifice and Struggle* (1989), alienated the group's pagan faction, of which Griffin was a leading light. A review of the pamphlet for *Nationalism Today*, quite possibly by Griffin, was telling.

> For myself, I found this [Holland's Catholic Traditionalism] intensely irritating at several points in what is otherwise a most inspiring book.... As a Pagan, I naturally share Derek's abhorrence of the 'City of Ruins' that is the modern world, and his

belief that we must counter the desiccated materialism of the Age with an intense spirituality which takes us above the material place. But while Christ may be Derek's Guide, He is not mine. And whilst I have great respect for the heritage of Christian Europe, I was not aware that we had adopted a Latin battle anthem.[438]

Indeed, the ITP increasingly resembled a fanatical 'pro-life' and homophobic fundamentalist sect, rather than a revolutionary nationalist party. This was undoubtedly because ITP leaders like Holland and Fiore were part of the Society of St Pius X (SSPX), a Traditionalist Catholic organisation founded in 1970 by the Catholic Archbishop Marcel Lefebvre following his refusal to accept changes wrought by the Second Vatican Council. SSPX held services at the Church of Saints Joseph and Padarn in north London that a group of ITP militants attended. The ITP journal, *Final Conflict*, conceived of politics in apocalyptic, millenarian terms, preaching the need for 'total war' to forestall the cultural desecration and racial ruination of white European civilisation and its absorption into a 'Kosher World'.[439]

Even though he had quickly became 'completely inactive' within the ITP,[440] for Griffin, the final breach came after a serious accident cost him an eye and, by his own account, 'made me pretty damn useless for about a year.'[441] During this enforced absence, the ITP completed its transformation into a 'clerical fascist organisation'. Upon returning to the group after his accident, Griffin perceived that 'there was nothing there that was of any value to me – they didn't want me and I didn't want them – so I went into the wilderness by myself for a period of about eighteen months in the early 90s.'[442]

Griffin later derided the ITP as a 'cult'[443] and agreed with the sentiment that Fiore was a 'nutter'.[444] Whilst he never recanted this 'ideologically crazy' period, Griffin would lament 'allowing my youthful enthusiasm for perfect ideas to run far beyond what's politically possible.'[445] The religious fanaticism of the ITP perturbed Griffin, but he also viewed its stance as prejudicial to white racial interests. The ITP, he argued, believe

> that England will be saved if enough people pray to the Virgin Mary to intercede on our behalf. I wonder whether the last pure whites in ancient India, in Egypt, in Athens and in Rome enjoyed similar fantasies as their civilizations floundered in a sea of alien blood.[446]

Griffin also attacked them for failing to adhere to the basic principles of 'biological racism', a position he himself had earlier rejected. Now, however, he attacked the ITP because one key activist had married 'a South American *mestizo*. But she's a Catholic, so that's all right by the leaders of the ITP.' Griffin also lambasted ITP support for the Front National, which allowed black and Arab members, provided they adhered to its vision of France – 'something the BNP will never emulate as long as I have a say in the matter,' he later wrote, before doing just that. Griffin now also fiercely criticised ITP support for the Palestinian cause, claiming, 'these people are so pro-Palestinian that they would rather have Zionists living in London than Tel Aviv. Sorry though I feel for the dispossessed Palestinians, I have to differ!'[447]

These disputes aside, Griffin increasingly focused his energies upon property development rather than politics. He took out large loans on several properties. His father guaranteed them. 'I made a fortune on paper,' Griffin recalled, 'probably £150,000 at one stage, with houses in Shropshire and France.'[448] The venture was doomed, however. High interest payments and negative equity, combined with Griffin's inaction following his accident in France, obliged his father to sell the family's Suffolk home and liquidate 'quite a lot of shares'. His mother also lost roughly £30,000 from the sale of her late mother's flat, ploughed into keeping her son's business venture afloat. 'We came out of it very badly,' Edgar Griffin told a journalist. 'My father had left me a rich man ... I was very comfortably off.' Griffin's debts caused a dissipation of the family's wealth.[449] The ordeal was not quite over yet. On 16 June 1994, Griffin – a 'Language Tutor and General Dealer' – declared Bankrupt at Welshpool and Newtown Court.[450] His total debts allegedly amounted to £70,000.[451] Griffin's financial ruination, combined with his determination to remain politically active, consigned him to a peripatetic existence. He worked for short periods chopping down trees with the Forestry Commission and spent several summers teaching English to foreign students. His wife worked as a nurse but the family lived on benefits when she took unpaid maternity leave.[452] By Griffin's own admission:

> Right up until the 2001 general election where we made our headline breakthrough in Oldham West, I was working three or four nights a week stacking shelves in a supermarket because there wasn't enough money to pay me to do politics.[453]

The Rune

After leaving the ITP in 1990, Griffin entered the political wilderness, taking a 'back seat' until 1993–1994. He began writing again, syndicating his output:

> I was writing for different little publications [including *Northern Way* and *The Sentinel*]: changing a few bits and pieces in the same article so it would appeal to the British Movement or the BNP, etc. I thought I would see what response I got, it was better than starting up a little publication myself.[454]

Griffin was not politically inert, however. In November 1991, he was part of the security team for a meeting organised by 'revisionist' author David Irving at Chelsea Town Hall.[455] The Chelsea meeting was a debacle, however. The authorities arrested and deported Fred Leuchter, Irving's star speaker, before he could speak.[456] Leuchter, an American engineer who sold execution equipment, had risen to prominence after the French Holocaust denier Robert Faurisson commissioned him to produce a 'scientific' report dismissing the existence gas chambers at Auschwitz for German-Canadian Holocaust denier Ernst Zündel, on trial again in 1988 for spreading 'false news' after circulating Richard Verrall's *Did Six Million Really Die?*

Zündel's trial, at which Irving also gave evidence, was a turning point. Staking his own already controversial reputation on the veracity of Leuchter's 'shattering' findings, Irving published *The Leuchter Report* in June 1989, contributing a foreword to it.[457] Its impact was writ large on the second edition of Irving's controversial book, *Hitler's War* (1977), which appeared in 1991.[458] The original, which viewed the Second World War 'from behind his [Hitler's] desk', had argued that there was no evidence Hitler ordered the annihilation of European Jewry; indeed, he knew nothing of the Holocaust until 1943. The new edition went further, replacing references made in 1977 to 'extermination' with vague allusions to 'the Jewish tragedy', 'the Nazi maltreatment of the Jews', or 'the entire tragedy'.[459] Irving was later forced to concede in court that *The Leuchter Report* was 'fundamentally flawed', whilst the judge's verdict admonished: 'I do not consider an objective historian would have regarded the Leuchter report as a sufficient reason for dismissing or even doubting ... the presence of homicidal gas chambers at Auschwitz.'[460]

Despite its lack of credibility, Griffin also found *The Leuchter Report* profound, promoting it as an authoritative 'scientific survey' using 'forensic evidence' to prove the gas chambers at Auschwitz were impossible.[461] The BNP also gave Leuchter their fulsome support, selling his report through its book service, and despatching a delegation led by John Peacock, the Leicestershire BNP organiser, to attend a 'European Leuchter Congress' in Munich, Germany, addressed by Leuchter, Faurisson and Irving.[462] Griffin's own penchant for Holocaust denial was increasingly manifest as his own politics continued to evolve, or devolve, depending on one's point of view, from the 'Third Position' towards a more orthodox national socialist position.

Different stories circulate regarding Griffin's decision to re-engage in racial politics. Griffin claimed that reports of a local school planning to celebrate a 'multi-faith' Christmas motivated him.[463] Steve Cartwright, the Scottish B&H organiser, recollected a different story. He stated that Griffin had remained in contact with 'Jim', the Scottish NA organiser, a former 'Gaddafi Front' activist who had joined the BNP. 'Jim' regularly sent Griffin taped copies of 'American Dissident Voices', William Pierce's shortwave radio programme which was billed as a 'clarion call to all White patriots to face, without evasion or compromise, the two greatest threats to our survival: the presence on non-Whites in our society and the control of our media by Jews.' Cartwright singled out 'Playing Cards on a Sinking Ship', broadcast on 25 June 1994, as having 'pricked Griffin's conscience'.[464] It clearly had an impact. Griffin subsequently published a transcript of the broadcast in *Spearhead* after he became assistant editor.[465] Thereafter, Cartwright stated, Griffin began making 'positive noises' to 'Jim' about political re-engagement, leading ultimately to his meeting with Cartwright and several other 'hard core' militants whose support would be crucial for his later BNP leadership challenge.[466] Neither story is mutually exclusive.

By 1993, Griffin was already in contact with newly minted Croydon and Merton BNP branch, comprising the remnants of the old NF branch he had involved with a decade beforehand.[467] Two of its activists, Paul Ballard and John Merritt, produced *The Rune*, an avowedly 'Nazi' journal.[468] *The Rune* praised Rudolf Hess as a 'martyr' whilst selling 'historic' postcards and posters of Hitler and the SS alongside VHS cassettes of Nazi 'classics' like *Triumph of the Will* and *The Eternal Jew* and books of a more recent vintage including *The Turner Diaries*. It revelled in tales of English folklore, Odinism ('our true religion'), racialised ruralism, and railed against 'race-mixing' and the racial inferiority of blacks; its writings on race distilled into a 'spotters guide to mongoloids'.[469]

Griffin began contributing to *The Rune* from Issue 5, using the pseudonym 'Geoff Peters'. His first article stressed the necessity of 'white counter-power', an idea recycled from *Nationalism Today*. His emphasis upon building a sound economic base for racial activism self-consciously drew inspiration from Codreanu's *For My Legionnaires*, Chesterton's Distributist League, William Pierce's racial communitarianism – 'based on the need to make an idealistic hardcore independent of the doomed system' – and also the 'ever incisive' Colin Jordan whose writings argued the same point.[470] Griffin's editorship of *The Rune* was publicly announced in Issue 10, after which he was 'wholly responsible' for its content.[471] The magazine's masthead featured the Odal Rune, which Griffin asserted 'stands for Unity and Inheritance. Intimately linked with ideas of ancestry, land and tribe, it is a symbolic version of the concept of Blood and Soil.'[472] *The Rune* was not widely read, having only 367 subscribers, Griffin later admitted.[473]

The Rune argued that not only were both world wars unnecessary 'Brothers Wars' but during the latter conflagration 'external forces' had given Churchill orders, 'to prolong a war which would lead Europe down a road to racial suicide.'[474] Issue 10, Griffin's first as editor, was, declared its front page, an 'SS Special!' 'Sick of Vera Lynn?' he asked rhetorically. 'See pages 18, 19, 21, 24 & 88.' Eighty-eight was not a page number. It denoted the eighth letter of the alphabet 'H' with '88' representing 'HH' – shorthand for 'Heil Hitler'. Inside, Griffin published an unsigned apologia for the Waffen-SS, praising the 'courage' and 'sacrifices' of its soldiers who believed they were fighting a 'Holy War'. The article concluded that: 'in an unbiased assessment of war-crimes ... the Waffen SS were undoubtedly no worse than the other troops of other nations – countless Allied war crimes are simply not publicised and the Soviets were far worse.'[475] *The Rune* also advertised and reproduced pictures from *The Fable of the Ducks and Hens* (1996), an anti-Semitic cartoon book aimed at children, which utilised a poem by murdered ANP leader George Lincoln Rockwell as its text. Visually, it evoked Philipp Rupprecht's notoriously anti-Semitic illustrations for *Der Giftpilz – The Toadstool* (1938), a children's book published by *Der Stürmer*.[476]

The Rune also mined Britain's native fascist tradition for inspiration. It featured an article on Mosley's BUF, titled 'Flames of Hope: The Legacy of the Blackshirts', arguing that a new generation of 'nationalists' were 'carrying on the same fight for a Greater Britain.'[477] Griffin also interviewed Ronald Creasy, the first elected BUF official who had won a town council election in Eye, Suffolk in November 1938. Griffin remembered Creasy as a 'grand old chap' having 'spent a number of late evenings while still a young activist sipping whisky and discussing his long eventful life.'[478] During the 1930s, Creasy had advertised his farmhouse, close to where Griffin grew up, as a place BUF activists could relax in a 'National Socialist atmosphere'. The British government had interned Creasy in 1940. MI5 retained him on their 'suspect list' until 1944 because, 'in the event of an Emergency his loyalty will not be beyond doubt.'[479] Griffin's interview with Creasy concluded that 'the best efforts of the BUF are sure to inspire the best of our folk in the years ahead.'[480] Griffin certainly perceived himself to be part of such a continuum, reportedly telling an interviewer 'there is a strong, direct link from Oswald Mosley to me.'[481] He offered only mild criticism of Mosley because he 'cut himself off from the people in symbolism and attitude' rather than through his fascist politics.[482]

Though the YNF had ultimately failed in its efforts to mobilise young people, Griffin still hoped to harness the 'skinhead revolt' and its unbridled racist machismo 'for the coming struggle for survival'.[483] To facilitate this, he sent *The Rune* to members of the British Hammerskins (BHS), for distribution through their networks.[484] Founded in 1995, BHS was the local franchise for the transnational Hammerskins network – 'run by skinheads for skinheads' – which emerged from the Hammerskin Nation, founded in Dallas, Texas in 1986, in an effort to impose a structure on the inchoate Nazi skinhead movement.[485] *The Rune* also advertised 'white power' music to its readership, which included everything from the Southern racist country compilation, *For Segregationists Only* (1971) to the latest Resistance Records' releases like *Fourteen Words* (1994) by Centurion, whose music was simply an 'audio incitement to violence'.[486] Griffin was especially impressed with *Cult of the Holy War* (1995) by RAHOWA – short for 'Racial Holy War' – a band fronted by Resistance Records founder George Eric Hawthorne. Griffin judged it 'simply the best White Power CD I've ever heard'. He was particularly enthused by its eugenicist lyrical content: 'Your love for the weak is a crime/I indict you for treason against Nature's design.' 'This to me sums up the biggest single reason for the relentless decline of our people in the last decades,' Griffin wrote. 'And the way in which super natural religions will seek to hinder the essential drive to reverse the de-evolutionary trend towards sub-humanity may well be the most important ideological battle-line of the next century.'[487]

The Rune also radiated the influence of the American Nazi underground upon Griffin, especially the '14 words' derived from the imprisoned former Klansman David Lane, then serving 190 years for racketeering and civil rights violations, following his involvement in The Order's 1984 murder of Jewish talk show host Alan Berg. Griffin had contemporaneously derided Berg as 'a particularly unpleasant anti-White media personality.'[488] 'The purpose of everything I do can be summed up in fourteen words,' Griffin told police in 1996.[489] *The Rune* published a long poem by Lane titled 'SS Lines & 14 words' and encouraged readers to write to him in prison where he languished, *The Rune* claimed, for activities against 'ZOG'.[490] Griffin subsequently contributed to Lane's *Focus Fourteen* newsletter, which introduced him as 'our friend and kinsman'. In apocalyptic tones, Griffin's article warned that the 'time of decision' was fast approaching. Either the white race would triumph or be doomed to 'extinction' in the mud, squalor and brutality of a 'global Haiti'. If white racial identity was to survive, the fight had to become transnational. 'This time, White nationalism is for export!' Griffin concluded: '14 WORDS WORLDWIDE!'[491] The implication of Griffin's remark, a play on Mussolini's comment that 'Fascism is not for export', is that 'white nationalism' and the fourteen words formed part of a historical continuum with fascism.

Joining the BNP

The Rune enabled Griffin to increase his involvement with the BNP. Despite regarding the BNP itself as 'an intellectually cretinous organisation',[492] Griffin viewed its Millwall victory in September 1993 with 'growing interest and admiration'.[493] He rejected the notion that democratic participation was a means in itself, however, reviling democracy as a 'hollow sham' that provided a 'constitutional rubber stamp' to make the 'change-over' of power palatable to the army and police. Taking aim at BNP 'modernisers' who had engineered its breakthrough, Griffin argued, that the future favoured 'strongly motivated fanatics' not 'electoralists'. Seek popularity, he contended, but understand: 'populism – which starts with thoughts of trimming policies, avoiding holding election rallies in areas which might cause Asian riots, sneering at skinheads and acquiescing in the Holocaust lie – is the kiss of death.' In Griffin's view:

> The electors of Millwall did not back a Post-Modernist Rightist Party, but what they perceived to be a strong, disciplined organisation with the ability to back up its slogan 'Defend Rights for Whites' with well-directed boots and fists. When the crunch comes, power is the product of force and will, not of rational debate.[494]

For Griffin, electoral success was 'the result of such power, not its cause' finding it 'significant' that Derek Beackon's election occurred following a violent attack upon an antiracist march in Bermondsey by BNP activists and Millwall football hooligans in August 1991.[495] Eddy Butler, the architect of the 'Rights for Whites' campaign, ridiculed Griffin's analysis. 'Nick Griffin was so reactionary,' Butler later recalled,

> that he failed to realise that we won for the very reason that *we did present ourselves as a post modernist rightist party* ... Nick Griffin came into the BNP to oppose me and what I was doing to try and modernise the party between 1993 and 1996.[496]

With the benefit of hindsight, BNP chairman John Tyndall perceived that Griffin simply saw the party as 'a good bandwagon to jump on'.[497] Griffin had begun corresponding with

Tyndall whilst working felling trees for the Forestry Commission in Central Wales.[498] Writing to Tyndall on 14 November 1994, Griffin highlighted his doubts about BNP electoral strategy. 'Bluntly, I am not at all sure I belong in the British National Party,' he stated:

> As you will have probably gathered from my *Rune* articles, my opinion of party political organisations with their primary focus on parliamentary elections is very similar to that espoused by Colin Jordan ... I believe that the BNP continues to put far too many eggs in the basket of mythical parliamentary democracy ... I cannot see why we should waste so much time appealing to dupes and morons when there is so much to be done recruiting, educating and equipping our power-winning machine. Further, I am not a *British* Nationalist. I am first and foremost a White Racialist, and second a Welsh Nationalist.[499]

Griffin's reference to Jordan spoke volumes. Griffin was also writing to Jordan during this period, offering to exchange copies of *The Rune* for *Gothic Ripples*.[500] 'I have found your series on the NS [National Socialist] Vanguard interesting and thought-provoking so far, and look forward to the remainder,' Griffin enthused.[501] Like Jordan, Griffin rejected mass political organisation as futile, believing the focus should be upon 'recruiting, training and equipping our elite "vanguard" so as to be able to channel and lead popular discontent when the crunch finally comes.'[502]

Whatever reservations he may or may not have because of such correspondence, Tyndall responded pragmatically to Griffin. With his leadership under acute pressure from two countervailing ideological tendencies – militant national socialists and party modernisers – Tyndall sought to use Griffin to burnish his own hard-line credentials. Despite his wife counselling him against it, Tyndall calculated that admitting Griffin to the BNP, thereby bringing 'new blood' into the party hierarchy, would bolster his leadership.[503] After all, *The Rune* gave Griffin a well-deserved reputation for ideological militancy. Significantly, from October 1995 onwards, *British Nationalist*, the BNP newspaper, began commending *The Rune* to its readership as 'Britain's fastest growing, liveliest Nationalist magazine'.[504]

Tyndall's efforts to tip the scales in favour of his own leadership reached their apogee when William Pierce addressed the November 1995 BNP rally, where 'several *Rune* staffers and contributors had time to talk with Dr. Pierce.'[505] Griffin also began contributing to Pierce's journal, *National Vanguard*, arguing that 'genetically as well as culturally,' the Celts 'played a major part in laying the foundations for the great achievements of the White race.'[506] Griffin's respect for Pierce remained undiminished, though their strategies diverged once Griffin embraced 'modernisation'. Following Pierce's death in July 2002, the BNP journal, *Identity*, which Griffin edited, published a fulsome obituary.[507]

In January 1996, Tyndall invited Griffin to contribute to *Spearhead*, which had become 'strident and unusually aggressive' in a bid 'to show impressionable youngsters' seduced by C18 that the party's 'peaceful and constitutional road was not boring or "soft"'.[508] Two months later, Tyndall appointed Griffin editor, allowing him to use the pseudonym 'Tom North'.[509] Although he edited the party's flagship publication, Griffin declined to join the BNP, however. He told Tyndall in July 1996 that he was not in sufficient 'ideological' agreement to do so.[510] Despite this, Tyndall treated Griffin as 'an integral part' of the party's leadership team from the outset. Griffin finally joined the BNP in February 1997.[511]

Griffin was 'useful' to Tyndall insofar as his own 'fairly extreme, hard-line background' helped him counter the ascendency of the 'moderating faction' led by Eddy Butler and Tony Lecomber, which also challenged his leadership.[512] Here, Tyndall was recycling a previous strategy. In 1977, he had appointed Richard Verrall, another ardent Holocaust denier, as *Spearhead* editor, signalling his rejection of 'populist' tendencies within the National Front.[513] Griffin rose to the occasion, attacking 'the spiral of sickly moderation' that had led successive nationalist groups 'to purge itself of "extremists", co-opt Winston Churchill as a posthumous honorary member and finally to drop the inconvenient commitment to compulsory repatriation just before its last members totter off to rejoin the Tory party.' 'We must never forget,' Griffin concluded, 'that, at the moment, it is more important to control the streets of a city than its council chamber.'[514] Lecomber retorted: 'All that kind of talk does is keep the BNP a small and isolated sect worshipping a long dead God, using long dead invocations and rituals.' Griffin's 'twin-track' strategy had already failed in Britain – C18 had 'flunked' the challenge – and the BNP was now firmly committed to a 'modern' European nationalist political strategy, argued Lecomber. 'Millwall showed the way – it's the Euro-Nationalist way!'[515]

To maintain ideological equilibrium, Tyndall ostensibly agreed with Lecomber, whilst simultaneously siding with Griffin on the necessity of controlling the streets.[516] Emboldened, Griffin continued arguing that anything other than a 'twin-track' strategy was 'a time-wasting fantasy'.[517] Violence, he contended, served a 'vital role' for building internal 'comradeship' and 'respect for our movement among the general public.' Moreover, when deployed against the 'right targets' and 'at times and places calculated to avoid unnecessary casualties,' violent confrontation with left-wing and ethnic minorities 'show us to be the disciplined defenders of the interests of the British people and not a gang of adventurist hooligans.' Physically controlling the streets was a prerequisite for political action because 'you can't knock on peoples' doors if you cannot walk down their streets' let alone engage in the 'serious business' of sinking communal roots.[518] *The Rune* subsequently boasted that Griffin's articles played a 'significant role' in Tyndall's 'firm action' to bring the 'populist experiment' to an end.[519] Griffin's vitriolic hectoring precipitated the departure of Butler and Michael Newland, the party treasurer, which bolstered Tyndall's position – or so he thought.[520]

In place of 'populism', Griffin advocated campaigning against the 'holohoax' – the defining feature of his anti-Semitism during this period. Issue 8 of *The Rune* titled 'Tales of the Holohoax Revisited' was almost entirely devoted to the subject. Famously, Griffin declared:

> I am well aware that the orthodox opinion is that 6 million Jews were gassed and cremated or turned into lampshades. Orthodox opinion also once held that the earth is flat ... I have reached the conclusion that the 'extermination' tale is a mixture of Allied wartime propaganda, extremely profitable lie, and latter-day witch-hysteria.[521]

Having established himself as one of the nation's most aggressive Holocaust deniers, Griffin rhetorically eviscerated those who prevaricated. David Irving's admission that an extermination programme *might* have existed at Treblinka, was tantamount to heresy. 'True Revisionists will not be fooled by this new twist to the sorry tale of the Hoax of the Twentieth Century,' Griffin raged.[522] In his view, the political purpose of Holocaust denial was to undermine Israel's moral legitimacy and, more broadly, that of European democracy too. As Griffin explained in *Spearhead* in February 1996:

> For the last fifty years the vision underlying all the vile sickness of this Age of Ruins has been the so-called 'Holocaust'. There is no need to elaborate on the way in which

the work of revisionist historians and forensic examinations have nailed the absurd lie that Nazi Germany, in the midst of a wartime shortage of labour and materials, gassed or otherwise systematically exterminated six million Jews. What does need to be stressed is the extent to which this nonsense underpins not just the Zionist state of Israel and Jewish power worldwide but the entire edifice of global liberalism.... The New World struggling to be born cannot do so until this lie is publicly exposed, ridiculed and destroyed ... members of the British National Party have a duty to be involved as active participants in the revisionist struggle.[523]

For Griffin: 'The Holocaust Lie is already dead – historically, legally and scientifically. But its rotting corpse still has to be buried. The academics [sic] have done their job. Now it is the duty of the publicists to spread their message.' Proselytising against the 'Holocaust Lie' was a 'historical and moral necessity' that 'every Nationalist should be involved in,' he argued. Publications like *Holocaust News* had also enabled NF and BNP activists to make 'common cause' regardless of party affiliations. 'That operation worked very well, but now needs updating,' Griffin contended. 'Surely basic co-operation in this crucial area is vital.'[524]

Griffin became an evangelist for Holocaust denial *sine qua non*. So much so in fact, that Tyndall later claimed to have advised him to put his time to better use:

I have a fat wad of private correspondence in my files consisting of letters from Nick in which he bangs on about the need to combat the 'Holocaust Myth' in letter after letter. In fact, I thought at the time that he had got the issue totally out of perspective, and I advised him that it would be better that he devote his time and energies to other matters. Enough good material, I said, had been written on the subject for us not to need any more.[525]

Unmoved, Griffin took his campaign to the streets. In July 1996, together with several BNP, NF, ITP and NA activists, he picketed a meeting in Coventry Cathedral staged by 'Action Reconciliation', an organisation seeking to foster reconciliation and atonement between Germans and Jews. Griffin and others handed out copies of a leaflet titled '95 Theses', authored by Manfred Roeder, the convicted German terrorist, which was obtained from a BNP supporter of 'German origin'.[526] The leaflet itself purportedly refuted 'the lie of German war "guilt"' for 'the events and non-events of WWII' – a coded reference to Holocaust denial. The government had previously excluded Roeder from Britain but 'that that didn't stop his ideas reaching Coventry,' gloated *The Rune*.[527]

The Rune trial

On 12 December 1996, Griffin was arrested for inciting racial hatred under Section 19(1) of the Public Order Act (1986) largely because of Issue 12 of *The Rune*.[528] Simultaneously, police arrested Paul Ballard in Surrey. The arrests followed a complaint from Griffin's former MP, Alex Carlisle QC, whom Griffin disparaged as 'this bloody Jew ... whose only claim to fame is that two of his grandparents died in the Holocaust.'[529] Whilst police searched his home, Griffin reassured a telephone caller that they were being respectful: 'They're very civilised. Not like the Mets. No Pakis and Jews.'[530] The police seized two computer hard disks, 106 floppy disks, the contents of a filing cabinet 'and many other papers, photos, books and tapes'. Griffin later boasted that 'the very first item I had seized by the political police was a calling card from David Lane's 14 WORD PRESS'.

Interviewed under caution, Griffin was granted bail until 3 March.[531] Unperturbed, Griffin appeared on a BBC Radio 5 Live phone-in on the following day, holding forth upon the 'hysterical' reaction of 'organised Jewry' to revelations that Waffen-SS soldiers had lived and worked in Britain since the end of the war.[532]

Undeterred by his impending prosecution, Griffin forged ahead with another project. He believed that an 'almost entirely Jewish' Hollywood was at 'the heart of the Race War – a war to turn the white nations of the world into a demoralised, atomized, mongrelised rabble.'[533] The 'Jewish' media, he argued, imparted a set of values that were in 'direct conflict with every instinct for self-preservation and every scrap of economic self-interest in the hearts, minds and blood of its targets.'[534] To prove that 'the Jews' controlled British media, Griffin penned an 'exposé' with his friend Mark Deavin, a recent doctoral graduate from the London School of Economics.[535] *Who Are the Mindbenders?* was launched at the annual BNP rally on 25 January 1997 – the centrepiece of 'Operation Daylight' through which the 'media conspiracy' ranged against the BNP would be exposed.[536] The BNP instructed local party units to concentrate upon getting *Mindbenders* 'into the hands of recent recruits who are starting to become active and to ask why the mass media are so consistently anti-BNP and anti-British.'[537] Griffin's unoriginal thesis, which accused Jews of 'providing us with an endless diet of pro-multiracial, pro-homosexual, anti-British trash,' drew upon a long lineage including, most recently, William Pierce's *Who Rules America?* (1996). *The Rune* described this booklet as a 'well researched expose of the extent to which the anti-White mass media is dominated by Jews.' Griffin quoted from it extensively.[538]

Whilst awaiting trial, and with Tyndall's blessing, Griffin secretly sought to facilitate a 'merger' between the BNP and the NF. Through his correspondence with Wayne Ashcroft, the West Midlands NF organiser, which began in July 1995,[539] Griffin tried to persuade NF activists of the advantages of pooling resources.[540] Whilst Ashcroft proved amenable to Griffin's entreaties, the initiative ultimately stumbled upon the intransigence of NF leader John McAuley, who saw nothing to gain from surrendering his party's name or resources to the BNP, an organisation he had already proscribed as 'nazi' in late 1994.[541]

Throughout this period, undercover journalists for the investigative current affairs television programme, *The Cook Report*, working in conjunction with the anti-fascist magazine, *Searchlight*, were also secretly filming Griffin. Prior to his arrest, two men posing as FN officials had approached Griffin in November 1996. Having convinced himself of their bona fides, Griffin spent the following five months outlining how, with the necessary finance, he could lead the extreme right out of the doldrums. His carefully costed 'shopping list' included plans for a 'White Europe radio station' in Eastern Europe, written with Steve Cartwright, the Scottish B&H organiser, which savoured of Mosley and Jordan's past efforts to create off-shore radio stations.[542] Tyndall was 'very taken' with the idea, though Griffin to wanted to ensure the venture to remain 'semi-autonomous' of the BNP.[543] Their proposals also included a bid to establish the British end of the *Resistance* music operation. 'I am in regular telephone contact with its founding editor [George Eric Hawthorne]. I would be delighted to organise a business liaison in this field,' Griffin revealed to his interlocutors.[544] At some juncture, Griffin realised the deception, decrying the programme as 'an MI5 operation, designed to create a split within the BNP.' He did not do so, however, before the journalists had secretly recorded him outlining his pretentions to lead the BNP, plans to merge the NF into the BNP, and his intention to update *Did Six Million Really Die?*[545] *The Truth Behind the Front* broadcast in June 1997. Griffin subsequently complained to the Broadcasting Standards Commission, which dismissed his claims of 'unfair and unjust treatment'.[546]

Whilst *The Cook Report* furthered Griffin's public profile as a racist extremist, conversely, it also enhanced his credentials internally. He continued running training seminars for BNP organisers and activists and was in demand as a speaker at regional BNP meetings, eager to hear him discuss his impending court case.[547] Though he no longer publicly espoused 'Blood and Soil' rhetoric, Griffin remained committed to his ruralised vision. He orchestrated BNP attendance at the Country Rally in September in an effort to broaden party appeal to rural areas and 'white flight' towns instead of remaining entrained upon 'multi-racial' urban areas.[548] He also helped produce a specialised newspaper, *The Countryman*, for distribution at the Countryside Alliance march in the following March and other rural events.[549] Following an appearance at Harrow Crown Court on the previous day, and ignoring advice from two lawyers not to attend, Griffin capped the year's activity by addressing the annual BNP rally on 22 November alongside Tyndall and Edmonds.[550] The New Year saw him addressing the party's annual planning conference on 24 January, emphasising the need for concentrating upon 'local' issues.[551]

To raise funds and generate publicity for his court case, Griffin sold extracts of his police interview on cassette tapes for a 'minimum donation' of £7 to his 'Publicity for Freedom' fund.[552] The Historical Review Press, run by Anthony Hancock, one of the principal purveyors of Holocaust denial material in Europe, sold the tapes.[553] Whilst Griffin revelled in the publicity, he was clearly unhappy that the trial, scheduled for 10 December 1997, was at Harrow Crown Court, West London. He had wanted the case heard in Wales 'where I could be judged by my peers' (i.e. whites) and not in Harrow, 'with its multiracial catchment area for jurors'.[554] Griffin pleaded not guilty, unlike Ballard. The judge adjourned the trial, rescheduling it for 27–30 April 1998. 'The delay is good for Nick,' argued *British Nationalist*, 'because the extra time involved will enable him to develop vital defence strategies and flesh out existing defence lines.'[555]

Griffin's strategy included issuing a challenge to the Crown Prosecution Service. He would plead guilty, if they could:

1 Either show me a picture of a Nazi gas chamber, and explain the process whereby it was used as an instrument of mass murder;
2 Or produce a single coloured person who was attacked assaulted or even insulted by a white who was incited to 'racial hatred' as a result of reading Issue 12 of *The Rune*;
3 Or provide a single 'eye-witness' to a homicidal mass gassing, or a single Exterminationist academic, whose evidence can stand up to a cross examination.

Griffin also arranged for Professor Robert Faurisson, the French Holocaust denier, to testify at his trial. Faurisson and his 'research assistant' had already flown over from France in December but would return in April.[556] Griffin hoped to turn his prosecution into the 'British Zündel Trial'.[557] Zündel himself offered encouragement and 'promised he will help his British cousins to the best of his abilities ... the groundwork laid by the two Zündel Trials should be of immense, time-saving and strategic as well as media value to the defense efforts.' To maximise publicity, Griffin announced he would fly in witnesses 'from all over the world' and subpoena 'Exterminationist propagandists' in order 'to rip up their disgusting Blood Libel against the German people and Europe civilisation to shreds in open court.'[558] His prosecution, the BNP claimed, was a latter day 'Witch Trial' against those who refused to believe the 'gas chamber hoax'. The BNP mobilised its activists to picket the offices of Amnesty International and Liberty for not defending Griffin.[559]

Griffin's defence strategy also included arguing that C18 produced material that was far more incendiary than *The Rune* which, he claimed, advocated democratic change, albeit in 'shrill' and 'impolite' language, in order to prevent activists joining C18.[560] This 'pacifist stance' led to threatening calls from C18, Griffin claimed, not to mention threats to do him physical harm in C18 publications.[561] Actually, rather than displaying hostility to Griffin, *The Order*, considered *The Rune* to be 'well worth getting'.[562] Steve Cartwright wrote,

> If observers look close enough, they will see that Griffin has had a pretty free ride off C18, particularly if you compare the pages and pages of anti-Tyndall nonsense that used to appear in C18 magazines like *Thor-Would* and *The Order*. This easy ride was simply down to an 'understanding' between Griffin and the leadership of C18.[563]

Though C18 remained proscribed by the BNP, Griffin's 'understanding' with its leadership extended to him requesting they help him prepare his defence strategy, something of an irony since he had recently derided its members as 'human shit' on *The Cook Report*. Through Cartwright, Griffin contacted one of C18's leading lights, Will 'The Beast' Browning, from whom he acquired literature and other materials to prove his case about the inflammatory nature of their publications. Cartwright recalled:

> Griffin told me to tell Will [Browning] that he regarded C18 as being on 'the same side' and that he would be eternally grateful (some hope) if he could furnish Griffin with the documents for his defence. Will agreed to help Griffin and within a few days a bumper pack of C18 stuff arrived in Wales. Griffin, phoned me up to confirm the package had arrived safely and to pass on his thanks to C18. Griffin was particularly tickled by the name of the parcel sender – Mr Beast, London.[564]

Whilst awaiting trial, Griffin continued fund-raising the £5,000 he believed necessary to turn his prosecution into a platform for his political views. By April, he had raised just £2,000.[565] Nottinghamshire BNP held a 'Dutch auction' for Griffin on 30 November 1997, whilst on 6 December the 'white power' bands Celtic Warrior and Whitelaw staged a benefit concert for him, attended by local BNP, BM and Hammerskins activists.[566]

Returning to Harrow Crown Court on 27 April 1998, Griffin insisted that the jury hear the full, unedited record of his police interview, which ran to one-and-three-quarter hours. On the following day, Faurisson provided 'expert' testimony that Griffin's 'apparently unorthodox opinions on certain aspects of the Second World War were in fact based on fact.' Ironically, a Parisian court convicted Faurisson of 'disputing a crime against humanity' on the very day he testified in Griffin's defence. Doubting the value of such testimony, the judge allotted Faurisson two-and-a-half minutes to sum up his case. Griffin's other defence witnesses, Michael Newland, the BNP press officer and Colin Smith, the Bexley and Dartford BNP organiser, sought to convince the jury that Griffin was not a racist and that, on his suggestion, the BNP worked with black people to promote repatriation.[567] To reinforce this point, Osiris Akkebala, the Black separatist, was Griffin's final witness. Akkebala appeared in court in full tribal robes, took his oath on the *Egyptian Book of the Dead*, and gave Griffin a character reference, explaining in 'almost identical words to express his views about the need for Black identity and survival as Nick had used in connection with the white people of Britain.'[568] Griffin's flawed reasoning was that if a Black separatist made identical arguments, then his own formulations were not racist.

Despite boasting 'the most professional and well organised defence team ever put together in a British Race Law case', the jury found Griffin guilty. The judge sentenced Griffin to nine months' imprisonment, suspended for two years, and fined him £2,300. Ballard who pled guilty, received six months, suspended for two years, and a £300 fine.[569] A court rejected Griffin's appeal, forcing him to pay off his fine at £100 a month.[570] The BNP claimed the verdict was a 'smashing victory'. *The Rune* never appeared again, however.[571]

Moderniser

Ironically, whilst his trial cemented his position as a hard-liner, Griffin was already repositioning himself as an evangelist for party 'modernisation'. As early as January 1997, he began pushing for further electoral engagement, thereby 'using the methods of democracy to fight the system which uses them as a cloak for the rule of vested interests.'[572] He attached himself to the clique surrounding *The Patriot*, a magazine founded in spring 1997 by Tony Lecomber, editor of the BNP newspaper, *British Nationalist*, whose 'populist' strategy Griffin had previously reviled. His volte-face was ironic insofar as Griffin's ideological extremity had been a catalyst for the modernising faction in the first place. 'I know you think that the BNP is a busted flush – because of J.T. [John Tyndall],' Lecomber wrote to Eddy Butler, whom he was trying to induce to re-join the party:

> But even so, it is easier to do good with the BNP than to start anew. J.T. and Griffin particularly last year were writing some real drivel – particularly Griffin. *Patriot*, I can tell you, has had a really *big* impact. I only conceived of it after Griffin's dribblings in *Spearhead*. If it weren't for that, I wouldn't have done it.[573]

BNP racial policy or, more accurately, the public's perception of it, became a key battleground between party 'modernisers' and 'hardliners'. Griffin weighed into the debate in November 1998, arguing in *Spearhead* for a 'gradualist approach' regarding the public presentation of race. Tyndall deemed the idea worthy of 'internal debate', provided there was no compromise on the 'bottom line' of restoring 'the white Britain our grandfathers knew'. Griffin agreed. Indeed, his personal position was more intransigent than the BNP manifesto, which only pledged to return Britain to the status quo ante prior to 1948. This was not enough for Griffin. He stated:

> I want to see Britain become the 99 per cent genetically white country she was just eleven years before I was born, and I want to die knowing that I have helped to set her on a course whereby her future genetic makeup will one day not even resemble that of January 1948, but that of July 1914, nothing will ever turn me from working for that final vision.[574]

Griffin belatedly recognised the policy of 'compulsory' repatriation was not 'saleable' to the British electorate. Moving the BNP away from its commitment to compulsory repatriation was undoubtedly key to overhauling public perceptions of the party but Griffin's advocacy of 'voluntary' repatriation was somewhat duplicitous since, as he put it, public understanding of the development, 'may very well be very different from the interpretation which you and I might give it.' It was a different means to the same end. The more non-whites who volunteered to go 'home', the more Britain would resemble a white 'homeland' leading to more departures. 'Why would any even *want* to say in a country which manifestly didn't want them,' asked Griffin? Despite the rhetorical shift, Griffin remained committed to the 'eventual ideal' of a mono-racial Britain. Quietly, the BNP would continue to educate its membership, 'in the realities of racial politics, even though they are of no great interest to the public at large.'[575]

Griffin's *Spearhead* article produced 'the largest postbag for some years', the majority in agreement with him. John Bean, leader of the first incarnation of the BNP, which many modernisers took as a model for emulation, added his support.[576] Griffin won the argument. *British Nationalist* began presenting BNP racial policy in terms of ethno-plurality rather than biology.[577] Human diversity 'is the thing which gives people their sense of identity and belonging,' Griffin explained. 'Now I can defend that on *Newsnight* or *Question Time* in a way that everyone of vaguely good will or independent thought out there will think "yeah, that's reasonable enough, that's not racist bigotry".'[578]

Tyndall assented to this policy change because, he later claimed, he recognised Griffin was using the issue to outmanoeuvre him politically, painting him as extreme and thus setting the stage for a leadership challenge. He, therefore, consented to the cosmetic change because behind it remained an 'unwritten subsidiary clause' that stipulated that 'if a voluntary policy did not succeed in ensuring the preservation of our British ethnic identity and eliminating inter-communal strife in the country, alternative policies would become an option.'[579] Writing in the following year after Griffin's leadership challenge had indeed materialised, Tyndall argued that no 'fundamental [ideological] differences' existed with him and his would-be usurper. 'The conflict arises solely out of the fact that he wants to be leader.'[580]

Griffin once derided the quest for 'respectability' as 'a hunt for fools' gold.' Now, however, he planted himself in the vanguard of those seeking to overhaul those aspects of BNP ideology and praxis 'which make us unelectable'. For Griffin, this meant professionalising the party's media strategy. Believing the BNP was engaged in 'a life and death struggle for white survival, not a fancy dress party', Griffin counselled 'more guile' and less 'careless extremism' was necessary in communicating core racial concerns to the electorate. 'As long as our own cadres understand the full implications of our struggle,' wrote Griffin, 'then there is no need for us to do anything to give the public cause for concern.' The BNP must project an image of 'moderate reasonableness', he essayed. This was the difference between having the 'will to win' and the 'will to do what is necessary to win.' Electability was the pragmatic goal of Griffin's modernisation drive. 'Of course we must teach the truth to the hardcore, for like you, I do not intend to allow this movement to lose its way,' Griffin told *The Patriot*: 'But when it comes to influencing the public, forget about racial differences, genetics, Zionism, historical revisionism and so on – all ordinary people want to know is what we can do for them that other parties can't or won't.'[581]

Racial nationalist ideology, red in tooth and claw, was concealed beneath four 'idealistic, unobjectionable, motherhood and apple pie concepts' – 'freedom', 'security', 'identity' and 'democracy' ('FSID'), which became the party's new 'media friendly' mantra. 'Identity' was the core concept because it re-framed 'all the issues connected with mass immigration without touching off the negative Pavlovian conditioning which decades of brainwashing have associated with the word "race".' The other three points were only possible, and indeed only had meaning for Griffin, if racially codified however, an argument that harked back to the central thesis of Joe Pearce's *Fight for Freedom* (1984).[582]

Refocusing the party's semantic strategy around 'FISD' saw the BNP seeking to mimic the 'mobility' of Front National (FN) ideological discourse which eschewed 'fixed' rhetorical 'signifiers' in favour of fluidity and ambiguity, enabling it to synthesise contradictory viewpoints and, in doing so, appeal to the broadest possible constituency without endangering party unity or alienating public support. With *Daily Express* opinion polls indicating a potentially large reservoir of support for a party like the FN in Britain,[583] Griffin, and strategists like Deavin, believed that although Jean-Marie Le Pen was committed to 'civic' nationalism, they too could ride the tiger of 'national-populism' whilst remaining faithful to racial nationalist ideals.[584] Griffin became conversant with the FN formula having read *The National Front and French Politics* (1995) during the filming of *The Cook Report* 'sting' in order to learn about his supposed French interlocutors. His study of FN strategy, as described in the book, turned Griffin, in his own words, from 'a crazy-eyed extremist into a born-again moderate'.[585] He penned a long appreciation of the FN in *Spearhead*, March 1997, concluding that 'our organisation and tactics will increasingly mirror those of the FN ... we too can get to Vitrolles' – a reference to the southern French town with a recently elected FN mayor.[586]

Keen to view FN success first-hand, Griffin attended its *Fête Bleu, Blanc Rouge* festival in Paris in May 1998. Duly impressed, it subsequently served as a model for his party's own Red, White and Blue (RWB) festival, which became the centrepiece of his attempts to project a family-friendly image of the BNP.[587] Griffin was careful, however, to downplay the 'imported parts of our worldview, ideology and tradition'. This could be 'politically damaging'. BNP activists were urged therefore to familiarise themselves with the 'very rich seam' of British anti-liberal thinkers like Anthony Ludovici.[588]

'New Leader, Same Cause'

Tyndall remained an implacable obstacle to Griffin's political ambitions of ruling the BNP as his own personal fiefdom. Griffin had long denied any desire to lead the BNP. Replying to this very question in July 1997, he asserted:

> It's a lonely and thankless task with a frightening burden of responsibility. I believe that I could do it, in some ways I'd like to try. But a combination of relative inexperience and family commitments means that this is not on the cards for quite some years to come.[589]

He scoffed at the presumption that someone such as himself, who had only been involved for a 'fraction' of the time as others, could 'leap frog' to the top.[590] Two years later, however, as the party embarked upon its European election campaign in February 1999, Griffin announced his leadership challenge standing as a 'moderate' and 'reformist' candidate. It was a superficial stance given that Germar Rudolf, a German Holocaust denier fleeing a fourteen-month prison sentence had visited him that month. Arriving in Britain, Rudolf had set up shop in Hastings from whence he ran his own 'revisionist' publishing outfit.[591] This was Griffin's gift, however. He appealed simultaneously to both the modernising and Nazi factions of the party. His 'reformist' image won over those desirous of an electorally credible party whilst his conviction for inciting racial hatred in 1998 established his personal credentials amongst the party's hard-core activists. 'I wouldn't have become BNP leader without it,' he conceded.[592]

Efforts to establish the BNP as a 'modern' party received a blow in the midst of its European election campaign when a former activist, David Copeland, planted several nail bombs targeting London's black, Asian and gay communities. His final terrorist attack on the Admiral Duncan pub in Soho, the heart of London's gay community, on 30 April killed three people, including a pregnant woman and her unborn child, and injured seventy-nine, four seriously. Speaking of his motivation for the atrocity, Copeland subsequently confessed:

> If you've read the *Turner Diaries*, you know the year 2000 there'll be the uprising and all that, racial violence on the streets. My aim was political. It was to cause a racial war in this country. There'd be a backlash from the ethnic minorities, then all the white people will go out and vote BNP.[593]

Though Copeland had drifted into the NSM before embarking upon his terrorist campaign, photographs quickly emerged of him standing with a bloodied Tyndall in the aftermath of an anti-fascist attack upon him and his wife as they made their way to the party's fifteenth anniversary dinner in Stratford, East London on 20 September 1997.[594] The photographs were particularly embarrassing for Tyndall personally, as he fought tooth and nail to fend off Griffin's challenge.[595]

Tyndall felt no responsibility for the atrocity. 'One isn't responsible for the oddballs. Anything on the fringe is likely to attract them,' he dismissively told a journalist.[596] The BNP moved to distance itself from Copeland, conspiratorially claimed the bombings could be 'the work of the state itself.'[597] Griffin muddied the waters in a similarly conspiratorial fashion.[598] He later portrayed Copeland as the real victim, 'driven to distraction by a modern multiracial society, he joined us as a possible way out and, seeing no progress at that time, he left and went mad. He really is not our responsibility.'[599] Griffin also went on the offensive against Copeland's victims. 'The footage of dozens of "gay" demonstrators flaunting their perversion in front of the world's journalists showed just why so many ordinary people find these creatures so repulsive,' he wrote.[600]

Appalled by Griffin's 'lying hypocrisy', Martin Webster re-emerged, publicly declaring that he had had a four-year homosexual relationship with Griffin, which had ended in 1981. *Come for an 'Outing' Down Memory Lane* appeared in September, the month of the leadership election.[601] The revelations, which Griffin strenuously denied as 'a pack of lies from a spiteful old man', made no difference either to his future stance on homosexuality (a 'behavioural deviancy' he wished to see 'pushed humanely but firmly back into the closet') or indeed the outcome of the vote.[602] The leadership campaign, which was characterised by mud-slinging and dirty tricks on both sides,[603] culminated in September 1999. Griffin won 62 per cent of the secret postal ballot, compared to Tyndall's 38 per cent on an 80 per cent turnout. Having only joined the BNP in February 1997, Griffin was now leader.[604] The party's modernising faction led by Lecomber rejoiced. 'It's going to be an exciting time for nationalism and the BNP!' declared *British Nationalist*.[605] *The Patriot* meanwhile proclaimed 'New Millennium, New Leader'.[606] Internally, however, BNP activists were reassured: 'New Leader, Same Cause'.[607] Indeed, Griffin hastily reaffirmed that the BNP 'was still committed to an all-White Britain.'[608] He also moved to cement his position by promoting supporters like Lecomber to key positions whilst side-lining Tyndall and his followers, many of whom resigned in protest. Further marginalising Tyndall's influence, Griffin replaced *Spearhead* as the official BNP organ with *Identity*, modelled on the FN journal *Identité* (1989–1996), which was firmly under his control. Ultimately, Griffin would force Tyndall out of the party altogether (see Chapter 5).

Oldham

The subsequent 'modernisation' of the BNP under Griffin's leadership need not detain us here since it has been more than adequately covered elsewhere.[609] Suffice to say that Griffin and his cohorts set about 'professionalising' the BNP apparatus, introducing: activist training programmes; structural decentralisation; 'community' campaigning with local 'patriot' leaflets; a 'Media Monitoring Unit' to rebut 'negative' media portrayals of the party; and the further development of satellite organisations or 'circles' as a mechanism for developing 'counter-power'. There was nothing 'new' here. Griffin simply recycled initiatives from his days as a 'political soldier' – including proposals to create an armed citizenry, which would appear in its 2005 general election manifesto, and the 'voting member' system which he would institute to safeguard ideological control over the party once it began experiencing a measure of public support.[610] That Griffin remained wedded to 'third position' politics was unsurprising. After all, Griffin had maintained his political relationship with Roberto Fiore who, he asserted in 2009, was a 'tremendous influence for good on this party [the BNP] and on the nationalist cause in Britain.'[611] Ironically, Fiore had recently declared that 'I have no difficulty in saying that I have sympathy for certain aspects of fascism.'[612]

Griffin's revamped BNP connected with two external events that transformed the party's fortunes: riots across a series of de-industrialised northern cities over the summer in 2001; and al-Qaeda's attack on the Twin Towers on 9/11. Tensions in the Lancashire town of Oldham, where the BNP had long talked up the prospects of 'race war', spilled over into rioting on 26 May as Asian and white youths fought one another in the streets. Griffin had been in the town earlier that day visiting a local pub where a 'white mob' had gathered. He was not welcome. C18 activist Mark Atkinson threatened to 'do him' whilst Griffin pleaded 'I don't have a problem with C18. We shouldn't fall out over petty things, after all, we're all on the same side. We should all pull together.'[613]

Following the riots, Griffin announced his candidacy for Oldham West and Royton on St George's Day. The BNP embarked upon an intensive doorstep campaign in the constituency, coupled with a drive for 'Equal Rights for Oldham Whites' that in one incidence saw Griffin leading a demonstration outside Oldham police station.[614] Griffin's solution for riot-scarred Oldham was, as it had been following riots in 1981 and 1985, racial segregation, though this time he claimed Belfast-style 'peace lines' between communities as his model to physically separate communities already leading 'parallel lives'.[615]

To shore up his campaign financially, Griffin and his wife, departed to the United States, to embark upon a six-day speaking tour, arranged for him by Mark Cotterill's American Friends of the BNP (AF-BNP), a last opportunity for foreign fund-raising before impending legal restrictions neutered such activities.[616] The trip also enabled Griffin to network with a plethora of American extreme right-wing activists. Those attending the second meeting, which took place in Arlington, Virginia, on 12 May, held a two minutes' silence for Byron De La Beckwith, the white supremacist who murdered Civil Rights leader Medgar Evers in 1963, who had recently died in prison. Griffin's tour raised 'several thousand dollars' for the BNP.[617]

The BNP stood thirty-three candidates in the 2001 general election. Overall, the results themselves were hardly startling; in Bethnal Green and Bow, the vote dropped from 7.5 per cent to 3 per cent. What garnered national headlines, however, were the results in Oldham and Burnley, which highlighted the impact of the riots across the North West. In Oldham West and Royton, Griffin polled 6,552 votes (16.4 per cent), the highest election result for the extreme right in a general election since October 1974 when the NF polled 7.83 per cent in Newham South.[618] The Returning Officer forbade speeches from the platform for fear the BNP would use it to intensify racial tension. Griffin appeared on the platform wearing a gag as a symbolic gesture, as did Mick Treacy, the Oldham organiser, who polled 5,091 votes (11.2 per cent) in neighbouring Oldham East and Saddleworth. In the nearby Lancashire mill-town of Burnley, the BNP polled 4,151 votes (11.3 per cent).

When rioting broke out in Burnley on 23–24 June and Bradford on 7 July, the latter following a confrontation between the ANL and NF activists earlier in the day, it was all grist to the BNP mill. *Identity*'s front cover featured a map of towns depicted by fiery icons to denote scenes of 'race riot' or 'race-related skirmish' and asked: 'Is this going to be a long hot summer?' It was a rhetorical question since Griffin already believed that as 'the liberal fantasy of multi-racial harmony is dead and gone forever ... the violence we have seen so far is likely to be dwarfed in its scale, ferocity and extent by the troubles of August and September.'[619]

Griffin's grim racial prognosticating received a considerable fillip when al-Qaeda attacked the World Trade Centre and the Pentagon on 11 September 2001. Serendipitously for Griffin, this occurred just as his normalisation strategy was embedding itself. Again, Griffin displayed ambivalence towards the victims of the atrocity, characterising the Twin Towers as 'a twin Tower of Babel – part of the power structure of a global capitalism which has no loyalty to our ethnic group.'[620] This did not stop him exploiting the tragedy to inflame anti-Muslim sentiment whilst simultaneously propagating the anti-Semitic conspiracy theory that the atrocity was an 'inside job'.[621] Griffin was quick to perceive 9/11 as a 'crucial turning point', one he believed would inaugurate a 'New Crusade for the Survival of the West'. The BNP ramped up its anti-Islam campaign, locally and nationally. Whilst Griffin supported military strikes against bin Laden and the Taliban because 'it was vital for the White Man to be seen to stand up and hit back' he opposed the expanding 'war on terror'.[622] This was because he viewed it as 'a cloak for the rapid advance of an assortment of globalist schemes designed to hasten the advent of the "New World Order".' Paradoxically, however, Griffin also believed that 'nothing could do a better job of highlighting the problems of immigration at home' than Britain becoming embroiled in a 'no-win' war abroad.[623]

Griffin mobilised immediately. He demanded the closure of 'every last' mosque in Britain influenced by Saudi-inspired Wahhabi Islam and the expulsion of 'anyone who adheres to this brutal creed'.[624] BNP activists began distributing leaflets describing 'Islam' as an acronym for 'Intolerance, Slaughter, Looting, Arson and Molestation of Women'.[625] 'Within hours of the horror,' boasted *Identity*, 'we had on our website a downloadable leaflet pointing out to parents their right to withdraw their children from Religious Instruction lessons if they don't want them taught about Islam or other foreign religions.'[626] Seeking to exacerbate ethnic cleavages, Griffin claimed that the violence was 'not an Asian problem, but a Muslim problem', making common cause in the process with a small handful of Hindu and Sikh extremists, producing a pamphlet and audiocassette aimed at educating people about the 'nature of the beast'.[627] Party recruitment accelerated fivefold over what it had been in the previous autumn.[628] At the annual Mansfield BNP Halloween/ Guy Fawkes' night festivity, Griffin celebrated with members, lighting a bonfire crowned with an effigy of bin Laden.[629]

Griffin's desire to concentrate *public* BNP propaganda against Islam rather than the Jews deepened the gulf between him and Tyndall who remained influential with the party's old guard. Despite viewing the 'Zionist distortion' of Western politics as the 'root' cause of

Islamic fundamentalism, Griffin perceived that even if Israel did not exist Islam would remain a 'mortal threat' to the West because of immigration. BNP publications denounced as 'reactionary' those who viewed Islam as a potential ally against Israel, a position Griffin once espoused as 'revolutionary'.[630] Tactically, anti-Muslim politicking was about 'the art of the possible' for Griffin. 'Which enemy is it in our political interest to be seen to be opposing more vigorously at the moment?' he asked rhetorically. 'To a party aiming to win seats in London, the West Midlands and the former mill-towns of Northern England, the answer should be pretty obvious.'[631] 'Islam' became the campaign issue *sine qua non*:

> *This* is the factor which is going to dominate politics for decades to come. *This* is the enemy that the public can see and understand. *This* is the threat that can bring us to power. *This* is the Big Issue on which we must concentrate in order to wake people up and make them look at what we have to offer all around.[632]

Griffin had hard words for those who refused to grasp the nettle, particularly in the United States. Addressing the 'white nationalist' American Renaissance conference in May 2002, Griffin's keynote address castigated his audience for failing to follow his lead. 'It's a disgrace, from what I've seen,' Griffin opined,

> that we made more out of September 11 in Britain in terms of finding ways to prise open cracks in multi-racial society and destroy it, which has to be our aim, we made more out of September 11 in Britain than American nationalists made in America and that is unbelievable. It really is. You should be ashamed of yourselves.[633]

Yet, even as Griffin sought to exploit jihadist terrorism for political gain, there was a certain symmetry in their respective world-views. Publicly debating the firebrand Islamist preacher Abu Hamza al-Masri (currently serving a life sentence without the possibility of parole for terrorism offences) in July 2002, Griffin found that their views converged. Abu Hamza 'surprised the liberal audience' by exhorting them to support the BNP, 'rather than encouraging homosexuality and justifying the exploitation of the third World and British mortgage payers by defending banking usury.' Abu Hamza stated that Muslims should leave Britain if it refused to become an Islamic state, but feared oppression in the Middle East. Griffin outlined BNP foreign policy to him, claiming it would break the exploitation of 'international banks and multinationals' and direct foreign aid and trade deals 'in such a way as to build up the economies of countries taking their countrymen back from Britain.' On this, they agreed too. 'Abu Hamsa acknowledged that he would be very happy with this and would regard it as a just end to the failed multiculti experiment,' reported the BNP website.[634]

'Hard talk, Hobbyism and Hitler'

Riots, racial violence and jihadist terrorism formed a backdrop for the BNP's subsequent electoral insurgency at the local level, though it by no means explained it.[635] Having won three council seats in the northern mill town of Burnley in the May 2002, four years later, it had fifty-six across the country. Whilst party activists created local legitimacy for themselves, Griffin was keen to safeguard this at a national level too. Griffin understood, rightly, that one of the party's worst enemies was itself and that future progress could very well be undermined by a propensity for 'Hard talk, Hobbyism and Hitler' amongst party activists.

With attaining further council seats being a real possibility, Griffin lambasted party activists who harboured 'a perverted nostalgia for the 1930s' and denounced Hitler as a 'disaster not just for Germany, but for the entire white race', which enraged and alienated BNP hardliners.[636] Griffin's attempt to fumigate the BNP ideologically included ousting John Tyndall from the party he had founded. Griffin eviscerated Tyndall in July 2003 as a 'Hollywood Nazi' out of step with 'modern' nationalism.[637] Tyndall's expulsion in October 2003 was widely supported. Many would later regret the decision, however. Tyndall's former colleague, John Bean, *Identity*'s editor, had supported Griffin's leadership, but with the benefit of hindsight 'came to realise that Tyndall's honesty and reliability might have offset some of his political baggage – which turned out to be not much heavier than Griffin's.'[638]

Griffin and his colleagues understood that whilst consolidating their gains in Burnley was important, they had to push beyond its confines. 'We must not become the Burnley party in the same way that we became the Tower Hamlets party in 1993–1994,' warned Lecomber. 'That way leads to ruin.'[639] Although Griffin personally failed to secure a seat in Oldham's Chadderton North ward in the 2003 local elections, the overall results were promising. The party won seats in West Yorkshire (Bradford, Calderdale and Kirklees); the West Midlands (Stoke-on-Trent, Dudley and Sandwell); and the South East (Broxbourne), subsequently extending into the outer East London districts of Barking and Dagenham and Epping Forest. The BNP would go on to consolidate its support in distinct geographical localities, a trend evident after the 2007 local elections which saw over half of the party's then forty-six councillors concentrated in just four areas: Barking and Dagenham, Epping Forest, Stoke-on-Trent, and Burnley.[640]

Within such localities, the BNP largely gained a foothold in wards that represented ethnically homogenous 'white enclaves' within ethnically diverse but economically deprived urban areas.[641] Much of its support came from mobilising a distinct support base of 'predominantly middle-aged working-class men with few educational qualifications' who were profoundly hostile to Muslim communities, the pace of demographic change and the political establishment: the archetypal 'angry white men'.[642] Despite applauding the gains, Griffin had no actual interest in local democracy. The growing cohort of BNP councillors were 'propagandists against the system, rather than social workers for it … Our job isn't to make it work a bit less unfairly, but to discredit and dismantle the entire edifice of treason and ethno-cultural destruction.'[643]

Whilst building up the party's local electoral machine, Griffin also opposed the invasion of Iraq in March 2003, arguing that it would stoke Muslim resentment abroad, whilst Labour's 'open door' immigration policy granted foreign jihadists 'the freedom to come here at will and organise terrorist attacks and violence against us.'[644] He predicted that war abroad would spark 'civil war' at home. Consequently, multiculturalism 'will die as the sounds of the dusty conflict in the Middle East echo through the streets of the West.'[645] This was 'our great opportunity,' Griffin argued.[646] The Iraq War also saw the party's conspiratorial anti-Semitism resurface through accusations that that conflict represented a 'Zionist' and neo-conservative conspiracy – a recycling of Mosley's 'Jews' war' thesis. 'It's a war about oil and Israel!' proclaimed *Voice of Freedom*.[647] Lord Levy, Labour's fund-raiser, represented a 'wealthy circle of Zionist backers who have bought the Labour party,' Griffin claimed.[648] In the same vein, *Voice of Freedom* declared that 'Tony Blair swapped British blood for donations from a clique of filthy-rich Zionist businessmen.'[649] This particular accusation invoked numerous anti-Semitic stereotypes: 'the Jew' as capitalist; rootless and disloyal; war-maker and profiteer; feasting vampire-like on British and *ergo* Christian 'blood' – the medieval canard of the 'blood libel'.[650]

Following the cessation of military action in May 2003, *Identity*'s editor, John Bean, declared Israel the 'only benefactor' of the conflict. The 2005 BNP manifesto enshrined this belief, pledging 'we will never again involve British troops in any more American "wars for oil" or neo-con adventures on behalf of the Zionist government of Israel.'[651] Ironically, by 2006, Bean perceived that the 'anti-Semitic hysteria' over the Iraq War, which the BNP willing fuelled, had deflected attention away from the responsibility Bush and Blair bore for the war. 'The real powers are quite likely laughing their heads off.'[652]

Griffin entered the 2004 European election campaign believing that the BNP could realistically return five MEPs though his 'best case scenario' was seven. Only the 'credibility gap' stood in the way of the BNP realizing up to 17 per cent of the vote, Griffin claimed.[653] He was concerned, however, that UKIP would split the vote. Griffin had once disparaged UKIP – as Leese and Jordan before him had derided the BUF and the NF – as a 'kosher' party.[654] Now, however, he tempered his rhetoric, simply denouncing UKIP as a 'Politically Correct safety valve'. This did not prevent Griffin from attempting to negotiate an electoral pact with them, however. UKIP rejected Griffin's entreaty out of hand. Griffin also conferred with FN leader Jean-Marie Le Pen in London who informed him that, if the BNP were elected, FN MEP's 'will be happy to show us the ropes and co-operate with us.'[655] Le Pen subsequently attended a BNP press conference in Cheshire in April. Griffin hoped that his presence would confer 'credibility' upon the BNP and his European dream. However, poor planning left Le Pen vulnerable to anti-fascist demonstrators ensuring that press coverage of the event centred upon the violence rather than the campaign. 'Griffin had dropped a right clanger,' recalled a former bodyguard.[656]

It was 'a day to make history,' Griffin proclaimed on the eve of the poll, hubristically predicting his party was on target to gain between 14–16 per cent of the vote and win three or four seats.[657] Griffin's optimism proved misplaced. The BNP won nothing, despite increasing its share of the vote from 1.1 per cent in 1999 to 4.9 per cent in 2004. UKIP was the clear winner, polling 16.1 per cent and returning twelve MEPs. Griffin was a long way from overcoming the 'credibility gap'. Just 8 per cent of respondents, according to one survey conducted during the elections, viewed the BNP positively highlighting the limits of BNP 'modernisation' strategies.[658] Griffin responded that the contest was 'gerrymandered and rigged' – a remark consonant with the party's continued efforts to question the integrity of democratic elections and to denigrate and undermine public trust in democratic institutions and processes more widely. Attempting to put a positive spin on the defeat, Griffin claimed it was actually a blessing in disguise since victory would have meant 'we'd have been too busy learning the ropes of the Brussels game and coping with a sudden influx of fair weather friends to pay much attention to getting our foundations right.'[659] It was a lesson he ignored five years later.

Keighley

Moving on from the party's lacklustre performance during the European elections, Griffin retrained his energies upon anti-Muslim politicking, particularly in the West Yorkshire towns of Keighley and Bradford where the issue of child sexual exploitation by gangs of predominantly Pakistani-heritage men provided a major campaign theme for extreme right-wing groups. For Griffin, sexual abuse by Muslim men constituted a form of original sin: 'It started with Muhammad, who raped a captive – a Jewish captive – whose husband he just had murdered,' he argued. 'He started that, and he is regarded by Muslims as the perfect man. His example colours what Muslims do.'[660] Speaking at a Keighley pub on 19 January 2004, Griffin proclaimed that Islam was a 'wicked, vicious faith' and that Muslims were turning Britain into a 'multi-racial hell hole'. His speech, covertly filmed by a BBC documentary team, aired in December, lead to Griffin's arrest on four counts of using words or behaviour intended or likely to stir up racial hatred. The BNP director of publicity, Mark Collett, who had dated Griffin's daughter, was filmed describing asylum seekers as 'cockroaches'. Police also arrested estranged party founder John Tyndall and fifteen other BNP activists who had been filmed committing or boasting about committing an array of criminal offences. Griffin dismissed the charges as 'an electoral scam to get the Muslim block vote back to the Labour party.'[661]

His arrest did not distract Griffin from organising for the 2005 general election. His strategy centred upon targeting Conservative seats, especially those held by right-wingers, in the hope of shifting the centre of gravity within the Tory party to the left, 'thereby opening up even more political space for us to its right.'[662] He was under no illusion, however, that the BNP would win a single seat. 'British nationalism's record in all those big set-piece contests since 1974 has been a cross between the Charge of the Light Brigade and a very expensive Chinese meal – one fart and its gone,' Griffin stated. Purged of pipe-dreams, Griffin believed the BNP could still use the election to acquire the assets and skills to enhance its 'community politics' through concentrating upon local issues and then playing these forward into local council elections 'which will remain our natural and main field of battle for some years to come yet.' Steeped in the movement's long history of internecine disputes, Griffin also began restructuring the BNP along 'political soldier' lines. As BNP membership expanded to incorporate a 'softer' element, attracted by the party's 'populist' stance on asylum, crime and the EU, but uncomprehending of the 'real' issues threatening 'the very extinction of Western civilisation and the people who created it' – mass immigration, de-culturalisation and globalisation, Griffin moved to ensure the party hard core remained in control. He resurrected the 'Voting Member' idea drawn from political soldier ideology to ensure political control whilst emphasising ideological development as the 'X-factor' that would allow activists 'to spend years locked in cells and come out even more committed to the Cause than when they went in'.[663]

The mainstay of Griffin's public campaign remained anti-Muslim prejudice. Muslims, he told an American extreme right-wing conference held shortly before the general election, were 'an appalling people, some of them are decent, but as a bloc they are an appalling, insufferable people to have to live with.'[664] Standing in Keighley, where the party already had two councillors, Griffin focused his campaign upon 'Muslim' grooming gangs.[665] His attempt to exploit child sexual abuse for political gain arguably made it harder to confront. Indeed, the mother of one victim who stood against the BNP in Keighley described it as 'unforgivable'.[666] Not everyone thought likewise. Griffin polled 4,240 votes (9.2 per cent). Overall, 118 BNP candidates polled a record 192,746 votes (4.2 per cent), a performance undoubtedly aided by widespread hostility towards asylum seekers, which was then reaching its apogee, framed by a broader 'common sense' racism.[667] The vote was a significant achievement for the BNP though, to put it into perspective, it was only 1,027 votes more than the NF had polled during its disastrous 1979 general election campaign, highlighting that it had taken the extreme right nearly twenty-six years to regain parity even with this debacle, such was its magnitude.

Though Griffin polled 9.2 per cent, his result fell short of his party's greatest achievement. Richard Barnbrook polled 16.9 per cent in Barking, East London, the highest vote polled by an extreme right candidate in a general election. It was portentous for both

Griffin and the BNP. Despite being dismissive about the efficacy of standing in general elections, the possibility that Barking might afford him the chance of becoming an MP seduced Griffin, contributing, ultimately, to his undoing.

The London 7/7 attacks

Two months after the general election, four jihadists perpetrated coordinated suicide attacks on the London transport network, murdering fifty-two people. 'All is changed, utterly changed,' Griffin announced in a jeremiad proclaiming, once more, 'the death of the multicultural fantasy'. He urged people to blame Prime Minister Tony Blair not 'ordinary Muslims' but the front page of *Identity* reiterated his claim that Islam was a 'vicious and wicked faith'. Inside, Griffin claimed that 'our culture ... is superior to that of other peoples and religions, including Islam', which was culturally incommensurable with 'the restless, Faustian spirit of the Western world' – phraseology redolent of Mosley. For Griffin, 7/7 was further evidence that Islamist terrorism was not a 'perversion' of the faith but ingrained in 'the very heart of Islam, drawing strength from the Koran.'[668]

Thereafter, the BNP made every effort to capitalise upon the situation. Griffin's rhetoric became increasingly militarised. The 'Clash of Civilisations' was no longer an abstract, but increasingly assumed the characteristics of a 'civil war' (a rhetorical repackaging of the 'race war' motif) to be fought out 'between angry neighbours on familiar streets.'[669] The English Civil War (1642 1651) would need to be termed the 'First English Civil War,' Griffin argued, 'to differentiate it from the one to come.'[670] Enoch Powell's 'Rivers of Blood' could only be avoided by returning Britain to a state of racial homogeneity and withdrawing from the Middle East: 'And those who would Islamify our European Christendom must in turn leave our shores – every last one of them.'[671] The BNP were the only 'safety valve' capable of diffusing further violence, Griffin was wont to claim. But, within days of the 7/7 atrocity, the party was using pictures of the bombed-out bus on its election literature for a Barking by-election with the caption: 'Maybe now it's time to start listening to the BNP.'[672] Party literature became increasingly incendiary. One leaflet featured a cartoon of the Prophet Muhammad derived from the Danish newspaper *Jyllands-Posten*, which had already provoked rioting and murder across the world.[673]

Islam was not the only enemy. Liberal parliamentary democracy, Griffin continued to claim, was a perversion, 'a rolling coup d'état by the followers of an extremist cult who will stop at nothing to impose their agenda on the society they hate.' It was Soviet communism's 'spiritual twin'. Though he remained committed to the BNP as a 'conventional political organisation', he recognised its limits, conceding that Labour had now figured out how to counteract its local campaigning. Thus, Griffin, argued, political struggle had to be converted into a 'civil rights struggle' carried out by a 'highly effective decentralised movement' which, through grassroots campaigning, could reverse the 'dhimmification' of liberal churches and turn Christianity 'into a weapon for Western survival' or at the very least 'a powerful symbolic rejection of multiculturalism'.[674]

An amicable divorce?

The hardening of the party's anti-Muslim stance after 7/7 obscured the ongoing revision of the party's anti-Semitic politics. In 2003, *Identity* was still denouncing multiculturalism and immigration as a conspiratorial 'project' for the 'phased destruction of our identities, freedoms and culture.'[675] Two years later, however, Griffin publicly eschewed this conspiratorial anti-Semitic framework. 'Capitalism knows no race or religion,' he asserted. 'Its motive forces are greed and shared ideological assumptions, not any "conspiracy" Learned Elder fantasy figures.'[676] Pointedly, the party's *Language & Concepts Discipline Manual* (2005) advised activists that, all things considered, 'it is best to simply never speak or write of Jews at all.'[677] That said, Griffin remained committed to 'teaching the truth to the hardcore,'[678] signalling obliquely to party activists, 'that certain minority groups [Jews] do punch far above their weight when it comes to the media,' referencing his 'now out-of-print survey *The Mindbenders*' as proof.[679] Nonetheless, the overall public downgrading of anti-Semitism attracted a Jewish activist who, having accepted the party's denial of anti-Semitism became a BNP councillor in Epping in 2004. The BNP held up this isolated instance as 'proof' that the party was no longer anti-Jewish.[680]

Tyndall found the party's transformation particularly risible given Griffin's own well-documented record of Holocaust denial. Tyndall wrote:

> I have in my office a large file of correspondence in which he [Griffin] has expressed his opinions on the subject to me in no uncertain terms. All this makes a complete nonsense of his current Jew-friendly postures. There may be people in the BNP who can with straight faces and complete honesty publicly proclaim their philo-Semitic credentials but Nick Griffin is not one of them.[681]

Griffin ignored Tyndall's criticism. Indeed, speaking at the 'Euro-American' conference in New Orleans in May 2005 organised by former Klansman David Duke, Griffin went one further. He called for 'an amicable divorce' between 'nationalist' politics and historical 'revisionism' – to the mutual benefit of both – if 'nationalist' politics was to advance its public appeal.[682]

The BNP dismissed accusations of Holocaust denial as 'smears' whilst countering weakly: 'Dredging up quotes from 10, 15, 20 years ago is really pathetic and, in a sense, rather fascist.'[683] Mindful of discussions in the European Parliament to have Holocaust denial declared illegal across all its member states, Griffin developed a new rhetorical strategy for deflecting questions about his Holocaust denial, whilst simultaneously signalling that he remained true to his hard-core beliefs. 'European law now says the Holocaust did happen, precisely as understood,' he told one journalist, 'so I accept European law, so yeah, I believe in the Holocaust.'[684] Whilst Griffin's double meaning was obvious, he also sought to clarify his political priorities by declaring, in an interview with Israeli newspaper *Ma'ariv*, that he had 'no time for anti-Semites' adding for good measure that 'four million Jews would be preferable to four million Pakistanis.'[685] By the end of the year, Griffin had told the *Think-Israel* website: 'The idea that "the Jew is the enemy" is simply over for us now, and not a moment too soon, because now we can get on with the real struggles.'[686]

Griffin's strategy to prioritise the party's electorally profitable anti-Muslim platform also meant playing down the party's racial ideology too. Party publications continued to rely upon racial science to affirm its rejection of the 'pernicious fantasy' of racial equality.[687] Pithy 'common sense' globules such as 'we simply want to be left with our own culture and identity intact,' peppered Griffin's public pronouncements, however.[688] Whilst the centrality of 'ethnic citizenship' has declined for Western states since 1945, for the BNP the idea was central to its understanding of the nation state as a racial state.[689] Non-Europeans, argued the BNP, could only remain in Britain as 'permanent guests'. They were not considered native citizens regardless of whether or not their families had resided in the country for 'generations' because status 'springs from blood' and 'not from printers' ink' on a passport. There could 'never' be such a thing category as 'Black British' for the BNP.⁶⁹⁰ To underscore the point, the party's merchandising arm sold reproductions of Queen Elizabeth I's 'Blackamoor' expulsion orders dating from 1596 and 1601 when the monarch sought to deport Britain's black populace.⁶⁹¹

Griffin remained implacably opposed to miscegenation and though he denied any future BNP government would make it a crime,

> neither do we subscribe to the convenient fiction that it's a good thing. It is not, it is a bad thing, and we condemn it, as genuine nationalists of all colours condemn it because it destroys their own people too.⁶⁹²

He pitied 'mixed race children' as 'the most tragic victims of enforced multiracialism' though this 'does not mean that we will accept miscegenation as moral or normal. We do not and we never will.'⁶⁹³ Nor did Griffin consider those with dual heritage to be 'white' since 'these unfortunates invariably identify with the non-European part of their ancestry.'⁶⁹⁴

He was not above using such 'unfortunates' to bolster the cosmetic overhaul of the party's image, however, though this proved more than some BNP stalwarts could stomach. In February 2003, *Voice of Freedom* featured a BNP activist with his black son-in-law under the heading 'How dare they call me a racist and a Nazi.'⁶⁹⁵ BNP membership was aghast. The article struck many activists, Griffin conceded, 'like a wet dead rat in the face'. Nonetheless, he was adamant that it reinforced the party's 'anti-racist' credentials. 'I'm asking people to put up with that.... And I'm asking people to understand that making political capital out of something doesn't mean that we necessarily approve of it.' To Griffin's mind, the party faced a choice. Either it remained an 'anti-asylum, racist sect' or it became a 'power-winning machine', which would allow it 'to protect our people and secure a future for white children. That has always been our aim, is our aim, and will always remain our aim.'⁶⁹⁶

Griffin had sanctioned a further repositioning of BNP racial ideology in light of British immigration policy. On 1 May 2004, Britain became one of only three European states allowing Polish and Hungarian workers unrestricted access to the labour market after their countries accessioned to the European Union. Non-EU migration had already doubled between 1997 and 2004 from 166,000 per annum to 370,000 whilst, in the aftermath of the EU's eastern enlargement, annual EU immigration rose from 66,000 to 269,000 by 2015. For the BNP, whose *raison d'être* was opposing *non-white* immigration, the rapid influx of large numbers of *white* immigrants created an ideological conundrum. To square the circle, in November 2005, BNP ideologues sought to shift the party membership from the universalism of 'racial nationalism' to a more nuanced 'ethno-nationalism' recognising the 'internal genetic diversity of the white race.' This, they believed, would enable the BNP to politically object to Polish immigration into Britain on the grounds that:

> A Europe with no Anglo-Saxons, or Germans, or Poles, or Spaniards but just one misceginated [sic] mass of mixed up 'white' tribal genes is as much a racial disaster for Europe and our peoples as a Europe swamped with African genes.⁶⁹⁷

The proposition met with hostility on extreme right internet forums.⁶⁹⁸ Again, little was 'new' in this ideological reformulation of earlier Nouvelle Droite arguments for 'ethno-plurality'.⁶⁹⁹

More innovative was the recalibration of racial nationalist arguments within the rhetorical parameters of liberal human rights. Griffin believed that these verbal 'judo tactics' were 'a hundred times more effective than a suicidal frontal assault trying to explain racial differences to people who have been convinced that such ideas are an unacceptable mixture of heresy and blasphemy.'[700] For Griffin, 'Britons' constituted a genetically defined 'indigenous' population with a 'primordial' claim on the nation, its identity, heritage and culture. Through immigration and multiculturalism, they were being 'ethnically cleansed' and subjected to 'genocide'.[701] As such, they deserved 'protected status', under the United Nations Charter on the Rights of Indigenous Peoples.[702] In support of this contention, the BNP began citing the Convention on the Prevention and Punishment of the Crime of Genocide, adopted by the United Nations General Assembly on 9 December 1948, which stated that genocide 'means any of the acts committed with intent to destroy, in whole or in part, a national, ethical, racial or religious group.' Section 2 (c) of this Convention further stated that 'deliberately inflicting on the group conditions of life, calculated to bring about its physical destruction in whole or in part' also constitutes genocide. By turning the language of multiculturalism and liberal humanitarianism against Liberalism, the BNP sought to validate its 'race realist' position without recourse to traditional racist argumentation.[703]

Beyond the BNP's 'populist' anti-immigration façade, Griffin viewed his party as a movement of 'white survivalists'.[704] Party publications had this 'survivalist discourse' embedded within them.[705] Though Griffin had overseen the presentational overhaul in how the BNP articulated its racial ideology in public, he also sanctioned the re-injection of a Nordicist racism into its core. This took place through the figure of Arthur Kemp, a Rhodesian-born activist arrested, though never charged, during the investigation into the assassination of leading ANC activist Chris Hani in South Africa in 1993. Kemp had compiled a list of nine names and addresses – he denied it was a 'hit list' – which he gave to Gaye Derby-Lewis for 'research purposes'.[706] Nelson Mandela's name was first on the list. Hani's was third. Her husband, Clive Derby-Lewis, the Conservative Party president, gave the list to Janusz Waluś, a Polish émigré active in the extreme right Afrikaner Weerstandsbeweging (AWB – Afrikaner Resistance Movement) who then shot Hani dead.[707] Kemp subsequently published a racist tome titled, *March of the Titans: A History of the White Race*, which denied the Holocaust.[708] It was required reading for BNP activists.[709] Thereafter, Kemp began playing a role in formulating BNP policy issues as well as overseeing the ideological development and training of party activists.[710] Griffin and Kemp co-authored *Folk and Nation: Underpinning the Ethnostate* (2008), an internal cadre-training manual, subsequently expanding it for a public audience, which recast racial nationalism as 'ethno-nationalism' defining the 'nation' in accordance with the dual concepts of the right to self-determination and racial heredity.[711]

Trial

Whilst Griffin worked to ensure the party's hard-core militants learned the 'truth', he continued to position himself in the in the vanguard of 'populist' anti-Muslim politics. His trial for inciting racial hatred at Leeds Crown Court, which began in January 2006, enhanced his efforts. Griffin styled himself and co-defendant Mark Collett as 'free speech martyrs', wagering that 'in historical terms, a lengthy prison sentence would be the best possible outcome of this trial.'[712] Instead, following a two-week trial, the jury acquitted Griffin and Collett of half the charges but failed to reach a verdict on the others. *Identity* proclaimed the trial 'our greatest publicity coup ever' whilst Griffin mocked the BBC for providing the 'largest bloc of donations we've ever had'.[713] Triumphant, Griffin lambasted the government 'for turning our once decent, stable country into a multicultural mess which looks increasingly like a future Bosnia.' Asked if he would moderate his language in future, Griffin replied: 'I don't think I will, no'.[714] The Crown Prosecution Service immediately announced it was seeking a retrial. Acquitted again on 10 November, Griffin told reporters: 'This party is now an icon of resistance to the forcibly imposed multi-cultural experiment which has failed.'[715] His celebration buffet included a 'halal-free' cake shaped like a pig.[716]

Rising support at the polls buoyed Griffin's defiance. Between his two trials, the BNP doubled its representation taking its tally to forty-six seats, including winning twelve on Barking and Dagenham council in outer East London, where the party's 'Africans for Essex' campaign explicitly racialising grievances about the perceived unfairness of local housing allocations had paid dividends. At a stroke, the BNP became the official opposition to Labour in the council chamber. Though race was the prism through which BNP support was articulated, this served as a cipher for a broader set of socio-economic grievances revolving around the trinity of 'homes, heritage and homogeneity',[717] which more prescient Labour MP's conceded their party had ignored.[718]

These grievances were not new of course. As Jeremy Seabrook observed in Blackburn during the late 1970s, there was a sense in such working-class communities 'that something has gone wrong, promises have been spoiled, improvements soured.' Industrial decline, depopulation and the weakening of working-class structures had fuelled a sense of grievance and victimhood directed towards immigrants that had enabled the extreme right to position itself as the champion of an increasingly marginalised white working class that felt itself politically abandoned by the Labour Party. 'The outages against immigrants, the anger and resentment have all the elements of a deformed crusade,' Seabrook reflected.

> In fact, the model for the growth of the parties of the far right echoes the struggles which the old talk of when they were fighting for socialism: the need to be secretive, the sense of persecution, the feeling of mission, the profound emotional attachment to a cause.[719]

Seeking to translate this inchoate and impotent sense of rage, insecurity and loss into electoral success, Griffin returned to the 'left-wing' roots of his national revolutionary phase. He positioned the BNP as a party that encapsulated the values of 'old Labour' or 'real Labour', whilst claiming brazenly that the BNP was 'the Labour Party your granddad voted for'. *Voice of Freedom*, the BNP newspaper, went so far as to list Labour Prime Minister Clement Attlee – who Griffin had previously reviled as a central figure in a plot to dilute racial purity through mass immigration[720] – as being amongst 'those who inspire our ideology'. Attlee, *Voice of Freedom* maintained, was 'the last radical patriot to lead any of the establishment parties and was Prime Minister of the last British Government we ever had that, on balance, did the British people and our country more harm than good.' Labour's nationalisation programme was also re-conceptualised as an assault on 'the inherently anti-British system of capitalism', the radical anti-capitalist nature of which only the BNP now embodied leading it to proclaim that 'today only the British National Party remains true to the basic principle of Attlee's Labour Clause Four.' The article concluded that:

> Clement Attlee were he alive today, would recognise his vision and principles not in Tony Blair's New Labour but in the BNP. His Labour party stood up for and sought

to improve the lives of working British people, whilst Blair's New Labour turns its back on them to serve its billionaire paymasters and curry favour with the Muslim vote.[721]

These themes featured prominently in BNP doorstep campaigns in outer East London. Local campaign literature featured a photograph of a BNP candidate outside Attlee's former home in Redbridge.[722] Griffin subsequently accused Labour of having 'sold out' whilst 'crushing ordinary people to ensure maximum profit for its corporate financiers' in the process – an anti-globalisation critique which, in this instance, was simply a variant of Griffin's earlier insistence that Labour and Capital were Siamese Twins servicing a Jewish world conspiracy. 'The old Labour Party is dead,' Griffin proclaimed. 'Long live the new party for British workers — the BNP.'[723]

As Griffin repositioned the BNP to take advantage of Labour's waning appeal for segments of the working class, he simultaneously misinterpreted his party's electoral advance as a sign of BNP strength rather than as an indication of the parlous state of local democracy and the advanced state of decay of local political parties.[724] The BNP had peaked in 2006. Whilst it would win further seats, overall progress began stagnating. Local elections in the following year offered Griffin little cause for celebration. Fielding a record 750 candidates in a bid to push its tally from forty-six to 100 councillors, the BNP made little headway. Despite some gains, the party lost three seats in Burnley, reducing its total from seven to four.

Dissatisfaction and loss of momentum bred intrigue, bringing about a damaging rift within the party as Griffin's leadership clique clashed with a section of the party's middle management. Griffin's decision to purge these 'rebels' in December threatened a serious split. Dozens of seasoned activists and organisers rushed to their defence. Griffin responded by branding his critics as extremists and denouncing 'the grim, raucous, counter-productive hatred of the old, neo-Nazi Blood and Honour scene' and the spectre of 'grown men Sieg Heiling.'[725] Those he had criticised lost no time reminding Griffin of his own 'neo-Nazi' dalliances with the 'white power' music scene that had continued after he became BNP chairman. 'Whenever Blood and Honour Scotland had a gig or a social, sizeable donations were given to Griffin's BNP,' recalled Cartwright. 'There was never any directive sent down from the Griffin leadership that such monies were to be refused. I guess "neo-Nazi" money was as good as any other money.'[726] Griffin's attack upon '"14 Words" cultists' also raised eyebrows given his own professed allegiance to the 'Fourteen Words' only three years beforehand.[727] Griffin continued to feel the pressure from the 'rebels', even after he had expelled them. In November 2008, one 'rebel', a former member of Griffin's security team, leaked the entire BNP membership list online causing the party protracted embarrassment. This schism also highlighted the volatility of Griffin's leadership when compared to that of his predecessor. From 2007 onwards, Griffin faced five leadership challenges. Until Griffin, Tyndall had not faced one.

Griffin's leadership also faced a broader external challenge from March 2009 onwards following the emergence of the English Defence League (EDL), a burgeoning anti-Muslim street movement, which challenged BNP hegemony on the right. The EDL, led by Luton Town football 'casual' Stephen Yaxley-Lennon ('Tommy Robinson'), began holding noisy and often violent demonstrations across the country in reaction to the heckling of a soldier's homecoming parade after a tour of duty in Afghanistan by a group of Islamist extremists in Luton. Lennon was briefly a BNP member but soon distanced himself from the group. 'Race' represented the key fault line. In contrast to the BNP, the EDL leadership made efforts to position itself as 'non-racist'. Whilst this stance was more often honoured in the breach than the observance by some activists, the enactment of this identity, even if 'uneven and erratic', still played a significant role in shaping the overall trajectory of the group away from the political ghetto of racial nationalist politics.[728]

The contrasting views Griffin and 'Robinson' held on multicultural society was epitomised in their respective responses to a speech by Prime Minister David Cameron on 5 February 2011 which had argued that the passive tolerance of 'state multiculturalism' fuelled segregation and exacerbated extremism and therefore requiring replacing with an pro-active 'muscular liberalism' that extolled the inclusive values of liberal democracy.[729] For Griffin, the speech was an acknowledgement that 'multiculturalism' had failed and therefore a validation of his own position. Cameron's speech, he argued, was a 'British version' of *glasnost* and *perestroika*, the two concepts that prefigured the demise of Soviet Communism, heralding a 'further huge leap for our ideas into the political mainstream.'[730] Lennon's response was markedly different. 'David Cameron is wrong,' he stated. 'Multiculturalism has worked, it hasn't failed. My goddaughter's black, my niece is black, yeah, we live side by side, brothers and sisters. It hasn't failed. What's he on about? He don't know what he's talking about. Religion's failed.'[731] For Robinson, multicultural society was not the problem. It was the singular failure of 'Muslims' to integrate, a vastly different position to the one Griffin had maintained throughout his political career.

Whilst both groups maintained a virtually indistinguishable position vis-à-vis Islam, viewing it as a threat to European 'identity', 'culture' and 'civilisation', Griffin's view was inflected by his anti-Semitism. Lennon's anti-Muslim politicking saw him openly support Israel. For Griffin, this was an anathema. With the racial nationalist tradition losing ground across Europe to a new form of 'counter-jihad' politics, Griffin denounced the EDL as 'Zionist puppets' dancing to a neo-conservative, pro-war tune. He proscribed the group. Griffin's vitriolic campaign culminated in *What Lies Behind the English Defence League?* (2012), which he billed as an investigation 'into one part of the global battle for the soul of the nationalist movement.'[732] Ironically, for Griffin, this battle entailed reverting to the position he had previously excoriated Tyndall for holding a decade beforehand, namely, that 'Jews' represented the real threat. 'To become fixated on the Islamist threat is completely counter-productive,' Griffin now argued.[733] The EDL leadership were impervious to Griffin's criticism. 'They are a complete set of wankers, that lot,' Lennon commented derisively.[734]

The Emperor's new clothes

With the exception of Richard Barnbrook's election to the Greater London Assembly in 2008, BNP performance at the polls since 2006 had been underwhelming. This made the shock of Griffin's election as an MEP in the 2009 European elections even more palpable. Griffin used the position to amplify core party themes and position himself as herald of the white working class. 'I am now there to give political articulation to the concerns of the mainly indigenous population,' he claimed. 'The ethnic populations have always had Labour to speak up for them. Finally their neighbours have got someone who speaks up for them.'[735] He also made a series of provocative comments regarding the growing Mediterranean immigration crisis. His solution, he told one journalist, was 'to sink several of those boats.' Informed that the EU was not 'in the business of murdering people at sea', Griffin retorted: 'I didn't say anyone should be murdered at sea – I say boats should be sunk, they can throw them a life raft and they can go back to Libya.'[736]

Griffin's election was a pyrrhic victory, however. Shortly afterwards, the BBC invited him to appear on its flagship current affairs programme, *Question Time*, an invitation he had long coveted believing that it would confer mainstream legitimacy upon him as *L'Heure de Vérité* (*The Hour of Truth*) had done for Jean-Marie Le Pen in 1984. However, instead of confounding his critics as Le Pen had done, Griffin's leadership, and with it the precarious public credibility of the BNP itself, would fail the litmus test. Buoyed with hubris, Griffin had assured supporters his appearance would be 'THE key moment that propels the BNP into the big time.'[737] Instead, it exposed the Emperor's new clothes to nationwide ridicule. Prior to broadcast, the programme's presenter, David Dimbleby, had stressed to the studio audience that it should 'not just be the Nick Griffin show'.[738] His entreaty was in vain. From the outset, the show, driven by audience questions, focused almost exclusively upon Griffin's personal record. Facing a barrage of hostile questions and broadsides from the panel, Griffin delivered a less than polished performance. He was 'trembling' at points, asserted a fellow panellist.[739] When he spoke, his rhetorical strategy of 'calculated ambivalence' simply appeared shifty and evasive; an impression reinforced by his lack of candour when confronted with past pronouncements.[740] BNP members in the audience offered little succour to their beleaguered leader.[741]

Instead of using the programme to dispel public preconceptions of the BNP, Griffin squandered the opportunity attacking Islam and branding the sight of homosexuals kissing as 'really creepy'. His claim that David Duke's Ku Klux Klan was 'almost totally non-violent' met with universal derision from the studio audience not least because it was palpably untrue: putting aside the Klan's well-documented history of racial terrorism, Duke had a conviction for inciting a riot. Griffin's greatest gaffe, however, was his response to questions about his Holocaust denial. Griffin stated that he 'did not have a conviction for Holocaust denial' which was of course true. His conviction was for inciting racial hatred. He refused to elaborate on the subject, however, claiming, 'I cannot tell you why I said those things in the past, or why I have changed my mind,' because European law prevented him from doing so. Fellow panellist Jack Straw, the government's Justice Secretary, assured Griffin that there was no such law. He refused to elaborate, however. Griffin's persistent smirk during the exchanges led Dimbleby to enquire: 'Why are you smiling, it is not a particularly amusing issue?' Griffin's riposte, that the BBC was 'part of a thoroughly unpleasant, ultra-leftist establishment which, as we have seen here tonight, doesn't even want the English to be recognised as an existing people,' fell flat.[742]

The programme recorded its highest viewing figures in its thirty-year history, 8.2 million viewers at its peak. Griffin's dismal performance won few converts, however. The verdict of the national press was almost universally withering.[743] Opinion polls conducted in the aftermath of the programme further highlighted that just 7 per cent would 'definitely' or 'probably' consider voting BNP (though a further 15 per cent identified themselves as 'possible' voters), highlighting the fact that the BNP 'brand' remained 'badly tainted'. Moreover, it signalled that Griffin had failed to assuage the 'very negative' feelings that some 62 per cent of Britons had for the BNP prior to the election.[744] Abstaining from self-reflection, Griffin simply decried the programme as a 'lynch mob' blaming the supposed racial complexion of the audience for his humiliation: 'That audience was taken from a city that is no longer British … That was not my country any more,' he stated.

> Why not come down and do it in Thurrock, do it in Stoke, do it in Burnley? Do it somewhere where there are still significant numbers of English and British people [living], and they haven't been ethnically cleansed from their own country.[745]

Griffin's lacklustre performance accelerated tensions within the party, fuelled by his prolonged absences in Brussels, which had loosened his grip on the BNP. Increased representation brought with it increased public scrutiny. In August, the Equality and Human Rights Commission (EHRC) brought a legal action against the party, which many activists felt Griffin badly mishandled. The EHRC case revolved around the party's racially restrictive membership clause. When confronted by interviewers about the party's 'whites only' constitution, Griffin pushed the language of indigeneity to its logical end, defending it has as having 'nothing to do with white'. 'We're talking about indigenous,' he continued. 'The fact that historically the indigenous British are white doesn't mean it's a colour issue … I don't give a damn about white. It really doesn't matter.'[746] Though the constitution did not explicitly use the word 'white', it did restrict membership by 'ethnic origin' to those described as 'indigenous Caucasian', which amounted to much the same thing and was illegal under British law.

The EHRC issued county court proceedings against Griffin and two other officials, which prohibited the BNP from recruiting new members in the interim. Griffin responded by embarking upon a protracted legal case to frustrate the EHRC, which was both costly and ultimately fruitless. Party members voted to remove the contentious clause from its constitution at an EGM in February 2010.[747] Spinning defeat as a victory, Griffin proclaimed unconvincingly that 'they can't call us racist anymore.'[748] Frustration spilt out during the proceedings. When the BNP security team assaulted a journalist from *The Times*, Griffin hailed the attack as proof the BNP was not 'going soft.… That's not the actions of a sniveling PC party, but of an organisation that has had enough of being lied about.'[749]

This legal defeat was largely symbolic, however. There was no influx of non-white members into the party, nor was there ever likely to have been. Although Griffin had defiantly declared in August 2004 that the BNP 'is not going to let in a single "token" non-white', following the ratification of the revised constitution, Rajinder Singh, an elderly Sikh who shared the party's antipathy towards Muslims, joined the BNP as its first non-white member.[750] Few, if any, followed Singh into the breach, however.[751] More importantly, Griffin's costly handling of the case only served to reinforce the party's racist image as the BNP entered the 2010 general election, placing further strain on his relationship with several key party strategists.

Griffin's *Götterdämmerung*

Despite simmering internal tensions, Griffin entered the 2010 general election campaign in a buoyant mood. He boasted he had turned the BNP 'from a potential footnote in history into a serious contender for power.'[752] The BNP fielded 338 candidates, more than the 303 fielded by the NF in 1979, and 739 local election candidates, a portent of the hubris saturating Griffin's strategy. Griffin stood against incumbent Labour MP Margaret Hodge in Barking, though to do so he had had to oust local party leader Richard Barnbrook. This exacerbated local dissatisfaction with his leadership, as did his marginalisation of party elections officer, Eddy Butler. Griffin centred the BNP election campaign on three major themes: Afghanistan, immigration and the global warming conspiracy, a peculiar decision given that only 'immigration' resonated with voters.[753]

Griffin's campaign team in Barking also favoured mobilising anti-Semitic prejudice, which they believed existed amongst the Black and Muslim electorate hoping that if they would not vote *for* the BNP they might at least vote *against* Hodge. The BNP distributed thousands of copies of *The Barking and Dagenham Sentinel* attacking Hodge's political record, underpinned by an assertion that she herself was a rich, foreign Jew. 'Hodge,' asserted the publication 'was born in Egypt as Margaret Oppenheimer, the daughter of a *refugee millionaire German Jewish steel trader* [my italics].'[754] It was a disastrously counter-productive piece of propaganda, recalled Butler. This 'anti-Semitic slur' had 'to be blacked out with marker pens' before it could be disseminated:

> This ridiculous newspaper destroyed the last week of the BNP's Barking and Dagenham campaign as it had to be censored (which took our activists days and days) and then they were ordered to distribute it. It will not have benefited our campaign in the slightest.[755]

Griffin's campaign was beset by a further series of self-imposed gaffes, including publicly accusing Mark Collett, his co-defendant in 2006 of plotting to 'kill' him; falling out with the party's webmaster who promptly removed the BNP website, its principal means of communication, only days before the election; as local party figures were captured on camera brawling with local Asian youth.[756] Griffin's own disparaging statements about London's white working class were another political own goal which returned to haunt him. Journalists reminded Griffin that he had once claimed that:

> [T]he people who have the brains and ability got out [of London] years ago, one way or another. The people who are left are either the 15 per cent of the population who are happy to put up with it, they're so decadent they actually like it, or they are too stupid to do anything about it. They will vote BNP, but you can't build a movement on those people.[757]

Why would he appeal to the very people he had once derided as 'too stupid to do anything about it,' journalists asked? Griffin claimed he was 'drunk'.[758] Griffin was also filmed whilst on the campaign trail deriding Barking as 'foreign' territory and commenting that campaigning there was 'like leafleting in central Nairobi.'[759] Whilst appealing to his base, it was unlikely to build wider support.

Griffin's insistence upon standing in Barking had serious consequences that rebounded upon the BNP. Tactically, the decision to shunt aside Richard Barnbrook proved a mistake. His candidacy became a lightning rod for anti-fascist campaigning in a constituency, which had offered the party its best hope. It bore an ill wind for the twelve BNP councillors facing re-election in local elections held on the same day. Whilst many increased their vote, they all lost their seats because of the increased anti-BNP vote. Predictably, Griffin's own election bid failed. He polled 6,620 votes (14.6 per cent), failing to beat the 16.9 per cent polled by Barnbrook in 2005. Following his defeat, Griffin declared Barking was 'finished'.[760] He also predicted that by the time of the next general election London, 'will be completely unassailable, colonised and in truth no longer part of Britain.' Griffin also hinted that the BNP might replace electoral activity with 'civil rights agitation' to protect the 'white minority' in 'occupied territories'.[761]

Overall, the BNP polled 564,321 votes (1.9 per cent), significantly more than the 192,746 votes (0.7 per cent) the party had polled five years previously. This was the best result recorded by an extreme right party in a general election in British history. Yet, the result delivered a 'mortal blow' to the party.[762] Despite its increased vote, the factors that had underpinned its rise and provided it with a window of opportunity had begun to change, most notably with regards public concern about immigration, which had peaked as an electoral issue in 2007. A resurgent Labour Party and the rise of UKIP also dramatically circumscribed BNP appeal on both its right and left flanks.[763]

For Griffin, the election was a political and personal disaster. It put his leadership under intense pressure, leading him to acquiesce to internal demands to step down as BNP leader at the end of 2013, after which he would concentrate upon gaining re-election as an MEP. 'It will be time to make way for a younger person who does not have any baggage which can be used against the party,' he stated, though gave no clue as to his potential successor.[764] This pronouncement failed to ameliorate the situation. In August, Griffin was challenged by Barnbrook and Butler, the latter arguing that the BNP required 'a complete relaunch' to survive.[765] Griffin withstood the challenge and promptly expelled Butler. Barnbrook simply resigned. This did little to quell growing disapproval of Griffin's leadership. He was challenged again, this time by Richard Edmonds following the 2011 local election, notable for its loss of every single BNP councillor in Stoke-on-Trent, a town once hailed as the party's 'jewel in the crown'. Stoke BNP's chances were hardly enhanced by the resignation of its branch leader, who publicly denounced 'a vein of Holocaust denying' within the party and the 'Nazi, Nazi-esque sympathies' held by senior BNP officials.[766]

In an attempt to revitalise the party, Griffin re-concentrated upon anti-Muslim politicking, particularly in the North-West where he would soon face re-election. This gained some traction because of a series of high-profile child sexual abuse cases involving vulnerable white girls and men largely, though not exclusively, of Pakistani heritage. Lacking activists, Griffin dropped his proscription of the EDL, though his entreaties only really appealed to its explicitly racist 'Infidel' splinter groups, who were running their own vociferously anti-Muslim campaigns in the region. Griffin centred his campaign upon 'Muslim paedophiles' or 'paedostanis', which in BNP parlance fused the crime and ethnic origin into one word. This also dovetailed with a campaign against 'Labour perverts' – the implication being that both the political establishment and ethnic minorities were predatory, sexual degenerates preying on white children. Reaction to the media's reporting of the 'Asian' grooming gang scandal reflected a further breakdown in inter-ethnic solidarity, which Griffin sought to leverage for political advantage. Several Sikh and Hindu organisations issued a communiqué stating that, as the perpetrators were in fact 'almost always of Pakistani origin', describing such criminals as 'Asian' was 'wholly inaccurate and unfair to other communities of Asian Origin.'[767] Griffin believed such statements legitimated the strategy he had adumbrated back in 2001, to isolate 'Muslims' from other 'Asians' proving he had been 'right all along'.[768]

BNP activists, frequently with Griffin at the helm, demonstrated outside the trials of Muslim men charged with raping and abusing children. The BNP had initially campaigned using banners and leaflets declaring 'Our Children are not Halal Meat'. It soon concluded, however, that this message, though forceful, was too negative and switched to using black banners declaring in *faux* Arabic script: 'Protect Children – Fight Grooming Gangs'. BNP 'support' for the victims of sexual abuse was of questionable value, however. Griffin himself jeopardised the outcome of one £2 million trial in Rochdale in 2012 after tweeting a guilty verdict before the jury had actually declared one providing the defendants' lawyers with the opportunity to call for a re-trial.[769] The father of one girl briefly joined the BNP but resigned shortly afterwards due to the 'downright nauseous' people he had met within the organisation.[770]

In Blackpool, Griffin achieved a measure of local legitimacy through his appearance at several demonstrations protesting the tragic case of Charlene Downes, a fourteen-year-old who disappeared in 2003, presumed murdered. Her parents joined the BNP demonstrations.

The BNP also protested another murdered Blackpool teenager, Paige Chivers, who had disappeared in 2007, though it subsequently transpired that her killer, Robert Ewing, had joined several of these BNP demonstrations too. Arrested in 2014, Ewing told police he was a 'neo-Nazi'.[771] Another militant active during these demonstrations was a local Young BNP member, Jack Renshaw. He subsequently joined National Action; the first extreme right group in British history banned as a terrorist group in December 2016 and was later jailed for plotting to murder his local Labour MP, Rosie Cooper, and a police officer who was investigating him for sexually grooming two underage boys.[772]

Though he claimed all paedophiles should be executed,[773] for Griffin, the issue of child sexual exploitation remained predominantly a means of defaming Muslims. When Jimmy Savile, a popular television and radio personality, was unmasked as a prolific child sex offender and rapist, following his death in 2011, Griffin claimed conspiratorially: 'I believe that the BBC Savile story was probably first rolled out to draw attention away from the issue of Muslim grooming gangs, which was dominating the news until then. It was meant as a propaganda red herring.'[774]

Despite their best efforts to exploit this ongoing scandal, BNP atrophy continued unabated. In 2012, the BNP lost all its remaining councillors in Burnley where, symbolically, its breakthrough had begun a decade earlier.[775] This neatly bookended the demise of the BNP's limited electoral insurgency – which, to put it in its proper perspective, saw the party, *at its peak*, win just fifty-six council seats out of the approximately 21,049 seats available across the United Kingdom.[776] The party's electoral implosion triggered a final challenge to Griffin's leadership, this time from fellow BNP MEP Andrew Brons whose supporters circulated a report alleging numerous instances of 'mismanagement'.[777] Griffin narrowly won by 1,157 votes to Brons' 1,148, a margin of nine votes. Despite previously claiming he would step down in 2013, Griffin now stated adamantly that he would remain chairman until at least 2015. 'I'm in charge and that's the end of it,' he told the BBC.[778] In the meantime, his relationship with Brons completely disintegrated. Having essentially ostracised his rival, Brons resigned in October 2012, claiming to have been 'constructively dismissed' from the BNP.[779] 'Policy hasn't been an issue – our difference was the way it was being run,' Brons lamented.[780] As he had done in 1986, Griffin resorted to claiming 'suspicion' surrounded Brons being 'a long-term plant'.[781] Brons responded with a joke: What is the difference between Griffin and prominent anti-fascist campaigner Nick Lowles? 'One of them has devoted his life to destroying the nationalist movement and the other is Nick Lowles.'[782]

For Butler, one of the original architects of the 'modernisation' strategy, Griffin's victory signalled that the BNP was 'finished' as a credible political vehicle. 'It is dead. It is over.' Cognisant of the academic literature, Butler recognised that the party's failure develop a 'reputational shield' had condemned the BNP to remain 'a tainted and toxic brand'. 'Organised nationalism has a bad public reputation in this country,' he admitted. 'Whether we like it or not, it is associated with Nazism, anti-Semitism, violence and hatred. That is some reputation to live down.'[783] The following anecdote spoke volumes about Griffin's failure to detoxify himself or his party. In 2011, Griffin had led a protest on the steps of South Shields Town Hall against the local council, which they accused of squandering taxpayer's money in a quest to unmask a mystery blogger called 'Mr Monkey', who had made scurrilous attacks on several councillors. 'To be honest, I saw the BNP and then saw a man in a monkey suit,' recalled an observer. 'I just assumed they were being derogatory towards certain races.'[784]

The BNP's failure to become a genuinely 'post-fascist' party was hardly surprising. Not only was its 'modernisation' project intellectually shallow but a genuine Herculean cleansing of the Augean stables, purging the party of its historical 'baggage' would have required the resignation of Griffin at the outset were it to have had any credibility. Butler's post-mortem placed the blame squarely at Griffin's door. The culture of 'careless extremism' that he had railed against in 2001 had remained pervasive. Indeed, Griffin's own predilection for such hard talk 'creates the climate where a BNP member has been arrested for burning the Koran,' stated Butler.[785] This failure to overhaul the centre, gave license to a more concrete expression of racist extremism on the periphery, which in turn fuelled the party's reputation for racism. The effect, Butler argued, was cumulative. Griffin's extremism 'creates a breeding ground for freaks and justifies nutters doing all manner of things.'[786]

Dashed electoral hopes, an acute financial crisis and debilitating schisms, combined to accelerate the departure of most of the party's paid staff and almost its entire activist base. Membership, already in decline, went into freefall: 12,632 (2009); 10,256 (2010); 7,651 (2011); 4,872 (2012); 4,200 (2013); and 2,992 (2014). Baseline membership was probably even lower since these figures included over 1,000 'life members' who remained 'members' regardless of whether they still supported the party or not.[787] BNP membership was reportedly lower than at any time since 1993, when the BNP boasted 1,353 members.[788]

Annus horribilis

The New Year started badly for Griffin, and got worse. On 3 January 2014, Welshpool County Court declared Griffin bankrupt, for a second time, after his former solicitors petitioned the court for £120,000 in unpaid legal fees relating to the opening rounds of the EHRC case. Glossing the humiliation, Griffin declared that he was turning his experience 'to the benefit of hard-up constituents by producing a booklet on dealing with debt.' It never appeared.[789] His modernisation strategy in tatters, Griffin ramped up the extremity of his rhetoric. In March, he told the European Parliament: 'An unholy alliance of capitalists and Zionist supremacists have schemed to promote immigration and miscegenation with the deliberate aim of breeding us out of existence in our homelands.'[790]

Standing for re-election to the European Parliament, Griffin sought to exploit the death of Lee Rigby, a young soldier murdered in a Woolwich street by Islamist terrorists, days before the election. He led a group of BNP activists in protest complete with a mock gallows outside the court demanding the death penalty for the killers.[791] The rowdy protest contrasted with the quiet dignity of Lee Rigby's family. The BNP election campaign, which utilised images of a British bulldog, served to make the BNP something of a reactionary caricature. It was revealing of how far Griffin had strayed from his radical roots. The European elections represented 'Judgement Day' with party fund-raising emails declaring that this was 'the most important appeal in our history NOW is the time!'[792]

The election was a debacle. Both Griffin and Brons, who had already announced he was stepping down, lost their seats. The BNP vote imploded. Having gained 943,000 votes (6.3 per cent) in 2009, five years later, this had plunged to 180,000 (1 per cent). Griffin polled a mere 32,826 votes (1.87 per cent) in the North West, where previously he had polled 132,094 votes (8 per cent). The BNP took cold comfort from the re-election of BNP councillor in Pendle, its first electoral 'victory' in three years and quite possibly its last. The rise of UKIP, which polled first place, accentuated the fact that the BNP's electoral decline appeared irreversible. Griffin put a brave face on the defeat, claiming this 'huge vote' would 'come back to us in due course' once the UKIP and its 'ultra Tory agenda' had disappointed its voters. Bereft of political support, Griffin reverted to type. Having previously derided the NF as 'boneheaded Nazi cranks' and 'perpetual losers',[793] Griffin now posed for photographs with its activists clutching a 'Fourteen Words' banner at a small anti-mosque demonstration in Bolton in a bid to re-establish his hard-line credibility.[794] Internationally, he had sought to burnish these credentials by making alliances with the overtly Nazi Golden Dawn resulting in anti-Semitic tropes creeping back into party pronouncements.[795]

Two months after losing the election, Griffin was ousted as BNP chairman at an Executive Council meeting on 19 July 2014. He issued a statement vaguely acknowledging the 'perception' that he was responsible for the party's poor electoral performance. To avoid a damaging period of 'internal friction', he declared that he was standing down to devote himself more fully to his transnational campaign, 'to build resistance to the neo-con drive to make the world safe for US oil giants, the internal banks, global corporations and Zionist supremacism.' Elevated to the position of 'Honorary President', Griffin reassured the membership that 'I am most definitely staying with the British National Party as an active member.'[796] This proved fanciful. Griffin's 'erratic and disruptive' behaviour, embodied in his authorship of *British National Party: Problems for the New Leader – Problems for us all and the Simple Solutions*, which made numerous accusations against the party officials who had ousted him (and was thus redolent of his 1986 tirade, *Attempted Murder*), led to Griffin's expulsion from the BNP only three months later.[797] Removing Griffin did nothing to revive the party's fortunes. The BNP has since plunged headlong into political oblivion. It polled just 1,667 votes (0 per cent) in the 2015 general election, plummeting from the 564,331 (1.9 per cent) only five years previously – a 99.7 per cent drop in its vote. The last time its vote was so low was 1987, a year in which settled immigration was at its lowest level since immigration controls were imposed in 1961.[798]

Legacy

Given Griffin's continued political activity, pronouncing judgement upon his 'legacy' seems premature. Whilst he helped transform the BNP into the most electorally successful extreme right-wing party in British history, paradoxically, he was also largely responsible for propelling it into political oblivion thereafter. Lacking an organisational legacy, Griffin has also yet to pen a major ideological treatise – unlike every other figure studied here – making the longevity of his intellectual influence upon the tradition even harder to discern. Since the demise of the BNP, Griffin has returned to the political margins. Following his expulsion, he briefly flirted with 'British Voice', a support group, which he soon exchanged for 'British Unity', 'a grass-roots Social Media and street protest movement', subsequently rebranded as a 'grass-roots National Revolutionary movement'. Organisationally, however, this was little more than a Facebook page, barely registering within the wider milieu of anti-Muslim politics. Portraying himself as a 'National revolutionary strategist & author' and 'Lifelong white rights fighter', Griffin increasingly retreated from the domestic sphere, seeking succour in his radical national revolutionary roots.[799]

His national profile now negligible, Griffin turned, as Mosley had done, to transnational activism. Following the collapse of the Alliance of European Nationalist Movements (AENM), a European political party to which the BNP belonged within the European Parliament, Griffin channelled his efforts into the Alliance for Peace and Freedom (AFP), a Third Position umbrella organisation presided over by his old friend Roberto Fiore.[800] Presumably supported by a stipend, Griffin currently acts as a tribune for the AFP, notable for its support for Russia's authoritarian leader Vladimir Putin and his Syrian satrap Bashar al-Assad, a position reflecting Griffin's own ongoing identification with anti-liberal despotisms since the 1980s.

Regarding Putin as a 'providential figure' who 'towers above all the other national leaders of this century,'[801] Griffin, like many extreme and radical right leaders in Europe, has aligned himself with Russia.[802] Griffin's VK page – The Russian equivalent of Facebook – currently describes him as 'Working with the Alliance for Peace & Freedom British Unity for peace between Russia and the occupied West.'[803] This trend had already been evident for several years. In 2011, Griffin, as part of his role as an MEP, had served as an election observer at the State Duma elections which, having visited a mere three polling stations, he declared to be 'much fairer than Britain's'.[804] Thereafter, he returned to Russia in November 2013, claiming, at a conference in Moscow, that Western 'controlled media' were 'hypocritical' to accuse Putin of human rights abuses when European countries jailed 'revisionists' for holding 'politically incorrect' views of history, illustrating his case with reference to Ernst Zündel and Manfred Roeder, whom he lauded as 'Prisoners of Conscience'.[805] He made a third visit in March 2015 to participate in an International Russian Conservative Forum in St Petersburg. 'I see this forum,' Griffin told those assembled, 'as a way of pushing the fight back against liberalism and what we call modernism, the destruction of traditional values, including Christianity, throughout the modern world.'[806] Furthermore, Griffin argued, 'the survival of Christendom' was 'absolutely impossible without the rise of the Third Rome: Moscow.' Fiore, who also spoke at the conference, reiterated this point, adding: 'It's not me saying this – it's God saying it.'[807]

During the closing months of his BNP leadership, Griffin had begun actively proselytising for Assad's Syrian regime within the European Parliament. He came to regard Assad as 'of all the world figures the bravest, and the one whose steadfast courage has done most to block and reverse the previously apparently unstoppable creep of globalism.'[808] Griffin visited Damascus in June 2013 as part of a twenty-eight-strong group of MEPs and MPs.[809] This 'fact finding' delegation was officially invited by President al-Assad and the Arab Socialist Baath Party, Syria's ruling party since the 1963 coup, whose initial reference points 'resonated with tropes that were attributed to National Socialist thought.'[810] Griffin owed his invitation to 'Russian connections' forged whilst serving as an election observer, he stated.[811] Arriving in the Lebanese capital Beirut on 9 June, Griffin claimed 'it's much less alien than the streets of London these days.'[812] Notably, he also appeared to praise Assad's Lebanese allies, Hezbollah ('The Party of God'), who, he stated, were 'doing better job than the Met dealing with "British" Jihadi cut-throats in Syria.'[813] Thereafter, having travelled through Hezbollah-controlled territory to reach Damascus, Griffin met Syria's Prime Minister Wael Nader al-Halqi and Information Minister Omran al-Zoubi. He reported that aside from 'occasional explosions' in the distance, life in the capital was 'normal'.[814] He was also chaperoned to a police station where a jihadi suicide bomber had killed fourteen people. 'This is done by the people David Cameron wants to arm,' Griffin claimed. 'It's an absolute disgrace.'[815] During the same visit, Griffin also filmed an interview with 'a failed "Free Syrian Army" suicide bomber', who allegedly told him that 'Christians' were a greater enemy than the Jews.[816]

Griffin subsequently spoke with *Russia Today*, the Kremlin-backed broadcaster, claiming that Syria was simply a 'secular, tolerant state' and that the 'majority' of those fighting to topple Assad's regime were 'foreign terrorists, tens of thousands of them', who would inevitably return to Western Europe 'to continue their jihad.' Griffin also railed against American intervention as 'a criminal action' aiming to secure energy supplies for the USA and to 'contain Russia'.[817] Syrian state media subsequently recycled the interview as propaganda for Assad's regime.[818]

Echoing his blinkered denial of Libyan terrorism thirty years earlier, Griffin also defended the Syrian despot against accusations he had used chemical weapons against his own people. Griffin dismissed, and continues to dismiss, such reports as the '#SyriaHoax' fabricated by a 'Lying Press' (an iteration of the Nazis' 'Lügenpresse' slur).[819] Griffin's position was consonant with that of *Russia Today*, which accused the BBC in March 2014 of fabricating such reports, leading Ofcom, the broadcasting regulator, to sanction it.[820] Undeterred, Griffin proclaimed *Russia Today* was 'For people who want the truth'.[821] Amidst increasing calls for British military intervention, Griffin returned to Syria in August on a self-funded 'peace mission', meeting with the Speaker of the People's Assembly, Mohammad Jihad al-Laham, and the Minister for National Reconciliation Ali Haidar. Al-Laham subsequently penned an open letter to British MPs urging them to 'turn Great Britain from the warpath'. Griffin claimed its contents had been 'influenced by my discussions' with al-Laham and others, insisting that it had helped sway some MPs to vote against a motion regarding military intervention, which saw the government defeated by thirteen votes. There was scant evidence, however, that the letter, or Griffin's supposed hand in it, had played any role in the outcome whatsoever. Branded an apologist for Assad's regime, a charge he rejected, Griffin conceded it was 'probably not the nicest, but at least it is on our side.' Despite professing sympathy for those displaced by the civil war, particularly Syrian Christians, Griffin remained adamant: 'I still wouldn't want people coming to Britain as refugees.'[822]

Griffin returned to Damascus in November 2014, attending a conference, organised by the Syrian Justice Ministry, which he characterised as being 'Against US-licenced Wahhabi terror'.[823] He was the only British attendee. Griffin claimed to have done 'nearly a dozen interviews' with Syrian media including an hour-long Syrian television broadcast.[824] 'Only when here can you really see the full criminality of US/EU/UK plan to use Isis as excuse to bomb Syrian army & put Islamists in power,' he claimed conspiratorially.[825] Returning for a fourth time in June 2015, this time as part of an eight-strong AFP delegation, which included Roberto Fiore, Hervé van Laethem of the Belgian 'Nation' group and Udo Voigt and Jen Pühse of the NPD, Griffin again met with Speaker of the People's Assembly and the Information Minister. The Deputy Foreign and Expatriates Minister Fayssal Mikdad joined them too. Fiore also met with the Assistant Regional Secretary of al-Baath Arab Socialist Party, Hilal al-Hilal. Perhaps the most important figure they met was General Michel Aoun in Beirut, a Maronite Christian who became president of Lebanon in October 2016. Fiore stated:

> Thanks to this providential election, another piece of American policy in Middle East is failing, since US are interested in a Lebanon torn by fratricidal and inter-confessional struggle. Thus Syria has strengthened its alliances in the area, while nationalists and European peoples have a one more nation to look at with a great confidence.[826]

Griffin also highlighted that the 'non-white leader who puts all of us to shame with his insight, political and organizational skills, and utter fearlessness' was Hezbollah's leader Hassan Nasrallah.[827] He forged further contacts with the Iran-backed group, which was providing military support to Assad, after returning to Lebanon on 16 March 2019 as part of an AFP delegation, led by Fiore. Ammar al-Moussawi, the foreign affair's chief of Hezbollah, received the delegation, only weeks after the British government had designated the group as a terrorist organisation. This did not deter the delegation from visiting the memorial garden for martyrs in southern Dehieh in Beirut, where they 'placed a wreath of flowers on the graves of [Hezbollah] martyrs. They said that these sacrifices have brought about victory, and have defended Lebanon and the region,' reported Al-Manar TV.[828] Griffin met again with the Lebanese president, Michel Aoun.[829]

In 2008, it had suited Griffin's domestic anti-Muslim agenda to praise Israel during its ground invasion of Gaza. Now, however, it was politically expedient for him to accuse Israel of wanting to 'destroy all resistance to their Eretz (Greater) Israel [by] ethnic cleansing of Palestinian land, to isolate Iran prior to launching another war there, and to reduce the whole Middle East into a howling wilderness of sectarian hatred.'[830] Thus, for Griffin, the Syrian Civil War was not only a conflict designed to bolster Israel, but one which would serve as a 'stepping stone' for a 'globalist' attack upon Iran and thence Russia, 'the last bastion of the white race'.[831] This final racial redoubt was again facing an existential threat from its seemingly eternal foe: 'Rothschilds v Russia', Griffin stated. 'Before Putin the target was the Romanovs.'[832] Reverting to the overtly anti-Semitic 'Jews' War' frame, characteristic of his earlier career, Griffin marked the centennial of the Bolshevik revolution, by proclaiming:

> The essentially alien and imported nature of the misnamed 'Russian' Revolution has close parallels with the creation and rise of Islamic State in Syria and Iraq. This is no accident, for both were there for very similar purposes, and had very similar origins.[833]

He has also returned to promoted Holocaust denial, something he demurred from countenancing when his political star was in the ascendant.[834]

Most recently, Griffin's activities have centred upon Eastern Europe, particularly Hungary, Bulgaria and Serbia, which he visited under the auspices of the AFP. Much of this activity took place under the umbrella of the 'Knights Templar International', an organisation run by Jim Dowson, a militant anti-abortion activist who had previously worked as the BNP fund-raiser. Griffin credits Dowson as being 'the man who really brought home to me both the crucial role of business organization and money in effecting change and the absolutely core issue of our own catastrophically law birthrate in the "Great Replacement"'.[835] Both men were pictured delivering supplies to anti-refugee vigilante groups on the Bulgarian border at the height of the refugee crisis. Interviewed in February 2016, Griffin reaffirmed his belief that Western Democracy was ending and that ensuing war would force people to move to 'Hungary, Poland, or Russia' – including himself.[836] Griffin planned to relocate to Hungary himself, having hitherto praised the hard-line immigration policies of Hungary's illiberal authoritarian Prime Minister Viktor Orbán throughout the refugee crisis. He had addressed several meetings in the country, having previously forged contacts with the Jobbik party. However, the Hungarian authorities scotched Griffin's plans by declaring him and Dowson *persona non grata* in May 2017. Griffin blamed the Jews, his anti-Semitism having become increasingly voluble following his departure from the BNP: 'Just shows the power of #Soros – been going to #Hungary for 18 months with no problems. Criticised him – banned!'[837]

Having previously rejected Christianity, Griffin now argued – in line with the Knights Templar's focus – that 'only' Christianity had the 'moral power' to 'bring to an end the worship of Mammon and to inspire the New Crusade which is the only thing that can drive Islamism back into the desert from which it emerged.' Providing the 'moral and spiritual heart of our world,' Christianity would provide the basis for 'future Resistance and Reconquista' in the lands of the West, inspiring a 'victorious counter-revolution'. Having 'vanquished' Bolshevism in the East, Griffin argued that '[t]he same will happen in the West, in the Long War against not just the Islamist plague, but also to destroy the liberal virus that unleashed it.'[838]

The ebb and flow of Griffin's seemingly ideological inconsistent and often contradictory political career represents something of a conundrum compared to the other ideologues scrutinised in this volume. After he became BNP chair in 1999 and began adumbrating a 'national populism' stance, former colleagues were puzzled.

> He has been a conservative, a revolutionary nationalist, a radical National Socialist, a Third Positionist, a friend of the 'boot boys' and the skinhead scene, a man committed to respectable politics and electioneering, a 'moderniser'. Which is he in reality?[839]

asked the ITP, which Griffin had helped found. 'Perhaps he has been all these quite sincerely – in which case his judgement is abysmal; or perhaps he has been none of them sincerely – which speaks for itself!'[840] Tyndall's long-term ally, John Morse, deposed as editor of *British Nationalist* in 1999, had been equally dismissive. 'Nick's words seem to be whatever flavoured chewing gum for the ears that he calculates his audience of the moment might prefer,' he wrote. 'It's all done for effect.'[841] Griffin's critics undoubtedly feel vindicated. Twenty years later, Griffin turned volte-face again, jettisoning 'modernisation' in order to re-embrace third position politics, albeit the religious fundamentalist variant that he had previously denounced. If nothing else, such shifts signal that the 'national populist' strategy, which won the BNP unprecedented support, was little more than a ruse, a thin veneer behind which stood Griffin's ongoing commitment to the racial nationalist and fascist politics of his youth.

The collapse of the BNP and his own unceremonious dismissal from the party led Griffin to abandon thoughts of engaging in electoral activity to achieve racial nationalist goals. Even being an MEP, a position he had long coveted, brought him to the realisation, he claimed in retrospect, that he was simply a 'totally powerless fig leaf' because real power lay with the European Commission. 'It's a complete farce,' he opined.[842] In several recent racially apocalyptic jeremiads, Griffin has proclaimed that there was 'no point' in doing politics anymore, 'it's too late'.[843] Demographic change in Europe had been 'so catastrophic that there is no possible political solution.'[844] Since 'our people' have stubbornly refused to 'wake up' and vote for racial nationalist panaceas 'they'll be woken up with pain, and plenty of it.' Only then, argued Griffin, will they begin to 'fight back' and reclaim Europe from the Muslim 'invasion' – 'Reconquista 2.0'.[845] The annihilation of his domestic political prospects did not deter Griffin. 'My firm belief,' he wrote about himself in 2018, 'is that Nick Griffin's long-term influence will not be anything I've already done, but what comes next.'[846] Whilst it is unlikely that he will again ever enjoy the political prominence he attained between 2001 and 2010, as Griffin's recent proselytising against 'Anglo-Zionists' in the Middle East suggests, he clearly continues to envision a role for himself within the racial nationalist milieu.

Notes

1 'BNP: Nick Griffin Victory Speech in Manchester', YouTube, 15 June 2009, www.youtube.com/watch?v=GPKDMjfrIr4 (accessed 25 May 2015).
2 Srdja Trifkovic, 'Nick Griffin's Long March', *American Renaissance*, 14 June 2006, reprinted from *Chronicles Magazine*, 8 June 2006, www.amren.com/news/2006/06/nick_griffins_l/ (accessed 16 March 2017).

3 Not to mention an annual income of nearly £2 million by 2009 (up from £80,000 in 2001), a dozen full-time, paid staff and a membership of approximately 12,500.
4 Robert Ford and Matthew Goodwin, *Revolt on the Right: Explaining Support for the Radical Right in Britain* (Abingdon: Routledge, 2014); and Matthew Goodwin and Caitlin Milazzo, *UKIP: Inside the Campaign to Redraw the Map of British Politics* (Oxford: Oxford University Press, 2015).
5 'Nick Griffin Expelled from BNP Membership', www.bnp.org.uk/news/national/nick-griffin-expelled-bnp-membership (accessed 1 October 2014).
6 Matthew Goodwin, 'Nick Griffin Supports the Golden Dawn in Athens as the BNP Falls Apart', the *Spectator*, 10 January 2014, http://blogs.spectator.co.uk/coffeehouse/2014/01/nick-griffin-supports-the-golden-dawn-in-athens-as-his-party-collapses/ (accessed 11 January 2014).
7 *Daily Mail*, 24 October 2009.
8 *Daily Mail*, 29 April 2006.
9 The *Observer*, 1 September 2002.
10 See the interview with Nick Griffin, 'High Profile: Far from Right?', *Third Way*, 24 May 2004, https://thirdway.hymnsam.co.uk/editions/archive/high-profile/far-from-right.aspx (accessed 21 February 2012).
11 On this theme, see John W.P. Veugelers, 'Dissenting Families and Social Movement Abeyance: The Transmission of Neo-Fascist Frames in Post-War Italy', *The British Journal of Sociology*, vol. 62, no. 2, 2011, pp. 241–261.
12 *Daily Mail*, 25 October 2009. @NickGriffinBU, Twitter, 9 November 2014, https://twitter.com/nickjgriffinbnp/status/531521587024265219 (accessed 9 November 2014).
13 *Daily Mail*, 25 October 2009. The interviewer Dominic Carmen had been researching a biography of Griffin which Griffin disputed here, see 'The Times Sinks to Gutter Level with "Devil's Brew" of Deliberate Lies and Incompetent Research', 14 June 2009, http://bnp.org.uk/2009/06/the-times-sinks-to-gutter-level-with-"devil's-brew"-of-deliberate-lies-and-incompetent-research (accessed 10 October 2009); and 'Professional Liar Dominic Carmen Slanders Nick Griffin', 22 October 2009, https//britishnationalpartynews.blogspot.com/2009/10/professional-liar-dominic-carmen (accessed 21 October 2009). Griffin subsequently complained to the Press Complaints Commission about another article, this time in the *Daily Mail*, which agreed to remove the disputed claim – that Griffin had an admiration for Hitler – from the online version of the article and to note Griffin's position for the future, on which, see www.pcc.org.uk/cases/adjudicated.html?article=NjMxNA==&type= (accessed 10 October 2009).
14 *Daily Mail*, 25 October 2009.
15 *Ibid*.
16 *Instauration*, vol. 10, no. 8, July 1985.
17 *Moving On, Moving Up* (Ilford: Nick Griffin election campaign, 1999).
18 'Obituary: Bill Fitt, the Man Who Introduced Nick Griffin to Nationalism', 1 June 2010, www.bnp.org.uk/?q=news/obituary-bill-fitt-man-who-introduced-nick-griffin-nationalism (accessed 1 June 2010). Fitt, a founding member of Norwich NF (*Spearhead*, no. 92, March 1976), remained in the party, sitting on its Directorate until 1998 when the branch disbanded and merged into the BNP (*British Nationalist*, no. 202, April 1999). Griffin addressed the inaugural meeting of Norwich BNP in March 1999. Thereafter, Fitt served as Norfolk BNP organiser until 2002. He died in 2010.
19 John Q. Publius, 'Racial Profiles: Nick Griffin', *Republic Standard*, 14 October 2018, https://republicstandard.com/racial-profiles-nick-griffin/ (accessed 18 October 2018). On Britton, who also edited *American Nationalist*, see FBI file 105–22921–7.
20 *Western Mail*, 25 August 2001.
21 Martin Webster, interview with the author, 21 July 2009.
22 *Electronic Loose Cannon*, no. 20, 13 June. Williams sold badges emblazoned with 'National Front' or 'Race and Nation' c/o Griffin's family home, see *Spearhead*, no. 111, November 1977.
23 *Spearhead*, no. 110, October 1977. *National Front News*, no. 12, March 1978 reported 'Red thugs' had attacked Edgar Griffin as he returned from an NF meeting at Ipswich Town Hall on 4 February 1978.
24 *The Mirror*, 24 August 2001. The Conservative Party expelled Griffin for answering the BNP hotline at his home usually manned by his wife, Jean, the party's Enquiries Secretary. Vice-chairman of the Montgomeryshire Conservative Association, Edgar Griffin had also become a

vice-president in Ian Duncan Smith's Conservative Party leadership campaign. Ironically, Jean Griffin had stood against Smith in the 2001 general election earlier that year having previously contested Enfield North for the BNP in 1997.

25 *Patriot*, no. 4, spring 1999.
26 *Spearhead*, no. 103, March 1977.
27 *Spearhead*, no. 106, June 1977.
28 Ryan Shaffer, *Music, Youth and International Links in Post-War British Fascism* (London: Palgrave, 2017), p. 69.
29 *Spearhead*, no. 108, August 1977; and *National Front News*, no. 11, December 1977. Andrew Brons proposed the motion to form the YNF at the NF AGM in October 1977, which also saw a Constitutional amendment lowering the minimum age limit for joining the NF from sixteen to fourteen.
30 Nick Griffin to John Cosier, 17 October 1997 in MSS 412/WA/3/1, Wayne Ashcroft papers, Modern Records Centre, Warwick University, hereafter Ashcroft papers.
31 *National Front News*, no. 10, August 1977.
32 NF Directorate, minutes, 3 December 1977, MSS 321/1, Harrington papers.
33 *Bulldog*, no. 5, n.d. notes the YNF Secretariat consisted of Andrew Fountaine (chairman); Joe Pearce (National Activities organiser); Kevin Randall (press officer); Tim White and Roger Denny (Administrative staff); Dave Goddard, Steve Smith, Bill Wright, Nick Griffin and Nick Wakeling (Regional Representatives).
34 Joseph Pearce, *Race with the Devil: My Journey from Racial Hatred to Rational Love* (Charlotte, NC: Saint Benedict Press, 2013), pp. 61–62.
35 *Spearhead*, no. 115, March 1978.
36 *Bulldog*, no. 5, n.d.
37 For an overview, see John Pollard, 'Skinhead Culture: The Ideologies, Mythologies, Religions and Conspiracy Theories of Racist Skinheads', *Patterns of Prejudice*, vol. 50, nos 4–5, 2016, pp. 398–319.
38 Paul Wilkinson, *The New Fascists* (London: Pan Books, 1983), p. 201.
39 Pearce, *Race with the Devil*, p. 63.
40 Colin Ward and 'Chubby' Chris Henderson, *Who Wants It?* (Edinburgh: Mainstream, 2001), p. 71. Griffin claimed that Leeds NF sold 700 copies of *Bulldog* every issue, see *Nationalism Today*, no. 25.
41 John E. Richardson, *British Fascism: A Discourse – Historical Analysis* (Stuttgart: ibidem-Verlag, 2017), p. 279.
42 *Spearhead*, no. 111, November 1977; *The True Facts About Race* (YNF leaflet); and George Marshall, *Spirit of '69: A Skinhead Bible* (Dunoon: STP, 1994), p. 134.
43 NF Directorate Meeting, Minutes, 30 October 1977, Harrington papers.
44 Stan Taylor, *The National Front in English Politics* (London: Macmillan, 1989), p. 142; and *Spearhead*, no. 113, January 1978.
45 M. Harrop, J. England and C.T. Husbands, 'The Bases of National Front Support', *Political Studies*, vol. 28, 1980, p. 278; Michael Billig and Raymond Cochrane, 'The National Front and Youth', *Patterns of Prejudice*, vol. 15, no. 4, October 1981, pp. 9–10; and Michael Billig and Raymond Cochrane, 'Adolescent Support for the National Front: A Test of Three Models of Political Extremism', *Journal of Ethnic and Migration Studies*, vol. 10, no. 1, 1982, pp. 86–94.
46 *Combat*, no. 2, May 1978.
47 *The Nazi Threat in Norwich* (Norwich: Norwich ANL, 1979).
48 *Anglian News*, no. 7, August 1978.
49 *Anglian News*, no. 10, December 1978; and *Anglian News*, 13, September–October 1979.
50 *Spearhead*, no. 122, October 1978; and *Spearhead*, no. 129, July 1979 highlights YNF football competitions, that the YNF organised its own sporting activities including a five-a-side football tournament – the 'John Tyndall Shield' – which was won by Hackney YNF. *Spearhead*, no. 129, July 1979 notes that thirty teams were involved in the tournament in the following year.
51 *Bulldog*, no. 6, n.d.
52 *Bulldog*, no. 14; *Bulldog*, no. 15; and *Spearhead*, no. 130, August 1979.
53 *Spearhead*, no. 114, February 1978; *Spearhead*, no. 117, May 1978; and *National Front News*, no. 15, September 1978.
54 *Spearhead*, no. 130, August 1979.

55 *National Front News*, no. 20, March 1980.
56 Pearce, *Race with the Devil*, pp. 82–90.
57 *Nationalism Today*, no. 31, n.d.
58 *Keith Allen meets Nick Griffin*, Channel 4 documentary, 5 March 2012.
59 *Bulldog*, no. 6, March 1978. He had no sympathy for left-wing students. When German student leader Rudi Dutschke died from an epileptic seizure in 1979, the result of injuries received during a botched assassination attempt by an extreme right student in 1968, Griffin mocked his passing in *Spearhead*, no. 135, January 1980.
60 Daniel Trilling, *Bloody Nasty People: The Rise of Britain's Far Right* (London: Verso, 2012), p. 41.
61 Kenneth Leech, *Brick Lane 1978: The Events and Their Significance* (London: Stepney Books, 1994); and *Brick Lane 1978: The Case for Defence* (London: Tower Hamlets Trades Council/Hackney Legal Action Group, 1979).
62 *Spearhead*, no. 124, December 1978.
63 *Spearhead*, no. 126, February 1979. His proposal was seconded by the new YNF chairman, Philip Gegan, who succeeded Andrew Fountaine (*Bulldog*, no. 10, November 1978). Gegan was 'regional agent for East Anglia' NF and worked with Anthony Reed-Herbert, organiser of the NF Leicester branch, for the Leicestershire-based solicitors Reed-Herbert, Gegan & Co., who frequently defended NF members in court.
64 *Spearhead*, no. 120, August 1978; and *Bulldog*, no. 10, November 1978. *Frontpage*, no. 1. This incorporated *Rite Up*, the journal of the Cambridge University NF group, which had run to three issues – one a year since 1974.
65 *Nationalism Today*, no. 46, July 1989 complained that both the YNF students' organisation and the NF trade union group ran in parallel to the party's geographical unit of organisation, which had priority. The result was that such initiatives, being outside the branch structure, were treated as a sideline and 'marginalised'.
66 *Bulldog*, no. 10, November 1978.
67 *Spearhead*, no. 129, July 1979.
68 *Spearhead*, no. 121, September 1978.
69 *Spearhead*, no. 130, August 1979; and *Instauration*, vol. 4, no. 4, April 1979. *Identity*, no. 11, July 2001 reviewed *Dispossessed Majority* (1972) indicating the continued appeal of its arguments for the BNP.
70 Mitch Berbrier, 'Impression Management for the Thinking Racist: A Case Study of Intellectualization as Stigma Transformation in Contemporary White Supremacist Discourse', *Sociological Quarterly*, vol. 40, no. 3, 1999, pp. 411–433.
71 *Spearhead*, no. 134, December 1979.
72 For list of party positions, see *National Front Members' Bulletin*, August–September 1974.
73 A.H.W. Brons to Mrs. Jordan, 15 June 1965 in SCH/01/Res/BRI/20/001, Searchlight archive.
74 *The Times*, 1 March 1980.
75 *New Nation*, no. 1, summer 1980; and *Spearhead*, no. 136, February 1980. *National Front News*, no. 20, March 1980 records that while the NF had 'sound analysis' of issues like race and immigration, 'it had not yet developed and articulated the broad philosophical basis on which the ideology of British Nationalism rests.'
76 *National Front Members' Bulletin*, July 1980. This was not simply a reaction to the fateful 1979 general election. Brons had been pursuing such an agenda since 1976 when he was appointed by the NF Directorate as the NF Education Officer in which capacity, recorded *Spearhead*, no. 97, September 1976, he was responsible 'for the promotion of political education and training courses for members, particularly prospective candidates and local party leaders.'
77 *Nationalism Today*, no. 3.
78 *Nationalism Today*, no. 26.
79 Tyndall was not averse to Distributism or the idea of workers' cooperatives per se but argued in *Spearhead*, no. 184, February 1984 that ideological refinement played a secondary role to the 'immediate questions concerned with the advancement of the political power and influence of the Nationalist movement itself.' Eddy Butler, a Tower Hamlets BNP activist, implied in *Spearhead*, no. 214, December 1986 that the basic principles of Distributism (that property should be more widely shared out with a great number of small businesses) were already enshrined in *Beyond Capitalism and Socialism* and the 1979 NF general election manifesto, both of which Tyndall had been largely responsible for writing.

80 *Nationalism Today*, no. 45 interviewed Father Brocard Sewell, a Carmelite friar and Distributist who had worked on *G.K.'s Weekly*, providing a living link to this tradition. Sewell, who edited *Aylesford Review*, admired Mosley and was one of the select few to attend his burial in Paris in 1980.
81 Julia Stapleton, 'The Limits of Pro-Fascism and Anti-Fascism: G.K. Chesterton and Arthur Bryant', in Nigel Copsey and Andrzej Olechnowicz, *Varieties of Anti-Fascism: Britain in the Interwar Period* (London: Palgrave, 2010), pp. 224–244.
82 *Nationalism Today*, no. 19.
83 *New Nation*, no. 2, autumn 1980; and *National Front News*, no. 37, December 1981.
84 *We are the National Front* (London: Newport Fotos, 1981).
85 *Spearhead*, no. 357, November 1998.
86 'Breaking News! Police Investigating Nick Griffin over Twitter Comment', 3 October 2012, www.bnp.org.uk/news/national/breaking-news-police-investigating-nick-griffin-over-twitter-comment (accessed 17 September 2013).
87 *National Front News*, no. 23, June 1980.
88 *New Nation*, no. 3, autumn 1982.
89 Dawkins' fiercely refuted the NF interpretation of his work, see Frank Miele, 'Darwin's Dangerous Discipline: An Interview with Richard Dawkins', *Skeptic*, vol. 3, no. 4, 1995, pp. 80–85, http://scepsis.net/eng/articles/id_3.php (accessed 31 January 2018).
90 Pearce, *Race with the Devil*, pp. 80–81.
91 New Nation, no. 1, summer 1980. Griffin's commentary was accompanied by a quotation from William Gayley Simpson's *Which Way Western Man?* (1978), dubbed the 'survival manual of the white race':

> The everlasting truth about race is that breed is everything. Or, to put it more in terms of the scientist, the gene pool of our race is its supreme treasure … And the first right under heaven, the right before which every other right must give way, is that our race should fight – with its every and uttermost resource – to keep its gene pool holy, unsullied and inviolable'.

92 *New Nation*, no. 1, summer 1980.
93 Pearce, *Race with the Devil*, p. 74.
94 *Spearhead*, no. 132, October 1979 records Wakeling's election to the NF Directorate. Shaffer, *Music, Youth and International Links in Post-War British Fascism*, p. 84.
95 *Nationalism Today*, no. 2.
96 *Nationalism Today*, no. 1, March 1980.
97 *Nationalism Today*, no. 5.
98 Griffin acknowledged the transition in *Identity*, no. 19, April 2002.
99 *Nationalism Today*, no. 2. In *Nationalism Today*, no. 13 Griffin asked why the Communists had also

> wallowed in the blood, not only of their 'class enemies', but also of the workers they claim to admire.… One reason is obvious. From Marx, Engels, Trotsky (Bronstein), Bela Kuhn in Hungary and Rosa Luxemburg in Germany, right up to Tony Cliff (Ygael Gluckstein) and the rest of his family running the SWP in Britain today, the most fanatical Communist leaders have been Jews. Imbued as they are with messianic urges and an age-old contempt for Gentiles, this is not surprising.

100 *Nationalism Today*, no. 1, March 1980; and *Nationalism Today*, no. 2.
101 *Nationalism Today*, no. 8.
102 *Nationalism Today*, no. 10.
103 *Spearhead*, no. 128, May 1979. Tyndall later attacked Webster's 'working class' strategy as 'infantile leftism' in *Spearhead*, no. 146, December 1980.
104 *New Nation*, no. 2, autumn 1980.
105 *Nationalism Today*, no. 18. Canadian 'left-nationalist' John Jewell also influenced Griffin's thought in this regard, as did some of the figures associated with the National Party.
106 Knights Templar International, January 2018, https://knightstemplarinternational.com/2018/01/white-sharia-ultimate-treason-important-audio-talk-2/ (accessed 10 March 2018).
107 Peter D. Stachura, *Gregor Strasser and the Rise of Nazism* (Abingdon: Routledge, 2015).

108 David Baker, 'A.K. Chesterton, the Strasser Brothers and the Politics of the National Front', *Patterns of Prejudice*, vol. 19, no. 3, 1985, pp. 23–33; and Philip M. Coupland, '"Left-Wing Fascism" in Theory and Practice: The Case of the British Union of Fascists', *Twentieth Century British History*, vol. 13, no. 1, 2002, pp. 38–61.
109 *Yesterday & Tomorrow: Roots of National-Revolution* (London: Rising Press, 1983). Authors included the Strasser brothers; Nazi economist Gottfried Feder; the Nazis' original Twenty-Five point and agrarian programmes; writings by the British socialists Robert Blatchford and William Morris; Catholic author G.K. Chesterton; and the revolutionary syndicalism of BUF ideologue Alexander Raven Thomson.
110 *Spearhead*, no. 161, March 1982.
111 *Nationalism Today*, no. 12; and *Nationalism Today*, no. 18.
112 *National Review*, no. 41, June 1983.
113 *Spearhead*, no. 180, October 1983.
114 *Spearhead*, no. 193, November 1984.
115 *Spearhead*, no. 206, December 1985.
116 *Gothic Ripples*, no. 7, November 1981.
117 Arnold Leese to Anthony Gittens, 29 October [n.d.], Leese papers.
118 *Gothic Ripples*, no. 108, 12 September 1953.
119 *Nationalism Today*, no. 23.
120 *National Front News*, no. 62, January 1985, for instance.
121 *Nationalism Today*, no. 22.
122 *Nationalism Today*, no. 24, September 1984; and *Nationalism Today*, no. 38, April 1986.
123 *Nationalism Today*, no. 11.
124 *Nationalism Today*, no. 39, 1986. Schumacher's influence endured. *Voice of Freedom*, no. 74, the BNP newspaper, listed him as one of 'those who inspire our ideology' and recorded that *Small is Beautiful* presented readers with 'that third choice, neither Capitalist nor Communist, which is at the heart of modern British Nationalist economic thought.'
125 *Nationalism Today*, no. 26.
126 *Nationalism Today*, no. 14.
127 *Nationalism Today*, no. 4.
128 *Nationalism Today*, no. 5.
129 The *Mail on Sunday*, 21 July 1985. Serena Depisa, another Italian militant, lived with the group before being arrested and imprisoned whilst fighting deportation to Italy. In September 1982, police also arrested Luciano Petrone, a bank robber wanted for murdering two policemen, who was secretly living in London with his English girlfriend. He was extradited to Italy to serve a long jail sentence. Ray Hill with Andrew Bell, *The Other Face of Terror: Inside Europe's Neo-Nazi Network* (London: Grafton, 1988), pp. 190–193 highlights Petrone's closeness to the London NAR group.
130 Richard Drake, *The Revolutionary Mystique and Terrorism in Contemporary Italy* (Bloomington, IN: Indiana University Press, 1989), p. 115.
131 CIA, *Terrorism Review*, 26 May 1983 available at www.cia.gov/library/readingroom/docs/CIA-RDP84–00893R000100170001–2.pdf (accessed 23 January 2017).
132 *Nationalism Today*, no. 46.
133 Larry O'Hara, 'Notes from the Underground: British Fascism, 1974–92. Part 2', *Lobster*, no. 24, December 1992.
134 *Nationalism Today*, no. 47, 1987.
135 For the NF position, see *National Front News*, no. 28, November–December 1980.
136 Nick Griffin interview, *The Lost Race*, BBC 2, 24 March 1999.
137 Pearce, *Race with the Devil*, p. 114.
138 *Voice of St. George*, no. 17, n.d.
139 TNA HO 306/269, the files relating to the Italian extradition request for Roberto Fiore, Marcello di Angelis, Stefano Tiraboschi and Massimo Morsello, remain classified.
140 The *Guardian*, 29 February 2009.
141 *Nationalism Today*, no. 46.
142 For broader context, see Anna Cento Bull, *Italian Neofascism: The Strategy of Tension and the Politics of Nonreconciliation* (New York: Berghahn, 2007).

143 *Nationalism Today*, no. 34. *Nationalism Today*, no. 63, February 1985 blamed the bombing on the Italian security services, alleging they had orchestrated it to deflect public attention from the P2 Masonic scandal, 'an organization to which many top secret servicemen belonged.'
144 *Nationalism Today*, no. 40.
145 *Nationalism Today*, no. 18.
146 *Nationalism Today*, no. 33, September 1985. 'Terrorism? – No Thanks', declared *National Front News*, no. 68, July 1985. Its condemnation was ambiguous, however:

> If *all* avenues for political expression are closed, direct action against tyrants is the right and duty of an oppressed nation, but there can never be justification for *indiscriminate* [my emphasis] bombing and terror – whether on the scale of Coventry and Dresden, or Bologna railway station.

For the time being, however, 'there is wide scope for legal and peaceful activity.'
147 *Nationalism Today*, no. 47, 1987.
148 *Nationalism Today*, no. 40, 1986.
149 Drake, *The Revolutionary Mystique*; and Paul Furlong, *Social and Political Thought of Julius Evola* (Abingdon: Routledge, 2011).
150 *Rising*, no. 1, 1982.
151 *Rising* no. 2, 1982.
152 *Rising*, no. 3, 1983 and no. 4, 1983. *Rising*, no. 5, summer 1985 suggested imminent publication. Troy Southgate, email to the author, 27 February 2013 suggests the *Rising* group only had access to a 'partial translation' of *The Aryan Doctrine of Fight and Victory*.
153 Tradition and Revolution forum, http://traditionandrevolution.freeforums.org/the-influence-of-baron-evola-in-the-english-speaking-world-t3228.html (accessed 18 November 2009). Evola's ideas were also discussed contemporaneously in *The Scorpion*, no. 6, winter/spring 1984; *The Scorpion*, no. 7, summer 1984; *The Scorpion*, no. 8, spring 1985; and *The Scorpion*, spring 1986, for instance.
154 Jonathan Bowden, *Collected Works, vol. 4* (London: Avant-Garde Publishing, 1995), p. 358.
155 *Nationalism Today*, no. 42; and *Rising*, no. 4, 1983, which promised a translation and critique of Freda's book. In 2001, three fascist militants were jailed, though later acquitted, for the bombing. The *Guardian*, 2 July 2001 recorded that the court in this new trial appeared to recognise that Freda and another fascist, Giovanni Ventura, who had previously been tried and acquitted for the bombing, 'were parties to the plot'. They could not be tried a second time for the same offence, however.
156 *Nationalism Today*, no. 26; and *Nationalism Today*, no. 40.
157 Corneliu Zelea Codreanu, *For My Legionaries* [*The Iron Guard*] (Madrid: Editura 'Libertatea', 1976).
158 Radu Ioanid, 'The Sacralised politics of the Romanian Iron Guard', *Totalitarian Movements and Political Religions*, vol. 5, no. 3, 2004, pp. 419–453.
159 Stephen Fischer-Galati, 'Codreanu, Romanian National Traditions and Charisma', in António Costa Pinto, Roger Eatwell and Stein Ugelvik Larsen (eds), *Charisma and Fascism in Interwar Europe* (Abingdon: Routledge, 2007), pp. 107–113.
160 Eugen Weber, 'Romania', in Hans Rogger and Eugen Weber (eds), *The European Right: A Historical Profile* (London: Weidenfeld & Nicholson, 1965), pp. 524, 527 and 570. Michael Mann, *Fascists* (Cambridge: Cambridge University Press, 2004), p. 269 similarly observes the Iron Guard 'resembled a church'.
161 Raffaello Pantucci, *'We Love Death as You Love Life': Britain's Suburban Terrorists* (London: Hurst, 2015).
162 This narrative of sacrifice and martyrdom was reinforced through sales of Dumitru Bacu's *The Anti-Humans* (Englewood, CO: Soldiers of the Cross, 1971), detailing the suffering and privation experienced by Romanians imprisoned by the Soviets after the Second World War.
163 Franco Ferraresi, *Threats to Democracy: The Radical Right in Italy after the War* (Princeton, NJ: Princeton University Press, 1996), p. 168.
164 *Legion* (Rising Press/Nationalist Books, n.d.).
165 Corneliu Zelea Codreanu, *The Nest Leader's Manual* (Madrid: Editura 'Libertatea', 1987), p. viv.
166 *New Nation*, no. 7, summer 1985. *Liberty Bell*, vol. 13, no. 4, December 1985 reprinted the interview for an American audience. It is also online, a testimony to its continued inspiration:

'Jianu Dianieleau gives an Insight into the Pre-War Rumanian Nationalist Movement', *Iron Guard*, http://miscarea.net/iron-guard.html (accessed 24 February 2016).
167 'Romania', *Holocaust Encyclopedia*, United States Holocaust Memorial Museum', www.ushmm.org/wlc/en/article.php?ModuleId=10005472_Romania (accessed 21 April 2015).
168 TNA FO 950/266; and TNA FO 950/97.
169 *Rising*, no. 4, 1983.
170 *Nationalism Today*, no. 18.
171 *Candour*, vol. 35, nos 2 and 3, February–March 1984.
172 *Candour*, vol. 45, nos 9, 10 and 11, September, October and November 1993.
173 Pearce, *Race with the Devil*, p. 114. De Bounevialle later placed her property in trust. Fiore was one trustee. NF activist Colin Todd, *Candour*'s current editor, was another. De Bounevialle became actively involved in the ITP towards the end of her life and was 'proud to help a cause which she saw as true to her beliefs and which brought a new, younger generation to Forest House.' When she died in 1999, ITP activists, including Fiore, provided 'a phalanx of smartly presented coffin bearers to take her to the graveside,' see *Candour*, vol. 73, no. 1, July 2000; and *Voice of St. George*, no. 20, n.d. [2000].
174 *Heritage and Destiny*, no. 1, spring 1980.
175 *The Scorpion*, no. 4, spring 1983; and Michael Walker, Podcast No. 210, *Counter-Currents Publishing*, January 2018, www.counter-currents.com/2018/01/counter-currents-radio-weekly-interview-with-michael-walker/ (accessed 20 March 2018).
176 *The Scorpion*, no. 9, autumn 1986.
177 For criticism of Italy's MSI and Spain's Fuerza Nueva as 'reactionary', see *Nationalism Today*, no. 13.
178 'French "New Right" Philosopher Alain de Benoist on America', *French Dissidents*, 20 February 2012, http://frenchdissidents.wordpress.com/2012/02/20/french-new-right-philosopher-alain-de-benoist-on-america-2/ (accessed 9 April 2014).
179 Tamir Bar-On, *Where have all the Fascists Gone?* (Aldershot: Ashgate, 2007), pp. 142 and 144.
180 Nicholas Goodrick-Clarke, *Black Sun: Aryan Cults, Esoteric Nazism and the Politics of Identity* (New York: New York University Press, 2002), pp. 68–70. *The Scorpion*, no. 6, winter–spring 1984 featured an introduction to Evola's life and work by 'Mario Aprile'. *Searchlight*, no. 110, August 1984 suggests this was Fiore's pseudonym.
181 Michael Walker, Podcast No. 210, *Counter-Currents Publishing*, January 2018, www.counter-currents.com/2018/01/counter-currents-radio-weekly-interview-with-michael-walker/ (accessed 20 March 2018); and also Nigel Copsey, '*Au Revoir* to "Sacred Cows"? Assessing the Impact of the *Nouvelle Droite* in Britain', *Democracy and Security*, vol. 9, no. 3, 2013, pp. 287–303.
182 *Identity*, no. 53, March 2005.
183 *Searchlight*, no. 99, September 1983.
184 *Nationalism Today*, no. 22. The Heritage Group was an adjunct to the NF Nationalist Education Group, founded in March 1985 by NF activist Eddy Butler, see *National Front News*, no. 66, May 1985; *Nationalism Today*, no. 31, July 1985; and *Nationalism Today*, no. 36, February 1986. After a Heritage Group visit to Bosworth Field, where Richard III died in August 1485, Griffin penned a defence of the monarch. 'The blackening of this brave man's name by artists, playwrights and historians goes to show that the 20th century is not the only one to have been duped by a propaganda hoax.'
185 Pearce, *Race with the Devil*, p. 73.
186 Brady was previously an NF member but joined the NP during the 1976 split.
187 *NA Bulletin*, May 1980; *NA Bulletin*, June 1980; and *NA Bulletin*, September 1980.
188 *NA Bulletin*, October 1980.
189 *Nationalism Today*, no. 4; *Nationalism Today*, no. 5; and *Nationalism Today*, no. 7.
190 *Nationalism Today*, no. 4.
191 *National Front News*, no. 28, November–December 1980.
192 *National Front News*, no. 34, July 1981.
193 *Nationalism Today*, no. 17.
194 The *Croydon Patriot*, no. 1, September 1981. During this period, racist literature circulated in Sutton and Croydon bearing the imprint of the 'White Defence Force', see *The Times*, 23 September 1981.
195 The *Guardian*, 10 October 1981.

196 *National Front News*, no. 36, October 1981.
197 *National Front Members' Bulletin*, autumn 1983; and *National Front News*, no. 51, November 1983. See also Thomas Linehan, 'Cultures of Space: Spatialising the National Front', in Nigel Copsey and John E. Richardson (eds), *Cultures of Post-War British Fascism* (Abingdon: Routledge, 2015), pp. 49–67.
198 *National Front News*, no. 37, December 1981. An NFCM candidate polled 111 votes (0.3 per cent) splitting Griffin's potential vote.
199 *National Front News*, no. 24, July 1980; and *National Front News*, no. 32, May 1981.
200 Pearce, *Race with the Devil*, p. 63.
201 *NF Members' Bulletin*, spring 1982. During one protest, Martin Webster led a group of NF activists in barracking the Home Secretary, William Whitelaw, about Pearce. One activist threw a smoke bomb towards Whitelaw. Webster received a one-month jail sentence, suspended for two years with £500 costs, see *The Times*, 20 October 1982. He appealed but the court increased his sentence to three months, suspended for one year, with £1,250 costs in addition to the original £500, see *The Times*, 19 February 1983.
202 *Nationalism Today*, no. 8, 1982.
203 'Helping to Keep our Feet on the Ground', *Martin Wingfield blog*, 8 April 2009, http://martinwingfield.blogspot.com/2009/04/i.html (accessed 1 June 2015).
204 Joe Pearce, *Fight for Freedom* (Croydon: Nationalist Books, 1984), pp. 3–5.
205 *Nationalism Today*, no. 11.
206 *Nationalism Today*, no. 15.
207 *Nationalism Today*, no. 11.
208 *Nationalism Today*, no. 15 – 'Victory to Palestine! Israel – The Hate State' supplement.
209 *Nationalism Today*, no. 10.
210 *Nationalism Today*, no. 12.
211 *Nationalism Today*, no. 17. Other authors were Ian Anderson, Martin Webster, Philip Gegan and Joe Pearce.
212 National Front, *Let Britain Live* (London: National Front, 1983).
213 Thomas Finnegan, the Conservative Party candidate (Stockton South) in the 1983 general election had previously stood as an NF candidate in both 1974 general elections but left in the following year after becoming 'disillusioned'. His past associations exposed, Finnegan publicly denounced the 'totally wrong-minded and repugnant' policies of the NF, see 'Statement made by Mr. Finnegan, Stockton South, 25 May 1983' in THCR 2/7/3/40 f41, Thatcher MSS, Churchill Archive Centre, Churchill College, Cambridge. Margaret Thatcher, *The Downing Street Years* (London: Harper Collins, 1993), p. 296 dismissed the episode as a 'peripheral embarrassment' to the party.
214 *National Front News*, no. 48, July 1983. The BNP stood fifty-four candidates who averaged 0.5 per cent.
215 Martin Webster, memo to Andrew Brons, 26 September 1983 in NF Directorate correspondence, MSS 321/3, Patrick Harrington papers, Modern Records Centre, Warwick University.
216 *Spearhead*, no. 183, January 1984.
217 *National Front News*, no. 53, February 1984.
218 Richard Thurlow, *Fascism in Britain* (London: I.B. Tauris, 1998), p. 260.
219 Cabinet Interdepartmental Group on Subversion in Public Life, 21 August 1985 in TNA CAB 301/485.
220 *NF Organisers' Bulletin*, no. 20, 2 November 1984. *Heritage and Destiny*, no. 34, October–December 2008 stated that Directorate member Roger Denny heckled Webster with the words 'this is the National Front, not the Gay Front' at the NF EGM, which confirmed his expulsion and that of his partner, Martin Salt.
221 The *Mail on Sunday*, 21 July 1985.
222 *Time Out*, 23–29 January 1986.
223 Ibid.
224 'Derek Holland Interview with Swedish Radio', YouTube, www.youtube.com/watch?v=VAoztg8KxaE (accessed 1 February 2018).
225 *Liberty Bell*, vol. 13, no. 3, November 1985 published it in full. *The Political Soldier* has been translated into numerous languages, most recently Polish *Polityczny Żołnierz* (1999); Swedish *Den Politiske Soldaten* (2015); and French *Le Soldat politique* (2016). It was also the central

text for *Winds of Change: Notes for the Reconquista* (Brussels: AFP, 2016), pp. 45–70, a collection of extreme right-wing essays simultaneously translated into German as *Zeiten des Wandels: Beiträge zur Reconquista* (2017).
226 *Nationalism Today*, no. 26. Holland used the same words about the Iron Guard in *Rising* no. 5.
227 *Ibid.*
228 *Nationalism Today*, no. 32, August 1985.
229 *Nationalism Today*, no. 24, September 1984. 'The Political Soldier', in *Nationalism Today*, no. 26, February 1986 also lauded Graham Gilmore, a Hammersmith and Fulham NF activist who fought against African 'communist' insurgents in Rhodesia and South Africa.
230 Otto Skorzeny, *My Commando Operations* (Atglen, PA: Schiffer, 1995), p. 37.
231 *The Times*, 4 March 1981.
232 Sir David McNee, *McNee's Law* (London: Collins, 1983), p. 99.
233 *Nationalism Today*, no. 5. Not everyone agreed, see *Nationalism Today*, no. 10.
234 *Sussex Front*, no. 14, January 1982.
235 *Nationalism Today*, no. 9, April 1982.
236 *Nationalism Today*, no. 20.
237 Matthew Worley, 'Shot by Both Sides: Punk, Politics and the End of "Consensus"', *Contemporary British History*, vol. 26, no. 3, 2012, pp. 233–354; and Matthew Worley, 'Oi! Oi! Oi!: Class, Locality and British Punk', *Twentieth Century British History*, vol. 24, no. 4, 2013, pp. 606–636.
238 Matthew Worley and Nigel Copsey, 'White Youth: The Far Right, Punk and British Youth Culture, 1977–87', *JOMEC Journal*, no. 9, 2016, p. 42.
239 *Nationalism Today*, no. 20.
240 *Bulldog*, no. 33, May 1983; and *National Front News*, no. 47, May 1983.
241 *Skrewdriver Songbook* (A-Press: BSJ, 1997) contains its lyrics.
242 Shaffer, *Music, Youth and International Links in Post-War British Fascism*, p. 89.
243 Paul London, *Ian Stuart: Nazi Rock Star* (Göteborg: Midgård, 2002), p. 52.
244 *The Chairman's Bulletin*, no. 1, spring 1984; *National Front News*, no. 64, March 1985; and *National Front News*, no. 65, April 1985.
245 For a transcript and commentary upon video footage of the renovation, which attacks Griffin's apparently cavalier attitude towards health and safety, particularly with regards removing asbestos from the property, see [Martin Webster], *Nick Griffin's 'Community Centre Project'* (2005).
246 *Skrewdriver – Live in Suffolk, England, 1984: Classic British RAC, Vol. 4* (DVD: NS88); and *National Front News*, no. 61, November 1984. The Belfast skinhead band, Offensive Weapon, were also on the bill. Johnny Adair, who had previously 'helped' organise the NF march through Belfast in September 1983, was the frontman. Adair was fined for his involvement in 'heavy fighting' after a Skrewdriver gig in London a few months later. 'Infatuated' with the racist skinhead movement, Adair travelled to London to watch Skrewdriver play several times. He subsequently achieved infamy as leader of the Ulster Freedom Fighters (UFF), the Loyalist paramilitary group, which, together with the Ulster Defence Association (UDA) was responsible for murdering over 250 Catholics. Adair became the first person in Northern Ireland to be convicted of 'directing terrorism', see Johnny Adair, *Mad Dog* (London: John Blake, 2009), pp. 21–22; and David Lister and Hugh Jordan, *Mad Dog: The Rise and Fall of Johnny Adair and 'C Company'* (Edinburgh: Mainstream, 2003), pp. 26–32.
247 Skrewdriver, *Blood & Honour* (Rock-O-Rama: RCD 105 1985).
248 *White Noise*, no. 1. Shaffer, *Music, Youth and International Links in Post-War British Fascism*, p. 117 notes, at its peak, *White Noise*'s circulation reached 5,000.
249 *Nationalism Today*, no. 9, April 1982.
250 *National Front News*, no. 60, October 1984; and *No to Cruise! No to CND!* (1984).
251 *The Scorpion*, no. 7, summer 1984
252 *Yorkshire Evening Post*, 1 May 1984; and *NF Members' Bulletin*, June 1984.
253 *Instauration*, vol. 10, no. 8, July 1985.
254 Griffin assisted Brons editing *New Nation* from Issue 5 (spring 1984). He assumed editorship from Issue 7 (summer 1985). The publication folded shortly afterwards.
255 *The Times*, 11 April 1985. *National Front News*, no. 20, March 1980 contains a short profile of Anderson.
256 *Instauration*, vol. 10, no. 8, July 1985.

257 *Ibid.*
258 *Nationalism Today*, no. 29, no date but 1985.
259 *The Rune*, no. 12, 1996.
260 *Nationalism Today*, no. 31, July 1985. *The Crusader*, no. 18, January 1977 had announced Metzger's appointment as the California organiser or 'Grand Titan' for David Duke's Knights of the Ku Klux Klan. James Ridgeway, *Blood in the Face* (New York: Thunder's Mouth Press, 1995), pp. 188–190 notes that although Metzger had respect for the NF, he also claimed, 'they're too wrapped up in the Queen. That Queen worship stuff. I've told those people they've got to become working-class revolutionary types and damn the Queen just like the left does, but do it from an honest position.'
261 *League Review*, no. 36, December 1981; and *National Review*, no. 44, winter 1985.
262 Shaffer, *Music, Youth and International Links in Post-War British Fascism*, 133. *Searchlight*, no. 165, March 1989 states Hoy was on the production team for *The Scorpion*. Hoy, described as a freelance photojournalist and contributor to the *Washington Star*, had previously authored a chapter for Robert W. Whitaker (ed.), *The New Right Papers* (New York: St Martin's Press, 1982), pp. 84–103. *Searchlight*, no. 178, April 1990 described him as the NF's 'man in the USA'. His work also graced the pages of *The Spotlight*, organ of Willis Carto's Liberty Lobby, as a photo-essay introducing British skinhead culture to the US extreme right. *Advocate Bulletin*, vol. 2, no. 3, March 1988 notes Hoy's involvement with the David Duke Campaign.
263 *NA Bulletin*, February 1985; and *NA Bulletin*, March 1985.
264 *Our Plan for a New America: Objectives of the National Democratic Front* and *White Revolution: The Only Solution* in FBI file 100A-RH-12274. The NDF supported the White Patriot Party (WPP), a paramilitary group that emerged from the Carolina Knights of the Ku Klux Klan in 1985. The two organisations enjoyed 'close ties', noted the FBI. *Searchlight*, no. 265, January 1997 states Griffin had 'dealings' with WPP leader (Frazier) Glenn Miller who rebranded his organisation as the Southern National Front (SNF) in October 1986. When SNF folded in the following year, the NDF absorbed its membership. A vituperative anti-Semite, Miller murdered three people he believed to be Jewish – they were not – in Kansas in April 2014. He received a death sentence.
265 Shaffer, *Music, Youth and International Links in Post-War British Fascism*, p. 133.
266 *Instauration*, vol. 10, no. 8, July 1985.
267 *Nationalism Today*, no. 30, June 1985; and *Nationalism Today*, no. 31, July 1985. For Gallo's account of his 'inspirational trip', see *The Nationalist*, vol. 2, no. 1, January 1986. See also *Searchlight*, no. 122, August 1985.
268 *The Nationalist*, vol. 2, no. 2, February 1986; and *The Nationalist*, vol. 2, no. 4, May 1986. See also *Ideas for the Future: An Interview with Derek Holland of the National Front* (Arlington, VA: Friends of the Movement, 1987). Malone began editing *Third Way* after visiting the NF in 1987. The 'political soldiers' later broke with Gallo, *Nationalism Today*, no. 44, denounced him as a 'militarist'. Tyndall subsequently reprinted an article from Gallo's journal *The Nationalist* in *Spearhead*, no. 241, March 1989 further highlighting the breach.
269 *Instauration*, vol. 10, no. 8, July 1985.
270 *National Front News*, no. 68, July 1985 contained a notice of congratulations. *Nationalism Today*, no. 7 lists her as a 'contributor'. *Nationalism Today*, no. 33, September 1985 contains 'Women in the Front', in which she argued that female activists needed to increase their involvement. 'Surely a WHITE future is worth it??' she asked. She later contributed to *The Patriot*, no. 4, spring 1999 urging 'a more caring face for the BNP' as part of the push to have her husband elected BNP chairman.
271 Pearce, *Race with the Devil*, p. 76.
272 'Griffin: My "Armed Gang" Mate Roberto Fiore – BNP Leader', Dominic Carman YouTube channel, 31 January 2010, www.youtube.com/user/dominiccarman67#p/u/5/si8O3zVk5M8 (accessed 31 January 2010).
273 Les Back, 'Guess Who's Coming to Dinner? Investigating Whiteness in the Gray Zone', in Vron Ware and Les Back (eds), *Out of Whiteness: Colour, Politics and Culture* (Chicago, IL: University of Chicago Press, 2002), p. 55.
274 *New Nation*, no. 1, summer 1980.
275 *Nationalism Today*, no. 30, June 1985. This was not an isolated occurrence. *Nationalism Today*, no. 7, regaled readers with an anti-Semitic parody of Holocaust survivor testimony through a

review of a fictitious book called *Even the Dead Were Killed* whilst *Nationalism Today*, no. 8, mocked *The Diary of Anne Frank* in another crude anti-Semitic spoof titled *The Diary of Rebecca Iceberg*. Later issues of *Nationalism Today*, no. 38, April 1986 also advertised *The Six Million Reconsidered, Is the Diary of Anne Frank Genuine?* and *The Hoax of the 20th Century*.
276 *Nationalism Today*, no. 32. This appears was part of an increasing trend towards prosecution. *Time Out*, 23–29 January 1986 stated eighteen 'nationalists' had been charged under Section 5A of the Race Relations Act.
277 *NF Members' Bulletin*, summer 1985; and *National Front News*, no. 69 August 1985.
278 *New Nation*, no. 4, autumn 1983. NF hostility to the state was reflecting in the prohibition against its activists talking to the police 'except to co-operate when arranging specific public Party activities', whilst Special Branch, Griffin observed in *Nationalism Today*, no. 27, March 1985, 'is, and will remain, one of the deadliest enemies of the National Front.' Griffin rejected terrorism as an option, however, arguing in *Nationalism Today*, no. 33 that: 'Such enormous powers of surveillance and control on the part of the State push dissident activity inexorably in one direction and one direction alone: legitimate political activity.'
279 *New Nation*, no. 4, autumn 1983. *Nationalism Today*, no. 5 lists South London NF activist Jim Sneath as MPLDAF organiser and Bill Neary as treasurer. *Nationalism Today*, no. 17 claims it had raised £1,000.
280 *NF Members' Bulletin*, no. 4, 1985. *Nationalism Today*, no. 28, April 1985 records that *Marching On with the National Front: For Albert Marriner and the Future of Britain* (1985) was not just a 'memorial' for the Tower Hamlets NF activist, who had died in May 1983, several days after apparently being struck on the head with a brick at a Tottenham NF meeting; it was also 'a source of funds for the Association'. *Nationalism Today*, no. 41 (*c*.1987) listed seven 'political prisoners'.
281 *National Front News*, no. 72, November 1985. Wingfield joined the NF in 1975, becoming a party functionary in 1977. He edited *Sussex Front*, a regional NF publication from 1979 before taking over as editor of *National Front News* and becoming a full-time party worker in 1983, following Webster's dismissal.
282 *Nationalism Today*, no. 39, 1986.
283 Griffin and Holland ran 'Gandalf Graphics' (its name an homage to J.R.R. Tolkien's *Lord of the Rings* trilogy), a typesetting and page make-up company. Gandalf Graphics received a grant of £4,000 by the Manpower Services Commission, a government scheme to assist small businesses. This breached its guidelines, forbidding political involvement by recipients, see the *Guardian*, 17 October 1985 and the *Guardian*, 8 July 1986. 'East Suffolk Press', which produced *National Front News*, *Nationalism Today* and *New Dawn*, operated from nearby Halesworth.
284 *NF Members' Bulletin*, summer 1985.
285 *NF Members' Bulletin*, no. 4, 1985; *Nationalism Today*, no. 32; and *Nationalism Today*, no. 36.
286 *Nationalism Today*, no. 39, 1986.
287 Channel 4 Television, *Dispatches: The Disciples of Chaos* (1988).
288 *National Front News*, no. 72, November 1985.
289 *National Front News*, no. 71, October 1985. The case file TNA DPP 2/7144 is closed until 2066.
290 *Nationalism Today*, no. 41, September 1987.
291 Shaffer, *Music, Youth and International Links in Post-War British Fascism*, p. 104.
292 *New Dawn* also promoted several 'futurist' bands, Final Sound and Above the Ruins – the latter a conscious nod towards Julius Evola – which, *New Dawn* noted, 'are trying to do something different within the Nationalist Music scene. They deserve to be supported.'
293 *National Front News*, no. 74, January 1986.
294 *Nationalism Today*, no. 37, March 1986.
295 Joe Pearce, *Skrewdriver: The First Ten Years – The Way It's Got to Be* (London: Skrewdriver Services, 1987)
296 For the definitive overview, see James Loughlin, *Fascism and Constitutional Conflict: The British Extreme-Right and Ulster in the Twentieth Century* (Liverpool: Liverpool University Press, 2019).
297 *Nationalism Today*, no. 37.
298 *Nationalism Today*, no. 16.
299 Steve Bruce, *The Red Hand: Protestant Paramilitaries in Northern Ireland* (Oxford: Oxford University Press, 1992), p. 153. Henry McDonald and Jim Cusack, *UDA: Inside the Heart of*

Loyalist Terror (London: Penguin, 2004), pp. 109–110 and 167–172 states the UDA met with fascists largely for the purpose of obtaining guns and money, but opposed their racist politics. '[Andy] Tyrie and the rest of the UDA leadership were implacably opposed to the political standpoint of the fascists,' they note. 'On one occasion when the National Front sent a delegation to Belfast, Tyrie detailed Louis Scott, a Shankill Road UDA man of mixed-race parentage to meet them.' Jim Cusack and Henry McDonald, *UVF* (Dublin: Poolbeg, 1997), pp. 217–220 observes that in 1980 the UVF, seeking weapons, held discussions with the Belgian Vlaamse Militanten Orde (VMO – Flemish Militants Order), which, ironically, had previously supported Irish Republicanism. The VMO offered guns and explosives in return for the UVF attacking Jewish targets. The UVF leadership declined. Personal relationships between individual NF militants and Loyalist terrorists existed, however, for example, Tony Simms, *Match Day: Ulster Loyalism and the British Far-Right* (No publisher: 2016).

300 Christopher Andrew, *The Defence of the Realm: The Authorized History of MI5* (London: Penguin, 2010), p. 738. For further detail, see Frank Portinari, *Left-Right-Loyalist* (London: No publisher, 2016).

301 *Bulldog*, no. 39, 1984.

302 Martin Durham, 'The British Extreme Right and Northern Ireland', *Contemporary British History*, vol. 26, no. 2, June 2012, pp. 195–211; and James W. McAuley, 'Ulster Loyalism and Extreme Right Wing Politics' in Max Taylor, P.M. Currie and Donald Holbrook (eds), *Extreme Right-Wing Political Violence and Terrorism* (London: Bloomsbury, 2013), pp. 85–103. Shaun McDaid, *Template for Peace, Northern Ireland, 1972–75* (Manchester: Manchester University Press, 2013), pp. 10–11 notes that elements within the 1970s Ulster Vanguard movement countenanced an independent Ulster, as indeed did some within the UVF and UDA but it was never a widely held aspiration.

303 *National Front News*, no. 73, December 1985.

304 *National Front News*, no. 75.

305 See 'Behind the Smear', British National Party, www.bnp.net/cook1.html (accessed 3 May 1998).

306 Christopher Farrington, *Ulster Unionism and the Peace Process in Northern Ireland* (Basingstoke: Palgrave, 2006).

307 *Nationalism Today*, no. 37, March 1986.

308 See 'Behind the Smear', British National Party. *Identity*, no. 13, September 2001 records that McLorie subsequently became Ulster BNP organiser.

309 *New Dawn*, no. 3.

310 The *Guardian*, 14 March 1986 reported the jailing of two leaders of a Glaswegian UVF cell who ran a 'gun kitty' into which members paid money to buy firearms for Loyalist terrorists. NF supporter David Seawright was one of five men charged with conspiracy, though in his case the charge was 'not proven'. *An Introduction to the National Front* (Worthing: NF, 1988), p. 20 subsequently listed Seawright, as 'organising the National Front in Scotland'. His brother, DUP politician George Seawright, a member of the Ulster Assembly and Belfast Council, also supported the NF, giving an interview to *Nationalism Today*, no. 18. The NF welcomed his support though, as James Loughlin, *Fascism and Constitutional Conflict*, p. 250 notes, sought to distance themselves from his violent sectarianism. Irish Republicans murdered George Seawright in 1987. The UVF admitted he was a member in 2006, see '"Burn Catholics" Man was in UVF', BBC News, 23 August 2006, http://news.bbc.co.uk/1/hi/northern_ireland/5279276.stm (accessed 10 May 2015). Extreme right support endured. *True Brit*, no. 5, December 1997 memorialised Seawright on its cover – 'The Fight Goes On' – on the tenth anniversary of his murder.

311 'Behind the Smear', British National Party. *Today*, 15 July 1986 reproduced in *Searchlight*, no. 134, August 1986.

312 *Nationalism Today*, no. 37. In *National Front News*, no. 92, 1 July 1987 Griffin subsequently explained that the political soldiers had invested themselves in campaigning for an independent Ulster because:

> If one of the British nations can be wrested from the grip of the American/Zionist/Capitalist axis, then the liberation of the rest will not be far behind. And when Britain awakes, Europe's long drugged sleep will be at an end. Ulster is where it will begin.

For a further insight, see *A Nation in Struggle: A Photo-Study* (Cardiff: Cardiff NF, 1987).

313 'Behind the Smear', British National Party; and *Nationalism Today Subscribers' Bulletin*, April 1986.
314 *Nationalism Today*, no. 39.
315 David Kerr, 'The History of the National Front in Ulster', *Civil Liberty*, www.civilliberty.org.uk/resources/nf_ulster.html (accessed 23 April 2015). *Heritage and Destiny*, no. 35, January–March 2009 makes the point about the evolution of UDA politics.
316 *Searchlight*, no. 141, March 1987; and *Searchlight*, no. 142, April 1987.
317 Loughlin, *Fascism and Constitutional Conflict*, p. 276.
318 *Nationalism Today*, no. 22.
319 Yann Fouéré, *Towards a Federal Europe: Nations or States?* (Swansea: Christopher Davies, 1980). Many of these Breton autonomists, from whom the NF derived their ideas on regional nationalism, had collaborated with the Vichy regime during the Second World War. Fouéré, who fled trial in March 1946 and was subsequently sentenced *in absentia* to a life term in prison for his collaborationist activities, lived in exile in Wales and Ireland, on which, see Daniel Leach, *Fugitive Ireland: European Minority Nationalists and Irish Political Asylum, 1937–2008* (Dublin: Four Courts Press, 2009), pp. 81–88.
320 Richard Lawson reviewed the book in *The Scorpion*, no. 9, spring 1986. *The Scorpion*, no. 12, winter 1988–1989 was devoted to the theme 'For Europe of a Hundred Flags'. This also became the title of the third Scorpion/IONA conference on 24 October 1988, which Fouéré attended.
321 National Front, 1984 Annual General Meeting – 'list of motions'.
322 *Nationalism Today*, no. 35, November–December 1985 and Richard Wyn Jones, *The Fascist Party in Wales? Plaid Cymru, Welsh Nationalism and the Accusation of Fascism* (Cardiff: University of Wales Press, 2014), pp. 28–29, 42–43, 46 and 87.
323 *The Times*, 29 March 1989.
324 Alberto Spektorowski, 'Ethnoregionalism: The Intellectual New Right and the Lega Nord', *Global Review of Ethnopolitics*, vol. 2, no. 3, 2003, pp. 55–70 makes a similar point.
325 The *Guardian*, 3 August 2009. Griffin's stance represented an evolution in the view expressed eight years previously in *Identity*, no. 5, January 2001 that 'there can never be such a thing as "Black British"'.
326 *Spearhead*, no. 269, July 1991. Liverpool BNP chairman, David Collingwood, sent Ulster NF an abusive letter, reprinted in *Ulster Nation*, no. 3 [no. date], stating:

> Do you really believe in loving niggers and arabs your [sic] going to obtain power. If your [sic] got any sense what so ever you'll become a proper Ulsterman, instead of mixing with the crap in London ie 'Holland' and 'Pat Harrington', both communist. Take my tip go back to glue sniffing.

Ulster Nation dismissed the BNP as 'a reactionary band of Hitlerites, race-haters and imperialists.'
327 *Spearhead*, no. 274, December 1991. For a broader discussion, see David Irwin, '"Dire Deeds Awake, Dark is it Eastward": Citizenship and Devolution, and the British National Party', in John Wilson and Karyn Stapleton (eds), *Devolution and Identity* (Aldershot: Ashgate, 2006), pp. 173–182.
328 'Behind the Smear', British National Party.
329 The *Guardian*, 23 March 1986.
330 For more detail on the split, see Larry O'Hara, 'The 1986 National Front Split', *Lobster*, no. 29, July 1995.
331 *NF Organisers' Bulletin*, 9 May 1986 cited in Lawrence Michael O'Hara, 'Creating Political Soldiers: The National Front, 1986–1990' (Unpublished PhD thesis), p. 229.
332 'Softly ... Softly, it's Shahid Malik', Martin Wingfield, 12 May 2009, http://martinwingfield.blogspot.co.uk/2009/05/softly-softly-its-shahid-malik.html (accessed 26 May 2015).
333 Pearce became disillusioned, dropping out of the NF and converting to Catholicism. Reinventing himself 'Joseph' Pearce, he moved to the United States, becoming a lecturer at Ave Maria University, writing several biographies of notable Catholic literary figures including Chesterton and Belloc. His 'mentor' in the conversion process had been Aidan Mackey, a former devotee of A.K. Chesterton and a leading authority on his second cousin, G.K. Chesterton, of whom Pearce wrote a biography, which skated over his anti-Semitism. He co-edited another book, *In Defence of Sanity: The Best Essays of G.K. Chesterton* (2011) with, amongst others, Mackey.

334 [Nick Griffin], *Attempted Murder: The State/Reactionary Plot against the NF* (Norwich: N.T. Press, 1986). Though he didn't believe it invalidated his portrayal of the division, Griffin later conceded that what was missing from the pamphlet, 'was an understanding of the contributing damage done by bad leadership decisions and attitudes on the "radical" side – not least my own. Equally unknown were the extremely manipulative nature and dishonesty of at least one of my allies,' see 'Behind the Smear', British National Party.

335 See 'Helping to Keep our Feet on the Ground', Martin Wingfield, 8 April 2009, http://martinwingfield.blogspot.com/2009/04/i.html (accessed 12 September 2011). Budden's racist effusions were particularly noxious. *Sussex Front*, no. 24, November 1983, edited by Wingfield, saw Budden attacking slain civil rights leader Martin Luther King as the 'reverend sootball' murdered by a 'pest exterminator'. He went on to lambast 'liberals' for accepting 'black savages in clerical collars whose negrified version of Christianity is diluted with obscene ritual and whose translation of Christ's message is, "Suffer little children to come unto me – I'm feeling peckish."' Griffin's objection to Budden proved transitory, however. When Budden fell out with Ian Anderson in 1996 and stopped writing for *The Flag*, he offered to write for *Spearhead* and *British Nationalist*, 'and will be taken up on this', noted Nick Griffin to Wayne Ashcroft, November–December 1996 in MSS 412/WA/3/1, Ashcroft papers.

336 Pearce, *Race with the Devil*, p. 188.

337 '*Attempted Murder*' – *Absolute Insanity* – *NFSG Newsletter* (1986).

338 *Vanguard*, no. 1, August 1986; Joe Pearce, *Nationalist Doctrine* (London: Freedom Books, 1987); and Steve Brady, *The Roots of the British: A Study of the Origins and Development of the British People* (Worthing: NF, 1990). *Vanguard*, no. 7, April 1987 reasserted the 'scientific' position on race.

339 *Vanguard*, no. 1, August 1986; and *Vanguard*, no. 15, January 1988.

340 *Vanguard*, no. 4, December 1986; and *Vanguard*, no. 6, February 1987.

341 *Spearhead*, no. 214, December 1986. This echoed an earlier, mocking critique of NF 'ruralism' in *Spearhead*, no. 190, August 1984, which conjured:

> the image of NF skinheads skipping down our country lanes each with a shovel under one arm and a copy of 'Skrewdriver's' latest record under the other, whilst happily chewing a piece of straw (a pleasant change from sniffing glue, don't you think?).

342 Butler joined the Hackney and Tower Hamlets BNP branch, formed in spring 1984, see *Spearhead*, no. 187, May 1984.

343 Roger Eatwell, 'The Esoteric Ideology of the National Front in the 1980s', in Mike Cronin (ed.), *The Failure of British Fascism: The Far Right and the Fight for Political Recognition* (Basingstoke: Macmillan, 1996), p. 102.

344 See 'Meeting by the Lake', Martin Wingfield, 12 December 2008, http://martinwingfield.blogspot.co.uk/2008/12/meeting-by-lake.html (accessed 12 December 2008).

345 *Nationalism Today*, no. 40.

346 *Ibid*.

347 *National Front News*, no. 78; and *National Front News*, no. 79. Two decades later, Griffin performed a U-turn arguing that to preserve as much British independence as possible 'we are probably better off allowing U.S. bases in Britain to stay, for as long as the United States agrees not to interfere in our political affairs,' see Srdja Trifkovic, 'Nick Griffin's Long March'.

348 For anti-fascist accounts of the day, see Sean Birchall, *Beating the Fascists: The Untold Story of Anti-Fascist Action* (London: Freedom Press, 2010), pp. 117–120; and K. Bullstreet, *Bash the Fash: Anti-Fascist Recollections, 1984–1993* (London: KSL, 2001), pp. 8–10.

349 *Red Action*, no. 26, September 1986.

350 *Vanguard*, no. 15, January 1988.

351 *Jewish Chronicle*, 5 June 1987.

352 The NFSG also declined to field any candidates though one, Paul Kingston, stood unofficially in Bristol East where he polled just 286 votes (0.6 per cent). The other two were BNP candidates.

353 Troy Southgate, *Nazis, Fascists, or Neither? Ideological Credentials of the British Far Right, 1987–1994* (Shamley Green: Palingensis Project: 2010), p. 44.

354 Matthew Collins, *Hate: My Life in the British Far Right* (London: Biteback, 2011), pp. 73–77.

355 *Nationalism Today*, no. 42. *Nationalism Today*, no. 30, June 1985 was the last issue to list editorial staff. Thereafter, *Nationalism Today* only listed 'Keiron Richards' as editor.

356 *Nationalism Today*, no. 46, July 1989. The *Disciples of Chaos* documentary claimed the NF 'cadre' was only 120-strong.
357 *White Noise*, no. 2, 1986; and *The Rune*, no. 12, 1996.
358 *Nationalism Today*, no. 40.
359 Bill Buford, *Among the Thugs* (London: Mandain, 1992), pp. 131–159. *Nationalism Today*, no. 1, March 1980 had advertised the 'Front Roadshow' for those inclined to hire an NF DJ for a party. Griffin's address was the point of contact.
360 *White Noise*, no. 3, 1987 notes this was the first of two proposed RAC festivals that summer. The second took place in Sweden in June.
361 *White Noise*, no. 4, 1987.
362 London, *Ian Stuart*, p. 75; and Shaffer, *Music, Youth and International Links in Post-War British Fascism*, p. 119. Metzger's *WAR*, vol. 3, no. 4, 1984 was already selling 'White Noise' cassettes.
363 White Noise Club originally operated from NF headquarters and shared the same 'BCM Noise' mailing address as 'Skrewdriver Services', see *White Noise*, no. 1, 1986 and *White Noise*, no. 3, 1987.
364 *Disciples of Chaos*, Despatches documentary, 5 October 1988.
365 *Diamond in the Dust: The Ian Stuart Biography*, states:

> Totally disgusted with the way Harrington, Griffin and Holland had gone about things with their gross dishonesty, Ian handed his letter of resignation to White Noise magazine and the National Front, with most of the other White rock bands following him.

366 Paul Jackson, 'White Warriors and Blood & Honour Magazine', 16 October 2016, https://paulnicholasjackson.wordpress.com/2016/10/16/white-warriors-and-blood-honour-magazine/ (accessed 18 October 2016).
367 *National Front News*, no. 100, January 1988.
368 *Blood & Honour*, no. 7.
369 *Welsh Leak*, no. 1, n.d. Shaffer, *Music, Youth and International Links in Post-War British Fascism*, p. 130 notes the NF disbanded WNC in February 1989.
370 *Keith Allen meets Nick Griffin*, Channel 4 documentary, 5 March 2012.
371 @ NickGriffinBU , Twitter, 25 September 2018, https://twitter.com/NickGriffinBU/status/1044508313780662273 (accessed 25 September 2018).
372 *Ideas for the Future: An Interview with Derek Holland of the National Front* (Arlington, VA: Friends of the Movement, 1987).
373 *Nationalism Today*, no. 35, November–December 1985.
374 *Nationalism Today*, no. 29, May 1985.
375 *Nationalism Today*, no. 37, March 1986.
376 Bean, *Many Shades of Black*, p. 169; and *Spearhead*, no. 48, December 1971.
377 *Nationalism Today*, no. 39.
378 *Nationalism Today*, no. 44; and *Nationalism Today*, no. 46. Mattias Gardell, *In the Name of Elijah Muhammad: Louis Farrakhan and the Nation of Islam* (Durham, NC: Duke University Press: 1997), p. 277 highlights that NDF leader Gary Gallo also contributed to the NOI newspaper, *Final Call* (March 1990), and had promised that his group, 'will divide the US into completely independent nations based on race.'
379 *Nationalism Today*, no. 43, April 1988. Patrick Harrington also remained in touch with these groups. Akkebala attended the October 1990 conference of his Third Way group, a small racial separatist *groupuscule* founded after the dissolution of the 'official' NF. *Third Way*, no. 4 October 1990 featured an interview with Akkebala, whilst *Third Way*, no. 7, May 1991 published a glowing review of *Black Man: Pathway to Freedom* by 'Comrade Osiris'. *Third Way*, no. 2, n.d.; *Third Way*, no. 3, August 1990; and *Third Way* no. 11, March 1992 also contained overviews of the music of Public Enemy, the politics of Malcolm X (in an article that stated he died in 'mysterious circumstances' rather than at the hands of NOI gunmen) and Black Nationalist philosophy.
380 *National Front News*, no. 102, February 1988. Anger was formerly deputy leader in Gary Gallo's NDF.
381 *Heritage and Destiny*, no. 37, July–September 2009 intimates that these alliances cost Griffin the support of several Greater Manchester area organisers.

382 *Ideas for the Future* (Arlington, VA: Friends of the Movement, 1987).
383 *National Front News*, no .93, August 1987.
384 *National Front News*, no. 27, October 1980. *National Front News*, no. 23, June 1980 notes that the party had held a march in London on 15 June under the banner 'Kick Iranian & Libyan Loonies Out of Britain!'
385 *Nationalism Today*, no. 21. One activist recalled of this period:

> I'd thought for a while that things were getting weird. But Brons and Anderson were a safe pair of hands. Then, it felt like suddenly, things went totally off the rails. We were being asked to prayer for foreign 'martyrs', to give a fuck about Palestinians and Iranians. The ayatollah and stuff like that. It was really weird – quite dark, actually. You had to check on your way out of some meetings that it had been a National Front meeting and not a Workers Revolutionary Party meeting or something like that. But at the same time, I suppose, it made us almost electric ... different. Frightening? But mainly bloody weird, I suppose. They wanted us to still go out and fight in the streets, but to martyr ourselves while doing it. For someone off a council estate in Forest Gate who had never read a book in his life, not even when in prison, it was also quite exciting.

See Matthew Collins, 'The National Front at 50: Part II – Hope Not Hate Magazine', *Hope Not Hate*, 15 December 2015, www.hopenothate.org.uk/2017/12/15/national-front-50-part-ii-hope-not-hate-magazine/ (accessed 30 January 2018).
386 *Nationalism Today*, no. 30, June 1985.
387 *Nationalism Today*, no. 28, April 1985.
388 *Nationalism Today*, no. 31, July 1985.
389 *Mother Jones*, vol. 12, no. 4, May 1987, p. 45. This was not entirely new either. Mosley had once postulated that the Viet Cong were the archetypal 'Thought-Deed Man'.
390 Compare *Kayhan International*, 6 February 1988 with *National Front News*, nos 82 to 84, for example.
391 *Nationalism Today*, no. 43.
392 *Nationalism Today*, no. 39.
393 *National Front News*, no. 94, August 1987.
394 *National Front News*, 1 March 1988.
395 *Searchlight*, no. 157, July 1988; and 'Political Soldiers and the New Man: Part Two', CST, 27 April 2010, https://cst.org.uk/news/blog/2010/04/27/political-soldiers-and-the-new-man-part-two (accessed 23 November 2015).
396 CST, 'Political Soldiers and the New Man: Part Two'.
397 'Political Soldiers and the New Man: Part One', CST, 26 April 2010, https://cst.org.uk/news/blog/2010/04/26/political-soldiers-and-the-new-man-part-one (accessed 23 November 2015).
398 *Time Out*, 2–8 August 1984. *Searchlight*, no. 109, July 1984 reproduces part of a letter making such claims.
399 Conveniently forgetting this period in extreme right history, Griffin's BNP laid a wreath in her memory thirty years later, see 'Remembering Yvonne', 22 April 2014, www.bnp.org.uk/news/regional/remembering-yvonne (accessed 29 April 2015).
400 David Blundy and Andrew Lycett, *Qaddafi and the Libyan Revolution* (Boston, MA: Little Brown & Co., 1987).
401 Muammar Al Qathafi, *The Green Book* (Malaysia: World Center for Researches and Studies of the Green Book: n.d.).
402 *Nationalism Today*, no. 41; and for an earlier supportive article, see *Nationalism Today*, no. 24, September 1984.
403 *Nationalism Today*, no. 39.
404 *Ibid.*
405 *National Front News*, no. 111.
406 'We've Been Here Before: John Tyndall Compares his Expulsion with Past Events', *Spearhead*, no date, www.spearhead.co.uk/0310-jt1.html (accessed 29 April 2015); and *Spearhead*, no. 211, May 1986. The NF had evinced an interest in Libyan affairs as early as 1975, noting the formation of a Committee for the Prohibition of Usury. 'Could this move herald the beginning of another debt free monetary system outside the control of International Finance? Developments will be watched with interest,' noted *Britain First*, no. 31, August 1975.

407 'Four Jailed for Berlin Disco Bombing', BBC News, 13 November 2001, http://news.bbc.co.uk/1/hi/world/europe/1653575.stm (accessed 29 April 2015).
408 *Nationalism Today*, no. 44. *Searchlight*, no. 165, 1989 stated that the political soldiers appear to have made contact with Libya in January 1987 after writing to Robert Pash, a former leader of the Aryan Nations in Australia who had converted to Islam, and who maintained links with the regime.
409 *National Front News*, no. 111.
410 *Nationalism Today*, no. 44.
411 *National Front News*, no. 111.
412 Griffin currently maintains that the CIA or Mossad were responsible for the Lockerbie attack: '#Neocon #fakenews media used the #Lockerbie tragedy as excuse for the disastrous against Libya. Now cynically recycling it as causus belli against #Iran. Truth is it was probably CIA or Mossad asset all along. #notinmyname', see @NickGriffinBU, Twitter, 30 September 2018, https://twitter.com/NickGriffinBU/status/1046318456440786944 (accessed 30 September 2018).
413 'The 38-Year Connection Between Irish Republicans and Gaddafi', BBC News, 23 February 2011, www.bbc.co.uk/news/uk-northern-ireland-12539372 (accessed 29 April 2015).
414 *Vanguard*, no. 11, August 1987. Harrington's refusal to condemn the IRA as 'terrorist' in the television documentary *Disciples of Chaos* (1988) probably did not endear him to fellow right-wing extremists.
415 Nick Griffin interview, *The Lost Race*, BBC 2, 24 March 1999. His hopes were not outlandish. Libya had funded the Toronto-based Nationalist Party of Canada, see Warren Kinsella, *Web of Hate: Inside Canada's Far Right Network* (Toronto: HarperCollins, 1994), p. 55.
416 Iain Dale, *Talking Politics: Political Conversations with Iain Dale* (London: Biteback, 2010), p. 219. No reader ever checked out the copy deposited at Isleworth Library.
417 *Vanguard*, no. 14, November–December 1987. As *Vanguard*, no. 22, September 1988 warned:

> Europe must realize that the biggest threat to its survival doesn't come from the white Russians to the East or from the mainly white Americans to the West. It comes from the rising brown tide of Islam to the South.

418 *Vanguard*, no. 15, January 1988.
419 *Spearhead*, no. 336, February 1997.
420 Martin Penrose, 'Why the US Needs Something Like the BNP: Interview with Nick Griffin', *Counter-Currents Publishing*, 15 January 2011, www.counter-currents.com/2011/01/interview-with-nick-griffin/ (accessed 23 April 2015).
421 'Interview: Judaism, Culture and the Gentile World: A Conversation with Rabbi Mayer Schiller', *The Jewish Review*, vol. 3, no. 5, April 1990, www.thejewishreview.org/articles/?id=182 (accessed 23 April 2015).
422 Griffin highlighted his continued contact with Rabbi Schiller who, he stated, donated £200 to the BNP in 2001, see *Spearhead*, no. 398, April 2002.
423 *Final Conflict*, no. 11, autumn 1996 reported the ITP's subsequent efforts to found another far right commune in the derelict hamlet of Los Pedriches, 60 miles from Valencia, Spain. They envisaged it as the first of several all white communes across Europe. Fiore financed the project to the tune of £12,000 according to *The Newcastle Journal*, 12 August 2000.
424 Dave Gobell to Nick Griffin, November 1989, quoted in O'Hara, 'Creating Political Soldiers', p. 277.
425 *Jewish Chronicle*, 13 October 1989.
426 Nick Griffin interview, *The Lost Race*, BBC 2, 24 March 1999.
427 O'Hara, 'Creating Political Soldiers', p. 243.
428 Community Security Trust, 'Nick Griffin Describing his Religion as "Eco-Pagan"', YouTube, 26 April 2010, www.youtube.com/watch?v=kx5fErVb4Sw (accessed 4 September 2011).
429 The ITP were not alone. *National Socialist Witness*, no. 6, 14 December 1990 reprinted Colin Jordan's letter to Saddam Hussein on 3 November, in which he decried the campaign of vilification against him by 'the same sickly brood as of 50 years or so who then clamoured to engage us in war against Hitler to our catastrophic detriment for the benefit of the Jews.' Dismissive of the British hostages Hussein held, Jordan wrote: 'What most of all needs emphasis is that the

British and American nations in general are being in effect made permanent hostages of Israel by the subservient policy of its ruling adherents in both countries.'
430 Southgate, *Nazis, Fascists, or Neither?*, p. 88; and Shaffer, *Music, Youth and International Links in Post-War British Fascism*, p. 182. Southgate states the ITP did obtain funds but that Afzal promptly absconded with them.
431 Southgate, *Nazis, Fascists, or Neither?*, p. 88.
432 *Sunday Telegraph*, 3 February 1991.
433 Christopher T. Husbands, *Racial Exclusionism and the City: The Urban Support of the National Front* (London: George Allen & Unwin, 1983).
434 *The Rune*, no. 6, n.d.
435 Alexander Raven Thomson, *The Coming Corporatist State* (London: BUF Publications, 1935), p. 48.
436 The *Observer*, 1 September 2002.
437 *Identity*, no. 40, January 2004.
438 *Nationalism Today*, no. 45, April 1989.
439 *The Stormer*, no. 7, October 2004.
440 Southgate, *Nazis, Fascists, or Neither?*, p. 79.
441 Penrose, 'Why the US Needs Something Like the BNP'.
442 *Ibid*. The ITP split again in 1992, see Graham Macklin, 'Co-Opting the Counter-Culture: Troy Southgate and the National Revolutionary Faction', *Patterns of Prejudice*, vol. 39, no. 3, September 2005, pp. 301–326.
443 'Griffin: I was a Cult Member', Dominic Carman YouTube channel, 15 April 2010, www.youtube.com/watch?v=ohLMemktE18 (accessed 19 April 2010).
444 Nick Griffin to Wayne Ashcroft, 14 January 1996 in MSS 412/WA/3/1, Ashcroft papers, stated:

> I'm not surprised that [John] McAuley [the NF chairman] found Roberto Fiore a nutter. The ITP has moved so far away from what was intended when it was first formed that it is now little more than a Catholic front group. A recent poster of theirs read 'Fornication and Drugs Will Destroy the World'. Even if one believed this, the idea of risking activists' necks and cash to put something so utterly valueless for recruiting purposes is absurd.

445 *The Times*, 10 April 1999.
446 *Spearhead*, no. 357, November 1998.
447 *Ibid.*
448 *Daily Mail*, 29 April 2006.
449 'Griffin's Dad: Our Son Destroyed Us', Dominic Carman YouTube Channel, 20 April 2010, www.youtube.com/watch?v=qZ9mJq-prNA (accessed 4 September 2011).
450 *London Gazette*, 23 June 1994, p. 9112.
451 *Spearhead*, no. 367, September 1999.
452 'Chairman's 2010 Summer School Address', 23 August 2010, http://bnptv.org.uk/2010/08/chairmans-2010-summer-school-address/ (accessed 25 August 2010); and 'Griffin: BNP Bradford Would-Be Bomber is Useful', Dominic Carman YouTube channel, 12 February 2010, www.youtube.com/user/dominiccarman67#p/a/u/0/GnLSdWRzrOA (accessed 22 April 2010).
453 'Top Tory Accused of "Expenses Irregularities"', 11 February 2012, www.bnp.org.uk/news/regional/top-tory-accused-expenses-irregularities (accessed 13 February 2012).
454 Quoted in *Searchlight*, no. 264, June 1997.
455 *Spearhead*, no. 274, December 1991. See 'BNP Mrs Griffin: No Sex for Years, Says Wife of BNP Leader', Dominic Carman YouTube channel, 19 January 2010, www.youtube.com/watch?v=lHIDXCwlFqw (accessed 28 January 2010) in which Griffin discusses the incident.
456 *This Man is the World's Leading Expert on Gas Chambers ...* (London: Academics for Free Speech, 1991).
457 Fred Leuchter, *The Leuchter Report: The First Forensic Examination of Auschwitz* (London: Focal Point, 1989).
458 Irving published an advance copy of the book's new introduction, written in January 1989, in *The Journal of Historical Review*, vol. 10, no. 4, winter 1990, pp. 389–416, organ of the Institute of Historical Review, the major engine of Holocaust denial.
459 Richard Evans, 'David Irving, Hitler and Holocaust Denial', www.hdot.org/evans/ (accessed 23 February 2018).

460 *The Irving Judgement: Mr. David Irving v. Penguin Books and Professor Deborah Lipstadt* (London: Penguin Books, 2000), pp. 318–319; and Richard J. Evans, *Telling Lies About Hitler: The Holocaust, History and the David Irving Trial* (London: Verso, 2002).
461 *The Rune*, no. 8.
462 *Spearhead*, no. 265, March 1991; and *Spearhead*, no. 267, May 1991.
463 Matthew Goodwin, 'In Search of the Winning Formula: Nick Griffin and the "Modernization" of the British National Party', in Roger Eatwell and Matthew Goodwin (eds), *The New Extremism in 21st Century Britain* (Abingdon: Routledge, 2010), p. 175.
464 'B&H Responds: Rock Against Griffinism', *Final Conflict*, 9 January 2008, http://finalconflict-blog.blogspot.com/2008/1/b-responds-rock-against-griffinism.html (accessed 27 March 2012); and *National Vanguard*, www.natvan.com/cgi-bin/audio.cgi?year=1994 (accessed 27 March 2012). 'Jim' is most likely Scottish BNP activist Jim White who worked as an excise officer in London before returning to Scotland, see *Searchlight*, no. 207, September 1992. Griffin was certainly aware of the ADV broadcasts. *The Rune*, no. 9, advertised Life Rune Books, run by John Cato, the NA-UK organiser, from whom, it noted, British radio listeners could obtain its radio frequencies.
465 *Spearhead*, no. 331, September 1996.
466 'B&H Responds: Rock Against Griffinism', *Final Conflict*, 9 January 2008. Griffin was close to Cartwright and his colleagues. In August 1996, he addressed a BNP meeting in Govan, Glasgow alongside Cartwright, until recently the Scottish B&H organiser, see *Spearhead*, no. 331, September 1996. *Highlander*, no. 1, 1996 observed:

> When the meeting was concluded a White Power social followed.... A large selection of NS/Racialist literature and CD's were distributed. The evening was brought to a boisterous end with a highly enjoyable rendition of 'Ye Olde Finklestein Song' (sometimes known as 'Perish Judah') and an equally as passionate 'Tomorrow Belongs To Me'.

Cartwright stated that Griffin was photographed Sieg Heiling at this event but did not produce it. *Highlander*, no. 3, 1997 voiced its support for Griffin during *The Rune* trial. Griffin continued cooperating with the group, helping the BNP Highlands and Islands group, run by Kenny Smith, produce anti-abortion leaflets, see *British Nationalist*, no. 193, July 1998.
467 *Spearhead*, no. 280, June 1992; and *The Rune*, no. 1. Croydon BNP was founded in June 1992.
468 Ballard was the son of Croydon NF activist Margaret Ballard, active on Griffin's behalf during his 1981 election campaign in Croydon. Ballard was a former British Movement activist. When he stood for election in Croydon's Waddon ward in May 1986, *Croydon Property News*, 1 May 1986, described Ballard 'as a private tutor in Croydon. Has a degree in Geology, was Treasurer of Croydon group for four years. Interested in improving local transport.' *Croydon Advertiser*, 2 May 1986 noted Ballard 'was a town planning assistant but now manages his own educational agency.' He had been active thereafter in the BNP as well as on the fringes of C18 and, according to *Searchlight*, no. 214, April 1993, was active with the 'Surrey Border Front', a small racist groupuscule.
469 *The Rune*, no. 3; *The Rune*, no. 4; *The Rune*, no. 5; and *The Rune*, no. 7.
470 *The Rune*, no. 5.
471 Nick Griffin, police interview, 12 December 1996, released under FOI.
472 *The Rune*, no. 11, 1995. The Odal Rune subsequently became the emblem of the Young BNP, see www.youngbnp.com/The%20Odal%20Rune.htm (accessed 3 February 2003).
473 *Identity*, no. 56, July 2005.
474 *The Rune*, no. 6, n.d.
475 *The Rune*, no. 10, 1995.
476 *The Rune*, no. 12, 1996; *The Fable of the Ducks and the Hens: A Dramatic Saga of Intrigue, Propaganda & Subversion* (Uckfield: Media Concept, 1996); and G.L. Rockwell, *The Fable of the Ducks and the Hens* (London: Stevens Books, n.d.). Colin Jordan had also published an own edition of *The Fable* in 1988.
477 *The Rune*, no. 11, 1995.
478 Publius, 'Racial Profiles'.
479 TNA HO 45/25568/43 and 47.
480 *The Rune*, no. 12, 1996.
481 *Daily Mail*, 25 October 2009.

482 'Circumstances will Play into British National Party's Hands', 12 February 2011, http://bnptv.org.uk/2011/02/circumstances-will-play-into-british-national-party's-hands/ (accessed 27 February 2012).
483 *The Rune*, no. 7.
484 *The Rune*, no. 12, 1996 contains a thank you letter from 'Darren' on behalf of BHS.
485 British Hammerskins, 'Who We Are and What We Stand For', www.hammerskins.co.uk/who.htm (accessed 23 September 2001).
486 Arno Michaelis, Fritt Ord, Oslo, Norway, 17 September 2018. Michaelis was the group's vocalist.
487 *The Rune*, no. 11, 1995; and *The Rune*, no. 12, 1996.
488 *Nationalism Today*, no. 29.
489 Nick Griffin, Record of Taped Interview, 12 December 1996, p. 3, released under FOI. The following year *British Nationalist*, no. 183, September 1997 records Griffin stated that 'everything the *party* did was geared to the 14 words' [author's emphasis]. *British Nationalist*, no. 188, February 1998 began advertising Fourteen Words (UK) the official distributors of 'videos and other items' from its American parent, the Fourteen Words Press: 'Watch videos of the late Robert Matthews and other former members of "The Order", including dramatic footage of their final confrontation with the "Feds".' Coventry BNP organiser, Mark Payne, who ran Fourteen Words (UK) later changed his name to 'Matthews' in homage states *Searchlight*, no. 301, July 2000.
490 *The Rune*, no. 5, n.d.; and *The Rune*, no. 12, 1996.
491 Nick Griffin 'The Domino Effect' in *Deceived, Damned and Defiant: The Revolutionary Writings of David Lane* (St Maries, ID: Fourteen Words Press, 1999), pp. 335–343.
492 Penrose, 'Why the US Needs Something Like the BNP'.
493 *British Nationalist*, no. 176, February 1997.
494 *The Rune*, no. 11, 1995.
495 *Spearhead*, no. 317, July 1995. On Bermondsey, see Collins, *Hate*, pp. 251–260; and Birchall, *Beating the Fascists*, pp. 244–248.
496 'Reconciliation', *Eddy Butler blog*, 20 March 2011, http://eddybutler.blogspot.com/2011/03/reconciliation.html (accessed 21 March 2011).
497 *Spearhead*, no. 417, November 2003.
498 *Spearhead*, no. 407, January 2003.
499 Nick Griffin to John Tyndall, 14 November 1994 quoted in *The Griffin File: Spotlight on an Erratic Record* (Leeds: Imperium Press, n.d.).
500 *The Rune*, no. 5, praised Jordan as an 'indefatigable patriot' whilst claiming his racist satire, *Merrie England 2,000*, was 'destined to become a classic'. Jordan praised Griffin's pamphlet *Who Are the Mindbenders?* as 'truly outstanding'.
501 Nick Griffin to Colin Jordan, 22 July 1995, quoted in *The Griffin File*.
502 *The Rune*, no. 9. Even after becoming *Spearhead*'s editor, Griffin published adverts for Jordan's *National Socialism: Vanguard of the Future* (1993), see *Spearhead*, no. 331, September 1996; and *Spearhead*, no. 334, December 1996.
503 Nick Lowles, *White Riot: The Violent Story of Combat 18* (London: Milo, 2001), p. 188. For Valerie Tyndall's advice, see 'Death of Valerie Tyndall', 25 June 2011, http://efp.org.uk/death-of-valerie-tyndall/ (accessed 30 June 2016); and John Tyndall, 'The Problem is Mr Griffin: It is Not Policies Which Divide the BNP, Says John Tyndall', *Spearhead*, www.spearhead.co.uk/0310-jt2.html (accessed 30 June 2016).
504 *British Nationalist*, no. 160, October 1995.
505 *The Rune*, no. 11, 1995; and *The Rune*, no. 12, 1996. *The Rune* also advertised *The Oak*, mouthpiece of the NA-UK.
506 *National Vanguard*, no. 115, November–December 1995; and *National Vanguard*, no. 116, August–September 1996. *Identity*, no. 31, April 2003, *Identity*, no. 32, May 2003; and *Identity*, no. 38, November 2003, subsequently reprinted these articles, highlighting their continued validity for Griffin.
507 *Identity*, no. 23, August 2002.
508 *Spearhead*, no. 352, June 1998.
509 Under Griffin's editorship, *Spearhead* published advertisements for numerous racist and anti-Semitic publishers including: Sons of Liberty books; Life Rune Books (advertising a new edition of *White Power* by George Lincoln Rockwell); and *The Barnes Review*, an American

Holocaust denial journal, edited by Willis Carto. It also advertised *Nature's Eternal Religion* and *The White Man's Bible*, authored by the late Ben Klassen, founder of the Church of the Creator, see *Spearhead*, no. 349, March 1998; *Spearhead*, no. 350, April 1998; *Spearhead*, no. 357, November 1998; and *Spearhead*, no. 358, December 1998.
510 *Spearhead*, no. 366, August 1999.
511 Nick Griffin to Wayne Ashcroft, n.d. (annotated 1997 'Post Cook Report') in MSS 412/WA/3/1, Ashcroft papers.
512 Penrose, 'Why the US Needs Something Like the BNP'.
513 *Spearhead*, no. 323, January 1996; and *Spearhead*, no. 326, April 1996.
514 *Spearhead*, no. 324, February 1996.
515 *Spearhead*, no. 325, March 1996.
516 *Ibid*.
517 *Spearhead*, no. 330, August 1996.
518 *Spearhead*, no. 333, November 1996; and *Spearhead*, no. 336, February 1997.
519 *The Rune*, no. 12, 1996.
520 Lowles, *White Riot*, p. 198.
521 *Carlisle Two Defence Fund Bulletin*, cited in *Searchlight*, no. 299, May 2000.
522 *The Rune*, no. 11, 1995 and *The Rune*, no. 12, 1996 in which Griffin clashed with Michael A. Hoffman II, editor of *Independent History and Research Newsletter* who defended Irving.
523 *Spearhead*, no. 324, February 1996. *The Rune*, no. 8, had also asserted that 'the contemporary conduct of European political affairs is intimately bound into a complex of ideas, justified by the legend of the Holocaust.'
524 *The Rune*, no. 8, n.d.; and *The Rune*, no. 11, 1995.
525 *Spearhead*, no. 402, August 2002.
526 Graham Macklin, 'Transnational Networking on the Far Right: The Case of Britain and Germany', *West European Politics*, vol. 36, no. 1, 2013, pp. 176–198.
527 *The Rune*, no. 12, 1996; and *Spearhead*, no. 360, August 1996.
528 Nicholas John Griffin, indictment, released under FOI.
529 *Searchlight*, no. 264, June 1997. 'Mr Carlisle changed his surname before entering politics,' sneered *Spearhead*, no. 335, January 1997, 'he had previously rejoiced in the name of Alex Fallick, and his family come from much further away from Wales than the Scottish border.'
530 WPC Carol Kendall, Witness statement, 12 December 1997, released under FOI.
531 *Spearhead*, no. 335, January 1997. Griffin wore this as a badge of honour, repeating the boast in his contribution to an anthology of Lane's writings, see Nick Griffin 'The Domino Effect', p. 343. *Spearhead*, no. 339, May 1997, edited by Griffin, reprinted an article from Lane's 14 Words Press (publishing its contact details as well) whilst referring to Lane as a 'political prisoner'. He published a further article authored by Lane in *Spearhead*, no. 340, June 1997.
532 *Spearhead*, no. 335, January 1997.
533 *Spearhead*, no. 323, January 1996.
534 *Spearhead*, no. 327, May 1996.
535 Mark Deavin, 'Harold Macmillan and the Origins of the 1961 British Application to Join the EEC' (London School of Economics: Unpublished PhD thesis, 1996), pp. 13 and 28 contain numerous conspiratorial allusions. *Searchlight*, no. 264, June 1997, quotes *The Grand Plan: The Origins of Non-White Immigration*, a document Deavin handed to *The Cook Report*, stating explicitly that the drive for 'World Government' was 'Jewish in origin and Zionist in motivation.' David Irving's Focal Point subsequently advertised Deavin's book, *Macmillan's Hidden Agenda* (1998) but it never appeared, see 'The New Book by Mark Deavin: Macmillan's Hidden Agenda', *Focal Point*, summer 1998, www.fpp.co.uk/Authors/Deavin.html (accessed 5 February 2018).
536 *British Nationalist*, no. 176, February 1997; and *Spearhead*, no. 336, February 1997.
537 *Spearhead*, no. 346, December 1997. Long after he had supposedly disavowed anti-Semitism, Griffin wrote in *Identity*, no. 53, March 2005, 'it is indeed true that certain minority groups do punch far above their weight when it comes to influence within the media ... which liberal propagandists still berate for pointing out in my now out-of-print survey *The Mind-Benders*.'
538 [Nick Griffin], *Who are the Mind-Benders?* (Welling: BNP, 1997); and *The Rune*, no. 12, 1996.
539 Wayne Ashcroft to Nick Griffin, 19 July 1995 in MSS 412/WA/3/1, Ashcroft papers. In *The Rune*, no. 11, 1995, Griffin quoted several excerpts from *Mein Kampf* in support of his assertion

that the BNP should not join with other groups but should absorb them by demonstrating the success of their own techniques.
540 Nick Griffin to Wayne Ashcroft, 1997 ('Post Cook Report'); and Nick Griffin to Wayne Ashcroft, n.d. (late 1997) in MSS 412/WA/3/1, Ashcroft papers.
541 'New Year Message & 1997 Review from Party Chairman John McAuley' in MSS 412/HQ/3/1/25(i), Ashcroft papers; and *NF Members' Bulletin*, n.d. (late 1994). John Tyndall to Wayne Ashcroft, 5 May 1998 in MSS 412/WA/3/1, Ashcroft papers suggested that, despite the failure of the merger, Ashcroft might wish to continue efforts aimed at 'unifying all nationalist elements' under the BNP umbrella as well as assisting Griffin in his task as Director of Publicity for the BNP.
542 For Cartwright's co-authorship, see 'B&H Responds: Rock Against Griffinism', *Final Conflict*, 9 January 2008.
543 Nick Griffin to Wayne Ashcroft, 8 July 1998 in MSS 412/WA/3/1, Ashcroft papers. Griffin advertised 'Radio White Europe' as a 'discussion document' in *Spearhead*, no. 338, April 1997.
544 *Searchlight*, no. 264, June 1997.
545 *Searchlight*, no. 264, June 1997. Roger Cook, *More Dangerous Ground* (Brighton: Book Guild, 2007), p. 372 refers to the broadcast cursorily in contrast to Griffin's lengthier responses 'The Cooked Report' and 'Behind the Smear' at British National Party, www.bnp.net/cooked.html; and 'Behind the Smear', British National Party.
546 'Regulator Archives', *Ofcom*, 24 June 2010, www.ofcom.org.uk/static/archive/bsc/pdfs/bulletin/bulletin12.pdf (accessed 3 June 2015).
547 *British Nationalist*, no. 183, September 1997; and *British Nationalist*, no. 186, December 1997.
548 *British Nationalist*, no. 185, November 1997; and *Spearhead*, no. 359, January 1999.
549 *British Nationalist*, no. 188, February 1998; and *British Nationalist*, no. 193, July 1998. The Countryside Alliance repudiated BNP support, see *Spearhead*, no. 368, October 1999.
550 *British Nationalist*, no. 185, November 1997.
551 *British Nationalist*, no. 188, February 1998.
552 *Nick Griffin – Police Interview: The Tyrannical Defence of the Impossible. Race Laws + 'Holocaust' = Persecution* (Welling: Carlisle Two Defence Fund Cassette Tape, 1997).
553 *New! Britain's Thought Police in Action!: Unique Cassette Tape* (Uckfield: Historical Review Press, 1997).
554 *British Nationalist*, no. 186, December 1997. Two genuine FN observers attended the initial hearing.
555 *British Nationalist*, no. 187, January 1998.
556 *Ibid. Spearhead*, no. 344, October 1997 highlights a £40 donation to Griffin's defence fund from a French reader of *Spearhead*, Jean-Louis Pesteil.
557 *Spearhead*, no. 342, August 1997.
558 'Good Morning from the Zundelsite', 31 August 1997, www.webcom.com/ezundel/english/zgrams/zg1997/zg9708/970831.html (accessed 17 December 1997). Zündel later listed Griffin amongst this 'Victims of Zion', see www.zundelsite.org/archive/victims/victims_of_zion.html (accessed 27 May 2015). Michael A. Hoffman II's *Hoffman Wire*, 23 November 1997 praised Griffin as a pioneer of 'online radical revisionism', see 'The Hoffman Wire', 23 November 1997, https://groups.google.com/forum/?hl=en#!msg/soc.culture.usa/K5mtomFqsYY/XpF2Vvkdo V0J (accessed 27 May 2015).
559 *British Nationalist*, no. 187, January 1998; and *Come one, Come all! The Grand Heresy Trial* (Welshpool: Publicity for Freedom, 1998).
560 *Searchlight*, no. 264, June 1997.
561 *Croydon Advertiser*, 8 May 1998.
562 *The Order*, no. 7, n.d. Less effusively, *Putsch*, no. 30, November 1995 noted Griffin's reappearance on the political scene, 'stirring up trouble everywhere he goes, West Yorkshire in particular.'
563 'B&H Responds: Rock Against Griffinism', *Final Conflict*.
564 *Ibid.*
565 *Spearhead*, no. 350, April 1998.
566 *British Nationalist*, no. 187, January 1998; and *Spearhead*, no. 347, January 1998.
567 *British Nationalist*, no. 172, October 1996. Smith had recently organised a demonstration with Archie O'Brien, a Bermudian-born Rastafarian petitioning the Home Office for financial assistance to emigrate to Ghana.

568 *British Nationalist*, no. 191, May 1998.
569 *Ibid*.
570 *Spearhead*, no. 356, October 1998. Griffin raised some funds to pay off his fine by selling far right music. *British Nationalist*, no. 197, November 1998 advertised for sale two albums by 'patriotic balladeer' Carl Klang, a Christian Identity adherent based in Oregon. Cheques were payable to Griffin's 'Publicity for Freedom' fund. He also sold a sampler tape of Klang's works, with his own commentary, see *Spearhead*, no. 350, April 1998.
571 *Spearhead*, no. 339, May 1997 stated that material for the 'long delayed' Issue 13 was 'still in the hands of the police, who refuse to return it.' The Libertarian Alliance published a critique of the proceedings: David Botsford, 'The British State versus Freedom of Expression: The Case of R. v. Griffin', *Legal Notes*, no. 29, 1998.
572 *Spearhead*, no. 335, January 1997.
573 Eddy Butler, September 2011, http://eddybutler.blogspot.com/2011/09/i-hear-you-knocking-but-you-cant-come.html (accessed 14 September 2011).
574 *Spearhead*, no. 357, November 1998.
575 *Ibid*.
576 *Spearhead*, no. 358, December 1998. For Bean's contribution to BNP modernisation, see Graham Macklin, 'Modernizing the Past for the Future', in Nigel Copsey and Graham Macklin (eds), *British National Party: Contemporary Perspectives* (Abingdon: Routledge, 2011), pp. 19–37.
577 *British Nationalist*, no. 198, December 1998.
578 Matthew Goodwin, *New British Fascism: Rise of the British National Party* (Abingdon: Routledge, 2011), p. 66.
579 *Spearhead*, no. 417, November 2003.
580 *Spearhead*, no. 117, August 1999.
581 *Patriot*, no. 4, spring 1999.
582 *Ibid*. Mark Deavin had outlined the idea in *Spearhead*, no. 351, May 1998.
583 One *Daily Express* opinion poll in 1997 indicated that 9 per cent of Britons wanted the chance to vote for an FN in Britain with a further 17 per cent saying they would consider it.
584 Steve Bastow, 'The Ideological Mobility of Front National Discourse', *Essex Papers in Politics and Government*, 10 (October 1998), pp. 1–25; and *Identity*, no. 1, January–February 2000.
585 Penrose, 'Why the US Needs Something Like the BNP'. Exactly when Griffin and his colleagues read the book is not clear. In 'Behind the Smear', British National Party, Griffin states that: 'several months *before* [my emphasis] the approach by the phoney "FN", a close study of several books about the genuine French party convinced me that its approach was, *mutatis mutandis*, largely applicable to Britain.' *The Patriot*, no. 4, spring 1999 reviewed it, but only four years after its publication.
586 *Spearhead*, no. 337, March 1997. Griffin's newfound enthusiasm for the FN contrasted sharply with the marked hostility he had displayed for the FN during his 'national revolutionary' phase. Then, *Nationalism Today* had denounced the FN as a 'reactionary, right wing Tory organization', preferring instead the 'real' French nationalism of the Mouvement Nationaliste Révolutionnaire (MNR – National Revolutionary Movement) founded in 1979 by Jean-Gilles Malliarakis, who similarly disparaged Le Pen as insufficiently radical. Griffin was particularly taken with the Groupe d'union et de défense (GUD), an extreme right-wing militant group notable for fighting violent battles with left-wing opponents on university campuses. He wrote in *Nationalism Today*, no. 17:

> The real significance of such relatively short-loved mass movements is that while they themselves fade away, they give political education to all the participants and provide new recruits to the hardcore elite of dedicated activists who form the backbone of any worthwhile organisation.

587 Nigel Copsey, *Contemporary British Fascism: The British National Party and the Quest of Legitimacy* (London: Palgrave 2008), p. 109.
588 *Spearhead*, no. 337, March 1997. Before his death, Ludovici gave a copy of his unpublished autobiography, *Confessions of an Anti-Feminist* to his Suffolk neighbour, former BUF activist Ronald Creasy. He passed the book to Griffin 'who in turn lent it to people he knew were keen on publishing it.' It finally appeared in 2018, see John V. Day (ed.), *The Confessions of an*

Anti-Feminist: The Autobiography of Anthony M. Ludovici (San Francisco, CA: Counter-Currents, 2018), p. iv.
589 *Spearhead*, no. 341, July 1997.
590 *Ibid.*
591 See Germar Rudolf, 'Fleeing from England', http://germarrudolf.com/persecution/germars-persecution/fleeing-from-england/ (accessed 1 June 2015). Rudolf recalled:

> I actually had a nice stay at Griffin's house. We spoke a lot about his family and personal fate, the ethnic and language situation in Wales, and of course about Holocaust revisionism and censorship in England. It was there that I learned about his leading role in the BNP and that he was about to challenge the leader of the party.

592 'BNP Griffin: They Dare not Prosecute Me – Dominic Carman Interview', Dominic Carman YouTube channel, 3 November 2009, www.youtube.com/watch?v=R9KZ4qokJrs (accessed 3 November 2009).
593 'The Nailbomber', Panorama, BBC 1, http://news.bbc.co.uk/hi/english/static/audio_video/programmes/panorama/transcripts/transcript_30_06_00.txt (accessed 25 August 2016).
594 *Spearhead*, no. 344, October 1997.
595 *Daily Mirror*, 25 May 1999.
596 Nick Ryan, *Homeland* (Edinburgh: Mainstream, 2003), p. 271.
597 *British Nationalist*, no. 203, May 1999.
598 *Spearhead*, no. 364, June 1999.
599 See the interview with Nick Griffin, 'High Profile: Far from Right?', *Third Way*, 24 May 2004, https://thirdway.hymnsam.co.uk/editions/archive/high-profile/far-from-right.aspx (accessed 1 March 2012).
600 *Spearhead*, no. 364, June 1999.
601 *Loose Cannon*, no. 1, September 1999.
602 *Sunday Times*, 5 September 1999; and for a stance on homosexuality, see *Identity*, no. 39, December 2003.
603 'Membership Lists', www.tyndallexposed.com/member.htm (accessed 3 March 2005) claimed Tyndall allowed the BNP mailing list to facilitate distribution of Webster's newsletter, *Loose Cannon*, to the party's membership.
604 *British Nationalist*, no. 207, October 1999.
605 *Ibid.*
606 *Patriot*, no. 5, summer 1999.
607 *British Nationalist* [membership bulletin], October 1999.
608 *British Nationalist*, no. 207, October 1999.
609 Copsey, *Contemporary British Fascism*.
610 Copsey, *Contemporary British Fascism*, pp. 108–109 notes Griffin appropriated the idea of party 'circles' or satellite organisations from the FN but *Nationalism Today*, no. 46, July 1989 highlights the Apristas as its source. The two are not mutually exclusive, however.
611 'Italian Roberto Fiore of "Forza Nuova Party"', 29 August 2009, http://bnptv.org.uk/2009/08/italian-roberto-fiore-of-the-forza-nuova-party/ (accessed 31 July 2015).
612 *Corriere della Sera*, 21 March 2008.
613 Lowles, *White Riot*, pp. 320–321.
614 *Identity*, no 7, March 2001; and *Identity*, no. 10, June 2001.
615 The *Guardian*, 30 May 2001.
616 Mark Cotterill, interview with the author, 16 July 2009. For an overview, see Ryan Shaffer, 'Foreign Friends and British Fascism: Understanding the American Friends of the British National Party', *Contemporary British History* (2019), https://doi.org/10.1080/13619462.2019.1636651.
617 *Heritage and Destiny*, no. 8, May–June 2001.
618 The 16.02 per cent polled by Martin Webster in West Bromwich in 1973 was a parliamentary by-election not a general election, nor was there a Liberal candidate.
619 *Identity*, no. 11, July 2001. The magazine's book review that month was, tellingly, Wilmot Robertson's 1972 'classic' *The Dispossessed Majority*.
620 *Identity*, no. 16, December 2001.
621 'The Federal Prosecution of David Duke', www.bnp.org.uk/articles/davidduke_battle.htm (accessed 24 December 2002).

622 *Identity*, no. 16, December 2001.
623 *Identity*, no. 14, October 2001; and *Identity*, no. 16, December 2001.
624 *Identity*, no. 15, November 2001.
625 *The Truth about Islam* (BNP leaflet, 2001).
626 *Identity*, no. 16, December 2001.
627 George Michael, *The Enemy of My Enemy: The Alarming Convergence of Militant Islam and the Extreme Right* (Lawrence, KS: University Press of Kansas, 2006), p. 277.
628 *Identity*, no. 16, December 2001. *Identity*, no. 17, March 2002 reported that total income from membership renewals that month 'was a whopping 89% up on the same time a year ago', which it claimed reflected 'high morale' amongst its existing membership and growing 'soft' support.
629 *Identity*, no. 15, November 2001.
630 *Identity*, no. 15, November 2001; and *Identity*, no. 19, April 2002. For an overview, see George Michael, *The Enemy of My Enemy*.
631 *Identity*, no. 19, April 2002.
632 *Identity*, no. 64, March 2006.
633 *American Renaissance Conference 2002* (VHS cassette, 2002).
634 'July Activities: BNP Chairman gives Presentation to Britain's Radio Bosses', July 2002, http://bnp.org.uk/activities/2002_jul1.htm (accessed 3 July 2002).
635 For a superlative overview of the party's local politics, see James Rhodes, 'The Political Breakthrough of the BNP: The Case of Burnley', *British Politics*, vol. 4, no. 1, 2009, pp. 22–46; James Rhodes, 'The Banal National Party: The Routine Nature of Legitimacy', *Patterns of Prejudice*, vol. 43, no. 2, 2009, pp. 142–160; and James Rhodes, 'White Backlash, "Unfairness" and Justifications of British National Party (BNP) Support', *Ethnicities*, vol. 10, no. 1, 2001, pp. 77–99.
636 *Identity*, no. 22, June 2002. For a further rejection of the 'Nazi' label, see 'Why the Swastika Appeals to Many Young Britons', www.bnp.org.uk/articles/appeal_swastika.htm (accessed 6 June 2004).
637 *Identity*, no. 34, July 2003.
638 John Bean, *Many Shades of Black: Inside Britain's Far Right* (Bloomington, IN: Ostara, 2013), p. v.
639 *Identity*, no. 20, May 2002.
640 In the 2008 local elections, the BNP made further gains in Stoke, ending the contest with nine local councillors and continuing the pattern of localised breakthrough.
641 Benjamin Bowyer, 'Local Context and the Extreme Right Support in England: The British National Party in the 2002 and 2003 Local Elections', *Electoral Studies*, vol. 27, no. 4, 2008, pp. 611–620.
642 Robert Ford and Matthew J. Goodwin, 'Angry White Men: Individual and Contextual Predictors of Support for the British National Party', *Political Studies*, vol. 58, 2010, pp. 1–25.
643 *Identity*, no. 35, August 2003.
644 *Identity*, no. 29, February 2003.
645 *Identity*, no. 26, November 2002.
646 *Identity*, no. 64, March 2006.
647 *Voice of Freedom*, no. 31, October 2002.
648 *Identity*, no. 38, November 2003.
649 *Voice of Freedom*, August 2004.
650 Despite publicly eschewing anti-Semitism, in 2006, the BNP 'cultural' website IONA featured 'Hugh of Lincoln', an anti-Semitic folk song. This song commemorates the 'ritual murder' of a young boy whose body was discovered in the well of a local Jew in 1255, who subsequently 'confessed' that he had been crucified by several prominent local Jews. Based on this 'testimony', eighteen Jews hanged, see www.project-iona.co.uk/article.php?iona_id=238 (accessed 15 March 2006).
651 *Identity*, no. 32, May 2003; and *Rebuilding British Democracy: British National Party General Election 2005 Manifesto* (London: BNP, 2005), p. 52.
652 *Identity*, no. 66, May 2006.
653 *Identity*, no. 42, March 2004.
654 *The Rune*, no. 11, 1995.
655 *Identity*, no. 32, May 2003; and *Identity*, no. 33, June 2003.

656 Joe Owens, *Action! From Race War to Door Wars* (Lulu, 2007), pp. 261–266. Griffin branded the incident a 'Zimbabwe-style disgrace' and blamed the police, see *Identity*, no. 56, July 2005.
657 'A Day to Make History', 9 June 2004, www.bnp.org.uk/news/2004_june/news_june19.htm (accessed 20 June 2004).
658 Peter John, Helen Margetts, David Rowland and Stuart Weir, *The BNP: The Roots of its Appeal* (Colchester: Democratic Audit/Human Rights Centre, University of Essex, 2006), p. 8.
659 *Identity*, no. 45, July 2004.
660 'Debates', European Parliament, 4 February 2013, www.europarl.europa.eu/sides/getDoc.do?pubRef=-//EP//TEXT+CRE+20130204+ITEM-017+DOC+XML+V0//EN&language=en&query=INTERV&detail=1-078-000 (accessed 10 April 2017).
661 Steven Morris and Martin Wainwright, 'BNP Leader Held by Police over Racist Remarks', the *Guardian*, 15 December 2002, www.theguardian.com/uk/2004/dec/15/race.thefarright (accessed 10 April 2017).
662 *Identity*, no. 49, November 2004.
663 *Identity*, no. 50, December 2004; and *Identity*, no. 52, February 2005.
664 *European American Conference 2005* (DVD: David Duke Report, 2005).
665 Shamim Miah, 'The Groomers and the Question of Race', *Identity Papers*, vol. 1, no. 1, 2015, pp. 54–65 highlights that the widespread racialised 'cultural' narrative provided an 'entry point' for the BNP.
666 Matthew Taylor, 'Mother Out to Seize Stronghold of "Unforgivable" BNP', the *Guardian*, 23 March 2006, www.theguardian.com/politics/2006/mar/23/uk.localgovernment (accessed 25 March 2006_.
667 Rose Capdevila and Jane E.M. Callaghan, '"It's not Racist. It's Common Sense." A Critical Analysis of Political Discourse Around Asylum and Immigration in the UK', *Journal of Applied Community & Applied Social Psychology*, no. 18, 2008, pp. 1–16.
668 *Identity*, no. 57, August 2005; and *Identity*, no. 58, September 2005.
669 *Identity*, no. 57, August 2005. One of those for whom such rhetoric resonated with, Robert Cottage, a Lancashire BNP activist who was jailed for stockpiling explosive chemicals and ball bearings in 2007 in preparation for the coming 'civil war'.
670 Nick Griffin, 'Blackpool, Oxford and a Studio and Visit', *Chairman's Column*, 3 December 2007, http://chairmans-column.blogspot.com/ (accessed 1 July 2009).
671 *Identity*, no. 57, August 2005.
672 'BNP Campaign Uses Bus Bomb Photo', BBC News, 12 July 2005, http://news.bbc.co.uk/1/hi/uk_politics/4674675.stm (accessed 1 July 2009); and *Islamic Terror, Labour Failure* (BNP leaflet, 2005).
673 *Which Do You Find Offensive?* (BNP leaflet, 2005); and 'BNP Handing Out Prophet Leaflets', *This is Lancashire*, www.thisislancashire.co.uk/news/701062.BNP_handing_out_Prophet_leaflets/ (accessed 3 August 2015). Local Muslim men attacked BNP activists distributing the leaflets in Nelson, Lancashire, leaving one with a broken arm.
674 *Identity*, no. 58, September 2005; and *Identity*, no. 59, October 2005.
675 *Identity*, no. 35, August 2003; and *Identity*, no. 38, November 2003.
676 *Identity*, no. 51, January 2005.
677 'BNP Language & Concepts Discipline Manual' (BNP Policy Research), www.bnp.org.uk/organisers/store/general_guides/language_discipline.pdf (accessed on 12 January 2009).
678 For more on this theme, see Graham Macklin '"Teaching the Truth to the Hardcore": The Public and Private Presentation of BNP Ideology', in Matthew Feldman and Paul Jackson (eds), *Doublespeak: The Framing of the Far Right since 1945* (Hannover: ibidem-Verlag, 2014).
679 *Identity*, no. 53, March 2005.
680 *Evening Standard*, 26 March 2004.
681 John Tyndall, 'Do We Need Jewish Candidates: John Tyndall Addresses a Vexed Issue', *Spearhead*, www.spearhead.co.uk/0405-jt4.html (accessed 1 June 2015).
682 *European American Conference 2005* (DVD: David Duke Report 2005).
683 'BNP FAQs: Countering the Smears', www.bnp.org.uk/articles/countering_smears.html (accessed 12 March 2007).
684 *Lincolnshire Echo*, 15 March 2007.
685 'Matthew Bell: The IoS Diary', *The Independent*, 3 May 2010, www.independent.co.uk/voices/commentators/matthew-bell-the-iiosi-diary-1224213.html (accessed 10 March 2010).

686 'The British National Party Goes Straight: [Nick Griffin] Interview by Robert Locke', *Think-Israel*, September–25 October 2005, www.think-israel.org/locke.bnp.html (accessed 25 November 2014). For a further rejection of 'Judeo-obsessivism' – though *not* anti-Semitism, see *Identity*, no. 66, May 2006.
687 *Identity*, no. 17, March 2002. *Identity*, no. 33, June 2003 contained a long review of *Race, Genetics and Society: On the Scientific and Social Policy Implications of Racial Differences* (2002) by Professor Glayde Whitney.
688 *Identity*, no. 30, March 2003.
689 Andreas Fahrmeir, *Citizenship: The Rise and Fall of a Modern Concept* (New Haven, CT: Yale University Press, 2007).
690 *Identity*, no. 30, March 2003; and *Identity*, no. 5, January 2001.
691 See BNP online shop 'Excalibur', http://excalibur.bnp.org.uk/acatalog/What_s_New.html (accessed 23 November 2005).
692 *Identity*, no. 30, March 2003.
693 *Ibid.*
694 *Identity*, no. 39, December 2003.
695 *Voice of Freedom*, February 2003.
696 *Identity*, no. 30, March 2003.
697 Lee Barnes, 'Ethno-Nationalism and the Political Struggle', 21 November 2005, www.bnp.org.uk/columnists/brimstone2.php?leeId=67 (accessed 23 November 2005).
698 See 'Racial or Ethno Nationalism?', *Storm Front*, 21 November 2005, www.stormfront.org/forum/showthread.php?t=248740 (accessed 23 November 2005).
699 Srdja Trifkovic, 'Nick Griffin's Long March'.
700 *Identity*, no. 30, March 2003.
701 Sasha Williams and Ian Law, 'Legitimising Racism: An Exploration of the Challenges Posed by the Use of Indigeneity Discourses by the Far Right', *Sociological Research Online*, vol. 17, no. 2, 2, www.socresonline.org.uk/17/2/2.html (accessed 12 August 2012).
702 Arthur Kemp, *Four Flags: The Indigenous People of Britain* (Deeside: Excalibur Books, 2010).
703 'Cockneys Become First Victims of the Immigration Invasion Genocide', 2 July 2010, www.bnp.org.uk/news/cockneys-become-first-victims-immigration-invasion-genocide (accessed 7 November 2011).
704 Marleen Gambel and Roland Sturm, 'Extremism in Großbritannien', in Eckhard Jesse and Tom Thieme (eds), *Extremismus in den EU-Staaten* (Wiesbaden: Verlag für Sozialwissenschaften, 2011), p. 172.
705 Goodwin, *New British Fascism*, pp. 39, 158–159 and 164–166.
706 Arthur Kemp, *Victory or Violence: The Story of the AWB of South Africa* (Burlington, VA: Ostara, 2008), p. 160.
707 For Kemp's version of events, see Arthur Kemp, *The Lie of Apartheid and Other True Stories from Southern Africa* (Burlington, VA: Ostara, 2009), pp. 79–102.
708 Arthur Kemp, *March of the Titans: A History of the White Race* (Burlington, VA, Ostara: 2006), pp. 541–544.
709 *Identity*, no. 13, September 2001; and *Identity*, no. 71, October 2006.
710 *Identity*, no. 55, June 2005. In August 2007, Griffin announced Kemp's role in 'ideological training' for voting members, stating that 'Arthur is a highly skilled and very welcome addition to our central team.' See Nick Griffin, 'Catching Up', *Chairman's Column*, 11 August 2007, http://chairmans-column.blogspot.com/2007/08/first-my-sincere-apologies-for-long-gap.html (accessed 11 August 2007). Griffin appointed Kemp as editor of the BNP website, see 'Chairman's Blog: Another Prediction Comes True', 15 December 2007, www.bnp.org.uk/2007/12/another-prediction-comes-true/ (accessed 15 December 2007).
711 Arthur Kemp and Nick Griffin, *Folk and Nation: Underpinning the Ethnostate* (2008).
712 *Identity*, no. 62, January 2006.
713 Shaffer, 'Foreign Friends and British Fascism', p. 275; and *Identity*, no. 63, February 2006.
714 The *Guardian*, 3 February 2006.
715 '"Victory for Freedom" Claims BNP', BBC News, 10 November 2006, http://news.bbc.co.uk/1/hi/england/bradford/6137986.stm (accessed 15 November 2006). For CPS comment on the acquittal, see Crown Prosecution Service, www.cps.gov.uk/news/latest_news/165_06/ (accessed 15 November 2006).

716 'Free Speech 2: The Party Starts', 2 November 2006, http://bnptv.org.uk/2006/11/free-speech-2-the-party-starts/ (accessed 15 November 2006).
717 Michael Collins, *The Likes of Us: A Biography of the White Working Class* (London: Granta, 2004), p. 173.
718 Jon Cruddas and Jonathan Rutherford, 'Labour Must Fashion a New Patriotism', The *Guardian*, 1 July 2011, www.theguardian.com/commentisfree/2011/jul/01/labour-patriotism-immigration-identity (accessed 11 September 2018).
719 Jeremy Seabrook, *What Went Wrong? Working People and the Ideas of the Labour Movement* (London: Victor Gollancz, 1978), p. 157.
720 *Chronicles Magazine*, www.chroniclesmagazine.org/cgi-bin/newsviews.cgi/Old%20Europe?Nick_Griffin_… (accessed 14 June 2006).
721 *Voice of Freedom*, no. 76, 2006.
722 *Redbridge Patriot*, Winter 2008.
723 Peter Hoskin, 'How the BNP are Campaigning', *The Spectator*, 12 May 2009, http://blogs.spectator.co.uk/2009/05/how-the-bnp-are-campaigning/ (accessed 21 August 2016).
724 On this theme, see Stuart Wilks-Heeg, 'The Canary in a Coalmine? Explaining the Emergence of the British National Party in English Local Politics', *Parliamentary Affairs*, vol. 62, no. 3, 2009, pp. 377–398.
725 British National Party, www.bnp.org.uk/?p=389 (accessed 3 January 2008). Griffin had long since argued that B&H no longer added anything of value to the BNP. In *Identity*, no. 17, March 2002, he stated that the 'white power' scene was 'fossilised' and insular, failing to appeal to 'the huge potential youth audience produced by the radicalising effect of the 2001-and-after race riots.' *Blood & Honour* magazine had been generally positive towards the party, however.
726 For details of the contribution B&H activists to the BNP *after* Griffin became chairman, see 'B&H Responds: Rock Against Griffinism', *Final Conflict*, 9 January 2008.
727 'The BNP: Anti-Asylum Protest, Racist Sect or Power-Winning Movement?', www.bnp.org.uk/articles/race_reality.htm (accessed 21 February 2006). The BNP legal officer defined the '14 words' as the party's 'strategic goal' as late as 2007, see Barnes, 'Ethno-Nationalism and the Political Struggle'.
728 Joel Busher, 'Why Even Misleading Identity Claims Matter: The Evolution of the English Defence League', *Political Studies*, published online 25 September 2017.
729 'PM's Speech at Munich Security Conference', 5 February 2011, *Prime Minister's Office, 10 Downing Street*, www.number10.gov.uk/news/speeches-and-transcripts/2011/02/pms-speech-at-munich-security-conference-60293 (accessed 10 February 2011).
730 'Cameron's "War on Multiculturalism" Speech: Another Milestone in the "Griffinisation" of British Politics', 5 February 2011, www.bnp.org.uk/news/cameron's-'war-multiculturalism'-speech-–anothermilestone-'griffinisation'-british-politics (accessed 5 June 2015).
731 'Proud and Prejudiced', Channel 4 documentary, www.channel4.com/programmes/proud-and-prejudiced (accessed 29 February 2012).
732 For an explanation of why the BNP lifted the proscription, see www.bnp.org.uk/news/national/opportunity-to-be-seized-why-we-have-lifted-proscription–english-defence-league (accessed 1 March 2012); and Nick Griffin, *English Defence League? Neo-Cons, Ultra-Zionists and The Useful Idiots* (2012). Nick Griffin, *Alt-Right? Not Right!* (2017) reflects his antipathy towards another emerging milieu whose leading lights he attacked as a 'gay mafia'.
733 'A Deadly Threat and the Way Ahead', 9 July 2014, www.bnp.org.uk/news/national/deadly-threat-and-way-ahead. Griffin went so far as to conspiratorially claim in January 2013 that US 'Neocons' (i.e. Jews) had tried to 'bribe' him to just attack Islam, see 'Neocons Tried to Bribe Nick Griffin's BNP to Ignore Jewish Power & Only Attack Islam', *Renegade Tribune*, 21 January 2016, www.renegadetribune.com/neocons-tried-bribe-nick-griffins-bnp-ignore-jewish-power-attack-islam/ (accessed 11 March 2018).
734 Tommy Robinson, *Enemy of the State* (Plymouth: The Press News Ltd, 2015), p. 76.
735 *The Times*, 24 June 2009.
736 '"Sink Immigrants" Boats – Griffin', BBC News, 8 July 2009, http://news.bbc.co.uk/1/hi/uk_politics/8141069.stm (accessed 10 April 2017).
737 BNP email bulletin, 21 October 2009.
738 The *Independent*, 23 October 2009.

739 *Daily Mail*, 23 October 2009.
740 Nigel Copsey and Graham Macklin, 'THE MEDIA = LIES, LIES, LIES! The BNP and the Media in Contemporary Britain', in Nigel Copsey and Graham Macklin (eds), *British National Party: Contemporary Perspectives* (Abingdon: Routledge, 2011), pp. 81–103; and Paul Bull and Anne-Marie Simon-Vandenbergen, 'Equivocation and Doublespeak in Far Right-Wing Discourse: An Analysis of Nick Griffin's Performance on BBC's Question Time', *Text & Talk*, vol. 34, no. 1, 2014, pp. 1–22.
741 Carl Packman, 'Nick Griffin Not Alone in QT Audience', *Liberal Conspiracy*, 30 October 2009, www.liberalconspiracy.org/2009/10/30/nick-griffin-not-alone-in-qt-audience/ (accessed 13 November 2009).
742 BBC, Question Time, 22 October 2009, available at: www.bbc.co.uk/iplayer/episode/b00nft24/Question_Time_22_10_2009/ (accessed 13 November 2009).
743 'BNP leader Nick Griffin is … A Disgrace to Humanity' (*Daily Express*, 23 October 2009); 'Bigot at Bay' (*Daily Mail*, 23 October 2009); 'Griffin uses BBC to Attack Islam and Defend the Ku Klux Klan' (*Daily Telegraph*, 23 October 2009); 'I'm the Most Loathed Man in Britain (We Couldn't Have Put It Better, Mr Griffin' (*Sun*, 23 October 2009); 'BNP Chief Griffin is a Nutter … Even Wife Puts the Boot in' (*Daily Star*, 23 October 2009); 'Rat Run – BNP Bigot Scuttles Away After Humiliation on TV' (*Daily Mirror*, 23 October 2009); 'Question Time for BNP Leader. His Answer: "I am not a Nazi"' (*Guardian*, 23 October 2009); and 'The BBC gave him the Oxygen of Publicity. He Choked' (*Independent*, 23 October 2009).
744 Peter Kellner, 'The BNP Brand Remains Badly Tainted', *YouGov*, 16 May 2011, https://yougov.co.uk/topics/politics/articles-reports/2011/05/16/bnp-brand-remains-badly-tainted; and Robert Ford and Matthew Goodwin, 'What's the Difference Between BNP and UKIP Voters?', the *Guardian*, 14 April 2014, www.theguardian.com/commentisfree/2014/apr/14/bnp-ukip-voters-politics-immigration (accessed 19 March 2019).
745 Hélène Mulholland and agencies, 'Griffin: Unfair that Question Time was Filmed in "Ethnically Cleansed" London', the *Guardian*, 23 October 2019, www.theguardian.com/politics/2009/oct/23/bnp-nick-griffin-question-time (accessed 10 April 2017).
746 'Who's Afraid of the BNP?', presented by Kenan Malik, BBC, http://news.bbc.co.uk/nol/shared/spl/hi/programmes/analysis/transcripts/28_09_09.txt (accessed 10 April 2017).
747 For the full extent of the changes, compare *Constitution of The British National Party* (12th edn, February 2010) with the previous edition published in August 2009.
748 'BNP Votes to Ditch Whites-Only Membership Rule', BBC News, 14 February 2010, http://news.bbc.co.uk/1/hi/uk_politics/8514736.stm (accessed 10 April 2017).
749 Caroline Davies, 'Nick Griffin says Times Journalist's Ejection Shows BNP has Not Gone Soft', the *Guardian*, 15 February 2015, www.theguardian.com/politics/2010/feb/15/nick-griffin-bnp-not-going-soft (accessed 10 April 2017).
750 *Identity*, no. 46, August 2004.
751 In April 2010, the BNP welcomed the Reverend James Gitau, a Kenyan preacher affiliated to the Pentecostal United Holy Church of America. Gitau had campaigned with Nick Griffin in Barking and Dagenham. However, he had left the BNP after less than a month claiming it was still 'too racist' though their refusal to stand him as a candidate in Croydon may also have played a role in his defection, see Kirsty Whalley, 'BNP "Too Racist" for Black Vicar', *Sutton and Croydon Guardian*, 28 April 2010, www.croydonguardian.co.uk/news/8123879.BNP_too_racist__for_black_vicar/ (accessed 10 April 2017).
752 Tim Black, 'The Fall of Britain's Far-Right Party', *EU Observer*, 13 March 2014, http://euobserver.com/eu-elections/123438 (accessed 10 April 2017).
753 'BNP Unveils Its 2010 Campaign Issues: Afghanistan, Immigration and the Global Warming Conspiracy', 7 April 2010, http://bnp.org.uk/2010/04/bnp-unveils-its-2010-campaign-issues-afghanistan-immigration-and-the-global-warming-conspiracy (accessed 1 May 2010).
754 the *Barking and Dagenham Sentinel*, no. 1, 2010. The BNP excised the offending phrase from pdf copies of the newspaper circulated online.
755 'The Highly Irregular Lifestyle of Patrick Harrington', *Eddy Butler blog*, 8 March 2011, http://eddybutler.blogspot.co.uk/2011/03/highly-irregular-lifestyle-of-patrick.html (accessed 7 November 2011).

756 Prior to the poll, Griffin had also embroiled the BNP in a costly financial settlement with Anglo-Dutch multinational Unilever after breaching its copyright during an election broadcast, see Christopher Wadlow, 'The Marmite Election', *Journal of Intellectual Property Law and Practice*, vol. 6, no. 12, 2011, pp. 868–879.
757 The *Guardian*, 13 March 2010.
758 *Ibid.*
759 Russell Myers and Lee Sorrell, 'Nick Griffin: Barking's just like Central Nairobi', *the People*, 25 April 2010, www.people.co.uk/news/tm_headline=nick-griffin-barking-s-just-like-central-nairobi%26method=full%26objcctid=22210082%26siteid=93463-name_page.html (accessed 7 July 2012).
760 'Nick Griffin Talking About Barking & the Rest London After the Elections', 8 May 2010, YouTube, www.youtube.com/watch?v=fr0LmLz0jXk (accessed 7 November 2011).
761 'General Election 2010 Analysis by BNP Leader Nick Griffin', 9 May 2010, http://bnp.org.uk/news/general-election-2010-analysis-bnp-leader-nick-griffin (accessed 10 May 2010).
762 Nigel Copsey, 'Sustaining a Mortal Blow? The British National Party and the 2010 General and Local Elections', *Patterns of Prejudice*, vol. 46, no. 1, 2012, pp. 16–39.
763 João Carvalho, 'The End of a Strategic Opening? The BNP's Window of Opportunity in the 2000s and its Closure in the 2010s', *Patterns of Prejudice*, vol. 49, no. 3, 2015, pp. 271–293.
764 'UPDATED WITH AUDIO AND VIDEO: BNP Conference Plans Way Forward as Nick Griffin Announces Intention to Step Down in 2013', www.bnp.org.uk/news/updated-audio-and-video-bnp-conference-plans-way-forward-nick-griffin-announces-intention-step- (accessed 22 September 2015).
765 A pliant Griffin loyalist also stood, presumably to make the contest appear less hostile to Griffin.
766 'Former Stoke-on-Trent BNP Man Criticises Party', BBC News, 21 March 2010, http://news.bbc.co.uk/1/hi/england/staffordshire/8579023.stm (accessed 8 August 2010).
767 See newsletter of SGSS (Gurdwara Sri Guru Singh Sabha), www.sgss.org/newsletter/documents/joint_statement.pdf (accessed 3 September 2012).
768 'Nick Griffin was Right on Grooming – and on Who Does It', 24 May 2012, www.bnp.org.uk/news/national/nick-griffin-was-right-grooming-–-and-who-does-it (accessed 30 May 2012).
769 'How the Far Right Almost Wrecked £2m Trial of Rochdale Sex Grooming Gang', *Manchester Evening News*, 9 May 2010, www.manchestereveningnews.co.uk/news/greater-manchester-news/how-the-far-right-almost-wrecked-2m-687969 (accessed 13 September 2018).
770 The *Sun*, 29 February 2012.
771 Siobhan Fenton, 'Paige Chivers Murder: Neo-Nazi Paedophile Robert Ewing Found Guilty of Murdering School Girl', the *Independent*, 11 July 2015, www.independent.co.uk/news/uk/crime/paige-chivers-murder-neo-nazi-paedophile-robert-ewing-found-guilty-of-murdering-school-girl-10382489.html (accessed 13 September 2018).
772 Daniel de Simone, 'The Neo-Nazi Paedophile who Plotted to Kill', BBC News, 2 April 2019, www.bbc.com/news/stories-44798649 (accessed 2 April 2019).
773 @NickGriffinBU, Twitter, 25 September 2014, https://twitter.com/nickjgriffinbnp/status/515082231413743616 (accessed 13 September 2018).
774 'Hitting Back at the Rotten Establishment', http://campaigns.bnp.org.uk/s/1/bbqi/ejQgOhW/691xr (accessed 21 November 2012).
775 Matthew Goodwin, 'Forever a False Dawn? Explaining the Electoral Collapse of the British National Party (BNP)', *Parliamentary Affairs*, vol. 67, no. 4, 2014, pp. 887–906.
776 'Local Government Facts and Figures: England', *LGiU*, www.lgiu.org.uk/local-government-facts-and-figures/ (accessed 10 April 2017).
777 *Leadership Election 2011: Andrew Brons' Election Address* (2011); and *Party Overview: A Report on the Mismanagement of the BNP* (2011).
778 'BNP Conference: I'm in Charge Says Nick Griffin', BBC News, 29 October 2011, www.bbc.co.uk/news/uk-politics-15499611 (accessed 10 April 2017).
779 For Brons' statement, see http://andrewbrons.eu/index.php?option=com_k2&view=item&id=628:statement-from-andrew-brons-mep (accessed 16 October 2012).
780 Ruby Kitchen, 'MEP Andrew Brons to Stand Down at Election', *Harrogate Advertiser*, 3 April 2014,www.harrogateadvertiser.co.uk/news/local/mep-andrew-brons-to-stand-down-at-election-1-6538148 (accessed 10 April 2017).

781 Nick Griffin, *What Lies Behind the English Defence League? Neo-Cons, Ultra-Zionists and Their Useful Idiots*, 23 May 2013, www.bnp.org.uk/sites/default/files/what_lies_behind_the_english_defence_league.r2.pdf (accessed 5 June 2015).
782 Andrew Brons, 'National Politics: Where Do We Go from Here?', YouTube, 23 May 2015, www.youtube.com/watch?v=FKSiDjQ9VWg (accessed 5 June 2015).
783 'It Isn't all Greek to Me', *Eddy Butler's Blog*, July 2011, http://eddybutler.blogspot.com/2011/07/it-isnt-all-greek-to-me.html (accessed 7 November 2011).
784 'BNP Chief Leads Mr Monkey Protest at Town Hall', the *Shields Gazette*, www.shieldsgazette.com/news/local-news/bnp_chief_leads_mr_monkey_protest_at_town_hall_1_3527662 (accessed 10 April 2017).
785 'Those who Cannot Remember the Past are Condemned to Repeat it (Part 2)', *Eddy Butler's Blog*, 14 April 2011, http://eddybutler.blogspot.com/2011/04/those-who-cannot-remember-past-are.html (accessed 7 November 2011).
786 'Every Fishing Line is the Beginning of a New Race', *Eddy Butler's Blog*, July 2011, http://eddybutler.blogspot.com/2011/07/every-finish-line-is-beginning-of-new.html (accessed 7 November 2011).
787 Andrew Brons, 'Reports of My Resignation Have Been Greatly Exaggerated', 8 February 2012, http://bnpideas.com/?p=3621 (accessed 17 February 2012).
788 Matthew Collins, 'The State of Hate in 2013', *Hope Not Hate*, 21 January 2014, www.hopenothate.org.uk/blog/insider/article/3368/the-state-of-hate-in-2013 (accessed 23 February 2014); and *Identity*, no. 28, January 2003.
789 'BNP's Nick Griffin Declared Bankrupt', BBC News, 3 January 2014, www.bbc.co.uk/news/uk-england-25590155
790 British Nationalists EU Speech, 'White Genocide & Zionist Supremacists', YouTube, www.youtube.com/watch?v=AabxIT1GGYU.
791 Griffin had tweeted on prior to the trial: '#Edl #Infidels #Casuals #EVF #SEA etc all welcome at Lee Rigby trial demo. Old Bailey, 18th Nov. 9 a.m. onwards. #protectourtroops #BNP #BVG,' @NickGriffinBU , Twitter, 12 November 2013, https://twitter.com/NickGriffinBU/status/400300074187915264 (accessed 12 November 2013).
792 For the appeal, see www.bnp.org.uk/news/national/22nd-may-judgement-day.
793 *Identity*, no. 55, June 2005.
794 See www.demotix.com/photo/4766977/nick-griffin-bolton-oppose-new-mosques-farnworth (accessed 21 January 2015).
795 Graham Macklin, '"There's a vital lesson here. Let's sure we learn it": transnational mobilisation and the impact of Greece's Golden Dawn upon extreme right-wing activism in Britain', in Nigel Copsey and Matthew Worley (eds), *Tomorrow Belongs To Us: The British Far Right since 1967* (Abingdon: Routledge, 2017), pp. 185–207.
796 'BNP Leadership: A Personal Statement by Nick Griffin', 21 July 2014, www.bnp.org.uk/news/national/bnp-leadership---personal-statement-nick-griffin (accessed 21 February 2014).
797 'Nick Griffin Expelled from BNP Membership', 1 October 2014, www.bnp.org.uk/news/national/nick-griffin-expelled-bnp-membership (accessed 2 October 2014).
798 Graham Stewart, *Bang! A History of Britain in the 1980s* (London: Atlantic, 2013), p. 428.
799 @NickGriffinBU, Twitter, https://twitter.com/NickGriffinBU (accessed 10 April 2017).
800 For an overview of APF politics, see Ryan Shaffer, 'Pan-European Thought in British Fascism: The International Third Position and the Alliance for Peace and Freedom', *Patterns of Prejudice*, vol. 52, no. 1, 2018, pp. 78–99.
801 Publius, 'Racial Profiles'.
802 Anton Shekhovstov, *Russia and the Western Far Right: Tango Noir* (Abingdon: Routledge, 2016).
803 See Nick Griffin's VK page, https://vk.com/nickgriffin (accessed 1 February 2018).
804 'Russian Elections "Much Fairer Than Britain's": Initial Verdict from Nick Griffin', 9 December 2011, https://bnp.org.uk/news/national/russian-elections-"much-fairer-britain's"---initial-verdict-nick-griffin (accessed 15 December 2011).
805 For the remarks, see 'For Those Who Cannot Speak!', www.bnp.org.uk/news/national/those-who-cannot-speak-video (accessed 18 December 2013). Tellingly, this was the title of a famous piece of Holocaust denial literature published by British Movement leader Michael McLaughlin in 1979.

806 Dominic Kennedy, 'Russia's Role in Fostering Extremism Under Scrutiny', *The Times*, 6 February 2017, www.thetimes.co.uk/article/russia-s-role-in-fostering-extremism-under-scrutiny-5ckh2qpgh (accessed 10 March 2018).

807 Alan Cullison, 'Far-Right Flocks to Russia to Berate the West', *Wall Street Journal*, 23 March 2015, www.wsj.com/articles/far-right-flocks-to-russia-to-berate-the-west-1427059613 (accessed 10 March 2018). In line with this appeal to traditionalist 'Christian' values in Russia, and elsewhere, the AFP published, *The Attack on the Family and the European Fightback* (Brussels: AFP, 2016) excoriating feminism, abortion and homosexuality. 'We have it translated into Russian already but need advice on advertising on VK and Odnoklassniki. If you can help please message me. Thank you,' Griffin posted on his VK page in September 2016, see https://vk.com/nickgriffin?w=wall292118168_234%2Fall (accessed 10 March 2018).

808 Publius, 'Racial Profiles'.

809 'Polish Fascists are Joining with Pro-Russian Right-Wing Extremists', *Anton Shekhovtsov's Blog*, 6 June 2014, http://anton-shekhovtsov.blogspot.no/2014/06/polish-fascists-are-joining-pro-russian.html (accessed 10 March 2018) provides an incomplete list of the delegation: Bartosz Bekier, leader of Falanga (Poland); Frank Creyelman and Filip Dewinter, leading figures in Vlaams Belang (Belgium); Roberto Fiore, leader of Forza Nuova (Italy); Luc Michel, leader of the Parti Communautaire National-Européen and founder of the Eurasian Observatory for Democracy & Elections (Belgium); and Mateusz Piskorski, of Samooborona (Poland).

810 Götz Nordbruch, *Nazism in Syria and Lebanon: The Ambivalence of the German Option, 1933–1945* (Abingdon: Routledge, 2009), pp. 117–120.

811 Ryan Shaffer, 'Pan-European Thought in British Fascism', p. 299.

812 @NickGriffinBU, Twitter, 9 June 2013, https://twitter.com/NickGriffinBU/status/343829470530113537 (accessed 10 March 2018).

813 @NickGriffinBU, Twitter, 9 June 2013, https://twitter.com/NickGriffinBU/status/343832151290167296 (accessed 10 March 2018).

814 'Shocking: Carnage in Syria', YouTube, 16 June 2013, www.youtube.com/watch?v=IBKwig2blkQ (accessed 10 March 2018).

815 'Jihad Attack on Police Station', YouTube, 14 June 2013, www.youtube.com/watch?v=bEbqN5czb9s (accessed 10 March 2018).

816 'Exclusive: Interview with a Suicide Bomber', YouTube, 19 June 2013, www.youtube.com/watch?v=xOYjCyAjnKY (accessed 10 March 2018).

817 '"Syrians Want to go on Living in Secular, Tolerant State"', *RT*, 12 June 2013, www.rt.com/op-edge/syria-secular-us-weapons-581/ (accessed 10 March 2018).

818 '"A State Under Attack, Not a State in Crisis"', *Syria Times*, 12 June 2013, http://syriatimes.sy/index.php/editorials/opinion/5939-a-state-under-attack-not-a-state-in-crisis (accessed 10 March 2018).

819 @NickGriffinBU, Twitter, 6 April 2017, https://twitter.com/NickGriffinBU/status/849896285830361089; and @NickGriffinBU, Twitter, 9 April 2017, https://twitter.com/NickGriffinBU/status/851010710675095552 (accessed 10 March 2018). In a similar vein, Griffin dismissed accusations that Putin was behind the attempted murder of a Russian defector and his daughter in Salisbury in March 2018 using a nerve agent as 'fake news' and a 'false flag', see @NickGriffinBU, Twitter, 14 March 2018, https://twitter.com/NickGriffinBU/status/973876248345743360 (accessed 23 March 2018).

820 Jasper Jackson, 'RT Sanctioned by Ofcom over Series of Misleading and Biased Articles', the *Guardian*, 21 September 2015, www.theguardian.com/media/2015/sep/21/rt-sanctioned-over-series-of-misleading-articles-by-media-watchdog (accessed 10 March 2018).

821 @NickGriffinBU, Twitter, 1 December 2014, https://twitter.com/nickgriffinbu/status/539475874501115904 (accessed 10 March 2018).

822 Brian Wheeler, 'BNP's Nick Griffin Claims He "Influenced" Syria Vote', BBC News, 4 September 2013, www.bbc.com/news/uk-politics-23942041 (accessed 10 March 2018).

823 @NickGriffinBU, Twitter, 30 November 2014, https://twitter.com/NickGriffinBU/status/538984327573688321 (accessed 10 March 2018).

824 @NickGriffinBU, Twitter, 29 November 2014, https://twitter.com/NickGriffinBU/status/538796559899832320 (accessed 10 March 2018).

825 @NickGriffinBU, Twitter, 30 November 2014, https://twitter.com/NickGriffinBU/status/539096081636659201 (accessed 10 March 2018).

826 'Alliance of Peace and Freedom Delegation: Europe Must Take Syria's Side and Fight Terrorism', *Syria Times*, 6 June 2015, http://syriatimes.sy/index.php/news/local/18192-alliance-of-peace-and-freedom-delegation-europe-must-take-syria-s-side-and-fight-terrorism; and 'Lebanon Michel Aoun Elected President Fiore Great Hope for the Entire Middle East', *APF*, October 2016, https://apfeurope.com/2016/10/lebanon-michel-aoun-elected-president-fiore-great-hope-for-the-entire-middle-east/ (accessed 10 March 2018); and Publius, 'Racial Profiles'.

827 Publius, 'Racial Profiles'. Griffin also highlighted that the AFP maintained 'good relations' with the Syrian Social Nationalist Party, see Nahed al-Husaini, 'VT Damascus: Interview with UK Activist, Nick Griffin', *Veterans Today*, 19 November 2018, www.veteranstoday.com/2018/11/19/vt-damascus-interview-with-uk-activist-nick-griffin/ (accessed 20 November 2018).

828 'Hizbullah Official in Beirut Receives Visiting Far-Right "Alliance for Freedom and Peace" Party Members from UK, Italy, Belgium, Germany, and Croatia – Who Express Support for Hizbullah's Fight Against Israel', *Middle East Media Research Institute*, 19 March 2019, www.memri.org/reports/hizbullah-official-beirut-receives-visiting-far-right-alliance-freedom-and-peace-party (accessed 19 March 2019).

829 @NickGriffinBU, Twitter, 18 March 2019, https://twitter.com/NickGriffinBU/status/1107771388331520000 (accessed 18 March 2019).

830 Marcus Dysch, 'BNP Leader Out of Love with Israel', *Jewish Chronicle*, 13 June 2013, www.thejc.com/news/uk-news/bnp-leader-out-of-love-with-israel-1.45841 (accessed 10 March 2018).

831 'Syria: Stepping Stone to Russia', YouTube, 30 June 2013, www.youtube.com/watch?v=lHtMzrnTI6Y (accessed 10 March 2018).

832 See @NickGriffinBU, Twitter, 13 September 2015, https://twitter.com/nickgriffinbu/status/643023911005868032 (accessed 10 March 2018).

833 Nick Griffin, 'Bolshevik Revolution: Myth and Reality', *APF*, 7 November 2017, https://apfeurope.com/2017/11/bolshevik-revolution-myth-and-reality/ (accessed 10 March 2018).

834 During 2018, for instance, he promoted the work of Germar Rudolf and praised the then recently deceased French Holocaust denier Robert Faurisson as 'undoubtedly one of the bravest men I have ever met.' See @NickGriffinBU, Twitter, 22 September 2018, https://twitter.com/NickGriffinBU/status/1043414397597696000; and @NickGriffinBU, Twitter, 22 October 2018, https://twitter.com/NickGriffinBU/status/1054288858639228928 (accessed 19 March 2019).

835 Publius, 'Racial Profiles'.

836 LBC Radio, www.lbc.co.uk/ex-bnp-leader-im-emigrating-to-eastern-europe-122816; and Josh Barrie, 'Far-Right British Nationalist Nick Griffin says He Now Wants to Emigrate to, Er, Eastern Europe', *Indy100*, 9 January 2016, www.indy100.com/article/farright-british-nationalist-nick-griffin-says-he-now-wants-to-emigrate-to-er-eastern-europe–bkMP9b9TM3l (accessed 10 March 2018).

837 @NickGriffinBU, Twitter, 26 May 2017, https://twitter.com/NickGriffinBU/status/868093230822412288 (accessed 10 March 2018).

838 For Griffin's remarks, see Knights Templar International, January 2018, https://knightstemplarinternational.com/2018/01/white-sharia-ultimate-treason-important-audio-talk-2/ (accessed 7 March 2018).

839 'Nick Griffin: Right-Wing Chameleon', BBC News, 29 June 2001, http://news.bbc.co.uk/1/hi/uk/1412785.stm (accessed 25 August 2016).

840 *Ibid*.

841 *Spearhead*, no. 118, September 1999.

842 Adam Smith, 'Nationalism in the Shadow of Empire: Nick Griffin', *Myth of the 20th Century*, 12 September 2018, https://myth20c.wordpress.com/2018/09/12/nationalism-in-the-shadow-of-empire-nick-griffin/ (accessed 19 September 2018).

843 *Ibid*.

844 Publius, 'Racial Profiles'.

845 Smith, 'Nationalism in the Shadow of Empire: Nick Griffin'.

846 Publius, 'Racial Profiles'.

Conclusion

Continuity and change on the British fascist fringe

This book has illuminated the ideological and strategic evolution of the British fascist tradition, and some of the overarching patterns of continuity and change within it, since it cohered into a recognisable political movement in the early 1920s. Where appropriate, it has viewed these developments through a transnational lens, to highlight that even small *groupuscules* and marginal actors were part of wider networks, which were shaped by an international context as much as a national or indeed local one. The biographical approach has enabled this study to explore both these individual ideological trajectories, taking a whole-life approach rather than focusing simply of the periods in which they achieved their greatest notoriety, using them as a prism through which to understand how their activities contributed to the milieu's overarching progression. This study has also been at pains to stress the essential ideological continuity underpinning the tradition, however. Indeed, it has resisted the seductive temptation to view every change in emphasis or a novel political development within the movement as constituting a radical 'new' departure, particularly once considered within the broader arc of the movement's history.

Taken collectively, these mutually entangled personal and political histories and the cleavages that they have generated highlight that British fascism was never a single, politically or ideologically homogenous entity, at any point during the last century. They also demonstrate how the personal agency of these activists, ideologues and leaders, which was often as destructive as it was creative, was as much responsible for shaping the movement, its ideas and its political structures, as were other externally imposed factors. Furthermore, it highlights an overarching resilience, often obscured by the tradition's tendency to factional squabbles, personal animosities and ruinous organisational rivalries. Its durability, over the course of a century, is due in large part, not to political parties, which have periodically disintegrated and disappeared, but to a subcultural, *groupuscular* milieu that has sustained and nourished the movement through several long periods of abeyance.

During the 1990s, there was a distinct strain of historical interpretation that appeared predicated upon a basic incredulity that anyone would bother to study British fascism in the first place such was its perceived marginality. Stanley Payne famously argued that British fascism represented a 'political oxymoron' that had generated a voluminous literature that was 'inversely proportionate to its significance'. His magisterial *A History of Fascism* contained 613 pages. British fascism merited a mere three of these, one of which consisted of photographs.[1] Other verdicts were equally withering. 'Seldom indeed, has so much ever been written about so little,' lamented W.D. Rubinstein.[2] Even Richard Thurlow, author of the seminal study, *Fascism in Britain*, which first appeared in 1987, and was revised in 1998, felt compelled to agree, stating that 'rarely can such an apparently insignificant topic have been responsible for such an outpouring of ink.' Such reservations did not preclude him from adding a further 298 pages to the topic, however.[3] Subsequent scholars have since mused that British fascism's historiographical cannon was now so 'vast' that it 'even surpasses the attention conferred on the Blackshirts during the 1930s.'[4]

None went as far as Vernon Bogdanor, however, who, in a somewhat scathing review of an edited collection titled *The Failure of British Fascism* in 1998 (which, amongst other things, called for a new research agenda that moved beyond traditional understandings of success and failure) dismissed the necessity for further study of the subject out of hand. Bogdanor declared imperiously:

> It is unlikely, however, that the conclusions already established by [Colin] Cross, [Robert] Benewick, [D.S.] Lewis and [Richard] Thurlow will be much challenged, and further research on the minuscule fascist movements in Britain is likely to yield only diminishing returns.[5]

Two decades later, Bogdanor's pronouncement appears no less absurd now than it was then. Far from there being nothing more to say, scholarly knowledge of British fascism's history has increased exponentially, advancing hand-in-hand with new archival releases and deposits and of course scholarship continues to evolve as the tradition itself generates new political forms. The present study, by no means definitive, has synthesised nearly twenty years' worth of archival releases together with access to several unique collections of private papers as a means of advancing the field so that – regardless of whether or not future scholars agree with its conclusions – they can at least take advantage of, and build upon, its empirical insights. The study of British fascism has also greatly profited from the introduction of a variety of theoretical and methodological innovations not least of which was the broader 'cultural turn' within 'Fascist Studies', which occasioned a range of penetrating and illuminating studies,[6] analytically reinvigorating the field and redirecting it away from the well-trodden debates about 'failure'. Whilst the present study has made use of this cultural reading where appropriate, it has also sought to tilt the pendulum back in the other direction, towards a more explicit understanding of British fascism as a 'political' movement underpinned by ideology, propaganda and violence.[7]

Enoch Powell famously remarked that: 'All political lives, unless they are cut off in midstream at a happy juncture, end in failure, because that is the nature of politics and of human affairs.'[8] In the case of British fascism, it is self-evident that the political lives of Leese, Mosley, Chesterton, Jordan, Tyndall and Griffin did not simply end in 'failure' but began there too, though in Mosley's case, it might be more accurate to state that his early political promise was derailed by his own impatience which played a large part in his decision to abandon his pursuit of power through democratic means. But to gauge the tradition's 'success' or 'failure' simply in terms of a group's impact at the ballot box, the 'size' of its membership or its ideological originality misses the mark not least because our own notions of what constitutes 'success' cannot always be easily aligned with the interpretations and perspectives of those involved in the 'scene'. Their impact might also be measured in different, less tangible ways such as their ability to have influence upon wider immigration debates or their role in communal polarisation.

Of course, British fascism failed in all these areas, and more, though one should be careful to extrapolate from this that it was an 'inevitable' failure, thereby validating ideas of British exceptionalism and reinforcing the myth of Britain as a 'tolerant country'.

Despite its broader marginality, the impecunious history of British fascism has still had a wider cultural impact, however – even if only as a means of providing a convenient 'other' to assuage Britons that fascism's racist panaceas are somehow 'alien' to and far removed from their own 'liberal' stance on race and immigration, positioned as reassuringly benign in comparison. 'The cultural, media and historical fixation suggests we somehow need the fascists,' argues Tony Kushner.[9] Moreover, extreme right activism has also had a profound, though curiously understudied, impact upon the lives of immigrants, ethnic and religious minorities, the LGBTQ community and political opponents of all stripes, ranging from inflammatory rhetoric and hate crimes to physical assaults and murders. Focusing on the revolutionary goals of the extreme right, which it remains as far from achieving now as it was a century ago, instead of its immediate harms, might also be regarded as examining the phenomenon through the wrong end of the telescope.

The implosion of the BNP in the aftermath of the 2010 general election and the decreasing momentum of the EDL after 2013, has reduced the farther shores of British right-wing politics to a state of seemingly unparalleled disarray. The BNP had polled 564,321 votes (1.9 per cent) during the 2010 general election, its peak electoral performance. Seven years later, however, contesting the 2017 general election, it could only muster 4,580 votes (0.01 per cent). Whereas Griffin could once boast that the BNP was 'the only game in town', the party – having already atrophied under his leadership – is now virtually moribund. Once the most electorally successful extreme right-wing group in British history, within only a few years, it had become one of the milieu's least dynamic players, marginal even amongst the kaleidoscopic profusion of racial nationalist, fascist, national socialist and anti-Muslim *groupuscules* that currently proliferate in the political hinterland.[10]

It is tempting to view the disagreement, division and disarray as a product of political collapse, which, in a literal sense, it most certainly is. As this study has highlighted, however, the bitter divisions that currently bedevil the movement are certainly one of the more obvious continuities within the British extreme right. These tensions have existed within the heart of the milieu since it coalesced into a recognisably 'fascist' form after 1919. It was evident during the early 1930s, when Leese first began labelling Mosley as a 'kosher fascist' as a means of distinguishing his 'authentic' and 'pure' brand of racial fascism from the 'sell out' variety of his infinitely more successful rival. It resurfaced with differing degrees of intensity periodically thereafter in the rivalry and rhetoric of Jordan and Tyndall in the 1970s, and again in Griffin's stance towards the UKIP 'safety valve' in the 2000s. Such divisions are currently replicated in the increasingly bitter feud on the far right between the remnants of UKIP and the newly founded Brexit Party, established by former UKIP leader Nigel Farage. UKIP had long struggled to accommodate a variety of ideological tendencies, the tension between those who wished to keep the party's focus on its Eurosceptic politics and another vocal faction who sought to fashion the party into a vehicle for anti-immigration and anti-Muslim politics, the latter becoming increasingly apparent after the party absorbed many former BNP voters after 2009 as part of its Northern electoral strategy. Whilst the embrace of anti-immigration politicking took place under Farage, it was after his departure, following the EU Referendum result, that the 'anti-Muslim' faction came to predominate, causing UKIP to lurch even further towards the far right, thereby entrenching its political marginalisation in the process.[11]

Stripped of its personal animosities and the specificities of their ideological inflections, these arguments, and derivations thereof, highlight an ongoing tension within the extreme right movement. This is between the 'mainstreamers' who have advocated legal, non-violent electoral strategies and the 'vanguardists' who have adopted extra-parliamentary approaches, which have often entailed violence and illegality, though this is not an either or question for movements, factions within movements or indeed individual activists themselves who often utilise both strategies simultaneously or emphasise different ones at different times depending on their requirements and needs.[12] For the time being at least, historical happenstance has served to negate the viability of the electoral option.

Nor, however, as the proscription of National Action (NA) as a 'terrorist' group made plain in December 2016, have 'revolutionary' strategies championed by a minority of militants proven any more successful for advancing the 'cause' than they were when espoused by similarly inclined activists from previous generations like Jordan.[13] Whilst the threat of extreme right terrorism remains of significant concern,[14] one emerging trend, which constitutes a clear challenge for detection and interdiction, relates to the changing positionality of such actors, vis-à-vis the milieu itself. Though NA represented a networked threat, something that had not existed since Combat 18 in the 1990s, contemporary lone actor terrorists appear only 'peripherally' involved in extreme right groups. Their involvement is increasingly mediated digitally through internet forums rather than through political organisations, in contrast to earlier cases where individuals like the London nailbomber David Copeland, despite acting alone, were, to some degree, 'embedded' within a broader milieu that had direct contact with extreme right political structures.[15]

The near total collapse of extreme right political structures and the nullification of its strategies, both electoral and revolutionary, in the past decade has plunged the racial nationalist tradition into the doldrums. Although it is currently at something of an impasse, having already endured several other spells in the political wilderness in the past century, the tradition's history would indicate that it will continue to endure in some form or another. Political parties might degrade but ideas – even once they have outlived their 'epoch' – continue to exhibit something akin to a radioactive half-live. Indeed, as another scholarly interlocutor of the extreme right observes, 'that these values are retrogressive, irrational and couched in the overwhelmed and anxious fears of apocalyptic conspiracism are no barrier to their longevity.'[16] Impervious to change, even as its dire racial and racist jeremiads remain stubbornly unfulfilled, the persistence of the racial fascist tradition, recalls the subjects of Leon Festinger's classic socio-psychological work of doomsday cults, *When Prophecy Fails* (1956), who readjusted to new realities rather than admitting error in their original prediction regarding the supposed immanency of the apocalypse.[17]

The current state of organisational disarray highlights another long-term structural continuity within the milieu: that 'mass' political parties like the BNP, NF and the BUF, have been the exception rather than the rule. The decentralised, fragmented and variegated field of *groupuscular* activity that currently defines the parameters of the extreme right hinterland reflects an equally 'natural' state of affairs as the structured, organised political endeavour. Indeed, as Kathleen Blee reminds us, this 'chaos' is 'central' to understanding how extreme right-wing organisations function within that liminal space between party political organisation and subcultural firmament.

Herein lies the importance of understanding and appreciating the important roles that *groupuscules* play within the extreme right subcultural 'scene'. When their hopes of a 'new dawn' were dashed for the foreseeable future in the early 2010s, the BNP and a range of other extreme right parties and organisations spectacularly collapsed; the BNP's not insubstantial electoral support shifting to the radical right UKIP (before that party also imploded in the wake of the EU Referendum in 2016). The extreme right did not simply cease to exist, however. Despite a paucity of viable 'political' vehicles, extreme right militancy continues to find expression through the *groupuscular* activities of the wider 'social movement'.¹⁸ These may appear marginal and ephemeral, possibly unworthy of scholarly attention but more broadly it is from within this stubborn and ideologically effervescent firmament – Campbell's 'cultic milieu' – that new challengers to the liberal democratic order will undoubtedly emerge in the future, regardless of orthodox measures of political 'success'.

The quest for relevance

Whilst this book has illuminated an essential continuity of the British fascist tradition, even during periods of fierce contestation and rivalry regarding people, ideas and strategies, there are several emerging discontinuities which, whilst their full import is yet to become clear, are perhaps worth pausing to reflect upon – albeit mindful of the fact that pontificating about the 'future' is a fool's errand. Five ongoing developments seem particularly salient with regard to the British case: the spread of a pervasive anti-Muslim politics on both sides of the Atlantic, and beyond; cultural, generational and demographic change; the ubiquity of social media tools; a changing policy context; and the potentially radical change in political, social and economic context post-Brexit, though the longer-term impacts of this shift in context are unknowable at present.

Perhaps the key disjuncture with regard to past patterns of prejudicial politics, particularly since 9/11, has been the entrenchment of an ostensibly culture-based, anti-Muslim politics as the 'master frame' through which such groups perceive and articulate their politics. Whilst anti-Muslim prejudice serves as the common denominator for an array of otherwise ideologically and politically diffuse groups, functioning, as anti-Semitism used to, as an ideological glue; for racial nationalists, the 'cultural' principle, as the basis of ideological analysis, remains a thin one since their ideas are inexorably wedded to biologically-based belief systems. This is not to argue that extreme right groups have not become completely reliant upon anti-Muslim politicking as the mainstay of their public platforms. Indeed, it has been a central and well-integrated component of their political repertoire for nearly two decades now.

Within extreme right ideological cosmology, the 'cultural' and the 'biological' sit alongside one another with relatively little tension. This is hardly surprisingly since arguments about cultural incommensurability of 'Muslims' with Western 'civilisation' were pioneered within the milieu, originally in defence of South African apartheid, before developing thereafter into comparatively more sophisticated arguments for 'ethno-plurality' and 'biodiversity', even if they amounted to much the same thing. The extreme right soon lost control of its own ideological narrative, however, to a younger generation of activists, who had come of age within a pluralistic and multiracial British society. These activists and others were more genuinely motivated by concerns and fears about 'religion' and 'culture' rather than 'biology' and had less interest in campaigning to return Britain to the status quo ante prior to 1948, a premise to which the older generation of racial nationalists remained committed.

It is of course possible to exaggerate this division, not least because the boundaries between such milieu and their activities are often porous rather than solidly demarcated. Moreover, the extent of the ideational transformation within far right groups, whose lexicon has shifted from a 'national' to a 'civilisational' defence of 'Europe' – employing Christianity (to emphasise 'belonging rather than believing'), Secularism (as a means of minimising the visibility of Islam in the public sphere) and Liberalism (to juxtapose the benefits of 'our' way of life against the perceived illiberalism and intolerance of Islam) – has, to date at least, been less genuinely transformative for many British groups.[19] Indeed, despite many younger activists, including former English Defence League (EDL) leader 'Tommy Robinson' (Stephen Yaxley-Lennon), adopting a more 'Identitarian' style rhetoric and discourse in recent years, efforts to directly emulate the organisational successes of Les Identitaries in France or the Identitäre Bewegung Österreichs (IBÖ – Identitarian Movement in Austria) have thus far fallen flat, reflecting, at least in part, an asymmetry between the popularity of such ideas on the Continent and their more limited appeal for broader extreme right and far right traditions in Britain.[20]

Whilst the prejudicial politics of both racial and civic nationalist groups converge at the intersection of Islam and immigration,[21] particularly in their shared conspiratorial narratives of 'white genocide' and a 'great replacement', there is still a discernable difference between the two camps regarding 'race'. This is not to suggest that this emergent variant of 'civic' nationalism – which might be more accurately described as 'cultural' nationalism – is a priori any more inclusive than racial nationalism.[22] It is not. However, broadly stated, the ideological distinction is reflected in the arguments of former UKIP leader Nigel Farage that his opposition to immigration is a matter of 'space, not race'[23] or those made by 'Tommy Robinson' that it is not multiculturalism that has 'failed' – as racial nationalists assert – but 'religion'.[24] Indeed Griffin, who fundamentally disagrees with the civic nationalist argument, currently views himself as being engaged in a 'global battle for the soul of the nationalist movement', against 'Zionist'-backed 'populists' who would subvert its revolutionary potential by siphoning off potential electoral support into 'safety valve' groups supportive of the status quo.[25]

Thus, after a century of racist, anti-immigration campaigning, the British fascist tradition presently finds itself facing an acute challenge not just from 'cultural' nationalist challengers but also from the inexorable march of history and the changing cultural and social mores that have accompanied it. Goodwin and Ford observed that many BNP activists were older, white working-class men with lower levels of educational achievement, politically socialised against immigration in the shadow of Enoch Powell during the 1970s. The problem, as other academic studies have highlighted, is that there has been a sharp, generationally observable decline in racial prejudice amongst young people who have grown up since the advent of mass immigration in the 1950s, although greater levels of prejudice are displayed towards 'more culturally distinct' Asian than black minorities.[26] Indeed, for a variety of reasons, British attitudes towards immigration, particularly amongst those born after 1960, show a 'small but steadily significant movement towards more positive attitudes immigration amongst younger generations.'[27] Whilst society remains dominated by those born before 1970, where anti-immigration attitudes still predominant, the diminishing generational interest in the extreme right's core ideological message represents a conundrum for the future viability of the racial nationalist tradition, both in terms of the purity of its racial vision and indeed in its ramifications for what any future British 'fascism' might look like ideologically and politically.

Intuitively, the salience of anti-Muslim politics could have offered an answer to these processes of generational and cultural attrition though after two decades of campaigning on the issue in the wake of 9/11, most British fascist groups are now paradoxically at their lowest ebb since perhaps the late 1940s, largely because, one might speculate, there are enough far right and even centre right actors mobilising around similar positions to make support for racial nationalist formations unnecessary. At the time of writing, the British extreme right was virtually inert during a period of widespread anger and angst across Europe relating to the 'refugee crisis' engendered by the Syrian Civil War, wherein migrants and refugees came to be portrayed by some sections of the European body politic as the 'embodiments of the collapse of order'.[28] Public attitudes towards refugees hardened in the wake of terrorist attacks in Paris in November 2015 in which Islamic State militants murdered 130 people, opinion polls indicating a sharp decrease in the willingness of the British public to accept refugees fleeing the conflict in Syria as a result.[29]

The passivity of the British extreme right in the face of such potential political 'opportunity' was indicative of the scale of its organisational implosion. It also stood in stark contrast to the revitalising effect that the refugee/migrant crisis had upon militants in Germany who orchestrated a wave of arson attacks against asylum hostels – a fourfold increase in the level of violence from the previous year. One extreme right activist went so far as to attempt to murder a Cologne mayoral candidate, Henriette Reker, noted for her support of refugees and who later won despite being hospitalised with serious injuries.[30] Walter Lübcke, a senior Christian Democratic Union politician in Hesse, likewise noted for his liberal attitude to asylum, was not so lucky. He was murdered by a suspected extreme right activist in June 2019.[31] In Britain, it was left to UKIP – not the BNP – to exploit the concerns about immigration and refugees, thereby helping to shape the political debate in the run up to the 2015 general election in which David Cameron, the British prime minister, would promise a referendum on Britain's EU membership in a woefully miscalculated bid to outflank the right-wing threat within and without the Conservative Party.

Another emergent disjuncture that this study has only hinted at, because it was not a factor historically, has been the shift of the racial nationalist milieu away from the traditional spaces of extreme right acculturation towards the digital realm. This is unsurprising since most social media platforms are of comparatively recent vintage. Generationally speaking, it was only Griffin who was in any position to tap the power of social media, though his pioneering efforts with regards to harnessing the power of the Internet from the early 1990s onwards have been dwarfed by the activities of a younger generation of technologically sophisticated, ideological entrepreneurs (not to mention 'trolls' and grifters) to have emerged during and since the 'Alt-Right' wave that played a role in electing Donald Trump as president, which in turn has emboldened the extreme, far and radical right on both sides of the Atlantic.[32]

Social media has had a transformative effect upon almost all forms of contentious politics, reducing the costs of communication between activists, accelerating the speed with which they can disseminate and receive information, increasing and amplifying the reach of their propaganda. It has also changed the very nature of strategic interaction and competitive adaptation between activists, as well as redefining their mobilisations, often in 'real time'.[33] Online platform providers like YouTube, the popular video sharing platform, also play a key role in this new extreme right media environment, their recommender systems narrowing the range of content to which users are exposed whilst simultaneously serving up a steady diet of similar material auto-selected by their algorithms.[34] Whilst scholars continue to debate whether social media fuels or reduces polarisation even those studies which argue that the effect of 'ideological bubbles' are overblown accept that a 'small segment of the population are likely to find themselves in an echo chamber'.[35] This most likely includes many of the individuals that most concern policy makers and security personnel, however.

If the importance of social media for extreme right-wing mobilisation and radicalisation processes has long been evident, its long-term impact upon its organisations is less clear. Whilst *groupuscular* organisation has played a pivotal role in preserving and transmitting key concepts and ideas across generations, social media in its various guises and platforms has come to assume much of this role, which arguably diminishes the importance of individual ideologues as mediators and educators of ideas which instead are communicated through memes and hashtags without reference to the weighty ideological tomes that might underpin them. It is too early to say, however, what effect such developments, when combined with the declining importance of organisations, might have upon traditional forms of ideological authority within the milieu which, as the preceding chapters indicate, have done much to shape the tradition in particular ways. The anonymity of the Internet and the accelerated access it provides militants to a veritable cornucopia of 'forbidden' knowledge – some of which, particularly in the tactical sphere, is at odds with the type of material traditionally made available by extreme right *parties* to their members – highlights the sort of shifts that technology is helping to facilitate. Indeed, if social media has lowered the bar for engaging with an increasingly diverse range of extreme right propaganda, whilst simultaneously raising the risk that its consumption is fuelling behavioural 'radicalisation' this might indicate, at least in part, the decreasing salience of organisational control mechanisms, often exerted by more experienced activists within the group, for whom an increase in violence – or rather the wrong violence at the wrong time – is not necessarily beneficial or indeed desired.[36]

It is still not clear how social media has benefited the extreme right organisationally, however. When coupled to certain 'celebrity' figures like 'Tommy Robinson' or to new groups like the Football Lads Alliance and the Democratic Football Lads Alliance, which spontaneously mobilised in the aftermath of several terrorist atrocities in 2017, social media has clearly played a key role in far right mobilisation. Some of the 'Free Tommy Robinson' demonstrations in 2018 – staged after he was imprisoned, though later released, for contempt of court – were estimated to have mobilised approximately 10,000, a scale hitherto unseen since the 1970s.[37] It is worth recalling, however, that the combination of social media and far right 'charisma' do not automatically equate to movement success. Robinson's attempt to establish a British branch of the German anti-Muslim movement, Patriotische Europäer gegen die Islamisierung des Abendlandes (PEGIDA – Patriotic Europeans Against the Islamisation of the Occident) failed miserably,[38] indicating that technological innovation and charisma alone are not enough. They are, however, necessary ingredients in the more complexly 'situated credibility contests', which take place between a variety of political and social actors over time and shape the extent to which such groups do, or do not, gain traction.[39]

Despite its self-evident potential as a tool for radicalisation and mobilisation, paradoxically social media has not provided a silver bullet for the extreme right: membership is at rock bottom and its electoral progress has flat-lined. Clearly, the horizontal, decentralised, democratising effect of social media has had some impact upon the traditional, vertically orientated and anti-democratic political structures of the extreme right, though the enduring consequences remain a subject for future historians to ponder. Social media conglomerates have themselves belatedly begun to take action against extreme right and far right accounts, as are payment service providers and, occasionally online retailers too, removing them from their platforms, an action which, whilst it might lead some activists to seek out darker, harder to monitor corners of the Internet, has served largely to deny many of these groups important organising and fund-raising tools and, moreover, a vital means of communicating with their perceived publics in a digital world.[40]

One final factor likely to impact upon the future of the extreme right concerns the outcome of the United Kingdom's Referendum on European Union membership on 24 June 2016. This saw the British electorate vote to leave the EU by a narrow margin, unleashing a wave of 'nationalist' sentiment in its wake and a spike in racist and religiously aggravated offences recorded by the police in England and Wales following the result.[41] The annual total of such offences rose to 94,098 in 2017/2018, an increase of 17 per cent compared with the previous year. This continued an upward trend. The number of hate crimes recorded by police had more than doubled since 2012/2013 (from 42,255 to 94,098 offences; an increase of 123 per cent). Whilst this undoubtedly reflected improvements in recording systems, the Home Office preface to their annual report was unequivocal in their analysis that: 'there has been spikes in hate crime following certain events such as the EU Referendum and the terrorist attacks in 2017.'[42]

Ironically, despite agitating to leave Europe since 5 June 1975 when the British electorate voted to join the European Community, the British extreme right was as marginal to the broader 'Leave' campaign as it had been to the campaign to prevent Britain joining Europe forty years earlier. Indeed, during the 2016 Referendum, the extreme right was completely eclipsed by the forces of the mainstream Conservative right and UKIP who, despite playing a key role in pressurising David Cameron to promise a referendum, found themselves subsumed in the wider 'Leave' campaign which, its ultimate success aside, came at the expense of the party's sense of purpose, cohesion and indeed its wider political relevance after attaining its core goal. Whilst the extreme right was a marginal actor on the broader stage of the EU Referendum campaign, it was still capable of exerting an outsized influence. In the midst of the increasingly toxic tone of what passed for political debate during the Referendum, a white supremacist, Thomas Mair, murdered his local MP, Jo Cox, whilst screaming 'Britain first, this is for Britain'. Asked for his name in court, Mair announced that it was 'Freedom for Britain, Death to Traitors' – words which were adopted as a slogan by NA who openly glorified the killing, which was a contributing factor to its proscription six months later.[43]

The ongoing potential of the extreme right to produce similar acts of violence has become a significant concern. Whilst it is too early to tell whether it is a short-term spike or a longer-term trend, let alone whether there is a causal relationship to the failure of its electoral strategies, the proportion of extreme right activists in custody for terrorism-related offences has increased steadily since 2016. As of 31 March 2018, 29 (13 per cent) of the 228 individuals in custody for terror-related offences adhered to extreme right ideologies, the number having doubled from nine in the previous year (several being clearly connected to the proscription of NA).[44] Understandably, the security services continues to focus its resources overwhelmingly upon the jihadist and dissident Irish Republican threat but since March 2017 they have disrupted seven extreme right plots compared to twenty-two Islamist plots during broadly the same period, leading to a range of official warnings about the growing magnitude of the threat.[45] 'I don't think we've woken up to it enough,' stated Mark Rowley, the Metropolitan Police's outgoing counter-terrorist officer in August 2018.

> Now I'm not going to say that it's the same level of threat as the Islamist threat ... no pretense that it's exactly the same order of magnitude, but it's very significant and growing, and what I've seen over the last couple of years is a lack of recognition of that.[46]

Terrorist-related arrests are only part of the present landscape, however. Referrals to the Prevent counter-terrorist programme have also steadily increased since the Prevent duty was retooled in 2011 to include a greater focus on right-wing extremism.[47] Whilst these figures are certainly concerning, they do highlight another discontinuity insofar as Prevent and other such countering violent extremism initiatives are concerned, which is that such interventions are comparatively new, having been previously non-existent in the lives of young people on a political trajectory towards violent right-wing extremism. Moreover, extreme right groups, as NA discovered to its cost, are now operating within a new policy and security context, the ramifications of which are not yet fully apparent.

The increased threat posed by extreme right terrorism is reflected in changes to the intelligence apparatus that is charged with monitoring it which in turn has constrained their room for manoeuvre, at least at the more violently inclined end of the spectrum. Following the recommendations of two previous Independent Reviewers of Terrorist Legislation, the government extended the remit of the Joint Terrorism Analysis Centre (JTAC), which had previously assessed all intelligence relating to international terrorism, overseas and at home, to include monitoring the threat of domestic extremism in 2017. Growing concern was also reflected in the October 2018 announcement that MI5 would take over as the lead intelligence agency investigating the right-wing terrorist threat, though, together with the police, it was already monitoring the milieu's trajectory.[48]

Whether or not the extreme right will profit politically from the increasingly polarised politics fuelled by 'Brexit' is unclear. Whilst it is unlikely that the overheated political rhetoric emanating from certain quarters decrying the supposed 'betrayal' of Brexit will crystallise into a British version of the *Dolchstoßlegende*, the angry and ill-tempered rhetoric surrounding the ongoing farrago has not only damaged trust in democratic processes and institutions but has also fuelled a 'permissive atmosphere'[49] in which – as the case of Jo Cox fatally illustrated – MPs on both sides of the political divide are branded as 'traitors' and 'saboteurs' and targeted accordingly. The net result is that many politicians are currently experiencing 'unprecedented' levels of threat and harassment as a result of their stance vis-à-vis 'Brexit'.[50]

Again, whilst it has been emboldened by this ugly shift, it is too early to tell whether or not the extreme right organisations will be politically rejuvenated, though given the depth of its current political paralysis one might speculate with reasonable confidence that the movement will continue to play second fiddle to the more publicly palatable forms of anti-Muslim politicking that presently predominate the wider far right 'scene'. UKIP's poor performance post-Referendum, first in the 2017 general election (its worst result since 2001), and most recently in the 2019 local elections, highlights, however, that the radicalisation of anti-Muslim platforms does not automatically translate into votes.[51] That said, the fracturing of mainstream British party politics and the anger that 'Brexit' is currently generating, might lead one to speculate that the weakening hold of social democratic parties, not just in Britain but in Europe more generally, might well provide future opportunities for the extreme right, either directly or indirectly, for instance, mobilising reactionary fears about the political 'left' as a potential beneficiary of Britain's decision to leave the EU.

British fascism took nearly three decades to recover from the collapse of the National Front in 1979. The implosion of the BNP is no less, and perhaps even more, profound. There is little doubt, however, that the tradition will endure, sustained by and nurtured through *groupuscular* organisations and its broader social movement, including its digital spaces. However, with its 'quest for legitimacy' at an end, demographic change, generational shifts in attitudes towards race, immigration and integration, and the popularity of emergent forms of anti-Muslim politics that do not share British fascism's stigmatised historical baggage, all combine to pose the extreme right with a new challenge – the quest for relevance.

Notes

1 Stanley Payne, *A History of Fascism, 1914–1945* (London: UCL Press, 1996), pp. 303–305.
2 W.D. Rubinstein, *A History of the Jews in the English Speaking World: Great Britain* (London: Macmillan, 1996), p. 314.
3 Richard Thurlow, *Fascism in Britain* (London: I.B. Tauris, 1998), p. x.
4 Julie V. Gottlieb, *Feminine Fascism: Women in Britain's Fascist Movement, 1923–1945* (London: I.B. Tauris, 2000), p. 2.
5 Vernon Bogdanor, 'Review of *The Failure of British Fascism: The Far Right and the Fight for Political Recognition* by Mike Cronin', *History*, vol. 83, no. 270, April 1998, p. 380.
6 These include Thomas Linehan, *British Fascism, 1918–1939: Parties, Ideology and Culture* (Manchester: Manchester University Press, 2000), which gives a cultural reading of the inter-war period, and Julie V. Gottlieb and Thomas P. Linehan, *The Culture of Fascism: Visions of the Far Right in Britain* (London: I.B. Tauris, 2004); Nigel Copsey and John E. Richardson (eds), *Cultures of Post-War British Fascism* (Abingdon: Routledge, 2015). For a broader study exploring the shifting representation of Nazism in contemporary culture, see Gavriel D. Rosenfeld, *Hi Hitler! How the Nazi Past is being Normalised in Contemporary Culture* (Cambridge: Cambridge University Press, 2015).
7 Roger Eatwell, 'Ideology, Propaganda, Violence and the Rise of Fascism', in António Costa Pinto (ed.), *Rethinking the Nature of Fascism: Comparative Perspectives* (London: Palgrave, 2011), pp. 165–185. For a nuanced discussion of the application of cultural analysis to British fascism, see John E. Richardson, 'British Fascism, Fascist Culture, British Culture', *Patterns of Prejudice*, vol. 53, no. 3, 2019, pp. 236–252.
8 Enoch Powell, *Joseph Chamberlain* (London: Thames and Hudson, 1977), p. 151.
9 Tony Kushner, 'The Fascist as "Other"? Racism and Neo-Nazism in Contemporary Britain', *Patterns of Prejudice*, vol. 28, no. 1, 1994, pp. 27–45.
10 For a snapshot of the current state of fragmentation, see Nick Lowles (ed.), *State of Hate 2019: People vs. the Elite?* (London: Hope Not Hate, 2019).
11 Jeanne Hanna and Joel Busher, 'UKIP and the UK's Radical Right: A Tale of Movement Party Success?', in Manuela Caiani and Ondřej Císař (eds), *Radical Right Movement Parties in Europe* (Abingdon: Routledge, 2019), pp. 46–62.
12 Betty A. Dobratz and Lisa K. Waldner, 'Repertoires of Contention: White Separatist Views on the Use of Violence and Leaderless Resistance', *Mobilization*, vol. 17, no. 1, 2012, pp. 49–66.
13 Graham Macklin, '"Only Bullets will Stop Us!" – The Banning of National Action in Britain', *Perspectives on Terrorism*, vol. 12, no. 6, December 2018, pp. 104–122. See also Matthew Collins and Robbie Mullen, *Nazi Terrorist: The Story of National Action* (London: Hope Not Hate, 2019).
14 For an overview, see Graham Macklin, 'The Evolution of Extreme Right Terrorism and Efforts to Counter It in the United Kingdom', *CTC Sentinel: Combating Terrorism Center at West Point*, vol. 12, no. 1, January 2019, pp. 15–20.
15 Lasse Lindekilde, Stefan Malthaner and Francis O'Connor, 'Peripheral and Embedded: Relational Patterns of Lone-Actor Terrorist Radicalization', *Dynamics of Asymmetric Conflict*, vol. 12, no. 1, 2019, pp. 20–41.
16 Andrew Fergus Wilson, 'The Bitter End: Apocalypse and Conspiracy in White Nationalist Responses to the Islamic State Attacks in Paris', *Patterns of Prejudice*, vol. 51, no. 5, 2017, p. 430.
17 Leon Festinger, Henry W. Riecken and Stanley Schachter, *When Prophecy Fails* (London: Pinter and Martin, 2008).
18 Fabian Virchow, 'Post-Fascist Right-Wing Social Movements', in Stefan Berger and Holger Nehring (eds), *The History of Social Movements in Global Perspective: A Survey* (London: Palgrave, 2017), pp. 619–646; and Pietro Castelli Gattinara and Andrea L.P. Pirro, 'The Far Right as Social Movement', *European Societies*, vol. 21, no. 4, 2019, pp. 447–462. The idea of the 'movement-party' – which contest elections whilst also mobilising around 'contentious issues' is analogous though seemingly utilised to understand groups at a slightly higher level of organisational development than those *groupuscules* under discussion here – many of which do not take part in elections. For more on this concept, see Manuela Caiani and Ondřej Císař (eds), *Radical Right Movement Parties in Europe* (Abingdon: Routledge, 2019).
19 Rogers Brubaker, 'Between Nationalism and Civilisationism: The European Populist Moment in Comparative Perspective', *Ethnic and Racial Studies*, vol. 40, no. 8, 2017, pp. 1191–1226.

20 For an introduction, see José Pedro Zúquete, *The Identitarians: The Movement against Globalism and Islam in Europe* (Notre Dame, IN: University of Notre Dame Press, 2018).
21 José Pedro Zúquete, 'The European Extreme-Right and Islam: New Directions?' *Journal of Political Ideologies*, vol. 13, no. 3, 2008, pp. 321–344.
22 Kristina Bakkær Simonsen and Bart Bonikowski, 'Is Civic Nationalism Necessarily Inclusive? Conceptions of Nationhood and Anti-Muslim Attitudes in Europe', *European Journal of Political Research*, vol. 59, no. 1, February 2020, pp. 114–136. If civic nationalism also encompasses groups like the Scottish Nationalist Party or the centre-left elements of the Catalan independence movement for example, then 'civic nationalism' becomes a very broad category which is not entirely consonant with the more exclusionary interpretation placed upon it here.
23 Nigel Farage, 'I've had Enough of People Insinuating that UKIP is Racist: It's Simply not True', *The Independent*, 16 April 2015, www.independent.co.uk/voices/comment/i-ve-had-enough-of-people-insinuating-that-ukip-is-racist-its-simply-not-true-10182747.html (accessed 1 May 2019).
24 'Proud and Prejudiced', Channel 4 documentary, www.channel4.com/programmes/proud-and-prejudiced (accessed 29 February 2012).
25 Nick Griffin, *English Defence League? Neo-Cons, Ultra-Zionists and The Useful Idiots* (2012).
26 Robert Ford, 'Is Racial Prejudice Declining in Britain?', *The British Journal of Sociology*, vol. 59, no. 4, 2008, pp. 609–636.
27 Lauren McLaren, Anja Neundorf and Ian Paterson, 'Anti-Immigration Attitudes are Disappearing Among Younger Generations in Britain', *The Conversation*, 5 July 2019, https://theconversation.com/anti-immigration-attitudes-are-disappearing-among-younger-generations-in-britain-119856 (accessed 5 July 2019).
28 Zygmunt Bauman, 'The Migration Panic and Its (Mis)uses', *Social Europe*, 17 December 2015, www.socialeurope.eu/2015/12/migration-panic-misuses/ (accessed 20 February 2019).
29 Will Dahlgreen, 'Brits less Accepting of Syrian Refugees in the Wake of Paris Attacks', *YouGov*, 18 November 2015, https://yougov.co.uk/news/2015/11/18/brits-less-accepting-syrian-refugees-wake-paris-at/ (accessed 20 February 2019).
30 "Anti-Refugee Attacks Rise Four-Fold in Germany, *DW*, 9 December 2015, www.dw.com/en/anti-refugee-attacks-rise-four-fold-in-germany/a-18907776 (accessed 20 February 2019).
31 Jenny Hill, 'German Politician's Murder Raises Spectre of Far-Right Attacks', BBC News, 23 June 2019, www.bbc.com/news/world-europe-48716944 (accessed 19 June 2019).
32 Useful introductions to the expanding literature on the digital dimension to 'Alt right' include: George Hawley, *Making Sense of the Alt-Right* (New York: Columbia University Press, 2017); George Hawley, *The Alt-Right: What Everyone Needs to Know* (Oxford: Oxford University Press, 2019), pp. 106–126; Angela Nagle, *Kill All Normies: Online Culture Wars from 4chan and Tumblr to Trump and the Alt-Right* (London: Zero Books, 2017); David Newert, *Alt America: The Rise of the Radical Right in the Age of Trump* (London: Verso, 2017); and Mike Wendling, *Alt-Right: From 4chan to the White House* (London: Pluto Press, 2018).
33 Thomas Zeithoff, 'How Social Media is Changing Conflict', *Journal of Conflict Resolution*, vol. 61, no. 9, 2017, pp. 1970–1991.
34 Derek O'Callaghan, Derek Greene, Maura Conway, Joe Carthy and Pádraig Cunningham, 'Down the (White) Rabbit Hole: The Extreme Right and Online Recommender Systems', *Social Science Computer Review*, vol. 33, no. 4, 2015, pp. 259–478.
35 Elizabeth Dubois and Grant Blank, 'The Echo Chamber is Overstated: The Moderating Effect of Political Interest and Diverse Media', *Information, Communication & Society*, vol. 21, no. 5, 2018, pp. 729–745.
36 Jacob N. Shapiro, *The Terrorist's Dilemma: Managing Violent Covert Organizations* (Princeton, NJ: Princeton University Press, 2013). For more on why 'extreme' political groups often do not carry out as much violence as they are clearly capable of, see Joel Busher, Donald Holbrook and Graham Macklin, 'The Internal Brakes on Violent Escalation: A Typology', *Behavioural Sciences of Terrorism and Political Aggression*, vol. 11, no. 1, 2019, pp. 3–25.
37 'At Free Tommy Robinson Demonstration', *Hope Not Hate*, 9 June 2018, www.hopenothate.org.uk/2018/06/09/big-numbers-violence-free-tommy-robinson-demonstration/ (accessed 1 May 2019).
38 Jamie Bartlett, *Radicals: Outsiders Changing the World* (London: Windmill, 2017), pp. 51–96.
39 Joel Busher, Gareth Harris and Graham Macklin, 'Chicken Suits And Other Aspects of Situated Credibility Contests: Explaining Local Trajectories of Anti-Minority Activism', *Social Movement Studies*, vol. 18, no. 2, 2019, pp. 193–214.

40 Zak Doffman, 'Facebook Responds to U.K. Regulation and Banns Far Right Groups EDL, BNP and Britain First', *Forbes*, 18 April 2019, www.forbes.com/sites/zakdoffman/2019/04/18/facebook-permanently-bans-u-k-far-right-including-bnp-edl-nick-griffin-and-paul-golding/; and Oliver Darcy, 'Louis Farrakhan, Alex Jones and Other "Dangerous" Voices Banned by Facebook and Instagram', CNN Business, 3 May 2019, https://edition.cnn.com/2019/05/02/tech/facebook-ban-louis-farrakhan-infowars-alex-jones-milo-laura-loomer/index.html (accessed 2 May 2019).

41 Matthew Weaver, 'Hate Crime Surge Linked to Brexit and 2017 Terrorist Attacks', the *Guardian*, 16 October 2018, www.theguardian.com/society/2018/oct/16/hate-crime-brexit-terrorist-attacks-england-wales (accessed 1 May 2019).

42 Home Office, *Hate Crime, England and Wales, 2017/2018 – Statistical Bulletin 20/18*, 16 October 2018, https://assets.publishing.service.gov.uk/government/uploads/system/uploads/attachment_data/file/748598/hate-crime-1718-hosb2018.pdf.

43 Brendan Cox, *Jo Cox: More in Common* (London: Two Roads, 2017).

44 Home Office, *Operation of Police Powers under the Terrorism Act 200 and Subsequent Legislation: Arrests, Outcomes, and Stop and Search, Great Britain, Financial Year Ending March 2018* (14 June 2018), p. 13, https://assets.publishing.service.gov.uk/government/uploads/system/uploads/attachment_data/file/716000/police-powers-terrorism-mar2018-hosb0918.pdf (accessed 1 May 2019).

45 'Neil Basu Leads Prevent Conversation at ICT Summit', *Counter Terrorism Policing*, 9 September 2019, www.counterterrorism.police.uk/neil-basu-leads-prevent-conversation-at-ict-summit/ (accessed 9 September 2019).

46 Mattha Busby, 'UK has not "Woken Up" to the Far-Right Threat, Says Ex-Counter-Terror Chief', the *Guardian*, 18 August 2018, www.theguardian.com/uk-news/2018/aug/18/former-counter-terrorism-chief-says-uk-has-not-woken-up-to-far-right-threat (accessed 1 May 2019).

47 Craig J.J. McCann, *The Prevent Strategy and Right-Wing Extremism: A Case Study of the English Defence League* (Abingdon: Routledge, 2019) for an overview. Statistics for the year to March 2018, the latest for which there are figures, record 7,318 Prevent referrals. 1,321 (18 per cent) of these related to right-wing extremism, a 36 per cent increase compared to the 2016/2017 period during which Islamist referrals decreased 14 per cent. The number of panel discussions regarding right-wing extremism taking place under the Channel programme, the part of Prevent focused upon providing support at an 'early stage' to those at risk of being drawn into terrorism also increased 58 per cent from 271 individuals in 2015/2016 to 472 in 2016/2017. 174 (44 per cent) of these individuals subsequently received specialist support from Channel, representing a 40 per cent increase on the previous year's figures. For the first time, a similar number of individuals have received Channel support for concerns relating to Islamist and right-wing extremism, see Home Office, *Individuals referred to and supported through the Prevent Programme, April 2017 to March 2018*, pp. 13–16, https://assets.publishing.service.gov.uk/government/uploads/system/uploads/attachment_data/file/763254/individuals-referred-supported-prevent-programme-apr2017-mar2018-hosb3118.pdf (accessed 1 May 2019).

48 Vikram Dodd, 'MI5 to Take Over in Fight Against Rise of UK Rightwing Extremism', the *Guardian*, 28 October 2018, www.theguardian.com/uk-news/2018/oct/28/mi5-lead-battle-against-uk-rightwing-extremists-police-action (accessed 1 May 2019).

49 Vikram Dodd, 'Far Right may Exploit Brexit Tensions, Says UK Counter-Terrorism Chief', the *Guardian*, 23 January 2019, www.theguardian.com/uk-news/2019/jan/23/no-deal-brexit-incredibly-damaging-security-says-uk-counter-terror-head-neil-basu (accessed 1 May 2019).

50 'Threats to MPs at "Unprecedented" Levels, Says Met Chief', BBC News, 8 May 2019, www.bbc.com/news/uk-politics-48205408 (accessed 8 May 2019).

51 'England Local Elections 2019', BBC News, www.bbc.com/news/topics/ceeqy0e9894t/england-local-elections-2019 (accessed 1 May 2019).

Select bibliography

The following section provides an overview of the archival collections consulted during the research for this study followed by a very short, select bibliography listing only some of the most important secondary works consulted.

The study drew upon a plethora of other sources too. Details of these are located in the footnotes.

Primary sources

Wayne Ashcroft papers, Modern Records Centre, Warwick University.
The Austin J. App Collection, American Heritage Centre, University of Wyoming, United States.
Adrien Arcand Collection, Library and Archives Canada, Ottawa, Canada.
George W. Armstrong papers, AUT Arlington Special Collections, Arlington, Texas, United States.
Henry Hamilton Beamish papers – private collection.
Lord Beaverbrook papers, House of Lords Record Office, London.
R.D. Blumenfeld papers, House of Lords Record Office, London.
Board of Deputies of British Jews papers, London Metropolitan Archives, London.
Britons archive – private collection.
A.K. Chesterton papers – private collection.
A.K. Chesterton papers, University of Bath Library, University of Bath.
Conservative Central Office papers, The Bodleian Library, Oxford.
Ernest Sevier Cox papers, David M. Rubenstein Rare Book & Manuscript Library, Duke University, United States.
Richard Crossman papers, Modern Records Centre, Warwick University.
Avendis Derounian papers, Mardigian Library, National Association for Armenian Studies and Research, Belmont, Massachusetts, United States.
Admiral Sir Barry Domvile papers, Greenwich Maritime Museum, London.
Per Engdahl papers, National Archives, Stockholm, Sweden.
Jeffrey Hamm papers, Cadbury Research Library, Special Collections, University of Birmingham, Birmingham.
Patrick Harrington papers, Modern Records Centre, Warwick University.
Hyman papers, William Cullen Library, University of Witwatersrand, Johannesburg, South Africa.
Jewish Chronicle Library Collection, Wiener Library, London.
Jewish Defence Committee papers, Wiener Library, London.
Arnold Leese papers – private collection.
Arthur Nelson Field papers, Alexander Turnbull Library, Wellington, New Zealand.
National Council for Civil Liberties papers, Hull University History Centre, Hull University Archives, Hull University.
Oswald Mosley papers, Cadbury Research Library, Special Collections, University of Birmingham.

Reverend James Parkes papers, Special Collections, University of Southampton.
Ezra Pound papers, Beinecke Library, Yale University, United States.
George Lincoln Rockwell papers, James M. Mason Collection, Kenneth Spencer Research Library, University of Kansas, Lawrence, Kansas, United States.
Robert Saunders papers, The University Library, Special Collections, The University of Sheffield.
Searchlight archive, University of Northampton Archive, University of Northampton.
G.L.K. Smith papers, Bentley Historical Library, University of Michigan, United States.
Keith Stimely papers, Special Collections and University Archives, Knight Library, University of Oregon, Oregon, United States.
Eric Stoneman collection, British Library Sound Archive, The British Library, London.
Myra Story papers, Imperial War Museum, London.
Adolf von Thadden papers, Niedersächsisches Landesarchiv, Hannover, Germany.
Margaret Thatcher papers, Churchill Archive Centre, Churchill College, Cambridge.
The National Archives, Kew, London.
H. Keith Thompson papers, Hoover Institution Archives, Stanford University, California, United States.
Trades Union Congress papers, Modern Records Centre, Warwick University.
Pedro del Valle papers, Special Collections and University Archives, Knight Library, University of Oregon, Oregon, United States.
Lord Robert Vansittart papers, Churchill Archive Centre, Churchill College, Cambridge.
Laurence Augustine Waddell papers, Special Collections, Glasgow University.
Patrick Wall papers, Hull University History Centre, Hull University Archives, Hull University.

Secondary literature – Books

Baker, David, *Ideology of Obsession: A.K. Chesterton and British Fascism*. London: I.B. Tauris, 2018.
Bar-On, Tamir, *Where have all the Fascists Gone?* Aldershot: Ashgate, 2007.
Beckett, Francis, *Fascist in the Family: The Tragedy of John Beckett MP*. Abingdon: Routledge, 2017.
Benewick, Robert, *The Fascist Movement in Britain*. London: Allen Lane, 1972.
Busher, Joel, *The Making of Anti-Muslim Protest: Grassroots Activism in the English Defence League*. Abingdon: Routledge, 2016.
Copsey, Nigel, *Contemporary British Fascism: The British National Party and the Quest for Legitimacy*. London: Palgrave, 2008.
Copsey, Nigel and Macklin, Graham (eds), *British National Party: Contemporary Perspectives*. Abingdon: Routledge, 2011.
Copsey, Nigel and Richardson, John E. (eds), *Cultures of Post-War British Fascism*. Abingdon: Routledge, 2015.
Copsey, Nigel and Worley, Matthew (eds), *Tomorrow Belongs to Us: The British Far Right since 1967*. Abingdon: Routledge, 2018.
Coogan, Kevin, *Dreamer of the Day: Francis Parker Yockey and the Postwar Fascist International*. New York: Autonomedia, 1999.
Cronin, Mike (ed.), *The Failure of British Fascism: The Far Right and the Fight for Political Recognition*. London: Macmillan, 1996.
Cross, Colin, *The Fascists in Britain*. London: Barrie and Rockliff, 1961.
Dietz, Bernhard, *Neo-Tories: The Revolt of British Conservatives against Democracy and Political Modernity, 1929–1939*. London: Bloomsbury, 2018.
Dorril, Stephen, *Blackshirt: Sir Oswald Mosley and British Fascism*. London: Viking, 2006.
Fielding, Nigel, *The National Front*. London: Routledge & Kegan Paul, 1981.
Ford, Robert and Goodwin, Matthew, *Revolt on the Right: Explaining Support for the Radical Right in Britain*. Abingdon: Routledge, 2014.

Goodrick-Clarke, Nicholas, *Hitler's Priestess: Savitri Devi, the Hindu-Aryan Myth and Neo-Nazism*. New York: New York University Press, 1998.
Goodrick-Clarke, Nicholas, *Black Sun: Aryan Cults, Esoteric Nazism and the Politics of Identity*. New York: New York University Press, 2002.
Goodwin, Matthew, *New British Fascism: Rise of the British National Party*. Abingdon: Routledge, 2011.
Gottlieb, Julie V. and Linehan, Thomas P., *The Culture of Fascism: Visions of the Far Right in Britain*. London: I.B. Tauris, 2004.
Griffin, Roger, *The Nature of Fascism*. Abingdon: Routledge, 1991.
Griffiths, Richard, *Fellow Travelers of the Right: British Enthusiasts for Nazi Germany, 1933–39*. Oxford: Oxford University Press, 1983.
Griffiths, Richard, *Patriotism Perverted: Captain Ramsay, the Right Club and British Anti-Semitism, 1939–40*. London: Constable, 1998.
Griffiths, Richard, *What Did You Do During the War? The Last Throes of the British pro-Nazi Right, 1940–45*. Abingdon: Routledge, 2017.
Holmes, Colin, *Searching for Lord Haw-Haw: The Political Lives of William Joyce*. Abingdon: Routledge, 2016.
Husbands, Christopher T., *Racial Exclusionism and the City: The Urban Support of the National Front*. London: George Allen & Unwin, 1983.
Jackson, Paul, *Colin Jordan and Britain's Neo-Nazi Movement: Hitler's Echo*. London: Bloomsbury, 2017.
Kaplan, Jeffrey and Lööw, Heléne (eds), *The Cultic Milieu: Oppositional Subcultures in an Age of Globalisation*. Walnut Creek, CA: AltaMira Press, 2002.
Linehan, Thomas, *East London for Mosley: The British Union of Fascists in East London and South-West Essex 1933–40*. London: Frank Cass, 1996.
Linehan, Thomas, *British Fascism, 1918–1939: Parties, Ideology and Culture* Manchester: Manchester University Press, 2000.
Loughlin, James, *Fascism and Constitutional Conflict: The British Extreme-Right and Ulster in the Twentieth Century*. Liverpool: Liverpool University Press, 2019.
Lowles, Nick, *White Riot: The Violent Story of Combat 18*. Bury: Milo, 2014.
Lunn, Kenneth and Thurlow, Richard (eds), *British Fascism: Essays on the Radical Right in Inter-War Britain*. London: Croon Helm, 1980.
McLagan, Graeme and Lowles, Nick, *Mr Evil: The Secret Life of Racist Bomber and Killer David Copeland*. London: Blake Publishing, 2000.
Macklin, Graham, *Very Deeply Dyed in Black: Sir Oswald Mosley and the Resurrection of British Fascism after 1945*. London: I.B. Tauris, 2007.
Paxton, Robert O., *The Anatomy of Fascism*. London: Penguin, 2005.
Pilkington, Hilary, *Loud and Proud: Passion and Politics in the English Defence League*. Manchester: Manchester University Press, 2016.
Pitchford, Mark, *The Conservative Party and the Extreme Right, 1945–1975*. Manchester: Manchester University Press, 2011.
Pugh, Martin, *Hurrah for the Blackshirts! Fascists and Fascism in Britain Between the Wars*. London: Cape, 2005.
Roberts, David D., *Fascist Interactions: Proposals for a New Approach to Fascism and its Era*. New York: Berghahn, 2016.
Shaffer, Ryan, *Music, Youth and International Links in Post-War British Fascism*. London: Palgrave, 2017.
Simonelli, Frederick J., *American Fuerher: George Lincoln Rockwell and the American Nazi Party*. Chicago, IL: University of Illinois Press, 1999.
Simpson, A.W. Brian, *In the Highest Degree Odious: Detention without Trial in Wartime Britain*. Oxford: Oxford University Press, 1994.
Skidelsky, Robert, *Oswald Mosley*. London: Macmillan, 1975.

Tauber, Kurt P., *Beyond Eagle and Swastika: German Nationalism since 1945, Vol. 1.* Middletown, CT: Wesleyan University Press, 1967.

Taylor, Stan, *The National Front in English Politics.* London: Macmillan, 1989.

Thurlow, Richard, *Fascism in Britain: From Oswald Mosley's Blackshirts to the National Front.* London: I.B. Tauris, 1998.

Tilles, Daniel, *British Fascist Anti-Semitism and Jewish Responses, 1932–40.* London: Bloomsbury, 2015.

Walker, Martin, *The National Front.* London: Fontana/Collins, 1977.

Willetts, Paul, *Rendezvous at the Russian Tea Rooms: The Spyhunter, the Fashion Designer & the Man From Moscow* London: Constable, 2016.

Index

62 Group 286, 291, 292, 416n236; activism and kidnapping 335n425, 359; and Jordan 332n364, 332n372; National Socialist Movement 333n389, 333n391
7/7 terror attacks, London 495
9/11 terror attacks 13, 20n78, 550, 551

Aaronsfeld, C.C 145
Åberg, Einar 60, 261
Abu Hamza al-Masri 491
Action 98, 102, 116, 117, 128, 132, 135, 140, 141–2, 191, 258
The Action Party 145, 174n335
Adair, Johnny 521n246
Adenauer, Konrad 171, 389
Africa 134, 144
African National Congress (ANC) 133, 216, 217, 269
Afrikaner Resistance Movement 498
Aims of Industry 194
Akkebala, Osiris 467–8, 484, 527n379
al-Assad, Bashir *see* Assad
Albert Hall 5, 99, 244n224
'Aldag, Peter' *see* Krüger, Dr Fritz
Aldermaston 211
Algeria 136, 140, 214, 215
Allen, Marilyn R. 62, 88n464
Allen, W.E.D. 'Bill' 95, 97, 100, 101
Alliance for Peace and Freedom 508
Alliance Racist Européene *see* Bund Völkischer Europäer/Alliance Racist Européene (BVE/ARE)
Almirante, Giorgio 141, 152, 170n368
al-Qaeda 489, 490
Altrincham, Lord 210
alt-Right 540n732, 552
Amaudruz, Gaston-Armand 'Guy' 108, 287, 437n509
America *see* USA
American Nationalist 82n341
American Nazi Party 88n472, 244n218, 301
American Review and Bookstore 83n362
Amery, John and Leopold 198

Amin, Idi 367
anarchists 445
Anderson, Ian 456, 463, 526n335
Anderson, Dr Ian 214
ANC *see* African National Congress
Anglo-German Academic Bureau 36
Anglo-German Domestic Agency 187
Anglo-German Fellowship 242n184
Anglo-Irish Agreement 459–61
Anschluss 101
Anti-Apartheid Movement (AAM) 135, 216, 217, 221; boycott of South African goods 217
Anti-Fascist Action 465
anti-fascist activism 33, 43, 48, 112, 132, 142–3, 182, 224, 274, 280, 292, 298–9, 337n452, 359, 373, 380–1, 396, 399, 418n273, 440, 465, 488, 493, 504; Battle of Cable Street 99; informers 65, 291
anti-Muslim politicking 13, 428n532, 490, 550, 555
Anti-Nazi League (ANL) 439, 441, 455, 490
anti-Semitism 12, 550; anti-Semitic attacks and vandalism 47, 270–1, 274, 292, 297, 302
anti-terrorism *see* Prevent
Antonio, José 9
Anwar, Aamer 274
apartheid 134, 149, 216, 441, 550
App, Austin J. 166n280
Apristas 465
Arab League 60, 281
Arcand, Adrien 42, 60, 65–6, 68, 87n439, 89n478, 90n498, 249n341, 261, 316n50
Argentina 58, 110, 327n276
Arkell-Smith, Valerie ('Colonel Victor Barker') 25
Armstrong, George W. 61
Aryan Strike Force 315
Aryanism 11, 12, 28, 35, 38, 39–42, 127, 207, 276, 278, 283, 296, 310, 342n566, 387
Asafu-Adjaye, Sir Edward 133
Ashcroft, Wayne 482, 534n541
Assad, Bashir al- 509–10

Atkinson, Mark 314, 489
Attlee, Clement 260, 499–500
Auschwitz 196, 475–6
Australia 42, 54, 77n223, 83n355, 169n336
Austria 39, 101, 141, 170n377, 187, 273, 466, 551
'Axis model' 94
Axmann, Artur 109
Ayatollah Khomeini 392, 469, 528n385
Ayres, Barry 138

Ba'ath Party 472, 473, 509
Bailey, Fred 113
Baines, Derek Talbot 226
Baker, A.E. 'Blackie' 45
Ball, Sir Joseph 192
Ballard, Margaret 451, 531n468
Ballard, Paul 476, 481, 483, 485, 531n468
Bardèche, Maurice 84n392, 108, 112, 195
Barker, Paul 121
Barnbrook, Richard 494, 501, 503–5
Barnes, Major James S. 29
Barnett, Corelli 424n424
Baron, A.F.X. 55, 86n421, 322n189
Barrett, Benjamin 34, 49
Barrett, Hamilton 174n445
Baruch, Bernard 221
Bavaria 84, 136, 273
BBC 58, 81n385, 144, 159n77, 191, 201, 210, 222, 238n96; and Griffin 482, 494, 498, 502, 506, 510; and Mosley 147–8, 149; *Panorama* 269; *Question Time* 502; and Tyndall 346, 405
BBC *History* magazine 153
BDL *see* British Defence League
Beackon, Derek 395, 396–7, 398, 478
Beamish, Henry Hamilton 28, 34–5, 41, 317n62; anti-Semitism 27, 28, 35, 46, 74n154
Beamish, Rear Admiral Tufton 28
Bean, John 39, 113, 154, 202, 204, 210, 230, 349, 362, 374; arrests and imprisonment 285–6, 350, 351; British Nationalist Party 224, 233, 271, 274–5; and Chesterton 349–50; and Iraq war 493; and Jordan 264, 268–9, 276, 277; National Labour Party 144, 271, 153; racial nationalism 226, 353; and Tyndall 349, 361, 262, 492
The Beatles 354
Beauclaire, Robin 419n304, 431n606
Beaumont, William Comyns 90n501
Beaverbrook, Lord 244n224; and Chesterton 198, 200, 242n192
Beckett, John 55, 59, 100, 184, 185, 186, 188–9, 195, 200–1, 260
Bedford, Duke of 55, 200, 259, 260, 261
Begin, Menachem 274, 452
Belfast 97, 417n249, 460, 461, 489, 523n299

Belgium 109; Belgian Congo 133, 140, 214; Belgian transnational fascist networks 138, 140, 141–2, 287, 301, 323n204, 326n243, 466, 510, 523n299, 544n809, 545n828; Walloons 140, 330n324
Bell, David 368
Bell, Mark and Peter 120
Belloc, Hilaire 181, 183, 191, 442, 445
Belsen 56, 135, 351
Bene, Otto 32
Benn, Tony 132, 154
Bennett, Frank 323n194
Benson, Ivor 117, 214–15, 218, 409n30
Berence Press 294
Berg, Alan 310, 478
Berger, Elizabeth 51, 55, 84n371, 85n406
Berger, J.M. 19n53
'Berne trials' 35, 62
Bernhardt, Johannes 161n140
Bethnal Green 44, 48, 100, 113, 115, 142, 173n420, 350, 359, 395, 489
BF *see* British Fascists
Bidney, Harry 293
Biggs, Ben 231
Biggs-Davidson, John 370
Bilderberg Group 220, 227, 233, 251n401
Billig, Michael 440
Billing, Noel Pemberton 28
bin Laden, Osama 490
Binet, René 108
Bingham, Colonel Ralph 69n20
Bird, William 34, 51, 81n321
Birley, Sir Robert 218
Birmingham Nationalist Club (BNC) 261, 262, 263, 265
Black and White News 267, 269
Black Flag 445
Black Separatism 270, 467, 471, 484
Blackham, Terry 430n573
Blackpool 210–11, 455, 505–6
Blackshirt 98, 182, 183, 186, 187, 191
Blackshirt (USA) 80n309
Blair, Tony 493, 495
Blakeney, Brigadier-General R.B.D. 24, 29, 35, 72n101
Blatchford, Robert 442, 446, 517n109
Bleach, Kevan 255n538
Blee, Kathleen 15, 549
Blood and Honour (B&H) 312, 395, 398, 400, 402, 429n569, 466, 476, 482, 500, 540n725
'blood and soil' 5, 12, 189, 258, 446, 476, 483
BM *see* British Movement
BNF *see* British National Fascists
BNP *see* British National Party
BNSM *see* British National Socialist Movement
BNSP *see* British National Socialist Party

BNY *see* British National Youth
Board of Deputies of British Jews (BDBJ) 163n188, 270
Bocquet, Roland 35
Bogdanor, Vernon 151, 547
Bologna bombing 446, 447, 518n146
Bolshevism 110, 181
Boldt, Dr H.J. 52
Boothby, Sir Robert J.G. 'Bob' 107, 286
Borghese, Junio Valerio 'The Black Prince' 109, 138
Bormann, Martin 109, 245n242
Borth, Friedrich 'Fred' 172n401, 282, 364
Bothamley, Margaret 35, 58, 71n86, 85n406
Boulding, Alan 243n208
Bow Street Magistrates Court 43, 280, 284, 299
Bowie, Alexander and Margaret 185
Box, F.M. 96, 184
BPP *see* British People's Party
Brady, Steve 376, 384, 423n388, 447, 451
Brassilach, Robert 195
Bretton Woods agreement 194, 238n96
Brexit 550, 552, 554–5; post-Brexit rise in hate crimes 553–4
Brexit Party 548
Brick Lane 396, 440–1, 464
Brighton 173n429, 266, 295, 320n147
Briscoe, Nora 85n406

Britain First 105, 154, 180, 359, 362, 554
Britain First 374–9, 419n293, 450
British Caribbean Association 270
British Council against European Commitments (BCAEC) 50, 188
British Defence League (BDL) 299, 365
The British Edda 38
British Empire 38, 51
British Empire Party 67
British Fascism 32
British fascism 4–8, 10, 12–14, 16, 546–8, 555; British style of Nazism 305, 311; 'folkish' (*völkisch*) ideas 12, 28, 35–9, 41, 127, 189, 206, 294, 362, 442; 'Hollywood Nazis' 304, 315, 403, 492; pro-Nazi groups 31–3, 49, 51, 53, 145, 151, 188, 189, 195, 199, 225, 265, 270, 275, 352, 364; neo-Nazis 110, 231, 257, 376, 404, 438, 456, 477, 500; racial nationalism 12, 14, 127
British Fascisti 25, 58
British Fascists (BF) 24, 29, 94
British Free Corps 294, 424n421
British Guardian 28
British Hammerskins 398, 477, 484
British Housewives League 195, 205, 244n230
British League of Ex-Servicemen 55, 259
British Movement (BM) 297, 311; anti-immigration 299; court appearances 302; Nazi ideology 298, 301; violence 302, 303, 438, 484
British National Fascists (BNF) 24, 25, 26
British National Party (BNP) [1940s] 258–9
British National Party (BNP) [founder John Bean 1960–1966]: 253n456, 356; activism and violence 132, 168n322, 271–2; anti-immigration platform 271, 272; anti-Semitism 233, 272, 274–5; 'the fallen list' 44; ideological divisions and splits 277, 353; international rallies 272, 275; merger (1960) 132, 271, 352; merger into National Front (1966) 224, 360; pan-Nordic ideology 271, 272–3; The Spearhead 276–8, 279, 284, 325n223, 344n601, 353, 354; transnational links: Europe 272, 273, 394; and USA 62, 363–4
British National Party (BNP) [founder John Tyndall 1982–present]: 9, 14, 268, 314, 391, 436, 549, 555; activism and violence 391–3, 395–7, 481, 487–8, 490, 505–6; anti-immigration platform 497–8, 501, 503; and 'Rights for Whites' 393, 395–6, 452, 478; anti-Muslim politicking 393, 405, 471, 490, 491–6, 498, 505–6; anti-Semitism 482, 490, 492–3, 495–6, 503–4; campaign against Tyndall 402; and expulsion from party 403–5, 492; and Chesterton 233–4; and Combat 18, 397–400, 484; formation of 347, 352; ideological divisions, 'modernisation' and party splits 488, 500, 508, 548; racial nationalism 390, 391, 401, 485–7, 498; and ethno-nationalism 497–8; transnational links and affiliations: Europe 353, 392, 394, 476; and USA 394, 404, 427n493, 489, 496
British National Socialist Movement (BNSM) 311
British National Socialist Party (BNSP) 319n95
British National Youth 281–2
British Nationalist 233, 389, 393, 396–7, 402, 425n447, 464, 479, 483, 485, 486, 512, 526n335
British People's Party (BPP) 55, 59, 195, 200, 260–1, 314, 316n23, 322n175, 386
British Union of Fascists (BUF) (British Union of Fascists and National Socialists) 12, 30–1, 93–6, 99, 100, 104, 153, 184, 185, 477, 549; anti-Semitism 30, 48, 98–9, 102; anti-war policy 101–3; Battle of Cable Street 99–100; blackshirts and uniforms 30, 109, 158n43, 95, 98, 100, 186; Earl's Court rally 101; funded by Mussolini 93, 95, 96, 100; funded by Nazis 158n42, 97, 101; ideological differences and tensions 7, 93, 94, 184–5, 188; internments 104; Olympia rally 96, 99, 182; transnational links 95, 96, 97–8, 140, 142
British Union Constitution and Rules 94

British Union Quarterly 188
British Vigil 190
The Britons 28, 43, 55, 186, 199, 262, 270; HQ 55, 67, 267–8; links to Nazis 28, 176n494; Publishing Society 27, 28, 66, 75n164, 132, 206, 252n42, 267, 273, 294, 319n107, 348
Britton, Frank L. 88n456, 317n80, 437
Brixton 66, 112–13, 114–15, 162n159, 319n95, 381, 446; riots 454, 459, 465, 467
Brixton Prison 53, 104, 160n116, 447
broadcasts *see* radio broadcasts
Broadsheet 149
Brock, Robert 467
Brockway, Fenner 208
Brons, Andrew 234, 379, 385, 408, 425n442, 433n647, 436, 440, 441–2, 463, 515n76; arrest 456; and Griffin 453, 456, 463, 506, 507; ideology 442–3
Brooks, Austen 201, 202, 212–13, 225, 248n335, 249n340, 249n341, 326n252, 348
Brooks, Collin 192, 193, 194, 197, 238n96
Brown, Gordon 358, 418n273
Brown, S.E.D. 218, 233, 391
Browning, Will 'The Beast' 401, 484
Brunerie, Maxime 314
Bruning, Clement 158n47
Bruno, Harry 149
Bruschi, Pierfranco 140, 141, 172n401, 172n404
Bryson, Bill 253n451
Budden, Ted 463, 465, 526n335
BUF *see* British Union of Fascists
BUF Trust Ltd 95
Bulganin, Nikolai 264
Bulgaria 411n108, 511
Bulliet, Richard 69n5
Bullitt, William 175n486
Bund Völkischer Europäer/Alliance Racist Européene (BVE/ARE) 35
Burbidge, Philip 210
Burdett-Coutts, Martin 265
Burnley riot 490
Bush, George 393, 494
Bussell, Wolfe 293
Butler, Eddy 395, 399, 407, 464, 478–80, 485, 503, 504, 505–7, 515n79, 519n184
Butler, Eric D. 83n355, 249n359
Butler, R.A. 'Rab' 206, 325n236
The Bugler 281, 282
Bulldog 438–9, 440, 443, 452, 455, 459–60

C18 *see* Combat 18
Cadogan, Aubrey 333n396
Callaghan, James 380
Cambridge University 137; Cambridge University Conservative Association (CUCA) 137, 170n364; Cambridge University Nationalist Club (CUNC) 261, 316n57

Cameron, David 501, 552, 554
Campaign for Nuclear Disarmament (CND) 171n397, 211, 247n309, 329n164, 456
Campbell, Colin 15, 550
Campbell, Jim 460
Canada: fascist and far-right groups 60, 213, 361, 322n189, 420n328, 529n415
The Canadian Nationalist 60
Candour 180, 199–200, 201–2, 204, 206–7, 209–10, 212–13, 221, 223, 230, 232–23, 244n218, 264, 349, 365, 472
Candour League 231
Candour Leagues in Africa 208, 214, 215, 217
Capricorn Africa Society 208
Carlisle, Alex QC 481
Carlyle, Thomas 4
Carol, King of Romania 101
Carr, William Guy 248n334
Carthew, Beryl 'Bee' 417n242
Carthew, Sidney 413n164
Carto, Willis 219, 220, 267, 270, 394, 532n510
cartoons 42, 185, 445, 477; Muhammed cartoon, Denmark 495
Cartwright, Steve 476, 482, 484, 500
Castorina, Paolo 'Paul' 80n309
'Cassandra' 125
Catalan independence movement 557n22
Catholics and Catholicism 121, 180, 181, 185, 191, 201, 205, 213, 243n206, 341n546, 442–3, 445, 472–3, 474, 517n109, 521n246, 525n333, 530n444
Cato, John 312, 313, 398–9, 531n464
Cats Protection League 91n521
Celtic cross 277, 297, 324n220, 469
Chaggar, Gurdip Singh 377
Chamberlain, H.S. 40
Chamberlain, Neville 93, 192
Cheetham, Beryl 283
Chelsea FC 439
Chesterton, A.K. (Arthur Kenneth) ('Caius Marcius Coriolanus') ('Philip Faulconbridge') and Africa 181, 198, 214–15, 217; apartheid 216–18; Aryanism and mysticism 189; Candour League 231; conspiratorial anti-Semitism 183, 186, 188–90, 191, 193, 195, 198, 201, 203–4, 219–20, 223, 445; Empire and imperialist views 198–201, 202–4, 207, 208, 212, 214–15, 218–20; influence and legacy 180, 232, 234; as propagandist 183, 186, 189, 192; Rhodesia 214, 215; USA links 219
Chesterton and the National Front 186, 194–195; foundation of 224; resignation from 230

Chesterton, Cecil and Gilbert 180–1
Chesterton, Doris 182
Chesterton, G.K. 191, 219, 254n508, 442, 517n109, 525n333

child sexual exploitation 493–4, 505–6
Childs, Major-General Sir Wyndham 25
Chile 199, 200, 212, 390, 416n237
Chirac, Jacques 314
Chiume, Kanyama 269
Chivers, Paige 506
Chorlton, Manchester 44
Christian Anti-Jewish Party 62
Christian identity groups in USA 63, 89n475, 246n272, 535n570
Christian Nationalist Crusade 212, 261, 317n78
Christiansen, Arthur 197
Churchill, Sir Winston 175n486, 322n176, 476, 480
Clark, E.G. 'Mick' 48, 100
Clark, Dr J.H. 28
Clark, James 58
Clarke, Ken 137
Clarke-Goldthorpe, John 190, 239n120
Clausen, Frits 81n314
Clay, Teresa 58
Clifford, Frank 201
Clonfert Palace, Co. Galway 105–6
CND *see* Campaign for Nuclear Disarmament
Coast, John 51
Cobbett, William 442, 446
Cochrane, Kelso 119, 164n215, 269
Codreanu, Corneliu 9, 101, 449, 454, 476
Cold War 110, 111, 221
Collett, Mark 346, 409, 494, 504; trial and imprisonment 498
Colonna, Don Mario 73n122
The Coloured Invasion 117
Combat 18 (C18) 312–14, 323n191, 397–400, 479, 480, 484, 489, 531n469, 549
Commissars over Britain 195
Common Market 220, 244n224, 246n259, 299
Common Sense 87n449, 213
Commonwealth Immigration Act (1962) 227, (1968) 292
Comrade 153
Conference of Venice 138–9
Congo 133–5, 140, 214, 335n425
conscientious objectors 50, 103, 258
Conservative Commonwealth Council 203
Conservative Party 27–8, 192, 194, 513n24; elections 206, 229, 291, 368, 382–3; Falklands War 453; immigration 227–8, 291, 367–71, 382, 414n178, 416n238; imperial policy 134, 202–3, 204; League of Empire Loyalists 203–5, 210, 244n230; Monday Club 224, 232, 360–71, 417n242; and Mosley 93, 96, 105, 137, 170n364; National Front 369, 370, 382, 320n213; and Enoch Powell 227–8; National Socialist Movement 295, 299; neo-Tories 5, 94
Constitutional Research Association 195

Convention on the Prevention and the Punishment of the Crime of Genocide 498
Cook, Jacqueline *see* Griffin, Jacqueline
Cook, Roger 534n545
The Cook Report 482–3, 484, 487
Cooke, Roger Gresham 238
Cooper, F.T. 42
Cooper, Richard T. 71n65
Cooper, Rosie 506
Cooper, Terry 289, 293, 294, 295–6, 335n425, 357–8
Copeland, David 314, 487, 549
Cornilleau, Claude 335n425, 394, 396
Cotswold Agreement 283, 291
Cotter, Hilary 193
Cotterill 407, 489
Countryside Alliance 483
Courtney, David J. 298
Coventry 77n227, 184, 264, 283, 288, 481
Covington, Harold 306, 313
Cox, Earnest Sevier 270
Cox, Jo 554–5
Creasy, Ronald 176n494, 477
Crisp, Dorothy 195
The Cross and the Flag 61, 66, 212, 261
Cross, Colin 153
Crossman, Richard 148, 292, 297
Crowder, Captain J.F.E. 194
Crowley, Aleister 31
Cuba 117
Cuddon, Ron 361, 363
Cudlipp, Hugh 148
'cultic milieu' concept 15, 16, 38, 550
Curry, Desmond 143, 173n425
Curzon, Cynthia 93
Czechoslovakia 101, 189

Dachau concentration camp 34, 138
Daily Express 116, 197, 198, 487
Daily Herald 25
Daily Mail 95, 96, 98, 182, 282, 283
Daily Mirror 119, 125, 148
Daily Worker 143, 192
Daily Worker Defence League 258
Darby, Simon 342n574
Darlington, Cyril 130, 132, 167n304
Darwin-Fox, S.F. 59
Davenport, John 240n144
Davidson, Roy 272
Davidson-Houston, Major James 35
Davies, Alex 83n349
Davis Jnr, Sammy 133
Dawkins, Richard 443
Dawson, Peter 119–20, 133, 135, 168n318
de Benoist, Alain ('Fabrice Laroche') 14, 131, 450
de Bounevialle, Casimir Marmaduke 231

de Bouneviallle, Rosine 204–5, 211, 225, 231, 232, 255n539, 341n546, 363, 450, 519n173
de Fabre-Luce, Baron Robert 35
de Gaulle, Charles 136, 214, 215
de Gobineau, Count Arthur 40
de Guingand, Major-General Sir Francis 144
de Lagarde, Paul 46
de Léon, Alberto Mellini Ponce 137, 138
de Rivera, José Primo 109
Deavin, Mark 482, 487
Debbault, Jean-Robert ('James Wilson') 287–8
Deckert, Günther 396, 403
Decline and Fall of the Roman Empire 424n424
Deedes, W.F. 'Bill' 149, 175n477
Defence 261, 262, 263
Defenders of the American Constitution 212
Degrelle, Léon 109–10, 139, 305
del Valle, Lieutenant-General Pedro Augusto 212, 219
Dell, J.D. 82n326, 186, 430n587
Democratic Football Lads Alliance 553
Democratic Unionist Party (DUP) 461
Denmark 50, 272, 321n169, 495
Der Stürmer 23, 33–4, 73n139, 477
Derby-Lewis, Clive and Gaye 498
Deutsche Aktionsgruppen (DAG) 392
Deutsche Reichspartei (DRP) 109, 110, 111, 138–40, 282
Deveraux, Philip 69n20
Devi, Savitri 275–6, 290, 313, 323n204; and Dior 288–9, 295–6, 425n335; and Jordan 275, 282, 294, 296, 307, 308, 313; and Tyndall 290–1, 364
The Diary of Anne Frank 522n275
Die Braune Post 75n165
Dietrich, Otto 78n238
Dietz, George P. 63, 340n529, 425n457
Digby, Patrick 120
digital spaces *see* social media
Dimbleby, David 502
Dingley, M.J. 140
Dior, Christian 287
Dior, Françoise 287, 296, 332n360, 332n374, 335n425; criminal activity, arrests and imprisonment 292–3, 296; description of 288; National Socialist Movement 287–9, 293, 295, 334n422; Nazi contacts 288, 295–6; and Tyndall 285, 288, 290; wedding and marriage to Jordan 288–9, 291, 292, 294–5
DIsraeli, Benjamin 63
Distributism 239n115, 316n35, 442–3, 445, 472, 476
Doenitz, Admiral Karl 129
Domvile, Admiral Sir Barry 53, 60, 84n371, 219, 258, 281–2
Donaldson, Ian Stuart 312, 398, 455, 459, 466–7
Donovan, Captain B.D.E. 103

The Dorchester 135
Dorman, Geoffrey 191
Dorman-Smith, Sir Reginald 204
Dos Santos, M. Francisco 84n392, 85n411
Downe, Dowager Viscountess 69n21
Downes, Charlotte 505
Dowson, Jim 511
Dresden 196, 355
Dugdale, Sir Thomas 192
Duke, David 404, 431n606, 441, 496, 502
Dukes, Paul 293
Dundas, Ian Hope 72n101, 95, 96, 97
DUP *see* Democratic Unionist Party
Duprat, François 408n5
Dutschke, Rudi 515n59
Dylan, Bob 81n325

Eacott, Rose 74n145
Eckart, Dietrich 28
Eckersley, Frances 57–8
Eckersley, Peter 58, 159n77
EDL *see* English Defence League
Eden, Anthony 204, 265
Edmonds, Richard 391, 392, 395–6, 402, 405, 407, 433n642, 483, 505
Edmondson, Robert E. 61
Edward I 37, 46
Edward VIII 85n406
Eichmann, Adolf 196, 274, 275, 281
Eichmann, Horst 327n276
Elmhurst, Ernest 65, 90n490
El-Shazly, Colonel Saad Mohamed El Husseiny 281
Emanuel, Charles 48
Engdahl, Per 108, 161n140, 172n401, 321n169
England–Germany football match 1955 161n150
English Array 189
English Civil War 451, 495
English Defence League (EDL) 5, 500, 501, 505, 548, 558n40
English Mistery 189, 204
English Nationalist Association 259
Equality and Human Rights Commission (EHRC) 503
Erra, Enzo 108
ethno-nationalism 314, 462, 497, 498
ethno-plurality 14, 128, 131, 441, 468, 486, 497, 550
EU Referendum (2016) 548, 549, 554; *see also* Brexit
eugenics 4, 78n206, 128, 130, 296, 387
Europe-Action 131, 172n403
'Europe-a-Nation' *see* Mosley: Europe
The European 112, 124, 128, 129, 150, 160n116
European Commission of Human Rights 148
European Economic Community referendum (1975) 145, 202, 345

European Liberation Front (ELF) 263
European Social Movement (ESB) 108–9, 111, 112, 161n140, 321n169, 321n172, 323n202
European Union *see* Brexit; EU Referendum (2016)
Eusom, James van 51
Everitt, Richard 428n532
Evola, Julius 141, 448–9, 450–1, 523n292
Ewing, Robert 506
Excalibur House *see* NF Properties Ltd
Exodus 272, 325n223
Eyre, Giles E. 69n20
Eysenck, Hans 443

Faci, Michel 394, 396
Facing the Abyss 232–24
fake news 544n819
Falange 74n145, 109, 115
Falklands war 453
Farage, Nigel 548, 551
Farrakhan, Louis 467, 469, 558n40
fasces 24, 29, 32, 95, 98
Fasci d'Azione Rivoluzionaria (FAR) 108
Fascism and the Press 183
Fascism: definitions 10; 'Five Stages of Fascism' 16; the 'fascist minimum' 7, 19n53
Faulconbridge, Phillip *see* Chesterton, A.K
Faurisson, Robert 457–8, 475, 476, 483, 484
Féderation Ouest Européen (FOE) 288, 289, 291
Festinger, Leon 549
Fichte-Bund 52, 98
Field, Arthur Nelson 60, 219
Field, John 461
Fields, Dr Edward 62–2, 63, 155, 165n238, 363–4, 383, 393–4, 429n557
Final Conflict 474
Findlay, A.G. 188, 240n147
Finnegan, Thomas 520n213
Fiore, Roberto: arrest 447; beliefs 447–8; Bologna bombing 446; International Third Position 472, 474, 489, 508, 509, 510, 519n173, 529n423; National Front 447, 450–3, 463, 472
Firearms Act (1967) 298
First World War 28
Fitt, William 'Bill' 437
FitzGerald, Garret 459
Fleet Street Review 195
Fleischhauer, Colonel Ulrich 35
Fletcher, WPC Yvonne 469
Flockhart, Lawrence 'Alf' 113, 114–15, 143, 241n178; convictions 113–14, 115
FN *see* Front National
football hooliganism 267, 302, 439, 478, 500, 553
Football Lads Alliance 553
Forgan, Dr Robert 99
Fortune, Gladys 83n361

Foss, Mary 58
Foster, Ken 225
Fouéré, Yann 462, 525n320
Fountaine, Andrew: British National Party 224, 226, 275, 282; Chesterton 224, 226, 228–9; National Front 362, 377, 382, 385, 386, 423n393, 438, 456; National Labour Party 269, 271, 275, 277, 350–1
'fourteen (14) words' 32n566, 345n616, 478, 500, 508, 532n489; song 477
Fox, Seaton Elliott 85n406
Fox, Seton Henry 74n145
France 102, 104, 175n486, 330n324, 457, 472; fascist and far-right groups 108, 136, 140, 170n377, 214, 215, 288, 296, 314, 332n374, 388, 394, 466, 483, 525n319, 551
Franco, Francisco 109, 252n435
Frank, Anne and Otto 168n318, 522n275
Frankel, William 145–6
Fraser, Fitzgerald 120
Fraser-Harris, Commander D.S. 211, 244n230
The Fraudulent Conversion 263–4, 267
Freda, Franco 449, 518n155
Free Britain 67, 198, 199, 263
Freedman, Benjamin H. 213
Freeman, Lady Elizabeth 199, 231, 248n330
Freeson, Reginald 333n389, 333n391
Frei Korps 266, 269
Freie Demokratische Partei 110
Friends of Oswald Mosley 153, 165n238
Fritsch, Theodor (Ferdinand Roderich-Stoltheim) 37
Front National (FN) 347, 388, 394, 474, 482, 486; *see also* Le Pen
Frost, David 146–7
Frost, Stephen 311, 345n616
Fuller, Major-General J.F.C. 31, 97, 184

Gaddafi, Colonel Muammar 469–70
Gair, Robert *see* Gayre
Gaitskell, Hugh 132
Gallo, Gary 457, 527n378
Gandalf Graphics 523n283
Gannon, Anthony 64, 89n479
Gardiner, Rolf 5
Garvey, Marcus 270, 467
Gateley, Kevin 373
Gayre, Robert 5, 36, 131, 132, 207, 226
Gegan, Phillip 515n63
Geldard, Alistair 136
Genoud, François 110
George, Professor W.C. 132, 207
German Embassy, London 287
Germany: attacks on migrants 392, 552; fascist and far-right groups 110, 111, 128, 139, 282, 296, 323n204, 392, 553; *völkisch* nationalism 12, 28, 35, 39

Gibson, Keith 135, 136, 138, 141, 143
Gilbert, Oliver 411n121
Gitau, Reverend James 541n751
Gittens, Anthony (Tony) 49–50, 51, 52, 54, 55, 59, 67–8, 86n417, 91n509, 199, 206, 267, 268
Gleave, Eileen 86n417
Gleaves, Roger C. 247n309
Godfrey, Edward 258–9
Goebbels, Joseph 97, 99, 100, 101, 109, 185, 207
Golden Dawn 305, 508
Gonzalez-Moreno, Edward 252n435
Goodman, Charlie 43
Gordon-Canning, Captain Robert 53, 60, 97
Gore, Charles W. 48
Göring, Hermann 56–7
Gostick, Ron 87n437, 212, 249n341
Gothic Ripples 91n521; and Leese 54, 56, 59, 60–2, 64, 66, 68; and Jordan 303, 308, 310
Goulding, William 143, 173n425
Graham, Thomas 322n189
Gramsci, Antonio 450, 451
Grand Mufti of Jerusalem 60
Grant, Donald 58
Graves, Commander Frank 268
Graves, Phillip 27
Great Depression 26, 151
the 'Great Displacement' 511
The Great Sedition Trial 61, 62, 65, 149
The Greater Britain 30, 94, 98, 359
Greater Britain Movement (GBM) 225, 230, 253n456, 291, 357–8, 361, 362, 387, 410n103, 412n137, 418n273; activism and violence 359
Greater London Council (GLC) 174n445, 380
The Green Book see Gaddafi
Greene, Ben 188, 189, 201, 202, 206, 208, 238n90, 260
Greene, Graham 201, 243n208
Greene, Sir Hugh Carlton 201
Greene, Margaret 'Leslie' 199, 201, 202, 210, 242n181, 246n259, 263, 349; arrest 349
Greenslade, Peter 265, 266
Greenwood, Arthur 321n164
Gregor, A. James 10, 128–30
Grieb, Conrad K. 83n162, 88n464
Griffin, Edgar 436–7, 438, 475
Griffin, Jacqueline (née Cook) 456, 457, 522n270
Griffin, Jean (née Thomas) 436
Griffin, Nick 233–4, 311, 341n545, 346, 433n645, 464, 488; anti-Semitism 437, 483, 501, 511; arrests, court appearances and trials 346, 405, 481, 482, 484–5; and Distributism 443, 472; in Eastern Europe 511; and Fiore 446–7; heritage and culture 451, 462; as Holocaust denier 476, 480–1, 483, 496, 502; as racial nationalist 441, 444–6, 451, 458–9;
ruralism and paganism 447, 464, 473, 476, 483; Russia 509; Syria and Lebanon 509–11; television appearances: *The Cook Report* 482–4, 487, 534n545; *Question Time* 502; *Russia Today* 509; use of home for events and training 440, 443, 455–6, 466; visits to USA 456–7, 489, 491
Griffin, Roger 7, 10
Griffin, Susan 438
Griffiths, Peter 291
Gritz, Bo 89n475
Grundy, Trevor 116, 163n178
Guardia Nazionale Repubblicana (GNR) 141
Guilds 29, 446
Guinness, Diana *see* Mosley, Lady Diana
Guinness, Jonathan 174n489, 232, 370–1
Gulf War 393, 472
Gummer, John 137
Günther, Hans F.K. 'Rassen' 39–40, 66, 128, 129; racial categorisation 267

Hacking, Douglas 194
Hailsham, Lord 205
Hamburg 50, 111, 392
Hamm, Jeffrey 55, 112, 115, 116–17, 118, 120, 123, 132, 142, 134, 173n428, 259, 262
Hammerskins *see* British Hammerskins
Hani, Chris 498
Harmston, Denis 'Big Dan' 143, 155–6
Harrington, Patrick 340n533, 455, 458, 463, 465, 466, 469, 470, 472, 473, 529n414, 541n755
Harrison, Major W.J. 'Bill' 210
Harvey, John Hooper 37–9, 40–1, 51, 66, 294
'Harwood, Richard' *see* Verrall, Richard
Hawkins, Neil Francis 103, 185, 187, 183
Hay, Michael 31
Head, C.B.V. 59
Healey, Cahir 160n116
Healey, Dennis 220, 292
Heath, Edward 156, 227, 291–2, 299, 365, 367, 370
Heathrow Airport 368, 378
Heaton, Michael 314–15
Herrero, Emilio Gutiérrez 88n411
Hesketh, Walter 136, 138
Hess, Ilse 129
Hess, Rudolph 129, 273–4, 283, 285, 312, 476
Hess, Wolf Rüdiger 273, 274
Hezbollah *see* Griffin: Syria
Hick, Captain U.A. 236n59
Hill, Ray 299, 303, 389
Hilton, Major-General Richard 210, 244n230, 281
Hilton, Susan 193
Himmler, Heinrich 11, 101, 111, 273, 464
Hindu community 490, 505

Hiscox, Gertrude 85n406
Hitler, Adolf 11, 24, 28, 70n44, 77n203, 109, 237–64, 283; and the Mosleys 97, 99–101
Hoare, Oliver and Samuel 101
Hodge, Margaret 503–4
Hoffmann, Hans-Rolf 40–1, 43, 74n145
Holland *see* Netherlands
Holland, Derek ('Richard Murphy') 418n273, 438, 445, 557, 448–50, 457, 463, 466, 467, 470–1; and Palestine 452, 468, 473; spiritual dimension 449, 454, 473–4
Holocaust denial 11, 56, 135, 138, 150–1, 275, 308, 392, 394, 440, 452, 457–8, 576
Holroyd, Stuart 124
homosexuality 286, 307, 381, 386, 482, 544n807
Hopkins, Bill 124
Horsfall-Ertz, Dr Eugene R. 242n181, 242n182
Horst-Wessel-Lied 98, 279, 282, 288
Horton, Edwin Bassett 263
Howard, Anthony 69n20
Howard, Michael 137
Hoy, Robert 457, 467, 522n262
Huddleston, Reverend Trevor 132
Hughes, Diana 332n372
Hughes, Hugh 292, 293, 313
Hughes, Ingram 82n341
Hungary 9, 187, 287, 293, 311, 497, 511
Huntley, Michele 58
Hussein, Saddam 472–3
Hyde, Douglas 192

I'm Alright Jack 243n208
Iceland 81n314, 83n332
Identitarian movements 551
If Britain Had Fallen 149
IMF *see* International Monetary Fund
immigration 12, 25, 113, 115, 117, 123, 227–8, 282, 367, 378, 382, 497, 547–8; anti-immigration politicking 13–14, 113, 131, 154, 155–6, 202, 206, 263, 436; changing attitudes to 551–2
Immigration Acts (1968) 227, 292; (1971) 367
Immigration Control Association 367
Imperial Fascist League (IFL) 28–9, 35, 98, 267, 268, 411n121; activism 30, 49, 51–2; anti-Semitism 35, 47–9; Australian branch 42; links with Netherlands and Scandinavia 50; and USA 63; membership and funding 30, 47; and Mosley 30–1; and Nazis 32–6; pan-Aryan, Nordic and *völkisch* ideology 38–41, 42, 189; trials and imprisonment 57–9
Imperium 63–5, 391
Incitement to Disaffection Act (1934) 51
Institute of Economic Affairs 206, 210
International Association for the Advancement of Ethnology and Eugenics (IAAEE) 130, 131, 167n304

International Centre of Fascist Studies (CINEF) 29
International Monetary Fund (IMF) 194, 220
International Third Position (ITP) 472–5, 481, 412, 519n173, 52n423
Internment 8, 104, 190, 191
Iona 462
IRA *see* Irish Republican Army
Iran 390, 392, 468–9, 510, 511
Iraq 472–3, 492–3
Ireland 57, 105, 282, 523n319
Irish Guards 15, 51
Irish Republican Army (IRA) 160n116, 301–2, 524n310, 554; and Libya 471
Irland-Redaktion 193
Iron Guard 449–50
Irving, David 84n474, 151, 196, 396, 475, 476, 480
Islamists 436, 471, 191, 195, 500; terror attacks 507, 552, 554
Israel 204, 274, 281, 293, 452, 469
Israeli Embassy, London 204, 274
It Happened Here 323n194
Italy 447, 450; Italian Fascism and Salò Republic 11, 29, 94–5, 109, 141, 152; fascist and far-right groups 108, 140, 141, 171n398, 410n172, 446–7, 544n809, 545n828, 450, 453

'Jack King' *see* Roberts, Eric
Jacobson, Dan 121
Janne, Claude 288
Janner, Sir Barnett 325n223
Jeanne, Yves 288, 291, 330n324, 332n374, 335n425
Jebb, Reginald 'Rex' 191
Jeffrey, Robert K. 198–9, 212
Jeffries, Paul 312
Jeffries, Richard 442, 446
Jenkins, Roy 297, 379
Jeune Europe network (JE) 297, 379, 442, 446
Jewell, John 516n105
Jewish Defence Committee 47, 163n188, 260
The Jewish War of Survival 54, 56, 57, 63
Jews: accusations of ritual murder and blood libel 33–4, 37, 43, 44–5, 54, 57, 61–3, 68, 222–3, 537n650; expelled from England in 1290 37, 44, 46; ritual slaughter of animals (Shechita) 43, 59
Jihad *see* 7/7 attacks
John Birch Society 213, 255n533
Joly, Maurice 27
Jones, Alex 558n40
Jones, David 445
Jones, Harry 115
Jones, Ronald 49
Jordan, Bertha (*née* Beecham) 258, 289, 301

Jordan, Colin 68, 116, 132, 154, 351, 445, 482, 529n429; anti-Semitism, attacks and vandalism 260, 261–2, 264, 270–1, 272, 274–5, 281, 292–3; arrests, trials and imprisonment 265, 280, 284–5, 295, 297, 301, 302, 308; camps 272–3, 275, 276, 283; and Chesterton 225, 231, 263, 266, 300; and Françoise Dior 287–9, 291, 292, 293–5, 355; Holocaust denial 275; immigration 261–3, 265, 268, 291–2, 299, 300; and Nazi wedding ceremony 288; and Rudolf Hess 273–4; and Leese 259, 267, 303; legacy 311–15; Nazism 128, 142, 257–8, 268, 270, 276–7, 278–9, 296, 305, 307, 311; pan-Aryan philosophy 11, 77n227, 278, 310, 313, 359, 389; and *Panorama* 269; racial activism and violence 202, 260–1, 264, 266, 267, 269, 271–2, 276, 279–80, 292, 295; racial nationalism 39, 66; and Spearhead 276–8; transnational links and alliances: American far-right 265, 270, 282–3, 285, 297, 306, 310; Arab 281; European 270, 272–3, 277, 282, 287–8, 305, 311; pan-Nordic 261, 304–5

Joyce, Margaret 316n23

Joyce, William 43, 58, 59; and British Union of Fascists 98, 100, 184, 185; and Chesterton 184, 190, 193; and Leese 57, 445; and Mosley 57, 192; radio broadcasts 190, 192; trial 57

Jyllands-Posten and Muhammed cartoon 495

Kallis, Aristotle A. 9
Kaufman, Gerald 307–8
Kavanagh, Paul 381, 385, 386
Kellerman, Otto 84n372
Kemp, Arthur 76n194, 498
Kemsley, Lord 193
Kennedy, Joseph 175n486
Kenya 208–9
Kenyatta, Jomo 66, 209–10, 358
Kerby, Captain Henry 'Bob' 204
Kerlen, Kurt 28
Kernmayer, Erich 138
Kerr-Ritchie, Roland 284, 285, 286–7, 329n319
Kerstein, Wolfgang 324n219
KGB 286, 321n148
King, Dr Martin Luther 364, 413n164, 526n335
Kirmse, Joachim 86n417
Kissinger, Henry 233
Kitson, Arthur 27, 219
Kitt, Eartha 133
KKK *see* Ku Klux Klan
Kleist, Peter 138
Klingel-Schmidt, Jean-Louis Bernard 289
Knight, Charles Maxwell 58
Knight, Professor G. Wilson 181
Knight, George 242n184
Knight, J.D.F. 297, 298

Knights Templar International 511
Koehl, Matt 66, 297, 298, 306–7, 394
Kops, Bernard 165n258
Kramer, Joseph 56
Kray, Reggie and Ronnie 143
Krieger, Heinz 36
Krüger, Dr Fritz ('Peter Aldag') 36
Krushchev, Nikita 264
Kruyt, Major Cornelius Jacobus Aart 81n316
Ku Klux Klan (KKK) 26, 62, 265, 294, 319n95, 384, 404, 502
Kühnen, Michael 274

Labour Party 93, 118, 194, 260, 351, 380, 499, 505
Lamarck, Jean-Baptiste 126, 127, 132
Lambrianou, Tony 143
Lammers, Hans Heinrich 97
Lane, David 309–10, 313, 478, 481
Lanfré, Giovanni Nicola 138, 140, 170n368, 171n384
Lanza, Mario 81n325
Laqueur, Walter 10
Lawson, Richard 374, 376, 450, 462
Lazarus, David 416n238
Le Pen, Jean-Marie 388, 394, 427n496, 473, 487, 493, 502
League of Empire Loyalists (LEL) 68, 263, 264, 266, 348, 411n108, 442, 450; Central Africa Branch 208, 214; Conservative Party 202–3, 205, 210; funding 211–12; immigration 202, 206, 263, 265; merger into National Front 225, 360; protests against 411n108; South Africa 216–17; transatlantic links 214
League of St George 306, 376, 388, 447, 450
Lebanon 452, 510–11
Lecomber, Tony 397, 399, 401, 405, 479–80, 485, 488, 492; imprisonment 391, 426n463, 432n619
Leech, Hilda 86n415
Lees, Aubrey 55
Leese, Arnold 283, 303, 313, 359, 446, 548; Africa 191, 198, 208–9, 214; anti-Semitism 23, 27, 42–3, 44–8, 54–6, 61, 66, 73n139; anti-war stance 49–51; arrests, trials and imprisonment 43–4, 52–3, 58, 59–60; Christmas cards 47; and Edward I 46; and Hitler 51–2, 56; Holocaust denial 56, 196; 'Madagascar plan' 46, 47; and Mussolini 23–4, 26, 32; Nordicist and *völkisch* ideas 37, 128; as racial geneologist 45–6, 59–60; racial nationalism 14, 23, 66–7; racialised paganism 41–2; transatlantic influence 61–3; and disagreements with Yockey 63–6; transnational links 60, 81n314; Nazis 33–6, 41, 60, 57; Sweden 50, 60; as veterinarian and camel doctor 23, 43, 59

Leese, May Winifred (née King) 23, 52, 59, 268, 271, 290, 358
Lees-Milne, James 152
Leftwich, Joseph 197, 222, 223
Legg, Rodney 224, 362
Legge-Bourke, Sir Harry 204
LEL see League of Empire Loyalists
Lenchitsky, Zalig 44
'Leslie Fry' (Paquita de Shishmareff) 62
Leuchter, Fred 394, 475–6
Lovell, John W. 52, 59
Levin, Bernard 198
Lewis, Frederick 162n167
liberal democracy 13, 15, 24, 149, 390, 469, 501
Liberal Party 149, 205, 336
Liberty Lobby 219, 220, 267, 384, 394, 522n262
Libya 469–71
Liddell, Guy 86n415, 156n1, 238n98
Life Rune Books 312, 429n557, 464, 532n509
Lindbergh trial 44
Lindholm, Sven 50
Ling, Peter 261, 265, 268, 272, 283, 285, 287, 328n282
The Link 53, 77n208, 81n321
Lintorn-Orman, Rotha 24, 32
Lipton, Marcus 113
The Listener 149
Lockhart, Sir Robert Bruce 94
Lockwood, Harold 29, 42, 49, 55, 74n145
Lombardo, Antonio 141
Longmate, Norman 149–50
Lord Haw Haw *see* Joyce, William
Loredan, Count Alvise 137–8, 140–2
Low Countries *see* Netherlands
Lowles, Nick 400, 506
Loyalist paramilitaries, Northern Ireland 460–1, 521n246, 524n310
Lübcke, Walter 552
Lucas, H.F. 78n238
Lucas, Sir Jocelyn 203
Lucht, Lea 109
Lüdecke, Kurt 28
Ludendorff, General Erich 24
Ludovici, Anthony M. 391, 487
Ludtke, Bruno 287
Lumumba, Patrice 133
Lundoff, John M. 64
Luton Town FC 500
Lymington, Viscount 5, 50, 188, 189, 198
Lynd, Robert 197, 241n162
Lyons, Kirk 393, 394, 396, 427n493
Lysenko, Professor Trofim 63, 65

'MacDonald, Andrew' *see* Pierce, William
MacDonald, Lieutenant-Colonel F.W.P. 30
MacDonald, Ramsay 94

Mackey, Aidan 201, 212, 225, 228, 230, 231, 239n115, 254n508, 363
Macmillan, Harold 134, 171n379, 202, 210, 213–14, 224, 227, 285, 286, 369
'Madagascar plan' 34–5, 46, 47, 88n472
Madole, James 64, 66
Maertz, Homer 65, 90n489
Mair, Thomas 554
Major, John 396
Malawi 378
Malmö 108
Malone, Matt 457, 467, 522n268
Manchester airport 368
Mandela, Nelson 217, 218, 307, 391, 498
Mankind Quarterly 36, 131, 132, 207, 226
Manpower Services Commission 523n283
Marconi scandal 181
Marino, Tony 72n101
'Marita network' 58–9, 86n415, 86n417
Marlborough Gate Secretarial College 201
Marriner, Albert 445
Marsh & Ferriman 152, 192
Martell, Edward 205–6, 223–4
Marx, Karl 47, 373, 516n99
Marxism 376, 439, 440, 450
Mason, James 345n616
Matthews, Robert J. 309, 310, 313, 456n57, 532n489
Mau Mau insurgency 66, 209–10
Maudling, Reginald 436
Maxwell-Fyfe, David 45
McAuley, John 482, 530n444
McGinley, Conde 87n449, 213
McKechnie, H.G. 138
McLaughlin, Michael 231, 301–2, 303, 311, 338n484, 338n488, 338n495, 543n805
McLorie, Andy 460–1
McNab, J.A. 183, 185, 198
McVeigh, Timothy 309
McWhirter, Kennedy, Norris and Ross 211
The Meaning of Treason 198
Mein Kampf 32, 279, 288, 330n327, 533n539
Mendelian genetics 46, 63, 132
Merrie England – 2000 307–8, 532n500
Merritt, John 476
Mertig, Kurt 65
Metzger, Tom 313, 457, 466, 522n260
Mew, Joyce 205, 244n230
Militant Christian Patriots 49, 51, 78n229
Militant Patriots Legal Defence and Air Fund 458
Mills, Alexander Rud 41–2, 77n226, 77n227
Mills, H.T.V. 'Bertie' 51, 85n406
Miners' Strike 445
Mitchell, Dr William J. 332n360
Mitford, Deborah 105
Mitford, Diana *see* Mosley, Lady Diana

Mitford, Jessica 152
Mitford, Nancy 137
Mitford, Pamela 105
Mitford, Unity 33, 97, 152, 117n448, 237n64
Mok, Hing Shung 196
Monckton, Walter 148–9
Mond, Sir Alfred 28
Monday Club 224, 232, 235n254, 372, 416n236, 416n238, 437; and immigration 369–71
the Moot of the Anglekin Body 41–2
Morris, William 442, 446, 517n109
Morse, John 389, 396–7, 430n587, 512
Mosley, Alexander 119, 153
Mosley, Lady Diana (née Mitford) 97, 123, 144, 145, 148, 151, 153, 202; and Hitler 99, 101, 152; marriage 99–100; Nazi funding 100–1
Mosley, Max 119, 136, 138, 142, 153, 170n360
Mosley, Nicholas 121–2, 142; biography of father 153
Mosley, Sir Oswald ('The Leader') 7, 10, 14, 72n94, 100, 121, 123, 124, 137, 147, 153, 280, 547; Africa 106, 107, 117, 126, 134; anti-Semitism 98–9, 145–6, 152, 187; anti-war stance 101–2, 104; arrests and internment 104, 153, 458; autobiography 147, 149, 150, 187; and BBC 144, 147–9; Cable Street 99; and the cult of celebrity 95; 'Europe-a-Nation' and pan-European philosophy 11, 105, 106, 137–8, 180, 359, 462; immigration 113, 117–18, 123, 125, 154, 155; move to Ireland 105; marriages 93, 99–100; the New Party 30, 93; Olympia 96; race science and eugenics 127–8, 130–2; radio station plans 101; South African apartheid 106, 114, 117, 126, 131–3, 144–5; 'Thought-Deed' man 7, 126, 528n389; television appearances *The Frost Report* 146–7; *Panorama* 148; transnational links and networking: Conference of Venice 137–9, 140, 142, 172n401; Europe 81n314, 108–10, 136–41, 150–1; Hitler and Nazis 94, 96–7, 99, 100–1; Mussolini and Italian Fascists 94–5, 96, 100; South Africa 144–5; USA 149
Mosse, George 12
Mouvement d'Action Civique (MAC) 138–40
Movement for Colonial Freedom 208, 266, 350
Movimento Sociale Italiano (MSI) 109, 129, 137, 138–9, 140–2, 152, 172n401
Moxon, Oliver 124
Muggeridge, Malcolm 318n84
Mullally, Frederick 10, 260–1
Mullins, Eustace 62, 223
multiculturalism 392, 498, 501
Munich crisis 24, 49, 188
Mussolini, Benito (Il Duce) 11, 23, 29, 109, 137, 153, 273; funding for BUF 93, 96, 100, 185; parade for Mosley 95
My Answer 93, 179

My Life 147–8, 149, 150, 187
Nadeau, Jean-François 60
Narjes, Mabel 150
Nation Europa 111–12, 129, 138, 150, 265, 275, 407
Nation of Islam (NOI) 467
National Action 83n349, 315, 345n616, 408, 506, 549
National Alliance (UK) 398
National Alliance (USA) 308, 309, 312, 341n550, 384, 429n558, 451
National Council for the Reduction of Taxation 205
National Democrat 233, 234, 450
National Democratic Front 457
National Democratic Party 414n178
Nationaldemokratische Partei Deutschlands (NPD) 139, 150, 226, 253n456, 296, 392, 396, 403, 510
National Front (NF) 14, 15, 156, 224–5, 233, 297, 347, 360–2, 365, 373, 437, 439, 464, 555; activism and violence 298, 368, 372–3, 380, 382, 440–1, 458, 465; Distributism 442–3, 445; immigration 156, 224, 227–8, 297, 367–9, 375, 377–9, 451–5, 459, 490; internal tensions, 'leftist' stance 372, 445; links with: France 347; Germany 226; Italy 447–8; USA 347, 363–4, 383, 451, 457; power struggles and splits 228–9, 230, 368, 374–7, 385–6, 463, 471; Italian clique 447–8, 453; pan-European philosophy 462; pro-Muslim/anti-Muslim 468, 490, 495; racial nationalism 442, 464, 467; Ulster loyalist paramilitaries 417n249, 430n573, 459–61, 521n246, 523n299; white power music scene 455–6, 459, 466–7
National Front After Victory 194–5
National Front Constitutional Movement (NFCM) 386, 442
National Labour Party (NLP) 132, 144, 210, 268–9, 270–1, 350–2; merger into BNP 352

National Party 376, 383, 384
National Referendum Campaign 375
National Renaissance Party 64
National Review 149, 306
National Socialist Alliance 313, 400
National Socialist German Workers Party (NSDAP) 28, 32, 55, 150
National Socialist Group (NSG) 298–9
National Socialist League (NSL) 188–90, 260, 294

National Socialist Movement (NSM) 253n456, 325n240, 278, 297, 313–14, 353–4; activism 283, 287, 291–2; anti-Semitic campaigns 292–3; and Dior 287–8; funding 281; links to

neo-Nazi groups 282, 287; membership 279; rallies 279–80, 282; tensions and splits 287–90
National Socialist Party of America (NSPA) 306
National States Right Party (NSRP) 62, 76n194, 165n238, 275, 323n204, 363
National Union of Mineworkers (NUM) 445
National Workers Movement 55
Nationalist Centre 337n452, 358, 363, 412, 131
NATO 220
Naumann, Werner 109–11, 129, 176n489
Nazi propaganda 34, 35, 36, 40, 98; *see also* radio broadcasts
Nazis and Nazism 273, 280, 295, 313, 353, 366, 448; Aryanism and racial science 38, 129–30, 267, 359; racial hygiene 40; *völkisch* nationalism 12, 28, 39
Nazi-Soviet pact 51
Netherlands 50, 58, 141, 321n172, 339n506
New European Order (NOE) 108, 287, 427n509
'New Labour' *see* Labour Party
New Nation 443, 449, 456, 457–8
National Socialist White Peoples' Party (NSWPP) 301, 306
The New Party 30, 93, 98
New Pioneer Group 189
The New Unhappy Lords 180, 219–20, 221–2, 223, 232, 233, 234
New Zealand 421n328
Newland, Michael 480, 484
News from Germany 40, 98
NF *see* National Front
NF Properties 385
Nicols, John 278, 325n223, 328n286
Nicolson, Harold 93, 94, 98
Nicolson, Nigel 205
Nietzsche, Friedrich 387, 391
Nolte, Ernst 8
Nordicism 32, 36, 38–41, 45, 66, 127–9, 154, 206–7, 266, 267, 270–1, 288, 357, 498
Nordic League 33, 49, 51, 55, 189–90, 411n121
The Nordics 37, 39–41, 77n206
North and East London Co-Ordinating Anti-Fascist Committee 143
Northern European Ring (NER) 272–23, 275, 277, 283, 323n204, 327n266, 327n276, 353
Northern League 77n227, 207, 246n272, 266, 270, 327n266
Norway 50; invasion of 51, 104, 127
Notting Hill 121, 125; carnival 380, 452; far-right demos, riots and violence 116, 143, 267, 269; murder 119
Nouvelle Droite (ND) 13, 14, 131, 441, 450, 468, 497
NSM *see* National Socialist Movement
Nuclei Armati Rivoluzionari (NAR) 446, 517n29
Nuffield, Lord 160n116
Nugent, Alfonso 120
Nuremberg 47; rallies 34–5, 98; trials 56–7, 63, 147
Nyasaland 198, 269

The Oak 312, 298
O'Brien, Archie 53n567
O'Brien, John 230, 299, 365–56, 367, 374, 387
occultism 28, 85n406, 336n442
Odinism 41, 476
'oi' music *see* Skrewdriver; white power music scene
Oklahoma bombing *see* McVeigh, Timothy
Old Bailey trials 57, 59, 120, 284, 293
Olden, Mark 120
Oliver, Revilo P. 219, 232, 391, 394
Olympia *see* British Union of Fascists
One Nation 335n425
Orbán, Viktor 511
The Order (the Silent Brotherhood) 309–10, 401, 456, 478
Ordine Nuovo 141
Oredsson, Göran A. 321n169, 327n276
Organisation Armée Secrète 136
Oronsay 42
Orwell, George 192
Oswald Mosley: Portrait of a Leader 179, 184
The Outsider 121, 123, 124
Owen, Bill 322n189
Owen, Robert 442
Oxford University Debating Society 149, 151

Painter, Roy 371, 374–5, 376, 377
Paisley, Reverend Ian 461
Pakistani community 162n168, 493, 505
Palestine 41, 60, 452, 469, 471
Palestine Liberation Army (PLO) 473
'palingenetic myth' 7, 9, 13
Palmer, Ernest 143, 173n425
Pan-African International Movement (PAIN) 467
Pannell, Charles 272
Panorama 148, 269
Parachute Regiment (TA) 136
Paris 95, 101, 110, 152, 229, 296, 487; attacks (2015) 552
Parker, Charles and Violet 387, 421n349, 425n433
Parker, Valerie *see* Tyndall, Valerie 381, 388, 407, 433n645
Partei nationaliste français et européen (PNFE) 335n425
Pash, Robert 529n428
Passmore, Michael 412n137
Pateley Bridge 303
The Patriot 57, 59, 204, 401, 485, 522n270

Pavarotti, Luciano 81n325
Paxton, Robert O. 4, 13; 'Five Stages of Fascism' 16
Payne, Stanley 5, 10, 546
Peace Pledge Union (PPU) 50
Peake, Alan Francis 74n145
Pearce, Joe 393, 438–49, 440, 443–4, 447, 450, 451, 453, 455, 457, 468, 486, 525n333; imprisonment 452, 459, 463
Pearson, Roger 5, 88n474, 207, 270
PEGIDA 553
Pelley, William Dudley 82n341
People's League for the Defence of Freedom 205
The People's Post 57, 195, 200, 260
Pepler, H.D.C. 191
Père Lachaise cemetery, Paris 152
Perigoe, Marita 59, 86n417
Petáin, Marshal 175n186
Pfister, G.A. 97
Phoenix Bookshop 279, 281
Pierce, William ('Andrew MacDonald') 296, 298, 308–9, 311–12, 361–2, 364, 384, 387, 397–400, 451, 457, 476, 479, 482
Pile, George 66, 320n114, 322n175
Pioneer News Service 489
Pirie, Denis 225, 228, 273, 279–80, 284–5, 300, 335n425, 355–6
Pirow, Oswald 106
Pitt, Dr David 269
Pitt-Rivers, George Lane Fox 81n325, 83n361
Plaid Cymru 462
Pleasants, Eric 424n421
Plummer, Leslie 272, 355
Poke, Greville 191
Poland 55, 102, 294, 497, 544n809
The Political Soldier 454, 457, 473
Pollard, Peter 297
Polzin, Frederick 64–5
Pope Pius X 442
Popolo d'Ital'a 97
Populist Party 393–4
Portsmouth, Earl of 198, 208
Potocki, Count Geoffrey of Montalk 293–4, 237n87
Potter's Bar 34
Pound, Ezra 29, 62, 137–8, 223, 449
Powell, Enoch 229, 292, 367–9, 370–1, 374, 382, 416n238, 417n242, 417n244, 547, 551; and 'Rivers of Blood' speech 13, 155–6, 227–8, 299, 365, 437, 495
Pownall, Capel 36–7
Pownall, George 48, 80n293
Prevent 554–5
Prevention of Terrorism Act 314, 460
Priester, Karl-Heinz 111, 323n202
Prisoners of War Assistance Society 58

Private Eye 227
Profumo, John 286
The Protocols of The Elders of Zion 27, 35, 43–4, 62, 186, 197, 222–3, 260, 281, 352, 367, 378, 389–90, 468
Pryce-Jones, David 147, 152
Public Meeting Act (1908) 285
Public Order Act (1936) 100, 276, 280, 284, 285, 295, 354, 389, 421n351; (1986) 308, 481
punk music 312, 455; *see also* white power music scene
Purcell, Hugh 152–3
Purdy, Roy Walter 294
Putin, Vladimir 12, 509, 544n819

Queen Mother 175n474
Question Time 502
Queens Park Rangers FC 267
Quisling, Vidkun 50, 81n314

Race Relations Act 226, 297, 302, 303, 330n328, 369, 370, 379, 440, 458
race riots 267, 454, 459
racial essentialism 12
racial genealogy 6, 45
racial hygiene and purity 12, 23, 40, 45, 54, 62, 278, 464, 499
racial identity 12, 39, 226, 478
racial nationalism 12, 23, 55, 63, 66, 154, 273, 276, 365, 388, 407, 442, 464, 498, 551
racialised paganism 41–2, 288
racial segregation 132, 270, 363, 443, 467, 468, 489
The Racial Elements of Europe 39–40, 66
Racial Preservation Society 224, 226, 414n178, 415n217, 419n304; merger 360
Racial Volunteer Force 314
radio broadcasts: Italy 29, 137–8; Nazi Germany 35, 43, 57, 58, 71n86, 189, 193, 237n64
radio stations 101, 213, 214, 281, 310, 476, 482
Ramsay, Captain Archibald M.H. 'Jock' 51, 53, 81n321, 87n435, 104, 190, 214
Rauti, Guiseppe 'Pino' 141
Raven, Alice 199, 242n181, 242n184
Ray, James Earl 364
Read, John Kingsley 371, 374–5, 376–7
Read, Simon 432n398
Reed, Douglas 192, 195, 199
Reed-Herbert, Anthony 374–5, 386
refugees and asylum seekers 49, 510; attacks on 392, 494, 552; change in attitudes to 551–2
Reker, Henriette 552
Relf, Robert 292, 294–5, 302
Remer, Major-General Otto Ernst 65, 128–9, 307
Renshaw, Jack 506

repatriation 58, 113, 118, 224, 369, 451, 471, 484; compulsory 156, 227, 301, 370–1, 384, 453, 459, 480, 485; voluntary 227, 229, 299, 472
Representation of the People Act (1949) 136, 302
Research and Study Group for European Civilisation 131
Resistance Records 477
revisionism 10–11, 151, 275, 392, 394, 450, 496; *see also* Holocaust denial
Reynaud, Paul 175n486
Rhodesia 28, 117, 134, 198, 208, 214–16, 218, 295, 363, 369, 498
Ribbentrop, Joachim von 34, 97, 111, 176n489
Rich, Major Theodore 44
Richard III 519n184
Ridgwell, Wendy 44
Ridout, Phillip J. 47–8, 50, 62, 67, 88n468, 277, 327n266
Rigby, Lee 507
The Right Club 51, 53, 81n325, 85n406, 104, 190, 214
Rippon-Seymour, Lieutenant-Colonel Henry 24–5, 26
Risdon, Wilfred 185, 188
The Ritz 133, 187
Roberts, David D. 9, 13
Roberts, Eric ('Jack King') 58, 86n417
Robertson, Wilmot (Humphrey Ireland) 383–4, 393, 441, 457
'Robinson, Tommy' (Stephen Yaxley-Lennon) 5, 500–1, 551, 553
Rock against Communism 312, 455
Rock against Racism 455
Rockwell, George Lincoln 244n218, 278–9, 281–3, 285, 288, 290–1, 296, 301, 345n616, 354–6, 363, 394, 477; murder 297–8, 306
'Roderich-Stoltheim, Ferdinand' *see* Fritsch, Theodor
Roeder, Manfred 392, 481, 509
Romania 101, 449, 518n162
Romualdi, Pino 137–8, 170n368
Roosevelt, Franklin D. 189
Rose, Kenneth 148–9
Rosenberg, Albert 32–3, 206, 330n327
Rosenburg, Ethel and Julius 61
Rössler, Dr Fritz 109
Rothermere, Lord 95–6, 148, 182
Rothschild, Baron Louis 101
Rothschild, Lord Victor 58
Routh, Guy 271
Row, Robert 80n293, 115, 128, 133, 143, 169n332
Royal College of Veterinary Surgeons 23, 59
RSPCA 43
Rudel, Hans-Ulrich 110, 137, 138, 170n377, 276, 305, 364

Rudman, Ray Kirch 83n363
Rudolf, Germar 431n607, 487, 545n834
The Rune 476–8, 479–80, 481–5
ruralism 5, 446, 464, 476, 483
Rushbrook, J.F. 31, 33, 51, 72n101, 78n229
Rushdie, Salman 392–3
Rushton, Peter 399, 408
Ruskin, John 442
Russia 12, 27, 52, 106, 111, 264, 318n84, 402, 444, 544n819
Russia Today 509–10
Ryan, Michael 112–13
Rylands, G.K. 230, 231, 253n456

Sabine, A.M. 32
Safrany, Julia 311
Salamon, Sidney 260, 319n95
Salisbury poisoning 544n819
Salmon, Mr Justice 116
Salò Republic 11, 29, 109, 137, 141
Sanderson, William 5, 189
Sargent, Paul 'Charlie' 313, 398–9, 401
Sargent, Steve 313
The Satanic Verses 392
Saudi Arabia 60, 426n274, 490
Savile, Jimmy 506
Savoy Grill, London 94
Scandinavia 39, 50, 224
Scargill, Arthur 445
Schiller, Rabbi Mayer 471–2
Schilling, Walter 84n392
Schoep, Jeff 314
Schumacher, E.F. 446
Schütz, Waldemar 161n141
scientific racism 5
The Scorpion 233, 309, 340n533, 449, 450–1
Scott, George 198
Scott, Jean and Michael 211, 394
Scott, Lieutenant-Colonel John 'Jock' Creagh 199
Scott, Sir Harold 59–60
Scottish League for European Freedom 264
Scottish Nationalist Party (SNP) 557n22
Seabrook, Jeremy 499
The Sealed Knot 451
Searchlight 333n389, 341n544, 389, 405, 482
Seawright, David and George 524n310
Second World War 12, 15, 29, 51, 109, 294
Sewell, Father Brocard 516n80
Shakespeare 181–2, 195
Sharon, Ariel 452
Sharpeville massacre 133, 135, 136, 217
Shaw, George Bernard 126
Shechita *see* Jews: ritual slaughter
Sheffield 191, 298
Sheppard, Frederick J. 173n425
Sherrard, Leslie H. 29, 30

Shiffner, Sir Henry David 135
Sikh community 490, 503, 505
Silver Shirt Legion of America Inc. 82n341, 90n489
Silverman, Julius 262
Silverman, Lloyd and Sidney 237n73, 325n223
Simmons, Field Marshall Sir John Lintorn Arabin 24
Simpson, Harry 24, 70n38
Simpson, William Gayley 387
Singh, Rajinder 503
Sinn Féin 160n116
Skeels, Cecil Serocold 33, 238n98
Skidelsky, Robert 115, 126, 129, 130, 147, 151–2
skinheads 302–3, 429n569, 443, 455, 456, 466, 526n341; in USA 477
Skorzeny, Otto 138, 161n140, 170n375, 273, 284, 306, 454
Skrewdriver 312, 401, 455–46, 459, 466–7, 526n341, 527n363
Slánský trial 64
Slatter, Michael 285
Smedley, Oliver 205
Smith, Arthur 326n256
Smith, Colin 484
Smith, Eugene J. 82n341
Smith, Gerald L.K. 61–2, 66, 212–13, 261, 317n78
Smith, H.N. 261
Smith, Ian 117, 214–16, 295
Smith, Ian Duncan 513n24
Smith, Trevor Malcolm 419n289
Smithfield Market porters 143, 155–6, 227, 367–8
Snowdon, Lord Philip 31
SNP *see* Scottish Nationalist Party
social media 508, 550, 552–3
Socialist Workers Party (SWP) 379–80, 441
Somen, Israel 'Izzy' 197
Sontag, Susan 255n533, 390
South Africa 29, 54, 106, 117–18, 133–5, 144, 149, 169n332, 181, 216–18, 221, 265, 440, 498, 550; boycott movement 132, 168n322, 217, 271
South Shields 506
South Tyrol 141, 170n377, 282, 364
Sozialistische Reichspartei 65, 110, 128
Spain 9, 44, 109, 115, 252n435, 332n374, 449, 519n177
Spanish Civil War 161n140, 224, 302
Spartacan Society 124
Spearhead 233, 357–60, 366, 373, 377, 386, 390, 403–6
The Spearhead *see* British National Party [John Bean]
Spengler, Oswald 63, 126–7, 235n25, 388

Spens, Sir Patrick 119
Spivey, Kenneth 333n391
Spranklin, Philip 186
Stanford, Mary 71n86, 85n406
Stephenson, William 270
Sternhell, Zeev 4, 8
Steven Books 91n523, 155
Stevens, Geoffrey 203
Stewart, J.F. 264
Stirling, Colonel David 208
Stoddard, Lothrop 40, 377
Stoke-on-Trent 184
Stokes, Richard 53
Stonehouse, John 350
Stoner, Jesse B. 62, 364
Story, Ann 52, 54, 59, 268
Strachey, Lytton 29
Strasbourg 107, 148
Strasser, Gregor 192, 444
Strasser, Otto 112, 192, 195, 196, 202, 444–5, 448
Straw, Jack 308, 502
Streicher, Elmer 33
Streicher, Julius 23, 33–5, 43, 283, 353, 357; execution 57; and Mosley 97, 102, 146
Streicher, Lothar 33
Stuart, Ian *see* Donaldson, Ian Stuart
Südholt, Dr Gert 150–1
Suez crisis 204–5
sugar industry 117, 194
Sumerian civilisation 38
Sunday Express 198
The Sunday Pictorial 259
Sündermann, Helmut ('Heinrich Sanden') 150–1
sunwheel symbol 271, 273, 275, 276, 357, 456
Scutari, Richard 309–10
swastika 30, 32, 37, 41, 51, 278, 283, 288, 293–4, 296–7, 438; 'swastika epidemic' 270–1
Sweden 133, 455, 527n360; fascist and far-right groups 50, 60, 108, 304–5
Switzerland 29, 35, 108, 110–11, 141, 172n401, 287, 394, 427n509
synagogues, attacks on 168n318, 270, 293, 296–8, 323n194
Syria 12, 509–11; refugees from 551–2
Szabó, Albert 342n570
Szálasi, Ferenc 9

Taliban 490
Tall, Abdullah 87n435
Tarka the Otter 81n325
'Tasman H. Forth' *see* Mills, A.R
Tate & Lyle 184
Taviner, Mary 154
Taylor, A.J.P. 147
teachers, attacks on 439

Tear, Ron W. 324n219
teddy boys 116, 119
Tedeschi, Mario 172n400
Terza Posizione 446–9
Teutonic tribes 270
Thatcher, Margaret 305, 347, 382–3, 386, 388, 459, 470
Thatcherism 206
Thayer, George 355, 359
The 'Third Force' 11, 106, 109
Thiriart, Jean-François 138–42, 282, 364
Thomas, J.H. 93, 94
Thompson, H. Keith 65, 128–9, 133
Thomson, Alexander Raven 55, 97, 108, 111–13, 115, 127–30, 187, 262, 473
Thorkelson, Jacob 61
Thorpe, Jeremy 132, 149
Thule-Gesellschaft (Thule Society) 28
Todd, Colin 232, 472–3
Tolkien, J.R.R. 473, 523n283
Townsend, Ralph 149
Travers, Denis 295
Treachery Act (1940) 189–90
Treacy, Mick 490
Treason and Felony Act (1848) 299
Treaty of Rome 202
Tremlett, Rex 182, 191
Triumph of the Will 292, 392, 476
Trochu, André 295, 422
Truhill, Mana 65, 90n488
Trump, Donald 552
Tulloch, 'Brigadier-General' D. Erskine 29
The Turner Diaries 308–9, 384, 400, 451, 476
Twin Towers *see* 9/11
Tyler Kent affair 85n406
Tynan, Richard 'Dick' 265
Tyndall, John 11, 202, 346–7, 347–9, 548; Anglo-Saxon supremacy 359, 385; appearance and profile 353, 359, 386; arrests, trials and imprisonment 280, 284, 346, 350, 354, 360, 389, 405; The Beatles 354; British National Party 268, 276, 347; and expulsion from 403; and Chesterton 210, 225, 230–2, 233, 349–50; Combat 18, 398–401; conspiratorial anti-Semitism 357, 393; death and legacy 406–8; and Dior 285, 288–90, 355; and Griffin 401–3, 443–5, 479, 488, 492; immigration 352, 367–58, 369, 377; and Jordan 271, 290–1, 300, 310, 315, 356; liberal democracy 390–1; and Mosley 155, National Front 297, 300, 347, 352–3, 361, 363, 366–7, 376–9; National Socialist Movement 279, 290, 353; Nazism 347, 351, 353–4, 387, 391–2; USA links 355, 363–4, 383–5, 393–4, 396, 404; visits to Nazi Germany 273, 353
Tyndall, Valerie (nèe Parker) 381, 388, 407
Tyrie, Andrew 417n249, 523n299

Ugandan Asian immigrants 178n541, 367–8, 370, 373
UKIP *see* United Kingdom Independence Party
Ukraine 264
Ulster Defence Association (UDA), Ulster Freedom Fighters (UFF); *see* Loyalist paramilitaries
UNESCO 130
UM *see* Union Movement
Unilever 542n756
Union Movement (UM) 63, 80n293, 91n509, 105, 115, 120–1, 136, 154–6, 261, 263, 265–6; activism and violence 132, 133–6, 142–3; anti-immigration campaign 112–15, 116–18, 122–3, 135; pan-European philosophy 105, 112; transnational networks 108–9, 111, 131, 138, 140–1, 144–5
Union of European Muslims 473
Unionists, Northern Ireland 459, 461
United Arab Republic 281
United British Party 73n135
United Empire Fascist Party 73n135
United Kingdom Independence Party (UKIP) 9, 436, 494, 505, 507, 548, 549, 551–2, 554, 555; immigration 436
United Nations (UN) 109, 194, 205, 220, 271, 498
United Nations Charter on the Rights of Indigenous Peoples 498
Unity Band 82n339

van den Bergh, Brigadier Hendrik 217–18, 221
van der Byl, Pieter Kenyou 'PK' 215
van Rappard, Ernst 50
van Ryswyk, Jacobus Johannes 85n406
van Tienan, Paul 273
van Tonningen, Florentine 'Florrie' Rost 307, 339n526
'Varange, Ulick' *see* Yockey, Francis Parker
Vassal, John 286
Vaughan, David Esmé 238n98
Veale, F.J.P. 275, 355
Verrall, Richard 377–8, 386, 440, 443, 458, 475, 480
Verwoerd, Henrik 133, 135, 216
Victoria Grill restaurant 187
völkisch ideas *see* British fascism; Germany
Völkischer Beobachter 32, 36, 97
von Blomberg, Werner 97
von Göetz, Leslie *see* Greene, Margaret 'Leslie'
von Goetz, Richard 244n218
von Pfugel, Baroness Alice 63
von Thadden, Albert 109, 138–9, 142

Wace, Denyss Chamberlaine 158n47, 237n64
Waddell, Lieutenant-Colonel Lawrence Augustine 38–9, 41–2, 54, 61, 66

Wagner, Richard 97, 308
Wagner, Winifred 97, 136, 138
Waite, Terry 274
Wakeling, Nick 439, 443
Waldheim, General Kurt 367
Wales 462, 554
Walker, Martin 367, 372, 374–5
Walker, Michael 309, 385, 449–51, 462
Walker, Patrick Gordon 291–2
Waller, W.H. 71n65
Walters, Avril 210
Watts, Charlie 6–7
Waugh, Auberon 201–2
Webb, Michael and Patrick 294, 334n409
Webster, Martin 178n541, 202, 209, 225, 286, 325n340; arrest 358; and Griffin 488; and Jordan 298, 300, 356, 368; National Front 231–2, 233, 279, 283, 285, 363, 368, 372–4, 375, 376–7, 380–1, 418n273, 439, 442, 447; and expelled from 385, 453–4; 'One Nation' group 335n426; and Tyndall 286, 357, 381–3, 386, 423n402
Webster, Nesta 219
Webster, William 'Bill' 144, 351
Weiss, Frederick C. 65, 129
Welt-Dienst 35, 49, 98
West Ham United FC 267
West Indian National Association 295
West, Rebecca 198
Wheatley, Frank 82n339
Wheeler, Gerald Camden 77n204
Whinfield, Peter 75n171
White Aryan Resistance (WAR) 313, 457, 466
White Defence League (WDL) 116, 132, 154, 210, 266, 267, 268–71, 349, 351, 437; merger into BNP 352
White Noise Club *see* white power music scene
White Patriot Party (WPP) 522n264
white power music scene 302, 401, 495, 455, 459, 466, 477, 500
Whitehead, Walter 43, 66
Whitelaw, Willie 303, 520n201
Who are the Mindbenders 311, 482
Wicks, Henry W. 43
Wickstead, Inspector Bert 296
Williams, Gordon 333n389
Williams, Robert H. 61

Williams, Tony 307, 313, 438, 439, 440
Williamson, Henry 5
Wilmer, Brendan 281–2
Wilson, Colin 121, 123–5
Wilson, Harold 147, 214, 216, 291–2
Wilson, Lieutenant-Colonel H.C. Bruce 31–2
Wilton, Bert 71n77
Windsor, Duke and Duchess of 148
Wingfield, Martin 403, 458, 460, 463–4
Wolkoff, Anna 81n325
Women's Voice 62
Woods, Gordon 32, 50, 54
Wooler, Leslie 416n236
Woolford, Maurice ('Wolf Cleveland') 319n95
Worker's Revolutionary Party 391, 528n385
World in Action 412n133
World Union of National Socialists (WUNS) 282–3, 285, 287–8, 289–90, 296, 298–9, 314, 363, 383; WUNS-Europe 288
Wormwood Scrubs 43, 286
Wötzel, Erich 36
Wrigley, S.H. 47–8

Yates, George 52
Yaxley-Lennon, Stephen *see* 'Robinson, Tommy'
YNF *see* Young National Front
Yockey, Francis Parker 63–4; argument with Leese 64–6; and *Imperium* 63–5, 391; and Jordan 264; and Tyndall 391
Yorkshire Evening Post 69n22
Yorkshire Post 201
Young Conservatives *see* Conservative Party
Young National Front (YNF) 438–9; classroom campaign against 'Red' teachers 439; Griffin 441; links with US white nationalist groups 457; skinheads and white power music scene 455; summer camp 457
Young, G.K. 369, 371
Young, Wing-Commander Leonard 210
YouTube *see* social media

Ziegler, Dr Hans-Severus 138
'ZOG' ('Zionist Occupation Government') 83n349, 309, 314, 405, 478
Zündel, Ernst 308, 433n642, 458, 475, 483, 509

Printed in Great Britain
by Amazon